Fourth BlackboxNLP Workshop on Analyzing and Interpreting Neural Networks for NLP (BlackboxNLP 2021)

Punta Cana, Dominican Republic
11 November 2021

ISBN: 978-1-7138-9170-3

Printed from e-media with permission by:

Curran Associates, Inc.
57 Morehouse Lane
Red Hook, NY 12571

Some format issues inherent in the e-media version may also appear in this print version.

Printed with permission by Curran Associates, Inc. (2024)

For permission requests, please contact the Association for Computational Linguistics at the address below.

Association for Computational Linguistics
209 N. Eighth Street
Stroudsburg, Pennsylvania 18360

Phone: 1-570-476-8006
Fax: 1-570-476-0860

acl@aclweb.org

Additional copies of this publication are available from:

Curran Associates, Inc.
57 Morehouse Lane
Red Hook, NY 12571 USA
Phone: 845-758-0400
Fax: 845-758-2633
Email: curran@proceedings.com
Web: www.proceedings.com

BlackboxNLP 2021

Proceedings of the Fourth BlackboxNLP Workshop on Analyzing and Interpreting Neural Networks for NLP

November 11, 2021

Introduction

BlackboxNLP is the workshop on analyzing and interpreting neural networks for NLP.

In the last few years, neural networks have rapidly become a central component in NLP systems. The improvement in accuracy and performance brought by the introduction of neural networks has typically come at the cost of our understanding of the system: How do we assess what the representations and computations are that the network learns? The goal of this workshop is to bring together people who are attempting to peek inside the neural network black box, taking inspiration from machine learning, psychology, linguistics, and neuroscience.

In this fourth edition of the workshop, hosted by the 2021 conference on Empirical Methods in Natural Language Processing (EMNLP), we accepted 41 archival papers and eight extended abstracts. The workshop also provided a platform for authors of four Findings of ACL papers, and seven Findings of EMNLP papers, to present their work as a poster at the workshop. In addition, for the first time, the workshop worked in collaboration with the ACL Rolling Review system (ARR), accepting two more archival papers through that avenue.

BlackboxNLP would not have been possible without the dedication of its program committee. We would like to thank them for their invaluable effort in providing timely and high-quality reviews on a short notice. We are also grateful to our invited speakers for contributing to our program.

Jasmijn Bastings, Yonatan Belinkov, Emmanuel Dupoux, Mario Giulianelli, Dieuwke Hupkes, Yuval Pinter and Hassan Sajjad

Organizers:

Jasmijn Bastings, Google Amsterdam
Yonatan Belinkov, Technion – Israel Institute of Technology
Emmanuel Dupoux, Ecole Normale Supérieure and INRIA
Mario Giulianelli, University of Amsterdam
Dieuwke Hupkes, Facebook AI Research
Yuval Pinter, Ben-Gurion University of the Negev
Hassan Sajjad, Qatar Computing Research Institute

Program Committee:

Badr Abdullah – Saarland University
Heike Adel – Bosch Center for Artificial Intelligence
Sachin Agarwal – Apple
Željko Agić – Unity Technologies
Leila Arras – Fraunhofer Heinrich Hertz Institute
Kalyani Asthana – University of California Irvine
Pepa Atanasova – University of Copenhagen
Tania Avgustinova – Saarland University
Parsa Bagherzadeh – Concordia University
Niranjan Balasubramanian – Stony Brook University
Vinayshekhar Bannihatti Kumar – Amazon Web Services
Laurent Besacier – LIG
Nikolay Bogoychev – University of Edinburgh
Gemma Boleda – Universitat Pompeu Fabra / ICREA
Jonathan Brophy – University of Oregon
Lisa Bylinina – Bookarang
Stergios Chatzikyriakidis – University of Gothenburg
Hanjie Chen – University of Virginia
Ting-Rui Chiang – Carnegie Mellon University
Marta R. Costa-jussà – Universitat Politècnica de Catalunya
Benoit Crabbé – University of Paris
Verna Dankers – University of Edinburgh
Debajyoti Datta – University of Virginia
Roberto Dessì – Facebook AI Research Paris / UPF
Anne Dirkson – Leiden University
Radina Dobreva – University of Edinburgh
Yanai Elazar – Bar-Ilan University
Allyson Ettinger – University of Chicago
Jean-Philippe – Fauconnier Apple Inc.
Ghazi Felhi – Université Paris Nord
Antske Fokkens – VU Amsterdam
Robert Frank – Yale University
Richard Futrell – University of California, Irvine
Sebastian Gehrmann – Google Research
Michael Goodale – Ecole Normale Superieure, Department of Cognitive Studies
Loïc Grobol – École Normale Supérieure

Prachi Gupta – New York University Tandon School of Engineering
David Harwath – The University of Texas at Austin
Peter Hase – University of North Carolina at Chapel Hill
Simon Hegelich – TUM
John Hewitt – Stanford University
Dewei Hu – University of Copenhagen
Cassandra L. Jacobs – University of Wisconsin, Madison
Alon Jacovi – Bar Ilan University
Robin Jia – Facebook AI Research
Zhiying Jiang – University of Waterloo
Richard Johansson – University of Gothenburg
Jaap Jumelet – University of Amsterdam
Lis Kanashiro Pereira – Ochanomizu University
Eugene Kharitonov – Facebook AI
Germán Kruszewski – Naver Labs Europe
Kunal Kukreja – University of Washington
Jenny Kunz – Linköping University
Shalom Lappin – King's College London
Alessandro Lenci – University of Pisa
Minghan Li – University of Waterloo
Sheng Liang – Center for Information and Language Processing, LMU Munich
Jindřich Libovický – Ludwig Maximilian University of Munich
Tomasz Limisiewicz – Charles University in Prague
Nelson F. Liu – Stanford University
David Mareček – Charles University
R. Thomas McCoy – Johns Hopkins University
Houman Mehrafarin – Iran University of Science and Technology
Koji Mineshima – Keio University
Saliha Muradoglu – The Australian National University
Anmol Nayak – ARiSE Labs at Bosch
Joakim Nivre – Uppsala University
Bhargavi Paranjape – University of Washington
Siddharth Patwardhan – Apple
Paolo Pedinotti – University of Pisa
Frithjof Petrick – RWTH Aachen University
Karl Pichotta – Memorial Sloan Kettering Cancer Center
Aman Priyanshu – Manipal Institute of Technology
Sara Rajaee – Iran University of Science and Technology
Abhilasha Ravichander – Carnegie Mellon University
Rudolf Rosa – Charles University, Faculty of Mathematics and Physics, Institute of Formal and Applied Linguistics
Jan Rosendahl – RWTH Aachen University
Swarnadeep Saha – University of North Carolina at Chapel Hill
Wojciech Samek – Fraunhofer Heinrich Hertz Institute
Hendrik Schuff – Bosch Center for Artificial Intelligence
Robert Schwarzenberg – German Research Center For Artificial Intelligence (DFKI)
Djamé Seddah – Inria
Rico Sennrich – University of Zurich
Mattia Setzu – University of Pisa
Tatiana Shavrina – Sberbank, Sberdevices, HSE University
Sanchit Sinha – University of Virginia

Pia Sommerauer – Vrije Universiteit Amsterdam
Vinitra Swamy – EPFL
Aarne Talman – University of Helsinki
Arka Talukdar – New York University
shimin tao – huawei
Jörg Tiedemann – University of Helsinki
Ivan Titov – University of Edinburgh / University of Amsterdam
Jithendra Vepa – Observe AI
Sarah Wiegreffe – Georgia Institute of Technology
Adina Williams – Facebook, Inc.
Hao Yang – Huawei Co. Ltd
Naoki Yoshinaga – Institute of Industrial Science, the University of Tokyo
Fabio Massimo Zanzotto – University of Rome Tor Vergata
Sheng Zhang – North Carolina State University
Yichu Zhou – University of Utah

Invited Speakers:

Sara Hooker, Google Brain
Ana Marasović, Allen AI
Willem Zuidema, University of Amsterdam

Table of Contents

Conference Program

Thursday, November 11, 2021

Virtual Programme

2:00–2:15	***Opening Remarks***
2:15–3:00	*Invited Talk by Jelle Zuidema & Q&A*
3:15–4:00	*Oral Session 1*
4:30–6:00	*Poster Session 1*
6:15–7:00	*Oral Session 2*
7:30–8:00	*Invited Talk by Ana Marasović*
8:00–8:30	*Invited Talk by Sara Hooker*
8:30–8:45	***Closing***

Thursday, November 11, 2021 (continued)

Hybrid Programme

9:00–9:15 ***Opening Remarks & Best Paper Award***

9:15–10:00 *Invited Talk by Jelle Zuidema & Q&A*

10:00–10:30 *Oral Session 3*

11:00–12:00 *Poster Session 2*

13:00–13:45 *Invited Talk by Sara Hooker & Q&A*

13:45–14:15 *Oral Session 4*

14:45–16:15 *Poster Session 3*

16:45–17:15 *Oral Session 5*

17:15–18:00 *Invited Talk by Ana Marasović & Q&A*

18:00–18:15 ***Closing***

Oral Sessions

To what extent do human explanations of model behavior align with actual model behavior?
Grusha Prasad, Yixin Nie, Mohit Bansal, Robin Jia, Douwe Kiela and Adina Williams

Test Harder than You Train: Probing with Extrapolation Splits
Jenny Kunz and Marco Kuhlmann

Does External Knowledge Help Explainable Natural Language Inference? Automatic Evaluation vs. Human Ratings
Hendrik Schuff, Hsiu-Yu Yang, Heike Adel and Ngoc Thang Vu

The Language Model Understood the Prompt was Ambiguous: Probing Syntactic Uncertainty Through Generation
Laura Aina and Tal Linzen

On the Limits of Minimal Pairs in Contrastive Evaluation
Jannis Vamvas and Rico Sennrich

What Models Know About Their Attackers: Deriving Attacker Information From Latent Representations
Zhouhang Xie, Jonathan Brophy, Adam Noack, Wencong You, Kalyani Asthana, Carter Perkins, Sabrina Reis, Zayd Hammoudeh, Daniel Lowd and Sameer Singh

Poster Sessions

ALL Dolphins Are Intelligent and SOME Are Friendly: Probing BERT for Nouns' Semantic Properties and their Prototypicality
Marianna Apidianaki and Aina Garí Soler

ProSPer: Probing Human and Neural Network Language Model Understanding of Spatial Perspective
Tessa Masis and Carolyn Anderson

Can Transformers Jump Around Right in Natural Language? Assessing Performance Transfer from SCAN
Rahma Chaabouni, Roberto Dessì and Eugene Kharitonov

Transferring Knowledge from Vision to Language: How to Achieve it and how to Measure it?
Tobias Norlund, Lovisa Hagström and Richard Johansson

Thursday, November 11, 2021 (continued)

Discrete representations in neural models of spoken language
Bertrand Higy, Lieke Gelderloos, Afra Alishahi and Grzegorz Chrupała

Word Equations: Inherently Interpretable Sparse Word Embeddings through Sparse Coding
Adly Templeton

A howling success or a working sea? Testing what BERT knows about metaphors
Paolo Pedinotti, Eliana Di Palma, Ludovica Cerini and Alessandro Lenci

How Length Prediction Influence the Performance of Non-Autoregressive Translation?
Minghan Wang, GUO Jiaxin, Yuxia Wang, Yimeng Chen, Su Chang, Hengchao Shang, Min Zhang, Shimin Tao and Hao Yang

On the Language-specificity of Multilingual BERT and the Impact of Fine-tuning
Marc Tanti, Lonneke van der Plas, Claudia Borg and Albert Gatt

Relating Neural Text Degeneration to Exposure Bias
Ting-Rui Chiang and Yun-Nung Chen

Efficient Explanations from Empirical Explainers
Robert Schwarzenberg, Nils Feldhus and Sebastian Möller

Variation and generality in encoding of syntactic anomaly information in sentence embeddings
Qinxuan Wu and Allyson Ettinger

Enhancing Interpretable Clauses Semantically using Pretrained Word Representation
Rohan Kumar Yadav, Lei Jiao, Ole-Christoffer Granmo and Morten Goodwin

Analyzing BERT's Knowledge of Hypernymy via Prompting
Michael Hanna and David Mareček

An in-depth look at Euclidean disk embeddings for structure preserving parsing
Federico Fancellu, Lan Xiao, Allan Jepson and Afsaneh Fazly

Training Dynamic based data filtering may not work for NLP datasets
Arka Talukdar, Monika Dagar, Prachi Gupta and Varun Menon

Multi-Layer Random Perturbation Training for improving Model Generalization Efficiently
Lis Kanashiro Pereira, Yuki Taya and Ichiro Kobayashi

Screening Gender Transfer in Neural Machine Translation
Guillaume Wisniewski, Lichao Zhu, Nicolas Bailler and François Yvon

What BERT Based Language Model Learns in Spoken Transcripts: An Empirical Study
Ayush Kumar, Mukuntha Narayanan Sundararaman and Jithendra Vepa

Assessing the Generalization Capacity of Pre-trained Language Models through Japanese Adversarial Natural Language Inference
Hitomi Yanaka and Koji Mineshima

Investigating Negation in Pre-trained Vision-and-language Models
Radina Dobreva and Frank Keller

Not all parameters are born equal: Attention is mostly what you need
Nikolay Bogoychev

Not All Models Localize Linguistic Knowledge in the Same Place: A Layer-wise Probing on BERToids' Representations
Mohsen Fayyaz, Ehsan Aghazadeh, Ali Modarressi, Hosein Mohebbi and Mohammad Taher Pilehvar

Learning Mathematical Properties of Integers
Maria Ryskina and Kevin Knight

Probing Language Models for Understanding of Temporal Expressions
Shivin Thukral, Kunal Kukreja and Christian Kavouras

How Familiar Does That Sound? Cross-Lingual Representational Similarity Analysis of Acoustic Word Embeddings
Badr Abdullah, Iuliia Zaitova, Tania Avgustinova, Bernd Möbius and Dietrich Klakow

Perturbing Inputs for Fragile Interpretations in Deep Natural Language Processing
Sanchit Sinha, Hanjie Chen, Arshdeep Sekhon, Yangfeng Ji and Yanjun Qi

An Investigation of Language Model Interpretability via Sentence Editing
Samuel Stevens and Yu Su

Thursday, November 11, 2021 (continued)

Non-archival papers (posters)

Language Models Use Monotonicity to Assess NPI Licensing – Jaap Jumelet, Milica Denic, Jakub Szymanik, Dieuwke Hupkes and Shane Steinert-Threlkeld

BPE affects Training Data Memorization by Transformer Language Models – Eugene Kharitonov, Marco Baroni and Dieuwke Hupkes

Do contextual language embeddings distinguish between intersective and strictly subsective adjectives? – Michael Goodale and Salvador Mascarenhas

Generalization in neural sequence models: a case study in symbolic mathematics – Sean Welleck, Peter West, Jize Cao and Yejin Choi

Human Evaluation Study for Explaining Knowledge Graph Completion – Timo Sztyler and Carolin Lawrence

Transformers Scan both Left and Right – When they Have a Cue – Jan H. Athmer and Denis Paperno

Explaining NLP Models via Minimal Contrastive Editing (MiCE) – Alexis Ross, Ana Marasović and Matthew Peters

Probing structures in the visual region embeddings from multimodal BERT – Victor Milewski, Miryam de Lhoneux and Marie-Francine Moens

Putting Words in BERT's Mouth: Navigating Contextualized Vector Spaces with Pseudowords – Taelin Karidi, Yichu Zhou, Nathan Schneider, Omri Abend and Vivek Srikumar

On Neurons Invariant to Sentence Structural Changes in Neural Machine Translation – Gal Patel, Leshem Choshen and Omri Abend

Explaining Classes through Word Attributions – Samuel Rönnqvist, Amanda Myntti, Aki-Juhani Kyröläinen, Sampo Pyysalo, Veronika Laippala and Filip Ginter

Testing the linguistics of transformer generalizations – Saliha Muradoglu and Mans Hulden

To what extent do human explanations of model behavior align with actual model behavior?

Grusha Prasad[†]*, **Yixin Nie**[‡], **Mohit Bansal**[‡], **Robin Jia**[⋆], **Douwe Kiela**[⋆], **Adina Williams**[⋆]

[†] Johns Hopkins University; [‡] UNC Chapel Hill; [⋆] Facebook AI Research

grusha.prasad@jhu.edu, adinawilliams@fb.com

Abstract

Given the increasingly prominent role NLP models (will) play in our lives, it is important for human expectations of model behavior to align with actual model behavior. Using Natural Language Inference (NLI) as a case study, we investigate the extent to which human-generated explanations of models' inference decisions align with how models actually make these decisions. More specifically, we define three alignment metrics that quantify how well natural language explanations align with model sensitivity to input words, as measured by integrated gradients. Then, we evaluate eight different models (the base and large versions of BERT, RoBERTa and ELECTRA, as well as an RNN and bag-of-words model), and find that the BERT-base model has the highest alignment with human-generated explanations, for all alignment metrics. Focusing in on transformers, we find that the base versions tend to have higher alignment with human-generated explanations than their larger counterparts, suggesting that increasing the number of model parameters leads, in some cases, to *worse* alignment with human explanations. Finally, we find that a model's alignment with human explanations is not predicted by the model's accuracy, suggesting that accuracy and alignment are complementary ways to evaluate models.

1 Introduction

NLP models often make classification decisions in ways humans don't expect them to. For example, Question Answering (QA) models often choose the correct answer for one example, but fail catastrophically on other very similar examples (Ribeiro et al., 2018; Wallace et al., 2019; Selvaraju et al., 2020), such as answering "Is the rose red?" with no, but then "What color is the rose?"

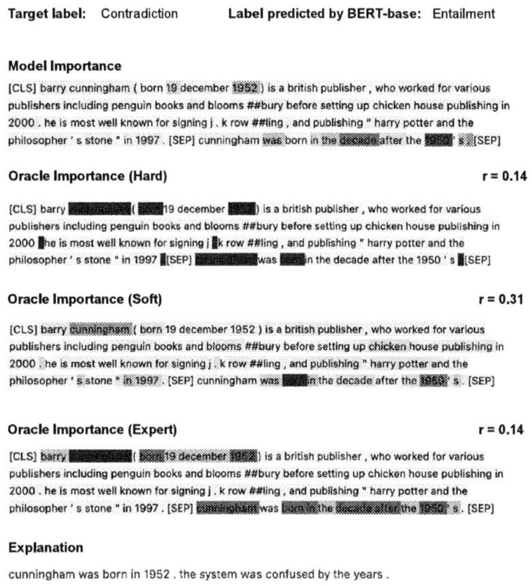

Figure 1: An example illustrating different token-level importance values. "Model Importance" is color coded by absolute value integrated gradients attribution for BERT-base. The other three rows show the oracle importance scores estimated by the hard, soft and expert oracles (darker values indicate more important).

with "red" (Ribeiro et al., 2019). VQA models often attend to different portions of images than humans do (Das et al., 2016). NLI models often rely on shallow heuristics, their predictions are inappropriately affected by particular words, and they sometimes perform unexpectedly well from only looking at the hypothesis (Gururangan et al., 2018; Poliak et al., 2018; Tsuchiya, 2018). Since people generally do not expect models to base decisions on spurious correlations in the data (cf. McCoy et al. 2019), models that make decisions in alignment with human expectations are less likely to make the right decisions for the wrong reasons.

In this paper, we measure how well model decisions are aligned with human expectations

*The work was conducted during an internship at Facebook AI Research.

Proceedings of the Fourth BlackboxNLP Workshop on Analyzing and Interpreting Neural Networks for NLP, pages 1–14
Online, November 11, 2021.

about those decisions. Building on work that aims to extract or generate interpretable or faithful descriptions of model behavior (Lipton, 2018; Rajani et al., 2019; Kalouli et al., 2020; Silva et al., 2020; Jacovi and Goldberg, 2020; Zhao and Vydiswaran, 2020), we use human-generated natural language explanations to determine which portions of the input people expected to be *important* in influencing models' decisions. We then use Integrated Gradients (IG, Sundararajan et al. 2017) to determine which portions actually influenced the models' decisions. We term the alignment between them as **Importance Alignment**. We formulate three different methods of using human-generated natural language explanations to quantify human expectations of model behavior, resulting in three different methods for calculating importance alignment.

As a case study, we applied our method to the Natural Language Inference task (Dagan et al., 2006; Bowman et al., 2015; Williams et al., 2018) in which models are tasked with classifying pairs of sentences according to whether the first sentence entails, contradicts, or is neutral with respect to the second. Concretely, we measured the extent to which the inference decisions of eight models (six state-of-the-art transformers, an LSTM model and a bag-of-words model) aligned with human-generated explanations from the Adversarial NLI dataset (ANLI, Nie et al. 2020).

In all three methods for calculating Importance Alignment, BERT-base had the highest importance alignment score. We also found that the smaller, 'base' versions of transformers tended to have higher importance alignment scores than the corresponding large versions. However, being smaller doesn't always result in higher importance alignment, since both small non-transformer models had lower importance alignment scores than 'base' transformers. Finally, we demonstrate that more accurate models (both for classic test accuracy and on the diagnostic dataset HANS; McCoy et al. 2019) do not necessarily have higher importance alignment, suggesting that accuracy and alignment with human expectations are orthogonal dimensions along which models should be evaluated.

2 Related Work

The term "alignment" has been used in several different contexts in AI: alignment of model behaviour with normative notions of human ethics ("value alignment"; Russell et al. 2015; Peng et al. 2020), alignment between tokens from source to target in machine translation, alignment between images and text in image-caption alignment models, etc. In this paper, we propose a new type of alignment, Importance Alignment: we want models to not only generate accurate outputs, but also to generate these accurate outputs for reasons that align with human expectations.

High importance alignment can be valuable because prior work has demonstrated that when people form correct mental models of AI decision boundaries, they make better AI-assisted decisions (Bansal et al., 2019a,b). For example, when annotators are provided with additional information about model decisions, such as model accuracy (cf. Yin et al. 2019) or model-generated explanations (Bansal et al., 2020b), it increases their level of trust and in some settings, can actually improve AI-assisted decision making (Zhang et al., 2020). Therefore, optimizing models to have high importance alignment is a worthy goal, even if it can initially result in models with lower accuracy. In the words of Bansal et al. (2020a), "predictable performance is worth a slight sacrifice in AI accuracy," especially on tasks with potentially serious social implications.

3 Measuring Importance Alignment

We assume that for some input example $x = \{x_1, x_2...x_n\}$ with n tokens and a gold label y, there exists an annotator-generated explanation of why the gold label is correct and/or why a model might output an incorrect prediction. We convert this natural language explanation into an **oracle importance score** ($\mathbb{I}_m^O(x, y)$) which quantifies the extent to which annotators expect each token in x to push the model's prediction towards or away from the gold label.[1] Then, to compute Importance Alignment we correlate the oracle importance score for x with the **model importance** ($\mathbb{I}_m(x, y)$), which quantifies the extent to which each token in x actually pushes the model's prediction towards or away from the gold label. A greater correlation between model and oracle importance scores indicates a greater alignment between how annotators expect models

[1] We refer to this as an "oracle", because we consider importance scores derived from human-generated explanations to be the ground truth.

to make decisions and how these models actually make decisions. In the remainder of this section we describe our methods to calculate oracle and model importance scores as well as the importance alignment metric from correlating these two scores.

3.1 Computing model importance scores

We compute model importance scores using *Integrated Gradients* (IG; Sundararajan et al. 2017). Concretely, we define model importance ($\mathbb{I}$) for some model m and some example x (e.g., the concatenation of the premise and hypothesis for NLI) with the gold label y, as follows,

$$\mathbb{I}_m(x, y) = |IG_m(x, y)| \quad (1)$$

where IG_m returns a vector of IG attribution scores with respect to the gold label for each token in x and $|\cdot|$ denotes component-wise absolute value.

For some token in the input x_i, a positive IG attribution score indicates that x_i pushed the model's prediction towards the gold label, whereas a negative IG attribution score indicates that x_i pushed the model's prediction away from the gold label. In a model with high importance alignment, we would expect positive attribution scores to be correlated with annotator expectations about why the gold label is correct, and negative attribution scores to be correlated with annotator expectations about why a model might output an incorrect prediction. In this paper, we are considering explanations which capture both of these annotator expectations without differentiating between them. Therefore, we use the absolute value of the IG attribution score.

Why Integrated Gradients? We use Integrated Gradients because they are axiomatically both interpretable and faithful (Sundararajan et al., 2017), unlike attention based methods which have been argued are not faithful explanations of models' decision making processes (Jain and Wallace 2019, but see Wiegreffe and Pinter 2019 for a counterpoint). Other perturbation methods which are more faithful than attention such as LIME (Ribeiro et al., 2016), SHAP (Lundberg and Lee, 2017), and their variants can be used, although these methods have been argued to be unreliable (Camburu et al., 2019; Slack et al., 2020; Camburu et al., 2021). No current consensus exists on which methods should be employed (Hase and Bansal, 2020; Ghorbani et al., 2019). Although we use IG, crucially, our method is not dependent on it; IG can be replaced with any method that can faithfully assign an importance score to each token in the input.

3.2 Computing oracle importance scores

We describe three methods of converting natural language explanations into oracle importance scores: hard oracle, soft oracle and expert oracle.

Hard oracle importance. Hard oracle importance is a binary measure of token overlap between the input and the explanation. This measure captures the intuition that if annotators thought that specific tokens in the input are important for pushing the model towards or away from the gold label, then they will use those words in their explanation. Formally, for some input x with gold label y and explanation e, we define hard oracle importance as follows, where the overlap function yields a binary vector in which the i-th component is valued 1 if $x_i \in e$ and x_i is not a stop word;[2] the i-th component of the vector is valued 0 otherwise.

$$\mathbb{I}^H_m(x, y, e) = overlap(x_m, e) \quad (2)$$

This measure is model specific only to the extent that the models differ in how they tokenize the input x; we assume that the annotator generated explanations themselves do not describe expectations about specific models.

Soft oracle importance. The hard oracle is very simple and does not capture synonyms, entities referred to with pronouns, paraphrases, etc. To overcome these shortcomings, we also define soft oracle importance where we compute importance scores from IG of explanation-informed models. The input for these explanation-informed models is the original input x concatenated with some explanation e. The task of the model is to predict not only the gold label for the original task y, but also a binary output indicating whether e was an explanation about the current example or about some other example. This task requires the model to perform not only the target task (e.g., NLI) but also requires the model to establish a relationship between the provided explanation and the input, thereby incorporating information from the natural language explanation.

[2]We used the list of stop words from NLTK (Bird et al., 2009)

Formally, for some input x with gold label y and explanation e, we define soft oracle importance as,

$$\mathbb{I}_m^S(x, y, e) = |IG_{m'}(x, e, y')| \tag{3}$$

where m' refers to the explanation-informed model and y' refers to the target output of m' which incorporates both y and a binary output indicating whether e is a matched explanation (e.g., for NLI, y' would have six possible values). This measure is also model specific both because of tokenization and because the explanation-informed model has the same model architecture as the target model.

Expert oracle importance. The hard and soft oracles are automatic ways of computing oracle importance scores. To validate these automatic measures, we also computed oracle importance scores from experts (three of the authors on this paper). Given the input, gold label, and annotator generated explanation for a given example, the expert annotators ($N = 3$) indicated which tokens of the input they believed that the original annotator (i.e., the one who generated the explanation) thought were important for the model's prediction. Since generating expert annotations was very time consuming, we computed this measure only for a random subset of 60 examples.

Formally, for some input x with gold label y and explanation e, we define expert oracle importance for any given token as the proportion of expert annotators who indicated that the token was important according to the annotator who generated the explanation. This is expressed as,

$$\mathbb{I}_m^E(x, y, e) = \frac{1}{N}\sum_k^N expert_k(x_m, e, y) \tag{4}$$

where $expert_k$ returns a binary vector in which the i-th element is valued 1 if annotator k indicated that the i-th token was important, and 0 otherwise.

Like with hard oracle importance, this measure is model specific only to the extent that the models differ in how they tokenize the input x.

We could not compute oracle importance scores from the original annotators and had to rely on expert annotators because this information was absent from the dataset of natural language explanations we used. Additionally, we argue below that collecting high-quality oracle importance annotations from naïve annotators can be very tricky.

Why start from human-generated natural language explanations? We convert natural language explanations to oracle importance scores instead of collecting oracle importance scores directly from naïve annotators for two reasons. First, there already exist data sets of natural language explanations, where annotators were required to reason about models' decision making in an adversarial setting (Nie et al., 2020), and more such data sets are being generated (Kiela et al., 2021). Second, we contend that for most non-expert annotators, asking them to provide verbal descriptions is easier and more natural than asking them to answer a question like, "For which words do you think the model's prediction would change the most if that word was blanked out?". In fact, to pursue this angle assiduously, one would ideally recruit annotators who know what IG is and ask them to predict IG scores—after all, since we are using IG scores to quantify how the models make decisions, the best way to quantify "how humans think models make decisions" would be to measure what humans think the IG scores will be. Unfortunately, such a task would be challenging for most non-expert annotators, making it infeasible to collect high quality annotations.

3.3 Importance Alignment Metric

For each example with input x, gold label y and explanation e, we compute importance alignment for some model m as the mean Fisher-transformed product-moment (i.e., Pearson's) correlation (r) between the model importance and oracle importance scores for that example as below, where the oracle O is either the hard (H), soft (S) or expert (E) oracles:

$$C_m(x, y) = \text{arctanh}(r(\mathbb{I}_m(x, y), \mathbb{I}_m^O(x, y, e))) \tag{5}$$

We Fisher-transform the correlation coefficient r to ensure that $C_m(x, y)$ is unbiased and does not violate normality assumptions required for the statistical analyses we use (Fisher, 1921).[3]

For each example, we also compute a random baseline for $C_m(x, y)$ where the oracle

[3]Fisher transformed correlation coefficients are approximately normally distributed when the correlation coefficients are calculated from sample pairs drawn from bivariate normal distributions. Although $\mathbb{I}_m(x, y)$ and $\mathbb{I}_m^O(x, y, e))$ are not normally distributed, visual examination of the resulting fisher transformed correlations revealed that $C_m(x, y)$ were in fact approximately normal.

importances are calculated by pairing the input with an explanation (e_R) which was written for a different input example and was chosen at random:

$$C_{m_R}(x, y) = \text{arctanh}(r(\mathbb{I}_m(x, y), \mathbb{I}^O_m(x, y, e_R))) \quad (6)$$

We compute this measure to control for spurious patterns that can drive the correlation between model and oracle importances: we can find a non-zero correlation between the importance scores if a certain model m, such as BERT, (explanation informed or not) always assigned high IG attribution values to tokens at specific indices; we can also find a non-zero correlation if certain tokens (e.g., "the") received high attribution irrespective of the context, and these tokens occurred frequently in the input and explanation.

To measure the extent to which model and oracle importances are correlated with each other over and above spurious correlations, we measure the mean difference ($\Delta\mathcal{A}$) between $C_m(x, y)$ and $C_{m_R}(x, y)$ for all examples in some dataset D and back-transform it to the correlation scale:

$$\Delta\mathcal{A} = \tanh\left(\frac{1}{\mid D \mid}\sum_{(x,y)\in D} C_m(x, y) - C_{m_R}(x, y)\right) \quad (7)$$

To measure whether $\Delta\mathcal{A}$ is significantly greater than 0, we use paired t-test between $C_m(x, y)$ and $C_{m_R}(x, y)$ for all examples in D. We compute a different measure of $\Delta\mathcal{A}$ for each oracle importance score.

4 Experimental details

4.1 Models

Target models. We measured the importance alignment for six pretrained Transformer language models: BERT base and large (Devlin et al., 2019); RoBERTa base and large (Liu et al., 2019); and ELECTRA base and large (Clark et al., 2020). We fine-tuned these models on the combination of the following NLI datasets: SNLI (Bowman et al., 2015), MultiNLI (Williams et al., 2018), NLI-recast FEVER (Thorne et al., 2019) and ANLI rounds 1–3 (Nie et al., 2020). We used the hyperparameters in the ANLI codebase for fine-tuning.[4]

We used the same datasets to also train two non-transformer models: a bag-of-words (BOW) model and a RNN based model we call **BInferSent** for 'BERT-InferSent'. The BOW model has a single max pooling layer on top of BERT token embeddings. The BInferSent model combines the InferSent architecture of Conneau et al. (2017) with Short-Stacked Sentence Encoders of Nie and Bansal (2017), using 3 layers of BiLSTMs (Hochreiter and Schmidhuber, 1997) with residual connections on top of BERT token embeddings.

	Target models	Explanation informed models
BERT-Base	48.02	44.85
RoBERTa-Base	50.47	60.93
ELECTRA-Base	52.33	51.93
BERT-Large	49.24	49.01
RoBERTa-Large	55.37	74.21
ELECTRA-Large	58.06	74.93
BInferSent	40.00	20.97
BOW	35.82	18.70

Table 1: Accuracy on the development partition of the ANLI dataset for target models (finetuned on MNLI + SNLI + ANLI + re-cast FEVER) and models used as the soft oracle (finetuned on 6-way NLI and reason classification on a subset of ANLI).

Explanation informed models. To compute soft oracle importance, we trained explanation informed models for each target model architecture on a six-way classification task. We trained three models per architecture using different random seeds. In this task, the input to the model was a context-hypothesis pair concatenated with an annotator-generated explanation. The output of the model was a joint label indicating whether the context entails, contradicts or is neutral with respect to the hypothesis, and whether the explanation matches the context-hypothesis pair.

We generated the training ($n = 19043$) and development ($n = 2116$) datasets for these classifiers by subsetting the portion of the ANLI training set for which an explanation was provided — i.e., the examples in the training set in which the ANLI annotators had successfully fooled the model. We presented each of the 19043 examples twice when training the explanation informed models: once with a matched explanation (i.e., the original one written by the annotator for that explanation) and once with a randomly selected explanation (see §3.3 above). We trained all models for two epochs.

The accuracy of these explanation informed models either matched or surpassed that of the target model despite being trained on only a

[4]https://github.com/facebookresearch/anli/blob/master/script/example_scripts/

Model	Importance Alignment		Acc.
	$\Delta\mathcal{A}^H$	$\Delta\mathcal{A}^S$	ANLI
BERT-Base	0.21^{***}	0.11^{***}	48.02
RoBERTa-Base	0.11^{***}	0.02^{*}	50.47
ELECTRA-Base	0.17^{***}	0.06^{***}	52.33
BERT-Large	0.18^{***}	-0.02	49.24
RoBERTa-Large	0.04^{*}	0.01	55.37
ELECTRA-Large	0.07	0.01	58.06
All Base Trans.	0.17	0.07	50.27
All Large Trans.	0.11	-0.003	54.56
BInferSent	0.12^{***}	<0.01	40.00
BOW	0.01^{***}	0.01^{***}	35.82

Table 2: Importance Alignment between model importance scores and oracle importance scores (both $\mathcal{A}^H$ and $\mathcal{A}^S$ metrics) across 5 random seeds on the ANLI dataset. **$\Delta\mathcal{A}$ was computed over the examples that the models got wrong**. Average model accuracy across seeds and different rounds of ANLI is also provided. '*'s indicate whether $\Delta\mathcal{A}$ is significantly greater than 0. '***' indicates $p < 0.001$, '**' indicates $p < 0.01$ and '*' indicates $p < 0.05$.

Model	Importance Alignment		
	$\Delta\mathcal{A}^H$	$\Delta\mathcal{A}^S$	$\Delta\mathcal{A}^E$
BERT-Base	0.21^{***}	0.14^{***}	0.39^{***}
RoBERTa-Base	0.10^{***}	0.04^{***}	0.31^{***}
ELECTRA-Base	0.15^{***}	0.09^{***}	0.33^{***}
BERT-Large	0.15^{***}	-0.03	0.27^{***}
RoBERTa-Large	0.02	-0.01	0.21^{***}
ELECTRA-Large	0.08	0.02	0.20^{*}
All Base Trans.	0.16	0.09	0.34
All Large Trans.	0.09	-0.01	0.23
BInferSent	0.14^{***}	-0.003^{***}	0.29^{***}
BOW	0.02	0.03	0.04

Table 3: Importance Alignment between model importance scores and oracle importance scores ($\mathcal{A}^H$, $\mathcal{A}^S$ and $\mathcal{A}^E$ metrics) across 5 random seeds on the ANLI dataset. **$\Delta\mathcal{A}$ was computed over the 60 examples with expert annotations.** '*'s indicate whether $\Delta\mathcal{A}$ is significantly greater than 0. '***' indicates $p < 0.001$, '**' indicates $p < 0.01$ and '*' indicates $p < 0.05$.

small subset of the original data (see Table 1). This suggests that these models did learn to incorporate information about explanations, and that the information present in the explanations was useful for NLI.

4.2 Evaluation Datasets

ANLI. We measured importance alignment on the development set of the ANLI dataset. In this dataset, annotators were given a context and a label and were asked to write a hypothesis that fooled a target model; if the model was fooled, annotators explained in natural language why the provided label was correct and why they thought model was fooled into generating an incorrect prediction. While other datasets with natural language explanations for NLI exist, (e.g., e-SNLI; Camburu et al. 2018), the explanations in these datasets only address why the gold label is correct, and not why the annotators thought the model generated an incorrect prediction. Additionally, the adversarial setting in which ANLI was collected encourages the annotators to reason about models' decision making. These two factors make ANLI more suitable for our purposes than other explanation datasets.

Since annotators provided explanations only when the model generated an incorrect prediction, to allow for an apples-to-apples comparison, we only compute importance alignment for examples in which our target models generate an incorrect prediction. As a consequence, the specific examples used to measure importance alignment differs across models: different models fail on different examples. To ensure that our results are not driven by the differences between examples, we repeated our analyses on a subset of examples that all models failed on, and we found that our results were nearly identical (compare Table 2 and Table 3).

We collected expert annotations (see §3.1) on 60 randomly sampled examples from the set of examples that all the models failed on, 20 from each round of ANLI. We computed the expert importance alignment score ($\mathcal{A}^E$) for this subset of examples and repeated our analyses.

HANS. We measured the extent to which importance alignment scores correlated with accuracy on the HANS diagnostic dataset (McCoy et al., 2019). This dataset measures the extent to which NLI models rely on non-human like heuristics when performing inference, such as inferring that the context entails the hypothesis if all of the words in the hypotheses are in the context: models which do not rely on these non-human like heuristics have higher accuracy on the this dataset. If we assume that naïve annotators in general do not expect NLI models to rely on such heuristics, then we might expect models with high importance alignment (i.e., models which make inference decisions in ways annotators expect them to) to also have high accuracy on the HANS dataset.

5 Results

In Table 2, we report the importance alignment scores for the hard and soft oracles computed over all the examples the models generated an incorrect prediction for, averaged across the five random seeds. In Table 3, we report the importance alignment scores for hard, soft and expert oracles computed over the subset of 60 examples with expert annotations. Since the importance alignment scores for the hard and soft oracles are nearly identical across both tables, we focus our discussion of the results from the subset of examples with expert annotations.We repeated the reported analyses with hard and soft oracles on all the examples, and found qualitatively similar results (see Appendix A).

Effect of model size on Importance Alignment. Across all three types of Importance Alignment scores ($\mathcal{A}^H$, $\mathcal{A}^S$ and $\mathcal{A}^E$) the base versions of the transformer models had higher importance alignment than their larger counterparts, with BERT-base having the highest importance alignment. To test the statistical significance of this this observation, we fit three linear mixed effect regression models: one for each type of oracle.

We predicted the pair-wise difference between $C_m(x, y)$ and $C_{m_R}(x, y)$ (see Equation 5 and Equation 6) as a function of the following predictors: model size (base vs. large), model type (BERT vs. ELECTRA and BERT vs. RoBERTa) and the interaction between the two. We included model type and its interaction with model size as predictors to measure the effect of model size over and above the differences between specific models. We also included a random intercept and random slope of model size for every example to incorporate the following assumptions: first, the difference $C_m(x, y)$ and $C_{m_R}(x, y)$ can differ for every example; second, the difference between base and large models can also differ for every example. The results described below were significant at a threshold of $p < 0.005$ unless specified otherwise. For further details see Appendix A.

The analyses indicated that across all measures importance alignment, $\Delta\mathcal{A}$ was significantly greater for the base models when compared to their larger counterparts. Additionally, $\Delta\mathcal{A}$ was significantly greater in BERT models than in RoBERTa and ELECTRA models (base and large).

Although the results suggest that smaller models have stronger importance alignment than their larger counterparts, our experiments with the BInfersent and BOW models suggest that smaller models do not always have higher importance alignment: the importance alignment for both these models is lower than the alignment for BERT-base model (the smallest of the transformer models when taking into consideration both the number of parameters and pre-training size).

To test the statistical significance of this numerical result, we fit another set of linear mixed effects model where we predicted the pair-wise difference between $C_m(x, y)$ and $C_{m_R}(x, y)$ as a function of model type (BERT-base vs. BInferSent and BERT-base vs. BOW). We also included a random intercept of item. As expected, the importance alignment for the BERT-base model was significantly greater than that for the BInferSent and BOW models for all the measures.

ANLI accuracy and Importance Alignment. Based on the results from Table 2 and Table 3, we wondered whether importance alignment might be negatively correlated with NLI accuracy: the base versions of the models which have higher importance alignment have lower accuracy on ANLI compared to their larger counterparts. To test this, we computed a separate value of $\mathcal{A}^H$, $\mathcal{A}^S$ and $\mathcal{A}^E$ for each random seed of the target model and for each round of ANLI. Then, we computed the product moment (i.e., Pearson's) correlation between model accuracy on NLI and $\mathcal{A}^H$, $\mathcal{A}^S$ and $\mathcal{A}^E$. We found a significant correlation between accuracy and $\mathcal{A}^E$ ($r = 0.42; p = 0.008$). However, this correlation was being driven entirely by the BOW models, which had both low accuracy and low importance alignment scores. When repeating the analysis with the BOW models excluded, we found that none of the measures of importance alignment were significantly correlated with NLI accuracy ($\mathcal{A}^H$: $r = -0.09$ and $p = 0.61$; $\mathcal{A}^S$: $r = 0.04$ and $p = 0.80$; $\mathcal{A}^E$ $r = -0.04$ and $p = 0.83$; see Figure 2a). We repeated the analyses for $\mathcal{A}^H$ and $\mathcal{A}^S$ for all wrong examples and found that only $\mathcal{A}^H$ was significantly correlated with accuracy ($r = 0.39, p = 0.01$; see Appendix A.2)

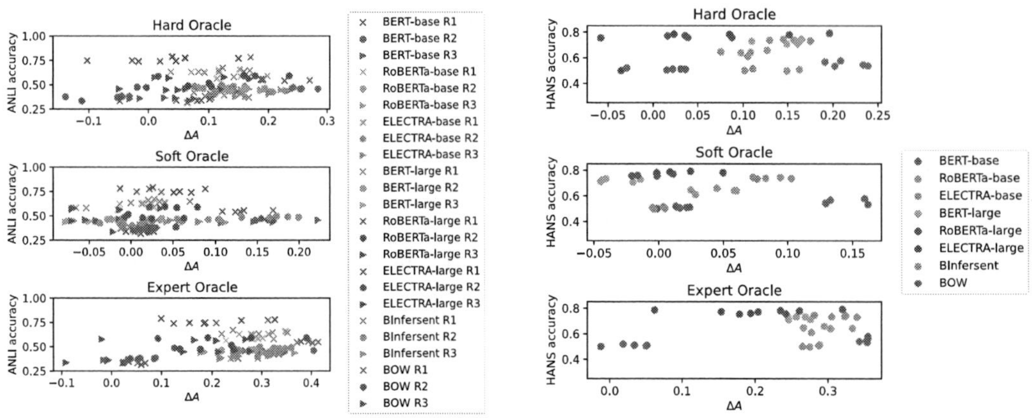

(a) Accuracy on ANLI is not correlated with importance alignment ($\mathcal{A}^H$ and $\mathcal{A}^S$). The cross, circle, and triangle refer to rounds 1, 2, and 3 of ANLI, respectively.

(b) Accuracy on HANS is not correlated with importance alignment. Alignment values are averaged across rounds because HANS is not divided into rounds.

HANS accuracy and Importance Alignment. As discussed earlier, we hypothesized that high importance alignment might result in models relying less on non-human-like heuristics, thereby resulting in higher accuracy on the HANS dataset. We found no such correlation, however ($\mathcal{A}^H$: $r = 0.04$ and $p = 0.82$; $\mathcal{A}^S$: $r = -0.21$ and $p = 0.21$; $\mathcal{A}^E$ $r = 0.23$ and $p = 0.17$; see Figure 2b).[5]

This lack of correlation is likely a result of the mismatch between how human-likeness is defined in HANS and in our importance alignment measures. In HANS, the targeted heuristics are simple (i.e., can be articulated with a rule), and describe general principles of how models ought not behave if they are to be human-like. In contrast, our measures of importance alignment are derived from example level explanations of how naïve annotators expected models to behave, and as such are not based on any overarching easy-to-articulate principles. When evaluating whether models make decisions as humans expect them to, jointly considering both these definitions of human-likeness can be useful.

Comparing the Importance Alignment Scores. We used hard and soft oracles to automatically measure oracle importance scores. To validate these methods, we computed the Spearman rank correlation between the importance scores derived from these methods and from the manually annotated expert oracle. The hard oracle was moderately correlated with the expert oracle ($r = 0.24$, $p < 0.0001$), whereas the soft oracle was more weakly correlated ($r = 0.14$, $p < 0.0001$). Additionally, the hard and soft oracle importance scores were also weakly correlated with each other ($r = 0.11$, $p < 0.0001$).[6] Taken together, these results suggest that neither the hard nor the soft oracle measures are perfect proxies for expert human importance scores. This imperfection does not impact the conclusions we draw in this paper, however: the results we discussed held true across all the measures.

6 Discussion

In this paper, we argued that it is important to not only evaluate models on how accurate they are on a given task, but also on whether the decisions that the models make align with how humans expect them to make these decisions. We introduced a measure called Importance Alignment which quantifies the extent to which the parts of the input that non-expert annotators expected to influence models' decisions actually influenced the decisions. To quantify which parts of the input influenced model decisions (*model importance*), we used Integrated Gradients. To quantify annotator expectations (*oracle importance*), we proposed three methods of quantifying annotator generated natural language explanations of model behaviour: two automatic and one that relied on expert input.

As a case study, we applied this method to measure Importance Alignment in eight NLI models (six transformers, an LSTM and a BOW model), using annotator generated explanations from the ANLI dataset. We found that, across

[5]When we considered the heuristics separately, we found some marginally significant correlations (see Appendix A.2)

[6]The results are comparable with Pearson's correlation.

all three measures of importance alignment, the base versions of the transformer models had significantly higher importance alignment than their larger counterparts, with BERT-base having the highest importance alignment. Smaller models do not always result in higher importance alignment, however: the BERT-base model had higher alignment than the LSTM and BOW models. Additionally, importance alignment scores were not correlated with model accuracy on ANLI or the HANS diagnostic dataset in most cases. This suggests that importance alignment and accuracy are complementary methods of evaluating models.

Future work. There are at least four directions in which this work can be extended. First, future work can evaluate whether our conclusions about model size in NLI models generalizes to smaller transformer models (Turc et al., 2019; Warstadt et al., 2020) and to models trained on other NLP tasks.

Second, future work can build on our methods of calculating model and oracle importance. The two methods of automatically computing oracle importance we proposed as a starting point were only moderately correlated with the method that relies of expert input. Future work can develop better methods of measuring oracle importance incorporating the strengths of both. Future work can also explore other existing ways of calculating model importance (e.g., LIME, SHAP and their variants).

Third, future work can generate more detailed datasets of natural language explanations of model behaviour. For example, in the dataset we used, the explanations the annotators provided were an amalgamation of both why the the label was correct and why the model might have been fooled. Additionally, annotators generated explanations only when the model generated an incorrect output. By disentangling these two types of explanations and collecting explanations for when models generate correct outputs future work can separately study whether models succeed and fail in ways people expect them to. Similarly in the dataset we used, each context-hypothesis-label triplet was associated with only one annotator generated explanation. However, it is possible that there are several explanations of model behaviour that are equally valid. Collecting more explanations per triplet can improve our understanding of how people expect models to succeed and fail.

Fourth, future work could explore which factors drive higher importance alignment. For example, we observed that transformer models with fewer parameters had higher importance alignment than models with more parameters. Does this finding apply to non-transformer architectures too? Is there a threshold for model parameters, where this inverse relationship between model size and alignment score breaks down? Additionally, can other factors like model architecture, type of training objective or the types of sentences the models were trained on influence importance alignment? Such exploration can not only result in models better aligned with human expectations, but also improve our understanding of what drives importance alignment.

7 Conclusion

We proposed a novel metric, Importance Alignment, to measure the extent to which human-generated explanations of model decisions align with how models actually make these decisions. As a case study, we used this metric to evaluate eight different models trained on NLI and found that the BERT-base model had the highest alignment with human-generated explanations. We also found that our metric was not correlated with model accuracy, suggesting that accuracy and Importance Alignment are complementary ways of evaluating models.

Acknowledgements

We would like to thank Luke Zettlemoyer, Ana Valeria Gonzalez, the Dynabench team, Roy Schwartz, Oana Maria Camburu, Tom McCoy, and Tal Linzen's Computation and Psycholinguistics lab for their invaluable comments and support.

References

Gagan Bansal, Besmira Nushi, Ece Kamar, Eric Horvitz, and Daniel S Weld. 2020a. Optimizing AI for teamwork. *arXiv preprint arXiv:2004.13102*.

Gagan Bansal, Besmira Nushi, Ece Kamar, Walter S Lasecki, Daniel S Weld, and Eric Horvitz. 2019a. Beyond accuracy: The role of mental models in human-ai team performance. *Proceedings of the AAAI Conference on Human Computation and Crowdsourcing*, 7(1):2–11.

Gagan Bansal, Besmira Nushi, Ece Kamar, Daniel S Weld, Walter S Lasecki, and Eric Horvitz. 2019b. Updates in human-AI teams: Understanding and addressing the performance/compatibility tradeoff. In *Proceedings of the AAAI Conference on Artificial Intelligence*, volume 33, pages 2429–2437.

Gagan Bansal, Tongshuang Wu, Joyce Zhou, Raymond Fok, Besmira Nushi, Ece Kamar, Marco Túlio Ribeiro, and Daniel S. Weld. 2020b. Does the whole exceed its parts? the effect of AI explanations on complementary team performance. *arXiV*, abs/2006.14779.

Steven Bird, Edward Loper, and Ewan Klein. 2009. *Natural Language Processing with Python*. O'Reilly Media Inc.

Samuel R. Bowman, Gabor Angeli, Christopher Potts, and Christopher D. Manning. 2015. A large annotated corpus for learning natural language inference. In *Proceedings of the 2015 Conference on Empirical Methods in Natural Language Processing*, pages 632–642, Lisbon, Portugal. Association for Computational Linguistics.

Oana-Maria Camburu, Eleonora Giunchiglia, Jakob Foerster, Thomas Lukasiewicz, and Phil Blunsom. 2019. Can I trust the explainer? verifying post-hoc explanatory methods. In *NeurIPS 2019 Workshop on Safety and Robustness in Decision Making*, Vancouver, Canada.

Oana-Maria Camburu, Eleonora Giunchiglia, Jakob Foerster, Thomas Lukasiewicz, and Phil Blunsom. 2021. The struggles of feature-based explanations: Shapley values vs. minimal sufficient subsets. In *Proceedings of the Explainable Agency in Artificial Intelligence Workshop at AAAI 2021*.

Oana-Maria Camburu, Tim Rocktäschel, Thomas Lukasiewicz, and Phil Blunsom. 2018. e-SNLI: Natural language inference with natural language explanations. In *Advances in Neural Information Processing Systems*, volume 31, pages 9539–9549. Curran Associates, Inc.

Kevin Clark, Minh-Thang Luong, Quoc V. Le, and Christopher D. Manning. 2020. ELECTRA: pre-training text encoders as discriminators rather than generators. In *8th International Conference on Learning Representations, ICLR 2020, Addis Ababa, Ethiopia, April 26-30, 2020*. OpenReview.net.

Alexis Conneau, Douwe Kiela, Holger Schwenk, Loïc Barrault, and Antoine Bordes. 2017. Supervised learning of universal sentence representations from natural language inference data. In *Proceedings of the 2017 Conference on Empirical Methods in Natural Language Processing*, pages 670–680, Copenhagen, Denmark. Association for Computational Linguistics.

Ido Dagan, Oren Glickman, and Bernardo Magnini. 2006. The PASCAL recognising textual entailment challenge. In *Machine learning challenges. evaluating predictive uncertainty, visual object classification, and recognising tectual entailment*, pages 177–190. Springer.

Abhishek Das, Harsh Agrawal, Larry Zitnick, Devi Parikh, and Dhruv Batra. 2016. Human attention in visual question answering: Do humans and deep networks look at the same regions? In *Proceedings of the 2016 Conference on Empirical Methods in Natural Language Processing*, pages 932–937, Austin, Texas. Association for Computational Linguistics.

Jacob Devlin, Ming-Wei Chang, Kenton Lee, and Kristina Toutanova. 2019. BERT: Pre-training of deep bidirectional transformers for language understanding. In *Proceedings of the 2019 Conference of the North American Chapter of the Association for Computational Linguistics: Human Language Technologies, Volume 1 (Long and Short Papers)*, pages 4171–4186, Minneapolis, Minnesota. Association for Computational Linguistics.

Ronald Aylmer Fisher. 1921. On the "probable error" of a coefficient of correlation deduced from a small sample. *Biometrika*, 10(4):507–521.

Amirata Ghorbani, Abubakar Abid, and James Zou. 2019. Interpretation of neural networks is fragile. *Proceedings of the AAAI Conference on Artificial Intelligence*, 33(01):3681–3688.

Suchin Gururangan, Swabha Swayamdipta, Omer Levy, Roy Schwartz, Samuel Bowman, and Noah A. Smith. 2018. Annotation artifacts in natural language inference data. In *Proceedings of the 2018 Conference of the North American Chapter of the Association for Computational Linguistics: Human Language Technologies, Volume 2 (Short Papers)*, pages 107–112, New Orleans, Louisiana. Association for Computational Linguistics.

Peter Hase and Mohit Bansal. 2020. Evaluating explainable AI: Which algorithmic explanations help users predict model behavior? In *Proceedings of the 58th Annual Meeting of the Association for Computational Linguistics*, pages 5540–5552, Online. Association for Computational Linguistics.

Sepp Hochreiter and Jürgen Schmidhuber. 1997. Long short-term memory. *Neural computation*, 9(8):1735–1780.

Alon Jacovi and Yoav Goldberg. 2020. Aligning faithful interpretations with their social attribution. *arXiV*, abs/2006.01067.

Sarthak Jain and Byron C. Wallace. 2019. Attention is not Explanation. In *Proceedings of the 2019 Conference of the North American Chapter of the Association for Computational Linguistics: Human Language Technologies, Volume 1 (Long and Short Papers)*, pages 3543–3556, Minneapolis, Minnesota. Association for Computational Linguistics.

Aikaterini-Lida Kalouli, Rita Sevastjanova, Valeria de Paiva, Richard Crouch, and Mennatallah El-Assady. 2020. XplaiNLI: Explainable natural language inference through visual analytics. In

Proceedings of the 28th International Conference on Computational Linguistics: System Demonstrations, pages 48–52.

Douwe Kiela, Max Bartolo, Yixin Nie, Divyansh Kaushik, Atticus Geiger, Zhengxuan Wu, Bertie Vidgen, Grusha Prasad, Amanpreet Singh, Pratik Ringshia, Zhiyi Ma, Tristan Thrush, Sebastian Riedel, Zeerak Waseem, Pontus Stenetorp, Robin Jia, Mohit Bansal, Christopher Potts, and Adina Williams. 2021. Dynabench: Rethinking benchmarking in NLP. In *Proceedings of the 2021 Conference of the North American Chapter of the Association for Computational Linguistics: Human Language Technologies*, pages 4110–4124, Online. Association for Computational Linguistics.

Zachary C Lipton. 2018. The mythos of model interpretability. *Queue*, 16(3):31–57.

Yinhan Liu, Myle Ott, Naman Goyal, Jingfei Du, Mandar Joshi, Danqi Chen, Omer Levy, Mike Lewis, Luke Zettlemoyer, and Veselin Stoyanov. 2019. Roberta: A robustly optimized BERT pretraining approach. *arXiv*.

Scott M. Lundberg and Su-In Lee. 2017. A unified approach to interpreting model predictions. In *Advances in Neural Information Processing Systems 30: Annual Conference on Neural Information Processing Systems 2017, December 4-9, 2017, Long Beach, CA, USA*, pages 4765–4774.

Tom McCoy, Ellie Pavlick, and Tal Linzen. 2019. Right for the wrong reasons: Diagnosing syntactic heuristics in natural language inference. In *Proceedings of the 57th Annual Meeting of the Association for Computational Linguistics*, pages 3428–3448, Florence, Italy. Association for Computational Linguistics.

Yixin Nie and Mohit Bansal. 2017. Shortcut-stacked sentence encoders for multi-domain inference. In *Proceedings of the 2nd Workshop on Evaluating Vector Space Representations for NLP*, pages 41–45, Copenhagen, Denmark. Association for Computational Linguistics.

Yixin Nie, Adina Williams, Emily Dinan, Mohit Bansal, Jason Weston, and Douwe Kiela. 2020. Adversarial NLI: A new benchmark for natural language understanding. In *Proceedings of the 58th Annual Meeting of the Association for Computational Linguistics*, pages 4885–4901, Online. Association for Computational Linguistics.

Xiangyu Peng, Siyan Li, Spencer Frazier, and Mark Riedl. 2020. Reducing non-normative text generation from language models. In *Proceedings of the 13th International Conference on Natural Language Generation*, pages 374–383, Dublin, Ireland. Association for Computational Linguistics.

Adam Poliak, Jason Naradowsky, Aparajita Haldar, Rachel Rudinger, and Benjamin Van Durme. 2018. Hypothesis only baselines in natural language inference. In *Proceedings of the Seventh Joint Conference on Lexical and Computational Semantics*, pages 180–191, New Orleans, Louisiana. Association for Computational Linguistics.

Nazneen Fatema Rajani, Bryan McCann, Caiming Xiong, and Richard Socher. 2019. Explain yourself! leveraging language models for commonsense reasoning. In *Proceedings of the 57th Annual Meeting of the Association for Computational Linguistics*, pages 4932–4942, Florence, Italy. Association for Computational Linguistics.

Marco Túlio Ribeiro, Carlos Guestrin, and Sameer Singh. 2019. Are red roses red? evaluating consistency of question-answering models. In *Proceedings of the 57th Conference of the Association for Computational Linguistics, ACL 2019, Florence, Italy, July 28- August 2, 2019, Volume 1: Long Papers*, pages 6174–6184. Association for Computational Linguistics.

Marco Túlio Ribeiro, Sameer Singh, and Carlos Guestrin. 2016. "Why should I trust you?": Explaining the predictions of any classifier. In *Proceedings of the 22nd ACM SIGKDD International Conference on Knowledge Discovery and Data Mining, San Francisco, CA, USA, August 13-17, 2016*, pages 1135–1144. ACM.

Marco Túlio Ribeiro, Sameer Singh, and Carlos Guestrin. 2018. Semantically equivalent adversarial rules for debugging NLP models. In *Proceedings of the 56th Annual Meeting of the Association for Computational Linguistics, ACL 2018, Melbourne, Australia, July 15-20, 2018, Volume 1: Long Papers*, pages 856–865. Association for Computational Linguistics.

Stuart Russell, Daniel Dewey, and Max Tegmark. 2015. Research priorities for robust and beneficial artificial intelligence. *Ai Magazine*, 36(4):105–114.

Ramprasaath R. Selvaraju, Purva Tendulkar, Devi Parikh, Eric Horvitz, Marco Túlio Ribeiro, Besmira Nushi, and Ece Kamar. 2020. Squinting at VQA models: Introspecting VQA models with sub-questions. In *2020 IEEE/CVF Conference on Computer Vision and Pattern Recognition, CVPR 2020, Seattle, WA, USA, June 13-19, 2020*, pages 10000–10008. IEEE.

Vivian S Silva, André Freitas, and Siegfried Handschuh. 2020. XTE: Explainable text entailment. *arXiv preprint arXiv:2009.12431*.

Dylan Slack, Sophie Hilgard, Emily Jia, Sameer Singh, and Himabindu Lakkaraju. 2020. Fooling LIME and SHAP: adversarial attacks on post hoc explanation methods. In *AIES '20: AAAI/ACM Conference on AI, Ethics, and Society, New York, NY, USA, February 7-8, 2020*, pages 180–186. ACM.

Mukund Sundararajan, Ankur Taly, and Qiqi Yan. 2017. Axiomatic attribution for deep networks. In *Proceedings of the 34th International Conference on Machine Learning, ICML 2017, Sydney, NSW, Australia, 6-11 August 2017*, volume 70 of *Proceedings of Machine Learning Research*, pages 3319–3328. PMLR.

James Thorne, Andreas Vlachos, Oana Cocarascu, Christos Christodoulopoulos, and Arpit Mittal. 2019. The FEVER2.0 shared task. In *Proceedings of the Second Workshop on Fact Extraction and VERification (FEVER)*, pages 1–6, Hong Kong, China. Association for Computational Linguistics.

Masatoshi Tsuchiya. 2018. Performance impact caused by hidden bias of training data for recognizing textual entailment. In *Proceedings of the Eleventh International Conference on Language Resources and Evaluation (LREC 2018)*, Miyazaki, Japan. European Language Resources Association (ELRA).

Iulia Turc, Ming-Wei Chang, Kenton Lee, and Kristina Toutanova. 2019. Well-read students learn better: The impact of student initialization on knowledge distillation. *CoRR*, abs/1908.08962.

Eric Wallace, Shi Feng, Nikhil Kandpal, Matt Gardner, and Sameer Singh. 2019. Universal adversarial triggers for attacking and analyzing NLP. In *Proceedings of the 2019 Conference on Empirical Methods in Natural Language Processing and the 9th International Joint Conference on Natural Language Processing (EMNLP-IJCNLP)*, pages 2153–2162, Hong Kong, China. Association for Computational Linguistics.

Alex Warstadt, Yian Zhang, Xiaocheng Li, Haokun Liu, and Samuel R. Bowman. 2020. Learning helpful inductive biases from self-supervised pretraining. In *Proceedings of the 2020 Conference on Empirical Methods in Natural Language Processing (EMNLP)*, pages 217–235, Online. Association for Computational Linguistics.

Sarah Wiegreffe and Yuval Pinter. 2019. Attention is not not explanation. In *Proceedings of the 2019 Conference on Empirical Methods in Natural Language Processing and the 9th International Joint Conference on Natural Language Processing (EMNLP-IJCNLP)*, pages 11–20, Hong Kong, China. Association for Computational Linguistics.

Adina Williams, Nikita Nangia, and Samuel Bowman. 2018. A broad-coverage challenge corpus for sentence understanding through inference. In *Proceedings of the 2018 Conference of the North American Chapter of the Association for Computational Linguistics: Human Language Technologies, Volume 1 (Long Papers)*, pages 1112–1122, New Orleans, Louisiana. Association for Computational Linguistics.

Ming Yin, Jennifer Wortman Vaughan, and Hanna Wallach. 2019. Understanding the effect of accuracy on trust in machine learning models. In *Proceedings of the 2019 CHI conference on human factors in computing systems*, pages 1–12.

Yunfeng Zhang, Q Vera Liao, and Rachel KE Bellamy. 2020. Effect of confidence and explanation on accuracy and trust calibration in ai-assisted decision making. In *Proceedings of the 2020 Conference on Fairness, Accountability, and Transparency*, pages 295–305.

Xinyan Zhao and V. G. Vinod Vydiswaran. 2020. LIREx: Augmenting language inference with relevant explanation. *arXiv preprint arXiv:2012.09157*.

A Details about statistical analyses

A.1 Effect of model size

Formula for Transformer models

```
smf.mixedlm("fisher_cor_diff ~ C(model_size, Treatment(reference='base'))
                              *C(model,Treatment(reference='bert'))",
            data = transformer_dat, groups = transformer_dat["ex_id"],
            re_formula="~model_size")
```

Formula for smaller models (BERT-base, InferSent and BOW)

```
smf.mixedlm("fisher_cor_diff ~ C(model,Treatment(reference='bert'))",
             data = small_dat, groups = small_dat["ex_id"],
             re_formula="~model_size")
```

Fit	Coefficient	All wrong examples		Expert annotated subset		
		$\Delta\mathcal{A}^H$	$\Delta\mathcal{A}^S$	$\Delta\mathcal{A}^H$	$\Delta\mathcal{A}^S$	$\Delta\mathcal{A}^E$
Transformer models	Large (vs. Base)	-0.32***	-0.142***	-0.057**	-0.173***	-0.115***
	ELECTRA (vs. BERT)	-0.044***	-0.057***	-0.048 **	-0.067***	-0.054*
	RoBERTa (vs. BERT)	-0.099***	-0.101***	-0.106***	-0.105***	-0.083***
	ELECTRA : Large	-0.070***	0.085***	-0.014	0.109***	-0.051
	RoBERTa : Large	-0.044***	0.127***	-0.016	0.134***	0.012
Smaller models	BOW (vs. BERT-base)	-0.203***	-0.104***	-0.184***	-0.125***	-0.184***
	BInferSent (vs. BERT-base)	-0.094***	-0.120***	-0.080***	-0.154***	-0.080***

Table 4: ***, **and *indicate $p < 0.0001$, 0.001 and 0.01 respectively and ':' indicates an interaction effect. A separate mixed effects regression model was fit for each column. Negative coefficients for the main effects indicate that the baseline value was greater than the comparison (e.g., Base was greater than Large).

A.2 Correlation with accuracy

Evaluation dataset	All wrong examples		Expert annotated subset		
	$\Delta\mathcal{A}^H$	$\Delta\mathcal{A}^S$	$\Delta\mathcal{A}^H$	$\Delta\mathcal{A}^S$	$\Delta\mathcal{A}^E$
ANLI Dev	0.39^*	0.10	0.23	0.10	0.42^{**}(-0.04)
HANS (all)	0.18	-0.19	0.04	-0.21	0.22
HANS (constituent)	0.30^+	-0.11	-0.19	-0.26	-0.18
HANS (lexical overlap)	0.20	-0.17	-0.25	-0.27	-0.19
HANS (subsequence)	-0.006	-0.31^+	-0.29^+	-0.39^*	-0.27

Table 5: '+', '*' and '**' indicate $p < 0.1$, 0.05 and 0.01 respectively. Values in parentheses indicate correlation without the BOW models in cases where they were outliers (see Figure 2a)

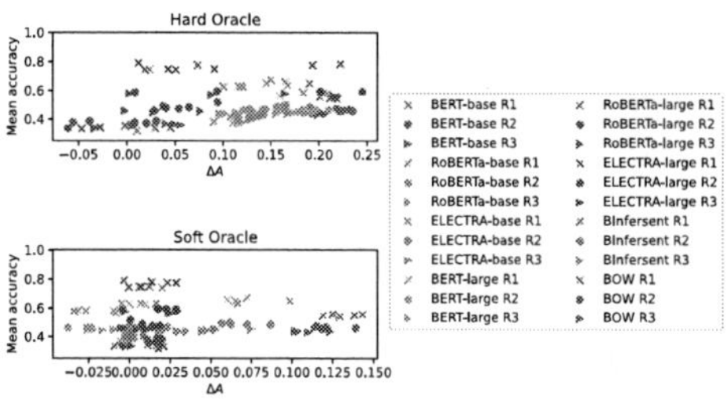

(a) Correlationg accuracy on ANLI with importance alignment ($\mathcal{A}^H$ and $\mathcal{A}^S$) for all wrong examples. The cross, circle, and triangle refer to rounds 1, 2, and 3 of ANLI, respectively.

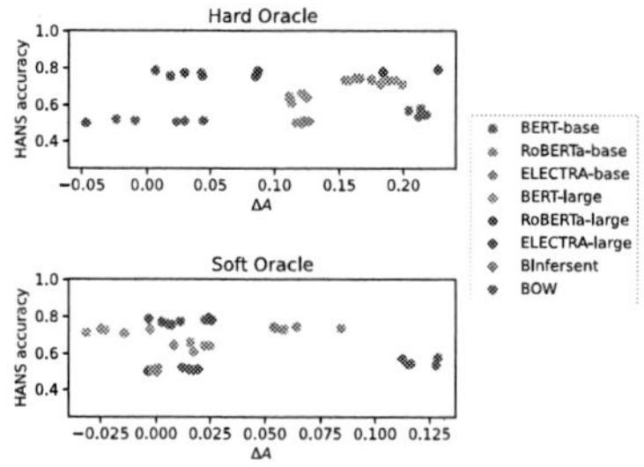

(b) Correlating accuracy on HANS with importance alignment for all wrong examples. Alignment values are averaged across rounds because HANS is not divided into rounds.

Figure 3

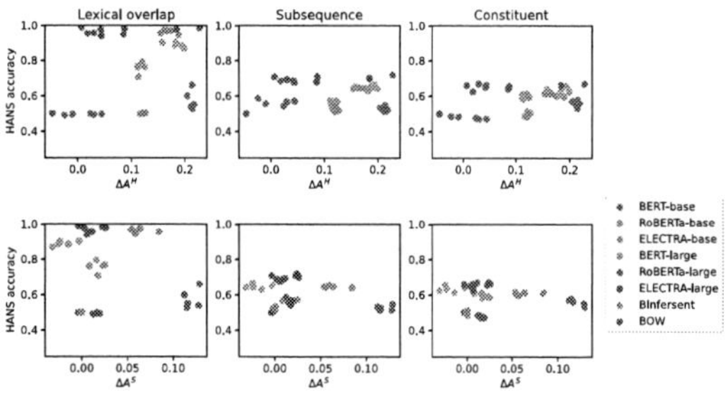

(a) Correlating accuracy on ANLI with importance alignment ($\mathcal{A}^H$ and $\mathcal{A}^S$) for all wrong examples. The cross, circle, and triangle refer to rounds 1, 2, and 3 of ANLI, respectively.

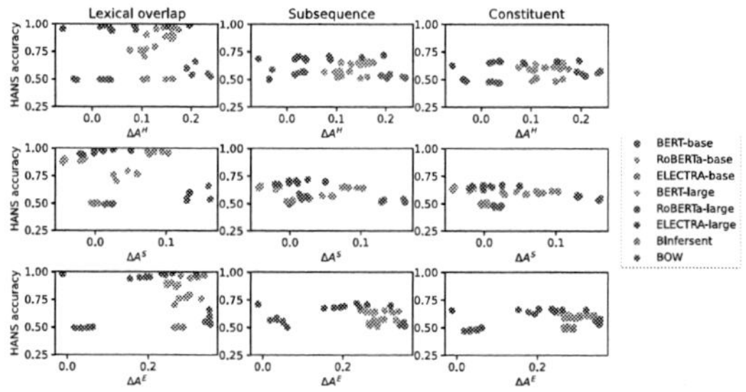

(b) Correlating accuracy on HANS with importance alignment for all wrong examples. Alignment values are averaged across rounds because HANS is not divided into rounds.

Figure 4

Test Harder than You Train: Probing with Extrapolation Splits

Jenny Kunz and **Marco Kuhlmann**
Dept. of Computer and Information Science
Linköping University
jenny.kunz@liu.se and marco.kuhlmann@liu.se

Abstract

Previous work on probing word representations for linguistic knowledge has focused on interpolation tasks. In this paper, we instead analyse probes in an extrapolation setting, where the inputs at test time are deliberately chosen to be 'harder' than the training examples. We argue that such an analysis can shed further light on the open question whether probes actually decode linguistic knowledge, or merely learn the diagnostic task from shallow features. To quantify the hardness of an example, we consider scoring functions based on linguistic, statistical, and learning-related criteria, all of which are applicable to a broad range of NLP tasks. We discuss the relative merits of these criteria in the context of two syntactic probing tasks, part-of-speech tagging and syntactic dependency labelling. From our theoretical and experimental analysis, we conclude that distance-based and hard statistical criteria show the clearest differences between interpolation and extrapolation settings, while at the same time being transparent, intuitive, and easy to control.

1 Introduction

The use of contextualised language models such as ELMo and BERT has brought about remarkable performance gains on a wide range of downstream tasks (Peters et al., 2018a; Devlin et al., 2019); but the question to what extent these models have acquired linguistic knowledge remains open. One way to investigate this question is through the use of *probing classifiers* trained to solve diagnostic prediction tasks that are considered to require linguistic information, such as parts-of-speech, syntactic structure, or semantic roles (Belinkov et al., 2017a; Conneau et al., 2018; Tenney et al., 2019). However, what conclusions can be drawn from probing experiments is disputed. In particular, a central point of debate is how to know whether probes 'decode linguistic knowledge' or simply 'learn to solve the diagnostic task' (Hewitt and Liang, 2019). We suggest that new methods that define more rigorous and harder challenges are needed to get further insights into the capabilities and limitations of probes and probing methodology.

In this paper, we propose to analyse probes in the context of an extrapolation setting, where the inputs at test time are deliberately chosen to be 'harder' than the training examples. While machine learning models and neural networks in particular have proved to be very effective learners in *interpolation* scenarios, where the examples at training time and those at test time are drawn from the same (idealised) underlying distribution, the ability of these models to *extrapolate* from the training data appears to be limited (Dubois et al., 2020). At the same time, extrapolation has been proposed as a litmus test for abstract reasoning in neural networks (Barrett et al., 2018). In the context of probing, we posit that the better the extrapolation capability of a probe, i.e. the higher its performance even in situations where the training and the test examples are substantially different, the more evidence we have for claiming that the probe actually uses abstract linguistic knowledge encoded in the input word representations.

To construct extrapolation challenges, we propose a conceptually simple approach where we start from standard probing datasets, stratify them based on the 'hardness' of examples, and then use the 'easy' examples for training and the 'hard' ones for testing (§ 3). The central decision in this approach is how to measure 'hardness'. Here we identify different scoring functions based on criteria grounded in linguistic theories, statistical properties of the base dataset, and learning behaviour. We apply these scoring functions to create extrapolation challenges from two standard probing tasks, part-of-speech tagging and syntactic dependency labelling (§ 4), and use the results of our experiments to discuss the merits of our approach (§ 5).

Proceedings of the Fourth BlackboxNLP Workshop on Analyzing and Interpreting Neural Networks for NLP, pages 15–25
Online, November 11, 2021.

2 Related Work

The method that we propose in this paper synthesises several strands of related work:

2.1 Probing (and its Limitations)

Probing aims at detecting linguistic knowledge in word representations. While this can be done in a zero-shot setting (Goldberg, 2019; Talmor et al., 2020) or as a structural probe (Hewitt and Manning, 2019), a dominant approach is to train and evaluate simple classifiers on relevant diagnostic tasks (Belinkov et al., 2017b; Hewitt and Liang, 2019), where the classifier receives one word representations at a time as its input. This is based on the idea that the accuracy of the trained probe can indicate to what extent the representations encode linguistic knowledge that is useful for the diagnostic task.

Recent work has questioned the validity of this methodology, suggesting that analysis should shift focus to measuring 'amount of effort' rather than task-based accuracy (Pimentel et al., 2020; Voita and Titov, 2020). Moreover, many probing tasks are relatively easy to learn with local context and strong independence assumptions. It thus remains unclear whether the probed word representations actually encode linguistic knowledge, contain predictive but superficial features extracted from the words' linear context (Kunz and Kuhlmann, 2020), or rather provide an effective initialisation for the probing classifier (Prasanna et al., 2020).

2.2 Interpolation and Extrapolation

A growing body of research suggests that, while deep neural models can reach remarkable performance in interpolation settings, they often fail to extrapolate, i.e. to generalise to inputs outside the range of the training data. For example, Barrett et al. (2018) show that in visual reasoning, popular models such as ResNets perform at levels barely above a random choice baseline in extrapolation settings. As the ability to extrapolate is generally considered a hallmark of intelligence, such findings raise the question whether deep models are capable of human-like reasoning. Similar concerns come from observations that performance can suffer greatly when models are confronted with adversarial examples (Goodfellow et al., 2015; Jia and Liang, 2017) or challenge sets (Zellers et al., 2018, 2019). Zellers et al. (2019) suggest that deep models may 'pick up on dataset-specific distributional biases' instead of learning the actual task.

In the domain of natural language understanding, authors have shown that Transformers lack the capability to extrapolate to longer sequences (Dubois et al., 2020) and number representations of higher values (Weiss et al., 2018); and that even large neural models such as RoBERTa can compare ages only within a restricted range (Talmor et al., 2020). Evidently, test data outside the training distribution is a great challenge, and contextualised language models are easily broken on such data.

2.3 What are Hard Examples?

Most of the aforementioned works on extrapolation and abstraction employ synthetic datasets or adversarial attacks to challenge a model. Here we propose a method based on the stratification of existing probing datasets according to a measure of expected difficulty or 'hardness'.

2.3.1 Readability Criteria

One way to quantify the difficulty of training examples is to use readability criteria, which are typically motivated on linguistic grounds or with reference to studies on human language processing (Kocmi and Bojar, 2017; Platanios et al., 2019). A widely used and widely applicable metric is sentence length, which is intuitive and straightforward to measure (Sherman, 1893), but only weakly correlated with processing complexity (Bailin and Grafstein, 2001). There are also many more specific measures, such as the respective averages of parse tree height, length of arcs in syntactic dependency trees, number of noun phrases and number of verb phrases, or word frequency. These measures often inform systems that help authors improve writing quality, and automatically transform texts to make them more understandable or accessibile (Zamanian and Heydari, 2012), but are also used to evaluate systems such as dependency parsers (McDonald and Nivre, 2007; Kulmizev et al., 2019).

2.3.2 Learning-Based Criteria

Instead of using inherent properties, another way to quantify the hardness of training examples is to look at the effort that a model has to put into learning them. Here we take inspiration from developments in curriculum learning, which moved from heuristic metrics on artificial datasets (Bengio et al., 2009) to learning-specific metrics. In particular, *self-paced learning* employs the loss of a model to rate and rank the difficulty of examples in a dataset (Kumar et al., 2010; Hacohen and Weinshall, 2019). This approach is widely used, but has also been criticised as being inherently model-specific (Lalor and Yu, 2020). Other approaches that have been successfully employed in curriculum learning are rankings based on the norms of word embeddings (Liu et al., 2020) and on model uncertainty (Zhou et al., 2020).

3 Experimental Setup

In this section we present our specific approach to creating extrapolation datasets, and the setup for our empirical evaluation.[1]

3.1 Word Representations

Our word representations come from the English BERT base (uncased) model (Devlin et al., 2019), accessed via the the Transformers library (Wolf et al., 2020). We probe on the hidden representations of words in all 13 layers, including the uncontextualised layer 0 as a baseline. For words that BERT tokenises into several word pieces, we use the last piece as the representation for the word.

3.2 Probing Classifier

The probing classifier is the same in all experiments: a feed-forward network with one hidden layer, 64 hidden units and ReLU activation. We train this classifier with cross-entropy loss for 5 epochs using the Adam optimizer (Kingma and Ba, 2015) with a learning rate of 0.001 and a batch size of 64. Our implementation uses PyTorch (Paszke et al., 2017).

3.3 Tasks and Datasets

We use two prototypical diagnostic tasks which have been widely studied in the probing literature: part-of-speech (POS) tagging and syntactic dependency labelling. The training and test data for both tasks comes from the English Web Treebank (EWT) as released by the Universal Dependencies project (Nivre et al., 2020) (v2.5). More specifically, we extract our examples from two 1,000-sentence sets $\mathcal{S}_{\text{train}}$ and $\mathcal{S}_{\text{test}}$, randomly sampled from the training and the development section of the EWT, respectively.[2] We write s_i^t to denote the ith sentence in $\mathcal{S}_t$, w_{ij}^t to denote its jth word, and x_{ij}^t to denote the BERT representation of w_{ij}. We omit the superscript when the base set (training or development) is understood or irrelevant.

T1: Part-of-speech tagging This is our prototypical single-word labelling task. Examples take the form $e = (x_{ij}, y_{ij})$, where x_{ij} is the representation of a single word w_{ij}, and y_{ij} is the corresponding gold-standard tag. The POS class of a word captures some of its most basic syntactic properties, and can be predicted with local or even without context information at a high accuracy. For our data, probes trained on contextualised word representations usually show a tagging accuracy above 95%, with the highest-performing layers being the lower middle or middle layers of a model (Peters et al., 2018b; Tenney et al., 2019).

T2: Syntactic dependency labelling In this task, which intends to capture the hierarchical structure of a sentence, we aim to predict the grammatical relation for a given dependency arc. Examples take the form $e = ((x_{ij}, x_{ik}), y_{ik})$, where x_{ij} and x_{ik} are word representations of the head and dependent, respectively, and y_{ik} is the gold-standard dependency label. The performance of simple probes on this task is usually lower than for POS tagging, as the syntactic information that is required to accurately predict the labels is more complex and depends on a larger context. Accuracy can however still exceed 90% in the highest-performing layers, which are usually the higher middle layers.

3.4 Scoring Functions

We next introduce the inventory of measures that we use to quantify the 'hardness' of training examples. Formally, each measure is a real-valued function m whose domain is the set of all task-specific examples. If $m(e) > m(e')$, we say that example e is *harder* than example e'.

3.4.1 Length-based Criteria

These scoring functions refer to two different notions of length:

Sentence length (T1, T2) The most basic length is that of the sentence s_i from which the example is derived. Using $|\cdot|$ to denote length,

$$m(x_{ij}, y_{ij}) = |s_i| \qquad \text{(for T1)}$$
$$m((x_{ij}, x_{ik}), y_{ik}) = |s_i| \qquad \text{(for T2)}$$

[1] All code necessary to reproduce our experiments is publicly available at https://github.com/jekunz/extrapolation.

[2] We sub-sample the full data to reduce training time and save resources. Preliminary experiments showed the same trends that we report here for the full data.

Arc length (T2) For dependency labelling, we may also consider the length of the dependency arc: $m((x_{ij}, x_{ik}), y_{ik}) = |j - k|$.

3.4.2 Statistical Criteria

For part-of-speech tagging, we consider criteria related to the distribution of the tags:

Tag proportions (T1) Here the hardness score of an example is the inverse relative frequency of the represented word's gold-standard POS tag in the training set. More formally, for a word w_{ij} from $\mathcal{S}_{\text{train}}$ and a tag t, let $f(w_{ij}, t)$ be the relative frequency of t among all possible tags for w_{ij}; then $m(x_{ij}, y_{ij}) = 1 - f(w_{ij}, y_{ij})$. For examples e that represent words which do not occur in $\mathcal{S}_{\text{train}}$, we let $m(e) = 1$; out-of-vocabulary words will thus always yield the hardest examples.

Most frequent tag (T1) In a related setup, we consider an example to be 'easy' if its gold-standard tag is the most frequent tag (mft) in the training set, and 'hard' otherwise. Formally,

$$m(x_{ij}, y_{ij}) = 1 - \mathbb{1}[y_{ij} \text{ is the mft for } w_{ij} \text{ in } \mathcal{S}_{\text{train}}] .$$

3.4.3 Learning-based Criteria

Here we implement ideas from curriculum learning. We first train an ensemble of 10 classifiers on all examples derived from $\mathcal{S}_{\text{train}}$. Each classifier has the same architecture and training regime as our probe (§ 3.2), but uses a different random seed. We then use this ensemble to define the hardness of each example e as follows:

Sample-specific loss (T1, T2) Here we let $m(e)$ be the sample-specific loss for e, relative to its gold-standard tag or label, averaged over the 10 classifiers in the ensemble.

Speed of learning (T1, T2) Here we want to classify an example as 'hard' if the probe needs a long time (a large number of updates) to learn it reliably. To implement this idea, at seven specified checkpoints early into training, we let each of the classifiers in the ensemble predict the tag or label of each example e, and define

$$m(e) = 1/(c + 1) ,$$

where c is the total number of correct predictions. For our checkpoints, we use the partially trained classifiers after 2^n batch updates, for $1 \leq i \leq 7$. As a consequence, the minimal value for c is 0 (never correctly classified), and the maximal value is $7 \cdot 10$ (correctly classified at every checkpoint, by every classifier).

3.5 Easy Sets and Hard Sets

The last step of our approach is to use our scoring functions to split the set of all task-specific examples into an 'easy' set and a 'hard' set. Here, for each specific experiment we choose two values m_1 and m_2 and let

$$\mathcal{D}_{\text{easy}} = \{e \,|\, m(e) < m_1\}$$
$$\mathcal{D}_{\text{hard}} = \{e \,|\, m(e) > m_2\}$$

The difference $m_2 - m_1$ denotes the *distance* between $\mathcal{D}_{\text{easy}}$ and $\mathcal{D}_{\text{hard}}$. The specific criteria according to which we choose the split points vary:

Linguistic criteria For sentence length we base our choice on the classification of Flesch and Gould (1949). Specifically, for $\mathcal{D}_{\text{easy}}$ we use the lengths less than 17 words ($m_1 = 17$), corresponding to (at most) 'fairly easy' readability, understood by 88% of adults in the referenced study. For $\mathcal{D}_{\text{hard}}$ we use the lengths greater than 29 words ($m_2 = 29$), classified as (at least) 'very difficult', understood by 4.5% of adults.

Distributional criteria For the remaining scoring functions, we choose split points based on the empirical distribution of the scores: We let m_1 be the 50th percentile (i.e., the median score), and m_2 be the 75th percentile. The only exception to this rule is for the most frequent tag criterion, as explained in § 3.4.2.

Note that, with our strategies of choosing split points, the sizes of the specific 'easy' and 'hard' sets that we use for each experiment differ from the full set, getting as low as half the number of all examples. To assess the impact of this reduction, in control experiments we randomly sub-sampled the 'standard' training sets down to 50% of their original size, but only observed a moderate drop in accuracy (at most 1%).

3.6 Evaluation

For each experiment, we consider two setups:

- In the *extrapolation setup*, we train on the examples in $\mathcal{D}_{\text{easy}}$ and test on those in $\mathcal{D}_{\text{hard}}$.
- In the *control setup*, we also test on the examples in $\mathcal{D}_{\text{hard}}$, but train on the full set of examples.

For both setups, we report the mean over 10 random seeds of the best accuracy of each classifier among the 5 epochs for which it was trained.

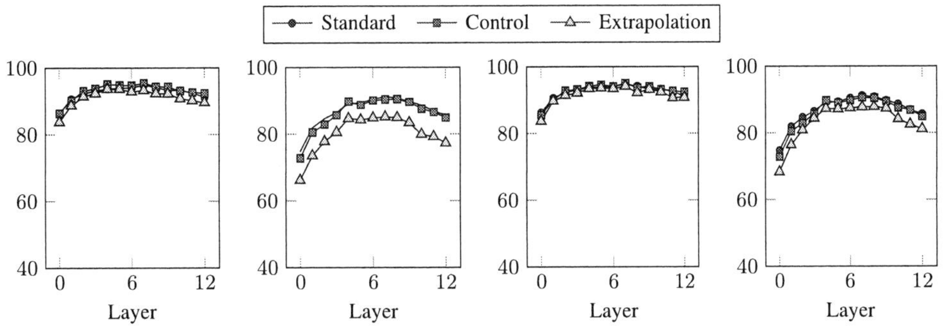

Figure 1: Extrapolation based on sentence length. From left to right: part-of-speech tagging (T1), linguistic criterion; dependency labelling (T2), linguistic; T1, distributional criterion; T2, distributional. In all plots, the x-axis corresponds to the BERT layer used for prediction, and the y-axis corresponds to the mean accuracy.

To interpret an experiment, we compare the two accuracy values: If the accuracy in the extrapolation setup is significantly lower than that of the control, we want to conclude that the probe lacks the ability to extrapolate from 'easy' examples, and that there is thus no evidence that the probe makes use of linguistic knowledge in the probed representations. On the other hand, similar scores in the two setups indicate that we have chosen a test set that is hard even for interpolation learning, in which case we do not want to draw this conclusion.

For comparison, we also report the mean accuracy in the *standard setup*, where we train and evaluate on the full datasets.

4 Results

We now present our experimental results for each of the scoring functions.

4.1 Sentence Length

The results for sentence length can be seen in Figure 1. The accuracies for the extrapolation setups are the highest among all scoring functions, and the differences to the standard setups are by far the smallest. Indeed, for part-of-speech tagging (T1) the difference is so small that a large part of it can probably be explained by the decreased number of training examples: the difference between the control and the extrapolation setup is mostly 1–2 points, and never exceeds 3 points. For dependency labelling (T2), the difference is more pronounced, but sentence length remains the measure with the smallest difference between the two setups.

The distributional split criterion gives $m_1 = 23$ and $m_2 = 34$, so both the longest sentences in the 'easy' set and the shortest sentences in the 'hard' set are longer than with the linguistic criterion. The linguistically motivated split shows a larger gap between the standard setups and the extrapolation setups. This is particularly clear for T2, with a gap as high as 8 points in layer 10.

4.2 Arc Length

The extrapolation accuracy of the probe based on arc length (Figure 2) is comparatively low, suggesting that this setup is more challenging than extrapolation based on sentence length. The control shows that the 'hard' set is clearly harder than the unfiltered test set; but there is an additional substantial accuracy drop in the extrapolation setup.

When using the distributional split criterion, we get $m_1 = 2$ and $m_2 = 4$, and the extrapolation accuracy does not exceed 46% in any layer. As $m_1 = 2$ results in a training set that only consists of arcs of length 1, we perform an additional experiment with a different split, decreasing the distance between $\mathcal{D}_{\text{easy}}$ and $\mathcal{D}_{\text{hard}}$ by setting $m_1 = 3$. This increases accuracy to at most 62%, which is considerably higher than before but still far below the control, which reaches up to 85% on the 'hard' set.

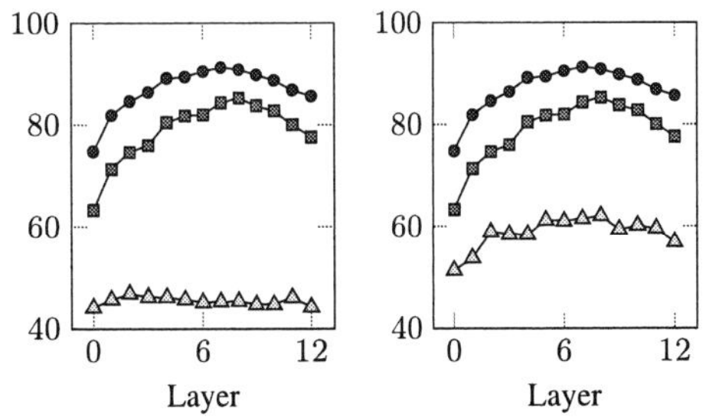

Figure 2: Extrapolation based on arc length. Left: Standard distributional setup. Right: Modified setup.

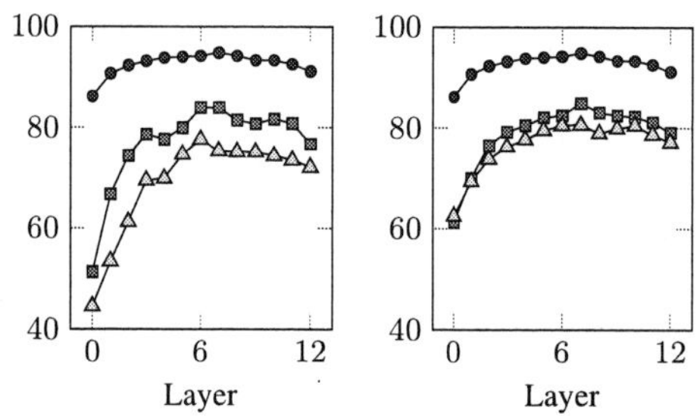

Figure 3: Extrapolation for T1 based on the most frequent tag (left) and tag proportions criteria (right).

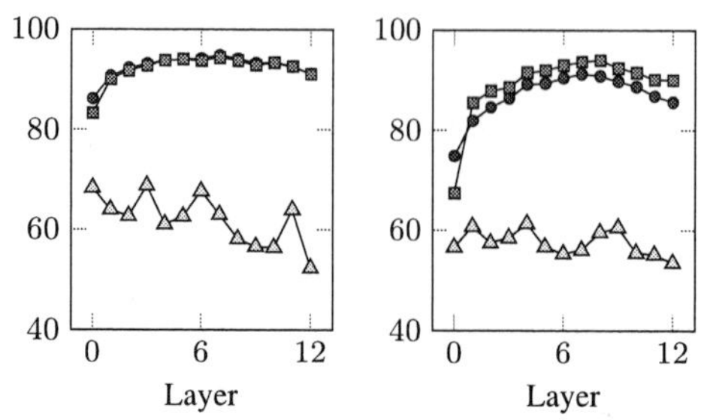

Figure 4: Extrapolation based on speed of learning. Left: Tagging (T1). Right: Dependency labelling (T2).

4.3 Most Frequent Tag and Tag Proportions

The results for the extrapolation splits based on the most frequent tag and the tag proportions criteria are shown in Figure 3.

Splitting based on the most frequent tag criterion leads to an extrapolation setup that is consistently more challenging than the standard setup. We observe a very low accuracy in the first layers, while the higher layers are significantly more predictive. The relative difference in accuracy between the extrapolation setup and the control is also most pronounced in the early layers, although the pattern is less clear in terms of absolute numbers. The gap to the standard (interpolation) setup is substantial: 11–35 points for the control, and 23–42 points for the extrapolation setup.

When using the tag proportions criterion for the extrapolation split, the 'hard' set is now easier, as around half of the examples have a tag that is the most frequent one for the word form. The simpler nature of this challenge is visible in the results: While the performance of the control only sees a modest increase (especially in the lower layers), the difference between the control and the extrapolation setup shrinks more clearly, presumably because the augmentation of the test set with easier examples has a high proportional effect on the previously very low results of the extrapolation probe.

4.4 Speed of Learning

Using the learning-based scoring function, the difference between the control and the extrapolation setup is the largest among all settings. The accuracy of the control is similar to that in the standard setup, suggesting that the 'hard' set may in fact not be (much) harder after all. For the dependency labelling task (T2), control accuracy even slightly *exceeds* accuracy on the standard set, in all layers but the uncontextualised layer 0.

Training the probe on the 'easy' set only, however, has a disastrous effect: in the extrapolation setup, the accuracy drops dramatically. Interestingly, accuracy continues to decrease in higher layers, whereas the typical curve for syntactic probes peaks in the middle layers (Tenney et al., 2019).

4.5 Sample-specific Loss

With the loss-based split (Figure 5), the results for the control setups are the lowest among all scoring functions. In this setting, by construction, the 'hard' set consists of the examples with the highest loss, making it challenging even in an interpolation setting. For the tagging task, we see an extreme drop of accuracy in layers 6–8, the layers on which the other two setups perform best.[3] The probes in these layers appear to be completely unable to extrapolate to the harder examples.

While for POS tagging (T1), extrapolation accuracy is generally very close to that of the control, for dependency labelling (T2) we observe a larger distance between all setups, but in particular between the extrapolation setup and the control.

[3] To put this into context, we recall that we tried to control for a too high model-specificness by averaging the losses of 10 different models.

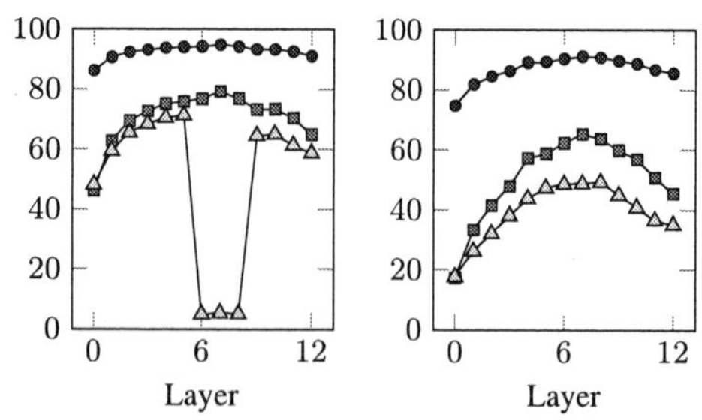

Figure 5: Extrapolation based on loss. Left: Tagging (T1). Right: Dependency Labelling (T2).

5 Discussion

While for all experiments, the accuracy in the extrapolation setup is substantially lower than in the standard interpolation setup, it is still above random guessing, which suggests that probes are able to extract *some* useful information from the word representations even under this experimental regime. However, the success of extrapolating from 'easy' to 'hard' examples varies depending on the choice of the scoring function. In this section we discuss these findings and the limitations of our method.

5.1 Scoring Functions

We start by arguing for the merits of the different scoring functions in the context of probing.

Sentence length Sentence length is the least discriminating metric in the experimental results, which is in line with our expectations and with previous work on curriculum learning discussed in § 2.3: for word-level tasks, sentence length is not a strong indicator for hard examples. In the case of part-of-speech tagging (T1), there is no considerable difference between interpolation and extrapolation accuracy. For dependency labelling (T2), such a difference is present; but it is small compared to other choices of scoring functions. The non-correlation between sentence length and hardness is quite intuitive: long sentences also contain many simple examples, and even short sentences may contain complex syntactic constructions. At the same time, the observed difference between the two tasks suggests that the higher-level the task is, and the wider the context it depends on, the more meaningful sentence length can be as a criterion for creating extrapolation challenges.

Arc length In contrast to sentence length, arc length provides a useful criterion for extrapolation. While the comparatively low accuracy in the control setup shows that longer arcs are a challenge in themselves, restricting the training set to short arcs limits the accuracy of the probe even further. Extrapolation capability is limited even in the softened setup where we decrease the distance between training and test set (Figure 2, right). Thus, under this scoring function, we find no evidence that the probe extracts useful linguistic knowledge from the word representations – a conclusion that establishes a difference between our extrapolation setup and results for interpolation-based learning (Tenney et al., 2020; Hewitt and Liang, 2019).

Most frequent tag and tag proportions Even the most frequent tag criterion is an informative setup. Our empirical results (Figure 3) suggest that the probe seems to heavily rely on word form-specific information at least in the first layers, while it focuses on more generalisable information in the later layers, and thus exhibits better extrapolation capabilities.

Based on the differences between the extrapolation setup and the control, we argue that the most frequent tag criterion is better motivated and provides more insights than tag proportions.

Speed of learning The 'speed of learning' criterion creates a very challenging extrapolation setup, compared to the standard setup (and the control). Probes trained on the full set perform well on the supposedly hard extrapolation test set, sometimes even better than on the standard test set. It is the training set that makes the difference: by only including fast-success examples, we are likely to miss patterns. The extrapolation setup favours patterns that are easy to learn, making it superfluous for the classifier to try harder and extract features that generalise better, even if these may not necessarily be extremely hard to learn – the number of such examples may simply be too small to learn the pattern in the first phase. As a consequence of this behaviour, the speed of learning criterion has a low interpretability. Without further qualitative analyses, we can only make assumptions about the nature of the 'easy' and 'hard' datasets, and in particular about the examples that are left out from either. And obviously, if patterns are completely missed, we cannot expect the model to extrapolate to harder examples of this very pattern.

Sample-specific loss The most opaque of all scoring functions is arguably the loss-based criterion. It is even less transparent than the learning-based criterion, where we can possibly identify the learned (and missed) patterns in an error analysis. With the loss-based criterion, we will be unlikely to identify commonalities between examples that share the same ranking with respect to the scoring function. While the loss-based criterion strongly discriminates between the standard setup and the extrapolation setup, this is largely an effect of the construction of the test set, which in the latter setup will contain all examples that are classified incorrectly. For tasks where the performance of a standard probe is already low, the test set will solely consist of misclassified examples. Applying the loss of fully trained probes on the test set can therefore be seen as circular.

Summary To summarise, from a perspective of transparency, controllability, and demonstrable success in separating the data into easier and harder examples, we argue that the most interesting metrics for the identification of extrapolation challenges are arc length and the most frequent tag criterion. The learning-based scoring functions, which have the potential to be less ad-hoc, are hard to interpret, give unsurprising results, and are therefore less useful as an analysis tool.

Another benefit of arc length and the most frequent tag criterion is that they are applicable to a wide range of tasks. The most frequent tag criterion can be applied to any word labelling task that has a limited number of labels. Examples for further tasks where it can be applied include named entity recognition and word sense disambiguation. Arc length can be applied to all tasks that can be formulated as operating on pairs of words. Besides other parsing tasks such as semantic dependency parsing, this is the case for e.g. coreference resolution or negation scope detection (Kurtz et al., 2020).

5.2 Contributions and Limitations

The strong differences between the standard setup and the extrapolation setup and the great variability of results across scoring functions illustrate that the interpretation of probing classifiers remains challenging. A more extensive analysis, be it with automated techniques such as our extrapolation splits or with a qualitative analysis, is a necessity for a deeper understanding of a probing classifier's results. Unlike previous restrictions of the model or the training data as proposed by Hewitt and Liang (2019), our approach offers (given an appropriate scoring function, such as arc length or the most frequent tag criterion), more control over and transparency about the nature of the restrictions imposed by the modification of the data.

While the extrapolation setup helps approximating the nature of the features the probe uses, it does not ultimately solve the problem of the lacking interpretability of probing classifiers themselves. Negative results in the extrapolation setup do not imply that the linguistic knowledge of interest is *not* present in the representation. The probe may just have focused on other features – the amount of predictors to approximate a given target function is infinite. However, classical interpolation-based setups using probing classifiers tend to overestimate the information present in the representations, as classifiers can learn a task even from randomly initialised word embeddings (Zhang and Bowman, 2018; Hewitt and Liang, 2019). Therefore we argue that, at this time, we need to be more aware of false positives than of false negatives in probing. Extrapolation probes have the potential to reduce the false positive rate while providing new insights into the generalisability of the features they use.

6 Conclusion

We identified and suggested several ways to define the difficulty of training and validation examples based on linguistic, statistical, and learning-based criteria, to create extrapolation splits for natural language datasets. We demonstrated the usefulness of these measures for the analysis of two linguistic tasks, and proposed an evaluation protocol with baselines and metrics.

Our experimental results suggest that a probe trained on BERT hidden representations is capable of applying patterns learned from easier examples to harder examples to some extent; but in well-motivated scenarios where the scoring function is an appropriate measure of difficulty of the examples, its competence is clearly limited compared to an interpolation probe. In our experiments, the most informative scoring functions are the distance-based arc length criterion that we applied to syntactic dependency labelling, and the word-specific most frequent tag criterion for part-of-speech tagging. These functions allow for a clear and transparent extrapolation setup, while at the same time being simple and also computationally efficient. Sentence length, as expected, did not turn out to be a strong indicator for hard examples, while learning-based criteria show a high margin between interpolation and extrapolation setups, but limited interpretability and qualitative insights.

We conclude that enriching probing experiments with automated extrapolation setups can be a valuable supplement to standard probing methods, as it gives us an instrument to test the generalisation capability of the probe, and thereby the robustness of the features it uses. In addition to interpretation purposes, well-chosen extrapolation splits can provide a cheap but valuable extension of the evaluation of a model, testing its generalisation capabilities and verifying the progress made.

References

Alan Bailin and Ann Grafstein. 2001. The linguistic assumptions underlying readability formulae: A critique. *Language & Communication*, 21(3):285–301.

David Barrett, Felix Hill, Adam Santoro, Ari Morcos, and Timothy Lillicrap. 2018. Measuring abstract reasoning in neural networks. In *Proceedings of the 35th International Conference on Machine Learning*, volume 80 of *Proceedings of Machine Learning Research*, pages 511–520. PMLR.

Yonatan Belinkov, Nadir Durrani, Fahim Dalvi, Hassan Sajjad, and James Glass. 2017a. What do neural machine translation models learn about morphology? In *Proceedings of the 55th Annual Meeting of the Association for Computational Linguistics (Volume 1: Long Papers)*, pages 861–872, Vancouver, Canada. Association for Computational Linguistics.

Yonatan Belinkov, Lluís Màrquez, Hassan Sajjad, Nadir Durrani, Fahim Dalvi, and James Glass. 2017b. Evaluating layers of representation in neural machine translation on part-of-speech and semantic tagging tasks. In *Proceedings of the Eighth International Joint Conference on Natural Language Processing (Volume 1: Long Papers)*, pages 1–10, Taipei, Taiwan. Asian Federation of Natural Language Processing.

Yoshua Bengio, Jérôme Louradour, Ronan Collobert, and Jason Weston. 2009. Curriculum learning. In *Proceedings of the 26th Annual International Conference on Machine Learning*, pages 41–48.

Alexis Conneau, German Kruszewski, Guillaume Lample, Loïc Barrault, and Marco Baroni. 2018. What you can cram into a single $&!#* vector: Probing sentence embeddings for linguistic properties. In *Proceedings of the 56th Annual Meeting of the Association for Computational Linguistics (Volume 1: Long Papers)*, pages 2126–2136, Melbourne, Australia. Association for Computational Linguistics.

Jacob Devlin, Ming-Wei Chang, Kenton Lee, and Kristina Toutanova. 2019. BERT: Pre-training of deep bidirectional transformers for language understanding. In *Proceedings of the 2019 Conference of the North American Chapter of the Association for Computational Linguistics: Human Language Technologies, Volume 1 (Long and Short Papers)*, pages 4171–4186, Minneapolis, Minnesota. Association for Computational Linguistics.

Yann Dubois, Gautier Dagan, Dieuwke Hupkes, and Elia Bruni. 2020. Location Attention for Extrapolation to Longer Sequences. In *Proceedings of the 58th Annual Meeting of the Association for Computational Linguistics*, pages 403–413, Online. Association for Computational Linguistics.

Rudolf Flesch and Alan J Gould. 1949. *The art of readable writing*, volume 8. Harper New York.

Yoav Goldberg. 2019. Assessing BERT's syntactic abilities. *arXiv preprint arXiv:1901.05287*.

Ian Goodfellow, Jonathon Shlens, and Christian Szegedy. 2015. Explaining and harnessing adversarial examples. In *International Conference on Learning Representations*.

Guy Hacohen and Daphna Weinshall. 2019. On the power of curriculum learning in training deep networks. In *International Conference on Machine Learning*, pages 2535–2544. PMLR.

John Hewitt and Percy Liang. 2019. Designing and interpreting probes with control tasks. In *Proceedings of the 2019 Conference on Empirical Methods in Natural Language Processing and the 9th International Joint Conference on Natural Language Processing (EMNLP-IJCNLP)*, pages 2733–2743, Hong Kong, China. Association for Computational Linguistics.

John Hewitt and Christopher D. Manning. 2019. A structural probe for finding syntax in word representations. In *Proceedings of the 2019 Conference of the North American Chapter of the Association for Computational Linguistics: Human Language Technologies, Volume 1 (Long and Short Papers)*, pages 4129–4138, Minneapolis, Minnesota. Association for Computational Linguistics.

Robin Jia and Percy Liang. 2017. Adversarial examples for evaluating reading comprehension systems. In *Proceedings of the 2017 Conference on Empirical Methods in Natural Language Processing*, pages 2021–2031, Copenhagen, Denmark. Association for Computational Linguistics.

Diederik P. Kingma and Jimmy Ba. 2015. Adam: A method for stochastic optimization. 3rd International Conference for Learning Representations.

Tom Kocmi and Ondřej Bojar. 2017. Curriculum learning and minibatch bucketing in neural machine translation. In *Proceedings of the International Conference Recent Advances in Natural Language Processing, RANLP 2017*, pages 379–386, Varna, Bulgaria. INCOMA Ltd.

Artur Kulmizev, Miryam de Lhoneux, Johannes Gontrum, Elena Fano, and Joakim Nivre. 2019. Deep contextualized word embeddings in transition-based and graph-based dependency parsing - a tale of two parsers revisited. In *Proceedings of the 2019 Conference on Empirical Methods in Natural Language Processing and the 9th International Joint Conference on Natural Language Processing (EMNLP-IJCNLP)*, pages 2755–2768, Hong Kong, China. Association for Computational Linguistics.

M. Kumar, Benjamin Packer, and Daphne Koller. 2010. Self-paced learning for latent variable models. In *Advances in Neural Information Processing Systems*, volume 23. Curran Associates, Inc.

Jenny Kunz and Marco Kuhlmann. 2020. Classifier probes may just learn from linear context features. In *Proceedings of the 28th International Conference on Computational Linguistics*, pages 5136–5146, Barcelona, Spain (Online). International Committee on Computational Linguistics.

Robin Kurtz, Stephan Oepen, and Marco Kuhlmann. 2020. End-to-end negation resolution as graph parsing. In *Proceedings of the 16th International Conference on Parsing Technologies and the IWPT 2020 Shared Task on Parsing into Enhanced Universal Dependencies*, pages 14–24, Online. Association for Computational Linguistics.

John P. Lalor and Hong Yu. 2020. Dynamic data selection for curriculum learning via ability estimation. In *Findings of the Association for Computational Linguistics: EMNLP 2020*, pages 545–555, Online. Association for Computational Linguistics.

Xuebo Liu, Houtim Lai, Derek F. Wong, and Lidia S. Chao. 2020. Norm-based curriculum learning for neural machine translation. In *Proceedings of the 58th Annual Meeting of the Association for Computational Linguistics*, pages 427–436, Online. Association for Computational Linguistics.

Ryan McDonald and Joakim Nivre. 2007. Characterizing the errors of data-driven dependency parsing models. In *Proceedings of the 2007 Joint Conference on Empirical Methods in Natural Language Processing and Computational Natural Language Learning (EMNLP-CoNLL)*, pages 122–131, Prague, Czech Republic. Association for Computational Linguistics.

Joakim Nivre, Marie-Catherine de Marneffe, Filip Ginter, Jan Hajič, Christopher D. Manning, Sampo Pyysalo, Sebastian Schuster, Francis Tyers, and Daniel Zeman. 2020. Universal Dependencies v2: An evergrowing multilingual treebank collection. In *Proceedings of the 12th Language Resources and Evaluation Conference*, pages 4034–4043, Marseille, France. European Language Resources Association.

Adam Paszke, Sam Gross, Soumith Chintala, Gregory Chanan, Edward Yang, Zachary DeVito, Zeming Lin, Alban Desmaison, Luca Antiga, and Adam Lerer. 2017. Automatic differentiation in PyTorch.

Matthew Peters, Mark Neumann, Mohit Iyyer, Matt Gardner, Christopher Clark, Kenton Lee, and Luke Zettlemoyer. 2018a. Deep contextualized word representations. In *Proceedings of the 2018 Conference of the North American Chapter of the Association for Computational Linguistics: Human Language Technologies, Volume 1 (Long Papers)*, pages 2227–2237, New Orleans, Louisiana. Association for Computational Linguistics.

Matthew Peters, Mark Neumann, Luke Zettlemoyer, and Wen-tau Yih. 2018b. Dissecting contextual word embeddings: Architecture and representation. In *Proceedings of the 2018 Conference on Empirical Methods in Natural Language Processing*, pages 1499–1509, Brussels, Belgium. Association for Computational Linguistics.

Tiago Pimentel, Josef Valvoda, Rowan Hall Maudslay, Ran Zmigrod, Adina Williams, and Ryan Cotterell. 2020. Information-theoretic probing for linguistic structure. In *Proceedings of the 58th Annual Meeting of the Association for Computational Linguistics*, pages 4609–4622, Online. Association for Computational Linguistics.

Emmanouil Antonios Platanios, Otilia Stretcu, Graham Neubig, Barnabas Poczos, and Tom Mitchell. 2019. Competence-based curriculum learning for neural machine translation. In *Proceedings of the 2019 Conference of the North American Chapter of the Association for Computational Linguistics: Human Language Technologies, Volume 1 (Long and Short Papers)*, pages 1162–1172, Minneapolis, Minnesota. Association for Computational Linguistics.

Sai Prasanna, Anna Rogers, and Anna Rumshisky. 2020. When BERT Plays the Lottery, All Tickets Are Winning. In *Proceedings of the 2020 Conference on Empirical Methods in Natural Language Processing (EMNLP)*, pages 3208–3229, Online. Association for Computational Linguistics.

Lucius Adelno Sherman. 1893. *Analytics of literature: A manual for the objective study of English prose and poetry*. Ginn.

Alon Talmor, Yanai Elazar, Yoav Goldberg, and Jonathan Berant. 2020. oLMpics-on what language model pre-training captures. *Transactions of the Association for Computational Linguistics*, 8:743–758.

Ian Tenney, Dipanjan Das, and Ellie Pavlick. 2019. BERT rediscovers the classical NLP pipeline. In *Proceedings of the 57th Annual Meeting of the Association for Computational Linguistics*, pages 4593–4601, Florence, Italy. Association for Computational Linguistics.

Ian Tenney, James Wexler, Jasmijn Bastings, Tolga Bolukbasi, Andy Coenen, Sebastian Gehrmann, Ellen Jiang, Mahima Pushkarna, Carey Radebaugh, Emily Reif, and Ann Yuan. 2020. The language interpretability tool: Extensible, interactive visualizations and analysis for NLP models. In *Proceedings of the 2020 Conference on Empirical Methods in Natural Language Processing: System Demonstrations*, pages 107–118, Online. Association for Computational Linguistics.

Elena Voita and Ivan Titov. 2020. Information-theoretic probing with minimum description length. In *Proceedings of the 2020 Conference on Empirical Methods in Natural Language Processing (EMNLP)*, pages 183–196, Online. Association for Computational Linguistics.

Gail Weiss, Yoav Goldberg, and Eran Yahav. 2018. On the practical computational power of finite precision RNNs for language recognition. In *Proceedings of the 56th Annual Meeting of the Association for Computational Linguistics (Volume 2: Short Papers)*, pages 740–745, Melbourne, Australia. Association for Computational Linguistics.

Thomas Wolf, Lysandre Debut, Victor Sanh, Julien Chaumond, Clement Delangue, Anthony Moi, Pierric Cistac, Tim Rault, Remi Louf, Morgan Funtowicz, Joe Davison, Sam Shleifer, Patrick von Platen, Clara Ma, Yacine Jernite, Julien Plu, Canwen Xu, Teven Le Scao, Sylvain Gugger, Mariama Drame, Quentin Lhoest, and Alexander Rush. 2020. Transformers: State-of-the-art natural language processing. In *Proceedings of the 2020 Conference on Empirical Methods in Natural Language Processing: System Demonstrations*, pages 38–45, Online. Association for Computational Linguistics.

Mostafa Zamanian and Pooneh Heydari. 2012. Readability of texts: State of the art. *Theory & Practice in Language Studies*, 2(1).

Rowan Zellers, Yonatan Bisk, Roy Schwartz, and Yejin Choi. 2018. SWAG: A large-scale adversarial dataset for grounded commonsense inference. In *Proceedings of the 2018 Conference on Empirical Methods in Natural Language Processing*, pages 93–104, Brussels, Belgium. Association for Computational Linguistics.

Rowan Zellers, Ari Holtzman, Yonatan Bisk, Ali Farhadi, and Yejin Choi. 2019. HellaSwag: Can a machine really finish your sentence? In *Proceedings of the 57th Annual Meeting of the Association for Computational Linguistics*, pages 4791–4800, Florence, Italy. Association for Computational Linguistics.

Kelly Zhang and Samuel Bowman. 2018. Language modeling teaches you more than translation does: Lessons learned through auxiliary syntactic task analysis. In *Proceedings of the 2018 EMNLP Workshop BlackboxNLP: Analyzing and Interpreting Neural Networks for NLP*, pages 359–361, Brussels, Belgium. Association for Computational Linguistics.

Yikai Zhou, Baosong Yang, Derek F. Wong, Yu Wan, and Lidia S. Chao. 2020. Uncertainty-aware curriculum learning for neural machine translation. In *Proceedings of the 58th Annual Meeting of the Association for Computational Linguistics*, pages 6934–6944, Online. Association for Computational Linguistics.

Does External Knowledge Help Explainable Natural Language Inference? Automatic Evaluation vs. Human Ratings

Hendrik Schuff[1,2] and **Hsiu-Yu Yang**[2] and **Heike Adel**[1] and **Ngoc Thang Vu**[2]
[1]Bosch Center for Artificial Intelligence, Renningen, Germany
[2]Institut für Maschinelle Sprachverarbeitung, University of Stuttgart
{Hendrik.Schuff,Heike.Adel}@de.bosch.com
{Hsiu-Yu.Yang,Thang.Vu}@ims.uni-stuttgart.de

Abstract

Natural language inference (NLI) requires models to learn and apply commonsense knowledge. These reasoning abilities are particularly important for explainable NLI systems that generate a natural language explanation in addition to their label prediction. The integration of external knowledge has been shown to improve NLI systems, here we investigate whether it can also improve their explanation capabilities. For this, we investigate different sources of external knowledge and evaluate the performance of our models on in-domain data as well as on special transfer datasets that are designed to assess fine-grained reasoning capabilities. We find that different sources of knowledge have a different effect on reasoning abilities, for example, implicit knowledge stored in language models can hinder reasoning on numbers and negations. Finally, we conduct the largest and most fine-grained explainable NLI crowdsourcing study to date. It reveals that even large differences in automatic performance scores do neither reflect in human ratings of label, explanation, commonsense nor grammar correctness.

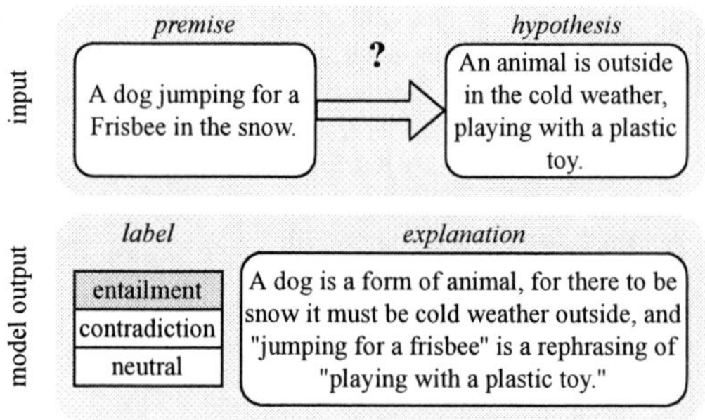

Figure 1: NLI example instance from e-SNLI (Camburu et al., 2018). The system needs to include commonsense knowledge, such as "snow → cold weather".

1 Introduction

Natural language inference (NLI) is closely related to real-world applications, such as fact checking. Given two sentences (premise and hypothesis), the task is to decide whether (a) the first sentence entails the second sentence, (b) the two sentences contradict each other or (c) they have a neutral relation. Figure 1 shows an example for an entailment relation. Solving the task requires models to not only reason over the provided information but also to link it with commonsense knowledge.

As for other natural language tasks, state-of-the-art NLI systems rely on deep neural architectures which do not easily expose their inner workings. However, following a model's reasoning process is valuable to machine learning engineers as well as end-users. The former can use the insights to improve models and the latter can base their decision on them whether to trust the system or not. One approach to gain insight into a system is to train it to generate explanations as an additional output (Camburu et al., 2018; Atanasova et al., 2020). Such self-explaining models are particularly interesting for NLI because the explanation can indicate the commonsense knowledge which was utilized during prediction. The integration of external knowledge was shown to improve NLI systems (Jijkoun and de Rijke, 2005; Chen et al., 2018; Li et al., 2019; Faldu et al., 2021). However, the following question remains: **Does the positive effect of external knowledge on the inference ability transfer to the generation of explanations? (R1)** Figure 1 shows an NLI example for which external knowledge potentially helps to infer the correct label and explanation. In the example, the system needs to link *dog* to *animal, jumping for a Frisbee* to *playing*, *Frisbee* to *plastic toy* and *snow* to *outside* as well as to *cold weather*. The predicted explanation needs to explicitly state this reasoning chain and thus would be expected to benefit from external knowledge.

Especially recently, pre-trained language models, such as BERT (Devlin et al., 2019) or GPT (Rad-

Proceedings of the Fourth BlackboxNLP Workshop on Analyzing and Interpreting Neural Networks for NLP, pages 26–41
Online, November 11, 2021. ©2021 Association for Computational Linguistics

ford et al., 2019), became popular. It was shown that they are able to learn and store commonsense knowledge implicitly (Petroni et al., 2019). As a result, an open question is: **How effective is the implicit commonsense knowledge of language models compared to symbolic sources of knowledge, such as knowledge base triplets? (RQ2)**

To evaluate NLI models, mainly automatic measures, such as accuracy, are used. However, model weaknesses can stay unnoticed using automatic scores alone. Moreover, Schuff et al. (2020) showed that automatic scores are not necessarily correlated to human-perceived model quality. Thus, human evaluation is a crucial step in the development of user-centered explainable AI systems. Therefore, we ask the question: **How do humans perceive explanation quality of state-of-the-art natural language inference models? (R3)**

In this paper, we investigate the three previously mentioned research questions R1–R3. To answer them, we analyze the impact of external knowledge from multiple sources, such as knowledge graphs, embeddings and language models and propose novel architectures to include and combine them into explainable NLI systems. Further, we conduct an extensive automatic analysis as well as a user study. To the best of our knowledge, our study exceeds previous human evaluations of explainable NLI models regarding the number of participants as well as the variety of rated explanation criteria.

For R1, we find that the positive effect of external knowledge on label accuracy in the standard NLI setting can also be observed in the explainable NLI setting and external knowledge can improve the BLEU scores of the generated explanations. In regard of R2, we observe that pre-trained language models are the most promising source of commonsense knowledge but at the same time identify weaknesses with respect to negations and numerical reasoning abilities which, however, can be mitigated through combination with additional knowledge sources. Despite the improvements in accuracy, BLEU or BLEURT scores, our user study shows for R3 that these do not reflect in human ratings of explanation correctness, commonsense inclusion or grammar and label correctness.

Our results urge caution to solely rely on automatic scores for explainability. Therefore, we expect our paper to motivate the development of dedicated evaluation tasks and scores and further emphasize the importance of the user within explainable AI. To facilitate future work, we release our model's predictions as well as the crowdsourced human ratings.[1]

2 Related Work

2.1 External Knowledge for NLI

External knowledge was shown to help across a wide variety of NLP tasks (Shi et al., 2016; Seyler et al., 2018; Pan et al., 2019; Lin et al., 2019). While early sources for external knowledge are WordNet and NomBank (Jijkoun and de Rijke, 2005; MacCartney et al., 2008), today a large variety of possibilities exist: From COMET (Bosselut et al., 2019) over ConceptNet (Speer et al., 2017) to language models. Chen et al. (2018) show that enriching an NLI system with external lexical-level semantic knowledge increases accuracy scores on SNLI and enhances transfer to MultiNLI. Wang et al. (2019) show the potential of knowledge from ConceptNet for NLI systems. Li et al. (2019) find that external knowledge from pretraining helps NLI and suggest to combine it with external knowledge from human-curated resources. Li and Sethy (2019) propose knowledge-enhanced attention modifications for Transformers and decomposable methods and show that their methods improve model robustness. Faldu et al. (2021) extend BERT by extracting entities from the input text and adding their projected KG embeddings derived from ConceptNet and WordNet as sequential input to a modified BERT layer. Bauer et al. (2021) present ERNIE-NLI, a modified ERNIE (Zhang et al., 2019) model using NLI-specific knowledge embeddings and find that it improves performance over a non-adapted ERNIE model using general-domain TransE embeddings. To compare different possibilities of integrating external knowledge, we propose various models in this paper. Further, we address the question whether external knowledge also improves explanation generation.

2.2 Explainable NLI

The task of explainable NLI consists of (i) predicting the correct entailment label and (ii) providing an explanation that allows the user to assess the model's reasoning. In general, such explanation can take various forms, such as weights and gradients over the input (Simonyan et al., 2014; Ribeiro et al., 2016; Lundberg and Lee, 2017) and

[1] https://github.com/boschresearch/external-knowledge-explainable-nli

text spans or snippets from the input or external text (Zaidan and Eisner, 2008; Lei et al., 2016; Yang et al., 2018). Beyond that, there exists various resources and approaches designed to generate textual explanations. Rajani et al. (2019) present a dataset that contains free-text explanations for multiple-choice commonsense reasoning and Bhagavatula et al. (2020) provide a dataset for abductive multiple choice answering as well as abductive NLG. Camburu et al. (2018) provide the e-SNLI dataset, which adds free-text explanations as an additional layer on the SNLI dataset (Bowman et al., 2015). As numerous models with and without external knowledge have been developed on the SNLI dataset, we use its explainable extension e-SNLI to conduct our analysis and train our models on. Various models have been proposed on e-SNLI including systems based on alignment (Swanson et al., 2020), label-specific explanation generators (Kumar and Talukdar, 2020) and fine-tuned text-to-text models (Narang et al., 2020). In contrast to those, our focus is not on proposing a new architecture or paradigm to develop a high-scoring system. Much more, we seek to conduct a broad comparison across knowledge sources and isolate their effect on automatic scores as well as human perception.

2.3 Evaluation and Human Ratings

Explainable NLI system performance is typically scored using (i) accuracy with respect to annotated gold labels on a reference dataset and (ii) BLEU scores (Papineni et al., 2002) between the generated explanations and the ground truth explanations (Camburu et al., 2018; Kumar and Talukdar, 2020; Narang et al., 2020). BLEU scores can only quantify explanation quality loosely (Narang et al., 2020). Therefore, previous work evaluates explanation quality either by manual annotation (Camburu et al., 2018; Kumar and Talukdar, 2020) or crowdsourcing (Narang et al., 2020). However, previous human evaluations regarding explainable NLI are limited to assess label and/or explanation correctness. In contrast, we additionally evaluate commonsense inclusion as well as grammatical correctness of explanations. As Clinciu et al. (2021) find automatic BLEURT scores to have distinctly stronger correlations to human ratings of generated textual explanations than BLEU, we investigate whether BLEURT is a viable replacement for a user study.

3 Method

In the following, we describe our base model and then present the models we analyze.

3.1 Base Model

We combine a state-of-the-art attention-based inference model with an explainable NLI model that predicts entailment labels and generates explanations. In particular, we use the encoder part of the enhanced sequential inference model (ESIM), which has a cross-attention layer to capture relevant semantics between premise and hypothesis (Chen et al., 2017) and the prediction part of the PRED-EXPL model of Camburu et al. (2018). We represent the input sentences with BERT embeddings (Devlin et al., 2019) which we fine-tune on the SNLI dataset.[2] Throughout the paper, we refer to this model as VANILLA.

3.2 Integration of Knowledge Sources

External knowledge can be found in various formats. We aim at covering a possibly broad variety and focus on state-of-the-art sources and methods. We include the natural language knowledge base COMET (Bosselut et al., 2019), the ConceptNet Numberbatch embeddings (Speer et al., 2017) and the GPT-2 language model (Radford et al., 2019).

3.2.1 Background Knowledge from COMET

As our example in Figure 1 shows, resolving natural language entailment can require reasoning over multiple concepts and relations, such as inferring *cold weather* and *outside* from *snow*. We seek to facilitate this resolvement by providing the model with related words (and phrases) that can be seen as a natural language extension of premise and hypothesis. We use the COMmonsEnse Transformers (COMET) (Bosselut et al., 2019) as a natural language knowledge base to query background knowledge for premise and hypothesis. COMET is based on a transformer language model that is fine-tuned on a knowledge base completion task on ConceptNet. Given an input sentence and a ConceptNet relation, it generates a phrase to complete the object in a knowledge statement expressed in the (subject, relation, object) format. Instead of feeding in the whole premise and hypothesis, we

[2] We pass inputs of the form *[CLS] premise [SEP] hypothesis* to BERT and use a softmax layer on top of the CLS token's embedding to predict the entailment label and fine-tune the model for up to 2 epochs.

find that chunking them into noun and verb sub-phrases based on POS tags patterns yields better object phrase generations.[3] Thus, for each sentence (premise/hypothesis) we generate #chunks × #relations object phrases.[4]

Afterwards, we embed each object phrase (with the respective relation string prependend) with Sentence-BERT (Reimers and Gurevych, 2019) and quantify its similarity to the embedding of the source sentence using cosine similarity. For each relation, we keep the object phrase with the highest similarity score.

Given the relation *HasA* and the chunked sentence *The dog* | *is walking in the snow*, for example, COMET will generate *bone* and *effect of freeze* for the two sub-phrases, respectively. We only preserve the object phrase *effect of freeze* as it has a higher similarity to the source sentence.

To condense the object phrases into a fixed-length vector representation, we average the respective Sentence-BERT embeddings. This procedure yields one vector representing the background knowledge regarding the premise and one regarding the hypothesis. We combine them with the local inference vector representation (Chen et al., 2017). Following Camburu et al. (2018), this vector is passed to the label prediction module as well as the explanation decoder. We refer to this model as COMET.

3.2.2 Modified Attention with ConceptNet

Following Li and Srikumar (2019), we use knowledge-driven rules to modify the attention weights within the cross-attention layer between premise and hypothesis in the encoder. This enforces the attention mechanism to align word pairs p_i and h_j from premise and hypothesis based on world knowledge. The rules proposed by Li and Srikumar (2019) are shown in Equation 1 and 2. In R_1, the antecedent K_{p_i,h_j} indicates that a word pair p_i and h_j is of a certain relation within ConceptNet. If the condition of the antecedent is true, the consequent A'_{p_i,h_j} that aligns the word pair follows. R_2 is a relatively conservative rule that additionally takes the model's own decision into account. The antecedent $K_{p_i,h_j} \wedge A_{p_i,h_j}$ in R_2 is a conjunctive condition that becomes true if a word pair is both in a relation and aligned by a model's original attention. If such a conjunctive condition is true, the word pair must be aligned which results in a new alignment as the consequent A'_{p_i,h_j} indicates.

$$R_1 : K_{p_i,h_j} \rightarrow A'_{p_i,h_j} \quad (1)$$

$$R_2 : K_{p_i,h_j} \wedge A_{p_i,h_j} \rightarrow A'_{p_i,h_j} \quad (2)$$

Different from the approach of Li and Srikumar (2019) that checks a word pair's relation in a binary fashion, we hypothesize that knowledge-aware embeddings might capture more fine-grained word relationship that exists in multi-hop relational edges. Considering *playground* and *playroom*, for example, the former is usually located outdoors whereas the latter is located indoors. We generalize the binary relational inclusion from Li and Srikumar (2019) to continuous relation scores. For this, we replace the binary rule antecedent with the absolute cosine similarity between the ConceptNet Numberbatch (Speer et al., 2017) vector representations of p_i and h_j. We empirically confirm that our continuous formulation outperforms the binary version regarding label accuracy as well as explanation correctness. In the following, we refer to these modified rules as continuous constraints and use CONT to refer to the respective model.

3.2.3 All-Text Prediction with GPT-2

Similar to Kumar and Talukdar (2020), we fine-tune a pre-trained GPT-2 language model on the e-SNLI dataset. In contrast to Kumar and Talukdar (2020), we use a single GPT-2 model to generate explanations for all three entailment labels instead of training a separate model for each of them. This allows us to directly integrate the label prediction into the language model instead of training an additional model which predicts the label on top of the three explanations. Therefore, we propose two models, which both are GPT-2-large models, but differ regarding their training setting. In the label-first setting (GPT-LF), the model is trained on text following the structure *Premise: <premise> Hypothesis: <hypothesis> [LAB] [label] [EXP] <explanation> EOS*. In the explanation-first setting (GPT-EF) it is trained on text following the structure *Premise: <premise> Hypothesis: <hypothesis> [EXP] <explanation> [LAB] <label> EOS*.

[3] We manually find that feeding in the whole sentence predominantly relates the output to the last tokens of the sentence and fails to include information from tokens earlier in the sentence.

[4] We consider the relations AtLocation, CapableOf, DefinedAs, HasA, HasProperty, HasSubevent, InheritsFrom, InstanceOf, IsA, LocatedNear, MadeOf, PartOf, SymbolOf, UsedFor and LocationOfAction.

3.3 Combined Models

COMET and ConceptNet. We combine COMET with CONT to benefit from both integrated background information from COMET and a knowledge-enhanced attention mechanism based on ConceptNet Numberbatch. We expect this to help the model focus on important relations between premise and hypothesis.

Knowledge-Enhanced Ensembles. We combine the world knowledge of BERT (VANILLA), ConceptNet Numberbatch (CONT), COMET (COMET) and the combined model COMET+CONT with the language model abilities of GPT-2 (GPT-LF and GPT-EF). For this, we propose an ensemble that not merely aggregates label votes, but combines the models with respect to their different strengths.

The label predictions of VANILLA, CONT, COMET, COMET+CONT as well as GPT-LF are passed to a majority voting. In the *basic ensemble*, the GPT-LF model is then conditioned on the voted label and generates the final explanation. We refer to this model as ENSEMBLE.

In the *filtered ensemble*, the majority voting only allows models to vote if their generated explanation lets the GPT-EF model predict the same label prediction as the original model. In other words, we fix the input as well as the generated explanation and only let the GPT-EF model predict the label. This step can be interpreted as a consistency filter which prevents models from voting if their label prediction does not match their explanation prediction. In the following, we refer to this model as FILTERED-ENS. We include a depiction of the model architecture in the appendix.

4 Automatic Evaluation

First, we evaluate the discussed knowledge-enhanced models with respect to commonly used scores on e-SNLI and a stress test evaluation. In addition to our constructed models, we also include PRED-EXPL (Camburu et al., 2018), which is basically our VANILLA baseline without cross-attention but with GloVe embeddings instead of fine-tuned BERT embeddings. Further, we include two recent models proposed for e-SNLI: NILE:post-hoc, which is the highest performing model from Kumar and Talukdar (2020), and WT5-11B from Narang et al. (2020), which holds the current state-of-the-art performance. While NILE:post-hoc is based on GPT-2 as well, WT5-11B is a fine-tuned version

Type	Model	Label Acc.	BLEU	BLEURT
non-LM	PRED-EXPL	84.21	19.77	-0.871
	VANILLA	89.20	19.71	-0.820
	COMET	88.97	18.84	-0.822
	CONT	89.02	20.1	-0.799
	COMET+CONT	89.07	19.66	-0.809
LM-based	GPT-EF	87.89	21.70	-0.624
	GPT-LF	89.70	26.90	-0.577
	ENSEMBLE	90.24	27.10	-0.576
	FILTERED ENS	90.24	27.09	-0.577
	NILE:POST-HOC	91.49	26.26	-0.577
	WT5-11B	**92.3**	**29.01**	**-0.511**

Table 1: Automatic evaluation metrics on the e-SNLI test set. Label accuracy quantifies NLI performance. BLEU and BLEURT score the similarity between predicted and ground truth explanation texts. Higher values are better.

of the T5 language model (Raffel et al., 2020). We train all non-LM models with five random seeds and report scores of the median model based on label accuracy. Table 2 shows predicted explanations for the subset of models that we investigate within the human evaluation in Section 5. Further examples are provided in the appendix.

4.1 Performance on e-SNLI

Following prior work on e-SNLI, we report label accuracy as well as BLEU scores (Papineni et al., 2002) for explanations. We additionally evaluate BLEURT scores (Sellam et al., 2020), which is a reference-based learned evaluation metric to model human judgements of text generation. BLEURT is of particular interest for explanation evaluation as Clinciu et al. (2021) compare how various automatic scores such as BLEU, ROUGE and METEOR correlate to human ratings of generated explanations and find that embedding-based methods and particularly BLEURT scores show distinctly higher correlations than, e.g., BLEU.

Table 1 shows the respective scores for all considered models.[5] The upper block lists models that share or extend the PRED-EXPL architecture. Compared to PRED-EXPL, the VANILLA model achieves a notable increase in label accuracy as well as BLEURT scores. Surprisingly, COMET reduces all scores and even decreases the BLEU score be-

[5]For NILE:post-hoc (Kumar and Talukdar, 2020) and WT5-11B (Narang et al., 2020) we report the label accuracy from their paper and calculate BLEU/BLEURT scores based on the explanation predictions provided by the authors. Narang et al. (2020) calculate BLEU scores using SacreBLEU v1.3. (Post, 2018) leading to a higher reported score of 33.7.

Model	Predicted Explanation
GROUND-TRUTH	a man is either playing the accordion or performs a mime act while happy people pass by or angry people glare at him.
VANILLA	a man can not be playing and a mime at the same time
COMET	the man is either playing the accordion or a mime
CONT	people can not be playing and angry at the same time
COMET+ CONT	the man can not be playing the accordion and the mime at the same time
GPT-LF	Happy people are not angry people.
WT5-11B	The man cannot be playing the accordion and performing a mime act at the same time.

Table 2: Explanation predictions of the models used within the human evaluation for the premise "*A man on a sidewalk is playing the accordion while happy people pass by*" and the hypothesis "*A man on the sidewalk performs a mime act while angry people glare at him*". All models correctly predict the class *contradiction* but generate different explanations. The predicted explanation of the FILTERED-ENS model is identical to the explanation of the GPT-LF model as GPT-LF is used to predict the ensemble's explanation.

low the PRED-EXPL score. In contrast, knowledge-enhanced cross attention (CONT) improves BLEU and BLEURT scores and reaches a label accuracy close to VANILLA. Combining CONT with COMET retains the CONT label accuracy but again slightly decreases BLEU and BLEURT scores. The lower block contains models that are or include language models. All language model-based models increase BLEU and BLEURT scores. All except GPT-EF outperform all non-language model models.

To analyze whether the performance differences of models can be really attributed to a better reasoning and commonsense knowledge ability instead of merely different model capacity, we next evaluate our models on the NLI stress test evaluation.

4.2 Stress Test Evaluation

Table 3 shows the results of our models on the NLI stress test evaluation proposed by Naik et al. (2018). The dataset contains multiple subsets of which each subset is used to evaluate the robustness of the system against a specific type of perturbation, e.g., spelling errors, negations, numerical reasoning and more. On average, all models distinctly improve performance compared to the PRED-EXPL baseline. With respect to VANILLA, all models except GPT-EF improve average performance. Further, both COMET and CONT improve average label accuracy, while their combination decreases performance. Surprisingly, GPT-LF outperforms the ensemble methods on average. While COMET+CONT reaches the best performance in terms of e-SNLI label accuracies, it performs worst on the stress tests. The same effect can be observed for the FILTERED-ENS. While it reaches top performance for the spelling error test, its performance drops for numerical reasoning, where it performs worse than any other model. These results show that combining different knowledge sources does not result in a consistent combination of their weaknesses and strengths. Instead, the sources of external knowledge have to be carefully adjusted to the target domain and our results paint a rather pessimistic picture regarding a cure-all solution. Further, a model's reasoning capabilities have to be assessed in detail as evaluation across different reasoning types easily masks model weaknesses.

Finally, we assess whether language models reach their higher performance due to better reasoning: For most of the assessed reasoning types — with exception of numerical reasoning and negation — the best non-ensemble model in fact is GPT-LF. Also, GPT-LF reaches the highest accuracy on average. Therefore one could generally recommend to include external knowledge in form of a pre-trained language model as the foremost option. However, our results also show that language models are not necessarily the best choice for all reasoning needs and can, e.g., severely decrease performance for numerical reasoning and negations, where models based on language models perform worse than all other models.

5 Human Evaluation

While automatic scores, such as BLEU, provide a valuable starting point for evaluating explanations, they fall short in capturing the model's real explanation capabilities. We, therefore, conduct a large-scale crowdsourcing study to complement our automatic evaluations on e-SNLI and the stress tests. Following related work (Narang et al., 2020), we assess explanation quality based on ratings from crowdworkers on Mechanical Turk. While previ-

Type	Model	Total	Competence Test		Distraction Test			Noise Test
			Antonymy	Numerical	Word Overlap	Length Mismatch	Negation	Spelling
non-LM	PRED-EXPL	48.69	36.36	36.55	47.17	53.44	45.31	52.42
	VANILLA	56.94	37.94	32.24	55.46	65.21	52.03	62.90
	COMET	57.05	34.54	35.48	57.31	64.15	52.85	62.33
	CONT	57.09	32.50	**40.28**	52.10	64.35	**53.38**	62.77
	COMET+CONT	56.26	44.43	34.16	51.34	64.39	49.36	63.03
LM-based	GPT-EF	52.74	51.81	31.33	55.91	60.97	38.44	58.20
	GPT-LF	**59.28**	**54.84**	28.80	**64.06**	**68.72**	42.82	67.07
	ENSEMBLE	59.19	37.97	34.03	58.13	67.45	52.51	65.92
	FILTERED-ENS	58.99	52.53	28.54	63.70	68.02	42.18	**67.10**

Table 3: Label accuracies (higher is better) for all categories in the NLI stress test tasks (Naik et al., 2018). The six rightmost columns show (i) the model's reasoning abilities (competence), (ii) how sensitive it is to lexical distractors (distraction) and (iii) how robust it is against noise from different perturbations (noise). Each column corresponds to one dataset. For datasets with matched and mismatched subsets, we report the accuracy over all labels within the group. Similarly, the total accuracy is calculated over all labels.

ous work limited evaluation to rating explanation correctness, we additionally ask participants to provide fine-grained ratings of commonsense inclusion and grammatical correctness. A screenshot of the interface is shown in the appendix. We release the full data of our study.

5.1 Conditions

In order to evaluate effects across the discussed sources of external knowledge, we include seven models in our human evaluation: VANILLA, COMET, CONT, COMET+CONT, GPT-LF, FILTERED-ENS and WT5-11B. Additionally we evaluate the e-SNLI ground truth labels and explanations. Table 2 displays the different explanations the models predict for an exemplary input as well as its ground truth explanation annotation.

5.2 Dependent Variables

We evaluate the models' predicted labels and explanations along four self-reported dimensions.

Label Correctness. Following Kumar and Talukdar (2020) and Narang et al. (2020), we ask participants to rate if the predicted label is correct.

Explanation Correctness. Similar to Camburu et al. (2018), Kumar and Talukdar (2020) and Narang et al. (2020), we collect subjective yes/no explanation correctness ratings.

Grammatical Correctness. We ask participants to rate if the generated explanation is grammatical.

Commonsense Inclusion. We ask participants whether the explanation includes commonsense knowledge that is needed to answer the question. We collect responses on an item with the options *yes*, *no* and *no need*.

5.3 Study Design

In order to evaluate the effect of the level of required external knowledge, we compile, like Kumar and Talukdar (2020) and Narang et al. (2020), a set of 100 premise-hypothesis pairs. In contrast to them, we compose the 100 pairs to contain 50 pairs that require a low level of external knowledge and 50 pairs that require a high level. To gather pairs of both categories, we let two annotators rate 250 premise-hypothesis pairs from the e-SNLI test set. We sample 50 pairs per level of external knowledge from the 179 pairs on which the annotators agree. We provide details on the annotation criteria in the appendix. During the study, we, like Narang et al. (2020), collect 5 crowdsourced ratings for each condition and for each of the 10 input pairs per batch, i.e., 500 ratings per model and a total of 4000 ratings for each variable. We provide ratings of exemplary model predictions in the appendix.

5.4 Analysis

We collect responses from 290 crowdworkers and discard those that were entered in less then 5 minutes (31%) as this might indicate arbitrary answer selection. Note that the repeated measures design of our study possibly introduces inter-dependencies within ratings as, e.g., certain participants can have a tendency to rate explanations as correct more often than others or a certain question might elicit more label correctness ratings. Thus, we use generalized linear mixed models (GLMM) to account for the potentially confounding variables (worker ID, question ID and level of required commonsense knowledge). As our response variables are binary,[6] we use binomial GLMMs. We include fixed effects (model and commonsense level) as well as random intercepts (worker and question IDs). Figure 2 shows effect displays for the collected ratings in relation to the predictor *model type*.

We conduct likelihood ratio tests between the full model and the model without the evaluated predictor to test the effects of *model type* and *commonsense level* on all four rating variables. As *model type* contains more than two factors, we additionally conduct single-step corrected Tukey HSD post-hoc tests for all four variables.

Label Correctness. We do not observe a significant main effect of *model type* ($\chi^2(7) = 13.00$, $p = 0.0723$) but a significant main effect of *commonsense level* ($\beta = 0.28$, $\chi^2(1) = 4.54$, $p < 0.0331$).[7]

Explanation Correctness. We observe a main effect of *model type* ($\chi^2(7)$=24.06, p<0.0012) and *commonsense level* ($\beta = 0.27$, $\chi^2(1) = 7.79$, $p < 0.0053$). For *model type*, a post-hoc Tukey test showed significant differences between FILTERED-ENS and VANILLA ($p < 0.0055$) as well as FILTERED-ENS and COMET+CONT ($p < 0.0029$).

Grammatical Correctness. We observe a main effect of *model type* ($\chi^2(7) = 14.20$, $p < 0.0479$). However, a post-hoc Tukey test did not reveal significant differences between any model type pair. No significant main effect of *commonsense level* was observed ($\beta = 0.02$, $\chi^2(1) = 0.02$, $p = 0.8803$).

Commonsense Correctness. We observe a main effect of *model type* ($\chi^2(7) = 20.63$, $p < 0.0044$). However, a post-hoc Tukey test did not reveal significant differences between any model type pair. No significant main effect of *commonsense level* was observed ($\beta = 0.07$, $\chi^2(1) = 0.25$, $p = 0.6163$).

Overall, these results show surprisingly few significant differences between the different model types and conflict with the large differences within automatic evaluation scores.

[6]We do not consider "no need" commonsense ratings during the respective model estimation.

[7]β refers to the estimate of a *high* commonsense level.

6 Discussion

R1: Effect of External Knowledge. We showed that external knowledge can increase label accuracies on e-SNLI as well as on the stress tests. In addition, we found external knowledge to increase BLEU/BLEURT scores and thus help explanation generation in terms of automatic evaluation.

R2: Implicit Knowledge in Language Models. While language models achieve the best scores on general e-SNLI performance, the stress tests showed that they do not succeed in all reasoning types. Thus, for choosing the best way of integrating commonsense knowledge, the final reasoning goal of the model needs to be considered.

R3: Perceived Explanation Quality by Humans. We expected the large differences in e-SNLI label accuracy (up to 3.23%), BLEU (up to 10.17) and BLEURT (0.31) to reflect in human ratings, but none of these maximal differences in scores leads to a significantly different rating for any dependent variable. Regarding the observed significant differences, FILTERED-ENS is not the best model included in the study with respect to e-SNLI (WT5-11B reaches distinctly higher values for all scores) and, similarly, neither VANILLA nor COMET+CONT are the worst models on any score in Table 1. Thus, large accuracy gains do not necessarily imply better models when used in real-world applications with users. In the following, we will further discuss these results.

Superhuman Model or Noisy Ground Truth? It is particularly remarkable that the ground truth ratings do not significantly differ from any other model's ratings. In fact, the ground truth condition ranks in the lower half across all four rating dimensions and yields the lowest probability of receiving label correctness ratings as shown in Figure 2a. Similarly, Narang et al. (2020) note that in their experiment the WT5-11B model reaches a 12%-higher explanation correctness rating than the ground truths. This indicates that e-SNLI might not be suitable to distinguish performances of today's high-performing models. While it remains valuable for training, models should be scored on specifically designed evaluation sets, for example an explainable extension of the NLI stress test dataset.

Limitations and Future Directions. Although we evaluated a total of 11 different model architectures and various different sources of external

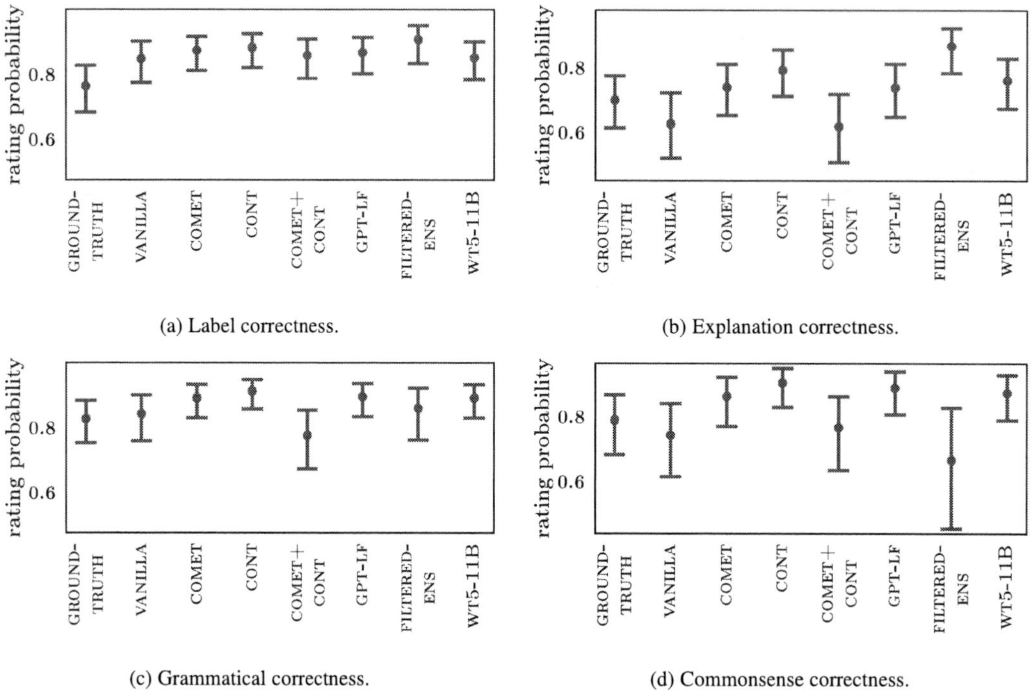

(a) Label correctness.

(b) Explanation correctness.

(c) Grammatical correctness.

(d) Commonsense correctness.

Figure 2: Effect displays for user ratings of label, explanation, grammatical and commonsense correctness depending on *model type* following Fox (2003). The rating probability is the probabality that a prediction of a respective model type is perceived to be correct by a human considering fixed effects. Error bars mark 95% confidence limits.

knowledge, this clearly does not exhaust all possible knowledge sources or architectures. While our analysis provides insight into the most common knowledge sources integrated into representative model architectures, future work should confirm our findings for additional sources and architectures. Although our user study already is the largest and most fine-grained evaluation of explainable NLI, future work should further expand the set of dependent variables to potentially reveal effects that are not visible through the lens of our experimental setup. While our work addresses the task of explainable NLI, we expect that the observed disconnect between automatic and human evaluation applies to further tasks and requires to re-assess model evaluation across explainability tasks.

7 Conclusion

In this paper, we addressed three research questions: whether integrating external knowledge can improve explainability for NLI, how effective knowledge implicitly stored in language models is for reasoning, and how humans perceive explanation quality of state-of-the-art natural language inference models. To answer these questions, we proposed different methods of integrating various knowledge sources into deep learning models. We found that fine-tuned language models reach the highest performance on e-SNLI as well as the highest average accuracy within the NLI stress test evaluation. However, their performance can break down on numerical reasoning and negations. In addition to automatic evaluation, we conducted a large-scale human crowdsourcing evaluation and found that high differences in accuracy, BLEU or BLEURT scores do not reflect in significant differences in human ratings of explanation correctness, commonsense inclusion, grammar or label correctness. This highlights an alarming disconnect between automatic evaluation scores and human ratings, that puts the real-world utility of recent model improvements into question and requires to re-think automatic evaluation across the field of explainable AI.

Acknowledgement

We thank the members of the BCAI NLP&KRR research group and the anonymous reviewers for their helpful comments. Ngoc Thang Vu is funded by Carl Zeiss Foundation.

References

Pepa Atanasova, Jakob Grue Simonsen, Christina Lioma, and Isabelle Augenstein. 2020. Generating fact checking explanations. In *Proceedings of the 58th Annual Meeting of the Association for Computational Linguistics*, pages 7352–7364, Online. Association for Computational Linguistics.

Lisa Bauer, Lingjia Deng, and Mohit Bansal. 2021. ERNIE-NLI: Analyzing the Impact of Domain-Specific External Knowledge on Enhanced Representations for NLI. In *Proceedings of Deep Learning Inside Out (DeeLIO): The 2nd Workshop on Knowledge Extraction and Integration for Deep Learning Architectures*, pages 58–69, Online. Association for Computational Linguistics.

Chandra Bhagavatula, Ronan Le Bras, Chaitanya Malaviya, Keisuke Sakaguchi, Ari Holtzman, Hannah Rashkin, Doug Downey, Wen-tau Yih, and Yejin Choi. 2020. Abductive Commonsense Reasoning. In *8th International Conference on Learning Representations, ICLR 2020, Addis Ababa, Ethiopia, April 26-30, 2020*. OpenReview.net.

Antoine Bosselut, Hannah Rashkin, Maarten Sap, Chaitanya Malaviya, Asli Celikyilmaz, and Yejin Choi. 2019. COMET: Commonsense transformers for automatic knowledge graph construction. In *Proceedings of the 57th Annual Meeting of the Association for Computational Linguistics*, pages 4762–4779, Florence, Italy. Association for Computational Linguistics.

Samuel R. Bowman, Gabor Angeli, Christopher Potts, and Christopher D. Manning. 2015. A large annotated corpus for learning natural language inference. In *Proceedings of the 2015 Conference on Empirical Methods in Natural Language Processing*, pages 632–642, Lisbon, Portugal. Association for Computational Linguistics.

Oana-Maria Camburu, Tim Rocktäschel, Thomas Lukasiewicz, and Phil Blunsom. 2018. e-snli: Natural language inference with natural language explanations. In *Advances in Neural Information Processing Systems 31: Annual Conference on Neural Information Processing Systems 2018, NeurIPS 2018, December 3-8, 2018, Montréal, Canada*, pages 9560–9572.

Qian Chen, Xiaodan Zhu, Zhen-Hua Ling, Diana Inkpen, and Si Wei. 2018. Neural natural language inference models enhanced with external knowledge. In *Proceedings of the 56th Annual Meeting of the Association for Computational Linguistics (Volume 1: Long Papers)*, pages 2406–2417, Melbourne, Australia. Association for Computational Linguistics.

Qian Chen, Xiaodan Zhu, Zhen-Hua Ling, Si Wei, Hui Jiang, and Diana Inkpen. 2017. Enhanced LSTM for natural language inference. In *Proceedings of the 55th Annual Meeting of the Association for Computational Linguistics (Volume 1: Long Papers)*, pages 1657–1668, Vancouver, Canada. Association for Computational Linguistics.

Miruna-Adriana Clinciu, Arash Eshghi, and Helen Hastie. 2021. A study of automatic metrics for the evaluation of natural language explanations. In *Proceedings of the 16th Conference of the European Chapter of the Association for Computational Linguistics: Main Volume*, pages 2376–2387, Online. Association for Computational Linguistics.

Jacob Devlin, Ming-Wei Chang, Kenton Lee, and Kristina Toutanova. 2019. BERT: Pre-training of deep bidirectional transformers for language understanding. In *Proceedings of the 2019 Conference of the North American Chapter of the Association for Computational Linguistics: Human Language Technologies, Volume 1 (Long and Short Papers)*, pages 4171–4186, Minneapolis, Minnesota. Association for Computational Linguistics.

Keyur Faldu, Amit P. Sheth, Prashant Kikani, and Hemang Akabari. 2021. KI-BERT: infusing knowledge context for better language and domain understanding. *CoRR*, abs/2104.08145.

John Fox. 2003. Effect Displays in R for Generalised Linear Models. *Journal of Statistical Software*, 8(15).

Valentin Jijkoun and Maarten de Rijke. 2005. Recognizing textual entailment using lexical similarity. In *Proceedings of the PASCAL Challenges Workshop on Recognising Textual Entailment*, pages 73–76.

Sawan Kumar and Partha Talukdar. 2020. NILE : Natural language inference with faithful natural language explanations. In *Proceedings of the 58th Annual Meeting of the Association for Computational Linguistics*, pages 8730–8742, Online. Association for Computational Linguistics.

Tao Lei, Regina Barzilay, and Tommi Jaakkola. 2016. Rationalizing neural predictions. In *Proceedings of the 2016 Conference on Empirical Methods in Natural Language Processing*, pages 107–117, Austin, Texas. Association for Computational Linguistics.

Alexander Hanbo Li and Abhinav Sethy. 2019. Knowledge enhanced attention for robust natural language inference. *CoRR*, abs/1909.00102.

Tao Li and Vivek Srikumar. 2019. Augmenting neural networks with first-order logic. In *Proceedings of the 57th Annual Meeting of the Association for Computational Linguistics*, pages 292–302, Florence, Italy. Association for Computational Linguistics.

Tianda Li, Xiaodan Zhu, Quan Liu, Qian Chen, Zhigang Chen, and Si Wei. 2019. Several experiments on investigating pretraining and knowledge-enhanced models for natural language inference. *CoRR*, abs/1904.12104.

Bill Yuchen Lin, Xinyue Chen, Jamin Chen, and Xiang Ren. 2019. KagNet: Knowledge-Aware Graph Networks for Commonsense Reasoning. In *Proceedings of the 2019 Conference on Empirical Methods in Natural Language Processing and the 9th International Joint Conference on Natural Language Processing (EMNLP-IJCNLP)*, pages 2829–2839, Hong Kong, China. Association for Computational Linguistics.

Scott Lundberg and Su-In Lee. 2017. A unified approach to interpreting model predictions. volume abs/1705.07874.

Bill MacCartney, Michel Galley, and Christopher D. Manning. 2008. A phrase-based alignment model for natural language inference. In *Proceedings of the 2008 Conference on Empirical Methods in Natural Language Processing*, pages 802–811, Honolulu, Hawaii. Association for Computational Linguistics.

Aakanksha Naik, Abhilasha Ravichander, Norman Sadeh, Carolyn Rose, and Graham Neubig. 2018. Stress test evaluation for natural language inference. In *Proceedings of the 27th International Conference on Computational Linguistics*, pages 2340–2353, Santa Fe, New Mexico, USA. Association for Computational Linguistics.

Sharan Narang, Colin Raffel, Katherine Lee, Adam Roberts, Noah Fiedel, and Karishma Malkan. 2020. Wt5?! training text-to-text models to explain their predictions. *CoRR*, abs/2004.14546.

Xiaoman Pan, Kai Sun, Dian Yu, Jianshu Chen, Heng Ji, Claire Cardie, and Dong Yu. 2019. Improving question answering with external knowledge. In *Proceedings of the 2nd Workshop on Machine Reading for Question Answering, MRQA@EMNLP 2019, Hong Kong, China, November 4, 2019*, pages 27–37. Association for Computational Linguistics.

Kishore Papineni, Salim Roukos, Todd Ward, and Wei-Jing Zhu. 2002. Bleu: a method for automatic evaluation of machine translation. In *Proceedings of the 40th Annual Meeting of the Association for Computational Linguistics*, pages 311–318, Philadelphia, Pennsylvania, USA. Association for Computational Linguistics.

Fabio Petroni, Tim Rocktäschel, Sebastian Riedel, Patrick Lewis, Anton Bakhtin, Yuxiang Wu, and Alexander Miller. 2019. Language models as knowledge bases? In *Proceedings of the 2019 Conference on Empirical Methods in Natural Language Processing and the 9th International Joint Conference on Natural Language Processing (EMNLP-IJCNLP)*, pages 2463–2473, Hong Kong, China. Association for Computational Linguistics.

Matt Post. 2018. A call for clarity in reporting BLEU scores. In *Proceedings of the Third Conference on Machine Translation: Research Papers*, pages 186–191, Brussels, Belgium. Association for Computational Linguistics.

Alec Radford, Jeffrey Wu, Rewon Child, David Luan, Dario Amodei, and Ilya Sutskever. 2019. Language models are unsupervised multitask learners. *OpenAI blog*, (8):9.

Colin Raffel, Noam Shazeer, Adam Roberts, Katherine Lee, Sharan Narang, Michael Matena, Yanqi Zhou, Wei Li, and Peter J. Liu. 2020. Exploring the limits of transfer learning with a unified text-to-text transformer. *J. Mach. Learn. Res.*, 21:140:1–140:67.

Nazneen Fatema Rajani, Bryan McCann, Caiming Xiong, and Richard Socher. 2019. Explain yourself! leveraging language models for commonsense reasoning. In *Proceedings of the 57th Annual Meeting of the Association for Computational Linguistics*, pages 4932–4942, Florence, Italy. Association for Computational Linguistics.

Nils Reimers and Iryna Gurevych. 2019. Sentence-BERT: Sentence embeddings using Siamese BERT-networks. In *Proceedings of the 2019 Conference on Empirical Methods in Natural Language Processing and the 9th International Joint Conference on Natural Language Processing (EMNLP-IJCNLP)*, pages 3982–3992, Hong Kong, China. Association for Computational Linguistics.

Marco Túlio Ribeiro, Sameer Singh, and Carlos Guestrin. 2016. "why should I trust you?": Explaining the predictions of any classifier. In *Proceedings of the 22nd ACM SIGKDD International Conference on Knowledge Discovery and Data Mining, San Francisco, CA, USA, August 13-17, 2016*, pages 1135–1144. ACM.

Hendrik Schuff, Heike Adel, and Ngoc Thang Vu. 2020. F1 is Not Enough! Models and Evaluation Towards User-Centered Explainable Question Answering. In *Proceedings of the 2020 Conference on Empirical Methods in Natural Language Processing (EMNLP)*, pages 7076–7095, Online. Association for Computational Linguistics.

Thibault Sellam, Dipanjan Das, and Ankur Parikh. 2020. BLEURT: Learning robust metrics for text generation. In *Proceedings of the 58th Annual Meeting of the Association for Computational Linguistics*, pages 7881–7892, Online. Association for Computational Linguistics.

Dominic Seyler, Tatiana Dembelova, Luciano Del Corro, Johannes Hoffart, and Gerhard Weikum. 2018. A study of the importance of external knowledge in the named entity recognition task. In *Proceedings of the 56th Annual Meeting of the Association for Computational Linguistics (Volume 2: Short Papers)*, pages 241–246, Melbourne, Australia. Association for Computational Linguistics.

Chen Shi, Shujie Liu, Shuo Ren, Shi Feng, Mu Li, Ming Zhou, Xu Sun, and Houfeng Wang. 2016. Knowledge-based semantic embedding for machine translation. In *Proceedings of the 54th Annual Meeting of the Association for Computational Linguistics*

(*Volume 1: Long Papers*), pages 2245–2254, Berlin, Germany. Association for Computational Linguistics.

Karen Simonyan, Andrea Vedaldi, and Andrew Zisserman. 2014. Deep inside convolutional networks: Visualising image classification models and saliency maps. In *2nd International Conference on Learning Representations, ICLR 2014, Banff, AB, Canada, April 14-16, 2014, Workshop Track Proceedings*.

Robyn Speer, Joshua Chin, and Catherine Havasi. 2017. Conceptnet 5.5: An open multilingual graph of general knowledge. In *Proceedings of the Thirty-First AAAI Conference on Artificial Intelligence, February 4-9, 2017, San Francisco, California, USA*, pages 4444–4451. AAAI Press.

Kyle Swanson, Lili Yu, and Tao Lei. 2020. Rationalizing text matching: Learning sparse alignments via optimal transport. In *Proceedings of the 58th Annual Meeting of the Association for Computational Linguistics*, pages 5609–5626, Online. Association for Computational Linguistics.

Xiaoyan Wang, Pavan Kapanipathi, Ryan Musa, Mo Yu, Kartik Talamadupula, Ibrahim Abdelaziz, Maria Chang, Achille Fokoue, Bassem Makni, Nicholas Mattei, and Michael Witbrock. 2019. Improving Natural Language Inference Using External Knowledge in the Science Questions Domain. In *AAAI*, pages 7208–7215.

Zhilin Yang, Peng Qi, Saizheng Zhang, Yoshua Bengio, William Cohen, Ruslan Salakhutdinov, and Christopher D. Manning. 2018. HotpotQA: A dataset for diverse, explainable multi-hop question answering. In *Proceedings of the 2018 Conference on Empirical Methods in Natural Language Processing*, pages 2369–2380, Brussels, Belgium. Association for Computational Linguistics.

Omar Zaidan and Jason Eisner. 2008. Modeling annotators: A generative approach to learning from annotator rationales. In *Proceedings of the 2008 Conference on Empirical Methods in Natural Language Processing*, pages 31–40, Honolulu, Hawaii. Association for Computational Linguistics.

Zhengyan Zhang, Xu Han, Zhiyuan Liu, Xin Jiang, Maosong Sun, and Qun Liu. 2019. ERNIE: Enhanced Language Representation with Informative Entities. In *Proceedings of the 57th Annual Meeting of the Association for Computational Linguistics*, pages 1441–1451, Florence, Italy. Association for Computational Linguistics.

A Ensemble Architectures

Figure 3 depicts the ensemble architectures discussed in Section 3.3.

B Study Interface

Figure 4 shows an example of the study interface used to collect human ratings as discussed in Section 5.

C Knowledge Requirement Annotation

Table 4 lists the annotation guidelines used to decide on low/high levels of required external knowledge as discussed in Section 5.3. Table 5 shows example annotations.

D Examples of Human Ratings

Table 6 displays various model prediction examples and corresponding examples of human ratings.

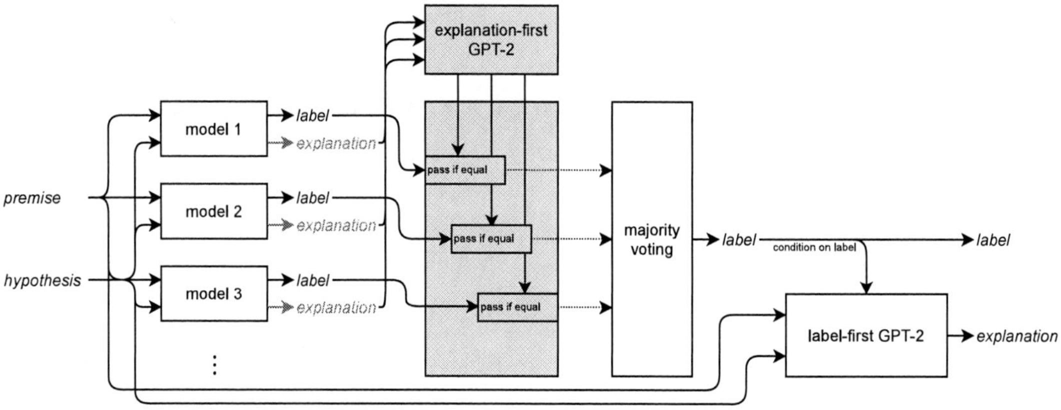

Figure 3: Ensemble architectures. The blue boxes show the consistency-filter extension.

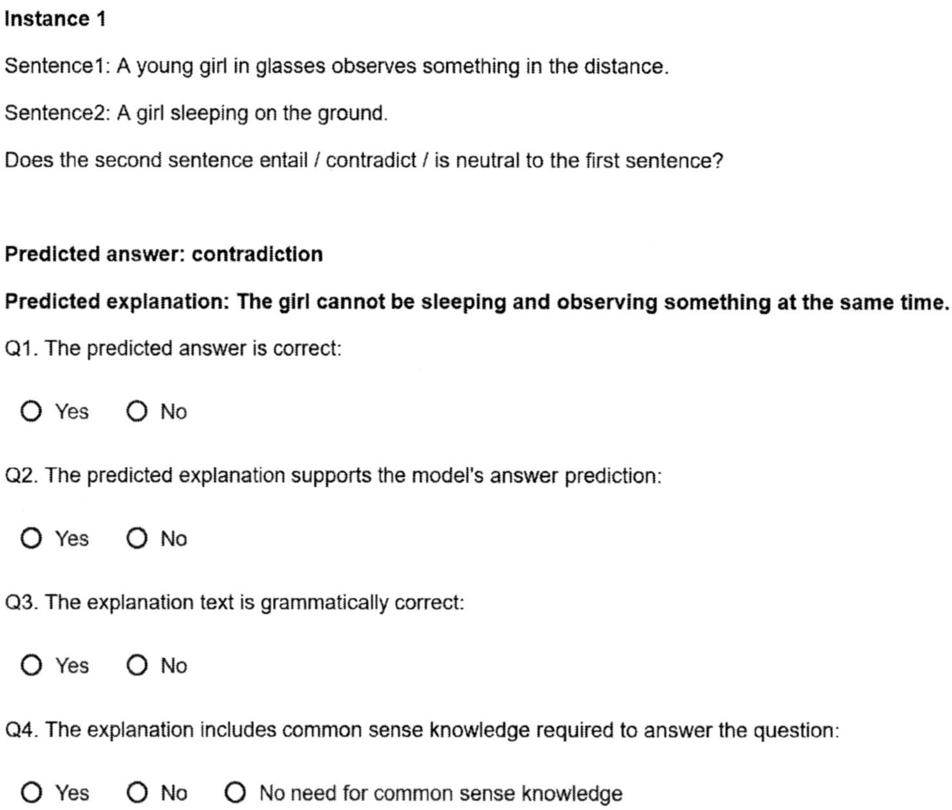

Instance 1

Sentence1: A young girl in glasses observes something in the distance.

Sentence2: A girl sleeping on the ground.

Does the second sentence entail / contradict / is neutral to the first sentence?

Predicted answer: contradiction

Predicted explanation: The girl cannot be sleeping and observing something at the same time.

Q1. The predicted answer is correct:

O Yes O No

Q2. The predicted explanation supports the model's answer prediction:

O Yes O No

Q3. The explanation text is grammatically correct:

O Yes O No

Q4. The explanation includes common sense knowledge required to answer the question:

O Yes O No O No need for common sense knowledge

Figure 4: Screenshot of the study interface presented to crowdworkers on Mechanical Turk.

Low Level	Pattern Matching	The entailment can be decided by matching identical parts in the premise and the hypothesis. Premise: *A water scene with a sunset in the background.* Hypothesis:*There is a water scene with the sunset in the back.*
	Unrelated Negation	The entailment can be decided by identifying an unrelated negation. Premise: *Children bathe in water from large drums.* Hypothesis: *The kids are not reading.*
	Rephrasing	The entailment can be decided by simple rephrasing (e.g. replacing a word with a synonym). Premise: *A boy dressed in an orange shirt and a helmet is riding a dirt bike in the woods.* Hypothesis: *A boy in orange rides his dirt bike.*
	Easily-Distinguishable Concepts	The entailment can be decided by identifying unrelated concepts that have no semantic relation. Premise: *Firefighters in full gear are walking up a ladder.* Hypothesis: *The firefighters are eating lunch.*
High Level	Complex Reasoning	The entailment can be decided by resolving more complex relations and reasoning using common sense knowledge. Premise: *Soccer players are playing a night game and the ball is in the air, while the two teams fight for it.* Hypothesis: *The sun was shining during the soccer match.*
	Abstract Concepts	The entailment can be decided using common sense knowledge about abstractions of concepts. Premise: *A girl reaches up to kiss a cat, which is sitting on the counter.* Hypothesis: *A girl is showing affection towards a cat.*

Table 4: Annotation guidelines used during the annotation of low/high levels of required external knowledge with examples.

Low Level	Premise: There is a group of children getting their picture taken with presents. Hypothesis: Two men carry a Christmas tree.
	Premise: A woman looks at a plate filled with steam. Hypothesis: The woman is out shopping at the mall.
	Premise: Man sitting on bench with a suitcase in front of PADDINGTON sign. Hypothesis: A man sitting with a sign.
	Premise: A man grilling a hamburger. Hypothesis: The man is swimming at the bottom of the ocean.
	Premise: The African American man protests against unlawful sex. Hypothesis: The man protests.
High Level	Premise: A boy in a red jacket and black hat sliding on his knees down a snowy hill Hypothesis: A child is playing outside.
	Premise: A man playing a piano. Hypothesis: The man's hands are on the keys of a piano.
	Premise: 3 girls chatting and laughing on the stairwell. Hypothesis: Girls are not having a good time.
	Premise: A man visiting a friend in the hospital. Hypothesis: A man and a patient in a hospital room.
	Premise: Two girls pose along a tree-lined path and blow kisses towards the camera. Hypothesis: Two girls are taking pictures outside.

Table 5: Pairs from the low/high external knowledge requirement annotations sampled from pairs for which annotators agreed.

Premise	Hypothesis	Common Sense	Model	Predicted Label	Predicted Explanation	Human Ratings			
						Label	Expl.	Grammar	Common Sense
By a table with several boxes and two coffee cups on it, a woman in a green sweater is opening a small box and another person (whose head cannot be seen) is operating a small handheld electronic device.	Members of congress opening care packages.	high	WT5-11B	neutral	Not all women are members of congress. Not all boxes are care packages.	✓	✓	✓	✓
In front is a guy singing and playing guitar and a white shirted drummer in the back.	Some people perform at a concert.	high	GPT-LF	neutral	Just because a guy singing and playing guitar and a white shirted drummer in the back does not mean they are performing at a concert.	✓	✓	✓	✓
A man in a black coat and hat and a woman in a blue coat with pink hat snowshoeing on the side of a road with a stoplight in the background .	A man and woman are outside in the snow .	high	COMET +CONT	entailment	in the snow is outside	✓	✓	✓	✓
Two individuals dressed up like animals are posing for the camera .	Two young boys dressed like cows are posing .	low	COMET +CONT	neutral	not all people are young	✗	✗	✓	✓
A man playing a piano	The man's hands are on the keys of a piano.	high	VANILLA	entailment	playing a piano requires one to be on the hands	✓	✓	✗	✓
Two women are hugging on a path through a grassy area with a cow visible past them.	There are women outside in this picture	high	WT5-11B	entailment	A grassy area is outside.	✓	✓	✓	✓
A woman in a spaghetti strap tank wearing a flower in her hair is staring towards the right .	The woman is sleeping on a pillow .	low	COMET +CONT	contradiction	the woman can not be looking towards a sleeping she is sleeping	✓	✗	✗	✓

Table 6: Examples of model predictions and human ratings of the predicted labels and explanations for various model types.

The Language Model Understood the *Prompt* was Ambiguous: Probing Syntactic Uncertainty Through Generation

Laura Aina
Universitat Pompeu Fabra
Barcelona, Spain
laura.aina@upf.edu

Tal Linzen
New York University
New York, NY
linzen@nyu.edu

Abstract

Temporary syntactic ambiguities arise when the beginning of a sentence is compatible with multiple syntactic analyses. We inspect to which extent neural language models (LMs) exhibit uncertainty over such analyses when processing temporarily ambiguous inputs, and how that uncertainty is modulated by disambiguating cues. We probe the LM's expectations by generating from it: we use stochastic decoding to derive a set of sentence completions, and estimate the probability that the LM assigns to each interpretation based on the distribution of parses across completions. Unlike scoring-based methods for targeted syntactic evaluation, this technique makes it possible to explore completions that are not hypothesized in advance by the researcher. We apply this method to study the behavior of two LMs (GPT2 and an LSTM) on three types of temporary ambiguity, using materials from human sentence processing experiments. We find that LMs can track multiple analyses simultaneously; the degree of uncertainty varies across constructions and contexts. As a response to disambiguating cues, the LMs often select the correct interpretation, but occasional errors point to potential areas of improvement.

1 Introduction

During sentence processing, humans incrementally derive analyses of linguistic expressions. At an initial stage, uncertainty regarding the analysis may be present if no contextual cues have been provided to allow for a unique interpretation; this results in a temporary ambiguity (Frazier, 1978). For instance, the initial sentence portion of (1) is ambiguous as to the syntactic function of *band*, which can be a direct object, as in (1a), or an embedded subject as in (1b):

(1) The audience knew the band ...

a) very well.

b) was going to come back on stage.

Like humans, autoregressive neural language models (henceforth, LMs) need to deal with temporary ambiguities, as they process text incrementally. In this work, we probe the degree of syntactic uncertainty that LMs maintain when processing temporary ambiguities, using generation (sampling) from those models as an analysis tool.

LMs are trained to output contextual probabilities of words in a next-word prediction task. In spite of this generic objective, these models have been shown to track syntactic information to a remarkable extent (Linzen and Baroni, 2021) and build context-sensitive internal representations, potentially resolving ambiguities in the input (e.g., Peters et al. 2018). The behavior of LMs on temporary syntactic ambiguities was previously investigated through the lens of word surprisal (e.g., Futrell et al. 2018), providing evidence for incremental syntactic processing in LMs. At the same time, the extent that a LM expects each interpretation of an ambiguous input, and therefore its degree of syntactic uncertainty, has not been quantified.

In this paper, we generate text from a LM, as a window into the LM's processing of an unfolding sentence. As (1) shows, the completion of a temporarily ambiguous fragment clarifies the intended interpretation. We can use the LM's output probabilities to complete an input – a *prompt* – and infer how it was initially interpreted. We generate a set of completions by drawing multiple samples from the LM's output distribution. The proportion of completions that are consistent with a certain parse of the prompt is taken to indicate the degree that that parse is expected by the LM.

We consider three types of temporary ambiguities in English; for each type, we derive prompts from sentences drawn from psycholinguistic experiments (Grodner et al., 2003; Frazier and Rayner, 1987). We compare the LM's uncertainty on ambiguous prompts as well as unambiguous prompts that vary in the number and location of disambiguat-

Proceedings of the Fourth BlackboxNLP Workshop on Analyzing and Interpreting Neural Networks for NLP, pages 42–57
Online, November 11, 2021. ©2021 Association for Computational Linguistics

ing cues. We infer the interpretation of a generated sentence from the labels predicted by a syntactic parser. The LMs we analyse are the LSTM model released by Gulordava et al. (2018) and the transformer GPT2 (Radford et al., 2019).[1]

We find that in the presence of temporary ambiguity LMs can track multiple interpretations in parallel, displaying syntactic uncertainty. The degree of bias towards one analysis varies across ambiguity types and across specific sentences within each type. Disambiguating cues often appropriately reduce the LMs' syntactic uncertainty in favor of the correct analysis. At the same time, we also identify evidence of disambiguation issues in the resolution of NP/Z and Noun/Verb ambiguities. We complement our analyses with a study on the effect of different decoding strategies on syntactic uncertainty, and a comparison of our method to scoring-based analysis.

2 Related Work

Temporary ambiguities have been studied extensively in psycholinguistics, as window into human incremental parsing: in case of ambiguities, is only one or a subset of the possible parses considered (Frazier and Fodor, 1978), or are all parses tracked in parallel, weighted by probability (Hale, 2001)? After disambiguation, how is the analysis revised (Grodner et al., 2003), and do traces of initial misinterpretations linger (Christianson et al., 2001)? We consider analogous questions, focusing on LMs instead of humans.

Several studies have examined the syntactic abilities of LMs, through targeted evaluations on specific syntactic phenomena (e.g., Linzen et al. 2016; Wilcox et al. 2018), or by analysing the degree to which syntactic information can be decoded from their internal representations (e.g., Giulianelli et al. 2018; Hewitt and Manning 2019). These studies show that LMs track syntax to a large extent, even when not explicitly trained to do so.

Some previous studies have investigated the behavior of LMs on temporary ambiguities focusing on the *garden-path effect* (Bever, 1970), where a high cognitive cost at disambiguation is taken to signal a preference for the alternative analysis. On the one hand, LMs' next-word probabilities can be used to model these effects (Van Schijndel and Linzen, 2018). On the other, one can test whether LMs themselves exhibit garden-path effects, looking at their surprisal at the disambiguation of the sentence (Futrell et al., 2019). This was taken to indicate that, as the sentence unfolds, the LM maintains a representation of its syntactic state, akin to an incremental parser.

As we do in the present work, Futrell et al. (2018) generated completions from language models, but that study focused on LMs' awareness of obligatory syntactic events (specifically in the case of relative clause completions). Finally, Van Schijndel and Linzen (2021) analyzed the syntactic predictions of LMs after temporary ambiguous sentence portions, but limited their analysis to the part-of-speech probabilities for the single word that is expected to follow the ambiguous portion. Although it is limited to one word, this approach is related to ours as the expectations of the LM are analyzed classifying its predictions based on syntactic information.

3 Temporary Ambiguities

This section describes the types of temporary ambiguity and the materials we use in our study (the full list of materials can be found in Appendix D). For each type of ambiguity, we refer to the ambiguous word whose syntactic role determines the analysis of the sentence as the **locus of the ambiguity**.

3.1 The NP/S Ambiguity

The sentence portion in (2) is compatible with the main verb *understood* taking either a noun phrase (NP) or a sentential (S) complement. This is reflected by the syntactic role of *contract* – the locus of the NP/S ambiguity – which could act as direct object of the main verb (2a), or as embedded subject in an upcoming subordinate clause (2b).

(2) The employees understood the contract ...

2a) NP:

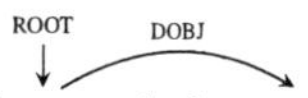

The employees understood the contract well.

2b) S:

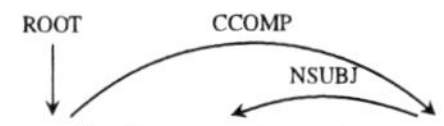

The employees understood the contract would be changed very soon.

An equivalent of (2b) without temporary ambiguity can be obtained by adding the complementizer *that*:

2c) S: The employees understood that the contract would be changed very soon.

[1]Our code is made available at https://github.com/amore-upf/syntactic-uncertainty-LMs.

We use the 20 NP/S sentence pairs from Grodner et al. (2003).[2] Each pair consists of a temporarily ambiguous sentence and its unambiguous counterpart, both of which eventually have an S interpretation (2b and 2c). From each sentence pair, we derive four types of **prompts**; i.e., the sentence portion which is passed to the LM as input for generation. Examples of prompts are shown in Table 1. NO CUE prompts are the sentence portions that exhibit temporary ambiguity. The other prompts contain at least one disambiguating cue, before or after the locus of ambiguity: *that* is the **pre-locus cue**, while the **post-locus cue** is the word immediately after the locus of ambiguity (varying across items).

Prompt type	
NO CUE	The employees knew the contract
POST-LOCUS CUE	The employees knew the contract **would**
PRE-LOCUS CUE	The employees knew **that** the contract
PRE&POST-LOCUS CUES	The employees knew **that** the contract **would**

Table 1: Examples of prompt types for NP/S; locus of ambiguity underlined, cues in bold.

3.2 The NP/Z Ambiguity

In (3), the verb *left* in the subordinate clause can be parsed as taking either a noun phrase complement (NP) or none (zero complement; Z). The locus of ambiguity is *party*, which can be direct object of *left* (3a) or subject of the upcoming main verb (3b).

(3) Even though the band left the party ...

3a) NP:

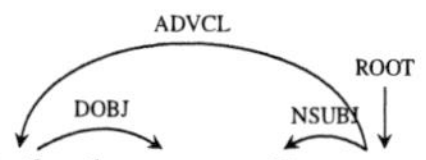

Even though the band left the party I stayed.

3b) Z:

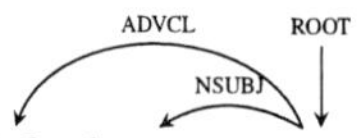

Even though the band left the party went on for another hour.

The unambiguous version of (3b) adds a comma between the subordinate and main clauses:

3c) Z: Even though the band left, the party went on for another hour.

We use the 20 "unmodified" (see Footnote 2) NP/Z sentence pairs from Grodner et al. (2003). Both sentences in each pair ultimately had the Z interpretation (3b and 3c). From a sentence pair, we derive prompts following the same criteria described for NP/S ambiguity; here, the pre-locus cue is the comma.

3.3 The Noun/Verb Ambiguity

The last ambiguity we investigate concerns words that can function as either a noun or a verb. Such words can lead to temporary structural ambiguities as in (4): if *suit*, the locus of this ambiguity, is a noun, *pants* acts as its modifier; otherwise, it serves as its subject.

(4) Mary thinks that the pants suit ...

4a) Noun

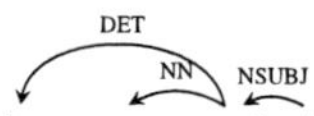

Mary thinks that the pants suit is pretty.

4b) Verb

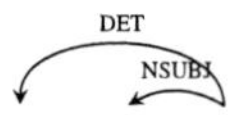

Mary thinks that the pants suit me well.

The temporary ambiguity in (4) can be preempted by replacing *the* with the determiners *this* and *these*, which, through number agreement, favor one of the interpretations:

4c) Noun: Mary thinks that this pants suit is pretty.
4d) Verb: Mary thinks that these pants suit me well.

We study this type of ambiguity using the data from Experiments 1 and 2 of Frazier and Rayner (1987). For each temporary ambiguity, two sentence pairs are provided, one with a Noun interpretation and one with a Verb interpretation (4a and 4c for Noun, and 4b and 4d for Verb). A minority of the sentences used by Frazier and Rayner were disambiguated by cues other than agreement; in our analyses, we discard those items and focus only on examples disambiguated by agreement. This leaves us with 26 sentence pairs (out of 32) each for Noun and Verb interpretations. We obtain prompts from the pairs, treating the determiner as the pre-locus cue. As we have one pair for each reading, for unambiguous prompt types (all but NO CUE), we derive two prompt subtypes, one for the Noun reading and another for the Verb reading.

[2]Grodner et al. (2003) considered two variants of sentences, with or without material between the locus of ambiguity and the post-locus cue (*modified* and *unmodified*, respectively). We only use the unmodified sentence pairs for both NP/S and NP/Z.

4 Methods

Language Models We evaluate two English language models: the **LSTM** model from Gulordava et al. (2018), which was trained on a 80M-tokens Wikipedia corpus, with 2 hidden layers of 650 units; and the transformer-based **GPT2** (*small*; Radford et al. 2019), which was trained on the 40GB WebText corpus, with 12 hidden layers of 768 units.[3] Both LMs are unidirectional: their predictions solely depend on the previous context. In the LSTM, this is achieved through recurrent connections, while in GPT2 through masked self-attention. Given previous evaluations, more fluent generation can be expected from GPT2, which surpasses the LSTM in both number of parameters and size of training corpus.

Generation Starting from a prompt, we generate a completion through stochastic decoding, sampling words from the LM's output distribution. The LM processes the prompt as input and outputs a probability distribution over the next token (1); we sample a word from this distribution sampled (2) and use this word as the next input token. The process is repeated to generate the next tokens.

$$P(X_{i+1}|x_{1:i}) = LM(x_{1:i}) \tag{1}$$

$$x_{i+1} \backsim P(X_{i+1}|x_{1:i}) \tag{2}$$

To obtain a sentence completion, we generate a fixed number of tokens from the prompt and crop the text to sentence boundaries identified using the Spacy Sentencizer.[4] More details are provided in Appendix A.

In our main experiments, we do not apply techniques that modify the LM's output distribution before sampling (e.g., nucleus sampling; Holtzman et al. 2019). In Section 8 we analyze how such decoding strategies affect syntactic uncertainty.

Syntactic Uncertainty Estimation We consider a scenario where the locus of ambiguity can be interpreted in one of two ways, i_1 or i_2. We aim to estimate the probability that the LM assigns to each interpretation based on the prompt; that is, a Bernoulli distribution, where $P(i_1|\text{prompt}) = 1 - P(i_2|\text{prompt})$. We derive an empirical estimate of this distribution by independently sampling a set of sentence completions of the prompt (C_p) and mapping them to their interpretations. We generate 100 completions of each prompt, sampled with replacement; in practice, the same completion is rarely generated more than once. Appendix B reports an analysis of the diversity of completions within a sample, in terms of lexical overlap and the proportion of unique sentences. The relative frequency of interpretations in the sample is then used to estimate their probabilities:

$$\hat{P}(i_1|\text{p}) = \frac{|\{c \in C_\text{p}|\text{interpretation}(c) = i_1\}|}{|C_\text{p}|} \tag{3}$$

This allows us to quantify the degree of preference of the LM for each interpretation of the prompt, and thus its uncertainty. For unambiguous prompts, it would be desirable for the probability of the correct interpretation to be 1, as the LM should only generate completions that are consistent with the correct interpretation. In the presence of ambiguity (NO CUE prompts), an LM that implicitly implemented a fully parallel parser (Hale, 2001) would distribute the probability mass across multiple interpretations.

Completion Classification This method requires us to classify completions based on the syntactic interpretation they imply for the locus of ambiguity. Manual classification is highly reliable, but less practical when a large set of sentences needs to be analyzed (in our case, at least 8K per ambiguity type). By contrast, automatic classification relies on the use of a syntactic parser, which may introduce noise in case the parser itself incorrectly disambiguates the sentence.

As a compromise, we use automatic annotations, and assess their quality by comparing them to manual annotations for a subset of sentences. We use the AllenNLP (Gardner et al., 2018) dependency parser, based on the model of Dozat and Manning (2016) (label attachment accuracy with predicted PoS tags $= 92.86\%$). For each ambiguity type we use a set of rules to classify completions based on the predicted labels. These are summarized in the next few sections, and described in more detail in Appendix C. If a completion cannot be traced back to either of the candidate interpretations, it is discarded from the sample; this rarely happens in practice.

For each type of ambiguity, a random sample of 80 sentences (20 for each prompt type) generated by GPT2 is manually annotated. This is carried out by three trained linguists, each of whom reviews

[3]GPT2 is used through the Transformers library (Wolf et al., 2020). For text generation, we adapt the code of the available decoding functions to also work with the LSTM.

[4]`https://spacy.io/api/sentencizer`

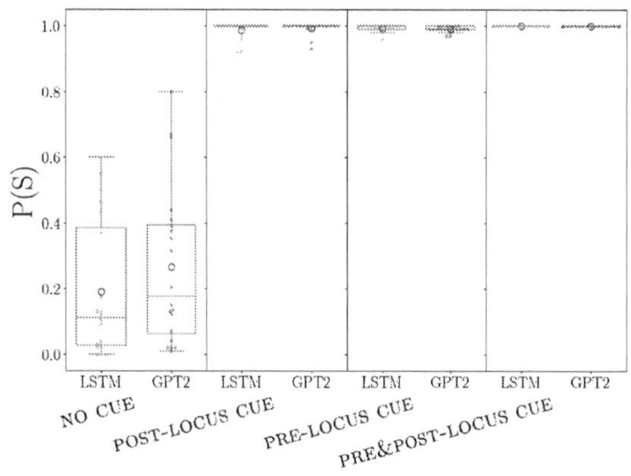

Figure 1: Distribution of $P(\mathrm{S})$ for each NP/S prompt type and LM; circle = mean across items.

Examples
(1) The scientist proved the theory a) *through two experiments.* (NP) b) *was correct.* (S)
(2) The tourists saw the palace was a) *on fire.* (S) b) *under construction.* (S)
(3) The journalist confirmed that the story a) *is false.* (S) b) *was being reported on his network.* (S)

Table 2: Examples of completions generated by GPT2 for NP/S prompts.

data from a different ambiguity type. There are four possible labels for each sentence: the two candidate interpretations, as well as *other* if the sentence has a different interpretation than the two candidate interpretation and *unclear* if the sentence cannot be interpreted. The annotators also judge the syntactic well-formedness of the sentences. We do not consider the semantic plausibility of the sentence. For all ambiguity types, between 61% and 66% of the generated sentences are judged to be fully well-formed; an additional fraction of the data (9–19%) are sentences that could be well-formed if it were not for punctuation errors and character errors. The lack of grammaticality of a sentence does not typically impair the ability to infer the interpretation of the locus of ambiguity (i.e., the annotators rarely used the labels *unclear*). We provide additional details on the annotation process in Appendix B.

5 The NP/S Ambiguity

Classification To classify a completion as a case of an NP or an S analysis, we inspect the dependency label of the locus of ambiguity (direct object $\rightarrow$ NP; subject $\rightarrow$ S). In some of the completions, the locus of ambiguity forms part of a complex NP (e.g., a modifier of another noun, as in *the contract clauses*): In this case, we use the dependency labels of the following words. To reduce noise from parser errors, we define a heuristic that corrects the most typical type of misclassification (NP instead of S).[5] If these rules do not identify the interpretation as either NP or S, the sentence is discarded from the completions; for both LMs, this is the case for 0.2% of the completions, across all prompt types. This classification method is reliable: First, the sentences from which the prompts were derived are all correctly classified as S. Second, there is near-perfect agreement between the manual and automatic annotations (Cohen's k = .96; accuracy of automatic classification with respect to manual: .99).

Results Based on the distribution of NP and S completions, we compute $P(\mathrm{S})$ for each prompt ($P(\mathrm{NP}) = 1 - P(\mathrm{S})$). The distribution across items for the different prompt types is shown in Figure 1, and examples of completions can be found in Table 2.

We focus first on the NO CUE prompts, which are ambiguous between NP and S. The LMs are often uncertain – to varying degrees – between the two interpretations. In most cases, they exhibit a preference for NP ($P(\mathrm{S}) < .5$), though this preference is typically not absolute, as S completions are also generated (e.g., (1) in Table 2). This indicates that, in the presence of the NP/S ambiguity, the LMs tend to consider multiple parses at the same time. In spite of the general preference for NP, $P(\mathrm{S})$ vary across items, with some cases even favoring an S analysis.

The other prompt types all contain at least one cue disambiguating the sentence as S; as such, we expect the LM to generate only completions that are consistent with S. In line with this prediction, for all these conditions and LMs, $P(\mathrm{S})$ is very close to 1. This indicates that the LMs are sensitive to the disambiguating cues and use them correctly to adapt their interpretation. A qualitative inspection of the sentences supports this observation: there is no evidence of disambiguation issues (e.g., (2-3) in Table 2). A minority of completions of unam-

[5] The misclassification consists in the locus of ambiguity being labeled as direct object while the finite verb that directly follows it is left without a preceding subject. This parse is ungrammatical in English. See Appendix C.1 for an example and more details.

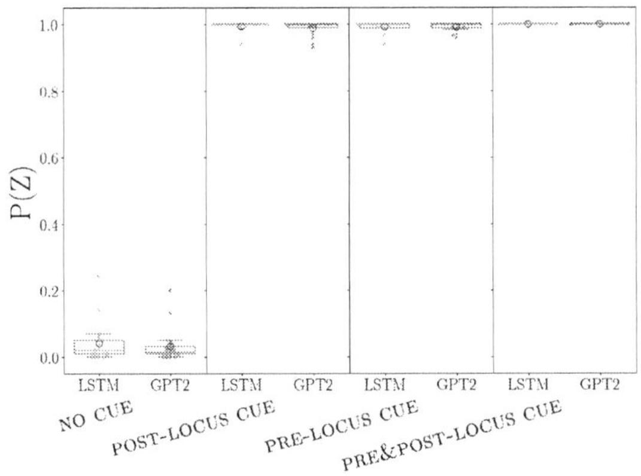

Figure 2: Distribution of $P(\text{Z})$ for each NP/Z prompt type and LM; circle = mean across items.

(1) In case the executive forgot the assistant a) *, the assistant was never fired and so on.* (NP) b) *explains the recommendations to this memo.* (Z)
(2) Because the train stopped the traffic was a) *much slower.* (Z) b) *suspended immediately.* (Z)
(3) Even though the girl phoned, the instructor a) *ignored her.* (S) b) *was too rude.* (S)

Table 3: Examples of completions generated by GPT2 for NP/Z prompts.

biguous prompts are recognized as NP. This occurs due to misclassifications, but also ill-formed completions whose interpretation is unclear (e.g., "The employees understood that *the contract.*"), or when NP is licensed despite the post-locus cue (e.g., "The army found the supplies saved *by the French.*").

6 The NP/Z Ambiguity

Classification As in the case of the NP/S ambiguity, the NP and Z interpretations can be distinguished based on the syntactic role (direct object or subject) of the locus of ambiguity. We therefore employ the same set of rules we used for NP/S. The rule correcting cases where a subject is labeled as direct object turns out to be crucial for this classification, as the parser is prone to errors on NP/Z sentences. A total of 0.6% of of GPT2 completions and 1.4% of LSTM completions cannot be identified as either NP or Z, and are thus discarded from analysis. The agreement between the automatic and manual annotations is high (Cohen's $k = .86$; accuracy of automatic classification with respect to manual: .95); the few divergences are cases where the annotator used the label *unclear*, which is not available to the parser.

Results Figure 2 shows $P(\text{Z})$ values ($P(\text{NP}) = 1 - P(\text{Z})$) for each prompt type. Examples of completions are reported in Table 3.

In the ambiguous NO CUE prompts, there is limited syntactic uncertainty: $P(\text{Z})$ stays close to 0 (on average, .03 and .04 for GPT2 and LSTM), as NP completions are generated much more often than Z ones. In spite of this default preference for NP, when there is at least one cue that biases the prompt in favor of the Z reading, $P(\text{Z})$ spikes to 1 or close to it, in line with the expected behavior on unambiguous prompts. Inspecting the completions, we find that most cases are correctly disambiguated (e.g., (2–3) in Table 3). The handful of NP completions are due to misclassifications or unclear cases, analogously to those reported for NP/S.

Alongside these encouraging results, we also observe the following curious behavior on a subset of completions to POST-LOCUS CUE prompts (examples from GPT2):

(5) As the couple danced the tango began *, the paparazzi swooned.*

(6) Once the child played the piano was *ours, it was somewhat expected.*

These completions suggest that even when the Z reading is selected, the LMs may not fully adapt to its structure. We estimate that this behavior affects 8% and 25% of POST-LOCUS CUE completions of the LSTM and GPT2, respectively (we detect these cases based on patterns in the dependency labels; see Appendix C.2). We interpret this phenomenon as evidence of confusion about the structure of the sentence, where the subordinate clause ends up ungrammatically incorporating two predicates. This points to a lingering effect of the initial NP analysis, and difficulty establishing the boundary between the subordinate and main clauses when that boundary is not marked by a comma.

We note that sentences such as (5) and (6) could, in principle, have a grammatical interpretation if the comma were to be interpreted as conjoining two clauses; under such an interpretation of (5), two things happened during the couple's dance: the tango began and the paparazzi swooned. However, this charitable interpretation is called into question by the fact that such comma-conjoined completions are very rare in other contexts: 0.01% of all PRE&POST-LOCUS CUE completions, for example, compared to 25% of POST-LOCUS CUE completions.

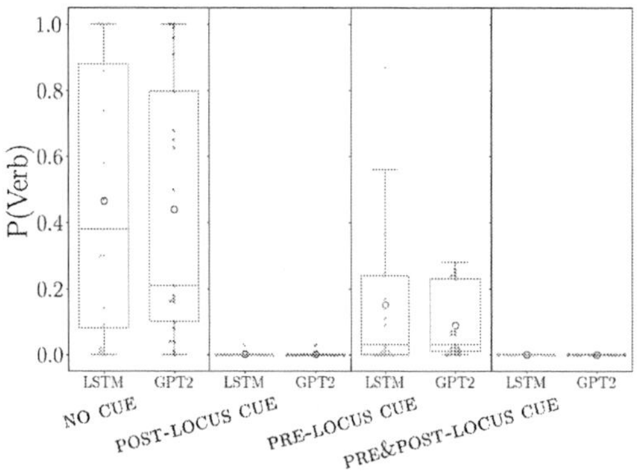

(a) Prompts with Noun interpretation

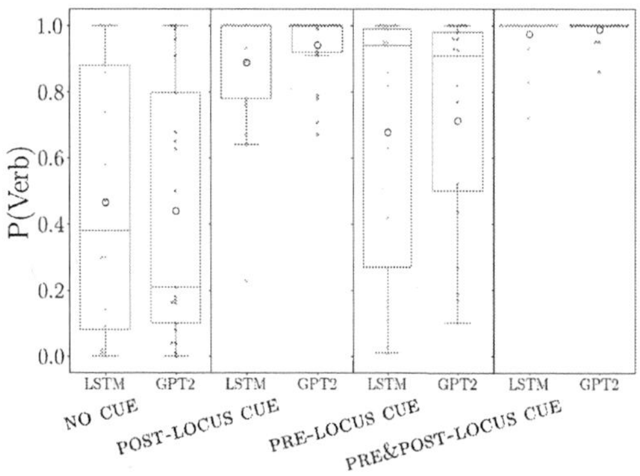

(b) Prompts with Verb interpretation

Figure 3: Distribution of $P(\text{Verb})$ for each Noun/Verb prompt type and LM; circle = mean across items.

7 The Noun/Verb Ambiguity

Classification To classify the generated sentences, we use the PoS label predicted by the parser for the locus of ambiguity. When run on the sentence pairs that the prompts are derived from, the classification sometimes fails. To minimize noise, we discard items where the tagger does not correctly interpret at least one of the sentences associated with that ambiguity (4 in total)—we reason that if the parser makes errors on the original sentences, this is likely to occur also on the sentences generated by the LMs from prompts taken from those sentences. This leaves us with 21 prompts for each subtype. The agreement between the automatic labels and the annotator's ones is high (Cohen's $k = .83$; accuracy of automatic classification with respect to manual: .91). Differences occur due to tagging errors and sentences annotated as *unclear* by the linguist.

Results $P(\text{Verb})$ values for each prompt type are shown in Figure 3, while examples of completions

(1) Nobody knows if it's true that the university fines a) *are ever issued.* (N) b) *people who don't study.* (V)
(2) Mrs. Baker is convinced that the school fears are a) *valid points.* (N) b) *unfounded.* (N)
(3) Mary thinks that the pants suit me a) *better.* (V) b) *really in a bad way.* (V)
(4) Despite last year's report, those city hopes a) *varied.* (N) b) *to become wealthier.* (V)
(5) I know that this desert trains a) *people to work!* (V) b) *are closed.* (N)

Table 4: Examples of completions generated by GPT2 for Noun/Verb prompts.

can be found in Table 4.

For ambiguous prompts – i.e., NO CUE – the dispersion of values is very high for both models. Though there is on average a preference for the Noun reading (mean $P(\text{Verb}) \approx .4$), the probability assigned to this interpretation varies across items. This indicates that the LMs' initial syntactic preferences on this temporary ambiguity are highly dependent on its instance.

For POST-LOCUS CUE prompts, $P(\text{Verb})$ adapts to the disambiguating cues, approaching 0 for the Noun reading and 1 for the Verb reading. In the latter case, we find dispersion of values, due to some completions labeled as NP. A qualitative inspection shows that this occurs due to tagger errors or when a Noun reading is licensed in spite of the post-locus cue (e.g., "some metal rings loudly *beat into our ears.*"). Overall, we do not find evidence of disambiguation issues on this type of prompt (e.g., (2-3) in Table 4).

By contrast, PRE-LOCUS CUE prompts, especially in the Verb subtype, pose more challenges to the LMs. $P(\text{Verb})$ values follow the expected trends – decreasing for the Noun cases, and increasing for the Verb cases – but exhibit variation. In some Verb cases, we do not even find a preference for the Verb reading (i.e., $P(\text{Verb}) < .5$). PRE-LOCUS CUE prompts are disambiguated by the number of the determiner: These results suggest that the LMs are not fully responsive this cue, especially when it points to a Verb reading. The LSTM shows greater dispersion than GPT2, indicating greater disambiguation difficulty. A qualitative analysis confirms these observations: besides a portion of tagger errors, we find several completions that persist in the incorrect interpretation, violating number agreement (e.g., (4b) and (5b) in Table 4).

In general, we find that classification errors occur more often with the Noun/Verb ambiguity than with the previously analysed ones. As errors introduce noise, our quantitative estimates should be considered approximate. However, as mentioned earlier, the trends they point to are reliable as they are all confirmed by qualitative analyses of the data.

8 Effect of Decoding Strategy

In our previous experiments, we generated completions by sampling from the LM's output distribution. We compare this approach to other decoding strategies, focusing on NP/S NO CUE prompts.

Stochastic Decoding Variants of stochastic decoding modify the LM output distribution before sampling words from it. Restricting or biasing the sampling process to high probability words can improve the quality of the generated text (Holtzman et al., 2019). In **nucleus sampling**, the LM distribution is truncated to top-probability words with cumulative probability p (e.g., $p = 0.9$). Another technique modifies the distribution by dividing the output scores by a parameter t – **temperature** – before softmax is applied: If $t \in [0, 1)$, the distribution is skewed towards high probability words.

We inspect how these decoding strategies affect the diversity of interpretations of the completions of an ambiguous prompt. For different combination of values of p and t, we generate set of completions from prompts and report the average $P(\mathrm{S})$ (Table 5). Standard sampling, used in our previous experiments, corresponds to $p = 1$ and $t = 1$. The values of $P(\mathrm{S})$ decrease as the hyperparameters are modulated to focus on high-probability words (t or p decreases), showing that fewer S completions are generated. This indicates that temperature and nucleus size can influence how temporary ambiguities manifest in generated text: Focusing on top-probability words increases the bias our method identifies towards the preferred interpretation (NP, in the case of NP/S).

Maximization-Based Decoding Is the preference for an analysis observed sampling multiple completions reflected by the analysis of the top-probability completion? We use **beam search** as our decoding strategy, returning the completion ranking highest in probability (beam size = 16). As in this case we consider only one completion per prompt, $P(\mathrm{S})$ for beam search in Table 5 reflects the proportion of prompts whose top-completion has an S interpretation. Most – though not all – have an NP interpretation. This mirrors what observed with sampling: in NP/S temporary ambiguities, there is a general preference for NP, but this does not apply uniformly to all instances.

	p	t	LSTM	GPT2
Pure sampling	1	1	.19	.27
Nucleus sampling	.9	1	.18	.24
	.75	1	.15	.23
	.6	1	.15	.22
With temperature	1	.9	.18	.24
	1	.75	.15	.24
	1	.6	.14	.23
Beam search - 16	-	-	.10	.25

Table 5: Average $P(\mathrm{S})$ for decoding strategies on NO CUE NP/S prompts (p: nucleus size; t: temperature).

9 Comparison to Surprisal-Based Analysis

Previous work has probed the syntactic state of a LM in a temporarily ambiguous sentence by measuring surprisal (negative log probability) at the disambiguation point (Futrell et al., 2019): If surprisal is higher than in the unambiguous sentence, we can infer that LM initially preferred the alternative, ultimately incorrect analysis. Focusing on NP/S sentence pairs, we compare this approach to our method to extract probabilities of analyses.

We calculate (1) the difference in word surprisal of the disambiguating word that follows the locus of ambiguity (i.e., the post-locus cue) between the ambiguous and unambiguous sentences of a pair; and (2) the estimated $P(\mathrm{S})$ values on NO CUE prompts. For both LMs, we find a strong negative correlation between the difference in surprisal and $P(\mathrm{S})$ (GPT2: Spearman's $\rho = -.70$; LSTM: $\rho = -.81$; both $p < .05$): As $P(\mathrm{S})$, as estimated through generation, increases, the LM is less surprised that the S analysis is introduced on the temporarily ambiguous sentence than on its unambiguous equivalent.

The fact that the two methods – surprisal and generation-based – are aligned in their estimates corroborates the findings derived from either approach. Both methods can be considered alternatives to probe the syntactic state of a LM, and one or the other may be favored depending on the study.

Surprisal estimates can be easily extracted from a LM, making them a more straightforward tool to apply. However, to analyse the expectations of a LM on an ambiguous input, the surprisal method requires a comparison to its unambiguous counterpart, which is not needed with our method. This allowed us to study a LM's behavior also on unambiguous inputs, providing insights about the sensitivity to disambiguating cues. Moreover, generating text exemplifies the LM's expectations over the sentence, which can reveal phenomena that may not be clear on the basis of surprisal estimates alone. An example are the ungrammatical blended continuations of NP/Z prompts (e.g., "*As the couple danced the tango began, *the paparazzi swooned.*").

10 Discussion and Conclusions

In this work, we have probed the syntactic uncertainty of LMs by generating sentence completions from the LMs. Our results contribute to research on the syntactic processing of LMs, quantifying the extent that one analysis of the input is implicitly entertained by the model.

We find that when processing temporary syntactic ambiguities, LMs typically exhibit uncertainty about the analysis of the input; that is, they simultaneously consider multiple analyses to be viable. In line with previous analyses of LMs on garden-path sentences, on NP/S and NP/Z sentences we detected a general preference for the NP analysis (e.g., Van Schijndel and Linzen 2018). But, while for NP/Z this preference was near-absolute and consistent across cases, on NP/S and Noun/Verb ambiguities the LMs' behavior varied across specific instantiations of the ambiguity. A promising direction for future work would be to determine whether this inter-item variation mirrors human expectations (Ford et al., 1982; Garnsey et al., 1997) and/or corpus statistics (for Noun/Verb, e.g., how often *suit* is used as Noun vs. Verb). A plausible hypothesis is that a LM acquires default preferences for analyses from regularities in the training data.

When disambiguating cues are given as part of the input, the LMs tend to display the correct behavior: we observe the appropriate shifts in uncertainty in favor of the disambiguated parse, providing further evidence of their context-sensitivity. At the same time, certain issues arise for NP/Z and Noun/Verb ambiguities, suggesting that there is room for improvement in the LMs' responsiveness and adaptation to disambiguating cues. On NP/Z ambiguities, some generated completions exhibit confusion over the sentence structure. This behavior calls to mind lingering effects of initial misinterpretations found in humans (Christianson et al., 2001). On Noun/Verb ambiguities, the LMs sometimes failed to use the number of a preceding determiner as cue for the correct parse. This may be due to difficulties in tracking number agreement in these constructions (in contrast to results by Linzen et al. (2016) and subsequent research on subject-verb agreement), or in generally overriding a default preference for the incorrect analysis.

Using generation proved to be an informative tool to inquire a LM's uncertainty over an unfolding sentence, and could be used also to inquire more types of ambiguities (e.g., semantic). Yet, there are some challenges to our proposed methodology. First, relying on an automatic classification of sentences can introduce noise: ambiguities can be difficult for NLP systems even when explicitly trained to analyse expressions (Elkahky et al., 2018). Second, we could not automatically detect ungrammatical completions or with an unclear analysis (the parser always returns an output), whereas it may be useful to be identify these cases. While these issues did not prevent us from inferring the main trends in the LMs behavior, all confirmed by qualitative inspections of the data, we look forward to future work that will attempt to overcome the aforementioned limitations.

Acknowledgements

We thank the members of the JHU/NYU Computation and Psycholinguistics Lab and of the UPF Computational Linguistics and Linguistic Theory group for valuable discussions and feedback. We are grateful to the annotators for their participation to this research. This work was supported in part by National Science Foundation grant BCS-2020945, and has received funding from the European Research Council (ERC) under the European Union's Horizon 2020 research and innovation programme (grant agreement No. 715154). This paper reflects the authors' view only, and the EU is not responsible for any use that may be made of the information it contains.

References

Thomas G. Bever. 1970. The cognitive basis for linguistic structures. In John R. Hayes, editor, *Cognition and the development of language*, pages 279–362. New York: John Wiley and Sons.

Kiel Christianson, Andrew Hollingworth, John F Halliwell, and Fernanda Ferreira. 2001. Thematic roles assigned along the garden path linger. *Cognitive Psychology*, 42(4):368–407.

Timothy Dozat and Christopher D Manning. 2016. Deep biaffine attention for neural dependency parsing. *arXiv preprint arXiv:1611.01734*.

Ali Elkahky, Kellie Webster, Daniel Andor, and Emily Pitler. 2018. A challenge set and methods for noun-verb ambiguity. In *Proceedings of the 2018 Conference on Empirical Methods in Natural Language Processing*, pages 2562–2572, Brussels, Belgium. Association for Computational Linguistics.

M. Ford, J. Bresnan, and R. Kaplan. 1982. A competence-based theory of syntactic closure. In *The mental representation of grammatical relations*, pages 727–796.

Lyn Frazier. 1978. *On comprehending sentences: Syntactic parsing strategies*. Doctoral dissertation, University of Connecticut.

Lyn Frazier and Janet Dean Fodor. 1978. The sausage machine: A new two-stage parsing model. *Cognition*, 6(4):291–325.

Lyn Frazier and Keith Rayner. 1987. Resolution of syntactic category ambiguities: Eye movements in parsing lexically ambiguous sentences. *Journal of memory and language*, 26(5):505–526.

Richard Futrell, Ethan Wilcox, Takashi Morita, and Roger Levy. 2018. RNNs as psycholinguistic subjects: Syntactic state and grammatical dependency. *arXiv preprint arXiv:1809.01329*.

Richard Futrell, Ethan Wilcox, Takashi Morita, Peng Qian, Miguel Ballesteros, and Roger Levy. 2019. Neural language models as psycholinguistic subjects: Representations of syntactic state. In *Proceedings of the 2019 Conference of the North American Chapter of the Association for Computational Linguistics: Human Language Technologies, Volume 1 (Long and Short Papers)*, pages 32–42, Minneapolis, Minnesota. Association for Computational Linguistics.

Matt Gardner, Joel Grus, Mark Neumann, Oyvind Tafjord, Pradeep Dasigi, Nelson Liu, Matthew Peters, Michael Schmitz, and Luke Zettlemoyer. 2018. AllenNLP: A deep semantic natural language processing platform. *arXiv preprint arXiv:1803.07640*.

S.M. Garnsey, N.J. Pearlmutter, E. Myers, and M.A. Lotocky. 1997. The contributions of verb bias and plausibility to the comprehension of temporarily ambiguous sentences. *Journal of Memory and Language*, 37(1):58–93.

Mario Giulianelli, Jack Harding, Florian Mohnert, Dieuwke Hupkes, and Willem Zuidema. 2018. Under the hood: Using diagnostic classifiers to investigate and improve how language models track agreement information. In *Proceedings of the 2018 EMNLP Workshop BlackboxNLP: Analyzing and Interpreting Neural Networks for NLP*, pages 240–248, Brussels, Belgium. Association for Computational Linguistics.

Daniel Grodner, Edward Gibson, Vered Argaman, and Maria Babyonyshev. 2003. Against repair-based reanalysis in sentence comprehension. *Journal of Psycholinguistic Research*, 32(2):141–166.

Kristina Gulordava, Piotr Bojanowski, Édouard Grave, Tal Linzen, and Marco Baroni. 2018. Colorless green recurrent networks dream hierarchically. In *Proceedings of the 2018 Conference of the North American Chapter of the Association for Computational Linguistics: Human Language Technologies, Volume 1 (Long Papers)*, pages 1195–1205.

John Hale. 2001. A probabilistic Earley parser as a psycholinguistic model. In *Second Meeting of the North American Chapter of the Association for Computational Linguistics*.

John Hewitt and Christopher D. Manning. 2019. A structural probe for finding syntax in word representations. In *Proceedings of the 2019 Conference of the North American Chapter of the Association for Computational Linguistics: Human Language Technologies, Volume 1 (Long and Short Papers)*, pages 4129–4138, Minneapolis, Minnesota. Association for Computational Linguistics.

Ari Holtzman, Jan Buys, Li Du, Maxwell Forbes, and Yejin Choi. 2019. The curious case of neural text degeneration. In *International Conference on Learning Representations*.

Tal Linzen and Marco Baroni. 2021. Syntactic structure from deep learning. *Annual Review of Linguistics*, 7.

Tal Linzen, Emmanuel Dupoux, and Yoav Goldberg. 2016. Assessing the ability of LSTMs to learn syntax-sensitive dependencies. *Transactions of the Association for Computational Linguistics*, 4:521–535.

Matthew Peters, Mark Neumann, Mohit Iyyer, Matt Gardner, Christopher Clark, Kenton Lee, and Luke Zettlemoyer. 2018. Deep contextualized word representations. In *Proceedings of the 2018 Conference of the North American Chapter of the Association for Computational Linguistics: Human Language Technologies, Volume 1 (Long Papers)*, pages 2227–2237, New Orleans, Louisiana. Association for Computational Linguistics.

Alec Radford, Jeff Wu, Rewon Child, David Luan, Dario Amodei, and Ilya Sutskever. 2019. Language models are unsupervised multitask learners.

Marten Van Schijndel and Tal Linzen. 2018. Modeling garden path effects without explicit hierarchical syntax. In *Proceedings of the 40th Annual Conference of the Cognitive Science Society*.

Marten Van Schijndel and Tal Linzen. 2021. Single-stage prediction models do not explain the magnitude of syntactic disambiguation difficulty. *Cognitive Science*, 45(6):e12988.

Ethan Wilcox, Roger Levy, Takashi Morita, and Richard Futrell. 2018. What do RNN language models learn about filler–gap dependencies? pages 211–221.

Thomas Wolf, Lysandre Debut, Victor Sanh, Julien Chaumond, Clement Delangue, Anthony Moi, Pierric Cistac, Tim Rault, Remi Louf, Morgan Funtowicz, Joe Davison, Sam Shleifer, Patrick von Platen, Clara Ma, Yacine Jernite, Julien Plu, Canwen Xu, Teven Le Scao, Sylvain Gugger, Mariama Drame, Quentin Lhoest, and Alexander Rush. 2020. Transformers: State-of-the-art natural language processing. In *Proceedings of the 2020 Conference on Empirical Methods in Natural Language Processing: System Demonstrations*, pages 38–45, Online. Association for Computational Linguistics.

Appendices

A Generation: Further Details

To generate completions from the prompt, we apply stochastic decoding as described in the paper. The LSTM employs a word-level encoding, with a fixed vocabulary size, whereas GPT2 uses Byte-Pair-Encoding, with a vocabulary of both word and subword units. From a prompt, we generate 30 and 50 tokens for the LSMT and GPT2, respectively. This is because GPT2 can generate subwords, and thus require more steps on average to reach the end of a sentence. For the analyses, we discard GPT2 completions where the last word of the prompt is followed by a subword, thus changing its identity (e.g., from *suit* to *suitable*). For the LSTM we penalize the generation of the unknown-word symbol, reducing its output score by a factor of 10^{16}.

A minority of words in NP/Z and Noun/Verb prompts were not in the vocabulary of the LSTM. We replace these words with equivalent ones that do not substantially affect the meaning of the sentence (e.g., *jogger* $\rightarrow$ *runner*) and use these modified prompts for the experiments on both LMs.

B Analysis of Generated Sentences

Diversity We analyse the diversity of the completions generated for each prompt. Completions were rarely completely identical: the average proportion of unique completions in a sample (pooling together all prompt types) is at least 98% for all ambiguity types and LMs. Of course, it is possible for two completions to be very similar, though not identical. To measure to extent of this phenomenon, we measure the lexical overlap across completions, focusing on unigrams and bigrams. We calculate individual Self-BLEU scores of each completion with respect to the others generated for the same prompt. Average unigram scores tend to be much higher than the bigram ones across ambiguity types and LMs (the former in the range .68-.71, while the latter .18-.25). This shows that individual words are often repeated across completions, but not so frequently in the same order.

Grammaticality During the manual annotation of the subset of GPT2 completions, the annotators are also requested to provide binary judgments of the syntactic well-formedness of each sentence. Since character and punctuation errors are frequent (e.g., a misspelled word, or the incorrect presence of a punctuation mark), annotators can specify when a sentence would count as grammatical without such errors. Overall, 66% of NP/S completions, 61% of NP/Z completions and 66% of of Noun/Verb completions are judged to be fully well-formed. If we ignore spelling and punctuation errors, these percentages increase to 75%, 74% and 85%.

C Classifying Completions

This appendix presents the rules employed to classify completions based on the inferred syntactic interpretation of the prompt.

C.1 NP/S and NP/Z Sentences

It is possible to distinguish between the NP and S interpretations and between the NP and Z interpretation by examining the syntactic role of the head of the noun phrase that contains the locus of ambiguity. In the simplest case, the locus of ambiguity is the direct object or subject; in other cases, it is part of a complex NP, where, for instance, it modifies another noun.

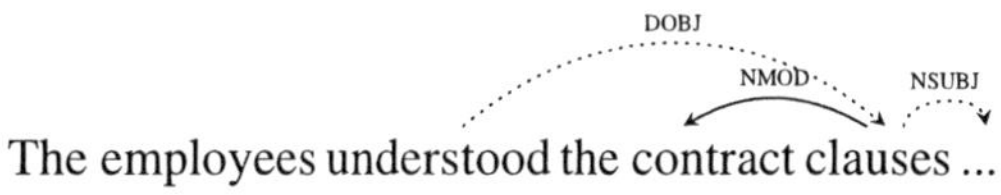

We define a set of rules that are based on the dependency labels predicted by the parser. The rules are applied recursively:

- In the base case, we check if the predicted label of a given token is that of direct object or subject. If it is a subject, we return S for NP/S and Z for NP/Z.
- If the label for the given token is neither subject nor direct object, we consider whether it could be part of a complex NP. If the predicted label is that of a modifier or possessive, we apply the function to the following tokens to identify the head of the NP and determine whether it is a subject or direct object. If this scenario does not apply, we return *other*.

The most common parser error involves a failure to detect S or Z cases, labeling the locus as direct object when followed by a finite verb:

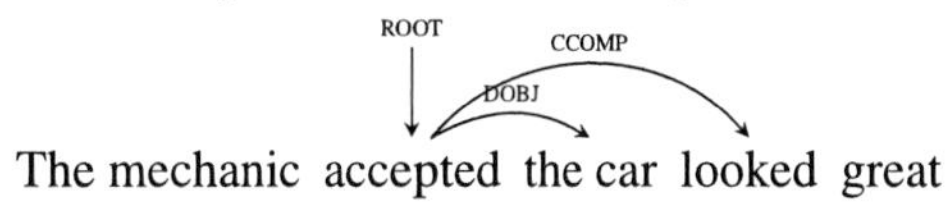

This parse is not only incorrect but also ungrammatical, as it leaves the verb after the locus without a subject. We modify the base case rule to detect and correct these cases:

- If the token is a direct object but it is followed by a token with a dependency label compatible with a finite verb (e.g., *root, ccomp*), we change the label to subject, and return S for NP/S and Z for NP/Z.

C.2 NP/Z Sentences with Disambiguation Issues

In Section 6, we described a subset of completions to POST-LOCUS CUE completions of NP/Z prompts that indicate that the LMs have not fully adapted to the Z interpretation. To identify this behavior and quantify it across the data, we consider patterns in the dependency labels predicted for a sentence. In particular, the following condition:

- The post-locus cue is not recognized as the main verb;
- A comma is placed between the post-locus cue verb and the main verb;
- The comma is not followed by a conjunction.

C.3 The Noun/Verb Ambiguity

For the Noun/Verb ambiguity, we read the interpretation off the PoS tag predicted by the parser for the locus of ambiguity (*NN, NNS* etc. $\rightarrow$ Noun; *VB, MD* etc. $\rightarrow$ Verb). Errors in the PoS tags predicted by the parser tend to cause incorrect dependency labels as well; as such, we do not rely on the dependency labels for this ambiguity.

D Prompts

Tables 6 through 8 show the full list of prompts used in our experiments on each ambiguity type.

NO CUE / PRE-LOCUS CUE	POST-LOCUS CUE / PRE&POST-LOCUS CUES	Locus
The employees understood (that) the contract	The employees understood (that) the contract would	contract
The mechanic accepted (that) the car	The mechanic accepted (that) the car looked	car
The old man recalled (that) the nurse	The old man recalled (that) the nurse had	nurse
The traveler heard (that) the clock	The traveler heard (that) the clock had	clock
The journalist confirmed (that) the story	The journalist confirmed (that) the story would	story
The worker maintained (that) the walls	The worker maintained (that) the walls fell	walls
The apprentice forgot (that) the bicycle	The apprentice forgot (that) the bicycle was	bicycle
The committee mentioned (that) the issue	The committee mentioned (that) the issue would	issue
The army found (that) the supplies	The army found (that) the supplies saved	supplies
The umpire warned (that) the spectators	The umpire warned (that) the spectators would	spectators
The coach discovered (that) the player	The coach discovered (that) the player tried	player
The woman noticed (that) the flyer	The woman noticed (that) the flyer had	flyer
The tourists saw (that) the palace	The tourists saw (that) the palace was	palace
The scientist proved (that) the theory	The scientist proved (that) the theory could	theory
The soldiers remembered (that) the town	The soldiers remembered (that) the town had	town
The priest recognized (that) two guests	The priest recognized (that) two guests were	guests
The reporter revealed (that) the politician	The reporter revealed (that) the politician received	politician
The owners insured (that) the house	The owners insured (that) the house would	house
The lawyer established (that) the alibi	The lawyer established (that) the alibi was	alibi
The store guaranteed (that) the television	The store guaranteed (that) the television would	television

Table 6: Prompts for NP/S ambiguity (pre-locus cue in parenthesis).

NO CUE / PRE-LOCUS CUE	POST-LOCUS CUE / PRE&POST-LOCUS CUES	Locus
Even though the band left(,) the party	Even though the band left(,) the party went	party
In case the executive forgot(,) the assistant	In case the executive forgot(,) the assistant would	assistant
Although the maid cleaned(,) the house	Although the maid cleaned(,) the house was	house
Because the class failed(,) the exam	Because the class failed(,) the exam was	exam
Once the child played(,) the piano	Once the child played(,) the piano was	piano
As the couple danced(,) the tango	As the couple danced(,) the tango began	tango
After the kids cheated(,) the teacher	After the kids cheated(,) the teacher had	teacher
After the thief attacked(,) the runner	After the thief attacked(,) the runner was	runner
Even though the girl phoned(,) the instructor	Even though the girl phoned(,) the instructor was	instructor
Even though the janitor cleaned(,) the carpet	Even though the janitor cleaned(,) the carpet was	carpet
Although the candidates debated(,) the issues	Although the candidates debated(,) the issues were	issues
Because the train stopped(,) the traffic	Because the train stopped(,) the traffic was	traffic
In case the team lost(,) the tiebreaker	In case the team lost(,) the tiebreaker was	tiebreaker
After the librarian called(,) the intern	After the librarian called(,) the intern began	intern
Even though the army surrendered(,) the territory	Even though the army surrendered(,) the territory was	territory
While the narrator read(,) the story	While the narrator read(,) the story was	story
Before the tribe worshipped(,) the idol	Before the tribe worshipped(,) the idol was	idol
In case the manager quit(,) the company	In case the manager quit(,) the company began	company
As the customer paid(,) the waitress	As the customer paid(,) the waitress could	waitress
While the artist painted(,) the furniture	While the artist painted(,) the furniture was	furniture

Table 7: Prompts for NP/Z ambiguity (pre-locus cue in parenthesis).

No cue / Pre-locus cue	Post-locus cue / Pre&post-locus cues	Locus
Mary thinks that the/those pants suit	Mary thinks that the/those pants suit me	suit
The local newspaper reported that the/this warehouse fires	The local newspaper reported that the/this warehouse fires numerous	fires
We all should have known that the/this metal rings	We all should have known that the/this metal rings loudly	rings
Susan was extremely surprised that the/this winter bears	Susan was extremely surprised that the/this winter bears no	bears
A lot of people know that the/a cashier checks	A lot of people know that the/a cashier checks the	checks
Local people are concerned that the/this theater shows	Local people are concerned that the/this theater shows lots	shows
I know that the/this desert trains	I know that the/this desert trains young	trains
In an old version of that movie, the/a detective cases	In an old version of that movie, the/a detective cases the	cases
Tom remarked that the/each summer flies	Tom remarked that the/each summer flies by	flies
Despite last year's report, the/this city hopes	Despite last year's report, the/this city hopes that	hopes
Every American knows that the/this government promises	Every American knows that the/this government promises it	promises
Nobody knows if it's true that the/this university fines visitors	Nobody knows if it's true that the/this university fines visitors	fines
Mrs. Baker is convinced that the/this school fears	Mrs. Baker is convinced that the/this school fears that	fears
We just found out that the/this post office packages	We just found out that the/this post office packages some	packages
Some of us weren't aware that the/this church pardons	Some of us weren't aware that the/this church pardons very	pardons
Nobody seems to complain about the fact that the/this department store buys	Nobody seems to complain about the fact that the/this department store buys only	stores
It is no secret that the/this official lies	It is no secret that the/this official lies all	lies
Mrs. Jones is pleased now that she has discovered that the/this greenhouse plants	Mrs. Jones is pleased now that she has discovered that the/this greenhouse plants lots	plants
We should have realized that the/this tractor wrecks	We should have realized that the/this tractor wrecks the	wrecks
The agency reported that the/this family worries	The agency reported that the/this family worries most	worries
Some people think it's ridiculous that the/this county buses	Some people think it's ridiculous that the/this county buses most	buses

Table 8: Prompts for Noun/Verb ambiguity, with Verb interpretation.

No cue / Pre-locus cue	Post-locus cue / Pre&post-locus cues	Locus
Mary thinks that the/this pants suit	Mary thinks that the/this pants suit is	suit
The local newspaper reported that the/these warehouse fires	The local newspaper reported that the/these warehouse fires harm	fires
We all should have known that the/those metal rings	We all should have known that the/those metal rings are	rings
Susan was extremely surprised that the/those winter bears	Susan was extremely surprised that the/those winter bears resemble	bears
A lot of people know that the/those cashier checks	A lot of people know that the/those cashier checks are	checks
Local people are concerned that the/many theater shows	Local people are concerned that the/many theater shows are	shows
I know that the/these desert trains	I know that the/these desert trains are	trains
In an old version of that movie, the/those detective cases	In an old version of that movie, the/those detective cases are	cases
Tom remarked that the/those summer flies	Tom remarked that the/those summer flies are	flies
Despite last year's report, the/those city hopes	Despite last year's report, the/those city hopes were	hopes
Every American knows that the/these government promises	Every American knows that the/these government promises are	promises
Nobody knows if it's true that the/those university fines	Nobody knows if it's true that the/those university fines are	fines
Mrs. Baker is convinced that the/these school fears	Mrs. Baker is convinced that the/these school fears are	fears
We just found out that the/these post office packages	We just found out that the/these post office packages are	packages
Some of us weren't aware that the/these church pardons	Some of us weren't aware that the/these church pardons are	pardons
Nobody seems to complain about the fact that the/those department store buys	Nobody seems to complain about the fact that the/those department store buys are	stores
Mrs. Jones is pleased now that she has discovered that the/those greenhouse plants	Mrs. Jones is pleased now that she has discovered that the/those greenhouse plants are	lies
We should have realized that the/these tractor wrecks	We should have realized that the/these tractor wrecks are	plants
The agency reported that the/these family worries	The agency reported that the/these family worries are	wrecks
Some people think it's ridiculous that the/those county buses	Some people think it's ridiculous that the/those county buses are	worries
John quickly learned that the/these hardware store prices	John quickly learned that the/these hardware store prices are	buses

Table 9: Prompts for Noun/Verb ambiguity, with Noun interpretations.

On the Limits of Minimal Pairs in Contrastive Evaluation

Jannis Vamvas[1] and **Rico Sennrich**[1,2]
[1]Department of Computational Linguistics, University of Zurich
[2]School of Informatics, University of Edinburgh
{vamvas,sennrich}@cl.uzh.ch

Abstract

Minimal sentence pairs are frequently used to analyze the behavior of language models. It is often assumed that model behavior on contrastive pairs is predictive of model behavior at large. We argue that two conditions are necessary for this assumption to hold: First, a tested hypothesis should be well-motivated, since experiments show that contrastive evaluation can lead to false positives. Secondly, test data should be chosen such as to minimize distributional discrepancy between evaluation time and deployment time. For a good approximation of deployment-time decoding, we recommend that minimal pairs are created based on machine-generated text, as opposed to human-written references. We present a contrastive evaluation suite for English–German MT that implements this recommendation.[1]

1 Introduction

Contrastive evaluation is one of the most widely used evaluation techniques for generative language models, both for causal models (Linzen et al., 2016) and sequence-to-sequence models (Sennrich, 2017). Various phenomena have been analyzed using this technique, including syntax (Marvin and Linzen 2018; among others), word sense disambiguation (Rios et al. 2017; among others), document coherence (Bawden et al. 2018; Beyer et al. 2021; among others), and grammatical acceptability in general (Warstadt et al., 2020; Xiang et al., 2021).

Contrastive evaluation allows for a targeted, automated evaluation of generative models but is restricted to a specific behavioral interface, namely the ranking of pre-defined *minimal pairs*. However, most models in application areas such as translation or conversation are deployed to produce 1-best sequences, exposing a different behavioral interface to users. While this limitation of contrastive evaluation is well known, its practical relevance has been unclear.

We show that under certain conditions, the gap between evaluation and deployment can indeed cause misleading results. As a main factor we identify the *distributional discrepancy* of contrastive evaluation datasets: Minimal pairs are usually derived from human-written references, but when deployed, a model is conditioned on its own output.

To measure the effect of this factor on evaluation, we focus on neural machine translation (NMT) systems. Our approach is to test *implausible research hypotheses* in addition to plausible ones. We find that distributional discrepancy increases the number of false positives regarding implausible hypotheses. They particularly occur when evaluating distilled NMT models (Kim and Rush, 2016), indicating that in such models, ranking behavior on noisy sequences diverges from generative behavior.

We also propose a way to reduce the distributional discrepancy of minimal pairs. Our experiments show that false positives can be largely avoided by using machine-generated text instead of human-written text. This inspires us to release **DistilLingEval**, a variant of the LingEval97 English–German MT evaluation suite (Sennrich, 2017) that uses MT-generated references.

We recommend that future efforts to create contrastive datasets for the evaluation of language generation models minimize distributional discrepancy between evaluation and deployment. Due to the possibility of false positives, linguistic conclusions about *knowledge* or *abilities* of models should be corroborated by additional evidence from a more natural setting.

2 Background and Related Work

2.1 Contrastive Evaluation

Contrastive evaluation compares the probability scores that a model assigns to two minimally dif-

[1]https://github.com/ZurichNLP/distil-lingeval

Proceedings of the Fourth BlackboxNLP Workshop on Analyzing and Interpreting Neural Networks for NLP, pages 58–68
Online, November 11, 2021.

ferent sequences. For example, the sentences *"The cats sleep"* and *"The cats sleeps"* differ in verb number only; if a model assigns higher scores to sentences of the first kind than to sentences of the second kind, it is said to prefer verb forms in agreement with the noun (Linzen et al., 2016).

An established method for scoring is to compute the score for a full sentence $X = x_0, x_1, ..., x_n$ as the sum of token log-probabilities predicted by the model θ (Marvin and Linzen, 2018):

$$\text{score}(X) = \sum_{i=0}^{n} \log p_\theta(x_i | x_{<i}) \quad (1)$$

When contrastive evaluation is applied to sequence-to-sequence models, two target sequences are scored given the same source sequence X (Sennrich, 2017). We follow previous work and normalize sequence-to-sequence scores by the length of the target sequence Y:

$$\text{score}(Y|X) = \frac{1}{|Y|} \sum_{i=0}^{|Y|} \log p_\theta(y_i | X, y_{<i}) \quad (2)$$

2.2 Limitations of Forced Choice

Since a limited set of variants is scored, contrastive evaluation presents the model with a forced choice. In fact, scoring a pre-defined sequence is related to *teacher forcing*, i.e., the conditioning of a model on a ground truth prefix during training. Whenever an application involves unconstrained generation, a discrepancy between evaluation and deployment arises that is comparable to the *exposure bias* of cross-entropy training (Ranzato et al., 2016).

With regard to syntactic evaluation of language models, Newman et al. (2021) point out that contrastive evaluation and evaluation of systematicity across a paradigm do not necessarily describe a model's likely behavior. They propose to analyze the complete search space, which, however, is difficult to implement in many use cases. We pursue a different strategy and create minimal pairs that are more similar to sequences the model will likely generate at deployment time.

3 Experiments

In previous work, contrastive evaluation has commonly been used to test *plausible* research hypotheses, for example the hypothesis that RNNs can predict long-distance number agreement (Gulordava et al., 2018), or the hypothesis that word dropout improves pronoun resolution in translation (Fernandes et al., 2021). In this paper, we are interested in *implausible* hypotheses and in how the testing of such hypotheses is affected by the limitations described in the previous section.

We formulate two implausible hypotheses about NMT systems, which we mark with an asterisk (*):

1. **Vague language:*
   NMT systems make liberal use of vague placeholder words. Specifically, English–German models use the German placeholder noun *Ding* ('thing') ubiquitously.

2. **Hypercorrection:*
   NMT systems have a tendency for hypercorrect language. Specifically, English–German models tend to use genitive case with prepositions that require dative case.

Examples are given in the next section. The two hypotheses are chosen because they seem implausible both theoretically and empirically. From a theoretical standpoint, both linguistic phenomena rarely occur in the training data and the model is unlikely to adopt them broadly. Furthermore, the cognitive and social factors that cause the phenomena in human speech do not apply to neural language models. Empirically, we find that both phenomena are indeed very rare in neural machine translations, independent of model quality.

For comparison, we also test two plausible hypotheses about NMT systems:

3. *Polarity affix deletion:*
   NMT systems sometimes omit negation affixes, changing the polarity of a word (Hossain et al., 2020). Specifically, English–German models sometimes omit the negation prefix *un-* from German words (Sennrich, 2017).

4. *Clause omission:*
   NMT systems sometimes omit a clause from the translated sentence (Tu et al., 2016).

3.1 Test Set Creation

For each of the four hypotheses, we create an English–German contrastive test set. For *vague language*, *polarity affix deletion* and *clause omission*, we use the newstest datasets 2009–2016 as a data source. For *hypercorrection*, we combine five data sources: newstest 2009–2019 as well as OpenSubtitles2016 (Lison and Tiedemann,

2016), TED2020 (Reimers and Gurevych, 2020), QED (Abdelali et al., 2014) and JW300 (Agić and Vulić, 2019), which are provided by OPUS (Tiedemann, 2012).

Vague language Contrastive variants are created by replacing a random noun in each reference with an uninflected *Ding* 'thing', which is a common replacement noun in spoken German (Vogel, 2020):

English: *Prague Stock Market falls to minus by the **end of the trading day***
German (correct): *Die Prager Börse stürzt gegen **Geschäftsschluss** ins Minus.*
German (contrastive): *Die Prager Börse stürzt gegen **Ding** ins Minus.*

Hypercorrection To create contrastive variants for hypercorrect genitives, we select references containing German propositions that require dative in Standard German, but are sometimes used hypercorrectly with a genitive case (Hentschel and Weydt, 2013).[2] We construct contrastive variants by converting the dative case into genitive case:

English: *I've loved you ever **since that day** in the rose garden.*
German (correct): *Ich liebe dich **seit dem Tag** im Rosengarten.*
German (contrastive): *Ich liebe dich **seit des Tags** im Rosengarten.*

Polarity affix deletion Contrastive variants are created by deleting the prefix *un-* from adjectives, adverbs and nouns in the German references in cases where this changes the polarity of the word, similar to the test set created by Sennrich (2017):

English: *The probes **unexpectedly** become faster or slower.*
German (correct): *Die Sonden werden **unerwartet** schneller oder langsamer.*
German (contrastive): *Die Sonden werden **erwartet** schneller oder langsamer.*

Clause omission Contrastive variants are created by deleting a clause from the reference. As clauses we treat token sequences segmented by the Stanza sentence splitter (Qi et al., 2020):

English: *And even if it could be proved for humans **- how would one want to prove it for rats?***
German (correct): *Und selbst wenn man das für den Menschen beweisen könnte: **Wie wollte man es bei Ratten nachweisen?***
German (contrastive): *Und selbst wenn man das für den Menschen beweisen könnte:*

3.2 Human-Written References

The above test sets are derived from naturally occurring parallel text, which is common practice when creating contrastive datasets for MT (Sennrich, 2017; Rios et al., 2017; Bawden et al., 2018; Müller et al., 2018; Voita et al., 2019; Raganato et al., 2019; Sugiyama and Yoshinaga, 2019; Nagata and Morishita, 2020; Shimazu et al., 2020; Lopes et al., 2020; He et al., 2020; Stojanovski et al., 2020). However, comparisons have shown that human-written references are different from machine translations in that they contain more noise and have more linguistic diversity (Zhang et al., 2018; Vanmassenhove et al., 2019).

We propose to measure the "distance" between a pre-defined target sequence and the 1-best translation $\hat{Y}$ generated by an MT system as the difference in log-scores (according to Equation 2) that the system assigns to the two sequences. Furthermore, we define the *distributional discrepancy* of a contrastive evaluation dataset as the mean difference in scores between the 1-best translation and the preferred variant:

$$\text{score\_preferred} = \max(\text{score}(Y^{correct}), \text{score}(Y^{contrast.}))$$

$$\text{discrepancy} = \frac{1}{n}\sum_{i=0}^{n} \text{score}(\hat{Y}_i) - \text{score\_preferred}_i$$

It should be noted that this definition of distributional discrepancy is mainly useful for comparing multiple test sets with respect to a single model. It is less useful for assessing a single test set with respect to multiple models, because score differences are not necessarily comparable between models.

3.3 Machine-Generated References

With the goal of reducing distributional discrepancy, we create versions of our test sets that use machine-generated references. First, we retranslate the sources from our test sets using commercial NMT systems.[3] We then repeat the steps described in Section 3.1 to create contrastive variants.

[2] We use the prepositions *entgegen, entsprechend, gegenüber, gemäß, nahe, nebst, (mit)samt* and *seit.*

[3] We used *Amazon Translate, DeepL Translator, Google Translate*, and *Microsoft Translator* for 25% sentences each.

Hypothesis	Test set type	Discrepancy of test set		Reported accuracy	
		TRANSFORMER	DISTILLED	TRANSFORMER	DISTILLED
**Vague language*	human references	1.2 ± 0.0	2.5 ± 0.1	99.1 ± 0.1	94.7 ± 0.4
	machine references	0.3 ± 0.0	0.7 ± 0.0	99.9 ± 0.0	98.7 ± 0.2
**Hypercorrection*	human references	1.3 ± 0.0	2.7 ± 0.1	95.4 ± 0.3	91.2 ± 0.5
	machine references	0.4 ± 0.0	1.1 ± 0.1	99.9 ± 0.1	99.6 ± 0.4
Polarity affix del.	human references	1.3 ± 0.0	2.7 ± 0.1	94.0 ± 1.1	78.3 ± 0.9
	machine references	0.3 ± 0.0	0.7 ± 0.1	96.7 ± 1.5	93.9 ± 1.1
Clause omission	human references	1.3 ± 0.0	2.8 ± 0.1	75.5 ± 3.7	71.3 ± 0.7
	machine references	0.3 ± 0.0	0.7 ± 0.0	87.7 ± 2.7	86.3 ± 2.7

Table 1: Results for four different hypotheses about English–German NMT systems. An asterisk (*) marks hypotheses that are a priori implausible. The table reports distributional discrepancies of different test set types, as well as the accuracy scores achieved by non-distilled and distilled systems when evaluated with the test sets. We report averages and standard deviations across three models trained independently with different random seeds.

Validation Since some machine-generated references contain errors, a validation step is needed. The validation should ensure that (a) the machine references are correct with respect to the linguistic phenomenon at hand, and that (b) no undesired bias is introduced into the evaluation.

We use a semi-automatic approach and look for lexical overlap with the human references regarding the phenomenon. For example, in the case of polarity affix deletion, we label the machine reference as correct if it contains the same polarity word as the human reference. Otherwise we manually check whether the machine reference might be incorrect, but only if it contains the same polarity word as the human contrastive variant. This occurs rarely, and most of the time we find that it is the original human reference that is incorrect while the machine reference is correct. In the rare cases where the machine reference is verifiably incorrect with regard to the phenomenon, we use it as the contrastive variant and derive the correct variant manually.

Machine references that have no phenomenon-specific lexical overlap to the human references are dropped from the test set because they cannot be automatically validated. This raises the question whether test sets created in such a way contain undesired bias.

Dataset Bias We discuss two kinds of bias that might be introduced. First of all, by only including machine references that can be classified automatically as either correct or incorrect based on the human references, the distribution of the machine-generated test set could become more similar to the human-written test set. However, our experiments show that the difference in distributional discrepancy between the two test sets is sufficiently large. Future work could avoid this bias by employing human annotators to validate machine references.

Secondly, it might be that machine references only use the phenomenon in unambiguous contexts. This would cut off the long tail of human-written test samples that is especially challenging for NLP models. While such a bias is likely to be introduced to a degree, we see it is a *desired* bias, since our goal is to reduce distributional discrepancy between a test set and the generative behavior of an evaluated system.

3.4 Experimental Setting

We evaluate two types of NMT systems:

1. TRANSFORMER: Transformer models of size 'big' (Vaswani et al., 2017).
2. DISTILLED: Transformer models of size 'small' distilled from (1) using sequence-level knowledge distillation (Kim and Rush, 2016).

Training For both types, we trained three models with different random seeds. To train the TRANSFORMER models, we used similar data and configuration as Ng et al. (2019), using Fairseq (Ott et al., 2019). We used the English–German parallel training data from the WMT19 news translation task (Barrault et al., 2019). Sentences longer than 250 tokens and pairs with a length ratio larger than 1.5 were filtered, resulting in 42.9M sentence pairs used for training and distillation. We selected the best checkpoint with respect to BLEU based on the *newstest* sets from the preceding years.

Distillation We then used each of the three TRANSFORMER models as a teacher to train an individual student model. A comparison of hyperparameters is provided in Appendix A.

For decoding we always use beam search with size 5.

Model Quality The models of type TRANSFORMER achieve an average BLEU score of 37.3 ± 0.3, while the DISTILLED models achieve 35.7 ± 0.4 BLEU when evaluated on newstest19.

3.5 Results

The left-hand side of Table 1 shows the distributional discrepancies of the test sets. As expected, the test sets derived from human-written references have a higher discrepancy, while those derived from machine-generated references are closer to what the evaluated model would generate.

The right-hand side of Table 1 shows the reported *accuracy* of the evaluated models, i.e. the ratio of test instances where the model prefers the correct variant over the contrastive variant. While all the accuracies are much better than random, the results for implausible hypotheses seem to indicate that models do occasionally generate the implausible phenomena, and that distilled models generate them more often than other models. Since this is not reflected by the actual generative behavior, the testing of implausible hypotheses shows the danger of false positives.

The test sets with machine-generated references produce far fewer false positives. The reported accuracy is higher with machine references also for the plausible hypotheses, but a gap to 100% accuracy remains, which is in line with previous work on these types of NMT errors (Hossain et al., 2020; Tang et al., 2021; Tu et al., 2016).

4 Dataset Release

Given the improved specificity of test sets with machine-generated references, we release corresponding test sets for other phenomena in the LingEval97 test suite (Sennrich, 2017), terming our dataset variant **DistilLingEval**.

LingEval97, the original test suite, is a collection of 97k contrastive translation pairs for 13 different error types in English–German translation. Building on LingEval97, we create test sets with machine-generated references for the following error types, in addition to the ones discussed in the previous section: *noun phrase agreement*, *subject-verb agreement* and other *polarity deletion* phenomena involving the German negation lexemes *kein* and *nicht*. Results for these test sets are reported in Table 3, and further results for a state-of-the-art NMT system are provided in Appendix C. Table 2 provides an overview of the test set sizes per error type in DistilLingEval.

Error type	Human Ref.	MT Ref.
clause_omission	1104	1025
hypercorrect_genitive	3404	635
np_agreement	24 055	10 595
placeholder_ding	18 647	18 659
polarity_affix_del	408	180
polarity_particle_kein_del	554	201
polarity_particle_nicht_del	2561	888
subj_verb_agreement	31 978	6701

Table 2: Number of samples per DistilLingEval error type. Error types with machine-generated references tend to have fewer samples, which is discussed in Section 3.3.

5 Discussion

By testing implausible hypotheses, we demonstrate the risk of drawing wrong inferences about generative behavior of (conditional) language models, especially if there is a large distributional discrepancy between minimal pairs and generated sequences.

This problem is especially apparent for distilled NMT models, which perform poorly on human-written minimal pairs because they were never exposed to such a distribution during training. While this indicates that distilled NMT models are less robust against improbable contexts, human-crafted minimal pairs also become less useful to predict their unconstrained generative behavior.

The danger of false positives from minimal pairs highlights the fact that behaviorist approaches to measuring knowledge are limited to the behavioral interface that is observed. Systematic assessments of linguistic *knowledge* or syntactic *abilities* of neural models should be qualified accordingly, in case minimal pairs are the primary analysis method. We suspect that whenever a broad range of hypotheses is tested, including phenomena that are rarely observed in actual machine-generated text, the risk of false positives is increased.

Error Type	Test set type	Discrepancy of test set		Reported accuracy	
		TRANSF.	DISTILLED	TRANSF.	DISTILLED
np_agreement	human references	2.0 ± 0.6	2.6 ± 0.1	95.9 ± 2.5	94.4 ± 0.8
	machine references	0.5 ± 0.2	0.7 ± 0.1	98.8 ± 0.8	99.0 ± 0.4
polarity_particle_kein_del	human references	1.3 ± 0.0	2.7 ± 0.1	95.3 ± 0.8	90.7 ± 0.9
	machine references	0.2 ± 0.0	0.6 ± 0.1	99.8 ± 0.3	99.8 ± 0.3
polarity_particle_nicht_del	human references	1.3 ± 0.0	2.6 ± 0.1	95.5 ± 0.2	87.9 ± 0.7
	machine references	0.3 ± 0.0	0.7 ± 0.0	99.7 ± 0.3	98.8 ± 0.1
subj_verb_agreement	human references	1.2 ± 0.0	2.6 ± 0.1	97.1 ± 0.3	91.4 ± 0.3
	machine references	0.3 ± 0.0	0.7 ± 0.0	99.2 ± 0.1	97.9 ± 0.3

Table 3: Test set discrepancies and model accuracies for the other four error types included in DistilLingEval (in addition to the four error types in Table 1).

We thus recommend that minimal pairs be constructed from machine-generated text in evaluation settings where unconstrained generation is the behavior of interest. This is relatively straightforward for sequence-to-sequence evaluation, as we demonstrated in our experiments. For other settings, e.g. the evaluation of dialogue models, obtaining useful machine-generated text might require more elaborate techniques, such as round-trip translation.

However, human-crafted minimal pairs remain valuable in other use cases. While machine-generated pairs may be more appropriate when the main interest is to study the model's behavior close to its mode, e.g. in a sequence-to-sequence task, human-written pairs (or pairs that are machine-generated to be different from the training distribution on purpose) may tell us more about the robustness of models outside the mode. For example, terminology-constrained or interactive applications depend on robustness against improbable contexts, and contrastive evaluation indicates that current NMT systems lack such robustness (Stojanovski et al., 2020). Similarly, syntactic evaluation of language models using randomly generated or nonsensical sentences (Gulordava et al., 2018; Warstadt et al., 2020) can be seen as method to assess the robustness of a model under improbable input, rather than as an assessment of generative capabilities in general.

6 Conclusion

We show that there are conditions where contrastive evaluation leads to false positives if generative behavior is inferred from behavior under forced choice. Experiments with English–German NMT indicate that the gap between the two behavioral interfaces is especially high when human-written text is used to create minimal pairs. Using machine-generated text largely reduces the gap. We recommend that human-written minimal pairs are mainly used for assessing the robustness of models, but that for predicting the generative behavior of language models, machine-generated minimal pairs are used.

Broader Impact

For language generation systems to be deployed, they should behave according to specified principles in a robust way. Typical requirements are linguistic acceptability, avoidance of undesirable societal biases (Sheng et al., 2021), and the avoidance of harmful speech acts. Contrastive evaluation is one of several methods that can help predict the behavior of language generation systems. However, to our knowledge the method has been mainly used to evaluate linguistic acceptability, and less to evaluate ethically sensitive aspects of generation.

It is crucial that evaluation methods have a high predictiveness regarding the behavior of a deployed system. On the one hand, lack of sensitivity can lead to unforeseen negative impact. On the other hand, lack of specificity – which we address in this paper – reduces the usefulness of comparisons between systems.

Acknowledgments

This work was funded by the Swiss National Science Foundation (project MUTAMUR; no. 176727) and made use of infrastructure services provided by S3IT, the Service and Support for Science IT team at the University of Zurich. We would like to thank Anne Beyer and the anonymous reviewers for helpful feedback.

References

Ahmed Abdelali, Francisco Guzman, Hassan Sajjad, and Stephan Vogel. 2014. The AMARA corpus: Building parallel language resources for the educational domain. In *Proceedings of the Ninth International Conference on Language Resources and Evaluation (LREC'14)*, pages 1856–1862, Reykjavik, Iceland. European Language Resources Association (ELRA).

Željko Agić and Ivan Vulić. 2019. JW300: A wide-coverage parallel corpus for low-resource languages. In *Proceedings of the 57th Annual Meeting of the Association for Computational Linguistics*, pages 3204–3210, Florence, Italy. Association for Computational Linguistics.

Loïc Barrault, Ondřej Bojar, Marta R. Costa-jussà, Christian Federmann, Mark Fishel, Yvette Graham, Barry Haddow, Matthias Huck, Philipp Koehn, Shervin Malmasi, Christof Monz, Mathias Müller, Santanu Pal, Matt Post, and Marcos Zampieri. 2019. Findings of the 2019 conference on machine translation (WMT19). In *Proceedings of the Fourth Conference on Machine Translation (Volume 2: Shared Task Papers, Day 1)*, pages 1–61, Florence, Italy. Association for Computational Linguistics.

Rachel Bawden, Rico Sennrich, Alexandra Birch, and Barry Haddow. 2018. Evaluating discourse phenomena in neural machine translation. In *Proceedings of the 2018 Conference of the North American Chapter of the Association for Computational Linguistics: Human Language Technologies, Volume 1 (Long Papers)*, pages 1304–1313, New Orleans, Louisiana. Association for Computational Linguistics.

Anne Beyer, Sharid Loáiciga, and David Schlangen. 2021. Is incoherence surprising? Targeted evaluation of coherence prediction from language models. In *Proceedings of the 2021 Conference of the North American Chapter of the Association for Computational Linguistics: Human Language Technologies*, pages 4164–4173, Online. Association for Computational Linguistics.

Patrick Fernandes, Kayo Yin, Graham Neubig, and André F. T. Martins. 2021. Measuring and increasing context usage in context-aware machine translation. In *Proceedings of the 59th Annual Meeting of the Association for Computational Linguistics and the 11th International Joint Conference on Natural Language Processing (Volume 1: Long Papers)*, pages 6467–6478, Online. Association for Computational Linguistics.

Kristina Gulordava, Piotr Bojanowski, Edouard Grave, Tal Linzen, and Marco Baroni. 2018. Colorless green recurrent networks dream hierarchically. In *Proceedings of the 2018 Conference of the North American Chapter of the Association for Computational Linguistics: Human Language Technologies, Volume 1 (Long Papers)*, pages 1195–1205, New Orleans, Louisiana. Association for Computational Linguistics.

Jie He, Tao Wang, Deyi Xiong, and Qun Liu. 2020. The box is in the pen: Evaluating commonsense reasoning in neural machine translation. In *Findings of the Association for Computational Linguistics: EMNLP 2020*, pages 3662–3672, Online. Association for Computational Linguistics.

Elke Hentschel and Harald Weydt. 2013. *Handbuch der deutschen Grammatik*. De Gruyter.

Md Mosharaf Hossain, Antonios Anastasopoulos, Eduardo Blanco, and Alexis Palmer. 2020. It's not a non-issue: Negation as a source of error in machine translation. In *Findings of the Association for Computational Linguistics: EMNLP 2020*, pages 3869–3885, Online. Association for Computational Linguistics.

Yoon Kim and Alexander M. Rush. 2016. Sequence-level knowledge distillation. In *Proceedings of the 2016 Conference on Empirical Methods in Natural Language Processing*, pages 1317–1327, Austin, Texas. Association for Computational Linguistics.

Tal Linzen, Emmanuel Dupoux, and Yoav Goldberg. 2016. Assessing the ability of LSTMs to learn syntax-sensitive dependencies. *Transactions of the Association for Computational Linguistics*, 4:521–535.

Pierre Lison and Jörg Tiedemann. 2016. OpenSubtitles2016: Extracting large parallel corpora from movie and TV subtitles. In *Proceedings of the Tenth International Conference on Language Resources and Evaluation (LREC'16)*, pages 923–929, Portorož, Slovenia. European Language Resources Association (ELRA).

António Lopes, M. Amin Farajian, Rachel Bawden, Michael Zhang, and André F. T. Martins. 2020. Document-level neural MT: A systematic comparison. In *Proceedings of the 22nd Annual Conference of the European Association for Machine Translation*, pages 225–234, Lisboa, Portugal. European Association for Machine Translation.

Rebecca Marvin and Tal Linzen. 2018. Targeted syntactic evaluation of language models. In *Proceedings of the 2018 Conference on Empirical Methods in Natural Language Processing*, pages 1192–1202, Brussels, Belgium. Association for Computational Linguistics.

Mathias Müller, Annette Rios, Elena Voita, and Rico Sennrich. 2018. A large-scale test set for the evaluation of context-aware pronoun translation in neural machine translation. In *Proceedings of the Third*

Conference on Machine Translation: Research Papers, pages 61–72, Brussels, Belgium. Association for Computational Linguistics.

Masaaki Nagata and Makoto Morishita. 2020. A test set for discourse translation from Japanese to English. In *Proceedings of the 12th Language Resources and Evaluation Conference*, pages 3704–3709, Marseille, France. European Language Resources Association.

Benjamin Newman, Kai-Siang Ang, Julia Gong, and John Hewitt. 2021. Refining targeted syntactic evaluation of language models. In *Proceedings of the 2021 Conference of the North American Chapter of the Association for Computational Linguistics: Human Language Technologies*, pages 3710–3723, Online. Association for Computational Linguistics.

Nathan Ng, Kyra Yee, Alexei Baevski, Myle Ott, Michael Auli, and Sergey Edunov. 2019. Facebook FAIR's WMT19 news translation task submission. In *Proceedings of the Fourth Conference on Machine Translation (Volume 2: Shared Task Papers, Day 1)*, pages 314–319, Florence, Italy. Association for Computational Linguistics.

Myle Ott, Sergey Edunov, Alexei Baevski, Angela Fan, Sam Gross, Nathan Ng, David Grangier, and Michael Auli. 2019. fairseq: A fast, extensible toolkit for sequence modeling. In *Proceedings of the 2019 Conference of the North American Chapter of the Association for Computational Linguistics (Demonstrations)*, pages 48–53, Minneapolis, Minnesota. Association for Computational Linguistics.

Peng Qi, Yuhao Zhang, Yuhui Zhang, Jason Bolton, and Christopher D. Manning. 2020. Stanza: A python natural language processing toolkit for many human languages. In *Proceedings of the 58th Annual Meeting of the Association for Computational Linguistics: System Demonstrations*, pages 101–108, Online. Association for Computational Linguistics.

Alessandro Raganato, Yves Scherrer, and Jörg Tiedemann. 2019. The MuCoW test suite at WMT 2019: Automatically harvested multilingual contrastive word sense disambiguation test sets for machine translation. In *Proceedings of the Fourth Conference on Machine Translation (Volume 2: Shared Task Papers, Day 1)*, pages 470–480, Florence, Italy. Association for Computational Linguistics.

Marc'Aurelio Ranzato, Sumit Chopra, Michael Auli, and Wojciech Zaremba. 2016. Sequence level training with recurrent neural networks. In *4th International Conference on Learning Representations, ICLR 2016, San Juan, Puerto Rico, May 2-4, 2016, Conference Track Proceedings*.

Nils Reimers and Iryna Gurevych. 2020. Making monolingual sentence embeddings multilingual using knowledge distillation. In *Proceedings of the 2020 Conference on Empirical Methods in Natural Language Processing (EMNLP)*, pages 4512–4525, Online. Association for Computational Linguistics.

Annette Rios, Laura Mascarell, and Rico Sennrich. 2017. Improving word sense disambiguation in neural machine translation with sense embeddings. In *Proceedings of the Second Conference on Machine Translation*, pages 11–19, Copenhagen, Denmark. Association for Computational Linguistics.

Rico Sennrich. 2017. How grammatical is character-level neural machine translation? Assessing MT quality with contrastive translation pairs. In *Proceedings of the 15th Conference of the European Chapter of the Association for Computational Linguistics: Volume 2, Short Papers*, pages 376–382, Valencia, Spain. Association for Computational Linguistics.

Emily Sheng, Kai-Wei Chang, Prem Natarajan, and Nanyun Peng. 2021. Societal biases in language generation: Progress and challenges. In *Proceedings of the 59th Annual Meeting of the Association for Computational Linguistics and the 11th International Joint Conference on Natural Language Processing (Volume 1: Long Papers)*, pages 4275–4293, Online. Association for Computational Linguistics.

Sho Shimazu, Sho Takase, Toshiaki Nakazawa, and Naoaki Okazaki. 2020. Evaluation dataset for zero pronoun in Japanese to English translation. In *Proceedings of the 12th Language Resources and Evaluation Conference*, pages 3630–3634, Marseille, France. European Language Resources Association.

Dario Stojanovski, Benno Krojer, Denis Peskov, and Alexander Fraser. 2020. ContraCAT: Contrastive coreference analytical templates for machine translation. In *Proceedings of the 28th International Conference on Computational Linguistics*, pages 4732–4749, Barcelona, Spain (Online). International Committee on Computational Linguistics.

Amane Sugiyama and Naoki Yoshinaga. 2019. Data augmentation using back-translation for context-aware neural machine translation. In *Proceedings of the Fourth Workshop on Discourse in Machine Translation (DiscoMT 2019)*, pages 35–44, Hong Kong, China. Association for Computational Linguistics.

Gongbo Tang, Philipp Rönchen, Rico Sennrich, and Joakim Nivre. 2021. Revisiting Negation in Neural Machine Translation. *Transactions of the Association for Computational Linguistics*, 9:740–755.

Jörg Tiedemann. 2012. Parallel data, tools and interfaces in OPUS. In *Proceedings of the Eighth International Conference on Language Resources and Evaluation (LREC'12)*, pages 2214–2218, Istanbul, Turkey. European Language Resources Association (ELRA).

Zhaopeng Tu, Zhengdong Lu, Yang Liu, Xiaohua Liu, and Hang Li. 2016. Modeling coverage for neural machine translation. In *Proceedings of the 54th Annual Meeting of the Association for Computational Linguistics (Volume 1: Long Papers)*, pages 76–85, Berlin, Germany. Association for Computational Linguistics.

Eva Vanmassenhove, Dimitar Shterionov, and Andy Way. 2019. Lost in translation: Loss and decay of linguistic richness in machine translation. In *Proceedings of Machine Translation Summit XVII Volume 1: Research Track*, pages 222–232, Dublin, Ireland. European Association for Machine Translation.

Ashish Vaswani, Noam Shazeer, Niki Parmar, Jakob Uszkoreit, Llion Jones, Aidan N Gomez, Łukasz Kaiser, and Illia Polosukhin. 2017. Attention is all you need. In *Advances in Neural Information Processing Systems*, volume 30, pages 5998–6008. Curran Associates, Inc.

Petra M. Vogel. 2020. *Dingsbums and Thingy: Placeholders for Names in German and Other Languages*, page 362–383. Cambridge University Press.

Elena Voita, Rico Sennrich, and Ivan Titov. 2019. When a good translation is wrong in context: Context-aware machine translation improves on deixis, ellipsis, and lexical cohesion. In *Proceedings of the 57th Annual Meeting of the Association for Computational Linguistics*, pages 1198–1212, Florence, Italy. Association for Computational Linguistics.

Alex Warstadt, Alicia Parrish, Haokun Liu, Anhad Mohananey, Wei Peng, Sheng-Fu Wang, and Samuel R. Bowman. 2020. BLiMP: The benchmark of linguistic minimal pairs for English. *Transactions of the Association for Computational Linguistics*, 8:377–392.

Beilei Xiang, Changbing Yang, Yu Li, Alex Warstadt, and Katharina Kann. 2021. CLiMP: A benchmark for Chinese language model evaluation. In *Proceedings of the 16th Conference of the European Chapter of the Association for Computational Linguistics: Main Volume*, pages 2784–2790, Online. Association for Computational Linguistics.

Dakun Zhang, Josep Crego, and Jean Senellart. 2018. Analyzing knowledge distillation in neural machine translation. In *Proceedings of the 15th International Workshop on Spoken Language Translation*, pages 23–30.

A Hyperparameters

Name	N	d_{model}	d_{ffn}	h	Parameters
TRANSFORMER (big)	6	1024	8192	16	269.7M
DISTILLED (small)	4	512	2048	4	50.9M

Table 4: Hyperparameters of the Transformer variants used for the experiments

B Examples

Example Inputs (English–German)	**Score Assigned by Model**
Source: *Yesterday evening, the committee wanted to vote on the* ***appointment****.*	
1-best translation by the evaluated system:	
Gestern Abend wollte der Ausschuss über die ***Ernennung*** *abstimmen.*	-0.09
Minimal pair based on a human-written reference:	
– Correct: *Gestern Abend wollte das Gremium über die* ***Personalie*** *abstimmen.*	-3.61
– Incorrect: *Gestern Abend wollte das Gremium über die* ***Ding*** *abstimmen.*	-2.34
Minimal pair based on a machine-generated reference (Amazon Translate):	
– Correct: *Gestern Abend wollte der Ausschuss über die* ***Ernennung*** *abstimmen.*	-0.09
– Incorrect: *Gestern Abend wollte der Ausschuss über die* ***Ding*** *abstimmen.*	-1.25
Source: *Why did Judah lose its land* ***and*** *temple?*	
1-best translation by the evaluated system:	
Warum hat Juda sein Land ***und*** *seinen Tempel verloren?*	-0.11
Minimal pair based on a human-written reference:	
– Correct: *Warum verlor Juda sein Land* ***mitsamt dem*** *Tempel?*	-2.58
– Incorrect: *Warum verlor Juda sein Land* ***mitsamt des*** *Tempels?*	-2.55
Minimal pair based on a machine-generated reference (DeepL):	
– Correct: *Warum hat Juda sein Land* ***und*** *seinen Tempel verloren?*	-0.11
– Incorrect: N/A	

Table 5: Examples of human-written and machine-generated minimal pairs for the **Vague language* hypothesis (top) and the **Hypercorrection* hypothesis (bottom). The log-scores are computed by an NMT model of type DISTILLED.
The first example demonstrates that a model often assigns a lower score to the correct human reference than to the incorrect machine reference. The human reference differs from the machine reference only in how the words *committee* and *appointment* are translated. The human word choice is fluent but has a lower probability under the model.
The second example shows that machine references often avoid the phenomenon altogether. Here, a simple conjunction is used instead of the more prestigious preposition *mitsamt* 'along with' in the human reference. This removes any risk of inserting a hypercorrect genitive. Since a contrastive variant cannot be derived from the machine reference, the sample is excluded from the machine-generated test set.

C State-of-the-art Accuracies for DistilLingEval

Error Type	Test set type	Discrepancy of test set	Reported accuracy
clause_omission	human references	0.91	78.1
	machine references	0.19	87.1
hypercorrect_genitive	human references	1.13	94.2
	machine references	0.18	100.0
np_agreement	human references	0.84	99.7
	machine references	0.15	100.0
placeholder_ding	human references	0.79	99.8
	machine references	0.16	100.0
polarity_affix_del	human references	0.87	98.8
	machine references	0.13	100.0
polarity_particle_kein_del	human references	0.88	97.5
	machine references	0.12	100.0
polarity_particle_nicht_del	human references	0.84	97.9
	machine references	0.14	99.9
subj_verb_agreement	human references	0.83	98.7
	machine references	0.14	99.8

Table 6: DistilLingEval results of a state-of-the-art NMT ensemble (Ng et al., 2019). The accuracies on machine references suggest that clause omission is an error type that still occurs with state-of-the-art NMT systems.

What Models Know About Their Attackers: Deriving Attacker Information From Latent Representations

Zhouhang Xie[1] Jonathan Brophy[2] Adam Noack[2] Wencong You[2] Kalyani Asthana[1]
Carter Perkins[2] Sabrina Reis[2] Zayd Hammoudeh[2] Daniel Lowd[2] Sameer Singh[1]
[1] University of California, Irvine CA
[2] University of Oregon, Eugene OR
{zhouhanx, sameer}@uci.edu

Abstract

Adversarial attacks curated against NLP models are increasingly becoming practical threats. Although various methods have been developed to detect adversarial attacks, securing learning-based NLP systems in practice would require more than identifying and evading perturbed instances. To address these issues, we propose a new set of adversary identification tasks, *Attacker Attribute Classification via Textual Analysis (AACTA)*, that attempts to obtain more detailed information about the attackers from adversarial texts. Specifically, given a piece of adversarial text, we hope to accomplish tasks such as localizing perturbed tokens, identifying the attacker's access level to the target model, determining the evasion mechanism imposed, and specifying the perturbation type employed by the attacking algorithm. Our contributions are as follows: we formalize the task of classifying attacker attributes, and create a benchmark on various target models from sentiment classification and abuse detection domains. We show that signals from BERT models and target models can be used to train classifiers that reveal the properties of the attacking algorithms. We demonstrate that adversarial attacks leave interpretable traces in the feature space of both of pre-trained language models and target models, making AACTA a promising direction towards more trustworthy NLP systems.

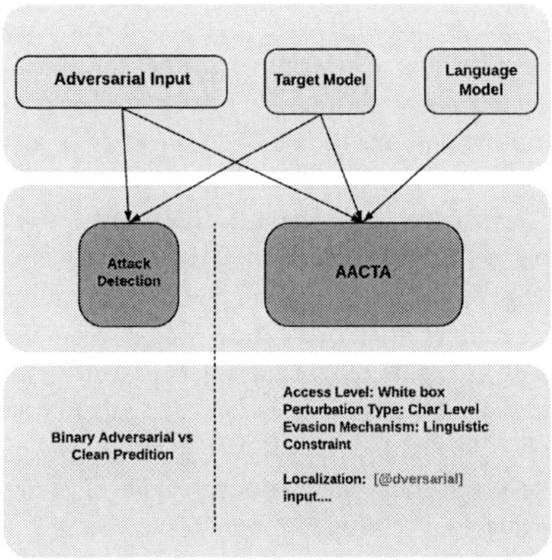

Figure 1: Illustration of AACTA compared to attack detection.

1 Introduction

Accompanying the success of deep learning in Natural Language Processing, there has been a prevalence of adversarial attacks in text. Attackers modify input sequences to NLP models such as text classifiers and machine translation models slightly so that the prediction of the target model will deviate from its original output (Zhang et al., 2020). These attacks are known to be generalizable across models (Yuan et al., 2021), and can hurt the performance of NLP models that are used in real-world tasks, such as commercial sentiment classification APIs (Garg and Ramakrishnan, 2020) and Google Translate (Wallace et al., 2020).

To address the potential threat of adversarial attacks in text, various defense methods have been proposed, such as training classifiers to determine whether a piece of text is perturbed by potential attackers (Zhou et al., 2019) and hiding the gradient of the model via prediction poisoning (Wallace et al., 2020; Orekondy et al., 2019). However, it is easier to defend against a threat when we know more about the attacker. For example, commercial model owners may need to take actions if the attackers have access to protected model weights. Similarly, model users may want to receive alerts when the system is attacked by elaborate attackers that employ language models with GPU resources. As an attempt to address this issue, previous work has shown that fine-grained analysis of adversarial images can reveal information about the attackers, such as the target labels of the attacks on image clas-

Proceedings of the Fourth BlackboxNLP Workshop on Analyzing and Interpreting Neural Networks for NLP, pages 69–78
Online, November 11, 2021.

sifiers (Pang et al., 2020a). However, this method requires access to all queries from the attacker and a known target model.

In this work, we take the next step towards understanding attackers through a task we call ***A**ttacker **A**ttribute **C**lassification via **T**extual **A**nalysis (AACTA).* AACTA includes a number of subtasks, including (1) attacker access level estimation, to determine what level of access the attacker has to the model being attacked; (2) perturbation type analysis, to determine the type of perturbation imposed by the attackers; (3) evasion mechanism determination, to determine whether the attackers used any constraints on generating imperceptible perturbations; and (4) attack localization, to determine which words or characters were changed.

To achieve these identification tasks, we exploit the fact that adversarial examples must make changes to the input text and thus the feature space of the target model. We draw signals from these traces as inputs to our classifiers, and formulate the task above as a series of classification subtasks. We conduct classification and localization over adversarial examples generated against multiple target text classifiers from various datasets. For classification sub-tasks, our method yields 74% accuracy on determining whether the *access level* of the attack is black-box or white-box, 75% accuracy on determining whether the attacking algorithm's *perturbation type* is word or character-level, and 78% accuracy on inferring whether the attackers attempt to construct *evasion method* by imposing linguistic constraints during attack construction. For attack localization, our model achieved 0.74 class-averaged f1 on flagging perturbed tokens[1].

2 Attacker Attribute Classification

2.1 Problem Statement

Consider an input space X and an NLP model parameterized by θ that maps the input space to an output space, i.e. $f_\theta(X) \to Y$. We refer to models under adversarial attacks as *target models*. The attacker's goal is to modify the output of the target model by making minor modifications to the input. For a given input $x \in X$, we define adversarial perturbations as samples x_{adv} that are close to x but with a different output from the target model:

$$\{\Delta(x, x_{\text{adv}}) \leq r, f_\theta(x) \neq f_\theta(\text{x}_{\text{adv}})\}$$

[1]Accuracy and f1 scores reported above are averaged scores across datasets.

Note that there can be various definitions of "closeness", corresponding to different distance metrics Δ. An adversarial attack $g : X \to X$ maps each input to an adversarial perturbation or to itself if no valid perturbation is found. Different attacking algorithms may use different constraints for "closeness" and different searching methods for generating perturbations.

In the context of AACTA, we aim to step beyond flagging adversarial samples from unperturbed texts. Specifically, we formulate AACTA as a series of classification and localization subtasks. For classification tasks, our goal is to infer whether the adversarial algorithm used to construct a sample x_{adv} belongs to a set of functions $A_{property}$, where *property* is a human-interpretable characteristic that is informative about the attackers. We accomplish this objective by training a classifier $h(X_{\text{adv}}) \to y_{property}$. For attack localization, the goal is to determine how the adversarial instance x_{adv} relates to the unseen source example x, namely, which token(s) in the sequence are modified by the attackers.

2.2 Classification Tasks

To perform sequence-level classification, we train logistic regression classifiers over two types of representations: a standard BERT sentence representation and a new target model representation, consisting of the layer-wise mean and variance of the node activations in each layer of the model. We show that the latter representation performs significantly better than the BERT representation in classifying the following properties:

1. *Target Model Access Level*: In this setup, the attacks are partitioned by the level of access to the target model (e.g. model weights and prediction probabilities). We formulate this sub-task as black-box vs. white-box classification. We consider an attack black-box if the attacker does not have any information about the target model; otherwise we consider the attack white-box. In some setups, adversarial attacks that require predicted probabilities of target models are considered grey-box attacks. Here we treat these attacks as white-box to ensure a wide enough range of attack algorithms populate both classes.

2. *Perturbation Type*: In this setup, we partition the attacks by perturbation type. This could include the level of perturbations (character or

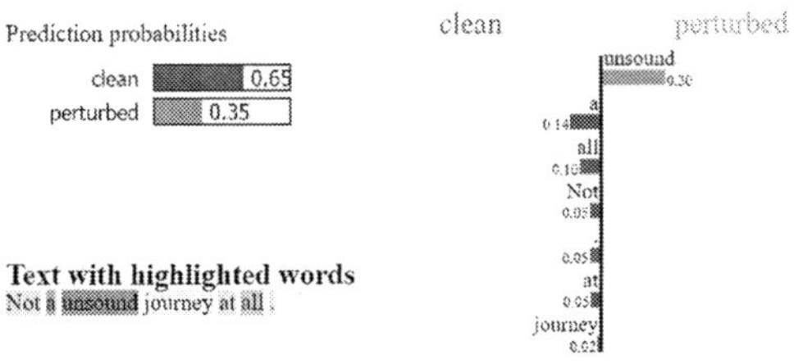

Figure 2: LIME explanation for a sentence-level classifier. The importance scores for the tokens could be used to localize perturbed tokens (see Algorithm 1). The localization algorithm does not fully depend on the classifier's ability to make correct predictions.

```
Input: Binary sequence classifier f, Interpretation
    framework LIME, Decision threshold ϵ ∈ [0, 1],
    Perturbed sequence x_adv
TokenScore ← GetImportance(f, x_adv, LIME)
Sort tokens by their importance score
i ← 0
for ;, i < NumTokens, i++ do
    if ImportanceOf(i) ≤ ImportanceOf(i-1)×ϵ then
        break
    end if
end for
PerturbedTokens = SortedTokens[:i]
return PerturbedTokens
```

Algorithm 1: Algorithm for Locating Perturbed Token with Binary Adversarial-or-Not Classifier

word level), or more fine-grained classes of adversarial edits such as in-word shuffling, intrude, and character deletion (Eger and Benz, 2020). In our experiments, we separate attacks into two groups: word-level and character-level perturbations. The attacks are recognized as character-level attacks if the attacks impose perturbations on both character and token levels.

3. *Evasion Mechanism*: In this setup, the attacks are partitioned by the constraints used by attackers in order to generate more indistinguishable attacks. Such constraints could be making visually imperceptible (Eger et al., 2019) and grammatically coherent (Zhao et al., 2018) adversarial attacks, or simply constraining the number of perturbations allowed per sentence.

   In our experiment, we label the adversarial instances by whether the attackers impose linguistic constraints on ensuring the coherency of perturbed sentences. For example, such constraints could involve language models on word or sentence level, distance metrics in word embedding space, and other constraints such as sememe. Upon training and evaluating our detection classifiers, adversarial attacks that impose any of the linguistic constraints are treated as one class, and attacks that do not consider coherency of perturbed sentences are treated as the other class.

2.3 Attack Localization

For attack localization, we incorporate signals from a target model and an external language model with two different approaches.

For classifiers using an external language model signal, we first obtain contextualized word embeddings for each token in a sequence, and then train a binary perturbed-vs-clean *token-level* logistic regression classifier to determine if a token is perturbed or not. As BERT contextualized representation works on sub-word level, the detector model using BERT representation as input makes predictions on sub-word level as well. To evaluate BERT-based localizers in a more realistic setup, we applied a hierarchical tokenization scheme at inference time. Specifically, for each space-separated token in a potentially perturbed sequence, we flag the token as malicious if our binary classifier detects any of the subwords contained in the token to be perturbed.

Since the target model activation signal is obtained with respect to the whole sequence, there is no way to directly train an activation-based classifier that makes token-level predictions. Thus, we cast attack localization as interpreting a sequence level classifier, i.e. identifying tokens that are important to the classifier's decision that some sentence is adversarial. Specifically, we train a binary *sequence-level* clean-vs-perturbed classifier that aims at flagging perturbed sentences, then we apply LIME (Ribeiro et al., 2016) to obtain an importance score for each token with respect to the adversarial class. The exact heuristic used to identify perturbed token(s) with LIME is described in Algorithm 1. When obtaining token importance via LIME, we always consider important tokens that skew the detection model's prediction to the *adversarial* class. Thus, the localization algorithm could identify perturbed tokens even when the detection model makes an inaccurate prediction on the sequence level. Meanwhile, such an interpretation approach could be applied to any general binary-sequence-level classifier.

	Acc. Lvl	Evasion Mec.	Perturb. Type
BAE	bb	yes	word
DeepWordBug	bb	no	char
FasterGenetic	bb	yes	word
Genetic	bb	yes	word
Hotflip	wb	yes	char
IgaWang	bb	yes	word
Pruthi	bb	no	word
Pso	bb	yes	word
Textbugger	wb	yes	word
Textfooler	bb	yes	word
Viper	bb	no	char

Table 1: **Adversarial attacks included.** From left to right: access level (black-box vs. white-box, denoted by bb/wb in the table), evasion mechanism (with/without linguistic constrains), and perturbation type (word vs. character-level).

3 Experiment Setup

Datasets We generate adversarial text instances against the target models with open-source adversarial evaluation codebases, OpenAttack (Zeng et al., 2020) and TextAttack (Morris et al., 2020). The incorporated attacks are DeepWordBug (Gao et al., 2018), FasterGenetic (Jia et al., 2019), Genetic (Alzantot et al., 2018), HotFlip (Ebrahimi et al., 2018), IGA (Wang et al., 2019), Pruthi (Pruthi et al., 2019), PSO (Zang et al., 2020), TextBugger (Li et al., 2018), TextFooler (Jin et al., 2019), and Viper (Eger et al., 2019). Table 1 details the attack partitioning.

Target Models The adversarial samples are constructed against BERT (Devlin et al., 2019), RoBERTa (Liu et al., 2019) and XLNet models (Yang et al., 2019) over two tasks: abuse detection and sentiment classification. For abuse detection, the models are trained on Hatebase, Civil Comments[2], and Wikipedia (Wulczyn et al., 2017; Dixon et al., 2018) datasets; for sentiment analysis, the models are trained on SST (Socher et al., 2013) and Twitter Climate Change Sentiment[3] datasets.

Evaluation Metrics We evaluate our localizers on f1 scores, and all classification models (including classification models trained for BERT localizers) by class-balanced accuracy scores. For localizers specifically, all predictions are truncated to space-separated token level (as described in Section 2.3).

Hyper-parameters For the LIME-based localizer, we set the decision threshold ϵ to 0.1 for all experiments (see Algorithm 1). For all classification tasks, we train logistic regression models with standard scaled data, and tune the model's hyper-parameters using grid search with 3-fold cross-validation.

4 Localization Results

We cover empirical and qualitative results of our localization models in this section, and provide case studies of localized adversarial instances by both BERT and LIME-based localizers.

4.1 Empirical Performance

In our localization experiments, both types of localizers using BERT contextualized embeddings and target model activations outperform the random baseline significantly. Namely, our BERT-based and LIME-based localizers achieve 74% and 63% class-balanced f1-score on localizing perturbed tokens, while the random baseline is 53%. This shows that information of perturbed tokens could be retrieved from either external language models and target models. Meanwhile, although LIME-based localizers have a lower general f1 score than BERT-based localizers, LIME localizers achieve better accuracy at identifying the perturbed tokens. This is because the optimization objective of sequence-level classifiers only requires the model to identify at least one of the perturbed tokens in a sequence. Consequently, the classifier tends to give accurate but conservative decisions when flagging perturbed tokens. On the other hand, BERT-based localizer is directly trained on binary classification and thus has better-balanced performance.

For LIME-based localizers specifically, the performance trade-off between clean and adversarial classes of the inference process could be adjusted by tuning the threshold hyper-parameter as described in the previous section. For our experiment, all localizers were set to conduct inference with a threshold of 0.1.

4.2 Qualitative Analysis

BERT-based Localizer In practice, BERT-based localizers tend to flag regions of perturbed text instead of individual tokens, potentially due to the usage of contextualized embeddings as input.

[2] https://www.kaggle.com/c/jigsaw-unintended-bias-in-toxicity-classification

[3] https://www.kaggle.com/edqian/twitter-climate-change-sentiment-dataset

	Original Texts	Perturbed Texts	Bert Localizer Outputs	Actv Localizer Outputs
1	Vile and tacky are the two best adjectives to describe Ghost Ship .	Hateful and dorky are the two best adjectives to describe ghost ship.	Hateful and dorky are the two best adjectives to describe ghost ship.	Hateful and dorky are the two best adjectives to describe ghost ship.
2	Its gorg out! RT @@anggxo: This bitch thinks its june or something @BriiiXO http://t.co/mFVCmym	Its gorg outside! Ti @@ anggxo : this blackguard thinks its june or something @ briiixo http :// t. Co / mfvcmym	Its gorg outside! Ti @@ anggxo : this blackguard thinks its june or something @ briiixo http :// t. Co / mfvcmym	Its gorg outside! Ti @@ anggxo : this blackguard thinks its june or something @ briiixo http :// t. Co / mfvcmym
3	It 's difficult to say whether The Tuxedo is more boring or embarrassing – I 'm prepared to call it a draw .	Ït 'ŝ difficuḷï to sây whetheř Ťhê Ťŭxeḍô îs moře borîng or embârrâsŝîňg – I 'ḿ prêp'ařêḍ tô caḷḷ iẗ a dřâw .	Ït 'ŝ difficuḷï to sây whetheř Ťhê Ťŭxeḍô îs moře borîng or embârrâsŝîňg – I 'ḿ prêp'ařêḍ tô caḷḷ iẗ a dřâw .	Ït 'ŝ difficuḷï to sây whetheř Ťhê Ťŭxeḍô îs moře borîng or embârrâsŝîňg – I 'ḿ prêp'ařêḍ tô caḷḷ iẗ a dřâw .
4	Wake up bitches	Following up fairies	Following up fairies	Following up fairies

Table 2: Selected examples of localizer predictions. Dark red denotes perturbed or correctly flagged tokens, blue denotes false negative predictions, and green denotes false positive predictions.

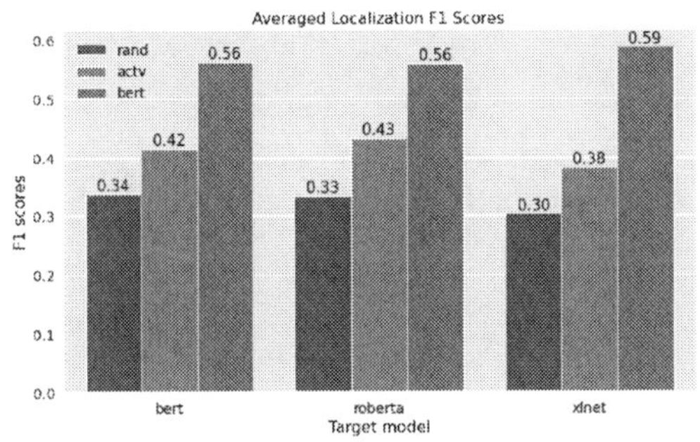

Figure 3: Average *adversarial* class f1 score over all datasets and target model combinations. Leftmost bars colored in blue denotes performance of a random token-level classifier.

For example (Table 2: instance 1), BERT localizer identified *"Hateful and dorky"* as consecutive perturbed tokens, although the word *"and"* is not perturbed. Similarly, in the perturbed phrase "*Ït 'ŝ difficuḷï* to *sây*" in instance 3, BERT localizer flagged the word *"to"* as perturbed.

On the other hand, the auto-correction scheme utilized by the off-the-shelf BERT tokenizer sometimes hinders the performance of the localizer. For example, BERT tokenizer will convert the visually attacked token *"îs"* to the regular token *"is"*; this makes it challenging for the BERT-embedding-based classifier to pick up such perturbed tokens.

In general, BERT-based localizers tend to give more aggressive predictions regarding perturbed tokens, thus yielding more false positives, as demonstrated in instance 1. However, the localizer struggles for instances where the original text contains many low-frequency tokens. For example, in instance 2, the only correctly identified perturbed token is a character level perturbation on the word "*blackguard.*" Perturbations on user ids and URLs are all overlooked.

LIME-based Localizer In contrast to the BERT-based localizer, the activation-based localizer achieves higher accuracy detecting perturbed tokens, as demonstrated empirically in Section 4.1. For example, in instance 1 of Table 2, the activation-based localizer did not yield false-positive labels on the phrase "*Hateful and dorky.*" However, the more conservative decision made by the LIME-based localizer makes it more likely to miss perturbed tokens. In instance 4, the localizer failed to recognize "*fairies*" as a perturbed token.

For both localizers, conducting classification on noisy inputs becomes a challenging task. Instance 2 in Table 2 shows an example where the input text contains user ids and hyperlinks. In this case, both localizers struggle to identify the perturbed tokens, while BERT-based localizers have the least accurate predictions. This may be explained by the failure of the pre-trained language model to capture the text properties corresponding to specific datasets, while target models are adapted to each of the datasets during training. We provide further discussion on this phenomena in Section 6.2.

5 Attack Attribute Classification

We evaluate the performance of our classification task by class-balanced accuracy scores. The results for classification tasks are shown in Figure 4 and Figure 5. For almost all target models and datasets, classifiers using target model activation as input signals consistently outperform classifiers using

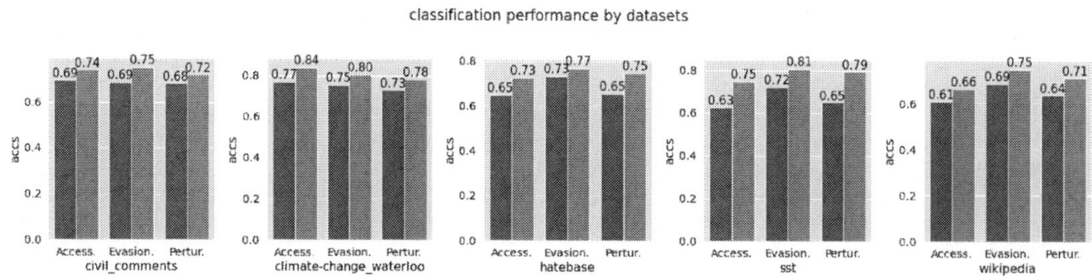

Figure 4: Accuracy score of each of the three classification task over all datasets. Blue bars denotes performance of BERT representation, orange bars denotes performance with target model activation. The three property being detected are access level, evasion mechanism and perturbation type.

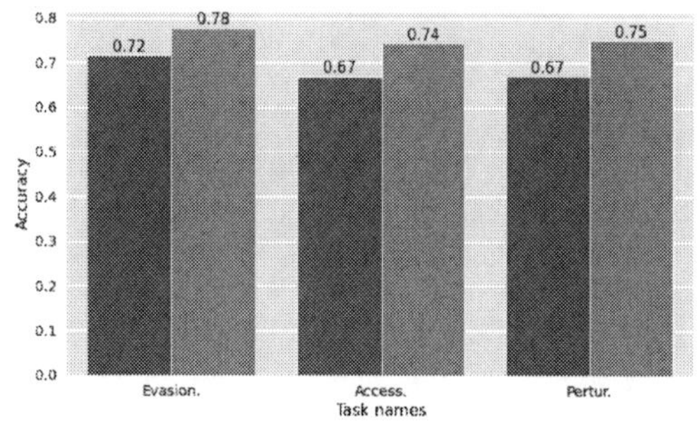

Figure 5: Average accuracy for different tasks across all datasets and target model combinations. The blue and orange bars denote BERT and activation-representation performance, respectively.

	wikipedia	sst	hatebase	climate.	civil.
civil.	57.4	59.0	54.1	58.5	na
climate.	57.2	57.6	55.3	na	60.1
hatebase	59.7	57.7	na	58.1	56.7
sst	58.4	na	55.1	62.5	60.6
wikipedia	na	58.2	61.0	59.8	62.8

Table 3: Averaged out-of-domain (dataset) generalization detection accuracy scores across all models for BERT-based classifiers.

BERT sentence representations.

Target Model Access Level On determining whether an adversarial attack is constructed with access to the target model, target model internal activation representations outperform BERT representations the most among the three tasks, demonstrating white and black box attacks will form different distributions in the representation space of target models. Interestingly, target model representation as a proxy to separate black and white-box attacks consistently achieve better performance in sentiment classification tasks (datasets) than abuse detection datasets.

Perturbation Type In classifying whether the attack algorithm operates on word or character-level, BERT and target model representation has the least significant performance gap among the three tasks. This shows pre-trained language models and target models capture information on the token level of perturbed texts to a similar extent. However, activation-based localizer still outperforms BERT-based localizer in all experiment setups, which could be explained by the phenomenon where general pre-trained language models fail to capture the nuances of specific datasets, as described in the previous section.

Evasion Mechanism We observe the highest accuracy for the task of determining whether attackers impose any linguistic constraints when curating adversarial samples. Similar to detecting black and white box attacks, detection models on sentiment classification datasets achieve higher scores in general than abuse detection datasets.

6 Discussion

This section is organized as follows: we first discuss out-of-domain performance of classifiers and localizers, then provide an analysis on the performance of BERT representations.

6.1 Out-of-Domain Generalization

We test our model's ability to generalize across target models and datasets by evaluating trained classifiers on (1) adversarial text instances targeted at different target models trained on the same dataset, (2) adversarial text instances targeted at the same target model trained on different datasets.

Generalization of BERT-based Classifiers Our results show BERT-representation-based classi-

	wikipedia	sst	hatebase	climate.	civil.
civil.	52.6	51.8	51.2	53.2	na
climate.	51.7	53.0	52.7	na	54.4
hatebase	51.4	50.9	na	52.4	51.5
sst	51.0	na	53.1	52.7	50.4
wikipedia	na	52.0	54.0	55.4	53.0

Table 4: Averaged out-of-domain (dataset) generalization accuracy scores across all models for activation-based classifiers

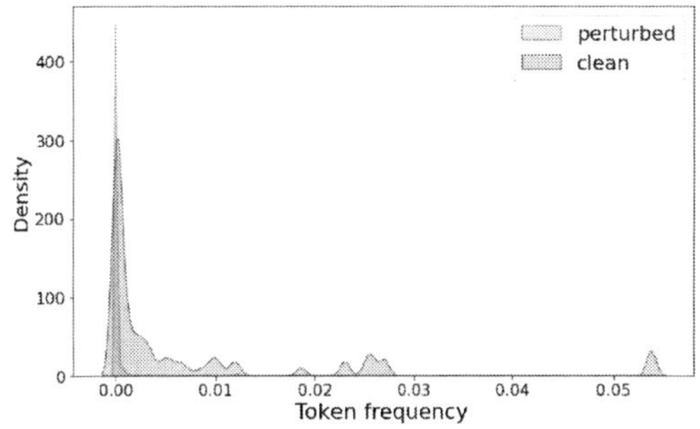

Figure 6: Frequency distribution of adversarial and clean tokens with respect to external corpus for all adversarial instances.

fiers demonstrate abilities to generalize to adversaries targeting different target models or datasets. Meanwhile, there is no significant difference between BERT-based classifiers' generalization performance to datasets for the same task and different tasks (i.e., abuse detection and sentiment classification).

Generalization of Activation-based Classifiers Compared to BERT-representation-based classifiers, classifiers that operate on target-model activation-representations do not generalize well to other datasets. In almost all cases, performance metrics for the classifier dropped to near-random performance on out-of-distribution data. This shows that although activation representations provide richer information about the attackers for in-distribution data, they are less dataset-agnostic than language-model representations.

Generalization of Localizers Similar to classifiers using two types of signals, BERT-based localizers outperform LIME (activation)-based localizers when given out-of-distribution data. When averaging over all out-of-domain datasets, the class-weighted f1 score of BERT-based localizer drops to 0.69, while performance of the LIME-based localizer drops to 0.28. This is consistent with the observations of classifiers using the two types of representations in previous sections: BERT representations tend to have better generalization ability across datasets, while signals from target models are highly dependent on specific domains.

6.2 BERT Feature Performance and Adversarial Token Frequencies

In sequence classification experiments, our proposed feature from target model activation statistics outperforms BERT representations. Similarly, previous works show that BERT does not work well in discriminating character-level attacks (Zhou et al., 2019). In this section, we demonstrate this might be due to perturbed tokens that are usually rare in natural texts; thus, pre-trained language models do not have enough signal to fully capture the feature of perturbed tokens.

To test the plausibility of this hypothesis, we apply an off-the-shelf word-frequency lookup library (Speer et al., 2018) to check the frequency of each token with respect to several external corpora[4], and show the distribution of token frequency with kernel density estimation. The plotted distribution of clean and adversarial tokens is shown in Figure 6. This gives some intuition on why target model activation achieves better results. Namely, tokens perturbed by attackers tend to have low occurrence in natural text, and thus forms out-of-distribution data to pre-trained language models. Thus, there might be more fine-grained signals that are lost during the encoding phase of BERT language model.

7 Related Work

This section is organized as follows: we first cover related literature in detecting and defending against adversarial input for deep neural networks. Then, we cover some closely connected lines of works and highlight their similarities and differences to our approach.

Adversarial Attacks for Deep Neural Networks Deep learning has achieved promising results in a wide range of domains such as CV and NLP. However, neural-network-based models are usually vulnerable to adversarial attacks. Although adversarial training could help, such a method is known to hurt the generalization ability and performance of the resulting models (Raghunathan et al., 2019) and

[4]Wikipedia, Google Books, Twitter and other commonly used corpora from various domains, see `https://github.com/LuminosoInsight/wordfreq`

requires additional data curation and training procedures. Exploiting the fact that adversarial examples are usually scattered in a different distribution than innocent inputs (Gong et al., 2017), people have achieved successful binary detection performance using external classifiers that directly operate on input data (Metzen et al., 2017; Feinman et al., 2017). Meanwhile, other works have shown that adversarial examples leave recognizable traces in latent spaces of the attacked models, enabling defensive methods that utilize model internals, such as using KNN on model states (Carrara et al., 2019).

Attack Detection in Text Different from detecting adversarial attacks in images, capturing text adversaries requires approaches that take into account the featurization of discrete text tokens. Previous works have shown that linear models that use BERT representation of each token as inputs could achieve good performance for word-level attacks and achieve competitive general detection accuracy over adversaries when combined with a spell checker (Zhou et al., 2019).

Obtaining Information about Attackers Via Adversarial Samples It is possible to learn even more about the attackers via analyzing a *batch* of adversarial exmaples, such as what class label the attacker interested in (Pang et al., 2020b). However, this method might not work for attacks that are only aimed at lowering the accuracy of target models. Additionally, our method could help in obtaining information about the attackers from more dimensions.

Deriving Interpretable Information From Latent Representations Previous studies have shown that interpretable linguistic information could be retrieved from representations of deep learning models, such as word embeddings and activation status of internal neurons (Belinkov, 2021). Our work borrows the general methodology from this literature but instead derives properties that are informative about the attackers from textural adversaries .

8 Conclusion

In this work, we introduce a new task, **A**ttacker **A**ttribute **C**lassification via **T**extual **A**nalysis (AACTA), that aims at deriving interpretable information about adversarial attack algorithms that are informative about the attackers. We demonstrate that characteristics of attacking algorithms leave traces in feature space of language models and target models, and that such information could be retrieved by training classifiers over latent representations.

Acknowledgements

This work was supported by the Defense Advanced Research Projects Agency (DARPA), agreement number HR00112090135. This work benefited from access to the University of Oregon high performance computer, Talapas.

References

Moustafa Alzantot, Yash Sharma, Ahmed Elgohary, Bo-Jhang Ho, Mani Srivastava, and Kai-Wei Chang. 2018. Generating natural language adversarial examples. In *Proceedings of the 2018 Conference on Empirical Methods in Natural Language Processing*, pages 2890–2896, Brussels, Belgium. Association for Computational Linguistics.

Yonatan Belinkov. 2021. Probing classifiers: Promises, shortcomings, and alternatives. *arXiv preprint arXiv:2102.12452*.

Fabio Carrara, Fabrizio Falchi, Roberto Caldelli, Giuseppe Amato, and Rudy Becarelli. 2019. Adversarial image detection in deep neural networks. *Multimedia Tools and Applications*, 78(3):2815–2835.

Jacob Devlin, Ming-Wei Chang, Kenton Lee, and Kristina Toutanova. 2019. BERT: Pre-training of deep bidirectional transformers for language understanding. In *Proceedings of the 2019 Conference of the North American Chapter of the Association for Computational Linguistics: Human Language Technologies, Volume 1 (Long and Short Papers)*, pages 4171–4186, Minneapolis, Minnesota. Association for Computational Linguistics.

Lucas Dixon, John Li, Jeffrey Sorensen, Nithum Thain, and Lucy Vasserman. 2018. Measuring and mitigating unintended bias in text classification. In *Proceedings of the 2018 AAAI/ACM Conference on AI, Ethics, and Society*, pages 67–73.

Javid Ebrahimi, Anyi Rao, Daniel Lowd, and Dejing Dou. 2018. HotFlip: White-box adversarial examples for text classification. In *Proceedings of the 56th Annual Meeting of the Association for Computational Linguistics (Volume 2: Short Papers)*, pages 31–36, Melbourne, Australia. Association for Computational Linguistics.

Steffen Eger and Yannik Benz. 2020. From hero to zéroe: A benchmark of low-level adversarial attacks. *arXiv preprint arXiv:2010.05648*.

Steffen Eger, Gözde Gül Şahin, Andreas Rücklé, Ji-Ung Lee, Claudia Schulz, Mohsen Mesgar, Krishnkant Swarnkar, Edwin Simpson, and Iryna

Gurevych. 2019. Text processing like humans do: Visually attacking and shielding NLP systems. In *Proceedings of the 2019 Conference of the North American Chapter of the Association for Computational Linguistics: Human Language Technologies, Volume 1 (Long and Short Papers)*, pages 1634–1647, Minneapolis, Minnesota. Association for Computational Linguistics.

Reuben Feinman, Ryan R Curtin, Saurabh Shintre, and Andrew B Gardner. 2017. Detecting adversarial samples from artifacts. *arXiv preprint arXiv:1703.00410*.

Ji Gao, Jack Lanchantin, Mary Lou Soffa, and Yanjun Qi. 2018. Black-box generation of adversarial text sequences to evade deep learning classifiers. *CoRR*, abs/1801.04354.

Siddhant Garg and Goutham Ramakrishnan. 2020. BAE: BERT-based adversarial examples for text classification. *CoRR*, abs/2004.01970.

Zhitao Gong, Wenlu Wang, and Wei-Shinn Ku. 2017. Adversarial and clean data are not twins. *arXiv preprint arXiv:1704.04960*.

Robin Jia, Aditi Raghunathan, Kerem Göksel, and Percy Liang. 2019. Certified robustness to adversarial word substitutions. In *Proceedings of the 2019 Conference on Empirical Methods in Natural Language Processing and the 9th International Joint Conference on Natural Language Processing (EMNLP-IJCNLP)*, pages 4120–4133.

Di Jin, Zhijing Jin, Joey Tianyi Zhou, and Peter Szolovits. 2019. Is BERT really robust? natural language attack on text classification and entailment. *CoRR*, abs/1907.11932.

Jinfeng Li, Shouling Ji, Tianyu Du, Bo Li, and Ting Wang. 2018. TextBugger: Generating adversarial text against real-world applications. *CoRR*, abs/1812.05271.

Yinhan Liu, Myle Ott, Naman Goyal, Jingfei Du, Mandar Joshi, Danqi Chen, Omer Levy, Mike Lewis, Luke Zettlemoyer, and Veselin Stoyanov. 2019. RoBERTa: A robustly optimized BERT pretraining approach. *CoRR*, abs/1907.11692.

Jan Hendrik Metzen, Tim Genewein, Volker Fischer, and Bastian Bischoff. 2017. On detecting adversarial perturbations. *arXiv preprint arXiv:1702.04267*.

John X Morris, Eli Lifland, Jin Yong Yoo, Jake Grigsby, Di Jin, and Yanjun Qi. 2020. TextAttack: A framework for adversarial attacks, data augmentation, and adversarial training in nlp. *arXiv preprint arXiv:2005.05909*.

Tribhuvanesh Orekondy, Bernt Schiele, and Mario Fritz. 2019. Prediction poisoning: Towards defenses against dnn model stealing attacks. *arXiv preprint arXiv:1906.10908*.

Ren Pang, Xinyang Zhang, Shouling Ji, Xiapu Luo, and Ting Wang. 2020a. AdvMind: Inferring adversary intent of black-box attacks. In *Proceedings of the 26th ACM SIGKDD International Conference on Knowledge Discovery Data Mining*, KDD '20, page 1899–1907, New York, NY, USA. Association for Computing Machinery.

Ren Pang, Xinyang Zhang, Shouling Ji, Xiapu Luo, and Ting Wang. 2020b. AdvMind: Inferring adversary intent of black-box attacks. In *Proceedings of the 26th ACM SIGKDD International Conference on Knowledge Discovery & Data Mining*, pages 1899–1907.

Danish Pruthi, Bhuwan Dhingra, and Zachary C. Lipton. 2019. Combating adversarial misspellings with robust word recognition. In *Proceedings of the 57th Annual Meeting of the Association for Computational Linguistics*, pages 5582–5591, Florence, Italy. Association for Computational Linguistics.

Aditi Raghunathan, Sang Michael Xie, Fanny Yang, John C Duchi, and Percy Liang. 2019. Adversarial training can hurt generalization. *arXiv preprint arXiv:1906.06032*.

Marco Tulio Ribeiro, Sameer Singh, and Carlos Guestrin. 2016. " why should i trust you?" explaining the predictions of any classifier. In *Proceedings of the 22nd ACM SIGKDD international conference on knowledge discovery and data mining*, pages 1135–1144.

Richard Socher, Alex Perelygin, Jean Wu, Jason Chuang, Christopher D Manning, Andrew Y Ng, and Christopher Potts. 2013. Recursive deep models for semantic compositionality over a sentiment treebank. In *Proceedings of the 2013 conference on empirical methods in natural language processing*, pages 1631–1642.

Robyn Speer, Joshua Chin, Andrew Lin, Sara Jewett, and Lance Nathan. 2018. Luminosoinsight/wordfreq: v2. 2.

Eric Wallace, Mitchell Stern, and Dawn Song. 2020. Imitation attacks and defenses for blackbox machine translation systems. *arXiv preprint arXiv:2004.15015*.

Xiaosen Wang, Hao Jin, and Kun He. 2019. Natural language adversarial attacks and defenses in word level. *CoRR*, abs/1909.06723.

Ellery Wulczyn, Nithum Thain, and Lucas Dixon. 2017. Ex machina: Personal attacks seen at scale. In *Proceedings of the 26th international conference on world wide web*, pages 1391–1399.

Zhilin Yang, Zihang Dai, Yiming Yang, Jaime Carbonell, Russ R Salakhutdinov, and Quoc V Le. 2019. XLNet: Generalized autoregressive pretraining for language understanding. *Advances in neural information processing systems*, 32.

Liping Yuan, Xiaoqing Zheng, Yi Zhou, Cho-Jui Hsieh, and Kai-Wei Chang. 2021. On the transferability of adversarial attacks against neural nlp models. In *EMNLP*.

Yuan Zang, Fanchao Qi, Chenghao Yang, Zhiyuan Liu, Meng Zhang, Qun Liu, and Maosong Sun. 2020. Word-level textual adversarial attacking as combinatorial optimization. In *Proceedings of the 58th Annual Meeting of the Association for Computational Linguistics*, pages 6066–6080, Online. Association for Computational Linguistics.

Guoyang Zeng, Fanchao Qi, Qianrui Zhou, Tingji Zhang, Bairu Hou, Yuan Zang, Zhiyuan Liu, and Maosong Sun. 2020. OpenAttack: An open-source textual adversarial attack toolkit. *arXiv preprint arXiv:2009.09191*.

Wei Emma Zhang, Quan Z Sheng, Ahoud Alhazmi, and Chenliang Li. 2020. Adversarial attacks on deep-learning models in natural language processing: A survey. *ACM Transactions on Intelligent Systems and Technology (TIST)*, 11(3):1–41.

Zhengli Zhao, Dheeru Dua, and Sameer Singh. 2018. Generating Natural Adversarial Examples. In *International Conference on Learning Representations (ICLR)*.

Yichao Zhou, Jyun-Yu Jiang, Kai-Wei Chang, and Wei Wang. 2019. Learning to discriminate perturbations for blocking adversarial attacks in text classification. In *Proceedings of the 2019 Conference on Empirical Methods in Natural Language Processing and the 9th International Joint Conference on Natural Language Processing (EMNLP-IJCNLP)*, pages 4906–4915.

ALL Dolphins Are Intelligent and SOME Are Friendly: Probing BERT for Nouns' Semantic Properties and their Prototypicality

Marianna Apidianaki
Department of Digital Humanities
University of Helsinki
Helsinki, Finland
marianna.apidianaki@helsinki.fi

Aina Garí Soler
Université Paris-Saclay
CNRS, LISN
91400, Orsay, France
aina.gari@lisn.fr

Abstract

Large scale language models encode rich commonsense knowledge acquired through exposure to massive data during pre-training, but their understanding of entities and their semantic properties is unclear. We probe BERT (Devlin et al., 2019) for the properties of English nouns as expressed by adjectives that do not restrict the reference scope of the noun they modify (as in *red car*), but instead emphasise some inherent aspect (*red strawberry*). We base our study on psycholinguistics datasets that capture the association strength between nouns and their semantic features. We probe BERT using cloze tasks and in a classification setting, and show that the model has marginal knowledge of these features and their prevalence as expressed in these datasets. We discuss factors that make evaluation challenging and impede drawing general conclusions about the models' knowledge of noun properties. Finally, we show that when tested in a fine-tuning setting addressing entailment, BERT successfully leverages the information needed for reasoning about the meaning of adjective-noun constructions outperforming previous methods.

Masking Properties	
SINGULAR	a balloon is [MASK].
PLURAL	balloons are [MASK].
SINGULAR + usually	a balloon is usually [MASK].
PLURAL + usually	balloons are usually [MASK].
SINGULAR+generally	a balloon is generally [MASK].
PLURAL + generally	balloons are generally [MASK].
SINGULAR + can be	a balloon can be [MASK].
PLURAL + can be	balloons can be [MASK].
most + PLURAL	most balloons are [MASK].
all + PLURAL	all balloons are [MASK].
some + PLURAL	some balloons are [MASK].
Masking Quantifiers	
[MASK] balloons are colourful.	(ALL-MOST-SOME)
[MASK] balloons are large.	(SOME-SOME-FEW)
[MASK] balloons are round.	(MOST-SOME-NO)

Table 1: Cloze statements for the noun *balloon* with its properties (McRae et al., 2005) and quantifiers masked. Parentheses in the lower part of the table contain the gold quantifiers in (Herbelot and Vecchi, 2015).

1 Introduction

Adjectival modification is one of the main types of composition in natural language (Baroni and Zamparelli, 2010; Guevara, 2010). Adjectives in attributive position[1] usually have a restrictive role on the reference scope of the noun they modify, limiting the set of things it refers to (e.g., *white rabbits* $\sqsubset$ *rabbits*). This property of adjectives has interesting entailment implications, generally leading to adjective-noun (AN) constructions where the entailment relationship with the head noun holds (AN $\models$ N) (Baroni et al., 2012). Entailment is directional (*white rabbit* $\models$ *rabbit* but *rabbit* $\not\models$ *white rabbit*) (Kotlerman et al., 2010), unless modification is not restrictive. When A is prototypical of the N it modifies (as in *soft silk, red lobster, small blueberry*), its insertion does not reduce the scope of N or add new information, but rather emphasises some inherent property (Pavlick and Callison-Burch, 2016). In these cases, N and AN denote the same set; they are in an equivalence relation (*red lobster* = *lobster*) and entailment is symmetric.

The notion of prototypicality has a prominent place in the computational linguistics literature, mainly by reference to relationships between nouns (Roller and Erk, 2016; Vulić et al., 2017). The prototypicality of adjectives has been understudied and is absent from lexico-semantic resources such as WordNet (Fellbaum, 1998) and HyperLex (Vulić et al., 2017). Alongside the theoretical interest of this linguistic property and its impact on the entailment properties of AN constructions, identifying prototypical adjectives has interesting practical implications. It can serve to retrieve information

[1]Adjectives that appear immediately before the noun they modify and form part of the noun phrase (e.g., *white rabbit*), as opposed to adjectives in predicative position that occur after the noun (e.g., this *rabbit* is *white*).

Proceedings of the Fourth BlackboxNLP Workshop on Analyzing and Interpreting Neural Networks for NLP, pages 79–94
Online, November 11, 2021.

about the general concept (*silk, blueberry*) when queries include such AN pairs (*soft silk, small blueberry*), or to discard adjectives that do not add new information about the noun they modify in summarisation or sentence compression.

We investigate the knowledge that the BERT model (Devlin et al., 2019) encodes about nouns' inherent properties as described in AN constructions. Although pre-trained language models have been shown to encode rich factual and commonsense knowledge (Petroni et al., 2019; Bouraoui et al., 2020), little is known about their understanding of the properties of the involved entities. We specifically explore whether BERT encodes information about the prototypical properties of the class of objects denoted by a noun (for example, that *all lobsters are red* and *blueberries are small*). We use a set of collected norms that describe important concept features (McRae et al., 2005) and their associated quantifiers (Herbelot and Vecchi, 2015). We rely on these data to derive cloze statements that we use to query BERT about noun properties, and to train BERT-based classifiers predicting these properties. We furthermore fine-tune BERT for entailment and test it in a task that involves AN constructions (Pavlick and Callison-Burch, 2016). Our cloze task results show that BERT has only marginal knowledge of noun properties and their prevalence, but can still successfully detect cases where the addition of an adjective does not alter the meaning of a sentence and where entailment is preserved.

2 Related Work

Compositionality in AN constructions has been a central topic in distributional and formal semantics. Mitchell and Lapata (2010) derive the meaning representation of a composite phrase from that of its constituents by performing algebraic operations (addition and multiplication) on distributional word semantic vectors, while Baroni and Zamparelli (2010) and Guevara (2010) derive composite vectors through composition functions learned from corpus-harvested phrase vectors. In our work, we represent AN phrases by combining the contextualised BERT representations of A and N in sentences where they occur, using algebraic operations. We also investigate the extent to which the representations of A and N in an AN phrase capture its meaning, since token-level BERT embeddings encode information from the surrounding context.

We furthermore address the entailment relationship between N and ANs (N $\models$ AN). In the opposite direction (AN $\models$ N) entailment generally holds, i.e. almost all ANs entail their head noun (*red car* $\models$ *car*) (Baroni et al., 2012; Kober et al., 2021). Determining whether N $\models$ AN holds, however, depends on the semantic properties described by the adjective. We base this analysis on the AddOne dataset proposed by Pavlick and Callison-Burch (2016). AddOne consists of sentence pairs that contain AN phrases annotated for entailment through crowdsourcing. This simplified entailment task differs from the classical RTE task (Dagan et al., 2005) in that the premise and hypothesis differ by only one atomic edit (insertion of A). We use this task as a proxy for prototypicality based on the assumption that adjectives describing typical properties of a noun do not modify its scope (e.g., *lobster* $\models$ *red lobster*, but *car* $\not\models$ *red car*). Prototypicality has been addressed in the literature mainly with respect to nouns, i.e. the typical hyponyms in a specific semantic class (e.g., *dog* $\models$ *animal*), or member concepts that are most central to a category (Roller and Erk, 2016). Vulić et al. (2017) also address verb prototypicality in terms of how typical of an action a verb is (e.g., "Is TO RUN a type of TO MOVE?"). Our work extends this notion to adjectives describing noun properties in AN phrases.

On the probing side, previous work explores the factual and commonsense knowledge present in pretrained language models (LMs). The LAMA (LAnguage Model Analysis) probe proposed by Petroni et al. (2019) contains sets of facts from various knowledge sources.[2] Each fact is converted into a "fill-in-the-blank" cloze statement that is used to query the LM for a missing token. A model is considered to know a fact ([SUBJECT, `relation`, OBJECT] triple) if it can successfully predict masked tokens in cloze statements expressing this fact (e.g., DANTE `was born` in ____). The `HasProperty` relation in LAMA (extracted from ConceptNet) is similar to our relation of interest as it links nouns to adjectives describing their properties. ConceptNet contains 3,894 such pairs, but a close inspection of the data reveals several problematic cases (e.g., *informal both*, *divine forgive*, *ten 10*). Additionally, the cloze statements proposed for this dataset were automati-

[2]Relations between entities stored in Wikidata, common sense relations between concepts from ConceptNet (Speer and Havasi, 2012), and knowledge aimed for answering natural language questions in SQuAD (Rajpurkar et al., 2016).

cally extracted from Open Mind Common Sense (OMCS)[3] sentences and are often too long, including irrelevant information that might confuse the model.[4] Jiang et al. (2020) demonstrate the impact of prompt quality on LM probing but focus on relations involving encyclopedic knowledge (e.g., born/died in, profession, subclass). Bouraoui et al. (2020) also explore the knowledge BERT has about lexical, morphological and commonsense relations (e.g., hypernymy, meronymy, plural, cause-effect) through fine-tuning, but neither they address noun properties.

3 Datasets

McRae et al. (2005) dataset (MRD): Semantic feature norms are used in the field of psycholinguistics for studying human semantic representation and computation. MRD contains feature norms for 541 living and nonliving concepts collected from 725 participants in an annotation task. The annotators proposed features they thought were important for each concept, covering physical (perceptual), functional and other properties. Among the collected 7,258 concept-feature pairs, we find that a dolphin is *intelligent, friendly*, and *lives in oceans*; and that a chandelier is *hanging from ceilings* and *is made of crystal*. The number of annotators who proposed each feature is also provided. The dataset has been extensively used to investigate and improve the knowledge about object properties encoded by distributional models (Rubinstein et al., 2015), word embeddings (Lucy and Gauthier, 2017; Yang et al., 2018) and, more recently, contextual LMs (Forbes et al., 2019; Hasegawa et al., 2020). These studies do not focus on adjectival attributes but rather consider all proposed properties, or specific subsets such as visual properties. In our experiments, we explore noun properties through the "IS_ADJ" features of noun concepts present in MRD.

Herbelot and Vecchi (2015) dataset (HVD) : HVD adds an extra level of quantification annotations to the MRD norms. Three native speakers of English selected a natural language quantifier among [NO, FEW, SOME, MOST, ALL][5] for each concept-feature (*C,f*) pair, expressing the ratio of *C* instances having feature *f* (e.g., ALL guitars are musical instruments, but SOME guitars are electric). Quantification is important for semantic inference; it can serve to understand set relations (such as synonymy and hyponymy) and to derive logically entailed sentences. We use the HVD dataset to probe BERT for the prevalence of noun properties.

Pavlick and Callison-Burch (2016) dataset (AddOne) : The Addone dataset is focused on AN composition. It contains 5,560 sentence pairs involving an AN pair (s_N, s_{AN}) which have been manually annotated for entailment ($s_N \models s_{AN}$) by crowd workers. Addone sentence pairs differ by one atomic edit, the insertion of A (s_N: "There are questions as to whether our culture has changed.", s_{AN}: "There are questions as to whether our traditional culture has changed."). Sentences were collected from corpora of different genres and each pair was annotated with a score in a 5-point scale from 1 (contradiction) to 5 (entailment). Only the pairs with high agreement (same score assigned by 2 out of 3 annotators) were retained. We use the AddOne dataset to assess BERT's ability to detect entailment in AN constructions. The dataset comes with a pre-defined split into training, development and test sets (83/10/7%) which we use in our experiments addressing entailment.

4 Cloze Task Experiments

We use the `bert-base-uncased` and `bert-large-uncased` models pre-trained on the BookCorpus (Zhu et al., 2015) and on English Wikipedia (Devlin et al., 2019). The models are trained using a cloze task where tokens of the input sequence are masked and the models learn to fill the slots, and a binary classification objective where they need to predict whether a particular sentence follows a given sequence of words.

4.1 Cloze Task Probing for Properties

We retrieve adjective modifiers of nouns in MRD found in the IS_ADJ features describing a concept (*bouquet*: IS_*colourful*; *panther*: IS_*black*). There are 509 noun concepts with at least one IS_ADJ feature in MRD. We exclude features involving multi-word attributes (*coconut*: IS_*white_inside*, *raft*: IS_*tied_together_with_rope*) which we do not expect BERT to be able to predict.[6] The average

[3] `https://github.com/commonsense/omcs`

[4] For example: "To understand the event "The monkey ate some bananas.", it is important to know that Banana is [MASK]". The ground truth adjective in this case is *yellow*.

[5] NO and FEW labels were rarely used by the annotators and we consider them as describing cases of non typical attributes.

[6] We use "multi-word" to refer to attributes that involve multiple words separated with underscores. These are not necessarily idiomatic expressions.

# features	1	2	3	4	5	6	7	8	9
# nouns	98	124	97	76	60	35	12	6	1

Table 2: Number of nouns with a specific number of IS_ADJ features in MRD.

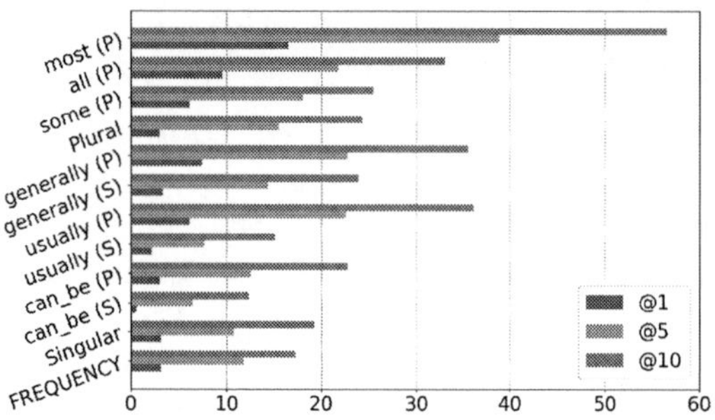

Figure 1: Accuracy at top-k with different query templates and BERT-`large`. The (S) and (P) markers denote singular and plural templates. Comparison to a frequency baseline.

number of features per noun is 3.12 (1,592 in total). Table 2 shows the number of nouns having a specific number of features. We define a set of templates and generate cloze statements for each noun that serve as our queries to probe BERT for these attributes. We define templates using both the singular and plural forms of a noun, as shown in Table 1.[7] We always use plural templates for 26 nouns given in plural form in MRD,[8] and singular templates for mass and uncountable nouns.[9] We evaluate the quality of the predictions made by BERT for each slot by checking the presence of ground-truth (reference) MRD adjectives in the top-1, top-5 and top-10 predictions ranked by probability. We compare BERT to a baseline that ranks by frequency all bigrams where a specific noun appears in the second position ("___ *bouquet*") in Google Ngrams (Brants and Franz, 2006), excluding bigrams that contain stop words and punctuation.

Similar to Ettinger (2020), we define accuracy as the percentage of items (nouns) for which the expected completion (one of the reference properties) is among the model's top-k predictions. The plot in Figure 1 shows the accuracy of predictions at top-k for BERT-`large`, with singular (S) and plural (P) queries. For $k = 1$, accuracy is very low, and naturally increases with $k = 5$ and $k = 10$. We observe that results differ considerably when different cloze statements are used for probing. Overall, BERT makes less accurate predictions with singular templates (e.g., a balloon usually is/can be [MASK]) than with plural templates (e.g., all/most balloons are [MASK]). Our assumption is that plural queries work better because they are more natural than singular ones,[10] and query naturalness seems to greatly influence prediction quality (Ettinger, 2020). The frequency baseline proposes correct properties for more nouns than the SINGULAR + `usually` and SINGULAR + `can be` templates. BERT-`large` gives slightly better results than BERT-`base` on this task. Best results are obtained with `most` + PLURAL queries (e.g., most balloons are [MASK]) where BERT-`large` proposes a correct attribute for 287 out of 509 nouns (56.4%). For BERT-`base`, best results are retrieved with PLURAL + `usually` queries (e.g., balloons are usually [MASK]), where a correct attribute is found in top-10 for 222 nouns. All results for BERT-`base` are given in Appendix B.1.

The results of this probing experiment suggest that BERT has marginal knowledge of noun properties as reflected in the MRD association norms, and highlight the difficulty to retrieve this kind of information from the representations using cloze task probes. This information (e.g., "bananas are yellow") is rarely explicitly stated in texts, in contrast to other types of lexical and encyclopedic knowledge (e.g., hypernymy: "a banana is a fruit") available in the Wikipedia texts that were used for model pre-training. Another issue with a cloze task evaluation for semantic properties is that contrary to structural properties (e.g., syntactic dependencies), there might be multiple correct answers for a query which might be partially covered by the resource used for evaluation. The quality of the resource, and the design of the task that served to gather the annotations, play an important role and should be taken into consideration for a fair interpretation of the results. We would, for example, expect annotators to propose a different set of properties if they were presented with cloze-type queries.

Although BERT does not always manage to predict the properties in MRD, we see from the quality of the proposed adjectives – quite high in some cases – that it encodes some knowledge about noun

[7]We use the plural form of nouns given by the `pattern` Python library and manually correct any errors.

[8]*beans, beets, curtains, earmuffs, jeans, leotards, mittens, onions, pajamas, peas, scissors, skis, slippers, shelves, sandals, bolts, gloves, nylons, boots, screws, pants, tongs, trousers, drapes, pliers, socks.*

[9]*rice, bread, football.*

[10]For example, "apples are red" has a higher frequency (919) than "an apple is red" (278) in Google Ngrams.

properties not present in the resource. For example, the predictions made for the probe "mittens are generally [MASK]" might not contain the gold MRD adjectives (*knitted*, *colourful*), but describe specific aspects such as their colour (*white, black, red, yellow*), shape and composition (*flat, thick, short, thin*), and the fact that they can be *removed* (i.e. a garment). Naturally, the quality of the predictions varies a lot across nouns. These often describe general knowledge about the described entity, as is the case in the predictions made for the query "all balloons are [MASK]": {*empty, free, flown, filled, lit, inflated, green, destroyed, closed, used*}. We also observe that most completions proposed by BERT are adjectives (more details in Appendix B.2).

BERT's predictions might contain synonyms of the adjectives present in MRD describing a correct property (for example, *deadly* instead of *lethal* for the noun *bomb*). We run an additional, more relaxed, evaluation where we also consider as correct the adjectives' synonyms in WordNet (Fellbaum, 1998).[11] As expected, we observe an increase in accuracy (cf. Appendix B.3). This highlights the limitation of the string matching approach and the need for a more flexible evaluation methodology.

We also conduct a human evaluation of the predictions made by BERT-`large` with the PLURAL + `most` template for 90 nouns. Two subjects (postgraduates in linguistics) annotated the top ten predictions made by the model as correct or wrong (independent of whether they were present in MRD or another resource). The task is different than the one that served to create MRD in that the annotators were not asked to propose adjectives for a noun, but instead they had to judge whether a prediction described some property of the noun. The micro-average inter-annotator agreement as measured with the Cohen's kappa (κ) coefficient was fair (0.39) (Landis and Koch, 1977; Artstein and Poesio, 2008). This demonstrates that deciding whether an adjective describes a property of a noun (instead of a state or some other marginal feature) is difficult for human annotators. We report the results of this evaluation in Appendix B.4.

Finally, we also investigate whether it is easier for BERT to propose correct properties for nouns that are not split into multiple tokens or WordPieces (Wu et al., 2016). The results (cf. Appendix B.5) confirm this intuition and show a slight decrease in the number of correctly predicted properties for nouns composed of multiple WordPieces.

[11]This is similar to synonym mapping in MT evaluation (Banerjee and Lavie, 2005; Marie and Apidianaki, 2015).

	Set A		Set B	
QUANT.	MRR	% of queries	MRR	% of queries
	BERT-base			
ALL	0.203	79.57	0.207	75.25
MOST	0.167	64.47	0.138	55.07
SOME	0.188	79.06	0.156	70.67
	BERT-large			
ALL	0.220	75.13	0.221	75.74
MOST	0.235	62.70	0.196	59.03
SOME	0.201	69.54	0.166	65.34

Table 3: MRR and proportion of queries in Sets A and B where a quantifier is predicted in top-10.

4.2 Cloze Task Probing for Quantifiers

In order to probe BERT for prototypicality, we split the AN pairs in HVD into two sets. Set (A) contains 788 pairs (for 386 nouns)[12] where the adjective describes a property that applies to most of the objects in the class denoted by the noun. These pairs are annotated with at least two ALL labels, or with a combination of ALL and MOST (*healthy banana* $\rightarrow$ [ALL-ALL-ALL]). We consider adjectives in Set (A) as describing prototypical properties of the nouns. Set (B), instead, contains 808 AN pairs (for 391 nouns) with adjectives describing properties of a smaller subset of the objects denoted by the noun. The labels assigned to these pairs contain SOME, FEW and NO's. For example, the annotations for *red apple* are [MOST-SOME-SOME], because there can be green and yellow apples.[13] We create cloze statements for the 788 pairs in Set (A), one for each pair, and for the 808 pairs in Set (B). A statement contains the noun in plural form and a masked slot for the quantifier (for example, "[MASK] *bananas are healthy*", "[MASK] *apples are red*"). We use each of the generated cloze statements to query BERT about prototypicality, checking whether it favours the expected (over the inappropriate) quantifier in its predictions. Given that BERT's predictions reflect the ranking of all words in the vocabulary according to whether they would be good fillers for the masked slot, we check the position of the quantifiers in the ranking.

[12]Some nouns have several AN pairs each.

[13]Note that a noun might be present in both Sets (A) and (B), depending on whether its ANs describe prototypical properties. We find, for example, *transparent jar* in Set (A), because all jars have this property, and *breakable jar* in Set (B), because not all jars can be easily broken.

We evaluate the predictions using Mean Reciprocal Rank (MRR) (cf. Appendix C). The results are shown in Table 3. The higher the MRR value is for a specific quantifier, the better its position in the ranking. If BERT encoded the knowledge needed to distinguish prototypical from other properties, we would expect ALL and MOST to be higher in the ranking produced for Set (A) queries, and SOME to come first in the ranking for Set (B) queries. We instead observe that ALL tends to occupy a higher position in the predictions for both sets. In Table 3, we also show the proportion of queries where a quantifier appears in the top-10 predictions. We observe that all three quantifiers are often proposed for queries in both sets. These results suggest that BERT does not distinguish properties on the basis of prototypicality.

When several quantifiers are found in the top-10 predictions, we also check their relative position in the ranking. We calculate the percentage of queries where BERT assigned a higher probability to the expected quantifiers, ranking them higher than the others. This corresponds to the "completion sensitivity test" proposed by Ettinger (2020), which serves to explore BERT's ability to prefer expected over inappropriate completions. No clear precedence pattern is detected: BERT-`base` assigns a higher probability to the expected (ALL) than to the incorrect completion (SOME) in 56% of Set (A) queries where both have been proposed; the inverse order is observed in 34% of queries in Set (B). We also run the sensitivity test on the ranking obtained for the whole vocabulary, but no meaningful patterns arise.[14] The use of a sensitivity threshold (Ettinger, 2020) turned out to be impractical in our setting because of the very low cloze probability assigned to the quantifiers in most cases. In our predictions, the definite article "*the*" is the most common top-1 prediction (in 85.7% of Set (A) queries, with an average probability of 0.629), followed by demonstrative and possessive determiners (e.g., *their, these*). The probability mass is concentrated on these words, hence the probability assigned to quantifiers is often close to zero.[15]

We also check whether the observed trends reflect the prior probability of the quantifiers and of the definite article in a large corpus. We approximate this using their frequency in Google Ngrams. We find that $freq(\text{THE}) > freq(\text{ALL}) > freq(\text{SOME}) > freq(\text{MOST})$. This is the same pattern obtained in our evaluation, with the exception of MRR results for BERT-`large`, where MOST is the highest ranked quantifier. This result suggests that BERT does not base prediction on the prevalence of noun properties but it, instead, largely follows the determiners' prior distribution.

5 Classification Experiments

We probe BERT representations for prototypicality in a classification setting, where models decide whether A describes a prototypical property of N. We use frozen embeddings (i.e. embeddings extracted from the pre-trained model) and fine-tuning.

5.1 Experimental Setup

Examples We consider as positive (prototypical) instances (`pos`) for this task AN phrases from HVD Set (A). As negative instances (`neg`) for a noun in Set (A), we use the AN pairs where it appears in Set (B). If $|\texttt{neg}| < |\texttt{pos}|$ for a noun, we collect additional negative instances from the ukWaC corpus (Baroni et al., 2009) where N is modified by an adjective A′ such that A′N $\notin$ HVD. We exclude cases where N is part of a compound (i.e. where it modifies another noun, as in *small sardine tin*).[16] We retain the most frequent ANs found for N in ukWaC as negative instances, until $|\texttt{neg}| = |\texttt{pos}|$.

Since common properties of nouns (e.g., *yellow banana, red strawberry*) are rarely explicitly stated in texts (Shwartz and Choi, 2020), we expect that the most frequent pairs found for a noun in ukWaC will not describe such properties. A manual exploration confirmed that the frequency-based filtering helps to retain good negative examples. The majority of the collected pairs do not describe prototypical properties (e.g., *useless pistol, organic celery*), with only a few (~10) exceptions (e.g., *silvery minnow*). The final dataset contains 1,566 instances in total, 783 for each class (positive and negative).[17]

Representations For each AN in `pos` and `neg`, we obtain a BERT representation from a sentence (s_{AN}) in ukWaC where A modifies N. We pair s_{AN} with a sentence s_N where A has been automatically

[14] Appendix B.6 contains the quantifier precedence results.

[15] More details on determiners are given in Appendix B.6.

[16] We obtain the dependency parse of a sentence using `stanza` (Qi et al., 2020).

[17] We omitted five positive AN pairs because not enough negative instances were found for the noun in Set (B) or in ukWaC.

deleted (e.g., "Then shape into balls about the size of a small tangerine" vs. "Then shape into balls about the size of a tangerine"). We choose sentences where A is not modified by an adverb (e.g., *very small ant*, where removing *small* would result in an ungrammatical sentence). When no sentences are found for an AN (588 out of 1,566 cases), we use as s_{AN} the plural pattern from the cloze task experiments (e.g., *raspberries are edible*) and the plural noun alone as s_N (*raspberries*). When N is an uncountable noun, we use the singular pattern instead.[18] We also feed the bigram in isolation into BERT (configuration that we call ISO).

Data Split We keep aside 10% of the data as our development set and perform 5-fold cross-validation on the rest. To minimise the impact of lexical memorisation where the model learns that a word is representative of a specific class (Levy et al., 2015), we observe a full lexical split by adjective between the development set and the data used for cross-validation, and also between the training and the test set in each fold. As a result, adjectives found in the test set at each iteration have not been seen in the training or in the development set. This is done to avoid that the model memorises an adjective as describing a common or prototypical property of nouns; for example, *small* is a feature for 120 out of 509 nouns in MRD. The split allows to evaluate the capability of the model to generalise to unseen adjectives.

5.2 Embedding-based Classification

We expect the vector of an AN phrase involving a prototypical adjective (*red strawberry*) to be more similar to the vector of N (*strawberry*), than that of a phrase A′N involving an adjective that expresses a non typical property of N (*rotten strawberry*). We extract three contextualised embeddings from each layer of the BERT-`base` model that we use to compare the representation of an AN phrase to that of the head N:

1. an embedding for N in sentence s_N where N occurs without the adjective ($\overrightarrow{Ns_N}$);
2. an embedding for N in sentence s_{AN} which contains the adjective ($\overrightarrow{Ns_{AN}}$);
3. an embedding for A in s_{AN} ($\overrightarrow{As_{AN}}$).

We obtain an AN representation ($\overrightarrow{AN}$) by combining the vectors pairwise: $\overrightarrow{Ns_N}$ and $\overrightarrow{Ns_{AN}}$; $\overrightarrow{Ns_N}$ and $\overrightarrow{As_{AN}}$; $\overrightarrow{Ns_{AN}}$ and $\overrightarrow{As_{AN}}$, using different composition operations: average, concatenation, difference, multiplication, and addition. We also experiment with the token-level contextualised representations $\overrightarrow{As_{AN}}$ and $\overrightarrow{Ns_{AN}}$ only, which we expect to also encode information about the noun and the adjective in the AN, respectively, since they occur in the same context. We use the different AN representations as features for a logistic regression classifier. Additionally, we calculate the cosine similarity and euclidean distance between the representation of a noun ($\overrightarrow{Ns_N}$ or $\overrightarrow{Ns_{AN}}$) and $\overrightarrow{AN}$ obtained through the vector combinations and composition operations described above, and feed them to the classifier as individual features or in combination. For comparison, we also run experiments using static word2vec (Mikolov et al., 2013) and fastText (Mikolov et al., 2018) embeddings as features, creating $\overrightarrow{AN}$ with the word embeddings $\overrightarrow{N}$ and $\overrightarrow{A}$, and using $\overrightarrow{A}$ alone. For each type of representation (BERT, word2vec, fastText), we select the configuration with the highest average accuracy on the development set over the five cross-validation runs. In Table 4, we report the average scores obtained on the test sets of the five folds for these configurations. Precision, recall and F1-score show how good a model is at detecting AN pairs that involve a prototypical adjective. As baselines, we provide results for a model that always predicts prototypicality (ALL-PROTO), and a model that assigns the majority label found in the training set at each fold (MAJORITY).

Model	Acc	F1	P	R
BERT	**0.658**	0.648	**0.676**	0.633
BERT (ISO)	0.586	0.548	0.605	0.506
fastText	0.593	0.481	0.639	0.411
word2vec	0.559	0.455	0.601	0.372
ALL-PROTO	0.507	**0.672**	0.507	**1.000**
MAJORITY	0.473	0.524	0.390	0.800

Table 4: Average accuracy, F1-score, precision (P) and recall (R) of embedding-based classifiers on HVD in the cross-validation experiment across five folds.

In terms of accuracy, BERT obtains the best results on this task (0.658) when cosine similarity and euclidean distance between $\overrightarrow{Ns_N}$ and $\overrightarrow{Ns_N}+\overrightarrow{Ns_{AN}}$ at the last (12th) layer are used as features. The simple ALL-PROTO baseline obtains the highest F1 score (0.672) but gets low accuracy in this balanced dataset. Using sentences containing the AN is more effective than feeding the AN

[18] Using sentences created with these patterns for all ANs hurts performance compared to the setting where sentences gathered from corpora are used.

Model	Acc	F1	P	R
BERT-CLS	0.696	**0.654**	0.763	**0.582**
BERT-TOK	**0.697**	0.646	**0.778**	0.561
BERT-CLS (ISO)	0.604	0.503	0.654	0.424
BERT-TOK (ISO)	0.636	0.591	0.701	0.539

Table 5: Average accuracy, F1 score, precision and recall in the cross-validation experiment across five folds for a BERT model fine-tuned on HVD using the CLS and TOK approaches.

bigram in isolation into BERT (ISO). Static representations, especially word2vec, perform worse than BERT but still manage to beat the baselines in terms of accuracy. The best configuration for word2vec and fastText was the use of the adjective representations ($\overrightarrow{A}$) as features, which shows that the models do not manage to extract the information needed for assessing prototypicality from the different $\overrightarrow{N}$ and $\overrightarrow{A}$ combinations. Instead, the best strategy is to learn the tendency of an adjective to be prototypical. When evaluated on unseen adjectives in our test sets, they base prototypicality judgments on the similarity of these adjectives to the ones seen in the training set. We observe a high variation in accuracy and F1 scores across folds for all models. For BERT, F1 scores range from 0.553 to 0.740 and the range is even larger for the fastText-based model (from 0.310 to 0.747). This suggests that prototypicality is not easy to detect for all AN pairs. Overall, BERT embeddings seem to be a better fit for estimating prototypicality than static representations. We report the detailed results by layer, and the best configurations per $\overrightarrow{AN}$ and composition type, in Appendix D.

5.3 Fine-tuning BERT

We compare our results with frozen embeddings to the performance of BERT fine-tuned for the prototypicality task. Specifically, we feed into BERT the two sentences in each (s_N, s_{AN}) pair separated by the [SEP] token. We experiment with a classifier on top of the [CLS] token, as is typically done in sentence-pair classification tasks (we call this approach BERT-CLS); and with a classifier on top of the concatenation of two token representations: ($\overrightarrow{Ns_N}$, $\overrightarrow{As_{AN}}$), ($\overrightarrow{Ns_N}$, $\overrightarrow{Ns_{AN}}$), ($\overrightarrow{Ns_N}$, $\overrightarrow{As_{AN}} + \overrightarrow{Ns_{AN}}$) (our BERT-TOK approach). The two classification heads consist of a linear layer with softmax and are trained with a cross entropy loss. We fine-tune each model for 3 epochs with 0.1 dropout, and choose the learning rate based on the accuracy on the development set. Results of this experiment are found in Table 5. BERT-CLS and BERT-TOK ($\overrightarrow{Ns_N}$, $\overrightarrow{As_{AN}}$) perform comparably on this task and obtain better results than embedding-based models (Table 4), with 0.697 accuracy. As in the experiment described in Section 5.2, using sentences yields better results than only feeding the AN (ISO).

6 Entailment in AN Constructions

6.1 Task Description

AN constructions are often in a forward entailment relation with the head noun (*white rabbit* $\models$ *rabbit*) (Baroni et al., 2012). Whether backward entailment holds depends on the properties of N described by A. For example, a *car* is not always *red* (the label would be "Unknown"), while *lobster* always entails *red lobster*. We explore BERT's capability to identify the AN cases where backward (N $\models$ AN) entailment holds using the Addone dataset (Pavlick and Callison-Burch, 2016).

We fine-tune BERT on Addone to assess whether it captures the entailment relationship in AN constructions. BERT has shown high performance in other textual entailment tasks (Devlin et al., 2019), but the Addone dataset has proved challenging for other models relying on recurrent architectures. We follow Pavlick and Callison-Burch (2016) and use Addone for a binary classification task, with the labels ENTAILMENT (for forward entailment and equivalence) and NOT ENTAILMENT (encompassing the contradiction, independence and reverse entailment relations). Similarly to the fine-tuning approach described in Section 5.3, we feed into BERT the two sentences in each pair (s_N, s_{AN}) separated by the special [SEP] token. We again use the CLS and TOK classification heads. We fine-tune the model for 5 epochs with 0.1 dropout and select the learning rate based on the F1 score calculated over the actual ENTAILMENT cases on the development set.[19]

6.2 Results

Results of our experiments on Addone are presented in Table 6. We include results reported by Pavlick and Callison-Burch (2016) (P&CB) for comparison. The MAJ and MAJ-BY-ADJ baselines assign the majority class in the training set (NON-

[19]We use F1 score as a criterion, and not accuracy, because the Addone dataset is highly imbalanced (only 23% of the instances belong to the ENTAILMENT class).

Model	Acc	F1	P	R
Human (P&CB)	0.933	0.730	0.840	0.640
MAJ-BY-ADJ (P&CB)	**0.922**	0.680	**0.860**	0.560
MAJ (P&CB)	0.853	-	-	-
BERT-TOK	0.912	**0.696**	0.709	0.684
BERT-CLS	0.147	0.257	0.147	**1.000**
RNN (P&CB)	0.873	0.510	0.600	0.440

Table 6: Results on the Addone test set. Best results for each metric are highlighted in boldface.

ENTAILMENT) and the majority class proposed for each adjective in the training set, respectively. We also report the human performance on this task as an upper bound, and compare to the best-performing model in Pavlick and Callison-Burch (2016) which relies on a RNN architecture (Bowman et al., 2015). BERT-CLS fails to learn the information needed for the task and predicts the ENTAILMENT label for all instances. This explains the low scores obtained with this model, since the majority label in this dataset is NON-ENTAILMENT. The default fine-tuning strategy used for textual entailment with BERT is, thus, not suitable for addressing cases of compositional entailment in the Addone dataset. It is much more effective to use the representations of the specific words that determine sentence entailment: BERT-TOK ($\overrightarrow{Ns_N}$, $\overrightarrow{As_{AN}}$) obtains higher results than the previous best model (RNN) and beats the MAJ baseline in terms of accuracy, as well as MAJ-BY-ADJ in terms of F1 and recall. This shows that BERT leverages the AN relations that are needed to solve this NLI task better compared to RNNs.

7 Discussion

Retrieving prototypical knowledge about entities is a real challenge for distributional models, not necessarily because of the models themselves and how advanced they are, but because this information is rarely stated in texts. This is described in the literature as the "reporting bias" phenomenon (Gordon and Van Durme, 2013) which poses challenges on knowledge extraction. According to this phenomenon, rare actions or properties are over-represented in texts at the expense of trivial ones. Shwartz and Choi (2020) show that the generalisation capability of pre-trained language models allows them to better estimate the plausibility of frequent but unspoken actions, outcomes and properties than previous models, but that they also tend to overestimate that of the very rare, amplifying the bias that already exists in their training corpus. In this study, using methodology commonly used for probing contextual models, we have precisely explored whether retrieving knowledge about noun properties constitutes a challenge for these models, or whether they manage to retrieve this knowledge due to their impressive generalisation capabilities.

Since prototypical properties are often visual or perceptual, in future work we plan to combine text and visual features (Silberer et al., 2013; Lazaridou et al., 2015; Lu et al., 2019; Li et al., 2019, 2021) for retrieving noun properties, in order to see how BERT can predict these properties when it has access to images alongside text. Another goal is to collect evaluation data using cloze task queries in specifically designed crowdsourcing tasks.

8 Conclusion

We have conducted a thorough investigation of the information encoded by BERT about nouns' intrinsic properties. Using datasets specifically compiled for psycholinguistics studies, we probed BERT for noun properties and their prototypicality, as well as for the entailment relationship involving AN constructions which indicates possible generalisations to the entire class denoted by the noun. Our results show that information about noun properties, as described in word association norms, is hard to retrieve using cloze tasks. We discuss the limitations of semantic cloze tasks evaluation against existing resources, and the need for more flexible evaluation scenarios. However, knowledge about properties can still be leveraged by BERT in a classification setting where the model is exposed to examples specifically encoding this information.

We make our code and datasets available to promote further research in this direction.[20]

Acknowledgements

This work has been supported by the French National Research Agency under project ANR-16-CE33-0013. The work is also part of the FoTran project, funded by the European Research Council (ERC) under the European Union's Horizon 2020 research and innovation programme (grant agreement № 771113). We thank the anonymous reviewers for their helpful feedback and valuable suggestions.

[20]The code and datasets are available at this URL: `https://github.com/ainagari/prototypicality`

References

Ron Artstein and Massimo Poesio. 2008. Survey Article: Inter-Coder Agreement for Computational Linguistics. *Computational Linguistics*, 34(4):555–596.

Satanjeev Banerjee and Alon Lavie. 2005. METEOR: An Automatic Metric for MT Evaluation with Improved Correlation with Human Judgments. In *Proceedings of the ACL Workshop on Intrinsic and Extrinsic Evaluation Measures for Machine Translation and/or Summarization*, pages 65–72, Ann Arbor, Michigan. Association for Computational Linguistics.

Marco Baroni, Raffaella Bernardi, Ngoc-Quynh Do, and Chung-chieh Shan. 2012. Entailment above the word level in distributional semantics. In *Proceedings of the 13th Conference of the European Chapter of the Association for Computational Linguistics*, pages 23–32, Avignon, France. Association for Computational Linguistics.

Marco Baroni, Silvia Bernardini, Adriano Ferraresi, and Eros Zanchetta. 2009. The WaCky wide web: a collection of very large linguistically processed web-crawled corpora. *Journal of Language Resources and Evaluation*, 43(3):209–226.

Marco Baroni and Roberto Zamparelli. 2010. Nouns are Vectors, Adjectives are Matrices: Representing Adjective-Noun Constructions in Semantic Space. In *Proceedings of the 2010 Conference on Empirical Methods in Natural Language Processing*, pages 1183–1193, Cambridge, MA. Association for Computational Linguistics.

Zied Bouraoui, José Camacho-Collados, and Steven Schockaert. 2020. Inducing Relational Knowledge from BERT. In *The Thirty-Fourth AAAI Conference on Artificial Intelligence*, pages 7456–7463, New York, NY, USA. AAAI Press.

Samuel R. Bowman, Gabor Angeli, Christopher Potts, and Christopher D. Manning. 2015. A large annotated corpus for learning natural language inference. In *Proceedings of the 2015 Conference on Empirical Methods in Natural Language Processing*, pages 632–642, Lisbon, Portugal. Association for Computational Linguistics.

Thorsten Brants and Alex Franz. 2006. Web 1T 5-gram Version 1. In *LDC2006T13*, Philadelphia, Pennsylvania. Linguistic Data Consortium.

Ido Dagan, Oren Glickman, and Bernardo Magnini. 2005. The PASCAL Recognising Textual Entailment Challenge. In *Proceedings of the First International Conference on Machine Learning Challenges: Evaluating Predictive Uncertainty Visual Object Classification, and Recognizing Textual Entailment*, MLCW'05, page 177–190, Berlin, Heidelberg. Springer-Verlag.

Jacob Devlin, Ming-Wei Chang, Kenton Lee, and Kristina Toutanova. 2019. BERT: Pre-training of Deep Bidirectional Transformers for Language Understanding. In *Proceedings of the 2019 Conference of the North American Chapter of the Association for Computational Linguistics: Human Language Technologies, Volume 1 (Long and Short Papers)*, pages 4171–4186, Minneapolis, Minnesota. Association for Computational Linguistics.

Allyson Ettinger. 2020. What BERT is not: Lessons from a new suite of psycholinguistic diagnostics for language models. *Transactions of the Association for Computational Linguistics*, 8:34–48.

Christiane Fellbaum, editor. 1998. *WordNet: An Electronic Lexical Database*. Language, Speech, and Communication. MIT Press, Cambridge, MA.

Maxwell Forbes, Ari Holtzman, and Yejin Choi. 2019. Do neural language representations learn physical commonsense? In *Proceedings of the 41th Annual Meeting of the Cognitive Science Society, CogSci 2019: Creativity + Cognition + Computation*, pages 1753–1759, Montreal, Canada.

Jonathan Gordon and Benjamin Van Durme. 2013. Reporting Bias and Knowledge Acquisition. In *Proceedings of the 2013 Workshop on Automated Knowledge Base Construction*, AKBC '13, page 25–30, New York, NY, USA. Association for Computing Machinery.

Emiliano Guevara. 2010. A Regression Model of Adjective-Noun Compositionality in Distributional Semantics. In *Proceedings of the 2010 Workshop on GEometrical Models of Natural Language Semantics*, pages 33–37, Uppsala, Sweden. Association for Computational Linguistics.

Mika Hasegawa, Tetsunori Kobayashi, and Yoshihiko Hayashi. 2020. Word Attribute Prediction Enhanced by Lexical Entailment Tasks. In *Proceedings of the 12th Language Resources and Evaluation Conference*, pages 5846–5854, Marseille, France. European Language Resources Association.

Aurélie Herbelot and Eva Maria Vecchi. 2015. From concepts to models: some issues in quantifying feature norms. *Linguistic Issues in Language Technology (LiLT)*, 2(4).

Zhengbao Jiang, Frank F. Xu, Jun Araki, and Graham Neubig. 2020. How Can We Know What Language Models Know? *Transactions of the Association for Computational Linguistics*, 8:423–438.

Thomas Kober, Julie Weeds, Lorenzo Bertolini, and David Weir. 2021. Data Augmentation for Hypernymy Detection. In *Proceedings of the 16th Conference of the European Chapter of the Association for Computational Linguistics: Main Volume*, pages 1034–1048, Online. Association for Computational Linguistics.

Lili Kotlerman, Ido Dagan, Idan Szpektor, and Maayan Zhitomirsky-Geffet. 2010. Directional distributional similarity for lexical inference. *Natural Language Engineering*, 16(4):359–389.

J. Richard Landis and Gary G. Koch. 1977. The measurement of observer agreement for categorical data. *Biometrics*, 33(1):159–174.

Angeliki Lazaridou, Nghia The Pham, and Marco Baroni. 2015. Combining Language and Vision with a Multimodal Skip-gram Model. In *Proceedings of the 2015 Conference of the North American Chapter of the Association for Computational Linguistics: Human Language Technologies*, pages 153–163, Denver, Colorado. Association for Computational Linguistics.

Omer Levy, Steffen Remus, Chris Biemann, and Ido Dagan. 2015. Do supervised distributional methods really learn lexical inference relations? In *Proceedings of the 2015 Conference of the North American Chapter of the Association for Computational Linguistics: Human Language Technologies*, pages 970–976, Denver, Colorado. Association for Computational Linguistics.

Liunian Harold Li, Mark Yatskar, Da Yin, Cho-Jui Hsieh, and Kai-Wei Chang. 2019. VisualBERT: A Simple and Performant Baseline for Vision and Language. *arXiv preprint:1908.03557*.

Liunian Harold Li, Haoxuan You, Zhecan Wang, Alireza Zareian, Shih-Fu Chang, and Kai-Wei Chang. 2021. Unsupervised vision-and-language pre-training without parallel images and captions. In *Proceedings of the 2021 Conference of the North American Chapter of the Association for Computational Linguistics: Human Language Technologies*, pages 5339–5350, Online. Association for Computational Linguistics.

Jiasen Lu, Dhruv Batra, Devi Parikh, and Stefan Lee. 2019. ViLBERT: Pretraining Task-Agnostic Visiolinguistic Representations for Vision-and-Language Tasks. In *33rd Conference on Neural Information Processing Systems (NeurIPS 2019)*, volume 32, Vancouver, Canada.

Li Lucy and Jon Gauthier. 2017. Are distributional representations ready for the real world? evaluating word vectors for grounded perceptual meaning. In *Proceedings of the First Workshop on Language Grounding for Robotics*, pages 76–85, Vancouver, Canada. Association for Computational Linguistics.

Benjamin Marie and Marianna Apidianaki. 2015. Alignment-based sense selection in METEOR and the RATATOUILLE recipe. In *Proceedings of the Tenth Workshop on Statistical Machine Translation*, pages 385–391, Lisbon, Portugal. Association for Computational Linguistics.

Ken McRae, George Cree, Mark Seidenberg, and Chris Mcnorgan. 2005. Semantic feature production norms for a large set of living and nonliving things. *Behavior research methods*, 37:547–59.

Tomas Mikolov, Kai Chen, Greg Corrado, and Jeffrey Dean. 2013. Efficient Estimation of Word Representations in Vector Space. *arXiv preprint:1301.3781v3*.

Tomas Mikolov, Edouard Grave, Piotr Bojanowski, Christian Puhrsch, and Armand Joulin. 2018. Advances in Pre-Training Distributed Word Representations. In *Proceedings of the Eleventh International Conference on Language Resources and Evaluation (LREC 2018)*, Miyazaki, Japan. European Language Resources Association (ELRA).

Jeff Mitchell and Mirella Lapata. 2010. Composition in distributional models of semantics. *Cognitive Science*, 34(8):1388–1429.

Ellie Pavlick and Chris Callison-Burch. 2016. Most "babies" are "little" and most "problems" are "huge": Compositional Entailment in Adjective-Nouns. In *Proceedings of the 54th Annual Meeting of the Association for Computational Linguistics (Volume 1: Long Papers)*, pages 2164–2173, Berlin, Germany. Association for Computational Linguistics.

Fabio Petroni, Tim Rocktäschel, Sebastian Riedel, Patrick Lewis, Anton Bakhtin, Yuxiang Wu, and Alexander Miller. 2019. Language models as knowledge bases? In *Proceedings of the 2019 Conference on Empirical Methods in Natural Language Processing and the 9th International Joint Conference on Natural Language Processing (EMNLP-IJCNLP)*, pages 2463–2473, Hong Kong, China. Association for Computational Linguistics.

Peng Qi, Yuhao Zhang, Yuhui Zhang, Jason Bolton, and Christopher D. Manning. 2020. Stanza: A Python Natural Language Processing Toolkit for Many Human Languages. In *Proceedings of the 58th Annual Meeting of the Association for Computational Linguistics: System Demonstrations*, pages 101–108, Online. Association for Computational Linguistics.

Pranav Rajpurkar, Jian Zhang, Konstantin Lopyrev, and Percy Liang. 2016. SQuAD: 100,000+ Questions for Machine Comprehension of Text. In *Proceedings of the 2016 Conference on Empirical Methods in Natural Language Processing*, pages 2383–2392, Austin, Texas. Association for Computational Linguistics.

Stephen Roller and Katrin Erk. 2016. Relations such as Hypernymy: Identifying and Exploiting Hearst Patterns in Distributional Vectors for Lexical Entailment. In *Proceedings of the 2016 Conference on Empirical Methods in Natural Language Processing*, pages 2163–2172, Austin, Texas. Association for Computational Linguistics.

Dana Rubinstein, Effi Levi, Roy Schwartz, and Ari Rappoport. 2015. How Well Do Distributional Models Capture Different Types of Semantic Knowledge? In *Proceedings of the 53rd Annual Meeting of the Association for Computational Linguistics and the 7th International Joint Conference on Natural Language Processing (Volume 2: Short Papers)*, pages 726–730, Beijing, China. Association for Computational Linguistics.

Vered Shwartz and Yejin Choi. 2020. Do neural language models overcome reporting bias? In *Proceedings of the 28th International Conference on Computational Linguistics*, pages 6863–6870, Barcelona, Spain (Online). International Committee on Computational Linguistics.

Carina Silberer, Vittorio Ferrari, and Mirella Lapata. 2013. Models of Semantic Representation with Visual Attributes. In *Proceedings of the 51st Annual Meeting of the Association for Computational Linguistics (Volume 1: Long Papers)*, pages 572–582, Sofia, Bulgaria. Association for Computational Linguistics.

Robyn Speer and Catherine Havasi. 2012. Representing General Relational Knowledge in ConceptNet 5. In *Proceedings of the Eighth International Conference on Language Resources and Evaluation (LREC'12)*, pages 3679–3686, Istanbul, Turkey. European Language Resources Association (ELRA).

Ivan Vulić, Daniela Gerz, Douwe Kiela, Felix Hill, and Anna Korhonen. 2017. HyperLex: A Large-Scale Evaluation of Graded Lexical Entailment. *Computational Linguistics*, 43(4):781–835.

Yonghui Wu, Mike Schuster, Zhifeng Chen, Quoc V. Le, Mohammad Norouzi, Wolfgang Macherey, Maxim Krikun, Yuan Cao, Qin Gao, Klaus Macherey, Jeff Klingner, Apurva Shah, Melvin Johnson, Xiaobing Liu, Łukasz Kaiser, Stephan Gouws, Yoshikiyo Kato, Taku Kudo, Hideto Kazawa, Keith Stevens, George Kurian, Nishant Patil, Wei Wang, Cliff Young, Jason Smith, Jason Riesa, Alex Rudnick, Oriol Vinyals, Greg Corrado, Macduff Hughes, and Jeffrey Dean. 2016. Google's Neural Machine Translation System: Bridging the Gap between Human and Machine Translation. *arXiv preprint:1609.08144*.

Yiben Yang, Larry Birnbaum, Ji-Ping Wang, and Doug Downey. 2018. Extracting Commonsense Properties from Embeddings with Limited Human Guidance. In *Proceedings of the 56th Annual Meeting of the Association for Computational Linguistics (Volume 2: Short Papers)*, pages 644–649, Melbourne, Australia. Association for Computational Linguistics.

A Masking Templates

Table 7 contains the templates that were used to construct the singular and plural queries for different nouns. SINGULAR_NOUN and PLURAL_NOUN are placeholders for the nouns in singular and plural form, respectively.

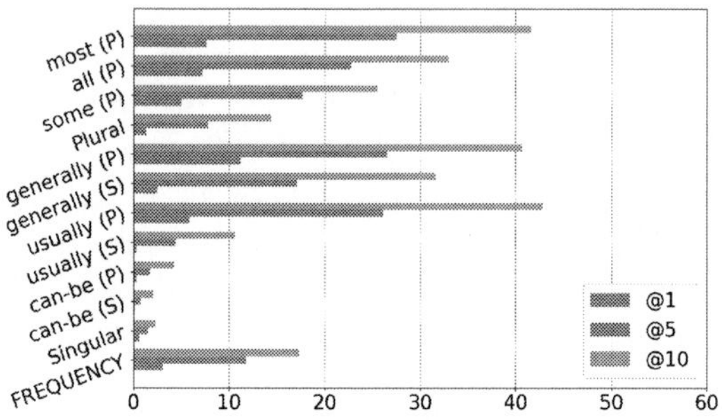

Figure 2: Accuracy at top-*k* for BERT-`base`. (S) and (P) stand for singular and plural templates. We compare to the results of a frequency baseline.

We generated the queries for the quantifiers using the template:

[MASK] `PLURAL-NOUN are ADJECTIVE.`

An example query generated using this template is:

[MASK] balloons are colourful .

B Additional Masking Results

In this section of the Appendix, we present in more detail the results that we obtained in the masking experiments for noun properties and quantifiers.

B.1 Property Masking Results

The plot in Figure 2 shows the accuracy of predictions at top-*k* for BERT-`base`. Figures 3 and 4 show the average recall at the top-1, top-5 and top-10 positions of the ranked BERT-`base` and `large` predictions, when using sentences constructed with the templates that correspond to the labels on the x axis. Average is calculated over the words for which at least one correct attribute is found at the specific rank.

B.2 Adjectives in BERT Predictions

Figure 5 shows the proportion of adjectives predicted by BERT-`large` using different templates. We count as adjectives all words that have a synset of this part of speech in WordNet. We observe that the majority of predictions pertain to this part-of-speech. Fewer adjectives are proposed for queries of the form SINGULAR + `can be` (e.g., a balloon can be [MASK]), where BERT tends to favour verbs in the past participle form.

B.3 WordNet-based Evaluation

Figure 6 presents the results of our more relaxed evaluation, which includes the WordNet synonyms of the adjectives in MRD. Specifically, we expand

SINGULAR	a SINGULAR_NOUN is [MASK].
PLURAL	PLURAL_NOUN are [MASK].
SINGULAR + usually	a SINGULAR_NOUN is usually [MASK].
PLURAL + usually	PLURAL_NOUN are usually [MASK].
SINGULAR + generally	a SINGULAR_NOUN is generally [MASK].
PLURAL + generally	PLURAL_NOUN are generally [MASK].
SINGULAR + can be	a SINGULAR_NOUN can be [MASK].
PLURAL + can be	PLURAL_NOUN can be [MASK].
PLURAL + most	most PLURAL_NOUN are [MASK].
PLURAL + all	all PLURAL_NOUN are [MASK].
PLURAL + some	some PLURAL_NOUN are [MASK].

Table 7: Masking templates with the noun in singular and plural form.

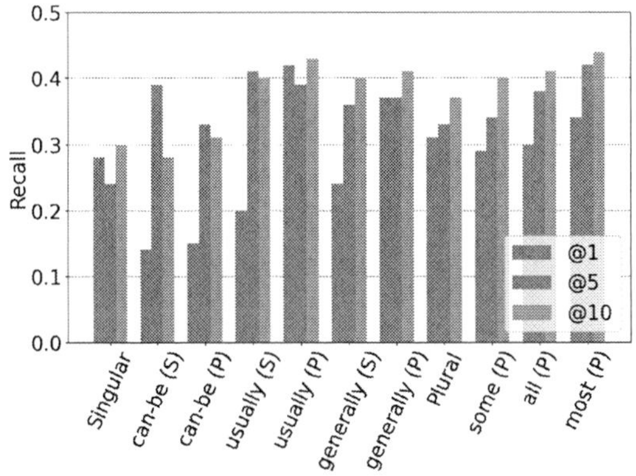

Figure 3: Average recall of MRD adjectives in the top-k predictions made by BERT–base.

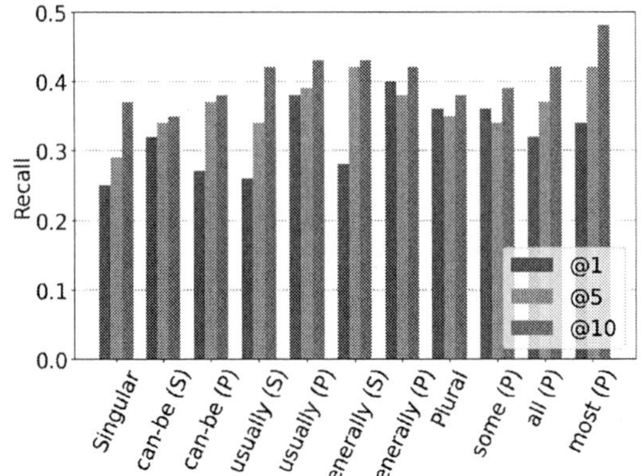

Figure 4: Average recall of MRD adjectives in the top-k predictions made by BERT–large.

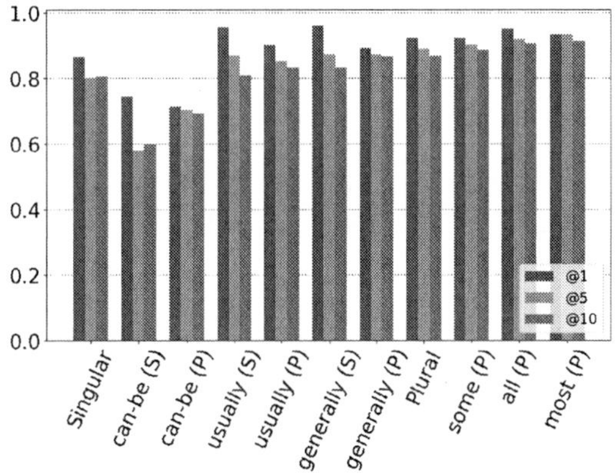

Figure 5: Proportion of adjectives among BERT-large predictions at different k.

the set of adjectives proposed in MRD for a noun (i.e. our reference) with their synonyms found in WordNet, and consider them all as correct. The lighter shades in the Figure show the improvement in accuracy at top-k with respect to our previous results (darker shades). This shows that the model sometimes predicts correct properties that cannot be captured in an evaluation based solely on string matching.

B.4 Manual Evaluation of Predicted Properties

In Table 8, we present the results of the manual evaluation. We show the number of properties that were marked as correct by each annotator (A#1 and A#2). We also report the number of properties for which the annotators agreed they were correct (Both). In the last column, we compare to the number of predictions that were found to be correct when evaluated solely against the reference properties in MRD. Since MRD has a different number of properties per noun – often fewer than ten – we indicate in parentheses the upper bound that could

	Manual evaluation			
	A#1	A#2	Both	MRD
@1	57	45	39	15 (90)
@5	228	166	130	50 (327)
@10	426	291	224	89 (355)

Table 8: Number of properties predicted by BERT-`large` with the "PLURAL + `most`" The last column shows the number of correct predictions when evaluating against properties in MRD. The upperbound for this evaluation is given in parentheses.

be reached if all reference properties for a noun were correctly predicted.

Agreement between the annotators is fair (0.39), which demonstrates that deciding whether an adjective describes a property of a noun is difficult. The annotators highlighted that there are some adjectives that BERT often proposes for nouns describing a specific class; for example, *nocturnal*, *solitary* and *shy* were proposed for different animals. We also find different colours proposed for *butterfly* (*white*, *black*, *brown*, *green*, *blue*) instead of the adjective *colourful* which describes a more general property of the insect (and which is one of its features in MRD).

B.5 Impact of Word Splitting on Performance

BERT uses WordPiece tokenization (Wu et al., 2016). The most frequent words are represented with a single token, but other words are split into multiple wordpieces. We investigate the impact of wordpiece splitting on the results. We run this analysis with BERT-`large` predictions at top-10. We classify nouns into two classes, `correct` and `incorrect`, depending on whether at least one of their properties was correctly predicted. We compare the proportion of multi-piece nouns (MPs) in the two classes using χ^2 tests. We observe a significant difference ($\alpha = 0.05$) with 4 out of our 11 templates. Table 9 contains the p-values and effect sizes (Cramer's V) for these templates. We also report the proportion of MPs in the `incorrect` class, which is slightly higher than that over all nouns in our dataset.[21] The effect size values are also weak, suggesting that word splitting has only a slight negative effect on BERT's performance on this cloze task.

[21]The number of MP nouns in singular and plural templates differs because plural forms of the nouns are more often split into multiple tokens.

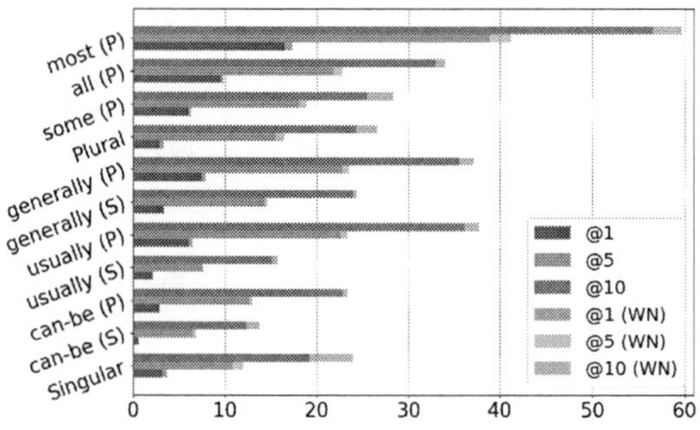

Figure 6: Improvement in accuracy at top-k for BERT-`large` predictions in the WordNet-based (WN) evaluation.

B.6 Additional Quantifier Probing Results

Table 10 shows the relative position of correct vs. incorrect quantifiers when they both appear in the top-10 predictions (columns 2 and 3), and in the ranking for the whole vocabulary (column 4). Correct (expected) completions for Set (A) queries are ALL and MOST; for Set (B), the correct answer is SOME.

The symbol ">" in the first column denotes precedence of a quantifier over another (i.e. higher probability). Column 3 shows the number of queries for which the two quantifiers were proposed in top-10, which served to calculate the proportion in column 2. ALL and SOME were, for example, proposed by BERT-`base` in top-10 for 532 Set (A) queries. ALL had a higher probability than SOME in 56% of these queries.

Table 11 shows the ranking results for other determiners (*the*, *these*, *their*) that are found in the first (top-1) position.

C Mean Reciprocal Ranking

Equation 1 contains the formula for Mean Reciprocal Ranking (MRR). RR measures the reciprocal of the rank of the first correct answer, and MRR is the average across queries. We use MRR in Section 4.2 to evaluate quantifier prediction. $|Q|$ corresponds to the number of queries.

$$MRR = \frac{1}{|Q|} \sum_{i=1}^{|Q|} \frac{1}{rank_i} \quad (1)$$

D Detailed Embedding-based Classification results

In Table 13, we report the best results obtained on the HVD development set for each type of BERT-

	p-value	effect size (Cramer's V)	% of MPs with no correct predictions	total % MPs
SINGULAR + `usually`	0.011	0.11	30.7%	
SINGULAR + `generally`	0.038	0.09	30.7%	28.2%
SINGULAR + `can be`	0.002	0.14	30.6%	
PLURAL	0.03	0.03	59.2%	56.4%

Table 9: Statistics of the χ^2 tests that showed a significant association between (a) a noun being multi-piece (MP), and (b) BERT predicting wrong properties for the noun (as evaluated against MRD). The last column shows the proportion of MP nouns in singular and plural templates.

	Results @10		Results @|V|
BERT-base			
QUANTIFIERS	% queries	# queries	% queries
Set (A)			
ALL > SOME	56.02%	532	53.43%
MOST > SOME	49.89%	451	37.31%
Set (B)			
SOME > ALL	34.48%	467	40.1%
SOME > MOST	83.87%	31	65.47%
BERT-large			
QUANTIFIERS	% queries	# queries	% queries
Set (A)			
ALL > SOME	55.19%	462	55.08%
MOST > SOME	58.00%	431	44.16%
Set (B)			
SOME > ALL	33.41%	449	35.02%
SOME > MOST	48.00%	25	51.98%

Table 10: Relative position of correct vs. incorrect quantifiers when they both appear in the top-10 predictions made by each model, and in the ranking for the whole vocabulary.

	Set (A)		Set (B)	
BERT-base				
	% queries	Avg. Prob.	% queries	Avg. Prob.
the	85.7%	0.629	90.5%	0.662
these	6.2%	0.350	3.8%	0.375
their	0.8%	0.523	1.0%	0.686
BERT-large				
	% queries	Avg. Prob.	% queries	Avg. Prob.
the	74.3%	0.664	79.9%	0.716
these	4.2%	0.419	3.1%	0.510
their	0.4%	0.398	0.7%	0.572

Table 11: Proportion of queries in each set where the determiners *the*, *these* and *their* are found at the first position in the ranking. We also report the average probability assigned to a determiner when found in this position.

$\overrightarrow{AN}$ type	Acc	composition	Acc
Ns_N, Ns_{AN}	0.712	addition	0.712
As_{AN}	0.675	difference	0.667
Ns_N, As_{AN}	0.667	concatenation	0.660
Ns_{AN}, As_{AN}	0.665	average	0.650
Ns_{AN}	0.613	multiplication	0.611

Table 12: Highest average accuracy obtained by the different types of AN representation (left) and composition operations (right) with BERT embedding-based classifiers on the HVD development set.

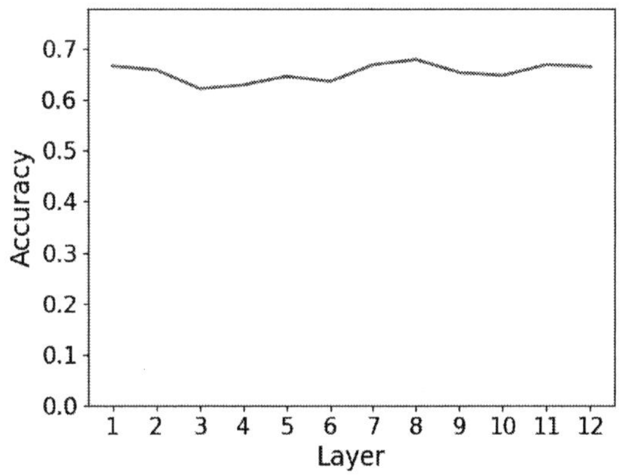

Figure 7: Highest average accuracy obtained by the embedding-based classifier on the HVD development set at every BERT layer.

based $\overrightarrow{AN}$ representation and composition operation. The combination of Ns_N and Ns_{AN} clearly outperforms the other vector combinations. Using the adjective token-level representation alone ($\overrightarrow{As_{AN}}$) also yields good results, definitely higher than $\overrightarrow{Ns_{AN}}$. In terms of composition functions, addition is the best performing operation for this task and multiplication the least useful.

Figure 7 shows the highest average accuracy obtained by each BERT layer on the HVD development set in these experiments.

$\overrightarrow{AN}$ type	Composition	Layer	Similarity	Accuracy
Ns_N, Ns_{AN}	addition	12	cosine & euclidean (Ns_N, $Ns_N + Ns_{AN}$)	0.712
As_N	-	8	-	0.675
Ns_N, As_{AN}	difference	12	-	0.667
Ns_{AN}, As_{AN}	difference	12	-	0.665
Ns_{AN}	-	11	cosine (Ns_N, Ns_{AN})	0.613
Composition type	**$\overrightarrow{AN}$ type**	**Layer**	**Similarity**	
addition	Ns_N, Ns_{AN}	12	cosine & euclidean (Ns_N, $Ns_N + Ns_{AN}$)	0.712
difference	Ns_N, As_{AN}	12	-	0.667
concatenation	Ns_{AN}, As_{AN}	7	-	0.660
average	Ns_N, As_{AN}	5	-	0.650
multiplication	Ns_N, As_{AN}	7	euclidean (Ns_N, $Ns_N \odot Ns_{AN}$)	0.611

Table 13: Best configurations for each type of $\overrightarrow{AN}$ (top) and composition operations (bottom) with BERT embedding-based classifiers. These are identified based on the accuracy obtained on the HVD development set.

ProSPer: Probing Human and Neural Network Language Model Understanding of Spatial Perspective

Tessa Masis
University of Massachusetts, Amherst
140 Governors Drive
Amherst, MA 01003, USA
tmasis@umass.edu

Carolyn Jane Anderson
Wellesley College
106 Central St
Wellesley, MA 02481, USA
carolyn.anderson@wellesley.edu

Abstract

Understanding perspectival language is important for applications like dialogue systems and human-robot interaction. We propose a probe task that explores how well language models understand spatial perspective. We present a dataset for evaluating perspective inference in English, ProSPer, and use it to explore how humans and Transformer-based language models infer perspective. Although the best bidirectional model performs similarly to humans, they display different strengths: humans outperform neural networks in conversational contexts, while RoBERTa excels at written genres.

1 Introduction

Point-of-view, or **perspective**, affects many aspects of language. This paper presents ProSPer, a dataset for probing how humans and neural language models track spatial perspective in text.

In recent years, neural network language understanding has been probed in a variety of syntactic and semantic tasks.[1] We propose a probe task for one of the most complex aspects of language: relative spatial language, or **spatial perspective**. We measure the ability to infer spatial perspective using a *come/go* prediction task: infer a missing motion verb from a passage of text (Figure 1).

This task combines aspects of previous probe tasks (long-distance dependencies, co-reference resolution), but also poses new challenges: (1) ranking the importance of individuals in a discourse, (2) reasoning over ambiguity, and (3) inferring spatial relations. This makes it challenging for any language user: as our behavioral data shows, human performance is not perfect. However, the task may be particularly hard for language models since they lack access to grounded information, which has been hypothesized to be important for spatial language acquisition (Glenberg and Gallese, 2012).

Rick changed the subject. "I heard that you were having some furniture delivered this afternoon," he said to Aunt Emily. "I thought I'd ___ by and see if you needed any help."

(1) go **(2) come**

Figure 1: Example PRoSPer item (target: *come*)

This paper explores human and neural network language model understanding of perspective. In Sections 2-3, we motivate and present our task and dataset. In Section 4, we measure human performance on ProSPer and find accuracy rates of 77-88%. In Section 5, we evaluate pre-trained neural language models and show that the BERT family (Devlin et al., 2019) achieves human-like accuracy.

In Section 6, we explore differences between human and model behavior. Drawing on psycholinguistic work on perspective (Harris, 2012), we outline three perspective inference strategies. Our evidence supports a **genre frequency bias**: humans perform best in conversation-like contexts, while RoBERTa excels in written genres, reflecting the language each encounters most during learning.

This paper contributes to the understanding of both neural network and human language capabilities. From a cognitive science perspective, our findings contribute to two open debates: the role of grounded information in language acquisition (Section 5) and the existence of cognitive biases in perspective inference (Section 6). From an applied perspective, our results motivate greater use of conversational data in applications where perspectival language is important, such as in navigation, story generation, and human-robot interaction.

[1] Including subject-verb agreement (Linzen et al., 2016; Giulianelli et al., 2018; Gulordava et al., 2018; Lin et al., 2019), question formation (Jumelet et al., 2019; McCoy et al., 2020), filler-gap dependencies (Wilcox et al., 2018), anaphora (Jumelet et al., 2019), category membership (Ettinger, 2020), and negative polarity items (Jumelet and Hupkes, 2018).

Proceedings of the Fourth BlackboxNLP Workshop on Analyzing and Interpreting Neural Networks for NLP, pages 95–135
Online, November 11, 2021.

Key contributions:

- ProSPer: a novel dataset for probing understanding of spatial perspectival language.
- Novel human behavioral data showing that humans achieve around 77-88% accuracy.
- Comparison of neural language models, showing that RoBERTa's accuracy is human-like.
- Fine-grained error analysis guided by previous psycholinguistic work, revealing a genre frequency bias for humans and RoBERTa.

2 Probing perspective inference

The perspectival motion verb prediction task is a compelling probe task because it is simple in design, but high in linguistic complexity.

2.1 Probe task description

The motion verbs *come* and *go* are identical in meaning except for point-of-view: *come* requires a discourse-important[2] person known as the **perspective-holder** to be at the destination of motion, while *go* does not. In Sentence (1) of Figure 2, for instance, motion to Boston is described with *come* because it is the location of the speaker, who is discourse-important, but motion to the beach is described with *go*.

Because *come* and *go* are synonymous except for perspective, they are an ideal test of perspective understanding for language models. If a model predicts *go* when the target is *come*, the model has failed to access an available perspective, or failed to realize the perspective-holder is at the destination. If the model predicts *come* instead of *go*, it has incorrectly inferred that the perspective-holder is at the destination.

2.2 Linguistic complexity

The perspective inference task incorporates aspects of previous probe tasks, including **long-distance dependencies** (Linzen et al., 2016), **named-entity recognition**, and **co-reference resolution** (Jumelet et al., 2019). However, perspective inference presents three additional challenges.

The first is **deciding who is important enough to be a perspective-holder**. Perspective-holders must be discourse-important, a property affected by many factors including topicality, subjecthood and definiteness (Kaiser and Lee, 2017; Hinterwimmer, 2017; Kaiser, 2020; Meuser et al., 2020). To infer

1. *Context: Sue is chatting with her sister Gina.* Sue: I'd love to see you if the flight isn't too much, but both are good options: if you **come** to Boston, you'll get a white Christmas, but if you stay in LA, you can **go** to the beach.
2. *Context: Poirot is in his flat, recounting a call from Chief Inspector Japp at Scotland Yard.* Poirot: Chief Inspector Japp thinks that the murderer will **come** to confess.

Figure 2: Constructed *come* and *go* examples

perspective, therefore, a model must **gather and evaluate contextual evidence** about characters.

Determining discourse-importance is especially challenging because it **changes dynamically**: at any one point in a sentence, there is a unique perspective-holder, but the perspective can shift as the discourse develops, even within a sentence.

Second, the perspectival motion verb task is challenging because there can be **surface ambiguity** about the perspective-holder, as in (2) in Figure 2, where the destination could be Poirot's flat or Scotland Yard, depending on whether the perspective-holder is Poirot or Japp. Unlike syntactic tasks like subject-verb agreement, our task involves ambiguous contexts where there is no one right answer.

Third, the perspectival motion verb task involves **inferring spatial relations**. To predict *come* and *go*, a model has to both identify the perspective-holder and figure out if they are at the destination of motion. This requires inferring the motion path from the text. In (1) in Figure 2, for instance, the model has to infer that Sue lives in Boston in order to guess that the first missing verb is *come*.

2.3 Related work

Spatial language understanding is a key topic for agent-based applications. Symbolic approaches generally restrict the set of terms and perspectives considered (Winograd, 1971; Zelle and Mooney, 1996; Cangelosi et al., 2007; Boteanu et al., 2017). Statistical approaches address naturalistic language (Misra et al., 2017), but still focus on contexts with a limited set of perspectives, such as navigation (Chen et al., 2019; Paz-Argaman and Tsarfaty, 2019; Platonov et al., 2019; Zheng et al., 2020).

By contrast, the psycholinguistic community is increasingly interested in narrative contexts where the set of available perspectives may be much larger (Harris, 2012; Meuser et al., 2020). These contexts are important for computational approaches to dis-

[2] The term **discourse prominence** is used in linguistics (Grosz et al., 1995; von Heusinger and Schumacher, 2019).

course like story generation (Jorge et al., 2019), character tracking (Rao et al., 2015; Toshniwal et al., 2020), and stance detection (Augenstein et al., 2016; Inkpen et al., 2017).

Spatial language is also a topic of importance to language acquisition. The extent to which grounded information is necessary for language acquisition is much debated within the cognitive science (Rehm et al., 2003; Glenberg and Gallese, 2012) and language modeling communities (Lucy and Gauthier, 2017; Bender and Koller, 2020; Bisk et al., 2020). Evidence from child language acquisition shows that learners rely on non-linguistic situational cues (Clark, 1973; Samuelson et al., 2011), but cannot establish if such information is necessary. If it is, spatial perspective is one of the most likely phenomena to require it, since it is relative and situational. Our proposed task explores this issue: successful perspective inference by text-based neural networks would imply that grounded information is not necessary for language acquisition.

Our task therefore brings together questions from several research communities. Using methods drawn from the neural network probe task and psycholinguistics communities, we gather novel empirical evidence that addresses two debated issues in cognitive science: grounding in language acquisition (Section 5), and cognitive biases in perspective shift (Section 6). In addition, our findings are relevant to several application areas, including work on embodied agents and story generation.

3 ProSPer: Probing Spatial Perspective

We present a new corpus for probing human and neural network ability to infer spatial perspective: ProSPer.[3]. The ProSPer dataset consists of two parts: the Automatic subset, a large set of examples extracted by string-matching, and the Annotated subset, a smaller set for fine-grained analysis. The Annotated items were hand-selected for linguistic diversity and annotated with linguistic features.

3.1 Task

PRoSPer probes perspective inference with a forced-choice task: given a passage with an omitted verb, decide if the missing word is *come* or *go*. Figures 1 and 3 show examples. In addition to the critical perspectival verbs, *come* and *go*, we also include three non-perspectival comparison verbs: *walk*, *drive*, and *arrive*. Each is compared with its closest semantic competitor: *come* and *go* with each other, *walk* and *drive*, and *arrive* with *come*.

3.2 Automatically selected subset

The Automatic subset consists of 47385 examples taken from the Open American National Corpus using all forms of *come*, *go*, *walk*, *arrive*, and *drive*.

3.3 Annotated subset

The Annotated subset consists of 600 examples from publicly available corpora of American English.[4] Examples were chosen to avoid non-perspectival uses (like *Come on, man!*) and to include a variety of genres. The examples were annotated by the authors with the following features:

Perspective-holder: Examples containing *come* were annotated by perspective-holder category: speaker, listener, attitude-holder, protagonist, theme, empathy center, home-base, or accompaniment. A quota system was used to ensure that each category was well-represented.

Subject: The perspective-holder is often ambiguous in sentences with non-perspectival verbs. Instead, the subject of the verb was recorded. These should not be confused: the perspective-holder is rarely the subject, since *come* requires the perspective-holder to be located at the destination of motion (Barlew, 2017).

Syntactic environment: Examples were categorized based on the verb's syntactic environment: top-level, within the scope of a speech verb, within the scope of a thought verb, quotation, or other. This is important because attitude verbs like *say* and *think* increase the importance of their subjects' perspectives. A quota system was used to ensure that each environment was represented.

Destination of motion: The destination of motion was recorded for all examples.

Tense: Examples in both subsets of ProSPer were sorted into coarse tense categories.

4 Human performance

We measured human performance on a representative subset of ProSPer using a forced choice task similar to bidirectional language modeling.[5]

[3]The ProSPer dataset and code can be found in the ProSPer Github repository. Files relating to the human experiments can be found in the ProSPer Open Science Foundation repository.

[4]The Corpus of Contemporary American English, the Corpus of Online Registers of English, and The Corpus of American Soap Operas (Davies, 2008, 2016, 2011).

[5]The IRB-approved design was preregistered through the Open Science Foundation. Experimental stimuli, results, and

Human format: *and they worked with her and got her walking and got her taking kind of taking care of herself and so she was able to __ back home*
Bidirectional format: *and they worked with her and got her walking and got her taking kind of taking care of herself and so she was able to* ***MASK*** *back home*
Unidirectional format: *and they worked with her and got her walking and got her taking kind of taking care of herself and so she was able to*

Figure 3: ProSPer presentation formats, target: *go*

4.1 Experimental design

Task: Participants were shown an item with the target omitted and asked to pick between two verbs (Figure 3). Each target verb was presented with its closest semantic competitor (see Section 3).

Items: Human judgments were collected on three subsets of ProSPer: the entire Annotated subset; 600 items from the Automatic subset, sampled randomly (Random); and the 300 most challenging items from the Automatic subset (NN Confounding).[6]

Participants: 300[7] monolingual American English speakers were recruited on Prolific. Each participant saw 20 Annotated items, 10 NN Confounding items, and 10 Random items, as well as 30 filler items. Participants were randomly assigned to item lists using a Latin square design. Each Annotated and NN Confounding item was seen by 10 participants, while Random items were seen by 5 participants.

4.2 Results

Mean accuracies by corpus and verb are shown in Figure 4. Participants did best on the Random subset (88.1% accuracy) and worst on the NN Confounding subset (47.2%). However, mean accuracies varied considerably by verb type, with *come* generally proving harder than other verbs.

5 Neural language model performance

We evaluated the performance of various neural network language models on the ProSPer dataset.

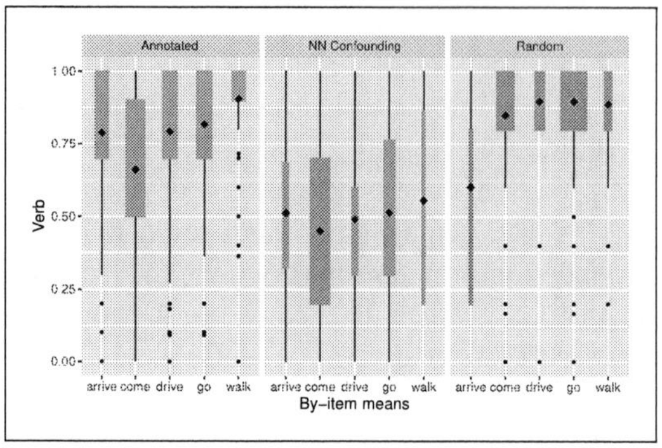

Figure 4: Human item means by verb type and corpus (diamond=mean, box=1st-3rd quartiles)

5.1 Baselines

We provide two baseline models trained on English Wikipedia: a Kneser-Ney smoothed trigram model and a unidirectional LSTM (Hochreiter and Schmidhuber, 1997).[8]

5.2 Transformer-based models

We compare the performance of pre-trained Transformer-based language models from the HuggingFace Transformers library (Wolf et al., 2019): Transformer-XL (Dai et al., 2019), BERT (Devlin et al., 2019), DistilBERT (Sanh et al., 2019), RoBERTa (Liu et al., 2019), GPT (Radford, 2018), and GPT-2 (Radford et al., 2018). Since our goal is to evaluate how much knowledge of spatial perspective models acquire from the language modeling task, we do not do fine-tune any of the models.

It is important to note that the different families of models are not directly comparable, since the BERT family of models are bidirectional and condition their predictions on a larger context. The models also differ in complexity and training data; retraining each model on the same dataset would be prohibitive in terms of computational cost.[9]

5.3 Task

The models' performance on ProSPer was measured in a two-way comparison, where the relative probability of the target word was compared to that of its closest semantic competitor. For unidirectional language models, we take the probabilities of each word at the target site. For bidirectional

analysis scripts can also be found there.

[6]We pooled the 1000 hardest items for each Transformer model and then selected the items missed by the most models.

[7]Excluding participants who did not meet the language criteria, had less than 80% accuracy on the attention check fillers, or gave an incoherent response to a bot check question.

[8]Implementations adapted from Rescia (2015) and Verwimp et al. (2018).

[9]Further description of the models can be found in the Appendix. Although the training data varies by model, we have verified that there is no overlap with ProSPer.

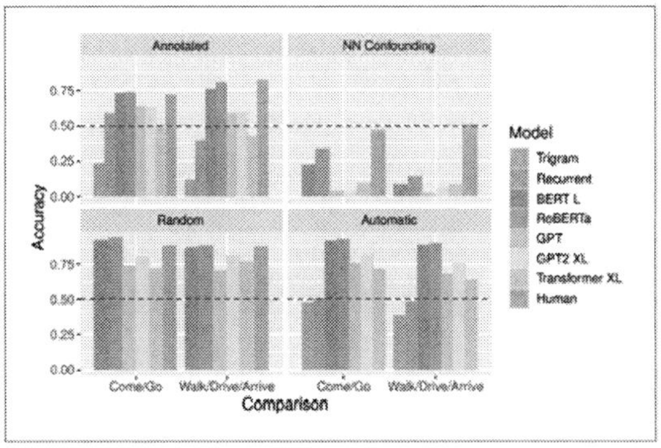

Figure 5: NN means by corpus[10]

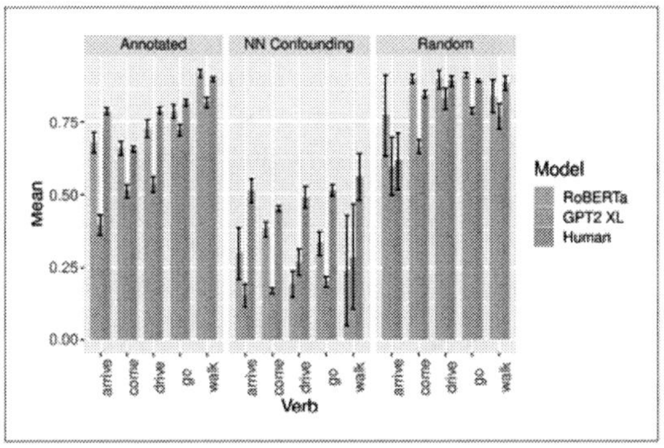

Figure 6: Human and NN means by corpus and verb

models, the target word was masked and the entire context was presented (Figure 3).

5.4 Results

Model performance on each subset of ProSPer is shown in Figure 5. The results suggest that neural language models are capable of tracking and using spatial perspective to some degree. Although all models find the Annotated subset more challenging than the Automatic one, the best-performing model, RoBERTa, performs similarly to human participants on the Annotated subset, and slightly better on the Random Automatic subset.

The GPT and GPT-2 models perform well above chance on the Automatic dataset but struggle on the harder Annotated dataset, suggesting that their success on the Automatic dataset may be built on non-perspectival uses of *come* and *go*. However, it is important to note that human performance was measured on the bidirectional task.

While the baseline models perform poorly,

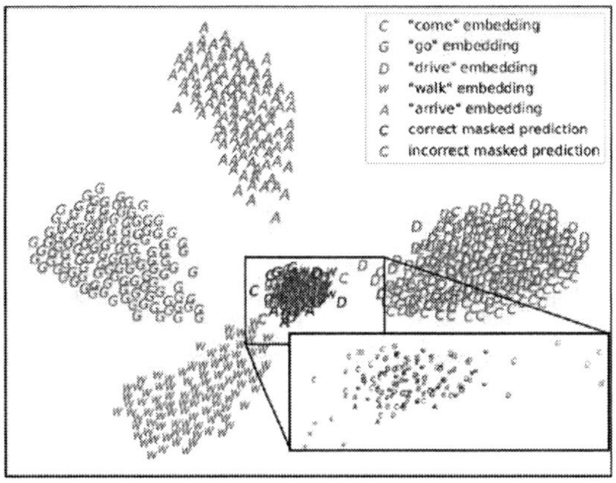

Figure 7: PCA of RoBERTa Automatic verb and Annotated MASK hidden layers. Inset: MASK cluster.

BERT models perform similarly to humans. This is impressive given the task's linguistic complexity: it suggests that models are able to use context clues to track the spatial perspectives and discourse-importance of characters. However, these results should not be over-interpreted: although we tried to control for possible confounds with the Annotated dataset, we cannot rule out the possibility that the models relying on some kind of simpler heuristic.[11]

5.5 Principal Components Analysis

To explore how neural networks represent the key motion verbs, we provide a principal components analysis of RoBERTa's hidden states retrieved after substituting each of the five target verbs into examples from the Automatic dataset.

Figure 7 shows the first two principal components for RoBERTa's hidden states when given each verb and when given masked examples from the Annotated dataset (*Susan is <mask> here*). We see that *come* and *go* are on opposing sides of the plot, reflecting their relationship as a minimal pair.

The masked tokens are clustered in the center of the plot and relatively equidistant from each verb cluster. We note that masked tokens from examples that RoBERTa classifies correctly have a slightly broader spread than incorrect ones. This may reflect the model's relative uncertainty.

6 How do human and neural network errors differ?

As Figure 6 shows, the best neural network model (RoBERTa) performs similarly to humans in the

[10]The below-chance NN Confounding results may be unintuitive, but since this subset was selected by poor model performance, it is expected (selection is causally dependent on low score).

[11]Bender and Koller (2020) discuss some cautionary tales.

Strong Egocentricity Hypothesis
- Low accuracy for *come* relative to other verbs.

Weak Egocentricity Hypothesis
- High accuracy with speaker perspectives.

Genre Frequency Bias Hypothesis
- Human accuracy improved by conversation-like contexts (spoken genres, quoted environments) and speaker or listener perspectives.
- RoBERTa accuracy improved by text-like contexts and attitude holder, empathy center, theme, and protagonist perspectives.

Figure 8: Perspective Inference Strategy Predictions

Random and Annotated subsets.[12] Although human participants found the NN Confounding subset difficult, with performance at about chance, they outperformed all models (unsurprising, since the subset was selected based on average model difficulty).

Averaging across neural network models, there is a medium correlation between by-item model and human performance (ρ=0.65); RoBERTa's predictions correlate a little more closely with human performance (ρ=0.71). The medium correlation suggests that despite their similar accuracy, there is considerable variance between human and RoBERTa predictions on ProSPer.

In the remainder of the paper, we explore possible explanations for these differences.

6.1 Three perspective inference strategies

To gain insight into how humans and neural network models infer perspective, we explore three possible perspective inference strategies.

Previous psycholinguistic work on perspective suggests that humans are **egocentric**: they are biased toward their own perspectives. The core idea is that accessing a self perspective is automatic, while accessing other perspectives involves a perspective shift operation (Epley et al., 2004; Lin et al., 2010). This causes slower, more errorful processing of non-self-oriented perspectival language.

Although there is converging evidence for egocentric cognitive bias from a variety of tasks,[13] there is ongoing debate over its strength (Brown-Schmidt and Heller, 2018). A strong version of the egocentricity hypothesis posits that participants are so self-biased that they struggle to access any other perspective, no matter how discourse-important. This **Strong Egocentricity Hypothesis** predicts low accuracy for human participants on all ProSPer *come* items.

Other psycholinguists propose an indirect egocentricity effect. If listeners are aware of speaker egocentricity, they may proactively take the speaker's perspective to facilitate processing (Harris, 2012; Anderson, 2020). We refer to this as the **Weak Egocentricity Hypothesis**: participants assume the perspective holder is the speaker because they know speakers tend to be egocentric. This hypothesis makes different predictions about human behavior on ProSPER. Rather than performing poorly on *come* in general, we expect accuracy to vary based on the perspective-holder: participants should predict *come* accurately when the speaker is the perspective holder, but underperform when non-speaker perspectives are discourse-important.

We introduce a third possibility: the **Genre Frequency Bias**. We note that although humans and RoBERTa both encounter a variety of data during language acquisition, its composition differs: children learn through conversation, while RoBERTa is primarily trained on news, non-fiction and third-person narratives. The only portion of RoBERTa's training data that contains conversation-like text is the Open Web Text corpus, and it differs in significant ways from in-person conversation (i.e., speakers lack mutual awareness of each other's spatial location). We hypothesize that this leads to advantages on different subsets of ProSPer.

Since humans acquire language through conversation, they may predict *come* best when anchored to the perspective of a conversation participant: a speaker or listener. They may also excel at transcribed speech. Conversely, RoBERTa may perform better in written genres and with third-person perspectives like protagonists and discourse themes. We also expect differences by syntactic environment: quotation is like conversation, while speech and belief contexts are more common in text.

The Annotated subset of ProSPer makes it easy to test the predictions of these three hypotheses (Figure 8). Note that they are not mutually exclusive: for instance, we could find evidence of both an egocentricity bias and a genre frequency bias

[12] To compare to human performance, the models' predicted probabilities for the two verb choices for each item have been renormalized to produce a prediction score from 0 to 1.

[13] Including two-player reference tasks (Horton and Keysar, 1996; Hanna et al., 2003; Heller et al., 2008), eye-tracking tasks (Brown-Schmidt and Hanna, 2011; Ferguson et al., 2017; Child et al., 2020), self-paced reading tasks (Millis, 1995), and interpretation tasks (Harris, 2012; Köder et al., 2015).

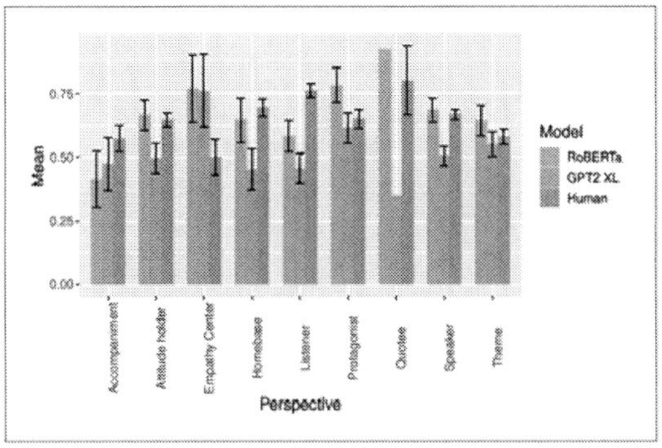

Figure 9: Annotated *come* means by perspective type

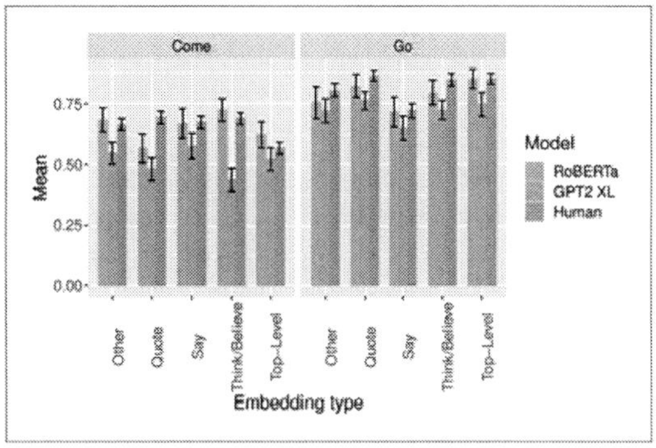

Figure 11: Annotated means by syntactic environment

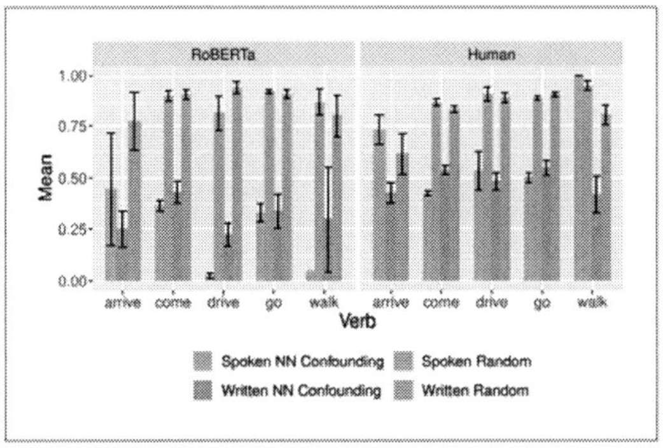

Figure 10: Means by modality and corpus

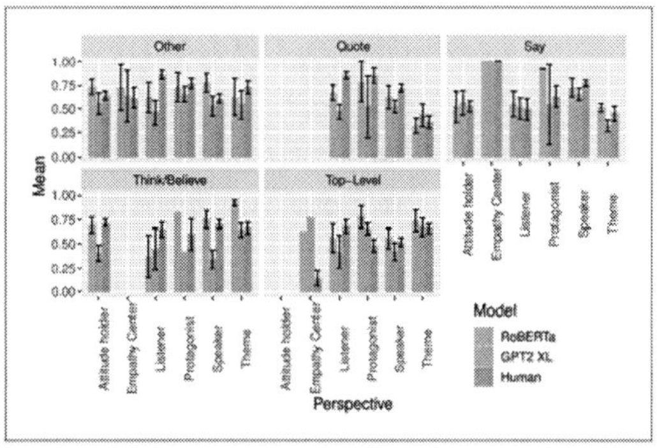

Figure 12: Annotated *come* means by perspective and syntactic environment

(lower *come* accuracy relative to other verbs, but mediated by perspective holder and genre). We explore the evidence for each, discussing only trends that are supported by statistically significant effects in regression models.[14]

6.2 Strong Egocentricity Evidence

The Strong Egocentricity Hypothesis predicts low accuracy for *come* items overall, due to interference from participants' own perspectives.

We do find that human performance on *come* is significantly lower than the verb group mean. However, we also find significantly lower accuracy on *come* for RoBERTa. It is unclear how the Strong Egocentricity Hypothesis could explain this, since neural networks do not hold a self-perspective. Our evidence is inconclusive: there may be a human Strong Egocentricity bias and another reason for RoBERTa's performance, or *come* items may challenge both groups for other reasons, such as the perspective ambiguity they introduce.

[14]Details of the regression models and full results are in the Appendix. Figure bars show standard error.

6.3 Weak Egocentricity Evidence

The Weak Egocentricity Hypothesis predicts that performance on *come* items will be highest when the perspective holder is the speaker. This prediction is not borne out by the human results. Although there were significant negative effects of empathy center, theme, and protagonist perspectives on human *come* performance, there was no significant positive effect of speaker perspective (Figure 9). Interestingly, there was an overall positive effect of speaker on RoBERTa's performance.

6.4 Genre Frequency Bias Evidence

The Genre Frequency Bias Hypothesis makes several predictions. First, it predicts that humans should excel in conversational contexts. We compared performance on the spoken and written subsets of the Random dataset. For humans, there was a significant positive effect of the spoken subset for *come* (Figure 10). The reverse was true for RoBERTa: accuracy at predicting *come* was significantly worse in the spoken subset.[15]

Second, the Genre Frequency Bias Hypothesis predicts that humans will perform best when the perspective holder is a speaker or listener, while RoBERTa will perform better with empathy center, attitude holder, theme, and protagonist perspectives. Our results support these predictions to some extent. Humans did significantly worse with empathy center, them, and protagonist perspectives, but RoBERTa did not do significantly better with them. Humans also performed better with listener perspectives than attitude holder perspectives, but there was no significant different between human performance with speaker and attitude holder perspectives. In addition, as noted above, there was a positive effect of speaker perspective for RoBERTa.

The Genre Frequency Bias Hypothesis also extends to syntactic environments: humans are expected to perform best in conversation-like contexts, such as quotation and top-level clauses. We observed that quoted environments had an overall positive effect on human performance, but found a negative effect of top-level contexts on *come* accuracy (Figure 11). However, this effect is complicated by the proportional representation of perspective holders in the Annotated subset. In a model including both perspective holder type and syntactic environment, a negative interaction with top-level environments is found only for empathy center, them, and protagonist perspectives (Figure 12).

RoBERTa's performance on *come* was improved by belief environments, and hurt by top-level and quoted environments. Mirroring the human data, we find a positive interaction between empathy center, theme, and protagonist perspectives and top-level and quoted environments for RoBERTa.

Thus, our data partially supports the Genre Frequency Bias. For humans, performance is better in conversation-like contexts and worse with third-person perspectives. For RoBERTa, performance is worse in conversation-like contexts. However, there was no preference for speaker perspectives over attitude holders for humans, as predicted, and RoBERTa performed well with speaker perspectives, which is unexpected if exposure to conversational contexts is what leads to speaker bias.

[15]This effect was significant in a RoBERTa-only model, but not in a human-RoBERTa model where RoBERTa was treated as a fixed effect. The human effects were significant in both.

6.5 Manual error analysis

To further explore possible perspective inference strategies, we examined *come/go* errors in the 10 hardest items for humans in the Annotated and Random subsets. Most of the Random errors involve incomplete sentences. The remaining 7 *come/go* examples in the Random and Annotated subsets involve errors consistent with the Genre Frequency Bias. In four, the target is *come*, but the speaker is the subject. This may lead speaker-biased participants astray: if the speaker is the perspective-holder, *go* must be used. One error involves *go* as a target for a context where the speaker is at the destination, which again, contradicts expectations if the speaker is the perspective-holder. The last two involve third-person perspective-holders.

7 Conclusion

In this paper, we present ProSPer, a dataset for probing how humans and language models infer spatial perspective from text. We use ProSPer's *come/go* prediction task to gather novel psycholinguistic data and evaluate Transformer-based language models. We find that the best bidirectional model, RoBERTa, performs similarly to humans, providing tentative evidence that grounded information is not required for spatial language acquisition.

Despite near-equal accuracy, we find only a medium correlation between RoBERTa and human scores, suggesting different perspective inference strategies. We explored two strategies proposed in prior psycholinguistic work, but ultimately argued in support of a novel Genre Frequency Bias effect: humans perform best in conversation-like contexts, while RoBERTa performs best in third-person narrative contexts. Although many of the observed trends support the Genre Frequency Bias, it did not explain the full pattern of results. We hope that ProSPer's Annotated subset will aid future work exploring perspective inference strategies.

The observed Genre Frequency Bias is important for both neural network and human language understanding. For cognitive scientists, it fuels an existing debate on cognitive biases in perspective inference. For applications where human-like use of perspectival language is important, like navigation, story generation, and human-robot interaction, it suggests that conversational training data may improve model robustness.

References

Carolyn Jane Anderson. 2020. *Shifting the perspectival landscape*. Ph.D. thesis, University of Massachusetts, Amherst.

Isabelle Augenstein, Tim Rocktäschel, Andreas Vlachos, and Kalina Bontcheva. 2016. Stance detection with bidirectional conditional encoding. In *EMNLP*.

Jefferson Barlew. 2017. *The semantics and pragmatics of perspectival expressions in English and Bulu: The case of deictic motion verbs*. Ph.D. thesis, The Ohio State University.

Emily M. Bender and Alexander Koller. 2020. Climbing towards NLU: On meaning, form, and understanding in the age of data. In *Proceedings of the 58th Annual Meeting of the Association for Computational Linguistics*, pages 5185–5198, Online. Association for Computational Linguistics.

Yonatan Bisk, Ari Holtzman, Jesse Thomason, Jacob Andreas, Yoshua Bengio, Joyce Chai, Mirella Lapata, Angeliki Lazaridou, Jonathan May, Aleksandr Nisnevich, Nicolas Pinto, and Joseph Turian. 2020. Experience grounds language. In *Proceedings of the 2020 Conference on Empirical Methods in Natural Language Processing (EMNLP)*, pages 8718–8735, Online. Association for Computational Linguistics.

Adrian Boteanu, Jacob Arkin, Siddharth Patki, Thomas M. Howard, and Hadas Kress-Gazit. 2017. Robot-initiated specification repair through grounded language interaction. *CoRR*, abs/1710.01417.

Sarah Brown-Schmidt and Joy E. Hanna. 2011. Talking in Another Person's Shoes: Incremental Perspective-taking in Language Processing. *Dialogue and Discourse*, 2:11–33.

Sarah Brown-Schmidt and Daphna Heller. 2018. Perspective-taking During Conversation. In G Gaskell and S. A. Rueschemeyer, editors, *Oxford Handbook of Psycholinguistics*. Oxford University Press.

A. Cangelosi, V. Tikhanoff, J. F. Fontanari, and Emmanouil Hourdakis. 2007. Integrating language and cognition: A cognitive robotics approach. *IEEE Computational Intelligence Magazine*, 2:65–70.

Howard Chen, Alane Suhr, Dipendra Kumar Misra, Noah Snavely, and Yoav Artzi. 2019. Touchdown: Natural language navigation and spatial reasoning in visual street environments. *2019 IEEE/CVF Conference on Computer Vision and Pattern Recognition (CVPR)*, pages 12530–12539.

Scarlett Child, Jane Oakhill, and Alan Garnham. 2020. Tracking your Emotions: an Eye-Tracking Study on Reader's Engagement with Perspective during Text Comprehension. *Quarterly Journal of Experimental Psychology*.

Eve V. Clark. 1973. Non-linguistic strategies and the acquisition of word meanings. *Cognition*, 2(2):161 – 182.

Zihang Dai, Zhilin Yang, Yiming Yang, Jaime Carbonell, Quoc Le, and Ruslan Salakhutdinov. 2019. Transformer-XL: Attentive language models beyond a fixed-length context. In *Proceedings of the 57th Annual Meeting of the Association for Computational Linguistics*, pages 2978–2988, Florence, Italy. Association for Computational Linguistics.

Mark. Davies. 2008. *The Corpus of Contemporary American English (COCA): 600 million words, 1990-present*. Available online at https://www.english-corpora.org/coca.

Mark. Davies. 2011. *Corpus of American Soap Operas: 100 million words*. Available online at https://www.english-corpora.org/soap.

Mark. Davies. 2016. *Corpus of Online Registers of English (CORE)*. Available online at https://www.english-corpora.org/core.

Jacob Devlin, Ming-Wei Chang, Kenton Lee, and Kristina Toutanova. 2019. BERT: Pre-training of deep bidirectional transformers for language understanding. In *Proceedings of the 2019 Conference of the North American Chapter of the Association for Computational Linguistics: Human Language Technologies, Volume 1 (Long and Short Papers)*, pages 4171–4186, Minneapolis, Minnesota. Association for Computational Linguistics.

Nicholas Epley, Boaz Keysar, Leaf Van Boven, and Thomas Gilovich. 2004. Perspective taking as egocentric anchoring and adjustment. *Journal of Personality and Social Psychology*, 87(3):327–339.

Allyson Ettinger. 2020. What BERT is not: Lessons from a new suite of psycholinguistic diagnostics for language models. *Transactions of the Association for Computational Linguistics*, 8:34–48.

Heather J. Ferguson, Ian Apperly, and James E. Cane. 2017. Eye tracking reveals the cost of switching between self and other perspectives in a visual perspective-taking task. *The Quarterly Journal of Experimental Psychology*, 70(8):1646–1660.

Mario Giulianelli, Jack Harding, Florian Mohnert, Dieuwke Hupkes, and Willem Zuidema. 2018. Under the hood: Using diagnostic classifiers to investigate and improve how language models track agreement information. In *Proceedings of the 2018 EMNLP Workshop BlackboxNLP: Analyzing and Interpreting Neural Networks for NLP*, pages 240–248, Brussels, Belgium. Association for Computational Linguistics.

Arthur. M. Glenberg and Vittorio Gallese. 2012. Action-based language: A theory of language acquisition, comprehension, and production. *Cortex*, 48.

Barbara J. Grosz, Aravind K. Joshi, and Scott Weinstein. 1995. Centering: a framework for modeling the local coherence of discourse. *Association for Computational Linguistics*, pages 203–225.

Kristina Gulordava, Piotr Bojanowski, Edouard Grave, Tal Linzen, and Marco Baroni. 2018. Colorless green recurrent networks dream hierarchically. In *Proceedings of the 2018 Conference of the North American Chapter of the Association for Computational Linguistics: Human Language Technologies, Volume 1 (Long Papers)*, pages 1195–1205, New Orleans, Louisiana. Association for Computational Linguistics.

Joy E. Hanna, Michael K. Tanenhaus, and John C. Trueswell. 2003. The effects of common ground and perspective on domains of referential interpretation. *Journal of Memory and Language*, 49(1):43–61.

Jesse A. Harris. 2012. *Processing Perspectives*. Ph.D. thesis, University of Massachusetts, Amherst.

Daphna Heller, Daniel Grodner, and Michael K. Tanenhaus. 2008. The role of perspective in identifying domains of reference. *Cognition*, 108(3):831–836.

Stefan Hinterwimmer. 2017. Prominent protagonists. *Journal of Pragmatics*.

Sepp Hochreiter and Jürgen Schmidhuber. 1997. Long short-term memory. *Neural Computation*, 9:1735–1780.

William S. Horton and Boaz Keysar. 1996. When do speakers take into account common ground? *Cognition*, 59(1):91–117.

Diana Inkpen, Xiao-Dan Zhu, and Parinaz Sobhani. 2017. A dataset for multi-target stance detection. In *EACL*.

A. Jorge, Ricardo Campos, A. Jatowt, and S. Bhatia. 2019. The 2nd international workshop on narrative extraction from text: Text2story 2019. In *ECIR*.

Jaap Jumelet and Dieuwke Hupkes. 2018. Do language models understand anything? on the ability of LSTMs to understand negative polarity items. In *Proceedings of the 2018 EMNLP Workshop BlackboxNLP: Analyzing and Interpreting Neural Networks for NLP*, pages 222–231, Brussels, Belgium. Association for Computational Linguistics.

Jaap Jumelet, Willem Zuidema, and Dieuwke Hupkes. 2019. Analysing neural language models: Contextual decomposition reveals default reasoning in number and gender assignment. In *Proceedings of the 23rd Conference on Computational Natural Language Learning (CoNLL)*, pages 1–11, Hong Kong, China. Association for Computational Linguistics.

Elsi Kaiser. 2020. Shifty behavior: Investigating predicates of personal taste and perspectival anaphora. In *Semantics and Linguistic Theory*, volume 30.

Elsi Kaiser and Jamie Herron Lee. 2017. Experience matters: A psycholinguistic investigation of predicates of personal taste. *Semantics and Linguistic Theory*, 27.

Franziska Köder, Emar Maier, and Petra Hendriks. 2015. Perspective shift increases processing effort of pronouns: a comparison between direct and indirect speech. *Language, Cognition and Neuroscience*, 30(8).

Shuhong Lin, Boaz Keysar, and Nicholas Epley. 2010. Reflexively mindblind: Using theory of mind to interpret behavior requires effortful attention. *Journal of Experimental Social Psychology*, 46:551–556.

Yongjie Lin, Yi Chern Tan, and Robert Frank. 2019. Open sesame: Getting inside BERT's linguistic knowledge. In *Proceedings of the 2019 ACL Workshop BlackboxNLP: Analyzing and Interpreting Neural Networks for NLP*, pages 241–253, Florence, Italy. Association for Computational Linguistics.

Tal Linzen, Emmanuel Dupoux, and Yoav Goldberg. 2016. Assessing the ability of LSTMs to learn syntax-sensitive dependencies. *Transactions of the Association for Computational Linguistics*, 4:521–535.

Yinhan Liu, Myle Ott, Naman Goyal, Jingfei Du, Mandar Joshi, Danqi Chen, Omer Levy, Mike Lewis, Luke Zettlemoyer, and Veselin Stoyanov. 2019. Roberta: A robustly optimized BERT pretraining approach. *CoRR*, abs/1907.11692.

Li Lucy and Jon Gauthier. 2017. Are distributional representations ready for the real world? evaluating word vectors for grounded perceptual meaning. In *Proceedings of the First Workshop on Language Grounding for Robotics*, pages 76–85, Vancouver, Canada. Association for Computational Linguistics.

R. Thomas McCoy, Robert Frank, and Tal Linzen. 2020. Does syntax need to grow on trees? sources of hierarchical inductive bias in sequence-to-sequence networks. *Transactions of the Association for Computational Linguistics*, 8:125–140.

Sara Meuser, Stefan Hinterwimmer, and Maximilian Hörl. 2020. Online Processing of Protagonists' Perspective-Taking. In *The CUNY Sentence Processing Conference*, volume 33.

Keith K. Millis. 1995. Encoding discourse perspective during the reading of a literary text. *Poetics*, 23(3):235–253.

Dipendra Kumar Misra, John Langford, and Yoav Artzi. 2017. Mapping instructions and visual observations to actions with reinforcement learning. *CoRR*, abs/1704.08795.

Tzuf Paz-Argaman and Reut Tsarfaty. 2019. RUN through the streets: A new dataset and baseline models for realistic urban navigation. In *Proceedings of the 2019 Conference on Empirical Methods in Natural Language Processing and the 9th International Joint Conference on Natural Language Processing (EMNLP-IJCNLP)*, pages 6449–6455, Hong Kong, China. Association for Computational Linguistics.

Georgiy Platonov, Benjamin Kane, Aaron Gindi, and Lenhart K. Schubert. 2019. A spoken dialogue system for spatial question answering in a physical blocks world. *CoRR*, abs/1911.02524.

Alec Radford. 2018. Improving language understanding by generative pre-training.

Alec Radford, Jeffrey Wu, Rewon Child, David Luan, Dario Amodei, and Ilya Sutskever. 2018. Language models are unsupervised multitask learners.

Sudha Rao, Allyson Ettinger, Hal Daumé III, and Philip Resnik. 2015. Dialogue focus tracking for zero pronoun resolution. In *Proceedings of the 2015 Conference of the North American Chapter of the Association for Computational Linguistics: Human Language Technologies*, pages 494–503, Denver, Colorado. Association for Computational Linguistics.

M. Rehm, K. Rohlfing, and K. U. Goecke. 2003. Situatedness: The interplay between context(s) and situation. *Journal of Cognition and Culture*, 3:132–156.

Giovanni Rescia. 2015. Procesamiento de lenguaje natural.

L.K. Samuelson, L.B. Smith, L.K. Perry, and J.P. Spencer. 2011. Grounding word learning in space. *PLoS ONE*, 6.

Victor Sanh, Lysandre Debut, Julien Chaumond, and Thomas Wolf. 2019. Distilbert, a distilled version of bert: smaller, faster, cheaper and lighter. *ArXiv*, abs/1910.01108.

Shubham Toshniwal, Allyson Ettinger, Kevin Gimpel, and Karen Livescu. 2020. PeTra: A Sparsely Supervised Memory Model for People Tracking. In *Proceedings of the 58th Annual Meeting of the Association for Computational Linguistics*, pages 5415–5428, Online. Association for Computational Linguistics.

Lyan Verwimp, Hugo Van hamme, and Patrick Wambacq. 2018. Tf-lm: Tensorflow-based language modeling toolkit. *Proceedings of LREC*.

Klaus von Heusinger and Petra B. Schumacher. 2019. Discourse prominence: Definition and application. *Journal of Pragmatics*, 154:117 – 127.

Ethan Wilcox, Roger Levy, Takashi Morita, and Richard Futrell. 2018. What do RNN language models learn about filler–gap dependencies? In *Proceedings of the 2018 EMNLP Workshop BlackboxNLP: Analyzing and Interpreting Neural Networks for NLP*, pages 211–221, Brussels, Belgium. Association for Computational Linguistics.

Terry Winograd. 1971. *Procedures as a representation of data in a computer program for understanding natural language*. PhD thesis, Massachusets Institute of Technology.

Thomas Wolf, Lysandre Debut, Victor Sanh, Julien Chaumond, Clement Delangue, Anthony Moi, Pierric Cistac, Tim Rault, Rémi Louf, Morgan Funtowicz, and Jamie Brew. 2019. Huggingface's transformers: State-of-the-art natural language processing. *ArXiv*, abs/1910.03771.

John M. Zelle and Raymond J. Mooney. 1996. Learning to parse database queries using inductive logic programming. In *Proceedings of the Thirteenth National Conference on Artificial Intelligence - Volume 2*, AAAI'96, page 1050–1055. AAAI Press.

Kaiyu Zheng, Deniz Bayazit, Rebecca Mathew, Ellie Pavlick, and Stefanie Tellex. 2020. Spatial language understanding for object search in partially observed cityscale environments.

A ProSPer composition

A.1 Automatic subset

All instances of each verb that occurred in the OANC and MASC corpora were included in the Automatic subset.

	Modality	OANC	MASC	Total
come	Spoken	5222	142	12650
	Written	6854	432	
go	Spoken	19337	427	28841
	Written	8471	606	
walk	Spoken	812	12	2098
	Written	1100	174	
arrive	Spoken	23	0	843
	Written	770	50	
drive	Spoken	1182	6	2953
	Written	1681	84	
Total		45452	1933	47385

Table 1: Summary of Automatic subset by source and modality

Source	*come*	*go*	*walk*	*arrive*	*drive*	Total
court transcript	40	115	3	0	1	159
debate transcript	56	136	5	0	3	200
face-to-face	591	1552	119	11	111	2384
telephone	4677	17961	697	12	1073	24420
blog	28	70	4	0	16	118
email	12	22	1	2	5	42
essays	22	25	0	0	9	56
ficlets	56	80	43	5	4	188
fiction	123	134	66	3	21	347
government	280	366	22	37	123	828
jokes	50	83	21	5	9	168
journal	4780	6739	440	338	921	13218
letters	171	26	18	3	8	226
movie script	29	55	42	10	0	136
newspaper	25	33	2	7	6	73
non-fiction	333	200	23	22	91	669
spam	23	26	0	2	0	51
technical	579	500	52	169	279	1579
travel guides	827	575	538	215	265	2490
twitter	25	66	2	2	8	103
Total	12650	28841	2098	843	2953	47385

Table 2: Summary of Automatic subset examples by genre

A.2 Annotated subset

The Annotated examples were selected using a quota system. A minimum of 15 examples were selected in each syntactic environment (25 for 'come'). A minimum of 20 examples of 'come' were selected for each main perspective-holder type, balanced across syntactic environments.

B ProSPer annotation schema

B.1 Perspective-holder categories for Annotated *come* items

Speaker: current speaker is the perspective-holder.

	None	*say*	*believe*	Quote	Other	Total
Speaker@ET	4	4	4	4	4	20
Speaker@UT	4	4	4	4	4	20
Protagonist	4	1	1	2	2	12
Listener	5	3	3	7	3	21
Attitude-holder	0	8	8	0	7	21
Home-base	1	1	1	1	1	5
Accompaniment	1	1	1	1	1	5
Other	6	3	3	6	3	21
Total	25	25	25	25	25	125

Table 3: Summary of *come* examples in Annotated subset by syntactic environment and perspective-holder

	None	*say*	*believe*	Quote	Other	Total
Speaker	4	3	3	4	3	17
Protagonist	3	0	0	1	1	5
Listener	3	3	3	5	2	16
Attitude-holder	0	5	5	0	4	14
3rd-person	3	2	2	3	3	13
Home-base	1	1	1	1	1	5
Accompaniment	1	1	1	1	1	5
Total	15	15	15	15	15	75

Table 4: Summary of non-*come* examples in Annotated subset by syntactic environment and subject

Example: *The sunlight falls into the room through the top windows. It's a big classroom, holds one fifty in a marble building. The oldest on campus. The pillars and doorways chiseled Grecian columns and archways. I would* ***come*** *to class even if I didn't like learning the stories and culture of southern Africa just to look at the sun glancing off the marble and dashing off the swaying bouncing leaves outside the windows. It's hot in here.*

Listener: the listener of the current speaker is the perspective-holder.

Example:

Attitude-holder: the subject of an attitude verb is the perspective-holder.

Example:

Protagonist: the main character of a story is the perspective-holder.

Example: *Walking home from Sudbury one night, he became aware of galloping horses, then he saw lights* ***coming*** *toward him and he stepped off the road to let the carriage pass . He saw distinctly one man or two in the box, driving; they had no heads, only hands and the lower part of the body. As he watched, the whole thing vanished.*

Theme: the person whose is the topic of the discourse is the perspective-holder.

Example: *Dante: Well, thank you for your patience, but we got to find the other Karen Anderson. It's pretty urgent. Karen: Oh. I hope for her sake there's no problem with her son. Dante: Actually, her son is in trouble, and we have reason to believe that he'll* ***come*** *to her for help.*

Empathy center: a person who the speaker cares strongly about (usually a family member) is the perspective-holder.

Example: *"We need your help." "She hasn't opened the blind in three days," he said. I raised my voice in case he couldn't hear me over the hurdy-gurdy music and the dull throb of the crowd. "Valerie is in labor." But he continued to stare at the window, black marble eyes filled with something like pain and hope, joy and terror and want. I imagined that death was the color of those eyes; I have often thought it since, but I yelled at him to* ***come*** *anyway, that Valerie was having a baby, that we needed him, that the baby was more important than this.*

Home-base: the motion is towards the home-base of the perspective-holder (i.e, house or workplace).

Example: *as i am new to this sport and am currently living in edinburgh it is easy for me to find some good routes to ride but i am* ***coming*** *home to nottingham soon for a couple of weeks and am very keen to ride whilst i am home. Could someone please suggest some routes around nottingham (if there are any) for me to ride my email is REDACTED.*

Accompaniment: the motion is alongside the perspective-holder.

Example: *Madagascar was one of those films that I really wanted to go and see at the cinema but nobody would* ***come*** *with me and my sister had already been to see it so I had to wait for the video.*

B.2 Syntactic environment categories for Annotated items

Top-level: verb appears in the matrix clause.

Example: *On Saturday I* ***went*** *with a friend and her husband to the Guggenheim Museum in Bilbao, a Basque city on the northern edge of Spain that has been revitalized by the stunning titanium and marble building by Frank Gehry. To call it a building does not do it justice. This is no ordinary museum. It is alive, a structure in motion, with titanium scales that move as the light washes over them.*

Speech verb: verb is in the scope of a speech verb like *say* or *tell*.

Example: *Mimi. I love your work. Found you through. Purl Bee. I visit your web site for inspiration and to "visit". I'm in California but daughters boyfriend is from Boston I've said if I ever **go** there I want to see your work or take a workshop.*

Thought verb: verb is in the scope of a thought verb like *think* or *believe*.

Example: *Stephanie: You saved a seat for me. Thank you. I thought I'd find you here. Nick: I'm not going, you know. They asked me to go, but I'm not going. Stephanie: You don't think I **drove** all the way down here to try and talk you into going, do you? Nick: If you came here for some Brooke bashing, you came to the wrong place. Let me tell you that right now. Stephanie: Actually, I came for a drink.*

Quotation: verb is part of a quotation.

Example: *Although he hasn't put all the pieces together yet, young Justin knows that words have power, too. "Once we stopped at a paint store with my mother," Laurie Bradley recalls. "She **went** in to get something while we waited in the car. Justin noticed the closed sign in the door of the store that the owner had forgotten to flip over. He said, "Mommy that's a c. That means kids aren't allowed. Don't you just hate that?""*

Other: verb is in the scope of a predicate that is not a speech or thought verb, such as *discover* or *learn*.

Example: *I see the mailman's truck go by and I know his routine so well; he'll be at my house in fifteen minutes. "I got ta go," I say, and standing, I take of my Thriftway apron. "I wanted to ask you to **go** to the movies," he says and I don't have time to think. I have fourteen minutes to check out with my boss and run home.*

B.3 Tense/aspect categories for Annotated and Automatic subsets

1: infinitive, 1st/2nd person habitual
come, go, walk, drive, arrive

2: progressive
coming, going, walking, driving, arriving

3: simple past
came, went, walked, drove, arrived

4: 3rd person habitual
comes, goes, walks, drives, arrives

5: past present
come, gone, walked, drove, arrived

C Human study

C.1 Data selection

Human performance was measured on the entire Annotated subset and two subsets of Automatic subset: the Random and NN Confounding subsets.

The Random subset was randomly sampled from the full Automatic subset; a handful of examples were excluded and resampled because they were deemed offensive or upsetting.

The NN Confounding subset consists of examples that proved challenging for neural network models. To select this subset, the items in the Automatic subset were ranked for each model by difficulty, and the top 100 most difficult items for each model were collated. These items were then re-ranked by how many lists they appeared on (how many models found them very difficult), and the top 100 were selected.

C.2 Participant instructions

The instructions to participants were as follows:

> You will see a passage of text where one of the words is missing (shown as a blank).
>
> You will be given several options for words that could fill in the blank. **Please select the word that you think is the best fit in the blank.** Don't worry about giving a perfect answer— just go with your first impression of the sentence.
>
> You can either click on the word to select it or use the number keys on your keyboard to select it: if you think the first word is the best fit, hit the "1" button on your keyboard.
>
> Most of the time, there will be only one word missing, but some times there will be two blanks. When that happens, you will have to choose a pair of words to fill in the blanks.
>
> **Note**: some sentences were automatically collected from online sources, including audio transcripts. **Because of this, you may notice spelling errors, incomplete sentences, speech hesitations ('uh', 'um') or weird punctuation.** Please try to ignore this.
>
> Here are a couple of practice items before the main experiment begins.

C.3 Practice items

Participants were given a chance to practice on the following items. They were not given feedback; this was just to acclimate them to the task format and response keys. The expected responses are in bold.

- One of the students in the class hadn't turned in his homework. Ms. Morris frowned and thought about what to do. After school, she called his mother to ___ her.
  (a) **tell** (b) fail

- I asked Harriet how the book was getting on and if Peter's suggestions had helped. Helen said, "Oh, yes, you write, don't you?" as if she'd never heard of her, and asked what the title was, so that she could get it from the library. Harriet said, quite gravely, "That is very kind of you, but do let me ___ you one– I am allowed six free copies, you know." First sign of temper, but I don't blame her.
  (a) **send** (b) buy
- "How about some breakfast?" asked Rupert, jerking a thumb back towards the tent. He fetched a box of wood chips from the back of the van and in a surprisingly short order had an admirable campfire crackling away in the churchyard. Next, he produced a coffeepot, a packet of bacon, a loaf of bread, and a couple of sharpened sticks to make a toast with. Nialla had even managed to find a jar of ___ somewhere in their baggage.
  (a) **marmalade** (b) almond butter

C.4 Data exclusion criteria

The data of participants who did not meet the language criteria, had less than 80% accuracy on the attention check fillers, or gave an incoherent response to a bot check question was excluded (the participants were, of course, still compensated). The attention check and bot check questions are given below (correct responses in bold).

C.4.1 Attention check items

- Davis handed Jasmine an large square box wrapped in festive paper and topped with an enormous pink bow. When she unwrapped it and opened the lid, she gasped. Inside was a beautiful crimson dress. The silk rustled as she lifted it carefully out of the box and held it up to the light. "It's perfect!" she declared. "How did you know that ___ is my favorite color?"
  (a) **red** (b) pink
- Polly's cat was a very finicky eater. At the pet store, she couldn't find the particular flavor of cat food that Percy liked: Seafood Surprise. After stopping by the grocery store, she got lunch ready: a tuna sandwich for ___ and a bowl of plain tuna for ___.
  (a) Percy/Polly (b) **Polly/Percy**
- Benjamin's favorite thing about where he lived was the desert. He could drive in it for hours, stopping his truck wherever he felt like it, and wait for night to fall. Lying in his truck bed, Benjamin could watch the ___ for hours, feeling utterly at peace.
  (a) fireworks (b) **stars**
- Betty had been working secretly on a beautiful patchwork quilt for months in her studio. When she gave it her mother at Christmas, Maia was amazed by its bright swirling colors. Since it had taken so long to make, Betty was very pleased that her mother liked the ___.
  (a) **blanket** (b) painting
- Throughout her writing, Anne had a unique talent for pushing literary boundaries and blending genres. She also tended to incorporate whatever strange new topic she had recently taken an interest in (the last one was Marilyn Monroe). Whatever she published, her readers knew to expect something ___.
  (a) **eccentric** (b) traditional
- Margaret celebrated her 80th birthday last month with unadulterated gaiety. During the party, she was often heard saying that the only thing she missed about being ___ was street hockey.
  (a) **young** (b) old
- Mr. Dougal hated catching cheaters, and Billy hated taking quizzes. This week, Billy was glad that he was sitting next to Sally, the best student in the class. After noticing how closely their answers matched, Mr. Dougal gave Billy an ___.
  (a) **F** (b) A
- Our mother, Harriet, to whom Buckshaw had been left by her uncle Tarquin de Luce, had died in a mountaineering accident in the Himalayas when I was a year old. Because she had left no ___, the vultures of His Majesty's Board of Inland Revenue had descended upon Father at once, and had been busily pecking out his liver ever since.
  (a) **will** (b) children
- Sheryl loved her son Clayton, but sometimes his forgetfulness drove her crazy. Thursdays were always extra busy at the bakery. Thursdays were also basketball nights, and Clayton had forgotten his uniform: again. Sheryl sighed. During her lunch break, ___ managed to sneak away and drop it off in the main office.
  (a) **she** (b) he
- Samantha was looking forward to her birthday party. It was going to be at the Cincinnati Zoo. Her dad was describing what kinds of animals there would be. He thought there ___ be any lions there. "That's ok. What I really want to see is a penguin."
  (a) would (b) **wouldn't**
- "So where are you taking me for brunch?" her mom asked. Abigail picked up her purse from the couch and said, "I was thinking we'd go to Green Bean. The French toast there is amazing!" "You remember that I'm allergic to nuts, right?" said her mom skeptically. "Yeah, but I don't think there'll be ___ in the French toast!"
  (a) some (b) **any**

C.4.2 Bot check questions

The bot check questions were designed to elicit free text responses from participants. Any participants who answered incoherently were excluded. We recognize that this is a subjective judgment. However, in practice, these participants almost always had low accuracy on the attention check items as well. Moreover, since we paid participants regardless of whether their data was ultimately included, we felt that it was acceptable to be overly strict.

- Imagine that you are back in elementary school. You've just made a new friend and invited him to come over to your house after school. How would you give him directions from your school to your house? (Please don't share any actual addresses or other identifying information; we're just interested in how people give directions.)
- What is your favorite insult and why?

We also excluded participants who gave incoherent answers to the demographic questions that were asked (for instance, "USA" in response to "What state do you currently live in?" or "None" in response to "How old are you?").

D Language model details

Model complexity and training data details are shown in Tables 5 and 6.

Family	Model	Layers	Attention heads	Embedding size
Transformer-XL	base	18	16	1024
BERT	base	12	12	768
	large	24	16	1024
RoBERTa	base	12	12	768
DistilBERT	base	6	12	768
GPT	base	12	12	768
GPT-2	base	12	12	768
	medium	24	16	1024
	large	36	20	1280
	extra-large	48	25	1600

Table 5: Model complexity

Family	Training data	# tokens (M)	Vocabulary
Transformer-XL	WikiText-103	100	26735
BERT	English Wikipedia, BooksCorpus	3300	30522
RoBERTa	English Wikipedia, BooksCorpus CC-News, Open Web Text, Stories	> 3300	50266
DistilBERT	English Wikipedia, BooksCorpus	3300	30522
GPT	BooksCorpus	800	40478
GPT-2	WebText	unknown	50257

Table 6: Model training data

E Detailed results

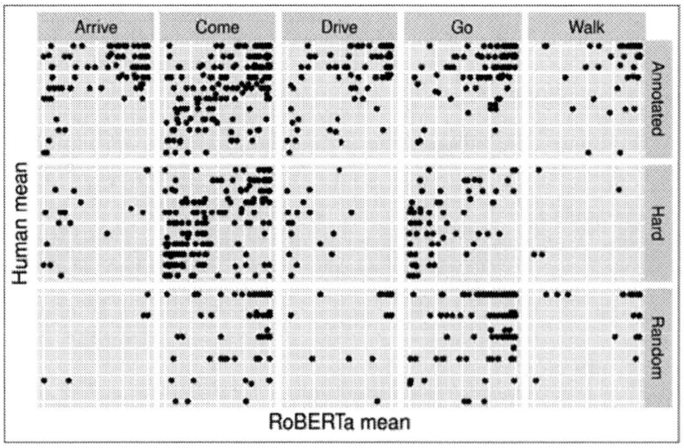

Figure 13: Human item means versus RoBERTa scores

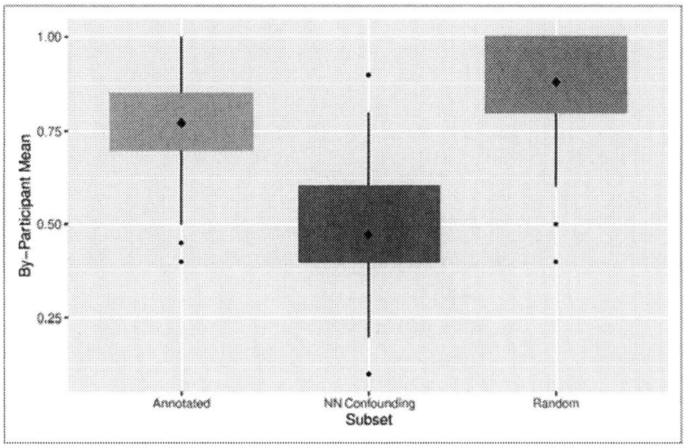

Figure 14: Participant means by subset, diamond=mean, interval=1st-3rd quartile

Condition	Overall mean	*come/go* mean	*walk/drive/ arrive* mean
Annotated	77.1%	73.8%	82.8%
Random	88.1%	87.2%	80.0%
NN Confounding	47.2%	48.3%	52.2%

Table 7: Human performance on ProSPer

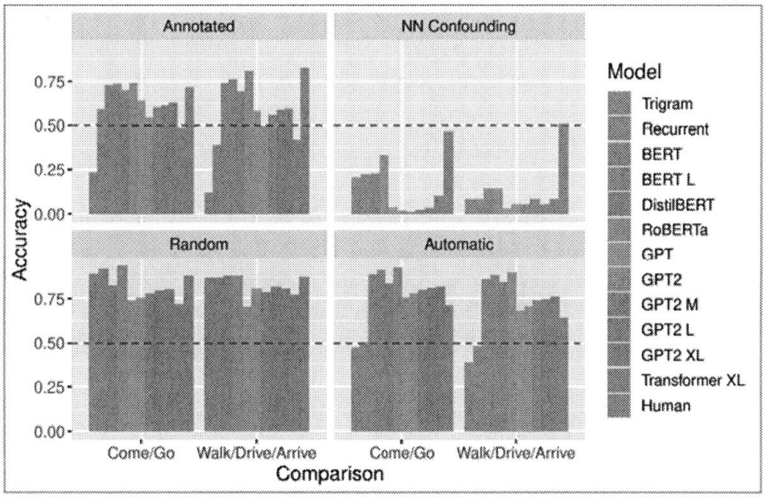

Figure 15: NN means by corpus

Family	Model	Corpus	Accuracy	*come/go* accuracy	*walk/drive/arrive* accuracy
random guess	-	-	20%	50%	50%
trigram	forward	Annotated	12.2%	23.3%	11.9%
		Automatic	40.7%	47.3%	38.6%
	backward	Annotated	27.5%	53.8%	27.0%
		Automatic	40.7%	46.9%	33.6%
RNN	wiki	Annotated	29.5%	59.0%	39.2%
		Automatic	21.6%	50.3%	48.2%

Table 8: Language model performance on ProSPer

Family	Model	Corpus	Accuracy	*come/go* accuracy	*walk/drive/arrive* accuracy
Transformer-XL	base	Annotated	28.0%	48.5%	42.0%
		Automatic	63.4%	71.2%	64.0%
		Random	-	71.7%	77.4%
		NN Confounding	-	9.8%	8.6%
BERT	base	Annotated	55.7%	72.8%	74.1%
		Automatic	85.0%	88.7%	86.3%
		Random	-	89.2%	86.9%
		NN Confounding	-	20.3%	8.6%
	large	Annotated	58.3%	73.4%	76.1%
		Automatic	88.2%	91.5%	88.7%
		Random	-	92.2%	86.9%
		NN Confounding	-	22.2%	8.6%
RoBERTa	base	Annotated	**63.5%**	**74.1%**	**80.9%**
		Automatic	**89.7%**	**93.0%**	**90.0%**
		Random	-	**93.9%**	**88.1%**
		NN Confounding	-	**33.2%**	**14.3%**
DistilBERT	base	Annotated	53.0%	69.8%	69.3%
		Automatic	78.7%	83.7%	84.6%
		Random	-	82.6%	**88.1%**
		NN Confounding	-	22.6%	**14.3%**
GPT	base	Annotated	39.8%	63.6%	58.0%
		Automatic	68.5%	75.6%	68.0%
		Random	-	73.8%	70.2%
		NN Confounding	-	3.8%	2.9%
GPT-2	base	Annotated	32.8%	54.4%	49.5%
		Automatic	71.7%	78.1%	70.6%
		Random	-	75.4%	81.0%
		NN Confounding	-	1.9%	5.7%
	medium	Annotated	38.5%	60.0%	55.6%
		Automatic	73.9%	80.0%	74.1%
		Random	-	77.9%	78.6%
		NN Confounding	-	1.1%	5.7%
	large	Annotated	40.2%	61.3%	58.7%
		Automatic	75.2%	81.1%	74.9%
		Random	-	79.8%	82.1%
		NN Confounding	-	2.3%	8.6%
	extra-large	Annotated	**41.0%**	**62.6%**	**59.4%**
		Automatic	**75.9%**	**81.8%**	**76.2%**
		Random	-	**80.6%**	**81.0%**
		NN Confounding	-	**3.4%**	**5.7%**

Table 9: Language model performance on ProSPer

F Detailed PCA results

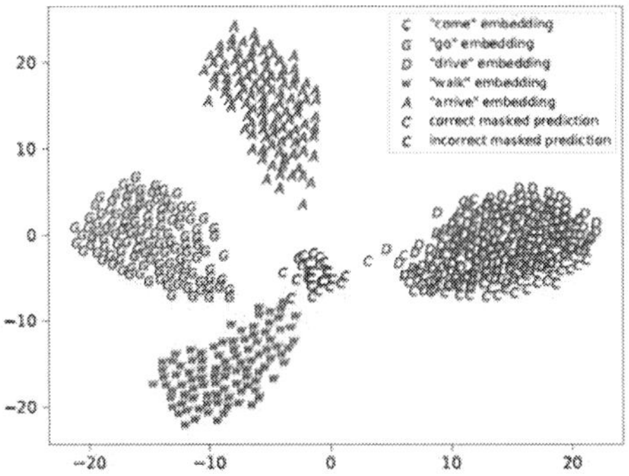

Figure 16: RoBERTa trained on Automatic subset and tested on masked "come" embeddings from Annotated corpus

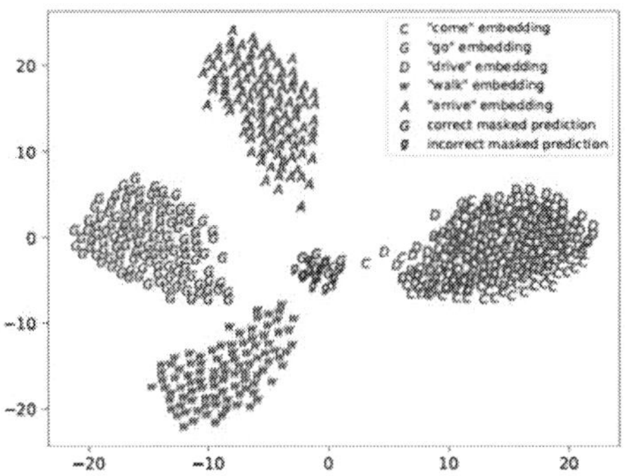

Figure 17: RoBERTa trained on Automatic subset and tested on masked "go" embeddings from Annotated corpus

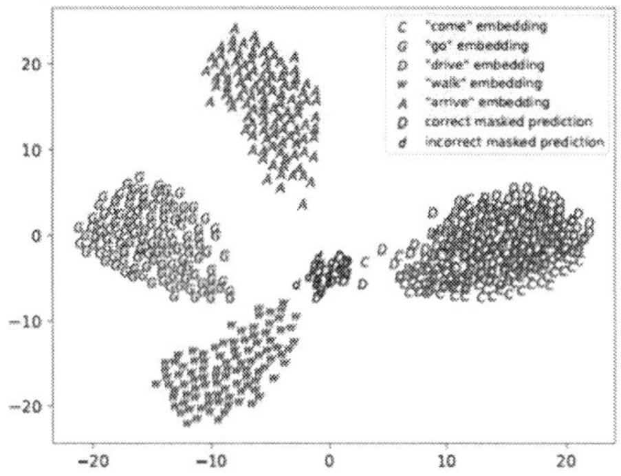

Figure 18: RoBERTa trained on Automatic subset and tested on masked "drive" embeddings from Annotated corpus

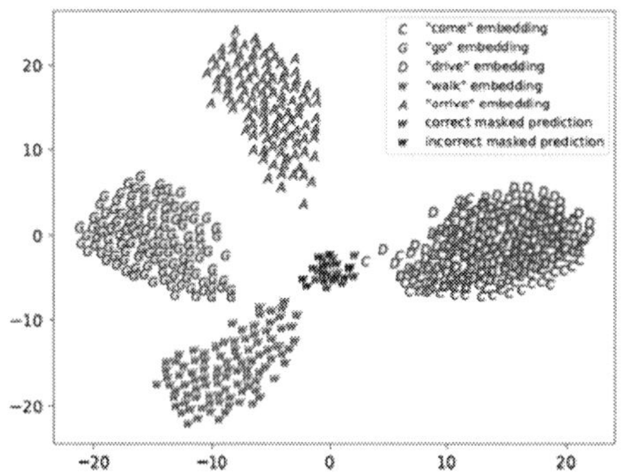

Figure 19: RoBERTa trained on Automatic subset and tested on masked "walk" embeddings from Annotated corpus

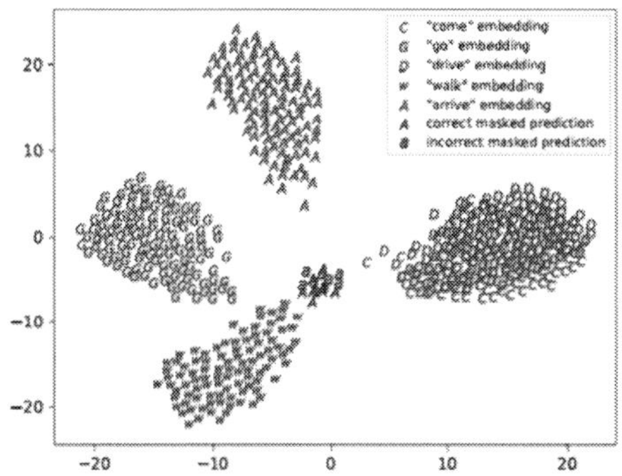

Figure 20: RoBERTa trained on Automatic subset and tested on masked "arrive" embeddings from Annotated corpus

G Regression results

G.1 Human models

Predictors of human scores were explored in a series of mixed-effects logistic regression models. Because our items were not controlled by condition, we do not include by-item random effects.

Fixed effects (n=12160)	Estimate	Std. Error	z value	Pr(>|z|)
(Intercept)	1.2	0.041	30.2	5.997e-200
come	-0.97	0.094	-10.4	3.2e-25
go	-0.51	0.1	-5.01	5.312e-07
drive	-0.57	0.1	-5.58	2.47e-08
arrive	-0.64	0.1	-6.3	3.071e-10
c.annotated.corpus	-0.59	0.075	-7.81	5.931e-15
n.annotated.corpus	-0.42	0.064	-6.56	5.502e-11
n.hard	-1.4	0.068	-20.9	1.177e-96
c.hard	-1.2	0.07	-17	6.038e-65

Table 10: Human performance by corpus and verb, corpus nested in *come*

Fixed effects (n=12160)	Estimate	Std. Error	z value	Pr(>|z|)
(Intercept)	1.2	0.054	22.5	3.324e-112
come	-1.2	0.15	-8.06	7.777e-16
go	-0.44	0.16	-2.8	0.005185
drive	-0.6	0.17	-3.46	0.0005442
arrive	-0.96	0.19	-5.11	3.271e-07
c.annotated.corpus	0.0031	0.055	0.0561	0.9553
c.spoken.corpus	-0.46	0.054	-8.64	5.677e-18
n.spoken.corpus	0.82	0.16	5.02	5.273e-07
n.annotated.corpus	0.65	0.076	8.6	8.02e-18
go:n.spoken.corpus	-1.4	0.3	-4.59	4.379e-06
go:n.annotated.corpus	-0.85	0.15	-5.75	9.016e-09
drive:n.spoken.corpus	-0.97	0.34	-2.9	0.003784
drive:n.annotated.corpus	-0.56	0.16	-3.63	0.0002838
arrive:n.spoken.corpus	-0.56	0.37	-1.51	0.1316
arrive:n.annotated.corpus	0.011	0.17	0.0621	0.9505

Table 11: Human performance by modality and verb, modality nested in *come* and Written treated as baseline

Fixed effects (n=6080)	Estimate	Std. Error	z value	Pr(>|z|)
(Intercept)	1.5	0.042	35.5	2.196e-276
come	-1.3	0.12	-10.5	7.954e-26
attitude.b	-0.059	0.15	-0.383	0.7016
listener.b	0.44	0.18	2.48	0.01325
anchor.b	-0.062	0.16	-0.389	0.6972
other.b	-0.32	0.13	-2.47	0.01354
go	-0.62	0.12	-5.3	1.141e-07
drive	-0.72	0.12	-6.21	5.212e-10
arrive	-0.78	0.11	-6.95	3.668e-12

Table 12: Human performance by perspective holder, Speaker treated as baseline

Fixed effects (n=12160)	Estimate	Std. Error	z value	Pr(>|z|)
(Intercept)	1.7	18	0.0937	0.9254
c.hard.spoken.corpus	-1.3	0.091	-13.8	2.276e-43
c.hard.written.corpus	-0.88	0.11	-8.07	7.115e-16
c.random.spoken.corpus	0.55	0.16	3.5	0.0004685
c.annotated.mod.corpus	-0.44	0.09	-4.9	9.687e-07
n.hard.spoken.corpus	3.5	1.4e+02	0.0242	0.9807
n.hard.written.corpus	-1.5	0.18	-7.9	2.812e-15
n.random.spoken.corpus	0.72	0.31	2.34	0.01953
n.annotated.mod.corpus	0.12	0.14	0.87	0.3845
come	-2.7	72	-0.0377	0.97
go	-2.3	72	-0.0321	0.9744
drive	-2.3	72	-0.0316	0.9748
arrive	-2.5	72	-0.035	0.972
n.hard.spoken.corpus:go	-9.7	2.9e+02	-0.0338	0.973
n.hard.spoken.corpus:drive	-9.5	2.9e+02	-0.0332	0.9735
n.hard.spoken.corpus:arrive	-7.8	2.9e+02	-0.0271	0.9784
n.hard.written.corpus:go	-0.16	0.34	-0.467	0.6403
n.hard.written.corpus:drive	-0.29	0.37	-0.768	0.4426
n.hard.written.corpus:arrive	0.66	0.43	1.54	0.1239
n.random.spoken.corpus:go	-1.1	0.41	-2.66	0.007775
n.random.spoken.corpus:drive	-0.8	0.51	-1.55	0.1202
n.annotated.mod.corpus:go	-1	0.24	-4.27	1.968e-05
n.annotated.mod.corpus:drive	-1.1	0.28	-3.79	0.0001536
n.annotated.mod.corpus:arrive	0.023	0.35	0.0653	0.9479

Table 13: Human performance by corpus, modality and verb, corpus+modality nested in *come* and Written Random treated as baseline

Fixed effects (n=6080)	Estimate	Std. Error	z value	Pr(>|z|)
(Intercept)	1.5	0.041	37	2.917e-300
come	-1.3	0.11	-12.3	5.884e-35
c.believe	0.095	0.12	0.787	0.4312
c.say	0.013	0.13	0.103	0.918
c.quote	0.11	0.13	0.823	0.4103
c.none	-0.36	0.12	-3.04	0.00239
go	-0.64	0.12	-5.21	1.85e-07
drive	-0.73	0.12	-6.03	1.665e-09
arrive	-0.77	0.12	-6.44	1.16e-10
n.believe	0.21	0.14	1.49	0.1363
n.say	0.12	0.15	0.801	0.4231
n.quote	0.28	0.15	1.88	0.06046
n.none	0.1	0.13	0.814	0.4159
go:n.believe	0.031	0.29	0.108	0.9139
go:n.say	-0.65	0.3	-2.17	0.0297
go:n.quote	-0.14	0.31	-0.434	0.664
go:n.none	0.22	0.27	0.831	0.4058
drive:n.believe	-0.33	0.28	-1.19	0.2354
drive:n.say	-0.091	0.31	-0.294	0.7687
drive:n.quote	-0.29	0.31	-0.931	0.3517
drive:n.none	0.16	0.26	0.609	0.5426
arrive:n.believe	0.32	0.3	1.06	0.2879
arrive:n.say	-0.5	0.3	-1.66	0.09612
arrive:n.quote	-0.56	0.31	-1.81	0.07074
arrive:n.none	0.045	0.26	0.174	0.8617

Table 14: Human performance by syntactic environment and verb, environment nested in *come* and Other treated as baseline

Fixed effects (n=6080)	Estimate	Std. Error	z value	Pr(>|z|)
(Intercept)	1.5	0.044	34.9	4.197e-266
come	-1.3	0.13	-10.1	5.596e-24
c.believe	0.31	0.25	1.25	0.2112
c.say	0.7	0.24	2.94	0.003318
c.quote	0.46	0.24	1.92	0.05508
c.none	-0.29	0.22	-1.31	0.1913
listener.b	0.27	0.19	1.41	0.1572
anchor.b	-0.1	0.17	-0.612	0.5405
other.b	-0.33	0.14	-2.42	0.01554
attitude.b	-0.1	0.2	-0.513	0.6077
go	-0.65	0.12	-5.23	1.654e-07
drive	-0.74	0.12	-6.06	1.325e-09
arrive	-0.78	0.12	-6.46	1.016e-10
n.believe	0.21	0.14	1.5	0.1339
n.say	0.12	0.15	0.816	0.4148
n.quote	0.28	0.15	1.86	0.06291
n.none	0.1	0.13	0.804	0.4217
c.believe:listener.b	-1.3	0.5	-2.52	0.0119
c.believe:anchor.b	0.67	0.41	1.63	0.1036
c.believe:other.b	-0.66	0.36	-1.84	0.06568
c.say:listener.b	-2.1	0.56	-3.84	0.0001251
c.say:anchor.b	0.76	0.46	1.64	0.09999
c.say:other.b	-1.4	0.36	-3.9	9.477e-05
c.quote:listener.b	-0.45	0.48	-0.935	0.3498
c.quote:anchor.b	0.46	0.46	1	0.3157
c.quote:other.b	-1.4	0.35	-3.96	7.405e-05
c.none:listener.b	-0.46	0.48	-0.958	0.3382
c.none:anchor.b	0.98	0.42	2.33	0.01977
c.none:other.b	-0.41	0.31	-1.34	0.1792
c.believe:attitude.b	0.015	0.34	0.0444	0.9646
c.say:attitude.b	-1.1	0.35	-3.22	0.001268
go:n.believe	0.024	0.29	0.085	0.9323
go:n.say	-0.65	0.3	-2.18	0.02892
go:n.quote	-0.14	0.31	-0.436	0.6629
go:n.none	0.22	0.27	0.822	0.411
drive:n.believe	-0.34	0.28	-1.21	0.2255
drive:n.say	-0.098	0.31	-0.316	0.7517
drive:n.quote	-0.29	0.31	-0.933	0.3506
drive:n.none	0.16	0.27	0.592	0.5542
arrive:n.believe	0.31	0.31	1.01	0.3102
arrive:n.say	-0.51	0.3	-1.69	0.0909
arrive:n.quote	-0.56	0.31	-1.83	0.06706
arrive:n.none	0.041	0.26	0.16	0.8727

Table 15: Human performance by perspective holder and syntactic environment, perspectives compared to group mean

Fixed effects (n=6080)	Estimate	Std. Error	z value	Pr(>|z|)
(Intercept)	1.5	0.042	36.7	2.444e-294
come	-1.3	0.12	-10.9	6.689e-28
c.believe	0.06	0.14	0.433	0.6648
c.say	-0.084	0.15	-0.544	0.5867
c.quote	0.28	0.19	1.48	0.1389
c.none	-0.076	0.17	-0.436	0.6626
listener	0.3	0.18	1.72	0.08627
speaker	0.084	0.14	0.612	0.5405
other	-0.18	0.14	-1.32	0.1875
attitude	0.29	0.21	1.4	0.1612
go	-0.65	0.12	-5.23	1.654e-07
drive	-0.74	0.12	-6.06	1.325e-09
arrive	-0.78	0.12	-6.46	1.016e-10
n.believe	0.21	0.14	1.5	0.1339
n.say	0.12	0.15	0.815	0.4148
n.quote	0.28	0.15	1.86	0.06292
n.none	0.1	0.13	0.804	0.4217
c.believe:listener	-1.5	0.43	-3.56	0.0003661
c.believe:speaker	-0.53	0.33	-1.63	0.1036
c.believe:other	-1.1	0.34	-3.16	0.001604
c.say:listener	-2.3	0.51	-4.53	5.971e-06
c.say:speaker	-0.6	0.37	-1.64	0.1
c.say:other	-1.7	0.38	-4.52	6.25e-06
c.quote:listener	-0.73	0.46	-1.6	0.1102
c.quote:speaker	-0.37	0.37	-1	0.3157
c.quote:other	-1.5	0.37	-3.97	7.175e-05
c.none:listener	-1.1	0.44	-2.62	0.008723
c.none:speaker	-0.78	0.34	-2.33	0.01977
c.none:other	-1.1	0.33	-3.41	0.0006576
c.believe:attitude	-0.52	0.32	-1.62	0.1053
c.say:attitude	-1.5	0.38	-3.98	6.748e-05
go:n.believe	0.024	0.29	0.085	0.9323
go:n.say	-0.65	0.3	-2.18	0.02892
go:n.quote	-0.14	0.31	-0.436	0.6629
go:n.none	0.22	0.27	0.822	0.411
drive:n.believe	-0.34	0.28	-1.21	0.2255
drive:n.say	-0.098	0.31	-0.316	0.7517
drive:n.quote	-0.29	0.31	-0.933	0.3507
drive:n.none	0.16	0.27	0.592	0.5542
arrive:n.believe	0.31	0.31	1.01	0.3102
arrive:n.say	-0.51	0.3	-1.69	0.0909
arrive:n.quote	-0.56	0.31	-1.83	0.06706
arrive:n.none	0.041	0.26	0.16	0.8727

Table 16: Human performance by perspective holder and syntactic environment, perspective compared to group mean

G.2 RoBERTa models

Predictors of RoBERTa scores were explored in a series of regression models.

Fixed effects (n=1495)	Estimate	Std. Error	z value	Pr(>|z|)
(Intercept)	0.64	0.02	32.3	9.901e-174
come	-0.043	0.055	-0.777	0.4375
c.annotated.corpus	-0.14	0.026	-5.23	1.938e-07
c.hard	-0.38	0.026	-14.6	2.428e-45
go	0.025	0.056	0.438	0.6614
drive	-0.085	0.061	-1.39	0.1641
arrive	-0.097	0.07	-1.38	0.1679
n.annotated.corpus	-0.0061	0.03	-0.206	0.8371
n.hard	-0.43	0.059	-7.2	9.836e-13
go:n.annotated.corpus	-0.089	0.048	-1.85	0.06428
go:n.hard	-0.0022	0.11	-0.0207	0.9835
drive:n.annotated.corpus	-0.14	0.055	-2.54	0.01134
drive:n.hard	-0.14	0.12	-1.16	0.2478
arrive:n.annotated.corpus	-0.075	0.084	-0.888	0.3749
arrive:n.hard	0.044	0.14	0.321	0.7484

Table 17: RoBERTa performance by corpus and verb, corpus nested in *come*

Fixed effects (n=1495)	Estimate	Std. Error	z value	Pr(>|z|)
(Intercept)	0.69	0.025	28.1	3.324e-139
come	-0.13	0.052	-2.52	0.01168
c.spoken.corpus	-0.15	0.03	-5.12	3.401e-07
c.annotated.mod.corpus	-0.026	0.037	-0.712	0.4768
n.spoken.corpus	0.022	0.055	0.396	0.692
n.annotated.mod.corpus	0.14	0.044	3.15	0.001693
go	0.041	0.052	0.786	0.4322
drive	-0.068	0.061	-1.11	0.2652
arrive	-0.27	0.089	-3.02	0.002565
n.spoken.corpus:go	-0.046	0.083	-0.554	0.5795
n.spoken.corpus:drive	-0.04	0.1	-0.394	0.6939
n.spoken.corpus:arrive	-0.12	0.16	-0.734	0.4628
n.annotated.mod.corpus:go	-0.13	0.084	-1.52	0.1276
n.annotated.mod.corpus:drive	-0.11	0.089	-1.2	0.2316
n.annotated.mod.corpus:arrive	0.018	0.1	0.175	0.8609

Table 18: RoBERTa performance by modality and verb, Written treated as baseline and modality nested in *come*

Fixed effects (n=1495)	Estimate	Std. Error	z value	Pr(>|z|)
(Intercept)	0.6	0.026	22.8	1.529e-98
come	0.032	0.074	0.439	0.6605
c.hard.spoken.corpus	-0.45	0.038	-11.9	3.209e-31
c.hard.written.corpus	-0.37	0.052	-7.03	3.223e-12
c.random.spoken.corpus	0.061	0.047	1.29	0.1962
c.annotated.mod.corpus	-0.14	0.037	-3.89	0.000106
n.hard.spoken.corpus	-0.57	0.13	-4.24	2.344e-05
n.hard.written.corpus	-0.47	0.085	-5.57	3e-08
n.random.spoken.corpus	0.023	0.072	0.314	0.7532
n.annotated.mod.corpus	0.0046	0.046	0.101	0.9194
go	0.068	0.074	0.913	0.3615
drive	-0.055	0.084	-0.654	0.5133
arrive	-0.028	0.096	-0.297	0.7666
n.hard.spoken.corpus:go	0.16	0.25	0.621	0.5345
n.hard.spoken.corpus:drive	-0.079	0.28	-0.277	0.7819
n.hard.spoken.corpus:arrive	0.26	0.29	0.876	0.3814
n.hard.written.corpus:go	-0.058	0.16	-0.353	0.724
n.hard.written.corpus:drive	-0.25	0.17	-1.44	0.1496
n.hard.written.corpus:arrive	-0.042	0.19	-0.219	0.8263
n.random.spoken.corpus:go	-0.0073	0.096	-0.0757	0.9396
n.random.spoken.corpus:drive	-0.084	0.12	-0.714	0.4756
n.annotated.mod.corpus:go	-0.11	0.081	-1.34	0.1817
n.annotated.mod.corpus:drive	-0.2	0.088	-2.29	0.02195
n.annotated.mod.corpus:arrive	-0.11	0.11	-0.968	0.3334

Table 19: RoBERTa performance by corpus, modality, and verb, Written Random corpus treated as baseline and corpus+modality nested in nested in *come*

Fixed effects (n=1495)	Estimate	Std. Error	z value	Pr(>|z|)
(Intercept)	0.79	0.017	45.2	1.349e-191
come	-0.24	0.042	-5.72	1.72e-08
c.believe	0.14	0.077	1.83	0.06844
c.say	0.099	0.08	1.23	0.2196
c.other_e	0.12	0.077	1.5	0.1348
c.none	0.022	0.078	0.279	0.7806
go	-0.078	0.046	-1.69	0.09241
drive	-0.16	0.047	-3.33	0.0009359
arrive	-0.2	0.048	-4.09	4.859e-05
n.believe	-0.0023	0.057	-0.0395	0.9685
n.say	-0.022	0.058	-0.374	0.7084
n.other_e	-0.011	0.058	-0.183	0.8548
n.none	0.024	0.054	0.439	0.6607
go:n.believe	0.018	0.12	0.153	0.8784
go:n.say	-0.033	0.12	-0.279	0.7806
go:n.other_e	0.00015	0.12	0.00124	0.999
go:n.none	0.072	0.11	0.646	0.5184
drive:n.believe	0.017	0.12	0.144	0.8852
drive:n.say	0.0084	0.12	0.0678	0.9459
drive:n.other_e	0.076	0.13	0.606	0.5449
drive:n.none	0.11	0.12	0.935	0.3501
arrive:n.believe	0.13	0.13	1.04	0.2995
arrive:n.say	-0.062	0.13	-0.494	0.6218
arrive:n.other_e	0.094	0.13	0.747	0.4551
arrive:n.none	0.17	0.12	1.45	0.1462

Table 20: RoBERTa performance by syntactic environment and verb, environment nested in *come*

Fixed effects (n=600)	Estimate	Std. Error	z value	Pr(>|z|)
(Intercept)	0.8	0.019	41.1	2.389e-175
come	-0.2	0.055	-3.69	0.000247
attitude.b	-0.035	0.092	-0.381	0.7033
listener.b	-0.062	0.098	-0.631	0.5285
anchor.b	-0.16	0.097	-1.69	0.0915
other.b	-0.015	0.079	-0.197	0.8441
go	-0.074	0.046	-1.63	0.1044
drive	-0.16	0.047	-3.32	0.0009536
arrive	-0.19	0.048	-4.07	5.382e-05

Table 21: RoBERTa performance by perspective-holder, Speaker treated as baseline and perspective nested in *come*

Fixed effects (n=1495)	Estimate	Std. Error	z value	Pr(>|z|)
(Intercept)	0.8	0.019	41.1	1.233e-170
come	-0.2	0.055	-3.69	0.0002461
c.believe	-1.6e-15	0.14	-1.11e-14	1
c.say	-0.011	0.13	-0.0852	0.9321
c.quote	-0.13	0.14	-0.925	0.3553
c.none	-0.24	0.14	-1.73	0.08406
listener.b	-0.12	0.11	-1.12	0.2616
anchor.b	-0.2	0.098	-2.08	0.03781
other.b	-0.017	0.081	-0.21	0.8341
attitude.b	-0.093	0.12	-0.776	0.4383
go	-0.078	0.046	-1.71	0.0884
drive	-0.16	0.047	-3.37	0.0008086
arrive	-0.2	0.048	-4.15	3.927e-05
n.believe	0.0084	0.058	0.147	0.8833
n.say	-0.011	0.058	-0.188	0.8507
n.quote	0.011	0.058	0.185	0.853
n.none	0.034	0.054	0.635	0.5259
c.believe:listener.b	-0.44	0.26	-1.69	0.09253
c.believe:anchor.b	0.2	0.25	0.814	0.4158
c.believe:other.b	0.33	0.21	1.58	0.1155
c.say:listener.b	-0.23	0.3	-0.756	0.45
c.say:anchor.b	0.25	0.26	0.985	0.3251
c.say:other.b	0.12	0.2	0.569	0.5696
c.quote:listener.b	0.11	0.23	0.493	0.6222
c.quote:anchor.b	-0.069	0.27	-0.257	0.7975
c.quote:other.b	-0.036	0.2	-0.175	0.8614
c.none:listener.b	0.08	0.25	0.323	0.7465
c.none:anchor.b	1.2e-15	0.26	4.61e-15	1
c.none:other.b	0.39	0.18	2.08	0.0376
c.believe:attitude.b	-0.086	0.2	-0.433	0.665
c.say:attitude.b	-0.29	0.21	-1.37	0.171
go:n.believe	0.018	0.12	0.148	0.8822
go:n.say	-0.033	0.12	-0.274	0.7845
go:n.quote	-0.00015	0.12	-0.00126	0.999
go:n.none	0.072	0.11	0.627	0.5306
drive:n.believe	-0.059	0.12	-0.49	0.6245
drive:n.say	-0.068	0.12	-0.545	0.5863
drive:n.quote	-0.076	0.12	-0.613	0.5398
drive:n.none	0.032	0.12	0.274	0.7842
arrive:n.believe	0.039	0.13	0.314	0.7533
arrive:n.say	-0.16	0.12	-1.27	0.2041
arrive:n.quote	-0.094	0.12	-0.757	0.4494
arrive:n.none	0.076	0.11	0.67	0.5032

Table 22: RoBERTa performance by syntactic environment and perspective-holder, Speaker treated as baseline and environment and perspective nested in *come*

Fixed effects (n=1495)	Estimate	Std. Error	z value	Pr(>|z|)
(Intercept)	0.78	0.018	43.5	2.628e-181
come	-0.28	0.046	-5.95	4.771e-09
c.believe	0.0014	0.077	0.0186	0.9852
c.say	-0.041	0.087	-0.47	0.6383
c.quote	-0.14	0.11	-1.34	0.1803
c.none	-0.15	0.1	-1.43	0.1539
listener	0.068	0.098	0.699	0.4849
speaker	0.16	0.079	2.08	0.03781
other	0.15	0.081	1.84	0.06583
attitude	0.075	0.12	0.605	0.5453
go	-0.078	0.046	-1.71	0.0884
drive	-0.16	0.047	-3.37	0.0008086
arrive	-0.2	0.048	-4.15	3.927e-05
n.believe	0.0084	0.058	0.147	0.8833
n.say	-0.011	0.058	-0.188	0.8507
n.quote	0.011	0.058	0.185	0.853
n.none	0.034	0.054	0.635	0.5259
c.believe:listener	-0.51	0.24	-2.18	0.03
c.believe:speaker	-0.16	0.2	-0.814	0.4158
c.believe:other	0.11	0.2	0.531	0.5957
c.say:listener	-0.38	0.28	-1.38	0.1675
c.say:speaker	-0.2	0.2	-0.985	0.3251
c.say:other	-0.11	0.21	-0.508	0.6118
c.quote:listener	0.15	0.23	0.625	0.5324
c.quote:speaker	0.055	0.22	0.257	0.7975
c.quote:other	0.027	0.22	0.122	0.9027
c.none:listener	0.064	0.24	0.268	0.7889
c.none:speaker	-5.3e-16	0.21	-2.56e-15	1
c.none:other	0.31	0.2	1.55	0.1229
c.believe:attitude	-0.23	0.19	-1.19	0.2348
c.say:attitude	-0.43	0.22	-1.99	0.0468
go:n.believe	0.018	0.12	0.148	0.8822
go:n.say	-0.033	0.12	-0.274	0.7845
go:n.quote	-0.00015	0.12	-0.00126	0.999
go:n.none	0.072	0.11	0.627	0.5306
drive:n.believe	-0.059	0.12	-0.49	0.6245
drive:n.say	-0.068	0.12	-0.545	0.5863
drive:n.quote	-0.076	0.12	-0.613	0.5398
drive:n.none	0.032	0.12	0.274	0.7842
arrive:n.believe	0.039	0.13	0.314	0.7533
arrive:n.say	-0.16	0.12	-1.27	0.2041
arrive:n.quote	-0.094	0.12	-0.757	0.4494
arrive:n.none	0.076	0.11	0.67	0.5032

Table 23: RoBERTa performance by syntactic environment and perspective-holder, perspectives nested in nested in *come* and compared to group mean

G.3 Combined models

Differences between RoBERTa and human scores were explored in a series of regression models.

Fixed effects (n=13632)	Estimate	Std. Error	z value	Pr(>|z|)
(Intercept)	0.76	0.0047	162	0
come	-0.23	0.012	-19.8	7.796e-86
c.roberta	0.015	0.02	0.787	0.431
n.roberta	-0.0033	0.02	-0.162	0.8716
go	-0.067	0.012	-5.59	2.357e-08
drive	-0.092	0.014	-6.61	3.984e-11
arrive	-0.11	0.015	-7.46	8.886e-14
n.roberta:go	0.017	0.037	0.472	0.6371
n.roberta:drive	-0.053	0.043	-1.21	0.2249
n.roberta:arrive	-0.094	0.047	-1.99	0.04693

Table 24: RoBERTa and human performance by verb, model nested in *come*

Fixed effects (n=13632)	Estimate	Std. Error	z value	Pr(>|z|)
(Intercept)	0.71	0.0085	83.5	0
come	-0.11	0.02	-5.42	6.109e-08
c.roberta	-0.017	0.019	-0.933	0.3507
c.annotated.corpus	-0.11	0.011	-9.92	4.268e-23
c.hard	-0.26	0.01	-24.9	1.708e-133
go	-0.033	0.021	-1.6	0.1107
drive	-0.046	0.023	-2	0.04577
arrive	-0.12	0.031	-3.74	0.0001831
n.roberta	-0.087	0.036	-2.43	0.01496
n.annotated.corpus	0.0028	0.015	0.184	0.8539
n.hard	-0.21	0.024	-8.75	2.469e-18
c.roberta:c.annotated.corpus	0.039	0.026	1.47	0.1411
go:n.roberta	0.055	0.066	0.829	0.4072
drive:n.roberta	-0.042	0.072	-0.583	0.5597
arrive:n.roberta	0.016	0.084	0.189	0.85
go:n.annotated.corpus	-0.05	0.021	-2.33	0.01999
go:n.hard	-0.029	0.04	-0.715	0.4744
drive:n.annotated.corpus	-0.064	0.025	-2.52	0.01178
drive:n.hard	-0.042	0.045	-0.937	0.3489
arrive:n.annotated.corpus	0.085	0.048	1.77	0.07666
arrive:n.hard	0.12	0.061	1.98	0.04805
n.roberta:n.annotated.corpus	-0.0061	0.037	-0.167	0.8675
n.roberta:n.hard	-0.22	0.07	-3.13	0.001759
go:n.roberta:n.annotated.corpus	-0.045	0.058	-0.771	0.4404
go:n.roberta:n.hard	0.027	0.13	0.207	0.8358
drive:n.roberta:n.annotated.corpus	-0.081	0.066	-1.22	0.2238
drive:n.roberta:n.hard	-0.095	0.14	-0.681	0.4961
arrive:n.roberta:n.annotated.corpus	-0.17	0.11	-1.56	0.1178
arrive:n.roberta:n.hard	-0.076	0.17	-0.462	0.644

Table 25: RoBERTa and human performance by verb and corpus, model nested in *come*

Fixed effects (n=13632)	Estimate	Std. Error	z value	Pr(>|z|)
(Intercept)	0.72	0.011	64.9	0
come	-0.13	0.027	-4.76	1.922e-06
c.roberta	-0.017	0.021	-0.8	0.4236
c.hard.spoken.corpus	-0.28	0.016	-17.5	1.089e-67
c.hard.written.corpus	-0.19	0.02	-9.36	9.063e-21
c.random.spoken.corpus	0.076	0.023	3.31	0.0009316
c.annotated.mod.corpus	-0.087	0.016	-5.55	2.925e-08
n.roberta	-0.16	0.048	-3.27	0.001076
n.hard.spoken.corpus	-0.042	0.05	-0.847	0.3972
n.hard.written.corpus	-0.28	0.034	-8.24	1.847e-16
n.random.spoken.corpus	0.069	0.035	1.98	0.04733
n.annotated.mod.corpus	0.028	0.023	1.26	0.2089
go	-0.066	0.027	-2.42	0.01542
drive	-0.075	0.031	-2.42	0.01559
arrive	-0.12	0.041	-2.97	0.003021
c.roberta:c.hard.spoken.corpus	-0.17	0.045	-3.76	0.0001689
c.roberta:c.hard.written.corpus	-0.18	0.061	-2.89	0.003908
c.roberta:c.random.spoken.corpus	-0.015	0.057	-0.26	0.7951
c.roberta:c.annotated.mod.corpus	-0.052	0.044	-1.19	0.2343
n.roberta:n.hard.spoken.corpus	-0.53	0.16	-3.35	0.0008145
n.roberta:n.hard.written.corpus	-0.2	0.1	-1.96	0.05016
n.roberta:n.random.spoken.corpus	-0.046	0.087	-0.53	0.5961
n.roberta:n.annotated.mod.corpus	-0.02	0.056	-0.365	0.7149
n.roberta:go	0.13	0.087	1.52	0.1297
n.roberta:drive	0.019	0.098	0.193	0.847
n.roberta:arrive	0.091	0.11	0.795	0.4267
n.hard.spoken.corpus:go	-0.38	0.091	-4.22	2.411e-05
n.hard.spoken.corpus:drive	-0.35	0.1	-3.41	0.0006463
n.hard.spoken.corpus:arrive	-0.049	0.11	-0.445	0.6567
n.hard.written.corpus:go	0.018	0.062	0.293	0.7696
n.hard.written.corpus:drive	-0.015	0.065	-0.224	0.8224
n.hard.written.corpus:arrive	0.13	0.082	1.55	0.1221
n.random.spoken.corpus:go	-0.1	0.046	-2.26	0.02414
n.random.spoken.corpus:drive	-0.081	0.059	-1.39	0.164
n.annotated.mod.corpus:go	-0.12	0.037	-3.25	0.001149
n.annotated.mod.corpus:drive	-0.13	0.041	-3.08	0.002064
n.annotated.mod.corpus:arrive	0.05	0.063	0.792	0.4286
n.roberta:n.hard.spoken.corpus:go	0.54	0.29	1.84	0.06537
n.roberta:n.hard.spoken.corpus:drive	0.27	0.33	0.824	0.4097
n.roberta:n.hard.spoken.corpus:arrive	0.31	0.35	0.887	0.3752
n.roberta:n.hard.written.corpus:go	-0.076	0.19	-0.394	0.6937
n.roberta:n.hard.written.corpus:drive	-0.23	0.2	-1.15	0.2497
n.roberta:n.hard.written.corpus:arrive	-0.17	0.23	-0.74	0.459
n.roberta:n.random.spoken.corpus:go	0.097	0.12	0.831	0.406
n.roberta:n.random.spoken.corpus:drive	-0.0026	0.14	-0.018	0.9857
n.roberta:n.annotated.mod.corpus:go	0.0045	0.098	0.0455	0.9637
n.roberta:n.annotated.mod.corpus:drive	-0.084	0.11	-0.786	0.4321
n.roberta:n.annotated.mod.corpus:arrive	-0.17	0.14	-1.18	0.24

Table 26: RoBERTa and human performance by modality, corpus, and verb, model nested in *come* and Written Random treated as baseline

Fixed effects (n=6657)	Estimate	Std. Error	z value	Pr(>|z|)
(Intercept)	0.79	0.0055	144	0
come	-0.2	0.013	-14.7	2.731e-48
c.roberta	0.0021	0.031	0.0682	0.9456
c.believe	0.02	0.023	0.87	0.3846
c.say	0.0074	0.024	0.31	0.7564
c.quote	0.024	0.024	0.999	0.3178
c.none	-0.079	0.023	-3.46	0.0005408
n.roberta	0.013	0.024	0.562	0.5742
go	-0.068	0.015	-4.66	3.232e-06
drive	-0.088	0.015	-5.9	3.846e-09
arrive	-0.09	0.015	-5.85	5.103e-09
n.believe	0.022	0.019	1.16	0.2455
n.say	0.0032	0.019	0.172	0.8637
n.quote	0.027	0.019	1.43	0.1539
n.none	0.015	0.017	0.84	0.4011
c.roberta:c.believe	0.019	0.076	0.254	0.7994
c.roberta:c.say	-0.025	0.079	-0.312	0.7552
c.roberta:c.quote	-0.14	0.081	-1.73	0.08389
c.roberta:c.none	-0.015	0.077	-0.195	0.8457
n.roberta:go	-0.02	0.049	-0.419	0.6751
n.roberta:drive	-0.08	0.05	-1.6	0.1087
n.roberta:arrive	-0.12	0.051	-2.34	0.01912
n.roberta:n.believe	-0.034	0.062	-0.557	0.5772
n.roberta:n.say	-0.035	0.062	-0.569	0.5691
n.roberta:n.quote	-0.037	0.062	-0.6	0.5486
n.roberta:n.none	-0.0017	0.058	-0.0294	0.9765
go:n.believe	0.012	0.039	0.313	0.754
go:n.say	-0.084	0.039	-2.16	0.03114
go:n.quote	0.0013	0.038	0.0329	0.9737
go:n.none	0.028	0.037	0.767	0.4431
drive:n.believe	-0.044	0.039	-1.15	0.2516
drive:n.say	0.0047	0.04	0.116	0.9078
drive:n.quote	-0.015	0.04	-0.373	0.7093
drive:n.none	0.022	0.038	0.577	0.5639
arrive:n.believe	0.043	0.04	1.06	0.2878
arrive:n.say	-0.058	0.04	-1.46	0.145
arrive:n.quote	-0.064	0.04	-1.6	0.1099
arrive:n.none	0.0011	0.037	0.0311	0.9752
n.roberta:go:n.believe	0.048	0.13	0.375	0.7079
n.roberta:go:n.say	0.094	0.13	0.725	0.4684
n.roberta:go:n.quote	0.041	0.13	0.324	0.7459
n.roberta:go:n.none	0.086	0.12	0.701	0.4832
n.roberta:drive:n.believe	0.028	0.13	0.217	0.8282
n.roberta:drive:n.say	-0.03	0.13	-0.224	0.823
n.roberta:drive:n.quote	-0.019	0.13	-0.141	0.8882
n.roberta:drive:n.none	0.053	0.13	0.423	0.6727
n.roberta:arrive:n.believe	0.039	0.13	0.291	0.7707
n.roberta:arrive:n.say	-0.056	0.13	-0.423	0.6725
n.roberta:arrive:n.quote	0.013	0.13	0.0942	0.9249
n.roberta:arrive:n.none	0.12	0.12	0.962	0.3358

Table 27: RoBERTa and human performance by syntactic environment and verb, model and evironment nested in *come*

Fixed effects (n=6657)	Estimate	Std. Error	z value	Pr(>|z|)
(Intercept)	0.79	0.0055	144	0
come	-0.13	0.0092	-14.4	1.87e-46
c.roberta	0.0021	0.032	0.0678	0.946
c.believe	0.02	0.023	0.864	0.3874
c.say	0.0074	0.024	0.308	0.7578
c.quote	0.024	0.024	0.993	0.3207
c.none	-0.079	0.023	-3.44	0.0005841
n.roberta	-0.00086	0.021	-0.04	0.9681
n.believe	0.019	0.017	1.14	0.2537
n.say	-0.009	0.017	-0.543	0.5875
n.quote	0.028	0.017	1.66	0.09772
n.none	0.023	0.016	1.44	0.151
c.roberta:c.believe	0.019	0.076	0.253	0.8006
c.roberta:c.say	-0.025	0.08	-0.31	0.7566
c.roberta:c.quote	-0.14	0.082	-1.72	0.08577
c.roberta:c.none	-0.015	0.077	-0.194	0.8466
n.roberta:n.believe	-0.017	0.056	-0.309	0.757
n.roberta:n.say	-0.026	0.055	-0.463	0.6437
n.roberta:n.quote	-0.024	0.055	-0.431	0.6662
n.roberta:n.none	0.023	0.053	0.428	0.669

Table 28: RoBERTa and human performance by syntactic environment, model and environment nested in *come*

Fixed effects (n=6657)	Estimate	Std. Error	z value	Pr(>|z|)
(Intercept)	0.79	0.0062	129	0
come	-0.19	0.017	-10.8	8.932e-27
c.roberta	0.033	0.057	0.586	0.5582
attitude.b	-0.022	0.029	-0.753	0.4514
listener.b	0.093	0.031	2.98	0.002853
anchor.b	-0.014	0.03	-0.469	0.6391
other.b	-0.069	0.025	-2.78	0.005398
n.roberta	0.013	0.023	0.559	0.5763
go	-0.067	0.015	-4.6	4.212e-06
drive	-0.089	0.015	-5.98	2.315e-09
arrive	-0.091	0.015	-6.03	1.696e-09
c.roberta:attitude.b	0.01	0.098	0.102	0.9185
c.roberta:listener.b	-0.15	0.1	-1.49	0.135
c.roberta:anchor.b	-0.15	0.1	-1.46	0.1432
c.roberta:other.b	0.053	0.083	0.643	0.5202
n.roberta:go	-0.016	0.048	-0.331	0.7408
n.roberta:drive	-0.075	0.049	-1.52	0.1289
n.roberta:arrive	-0.11	0.05	-2.21	0.02725

Table 29: RoBERTa and human performance by perspective-holder, perspective and model nested in *come*

Fixed effects (n=6657)	Estimate	Std. Error	z value	Pr(>|z|)
(Intercept)	0.79	0.0061	129	0
come	-0.13	0.015	-8.64	7.018e-18
c.roberta	0.039	0.057	0.686	0.4926
listener.b	0.045	0.034	1.32	0.1864
other.b	-0.066	0.026	-2.56	0.01052
anchor.b	-0.021	0.031	-0.678	0.4976
c.say	0.13	0.043	3.05	0.00231
c.believe	0.074	0.046	1.61	0.1073
c.quote	0.087	0.045	1.95	0.05123
c.none	-0.072	0.044	-1.63	0.1036
attitude.b	-0.026	0.038	-0.687	0.4924
n.roberta	-0.00086	0.021	-0.0403	0.9678
n.say	-0.009	0.016	-0.547	0.5846
n.believe	0.019	0.017	1.15	0.2501
n.quote	0.028	0.017	1.67	0.09519
n.none	0.023	0.016	1.45	0.1479
listener.b:c.say	-0.42	0.096	-4.36	1.292e-05
listener.b:c.believe	-0.24	0.083	-2.94	0.003271
listener.b:c.quote	-0.093	0.073	-1.28	0.2006
listener.b:c.none	-0.074	0.079	-0.947	0.3438
other.b:c.say	-0.25	0.065	-3.83	0.0001273
other.b:c.believe	-0.13	0.067	-1.97	0.04865
other.b:c.quote	-0.29	0.065	-4.4	1.075e-05
other.b:c.none	-0.072	0.058	-1.24	0.2156
anchor.b:c.say	0.18	0.081	2.19	0.02845
anchor.b:c.believe	0.14	0.078	1.8	0.07142
anchor.b:c.quote	0.14	0.085	1.65	0.09932
anchor.b:c.none	0.24	0.081	2.94	0.003329
c.say:attitude.b	-0.22	0.066	-3.35	0.0008274
c.believe:attitude.b	-0.017	0.064	-0.265	0.7913
c.roberta:listener.b	-0.16	0.11	-1.46	0.145
c.roberta:other.b	0.049	0.086	0.568	0.5703
c.roberta:anchor.b	-0.18	0.1	-1.76	0.07794
c.roberta:c.say	-0.14	0.14	-0.998	0.3182
c.roberta:c.believe	-0.074	0.15	-0.485	0.628
c.roberta:c.quote	-0.22	0.15	-1.46	0.1452
c.roberta:c.none	-0.17	0.15	-1.15	0.2521
c.roberta:attitude.b	-0.055	0.13	-0.434	0.6645
n.roberta:n.say	-0.026	0.055	-0.466	0.6412
n.roberta:n.believe	-0.017	0.055	-0.312	0.7552
n.roberta:n.quote	-0.024	0.055	-0.435	0.6639
n.roberta:n.none	0.023	0.052	0.431	0.6666
c.roberta:listener.b:c.say	0.19	0.32	0.6	0.5489
c.roberta:listener.b:c.believe	-0.2	0.28	-0.706	0.48
c.roberta:listener.b:c.quote	0.21	0.24	0.849	0.396
c.roberta:listener.b:c.none	0.15	0.26	0.589	0.5556
c.roberta:other.b:c.say	0.37	0.22	1.69	0.0905
c.roberta:other.b:c.believe	0.47	0.22	2.08	0.03774
c.roberta:other.b:c.quote	0.25	0.22	1.15	0.2486
c.roberta:other.b:c.none	0.46	0.2	2.34	0.01942

Table 30: RoBERTa and human performance by perspective-holder and syntactic environment, perspective and model nested in *come* and Speaker treated as baseline

Fixed effects (n=6657)	Estimate	Std. Error	z value	Pr(>|z|)
c.roberta:other.b:c.say	0.37	0.22	1.69	0.0905
c.roberta:other.b:c.believe	0.47	0.22	2.08	0.03774
c.roberta:other.b:c.quote	0.25	0.22	1.15	0.2486
c.roberta:other.b:c.none	0.46	0.2	2.34	0.01942
c.roberta:anchor.b:c.say	0.074	0.27	0.272	0.7856
c.roberta:anchor.b:c.believe	0.06	0.26	0.23	0.8183
c.roberta:anchor.b:c.quote	-0.21	0.29	-0.736	0.4616
c.roberta:anchor.b:c.none	-0.24	0.27	-0.873	0.3827
c.roberta:c.say:attitude.b	-0.063	0.22	-0.286	0.7745
c.roberta:c.believe:attitude.b	-0.023	0.21	-0.109	0.9133

Table 31: RoBERTa and human performance by perspective-holder and syntactic environment, perspective and model nested in *come* and Speaker treated as baseline

Fixed effects (n=6657)	Estimate	Std. Error	z value	Pr(>|z|)
c.roberta:listener:c.say	0.095	0.29	0.322	0.7475
c.roberta:listener:c.believe	-0.2	0.25	-0.819	0.4128
c.roberta:listener:c.quote	0.33	0.25	1.35	0.178
c.roberta:listener:c.none	0.31	0.25	1.24	0.2143
c.roberta:other:c.say	0.23	0.23	1.04	0.2993
c.roberta:other:c.believe	0.32	0.21	1.53	0.1272
c.roberta:other:c.quote	0.37	0.23	1.59	0.1111
c.roberta:other:c.none	0.56	0.21	2.64	0.008366
c.roberta:speaker:c.say	-0.059	0.22	-0.272	0.7856
c.roberta:speaker:c.believe	-0.048	0.21	-0.23	0.8183
c.roberta:speaker:c.quote	0.17	0.23	0.736	0.4616
c.roberta:speaker:c.none	0.19	0.22	0.873	0.3827
c.roberta:c.say:attitude	-0.11	0.23	-0.479	0.6318
c.roberta:c.believe:attitude	-0.066	0.2	-0.323	0.7464

Table 32: RoBERTa and human performance by perspective-holder and syntactic environment, perspective and model nested in *come* and perspectives compared to group mean

Fixed effects (n=6657)	Estimate	Std. Error	z value	Pr(>|z|)
(Intercept)	0.79	0.0057	140	0
come	-0.12	0.011	-11	6.28e-28
c.roberta	-0.054	0.041	-1.31	0.1916
listener	0.052	0.031	1.69	0.09179
other	-0.036	0.026	-1.38	0.1667
speaker	0.017	0.025	0.678	0.4976
c.say	-0.013	0.028	-0.458	0.6467
c.believe	0.024	0.025	0.966	0.334
c.quote	0.068	0.034	2.01	0.04476
c.none	-0.0058	0.032	-0.18	0.857
attitude	0.072	0.039	1.82	0.06935
n.roberta	-0.00086	0.021	-0.0403	0.9678
n.say	-0.009	0.016	-0.547	0.5846
n.believe	0.019	0.017	1.15	0.2501
n.quote	0.028	0.017	1.67	0.09519
n.none	0.023	0.016	1.45	0.1479
listener:c.say	-0.48	0.088	-5.42	6.315e-08
listener:c.believe	-0.31	0.075	-4.13	3.731e-05
listener:c.quote	-0.19	0.074	-2.53	0.01154
listener:c.none	-0.25	0.075	-3.32	0.0009119
other:c.say	-0.34	0.068	-5.05	4.523e-07
other:c.believe	-0.22	0.063	-3.44	0.000587
other:c.quote	-0.34	0.069	-4.93	8.419e-07
other:c.none	-0.25	0.062	-3.97	7.121e-05
speaker:c.say	-0.14	0.065	-2.19	0.02845
speaker:c.believe	-0.11	0.062	-1.8	0.07142
speaker:c.quote	-0.11	0.068	-1.65	0.09932
speaker:c.none	-0.19	0.065	-2.94	0.003329
c.say:attitude	-0.32	0.069	-4.67	3.068e-06
c.believe:attitude	-0.13	0.061	-2.05	0.03999
c.roberta:listener	0.016	0.1	0.154	0.8778
c.roberta:other	0.19	0.086	2.15	0.03129
c.roberta:speaker	0.15	0.083	1.76	0.07794
c.roberta:c.say	-0.028	0.092	-0.306	0.7596
c.roberta:c.believe	-0.013	0.082	-0.159	0.8735
c.roberta:c.quote	-0.21	0.11	-1.87	0.06177
c.roberta:c.none	-0.14	0.11	-1.3	0.1952
c.roberta:attitude	0.013	0.13	0.0978	0.9221
n.roberta:n.say	-0.026	0.055	-0.466	0.6412
n.roberta:n.believe	-0.017	0.055	-0.312	0.7552
n.roberta:n.quote	-0.024	0.055	-0.435	0.6639
n.roberta:n.none	0.023	0.052	0.431	0.6666

Table 33: RoBERTa and human performance by perspective-holder and syntactic environment, perspective and model nested in *come* and perspectives compared to group mean

H ProSPer examples with lowest human mean accuracy

H.1 Annotated subset

1. **Human mean: 0%**
   RoBERTa score: 1.6%
   Target: *come*
   "You should go to Jinyang too," she answered coldly. "There are already too many people," he answered. "My sister's house is full. And there's no work in Jinyang." "What do you want?" "I'll leave Lan Lan in Jinyang– none of the schools are open now, anyway– and my parents can take care of her." "And you?" "I thought I might **come** to Beijing." He said this weakly, and the next sentence was even more feeble. "There's nothing left here." Chrysanthemum was silent for a long time. Then she said, "Let me think about it." She hung up and suddenly realized no other plan of action was possible.
2. **Human mean: 0%**
   RoBERTa score: 39%
   Target: come
   As Luc lived alone in Lyon, his son tried hard to **come** there every week.
3. **Human mean: 0%**
   RoBERTa score: 1.0%
   Target: come
   Charles, I would like to go on record, the tux, not my idea. No, no. But they said if you want to **come** behind the scenes on the number one show in America, you got ta succumb to the dress code.
4. **Human mean: 0%**
   RoBERTa score: 51%
   Target: walk
   CORSON: Did he say where he was going when he got out? PAUL: Yes. CORSON: Where? PAUL: Paris. OSCAR: see what I mean? Stupid. PAUL: He just wanted to think about it. The Eiffel Tower, he wanted to see, aperitifs, he wanted to drink, the Follies Brassiere, he wanted to go to. Beautiful buildings, cafs, music, and women. I told him what I knew. Then he showed me a map. CORSON: A map? PAUL: He said I could **walk** to Paris. CORSON: From where? PAUL: From here. OSCAR: Aw, man. PAUL: He had it all worked out. You go up through Laos, then into Burma, some other country I forget, then India, Iran, Turkey, and Greece. The rest, he said, is easy.
5. **Human mean: 0%**
   RoBERTa score: 82%
   Target: walking
   It's hard to keep calm and carry on, not let anyone see me at my most vulnerable, when I'm away from home and I don't have hugs in the kitchen with my mum or chats by the fire with my dad to see me through the day. Sometimes it's just a case of putting on the saddest Taylor Swift song while you're **walking** home from the laundrette, crying quietly.
6. **Human mean: 0%**
   RoBERTa score: 3.6%
   Target: arrive
   Kristen wrote to him in a joyful, loopy scrawl from Middlebury on a postcard which bore a bright blue picture of the school's ski team. The card said Sophie wanted Frank to **arrive** home early because she was giving him a surprise graduation party. Kristen was meddling in her parents' lives with characteristic thoughtfulness, not wanting Frank to disappoint Sophie by being late, not wanting him to be so surprised himself that he couldn't enjoy the party.
7. **Human mean: 0%**
   RoBERTa score: 2.1%
   Target: drive
   So where does your husband live? I asked Marietta. She sat back in the armchair. On top of the hill, before you turn to 248, there's a white trailer, with many pots of flowers in the windows. You are welcome to stop by. To see him? Well, no, there's another trailer, a pink one, and that's mine, way back in the yard. You think I could just **drive** in and talk to you all? Your trailer doesn't have the flowers? No, I have cats. They're always sunbathing in the windows. Why wouldn't you stop by? If you usually don't even talk to each other? Oh, we do, I just hope we won't. We have a kid to take care of, so that keeps us pretty close.
8. **Human mean: 0%**
   RoBERTa score: 0.9%
   Target: arrive
   There was also a charming lady in her late thirties or perhaps early forties who was secretary to a member of Parliament. She was responsible for my enjoying a weekend at the country home of well-to-do friends of hers. She remarked at dinner once that she had an invitation to spend the weekend with friends but was unable to accept. So, playing the role of the brash American, I suggested that she tell them I would **arrive** as substitute. She did, and I did. Her friends entertained me extravagantly, I thought, and took me around to meet their friends, who also felt obliged to entertain me. One of them later visited us in Paris, and in return for his and his wife's hospitality I took him to dinner in Paris and then to the opera.
9. **Human mean: 0%**
   RoBERTa score: 22%
   Target: come
   We were still cheerful when we got back to Johannesburg next evening, in spite of the weather. It was one of those bitter Transvaal nights, with a sharp, icy drizzle. We arrived at the house about eight. For a moment we both thought we had **come** up the wrong street, because there on the lawn was a red tent – one of those long low ones they call patrol tents – tied against the kaya.
10. **Human mean: 0%**
    RoBERTa score: 10%

Target: came
YDSTIE: When you went to Rome, you brought along the beginnings of a World War II novel you were working on, but you got distracted. Tell us what happened? Mr-DOERR: Yes, or overwhelmed perhaps is the better word. I **came** there with about 50 pages in notes on this novel thinking that that would be my next project. I had just published my second book, a novel, and was trying to get a new project off the ground. And usually, I think I learned there that I prefer a very insulated environment where everything is pretty familiar for me to be able to enter and imagine this space and start writing fiction. And Rome invaded me on all sides, even from the first day.

H.2 Random subset

1. **Human mean: 0%**
   RoBERTa score: 10%
   Target: came
   and we'd go up to the Adirondacks and camp and it was so you know pick your own uh blueberries and make blueberry pancakes for breakfast uh also go ahead oh yes yes yes i **came** i
2. **Human mean: 0%**
   RoBERTa score: 87%
   Target: drove
   Dorians and Romans After the disaster, Mycenean Greeks from the Peloponnese moved in to control what remained of the Minoan settlements — they may even have precipitated the destruction. Around 1200 b.c., Dorian invaders from the Balkans **drove** south through the Greek mainland, the Aegean islands, and across to Crete. Many coastal dwellers migrated to remote mountain villages in order to escape their enemies. Others embarked on an overseas exodus that took them around the Mediterranean Sea. The island did not get directly involved in Greece's Persian and Peloponnesian Wars, however it became well-known as a valuable source of brave and energetic mercenaries.
3. **Human mean: 0%**
   RoBERTa score: 22%
   Target: coming
   Robe's collection of New Mexico legends contains thirty-four variants of the devil-at-the-dance tale. Although the legends in this collection are from rural northern New Mexico, collected in the 1950s and 1960s, we find contemporary versions of the devil-at-the-dance tales in south Texas and in Baja California from the 1980s. Limón and Herrera-Sobek discuss versions of the tale circulating in nightclubs and discotheques among urbanized young people. Of course, not everyone believes such stories. Martin's book contains a story by a man born in 1904, who says his friend played a trick on his community in Tucson by **coming** to a dance dressed in black, with a fake rooster foot. Eventually someone noticed his foot and yelled, "The Devil! The Devil!" The narrator says he was there when his friend played the trick, so he doesn't believe in the legend (50). References De Leon 1982; Glazer 1984,1994; Herrera-Sobek 1988; Limón 1994; Martin 1983; Robe 1951; Robe ed. 1980; West 1988
4. **Human mean: 0%**
   RoBERTa score: 77%
   Target: come
   supposed to convince the market that all was well, so eventually interest rates could **come** down. The trouble was that all that austerity was a hard sell politically–especially because the economy was going into a nasty recession
5. **Human mean: 0%**
   RoBERTa score: 52%
   Target: going
   uh above or around or uh from other places in in well if he got out of line too much from the old school they'd just knock him off i mean they're not **going** they're not
6. **Human mean: 0%**
   RoBERTa score: 71%
   Target: go
   um-hum hopefully next year get to **go** back because uh a lot of the family has not uh on her side my mother's side has not seen you know my daughter so
7. **Human mean: 0%**
   RoBERTa score: 56%
   Target: went
   Well, they **went** through, they broke a soldier's leg, you could hear his moaning. Then they
8. **Human mean: 17%**
   RoBERTa score: 0.8%
   Target: went
   contained both cocaine and an extract from the cola nut. The cocaine **went** out when it was declared a controlled substance early in this century. Interestingly,
9. **Human mean: 17%**
   RoBERTa score: 82%
   Target: come
   intent of attracting people to treatment because patients do not **come** to the emergency department with the intention of receiving substance abuse treatment.

I ProSPer examples with lowest RoBERTa accuracy

I.1 Annotated subset

1. **Human mean: 10%**
   RoBERTa score: 0.2%
   Target: drive
   "You want to turn back after lunch?" she offered. Hisako looked up from her snow picnic hesitantly. "I know how badly you want to go to the hot springs..." "Not so bad I'll drag you there when it's making you feel awful." "Really?" "It's a holiday, right?" "You won't be mad at me later?" "What do you take me for?" Megumi asked. "We can **drive** down to the public one. It's not as nice, but it'll be warm." "We've been walking for over three hours," Hisako looked at her watch. "It's getting kind of darker, don't you think." "It'll be faster going downhill," Megumi promised. sniffing and Megumi didn't know if it was only her nose, or if she was crying.
2. **Human mean: 50%**
   RoBERTa score: 0.6%
   Target: arrive
   ASSURAS: When you immigrated to the United States, you were 19 years old and you had huge expectations, didn't you? Mr-McCOURT: Well, this w– this was the golden land for– for most people who come here, so I– I– I thought I'd just– I– I thought I'd **arrive** here, get off the boat and– and go marching up Fifth Avenue like Fred Astaire and Ginger Rogers, and that music would play in the background because all the movies had music in the background. I thought that– that's how it was in America. ASSURAS: It didn't happen that way, though, did it? Mr-McCOURT: No, it didn't because somebody has to take out the garbage. And that's– that's the kind of job I got right away.
3. **Human mean: 0%**
   RoBERTa score: 0.9%
   Target: arrive
   "There was also a charming lady in her late thirties or perhaps early forties who was secretary to a member of Parliament, She was responsible for my enjoying a weekend at the country home of well-to-do friends of hers. She remarked at dinner once that she had an invitation to spend the weekend with friends but was unable to accept. So, playing the role of the brash American, I suggested that she tell them I would **arrive** as substitute. She did, and I did. Her friends entertained me extravagantly, I thought, and took me around to meet their friends, who also felt obliged to entertain me. One of them later visited us in Paris, and in return for his and his wife's hospitality I took him to dinner in Paris and then to the opera."
4. **Human mean: 0%**
   RoBERTa score: 1.0%
   Target: come
   Charles, I would like to go on record, the tux, not my idea. No, no. But they said if you want to **come** behind the scenes on the number one show in America, you got ta succumb to the dress code.
5. **Human mean: 27%**
   RoBERTa score: 1.6%
   Target: come
   The clout list shows an Anthony Scarpelli sought a city job in 1994 with help from Terry Teele, a former Daley aide. Scarpelli said he's not sure if that's him or his father, also a city worker on disability leave. Scarpelli, a cousin of the late mobster Gerald Scarpelli, said he also helped run a patronage army for Carmen Iacullo and Anthony Pucillo, two former transportation department officials. "I want to **come** back to work," said Scarpelli , who settled four previous cases for $28,000.
6. **Human mean: 0%**
   RoBERTa score: 1.9%
   Target: come
   "You should go to Jinyang too," she answered coldly. "There are already too many people," he answered. "My sister's house is full. And there's no work in Jinyang." "What do you want?" "I'll leave Lan Lan in Jinyang– none of the schools are open now, anyway– and my parents can take care of her." "And you?" "I thought I might **come** to Beijing." He said this weakly, and the next sentence was even more feeble. "There's nothing left here." Chrysanthemum was silent for a long time. Then she said, "Let me think about it." She hung up and suddenly realized no other plan of action was possible.
7. **Human mean: 0%**
   RoBERTa score: 2.1%
   Target: drive
   So where does your husband live? I asked Marietta. She sat back in the armchair. On top of the hill, before you turn to 248, there's a white trailer, with many pots of flowers in the windows. You are welcome to stop by. To see him? Well, no, there's another trailer, a pink one, and that's mine, way back in the yard. You think I could just **drive** in and talk to you all? Your trailer doesn't have the flowers? No, I have cats. They're always sunbathing in the windows. Why wouldn't you stop by? If you usually don't even talk to each other? Oh, we do, I just hope we won't. We have a kid to take care of, so that keeps us pretty close.
8. **Human mean: 70%**
   RoBERTa score: 2.4%
   Target: come
   "They talked about Harry Logan and Chatham and a new outbreak of Lyme disease that everyone was worrying about. Elliott said they knew a young girl about Grace's age who'd caught it and her life had been completely wrecked. Connie darted a look at him and he flushed a little and quickly changed the subject. As soon as the meal was over, Grace said she was tired and would they mind if she went to bed. Annie said she would **come** too but Grace wouldn't let her."
9. **Human mean: 10%**
   RoBERTa score: 2.4%

Target: came
The house of my paternal grandparents in central Switzerland: that was the "other" home of my childhood. And at the same time, it was another world. Back then, it took a long time to get there, and that universe had nothing to do with my life in Paris: it was completely surrounded by countryside, and I was rid of the school I hated. From early on, I **came** there alone. I was reunited with my Roman cousins and experienced a completely different lifestyle. I smelled different odors. I saw new lights both outside and inside the home where, once evening fell, the large lamps spread out on various pieces of furniture or hanging above the big dinner table made centers of luminous warmth.

10. **Human mean: 50%**
RoBERTa score: 2.6%
Target: arrive
I had a snapped torsion spring and needed it fixed. I also had an ancient Genie screw drive motor that I'm pretty sure the neighbors 3 blocks away could hear each time we opened our garage door. I called Art who answered right away, we talked about the cost to replace the springs and some options for openers. He said they'd **arrive** the next day between 9-10 after they finished a job they had that morning.

I.2 Random subset

1. **Human mean: 20%**
RoBERTa score: 0.6%
Target: arrive
More than 30,000 Cubans tried to cross shark-infested waters to Florida on improvised rafts. Facing a dramatic influx of Cubans, President Clinton abolished the US policy of automatic asylum to Cuban refugees, placing them in a makeshift tent settlement in Guantánamo Bay Naval Base. In the opinion of many, Cuba is an isolated socialist dinosaur. Yet it— and its aging leader— soldier on against all odds. The US embargo, denounced by an ever-increasing majority in the United Nations, is spurred on by vehement anti-Castro lobbying by Cubans in southern Florida. Still, changes in the status quo seem likely. But nearly four decades after the Cuban missile crisis, the world continues to wait, wondering whether a lifting of US trade and tourism sanctions or a change in leadership in Cuba will **arrive** first.
2. **Human mean: 17%**
RoBERTa score: 0.8%
Target: went
contained both cocaine and an extract from the cola nut. The cocaine **went** out when it was declared a controlled substance early in this century. Interestingly,
3. **Human mean: 40%**
RoBERTa score: 1.3%
Target: goes
that by the conservatives' lights, the bill spends too much and cuts taxes too little. The NYT even **goes** out of its piece saying that the vote revealed a severe split in the Republican Party that may be hard to patch up.
4. **Human mean: 20%**
RoBERTa score: 1.4%, target: went
Commercial enterprise, military power, and religious fervor **went** together. More than the divinity of Shiva, the 11th-century Temple of Brihadisvara boasts architecture celebrating the victory of
5. **Human mean: -[16]**
RoBERTa score: 2.1%
Target: drove
yeah well in um in Dallas um i don't know if you heard about the killing where the guy **drove** into Luby's and the story was uh
6. **Human mean: 20%**
RoBERTa score: 2.7%
Target: walks
. More generally, each organism has traits that are aected by many genes, the polygeny discussed above, and each gene aects many traits, the pleiotropy alluded to above. It is interesting to note that were organisms to evolve to a position below but near the biological reality that is the proper analogue of the Ksat phase transition, such a location might well achieve the gradualism and capacity to persistently evolve that Darwin noted and that we observe. Both the gradualism and capacity to evolve are related to the number of alternative assignments of true or false to the V variables that satisfy the Ksat normal disjunctive form. If there are connected pathways from one such assignment via -Hamming-mutant neighboring assignments that all satisfy the normal disjunctive form, then adaptive **walks** via alternatives genotypes are available, all of which roughly generate the same organism. Gradualism is achieved. Polygeny and pleiotropy tune landscape ruggedness and deformability, which tune coevolutionary dynamics, perhaps to a self-organized critical state of an ecosystem. There are, in short, dimly understood laws that allow the coevolutionary construction of accumulating complexity. And it appears that such coevolution typically is self-organized critical. The NK coevolutionary model is not the only example of a model exhibiting self-organized critical behavior of model ecosystems. Bak and colleagues, Ricard Solé, and others have created elegant models aiming in the same direction. In particular, Solé's model comes closest to fitting the actual slopes of the observed power laws, whi
7. **Human mean: 80%**
RoBERTa score: 3.8%
Target: drive
yes they are well most of them you're right but then i **drive** through Riodosa and i think well not all of them have it
8. **Human mean: 100%**
RoBERTa score: 3.9%

[16]Removed due to violent content.

Target: go
we've **go** t all of our trees from Calloway's and luckily they'll take them back any time for any reason if they die yeah i usually

9. **Human mean: 40%**
   RoBERTa score: 6.0%
   Target: went
   out the discerning sense of discriminating. Disinterested **went** next, the eulogy continued, becoming a posh synonym for uninterested , because
10. **Human mean: 20%**
    RoBERTa score: 6.3%
    Target: coming
    to slam a competitor via the most unprofessional means. The kind of SLATE I was to **coming** enjoy reading was one that would rip the Wall Street Journal apart using facts, ideas, and finely honed reasoning. There is no place in that

Can Transformers *Jump Around Right* in Natural Language? Assessing Performance Transfer from SCAN

Rahma Chaabouni[*†] **Roberto Dessì** **Eugene Kharitonov**[*]
Ecole Normale Superieure Facebook AI & Pompeu Fabra Facebook AI
{chaabounirahma, roberto.dessi11}@gmail.com kharitonov@fb.com

Abstract

Despite their failure to solve the compositional SCAN dataset, seq2seq architectures still achieve astonishing success on more practical tasks. This observation pushes us to question the usefulness of SCAN-style compositional generalization in realistic NLP tasks. In this work, we study the benefit that such compositionality brings about to several machine translation tasks. We present several focused modifications of Transformer that greatly improve generalization capabilities on SCAN and select one that remains on par with a vanilla Transformer on a standard machine translation (MT) task. Next, we study its performance in low-resource settings and on a newly introduced distribution-shifted English-French translation task.

Overall, we find that improvements of a SCAN-capable model do not directly transfer to the resource-rich MT setup. In contrast, in the low-resource setup, general modifications lead to an improvement of up to 13.1% BLEU score w.r.t. a vanilla Transformer. Similarly, an improvement of 14% in an accuracy-based metric is achieved in the introduced compositional English-French translation task. This provides experimental evidence that the compositional generalization assessed in SCAN is particularly useful in resource-starved and distribution-shifted scenarios.

1 Introduction

While sequence-to-sequence (seq2seq) models achieve remarkable performance in many tasks (Sutskever et al., 2014; Raffel et al., 2019; Adiwardana et al., 2020), they often fail to generalize in a systematic way (Baroni, 2019; McCoy et al., 2020; Hupkes et al., 2020; Kharitonov and Chaabouni, 2021; Dankers et al., 2021). These shortcomings are particularly obvious in the experiments on the SCAN domain (Lake and Baroni, 2018; Loula et al., 2018; Bastings et al., 2018).

In SCAN, inputs are instructions that describe trajectories and outputs define sequences of actions to follow them (see Table 1). To illustrate how SCAN probes a model for compositional generalization, imagine that we train it on a set of instructions {`jump`, `run`, `turn`, `turn twice`, `run twice`}, but test it on `jump twice`. Strictly speaking, nothing in the training data indicates that the model *must* output `JUMP JUMP` instead of e.g. `JUMP`. However, it is hypothesised that a bias for such compositional, human-like induction is beneficial (Lake and Baroni, 2018; Lake, 2019).

This hypothesis stumbles into a perplexing situation: despite failing at compositional generalization, considered as a core requirement for language understanding, seq2seq models have tremendous success in practice. Is the type of compositional generalization, that SCAN probes for, useful for NLP tasks? If so, in what scenarios?

In this work, we aim to answer this question. Firstly, we introduce focused modifications to Transformer that greatly improve accuracy performance on SCAN. To build such modifications, we exploit two observations: (i) Transformer's architecture is very similar to convolution-based seq2seq models (ConvS2S) (Gehring et al., 2017), (ii) ConvS2S performs well on SCAN (Dessì and Baroni, 2019). This capability (ii) is hypothesized to be due to explicitly localized representation of the sequences, where only deep layers of the model can access more distant tokens (Dessì and Baroni, 2019; Hupkes et al., 2020). Such a capability should also benefit to natural language processing as human languages are proved to favor local syntactic constructions (Futrell et al., 2015). Motivated by these observations, we focus on the major differ-

[*] Equal contribution. [†] work was done while R.C. was at Facebook AI.

Proceedings of the Fourth BlackboxNLP Workshop on Analyzing and Interpreting Neural Networks for NLP, pages 136–148
Online, November 11, 2021.

ences between ConvS2S and Transformer, namely the localized receptive field span and the gating mechanism, to inject into Transformer inductive biases useful for SCAN.

As a testbed, we use the machine translation (MT) domain as one of the most popular applications for seq2seq models. We consider both resource-rich (IWSLT'14 German→English) and low-resource (Nepali&Sinhala↔English) setups. Finally, to evaluate SCAN-style capabilities in natural language tasks, we build a dataset that probes whether models can systematically generalize w.r.t. noun-adjective ordering while translating from English to French. We construct this dataset by filtering the EuroParl corpus (a part of WMT'14).

Our results indicate that combining two ConvS2S-inspired changes improves accuracy on one SCAN split (SCAN-jump) from 3.4% to 43.0%, while maintaining a high accuracy on the other splits (SCAN-simple and SCAN-around-right). As expected, given that SCAN is an artificial diagnostic dataset, not all modifications lead to equal improvements on an MT task. We select one of the considered modifications that performs on par with the vanilla Transformer on IWSLT'14.

Testing the selected modification on low-resource data, we observe that it provides between 3.6% and 13.1% BLEU improvements over Transformer. On the noun-adjective ordering dataset, we find that our modification results into gains in generalization of 14%.

This leads to the following picture: the localized attention, augmented by a gating mechanism, provides a useful inductive bias that proves to be beneficial for SCAN-style generalization. Additionally, it turns out useful in low-resource and distribution-shifted settings. Thus, testing seq2seq models on SCAN while controlling for a non-degraded performance leads to improvement in domains where syntactic compositionality is crucial for a task success.

2 Transformers and ConvS2S

Architecture overview Both Transformer and ConvS2S are encoder-decoder architectures (Sutskever et al., 2014), where the decoder has an attention mechanism to peek into the encoder's representation (Bahdanau et al., 2014). These representations are obtained by embedding the inputs, adding a positional embedding, and passing them through a sequence of layers.

In Transformer's encoder, the output representations are the result of a sequential application of two (sub)layer types: self-attention and fully connected layers. The input representation can "skip" any sublayer via a residual connection. The output of the sublayer is passed through a dropout mechanism and added to the residual. This sum is then layer-normalized. Any relation between input tokens is modeled solely by self-attention modules.

In ConvS2S, the encoder is also a sequence of identical blocks. The inter-term dependencies are modeled by 1D convolutions with GLU activation functions (Dauphin et al., 2017).[1] In contrast to self-attention, convolutions have a finite kernel size, thus effectively capping the maximal distance of intermediate dependencies that can be modeled. The GLU activation function serves as a gate, allowing ConvS2S to control the balance between residuals and the output of the convolution. After the GLU operation, the intermediate representation is added to the residual and scaled. The output of the final convolution is then passed into a fully connected layer. In ConvS2S and Transformer, decoders have similar structures to those of encoders, with an additional decoder→encoder attention layer after the convolution and self-attention blocks, respectively.

Despite the similarities, there are numerous low-level differences between the two architectures: normalization (layer norm (Ba et al., 2016) vs. weight normalization (Salimans and Kingma, 2016)), optimization (Adam (Kingma and Ba, 2014) with a ramp-up vs. NAG (Sutskever et al., 2013)), etc. *A priori*, any of those can affect models' inductive biases. However, we concentrate on some of the most obvious architectural differences: the limited convolution span and GLU activations.

We believe these features can greatly affect models' performance on SCAN. Indeed, SCAN has only local dependencies between tokens, thus the ability to avoid spurious correlations with more distant tokens can be useful. Similarly, the ability to weight contributions from the token interactions into the intermediate representation is intuitively prerequisite to build compositional representation.

GLU (Dauphin et al., 2017) Given a vector input $\boldsymbol{x}$, GLU splits it in two equally sized halves $\boldsymbol{x}_1$ and $\boldsymbol{x}_2$; one is passed through a sigmoid ($\sigma(x) = (1 + e^{-x})^{-1}$). Then both parts are pointwise multiplied:

[1] GLU was introduced as a combination of a convolution network and an activation; we follow the Pytorch convention and consider it as separate blocks for convenience.

jump	⇒	JUMP
jump around right	⇒	RTURN JUMP RTURN JUMP RTURN JUMP RTURN JUMP
turn left twice	⇒	LTURN LTURN
jump opposite left after walk around left	⇒	LTURN WALK LTURN WALK LTURN WALK LTURN WALK LTURN LTURN JUMP

Table 1: Examples of SCAN trajectories and instructions, adopted from (Lake and Baroni, 2018).

$$GLU(\boldsymbol{x}) := \sigma(\boldsymbol{x}_1) \odot \boldsymbol{x}_2 \qquad (1)$$

This allows a network to implement a gating mechanism, where one half of its output gates the signal from the second.

Self-attention Instead of convolutions, Transformer uses multi-headed self-attention to model interactions between tokens. Given n embeddings, $\boldsymbol{x}_1, \boldsymbol{x}_2, ...\boldsymbol{x}_n$ of dimensionality d, the self-attention layer transforms them in the following way.

Firstly, each embedding $\boldsymbol{x}_i$ is projected by three matrices Q, K, and V to get query $\boldsymbol{q}_i$, key $\boldsymbol{k}_i$, and value $\boldsymbol{v}_i$ representations, respectively: $\boldsymbol{q}_i, \boldsymbol{k}_i, \boldsymbol{v}_i \leftarrow Q\boldsymbol{x}_i, K\boldsymbol{x}_i, V\boldsymbol{x}_i$. Next, a scaled dot-product between query $\boldsymbol{q}_i$ and key $\boldsymbol{k}_j$ is calculated as follow:

$$\alpha_{ij} = \frac{1}{\sqrt{d}} \boldsymbol{q}_i \cdot \boldsymbol{k}_j^T \qquad (2)$$

This dot-product defines the attention weights $w_{ij} = e^{\alpha_{ij}} / \sum e^{\alpha_{ij}}$ which are used to get the output representations: $\boldsymbol{o}_i = \sum_j w_{ij} \boldsymbol{v}_j$. This process is done in parallel for multiple heads, acting on independent slices of the input embeddings; their outputs are concatenated and passed through a fully connected layer.

3 Transformer Modifications

Self-attention gate (SAG) The simplest way to imitate the effect of GLU activation (Eq. 1) is to weight (gate) the output of self-attention by a learned scalar parameter. To ensure that it is non-negative and is scaled in $[0, 1]$, we parameterize it as a sigmoid of a real-valued learned parameter β. Algorithm 1 illustrates the introduced change. In comparison to Transformer, SAG adds one scalar parameter for each encoder and decoder layer.

We treat β_0, the value β is initialized with before training, as a hyperparameter. In the preliminary experiments, we found that after training, encoder layers often have small negative β values $(-2..-0.5)$, while decoder layers have positive values (0.2..4.5) that grow monotonically for higher layers.

A similar modification was considered in an effort to stabilize Transformer training in the Reinforcement Learning domain (Parisotto et al., 2020).

Convolution as self-attention In the limit case, we can entirely replace self-attention with convolutions. This modification introduces one hyperparameter (kernel size). However, convolutional layers have fewer parameters than the self-attention mechanism. One might consider this not to be a Transformer variant due to the lack of self-attention, but as self-attention generalizes convolutions (Cordonnier et al., 2020), we consider this as an extreme form of regularization.

Fixed-span self-attention A less extreme modification would be to use the regular multi-head self-attention mechanism, but without allowing attention to peek beyond some distance. This mimics the limited kernel size of convolutions in ConvS2S. We achieve this by adding a fixed bias term b_{ij} to the self-attention logits (Eq. 2):

$$\alpha_{ij} = \frac{1}{\sqrt{d}} \boldsymbol{q}_i \cdot \boldsymbol{k}_j^T + b_{ij} \qquad (3)$$

Setting b_{ij} to $-\infty$ when the difference $|i-j|$ exceeds some fixed value s and to 0 otherwise prevents the self-attention to look beyond distance s.

Fixed-span self-attention with a span parameter s has the same "receptive field" as 1D convolution with kernel size $2s+1$. This modification adds one hyperparameter (span size), but does not introduce new learned parameters.

T5 attention Further relaxing constraints on self-attention, we consider the case where we allow Transformer to learn how to (soft-)limit its self-attention. We introduce the bias term b_{ij} that is learned as a function of a (signed) difference $i-j$, capping it to $[-s, +s]$ (e.g., positions with difference above s would have the same bias b_s).

This modification is similar to one introduced by Raffel et al. (2019) in T5, with the only exception that we allow each head to have its own bias. Again, the span size is a new hyperparameter. In a model with n_h heads and n_l layers, this modification requires $(2s+1) \times n_l \times n_h$ new parameters, which is negligible in comparison with the sizes of fully connected layers. Examples of the learned b_{ij} parameters are shown in Supplementary when training on SCAN.

```
1: procedure COMPUTE_SELFATTENTION
2:     res ← x
3:     x ← self_attn(x)
4:     x ← x * σ(β)
5:     x ← layer_norm(res + dropout(x))
```

Algorithm 1: Self-attention gate (SAG). The only introduced change is on line 4. β is a learned per-layer scalar parameter.

Implementation details We used the fairseq (Ott et al., 2019) implementation of Transformer seq2seq as a foundation, with its initialization and default parameters. T5 and fixed-span attentions are implemented by providing additive attention masks to Transformer.

4 Datasets

4.1 SCAN

Introduced by Lake and Baroni (2018), SCAN is a collection of tasks used for studying systematic generalization of seq2seq models (see Table 1 for some input-output examples). A set of 4 primitive verbs are combined with different modifiers generating around 27k unique samples. Lake and Baroni (2018) and, later, Loula et al. (2018) prepared several non-i.i.d. splits of the data into training and test sets. To successfully generalize on such non-i.i.d. splits, a model has to generalize systematically, in a compositional way.

We experiment with three tasks, often focused on in the literature[2] (Dessì and Baroni, 2019). **SCAN-simple** splits all sequences in train and test sets uniformly at random. Hence, both train and test are identically distributed. Typically models succeed at it easily. In **SCAN-jump**, the test set contains all compositional uses of one of the primitives, `jump`. The train set contains all uses of other primitives, and inputs where `jump` is used in isolation. **SCAN-around-right** tests if a model is capable to generalize to combinations of two modifiers, `around` and `right`, that never co-occur in the training data. The test data contain all examples where the two modifiers are combined.

[2]We have also ensured that our best modification performs on par ($\approx$ 10%) with Transformer on SCAN-length; however SCAN-length is believed to require a different type of generalization (Gordon et al., 2019).

4.2 Machine Translation

We hypothesize that the type of systematic generalization that SCAN probes for could be most useful in data-poor tasks or tasks with train-test distribution shift. Hence, we complement the standard IWSLT'14 En-De dataset with a low-resource task, FLoRes. To study whether our models can perform SCAN-style generalization on natural language data, we also build a dataset that probes for compositional generalization in noun-adjective ordering in French, when translating from English.

IWSLT'14 En-De This is a standard MT dataset, that includes train, validation, & test sets. We apply preprocessing as in the fairseq example.[3]

FLoRes (Guzmán et al., 2019) FloRes is a low-resource dataset for English↔ Nepali and English ↔ Sinhala translation. The dataset is split into dev, devtest, and test subsets. We only use the provided supervised data.

Noun-adjective ordering We take inspiration from SCAN-jump to construct an MT dataset that probes for compositional generalization using noun-adjective ordering in French. In French, both *adjective noun* (forward) and *noun adjective* (backward) orders are used, unlike English that only has the forward order. Which order is used largely depends on the adjective. For example, to refer to a *specific response*, French speakers say *résponse spécifique* (backward order), while *new response* would be *nouvelle résponse* (forward).

To draw a parallel with SCAN-jump, we consider the nouns as primitives and adjectives as modifiers. Modifiers appear with different primitives, however, some primitives appear with only one modifier. For instance, if, in the training set, *response* only appears with *specific* (backward), we test models on translating sentences containing *new response*, where *new* modifies many other nouns in the training set in the forward order. Such generalization is required by humans when dealing with rare or too specific nouns.

To construct our dataset, we start from the English-French Europarl dataset (a part of WMT'14 En-Fr)[4] and select 8 nouns, $\mathcal{N}$ ={*response, institution, organisation, solution, source, decision, responsibility, population*}. We constrain our train set so that each of the nouns in $\mathcal{N}$ appears only with one adjective (hence in

[3]`https://github.com/pytorch/fairseq/tree/master/examples/translation`

[4]`http://www.statmt.org/europarl/`

backward order	forward order
('specific', 'response')	('new', 'source')
('particular', 'institution')	('good', 'decision')
('effective', 'organisation')	('big', 'responsibility')
('permanent', 'solution')	('first', 'population')

Table 2: (adjective, noun) pairs in the train set of the noun-adjective ordering dataset, classified by their order in French language.

one particular order) as shown in Table 2. For example, the noun *response* will only be composed with the adjective *specific*. However, *specific* (and all other adjectives in Table 2) appears with other nouns. To select these sentences, we use the CoreNLP parser (Manning et al., 2014).[5] Finally, all sentences with nouns that are not among the selected ones are kept. In other words, the training set may contain sentences that have neither the selected adjectives nor the selected nouns. This results to 1641681 sentence pairs split into train (1478195 pairs) and validation (163486 pairs) sets. The test set is composed of the filtered sentences of the original Europarl dataset: we select sentences where nouns in the backward column of Table 2 ({*response, institution, organism, solution*}) are only modified by the adjectives in the forward column ({*new, good, big, first*}). Similarly, we also consider the sentences where the nouns of the forward column are composed with the adjectives of the backward column of the Table.[6] This process will ensure that in the test set, the noun-adjective only appears in the reverse order compared to the train set. Unlike the training data, the test data contains only sentences with the target nouns and adjectives. In total, we test models on 659 sentences. Note that the train and validation sets are identically distributed, however, the test set is distribution-shifted w.r.t. train, akin to SCAN-jump.

We follow the preprocessing steps on the fairseq example page for WMT'14 English to French.[3]

5 Methodology

SCAN Lake and Baroni (2018) were concerned by the feasibility of systematic generalization in seq2seq models. Hence, in their experiments, they tuned the models on the train data and then directly evaluated them on test set, reporting test scores. We follow the same protocol: given a grid of hyperparameters, we fit models on the training data. Next, for each hyperparameter configuration, we average the performance of the models across random seeds. Such a setup demonstrates that, at least for some hyperparameter configurations, the introduced models can learn to generalize systematically. At evaluation time, we decode greedily.

IWSLT'14 De-En We run a grid search on train data; next we select the best performing checkpoint on the validation dataset. We report performance on the test data. We use the same training and evaluation protocols as suggested on the fairseq MT example page.[3] We use beam size 5.

FLoRes This dataset has dev, devtest, and test splits provided. We run a hyperparameter grid search training on the dev data. Next, we select the hyperparameter configuration that has the best average (across seeds) performance on devtest. We report the performance of the selected hyperparameter configuration on the test set, averaged across seeds. We use the training/evaluation scripts, tokenization and other parameters suggested on the dataset page: beam size 5 and length penalty 1.2.

Noun-adjective ordering We run the hyperparameter search similarly to IWSLT'14 De-En. The training and evaluation protocols are the ones suggested by the fairseq page for WMT'14 En-Fr.[3] We also use beam size 5.

As we aim to probe abilities for compositional generalization, we introduce an accuracy-based measure, *COMP*. When analyzing models' errors, we encountered 3 common errors: (1) removing the adjective (example 1 in Table 6), (2) replacing the adjective with a synonym and reversing the order (examples 2 and 3 in Table 6), and (3) producing a completely wrong generalization while removing the adjective. While (2) provides a good enough translation, it is a mistake in the noun-adjective order. However, when outputting the right noun and adjective, the order is always preserved. Hence, to measure if a model is compositional, we only look if both the target adjective and the target noun appear in the prediction, irrespective of their order. We define thus COMP as the ratio of predicted sentences that include *both* the target adjective and noun.[7]

[5]`https://stanfordnlp.github.io/`

[6]We use the Stanford parser to select these sentences.

[7]It happens that models use a synonym in the right order as shown in SAG+T5's prediction 2 in Table 6. In that case, models had generalized well but are still penalized by COMP. COMP is hence only a proxy measure for compositional generalization based on the common failures.

	jump	around-right	simple
Transformer	$3.4_{\pm 2.0}$	$97.6_{\pm 1.5}$	$100.0_{\pm 0.0}$
self-att. gate (SAG)	$17.2_{\pm 5.8}$	$85.2_{\pm 10.0}$	$100.0_{\pm 0.0}$
+ Conv as s.-a.	$25.7_{\pm 20.4}$	$38.4_{\pm 7.8}$	$99.8_{\pm 0.0}$
+ Fixed-span	$33.6_{\pm 9.5}$	$97.6_{\pm 1.3}$	$100.0_{\pm 0.0}$
+ T5	$43.0_{\pm 9.5}$	$92.6_{\pm 2.8}$	$100.0_{\pm 0.0}$
LSTM seq2seq (Lake and Baroni, 2018)	1.2	2.5	99.8
ConvS2S (Dessì and Baroni, 2019)	$69.2_{\pm 8.2}$	$56.7_{\pm 10.2}$	$100.0_{\pm 0.0}$

Table 3: Accuracy on SCAN tasks, %. For each architecture and task, we report the mean accuracy of the best hyperparameter configuration. ± denotes 1 SEM.

Hyperparameter search Transformer models have multiple hyperparameters (embeddings dimensionality, number of layers and attention heads, dropout probabilities, etc.). On top of those, our introduced models add the attention span s, and the initial gate state β_0. For MT tasks, we start from the existing strong baseline hyperparameter configurations (FLoRes: specified by Guzmán et al. (2019), De-En & En-Fr: following the fairseq example page) and only tune (a) the parameters introduced by our architectures, and (b) the attention dropout parameter (for all architectures, including Transformer). For SCAN, there is no baseline hyperparameter configuration, so we start with tuning Transformer and then base hyperparameters of the introduced architectures on it. We report full hyperparameter grids in Supplementary.

6 SCAN experiments

In our preliminary experiments, we found that our modifications of the self-attention mechanism do not lead to improvements over the standard Transformer when they are not combined with the self-attention gate (SAG). Hence, we focus our experiments on architectures that include SAG.

We report our results in Table 3. We also include results for LSTM- and Conv-based seq2seq models that were reported in earlier work (Lake and Baroni, 2018; Dessì and Baroni, 2019). From Table 3, we see that the unmodified Transformer has very low accuracy on `jump` (3.4%), which is only slightly above that of LSTM seq2seq (1.2%) and well below ConvS2S (69.2%). This indicates that Transformer models are indeed failing in compositional generalization on `jump`. However, they have a very high score on the `around-right` split (97.6%) and `simple` (≥ 99.8%). By introducing the different modifications described in Section 3, making Transformers closer to ConvS2S, we aim at preserving the high performance of Transformers on `around-right` and `simple` while significantly improving it on `jump`.

Transformer	SAG	+ Conv s.-a.	+ fix. span	+ T5
$34.64_{\pm 0.03}$	$34.28_{\pm 0.08}$	$33.44_{\pm 0.04}$	$34.32_{\pm 0.01}$	$34.66_{\pm 0.04}$

Table 4: BLEU on test set. IWSLT'14 German to English dataset. ± denotes 1 SEM.

Adding SAG increases accuracy on `jump` 5-fold (17.2%) at the expense of a small drop in `around-right` scores (not stat. sig.).

Further, we observe that changes of the self-attention mechanism (replacing it with Convs, limiting its span, and adding a relative position-dependent bias), can further increase the performance on `jump`. Apart from SAG+Conv as s.-a, the self-attention modifications do not significantly alter the performance on `around-right`.

We see that the architectural changes that we proposed improve the compositional capabilities of the Transformer models. As expected, the introduced hybrid architectures reach significantly better performance on `jump` (up to 12x improvements for SAG+T5) while keeping high performance on the `around-right` & `simple` tasks.

7 Machine Translation experiments

IWSLT'14 De-En In Table 4, we report BLEU scores on German-English translation. SAG + T5 performs slightly better (0.02 BLEU, not stat. sig.), but other modifications underperform w.r.t. Transformer. Replacing self-attention with convolutions resulted in the largest drop, 3%. Other differences are smaller, ≤ 1%. For the following parts, we only experiment with the SAG + T5 model as the only non-degraded one. However, results with the remaining models on FLoRes and the Noun-adjective ordering datasets are reported in Supplementary.

FLoRes, Si/Ne ↔ En We report results on

English↔Nepali and English↔Sinhala translation in Table 5. Following Guzmán et al. (2019), we use tokenized BLEU when translating from English. We run standard Transformer models as specified in Guzmán et al. (2019), but adding a search over the attention dropout probability. We verify that we have close results compared to Guzmán et al. (2019).[8] Table 5 shows that SAG + T5 outperforms Transformer on all language pairs and directions with relative improvements between 3.6% (si-en) and 13.1% (en-ne).

Noun-adjective ordering BLEU scores on the test set are reported in Table 5. SAG + T5 leads to a relative improvement of 1.39% compared to standard Transformer. BLEU, however, is not informative about the particular noun-adjective generalization. We hence also report COMP scores. From Table 5, we see that SAG + T5 demonstrates a significant improvement with 14% relative gain compared to the standard Transformer architecture. Our follow-up experiments show that the hybrid model recovers an average of 43.3% of cases where the best Transformer model (best seed w.r.t. COMP) failed in compositional generalization, whereas Transformer is only correct at 21.5% of SAG + T5's errors. We report in Table 6 examples comparing SAG + T5 and Transformer translations.

Discussion Upon analyzing our experiments on SCAN and machine translation tasks, we see the following picture. Indeed the hybrid models that we described in Section 2 have considerably higher accuracy on SCAN-`jump` w.r.t. Transformer and a comparable performance on the other SCAN splits. Hence, our results suggest the importance of both gating and (the ability of) limiting the attention span for SCAN generalization.

As expected, the improvement on SCAN do not consistently entail improvements on the resource-rich dataset, and only the combination of SAG and T5 showed a tiny improvement. This emphasizes the importance of testing models on realistic setups to model from being too SCAN-tailored.

Finally, we test SAG + T5 on low-resource and compositional tasks. The hybrid architecture shows consistent improvements on FLoRes for all translation directions, with at up to 13.1% relative improvement, and on the the natural language compositional task with 14% relative improvement on COMP. Our qualitative analysis also showed that SAG + T5 correctly handles noun-adjective ordering in most cases, while Transformer makes more mistakes.

[8]We got better BLEU scores due to the extra grid search.

8 Related Work

Compositionally-biased models Several approaches were proposed to build SCAN-capable architectures. They span from meta-learning (Lake, 2019), disentangling syntax and semantics (Russin et al., 2019), learning equivariant (Gordon et al., 2019) and disentangled representations (Li et al., 2019) or combining neural & symbolic computations (Chen et al., 2020). In contrast, we do not build new models that are specialized to SCAN. Instead, we show that a standard model can be incrementally modified so that performs well on SCAN and still performs well on a standard MT task. Having such incrementally improved models allows us to step back and wonder if SCAN (or similar artificial tasks) should be used as a guidance when developing new models.

Bastings et al. (2018) raised concerns due to SCAN being too artificial by showing that even degenerate architectures can perform well on some SCAN tasks. Our results echo their findings: by developing architectures tailored for SCAN, one can easily come up with models that perform worse on general tasks. However, we find that if one avoids this "SCAN overfitting" and endows a model with capabilities that SCAN probes for without harming its general performance, they can gain in low-resource scenarios and better handle relevant phenomena in language.

Changing attention mechanisms Self- and cross-attention mechanisms were tweaked in earlier work in order to inject useful biases, e.g., by adding information of relative positions of tokens (Shaw et al., 2018; Raffel et al., 2019) or accounting for the locality bias in cross-attention (Yang et al., 2018). Sukhbaatar et al. and Rae and Razavi (2020) demonstrated that having a short attention span on the lower layers of Transformer models is enough for good language modeling performance.

9 Conclusion

In this work, we primarily focused on whether and in which scenarios the inductive bias for compositional generalization, that SCAN looks for, can be useful in natural language tasks.

We ran study in two steps. As the first step, by exploiting ConvS2S/Transformer similarities, we came up with a modification of the Transformer

	FLoRes (BLEU)				Noun-Adj. ordering	
	ne-en	si-en	en-ne	en-si	BLEU	COMP
Transformer	$7.94_{\pm 0.05}$	$7.15_{\pm 0.07}$	$4.43_{\pm 0.01}$	$2.32_{\pm 0.08}$	$40.86_{\pm 0.34}$	$0.64_{\pm 0.01}$
SAG + T5	$\mathbf{8.40}_{\pm \mathbf{0.02}}$	$7.41_{\pm 0.10}$	$\mathbf{5.01}_{\pm \mathbf{0.10}}$	$\mathbf{2.54}_{\pm \mathbf{0.03}}$	$41.43_{\pm 0.29}$	$\mathbf{0.73}_{\pm \mathbf{0.01}}$

Table 5: Models performance on FLoRes and Noun-adjective ordering (English to French) dataset. For FLoRes, we report the BLEU dev-test scores for the different translation directions. For the Noun-adjective ordering dataset, we report both BLEU and COMP measures on the test set. In bold are values that stat. sig. improve over Transformer. $\pm$ denotes 1 SEM.

Target: Nous sommes face à une *responsabilité politique particulière*.
Prediction SAG+T5: Nous sommes accablés par une *responsabilité politique particulière*.
Prediction Transformer: Nous sommes accablés par une *responsabilité politique*.

Target: Nous voulons trouver une *bonne solution* à ce problème.
Prediction SAG+T5: Nous voulons trouver une *bonne solution* à ce problème.
Prediction Transformer: Nous voulons trouver une *solution adéquate* à ce problème.

Target: Ce qui nous déçoit par rapport à cette *décision particulière*, c'est que le projet aurait pu clairement voir le jour.
Prediction SAG+T5: Ce qui est triste dans cette *décision précise*, c'est que le projet aurait été clairement réalisé.
Prediction Transformer: Ce qui est triste dans cette *mauvaise décision*, c'est que le projet aurait clairement été.

Table 6: Generation Examples for Noun-adjective ordering dataset. Models are tested on the underlined and italic *(adjective, noun)*. For the first 2 examples, SAG+T5 predicted the right *(adjective, noun)* translation. In the last one, SAG+T5 replaced the adjective with a synonym but in the right target order (the one not seen in the training set). In the first example, Transformer removed the adjective *particulière*. In the two following examples, Transformer replaced the right adjective with a close synonym adjective to be conform with the training order. For instance, in the second example, *bonne* (an adjective that appears in the forward order) was replaced by *adéquate* (an adjective that appears in the backward order) as the *solution* appears only in the backward order at training.

architecture that performs considerably better than vanilla Transformer on SCAN-jump (43.0% vs 3.4% accuracy) and performs equally well on SCAN-simple, SCAN-around-right, and on a standard resource-rich MT task (IWSLT'14 De-En).

Next, we tested this modification in low-resource and distribution-shifted setups. In the low-resource MT setup (FLoRes Si/Ne↔En), we found that our considered architecture improves by up to 13.1% in BLEU score over the vanilla Transformer. Then, we introduced a new dataset that probes specifically for compositional reasoning in natural language. Unlike SCAN, our compositional dataset is built by filtering an existing natural language corpus (EuroParl En-Fr) to probe how models perform noun-adjective ordering under a (minimal) distribution shift. Thus, we are largely closer to testing the compositional generalization required by humans compared to SCAN, and succeeding on the test set requires both compositional reasoning and good language model performance (see examples in Table 6). We believe that such a dataset is beneficial for future research to test more complex compositionality skills. Finally, our experiments on our dataset demonstrated that better SCAN generalization leads to better results on noun-adjective ordering (14% on COMP).

Our findings indicate the following. Firstly, as hypothesized before (Dessì and Baroni, 2019; Hupkes et al., 2018), the limited attention span provides a useful inductive bias that allows models to perform better on compositional generalization induction, that SCAN probes for. Further, endowing a model with SCAN-style generalization capabilities *can* lead to improvements in low-resource and distribution-shifted scenarios as long as we ensure that we do not overfit to SCAN.

We believe that the contribution of diagnostic datasets like SCAN is of great value. As performance grows on tasks such as MT, identifying gaps where a model's performance lags will become fundamental and will guide us to develop architectures that cover genuine new linguistic grounds and not just overfit to peculiarities of standard datasets.

Acknowledgments

The authors are grateful to Marco Baroni and the reviewers for feedback that helped us to improve our .

References

Daniel Adiwardana, Minh-Thang Luong, David R So, Jamie Hall, Noah Fiedel, Romal Thoppilan, Zi Yang, Apoorv Kulshreshtha, Gaurav Nemade, Yifeng Lu, et al. 2020. Towards a human-like open-domain chatbot. *arXiv preprint arXiv:2001.09977.*

Jimmy Lei Ba, Jamie Ryan Kiros, and Geoffrey E Hinton. 2016. Layer normalization. *arXiv preprint arXiv:1607.06450.*

Dzmitry Bahdanau, Kyunghyun Cho, and Yoshua Bengio. 2014. Neural machine translation by jointly learning to align and translate. *arXiv preprint arXiv:1409.0473.*

Marco Baroni. 2019. Linguistic generalization and compositionality in modern artificial neural networks. *Philosophical Transactions of the Royal Society B: Biological Sciences*, 375(1791):20190307.

Jasmijn Bastings, Marco Baroni, Jason Weston, Kyunghyun Cho, and Douwe Kiela. 2018. Jump to better conclusions: Scan both left and right. In *MNLP Workshop BlackboxNLP: Analyzing and Interpreting Neural Networks for NLP.*

Xinyun Chen, Chen Liang, Adams Wei Yu, Dawn Song, and Denny Zhou. 2020. Compositional generalization via neural-symbolic stack machines.

Jean-Baptiste Cordonnier, Andreas Loukas, and Martin Jaggi. 2020. On the relationship between self-attention and convolutional layers. In *ICLR.*

Verna Dankers, Elia Bruni, and Dieuwke Hupkes. 2021. The paradox of the compositionality of natural language: a neural machine translation case study.

Yann N Dauphin, Angela Fan, Michael Auli, and David Grangier. 2017. Language modeling with gated convolutional networks. In *ICML.*

Roberto Dessì and Marco Baroni. 2019. CNNs found to jump around more skillfully than RNNs: Compositional generalization in seq2seq convolutional networks. In *ACL.*

Richard Futrell, Kyle Mahowald, and Edward Gibson. 2015. Large-scale evidence of dependency length minimization in 37 languages. *PNAS*, 112(33):10336–10341.

Jonas Gehring, Michael Auli, David Grangier, Denis Yarats, and Yann N. Dauphin. 2017. Convolutional sequence to sequence learning. In *ICML.*

Jonathan Gordon, David Lopez-Paz, Marco Baroni, and Diane Bouchacourt. 2019. Permutation equivariant models for compositional generalization in language. In *ICLR.*

Francisco Guzmán, Peng-Jen Chen, Myle Ott, Juan Pino, Guillaume Lample, Philipp Koehn, Vishrav Chaudhary, and Marc'Aurelio Ranzato. 2019. Two new evaluation datasets for low-resource machine translation: Nepali-english and sinhala-english.

Dieuwke Hupkes, Verna Dankers, Mathijs Mul, and Elia Bruni. 2020. Compositionality decomposed: How do neural networks generalise? *Journal of Artificial Intelligence Research*, 67:757–795.

Dieuwke Hupkes, Anand Singh, Kris Korrel, German Kruszewski, and Elia Bruni. 2018. Learning compositionally through attentive guidance. *arXiv preprint arXiv:1805.09657.*

Eugene Kharitonov and Rahma Chaabouni. 2021. What they do when in doubt: a study of inductive biases in seq2seq learners. In *ICLR.*

Diederik P Kingma and Jimmy Ba. 2014. Adam: A method for stochastic optimization. *arXiv preprint arXiv:1412.6980.*

Brenden Lake. 2019. Compositional generalization through meta sequence-to-sequence learning. In *NeurIPS.*

Brenden Lake and Marco Baroni. 2018. Generalization without systematicity: On the compositional skills of sequence-to-sequence recurrent networks. In *ICML.*

Yuanpeng Li, Liang Zhao, Jianyu Wang, and Joel Hestness. 2019. Compositional generalization for primitive substitutions. *arXiv preprint arXiv:1910.02612.*

Joao Loula, Marco Baroni, and Brenden M Lake. 2018. Rearranging the familiar: Testing compositional generalization in recurrent networks. *EMNLP 2018.*

Christopher Manning, Mihai Surdeanu, John Bauer, Jenny Finkel, Steven Bethard, and David McClosky. 2014. The Stanford CoreNLP natural language processing toolkit. In *ACL: System Demonstrations.*

R Thomas McCoy, Robert Frank, and Tal Linzen. 2020. Does syntax need to grow on trees? sources of hierarchical inductive bias in sequence-to-sequence networks. *TACL*, 8:125–140.

Myle Ott, Sergey Edunov, Alexei Baevski, Angela Fan, Sam Gross, Nathan Ng, David Grangier, and Michael Auli. 2019. fairseq: A fast, extensible toolkit for sequence modeling. In *NAACL-HLT 2019: Demonstrations.*

Emilio Parisotto, Francis Song, Jack Rae, Razvan Pascanu, Caglar Gulcehre, Siddhant Jayakumar, Max Jaderberg, Raphael Lopez Kaufman, Aidan Clark, Seb Noury, et al. 2020. Stabilizing transformers for reinforcement learning. In *ICLR.*

Jack Rae and Ali Razavi. 2020. Do transformers need deep long-range memory? In *ACL*.

Colin Raffel, Noam Shazeer, Adam Roberts, Katherine Lee, Sharan Narang, Michael Matena, Yanqi Zhou, Wei Li, and Peter J Liu. 2019. Exploring the limits of transfer learning with a unified text-to-text transformer. *arXiv preprint arXiv:1910.10683*.

Jake Russin, Jason Jo, Randall C O'Reilly, and Yoshua Bengio. 2019. Compositional generalization in a deep seq2seq model by separating syntax and semantics. *arXiv preprint arXiv:1904.09708*.

Tim Salimans and Durk P Kingma. 2016. Weight normalization: A simple reparameterization to accelerate training of deep neural networks. In *NeurIPS*.

Peter Shaw, Jakob Uszkoreit, and Ashish Vaswani. 2018. Self-attention with relative position representations. In *NAACL*, pages 464–468.

Sainbayar Sukhbaatar, Édouard Grave, Piotr Bojanowski, and Armand Joulin. Adaptive attention span in transformers.

Ilya Sutskever, James Martens, George Dahl, and Geoffrey Hinton. 2013. On the importance of initialization and momentum in deep learning. In *ICML*.

Ilya Sutskever, Oriol Vinyals, and Quoc V Le. 2014. Sequence to sequence learning with neural networks. In *NeurIPS*.

Baosong Yang, Zhaopeng Tu, Derek F Wong, Fandong Meng, Lidia S Chao, and Tong Zhang. 2018. Modeling localness for self-attention networks. *arXiv preprint arXiv:1810.10182*.

A Hyperparameter grids

A.1 SCAN

For each architecture, we used the same hyperparameter grids for all splits of SCAN.

All models were trained by Adam with default β_1 and β_2 parameters, for 250 epochs, with batch size 256, learning rate $5 \cdot 10^{-4}$, dropout and attention dropout 0.1, random seeds $\{0, 1, 2\}$. We vary the Encoder and Decoder parameters independently: number of attention heads $\{4, 8\}$, embedding dimensions $\{128, 256\}$, FFN dimensions $\{256, 512\}$, and the number of layers $\{4, 6, 8\}$; clip norm 1.0.

For hybrids models, add the following parameters.

SAG To reduce the search space, we did not vary β_0, setting it to -1.

SAG + CNN as self-attention Span: $\{2, 4, 6\}$, $\beta_0 = -1$, number of layers: $\{4, 6\}$.

SAG + fixed span self-attention Span: $\{2, 4, 6\}$, $\beta_0 = -1$, number of layers: 4.

SAG + T5 Span: $\{2, 4, 6\}$, $\beta_0 = -1$, number of layers: 4.

A.2 Machine Translation

De-En We start from the standard architecture suggested by Fairseq examples for IWSLT'14 De-En. That is we share decoder input and output embeddings. Both Encoder and decoder have an embedding size of 512 FFN dimensions of 1024, 4 attention heads, 6 encoder & decoder layers. We used adam optimizer with learning rate of 5e-4, no clip norm, warm-up learning rate 1e-7, inverse square root learning rate scheduler, 4000 warm-up updates, dropout 0.3, weight decay 1e-4, label smoothing 0.1, max. tokens per batch per GPU: 1024, 40 epochs. We used 4 GPUs for training.

For SAG-enabled architectures, we additionally searched for Encoder's β_0 in $\{-1, 0\}$ and $\{1, 0\}$ for Decoder. We varied attention span in $\{2, 4, 6\}$, ttention dropout in $\{0.0, 0.2\}$ and pre-block encoder and decoder normalization.

For model selection, we also follow Fairseq example and checkpoint the best model on validation set based on BLEU score. BLEU score is computed with a beam of size 5.

FLoRes We used shared embeddings between Encoder and Decoder, embedding dimenions of 512, FFN dimensions of 2048, 2 attention heads, 5 encoder & decoder layers. We used pre-block normalization[9], learning rate of 1e-3, no clip norm, warm-up learning rate 1e-7, inverse square root learning rate scheduler, 4000 warm-up updates, dropout 0.4, activation dropout 0.2, weight decay 1e-4, label smoothing 0.2, max. tokens per batch per GPU: 4000, 100 epochs. We searched for attention dropout in $\{0.0, 0.2\}$. We used 4 GPUs for training.

For SAG-enabled arcchitectures, we additionally searched for Encoder's β_0 in $\{-2, -1, 0\}$ and $\{2, 1, 0\}$ for Decoder. We varied attention span in $\{2, 4, 6\}$.

Noun-adjective order agreement We start from the standard architecture suggested by Fairseq examples for WMT'14 En-Fr. That is we share encoder, decoder and output embeddings. Both Encoder and decoder have an embedding size of 1024 FFN dimensions of 4096, 16 attention heads, 6 encoder & decoder layers. We used adam optimizer with learning rate of 7e-4, no clip norm, warm-up learning rate 1e-7, inverse square root learning rate scheduler, 4000 warm-up updates, dropout 0.1, label smoothing 0.1, max. tokens per batch per GPU: 4000, 30 epochs. We used 6 GPUs for training.

For SAG-enabled architectures, we additionally searched for Encoder's β_0 in $\{-1, 0\}$ and $\{1, 0\}$ for Decoder. We varied attention span in $\{2, 4, 6\}$, ttention dropout in $\{0.0, 0.2\}$ and pre-block encoder and decoder normalization.

Best checkpoint is based on the loss of the validation set.

B Other modifications on FloRes and Noun-adjective ordering datasets

In the main paper, we only experimented with SAG + T5 as the only non-degraded modification on the IWSLT'14 En-De dataset. Our intuition is that the remaining hybrid models are SCAN-tailored and would not lead to any improvement in the low-resource (FloRes) and domain-shifted (Noun-adjective ordering dataset) settings. In this section, we verify our intuition and report the results of all the introduced variants. The hyper-parameters search is reported in Section A.

FloRes We report results on English↔Nepali and English↔Sinhala translation in Table 7. We

[9] `--encoder-normalize-before` and `--decoder-normalize-before` in fairseq.

also report Guzmán et al. (2019) results under "Baseline".

Analyzing results of SAG, we notice that it is usually very close to Transformer's results on all tasks, apart from Nepali→English, where it lags behind. The fixed-span modification performs worse than Transformer on in all directions. Replacing self-attention with convolutions results in better scores on En→Ne and worse scores on Ne→En/En→Si.

Hence, as expected, only the SAG + T5 model outperforms Transformer on all language pairs and directions, highlighting the importance of verifying the generality of the model on realistic datasets.

Noun-adjective order agreement BLEU scores on the test set are reported in Table 8. SAG leads to a relative improvement of 1.44% compared to standard Transformer, closely followed by SAG + T5. Still, in total, the differences are very small across all models. On the other hand, all introduced variants outperform standard Transformer on COMP. However, only SAG + T5 demonstrates a significant improvement with 14% relative gain.

Overall, we observe that the SCAN-tailored variants do not degrade performances on the Noun-adjective order agreement dataset, but still do not lead to any significant improvement, contrary to SAG + T5.

C Visualizing attention biases

In this Section, we illustrate how a successful SAG + T5 model uses its b_{ij} terms (Eq. 1) to control its attention.

We take the most successful hyperparameter combination on SCAN-`jump` in Table 3 and select a model instance that has the best accuracy ($\approx$ 60%). Next, for each attention head of each encoder and decoder layer, we retrieve its learned relative-position bias b_d, where d is a (signed) relative distance between positions i and j, that is capped to be within $[-s, +s]$ (see Section 3). For each head, we apply a softmax, to find its "preference" $\hat{b}_d$ over relative positions d:

$$\hat{b}_d = \frac{\exp(b_d)}{\sum_d \exp(b_d)}$$

We report the results in Figure 1. Interestingly, quite a few attention heads have very strong preferences for fixed relative positions and some are even dominantly focused on particular positions (Encoder: head 7 in the layer 0; heads 4, 5 in layer 1, heads 3, 7 in layer 2; head 2 in layer 3; Decoder: head 4 in layer 0, head 2 in layer 1, heads 3,4,5 in layer 2; heads 2, 6, 7 in layer 3)[10]. More often than not, those "specialized" heads look within the span and not on the "border" values of d (due to d being capped, they also correspond to arbitrary distant positions to the left and right).

Hence we conclude that in a T5 model (among most successful on SCAN-`jump`), several heads leverage the ability pay attention locally; supporting our finding that local attention is connected with the compositional generalization needed to succeed at SCAN. At the same time, some heads have large relative-position bias for distant positions ($[s, +\infty[$ or $] - \infty, -s]$). This general ability to *optionally* look beyond a fixed span in T5 could be responsible for its better performance compared to the fixed span modification.

[10]T5 reduces to the vanilla Transformer if all b_d are equal to zero. That corresponds to the uniform bias $\hat{b}_d$.

	Baseline	Transformer	SAG	+ Conv s.-a.	+ fixed span	+ T5
ne-en	7.6	$7.94_{\pm 0.05}$	$7.58_{\pm 0.06}$	$7.59_{\pm 0.02}$	$7.44_{\pm 0.08}$	$\mathbf{8.40_{\pm 0.02}}$
si-en	7.2	$7.15_{\pm 0.07}$	$7.14_{\pm 0.10}$	$7.18_{\pm 0.10}$	$.78_{\pm 0.07}$	$7.41_{\pm 0.10}$
en-ne	4.3	$4.43_{\pm 0.01}$	$4.36_{\pm 0.08}$	$\mathbf{4.63_{\pm 0.03}}$	$4.12_{\pm 0.05}$	$\mathbf{5.01_{\pm 0.10}}$
en-si	1.2	$2.32_{\pm 0.08}$	$2.37_{\pm 0.10}$	$2.14_{\pm 0.03}$	$2.12_{\pm 0.04}$	$\mathbf{2.54_{\pm 0.03}}$

Table 7: BLEU dev-test scores on FLoRes. Baseline scores are taken from (Guzmán et al., 2019). In bold are values that stat. sig. improve over Transformer ($p < 10^{-3}$). $\pm$ indicates 1 SEM.

	Transformer	SAG	+ Conv s.-a.	+ fixed span	+ T5
BLEU	$40.86_{\pm 0.34}$	$41.45_{\pm 0.14}$	$39.89_{\pm 0.27}$	$41.01_{\pm 0.24}$	$41.43_{\pm 0.29}$
COMP	$0.64_{\pm 0.01}$	$0.70_{\pm 0.03}$	$0.67_{\pm 0.01}$	$0.68_{\pm 0.01}$	$\mathbf{0.73_{\pm 0.01}}$

Table 8: BLEU and COMP measures on test sets: compositional English to French dataset. In bold are values that stat. sig. improve over Transformer ($p < 0.05$). $\pm$ denotes 1 SEM.

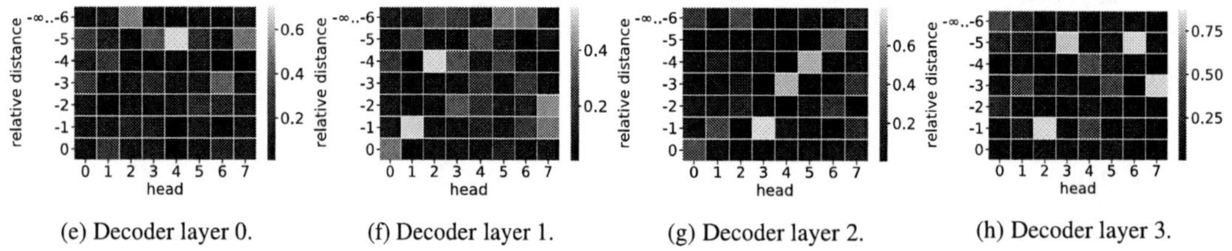

(a) Encoder layer 0. (b) Encoder layer 1. (c) Encoder layer 2. (d) Encoder layer 3.

(e) Decoder layer 0. (f) Decoder layer 1. (g) Decoder layer 2. (h) Decoder layer 3.

Figure 1: Relative attention biases for T5 + SAG architecture (after a softmax). Each cell indicates preference of a head to a position at a signed relative distance. The relative distances are capped. For the decoder we only represent relative attention biases for $d \leq 0$, as positions with positive relative distance are masked in the autoregressive decoder.

Transferring Knowledge from Vision to Language: How to Achieve it and how to Measure it?

Tobias Norlund[*†] **Lovisa Hagström**[*] **Richard Johansson**
Division of Data Science and Artificial Intelligence
Chalmers University of Technology
[†] Recorded Future
{tobiasno, lovhag, richajo}@chalmers.se

Abstract

Large language models are known to suffer from the hallucination problem in that they are prone to output statements that are false or inconsistent, indicating a lack of knowledge. A proposed solution to this is to provide the model with additional data modalities that complements the knowledge obtained through text. We investigate the use of visual data to complement the knowledge of large language models by proposing a method for evaluating visual knowledge transfer to text for uni- or multimodal language models. The method is based on two steps, 1) a novel task querying for knowledge of memory colors, i.e. typical colors of well-known objects, and 2) filtering of model training data to clearly separate knowledge contributions. Additionally, we introduce a model architecture that involves a visual imagination step and evaluate it with our proposed method. We find that our method can successfully be used to measure visual knowledge transfer capabilities in models and that our novel model architecture shows promising results for leveraging multimodal knowledge in a unimodal setting.

1 Introduction

Large language models have proved performant across a diverse set of tasks in NLP, and most recently even as unsupervised multitask learners (Radford et al., 2019; Brown et al., 2020). An important contributing factor to this is the capability of the models to hold large amounts of linguistic as well as factual knowledge in their parameters.

While impressive, without strong task-specific fine-tuning these models are prone to outputting false or inconsistent statements, often also referred to as *hallucination* (Logan et al., 2019). This has been particularly studied for generative tasks such as abstractive text summarization (Maynez et al., 2020) and dialog systems (Roller et al., 2021; Li et al., 2020a), but the problem is also apparent for models applied to cloze-style fill-in-the-blank tasks (Petroni et al., 2019; Jiang et al., 2020). Having truthful NLP systems is a core requirement for most applications, which is why this is an important problem to address.

Grounding has been proposed as a potential way to mitigate this problem, e.g by providing broader world information from for example multimodal perception (Bisk et al., 2020; Bender and Koller, 2020).

Information from multimodal perception may actually provide a significant amount of additional world information to an NLP model, since text data suffers from the problem of *reporting bias*. That is, humans generally communicate novel information rather than trivial, leading to a discrepancy between reality and what gets described in text (Gordon and Van Durme, 2013). Consequently, perceptual information may contain complementing world knowledge that cannot be found in text data, and has the potential to mitigate the aforementioned problem of hallucinating NLP models.

Previous works have evaluated how grounded language representations impact performance on common NLP benchmarks (Sileo, 2021; Kiela et al., 2018; Elliott and Kádár, 2017), but little has been done on investigating grounding specifically as an additional source of knowledge.

In this work, we take a focused look at how data from a visual modality can augment the knowledge a language model expresses. We design an experimental setup to enable the development of strategies for maximizing visual-to-textual knowledge transfer. In the setup, we create a small knowledge-centric cloze-style task in English named *Memory Colors* that is tailored to test for visual knowledge by querying for the typical colors of well-known items. We also build a large vision-and-language

[*]Equal contribution.

Proceedings of the Fourth BlackboxNLP Workshop on Analyzing and Interpreting Neural Networks for NLP, pages 149–162
Online, November 11, 2021.

dataset in the English language, where we carefully control for the modality from which the necessary visual knowledge can be learnt. Finally, we use this data to train self-supervised multimodal models, and compare strategies to query for the visual knowledge.

Based on intuitions of how humans are able to store and retrieve such knowledge, we also propose a querying strategy that involves "imagining" a visual representation from which the answer then can be decoded.

To summarize, our contribution is twofold:

1. We provide an experimental setup for evaluating visual knowledge transfer in English multimodal language models, including a novel task we denote *Memory Colors*.
2. We propose a language model querying strategy involving a visual imagination step and show that it can provide an efficient means of visual knowledge transfer compared to standard querying.

2 An experimental setup evaluating visual knowledge transfer

Humans have the ability to learn knowledge from non-linguistic modalities (such as visual perception) and express this in language, making them able to e.g. textually reason about what an elephant looks like because they have previously seen said animal in an image. Many models that integrate the textual and visual modalities exist, but the majority of them have been created with the purpose of reasoning about properties of *individual images* provided to the system: for instance, to ask about an elephant, you need to simultaneously provide the model with an image of an elephant.

We hypothesize that the capability to incorporate knowledge from different modalities and expressing it textually could improve on the common sense as well as in-domain knowledge that language models possess. To this end, we wish to create an experimental setup in which we can measure how well a model can acquire visual knowledge and then express it in text.

A simple way to evaluate a model for its capability to transfer visual knowledge into text is to query it about typical colors of certain objects – *memory colors* – while making sure that the model cannot acquire this knowledge through a text signal, i.e. it has not previously been told what the colors should be.

Consequently, we create a zero-shot cloze-style task of predicting memory colors of common objects, described in Section 2.1. We also collect a large vision-and-language dataset for model training in which we carefully control for whether the knowledge necessary for solving the memory color task is available strictly in the visual, textual, or both modalities, described in Section 2.2.

2.1 Memory Colors dataset

When human observers can agree on the typical color, or canonical color, of a certain object type through their experiences with instances of said object type, the color of that object is generally referred to as its *memory color* (Pérez-Carpinell et al., 1998). For example, a banana can be green or brown, but it is usually remembered as being yellow, such that *yellow* is the memory color of a banana. As explained by Newhall et al. (1957) "... color memory is a selective resultant of the relative impressiveness during perception of the various aspects of stimulation. More dominant, characteristic, and attractive aspects tend to be more impressive, and less dominant aspects tend to be less impressive. The more impressive aspects are more prone to survival in subsequent memory while other aspects are not."

As such, memory colors of typical objects are remembered by humans and a human can answer questions about what the typical color of such an object is despite not having the object in front of them when answering. Consequently, memory colors express visual knowledge and we can use them for a simple zero-shot evaluation of whether a model can display the same capability as a human of transferring a visual signal into memory and, later on, text.

Figure 1: One entry in the Memory Colors dataset.

For our visual knowledge transfer evaluation task we create a novel Memory Colors dataset in the English language, consisting of 109 object types paired with their memory color, an illustrating picture and a descriptor. Figure 1 shows an example, and the supplementary material includes the full dataset with additional statistics.

The Memory Colors dataset and a corresponding human baseline is obtained by annotating a set of randomly shuffled cloze questions based on well-known entities with typical colors. Examples of such entities are items, materials, animals, ingredients or plants that are observable in the real world, such as *tomato*, *elephant*, *cocoa* and *grass*. These entities were sourced from the web, including Wikidata[1] and ConceptNet,[2] as well as from the commonsense knowledge of the authors of this article.

The cloze questions of the Memory Colors dataset are created with the help of a predefined query template; see an example question in Table 2. The predefined query template is assigned to each annotator from a set of seven different templates to create differently formatted questions querying for the same visual knowledge.

The memory colors used for the items in the dataset are black, blue, brown, green, grey, orange, pink, purple, red, white and yellow. The annotators are asked to pick their answer from one of these 11 colors for each question. They are also asked to answer the questions to the best of their ability, without consulting other information sources.[3]

Memory color label The color label for each item is given by the majority vote of 11 annotators, and only items with a minimum of 8 annotators agreeing on a memory color are included in the dataset, resulting in the Memory Colors dataset consisting of 109 items and corresponding memory colors, with a majority vote distribution as indicated in Table 1.

Table 1: The count of the number of majority votes for each of the items in the Memory Colors dataset. A majority vote of 11 means that all annotators agreed on the color.

# of majority votes	Count
11	60
10	32
9	7
8	10

Arguably, our use of the term *memory color* may be somewhat less strict than that of the optical science field, in which very few memory colors are admitted due to high requirements on agreement between humans for a color to be classified as a memory color. However, for the sake of obtaining a dataset of a sufficent size, we decide to also include items and colors for which there is a majority, while not a perfect one.

Table 2: An example of a cloze-question provided to a human annotator, given by the query template *Q: What is the color of [DESCRIPTOR] [ITEM]? A: [MASK].*

Question	Answer
Q: What is the color of *a lemon*? A: [answer]	*yellow*

Descriptor The descriptor for each item in the dataset is manually added to make the cloze-questions grammatically correct and to resolve potential item reference ambiguities. For example, determiners such as "a", "an" or " the" are added as a descriptor for countable nouns and the addition "the animal" might be added for the occurence *seal* to clarify that we refer to the animal and not e.g. a letter seal.

Illustrating picture A picture of each item in the dataset is manually added by the authors by picking an image from the Internet that is deemed to correspond well to the item, and that to the authors' best ability reflects the labeled color.

Human baseline The human baseline for the task is taken as the mean of the accuracy scores of 11 annotators, where each accuracy score is calculated by comparing the annotator answers with the majority vote labels. The annotators achieved a mean accuracy score of 0.937 with a standard deviation of 0.051 on the Memory Colors dataset.

We hypothesize that a perfect accuracy score is not reached due to different perceptions of colors, varying knowledge of what the Memory Colors items refer to and that it perhaps is unavoidable that some disagreements exist for this fairly large dataset that has an apparent dependence on cultural background. Hypothetically, the phrasing of the question may also be a factor that explains some of the variation (Kalton and Schuman, 1982), although this seems unlikely in this case since the questions concern concrete physical objects.

Annotator agreement To verify our Memory Colors dataset and its human baseline we also evaluate the annotator agreement between the 11 annotators using Fleiss' kappa score (Fleiss, 1971).

[1] `www.wikidata.org`

[2] `www.conceptnet.io`

[3] All the query templates and annotator instructions are provided in the supplementary material.

Table 3: Total number of image and caption samples for the full and filtered versions of the training dataset.

	Total
Validation	
Captions	58,937
Images	38,234
Training-unfiltered	
Captions	4,720,971
Images	2,911,438
Training-filtered	
Captions	4,429,671
Images	2,749,612

The kappa score for the agreement between the annotators is found to be 0.863, indicating that the annotators agree fairly well.

2.2 Vision-and-language dataset

We combine four public image+text datasets to be used for self-supervised training in our experiments: MS COCO (Lin et al., 2014), SBU Captions (Ordonez et al., 2011), Visual Genome QA (Krishna et al., 2017) and Conceptual Captions (Sharma et al., 2018). In total it comprises 4.7M captions paired with 2.9M unique images.

At the core of this work is a method to measure visual knowledge transfer by means of the memory colors task described in Section 2.1. To this end, we construct a version of this vision-and-language dataset where we remove training examples in which a memory color is revealed in the caption. This way we can, with high confidence, attribute correct model predictions to originate from the visual modality rather than the captions. In the filtered version, an example is excluded if its caption matches either of two conditions:

1. It contains any object word and any color word from the memory colors dataset, by exact string match.
2. When tokenized and stemmed, it contains any stemmed object word and any stemmed color word from the memory colors dataset

The above filter matches about 6% of the captions in the training set. A summary of the statistics for the full and filtered versions of the training dataset are detailed in Table 3. Complete statistics for the dataset can be found in the supplementary material.

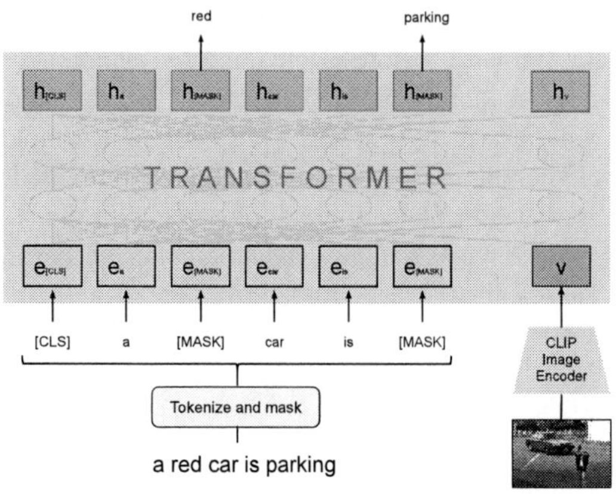

Figure 2: Training of the multimodal CLIP-BERT model using MLM. An image represented by CLIP is appended to the transformer input.

3 Models

When a human is asked a question like *What is the color of your house?* it typically requires retrieving a mental picture from memory of what the house looks like. Based on this mental picture, the answer can then easily be inferred. The mental picture provides an efficient means to store knowledge about the appearance of the house, as other questions like *How many floors does it have?* or *Does it have a garden?* can as easily be inferred. We hypothesize that this idea of visual imagination could also provide an efficient means of visual knowledge transfer, and propose a model for performing the "imagination" explicitly.

We take inspiration from recent works in vision-and-language modeling, where the transformer architecture (Vaswani et al., 2017) has become the de facto standard (Lu et al., 2019; Tan and Bansal, 2019; Qi et al., 2020; Li et al., 2020b). In a typical setup, an image representation is fed to the transformer encoder jointly with the text tokens, and the encoder is then pre-trained using various denoising and contrastive objectives.

In this work, we perform experiments on a simple yet novel variant to accomodate for the visual imagination. While common practice is to use visual features from an object detector (Ren et al., 2015), we extract visual representations using the image encoder of a pretrained CLIP model (Radford et al., 2021) instead. CLIP consists of two networks for encoding an image and a text sentence respectively, and is trained to align these representations in a joint space using a contrastive training objective. The resulting visual encoder is shown to

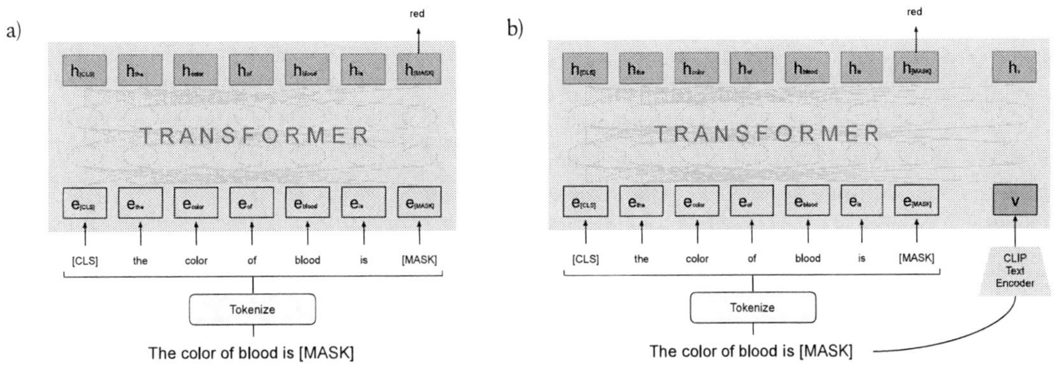

Figure 3: a) Inference from CLIP-BERT using the implicit transfer strategy, directly querying for knowledge through a masked token prediction. b) Inference from CLIP-BERT using the explicit transfer strategy, involving the prediction of visual latent features (visual imagination) as a preceding step.

have great discriminatory performance, for example when applied to zero-shot image classification. However, the main benefit of using CLIP to extract visual features is the joint feature space between its visual and textual encoder, enabling us to generate "visual" features from text.

In our experiments, we start from the popular pretrained BERT base model[4], and continue training on our visual-language dataset from Section 2.2, using only the Masked Language Modelling (MLM) objective with 15% random dynamic masking ratio. Specifically, we train two models on the filtered and unfiltered versions respectively:

BERT-base We continue training of BERT base using MLM *only on the captions part* of the visual-and-language dataset. This provides a baseline of the amount of color knowledge that can be picked up from text alone.

CLIP-BERT We continue training of BERT base using MLM but *on both the captions and the images* of the visual-and-language dataset. The image representation is transformed through a projection layer and appended to the transformer input without adding any positional or segment embeddings. The MLM objective is only applied on the textual positions. An illustration of the training of CLIP-BERT is shown in Figure 2.

3.1 Training

All models were trained for 16 hours using 32 16 GB T4 GPUs with a total batch size of 16,384. During this time between 44k to 58k gradient steps were taken, and all validation losses had converged. We used the Adam optimizer with a constant learning rate of 5e-5, and applied mixed-precision training for increased performance.

3.2 Querying strategies

The canonical way to query BERT-like models for knowledge in a zero-shot setting is to construct textual templates containing a `[MASK]` token to be predicted by the model in a cloze-style fashion (Petroni et al., 2019). Similarly, we manually construct templates to query for the color of objects in Memory Colors. Since it has been shown that language models can be sensitive to the exact phrasing of such templates (Jiang et al., 2020), we construct a set of 13 distinct alternatives paraphrasing each other. The templates provided to the human annotators (described in Section 2.1) are included in these alternatives, while the model templates are complemented with versions that also contain model-specific tokens, such as `[SEP]`. All model templates are listed in the supplementary material. We report the mean top-1 accuracy and standard deviation of each model over all templates, and we only consider the eleven valid color words from the full vocabulary of model predictions.

Since the goal of our work is to investigate how visual knowledge can be transferred into language models, we consider two mechanisms of knowledge transfer, denoted *implicit* and *explicit* transfer respectively. These mechanisms are investigated using two different querying strategies.

3.2.1 Implicit transfer

By *implicit transfer*, we refer to the effect of multimodal training on the word representations of a language model. To measure the implicit transfer

[4]`bert-base-uncased` in Huggingface Transformers.

capabilities of a model, we use a multimodal signal at training time but at test time, we query the model as described above using the method proposed by Petroni et al. (2019). We use the term *implicit*, as the visual knowledge (e.g. that blood typically has a red hue) needs to be memorized in the model weights as a part of MLM training, and later retieved textually (the correct masked token should be "red").

3.2.2 Explicit transfer by visual imagination

As an alternative to implicit transfer, we propose a more explicit transfer strategy where we as a preceeding step predict visual features of an imaginary image based on the text.[5] These predicted features are then appended to the transformer input that thus becomes complete with both the textual and visual features as seen during training. For this visual prediction, we use the textual encoder of CLIP as it is explicitly trained to align its representations with the visual counterpart.

To evaluate the quality of the predicted representations on the Memory Colors dataset, we also generate "true" visual representations with the visual encoder of CLIP using a ground truth image of each object, and evaluate each model using these as well. This setting more resembles visual question answering, and should be considered as an upper bound for what performance can be expected from the predicted features.

4 Results and analysis

We evaluate the transfer capabilities of our aforementioned models both to assess the functionality of our measurement method and to investigate the effect of implicit and explicit visual knowledge transfer. The results on Memory Colors for the different experiments are displayed in Table 4. We structure the analysis in this section around a set of interesting questions.

Are humans the top performers on the Memory Colors dataset? We can conclude that the human baseline results are better than those of any model, training procedure and querying strategy evaluated. This baseline is expected to be high because the task is inherently based on the notions of color according to the majority of the humans that were evaluated.

Furthermore, as language models lack much knowledge compared to humans, we expect them to perform worse than humans on this task.

[5] We refer to the raw text, including the [MASK] part.

Table 4: The mean and standard deviation of the accuracy scores of the models on the Memory Colors dataset for different query templates. CLIP-BERT-images is the only model that is given the pictures from the dataset during evaluation.

Training	Model	Accuracy
	Random baseline	0.091 ± 0.026
	Majority baseline	0.229 ± 0.000
	Human baseline	0.937 ± 0.051
None	BERT-base	0.252 ± 0.102
Unfiltered	BERT-base	0.724 ± 0.112
	CLIP-BERT	
	implicit	0.744 ± 0.080
	explicit	0.870 ± 0.086
	images	0.876 ± 0.063
Filtered	BERT-base	0.460 ± 0.083
	CLIP-BERT	
	implicit	0.541 ± 0.060
	explicit	0.733 ± 0.098
	images	0.785 ± 0.055

Not even the CLIP-BERT model provided with gold standard images and unfiltered textual information on colors matches the performance of the human annotators. There may be several reasons for this, for instance that the capacity of the multimodal models is not sufficient, or that humans are privy to additional information that helps them solve the Memory Colors task better.

Is the filtering of the training data necessary for our experimental setup of evaluating visual knowledge transfer? We see that the BERT-base model without any further training has a bad performance on the Memory Colors dataset, only slightly better than the majority baseline. On the other hand, the model shows significant performance improvement if it is trained on our unfiltered visual-and-language data. This suggests that the unfiltered training dataset contains much information about the objects' color *textually*. This is perhaps not surprising, as it is common that captions describe what colors the objects in the image have. However, for our purposes it is problematic as we wish to constrain this information to be learnt from the visual modality solely. Based on this, we conclude that the filtering of the training data is necessary in our experimental setup for evaluating visual knowledge transfer.

Does the filtering of the training data work as intended according to the Memory Colors dataset? If we filter the training data of the BERT-base model, the performance drops from 0.724 to 0.460, indicating that a large portion of the necessary information has been removed. However, the model performance does not drop to that of the original BERT-base model, so seemingly some color information still reaches the model through the text despite the data filtering. This leakage is undesirable from the perspective of evaluating visual knowledge transfer, since the model should not be able to perform well on Memory Colors without visual knowledge transfer capabilities.

Does the implicit transfer strategy improve performance on Memory Colors? The CLIP-BERT model using implicit transfer displays significantly better performance than the corresponding BERT-base baseline in the filtered case, while the performance difference is negligible in the unfiltered case. This indicates that the implicit strategy does work to some extent, at least when corresponding textual information is lacking.

Does the explicit transfer strategy improve performance on Memory Colors? The CLIP-BERT model using explicit transfer displays significantly better performance than the baseline and the implicit transfer model for both the unfiltered and filtered training methods. This suggests that the model has a strong visual knowledge transfer capability that enables it to improve the performance on Memory Colors, beyond the knowledge provided textually. However, we can observe that the rise from the baseline is larger for the filtered case than the unfiltered case, with a difference of 27 percentage units and 15 percentage units respectively. This is expected of our task, as the models need to rely more on their visual transfer capabilites to perform well in the filtered training case.

Is the explicit strategy better than the implicit? The fact that the performance is much improved over the text-only baseline also in the unfiltered case indicates that the explicit strategy indeed extends the textual knowledge in a complementary manner. Since we do not see a similar performance gain for the implicit strategy, we have reason to believe that the explicit strategy is more effective.

What is the quality of the predicted visual features compared to those of the gold standard visuals? Lastly, we have the results of the CLIP-BERT model that bases its predictions on the ground truth image of each object it is being queried on. As expected, this model acts as an upper bound for the model performance on both the unfiltered and filtered method cases, while the rise in performance is more significant in the filtered training case. This also agrees with the previously mentioned hypothesis on the performance difference between the filtered and unfiltered training case. It also implies that the predicted features of the CLIP-BERT-explicit model are not as good as if they were generated from the actual item pictures.

Are the models sensitive to the phrasing of the query templates? The standard deviation figures presented in Table 4 show the variation in the accuracy scores for the different query templates. We can observe that all of the models evaluated display a standard deviation between 5-11%, and that none are lower than the standard deviation of the human baseline. Consequently, the models are sensitive to the phrasing of the query templates, as already mentioned in Section 3.2.

5 Related work

There are multiple perspectives on how our contributions relate to previous work, and we elaborate on this in the subsequent sections.

5.1 Visual grounding for improved NLP

A body of previous work exists on the topic of visual grounding for improving performance on language tasks. For example, Chrupała et al. (2015) ground the language representations by adding an auxiliary visual feature prediction loss during training, and evaluate the learned representations on word and sentence similarity tasks. Similarly, Kiela et al. (2018) align language and corresponding visual representations through a contrastive ranking loss, and evaluate the learned representations on a suite of common NLP classification tasks. Visual grounding has also been explored for machine translation; for instance, Elliott and Kádár (2017) add an auxiliary visual prediction loss in addition to the regular seq2seq objective which is shown to improve performance. More recently, Sileo (2021) investigates the extent to which visual-linguistic pretraining of multimodal transformers can improve performance on a set of text-only tasks. While these approaches suggest that visual grounding can be helpful for language tasks, our work more explicitly targets the question of *how* the additional modality can complement the textual signal. We do this through a narrow focus on visual knowledge, in contrast to tasks requiring broader language understanding.

5.2 Augmenting input using feature prediction

Our work is not the first to implement the generation of imaginary features based on text for a unimodal text task. There is previous work investigating the potential of leveraging multimodal information during training to enable a model to generate or retrieve additional multimodal information at inference time for a pure text input.

Sileo (2021) uses the term *associative grounding*, which can be based on synthesis or retrieval. The main difference between our work and Sileo's is that he develops a model based on retrieval, while we use feature synthesis. Earlier work has used latent visual features to augment the input for improving word embeddings (Goyal et al., 2017).

The idea has been explored for non-visual information as well. For example in open-domain question answering, retrieving relevant source documents as a preliminary step prior to knowledge extraction has proved highly effective (Guu et al., 2020). Recently, Zellers et al. (2021) also proposed a similar explicit decoupling but for augmenting a language model with knowledge about physical dynamics. Also here, our work differs in that we augment the input with a visual signal and that we use it for a task focused on evaluating the capacity of visual knowledge transfer of a model.

5.3 Visual-linguistic tasks

Much recent work on vision-and-text models focuses on developing models for multimodal tasks. Here, the model is queried with both textual and visual input on tasks such as VQA, GQA and NLVR2 (Goyal et al., 2017; Hudson and Manning, 2019; Suhr et al., 2019). Recently developed models that can or could be found on the leaderboards of these tasks without using ensembling are e.g. ViLBERT, LXMERT, ImageBERT and OSCAR (Lu et al., 2019; Tan and Bansal, 2019; Qi et al., 2020; Li et al., 2020b). These models are typically based on the BERT transformer model architecture (Devlin et al., 2019) and they often extract features from the visual input using a Faster R-CNN model (Ren et al., 2015). Similarly to this previous work, we also base our model design on the BERT model architecture and extract features from the visual input using a pre-trained visual processing model. However, we differ from the previous work in that we utilize the CLIP model to extract visual features, which also enables us to predict visual features from a pure textual input using the shared feature space for textual and visual representations of CLIP. We also differ in that we aim to study the visual knowledge transfer capabilities of a model by evaluating it with a method that measures visual knowledge for a unimodal textual task.

6 Conclusions and future work

We have introduced a methodology for measuring visual knowledge transfer in multimodal language models. The centerpiece is a new benchmark *Memory Colors* designed to test how well such models incorporate knowledge about colors of common objects. We find that careful filtering of the underlying training data can provide an effective means to attribute the acquired knowledge to the individual source modalities.

Our results based on this methodology also showcase that vision-and-language pre-trained language models are able to *textually* express knowledge obtained from a separate (e.g. visual) modality.

We also found that there is some information leakage in our filtering method, as the performance of filtered BERT-base improves over the BERT-base baseline. This improvement in model performance cannot be explained based on the method and results of this work. Thus, it remains to be investigated what kind of information leakage takes place in spite of the filtering. Potential explanations are that the model learns the color of an item through second-order effects, e.g. by learning the color of a synonymous item that we have not filtered for, or that the original BERT-base model already contains textual knowledge relevant to Memory Colors, while it needs further training on a visual-language dataset to access that knowledge. Future work should ensure that the experimental setup for evaluating visual knowledge works as intended.

Additionally, it is worth investigating what other evaluation alternatives we have for measuring the cross-modal capabilities of NLP models. Can we create an evaluation methodology that is not task-based, can we find some other task to evaluate on, or can we improve on the statistical robustness of our evaluation methodology?

We observed that a model with implicit transfer performs better on our evaluation task than a unimodal language model, while a model with explicit transfer through prediction performs even better on the task. This implies that both implicit and explicit knowledge transfer are promising directions for efficient visual knowledge transfer to text, although the explicit transfer may be more promising.

While we here only investigate knowledge transfer from a visual modality, it is likely that this model design also can be successfully implemented for other modalities.

The experimental setup proposed in this work helped us discover and validate the potential of explicit transfer. We can conclude that more work on understanding how multimodal training of language models affect their predictions is an interesting direction towards more robust and trustworthy NLP systems.

Acknowledgments

This work was partially supported by the Wallenberg AI, Autonomous Systems and Software Program (WASP) funded by the Knut and Alice Wallenberg Foundation.

Additionally, the computations were enabled by resources provided by the Swedish National Infrastructure for Computing (SNIC), partially funded by the Swedish Research Council through grant agreement no. 2018-05973.

Lastly, we would like to thank the 11 individuals who helped us annotate our Memory Colors dataset. Their work was imperative for the creation of this article. We also thank the anonymous reviewers for their valuable feedback and knowledge sharing.

References

Emily M. Bender and Alexander Koller. 2020. Climbing towards NLU: On meaning, form, and understanding in the age of data. In *Proceedings of the 58th Annual Meeting of the Association for Computational Linguistics*, pages 5185–5198, Online. Association for Computational Linguistics.

Yonatan Bisk, Ari Holtzman, Jesse Thomason, Jacob Andreas, Yoshua Bengio, Joyce Chai, Mirella Lapata, Angeliki Lazaridou, Jonathan May, Aleksandr Nisnevich, Nicolas Pinto, and Joseph Turian. 2020. Experience grounds language. In *Proceedings of the 2020 Conference on Empirical Methods in Natural Language Processing (EMNLP)*, pages 8718–8735, Online. Association for Computational Linguistics.

Tom Brown, Benjamin Mann, Nick Ryder, Melanie Subbiah, Jared D Kaplan, Prafulla Dhariwal, Arvind Neelakantan, Pranav Shyam, Girish Sastry, Amanda Askell, Sandhini Agarwal, Ariel Herbert-Voss, Gretchen Krueger, Tom Henighan, Rewon Child, Aditya Ramesh, Daniel Ziegler, Jeffrey Wu, Clemens Winter, Chris Hesse, Mark Chen, Eric Sigler, Mateusz Litwin, Scott Gray, Benjamin Chess, Jack Clark, Christopher Berner, Sam McCandlish, Alec Radford, Ilya Sutskever, and Dario Amodei. 2020. Language models are few-shot learners. In *Advances in Neural Information Processing Systems*, volume 33, pages 1877–1901. Curran Associates, Inc.

Grzegorz Chrupała, Ákos Kádár, and Afra Alishahi. 2015. Learning language through pictures. In *Proceedings of the 53rd Annual Meeting of the Association for Computational Linguistics and the 7th International Joint Conference on Natural Language Processing (Volume 2: Short Papers)*, pages 112–118, Beijing, China. Association for Computational Linguistics.

Jacob Devlin, Ming-Wei Chang, Kenton Lee, and Kristina Toutanova. 2019. BERT: Pre-training of deep bidirectional transformers for language understanding. In *Proceedings of the 2019 Conference of the North American Chapter of the Association for Computational Linguistics: Human Language Technologies, Volume 1 (Long and Short Papers)*, pages 4171–4186, Minneapolis, Minnesota. Association for Computational Linguistics.

Desmond Elliott and Ákos Kádár. 2017. Imagination improves multimodal translation. In *Proceedings of the Eighth International Joint Conference on Natural Language Processing (Volume 1: Long Papers)*, pages 130–141, Taipei, Taiwan. Asian Federation of Natural Language Processing.

Joseph L Fleiss. 1971. Measuring nominal scale agreement among many raters. *Psychological bulletin*, 76(5):378.

Jonathan Gordon and Benjamin Van Durme. 2013. Reporting bias and knowledge acquisition. In *Proceedings of the 2013 workshop on Automated knowledge base construction*, pages 25–30.

Yash Goyal, Tejas Khot, Douglas Summers-Stay, Dhruv Batra, and Devi Parikh. 2017. Making the V in VQA matter: Elevating the role of image understanding in Visual Question Answering. In *Conference on Computer Vision and Pattern Recognition (CVPR)*.

Kelvin Guu, Kenton Lee, Zora Tung, Panupong Pasupat, and Ming-Wei Chang. 2020. REALM: retrieval-augmented language model pre-training. *CoRR*, abs/2002.08909.

Drew A Hudson and Christopher D Manning. 2019. GQA: A new dataset for real-world visual reasoning and compositional question answering. *Confer-*

ence on Computer Vision and Pattern Recognition (CVPR).

Zhengbao Jiang, Frank F. Xu, Jun Araki, and Graham Neubig. 2020. How can we know what language models know? *Transactions of the Association for Computational Linguistics*, 8:423–438.

Graham Kalton and Howard Schuman. 1982. The effect of the question on survey responses: A review. *J. R. Statist. Soc.*, 145:42–73.

Douwe Kiela, Alexis Conneau, Allan Jabri, and Maximilian Nickel. 2018. Learning visually grounded sentence representations. In *Proceedings of the 2018 Conference of the North American Chapter of the Association for Computational Linguistics: Human Language Technologies, Volume 1 (Long Papers)*, pages 408–418, New Orleans, Louisiana. Association for Computational Linguistics.

Ranjay Krishna, Yuke Zhu, Oliver Groth, Justin Johnson, Kenji Hata, Joshua Kravitz, Stephanie Chen, Yannis Kalantidis, Li-Jia Li, David A. Shamma, Michael S. Bernstein, and Li Fei-Fei. 2017. Visual genome: Connecting language and vision using crowdsourced dense image annotations. *Int. J. Comput. Vision*, 123(1):32–73.

Margaret Li, Stephen Roller, Ilia Kulikov, Sean Welleck, Y-Lan Boureau, Kyunghyun Cho, and Jason Weston. 2020a. Don't say that! making inconsistent dialogue unlikely with unlikelihood training. In *Proceedings of the 58th Annual Meeting of the Association for Computational Linguistics*, pages 4715–4728, Online. Association for Computational Linguistics.

Xiujun Li, Xi Yin, Chunyuan Li, Pengchuan Zhang, Xiaowei Hu, Lei Zhang, Lijuan Wang, Houdong Hu, Li Dong, Furu Wei, et al. 2020b. Oscar: Object-semantics aligned pre-training for vision-language tasks. In *European Conference on Computer Vision*, pages 121–137. Springer.

Tsung-Yi Lin, Michael Maire, Serge Belongie, James Hays, Pietro Perona, Deva Ramanan, Piotr Dollár, and C. Lawrence Zitnick. 2014. Microsoft COCO: Common objects in context. In *Computer Vision – ECCV 2014*, pages 740–755, Cham. Springer International Publishing.

Robert Logan, Nelson F. Liu, Matthew E. Peters, Matt Gardner, and Sameer Singh. 2019. Barack's wife Hillary: Using knowledge graphs for fact-aware language modeling. In *Proceedings of the 57th Annual Meeting of the Association for Computational Linguistics*, pages 5962–5971, Florence, Italy. Association for Computational Linguistics.

Jiasen Lu, Dhruv Batra, Devi Parikh, and Stefan Lee. 2019. ViLBERT: Pretraining task-agnostic visiolinguistic representations for vision-and-language tasks. In *Advances in Neural Information Processing Systems*, volume 32. Curran Associates, Inc.

Joshua Maynez, Shashi Narayan, Bernd Bohnet, and Ryan McDonald. 2020. On faithfulness and factuality in abstractive summarization. In *Proceedings of the 58th Annual Meeting of the Association for Computational Linguistics*, pages 1906–1919, Online. Association for Computational Linguistics.

SM Newhall, RW Burnham, and Joyce R Clark. 1957. Comparison of successive with simultaneous color matching. *JOSA*, 47(1):43–56.

Vicente Ordonez, Girish Kulkarni, and Tamara Berg. 2011. Im2Text: Describing images using 1 million captioned photographs. In *Advances in Neural Information Processing Systems*, volume 24. Curran Associates, Inc.

Joaquín Pérez-Carpinell, MD De Fez, Rosa Baldoví, and Juan Carlos Soriano. 1998. Familiar objects and memory color. *Color Research & Application: Endorsed by Inter-Society Color Council, The Colour Group (Great Britain), Canadian Society for Color, Color Science Association of Japan, Dutch Society for the Study of Color, The Swedish Colour Centre Foundation, Colour Society of Australia, Centre Français de la Couleur*, 23(6):416–427.

Fabio Petroni, Tim Rocktäschel, Sebastian Riedel, Patrick Lewis, Anton Bakhtin, Yuxiang Wu, and Alexander Miller. 2019. Language models as knowledge bases? In *Proceedings of the 2019 Conference on Empirical Methods in Natural Language Processing and the 9th International Joint Conference on Natural Language Processing (EMNLP-IJCNLP)*, pages 2463–2473, Hong Kong, China. Association for Computational Linguistics.

Di Qi, Lin Su, Jia Song, Edward Cui, Taroon Bharti, and Arun Sacheti. 2020. ImageBERT: Cross-modal pre-training with large-scale weak-supervised image-text data. *arXiv preprint arXiv:2001.07966*.

Alec Radford, Jong Wook Kim, Chris Hallacy, Aditya Ramesh, Gabriel Goh, Sandhini Agarwal, Girish Sastry, Amanda Askell, Pamela Mishkin, Jack Clark, Gretchen Krueger, and Ilya Sutskever. 2021. Learning transferable visual models from natural language supervision.

Alec Radford, Jeffrey Wu, Rewon Child, David Luan, Dario Amodei, Ilya Sutskever, et al. 2019. Language models are unsupervised multitask learners. *OpenAI blog*, 1(8):9.

Shaoqing Ren, Kaiming He, Ross Girshick, and Jian Sun. 2015. Faster R-CNN: Towards real-time object detection with region proposal networks. In *Advances in Neural Information Processing Systems*, volume 28. Curran Associates, Inc.

Stephen Roller, Emily Dinan, Naman Goyal, Da Ju, Mary Williamson, Yinhan Liu, Jing Xu, Myle Ott, Eric Michael Smith, Y-Lan Boureau, and Jason Weston. 2021. Recipes for building an open-domain chatbot. In *Proceedings of the 16th Conference of the European Chapter of the Association for Computational Linguistics: Main Volume*, pages 300–325, Online. Association for Computational Linguistics.

Piyush Sharma, Nan Ding, Sebastian Goodman, and Radu Soricut. 2018. Conceptual captions: A cleaned, hypernymed, image alt-text dataset for automatic image captioning. In *Proceedings of the 56th Annual Meeting of the Association for Computational Linguistics (Volume 1: Long Papers)*, pages 2556–2565, Melbourne, Australia. Association for Computational Linguistics.

Damien Sileo. 2021. Visual grounding strategies for text-only natural language processing. *arXiv preprint arXiv:2103.13942.*

Alane Suhr, Stephanie Zhou, Ally Zhang, Iris Zhang, Huajun Bai, and Yoav Artzi. 2019. A corpus for reasoning about natural language grounded in photographs. In *Proceedings of the 57th Annual Meeting of the Association for Computational Linguistics*, pages 6418–6428, Florence, Italy. Association for Computational Linguistics.

Hao Tan and Mohit Bansal. 2019. LXMERT: Learning cross-modality encoder representations from transformers. In *Proceedings of the 2019 Conference on Empirical Methods in Natural Language Processing and the 9th International Joint Conference on Natural Language Processing (EMNLP-IJCNLP)*, pages 5100–5111, Hong Kong, China. Association for Computational Linguistics.

Ashish Vaswani, Noam Shazeer, Niki Parmar, Jakob Uszkoreit, Llion Jones, Aidan N Gomez, Łukasz Kaiser, and Illia Polosukhin. 2017. Attention is all you need. In *Advances in Neural Information Processing Systems*, volume 30. Curran Associates, Inc.

Rowan Zellers, Ari Holtzman, Matthew Peters, Roozbeh Mottaghi, Aniruddha Kembhavi, Ali Farhadi, and Yejin Choi. 2021. PIGLeT: Language grounding through neuro-symbolic interaction in a 3D world. In *Proceedings of the 59th Annual Meeting of the Association for Computational Linguistics*.

A Supplementary material

The supplementary material of this work includes the instructions provided to the human annotators in Figure 4, the Memory Colors data in Table 5, the color label distribution of the data in Figure 5, the different query templates for human annotators and models in Table 6 and the full statistics for the Vision-and-Language dataset in Table 7.

```
Annotator Instructions
Thank you for helping us out by solving
this task!

You will be presented with 121
fill-in-the-gap color questions that
are to be answered with one answer,
where you can pick between the
following answer alternatives:

yellow
blue
green
white
red
orange
black
pink
brown
grey
purple

You should fill in your answer for the
gap [fill-in-this-word] under the
column Fill-in-word. Answer with the
alternative that first comes to your
mind. The cell you are to fill in will
turn green after you have specified one
of the possible answers in it. Make
sure that all cells in the column are
green and not red before you submit
your answers. Do not leave any cells
empty, just guess on the alterative you
find most likely even if you don't know
the answer.

It is important that you solve this
task by yourself, such that you do not
discuss the questions or the answers
with anyone else before you have
submitted your answers. Also, you
should not Google or look up anything
while answering the questions.

Thank you again!
```

Figure 4: The instructions provided to the human annotators before they annotated the predecessor to the Memory Colors dataset.

Table 5: The 109 entries in the Memory Colors dataset.

Index	Descriptor	Item	Color	Index	Descriptor	Item	Color
1	a	sunflower	yellow	56		plants	green
2	the	ocean	blue	57	a	suit	black
3		grass	green	58		cocoa	brown
4		butter	yellow	59		chocolate	brown
5		bone	white	60		concrete	grey
6		ivory	white	61		aluminium foil	grey
7	the	sky	blue	62	a	pea	green
8	the inside of a	pineapple	yellow	63	a	rainforest	green
9	a	tomato	red	64		rice	white
10	a	strawberry	red	65		pasta	yellow
11	a	rose	red	66		spinach	green
12		blood	red	67		broccoli	green
13	a	heart	red	68	a	lime	green
14	a	pumpkin	orange	69		guacamole	green
15	a	carrot	orange	70		salmon meat	pink
16		cheese	yellow	71		yoghurt	white
17	the	sun	yellow	72		cottage cheese	white
18	a	lemon	yellow	73		feta cheese	white
19		corn	yellow	74		matcha	green
20	a	frog	green	75		seaweed	green
21	a	leaf	green	76		garlic	white
22	a	blueberry	blue	77	an	aubergine	purple
23		jeans	blue	78		ivy	green
24	the animal	bat	black	79	a	ruby	red
25	a	crow	black	80		flour	white
26	a	raven	black	81		baking soda	white
27		coal	black	82	a	snowman	white
28		paper	white	83		gravel	grey
29		sugar	white	84	an	egg yolk	yellow
30		milk	white	85	an	egg	white
31		snow	white	86		moss	green
32		sheep	white	87		cinnamon	brown
33	a	flamingo	pink	88	the outside of a	coconut	brown
34		cherry blossoms	pink	89		scrambled eggs	yellow
35		soil	brown	90	a	cucumber	green
36		stone	grey	91	a	fire extinguisher	red
37	an	elephant	grey	92	a	duckling	yellow
38	the animal	seal	grey	93	a	panther	black
39	a	plum	purple	94	a	pine tree	green
40		lavender	purple	95	a	tooth	white
41	a	polar bear	white	96		feces	brown
42	the inside of a	watermelon	red	97		urine	yellow
43		honey	yellow	98	an	iceberg	white
44	a	banana	yellow	99	a	school bus	yellow
45	an	orange	orange	100	a	chick	yellow
46	a	pear	green	101		sails	white
47	the fruit	mandarin	orange	102		wood	brown
48	a	cherry	red	103	a	lady bug	red
49		salt	white	104	a	daffodil	yellow
50	a	swan	white	105	a	dandelion	yellow
51	a	snow leopard	white	106		cardboard	brown
52	an	arctic fox	white	107	a	blackboard	black
53		steel	grey	108		basil	green
54		clouds	white	109		parsley	green
55		rainclouds	grey				

Table 6: The query templates used to query both human annotators and models on the Memory Colors task.

(a) The question templates used to query the human annotators on the object-colors evaluation task.

Index	Template
1	Q: What is the color of [DESCRIPTOR] [ITEM]? A: It is [MASK].
2	What is the color of [DESCRIPTOR] [ITEM]? [MASK].
3	The color of [DESCRIPTOR] [ITEM] is [MASK].
4	The usual color of [DESCRIPTOR] [ITEM] is [MASK].
5	[DESCRIPTOR] [ITEM] usually has the color of [MASK].
6	What is the usual color of [DESCRIPTOR] [ITEM]? [MASK].
7	What is the typical color of [DESCRIPTOR] [ITEM]? [MASK].

(b) The question templates used to query the models on the object-colors evaluation task.

Index	Template
1	Q: What is the color of [DESCRIPTOR] [ITEM]? A: It is [MASK].
2	Q: What is the color of [DESCRIPTOR] [ITEM]? [SEP] A: It is [MASK].
3	Q: What is the colour of [DESCRIPTOR] [ITEM]? A: It is [MASK].
4	What is the color of [DESCRIPTOR] [ITEM]? [MASK].
5	What is the color of [DESCRIPTOR] [ITEM]? [SEP] [MASK].
6	What is the colour of [DESCRIPTOR] [ITEM]? [MASK].
7	The color of [DESCRIPTOR] [ITEM] is [MASK].
8	The usual color of [DESCRIPTOR] [ITEM] is [MASK].
9	[DESCRIPTOR] [ITEM] usually has the color of [MASK].
10	What is the usual color of [DESCRIPTOR] [ITEM]? [MASK].
11	What is the usual color of [DESCRIPTOR] [ITEM]? [SEP] [MASK].
12	What is the typical color of [DESCRIPTOR] [ITEM]? [MASK].
13	What is the typical color of [DESCRIPTOR] [ITEM]? [SEP] [MASK].

Table 7: Total number of image and caption samples, in each respective source dataset. In Visual Genome QA, the "caption" is the concatenation of the question and answer strings. Since some image links in SBU Captions and Conceptual Captions have become broken, the total number of samples don't match what was originally reported. There are more captions than images in the dataset since several different captions may refer to the same image.

	MS COCO	**SBU Captions**	**VG QA**	**Conc. Captions**	**Total**
Validation					
Captions	25,014	10,000	10,000	13,923	58,937
Images	5,000	10,000	9,311	13,923	38,234
Training-unfiltered					
Captions	591,753	852,504	1,435,322	1,841,392	4,720,971
Images	118,287	852,504	99,255	1,841,392	2,911,438
Training-filtered					
Captions	548,887	760,724	1,348,120	1,771,940	4,429,671
Images	117,897	760,724	99,051	1,771,940	2,749,612

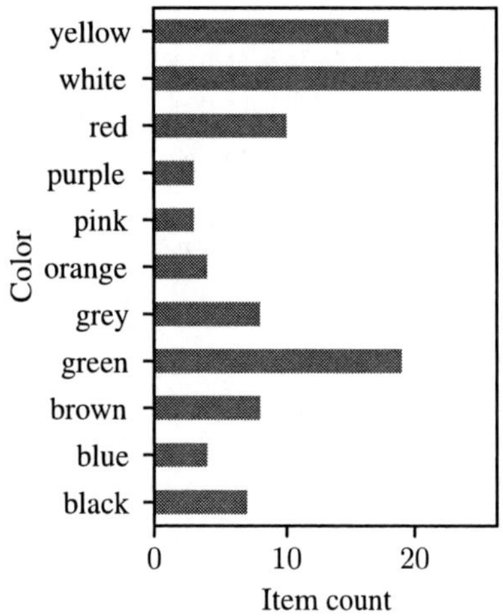

Figure 5: The color distribution of the 109 items in the Memory Colors dataset. The most frequent color in the dataset is *white* with a count of 25. The colors with the lowest frequency are pink and purple, which only occur for 3 items each.

Discrete representations in neural models of spoken language

Bertrand Higy
Cognitive Science and AI
Tilburg University
b.j.r.higy@tilburguniversity.edu

Lieke Gelderloos
Cognitive Science and AI
Tilburg University
l.j.gelderloos@tilburguniversity.edu

Afra Alishahi
Cognitive Science and AI
Tilburg University
a.alishahi@tilburguniversity.edu

Grzegorz Chrupała
Cognitive Science and AI
Tilburg University
grzegorz@chrupala.me

Abstract

The distributed and continuous representations used by neural networks are at odds with representations employed in linguistics, which are typically symbolic. Vector quantization has been proposed as a way to induce discrete neural representations that are closer in nature to their linguistic counterparts. However, it is not clear which metrics are the best-suited to analyze such discrete representations. We compare the merits of four commonly used metrics in the context of weakly supervised models of spoken language. We compare the results they show when applied to two different models, while systematically studying the effect of the placement and size of the discretization layer. We find that different evaluation regimes can give inconsistent results. While we can attribute them to the properties of the different metrics in most cases, one point of concern remains: the use of minimal pairs of phoneme triples as stimuli disadvantages larger discrete unit inventories, unlike metrics applied to complete utterances. Furthermore, while in general vector quantization induces representations that correlate with units posited in linguistics, the strength of this correlation is only moderate.

1 Introduction

The dominant machine learning paradigm for processing spoken language is based on neural network architectures, such as recurrent nets and transformers, inducing a hierarchy of hidden representations which are distributed and continuous. In contrast, human history has repeatedly seen the discovery and wide adoption of discrete, symbolic representations of speech in the form of writing. These systems commonly represent basic units of language such as morphemes, syllables or phonemes while discarding other information contained in the speech signal such as emotion or speaker identity.

Symbolic representation of speech has proven tremendously useful for storage and transmission of information, and it also plays a crucial role in systems dealing with spoken language such as spoken dialog systems: these typically employ an automatic speech recognition (ASR) module to transcribe the speech signal into written form, which is then used as input to upstream language understanding modules. While some attempts have been made to train such systems end-to-end, pipelines are still very competitive (see Haghani et al., 2018; Higy et al., 2020), which strengthens the point that a symbolic encoding of spoken language contains most of the information relevant for this task.

It may thus be desirable to incorporate similar representations in neural architectures. Accordingly, multiple efforts have been made to design neural networks with discrete hidden representations and to apply them to spoken language data. This is evident in the recent editions of the ZeroSpeech challenge (Dunbar et al., 2019) on unit discovery, which have featured many such approaches. Specifically, Vector Quantization (VQ) has proven to be a simple and effective method to induce discrete neural representations (e.g., van den Oord et al., 2017; Harwath et al., 2020a; Chung et al., 2020; Liu et al., 2021). VQ layers are added to neural architectures in order to map continuous activation vectors onto a finite set of discrete units, often referred to as *codes*, via a dictionary (or *codebook*) associating these codes with their vector embeddings; the number of entries in the codebook is the *codebook size*. Such symbolic codes have been claimed to correspond to phonemes and/or words. What is still lacking though is a detailed analysis of how much the reported equivalence is affected by details of the architectures such as the size and placement of the VQ layers, learning objectives and dataset, as well as by the evaluation metrics used to quantify it. The present study aims

Proceedings of the Fourth BlackboxNLP Workshop on Analyzing and Interpreting Neural Networks for NLP, pages 163–176
Online, November 11, 2021.

to fill this gap.

We study two approaches to modeling spoken language: learning driven by language-internal structure, and learning driven by grounding in the extra-linguistic world. These two approaches are exemplified by two types of models with VQ layers: the self-supervised model for unit discovery of van Niekerk et al. (2020), and a visually grounded model similar to Harwath et al. (2020a). The datasets used to train each model, Zerospeech 2020 (Dunbar et al., 2020) and Flickr8K (Harwath and Glass, 2015; Rashtchian et al., 2010) are also typical of the task they are used for. Using these two models as our test cases, we systematically investigate the impact of the following factors: (i) the codebook size for the VQ layer, and (ii) the level of placement of the VQ layer. Furthermore, we apply and check the consistency across four different metrics for evaluating the correspondence of the representations with phonemes.

Findings The self-supervised model shows high variability, but with some of the evaluation metrics (especially ABX and RSA, see Section 3.3 for the definition of the metrics) there is a trend for better correspondence to phonemes for smaller codebook sizes (32-128). The visually grounded model, on the other hand, generally shows the closest match with phonemes for the *largest* codebook sizes (512 or 1024) when evaluated on full utterances. In contrast, smaller codebooks score higher for the short utterance segments used by the ABX metric (i.e. minimal pairs of phoneme triples). We also observe inconsistencies in the relative performance of VQ layers placed at different levels in the model for RSA vs. the other metrics. As discussed in Section 5, we attribute those inconsistencies to the properties of the different metrics. Thus, the conclusions drawn using a single metric, even a widely used one like the ZeroSpeech ABX metric, should be treated with caution, and further corroborated.

2 Related work

The domain of speech processing has seen recent efforts to modify existing neural architectures to enable the induction of discrete latent representations. These developments are promising for boosting performance, improving interpretability, and modeling the acquisition and processing of linguistic knowledge in humans.

Applying Vector Quantization (VQ) techniques for this purpose was pioneered by van den Oord et al. (2017), who propose generative models based on the variational auto-encoder (VAE) architecture and use VQ to induce discrete latent representations. They apply this method to images, videos, and speech, and show that the models can learn discrete latent representations without supervision. When applied to raw speech, the VQ-VAE architecture learns high-level discrete representations that are invariant to low-level features of the audio signal such as prosody and speaker identity, and mostly encode the content of the speech. Classification of the discrete representations into phoneme classes (based on majority ground truth label) suggests they capture phonemes to some extent.

Learning discrete instead of (or in addition to) continuous representations can facilitate unit discovery in unsupervised models of speech. In the 2015 Zero Resource Speech Challenge (Versteegh et al., 2015), Badino et al. (2015) present a binarized auto-encoder, certain variants of which outperform its continuous counterpart. In the 2017, 2019, and 2020 editions of this challenge (Dunbar et al., 2017, 2019, 2020), following the work of van den Oord et al. (2017), several models include at least one VQ layer (see e.g. Chorowski et al., 2019; Eloff et al., 2019; Tjandra et al., 2019, 2020). These studies demonstrate the benefit of using VQ layers for phoneme classification and for learning speaker-invariant representations, focusing on the ABX phoneme discrimination metric to evaluate the encoding of phonemic information. However, little analysis on the impact of the size and configuration of the employed VQ layers is performed. For example, van Niekerk et al. (2020) train a VQ-VAE model for reconstructing audio waveforms, and a VQ-CPC (Contrastive Predictive Coding) model for predicting future acoustic units. They evaluate these architectures on the ABX phoneme discrimination task, voice conversion and speaker classification and show that VQ-CPC performs better than VQ-VAE overall, but they do not manipulate the configuration or the dimension of the VQ layers.

Chung et al. (2020), however, report the impact on phoneme and speaker classification of systematic manipulation of VQ-related factors. They train an Autoregressive Predictive Coding (APC) model to predict upcoming frames, and use VQ as a methodology to limit the model's capacity. Using a frame-wise diagnostic classifier (namely linear logistic regression), they show that under restricted configurations (only one VQ layer inserted at the

Table 1: A comparison of studies of VQ-based speech models. RAW (Reconstructing Audio Waveform); VAE (Variational Autoencoder); APC (Autoregressive Predictive Coding); CPC (Contrastive Predictive Coding); DC (Diagnostic Classifier).

Study	Objective	Model	Analysis	Manipulated factors
van den Oord et al. (2017)	RAW	VAE	Phoneme (majority label)	None
Chorowski et al. (2019)	RAW	(V)AE, VQ-VAE	Phoneme (ABX, frame-wise DC), gender, speaker	VAE latent dimensions
Chung et al. (2020)	Predicting next frame	APC	Phoneme (frame-wise DC), speaker	VQ layer number, position, codebook size
van Niekerk et al. (2020)	RAW, predicting future frames	VQ-VAE, VQ-CPC	Phoneme (ABX), speaker, voice conversion	None
Harwath et al. (2020a)	Visual grounding	ResDAVEnet	Phoneme (ABX), bitrate, word (F1 scores)	VQ layer number, position, training regime

top), phoneme prediction using discrete representations improves over using continuous representations learned by an APC model without VQ. In this configuration, larger codebook sizes lead to better performance in phoneme classification but not in speaker identification.

In contrast to the work cited above, which discusses uni-modal speech models, Harwath et al. (2020a) use VQ layers within the setting of learning spoken language via grounding in the visual modality, where the speech signal is associated to images (for an overview of visually grounded speech models, see Chrupała, 2021). They hypothesize that discrete representations learned by such models are more likely to capture higher-level semantic information. Their analyses suggest that the trained multimodal models can learn discrete linguistic units at both word and sub-word levels, with quantization layers inserted at the lower levels of the network showing correspondence to sub-word (i.e. phonemic) units, and those inserted at the higher level corresponding to word-level units. Analyses are based on the Zerospeech ABX metric for phoneme encoding and F1 scores for word detection. Similarly, Liu et al. (2021) propose a framework based on VQ to discover discrete concepts in models of visually grounded language trained on video and text, video and audio or image and audio. Evidence of a correspondence between the learned concepts and visual entities/actions or words are given but no detailed analysis is performed.

When evaluating the encoding of phonemic information in continuous representations from models of spoken language, recent work has shown that different metrics may yield different outcomes. Chrupała et al. (2020) show that representational similarity analysis (RSA) and diagnostic classifier (DC) applied to pooled representations disagree with the results of DC applied on local representations for RNN-based architectures, while they are all in agreement when applied to transformer-based representations. Algayres et al. (2020) compare the aforementioned ABX metric and the mean-average-precision (MAP) metric (which uses representations to predict whether two stimuli have the same ground-truth label) to each other and to a down-stream frequency estimation task. Performance on the three metrics is correlated, but not to a high degree, and marked discrepancies are found for particular models.

Table 1 summarizes some of the representative studies that use VQ layers and their specifications and reported analyses. As can be seen from this summary, existing work on learning VQ-based discrete representations does not easily lead to a coherent picture due to the wide range of the training objectives and modeling architecture they use, the analyses they perform, the evaluation metrics they employ and the VQ-related factors they manipulate. In this paper, we aim to provide this overview by employing different discretized speech modeling approaches and consistently comparing architectural parameters and evaluation metrics.

3 Methods

3.1 Vector quantization

We investigate evaluation metrics for the analysis of discrete representations induced through vector quatization. Since phoneme classification/identification has been the dominant analysis task for discrete representations of speech, we use this as our main task. We do so through the specific case of speech representations learned by two different models: a self-supervised model of speech trained to reconstruct the audio waveform, and a visually-supervised model of spoken language which maps audio representations of spoken utterances and visual representations of their corresponding images to a shared semantic space. Both models employ VQ layers in their architecture to induce discretized representations. A VQ layer takes as input a continuous distributed representation in the form of a vector $h \in \mathbb{R}^d$, and returns the closest of K prototype vectors contained in a trainable codebook $\{e_1, e_2, \ldots, e_K\}$ where $e_i \in \mathbb{R}^d$. For a sequence of continuous vectors $(h_1, h_2, \ldots, h_n)$ the discrete codes are given by the sequence of indices of the prototype vectors returned by the VQ layer. Since the $\arg\max$ operation needed to select the nearest vector is not differentiable, the gradient for backpropagation is approximated by using the straight-through estimator (Bengio et al., 2013), which replaces each non-differentiable operation with the identity function for the backward pass. For further details, consult van den Oord et al. (2017).

3.2 Target models

Self-supervised Our self-supervised model is the VQ-VAE model introduced in van Niekerk et al. (2020).[1] The model consists of an *encoder* built out of a stack of five convolutional layers, a *bottleneck* comprising a linear projection and a VQ layer, and a *decoder* comprising an embedding layer and a stack of upsampling and recurrent layers; the decoder attempts to reconstruct the original waveform. For details of the architecture, see van Niekerk et al. (2020). In the experiments reported here, we vary the size of the codebook, but keep the placement of the VQ layer constant as the encoder contains only one fully connected layer after which the VQ layer can be placed.

Visually-supervised A visually-supervised model of spoken language with discrete representations was introduced by Harwath et al. (2020a): they adapted an existing model (Harwath et al., 2020b) by inserting one or more VQ layers within the speech encoder stack. We similarly adapt the architecture used in Merkx et al. (2019) and Chrupała et al. (2020) by inserting a single VQ layer at one of three levels: either following the first, second or third GRU layer of the speech encoder. In addition to VQ layer placement, we also vary the size of the codebook. Note that unlike Harwath et al. (2020a) we do not use a pre-training stage which by-passes the VQ layers; rather, we train the complete network from scratch. This model thus consists of an image encoder, which takes as input image features extracted via a pre-trained ResNet-152 model (He et al., 2016) and maps these features via a learned affine transform into a joint visual-language space. The audio input are MFCC features with total energy and delta and double-delta coefficients with combined size 39. The speech encoder consists of one 1D convolutional layer (with 64 output channels) which subsamples the input by a factor of two, four bidirectional GRU layers (each of size 2048), with a VQ layer inserted between a single pair of GRU layers. This stack is followed by a self-attention-based pooling layer. The objective function is a version of the triplet loss with negative examples from the current batch. The model is trained with the Adam optimizer (Kingma and Ba, 2015) with a cyclical learning rate schedule (Smith, 2017).

3.3 Evaluation methods

Different evaluation methods have been used for analyzing the nature of information captured by VQ-based discrete representations in different studies. We present here a thorough examination of their formal similarities and differences as well as their sensitivity to different conditions. In this section we introduce the methods commonly used to evaluate the learned representations.

Chrupała et al. (2020) study the effect representation scope, i.e. activation vectors retrieved at the level of frames (local) or pooled over whole utterances (global), concluding that it can affect results. Following their recommendations, and for the sake of simplicity, we include one measure for each scope. Since their findings suggest that local RSA lacks sensitivity, we use local DC (which is also the most widely used) as well as global RSA in our experiments. Global RSA has the double advantage of not using any trainable parameters and not requiring any alignments.

Normalized Mutual Information (NMI) An information-theoretically motivated measure of the association between two random variables is mutual information. In the general case of vector-valued neural representations, computing mutual information with the target annotation is intractable. In the special case where the representation is discrete-valued, we can use the standard empirical estimate. Given discrete random variables X

[1] We use the authors' implementation available at github.com/bshall/ZeroSpeech.

with image $\mathcal{X}$ and Y with image $\mathcal{Y}$ (i.e. frame-wise codes and phoneme labels in our case), the mutual information $I(X;Y)$ is

$$I(X;Y) = \sum_{x \in \mathcal{X}} \sum_{y \in \mathcal{Y}} P(x,y) \log \frac{P(x,y)}{P(x)P(y)} \quad (1)$$

It is often more informative to use mutual information normalized by the arithmetic mean of the entropies of the two random variables:

$$\text{NMI}(X;Y) = 2\frac{I(X;Y)}{H(X)+H(Y)} \quad (2)$$

where $H(X)$ is the entropy of X. This definition of normalized mutual information (NMI) is equivalent to the V-measure (Rosenberg and Hirschberg, 2007).

Diagnostic Classifier (DC) A diagnostic model, also known as a *probe*, is a classifier or regressor trained to predict some information of interest (such as a linguistic annotation) given a neural representation. To the extent that the model successfully predicts the annotation, we conclude that the neural representation encodes this information. Informally, such a diagnostic classifier can be seen as quantifying the amount of easily-accessible – or in the extreme case, linearly decodable – information about the target annotation (Adi et al., 2017; Alishahi et al., 2017; Hupkes et al., 2018; Conneau et al., 2018, among others).

As argued by Pimentel et al. (2020), without the qualification that information be easily accessible, probing should aim to approximate the mutual information between the neural representation and the target annotation, and thus should use the best-performing probe possible. Furthermore, it is not possible for the neural representation to contain more information about the target annotation than the source utterance itself, due to the information processing inequality, and thus, in the general case, probing with an unrestricted classifier is not a well-founded exercise. In the special case of probing a discrete-valued variable (as is the case in our study) the situation is simpler: the accuracy of a linear classifier is closely related to the empirical estimate of the mutual information between the representation and the target annotation; see the formal argument in Appendix A.1 as well as our empirical results.

Representational Similarity Analysis (RSA) RSA is a second-order technique originating in neuroscience (Kriegeskorte et al., 2008) where similarities between pairs of stimuli are measured in two representation spaces: e.g. neural activation pattern space and a space of symbolic linguistic annotations such as sequences of phonemes or syntax trees. The correlation between these pairwise similarity measurements quantifies how much the two representations are aligned. This approach requires a similarity or distance metric for pairs of stimuli within each representation space, but does not need a way of mapping from one space to the other. It generally does not have any trainable parameters. As a consequence, it is sensitive to the purity of the representation with regard to the variable of interest: unlike DC, the RSA metric will penalize representations for encoding any information unrelated to the target variable. See for example Bouchacourt and Baroni (2018); Chrupała and Alishahi (2019); Abnar et al. (2019); Abdou et al. (2019); Chrupała et al. (2020); Fereidooni et al. (2020); Davis and van Schijndel (2020) for uses in NLP and speech processing.

When the neural representations of the stimuli evaluated are sequences of vectors, we need to make a choice regarding how to measure similarities or distances between them. Here we focus on neural representations which take the form of sequences of symbolic codes, which makes measuring distances simple: a natural choice is the Levenshtein edit distance normalized by the length of the longer string. We can thus apply the same edit-distance metric on both the neural representations and on the reference sequences of phonemes or words (for efficiency we collapsed code repetitions).

ABX discriminability (ABX) The ABX phoneme discriminability metric (Schatz, 2016) as used in the Zerospeech challenge (Dunbar et al., 2019) is based on triples of stimuli (A, B, X) where A and X belong to the same category and B and X belong to different categories. The ABX error is a function of $d(A, X)$ and $d(B, X)$ where $d(\cdot, \cdot)$ is a distance metric for the representation being evaluated:[2]

$$\text{abx}(A,B,X) = \begin{cases} 1 & \text{if } d(A,X) > d(B,X) \\ \frac{1}{2} & \text{if } d(A,X) = d(B,X) \\ 0 & \text{otherwise} \end{cases} \quad (3)$$

[2]The ABX error is thus similar to a discretized version of the triplet loss.

Metric	Triples	Align	Train	Distance
RSA				✓
ABX	✓	✓		✓
NMI		✓		
DC		✓	✓	

Table 2: Summary of the main features of the evaluation metrics used.

The categories are determined by gold annotation: in the case of Zerospeech they are phoneme labels. The stimuli are presented in context in the form of minimal pairs: (A =/beg/$_1$, B =/bag/, X =/beg/$_2$), where /beg/$_1$ and /beg/$_2$ are two different utterances of this phoneme sequence. In our use case, alignments between the gold phoneme transcriptions and the evaluated representations are required to extract the stimuli for ABX. Here we use the same distance metric as for RSA: Levenshtein edit distance normalized by the length of the longer string.

The ABX error is loosely related to the RSA score. With RSA, pairwise distances are measured between gold representations of stimuli (e.g. their phonemic transcriptions) as well as between system representations of the same set of stimuli. The correlation coefficient between these two sets of distance measurements is the RSA score. With RSA there is no notion of a stimulus triple, but rather the score reflects distances between all pairs of stimuli. Likewise, the representation of stimuli according to the gold standard is typically not in the form of atomic categorical labels but can be any representation with an associated distance (or similarity) metric. Thus RSA can be seen as more general than ABX, while being less controlled.

Summary of metrics Table 2 summarizes the main characteristics of the evaluation metrics described above in the context of analyzing neural representations of speech, along the following facets: the need to arrange input in the form of minimal-paired stimulus triples, the need for alignment between input/codes and phonemic transcriptions, the presence of trainable parameters, and reliance on a distance metric between stimuli. According to these criteria, RSA and NMI are the least restricted in their applicability, requiring only a distance function or alignment, respectively. In addition to a distance metric, ABX needs minimal-paired stimulus triples to be extracted. In addition to alignment DC has trainable parameters, and in the case of analyzing discrete codes, it behaves like an approximation to the NMI metric.

3.4 Evaluation procedure

We evaluate the induced discrete representations by applying the trained networks on the relevant examples – either full utterances, or speech segments corresponding to sequences of three phonemes (triplets) – and extract the sequences of codes from the VQ layer. We do the same for randomly initialized (untrained) versions of the networks, in order to provide a baseline score, following the methodology of Chrupała et al. (2020). In Section 4, we include in the plots both the baseline scores and the scores with the trained models. For the self-supervised target model we vary only the size of the codebook in the VQ layer,[3] using sizes 2^n for $n \in [5, 10]$. For the visually-supervised target model we use the same sizes and also vary the placement of the VQ layer between one of three levels (following first, second or third GRU layer). For both target models, each variant was trained three times with a different random initialization; the scatter plots in Section 4 show each of these runs, as well as a LOESS fit (Cleveland, 1979) to each combination of codebook size and level.

3.5 Datasets

Training target models Following van Niekerk et al. (2020) we train the self-supervised model on about 15 hours of speech from over 100 speakers provided by Zerospeech 2020 (Dunbar et al., 2020).[4] The visually-supervised model is trained on the Flickr8K Audio Caption Corpus (Harwath and Glass, 2015; Rashtchian et al., 2010)[5], which consists of 8,000 images of daily scenes each paired with five spoken captions. The training portion of this dataset contains 6,000 images and about 34 hours of speech.

Evaluation We encode the development captions of Flickr8K (5,000 captions) using the encoders of the trained and untrained target models, and for each utterance extract the sequence of codes output by the VQ layer. We split this data in half, and use

[3]The self-supervised model has the VQ layer as part of its original architecture, in a *bottleneck* composed of only one linear layer making it hard to manipulate the level of the layer without disrupting the model.

[4]https://zerospeech.com/2020/

[5]https://groups.csail.mit.edu/sls/downloads/flickraudio/

one half for training the DC, and the other half for computing the scores for DC, RSA and NMI.

As ABX (and one experiment with RSA) is not computed on full utterances but on phoneme trigrams, we prepare this data by sampling 1,000 captions from the Flickr8K development set, and cutting the audio into non-overlapping segments corresponding to a sequence of three phonemes. We then use the ZeroSpeech code to generate minimal-pair stimulus triples.

In order to obtain reference phonemic transcriptions we use forced alignment with the Gentle toolkit,[6] based on Kaldi (Povey et al., 2011). This fails for a small number of utterances, which we remove from the data.

3.6 Repository

The code for replicating our experiments is available at https://github.com/bhigy/discrete-repr under Apache License 2.0.

4 Experimental results

Here we report experiments examining how VQ layers encode phonemes in each target model according to different evaluation metrics. The impact of VQ layers on performance of the visually-supervised model in image retrieval is reported in Section A.2 of the Supplementary Material.

4.1 Visually-supervised representations

We extract codes from visually-supervised VQ models trained on the Flickr8K data while varying VQ layer placement and codebook size. We evaluate how much these codes correspond to phonemes according to four metrics: DC, NMI, RSA and ABX. These results are shown in Figure 1.

DC vs. NMI As expected on theoretical grounds, diagnostic classifiers and mutual information give very similar results. Overall, VQ layers at level 1 and 2 perform significantly better than VQ layers at level 3 or equivalent untrained models. Larger codebook sizes also tend to perform better than smaller ones.

DC and NMI vs. RSA RSA differs from the other two metrics on three main aspects: (i) VQ layers at level 3 perform comparably to level 2, (ii) medium codebook sizes give better performances for VQ layers at level 1, and (iii) untrained models show very poor performance. The three points can be explained by the sensitivity of RSA to the purity of the representations. Focusing on the last point first, while representations extracted from untrained models can still contain meaningful information, it will be less explicit and mixed with information that is not relevant for the task of interest. A similar explanation might also hold for the first two points; in particular, we observed that the VQ layers at level 1 retain much more information on the speaker than the other two levels and that the encoding of speaker information increases with the size of the codebook (see Section A.4 of the Supplementary Material for related experiments).

[6]http://lowerquality.com/gentle/

Model	RSA input	r
VS	triplet	0.93
VS	complete	0.16
SS	triplet	0.92
SS	complete	0.93

Table 3: Correlation between the ABX and RSA scores, with RSA computed on complete utterances and phoneme triplets, for the visually supervised (VS) and self-supervised (SS) models.

ABX vs. rest ABX is the most divergent metric. While VQ layers at level 1 and 2 still perform better, the gap with equivalent untrained models is smaller. The effect of codebook size is also much less pronounced and layer-specific. The difference in patterns of results between the metrics might be due to the different testing stimuli used by ABX versus the other three metrics: whereas DC, NMI and RSA are tested on full utterance audio files, ABX is tested on small phoneme trigram files.

Role of stimulus size To disentangle the impact of the metric and the size of the stimulus it is applied on, we run two additional experiments. First, we re-calculate RSA using the same phoneme trigram files used for ABX. The correlation coefficient between ABX and this version of RSA is much stronger (see Table 3), suggesting that the type of stimulus used to test the model does play a role.

The other experiment goes in the opposite direction and brings the ABX evaluation closer to the other three metrics. Training the target model on full sentences but applying it to short segments could play a role. Thus, we run an additional set of experiments where we apply the models to full utterances and generate the representation used in

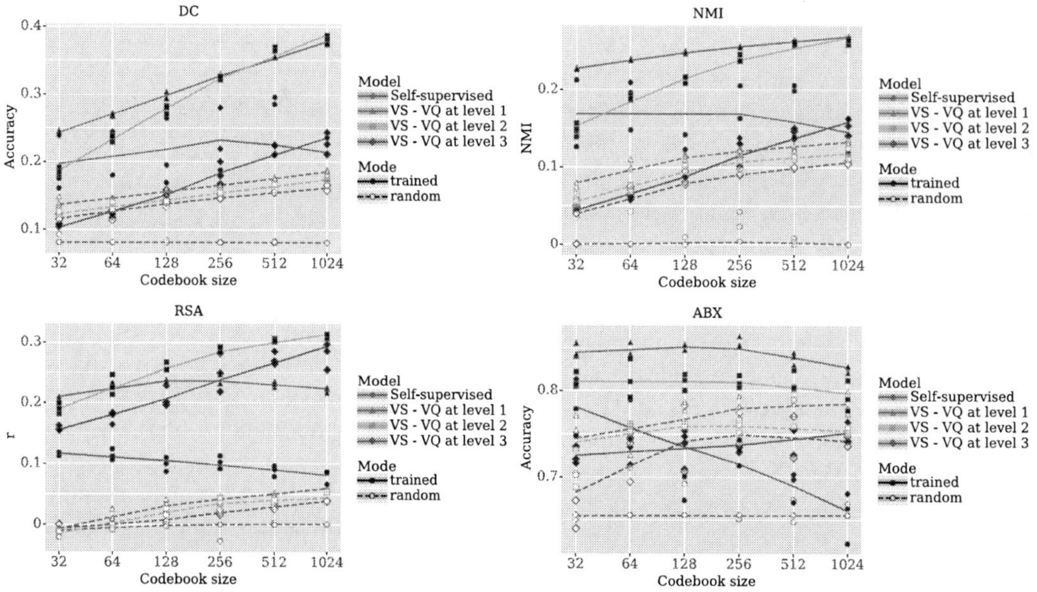

Figure 1: Correspondence of codes to phonemes according to four different metrics as a function of codebook size, type of model, and level of VQ layer placement (in the visually-supervised case).
Top left: Accuracy of the DC.
Top right: NMI between codes and phoneme labels.
Bottom left: RSA score measured against phonemic transcriptions.
Bottom right: Accuracy on the ABX task.
RSA is computed on full utterances; ABX on phoneme-triple segments. DC and NMI are computed frame-wise on full utterances forced-aligned to the phonemic transcriptions. Higher scores are better for all metrics. Trained models are represented by black icons and solid lines. Dashed lines and white filled icons represent randomly initialized models.

ABX by extracting the portion of the code sequence corresponding to each phoneme trigram from the full sequence of activations. The correlation with RSA is still low (0.14) indicating that the problem is intrisic to the evaluation relying on phoneme triplets and not train/test mismatch. This impact of stimulus size on results is likely related to the fact that, with very short stimuli, most normalized edit distances will be maximum, or near maximum, and this will especially be the case for large codebook sizes, giving very skewed and long-tailed edit distance distributions (see details in Section A.3 in the Supplementary Material).

4.2 Self-supervised representations

We extract codes from a number of self-supervised VQ-VAE models trained on the Zerospeech 2019 challenge dataset with varying codebook sizes (note that the VAE model has only one possible placement for the VQ layer). We compare how well these codes correspond to phonemes according to the same four metrics, as displayed in Figure 1. In contrast to what we see for visually-supervised representations, here RSA and ABX scores are largely consistent and suggest that a larger codebook leads to weaker encoding of phonemic information. The effect is more pronounced for ABX though with the largest codebook performing similarly to the baseline. DC and NMI are relatively insensitive to the size of the codebook.

The self-supervised model does not show the discrepancy observed with the visually-supervised model when RSA and ABX scores are run on testing input of different size. This is confirmed by the correlation coefficients between the ABX score and RSA computed on complete utterances and phoneme triplets shown in Table 3. The VQ layer in the self-supervised model only has access to a limited context, which provides enough information to subsequently reconstruct the input audio frame. The visually-supervised architecture on the other hand builds a representation for the whole utterance, supported by recurrent layers. This core difference may explain the pattern of results we report here.

5 Discussion

To summarize, the different metrics we compared give divergent views of the same representations. This should not necessarily be interpreted as one metric being right while the others are flaweded. It is likely that the different metrics account for somewhat different properties of the representation. The differences between RSA and DC/NMI are probably related to the purity of the representation. RSA is based on the correlation of distances between pairs of stimuli and is thus sensitive to the presence of additional information in the representation. If the model's representation contains information that is not related to the representation that is the target of the analysis (in our case phonemes identification), this will be reflected in lower RSA scores.

An obvious example of such information that a model of speech is likely to encode is speaker identity. As pointed out in Section 4.1, the pattern of results obtained with a classifier trained to predict speaker identity supports this view. The encoding of speaker information could lead to comparatively lower scores with RSA, especially for level 1 and large codebooks where speaker identity is better encoded.

In general, our results suggest that different metrics might be preferred depending on the question that one is trying to answer. RSA scores are a better indicator of the exact match between two representations while DC/NMI better evaluate the extent to which a given information can be extracted from a model's representation, irrespective of other sources of information that might be encoded at the same time. This could be confirmed through white-box experiments, where the different metrics would be applied to hand-crafted representations with different properties (e.g. in term of purity). We leave this to future work.

The only remaining point of concern that arises from our results is the interaction between codebook size and input size. Larger codebook sizes tend to be disadvantaged when short input segments are used as input, such as minimal pairs of phoneme triplets. This is particularly relevant for ABX where the use of minimal pairs of phoneme triplets is a common practice. Analysis of discrete representations using short segments should preferably be carried with diagnostic classifiers or NMI, especially if codebooks or different sizes are compared.

It is also important to highlight that the importance of this effect is dependent on the architecture and the training objective of the model, as our experiments with a self-supervised model show.

6 Conclusion

We compared four different metrics for discrete representations induced by VQ layers in weakly-supervised models of spoken language, and while the results are broadly consistent, some differences did emerge. RSA tends to show a bigger gap between trained and untrained models as it is more sensitive to the purity of representations with respect to the information of interest. More surprising is the divergent results we observe when evaluation is performed on minimal pairs of phoneme trigrams: this is likely due to the skew of distance distributions with large codebooks sizes.

This is an important finding as some previous work on discrete representations focused exclusively on the ABX metric. In contrast, we recommend corroborating results with multiple analytical approaches, as currently their behavior in different settings is incompletely understood.

Overall, our findings do support the idea that vector quantization is an effective way to induce discrete representations, and that these correlate with symbolic representations assumed in linguistics. However, it is worth noting that the absolute values of our metrics measuring correspondence to phonemes are moderate at best.[7] It is thus important to keep in mind that these symbolic units are not exact analogs of the concepts familiar from linguistic theory and psycholinguistic studies.

Acknowledgements

Bertrand Higy was supported by a NWO/E-Science Center grant number 027.018.G03.

We would also like to thank multiple anonymous reviewers for their useful comments which helped us improve this paper.

References

Mostafa Abdou, Artur Kulmizev, Felix Hill, Daniel M. Low, and Anders Søgaard. 2019. Higher-order comparisons of sentence encoder representations. In

[7]The highest RSA correlations are around 0.3 and NMI values slightly above 0.25.

Proceedings of the 2019 Conference on Empirical Methods in Natural Language Processing and the 9th International Joint Conference on Natural Language Processing (EMNLP-IJCNLP)*, pages 5838–5845, Hong Kong, China. Association for Computational Linguistics.

Samira Abnar, Lisa Beinborn, Rochelle Choenni, and Willem Zuidema. 2019. Blackbox meets blackbox: Representational similarity & stability analysis of neural language models and brains. In *Proceedings of the 2019 ACL Workshop BlackboxNLP: Analyzing and Interpreting Neural Networks for NLP*, pages 191–203, Florence, Italy. Association for Computational Linguistics.

Yossi Adi, Einat Kermany, Yonatan Belinkov, Ofer Lavi, and Yoav Goldberg. 2017. Fine-grained analysis of sentence embeddings using auxiliary prediction tasks. In *5th International Conference on Learning Representations, ICLR 2017, Toulon, France, April 24-26, 2017, Conference Track Proceedings*. OpenReview.net.

Robin Algayres, Mohamed Salah Zaiem, Benoît Sagot, and Emmanuel Dupoux. 2020. Evaluating the reliability of acoustic speech embeddings. In *INTERSPEECH 2020 - Annual Conference of the International Speech Communication Association*, Shanghai / Vitrtual, China.

Afra Alishahi, Marie Barking, and Grzegorz Chrupała. 2017. Encoding of phonology in a recurrent neural model of grounded speech. In *Proceedings of the 21st Conference on Computational Natural Language Learning (CoNLL 2017)*, pages 368–378, Vancouver, Canada. Association for Computational Linguistics.

Leonardo Badino, Alessio Mereta, and Lorenzo Rosasco. 2015. Discovering discrete subword units with binarized autoencoders and hidden-markov-model encoders. In *Sixteenth Annual Conference of the International Speech Communication Association*.

Yoshua Bengio, Nicholas Léonard, and Aaron Courville. 2013. Estimating or propagating gradients through stochastic neurons for conditional computation. *arXiv preprint arXiv:1308.3432*.

Diane Bouchacourt and Marco Baroni. 2018. How agents see things: On visual representations in an emergent language game. In *Proceedings of the 2018 Conference on Empirical Methods in Natural Language Processing*, pages 981–985, Brussels, Belgium. Association for Computational Linguistics.

Jan Chorowski, Ron J. Weiss, Samy Bengio, and Aäron van den Oord. 2019. Unsupervised Speech Representation Learning Using WaveNet Autoencoders. *IEEE/ACM Transactions on Audio, Speech, and Language Processing*, 27(12):2041–2053. Conference Name: IEEE/ACM Transactions on Audio, Speech, and Language Processing.

Grzegorz Chrupała and Afra Alishahi. 2019. Correlating neural and symbolic representations of language. In *Proceedings of the 57th Annual Meeting of the Association for Computational Linguistics*, pages 2952–2962, Florence, Italy. Association for Computational Linguistics.

Grzegorz Chrupała, Bertrand Higy, and Afra Alishahi. 2020. Analyzing analytical methods: The case of phonology in neural models of spoken language. In *Proceedings of the 58th Annual Meeting of the Association for Computational Linguistics*, pages 4146–4156, Online. Association for Computational Linguistics.

Grzegorz Chrupała. 2021. Visually grounded models of spoken language: A survey of datasets, architectures and evaluation techniques. *CoRR*, abs/2104.13225.

Yu-An Chung, Hao Tang, and James Glass. 2020. Vector-quantized autoregressive predictive coding. *arXiv preprint arXiv:2005.08392*.

William S Cleveland. 1979. Robust locally weighted regression and smoothing scatterplots. *Journal of the American statistical association*, 74(368):829–836.

Alexis Conneau, German Kruszewski, Guillaume Lample, Loïc Barrault, and Marco Baroni. 2018. What you can cram into a single $&!#* vector: Probing sentence embeddings for linguistic properties. In *Proceedings of the 56th Annual Meeting of the Association for Computational Linguistics (Volume 1: Long Papers)*, pages 2126–2136, Melbourne, Australia. Association for Computational Linguistics.

Forrest Davis and Marten van Schijndel. 2020. Discourse structure interacts with reference but not syntax in neural language models. In *Proceedings of the 24th Conference on Computational Natural Language Learning*, pages 396–407, Online. Association for Computational Linguistics.

E. Dunbar, X. N. Cao, J. Benjumea, J. Karadayi, M. Bernard, L. Besacier, X. Anguera, and E. Dupoux. 2017. The zero resource speech challenge 2017. In *2017 IEEE Automatic Speech Recognition and Understanding Workshop (ASRU)*, pages 323–330.

Ewan Dunbar, Robin Algayres, Julien Karadayi, Mathieu Bernard, Juan Benjumea, Xuan-Nga Cao, Lucie Miskic, Charlotte Dugrain, Lucas Ondel, Alan W Black, et al. 2019. The zero resource speech challenge 2019: Tts without t. *arXiv preprint arXiv:1904.11469*.

Ewan Dunbar, Julien Karadayi, Mathieu Bernard, Xuan-Nga Cao, Robin Algayres, Lucas Ondel, Laurent Besacier, Sakriani Sakti, and Emmanuel Dupoux. 2020. The Zero Resource Speech Challenge 2020: Discovering Discrete Subword and Word Units. In *Proc. Interspeech 2020*, pages 4831–4835.

Ryan Eloff, André Nortje, Benjamin van Niekerk, Avashna Govender, Leanne Nortje, Arnu Pretorius, Elan van Biljon, Ewald van der Westhuizen, Lisa van Staden, and Herman Kamper. 2019. Unsupervised acoustic unit discovery for speech synthesis using discrete latent-variable neural networks. *arXiv:1904.07556 [cs, eess]*. ArXiv: 1904.07556.

Sam Fereidooni, Viola Mocz, Dragomir Radev, and Marvin Chun. 2020. Understanding and improving word embeddings through a neuroscientific lens. *bioRxiv*.

Parisa Haghani, Arun Narayanan, Michiel Bacchiani, Galen Chuang, Neeraj Gaur, Pedro Moreno, Rohit Prabhavalkar, Zhongdi Qu, and Austin Waters. 2018. From Audio to Semantics: Approaches to End-to-End Spoken Language Understanding. In *2018 IEEE Spoken Language Technology Workshop (SLT)*, pages 720–726. ISSN: null.

David Harwath and James Glass. 2015. Deep multimodal semantic embeddings for speech and images. In *2015 IEEE Workshop on Automatic Speech Recognition and Understanding (ASRU)*, pages 237–244. IEEE.

David Harwath, Wei-Ning Hsu, and James R. Glass. 2020a. Learning hierarchical discrete linguistic units from visually-grounded speech. In *8th International Conference on Learning Representations, ICLR 2020, Addis Ababa, Ethiopia, April 26-30, 2020*. OpenReview.net.

David Harwath, Adrià Recasens, Dídac Surís, Galen Chuang, Antonio Torralba, and James Glass. 2020b. Jointly discovering visual objects and spoken words from raw sensory input. *International Journal of Computer Vision*, 128(3):620–641.

Kaiming He, Xiangyu Zhang, Shaoqing Ren, and Jian Sun. 2016. Deep residual learning for image recognition. In *2016 IEEE Conference on Computer Vision and Pattern Recognition, CVPR 2016, Las Vegas, NV, USA, June 27-30, 2016*, pages 770–778. IEEE Computer Society.

Bertrand Higy, Desmond Elliott, and Grzegorz Chrupała. 2020. Textual Supervision for Visually Grounded Spoken Language Understanding. In *Findings of the Association for Computational Linguistics: EMNLP 2020*, pages 2698–2709, Online. Association for Computational Linguistics.

Dieuwke Hupkes, Sara Veldhoen, and Willem Zuidema. 2018. Visualisation and 'diagnostic classifiers' reveal how recurrent and recursive neural networks process hierarchical structure. *Journal of Artificial Intelligence Research*, 61:907–926.

Diederik P. Kingma and Jimmy Ba. 2015. Adam: A method for stochastic optimization. In *3rd International Conference on Learning Representations, ICLR 2015, San Diego, CA, USA, May 7-9, 2015, Conference Track Proceedings*.

Nikolaus Kriegeskorte, Marieke Mur, and Peter A Bandettini. 2008. Representational similarity analysis-connecting the branches of systems neuroscience. *Frontiers in systems neuroscience*, 2:4.

Alexander H. Liu, SouYoung Jin, Cheng-I. Jeff Lai, Andrew Rouditchenko, Aude Oliva, and James Glass. 2021. Cross-Modal Discrete Representation Learning. *arXiv:2106.05438 [cs]*. ArXiv: 2106.05438.

Danny Merkx, Stefan L. Frank, and Mirjam Ernestus. 2019. Language Learning Using Speech to Image Retrieval. In *Proc. Interspeech 2019*, pages 1841–1845.

Tiago Pimentel, Josef Valvoda, Rowan Hall Maudslay, Ran Zmigrod, Adina Williams, and Ryan Cotterell. 2020. Information-theoretic probing for linguistic structure. In *Proceedings of the 58th Annual Meeting of the Association for Computational Linguistics*, pages 4609–4622, Online. Association for Computational Linguistics.

Daniel Povey, Arnab Ghoshal, Gilles Boulianne, Lukas Burget, Ondrej Glembek, Nagendra Goel, Mirko Hannemann, Petr Motlicek, Yanmin Qian, Petr Schwarz, Jan Silovsky, Georg Stemmer, and Karel Vesely. 2011. The kaldi speech recognition toolkit. In *IEEE 2011 Workshop on Automatic Speech Recognition and Understanding*. IEEE Signal Processing Society. IEEE Catalog No.: CFP11SRW-USB.

Cyrus Rashtchian, Peter Young, Micah Hodosh, and Julia Hockenmaier. 2010. Collecting image annotations using Amazon's Mechanical Turk. In *Proceedings of the NAACL HLT 2010 Workshop on Creating Speech and Language Data with Amazon's Mechanical Turk*, pages 139–147, Los Angeles. Association for Computational Linguistics.

Andrew Rosenberg and Julia Hirschberg. 2007. V-measure: A conditional entropy-based external cluster evaluation measure. In *Proceedings of the 2007 Joint Conference on Empirical Methods in Natural Language Processing and Computational Natural Language Learning (EMNLP-CoNLL)*, pages 410–420, Prague, Czech Republic. Association for Computational Linguistics.

Thomas Schatz. 2016. *ABX-discriminability measures and applications*. Ph.D. thesis, Université Paris 6 (UPMC).

Leslie N Smith. 2017. Cyclical learning rates for training neural networks. In *2017 IEEE Winter Conference on Applications of Computer Vision (WACV)*, pages 464–472. IEEE.

Andros Tjandra, Sakriani Sakti, and Satoshi Nakamura. 2020. Transformer VQ-VAE for Unsupervised Unit Discovery and Speech Synthesis: ZeroSpeech 2020 Challenge. *arXiv:2005.11676 [cs, eess]*. ArXiv: 2005.11676.

Andros Tjandra, Berrak Sisman, Mingyang Zhang, Sakriani Sakti, Haizhou Li, and Satoshi Nakamura. 2019. VQVAE Unsupervised Unit Discovery and Multi-scale Code2Spec Inverter for Zerospeech Challenge 2019. *arXiv:1905.11449 [cs, eess]*. ArXiv: 1905.11449.

Aäron van den Oord, Oriol Vinyals, and Koray Kavukcuoglu. 2017. Neural discrete representation learning. In *Advances in Neural Information Processing Systems 30: Annual Conference on Neural Information Processing Systems 2017, December 4-9, 2017, Long Beach, CA, USA*, pages 6306–6315.

Benjamin van Niekerk, Leanne Nortje, and Herman Kamper. 2020. Vector-quantized neural networks for acoustic unit discovery in the zerospeech 2020 challenge. *arXiv preprint arXiv:2005.09409*.

Maarten Versteegh, Roland Thiolliere, Thomas Schatz, Xuan Nga Cao, Xavier Anguera, Aren Jansen, and Emmanuel Dupoux. 2015. The zero resource speech challenge 2015. In *Sixteenth annual conference of the international speech communication association*.

A Supplementary material

A.1 Loss of a logistic diagnostic classifier

The most general measure of the amount of information about the value of a random variable Y obtained through the observation of the value of random variable X is mutual information $I(Y;X)$. Here we relate the loss of a logistic diagnostic classifier predicting Y from X in the special case where both Y and X are discrete, with image $\mathcal{Y}$ and $\mathcal{X}$ respectively.

We can construct a logistic classifier which outputs the empirical probability $\hat{P}(Y = y|X = x)$ with $y \in \mathcal{Y}$ and $x \in \mathcal{X}$, by using a one-hot encoding of the categorical predictor variable X as $\mathbf{x}$ and by setting the classifier coefficients $\mathbf{W}$ as

$$W_{y,x} = \ln \hat{P}(Y = y|X = x). \tag{4}$$

The softmax of the logistic classifier with these coefficients simplifies to the empirical estimates of conditional probabilities of Y:

$$p_{y|\mathbf{x}} = \frac{\exp(\ln \hat{P}(Y = y|X = x))}{\sum_{z\in\mathcal{Y}} \exp(\ln \hat{P}(Y = z|X = x))} \tag{5}$$

$$= \hat{P}(Y = y|X = x). \tag{6}$$

The cross entropy of the predictions of this classifer is then:

$$J(\mathbf{w}) = -\frac{1}{N}\sum_{n=1}^{N} \ln \hat{P}(Y = y_n|X = x_n) \tag{7}$$

where y_n and x_n are the values taken by the random variables Y and X for the nth example. The loss is equivalent to the empirical estimate of the conditional entropy $H(Y|X)$, and related to the mutual information between $I(Y;X)$ via:

$$I(Y;X) = H(Y) - H(Y|X). \tag{8}$$

To the extent that the scores of the logistic diagnostic classifier and normalized mutual information applied to the same data are not perfectly correlated, this would be due to the stochasticity of training, regularization, as well as the use of accuracy rather than cross entropy to measure performance.

A.2 Overall performance of the visually supervised model

Since the visually-supervised model is trained and optimized for matching images and their corresponding spoken captions, we measure the recall@10 of retrieving the correct image for a given spoken utterance as a function of the size of the learned codebook and the placement of the VQ layer. Figure 2 shows these results. We observed the following patterns:

- Most models perform worse than a model without the VQ layer, with the exception of the models with the VQ layer at level 1 and a codebook of size 512 or 1024.
- Performance on the image retrieval task is negatively correlated with the level of placement of the VQ layer.
- VQ layers with larger codebooks perform better.

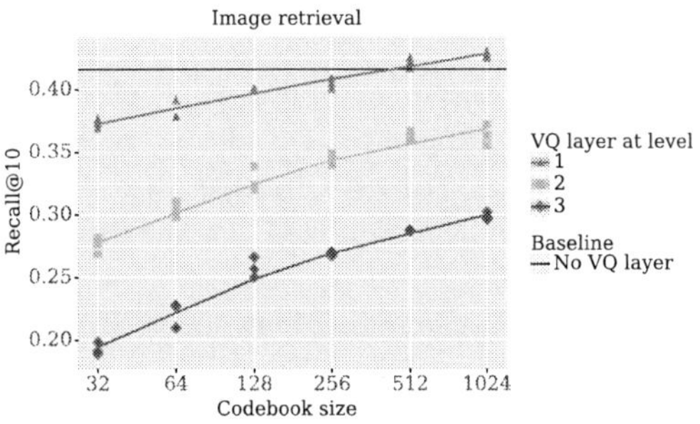

Figure 2: Recall@10 as a function of codebook size and level of placement.

Model	Input	Size	Skew	Kurtosis
SS	complete	32	0.14	0.21
SS	triplet	32	-0.67	0.55
SS	complete	1024	-0.20	0.29
SS	triplet	1024	-2.79	8.99
VS	complete	32	0.04	0.35
VS	triplet	32	-1.66	3.20
VS	complete	1024	-1.40	4.71
VS	triplet	1024	-7.92	87.20

Table 4: Skew and excess kurtosis of edit distance distributions, for the self-supervised (SS) and visually-supervised level 1 (VS) models.

A.3 Edit distance distribution

Table 4 presents skew and excess kurtosis of edit distance distributions for both target models, using codebooks of size 32 and 1024 and trained on long and short segments, confirming the hypothesis that the combination of short segments and large codebooks leads to skewed distributions.

A.4 Speaker identification

Figure 3 shows accuracy of diagnostic classifiers trained on code sequences encoded as vectors of code frequencies. For visually-supervised models, speaker identity is represented to some degree in untrained models, for codebooks of all sizes and at all levels, and most strongly for large codebook sizes at level 1. After training, we observe differentiated patterns for VQ layers at level 1 versus 2 and 3. While speaker identity is emphasized in codebooks at level 1 compared to the untrained models, it is weakened for subsequent layers, to the point of being effectively removed at level 3. These results indicate that VQ layers at level 1 represent speaker-dependent information, possibly encoding acoustic rather than phonemic information. The self-supervised models show results similar to the visually-supervised models with the VQ layer at level 1 when trained, but capture nearly no speaker information before training.

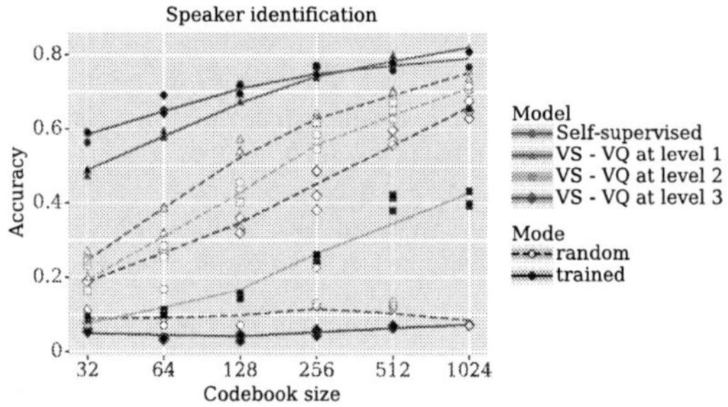

Figure 3: Accuracy of speaker classification on codebooks for the self-supervised and visually-supervised models. Trained models are represented by black icons and solid lines. Dashed lines and white filled icons represent randomly initialized models.

Word Equations: Inherently Interpretable Sparse Word Embeddings through Sparse Coding

Adly Templeton
Williams College
adlytempleton@gmail.com

Abstract

Word embeddings are a powerful natural language processing technique, but they are extremely difficult to interpret. To enable interpretable NLP models, we create vectors where each dimension is *inherently interpretable*. By inherently interpretable, we mean a system where each dimension is associated with some human-understandable *hint* that can describe the meaning of that dimension. In order to create more interpretable word embeddings, we transform pretrained dense word embeddings into sparse embeddings. These new embeddings are inherently interpretable: each of their dimensions is created from and represents a natural language word or specific grammatical concept. We construct these embeddings through sparse coding, where each vector in the basis set is itself a word embedding. Therefore, each dimension of our sparse vectors corresponds to a natural language word. We also show that models trained using these sparse embeddings can achieve good performance and are more interpretable in practice, including through human evaluations.

1 Introduction

Word embeddings represent each word in a natural language as a vector in a continuous high dimensional space. Many different pretrained embeddings are readily available (Mikolov et al., 2013; Pennington et al., 2014; Bojanowski et al., 2017), and are used in a range of applications (Li and Yang, 2018). This vector representation can be said to encode the meaning of the word; not only are similar words close together but linear relationships between words are thought to have conceptual meaning. In the famous example, the vector difference between 'man' and 'woman' is similar to the vector difference between 'king' and 'queen' (Landauer and Dumais, 1997; Mikolov et al., 2013). This observation suggests that the vector difference between 'woman' and 'man' represents a concept of gender within the vector space, implying that dimensions or linear combinations of dimensions in the vector space are related to human-understandable concepts. However, in practice, interpreting these vector spaces is extremely difficult. This obscures the behavior of any NLP model built on top of word embeddings.

To enable interpretable NLP models, we create vectors where each dimension is *inherently interpretable*. By inherently interpretable, we mean a system where each dimension is associated with some human-understandable *hint* that can describe the meaning of that dimension. This allows us to directly interpret the coefficients of simple models trained on these vectors. By comparison, most other systems of interpretable word embeddings aim to create dimensions that humans may be able to manually interpret after the fact.

To create our vectors, we represent word embeddings as the sparse linear combination of a basis set of other word embeddings. Our primary contribution is that, instead of learning an optimal basis for our sparse vector space, we draw the columns of the basis from the original set of dense word embeddings. This strategy provides a natural label for each sparse dimension and allows us to represent each natural language word as the linear combination of a small number of other natural language words. This representation is itself a more 'interpretable' word embedding. This technique produces representations of words that have interpretable dimensions. We show that these representations are more interpretable and that models trained on these embeddings perform almost as well as models trained on standard dense embeddings. We show how the creation of inherently interpretable vectors can help us understand the behavior and structure of the original word embeddings.

Proceedings of the Fourth BlackboxNLP Workshop on Analyzing and Interpreting Neural Networks for NLP, pages 177–191
Online, November 11, 2021.

Recent work has created more interpretable vectors through a variety of methods. However, relatively few approaches create *inherently interpretable* dimensions. Therefore, we believe that our work, which creates inherently interpretable embeddings through a simple novel method can be the basis of future NLP tools where interpretability is crucial.

As an example, we present one randomly selected embedding from our system. More examples can be found in the appendix.

$$\begin{aligned}
&\text{carbon} = 0.79 * \text{nitrogen}\\
&- 0.38 * \text{CAPITALIZATION} + 0.3 * \text{fossil}\\
&- 0.21 * \text{POS-NOUN} + 0.16 * \text{POS-ADJ}\\
&+ 0.14 * \text{C0} - 0.14 * \text{PAST-TENSE}\\
&+ 0.13 * \text{wood} + 0.11 * \text{global}\\
&+ 0.1 * \text{atoms} - 0.095 * \text{POS-ADV}\\
&+ 0.092 * \text{aluminum}\\
&- 0.078 * \text{PLURAL-NOUN}\\
&+ 0.073 * \text{greenhouse}\\
&- 0.072 * \text{POS-PROPN}\\
&- 0.048 * \text{POS-VERB} + 0.046 * \text{forestry}\\
&+ 0.03 * \text{PARTICIPLE} + 0.017 * \text{sink}\\
&+ 0.012 * \text{POS-NUM}
\end{aligned}$$

2 Previous Work

Park et al. (Park et al., 2017) find a more interpretable rotation of word embeddings using techniques associated with factor analysis. Other work (Dufter and Schütze, 2019; Rothe and Schütze, 2016) rotates dense vectors using different methods.

Koc et al. (Şenel et al., 2020) tie concepts to dimensions in a more direct way. They select a concept for each dense dimension and identify words that are associated with these concepts. A penalty term pushes coefficients for these words towards the fixed values.

Other work has focused on interpretability through sparsity. Subramian et al. (Subramanian et al., 2018) created more interpretable embeddings by passing pretrained dense embeddings through a sparse autoencoder.

Panigrahi et al. (Panigrahi et al., 2019) proposed Word2Sense, a generative approach that models each dimension as a 'sense' and word embeddings as a sparse probability distribution over the senses.

The mathematical technique we use in this paper, *Sparse coding*, which is defined as the representation of vectors as the sparse linear combination of an overcomplete basis, is a well-studied optimization problem (Coates and Ng, 2011; Hoyer, 2002; Lee et al., 2007). Previous work (Coates and Ng, 2011) has also shown that basis vectors can be efficiently selected from the set that is being encoded.

Faruqui et al. (Faruqui et al., 2015) used non-negative sparse coding to recode dense word embeddings into more interpretable sparse vectors while learning a basis. However, because they create their basis through direct optimization, the basis vectors (and, consequently, the dimensions in their transformed sparse space) do not have any inherent interpretation and must be manually interpreted.

Zhang et al. (Zhang et al., 2019) also used non-negative sparse coding to learn a set of *word factors* to recode word2vec embeddings. The basis vectors created in this way are highly redundant, so they then use spectral clustering to remove near-duplicate factors. Then, they are able to manually infer reasonable post hoc interpretations for most of the factors.

Concurrently with our work, Mathew et al. create an inherently interpretable subspace from pairs of antonyms. They then project embeddings into that subspace, producing lower-dimensional dense vectors (Mathew et al., 2020).

3 Model

Our work uses *sparse coding* to transform a set of word embeddings from a dense and uninterpretable space into a sparse and interpretable space. Let v_D represent a dense word embedding, and let $\mathcal{B}$ represent a matrix with basis vectors along the columns. $\mathcal{B}$ has size (n_S, n_N) where n_d is the dimensionality of the dense vectors and n_S is the dimensionality of the sparse vectors. We achieve sparse coding using regularized regression, inducing sparsity using the L_1 norm. Formally, this corresponds to finding the sparse vector v_S that minimizes the following objective function

$$\arg\min_{v_S} \ ||v_D - v_S\mathcal{B}||_2^2 + \alpha||v_S||_1 \qquad (1)$$

α is a hyperparameter that controls the level of sparsity. The first term in Equation 1 ensures the sparse vector corresponds to a vector in the dense space that is similar to the original vector. The second term is a sparsity-inducing penalty.

Note that by 'basis' we mean a set of vectors in the dense space, each one corresponding to a dimension in the transformed, sparse, space. Out of necessity, these vectors are *overcomplete* (there are more dimensions than vectors) and so they do not form a basis according to the traditional definition.

Previous work using sparse coding to create interpretable word embeddings has considered the basis $\mathcal{B}$ to be part of the optimization problem (Faruqui et al., 2015; Zhang et al., 2019). Our primary contribution is that, instead of learning an optimal basis, we draw the columns of the basis from the original set of dense word embeddings. This strategy provides a natural label for each sparse dimension.

3.1 Grammatical Basis

We can roughly divide the 'meaning' carried by a word embedding into *grammatical* and *non-grammatical* properties. Here we use 'grammatical properties' to mean properties that describe how that word fits into the grammar of the language, such as its part-of-speech, tense, or number. We use 'non-grammatical properties' to mean all other aspects of the meaning of a word. For instance, we expect the embedding for the word 'swimming' to include a grammatical component representing that this word is a present-tense participle and a non-grammatical component that represents the meaning 'to swim'. Of course, this deconstruction is imperfect. Nevertheless, this approach provides a useful insight towards decomposing the meaning of a word embedding.

Preliminary experiments showed that, without special consideration, grammatical properties would be captured in an unintuitive way. The grammatical components could not be easily isolated to one subset of the nonzero dimensions. Ideally, the grammatical information would be captured in a small number of interpretable dimensions. Instead, each basis vector would capture part of the grammatical component and part of the semantic component. This duality creates difficulty when interpreting our representations.

To address this, we construct a small number of *grammatical basis vectors* and add them to the basis set. For instance, we construct a 'POS-NOUN' vector by taking the mean of all word embeddings corresponding to nouns. For this work, we use a set of 11 grammatical basis vectors, though the number and the construction of these are arbitrary. A description of the grammatical basis vectors is in the appendix.

Next, we make the grammatical basis vectors orthogonal using the Gram-Schmidt process. Finally, we subtract the projection along the grammatical basis vectors from all other ('non-grammatical') basis vectors we use and renormalize them. This procedure separates the grammatical meaning from our non-grammatical basis vectors, ensuring that non-grammatical bases are not also coding for grammatical concepts.

Note that we only perform this orthogonalization with respect to a very small number of grammatical basis vectors. We find that this procedure does not remove more than 50% of the length of any individual vector and 50% of vectors have less than 20% of their length removed.

When encoding a dense vector, instead of finding the grammatical coefficients using sparse coding, we set each grammatical coefficient to the projection along the corresponding grammatical basis vector, which is equal to the dot product similarity between the original vector and the grammatical basis vector. Because the grammatical basis is orthogonal, we can do this for every grammatical basis vector simultaneously. This residual is then transformed using Equation 1.

Note that, although we do require hand-crafted features to create the grammatical basis vectors, our system does not use hand-crafted features in the representation of new words. Once the grammatical feature vectors are defined, words can be represented in our sparse space using no more information than their *fasttext* dense vectors.

3.2 Basis Selection

We cannot practically use all words as our basis set, so we have to select a subset. First, we start with the 30,000 most frequent words. We filter out any words that are capitalized or that are not in a standard English vocabulary (using the vocabulary of the spaCy *en_core_web_sm* model). Next, we filter out any words that are not nouns, verbs, or adjectives. This process removes many basis vectors that may be hard to interpret. This gives us approximately 11,000 remaining potential basis words. From these, we will select 3,000 words to use in the final basis.

We use an iterative algorithm that takes, at each step, the potential basis vector with the highest mean cosine similarity to all other vectors. To encourage diversity, this mean is weighted by the lowest cosine dissimilarity that each vector has with any already-selected basis vector. Formally, at each step, we grow the set of basis vectors B by adding the potential basis vector x from the set of unchosen potential basis vectors $\mathcal{F} \setminus B$ that satisfies

$$\arg\max_{x \in \mathcal{F} \setminus B} \sum_{v \in V_D} (x \cdot v) \max_{b \in B}(1 - b \cdot v)$$

Where V_D is the set of dense vectors for the 30,000 most frequent words.

Note that, despite our use of the word 'basis', this is not a basis in the traditional sense; the set of basis vectors are not linearly independent, and there are more basis vectors than dimensions in the original space. However, because of the L1 penalty term, our objective function still allows for optimal decompositions.

3.3 End-to-end Process

In order to find the sparse vector representation, we follow the following process, combining the above elements.

1. Find the dense vector representation of the word.
2. Compute the projection along each vector orthogonal grammatical basis. Store these projections as the first part of the resulting vector. Subtract the projection along this basis before moving on to the next step.
3. Optimize Eq. 1 using the FISTA algorithm (Chalasani et al., 2013). Store the learned sparse vector as the second part of the resulting vector.

4 Results

We will evaluate this model in multiple ways. In particular, we care about two contradictory properties of our transformed vector space. First, we want our vector space to be useful in downstream machine learning applications. We expect that, in most applications, increased interpretability comes with some performance cost. Therefore, we care about the performance loss when moving from dense vectors to our sparse vectors.

The other goal is that our sparse vectors should be interpretable. It is much harder to articulate exactly what interpretability is or how we can measure it. Metrics such as the Word Intrusion Task (Section2) can act as a useful proxy for interpretability, and we use it as our primary quantitative measure of interpretability. But part of interpretability is, by definition, subjective and any metric is imperfect.

4.1 implementation

We use the FastText (Bojanowski et al., 2017) pretrained 300 dimensional English vectors (without subword information) trained on Wikipedia 2017, UMBC webbase corpus and statmt.org news dataset as the dense vectors that we input into our models. Unless otherwise mentioned, we only consider the 30,000 most frequent words, for computational reasons. We normalize all vectors to have mean 0 and unit length. After learning sparse vectors, we normalize each sparse vector so that it corresponds to a dense vector of unit length. When comparing with the original dense vectors (FastText (Bojanowski et al., 2017)), we subtract the mean of all vectors, to match our preprocessing.

In practice, the sparse penalty term will only push coefficients very close to 0. We clamp any coefficient with a magnitude of less than .001 to 0. We found this threshold by taking the lowest cutoff that does not introduce significant irregularities into the tradeoff curves in Section 4.3.

We solve the regularized optimization problems using the FISTA algorithm (Chalasani et al., 2013), as implemented in the Python Lightning package (Blondel and Pedregosa, 2016), using default hyperparameters. FISTA is an optimization algorithm that can efficiently solve sparse coding problems. We use the spaCy library (Honnibal and Montani, 2017) to check for out of vocabulary words and perform part-of-speech tagging. We use the numpy (Oliphant, 2006), CuPy (Okuta et al., 2017), and Scikit learn (Pedregosa et al., 2011) libraries for various linear algebra implementations. We use the open-source Gensim library (Rehurek and Sojka, 2010) to manipulate word embeddings. For the word analogy task evaluation, we use the *3CosAdd* method, as implemented by Gensim. Models processed 30,000 words within a few hours, running across 32 2.5 GHz processors with no GPU.

4.2 Comparison with Previous Work

To compare our work against other sparse coding approaches, we will often reference the vectors created by Faruqui et al. (Faruqui et al., 2015). That work generates more interpretable vectors using

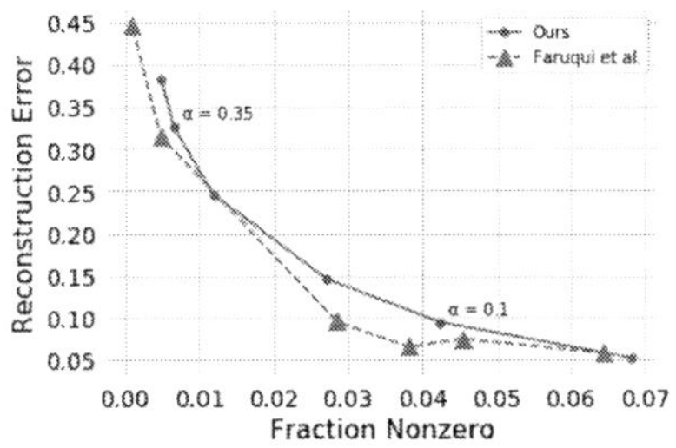

Figure 1: The tradeoff curve between sparsity and reconstruction error. The dashed line shows the tradeoff curve achieved by Faruqui et al. using sparse coding without inherently interpretable dimensions (Section 4.2).

sparse coding but without inherently interpretable dimensions.

4.3 Reconstruction Error and Sparsity

Note that, because of the penalty term in Equation 1, $V_S\mathcal{B}$ (the *reconstructed vectors*) are not exactly equal to the original dense vectors V_D. Therefore, we expect a tradeoff between sparsity and this difference (which we call *reconstruction error).*

This tradeoff curve is displayed in Figure 1. Despite the additional constraints of an inherently interpretable system, we suffer only a minor increase in reconstruction error compared to traditional sparse coding. This *reconstruction error* is the primary drawback of our system; reconstruction error adds a small amount of noise to every model built on top of our sparse vectors. For the remainder of this work, unless otherwise mentioned, we will consider the vectors made with $\alpha = 0.35$. These vectors have, on average, 20 nonzero entries.

4.4 Analogy Task

In the word2vec vector space, famously, the vector for 'king' plus the vector for 'woman' minus the vector for 'man' is close to the vector for 'queen'. Analogy tasks quantitatively test these properties. The task consists of analogies of the form *A is to A' as B is to B'*. The vector space is evaluated on its ability to correctly determine the value of B'.

The performance of our vector space at this task is displayed in Table 1. Our model performs poorly on this task. This degradation comes from two sources. First, the drop from the original vectors to the reconstructed vectors that is due to reconstruction error. Second, an additional degradation is caused by the transformation from dense vectors to sparse vectors, especially with cosine similarity.

	Nonzero	Total	Gram.	Sem.
FastText	300	0.88	0.85	0.94
Faruqui $\lambda = 0.75$	136	0.65	0.60	0.73
Ours $\alpha = 0.1$	127	0.50	0.46	0.59
Recons. $\alpha = 0.1$	300	0.83	0.80	0.88
Ours $\alpha = 0.35$	20	0.20	0.22	0.15
Recons. $\alpha = 0.35$	300	0.33	0.38	0.25

Table 1: Accuracy on the word2vec analogy evaluation set for various vector spaces. The first column shows the average number of nonzero entries in each sparse vector. Accuracy is also broken down by nongrammatical and grammatical categories. 'Recons' denotes the performance of the reconstructed dense vectors. All results are on a 50% held-out test set.

4.5 Classification

Next, we demonstrate that our model can be used to build interpretable machine learning systems. To this end, we train classifiers using our word embeddings as input. We demonstrate that these classifiers are not only effective but also interpretable.

We evaluate our vectors on two datasets, the IMDB sentiment analysis dataset (Maas et al., 2011) and the TREC question classification dataset (Li and Roth, 2002). For both of these datasets, we use a logistic regression model and a bag of words representation.

4.5.1 IMDB Sentiment Analysis Dataset

The IMDB movie review dataset consists of 50,000 passages taken from IMDB movie reviews, evenly split between positive and negative reviews. The task is to determine the sentiment of each passage (Maas et al., 2011).

We train classifiers using various word embedding spaces as inputs. While we could train deep neural modesl on these vector spaces, neural models do not directly produce interpretable coefficients, and therefore we provide a demonstration on simple logistic regression models. The results are presented in Table 2. Our vector spaces demonstrate improvement over the original dense vectors (FastText (Bojanowski et al., 2017)), as well as the traditional sparse coding approach of Faruqui et al. This result holds despite a slight decrease in performance caused by the reconstruction error (as demonstrated by the low performance with reconstructed vectors).

We can directly interpret our classifier's coefficients. Here, we present the most significant coeffi-

	IMDB	TREC
FastText	85.35	84.2
Faruqui $\lambda = .75$	85.54	84.4
Ours $\alpha = 0.1$	**87.51**	**86.2**
Ours Recons. $\alpha = 0.1$	85.08	81.4
Ours $\alpha = 0.35$	86.46	84.0
Ours Recons. $\alpha = 0.35$	83.00	75.8

Table 2: Accuracy on the IMDB sentiment analysis dataset and the TREC question classification dataset. We use a logistic regression classifier, which uses as input a bag-of-words sum of various word embeddings.

cients ($\alpha = 0.1$) [1]:

$$\ln \frac{P(\text{positive})}{1 - P(\text{positive})} = -157 \cdot \text{dreadful}$$
$$- 153 \cdot \text{horrible} + 150 \cdot \text{fabulous} - 140 \cdot \text{dull}$$
$$- 132 \cdot \text{dreary} - 107 \cdot \text{worsen}$$
$$- 105 \cdot \text{ridiculous} + \ldots$$

Note that these are not coefficients on the frequencies of individual words. Instead, these are coefficients on vectors in the basis set. We can consider them to be coefficients on concepts, which are labeled by the displayed words. The coefficients make sense: positive concepts have positive coefficients, while negative concepts have negative coefficients. This pattern continues for much longer than displayed above, and we have omitted other terms for space reasons. The first term to not fall into this clear interpretation is the 24th-most significant: ... $+ 74 \cdot$ shall + ..‘

At first, this term appears nonsensical. Looking more closely at this dimension can reveal more about our system. The top five words in the dimension represented by ‘shall’ are the following: ‘henceforth’, ‘herein’, ‘hereafter’, ‘thereof’, ‘hereby’. We can see here how both our vector space and our regression model pick up on tone. This dimension appears to correspond to a formal and somewhat archaic tone, which is likely not found in a negative internet comment.

4.5.2 TREC Question Classification Dataset

Our next classification task is more complex. The TREC question classification dataset consists of 6,000 questions that are divided into 6 categories based on the expected answer: abbreviations, descriptions, entities, humans, locations, and numeric.

Accuracy for various vector spaces is presented in Table 2. Again, our model does better than the unmodified input vectors we start with, despite some loss from the reconstruction error. Both results suggest that our vector spaces are efficient in regression-based settings, though the performance at the word-analogy task suffers a serious degradation. It is likely that different qualities are needed for these different tasks. The exact-match evaluation of the word analogy task severely punishes even slight noise in the vector space, and cosine similarities are noisy in sparse vectors.

Once again, we directly interpret the coefficients learned by logistic regression. For space, we display the most significant terms for the HUM category. Questions in this category expect the name of a human as the answer:

$$\ln \frac{P(\text{HUM})}{1 - P(\text{HUM})} = -77 \cdot \text{wonder}$$
$$+ 66 \cdot \text{organizations} + 54 \cdot \text{companies}$$
$$+ 51 \cdot \text{poet} + 49 \cdot \text{songwriter}$$
$$+ 48 \cdot \text{identities} + 42 \cdot \text{fan} - 42 \cdot \text{movie}$$
$$- 39 \cdot \text{resulting} + 36 \cdot \text{university}$$
$$- 36 \cdot \text{diseases} + 36 \cdot \text{successive} +$$
$$35 \cdot \text{consist} + 35 \cdot \text{cabinets} + \ldots$$

Some of these coefficients, such as ‘songwriter’ or ‘identities’ are intuitive and reveal interesting behavior of the classifier. Others, such as ‘wonder’, are not. Manual inspection reveals that ‘wonder’ is used to represent words such as ‘How’ or ‘why’ but not ‘who’, though this behavior is likely noise.

4.5.3 Word Intrusion Task

To quantitatively measure interpretability, we use human experiments. In particular, we use the word intrusion task (Chang et al., 2009). In this task, humans are presented with five words, four of which are associated highly with a particular dimension. Participants are asked to choose the word that does not belong. We use our vectors both with and without providing the label of the dimension as a ‘hint’.

We use the following procedure for generating questions. First, we filter candidate words, starting with the 20,000 most frequent words and filtering out words that are not lowercase, words that are

[1] These weights are real-values and truncated for space. Note that the weights are very large because they correspond to sparse low-magnitude features.

Figure 2: An example of the user interface given to annotators. The following instructions were given to the annotators: 'You will be presented with a group of 5 words. Four of these words are similar in some way and the other one is not. Pick out the word which is dissimilar. You may be provided with a hint about how the words are similar.'

	Accuracy	CI
FastText	0.31	[0.27,0.34]
Faruqui	0.77	[0.74,0.80]
Ours	0.80	[0.77,0.83]
Ours (with Hints)	0.84	[0.81,0.86]

Table 3: Results on the word intrusion task. 95% normal confidence intervals are displayed.

not made up of only ASCII alphabetic characters, and words with only one letter. Then we randomly select a dimension. We pick the 4 highest words along that dimension, and one word randomly selected from the bottom 50% of words in that dimension, then randomize the order. Each example is presented to three different Mechanical Turk annotators. An example of the interface presented to annotators is seen in Figure 2.

The results of the word intrusion task are presented in Table 3. When hints are provided, we see a statistically significant improvement in accuracy between our vectors and the sparse coding baseline ($p = .00055$). In addition, using hints produces a statistically significant improvement ($p = .040$), validating our motivation for inherently interpretable dimensions. Of course, any quantitative metric of interpretability is imperfect. To qualitatively assess interpretability, randomly selected vectors are presented in the appendix.

4.6 Summary

Our method still has some serious drawbacks. Sparse coding, by its nature, introduces a substantial amount of noise in the form of reconstruction error and sparse coding has the potential to assign very different sparse vectors to similar dense vectors. We hope that future work will produce sparse embeddings that are interpretable by construction without some of the shortcomings of our work.

4.7 Conclusions and Future Work

In this work, we presented a method to create word embeddings that are interpretable by construction. Each dimension of these embeddings corresponds precisely to a natural language word. These embeddings can be presented in a human readable form, and we have shown that most of these representations are intuitive. We have also shown that these embeddings can be used to produce an extremely interpretable classification model that still delivers performance comparable to or better than a classification model based on the original embeddings.

Unlike most previous work on interpretable word embeddings, our method does not require humans to interpret and label each dimension. We have previously seen how this feature allows us to easily create interpretable classification models. It also allows us to gain a deeper understanding of the original dense vector space. Previous approaches may have obscured nuanced or hard to interpret behavior. In particular, a human manually interpreting a dimension may not appreciate subtle behavior of the system. Several sections of this work, which have manually examined individual word representations in our system, have revealed the nuanced behavior that our system demonstrates.

Our method still has some serious drawbacks. While we have examined a number of these flaws, many are tied closely to the sparse coding method we have chosen to use. Sparse coding, by its nature, introduces a substantial amount of noise in the form of reconstruction error. In addition to the reconstruction error, sparse coding has the potential to assign very different sparse vectors to similar dense vectors. We hope that future work will produce sparse embeddings that are interpretable by construction without some of the shortcomings of our work.

Much of the promise of sparse coding methods remains to be proved. In particular, we believe it will be fruitful to study the representation of syntactic concepts. We have seen that our attempts to disentangle syntactic concepts from our semantic basis vectors were not entirely successful. We would also like to better understand how these methods are applicable in deep learning models.

There is still a large amount of analytical work left to be done on evaluation. The word intrusion task, while an effective quantitative method, does not offer a complete view of interpretability. Part of this problem is that we do not have any way to quantify interpretability where it is most useful: when building downstream classification models. More fundamentally, we do not have any underlying framework for understanding what it means for a word embedding to be interpretable.

We believe that interpretable word embeddings have great potential for helping us understand and interpret models in a wide range of NLP tasks.

Acknowledgements

Thanks to Duane Bailey for his extensive support and advice, and for advising the thesis on which this paper is based.. Thanks to Andrea Danyluk for her guidance as the second reader of that thesis.

References

Mathieu Blondel and Fabian Pedregosa. 2016. Lightning: large-scale linear classification, regression and ranking in Python.

Piotr Bojanowski, Edouard Grave, Armand Joulin, and Tomas Mikolov. 2017. Enriching word vectors with subword information. *Transactions of the Association for Computational Linguistics*, 5:135–146.

Rakesh Chalasani, Jose C Principe, and Naveen Ramakrishnan. 2013. A fast proximal method for convolutional sparse coding. In *The 2013 International Joint Conference on Neural Networks (IJCNN)*, pages 1–5. IEEE.

Jonathan Chang, Sean Gerrish, Chong Wang, Jordan L. Boyd-Graber, and David M. Blei. 2009. Reading tea leaves: How humans interpret topic models. In *Advances in Neural Information Processing Systems*, pages 288–296.

Adam Coates and Andrew Y. Ng. 2011. The importance of encoding versus training with sparse coding and vector quantization. In *Proceedings of the 28th International Conference on Machine Learning (ICML-11)*, pages 921–928.

Philipp Dufter and Hinrich Schütze. 2019. Analytical methods for interpretable ultradense word embeddings. *arXiv preprint arXiv:1904.08654*.

Manaal Faruqui, Yulia Tsvetkov, Dani Yogatama, Chris Dyer, and Noah A Smith. 2015. Sparse overcomplete word vector representations. In *Proceedings of the 53rd Annual Meeting of the Association for Computational Linguistics and the 7th International Joint Conference on Natural Language Processing (Volume 1: Long Papers)*, pages 1491–1500.

Matthew Honnibal and Ines Montani. 2017. spaCy 2: Natural language understanding with Bloom embeddings, convolutional neural networks and incremental parsing.

Patrik O. Hoyer. 2002. Non-negative sparse coding. In *Proceedings of the 12th IEEE Workshop on Neural Networks for Signal Processing*, pages 557–565. IEEE.

Thomas K. Landauer and Susan T. Dumais. 1997. A solution to Plato's problem: The latent semantic analysis theory of acquisition, induction, and representation of knowledge. *Psychological Review*, 104(2):211.

Honglak Lee, Alexis Battle, Rajat Raina, and Andrew Y. Ng. 2007. Efficient sparse coding algorithms. In *Advances in Neural Information Processing Systems*, pages 801–808.

Xin Li and Dan Roth. 2002. Learning question classifiers. In *Proceedings of the 19th International Conference on Computational Linguistics-Volume 1*, pages 1–7. Association for Computational Linguistics.

Yang Li and Tao Yang. 2018. Word embedding for understanding natural language: a survey. In *Guide to Big Data Applications*, pages 83–104. Springer.

Andrew L. Maas, Raymond E. Daly, Peter T. Pham, Dan Huang, Andrew Y. Ng, and Christopher Potts. 2011. Learning word vectors for sentiment analysis. In *Proceedings of the 49th Annual Meeting of the Association for Computational Linguistics: Human Language Technologies*, pages 142–150, Portland, Oregon, USA. Association for Computational Linguistics.

Binny Mathew, Sandipan Sikdar, Florian Lemmerich, and Markus Strohmaier. 2020. The polar framework: Polar opposites enable interpretability of pre-trained word embeddings. *arXiv preprint arXiv:2001.09876*.

Tomas Mikolov, Ilya Sutskever, Kai Chen, Greg S Corrado, and Jeff Dean. 2013. Distributed representations of words and phrases and their compositionality. In *Advances in Neural Information Processing Systems*, pages 3111–3119.

Ryosuke Okuta, Yuya Unno, Daisuke Nishino, Shohei Hido, and Crissman Loomis. 2017. CuPy: A NumPy-compatible library for nvidia gpu calculations. In *Proceedings of Workshop on Machine Learning Systems (LearningSys) in The Thirty-first Annual Conference on Neural Information Processing Systems (NIPS)*.

Travis E. Oliphant. 2006. *A guide to NumPy*, volume 1. Trelgol Publishing USA.

Abhishek Panigrahi, Harsha Vardhan Simhadri, and Chiranjib Bhattacharyya. 2019. Word2sense: Sparse interpretable word embeddings. In *Proceedings of the 57th Annual Meeting of the Association for Computational Linguistics*, pages 5692–5705.

Sungjoon Park, JinYeong Bak, and Alice Oh. 2017. Rotated word vector representations and their interpretability. In *Proceedings of the 2017 Conference on Empirical Methods in Natural Language Processing*, pages 401–411.

Fabian Pedregosa, Gaël Varoquaux, Alexandre Gramfort, Vincent Michel, Bertrand Thirion, Olivier Grisel, Mathieu Blondel, Peter Prettenhofer, Ron Weiss, Vincent Dubourg, et al. 2011. Scikit-learn: Machine learning in Python. *Journal of Machine Learning Research*, 12(Oct):2825–2830.

Jeffrey Pennington, Richard Socher, and Christopher D Manning. 2014. Glove: Global vectors for word representation. In *Proceedings of the 2014 Conference on Empirical Methods in Natural Language Processing (EMNLP)*, pages 1532–1543.

Radim Rehurek and Petr Sojka. 2010. Software framework for topic modelling with large corpora. In *In Proceedings of the LREC 2010 Workshop on New Challenges for NLP Frameworks*. Citeseer.

Sascha Rothe and Hinrich Schütze. 2016. Word embedding calculus in meaningful ultradense subspaces. In *Proceedings of the 54th Annual Meeting of the Association for Computational Linguistics (Volume 2: Short Papers)*, pages 512–517.

Lütfi Kerem Şenel, Ihsan Utlu, Furkan Şahinuç, Haldun M Ozaktas, and Aykut Koç. 2020. Imparting interpretability to word embeddings while preserving semantic structure. *Natural Language Engineering*, pages 1–26.

Anant Subramanian, Danish Pruthi, Harsh Jhamtani, Taylor Berg-Kirkpatrick, and Eduard Hovy. 2018. Spine: Sparse interpretable neural embeddings. In *Thirty-Second AAAI Conference on Artificial Intelligence*.

Juexiao Zhang, Yubei Chen, Brian Cheung, and Bruno A. Olshausen. 2019. Word embedding visualization via dictionary learning. *arXiv preprint arXiv:1910.03833*.

5 Appendix

A Gramtacic Basis Descriptions

Our approach makes use of four types of grammatical basis vectors:

1. We use the first principal component of the embeddings of the 30,000 most frequent words. Previous work on word embedding has referred to this as the *common discourse vector*, or c_0, and has shown that this vector encodes words that appear commonly in all contexts, such as 'the'.

2. We take the mean of all vectors of capitalized words and use this as a grammatical basis vector to represent capitalization.

3. For a variety of parts-of-speech, we use the mean vectors for words with that part-of-speech (POS). Specifically, we encode a vector for each of the following: nouns, verbs, adjectives, adverbs, and numbers.

4. We create mean vector differences for the following grammatical concepts: the relationship between singular and plural nouns, the relationship between present-tense verbs and their present participle form, and the relationship between present-tense verbs and their past-tense forms. For each of these relationships, we manually collect approximately 50 example word pairs that fit that relationship. We manually filter for word pairs where either the grammatical relationship does not change the form of the word (i.e., 'deer') or for word pairs where the grammatical change is likely to produce a more complicated change in meaning (i.e., 'math' and 'maths'). We average the differences between pairs of each relationship type and use it as the vector for that relationship.

The choice and construction of these grammatical basis vectors is highly arbitrary, and different grammatical basis vectors could easily be used in different applications or in follow up work.

B Implementation

B.1 Comparison to Faruqui et al.

To compare to the sparse coding approach of Faruqui et al., we use their publicly available implementation with the following settings: We use the same input vectors without preprocessing, a dimensionality of 3000, L_2 regularization penalty $\tau = 10^{-5}$, as suggested in their paper, and various L_1 regularization penalties (λ).

B.2 Word Intrusion Task Implementation

C Randomly Selected Word Representations

We randomly select 25 words and display their complete sparse vector representations here:

carbon $= 0.79 *$ nitrogen
$- 0.38 *$ CAPITALIZATION $+ 0.3 *$ fossil
$- 0.21 *$ POS-NOUN $+ 0.16 *$ POS-ADJ
$+ 0.14 *$ C0 $- 0.14 *$ PAST-TENSE
$+ 0.13 *$ wood $+ 0.11 *$ global
$+ 0.1 *$ atoms $- 0.095 *$ POS-ADV
$+ 0.092 *$ aluminum
$- 0.078 *$ PLURAL-NOUN
$+ 0.073 *$ greenhouse
$- 0.072 *$ POS-PROPN
$- 0.048 *$ POS-VERB $+ 0.046 *$ forestry
$+ 0.03 *$ PARTICIPLE $+ 0.017 *$ sink
$+ 0.012 *$ POS-NUM

reefs $= 0.68 *$ islands
$- 0.66 *$ CAPITALIZATION $+ 0.4 *$ C0
$+ 0.35 *$ PLURAL-NOUN
$+ 0.28 *$ POS-VERB
$+ 0.25 *$ rocks
$+ 0.19 *$ dredging
$+ 0.18 *$ oysters $+ 0.12 *$ POS-ADJ
$+ 0.096 *$ POS-NUM $+ 0.096 *$ POS-ADV
$+ 0.089 *$ POS-PROPN $+ 0.086 *$ tropical
$+ 0.075 *$ underwater $+ 0.068 *$ dunes
$+ 0.063 *$ seas $+ 0.06 *$ diver
$- 0.058 *$ PAST-TENSE
$+ 0.042 *$ sandstone
$- 0.025 *$ demon $+ 0.02 *$ marine
$- 0.019 *$ PARTICIPLE
$- 0.014 *$ POS-NOUN
$- 0.012 *$ french $- 0.0041 *$ witches

$$\text{Coulson} = 0.85 * \text{hacking} + 0.72 * \text{C0} + 0.59 * \text{POS-PROPN} + 0.25 * \text{CAPITALIZATION} - 0.23 * \text{POS-ADJ} - 0.19 * \text{POS-NOUN} + 0.17 * \text{butler} - 0.17 * \text{southern} + 0.15 * \text{POS-VERB} - 0.14 * \text{website} - 0.12 * \text{com} - 0.12 * \text{roaring} + 0.1 * \text{solicitors} - 0.094 * \text{POS-ADV} + 0.074 * \text{oats} - 0.068 * \text{cathedral} - 0.064 * \text{PARTICIPLE} + 0.061 * \text{inquiry} - 0.06 * \text{dances} - 0.056 * \text{fan} + 0.042 * \text{POS-NUM} - 0.029 * \text{provinces} - 0.029 * \text{finals} - 0.02 * \text{dance} - 0.017 * \text{waters} - 0.013 * \text{tango} - 0.013 * \text{shame} - 0.012 * \text{PAST-TENSE} - 0.005 * \text{PLURAL-NOUN}$$

$$\text{roundabout} = 0.72 * \text{bypass} + 0.4 * \text{roadway} - 0.28 * \text{CAPITALIZATION} + 0.22 * \text{plaza} - 0.16 * \text{PLURAL-NOUN} + 0.11 * \text{POS-ADJ} + 0.11 * \text{clumsy} + 0.1 * \text{airfield} + 0.088 * \text{POS-ADV} - 0.08 * \text{biological} + 0.079 * \text{C0} + 0.051 * \text{POS-NOUN} + 0.043 * \text{PAST-TENSE} + 0.039 * \text{PARTICIPLE} + 0.028 * \text{caravan} + 0.025 * \text{ironic} + 0.021 * \text{POS-VERB} - 0.021 * \text{POS-NUM} - 0.0038 * \text{POS-PROPN} + 0.003 * \text{nonsensical}$$

$$\text{Hub} = 0.49 * \text{bustling} + 0.47 * \text{C0} + 0.4 * \text{portal} + 0.39 * \text{infrastructure} + 0.32 * \text{POS-NOUN} + 0.31 * \text{CAPITALIZATION} + 0.31 * \text{central} - 0.13 * \text{POS-PROPN} - 0.1 * \text{PLURAL-NOUN} + 0.069 * \text{outage} + 0.068 * \text{centre} + 0.061 * \text{POS-NUM} + 0.058 * \text{connectivity} + 0.058 * \text{PARTICIPLE} - 0.057 * \text{POS-ADJ} + 0.043 * \text{PAST-TENSE} - 0.043 * \text{POS-VERB} + 0.027 * \text{POS-ADV}$$

$$\text{environmental} = 0.43 * \text{sustainability} + 0.43 * \text{economic} + 0.38 * \text{POS-ADJ} - 0.3 * \text{CAPITALIZATION} - 0.27 * \text{POS-VERB} + 0.27 * \text{regulatory} - 0.2 * \text{PAST-TENSE} + 0.18 * \text{biological} + 0.17 * \text{campaigner} + 0.17 * \text{POS-NUM} + 0.14 * \text{thermal} - 0.14 * \text{POS-ADV} - 0.12 * \text{POS-NOUN} + 0.1 * \text{health} - 0.1 * \text{C0} + 0.087 * \text{PARTICIPLE} + 0.087 * \text{POS-PROPN} - 0.084 * \text{PLURAL-NOUN} + 0.073 * \text{outdoor} + 0.055 * \text{chemical} + 0.0055 * \text{cultural}$$

$$\text{Churchill} = 0.84 * \text{wartime} + 0.6 * \text{C0} + 0.41 * \text{CAPITALIZATION} + 0.4 * \text{quotation} + 0.38 * \text{POS-PROPN} + 0.36 * \text{statesman} - 0.21 * \text{PARTICIPLE} - 0.14 * \text{astronomer} - 0.14 * \text{POS-NOUN} - 0.11 * \text{POS-ADJ} - 0.1 * \text{PAST-TENSE} + 0.082 * \text{POS-VERB} + 0.078 * \text{POS-NUM} + 0.064 * \text{POS-ADV} + 0.045 * \text{advising} - 0.025 * \text{architectures} + 0.022 * \text{PLURAL-NOUN} + 0.017 * \text{pint} + 0.013 * \text{fascism}$$

$$\text{resident} = 0.54 * \text{citizens} + 0.49 * \text{native} + 0.37 * \text{visiting} - 0.19 * \text{PLURAL-NOUN} + 0.12 * \text{PAST-TENSE} + 0.11 * \text{caretaker} - 0.099 * \text{CAPITALIZATION} - 0.094 * \text{C0} + 0.082 * \text{PARTICIPLE} + 0.082 * \text{ward} + 0.077 * \text{POS-NOUN} - 0.039 * \text{POS-ADV} + 0.022 * \text{proprietor} + 0.022 * \text{POS-VERB} - 0.0065 * \text{POS-NUM} + 0.0045 * \text{POS-PROPN} + 0.0036 * \text{POS-ADJ}$$

backers = 0.64 ∗ sponsors
+ 0.4 ∗ POS-NOUN − 0.4 ∗ CAPITALIZATION
+ 0.33 ∗ advocates + 0.28 ∗ PLURAL-NOUN
+ 0.19 ∗ POS-PROPN + 0.18 ∗ businessman
+ 0.18 ∗ businessmen + 0.16 ∗ fans
− 0.15 ∗ POS-ADJ + 0.12 ∗ PARTICIPLE
+ 0.12 ∗ PAST-TENSE − 0.12 ∗ POS-ADV
+ 0.092 ∗ whose + 0.082 ∗ opposition
+ 0.065 ∗ POS-VERB + 0.056 ∗ candidacy
+ 0.055 ∗ touted + 0.047 ∗ startups
− 0.024 ∗ POS-NUM + 0.024 ∗ rebels
+ 0.014 ∗ reformist + 0.013 ∗ investment
− 0.002 ∗ C0

re-add = −0.65 ∗ PARTICIPLE
− 0.47 ∗ POS-NUM + 0.44 ∗ deleted
+ 0.43 ∗ POS-VERB + 0.41 ∗ cruft
− 0.41 ∗ C0 − 0.3 ∗ PAST-TENSE
+ 0.28 ∗ section + 0.19 ∗ CAPITALIZATION
+ 0.17 ∗ categorization + 0.16 ∗ unblock
+ 0.15 ∗ POS-ADV + 0.11 ∗ POS-PROPN
+ 0.098 ∗ reversion − 0.09 ∗ POS-ADJ
+ 0.09 ∗ POS-NOUN + 0.061 ∗ inserting
+ 0.046 ∗ reference + 0.043 ∗ sourcing
+ 0.034 ∗ template + 0.027 ∗ encyclopedic
+ 0.013 ∗ modify − 0.0088 ∗ battleship
− 0.0071 ∗ cow + 0.006 ∗ PLURAL-NOUN

rudimentary = 0.84 ∗ basics
− 0.65 ∗ C0 + 0.49 ∗ POS-ADJ
− 0.41 ∗ POS-VERB + 0.41 ∗ apparatus
− 0.36 ∗ POS-NOUN + 0.35 ∗ improvised
+ 0.15 ∗ POS-ADV + 0.099 ∗ CAPITALIZATION
+ 0.072 ∗ PARTICIPLE + 0.069 ∗ PLURAL-NOUN
+ 0.062 ∗ POS-NUM + 0.059 ∗ develop
+ 0.05 ∗ PAST-TENSE + 0.043 ∗ POS-PROPN

visuals = 0.47 ∗ cinematography
− 0.47 ∗ CAPITALIZATION + 0.29 ∗ evocative
+ 0.25 ∗ multimedia + 0.21 ∗ videos
+ 0.19 ∗ POS-NOUN + 0.15 ∗ PLURAL-NOUN
+ 0.14 ∗ POS-PROPN + 0.12 ∗ hallucinations
+ 0.11 ∗ awesome + 0.1 ∗ PARTICIPLE
+ 0.08 ∗ video − 0.079 ∗ POS-VERB
+ 0.076 ∗ sounds + 0.076 ∗ POS-ADJ
+ 0.076 ∗ slick + 0.075 ∗ POS-ADV
+ 0.066 ∗ C0 + 0.062 ∗ dazzling
+ 0.052 ∗ colorful + 0.044 ∗ interactive
+ 0.027 ∗ jarring + 0.019 ∗ visualization
+ 0.0047 ∗ PAST-TENSE + 0.00025 ∗ POS-NUM

admire = 0.73 ∗ admirable
− 0.66 ∗ PARTICIPLE − 0.65 ∗ C0
+ 0.31 ∗ magnificent + 0.23 ∗ CAPITALIZATION
+ 0.16 ∗ criticize + 0.16 ∗ POS-NOUN
− 0.16 ∗ PAST-TENSE + 0.14 ∗ loves
+ 0.1 ∗ POS-PROPN + 0.1 ∗ beauty
− 0.098 ∗ POS-NUM − 0.068 ∗ PLURAL-NOUN
+ 0.066 ∗ devotion − 0.061 ∗ POS-ADV
− 0.058 ∗ POS-ADJ + 0.039 ∗ openness
+ 0.02 ∗ charming − 0.00015 ∗ POS-VERB

Conflict = 0.61 ∗ POS-NOUN
− 0.49 ∗ POS-PROPN + 0.44 ∗ warfare
+ 0.4 ∗ escalation + 0.4 ∗ peace
+ 0.36 ∗ C0 + 0.24 ∗ guideline
+ 0.23 ∗ CAPITALIZATION + 0.21 ∗ PARTICIPLE
+ 0.19 ∗ ethnic − 0.19 ∗ POS-VERB
+ 0.16 ∗ resolved + 0.12 ∗ POS-NUM
− 0.099 ∗ PLURAL-NOUN + 0.078 ∗ PAST-TENSE
+ 0.07 ∗ divergence + 0.065 ∗ geopolitical
− 0.05 ∗ stationary + 0.038 ∗ POS-ADJ
− 0.032 ∗ shops + 0.03 ∗ polarized
− 0.012 ∗ POS-ADV

$$\begin{aligned}\text{hitter} = &-0.54 * \text{CAPITALIZATION}\\ &+ 0.45 * \text{C0} - 0.42 * \text{PLURAL-NOUN}\\ &+ 0.42 * \text{shortstop} + 0.36 * \text{designated}\\ &+ 0.32 * \text{batting} + 0.3 * \text{POS-VERB}\\ &+ 0.21 * \text{POS-NOUN} + 0.18 * \text{POS-ADV}\\ &+ 0.17 * \text{pitchers} + 0.17 * \text{pitcher}\\ &+ 0.14 * \text{catcher} - 0.12 * \text{PARTICIPLE}\\ &- 0.1 * \text{POS-NUM} - 0.096 * \text{inane}\\ &+ 0.087 * \text{guy} + 0.073 * \text{POS-PROPN}\\ &+ 0.048 * \text{exert} - 0.014 * \text{PAST-TENSE}\\ &+ 0.0071 * \text{outs} - 0.0064 * \text{POS-ADJ}\\ &+ 0.0019 * \text{swings}\end{aligned}$$

$$\begin{aligned}\text{fence} = &\ 0.52 * \text{wire}\\ &+ 0.43 * \text{gates} - 0.41 * \text{CAPITALIZATION}\\ &+ 0.35 * \text{yard} - 0.32 * \text{PLURAL-NOUN}\\ &+ 0.21 * \text{shrubs} + 0.14 * \text{barn}\\ &+ 0.14 * \text{ditch} + 0.09 * \text{POS-VERB}\\ &+ 0.085 * \text{side} - 0.07 * \text{PARTICIPLE}\\ &- 0.052 * \text{POS-ADJ} + 0.042 * \text{POS-NUM}\\ &- 0.032 * \text{POS-PROPN} - 0.02 * \text{PAST-TENSE}\\ &- 0.012 * \text{C0} + 0.0068 * \text{nailed}\\ &- 0.0047 * \text{POS-ADV} + 0.00013 * \text{POS-NOUN}\end{aligned}$$

$$\begin{aligned}1978 = &\ 0.97 * \text{1970s}\\ &- 0.89 * \text{POS-ADJ} - 0.6 * \text{POS-PROPN}\\ &+ 0.49 * \text{POS-NUM} - 0.42 * \text{POS-NOUN}\\ &+ 0.21 * \text{C0} - 0.18 * \text{PLURAL-NOUN}\\ &- 0.12 * \text{POS-ADV} - 0.081 * \text{PARTICIPLE}\\ &- 0.073 * \text{CAPITALIZATION}\\ &+ 0.067 * \text{POS-VERB}\\ &+ 0.041 * \text{PAST-TENSE} + 0.039 * \text{seventies}\\ &+ 0.026 * \text{contends}\end{aligned}$$

$$\begin{aligned}\text{heroine} = &\ 0.66 * \text{hero}\\ &+ 0.35 * \text{protagonist}\\ &- 0.34 * \text{CAPITALIZATION}\\ &- 0.25 * \text{PLURAL-NOUN} + 0.14 * \text{actress}\\ &+ 0.13 * \text{girl} + 0.1 * \text{C0}\\ &+ 0.1 * \text{PAST-TENSE} + 0.071 * \text{POS-PROPN}\\ &+ 0.07 * \text{POS-NOUN} + 0.063 * \text{POS-ADV}\\ &- 0.058 * \text{POS-NUM} + 0.051 * \text{protagonists}\\ &- 0.029 * \text{POS-VERB} + 0.026 * \text{PARTICIPLE}\\ &+ 0.015 * \text{POS-ADJ} + 0.014 * \text{goddess}\end{aligned}$$

$$\begin{aligned}\text{structure} = &\ 0.91 * \text{structures}\\ &- 0.35 * \text{CAPITALIZATION}\\ &- 0.25 * \text{PLURAL-NOUN}\\ &+ 0.17 * \text{structuring} + 0.16 * \text{POS-NOUN}\\ &- 0.085 * \text{POS-VERB} - 0.078 * \text{PAST-TENSE}\\ &+ 0.05 * \text{POS-ADV} - 0.039 * \text{POS-ADJ}\\ &- 0.034 * \text{POS-PROPN} + 0.029 * \text{POS-NUM}\\ &+ 0.026 * \text{structural} + 0.022 * \text{reorganization}\\ &- 0.022 * \text{C0} + 0.0079 * \text{PARTICIPLE}\end{aligned}$$

$$\begin{aligned}\text{wizards} = &\ 0.65 * \text{magic}\\ &+ 0.41 * \text{witches}\\ &- 0.41 * \text{CAPITALIZATION}\\ &+ 0.36 * \text{PLURAL-NOUN}\\ &+ 0.19 * \text{POS-NOUN}\\ &- 0.19 * \text{POS-NUM} + 0.15 * \text{POS-ADJ}\\ &+ 0.15 * \text{tech} + 0.13 * \text{POS-ADV}\\ &+ 0.098 * \text{PAST-TENSE} + 0.09 * \text{wannabe}\\ &+ 0.084 * \text{dragons} + 0.084 * \text{knights}\\ &+ 0.052 * \text{C0} - 0.036 * \text{POS-PROPN}\\ &+ 0.022 * \text{PARTICIPLE} + 0.015 * \text{err}\\ &- 0.013 * \text{POS-VERB} + 0.0041 * \text{guru}\end{aligned}$$

$$\begin{aligned}\text{autistic} = &\ 0.49 * \text{preschool}\\ &+ 0.37 * \text{epilepsy} - 0.35 * \text{POS-NOUN}\\ &+ 0.33 * \text{POS-ADJ} - 0.25 * \text{papal}\\ &+ 0.22 * \text{son} + 0.21 * \text{POS-PROPN}\\ &+ 0.16 * \text{twins} + 0.12 * \text{PAST-TENSE}\\ &+ 0.12 * \text{therapist} + 0.12 * \text{PARTICIPLE}\\ &- 0.1 * \text{CAPITALIZATION} + 0.084 * \text{teenage}\\ &+ 0.072 * \text{trait} + 0.069 * \text{psychologist}\\ &+ 0.067 * \text{behaviors} + 0.056 * \text{kid}\\ &+ 0.054 * \text{hospitalized} - 0.053 * \text{C0}\\ &+ 0.052 * \text{manipulative} - 0.038 * \text{POS-NUM}\\ &+ 0.037 * \text{granddaughter} - 0.03 * \text{rounds}\\ &+ 0.03 * \text{PLURAL-NOUN} + 0.027 * \text{campers}\\ &+ 0.026 * \text{POS-VERB} + 0.0092 * \text{dementia}\\ &- 0.0054 * \text{regional} - 0.0052 * \text{POS-ADV}\\ &- 0.0023 * \text{sedan}\end{aligned}$$

$$\text{tornado} = 0.72 * \text{hurricane} + 0.49 * \text{C0} - 0.47 * \text{CAPITALIZATION} + 0.28 * \text{typhoon} - 0.26 * \text{PLURAL-NOUN} + 0.23 * \text{tractor} + 0.21 * \text{POS-VERB} + 0.16 * \text{POS-ADJ} + 0.12 * \text{POS-NUM} + 0.1 * \text{flattened} - 0.1 * \text{ports} - 0.097 * \text{opium} + 0.072 * \text{POS-ADV} + 0.053 * \text{POS-PROPN} + 0.053 * \text{avalanche} + 0.052 * \text{tape} + 0.05 * \text{earthquake} - 0.045 * \text{colonial} - 0.043 * \text{POS-NOUN} + 0.028 * \text{musical} - 0.025 * \text{handsets} + 0.014 * \text{terrifying} + 0.013 * \text{PAST-TENSE} + 0.013 * \text{occurrences} - 0.0067 * \text{labour} + 0.0025 * \text{PARTICIPLE}$$

$$\text{recycle} = -0.65 * \text{PARTICIPLE} + 0.61 * \text{bin} + 0.49 * \text{rubbish} - 0.48 * \text{C0} - 0.47 * \text{PAST-TENSE} + 0.27 * \text{POS-VERB} + 0.18 * \text{POS-NOUN} + 0.15 * \text{utilize} + 0.14 * \text{plastic} - 0.12 * \text{POS-NUM} + 0.1 * \text{excess} + 0.088 * \text{sustainability} + 0.083 * \text{POS-PROPN} + 0.066 * \text{aluminum} + 0.042 * \text{gramthesize} - 0.037 * \text{PLURAL-NOUN} + 0.036 * \text{POS-ADJ} + 0.035 * \text{refurbished} + 0.034 * \text{POS-ADV} + 0.03 * \text{converter} + 0.026 * \text{nitrogen} - 0.004 * \text{CAPITALIZATION} + 0.0024 * \text{saving}$$

$$1852 = 0.85 * \text{1800s} - 0.81 * \text{POS-PROPN} - 0.78 * \text{POS-ADJ} - 0.61 * \text{POS-NOUN} + 0.45 * \text{POS-NUM} + 0.43 * \text{C0} - 0.31 * \text{CAPITALIZATION} + 0.29 * \text{renders} + 0.25 * \text{POS-VERB} - 0.19 * \text{PLURAL-NOUN} + 0.16 * \text{noted} - 0.15 * \text{PARTICIPLE} + 0.13 * \text{underscored} - 0.082 * \text{POS-ADV} + 0.063 * \text{insisting} + 0.029 * \text{PAST-TENSE}$$

$$\text{gloom} = 0.66 * \text{gloomy} - 0.46 * \text{CAPITALIZATION} - 0.32 * \text{POS-VERB} + 0.28 * \text{pessimism} + 0.28 * \text{darkness} + 0.15 * \text{PAST-TENSE} - 0.14 * \text{PLURAL-NOUN} + 0.14 * \text{POS-NOUN} + 0.12 * \text{PARTICIPLE} + 0.11 * \text{POS-NUM} - 0.058 * \text{C0} - 0.058 * \text{POS-ADV} + 0.052 * \text{misery} + 0.051 * \text{POS-PROPN} + 0.037 * \text{slump} - 0.025 * \text{POS-ADJ}$$

A howling success or a working sea? Testing what BERT knows about metaphors

Paolo Pedinotti and **Eliana Di Palma** and **Ludovica Cerini** and **Alessandro Lenci**
University of Pisa
paolo.pedinotti@phd.unipi.it, e.dipalma@studenti.unipi.it,
ludovica.cerini@phd.unipi.it, alessandro.lenci@unipi.it

Abstract

Metaphor is a widespread linguistic and cognitive phenomenon that is ruled by mechanisms which have received attention in the literature. Transformer Language Models such as BERT have brought improvements in metaphor-related tasks. However, they have been used only in application contexts, while their knowledge of the phenomenon has not been analyzed. To test what BERT knows about metaphors, we challenge it on a new dataset that we designed to test various aspects of this phenomenon such as variations in linguistic structure, variations in conventionality, the boundaries of the plausibility of a metaphor and the interpretations that we attribute to metaphoric expressions. Results bring out some tendencies that suggest that the model can reproduce some human intuitions about metaphors.

1 Introduction

Metaphor is a blooming affair. Since the publication of Lakoff and Johnson (1980) *Metaphors we live by*, it has been shown that metaphors represent a core cognitive mechanism, identified as a process that aids human beings in the comprehension of abstract concepts. Metaphors could be described as a process to endow linguistic expressions with new meaning: A concept of a *target* domain A is understood in terms of a *source* domain B.

Metaphors are pervasive in language, and they are a complex phenomenon to describe and categorize. We can distinguish metaphors for their degree of conventionalization, their linguistic structure (e.g., "A is B", "A of B", etc.), and for the semantic effect they create (Newmark, 1980; Charteris-Black, 2004), namely concretizing metaphors, animating and personifying metaphors, and synaesthetic metaphors. All these categories can tell us something about the degree of metaphoricity that an expression conveys. Many psycholinguistic studies have been carried out to understand how metaphors are perceived by humans and to what extent a metaphor is recognized as such (Lai et al., 2009; Glucksberg, 2003; Al-Azary and Buchanan, 2017).

A key aspect is surely the distinction between **conventional** metaphors (e.g., *Her lawyer is a shark*) and **novel** (or **creative**, Birdsell (2018)) metaphors (e.g., *Her mouth was a fountain of delight.*). These types of metaphors are processed differently by humans (Glucksberg et al., 1982; Gentner and Bowdle, 2008). Moreover, the latter constitutes an open class, as we have the ability to create new metaphors and make sense out of them. However, this ability is not erratic, but it is ruled by cognitive mechanisms: For example, metaphors have been shown to be justified by analogies between conceptual domains. This ability has also clear boundaries: Due to the same mechanisms we can evaluate the plausibility of a given expression, and distinguish creative meanings from nonsense expressions. For instance, even if both *An ambassador is a peacock* and *An ambassador is a fish* constitute semantic violations, we accept only the first as a plausible metaphor. Another example are the sentences *The wind was a howling wolf* and *The wind was a jumping seat* (McGregor et al., 2019).

Transformer Language Models such as BERT (Devlin et al., 2019) have brought important improvements in metaphor-related tasks (see section 2). However, such models have been used only in application contexts, while analysis aimed at investigating directly what the models capture about this phenomenon has not been conducted. In the first part of our work, we tested whether BERT predicts metaphors differing for linguistic structure and conventionality, with a particular focus on whether the model is able to identify the boundaries of metaphoric creativity. Of particular relevance for the second aspect is the comparison of novel, unconventional metaphors with nonsense expressions.

Proceedings of the Fourth BlackboxNLP Workshop on Analyzing and Interpreting Neural Networks for NLP, pages 192–204
Online, November 11, 2021.

Our ability with figurative language also allows us to assign new meanings to words when they are used metaphorically, independently from the conventionality of a metaphor. Therefore, we expect to find information about these meanings in the model's representations of different types of metaphors.

To test these aspects, we collected a dataset of conventional and creative metaphors, matched with control literal and nonsense sentences, evaluated by English native speakers for their degree of metaphoricity and semantic plausibility. We carried out two experiments. In **Experiment 1** we modeled the dataset of human judgments using BERT as a **language model**, to evaluate whether its pseudo-log-likelihood values correlate with the human semantic plausibility scores. Our results show that BERT seems to distinguish the literal, metaphorical and nonsense expressions. In **Experiment 2**, we used the **landmark method** introduced by Kintsch (2000) to test the representation of metaphorical meanings in BERT contextualized embeddings. Despite limitations given by the size of our dataset, we show that some consistent trends about how the model processes metaphors can be identified by analyzing the model's representations. We observed that several factors such as the layer and the representations analyzed could influence the model's performance.

To sum up, we collected various evidence related to what BERT learns about metaphorical language. Such results pave the way for future investigation, and can be of interest for those who use Transformers Language Models in NLP applications or in metaphor-related tasks.

2 Related works

The computational literature on metaphors has focused on two distinct tasks. Metaphor identification involves deciding whether a sequence or a single word is an instance of a metaphor or not. On the other hand, Metaphor interpretation concerns the description of the meaning of metaphorical expressions, and is typically cast as a paraphrasing (Shutova, 2010) or a classification (Bizzoni and Lappin, 2017) task. Even if some recent work has approached the interpretation task (Su et al., 2016; Mao et al., 2018; Rosen, 2018), much of the literature in the last years has been devoted to metaphor identification (Leong et al., 2018; Gao et al., 2018; Dankers et al., 2019, 2020; Leong et al., 2020). The use of deep learning for this task has become widespread and has contributed to advance the state-of-the-art. While the most recent models proposed for this task differ with respect to the information they exploit, most of them use Transformers Neural Language Models like BERT in order to obtain an initial representation of the processed sequence. This strategy is now very common and has led to general improvements in performance: Four out of the six best systems that participated in the 2020 shared task on the VUA corpus (Steen et al., 2010) used it, and a system based only on BERT and an additional layer outperformed many other systems which were based on explicit linguistic information (Leong et al., 2020). These results strongly suggest that models like BERT already possess some knowledge that is relevant to the detection of metaphors. However, to the best of our knowledge, there is no study directly investigating what these models know about metaphors and if this knowledge shares some aspects with that of humans.

The application of this last question to other aspects of language has characterized the field of study known as BERTology (Rogers et al., 2020). Researchers in this field intrinsically evaluate BERT and its variants on challenge sets (Belinkov and Glass, 2019), annotated datasets of various sizes that target specific linguistic phenomena. Part of the literature on this subject made use of methods which we will adopt in our work. A first method is to study the probabilities assigned by the language model to the instances of a specific linguistic phenomenon, to establish whether the model is able to predict such phenomenon (Goldberg (2019); Ettinger (2020) among others). This methodology can provide interesting insights when applied to figurative language. Since these phenomena can be seen as exceptions to general linguistic rules, they require the model to apply some special ability, which is independent and often in contrast with the signals it has been exposed to during training.

Another possibility is to directly investigate the model's embeddings which are then used for tasks like metaphor identification. Since these representations have been shown to be transferable to a high number of linguistic tasks (Liu et al., 2019), they must encode some sort of general knowledge about linguistic expressions. Previous work (Bommasani et al., 2020; Chronis and Erk, 2020) hypothesizes that they encode knowledge about meaning, and therefore BERT and its variants can be seen as Distributional Semantics Models (**DSMs**), (Lenci, 2018). Consequently, they applied the same methods used in distributional semantics to BERT, for example comparing the model's representations via cosine similarity to see whether they reproduce human judgments of similarity. However, BERT as a DSM has a crucial property which previous DSMs lack: The ability to produce **contextualized embeddings** for each word token. As such, it can positively contribute to the modeling of the meaning of figurative expressions like metaphors, where words acquire new senses which are highly context-dependent. This is why BERT can be compared with previous distributional models of metaphors, and the evaluation methods used for these models can be adapted to test BERT. In this work, we use the landmark method proposed by Kintsch (2000), which tested whether distributional representations of metaphors reflect human intuitions about the meaning of the expressions they model. We will describe the method in more detail in section 3.2.

3 Data and Experiments

3.1 Dataset

We found that existing datasets of metaphors (see Parde and Nielsen (2018) for a review) are not particularly well-suited to test how the model deals with expressions with different structures and different degrees of metaphoricity and plausibility, and more specifically with their interpretation. In fact, to the best of our knowledge none of the existing datasets presents, for different types of structures, annotation regarding both the conventionalization of a metaphor and its interpretation. Moreover, nonsense sentences have never been included in datasets used for computational modeling of such phenomenon.

We therefore decided to create a new dataset. Our dataset contains 47 conventional metaphors and 53 creative metaphors. Metaphors have different linguistic structures: Attributive, or "A is B" like in *An ambassador is a peacock* (Cacciari and Glucksberg, 1994), Genitive or "A of B", like in *There was an invisible necklace of now* (Bambini et al., 2014), Complex like in *He planted the seeds of doubt in my mind* (Newmark, 1980) and Single-Word or one-word-metaphors, like in *The mother broke the silence* (Newmark, 1980). The conventional metaphors were selected from BNC

	Test sentence
Met	I could almost taste victory.
Lit	I can taste ginger in this cake.
Nonsense	I could almost wash victory.

Table 1: Example of test sentences from the dataset.

and the English Web Corpus (2015, 2018) while the creative metaphors from Katz et al. (1988), Rasse et al. (2020), poetries, and the Web. We matched each sentence with two control items (literal and nonsense) with the same structure as the metaphors (an example of a sentence with the corresponding control items can be seen in Table 1).

The final dataset includes 300 items that have been rated for their degree of **semantic plausibility** and **metaphoricity** by human subjects recruited through the Prolific crowdsourcing platform.

Semantic Plausibility test To assess the semantic plausibility of our sentences, we submitted a survey to 20 English speakers. The participants were asked to judge how meaningful a given sentence was (metaphoric, literal, or nonsense), on a Likert scale from 1 (meaningless) to 7 (meaningful). Pairwise Wilcoxon comparisons showed that each group was significantly different from the others (p-value < 0.001). The participants rated conventional metaphors as less meaningful (M= 4.86) than literal expressions (M=5.45), but more plausible than creative metaphors. Creative metaphors were judged (M= 3.69) as more meaningful than nonsense expressions (M= 2.7). Crucially, this test shows that, on the one hand, subjects perceive that metaphorical sentences somehow "deviate" from literal ones, but on the other hand, they recognize that metaphorical sentences, even the most creative ones, differ from purely nonsense structures.

Metaphoricity test To assess the metaphoricity of our sentences, we submitted a second survey to 20 English speakers. The participants were asked to judge how metaphoric a given metaphorical or literal expression was, on a Likert scale from 1 (literal) to 7 (metaphorical). Significance values for the pairwise comparisons were corrected for multiple comparisons using the Bonferroni correction. The results showed that creative metaphors were rated as more metaphoric (M= 5.59) than conventional metaphors (M= 4.64, p-value < 0.001), and conventional metaphors obtained a significantly higher score of metaphoricity than literal expressions (M= 1.94, p-value < 0.001). Therefore, this test reveals that the conventionalized nature of conventional metaphors does not alter their figurative power with respect to literal sentences.

3.2 Models and Experiments

We carried out our experiments with the base (number of layers = 12, hidden size = 768) and the large (number of layers = 24, hidden size = 1024) cased versions of BERT. We used the pretrained model that is provided by the HuggingFace library Transformers (Wolf et al., 2020).

Experiment 1: Sentence plausibility scores To get an estimate of how much BERT considers an expression as plausible, we computed a probability score for each sentence in our dataset. Then we examined whether the scores vary with the sentence types (metaphorical conventional, metaphorical creative, literal, nonsense), and whether they mirror human plausibility judgments.

As a measure of sentence plausibility, we used the **pseudo-log-likelihood score** (PLL) (Wang and Cho, 2019). The probability of a sentence cannot be computed using autoencoding models like BERT. In fact, these models are inherently bidirectional, that is, they are trained to predict a word given all the other words in the left and the right context. Therefore, they cannot be used for estimating probabilities of sequences via the chain rule, since this requires to compute the probability of any word given the *previous* words in a sequence. The PLL of a sentence W is obtained by masking one token w at a time, calculating the token's probability given all the other context words, and summing the log-probabilities for all the tokens as in Equation 1. Salazar et al. (2020) showed that the PLL score, even if strictly speaking it is not a probability, outperforms scores from autoregressive models in a variety of tasks related to the acceptability of sentences. This is probably due to the fact that the PLL eliminates the discrepancy between the probabilities of the first elements of a sequence and those of the last elements.

$$PLL(W) = \sum_{t=1}^{|W|} \log P(w_t \mid W_{\setminus t}) \quad (1)$$

Experiment 2: The landmark method To determine whether the model's representations of metaphorical expressions reproduce the shift from a source literal domain to a new target one, we applied the landmark method, which was proposed by Kintsch (2000) to test a model producing distributional representations of predicate-argument metaphors (e.g., *My lawyer is a shark*). His aim was to test to which extent these vectors encoded information about the meaning of the argument (*lawyer*), the inappropriate literal sense of the predicate (*shark*) and the appropriate metaphorical sense of the predicate (e.g., *ferocious*). To this end, he selected three different sets of words, where the words in each set were related to only one of those meanings based on the author's intuitions. For example, *justice* and *crime* were selected because they are related to *lawyer*, *fish* is related to the literal sense of *shark* and *viciousness* is related to the metaphorical sense of *shark*. These words were used in Kintsch (2000) as **landmarks**, in that their vector representations were compared to the model's representations of metaphors.

The landmark method gives us a straightforward way of examining BERT's internal representations (i.e., the contextualized embeddings generated by its layers) with regards to metaphorical meaning. Since the essence of BERT is that each word token is associated with a context sensitive embedding, if the model is somehow "aware" of the figurative interpretation of a metaphorical sentence, this should be reflected in the embeddings of its words. We performed two versions of our experiment, which mainly differ for the representations that are examined. In the **MetSentences** version, we tested the global metaphorical interpretation of a sentence, by representing it with an embedding obtained by summing the embeddings of its words. In the **MetWords** version, we examined the representations of specific words that undergo the metaphorical shift. For example, in *This fighter is a lion*, the word *lion* is used metaphorically, while the other words keep their literal meaning. In cases where the shift involves more than one word (e.g., *The heart is the legendary muscle that wants and grieve*), we summed the embeddings of the metaphorical words to obtain a representation that capture the information that is common to both words.

We tested these two types of representations with respect to the literal and metaphorical sense of the word(s) that carry the metaphorical meaning. Such information is crucial in determining whether BERT interprets metaphorical expressions successfully. We therefore defined two sets of landmarks for each metaphorical sentence of our dataset

Sentence	metaphorical landmarks literal landmarks
A smile is an **ambassador**.	message confident express official embassy envoy
The flowers **nodded** in the wind	movement wave sway assent head greeting

Table 2: Landmarks for two sentences from the dataset

(two examples of sentences from our datasets with the corresponding sets of landmarks can be seen in Table 2). The metaphorical landmarks are elements of the target conceptual domain to which the metaphorical words in a sentence point. For example, the words *want* and *grieve* in the sentence *The heart is the legendary muscle that wants and grieve* point to the target domain of emotion. The literal landmarks can be synonyms, associates or words morphologically derived from the literal sense of one of the metaphorical words in the sentence. If a sentence contains more than one metaphorical word, we defined the set of literal landmarks so that it contains at least one related word for each metaphorical word in the sentence.

To obtain BERT contextualized embeddings of the landmarks, we extracted a sentence from the landmark's lexical entry in WordNet or the Cambridge Dictionary and we passed it to BERT. Each landmark set was then represented with the averaged embeddings of its words.

Given the limited size of our dataset, we chose not to use the representations of the model as input for another layer specifically optimized for choosing the right set of landmarks. Therefore, we analyzed directly the model's output. Specifically, we compared the similarity (via cosine similarity) of the representations of the metaphorical expressions and the representations of the metaphorical/literal landmarks. To see whether conclusions can be derived from a simple analysis of the representations, we evaluated the model in two ways. First, we checked whether the similarity between the expressions and the metaphorical landmarks is in general significantly higher than the literal landmarks. We also evaluated the model on a binary classification task, measuring the accuracy in producing embeddings that are more similar to the metaphorical landmarks than to the literal ones. To estimate the added value of BERT contextualized embeddings with respect to traditional static embeddings, we compared BERT performance with a baseline computed with GloVe vectors (Pennington et al., 2014) (context window=2, dimension=300).

Since we are interested in exploring the inner behavior of the model, we compared the representations for each BERT layer. Recent studies (Liu et al., 2019; Jawahar et al., 2019) have shown that upper-intermediate layers produce general purpose representations which are less dependent on the language modeling objective and approximate linguistic knowledge better. We surmise that this ability could also reflect on the interpretation of metaphors.

4 Results

Experiment 1 We calculated the Spearman ρ correlation between the PLL and the semantic plausibility human ratings. Both models show a fair correlation: BERT base $\mathbf{0.504}$ and BERT large $\mathbf{0.496}$.

We then verified whether BERT mirrors the human perceived contrast between conventional metaphorical and literal sentences, and between creative metaphorical and nonsense sentences.

The models' results (first two boxplots of figure 4.1) show that the creative metaphors (BERT base: M= -4.1; BERT large: M= -4.04) were rated by the models with significantly higher scores than nonsense expressions (BERT base: M= -4.96; BERT large: M= -4.93, p-value < 0.003). Furthermore, the conventional metaphors (BERT base M= -3.62 ; BERT large M= -3.46) were considered less likely than literal ones (BERT base M=-3.01; BERT large M= -3.04), but they were rated with higher scores than creative metaphors, though these two differences are not statistically significant (p-value > 0.05). These results partially reflect human judgments (right boxplot of figure 4.1).

Experiment 2 In the **MetSentences** setting, the embeddings of both models (base, large) for the metaphorical sentences have significantly higher cosine similarity with the embeddings of the metaphorical landmarks (e.g. layer 10 (base) M= 0.83582; layer 20 (large) M = 0.58177) than with the embeddings of the literal landmarks (e.g. layer 10 (base) M= 0.82691, p-value < 0.03 ; layer 20 (large) M = 0.56087, p-value < 0.01) in the upper intermediate layers (base: 9,10,11; large: 11-22, p-value < 0.05). The accuracy of the models (which is shown in figure 4.2) varies along the layers with the same tendency.

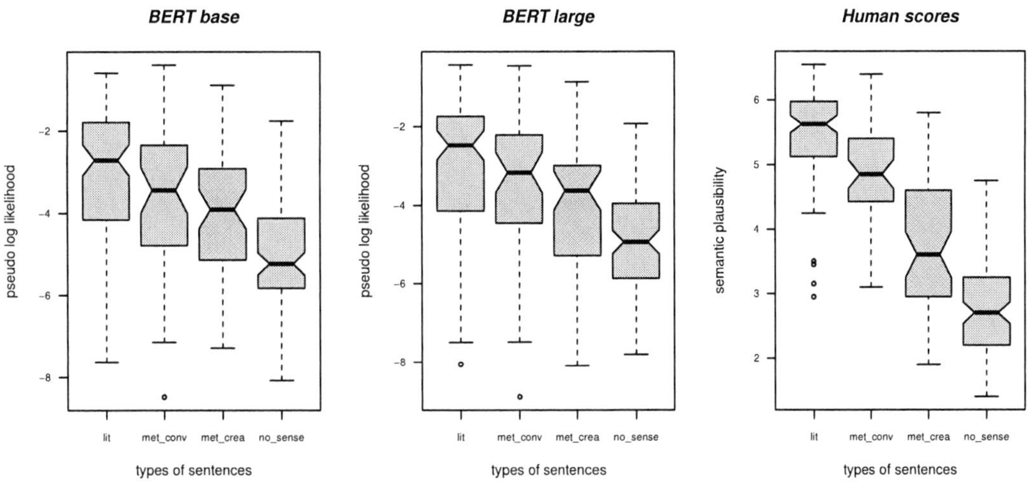

Figure 4.1: Boxplots of BERT pseudo-log-likelihood scores and the human ratings of semantic plausibility. For each distribution, the boxplot indicates the median, the quartiles, the maximum and the minimum of the distribution and the outliers when they are present.

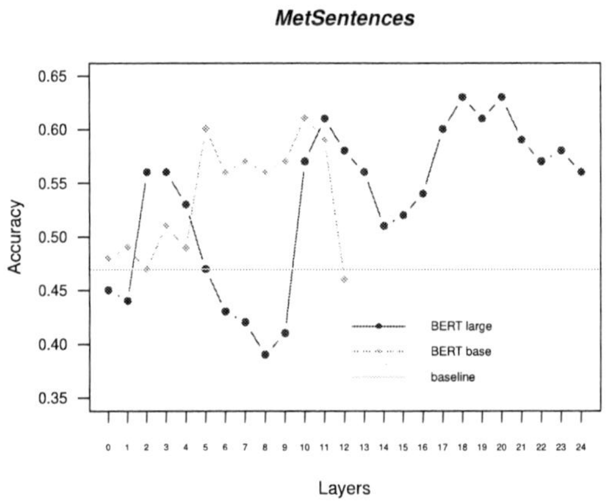

Figure 4.2: Models' accuracy for **MetSentences**

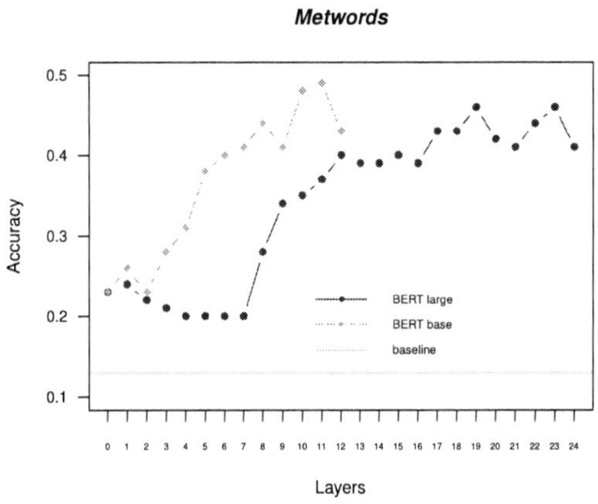

Figure 4.3: Models' accuracy for **MetWords**

As can be seen in Figure 4.2, BERT accuracy outperforms the GloVe baseline (0.47) in the layers 0-1, from 3 to 11 (BERT base), from 2 to 4 and from 10 onward (BERT large). This baseline is outperformed by more than 10 percentage points in some layers (10-11 BERT base; 10-12,17-21,23 BERT large). The layers 10 (base) and 20 (large) produce the highest accuracy values: 0.61 (base) and 0.63 (large). Examples of sentences that are classified correctly (the model's representations are more similar to the metaphorical landmarks than to the literal ones) and sentences that are classified wrongly by the best BERT large layer are reported in Table 3.

In the **MetWords** setting and in both models, the similarities to the two landmark sets are not significantly different (p-value > 0.05). The only exceptions are the first layers where, in contrast with our expectations, the metaphorical expression embeddings are significantly more similar to the literal landmarks embeddings than to the metaphorical ones. As can be seen from figure 4.3, the accuracy generally increases along the layers apart from the final ones, in the same way as we saw for **MetSentences**.

In **MetWords** (cf. figure 4.3), BERT accuracy overcomes the correspondent GloVe baseline (acc= 0.13) by a margin ranging from 10 (layers 0,2) to

Best perfomance Acc.0.63	Conventional Creative
Correct	What is the source of your anger? Laughter is the mind sneezing.
Wrong	Lawyers are real sharks. Prejudice is the child of ignorance.

Table 3: Examples of correct and wrong sentences from the layer with the best performance (20 BERT large)

36 (layer 11) points in BERT base and from 07 (layers 4-7) to 33 (layers 19,23) points in BERT large. Instead, BERT accuracy almost never goes beyond the **MetSentences** version of the baseline, except the layers 10-11 of BERT base with a difference no higher than 2 points.

We also evaluated the influence of the conventionality of a metaphor on the success of the models' interpretation[1]. Data (see the right plot in figure .4) show that, in BERT-large, the proportion of the correct conventional metaphors is higher than the proportion of the correct creative ones up to a margin of 10 points in **MetSentences** (layers 2-5, 10, 16-17, 24 BERT large). In this setting, this disparity decreases along the layers of the model and it disappears in the layers close to 20 (BERT large). In BERT base (cf. the left plot in figure .4), the proportion of correct creative metaphors overcomes the proportion of correct conventional metaphors at the layers 0, 3-4, 6-12. On the other hand, the wrong cases in **MetSentences** (see figure .7) are mostly creative metaphors. As well as for the correct representations, the disparity tends to decrease along the layers of both models and in BERT large it disappears at the layer 23, in BERT large at the layer 7). On the other hand, these differences persist in the **MetWords** version at all layers and in both models (see figures .5 and .6).

5 Discussion

Likelihood of metaphors with respect to other expressions. The likelihood scores that the models assign to metaphorical expressions lie halfway between those of literal and nonsense sentences, in line with human judgments of semantic plausibility (compare the first two plots in Figure 4.1 with the last one). Most importantly, BERT discriminates unconventional creative metaphors from nonsense sentences and seems to discriminate highly conventionalized metaphors from literal expressions, even though the difference is not significant in the second case.

This result raises some interesting questions that need to be further investigated. Where does BERT's ability to discriminate metaphorical expressions come from? How does BERT know that, for example, the sentence *A smile is an ambassador* (PLL=-6.02) is more plausible than the sentence *A smile is a fishing man* (PLL=-6.89)? It is likely that the model has not received explicit training on this, since it has probably never or rarely encountered any of such expressions during learning. Does this ability share some aspects with the human ability of producing novel metaphors? A possible answer is that the creative metaphors that are in our dataset are grounded on associations that manifest themselves more frequently in language. For example, the creative metaphor *The sea whispered on the sand* represents a personifying mapping which is expressed by other more frequent expressions such as *whispering wind*. The model might learn these mappings from training data in the form of associations between groups of words, and then extend them to similar constructions.

An analysis of the model's representations, although it does not allow us to draw firm conclusions about BERT capability to capture our intuitions about metaphorical meaning, brings out fairly clear trends with respect to the model's interpretation of metaphors, some of which are consistent with findings in the previous literature.

General evaluation of BERT. Our second experiment reveals that in some cases BERT representations of metaphorical expressions are significantly more similar to the metaphorical landmarks than to the literal ones. This result is not stable but varies considerably across configurations (see below). Moreover, in both versions of Experiment 2, BERT is almost always above the GloVe baseline (as can be seen from the plots in Figures 4.2 and 4.3). For **MetWords** this is not surprising, since in that case we examined only the static vector of a word, which is obviously more similar to the literal than to the metaphoric landmarks. However, it is less obvious for **MetSentences**, where the baseline is outperformed by 16% in some layers (BERT classified correctly 16 more sentences out of 100).

Analysis of internal representations. At upper-intermediate layers, we find significantly more metaphorical than literal information in the model's representations, and the accuracy in the

[1]These data are reported in the Appendix due to space constraints

landmark task typically rises until it reaches its peak (see the plots in Figures 4.2 and 4.3). This behavior is probably explained by the fact that, at higher layers, the model produces more contextualized embeddings (Ethayarajh, 2019), and contextual information is relevant to understanding metaphorical meaning shifts. This also explains why BERT large achieves higher scores than the base version: The deeper the model, the stronger the contextualization.

This result is consistent with the previous findings about the distribution of linguistic abilities in different layers of the model. It has been shown (Liu et al., 2019; Jawahar et al., 2019) that upper-intermediate layers are the ones that perform best in probing tasks involving different types of linguistic knowledge. Our results are also consistent with findings from metaphor identification (Liu et al., 2020). The error analysis of our results shows that the first layers of the model do not encode much information that is useful for the task and is not present in the subsequent layers. In the **MetSentences** setting, 27 out of the 37 errors made from the layer 20 of BERT large (the layer with the highest accuracy) are common to layer 1.

Sentence vs. word representations. In **MetWords** (where we examined only the embeddings of the specific words that are used metaphorically), BERT representations are never significantly biased in favor of the metaphorical reading. As can be seen by comparing the plots in Figures 4.2 and 4.3, results are almost always worse than in the **MetSentences** setting and below the additive GloVe baseline. In **MetWords**, the performance is affected by the fact that the BERT embeddings of a single word token encode a significant amount of information about its literal sense. The salience of this information diminishes as the representation is fed to the higher layers of the models, but it is not enough for the models to achieve performances comparable to those in the **MetSentences** version.

Another major difference between the two approaches concerns metaphor conventionality. In the **MetSentences** setting, the improvements that we observe when using higher layers mainly concern creative metaphors (this can be seen from the plots in .4 and .7). While in the first layers the models generally classify correctly more conventional than creative metaphors, the difference tends to reduce as we climb up the layers. In other words, the interpretation of creative metaphors seems to benefit the most from the process of contextualization. On the other hand, this does not occur in the **MetWords** version (see .5 and .6), where the number of conventional metaphors among the items that were correctly classified by the model is always higher than the number of creative metaphors.

An important difference between conventional and creative metaphors can account for both these results. Since creative metaphors are idiosyncratic and context-dependent, it is more likely that the model needs global information about all sentence components to "understand" metaphorical aspects of their meaning. This ability manifests itself more clearly in the later layers of the model, where a larger amount of contextual information has been processed through the repetition of the self-attention mechanism. Accordingly, the information crucial to the interpretation of these metaphors will more likely be a feature of the representation of the entire sequence. In contrast, conventional metaphors occur more systematically in language and eventually become lexicalized. As such, they should be already encoded in the general representations that the model creates for single words, since these representations account for the behavior of a word in all the contexts in which it has been encountered. The process of interpreting highly conventionalized metaphors is thus akin to disambiguation, since the relevant meaning is already encoded in the original embedding of a word and the model only needs to recover it by using contextual information. Therefore, the process is likely to be successfully accomplished earlier by the model.

6 Conclusion

In this paper, we adopted different methods used in the literature on the analysis of neural language models to explore how BERT captures various human evidence about a linguistic phenomenon that is relatively underexplored in this field, namely metaphors. In **Experiment 1**, starting from the assumption that metaphorical sentences are more plausible than nonsense sentences (even if they are "deviant" from literal ones), we tested whether BERT can make a distinction between literal, nonsense and metaphorical expressions with various degrees of conventionality. We show that BERT can distinguish between these types of expressions, assigning them different degrees of plausibility in much the same way as humans do.

In **Experiment 2**, we wanted to test BERT's

ability to understand the figurative meaning of metaphorical sentences and the lexical meaning shifts these sentences activate, in comparison with their literal meaning. Despite the limited size of our dataset, we can derive some trends. In particular, we observed that the shift is captured by the model's representations (without fine-tuning and when compared via cosine similarity) to a fair extent, especially when it can exploit more contextual information (in upper layers and at the sentence level). We take the results of this experiment as the starting point for future work aimed at investigating how the model can perform when it receives explicit training on this specific task.

There are many directions for future works, including testing the model using landmarks which do not derive from subjective intuitions, but which are obtained from human judgments. Some of the hypotheses formulated here (for example, BERT ability to derive metaphorical mappings from training) need to be verified on a larger dataset of metaphors, where different conceptual domains involved in the phenomenon can be explored. Moreover, the use of datasets made of longer portions of texts could help BERT in improving its ability to encode metaphorical meanings, since we have shown that contextualization improves the model's ability, with positive effects in particular on the interpretation of creative metaphors.

References

H. Al-Azary and L. Buchanan. 2017. Novel metaphor comprehension: Semantic neighbourhood density interacts with concreteness. *Memory Cognition*, 45:296–307.

Valentina Bambini, Donatella Resta, and Mirko Grimaldi. 2014. A Dataset of Metaphors from the Italian Literature: Exploring Psycholinguistic Variables and the Role of Context. *PLoS ONE*, 9(9).

Yonatan Belinkov and James Glass. 2019. Analysis Methods in Neural Language Processing: A Survey. *Transactions of the Association for Computational Linguistics*, 7:49–72.

Brian J. Birdsell. 2018. Conceptual Wandering and Novelty Seeking: Creative Metaphor Production in an L1 and L2. *Journal of Cognitive Science*, 19(1):35–67.

Y. Bizzoni and S. Lappin. 2017. Predicting human metaphor paraphrase judgments with deep neural networks. *Memory Cognition*, 45:296–307.

Rishi Bommasani, Kelly Davis, and Claire Cardie. 2020. Interpreting Pretrained Contextualized Representations via Reductions to Static Embeddings. In *Proceedings of ACL*.

Cristiana Cacciari and Sam Glucksberg. 1994. Understanding figurative language. In *Handbook of psycholinguistics*, page 447–477. Academic Press.

J. Charteris-Black. 2004. *Corpus Approaches to Critical Metaphor Analysis*. Palgrave Macmillan.

Gabriella Chronis and Katrin Erk. 2020. When Is a Bishop Not Like a Rook? When It's Like a Rabbi! Multi-prototype BERT Embeddings for Estimating Semantic Relationships. In *Proceedings of CONLL*.

Verna Dankers, Karan Malhotra, Gaurav Kudva, Volodymyr Medentsiy, and Ekaterina Shutova. 2020. Being neighbourly: Neural metaphor identification in discourse. In *Proceedings of the Second Workshop on Figurative Language Processing*, page 227–234.

Verna Dankers, Marek Rei, Martha Lewis, and Ekaterina Shutova. 2019. Modelling the interplay of metaphor and emotion through multitask learning. In *Proceedings of the 2019 Conference on Empirical Methods in Natural Language Processing and the 9th International Joint Conference on Natural Language Processing (EMNLP-IJCNLP)*, page 2218–2229.

Jacob Devlin, Ming-Wei Chang, Kenton Lee, and Kristina Toutanova. 2019. BERT: Pre-training of Deep Bidirectional Transformers for Language Understanding. In *Proceedings of NAACL*.

Kawin Ethayarajh. 2019. How Contextual Are Contextualized Word Representations? Comparing the Geometry of BERT, ELMo, and GPT-2 Embeddings. In *Proceedings of EMNLP*.

Allyson Ettinger. 2020. What BERT Is Not: Lessons from a New Suite of Psycholinguistic Diagnostics for Language Models. *Transactions of the Association for Computational Linguistics*, 8.

Ge Gao, Eunsol Choi, Yejin Choi, and Luke Zettlemoyer. 2018. Neural Metaphor Detection in Context. In *Proceedings of the 2018 Conference on Empirical Methods in Natural Language Processing*, page 607–613.

Dedre Gentner and Brian Bowdle. 2008. Metaphor as structure-mapping. In Raymond W.Editor Gibbs, Jr., editor, *The Cambridge Handbook of Metaphor and Thought*, Cambridge Handbooks in Psychology, page 109–128. Cambridge University Press.

Sam Glucksberg. 2003. The psycholinguistics of metaphor. *Trends in Cognitive Sciences*, 7(2):92–96.

Sam Glucksberg, Patricia Gildea, and Howard B. Bookin. 1982. On understanding nonliteral speech: Can people ignore metaphors? *Journal of Verbal Learning and Verbal Behavior*, 21(1):85–98.

Yoav Goldberg. 2019. Assessing BERT's Syntactic Abilities. arXiv:1901.05287.

Ganesh Jawahar, Benoît Sagot, and Djamé Seddah. 2019. What Does BERT Learn about the Structure of Language? In *Proceedings of the 57th Annual Meeting of the Association for Computational Linguistics*, page 3651–3657.

Albert N. Katz, Allan Paivio, Marc Marschark, and James M. Clark. 1988. Norms for 204 Literary and 260 Nonliterary Metaphors on 10 Psychological Dimensions, Metaphor and Symbolic Activity. *Metaphor and Symbolic Activity*, 3:4:191–214.

Walter Kintsch. 2000. Metaphor comprehension: A computational theory. *Psychonomic Bulletin Review*, 7:257–266.

VT Lai, T Curran, and L. Menn. 2009. Comprehending conventional and novel metaphors: an ERP study. *Brain Research*, 1284:145–55.

G. Lakoff and M. Johnson. 1980. *Metaphors We Live By*. University Of Chicago Press.

Alessandro Lenci. 2018. Distributional Models of Word Meaning. *Annual Review of Linguistics*, 4:151–171.

Chee Wee (Ben) Leong, Beata Beigman Klebanov, Chris Hamill, Egon Stemle, Rutuja Ubale, and Xianyang Chen. 2020. A Report on the 2020 VUA and TOEFL Metaphor Detection Shared Task. In *Proceedings of the Second Workshop on Figurative Language Processing*, page 18–29.

Chee Wee (Ben) Leong, Beata Beigman Klebanov, and Ekaterina Shutova. 2018. A Report on the 2018 VUA Metaphor Detection Shared Task. In *Proceedings of the Workshop on Figurative Language Processing*, page 56–66.

Jerry Liu, Nathan O'Hara, Alexander Rubin, Rachel Draelos, and Cynthia Rudin. 2020. Metaphor Detection Using Contextual Word Embeddings From Transformers. In *Proceedings of the Second Workshop on Figurative Language Processing)*, page 250–255.

Nelson F. Liu, Matt Gardner, Yonatan Belinkov, Matthew E. Peters, and Noah A. Smith. 2019. Linguistic Knowledge and Transferability of Contextual Representations. In *Proceedings of the 2019 Conference of the North American Chapter of the Association for Computational Linguistics: Human Language Technologies, Volume 1 (Long and Short Papers)*, page 1073–1094.

Rui Mao, Chenghua Lin, and Frank Guerin. 2018. Word Embedding and WordNet Based Metaphor Identification and Interpretation. In *Proceedings of the 56th Annual Meeting of the Association for Computational Linguistics (Volume 1: Long Papers)*, page 1222–1231.

S. McGregor, K. Agres, K. Rataj, M. Purver, and G. Wiggins. 2019. Re-Representing Metaphor: Modeling Metaphor Perception Using Dynamically Contextual Distributional Semantics. *Frontiers in Psychology*, 10(765).

Peter Newmark. 1980. The Translation of Metaphor. *Babel*, 26(2):93–100.

Natalie Parde and Rodney Nielsen. 2018. A Corpus of Metaphor Novelty Scores for Syntactically-Related Word Pairs. *Proceedings of the Eleventh International Conference on Language Resources and Evaluation (LREC 2018)*.

Jeffrey Pennington, Richard Socher, and Christopher Manning. 2014. Glove: Global Vectors for Word Representation. In *Proceedings of EMNLP*, pages 1532–1543.

Carina Rasse, Alexander Onysko, and Francesca M. M. Citron. 2020. Conceptual metaphors in poetry interpretation: A psycholinguistics approach. *Language and Cognition*, 12(2):310–342.

Anna Rogers, Olga Kovaleva, and Anna Rumshisky. 2020. A Primer in BERTology: What We Know About How BERT Works. *Transactions of the Association for Computational Linguistics*, 8:842–866.

Zachary Rosen. 2018. Computationally Constructed Concepts: A Machine Learning Approach to Metaphor Interpretation Using Usage-Based Construction Grammatical Cues. In *Proceedings of the Workshop on Figurative Language Processing*, page 102–109.

Julian Salazar, Davis Liang, Toan Q. Nguyen, and Katrin Kirchhoff. 2020. Masked Language Model Scoring. In *Proceedings of the 58th Annual Meeting of the Association for Computational Linguistics*, page 2699–2712.

Ekaterina Shutova. 2010. Automatic Metaphor Interpretation as a Paraphrasing Task. In *Human Language Technologies: The 2010 Annual Conference of the North American Chapter of the Association for Computational Linguistics)*, page 1029–1037.

Gerard J. Steen, Aletta G. Aletta G. Dorst, J. Berenike Herrmann, Anna A. Kaal, Tina Krennmayr, and Trijntje Pasma. 2010. *A method for linguistic metaphor identification. From MIP to MIPVU.* John Benjamins, Amsterdam, Netherlands.

Chang Su, Shuman Huang, and Yijiang Chen. 2016. Automatic detection and interpretation of nominal metaphor based on the theory of meaning. *Neurocomputing*, 219.

Alex Wang and Kyunghyun Cho. 2019. BERT has a Mouth, and It Must Speak: BERT as a Markov Random Field Language Model. In *Proceedings of the Workshop on Methods for Optimizing and Evaluating Neural Language Generation*, page 30–36.

Thomas Wolf, Lysandre Debut, Victor Sanh, Julien Chaumond, Clement Delangue, Anthony Moi, Pierric Cistac, Tim Rault, Remi Louf, Morgan Funtowicz, Joe Davison, Sam Shleifer, Patrick von Platen, Clara Ma, Yacine Jernite, Julien Plu, Canwen Xu, Teven Le Scao, Sylvain Gugger, Mariama Drame, Quentin Lhoest, and Alexander Rush. 2020. Transformers: State-of-the-Art Natural Language Processing. In *Proceedings of the 2020 Conference on Empirical Methods in Natural Language Processing: System Demonstrations*, page 38–45.

Figure .4: Experiment 2. Distribution of correct answers with respect to the conventionality of the metaphor along the layers in BERT base (on the left) and BERT large (on the right) in MetSentences version.

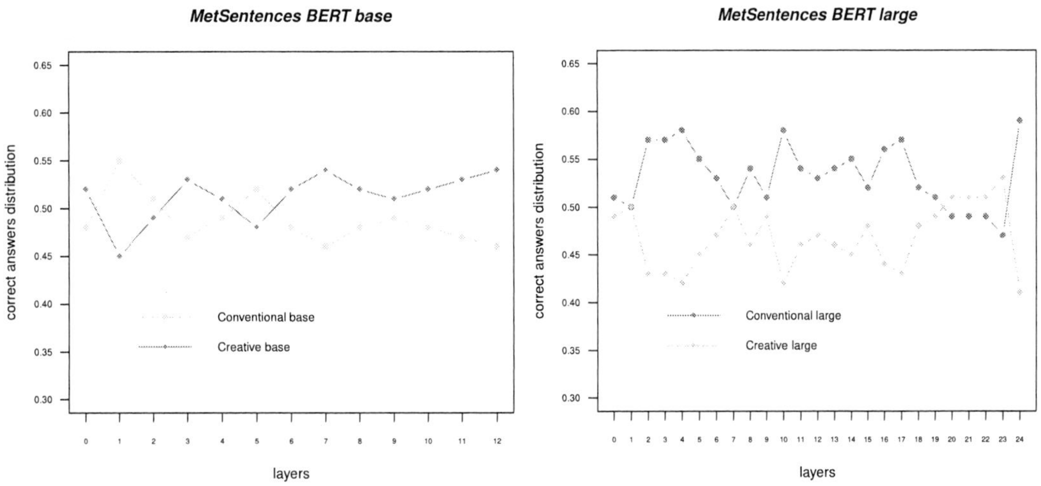

Figure .5: Experiment 2. Distribution of correct answers with respect to the conventionality of the metaphor along the layers in BERT base and BERT large in MetWords version.

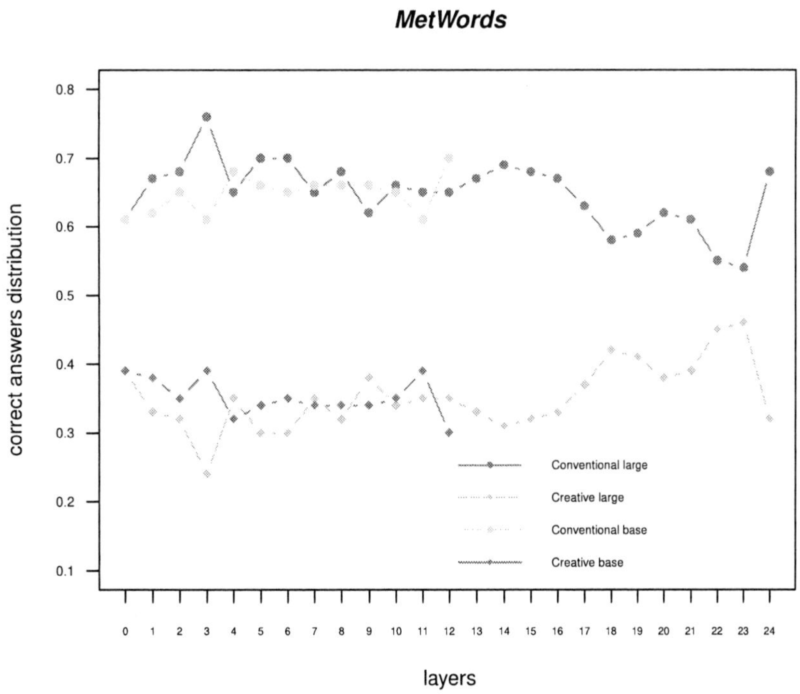

Figure .6: Experiment 2. Distribution of wrong answers with respect to the conventionality of the metaphor along the layers in BERT base and BERT large in MetWords setting.

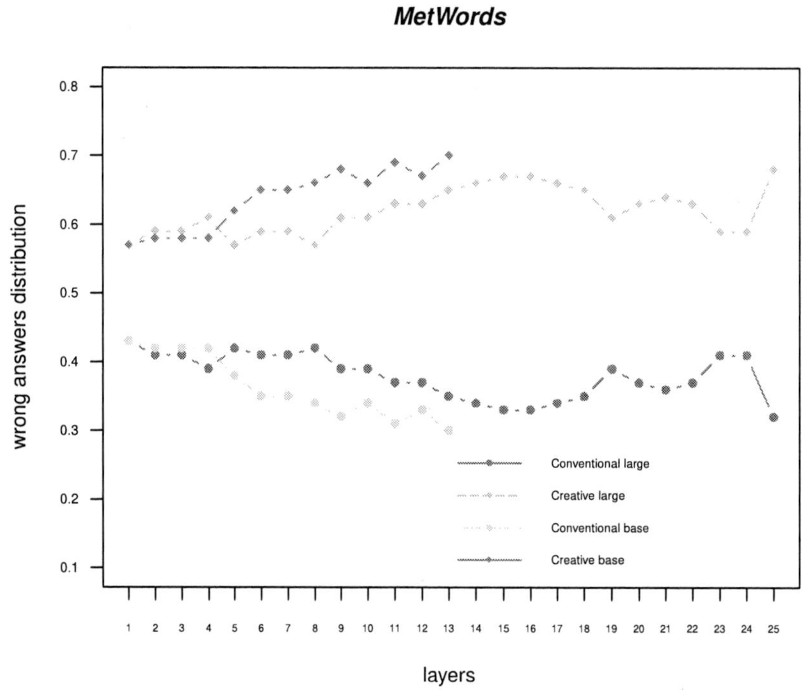

Figure .7: Experiment 2. Distribution of wrong answers with respect to the conventionality of the metaphor along the layers in BERT large and BERT base in MetSentences version.

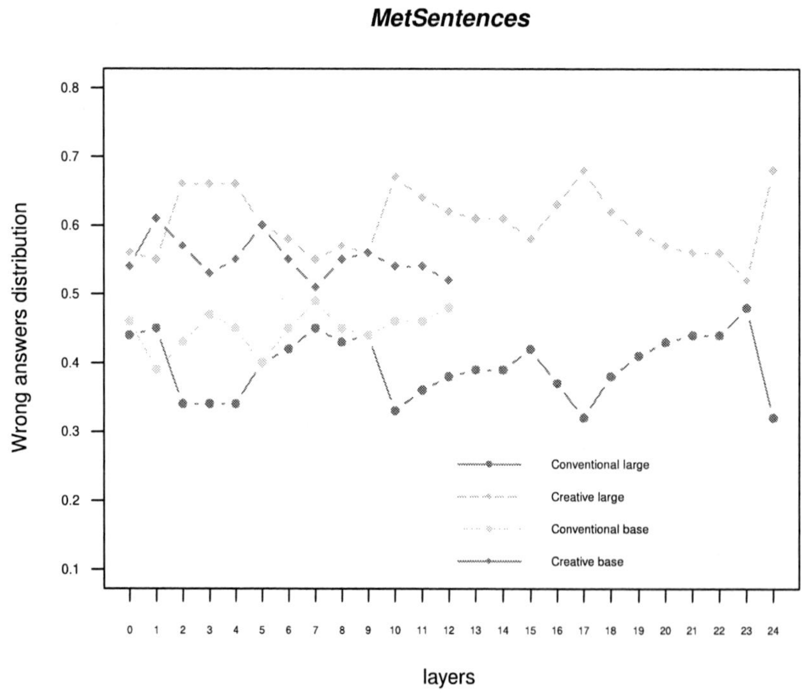

How does Length Prediction Influence the Performance of Non-Autoregressive Translation?

Minghan Wang[1], Jiaxin Guo[1], Yuxia Wang[2], Yimeng Chen[1], Chang Su[1], Hengchao Shang[1], Min Zhang[1], Shimin Tao[1], Hao Yang[1]
[1]Huawei Translation Services Center, Beijing, China
[2]University of Melbourne, Melbourne, Australia
{wangminghan,guojiaxin1,chenyimeng,suchang8, shanghengchao,zhangmin186,taoshimin,yanghao30}@huawei.com
yuxiaw@student.unimelb.edu.au

Abstract

Length prediction is a special task in a series of NAT models where target length has to be determined before generation. However, the performance of length prediction and its influence on translation quality has seldom been discussed. In this paper, we present comprehensive analyses on length prediction task of NAT, aiming to find the factors that influence performance, as well as how it associates with translation quality. We mainly perform experiments based on Conditional Masked Language Model (CMLM) (Ghazvininejad et al., 2019), a representative NAT model, and evaluate it on two language pairs, En-De and En-Ro. We draw two conclusions: 1) The performance of length prediction is mainly influenced by properties of language pairs such as alignment pattern, word order or intrinsic length ratio, and is also affected by the usage of knowledge distilled data. 2) There is a positive correlation between the performance of the length prediction and the BLEU score.

1 Introduction

Though Transformer (Vaswani et al., 2017) has promoted conventional autoregressive generation (AR) by leveraging multi-head self-attention to avoid recurrence at training, decoders that generate each token conditioned on previously generated tokens still make it impossible to take full advantage of parallelism during inference: $p(Y|X) = \prod_i^T p(y_i|y_{\leq i}|X)$. Non-autoregressive Machine Translation (NAT) (Gu et al., 2018; Kaiser et al., 2018) was proposed to parallelize the generation by allowing the prediction of each token independently, known as the conditional independence assumption i.e. $p(Y|X) = \prod_i^T p(y_i|X)$. However, it always results in significant performance degradation. Therefore, how to improve NAT performance remains an open question.

There are basically two directions of NAT models. One is insertion-based models where multiple tokens can be inserted into an existing unfinished sentence, and the sentence length dynamically changes during insertion (Stern et al., 2019; Gu et al., 2019; Chan et al., 2019). Another predetermines the target side length N and generates tokens in a fixed length space conditioned on well-predicted tokens and optionally copied source embedding within N iterations (Gu et al., 2018; Lee et al., 2018; Ghazvininejad et al., 2019). In this paper, we mainly focus on the critical component in the second direction — length prediction which has been rarely discussed. Specifically, we investigate *RQ1: what influences accuracy of length prediction*, and *RQ2: how accuracy of target sentence length prediction affects the translation quality*.

To answer these questions, we first analyze intrinsic properties of sentence lengths for different language pairs. Then we evaluate various length prediction strategies and dig into potential influential factors. Finally the correlation between accuracy of length prediction and translation quality is investigated.

2 Related Work

Gu et al. (2018) predict target length with fertility which essentially is an alignment of source and target tokens generated by a tool named IBM Model 2 (Brown et al., 1993). The hidden state of each source token is used to predict the number of the aligned target token. Then each source token is copied one or multiple times as decoder input, depending on the corresponding predicted length during inference. However, it may introduce noise during training as no ground truth alignment is available. As such, noisy parallel decoding (NPD) was proposed to ameliorate this issue, by applying an autoregressive teacher model to select the best translation from generated candidates sampled in fertility space.

Instead of predicting aligned length token by token mentioned above, naive linear projection has

Proceedings of the Fourth BlackboxNLP Workshop on Analyzing and Interpreting Neural Networks for NLP, pages 205–213
Online, November 11, 2021.

been applied extensively due to its simplicity (Guo et al., 2019; Wang et al., 2019; Li et al., 2019), that is to learn a ratio α from the training set, mapping source length M to the length of the target side: $N = \alpha \cdot M$. Obviously the frequentist statistical notion of α neglects the uniqueness of each individual instance. Thus, classifiers based on the source representation are used to predict target length or length offset (Lee et al., 2018; Ghazvininejad et al., 2019), but the fixed length determined in advance still limits the flexibility during inference.

Aiming to alleviate this issue, insertion-based models are proposed, they implicitly learn the latent variable length by dynamic insertion. Stern et al. (2019) generates text by inserting multiple tokens to readily existing unfinished sentence. Levenshtein Transformer (LevT) (Gu et al., 2019) extends the model by incorporating the deletion operation and decomposing the insertion operation into two steps — first predicting insertion positions and then specific tokens given the position.

Though various approaches are proposed to address the length prediction either explicitly or implicitly, comprehensive comparison, analysis on potential factors affecting their accuracy and the impact on final translation quality are not fully explored. In this work, we shall fill this gap.

3 Model and Dataset

In this section, we first introduce Conditional Masked Language Model (CMLM) framework (Ghazvininejad et al., 2019), on which we perform all experiments throughout this work, followed by datasets details and the experimental setup.

3.1 Conditional Masked Language Model

CMLM is a representative NAT model due to both the simple implementation and the impressive performance. It's built up on the standard Transformer architecture without the decoder self-attention mask.

Formally, given source and target sentence $X = (x_1, ..., x_k)$ and $Y = (y_1, ...y_n)$, the model first predicts target length with hidden state of the source sentence: $p(L|X)$, and initializes a sequence of [MASK] $\times L$ accordingly as decoder input. Then it repeats an alternative between predicting and re-masking tokens in sequence until all tokens are well-predicted with high confidence, this mechanism is referred as iterative refinement with mask-predict.

Notably, at step t, for an unfinished sentence that contains observed tokens $Y^{(t)}_{\text{obs}}$ and masked tokens $Y^{(t)}_{\text{mask}}$, the model predicts masked token under the condition of observed and source tokens:

$$\mathcal{L} = \sum_{y_i \in Y^{(t)}_{\text{mask}}} logP(y_i|X, Y^{(t)}_{\text{obs}}; \theta). \tag{1}$$

During training, the target sentence is corrupted by randomly replacing tokens with [MASK], and the model should learn to recover it. During inference, at step t, it predicts tokens of Y_{mask} with the argmax operation:

$$y^{(t)}_i = \arg\max P(y_i = w|X, Y^{(t)}_{\text{obs}}) \tag{2}$$

$$p^{(t)}_i = \max P(y_i = w|X, Y^{(t)}_{\text{obs}}), \tag{3}$$

and keeps the probability and token unchanged for Y_{obs}. When prediction finishes, k tokens with the lowest probabilities are re-masked, and the remaining tokens are considered as observation in the next iteration:

$$Y^{(t+1)}_{\text{mask}} = \arg\min(p^{(t)}_i, k) \tag{4}$$

$$Y^{(t+1)}_{\text{obs}} = Y^{(t)} \setminus Y^{(t+1)}_{\text{mask}}, \tag{5}$$

where k is determined by a linear decay function with respect to current t and max step T:$k = L \times \frac{T-t}{T}$. For the first step, the model creates a sequence full of [MASK]s with length of L and predicts entire target sequence with it.

3.2 Datasets

We perform experiments on two commonly-used corpora for convenient comparison, including WMT14 En↔De (train=4.5M / valid=3k / test=3k) and WMT16 En↔Ro (train=2.8M/ valid=2k/ test=2k). Following Gu et al. (2018); Zhou et al. (2020), we employ knowledge distilled (KD) data to train our NAT model. The KD data is generated with a pre-trained autoregressive Transformer-big teacher model by completely translating the source text into the target language. We set beam size as five in distillation and only keep the first candidate to make KD data equally sized with raw data. Corpus for all language pairs are tokenized into subwords with BPE (Sennrich et al., 2016), the vocabulary sizes are 42k and 40k for En↔De and En↔Ro respectively.

3.3 Experimental setup

We use the implementation of fairseq (Ott et al., 2019) for AT and NAT models, with similar model

	En-De	De-En	En-Ro	Ro-En
$\alpha_{\text{ref,train}}$	1.0982	1.0043	1.0665	0.9580
$\alpha_{\text{KD,train}}$	1.0333	0.9312	1.0258	0.9410
$\alpha_{\text{ref,test}}$	1.0401	0.9894	1.0704	0.9570
$\alpha_{\text{KD,test}}$	1.0606	0.9620	1.0757	0.9341
$\alpha^{\text{D}}_{\text{hyp,test}}$	1.0530	0.9419	1.0700	0.9275
$\alpha^{\text{R}}_{\text{hyp,test}}$	1.0779	0.9613	1.0824	0.9267

Table 1: The average length ratio for each language pairs: $\alpha^{\{\text{D}|\text{R}\}}_{\{\text{ref}|\text{KD}|\text{hyp}\},\{\text{train}|\text{test}\}} = L_{\text{tgt}}/L_{\text{src}}$, where subscripts represent for the length of reference, knowledge distilled (KD) data or hypothesis, computed on training or testing set, and the superscripts represent for model trained on KD or raw (R) data.

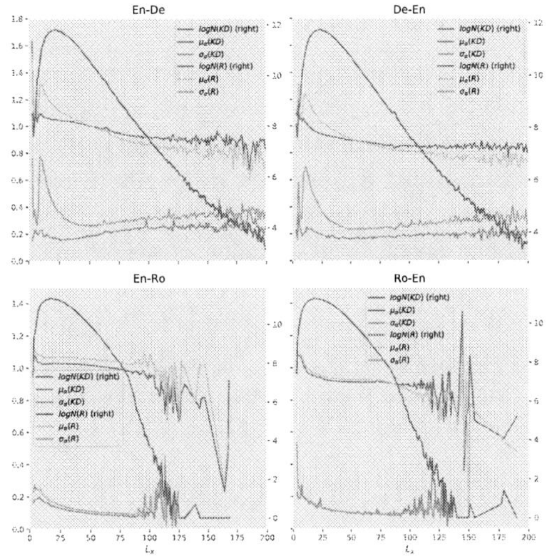

Figure 1: The distribution of the length ratio α with respect to the source length L_x (L_{src}) for raw and KD training set, where frequency is converted with logarithm. Outliers with more than 200 tokens are removed. μ and σ are mean and standard deviation of α where values are shown on the left axis. Right axis is the log frequency.

configuration in (Vaswani et al., 2017; Ghazvininejad et al., 2019). Transformer-big with 6/6 layers, 16 heads and 1024/4096 dimensions is used as our AT model. The NAT model is CMLM-base with 6/6 layers, 8 heads and 512/2048 dimensions.

All models are trained on 4 Tesla-V100 GPUs with gradient accumulation for 2 batches per update. Batch size is set to be maximum of 8k tokens per card. All AT models are trained for 100k updates and NAT models are trained for 300k updates. Adam (Kingma and Ba, 2015) is used as optimizer and inverse-sqrt is used as scheduler. The max learning rate and number of warmup steps are set to be 1e-4 and 4000 for AT models, 5e-4 and 20000 for NAT models.

4 Length Prediction Method

Modelling target length can be implemented in either simple or complex manners depending on learnable parameters, but it's mathematically defined as below:

$$J_L(\theta) = P(L|X;\theta), \tag{6}$$

As such, it can be solved by any maximum likelihood estimation (MLE) algorithms.

4.1 Length to Length

The most straightforward intuition is to estimate a mapping from the length of source to target in training set: $L_y = \alpha L_x$, which can be inferred by optimization and also directly measured through a statistical ratio α from the averaged length of source sentences to averaged length of target sentences of training set. We discuss four interesting findings below, acting as prior knowledge for further investigation on length prediction.

Analysis of Statistical Length Ratio Table 1 and Figure 1 show the statistical results and the distribution of the length ratio $\alpha = L_{\text{tgt}}/L_{\text{src}}$. We summarize our findings as follows:

- De and Ro sentences are usually longer than En sentences.
- For all language pairs, the length ratio changes (often decreases) with the increase of source length, which means using a linear model to fit the ratio is not enough.
- There is usually a gap between the length ratio of training and testing set which might be a causality of the length prediction error.
- For En↔De language pair, the standard deviation and the slope of the mean value for raw data is consistently larger than distilled data, demonstrating the cleanness and simplicity of the distilled data. For En↔Ro the gap of mean and standard deviation is not that big.

This method is simple and time-efficient, but the frequentist α is too generalized to ignore the distinction of each instance. Furthermore, the length of target side is not merely associated with the length of source, but various linguistic properties, such as syntax and semantics.

4.2 Latent Features to Length

Naturally, the hidden state of source sentence embedded rich information is used to incorporate latent linguistic features into target length prediction, instead of just the property of length. They explicitly or implicitly model the target length conditioned on the representation of source X, for example, $L_y = f(X;\theta)$ to predict the absolute length, $L_y = f(X;\theta)L_x$ to predict length ratio and length offset by $L_y = L_x + f(X;\theta)$, as well as fine-grained manners such as the fertility (Gu et al., 2018): $L_y = \sum_i^N f(x_i)$.

4.3 Latent Features to Latent Variables

If we consider two paradigms above as $1 \to 1$ and $N \to 1$ respectively, the third direction is to model $N \to N$. That is, each source sentence is translated into multiple targets in different lengths, which largely increases the potential to generate optimal translations by multiple candidates. In practice, it is implemented by introducing a latent variable to control length prediction $p(L_y|X,Z)p(Z|X)$ which has not been fully investigated yet due to the limitation of reference number in existing open sourced corpora. The closest prior work is sampling from length space and then selecting such as length beam and NPD (Gu et al., 2018).

The second category of approaches are extensively explored partially because current dataset and evaluation metrics applied are more friendly to them, i.e. higher performance is liable to be obtained in comparison, but in our view, the third one is a significantly promising direction to investigate.

5 Error Analysis

In this section, we analyse the predicted length of NAT models trained on distilled (denoted as D) and raw (denoted as R) data, as well as the length of the hypothesis from the teacher model (denoted as KD). We define the following metrics to quantify the error for each sentence and average them over the corpus:

$$\epsilon = L_y - \hat{L}_y \tag{7}$$

$$\epsilon^{+} = |L_y - \hat{L}_y| \tag{8}$$

$$\epsilon^{\%} = 1 - \frac{\hat{L}_y}{L_y} \tag{9}$$

$$\epsilon^{\%+} = |1 - \frac{\hat{L}_y}{L_y}| \tag{10}$$

Error	Model	En-De	De-En	En-Ro	Ro-En
ϵ	D	-0.0513	1.2188	-0.0426	0.7382
	R	0.0793	0.8418	-0.4727	0.8671
	KD	-0.4392	0.6890	-0.1943	0.6735
ϵ^{+}	D	2.5534	2.6787	2.6124	2.6359
	R	2.7093	2.9790	2.6610	2.6444
	KD	2.8528	2.7995	2.7802	2.7277
$\epsilon^{\%}$	D	-0.0170	0.0341	-0.0119	0.0180
	R	-0.0176	0.0224	-0.0241	0.0191
	KD	-0.0319	0.0143	-0.0168	0.0116
$\epsilon^{\%+}$	D	0.0950	0.0965	0.0933	0.0961
	R	0.1003	0.1065	0.0949	0.0974
	KD	0.1069	0.1026	0.0985	0.1015

Table 2: The average value of four error types of all language pairs. In the model column, D and R indicate models trained with the distilled or raw data, and KD represents for the performance of the teacher model.

where the ϵ is the length error, ϵ^{+} is the absolute error regardless of the skew, $\epsilon^{\%}$ is the error ratio that excludes the influence of the sentence length (e.g. 3 tokens error in a 5 tokens target and a 50 tokens target is different), and $\epsilon^{\%+}$ is the absolute error ratio. All errors are measured in the subtokens level.

Table 2 is the statistical result for each error type. The ϵ^{+} shows that NAT models usually have better performance, and the model trained with distilled data outperforms the teacher in a large margin. We speculate that NAT explicitly models the distribution of length. It is reasonable for NAT to have better performance compared with the implicit way of AT model. Intuitively, the model trained with raw data should perform better in length prediction because of the identical distribution in the training and testing set. But the result is the opposite. The reason behind we guess is that distilled data is cleaner and more monotonous than the raw data. Although length error is larger, it still makes the model easier to fit the length distribution compared with the raw data. Figure 2 shows the distribution of length error, indicating that the most errors (75%) are within 5 tokens, and there are slight differences between distributions of D, R and KD especially in the large error zone.

6 Influence on Translations

After investigating the performance of length prediction, we move forward to associate it with the performance of translation and try to answer the question of how length prediction influences the translation. In this section, we use BLEU (Pap-

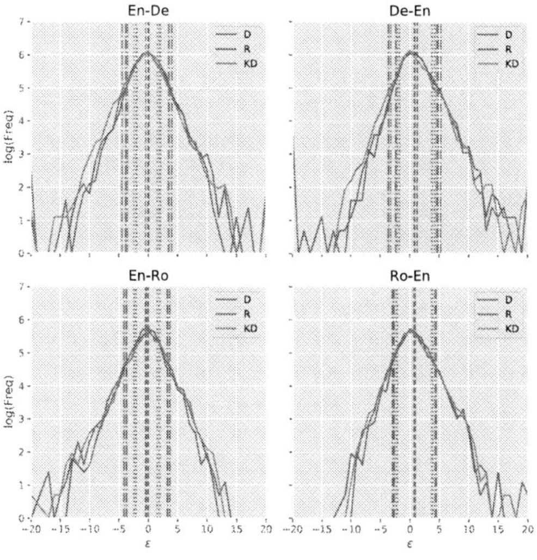

Figure 2: The distribution of the length error on the test set for each language pair, note that the error has been clipped between -20 to 20 and the logarithm of the frequency is used for clearness. The dashed line, dashed dot line and dotted line represents for the mean, $1 \times$ std and the 75% quantile.

Lang	Data	(0, 10]	(10, 20]	(20, 30]	(30, 40]	(40, 150]
En-De	D	22.67	24.52	24.35	25.68	26.30
	R	20.23	22.67	23.14	24.39	23.81
	KD	22.36	26.36	27.41	28.01	29.51
De-En	D	22.73	29.82	28.97	31.35	30.56
	R	21.17	27.40	27.66	29.41	28.14
	KD	24.12	31.63	31.22	34.14	33.32
En-Ro	D	25.02	27.63	28.74	29.59	31.99
	R	25.31	27.17	27.87	28.52	31.05
	KD	27.29	29.31	29.51	31.39	33.41
Ro-En	D	24.18	31.72	31.94	32.13	33.12
	R	22.05	29.46	30.88	31.40	32.45
	KD	25.85	31.85	32.30	32.36	33.63

Table 3: The BLEU scores for the length interval on test set for NAT and AT model.

ineni et al., 2002) and TER (Snover et al., 2006) as the corpus and sentence level metrics, respectively. Two additional factors are also discussed including the sentence length and the number of refinements.

6.1 Correlation to the Source Length

First of all, we use source length to group hypothesises into several buckets with equal interval size, then calculate BLEU for each bucket to find out to what extent source length can affect translation result. Table 3 shows the BLEU of each interval. We find that the first interval has relatively low BLEU which is caused by the imbalanced sample size. Later intervals don't show clear trends which means the translation performance is not quite sensitive to the sentence length thanks to the capability of Transformer architecture for modelling long term dependency (Vaswani et al., 2017), as well as the robustness of CMLM tested in (Ghazvininejad et al., 2019). From this result, we can basically exclude the influence of source length or consider it as a minor factor.

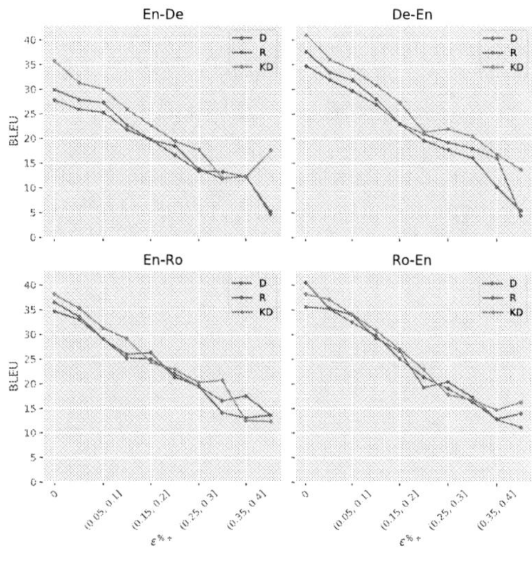

Figure 3: The BLEU scores for each error interval on test set for NAT and AT model.

6.2 Correlation to the Length Error

Then, we group hypotheses with the $\epsilon^{\%+}$ and cut several equal sized intervals to calculate BLEU and TER for each of them. Figure 3 reveals the clear trend that with the increase of the error, the BLEU score decreases almost linearly. This result is consistent with intuition that the negative correlation between length error and the BLEU is not only applicable for AT model but also for the NAT model.

6.3 Upper-Bound of Translations

We basically conclude that incorrect length prediction has negative impact on the translation, but another question arises: if the oracle length is provided, what is the upper-bound the model could reach?

Table 4 shows the overall performance of the model trained and tested on KD or raw data with predicted ($\hat{L}$) or oracle length (L^*). Except for Ro-En result, there are clear improvements on the BLEU and TER for both types of models. In terms of the Ro$\rightarrow$En, the contradictory result happens only on the raw test set. And noticeable unreason-

		Lang	En-De		De-En		En-Ro		Ro-En	
		Length Type	L^*	$\hat{L}$	L^*	$\hat{L}$	L^*	$\hat{L}$	L^*	$\hat{L}$
Trained on	Metric	Tested on								
D	BLEU	R	25.84	25.32	31.01	30.15	30.50	30.04	31.99	32.41
		D	56.41	53.09	61.81	57.95	59.32	55.93	79.09	74.88
	TER	R	0.54	0.58	0.48	0.50	0.50	0.53	0.48	0.50
		D	0.26	0.30	0.23	0.27	0.24	0.28	0.11	0.15
R	BLEU	R	24.56	23.58	29.21	28.17	29.81	29.09	31.66	31.42
		D	48.98	45.59	54.20	49.83	54.19	50.31	72.88	68.74
	TER	R	0.54	0.59	0.49	0.53	0.50	0.54	0.48	0.51
		D	0.31	0.36	0.28	0.34	0.27	0.32	0.14	0.19
Transformer-big		R	28.03		32.64		32.21		32.76	

Table 4: The overall performance of the NAT model trained and tested on distilled (D) or raw (R) data, with predicted ($\hat{L}$) or oracle (L^*) length. The last row shows the BLEU score of the autoregressive teacher model.

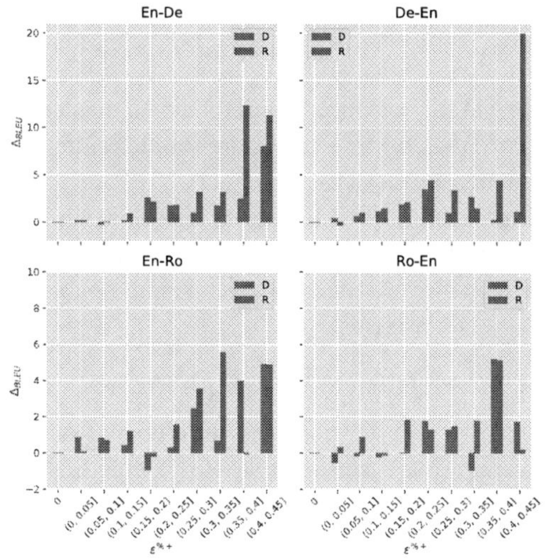

Figure 4: The difference value of the BLEU ($\Delta_{\text{BLEU}} = \text{BLEU}_{L^*} - \text{BLEU}_{\hat{L}}$) with or without oracle length for each error interval.

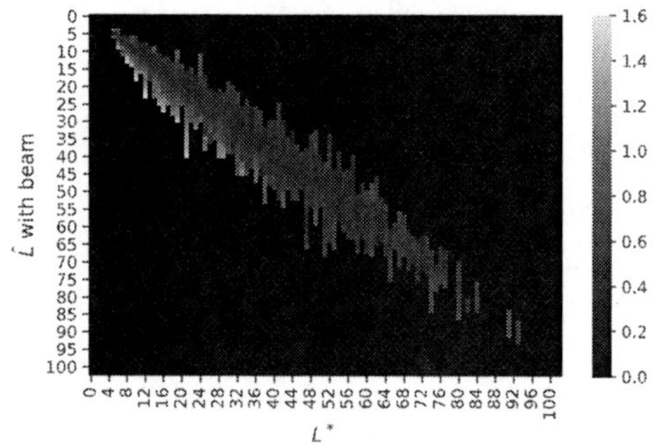

Figure 5: The heatmap of the averaged TER for candidates of length beam with respect to the oracle length.

able translations are observed in generated outputs amongst samples with higher TER, their L^* causes negative influences. This suggests that the modeling of length and token prediction are strongly related, as the length can be considered a discrete latent variable. We suspect that this counter-intuitive result is due to the overfitting of the model to the KD data and resulting in inability to correctly use the latent variable (length) from the unseen distribution (ground truth).

To further investigate the upper-bound of the performance beyond the oracle length, we perform another set of experiments with length beam to find the maximum BLEU at which a model could peak. To control the search space, we narrow search candidates within the area between the predicted length and oracle length i.e. with the beam size of $|L^* - \hat{L}|$ including L^* and $\hat{L}$. We take En→De as the example and plot the averaged TER for translations with same reference length for each beam candidates in Figure 5. In the heatmap, x axis is the oracle length and y axis is the predicted length, averaged TER for beam candidates are plotted as an vertical area. Without choosing the one with highest probability, we directly calculate the TER for all candidates towards the reference. Then, we filter hypothesises with the lowest TER for each sentence pair and calculate the corpus BLEU, which is 28.688, and the averaged ϵ^+ is 1.567. The searched upper-bound is better than those hypothesis with oracle length with approximately 3 BLEU (28.69 to 25.84), and the ϵ^+ is small than the predicted length. Through the empirical experiment results, it should be highlighted

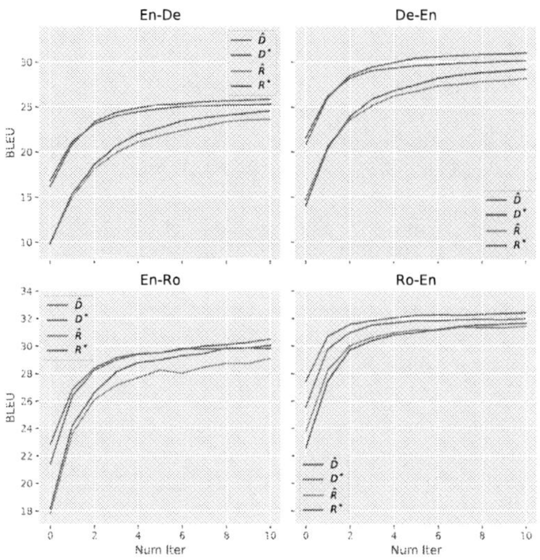

Figure 6: BLEU scores of each run when setting max refinement steps ranging from 0 to 10 with or without oracle length (asterisk or hat), where R and D represents for training on raw or distilled data.

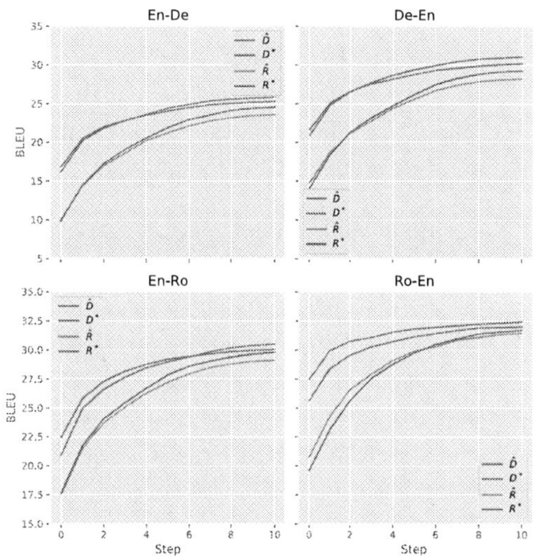

Figure 7: BLEU scores of each step with or without oracle length (asterisk or hat) when max refinement step is set to 10. R and D represents for training on raw or distilled data.

that potential improvements can be obtained if the optimal length for the model can be inferred.

6.4 Correlation to Refinement

It has been known that with multiple iterations of refinement in decoding, the translation performance could be dramatically improved. Therefore, we want to investigate the role of the length prediction during refinement. In CMLM, the refinement is achieved by re-masking predicted tokens with low confidence. Assuming we set the max step to T, at step i, $(1 - \frac{i+1}{T}) \times 100\%$ of tokens will be re-masked and predicted again at next step, note that the prediction of i-th step for different max step T might be different. In the experiment, we set maximum step as 10, run the model from 1 to 10 refinement iterations and compute the BLEU in each iteration. We also observe the translation for each iteration in 10-th run.

Figure 6 depicts the BLEU score of each run. We find that decoding with fewer iteration can be negatively scored with L^* compared to $\hat{L}$. This also happens in step wise BLEU shown in Figure 7. From this case study, we find that translations at initial several steps or with fewer refinement iterations, often have many repeated tokens. We then statistics the average repetition rate of the first step, the result shows that translations with L^* have higher repetition rate compared with using $\hat{L}$ (15.43% to 12.84% for En$\rightarrow$De), which confirms our assump-

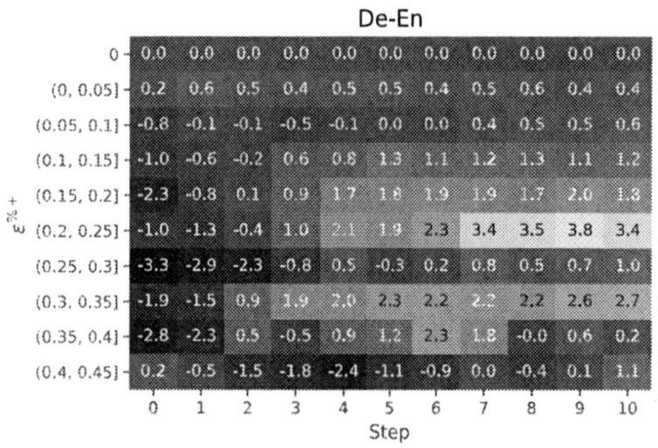

Figure 8: The heat map of the delta BLEU for each error interval and each refinement step while given the oracle length or not (max refinement step = 10).

tion that when given the oracle length, the model may not be able to correctly use it. However, after few steps of refinement, the incompatibility to the oracle length can be eliminated thereby makes translations with correct length can be more similar to the reference. Figure 8 is the increase of BLEU $\Delta_{\text{BLEU}} = \text{BLEU}_{L^*} - \text{BLEU}_{\hat{L}}$ for each error interval at each step, which also reveals that increases in later steps are more significant.

7 Conclusion

From the analysis of length prediction as well as related factors, we have a deeper understanding of it and draw following conclusions:

- Length is an important latent variable for full or iterative based NAT models, it strongly affects the ultimate translation quality, so it should be paid more attention and emphasised in future work of the community.
- Accurately predicting the target side length is beneficial to achieving better BLEU, but it's far from the upper-bound BLEU score bonus brought by length variable.

  Specifically, even if 100% accuracy is achieved, it still can't peak the best BLEU when only judged by reference translation which is not the unique ground truth, because it ignores the linguistic diversity. We find significant improvement can be obtained by a flexible length beam search by over 3 BLEU.

This reveals that, with regard to improving the NAT translation, flexible decoding strategies are more effective than exhausting towards accurate length prediction, since essentially no ground truth of length exists owing to the complexity and diversity of languages. Elegant parallel decoding methods are more promising, such as dynamically changing the length as we evaluated, and meanwhile retaining the simplicity of mask predicting of NAT.

References

Peter F. Brown, Stephen Della Pietra, Vincent J. Della Pietra, and Robert L. Mercer. 1993. The mathematics of statistical machine translation: Parameter estimation. *Comput. Linguistics*, 19(2):263–311.

William Chan, Nikita Kitaev, Kelvin Guu, Mitchell Stern, and Jakob Uszkoreit. 2019. KERMIT: generative insertion-based modeling for sequences. *CoRR*, abs/1906.01604.

Marjan Ghazvininejad, Omer Levy, Yinhan Liu, and Luke Zettlemoyer. 2019. Mask-predict: Parallel decoding of conditional masked language models. In *Proceedings of the 2019 Conference on Empirical Methods in Natural Language Processing and the 9th International Joint Conference on Natural Language Processing, EMNLP-IJCNLP 2019, Hong Kong, China, November 3-7, 2019*, pages 6111–6120. Association for Computational Linguistics.

Jiatao Gu, James Bradbury, Caiming Xiong, Victor O. K. Li, and Richard Socher. 2018. Non-autoregressive neural machine translation. In *6th International Conference on Learning Representations, ICLR 2018, Vancouver, BC, Canada, April 30 - May 3, 2018, Conference Track Proceedings*. OpenReview.net.

Jiatao Gu, Changhan Wang, and Junbo Zhao. 2019. Levenshtein transformer. In *Advances in Neural Information Processing Systems 32: Annual Conference on Neural Information Processing Systems 2019, NeurIPS 2019, December 8-14, 2019, Vancouver, BC, Canada*, pages 11179–11189.

Junliang Guo, Xu Tan, Di He, Tao Qin, Linli Xu, and Tie-Yan Liu. 2019. Non-autoregressive neural machine translation with enhanced decoder input. In *The Thirty-Third AAAI Conference on Artificial Intelligence, AAAI 2019, The Thirty-First Innovative Applications of Artificial Intelligence Conference, IAAI 2019, The Ninth AAAI Symposium on Educational Advances in Artificial Intelligence, EAAI 2019, Honolulu, Hawaii, USA, January 27 - February 1, 2019*, pages 3723–3730. AAAI Press.

Lukasz Kaiser, Samy Bengio, Aurko Roy, Ashish Vaswani, Niki Parmar, Jakob Uszkoreit, and Noam Shazeer. 2018. Fast decoding in sequence models using discrete latent variables. In *Proceedings of the 35th International Conference on Machine Learning, ICML 2018, Stockholmsmässan, Stockholm, Sweden, July 10-15, 2018*, volume 80 of *Proceedings of Machine Learning Research*, pages 2395–2404. PMLR.

Diederik P. Kingma and Jimmy Ba. 2015. Adam: A method for stochastic optimization. In *3rd International Conference on Learning Representations, ICLR 2015, San Diego, CA, USA, May 7-9, 2015, Conference Track Proceedings*.

Jason Lee, Elman Mansimov, and Kyunghyun Cho. 2018. Deterministic non-autoregressive neural sequence modeling by iterative refinement. In *Proceedings of the 2018 Conference on Empirical Methods in Natural Language Processing, Brussels, Belgium, October 31 - November 4, 2018*, pages 1173–1182. Association for Computational Linguistics.

Zhuohan Li, Zi Lin, Di He, Fei Tian, Tao Qin, Liwei Wang, and Tie-Yan Liu. 2019. Hint-based training for non-autoregressive machine translation. In *Proceedings of the 2019 Conference on Empirical Methods in Natural Language Processing and the 9th International Joint Conference on Natural Language Processing, EMNLP-IJCNLP 2019, Hong Kong, China, November 3-7, 2019*, pages 5707–5712. Association for Computational Linguistics.

Myle Ott, Sergey Edunov, Alexei Baevski, Angela Fan, Sam Gross, Nathan Ng, David Grangier, and Michael Auli. 2019. fairseq: A fast, extensible toolkit for sequence modeling. In *Proceedings of NAACL-HLT 2019: Demonstrations*.

Kishore Papineni, Salim Roukos, Todd Ward, and Wei-Jing Zhu. 2002. Bleu: a method for automatic evaluation of machine translation. In *Proceedings of the 40th Annual Meeting of the Association for Computational Linguistics, July 6-12, 2002, Philadelphia, PA, USA*, pages 311–318. ACL.

Rico Sennrich, Barry Haddow, and Alexandra Birch. 2016. Neural machine translation of rare words with subword units. In *Proceedings of the 54th Annual Meeting of the Association for Computational Linguistics, ACL 2016, August 7-12, 2016, Berlin, Germany, Volume 1: Long Papers*. The Association for Computer Linguistics.

Matthew G. Snover, Bonnie J. Dorr, Richard M. Schwartz, Linnea Micciulla, and John Makhoul. 2006. A study of translation edit rate with targeted human annotation. In *Proceedings of the 7th Conference of the Association for Machine Translation in the Americas: Technical Papers, AMTA 2006, Cambridge, Massachusetts, USA, August 8-12, 2006*, pages 223–231. Association for Machine Translation in the Americas.

Mitchell Stern, William Chan, Jamie Kiros, and Jakob Uszkoreit. 2019. Insertion transformer: Flexible sequence generation via insertion operations. In *Proceedings of the 36th International Conference on Machine Learning, ICML 2019, 9-15 June 2019, Long Beach, California, USA*, volume 97 of *Proceedings of Machine Learning Research*, pages 5976–5985. PMLR.

Ashish Vaswani, Noam Shazeer, Niki Parmar, Jakob Uszkoreit, Llion Jones, Aidan N. Gomez, Lukasz Kaiser, and Illia Polosukhin. 2017. Attention is all you need. In *Advances in Neural Information Processing Systems 30: Annual Conference on Neural Information Processing Systems 2017, December 4-9, 2017, Long Beach, CA, USA*, pages 5998–6008.

Yiren Wang, Fei Tian, Di He, Tao Qin, ChengXiang Zhai, and Tie-Yan Liu. 2019. Non-autoregressive machine translation with auxiliary regularization. In *The Thirty-Third AAAI Conference on Artificial Intelligence, AAAI 2019, The Thirty-First Innovative Applications of Artificial Intelligence Conference, IAAI 2019, The Ninth AAAI Symposium on Educational Advances in Artificial Intelligence, EAAI 2019, Honolulu, Hawaii, USA, January 27 - February 1, 2019*, pages 5377–5384. AAAI Press.

Chunting Zhou, Jiatao Gu, and Graham Neubig. 2020. Understanding knowledge distillation in non-autoregressive machine translation. In *8th International Conference on Learning Representations, ICLR 2020, Addis Ababa, Ethiopia, April 26-30, 2020*. OpenReview.net.

On the Language-specificity of Multilingual BERT and the Impact of Fine-tuning

Marc Tanti[1] **Lonneke van der Plas**[2] **Claudia Borg**[3] **Albert Gatt**[4]

[1]University of Malta, Institute of Linguistics and Language Technology
[2]Idiap Research Institute
[3]University of Malta, Department of AI
[4]Utrecht University, Information and Computing Sciences
{marc.tanti,claudia.borg}@um.edu.mt
lonneke.vanderplas@idiap.ch, a.gatt@uu.nl

Abstract

Recent work has shown evidence that the knowledge acquired by multilingual BERT (mBERT) has two components: a language-specific and a language-neutral one. This paper analyses the relationship between them, in the context of fine-tuning on two tasks – POS tagging and natural language inference – which require the model to bring to bear different degrees of language-specific knowledge. Visualisations reveal that mBERT loses the ability to cluster representations by language after fine-tuning, a result that is supported by evidence from language identification experiments. However, further experiments on 'unlearning' language-specific representations using gradient reversal and iterative adversarial learning are shown not to add further improvement to the language-independent component over and above the effect of fine-tuning. The results presented here suggest that the process of fine-tuning causes a reorganisation of the model's limited representational capacity, enhancing language-independent representations at the expense of language-specific ones.

1 Introduction

Since the introduction of transformer architectures and the demonstration that they improve the state of the art on tasks such as machine translation and parsing (Vaswani et al., 2017), there has been a decisive turn in NLP towards the development of large, pre-trained transformer models, such as BERT (Devlin et al., 2019). Such models are pre-trained on tasks such as masked language modelling (MLM) and next-sentence prediction (NSP) and are intended to be task-agnostic, facilitating their transfer to new tasks following fine-tuning with limited amounts of data.

Extending such models to multiple languages is a natural next step, as evidenced by the recent proliferation of multilingual transformers, including multilingual BERT (mBERT), XLM (Conneau and Lample, 2019), and XLM-R (Conneau et al., 2020a). These follow from a line of earlier work which sought to achieve transferable multilingual representations using recurrent network-based methods (e.g. Artetxe et al., 2019, *inter alia)*, as well as work on developing multilingual embedding representations (Ruder et al., 2017).

The considerable capacity of these multilingual models and their success in cross-lingual tasks has motivated a lot of research into the nature of the representations learned during pre-training. On the one hand, there is a significant amount of research suggesting that models such as mBERT acquire robust language-specific representations (Wu and Dredze, 2019; Libovický et al., 2020; Choenni and Shutova, 2020). On the other hand, it has been suggested that in addition to language-specific information, models like mBERT also have language-neutral representations, which cut across linguistic distinctions and enable the model to handle aspects of meaning language-independently. This also allows the model to be fine-tuned on a monolingual labelled data set and achieve good results in other languages, a process known as cross-lingual zero-shot learning (Pires et al., 2019; Libovický et al., 2020; Conneau et al., 2018; Hu et al., 2020). These results have motivated researchers to try and disentangle the language-specific and language-neutral components of mBERT (e.g. Libovický et al., 2020; Gonen et al., 2020).

This background provides the motivation for the work presented in this paper. We focus on the relationship between language-specific and language-neutral representations in mBERT. However, our main goal is to study the impact of fine-tuning on the balance between these two types of representations. More specifically, we measure the

Proceedings of the Fourth BlackboxNLP Workshop on Analyzing and Interpreting Neural Networks for NLP, pages 214–227
Online, November 11, 2021.

effect of fine-tuning on mBERT's representations in the context of two different tasks – part-of-speech (POS) tagging and natural language inference (NLI) – which lay different demands on the model's semantic and language-specific knowledge. While NLI involves reasoning about deep semantic relations between texts, POS tagging requires a model to bring to bear knowledge of a language's morphosyntactic features. Though many languages share such features as a result of typological relations (which mBERT is known to exploit; see, e.g. Pires et al., 2019; Choenni and Shutova, 2020; Rama et al., 2020), there are also language-specific features to which, we hypothesise, mBERT needs to dedicate a greater share of its representational capacity, compared to the NLI task.

We show that the model accommodates language-specific and language-neutral representations to different degrees as a function of the task it is fine-tuned on. This is supported by results from language identification (LID) experiments, conducted both on task-specific data and on a new data set extracted from Wikipedia. We then consider two alternative strategies that force the model to 'unlearn' language-specific representations, via gradient reversal or iterative adversarial learning. These are shown not to further improve the language-independent component for cross-lingual transfer, over and above the effect of fine-tuning. Thus, we conclude that the reorganisation of mBERT's representations that happens with fine-tuning is already taking on this role. Note that our goal is not to improve mBERT's multilinguality but to acquire a better understanding of it, extending previous work along these lines.

Our main contributions are (a) to provide further support for the distinction between language-specific and language-neutral representation in mBERT; (b) to show that fine-tuning results in a reorganisation of mBERT's representations in a way that destroys existing language clusters; (c) to study two methods to enhance language-neutrality in mBERT, both of which are shown not to improve performance on fine-tuned tasks; (d) a new Wikipedia-based language identification data set.

2 Tasks and data

To perform cross-lingual zero-shot learning, we fine-tune mBERT on English only and evaluate it on multiple languages at once. We focus on two tasks: the low-level structured prediction task of cross-lingual POS tagging and the high-level semantic task of cross-lingual NLI. We chose these two tasks, because each task requires a different type of linguistic knowledge. Cross-lingual POS tagging requires a model to bring to bear language-specific knowledge related to morphosyntactic properties, word order, etc., in determining the correct part-of-speech to assign to a token in context. Previous work, for example by Pires et al. (2019), showed good results on this task for mBERT in a cross-lingual zero-shot setting. In contrast, NLI requires a model to determine the semantic relationship between two texts, determining whether it is one of entailment, contradiction or neutrality (Sammons, 2015; Bowman et al., 2015). We expected this task to require more language-neutral, semantic knowledge, compared to POS tagging.[1]

In addition to results on these two tasks, we report results on language identification (LID) experiments. These are reported both on the test data for the tasks themselves, as well as on an independent data set consisting of Wikipedia texts, described below.

In all the experiments reported, we reserve a development set for hyperparameter tuning and a validation set to monitor progress during training. Data set statistics are provided in the Appendix. Following the practice of Hu et al. (2020) for the XTREME benchmark, all texts were truncated to their first 128 tokens (with XNLI having a combined premise-hypothesis length of 128). All the data was tokenised using the `bert-base-multilingual-cased` tokeniser.[2] Data containing unknown tokens (according to the tokeniser) was omitted. All our experiments are conducted on data for 33 languages, the same set of languages included in the UD-POS task of the XTREME benchmark (Hu et al., 2020).[3] The exception is XNLI, for which cross-lingual test data exists for only 15 of these lan-

[1] We note that one task is word-level and one is sentence-level. Ideally the two tasks would have the same level of granularity, but, to our knowledge, no two tasks conform to this goal while at the same time addressing the morphosyntax-versus-semantics requirements.

[2] `https://huggingface.co/bert-base-multilingual-cased`

[3] ISO 639-1 language codes used: af, ar, bg, de, el, en, es, et, eu, fa, fi, fr, he, hi, hu, id, it, ja, kk, ko, mr, nl, pt, ru, ta, te, th, tl, tr, ur, vi, yo, and zh.

guages (Conneau et al., 2018).

UDPOS For POS tagging, we use data from the Universal Dependencies Treebank (UDPOS; Marneffe et al., 2020) v2.7, using the train/dev/test splits provided. A validation set is randomly sampled from the training set. Since we are interested in cross-lingual zero-shot learning, we removed all non-English data from the train/val splits.

XNLI For NLI, we use the monolingual English MultiNLI data set (Williams et al., 2018) as a training set, and the Cross-lingual Natural Language Inference data (XNLI; Conneau et al., 2018) for the development set and test set. Again, a validation set is randomly sampled from the training set.

Wikipedia An independent data set for LID was extracted from Wikipedia. For each language, we randomly selected 5 000 paragraphs which are at least 100 characters in length. Further details are provided in the Appendix.

3 Model architecture

The general architecture used in our experiments is shown in Figure 1. We use a pre-trained mBERT model to encode the input using its final hidden layer, because we are interested in the linguistic capabilities of mBERT's typical use case, which is also the practice in the XTREME benchmark (Hu et al., 2020). The same mBERT model is shared between two single-layer softmax classifiers, both trained using a categorical cross-entropy loss. One of these assigns a task-specific label (a POS tag or an NLI class). This is trained on UDPOS or XNLI data. We will sometimes refer to this as the *target* task. The other is a language classifier that predicts which of the 33 languages (see above) the input text is written in. The language classifier is trained on the Wikipedia data.

We conduct separate experiments for each target task (UDPOS and XNLI). In the case of UDPOS, the classification is for individual tokens. For XNLI, the classification is for sentence pairs, represented as a single text consisting of the concatenation of the premise and hypothesis, separated by a `[SEP]` token.

The language classifier is also trained to either predict the language of each token or of an entire text according to the target task. In this way, we are also able to test this classifier for predictions both on the independent Wikipedia data and on the test data from the target task (which is also labelled by language).

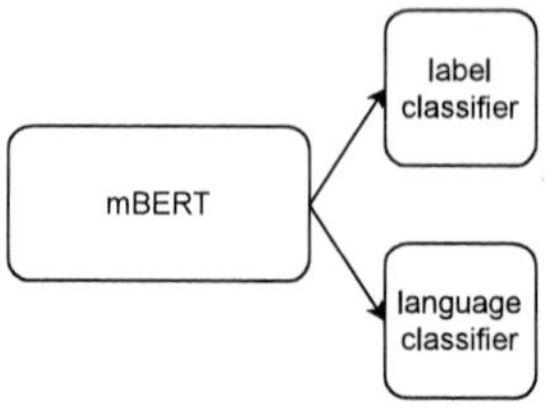

Figure 1: The basic model architecture.

Unless otherwise specified, gradients from the language classifier are not propagated to the pre-trained mBERT model. Thus, the mBERT model parameters are only fine-tuned on the target task data set whilst the language classifier is fine-tuned in isolation. This allows us to monitor how much language-specific information exists in the mBERT encoding, without directly influencing it.

More information about how the model was trained together with the hyperparameters used can be found in the Appendix.[4]

3.1 Modifying mBERT's language-specific representations

To explain the rationale for our experiments on language-specificity, we distinguish *language-neutrality* from *language confusion*.

Let T_{L1} be a text in language L1, and its translation T_{L2} in language L2, and let $E(\cdot)$ be an encoding extracted from a model $\mathcal{M}$. We say that $E(\cdot)$ is language-neutral if $E(T_{L1})$ is close to, or identical with, $E(T_{L2})$. Thus, $\mathcal{M}$ treats semantically equivalent texts in different languages in the same way. In contrast, language confusion places a weaker requirement on a model: here, $E(T_{L1})$ and $E(T_{L2})$ need not be identical, but the encoding itself does not support language identification. In short, language confusion arises when language-specific information is missing from an encoding.

Here, we focus on reducing language-specificity using methods to enhance language confusion, inspired by work on domain adaptation. In a domain adaptation setting, Ganin and Lempitsky (2015) successfully enhanced domain invariance by enhancing domain confusion. We want to see if this works for language as well, that is, whether reducing the language-specificity

[4]Our implementation can be found on the GitHub repo `https://github.com/mtanti/mbert-language-specificity`.

of representations leads to better cross-lingual generalisation on target tasks. To this end, we consider two methods which are intended to enhance the model's language confusion: gradient reversal and iterative entropy maximisation.[5]

Gradient reversal Gradient reversal has been used to train a classifier in a multi-domain setting, using only labelled data in a single domain (Ganin and Lempitsky, 2015). A small labelled data set in one domain and a large unlabelled data set in another domain can be used to encourage the features learned by the model to be domain-invariant by training the model to confuse a domain classifier, thus avoiding any features that are specific to the labelled data set's domain. We make use of Ganin and Lempitsky's gradient reversal layer, which multiplies gradients from the language classifier by a factor $-\lambda$ before backpropagating them to the mBERT model. In effect, this updates the language classifier layer itself to perform better at LID whilst the mBERT parameters are updated to make the language of an encoded text progressively harder to classify. A similar strategy was proposed by Libovický et al. (2020), who used gradient reversal from LID during additional pre-training of mBERT using masked language modelling. Here, we consider its use in the context of fine-tuning on a target task, such as UDPOS or NLI. Hyperparameters, including λ, are listed in the Appendix.

Entropy maximisation Iterative entropy maximisation is closer in spirit to the strategies employed by generative adversarial networks (GANs), in that training is performed iteratively in two alternating phases, each lasting one epoch. In the first phase, the language classification layer is trained in isolation for one epoch on the Wikipedia data set. In the second phase, the target classifier is trained together with mBERT with two goals: (a) maximise the accuracy of the label classifier and (b) maximise the entropy of the language classifier's output probabilities. The entropy maximisation step is intended to make the language classifier approach a uniform distribution, thus training the mBERT model to make the encodings as confusing as possible to the language classifier.

The loss in the second phase is a combination of the label classifier's loss and the language classifier's negative entropy. This loss is calculated as follows:

$$L = (1 - w)(\mathrm{XE}(y_a)) + w\left(-\sum \ln y_b\right) \quad (1)$$

where y_a is the label classifier output, y_b is the language classifier output, XE is the cross entropy function, and w is the weight assigned to the loss for the language classifier. Hyperparameters, including w, are listed in the Appendix.

4 Experiments

In what follows, we first discuss the language clustering and LID capabilities of mBERT both in its unmodified form, and after fine-tuning on UDPOS and XNLI. Then, we consider the impact of gradient reversal and entropy maximisation, both of which seek to shift mBERT representations towards greater language neutrality.

4.1 The effect of fine-tuning on language-specific representations

In this section we focus on how much language-specific information is readily available in mBERT representations before and after fine-tuning it. We measure this in two steps.

First, we train the label and language classifiers on the unmodified pre-trained mBERT model, without modifying mBERT's parameters. We measure the model's performance on the target task using the label classifier and on the LID task using the language classifier. We measure LID performance on both the target task test data and on the Wikipedia test data.

Second, we reinitialise both classifiers and train the label classifier together with the pre-trained mBERT model, after which we freeze mBERT's parameters and train the language classifier. Again, we measure the label and language classifiers' performance as explained above.

In addition, we show 2D t-SNE projections of mBERT's representations of a sample of data items (tokens or texts) from the target task test set and from the Wikipedia test set. Sample sizes are given in the Appendix. We colour the 2D points according to label (target test set) or language (target test set and Wikipedia test set). This allows us to compare the way in which mBERT organises representations prior to and after fine-tuning. As a numerical measure of organisation we cluster the full representations (prior to t-SNE compression) using k-means and measure the agreement of the

[5] Note that we do not change the architecture or the pre-trained mBERT model in these experiments.

	UDPOS		XNLI	
	Init.	Fine-T.	Init.	Fine-T.
Target task	51.2	59.6	29.7	66.3
Lang. ID (Target)	78.3	0.3	49.8	39.2
Lang. ID (Wiki)	59.3	0.5	97.0	97.2

Table 1: Macro F1 scores (%) for target tasks (UDPOS and XNLI) and language identification before (Init.) and after fine-tuning (Fine-T.). Note that 'Lang. ID (Target)' refers to language classification on the target data set.

clusters for labels/languages using the V-measure (Rosenberg and Hirschberg, 2007). We take the average V-measure from ten independent runs of k-means clustering (from scratch).

Table 1 gives the macro F1 scores of the classifier predictions. For both target tasks, performance improves after fine-tuning, as expected. This occurs to a greater extent on XNLI than on UDPOS.[6] For LID, we observe the reverse trend: on both the target test sets and Wikipedia, the classifier's performance in detecting the language of the input drops significantly after fine-tuning for UDPOS, less so for XNLI (with Wikipedia LID remaining unchanged on XNLI).

	UDPOS		XNLI	
	Grad.	Ent.	Grad.	Ent.
Target task	53.5	56.8	62.2	62.1
Lang. ID (Target)	0.1	5.5	1.3	3.4
Lang. ID (Wiki)	0.1	3.1	1.5	54.3

Table 2: Macro F1 scores (%) for target tasks (UDPOS and XNLI) and language identification after training using gradient reversal (Grad.) and entropy maximisation (Ent.). Note that 'Lang. ID (Target)' refers to language classification on the target data set.

Figure 3 and Figure 4 show the t-SNE projections of the token-based UDPOS representations and the text-based XNLI representations respectively, together with the corresponding V-measure. For labels in both target tasks, mBERT starts off with no discernible structure, whereas fine-tuning results in clear clusters by label (compare Figures 3a vs 3b; and 4a vs 4b).[7]

On the other hand, the opposite is observed for languages. Here, mBERT starts off with fairly clear-cut language clusters which then become mixed (compare Figures 3c vs 3d; and 4c vs 4d). This is less evident in the Wikipedia data set. In general, we observe a loss of language-specific representational capacity following fine-tuning on both tasks, in line with the drop in LID performance in Table 1.

In the case of the Wikipedia plots for XNLI (Figures 4e and 4f), there seems to be negligible clustering present (even according to V-measure) but a very high LID performance. Given that the language classifier is single layer deep, this indicates that, although the representations are not clustered, they are still linearly separable (before being compressed by t-SNE).

With the exception of LID on Wikipedia after XNLI fine-tuning, there is a drop in LID performance, which we take as evidence that as mBERT is fine-tuned on a task, its representations become more language invariant. Put differently, fine-tuning requires mBERT's finite representational capacity to be dedicated to the task requirements, at the expense of accurately distinguishing between languages. In this sense, language-specific and language-neutral representations are competing with each other in the context of fine-tuning.

However, the results also show interesting differences between tasks: fine-tuning results in a steeper increase in F1 score for XNLI compared to UDPOS, suggesting that cross-lingual transfer on semantic tasks may benefit more if language specificity decreases, compared to tasks involving morphosyntax. In a related vein, Lauscher et al. (2020) show that POS tagging and dependency parsing are impacted by structural language similarity.

4.2 The impact of increasing language confusion

In this section, we address whether, by using explicit means to enforce language confusion in mBERT representations, we can observe better performance on the target tasks in a cross-lingual zero-shot transfer setting. Unlike the fine-tuning experiments, the language classifier in this case is not trained in isolation, but is trained together with the rest of the system in order to allow the mBERT model to learn to confuse the language classifier. The language classifier is then retrained from scratch in isolation in order to be able to mea-

[6]Note that we report macro F1 scores. The results reported in related work, such as the XTREME benchmark (Hu et al., 2020), report accuracies for NLI and micro F1 scores for POS. They are comparable to those in Table 1: we obtain micro F1 for POS of 73.4%, compared to 70.3% reported by Hu et al. (2020); and accuracy of 66.3% on XNLI, where the equivalent result reported by Hu et al. (2020) is 65.4%.

[7]Note that fine-tuning was done on English data, while the plots are generated on the multilingual test data, meaning that data for languages that were not used for fine-tuning nevertheless cluster by labels in line with the English data.

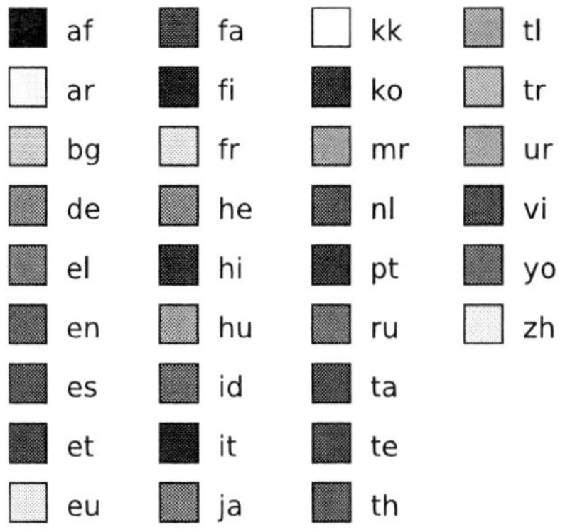

(a) Colour legend for languages.

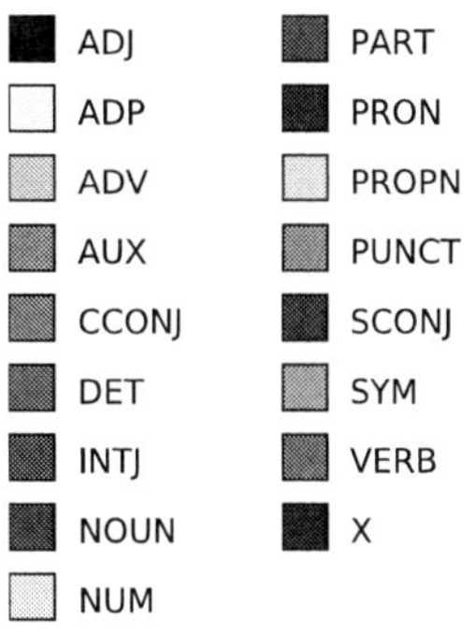

(b) Colour legend for UDPOS labels.

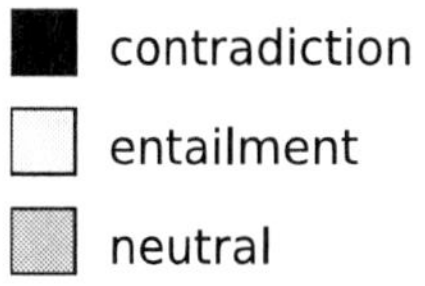

(c) Colour legend for XNLI labels.

Figure 2: Legends for t-SNE visualisations.

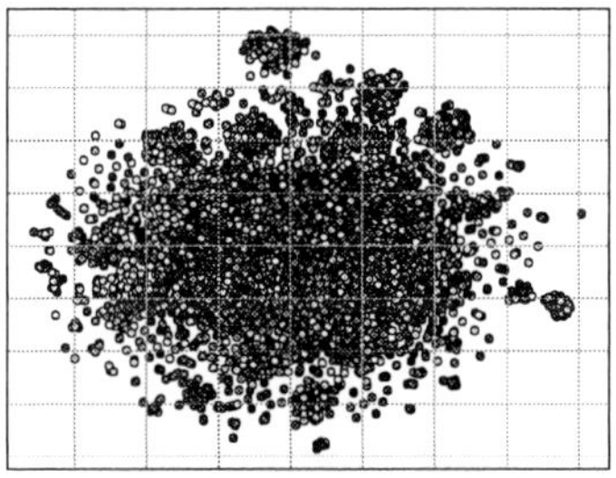

(a) UDPOS labels with initial mBERT (macro F1: 51.2%, V-measure: 13.0%).

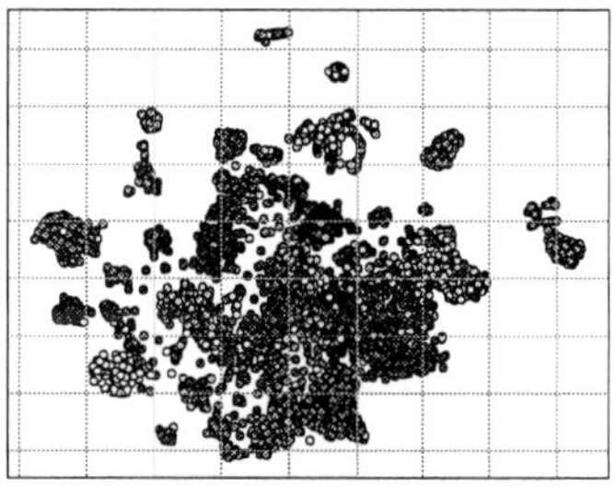

(b) UDPOS labels with fine-tuned mBERT (macro F1: 59.6%, V-measure: 47.5%).

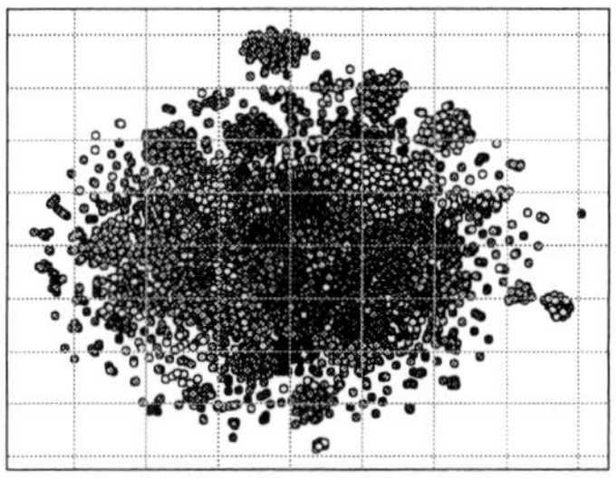

(c) UDPOS languages with initial mBERT (macro F1: 78.3%, V-measure: 49.2%).

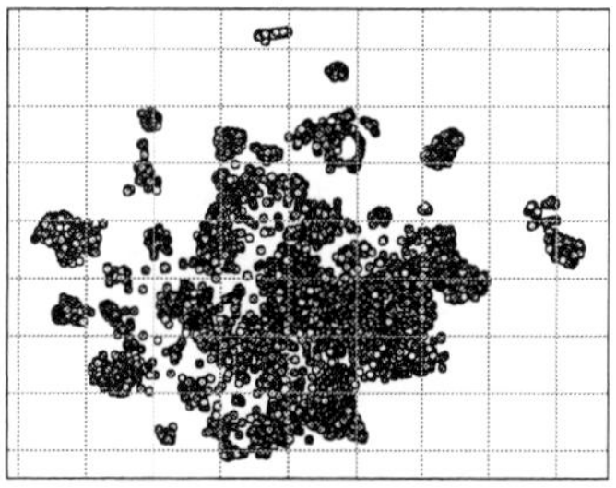

(d) UDPOS languages with fine-tuned mBERT (macro F1: 0.3%, V-measure: 10.4%).

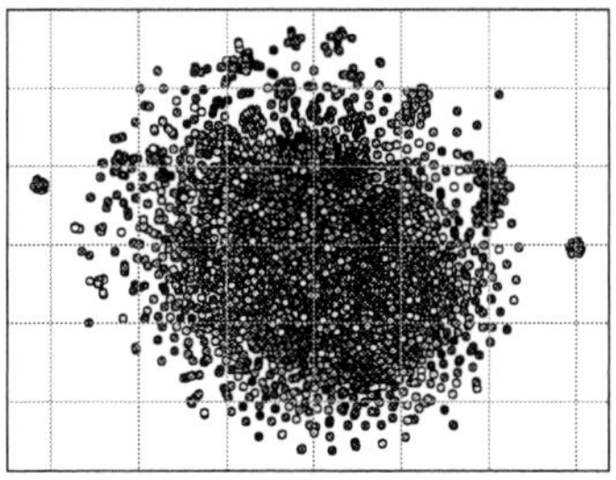

(e) Wikipedia languages with initial mBERT (macro F1: 59.3%, V-measure: 22.3%).

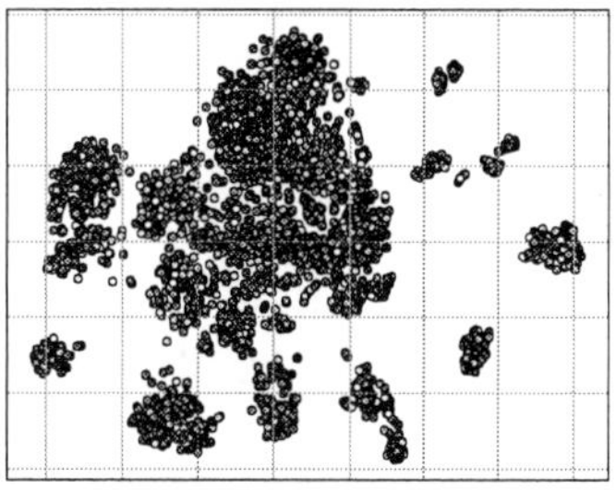

(f) Wikipedia languages with fine-tuned mBERT (macro F1: 0.5%, V-measure: 11.6%).

Figure 3: 2D t-SNE projections before and after fine-tuning, with UDPOS as target task. Macro F1 scores for label/language classification of mBERT embeddings are also given. Points represent tokens. See Figure 2a (languages) and Figure 2b (labels) for colour legends.

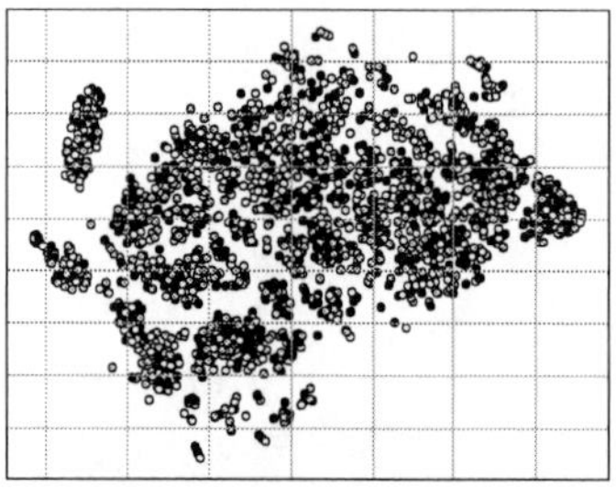

(a) XNLI labels with initial mBERT (macro F1: 29.7%, V-measure: 0.1%).

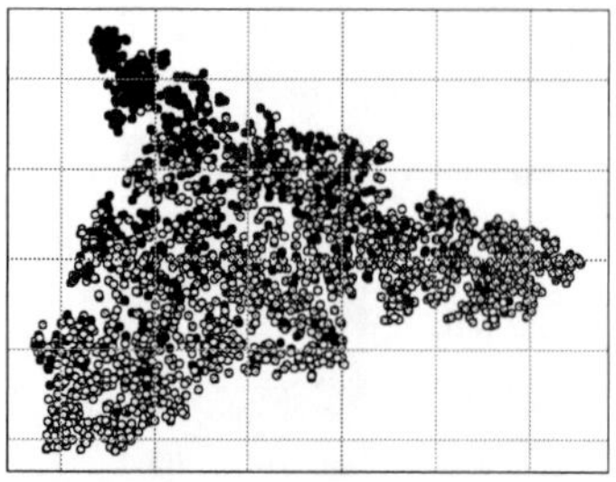

(b) XNLI labels with fine-tuned mBERT (macro F1: 66.3%, V-measure: 20.3%).

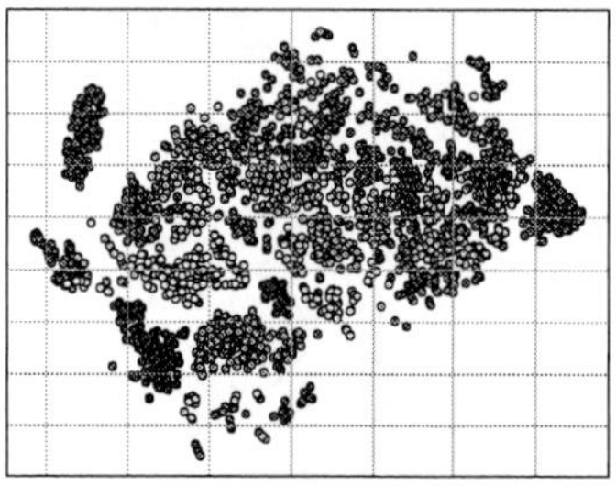

(c) XNLI languages with initial mBERT (macro F1: 49.8%, V-measure: 35.1%).

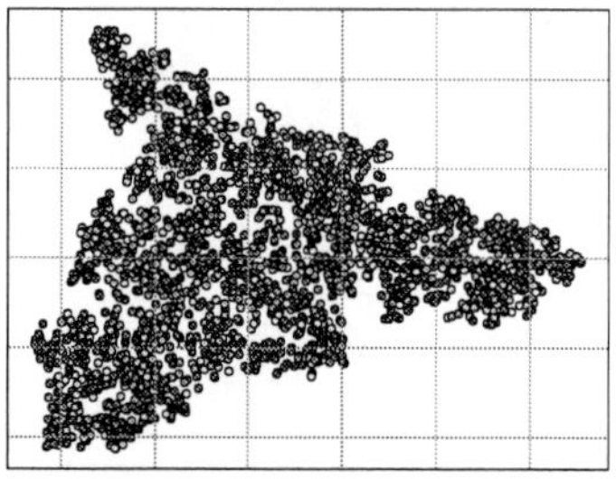

(d) XNLI languages with fine-tuned mBERT (macro F1: 39.2%, V-measure: 6.8%).

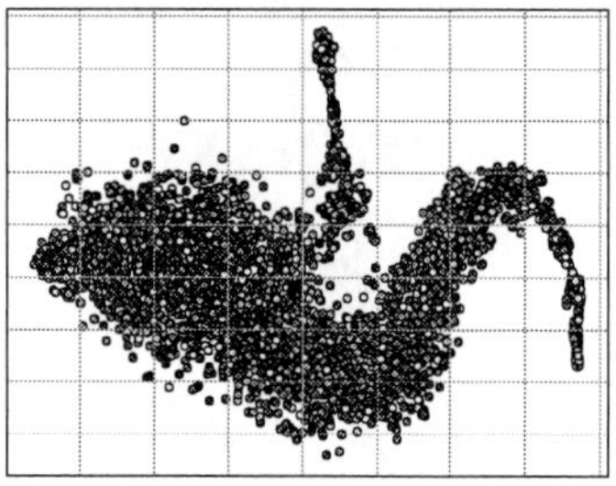

(e) Wikipedia languages with initial mBERT (macro F1: 97.0%, V-measure: 11.7%).

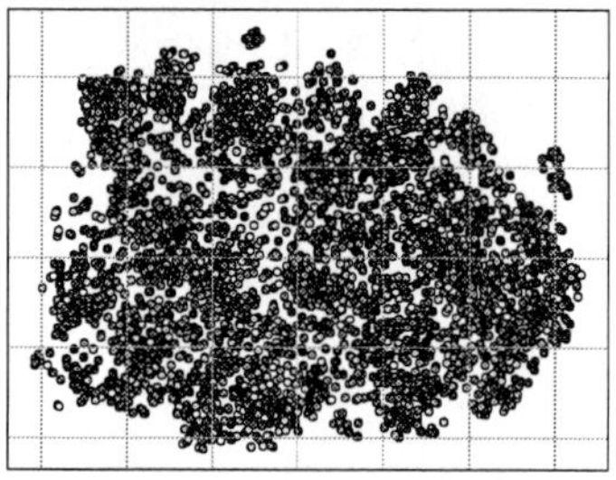

(f) Wikipedia languages with fine-tuned mBERT (macro F1: 97.2%, V-measure: 8.9%).

Figure 4: 2D t-SNE projections before and after fine-tuning, with XNLI as target task. Macro F1 scores for label/language classification of mBERT embeddings are also given. Points represent pairs of sentences. See Figure 2a (languages) and Figure 2c (labels) for colour legends.

sure the amount of language sensitive information in the mBERT representations.

Table 2 gives the macro F1 scores of the classifier predictions. Compared to the simple fine-tuning setup in Table 1, it is clear that both gradient reversal and entropy maximisation have a negative impact on target task performance.

t-SNE plots for the mBERT representations after language unlearning are shown in the Appendix, but we show the V-measure values in Table 3. In general, gradient reversal and entropy maximisation yield a comparable degree of clustering to that observed above after fine-tuning. The exception is XNLI, where the V-measure is higher and suggests more well-defined clusters compared to the fine-tuned case.

	UDPOS		**XNLI**	
	Grad.	Ent.	Grad.	Ent.
Target labels	22.8	30.1	1.1	12.2
Language (Target)	12.5	12.1	18.8	20.0
Language (Wiki)	7.9	9.6	12.2	14.7

Table 3: V-measures (%) of full vector test set samples after clustering for target labels (UDPOS and XNLI) and languages after training using gradient reversal (Grad.) and entropy maximisation (Ent.). Note that 'Language (Target)' refers to languages in the target data set.

These results suggest that fine-tuning of multilingual models such as mBERT involves an interplay between language-specific and language-neutral representations. They also indicate that the task matters: classifying tokens with morphosyntactic information results in greater loss of language specificity and in the ability to identify languages than classifying entire texts. Furthermore, strategies to enforce language confusion in representations result in a deterioration of performance, interfering with the ability of the model to balance the two sources of information as a function of the task it is being fine-tuned on.

5 Related work

Several studies have shown that mBERT performs well in zero-shot transfer settings in low-level structured prediction tasks (Pires et al., 2019) and in comparison to models that use explicit multilingual information for a variety of tasks and languages (Wu and Dredze, 2019). Another focus of research has been the correlation between cross-lingual performance and shared vocabulary (e.g. as measured by wordpiece overlap). K et al. (2020) find no such correlation, suggesting that mBERT's success in zero-shot transfer must be due to cross-lingual mappings at a deeper linguistic level. However, it is not clear how this finding should be interpreted in light of the further finding that mBERT performs well (ca. 96%) at language identification on the WiLI data set[8].

Other work has taken this further by focusing on the hypothesis that mBERT encodings contain both a language-specific and a language-neutral component (Libovický et al., 2020). Gonen et al. (2020) set out to disentangle both components and find that in 'language identity subspace', t-SNE projections show large improvement in clustering with respect to language. In language-neutral space, semantic representations are largely intact. Dufter and Schütze (2020) show that smaller models result in better cross-lingual zero-shot learning. This could be due to there being less representational space allocated to language-specific information.

Some previous work has also shed light on the impact of training strategies on cross-lingual zero-shot learning. Tan and Joty (2021) show that training on code-switched data improves cross-lingual transfer, while Phang et al. (2020) show that intermediate task training, prior to fine-tuning proper, also results in better transfer with XLM-R (Conneau et al., 2020b). This is related to the present finding that mBERT representations become less language-specific after fine-tuning.

In this paper, we also experiment with techniques that specifically enforce language confusion, using entropy maximisation or gradient reversal. The latter has been used successfully for domain adaptation (Ganin and Lempitsky, 2015), while Libovický et al. (2020) use it for additional pre-training.

6 Conclusions

This paper explored the interplay between language-specific and language-neutral representations in the multilingual transformer model mBERT. Our results show that fine-tuning on specific tasks has a differential impact on how much language-specific information is retained. On the other hand, gradient reversal and iterative entropy maximisation interfere with fine-tuning and do not improve task performance.

Fine-tuning for tasks requiring identification of morphosyntactic properties, such as POS tagging, can result in greater loss of language-specific information, compared to deeper semantically-oriented tasks such as NLI[9].

However, there are also differences in the input data of these two tasks which could have impacted the results reported here. The data sets differ in their homogeneity (unlike XNLI, UDPOS is constructed from multiple sources) and size. The tasks also differ in their granularity, in that NLI is text-level, while POS is token-level. Furthermore, NLI is known to be susceptible to 'shortcut learning', whereby models rely on recurrent biases in training to solve the task (D'Amour et al.) whereas shortcuts in part of speech tagging are less known. These considerations are worthy of further investigation.

We believe these results contribute towards greater understanding of fine-tuning on multilingual model representations. This results in a reorganisation of the representation space, suggesting that language-specific and language-independent subspaces are dependent on task.

7 Ethical considerations

The experiments reported here rely on previously available data sets and/or data extracted from pub-

[8] `https://zenodo.org/record/841984`

[9] It could be argued that the model's loss of language-specific information is not due to the nature of fine-tuning, but due to the fact that fine-tuning is carried out using monolingual data (English). This could, in principle, imply that the model is not being given any indication that language-specific information should be retained. However, we find this an unlikely explanation since it does not account for the substantial difference in LID performance after fine-tuning on *different* tasks.

licly available sources. To ensure reproducibility, we will release all code, including scripts to regenerate the Wikipedia data set for language identification.

Acknowledgements

This research was supported by a Malta Enterprise Research and Development grant. We thank our collaborators, CityFalcon Ltd. Comments and questions by four anonymous reviewers are also gratefully acknowledged.

References

Mikel Artetxe, Sebastian Ruder, and Dani Yogatama. 2019. On the cross-lingual transferability of monolingual representations. In *Proceedings ofthe 58th Annual Meeting ofthe Association for Computational Linguistics (ACL'20)*, pages 4623–4637. Association for Computational Linguistics.

Samuel R Bowman, Gabor Angeli, Christopher Potts, and Christopher D Manning. 2015. A large annotated corpus for learning natural language inference. In *Proceedings of the 2015 Conference on Empirical Methods in Natural Language Processing*, pages 632–642, Lisbon, Portugal. Association for Computational Linguistics.

Rochelle Choenni and Ekaterina Shutova. 2020. What does it mean to be language-agnostic? probing multilingual sentence encoders for typological properties. *CoRR*, abs/2009.12862.

Alexis Conneau, Kartikay Khandelwal, Naman Goyal, Vishrav Chaudhary, Guillaume Wenzek, Francisco Guzman, Edouard Grave, Myle Ott, Luke Zettlemoyer, and Veselin Stoyanov. 2020a. Unsupervised Cross-lingual Representation Learning at Scale. In *Proceedings ofthe 58th Annual Meeting ofthe Association for Computational Linguistics (ACL'20)*, pages 8440–8451.

Alexis Conneau, Kartikay Khandelwal, Naman Goyal, Vishrav Chaudhary, Guillaume Wenzek, Francisco Guzmán, Edouard Grave, Myle Ott, Luke Zettlemoyer, and Veselin Stoyanov. 2020b. Unsupervised cross-lingual representation learning at scale. In *Proceedings of the 58th Annual Meeting of the Association for Computational Linguistics*, pages 8440–8451, Online. Association for Computational Linguistics.

Alexis Conneau and Guillaume Lample. 2019. Cross-lingual Language Model Pretraining. In *Proceedings of the 2019 Conference on Advances in Neural Information Processing Systems (NeurIPS'19)*, Online. Curran Associates, Inc.

Alexis Conneau, Ruty Rinott, Guillaume Lample, Adina Williams, Samuel Bowman, Holger Schwenk, and Veselin Stoyanov. 2018. XNLI: Evaluating cross-lingual sentence representations. In *Proceedings of the 2018 Conference on Empirical Methods in Natural Language Processing*, pages 2475–2485, Brussels, Belgium. Association for Computational Linguistics.

Alexander D'Amour, Katherine Heller, Dan Moldovan, Ben Adlam, Babak Alipanahi, Alex Beutel, Christina Chen, Jonathan Deaton, Jacob Eisenstein, Matthew D. Hoffman, Farhad Hormozdiari, Neil Houlsby, Shaobo Hou, Ghassen Jerfel, Alan Karthikesalingam, Mario Lucic, Yian Ma, Cory McLean, Diana Mincu, Akinori Mitani, Andrea Montanari, Zachary Nado, Vivek Natarajan, Christopher Nielson, Thomas F. Osborne, Rajiv Raman, Kim Ramasamy, Rory Sayres, Jessica Schrouff, Martin Seneviratne, Shannon Sequeira, Harini Suresh, Victor Veitch, Max Vladymyrov, Xuezhi Wang, Kellie Webster, Steve Yadlowsky, Taedong Yun, Xiaohua Zhai, and D. Sculley. Underspecification presents challenges for credibility in modern machine learning. *CoRR*.

Jacob Devlin, Ming-Wei Chang, Kenton Lee, and Kristina Toutanova. 2019. BERT: Pre-training of deep bidirectional transformers for language understanding. In *Proceedings of the 2019 Conference of the North American Chapter of the Association for Computational Linguistics: Human Language Technologies, Volume 1 (Long and Short Papers)*, pages 4171–4186, Minneapolis, Minnesota. Association for Computational Linguistics.

Philipp Dufter and Hinrich Schütze. 2020. Identifying elements essential for BERT's multilinguality. In *Proceedings of the 2020 Conference on Empirical Methods in Natural Language Processing (EMNLP)*, pages 4423–4437, Online. Association for Computational Linguistics.

Yaroslav Ganin and Victor Lempitsky. 2015. Unsupervised domain adaptation by backpropagation. In *Proceedings of the 32nd International Conference on Machine Learning*, volume 37 of *Proceedings of Machine Learning Research*, pages 1180–1189, Lille, France. PMLR.

Hila Gonen, Shauli Ravfogel, Yanai Elazar, and Yoav Goldberg. 2020. It's not Greek to mBERT: Inducing word-level translations from multilingual BERT. In *Proceedings of the Third BlackboxNLP Workshop on Analyzing and Interpreting Neural Networks for NLP*, pages 45–56, Online. Association for Computational Linguistics.

Junjie Hu, Sebastian Ruder, Aditya Siddhant, Graham Neubig, Orhan Firat, and Melvin Johnson. 2020. Xtreme: A massively multilingual multi-task benchmark for evaluating cross-lingual generalization. *CoRR*.

Karthikeyan K, Zihan Wang, Stephen Mayhew, and Dan Roth. 2020. Cross-lingual ability of multilingual bert: An empirical study. In *International Conference on Learning Representations*.

Anne Lauscher, Vinit Ravishankar, Ivan Vulić, and Goran Glavaš. 2020. From zero to hero: On the limitations of zero-shot language transfer with multilingual Transformers. In *Proceedings of the 2020 Conference on Empirical Methods in Natural Language Processing (EMNLP)*, pages 4483–4499, Online. Association for Computational Linguistics.

Jindřich Libovický, Rudolf Rosa, and Alexander Fraser. 2020. On the language neutrality of pre-trained multilingual representations. In *Findings of the Association for Computational Linguistics: EMNLP 2020*, pages 1663–1674, Online. Association for Computational Linguistics.

Marie-Catherine de Marneffe, Filip Ginter, Yoav Goldberg, Jan Hajič, Christopher Manning, Ryan McDonald, Joakim Nivre, Slav Petrov, Sampo Pyysalo, Sebastian Schuster, Natalia Silveira, Reut Tsarfaty, Francis Tyers, and Dan Zeman. 2020. Universal dependencies v2.7.

Jason Phang, Iacer Calixto, Phu Mon Htut, Yada Pruksachatkun, Haokun Liu, Clara Vania, Katharina Kann, and Samuel R. Bowman. 2020. English intermediate-task training improves zero-shot cross-lingual transfer too. In *Proceedings of the 1st Conference of the Asia-Pacific Chapter of the Association for Computational Linguistics and the 10th International Joint Conference on Natural Language Processing*, pages 557–575, Suzhou, China. Association for Computational Linguistics.

Telmo Pires, Eva Schlinger, and Dan Garrette. 2019. How multilingual is multilingual BERT? In *Proceedings of the 57th Annual Meeting of the Association for Computational Linguistics*, pages 4996–5001, Florence, Italy. Association for Computational Linguistics.

Taraka Rama, Lisa Beinborn, and Steffen Eger. 2020. Probing multilingual BERT for genetic and typological signals. In *Proceedings of the 28th International Conference on Computational Linguistics*, pages 1214–1228, Barcelona, Spain (Online). International Committee on Computational Linguistics.

Andrew Rosenberg and Julia Hirschberg. 2007. V-measure: A conditional entropy-based external cluster evaluation measure. In *Proceedings of the 2007 Joint Conference on Empirical Methods in Natural Language Processing and Computational Natural Language Learning (EMNLP-CoNLL)*, pages 410–420, Prague, Czech Republic. Association for Computational Linguistics.

Sebastian Ruder, Ivan Vulić, and Anders Søgaard. 2017. A Survey Of Cross-lingual Word Embedding Models. *CoRR*, pages 1–55.

Mark Sammons. 2015. Recognizing textual entailment. In Chris Lappin, Shalom and Fox, editor, *The Handbook of Contemporary Semantic Theory*, 2 edition, chapter 17, pages 523–557. John Wiley & Sons Ltd.

Samson Tan and Shafiq Joty. 2021. Code-mixing on sesame street: Dawn of the adversarial polyglots. In *Proceedings of the Fifth Workshop on Computational Approaches to Linguistic Code-Switching*, page 141, Online. Association for Computational Linguistics.

Ashish Vaswani, Noam Shazeer, Niki Parmar, Jakob Uszkoreit, Llion Jones, Aidan N. Gomez, and Łukasz Kaiser. 2017. Attention Is All You Need. In *Proceedings of the 31st Conference on Neural Informaton Processing Systems (NeurIPS'17)*, Long Beach, CA.

Adina Williams, Nikita Nangia, and Samuel Bowman. 2018. A broad-coverage challenge corpus for sentence understanding through inference. In *Proceedings of the 2018 Conference of the North American Chapter of the Association for Computational Linguistics: Human Language Technologies, Volume 1 (Long Papers)*, pages 1112–1122, New Orleans, Louisiana. Association for Computational Linguistics.

Shijie Wu and Mark Dredze. 2019. Beto, bentz, becas: The surprising cross-lingual effectiveness of BERT. In *Proceedings of the 2019 Conference on Empirical Methods in Natural Language Processing and the 9th International Joint Conference on Natural Language Processing (EMNLP-IJCNLP)*, pages 833–844, Hong Kong, China. Association for Computational Linguistics.

Appendix

A Data set details

When splitting data sets, a stratified split was used to preserve the proportions of different languages between splits.

UDPOS After filtering data so that only the 33 selected languages are used, we split the initial training set into a smaller training set (90%) and a validation set (10%). Non-English data was removed from the training set and validation set. The training set contains 18 906 sentences, the validation set contains 2 100 sentences, development set contains 66 062, and the test set contains 95 065 sentences.

XNLI We split the training set (which contains only English text) into a smaller training set (90%) and a validation set (10%). The training set contains 351 340 pairs of sentences, the validation set contains 39 037 pairs, development set contains 33 484, and the test set contains 67 459 pairs.

Wikipedia After randomly sampling 5 000 paragraphs per language from the 33 selected languages, we split the paragraphs into train/val/dev/test splits using 70/10/10/10% splits. The training set contains 115 500 paragraphs, the validation set contains 16 500 paragraphs, development set contains 16 500, and the test set contains 16 500 paragraphs. Text was extracted from the `20200420` Wikimedia dump using `wikiextractor`.[10]

B t-SNE/V-measure data sample

For t-SNE plots and V-measure computation, we use a random sample of data points. The samples were chosen such that a maximum number of points is shown from each label-language pair in the target data set, or from each language in the Wikipedia data set. Since different data sets have different numbers of label-language pairs, a different maximum is chosen for each data set in order to keep them similarly sized in total.

For UDPOS, which has the largest number of language-label pairs, only a maximum of 10 points are shown from each pair. This results in 5 013 points in total.

XNLI has three different labels, so a maximum of 50 points is shown from each pair. This results in 2 100 points in total.

Wikipedia has no labels and a maximum of 100 points is shown from each language. This results in 3 300 points in total.

C Model training details

All experiments are conducted on a 64GB RAM server with an Intel(R) Xeon W-2123 8-core CPU (3.60GHz) and a GeForce Titan RTX2080 Ti GPU.

Experiments are conducted using PyTorch and the implementation of Multilingual BERT in the `transformers` Python library.[11] We use the Adam optimiser with a different learning rate for the mBERT model and for the classification layers, although both classification layers use the same learning rate.

The classification layers are initialised randomly using a normal distribution with mean zero. The mBERT encodings are passed through a dropout layer with a dropout rate of 0.1 before being passed to the classification layers.

We train the model for 5 epochs. A validation set is used to measure the model's performance after each epoch; we reserve the model at the best epoch out of the five.

When optimising the label classifier, the macro F1 score performance on the English data of the target task validation set is measured (only English is considered in order to be faithful to a cross-lingual zero-shot learning setting).

On the other hand, when optimising the language classifier, the macro F1 score performance on all of the Wikipedia validation set is measured (language labels are assumed to be available during zero-shot learning).

In the gradient reversal experiments, only the target task validation set is used for determining which epoch gave the best model. Two mini-batches of the same size from the labelled data and the language data are used for each parameter update.

D Hyperparameter tuning

Hyperparameter tuning is conducted via random search over a fixed set of values per hyperparameter. Due to time constraints, only 20 random sets

[10] `https://github.com/attardi/wikiextractor`.

[11] `https://huggingface.co/bert-base-multilingual-cased`

Hyperparameter	Values
Init. standard deviation	1e-1, 1e-2, 1e-3
Minibatch size	64, 32, 16
Classifier learning rate	1e-1, 1e-2, 1e-3, 1e-4
mBERT learning rate	1e-3, 1e-4, 1e-5, 1e-6
Gradient reversal lambda	0.1, 0.3, 0.5, 0.7
Entropy max. weighting	0.1, 0.3, 0.5, 0.7

Table 4: Sets of hyperparameter values sampled from during hyperparameter tuning.

of hyperparameters are sampled for each experiment. The development set is used to evaluate hyperparameters during hyperparameter tuning and only the label classifier is evaluated. Hyperparameters that best fit the label classifier are also used in the language classifier.

The hyperparameter values used in the random search are given in Table 4. Selected hyperparameter values for each model are given in Table 5.

E Results on XNLI after language unlearning

In Figure 5 and Figure 6 we reproduce the visualisations after gradient reversal and entropy maximisation, when the model is fine-tuned on UD-POS and XNLI respectively.

Experiment	Hyperparameters
UDPOS frozen	init. stddev.: 1e-01, minibatch size: 16, class. learning rate: 1e-03
UDPOS fine-tuned	init. stddev.: 1e-02, minibatch size: 64, mBERT learning rate: 1e-04, class. learning rate: 1e-01
UDPOS grad. rev.	init. stddev.: 1e-03, minibatch size: 32, mBERT learning rate: 1e-06, class. learning rate: 1e-03, grad. rev. λ: 0.1
UDPOS ent. max.	init. stddev.: 1e-02, minibatch size: 32, mBERT learning rate: 1e-06, class. learning rate: 1e-02, entropy max. w: 0.7
XNLI frozen	init. stddev.: 1e-02, minibatch size: 64, class. learning rate: 1e-02
XNLI fine-tuned	init. stddev.: 1e-03, minibatch size: 64, mBERT learning rate: 1e-05, class. learning rate: 1e-02
XNLI grad. rev.	init. stddev.: 1e-03, minibatch size: 32, mBERT learning rate: 1e-06, class. learning rate: 1e-03, grad. rev. λ: 0.1
XNLI ent. max.	init. stddev.: 1e-01, minibatch size: 32, mBERT learning rate: 1e-06, class. learning rate: 1e-04, entropy max. w: 0.1

Table 5: Selected hyperparameter values used in training.

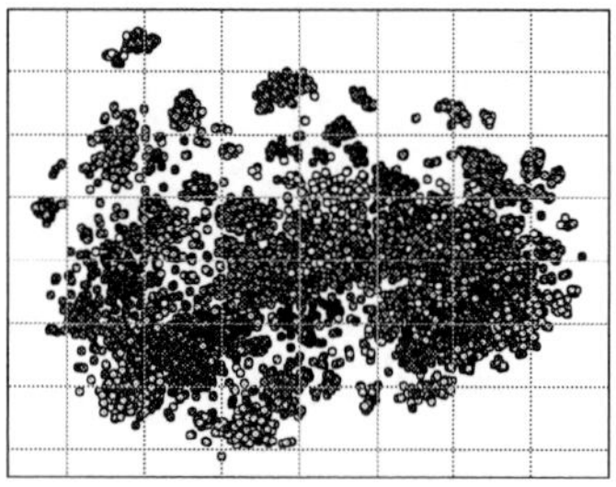

(a) UDPOS labels with gradient reversal (macro F1: 53.5%, V-measure: 22.8%).

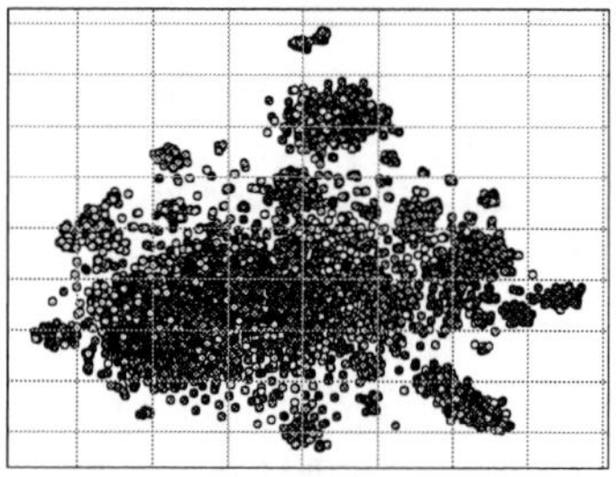

(b) UDPOS labels with entropy maximisation (macro F1: 56.8%, V-measure: 30.1%).

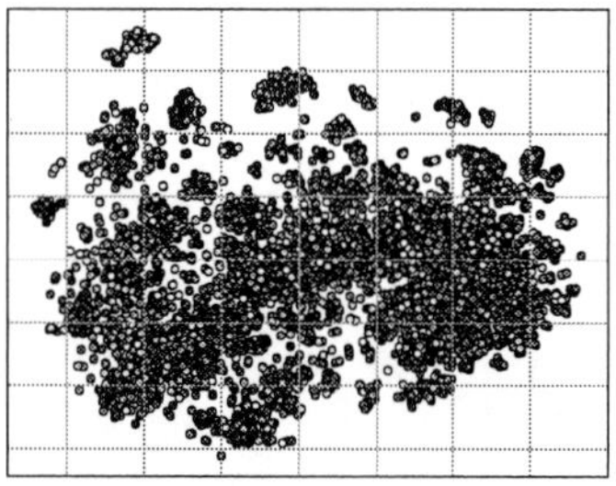

(c) UDPOS language clusters after gradient reversal (macro F1: 0.1%, V-measure: 12.5%).

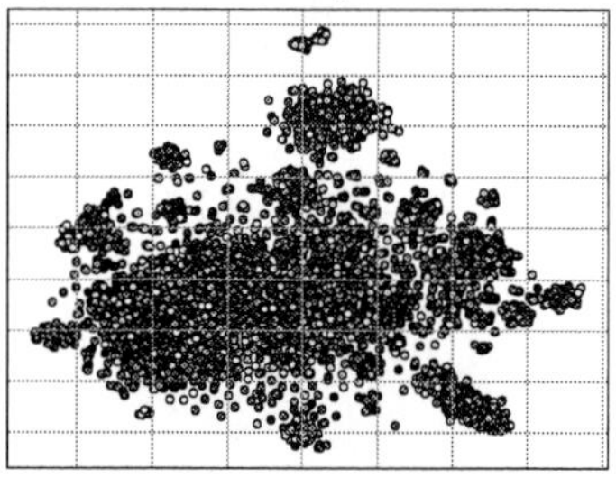

(d) UDPOS language clusters after entropy maximisation learned mBERT (macro F1: 5.5%, V-measure: 12.1%).

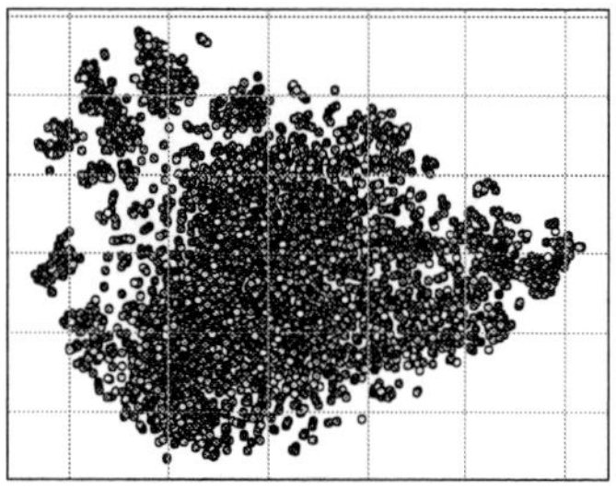

(e) Wikipedia language clusters after gradient reversal (macro F1: 0.1%, V-measure: 7.9%).

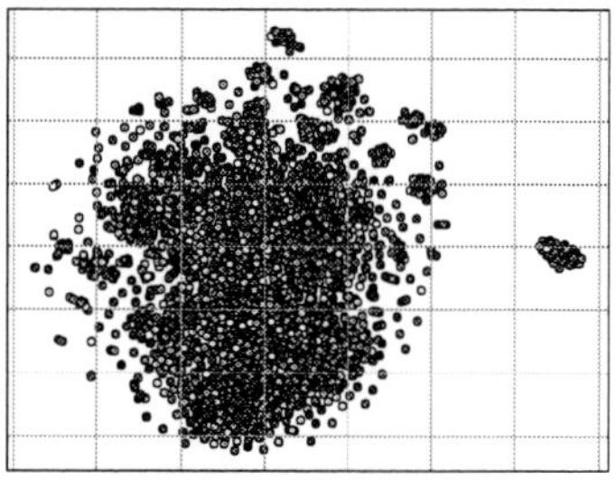

(f) Wikipedia language clusters after entropy maximisation (macro F1: 3.1%, V-measure: 9.6%).

Figure 5: Token based t-SNE plots of target task label and language clusters, after fine-tuning on UDPOS with gradient reversal or entropy maximisation. Each point is a randomly sampled token. Macro F1 scores for classification of mBERT embeddings is also given.

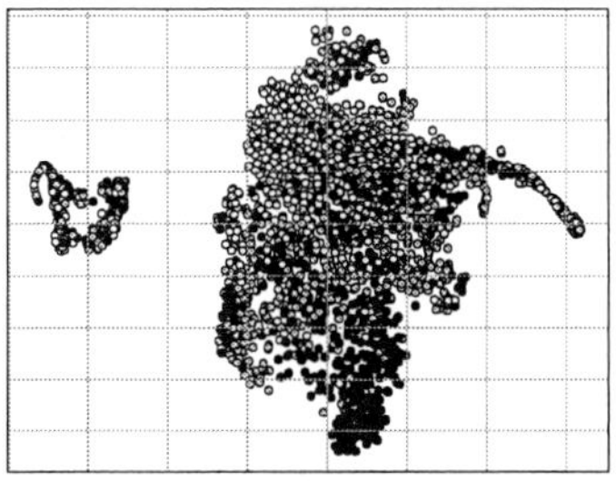

(a) XNLI labels with gradient reversal (macro F1: 62.2%, V-measure: 1.1%).

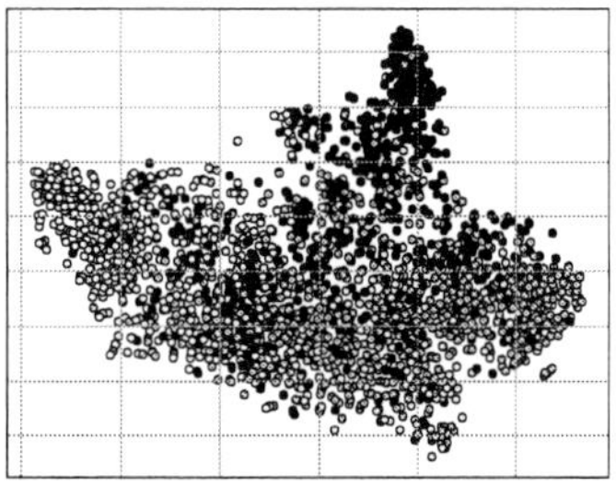

(b) XNLI labels with entropy maximisation (macro F1: 62.1%, V-measure: 12.2%).

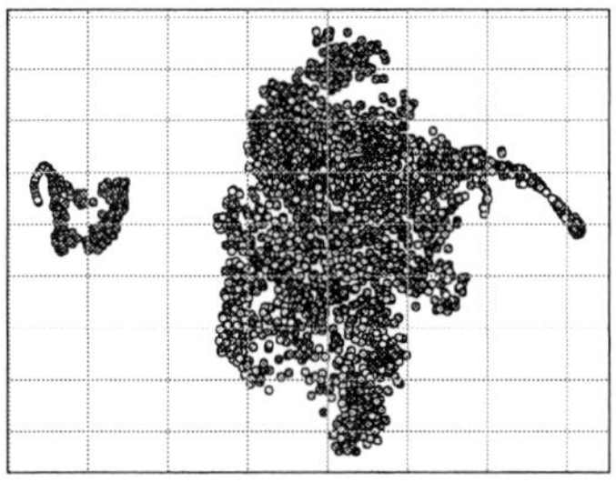

(c) XNLI languages with gradient reversal (macro F1: 1.3%, V-measure: 18.8%).

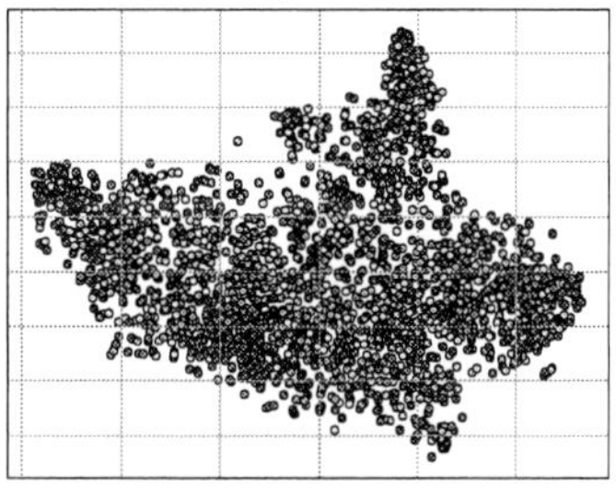

(d) XNLI languages with entropy maximisation (macro F1: 3.4%, V-measure: 20.0%).

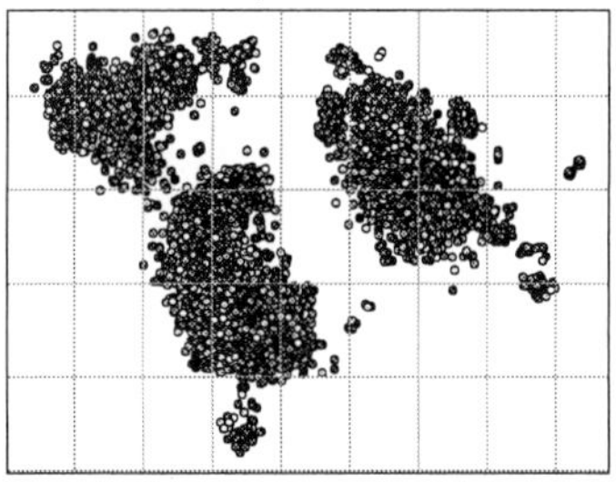

(e) Wikipedia languages with gradient reversal learned mBERT (macro F1: 1.5%, V-measure: 12.2%).

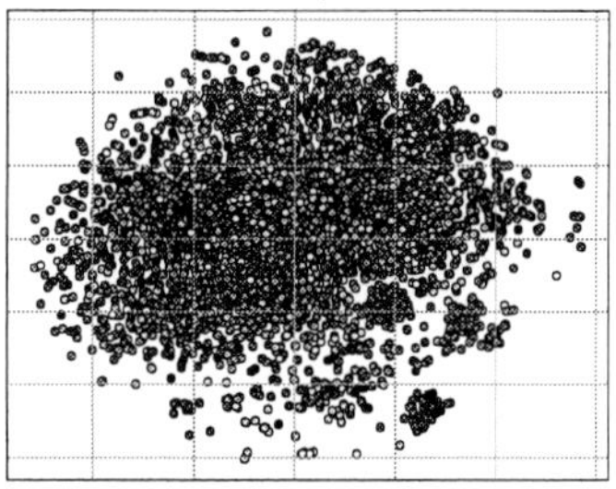

(f) Wikipedia languages with entropy maximisation learned mBERT (macro F1: 54.3%, V-measure: 14.7%).

Figure 6: Text-based t-SNE plots of language clusters, after fine-tuning on XNLI with gradient reversal or entropy maximisation. Macro F1 scores for classification of mBERT embeddings is also given.

Relating Neural Text Degeneration to Exposure Bias

Ting-Rui Chiang
Carnegie Mellon University
tingruic@andrew.cmu.edu

Yun-Nung Chen
National Taiwan University
y.v.chen@ieee.org

Abstract

This work focuses on relating two mysteries in neural-based text generation: exposure bias, and text degeneration. Despite the long time since exposure bias was mentioned and the numerous studies for its remedy, to our knowledge, its impact on text generation has not yet been verified. Text degeneration is a problem that the widely-used pre-trained language model GPT-2 was recently found to suffer from (Holtzman et al., 2020). Motivated by the unknown causation of the text degeneration, in this paper we attempt to relate these two mysteries. Specifically, we first qualitatively and quantitatively identify mistakes made before text degeneration occurs. Then we investigate the significance of the mistakes by inspecting the hidden states in GPT-2. Our results show that text degeneration is likely to be partly caused by exposure bias. We also study the self-reinforcing mechanism of text degeneration, explaining why the mistakes amplify. In sum, our study provides a more concrete foundation for further investigation on exposure bias and text degeneration problems.

1 Introduction

One mythology in neural text generation is *exposure bias* (Bengio et al., 2015; Pomerleau, 1989; Thrun, 1995). In the context of text generation, exposure bias refers to mistakes made by the model at the beginning of text generation, which may amplify, and lead the model to a state unseen in training time, and may thus cause misbehavior in the following generation. Phenomena related to exposure bias were first observed in (Pomerleau, 1989) in the self-driving vehicles field. After that, exposure bias was mainly discussed in the context of imitation learning (Thrun, 1995; Ross and Bagnell, 2010; Ross et al., 2011). In 2015, Bengio et al. (2015) introduced it in the context of neural text generation. However, its impact on text generation is questionable from both the empirical and the theoretical perspectives. Empirically, despite the number of studies for its remedy (Bengio et al., 2015; Huszár, 2015; Ranzato et al., 2016; Lamb et al., 2016; Yu et al., 2017; Wiseman and Rush, 2016; Schmidt, 2019; Zhang et al., 2019a), phenomena resulted from exposure bias have not yet been explicitly identified. On the other hand, theories attained in the context of imitation learning may not be applicable to the above text generation tasks. For example, (Ross and Bagnell, 2010) shows a $O(T^2)$ trend of cost with respect to the number of steps T in an episode. It implies that the cost grows quadratically when T is large. However, most of natural language process tasks, e.g. machine translation and image captioning, do not generate very long text. The impact of exposure bias is thus not clear for text generation tasks.

A younger mystery is the recently discussed enigma of *text degeneration* (Holtzman et al., 2020). It refers to the phenomenon in which bland or strange repetitive texts may be generated when the likelihood is the objective of generation, for example, when some commonly used strategies, such as greedy decoding and beam-search decoding, are used. Especially, the prior work (Holtzman et al., 2020) observed such problems in GPT-2 (Radford et al.), a pre-trained language model that has been shown useful in many NLP tasks (Radford, 2018; Zhang et al., 2019b; Petroni et al., 2019; Talmor et al., 2019; See et al., 2019). Despite many attempts proposed to address this issue (Holtzman et al., 2020; Welleck et al., 2020; Li et al., 2019), its root cause remains unknown.

Motivated by the unknown issues, we wonder whether text degeneration can be connected to the well-known exposure bias. If text degeneration is the misbehavior caused by exposure bias, it actually provides us a perfect opportunity to identify the existence of exposure bias. One of misbehavior of text degeneration is the occurrence of repetitive loops. It is a phenomenon that a model tends to

Proceedings of the Fourth BlackboxNLP Workshop on Analyzing and Interpreting Neural Networks for NLP, pages 228–239
Online, November 11, 2021.

GraphQL is an interesting technology originating at Facebook. ***It is a query language** that allows you to query a database and then query the database for the results.\n \n The query language is called QueryQL.* It is a query language ...
We first saw Anki Overdrive, the company's follow-up to the original game, in the early 2000s. It was a game that was a bit of a hit, and it was a game *that was a bit of a hit* that was a bit of a hit that was a hit that ...

Table 1: Randomly sampled examples generated by GPT-2 by greedy decoding. The **bold** part are the text conditioned on, and the *italic* part are the text in the repetitive loop.

repeat a span of text during generation (an example is shown in Table 1. This phenomenon is salient enough to be detected automatically, and occurs when greedy decoding strategy is used with high probability[1]. The easiness of spotting can help the identification of exposure bias. Therefore, this work aims at looking for the indications of exposure bias when repetitive loops are generated by the greedy decoding strategy. We will focus on GPT-2, because it is the only publicly available language model trained on a massive amount of data at the time this work is done, and is widely used by the community.

To the best of our knowledge, this paper is the first work that attempts to relate text degeneration to exposure bias. We first conclude two necessary conditions of its occurrence based on the intuition of exposure bias in literature in Section 3.4. We then inspect the two necessary conditions qualitatively and quantitatively. In Section 4.1, we find that before text repeating starts, GPT-2 generates unnatural text. In Section 4.3, we show that the hidden states of GPT-2 deviate to an area less similar to the states generated by encoding real text. The above observations satisfy the intuition of exposure bias that mistakes are made in the early stage and are amplified afterward. According to the indications we discover, we conclude that exposure bias is likely to co-occur with repetitive loops. Finally, we investigate how the mistakes are amplified after repetitive loops occur in Section 5. We discover the self-reinforcing mechanism of text degeneration. The results provide a possible outline of how a model is trapped in repetitive loops. These findings should be helpful for future studies on exposure bias and remedies for text degeneration.

[1]93% in our experiment.

2 Related Work

2.1 Exposure Bias in Imitation Learning

Imitation learning aims at imitating an expert policy π^* by learning from trajectories generated by the expert, namely finding the policy

$$\hat{\pi} = \arg\min_{\pi} \mathbb{E}_{s \sim d_{\pi^*}} I[\pi(s) = \pi^*(s)], \quad (1)$$

where d_{π^*} is the distribution of states visited by the expert policy π^*. It is very similar to training a language model with maximum likelihood objective, and has succeeded in many applications (Pomerleau, 1989; Schaal, 1999; Muller et al., 2006; Ratliff et al., 2006). However, it was mentioned in (Pomerleau, 1989) that when a model makes a mistake and thus encounters a state that the expert rarely encounters, it may fail to recover from the mistake. It was the first time the concept of exposure bias was mentioned. Similar issues were also considered in (Thrun, 1995; Daumé et al., 2009). Ross and Bagnell proved that the cost in a trajectory grows at the rate $O(T^2)$ instead of $O(T)$ if mistakes are made with a non-zero probability. It can be seen as a theoretical analysis of exposure bias. Nevertheless, in the context of text generation, the total number of steps in a trajectory is finite and is usually not large. Therefore, it is still not clear how meaningful this growth rate of cost is for text generation tasks. In Ross and Bagnell (2010); Ross et al. (2011), theoretically-grounded algorithms are proposed. However, they require the access of expert policy to annotate the trajectories generated by the learnt agent. It is generally not feasible in text generation tasks.

2.2 Exposure Bias in Text Generation

Then the concept of exposure bias is introduced in the context of text generation by (Bengio et al., 2015; Ranzato et al., 2016). Since then, there have been many methods proposed to tackle this problem (Bengio et al., 2015; Huszár, 2015; Ranzato et al., 2016; Lamb et al., 2016; Yu et al., 2017; Wiseman and Rush, 2016; Schmidt, 2019; Zhang et al., 2019a; Wang and Sennrich, 2020). They proposed their remedies based on the assumption that exposure bias is causing problems, and their approaches were justified by the improvement of performance when they are adopted. However, to our knowledge, He et al. (2019) is the only study attempting to verify the impact of exposure bias, where they proposed metrics for estimating the impact of exposure bias in models. Different from the prior work, this paper focuses on directly checking whether a specific phenomenon is the result of exposure bias.

2.3 Neural Text Degeneration

The term neural text degeneration was first defined recently in Holtzman et al. (2020), which focused on GPT-2. Similar phenomenon was also observed in LSTM language models (Strobelt et al., 2018). Regarding its causation, Welleck et al. (2020) summarized three possible reasons about repetitive loops generated by GPT-2: i) The Transformer architecture of GPT-2 prefers repeating. ii) Repeating is an intrinsic property of human language. iii) The model is unable to model real language usage due to the fixed training corpora. However, none of them have been proven theoretically or verified empirically.

Before this work, this phenomenon has not been linked to exposure bias, and thus remedies different from those for exposure bias are proposed. Holtzman et al. (2020) proposed sampling from the language model with nucleus sampling. Welleck et al. (2020) proposed to train neural language models with an unlikelihood as a regularization. Li et al. (2019) further applied unlikelihood training on dialogue tasks. Since in this work we discover the linkage between exposure bias and text degeneration, new approaches that specifically tackle exposure bias may be found effective for text degeneration in the future.

3 Background and Notations

To better elaborate the investigation of the above problems, background knowledge and notations are briefly introduced here.

3.1 Real and Artificial Passages

Considering that this paper focuses on analyzing the issues in text generation, we first define *real* passages as natural language and *artificial* passage as the generated language for following study.

Real Passages and Real Distribution *Real passages* and *real distribution* are related to training data. Given Y denoting the training set, a *real passage* $y \in Y$ is a sequence of tokens $\{y_1, y_2, \cdots, y_T\}$, and *real distribution* P_Y is the distribution passages $y \in Y$ are drawn from, and it can be factorized as

$$P_Y(y) = P_Y(y_1) \prod_{t=2}^{T} P_Y(y_t \mid y_1, y_2, \cdots, y_{t-1}). \quad (2)$$

Artificial Passages and Artificial Distribution A *artificial passage* $\hat{y}$ is a sequence of tokens $\{\hat{y}_1, \hat{y}_2, \cdots, \hat{y}_T\}$ generated by a model. We denote the set of generated passages as $\hat{Y}$, where each $\hat{y}$ is generated based on the conditional probability, $P_M(\hat{y}_t \mid \hat{y}_1, \hat{y}_2, \cdots, \hat{y}_{t-1})$, predicted by an auto-regressive language model M such as GPT-2. We define *artificial distribution* $P_{\hat{Y}}$ as the distribution of $\left\{\hat{y} \in \hat{Y}\right\}$ detailed below. Note that $P_{\hat{Y}}$ could be different from P_M, depending on the decoding strategy used. A decoding strategy is how a token $\hat{y}_t$ is chosen based on the conditional probability $P_M(\hat{y}_t \mid \hat{y}_1, \hat{y}_2, \cdots, \hat{y}_{t-1})$. In this work, we considered the greedy strategy and the sampling-based strategies, including the top-k candidates at each step (Fan et al., 2018), nucleus sampling (Holtzman et al., 2020). Details are included in the appendix.

3.2 States of GPT-2

GPT-2 is a pre-trained language model constituted with L layers of Transformer blocks (Vaswani et al., 2017). Considering that exposure bias is described as a general problem of neural text generation models, we pick GPT-2 as an example model for the study. When the tokens $\{y_t\}_{t=1,2,\cdots,T-1}$, which we refer to as the *conditioned passage*, are fed in, we denote the states outputted by each layers as

$$[h^{(y)}_{1,1}, h^{(y)}_{1,2}, \cdots, h^{(y)}_{1,T}] = \text{transformer}_1(\text{embedding}([y_1, \cdots, y_T])), \quad (3)$$

$$[h^{(y)}_{l,1}, h^{(y)}_{l,2}, \cdots, h^{(y)}_{l,T}] = \text{transformer}_l([h^{(y)}_{l-1,1}, \cdots, h^{(y)}_{l-1,T}]) \quad \forall l = 1, 2, ..., L. \quad (4)$$

It predicts the conditional probability as

$$P(y_T \mid \{y_t\}_{t=1 \dots T-1}) = \text{softmax}(\text{MLP}(h^{(\hat{y})}_{L,T-1}). \quad (5)$$

We refer to *real states* as the states outputted when $y \sim Y$ is fed in, and *artificial states* as the states when $\hat{y} \sim \hat{Y}$ is fed in. *States of a token y_t* refer to the set of states $\left\{h^{(y)}_{l,t}\right\}_{l=1,2,\cdots,L}$.

3.3 Repetitive Loops

Let the time step at which a passage $\hat{y}$ starts to repeat be ρ, and the length of the repeated part be λ. Then a passage $\hat{y}$, where a repetitive loop occurs, is of the form

$$\begin{aligned}\hat{y} =& \hat{y}_1, \hat{y}_2, \cdots, \hat{y}_{\rho-1}, \hat{y}_\rho, \cdots \hat{y}_{\rho+\lambda}, \\ & \hat{y}_\rho, \cdots \hat{y}_{\rho+\lambda}, \hat{y}_\rho, \cdots \hat{y}_{\rho+\lambda}, \cdots \end{aligned} \tag{6}$$

We refer to the repeated part $\hat{y}_\rho, \cdots \hat{y}_{\rho+\lambda}$ as a *looping sequence*.

3.4 Exposure Bias

In the literature, exposure bias was conceptually proposed (Bengio et al., 2015), which is described as the discrepancy between the way the model is used during training and the way during inference. When training, at the time step t, the model objective is to maximize the probability of the correct token y_t conditioning on the *real* past tokens $y_1, y_2, \cdots, y_{t-1}$. However, during inference, $\hat{y}_t$ is predicted conditioning on the *generated* past tokens $\hat{y}_1, \hat{y}_2, \cdots, \hat{y}_{t-1}$. Therefore, mistakes in the early stage may lead the model to a state unseen in training time, and errors may consequently amplify quickly.

More explicitly, based on the description of bias in Bengio et al. (2015), we summarize the necessary conditions as follow: If some misbehavior, such as repetitive loop, starts at time ρ is the result of exposure bias, then the two indications must be observed:

1. **Mistakes are made in the early phase:** In the context of text generation, qualitatively, it means the unnatural sequence is generated before time step ρ. Quantitatively, it means that $P_Y(\hat{y}_1, \hat{y}_2, \cdots, \hat{y}_{\rho-1})$, the likelihood that the previous generated text is real, is low.

2. **Mistakes are significant to the model:** The mistakes must be significant enough to lead the model to a state unseen in training time. Specifically, here we analyze the hidden states of GPT-2. We posit that, if some misbehavior is due to exposure bias, then the mistakes in the early stage should be significant enough to cause the model to generate an unseen state.

4 Relating Text Degeneration to Exposure Bias

In this section, we investigate whether the conditions in Section 3.4 are satisfied when text degeneration occurs.

4.1 Experimental Setting

As in Holtzman et al. (2020), we focus on the pretrained language model GPT-2[2]. GPT-2 is trained on the WebText dataset. We use the training, validation and testing subsets of WebText released by OpenAI [3].

When generating passages, first 50 tokens from passages $y \in Y$ are given as the condition. Therefore, for different conditions y, even if the decoding strategy is deterministic, the generated passages $\hat{y}$ could be different. We empirically observe that repetitive loops tend to occur later when the number of conditioned tokens is greater. We choose to condition on 50 tokens, so the sequences before repetitive loops are lengthy enough for analysis while the computation power required is affordable.

4.2 Qualitative Inspection on Generated Tokens Prior to Repetitive Loops

We inspect the first condition about exposure bias by *subjectively* examining the passages generated before a repetitive loop occurs. For each passage $\hat{y}$ generated by conditioning on $\{y\}_{t=1,2,\cdots,50}$, we compare the pair $\hat{y}_{t=51,\cdots,\rho-1}$ (generated) and $y_{t=51,\cdots,\rho-1}$ (real), where ρ is the time step where the repeating sentence first appears. We want to check if the model does make mistakes during $t = 51, \cdots, \rho - 1$. We manually examine 50 randomly sampled pairs [4]. We observe that the generated passages are often less informative, less relevant or coherent to $\{y\}_{t=1}^{50}$. As a result, without knowing which passage in the pair is real, we can still correctly identify the generated ones for 78% of them. We also inspect the sequence pairs from time 0 to $\rho + \lambda - 1$, the time step *after* which the model starts to repeat. In that case, our correctness is even higher, up to 92%. Note that even though the annotation is not done by many people, the fact that the fake sentences can be identified accurately is suffice to claim that a portion of passages generated in the early stage are perceivably dissimilar to real language. Namely $P_Y(\hat{y}_1, \hat{y}_2, \cdots, \hat{y}_{\rho-1})$ and

[2]We use the implementation from Hugging Face (`https://huggingface.co/transformers/index.html`).

[3]`https://github.com/openai/gpt-2-output-dataset`

[4]We didn't use crowdsource, since this inspection needs to be done very carefully, and workers could be uncareful.

$P_Y(\hat{y}_1, \hat{y}_2, \cdots, \hat{y}_{\rho+\lambda-1})$ is low from human judgement. Thus, qualitatively we can say mistakes are made before the repeating loop occurs. It satisfies the first condition of expsure bias.

4.3 Quantitative Inspection on Generated Tokens Prior to Repetitive Loops

We further inspect the first condition of exposure bias *quantitavely* and *objectively*. We want to estimate $P_Y(\hat{y}_1, \hat{y}_2, \cdots, \hat{y}_{\rho-1})$, the likelihood $\hat{y}_1, \hat{y}_2, \cdots, \hat{y}_{\rho-1}$ is real. However, the true P_Y is not tractable. Using an auto-regressive model to estimate the likelihood is not feasible either, since they may give higher probability to passages that is also generated by auto-regressive models and thus favor GPT-2. Thus we use a pre-trained masked language model RoBERTa-Large (Liu et al., 2019). It is trained non-autoregressively, so it does not favor auto-regressively generated passages. Therefore it should be a good proxy estimating the realness of the passages generated by GPT-2.

Specifically, to estimate the likelihood of tokens in a passage, real passages and artificial passages with repetitive loops are fed in RoBERTa with 15% randomly selected tokens masked. Log likelihood of recovering the masked tokens is calculated. To anneal the randomness due to the selection of masked tokens, this process is repeated 10 times for each passage. Finally, the likelihood for each time step is averaged.

Figure 1 shows that the likelihood of the generated passages is generally lower than real text starting from the time step where the conditioned passages end (dashed line). Especially, even though the likelihood of the text generated with greedy decoding strategy grows after a few time steps, the likelihood drop significantly at the beginning. Considering that the mask language model is sensitive to the context around the masked token, it may indicate that the text generated at the beginning is very unnatural.

4.4 Significance of Mistakes Prior to Repetitive Loops

We then check how significant the mistakes are to the GPT-2 model. Though the previous sections have shown the existence of the mistakes in the early stage. However, to cause misbehavior, the mistakes must be significant enough to cause GPT-2 to behave differently. Therefore, we check how differently GPT-2 processes the generated text compared to the way it processes the real ones.

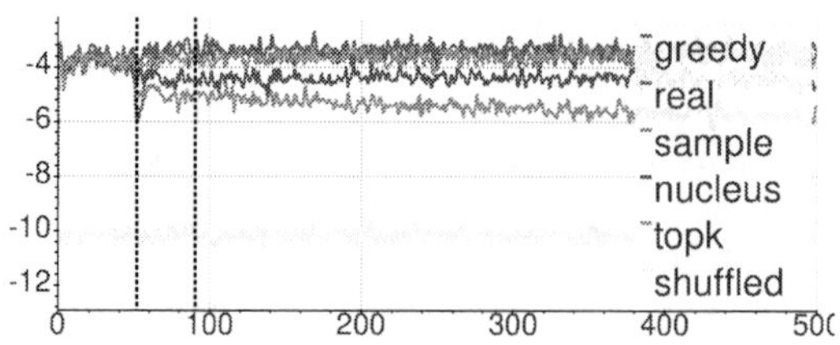

Figure 1: The average log likelihood (y-axis) predicted by RoBERTa at each time step (x-axis). The first dotted line is the averaged length of prefix, and the second one is the averaged ρ.

4.4.1 Measuring the Significance of Mistakes

To measure the significance of mistakes, we inspect the hidden states of GPT-2 when generating passages. For each layer $l > 1$ and time step t, the artificial state $h_{l,t}^{(\hat{y})}$ is the result of applying the transformer function $l - 1$ times over the input sequence $\{\hat{y}_{l-1,\tau}\}_{\tau=1\ldots t-1}$, which is the prefix of the artificial passage. Therefore, if a artificial state $h_{l,t}^{(\hat{y})}$ is significantly dissimilar to any real states, then it implies that the generated passage $\{\hat{y}_{l-1,\tau}\}_{\tau=1\ldots t-1}$ contains mistakes that are significant to the model, and that the mistakes do lead the model to an unseen state. Thus, the similarity between the artificial states and the real state indicates how significant the mistakes in the passage are.

Specifically, we measure how many real state is similar to a artificial state. It is done by counting the number of real states in the neighbor of the artificial state. A lower number of real neighborhoods suggests that the artificial state is more unseen, and thus implies higher significance of the mistakes.

Formally, given a hidden state $h_{l,t}^{(\hat{y})}$ at the time step t in the layer l, we count the number of real states in a support set $H_{l,t}^{Y}$ which is close to $h_{l,t}^{(\hat{y})}$:

$$N(h_{l,t}^{(\hat{y})}) = \left|\left\{ \left\| h_{l,t}^{(\hat{y})} - h \right\|_2 < r \middle| h \in H_{l,t}^{Y} \right\}\right| \quad (7)$$

where r is the predefined radius.

We use different $H_{l,t}$ depending on the layer l and the time step t of the hidden state $h_{l,t}^{(\hat{y})}$ to be considered. We compare $h_{l,t}^{(\hat{y})}$ only with the real states of the same layer, $H_{l,t}^{Y}$ only contains state of the same layer. To reduces the required computation power, we also limit the set $H_{l,t}$ to the state of the tokens whose time step differ to t by less than δ[5]. This limitation is reasonable, because we found

[5] We use $\delta = 5$.

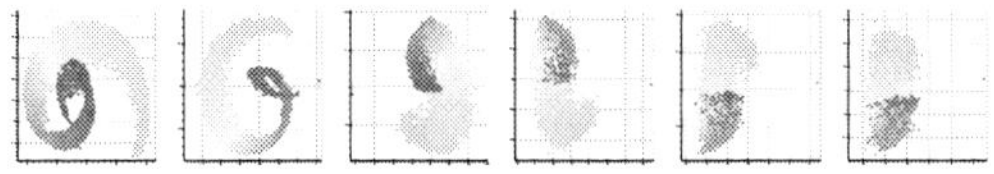

Figure 2: Hidden states projected to their first two principal components. Figures from left to right include states in layers 1, 3, 5, 7, 9, 11. Colors from red to green indicate the time steps from 0 to 512.

the position of the states are time-step-dependent. We found this by projecting the real states to their first two principle components with PCA (Pearson, 1901). As shown in figure 2, states of nearby time steps are clustered together. Formally, the support set of real neighbors is written as

$$H_{l,t}^{Y} = \{h_{l,\tau}^{(y)} \mid \tau \in [t-\delta, t+\delta], y \in Y\}. \quad (8)$$

Note that the constitution of $H_{l,t}^{Y}$ depends on a set of real passages Y. We will discuss the choice of Y in the next section.

4.4.2 Experimental Setting

Roughly speaking, we perform our experiment with two sets of passages Y_{sup} and Y_{cond}. We use Y_{cond} to generate real states, and from them we build $H_{l,t}^{Y_{cond}}$ for all layer l and time step t. $H_{l,t}^{Y_{cond}}$ can be used to evaluate any state of layer l and t. As for Y_{cond}, we use it to generate states to be evaluated. By using the prefix of $y \in Y_{cond}$ as condition, we can use it to generate artificial passage $\hat{Y}$ and artificial states. We also generate real states by encoding the whole $y \in Y_{cond}$ with GPT-2. We expect that the states of $y \in Y_{cond}$ to be similar to the states of $y \in Y_{sup}$, while the artificial state $\hat{y} \in \hat{Y}$ to be dissimilar to the artificial ones. Specifically, we conduct the experiment with the following steps:

1. We prepare two disjoint sets of sequences Y_{cond} and Y_{sup}. There two sets are parts of the union of the training, validation and testing subsets of WikiText released by OpenAI (as described in Section 4.1).
2. For all y in Y_{sup}, we collect a set of real states h_{sup} by using GPT-2 to encode y. These real states are used to construct the $H_{l,t}$ as mentioned in 8.
3. For all y in Y_{cond}, we generate artificial sequences $\hat{y}$ by conditioning GPT-2 on the first 50 tokens of $y_{cond} \in Y_{cond}$. We experiment with the generation strategies mentioned in Section 3.1. The hidden states $\hat{h}$ are also collected.
4. For all y in Y_{cond}, we also use GPT-2 to encode the whole passage y and collect the states h_{cond}. Since the sequences $y \in Y_{cond}$ are real, the states h_{cond} are real too.
5. Finally, we evaluate how the states collected with Y_{cond} are similar to the real states from Y_{real}. We calculate $N(\hat{h})$, the numbers of artificial states' real neighbor in h_{sup}. We also use y_{cond} calculate $N(h_{cond})$. It is referred to as "real" in Figure 3 and 4.

We prepare Y_{sup} and Y_{cond} in two ways:

compare-seen The training split is used as Y_{sup}. It is *seen* when training. Real passages in the validation split and the testing split are used as Y_{cond}.

compare-unseen The union of the validation split and the testing split is split into two disjoint subsets by ratio 9:1. They are used as Y_{sup} and Y_{cond} respectively. Y_{sup} is *unseen* when training.

4.4.3 Sanity Check

We experiment with a set of *shuffled* states as a sanity check of our approach. It verifies whether the number of neighbors is an indicative measure of the significance of mistakes. The *shuffled* set is constructed by first shuffling the real passages in the Y_{cond}, and is then encoded with GPT-2. The shuffled passages have the same 1-gram distribution as real natural language, but have low likelihood to be real. We expect them to have low numbers of real neighbors.

The results show that the number of real neighbors is a good indication of mistakes for middle layers from layer 5 to layer 9 when $r = 1024$ for both the compare-seen and compare-unseen settings. For smaller $r \in 32, 64, 128, 256, 512$, the results are not stable. The average number of neighbors for different time steps at the seventh layer is plot in figure 3. We include the results of other layers in the appendix. The figure shows that the number of neighbors of the *shuffled* states are consistently low for all time steps. It implies that the number of neighbors is indicative for detecting unreal passages. However, it is less indicative when R is small. We posit that it is due to the high sparsity of the states due to their high dimensionality [6].

4.4.4 Results

Figure 3 also plots the number of real neighbors (h) for states generated with greedy strategy and the sampling-based strategies ($\hat{h}$). For the greedy strategy, the number of neighbors declines rapidly

[6]Each state $\in \mathcal{R}^{1536}$

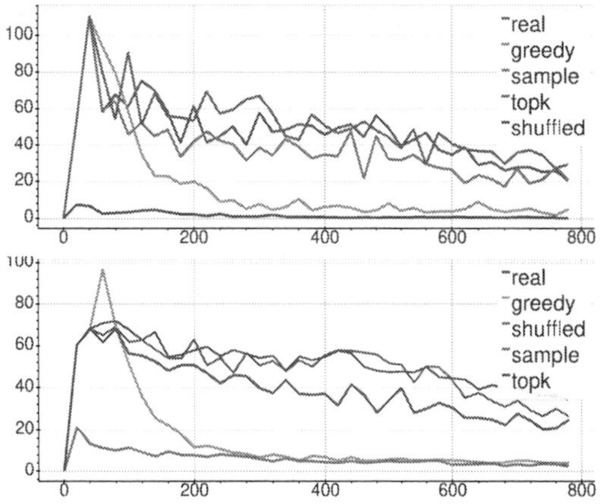

Figure 3: Number of neighbors in the *seen-case* (top) and *unseen-case* (bottom) at layer 7. The x-axis is the time step of the tokens. The y-axis is the number of real neighbors with the radius.

when the time step increases. Note that we observe that repetitive loops occur in about 93% of the sequences. It shows that GPT-2 indeed fails to recover from mistakes, and the mistakes are amplified through time. It is aligned with the description of exposure bias. On the other hand, compared with real sequences (the control group), the number only decreases slightly when sampling-based strategies are used. In contrast to the case of greedy decoding, repetitive loops are rarely observed when those sampling-based methods are used ($< 1\%$ for all of the strategies). It implies that if GPT-2 has misbehavior when using those strategies, the misbehavior is less likely to be related to exposure bias.

We further inspect the number of neighbors of the artificial state prior to the time step $\rho + \lambda$, when a repetitive loop starts. We want to know whether the model does make significant mistakes before $\rho + \lambda$. It is not shown in Figure 3, as it only shows the significance of mistakes in the late stage. To this end, we plot the number of neighbors again in Figure 4. Different from Figure 3, in Figure 4, the x-axis is the time step *relative to* $\rho + \lambda$, so the significance of mistakes before repetitive loops can be manifested. In particular, we compare the number of real neighbors around the real states and the artificial states. Formally, for each artificial passage $\hat{y}$ conditioning on $y_{1,2,\cdots,50}$, we compare the number of neighbors around the state of $n_{l,t}^{(\hat{y})}$, and the state of the real passage following the condition $n_{l,t}^{(y)}$. Here we set the y-axis of Figure 4 to be the difference $(n_{l,t}^{(\hat{y})} - n_{l,t}^{(y)})$.

Surprisingly, in Figure 4, the *compare-seen* and *compare-unseen* settings show different trends. At the beginning, the number of neighbors decreases relatively slowly in both of the two settings. At around $x = -10$, the number in both of them drop to less than zero. It indicates that at this time step, some significant mistakes are made. However, the number in the *compare-seen* setting dramatically grows while the number continues decreasing in the *compare-unseen* setting. The low number of neighbors in the *compare-unseen* indicates the low realness of the generated passages. The high number of neighbors in the *seen-setting* indicates that the model encodes those unreal passages to space close to the states of training data. It may imply that, at this moment, the model fails to generalize, so it incorrectly encodes the unreal passages as seen ones. Finally, the mistakes are amplified. Consequently, the number in both of the settings drops to less than zero. In sum, Figure 4 shows the significance of mistakes made before it starts repeating a looping sequence. Therefore, the second indication of exposure bias is observed.

Table 2: Similarity between the conditioned passage and the generated passage of the same length.

Conditioned Sentences	Similarity (mean/std)
Looping sequences	0.7327 / 0.3226
First sentences	0.2157 / 0.1911
Last sentences	0.1837 / 0.1848

Repeat #	Looping Seq.	First Sent.	Last Sent.
1	0.451 / 0.368	0.148 / 0.155	0.131 / 0.144
2	0.681 / 0.423	0.331 / 0.373	0.337 / 0.377
3	0.888 / 0.282	0.492 / 0.435	0.578 / 0.431

Table 3: The ROUGE-L (mean/std) between the sentences in the generated repetitive loops and x, when GPT-2 conditions on the pattern $c, x, \cdots, x$.

5 Mechanisms after a Repetitive Loop Starts

While the above experiments show the indications of exposure bias, in this section we further investigate how the early stage mistakes cause the model to degenerate. Figure 4 indicates some mistakes are made prior to time step $\rho + \lambda$. Thus, in this section, we investigate the characteristics of the

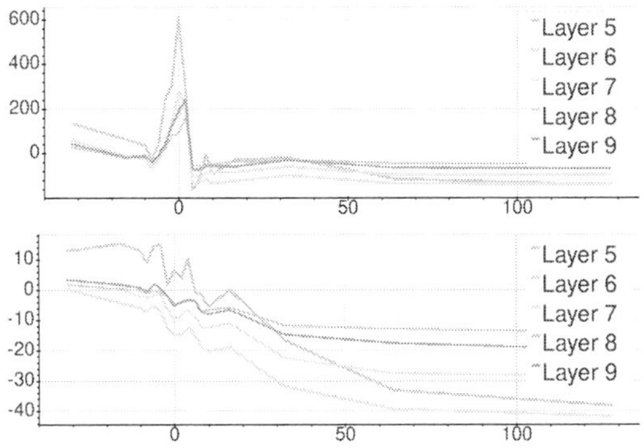

Figure 4: Number of neighbors for setting *compare-seen* (upper) and *compare-unseen* (lower). The x-axis is the time step of the tokens *relative to* $\rho + \lambda$. The y-axis is $(n_{l,t}^{(\hat{y})} - n_{l,t}^{(y)})$.

sequence generated prior to $\rho + \lambda$, the looping sequence $\hat{y}_\rho \cdots \hat{y}_{\rho+\lambda}$ (as defined in Section 3.3).

5.1 The Looping Sequence is Loop-Inducing

We investigate how the looping sequences are loop-inducing by using them as conditions when generating text. We construct a *looping sequence* set that is constituted with all looping sequences generated when conditioning on the first 50 tokens of real sequences. In a generated sequence $\hat{y}$, since $\hat{y}_\rho$ may not be a start point of a grammatical sentence, we use the sequence $\hat{y}_{\rho+\delta+1}, \cdots, \hat{y}_{\rho+\lambda}\hat{y}_\rho \cdots \hat{y}_{\rho+\delta}$, where δ is chosen based on the punctuation in it [7]. As control groups, we also construct two real sequence sets, *first sentence* set and *last sentence* set. They consist of the first sentence and the last sentence of the articles in WikiText validation split and testing split.

To measure how those sequences are looping-inducing, we calculate the similarity between x and $\hat{y}$, where x is the sequence used as condition, and $\hat{y}$ is the generated passage. Specifically, we measure ROUGE-L (Lin, 2004)[8] between x and the first $\text{length}(x)$ tokens of $\hat{y}$. A higher score implies higher similarity, and thus more looping-inducing. Results shown in Table 2 indicate that looping sequences are indeed more loop-inducing.

5.2 Any Repeating Sequence is Loop-Inducing

We further discover that any sequence that is repeated is loop-inducing, regardless of contexts. We create the conditioned sequence by concatenating c with x repeated from 1 to 3 times, where c is the first 5 sentences from a random article of WebText, and x is either from the *looping sequence* set or the real sets. Measurement, the same as in Section 5.1 is applied on x and the generated passages. The results are shown in Table 3, and it shows that even when the conditioned sequence is real, it is more loop-inducing if it is repeated more times.

5.3 The Self-Reinforcing Mechanism of Text Degeneration

In sum, in this section, we discover the self-reinforcing mechanism of text degeneration. First, Section 5.1 a looping sequence is loop-inducing. Thus, after a looping sequence is generated, it is likely to be repeated. Second, Section 5.2 shows that when a sequence is repeated, then GPT-2 would be more likely to continue repeating it. Therefore, it shows how GPT-2 fails to recover from the mistake.

6 Conclusion

In conclusion, we provide a deeper insight into the relation between exposure bias and text degeneration. We qualitatively and quantitatively show that mistakes are indeed made in the early stage of generation. In Particular, some significant mistakes are made prior to $\rho + \lambda$, the time step when the model starts repeating. We then show why the model fails to recover from the mistakes. The looping sequence, which is the sequence generated prior to $\rho + \lambda$, and repeated sequences are looping-inducing. That is how the model fails to recover from the mistakes, and how the mistakes amplify.

Our contributions are four-fold: 1) We explicitly formulate the necessary indications for the detection of exposure bias. 2) For each condition, we design the associated experiments for validation. 3) By the experiments, we show that text degeneration is likely to be partly caused by exposure bias. 4) Finally, we provide a possible explanation how GPT-2 fails to recover from the mistake. Our formulation and the conducted experiments build a solid foundation for future study on exposure bias.

[7]For example, if the looping sequence is "an apple. It is", we use "It is an apple."

[8]We use the implementation in https://github.com/google-research/google-research/tree/master/rouge.

Acknowledgements

We would like to than Ting-Yun Chang for in-depth discussions. We are thankful to the anonymous reviewers for their insightful comments on the paper. This work was financially supported from the Young Scholar Fellowship Program by Ministry of Science and Technology (MOST) in Taiwan, under Grant 110-2636-E-002-003.

References

Samy Bengio, Oriol Vinyals, Navdeep Jaitly, and Noam Shazeer. 2015. Scheduled sampling for sequence prediction with recurrent neural networks. In *Advances in Neural Information Processing Systems*, pages 1171–1179.

Hal Daumé, John Langford, and Daniel Marcu. 2009. Search-based structured prediction. *Machine learning*, 75(3):297–325.

Angela Fan, Mike Lewis, and Yann Dauphin. 2018. Hierarchical neural story generation. *arXiv preprint arXiv:1805.04833*.

Tianxing He, Jingzhao Zhang, Zhiming Zhou, and James Glass. 2019. Quantifying exposure bias for neural language generation. *arXiv preprint arXiv:1905.10617*.

Ari Holtzman, Jan Buys, Li Du, Maxwell Forbes, and Yejin Choi. 2020. The curious case of neural text degeneration. In *International Conference on Learning Representations*.

Ferenc Huszár. 2015. How (not) to train your generative model: Scheduled sampling, likelihood, adversary? *arXiv preprint arXiv:1511.05101*.

Jeff Johnson, Matthijs Douze, and Hervé Jégou. 2017. Billion-scale similarity search with gpus. *arXiv preprint arXiv:1702.08734*.

Alex M Lamb, Anirudh Goyal Alias Parth Goyal, Ying Zhang, Saizheng Zhang, Aaron C Courville, and Yoshua Bengio. 2016. Professor forcing: A new algorithm for training recurrent networks. In *Advances In Neural Information Processing Systems*, pages 4601–4609.

Margaret Li, Stephen Roller, Ilia Kulikov, Sean Welleck, Y-Lan Boureau, Kyunghyun Cho, and Jason Weston. 2019. Don't say that! making inconsistent dialogue unlikely with unlikelihood training. *arXiv preprint arXiv:1911.03860*.

Chin-Yew Lin. 2004. ROUGE: A package for automatic evaluation of summaries. In *Text Summarization Branches Out*, pages 74–81, Barcelona, Spain. Association for Computational Linguistics.

Yinhan Liu, Myle Ott, Naman Goyal, Jingfei Du, Mandar Joshi, Danqi Chen, Omer Levy, Mike Lewis, Luke Zettlemoyer, and Veselin Stoyanov. 2019. Roberta: A robustly optimized bert pretraining approach. *arXiv preprint arXiv:1907.11692*.

Urs Muller, Jan Ben, Eric Cosatto, Beat Flepp, and Yann L Cun. 2006. Off-road obstacle avoidance through end-to-end learning. In *Advances in neural information processing systems*, pages 739–746.

Karl Pearson. 1901. Liii. on lines and planes of closest fit to systems of points in space. *The London, Edinburgh, and Dublin Philosophical Magazine and Journal of Science*, 2(11):559–572.

Fabio Petroni, Tim Rocktäschel, Sebastian Riedel, Patrick Lewis, Anton Bakhtin, Yuxiang Wu, and Alexander Miller. 2019. Language models as knowledge bases? In *Proceedings of the 2019 Conference on Empirical Methods in Natural Language Processing and the 9th International Joint Conference on Natural Language Processing (EMNLP-IJCNLP)*, pages 2463–2473, Hong Kong, China. Association for Computational Linguistics.

Dean A Pomerleau. 1989. Alvinn: An autonomous land vehicle in a neural network. In *Advances in neural information processing systems*, pages 305–313.

Alec Radford. 2018. Improving language understanding by generative pre-training.

Alec Radford, Jeffrey Wu, Rewon Child, David Luan, Dario Amodei, and Ilya Sutskever. Language models are unsupervised multitask learners.

Marc'Aurelio Ranzato, Sumit Chopra, Michael Auli, and Wojciech Zaremba. 2016. Sequence level training with recurrent neural networks. In *4th International Conference on Learning Representations, ICLR 2016, San Juan, Puerto Rico, May 2-4, 2016, Conference Track Proceedings*.

Nathan D Ratliff, J Andrew Bagnell, and Martin A Zinkevich. 2006. Maximum margin planning. In *Proceedings of the 23rd international conference on Machine learning*, pages 729–736.

Stéphane Ross and Drew Bagnell. 2010. Efficient reductions for imitation learning. In *Proceedings of the thirteenth international conference on artificial intelligence and statistics*, pages 661–668.

Stéphane Ross, Geoffrey Gordon, and Drew Bagnell. 2011. A reduction of imitation learning and structured prediction to no-regret online learning. In *Proceedings of the fourteenth international conference on artificial intelligence and statistics*, pages 627–635.

Stefan Schaal. 1999. Is imitation learning the route to humanoid robots? *Trends in cognitive sciences*, 3(6):233–242.

Florian Schmidt. 2019. Generalization in generation: A closer look at exposure bias. In *Proceedings of the 3rd Workshop on Neural Generation and Translation*, pages 157–167, Hong Kong. Association for Computational Linguistics.

Abigail See, Aneesh Pappu, Rohun Saxena, Akhila Yerukola, and Christopher D. Manning. 2019. Do massively pretrained language models make better storytellers? In *Proceedings of the 23rd Conference on Computational Natural Language Learning (CoNLL)*, pages 843–861, Hong Kong, China. Association for Computational Linguistics.

Hendrik Strobelt, Sebastian Gehrmann, Michael Behrisch, Adam Perer, Hanspeter Pfister, and Alexander M Rush. 2018. Seq2seq-vis: A visual debugging tool for sequence-to-sequence models. *IEEE transactions on visualization and computer graphics*, 25(1):353–363.

Alon Talmor, Jonathan Herzig, Nicholas Lourie, and Jonathan Berant. 2019. CommonsenseQA: A question answering challenge targeting commonsense knowledge. In *Proceedings of the 2019 Conference of the North American Chapter of the Association for Computational Linguistics: Human Language Technologies, Volume 1 (Long and Short Papers)*, pages 4149–4158, Minneapolis, Minnesota. Association for Computational Linguistics.

Sebastian Thrun. 1995. Learning to play the game of chess. In *Advances in neural information processing systems*, pages 1069–1076.

Ashish Vaswani, Noam Shazeer, Niki Parmar, Jakob Uszkoreit, Llion Jones, Aidan N Gomez, Łukasz Kaiser, and Illia Polosukhin. 2017. Attention is all you need. In *Advances in neural information processing systems*, pages 5998–6008.

Chaojun Wang and Rico Sennrich. 2020. On exposure bias, hallucination and domain shift in neural machine translation. In *Proceedings of the 58th Annual Meeting of the Association for Computational Linguistics*, pages 3544–3552, Online. Association for Computational Linguistics.

Sean Welleck, Ilia Kulikov, Stephen Roller, Emily Dinan, Kyunghyun Cho, and Jason Weston. 2020. Neural text generation with unlikelihood training. In *International Conference on Learning Representations*.

Sam Wiseman and Alexander M. Rush. 2016. Sequence-to-sequence learning as beam-search optimization. In *Proceedings of the 2016 Conference on Empirical Methods in Natural Language Processing*, pages 1296–1306, Austin, Texas. Association for Computational Linguistics.

Lantao Yu, Weinan Zhang, Jun Wang, and Yong Yu. 2017. Seqgan: Sequence generative adversarial nets with policy gradient. In *Thirty-First AAAI Conference on Artificial Intelligence*.

Wen Zhang, Yang Feng, Fandong Meng, Di You, and Qun Liu. 2019a. Bridging the gap between training and inference for neural machine translation. In *Proceedings of the 57th Annual Meeting of the Association for Computational Linguistics*, pages 4334–4343, Florence, Italy. Association for Computational Linguistics.

Yizhe Zhang, Siqi Sun, Michel Galley, Yen-Chun Chen, Chris Brockett, Xiang Gao, Jianfeng Gao, Jingjing Liu, and Bill Dolan. 2019b. Dialogpt: Large-scale generative pre-training for conversational response generation. *arXiv preprint arXiv:1911.00536*.

A Sample-based Decoding Strategies

- Sampling: $\hat{y}_t$ is directly sampled from the conditional probability $P_M(\hat{y}_t \mid \hat{y}_1, \hat{y}_2, \cdots, \hat{y}_{t-1})$.
- Top-k sampling (Fan et al., 2018): At the time step t, $\hat{y}_t$ is sampled from the conditional probability:

$$P_Y(\hat{y}_t \mid \hat{y}_1, \hat{y}_2, \cdots, \hat{y}_{t-1}) \propto \begin{cases} P_M(\hat{y}_t \mid \hat{y}_1, \hat{y}_2, \cdots, \hat{y}_{t-1}) & \text{if } \hat{y}_t \in \text{top-}k, \\ 0 & \text{otherwise.} \end{cases} \tag{9}$$

- Nucleus sampling (Holtzman et al., 2020): At the time step t, $\hat{y}_t$ is sampled from the conditional probability

$$P_Y(\hat{y}_t \mid \hat{y}_1, \hat{y}_2, \cdots, \hat{y}_{t-1}) \propto \begin{cases} P_M(\hat{y}_t \mid \hat{y}_1, \hat{y}_2, \cdots, \hat{y}_{t-1}) & \text{if } \hat{y}_t \in V^{(p)} \\ 0 & \text{otherwise.} \end{cases}, \tag{10}$$

and for a predefined $p \in (0, 1]$, $V^{(p)}$ is the minimal set that satisfies

$$\sum_{v \in V^{(p)}} P_M(v \mid \hat{y}_1, \hat{y}_2, \cdots, \hat{y}_{t-1}) \geq p \tag{11}$$

B Dataset

We use the subsets of WebText released by OpenAI (`https://github.com/openai/gpt-2-output-dataset`). It is an English dataset. There are 25000, 5000, 5000 passages in the train, validation, testing splits respectively. For experiments in Section 4.3 and Section 4.4), we only use the passages with more than 512 tokens. After passages with less than 512 tokens are removed, there are 5269 passages in the union of the validation split and the testing split.

C Detail of Experiments

C.1 Quantitative Inspection of Generated Tokens Priors to Repetitive Loops (Section 4.3)

Implementation of RoBERTa from Python package transformers 2.8.0 by Hugging Face (`https://huggingface.co/transformers/`) is used.

C.2 Significance of Mistakes Prior to Repetitive Loops (Section 4.4)

We use Faiss (Johnson et al., 2017) to calculate the number of neighbor vectors within a radius. For Figure 3, the number of neighbors is calculated for 20 time steps. For Figure 4, the number of neighbors is calculated at time steps {-32, -16, -10, -8, -6, -4, -2, 0, 2, 4, 6, 8, 10, 16, 32, 64, 128} relative to $\rho + \lambda$.

Seen-setting: We sampled 2500 passages from the WebText training split. Each line in Figure 4 is the average over 500 passages generated by each decoding strategy. The result in Figure 4 is the average over 1000 passages.

Unseen-setting: We first combine the validation split and the testing split as the set of all real unseen text $\bar{Y}$. Then we split it into 10 equal-sized subsets $\bar{Y}_1, \bar{Y}_2, \cdots, \bar{Y}_{10}$. We repeat the following process 3 times:

- From $\{\bar{Y}_1, \bar{Y}_2, \cdots, \bar{Y}_{10}\}$, a subset Y_{real} is selected, and the rest $\bar{Y} \backslash Y_{real}$ is used as the support set $Y_{support}$.
- Real states are collected by encoding passages in $Y_{support}$ with GPT-2. When we are calculating the number of neighbors, only these real states are counted.
- Artificial passages are generated by conditioning on the first 50 tokens for passages in Y_{real} using the decoding strategies.
- The number of neighbors is calculated for each decoding strategies.

Finally, the result is averaged to plot Figure 3 and Figure 4.

C.3 Automatic Detection of Looping Sequence

Given a passage $x_1, x_2, \cdots, x_T$, we first search for the length of a repetitive loop by comparing $x_{T-\lambda+1}, \cdots x_T$ and $x_{T-2\lambda+1}, \cdots x_{T-\lambda}$ for $\lambda = 4, 5, \cdots, l/2, 1, 2, 3$. If there exists some λ such that $x_{T-\lambda+1}, \cdots, x_T = x_{T-2\lambda+1}, \cdots, x_{T-\lambda}$, then we search ρ as the first place such that $x_{\rho+i\lambda}, \cdots, x_{\rho+(i+1)\lambda-1} = x_{T-2\lambda+1+\delta}, \cdots, x_{T-\lambda+\delta}$ for some $\delta \in [0, \lambda - 1]$ and all i such that $\rho + i\lambda < T$.

D Computing Infrastructure

Each of our experiments were run on a workstation with 187 GiB RAM. A workstation is equipped with either two Intel Xeon 5218 CPUs or two Intel Xeon 4110 CPUs. Every experiment can be run with 1 Nvidia GTX 2080Ti GPU.

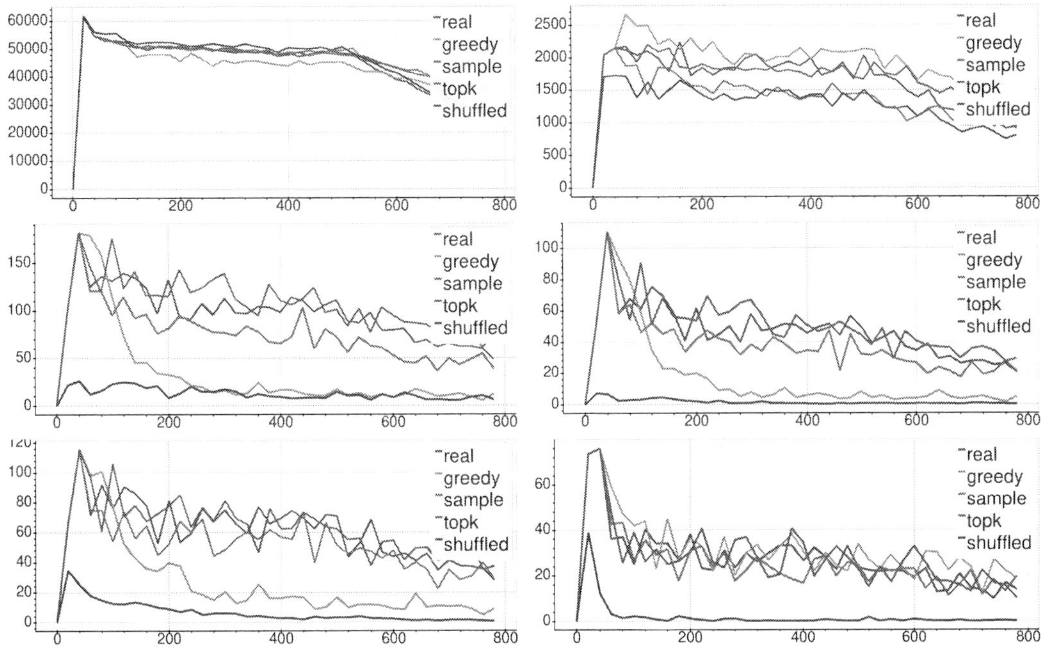

Figure 5: Number of neighbors for *compare-seen* setting. The figures are the number of layer 1, 3, 5, 7, 9, 11, from left to right, top to bottom. The x-axis is the time step of the tokens. The y-axis is the number of real neighbors with the radius.

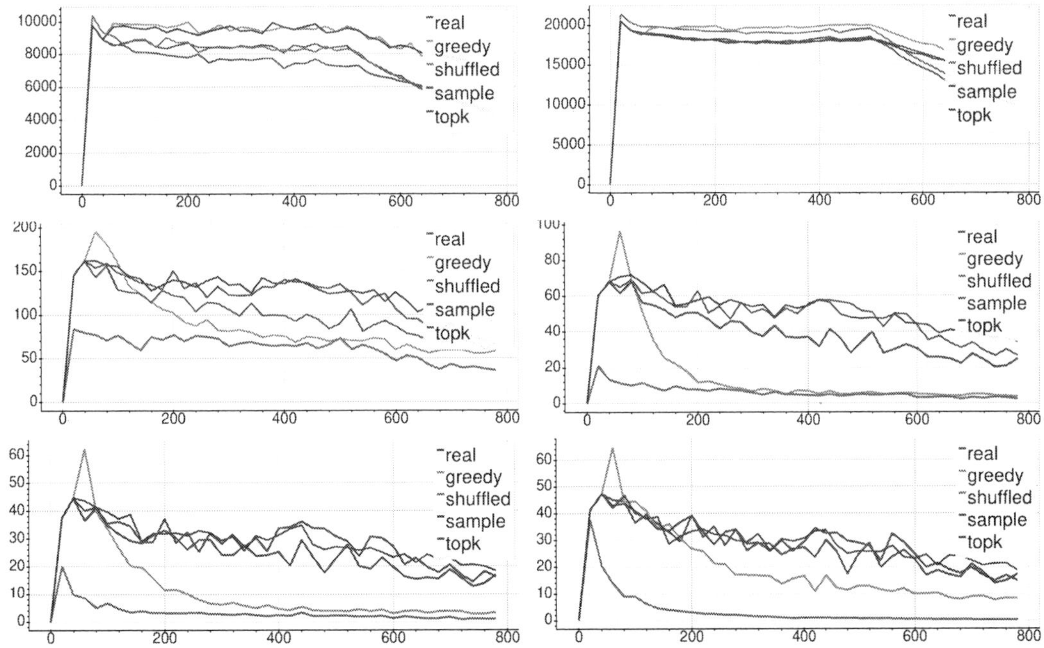

Figure 6: Number of neighbors for *compare-unseen* setting. The figures are the number of layers 1, 3, 5, 7, 9, 11, from left to right, top to bottom. The x-axis is the time step of the tokens. The y-axis is the number of real neighbors with the radius.

Efficient Explanations from Empirical Explainers

Robert Schwarzenberg[1] **Nils Feldhus**[1] **Sebastian Möller**[1,2]
[1]German Research Center for Artificial Intelligence (DFKI)
[2]Technische Universität Berlin (TU Berlin)
{firstname.lastname}@dfki.de

Abstract

Amid a discussion about Green AI in which we see explainability neglected, we explore the possibility to efficiently approximate computationally expensive explainers. To this end, we propose feature attribution modelling with Empirical Explainers. Empirical Explainers learn from data to predict the attribution maps of expensive explainers. We train and test Empirical Explainers in the language domain and find that they model their expensive counterparts surprisingly well, at a fraction of the cost. They could thus mitigate the computational burden of neural explanations significantly, in applications that tolerate an approximation error.

1 Introduction

In recent years, important works were published on the ecological impacts of artificial intelligence and deep learning in particular, e.g. Strubell et al. (2019), Schwartz et al. (2020), Henderson et al. (2020). Research is focused on the energy hunger of model training and subsequent inference in production. Besides training and in-production inference, explainability has become an integral phase of many neural systems.

In the ongoing discussion about Green AI we see explainability neglected. Conversely, in the explainability community, even though research on efficiency is an active area, apparently the discussion is currently shaped by other aspects, such as faithfulness and plausibility (Jacovi and Goldberg, 2020). This is surprising because to explain a single model output, many prominent explanation methods, in particular many feature attribution methods (cf. below), require a multiple of computing power when compared to the prediction step.

1.1 Motivation: Expensive Explainers

Take, for instance, the demonstrative but arguably realistic case of a classifier that was trained on $100k$ instances for 10 epochs. The training thus amounts to at least $1M$ forward passes and $1M$ backward passes. To produce explanations, in this paper, we consider feature attribution methods and focus on Integrated Gradients (IG) (Sundararajan et al., 2017) and Shapley Values (SV) (Castro et al., 2009), which are popular and established but also computationally expensive. To compute the exact IG or SV is virtually intractable, which is why sampling-based approximations were devised. For IG

$$\phi_{f,i}(x) = \frac{x_i - \bar{x}_i}{s} \sum_{k=1}^{s} \frac{\partial f(\bar{x} + \frac{k}{s}(x - \bar{x}))}{\partial x_i}$$

is computed, where x is the input to model f, $\bar{x}$ is a user-defined baseline, s denotes the number of samples (a hyperparameter), and $\phi_{f,i}(x)$ denotes the attribution score of feature i. For SV, s permutations of the input data $O_1, O_2, \ldots O_s$ are drawn and then features from x are added to a user-defined baseline,[1] in the order they occur in the permutation. Let $\text{Pre}^i(O)$ denote the baseline including the features that were added to the baseline prior to i. The Shapley value can then be approximated by

$$\phi_{f,i}(x) = \frac{1}{s} \sum_{k=1}^{s} f(\text{Pre}^i(O_k) \cup x_i) - f(\text{Pre}^i(O_k))$$

Sundararajan et al. (2017) report that s between 20 and 300 is usually enough to approximate IG. Let us set $s := 20$. This requires 40 passes (forward and backward) through model f to explain a single instance in production and furthermore, after only 50k explanations the computational costs of training are also already surpassed. In the case of SV, again setting $s := 20$ and assuming only 512 input features (i.e. tokens to an NLP model),

[1]There are several variants of Shapley Value Sampling. This sampling method is based on PyTorch's Captum (Kokhlikyan et al., 2020) library, that we also use for our experiments: `https://captum.ai/api/shapley_value_sampling.html`, last accessed March 26, 2021.

Proceedings of the Fourth BlackboxNLP Workshop on Analyzing and Interpreting Neural Networks for NLP, pages 240–249
Online, November 11, 2021.

[CLS] While I can ' t say whether or not Larry Ham ##a ever saw any of the old cartoons , I would think that writing said cartoons , file cards , and some of the comics would count for something . br / br / For fans of the old cartoon , this is pretty much a continuation of the same , except with a few new characters - and a more insane Cobra Commander . br / br / We still have all the old favorites too , but on a personal note , one thing that always irritated me was this " Duke in charge " stuff , when there are tons of other * officers * around instead . br / br / The battle sequences are similar to the old series as well ; the main trick here seems to be the C ##GI . It ' s overall pretty good , if not a little over - the - top . [SEP]

[CLS] While I can ' t say whether or not Larry Ham ##a ever saw any of the old cartoons , I would think that writing said cartoons , file cards , and some of the comics would count for something . br / br / For fans of the old cartoon , this is pretty much a continuation of the same , except with a few new characters - and a more insane Cobra Commander . br / br / We still have all the old favorites too , but on a personal note , one thing that always irritated me was this " Duke in charge " stuff , when there are tons of other * officers * around instead . br / br / The battle sequences are similar to the old series as well ; the main trick here seems to be the C ##GI . It ' s overall pretty good , if not a little over - the - top . [SEP]

Figure 1: Explanations (attribution maps) for a BERT-based sentiment classification (best viewed digitally). The input is taken from the test split and was classified into `Positive`. **Top**: Integrated Gradients ($s = 20$, 40 passes through classifier required). **Bottom**: Empirical Integrated Gradients (1 pass through Empirical Explainer required). Attribution scores were normalized on sequence level. Red: positive; blue: negative.

one already needs to conduct $20 * 512 = 10240$ passes to generate an input attribution map for a single classification decision. This means that SV surpasses the training costs specified above after only 195 explanations.

This may only have a small impact if the number of required explanations is low. However, there are strong indications that explainability will take (or retain) an important role in many neural systems: For example, there are legal regulations, such as the EU's GDPR which hints at a "right to explanation" (Goodman and Flaxman, 2017). For such cases, a 1:1 ratio in production between model outputs and explanations is not improbable. If the employed explainability method requires more than one additional pass through the model (as many do, cf. below), there then is a tipping point at which the energy need of explanations exceeds the energy needs of both model training and in-production inference.

IG and SV are not the only tipping point methods. Other expensive prominent and recent methods and variants are proposed by Zeiler and Fergus (2014); Ribeiro et al. (2016); Lundberg and Lee (2017); Smilkov et al. (2017); Chen et al. (2019); Dhamdhere et al. (2020); Erion et al. (2019); Covert and Lee (2020); Schwarzenberg and Castle (2020); Schulz et al. (2020); Harbecke and Alt (2020).

All of the above listed explainers require more than one additional pass through the model. This is why in general the following should hold across methods: *The smaller the model, the greener the explanation.* In terms of energy efficiency, explainability therefore benefits from model compression, distillation, or quantization. These are dynamic fields with a lot of active research which is why in the remainder of this paper we instead focus on something else: The mitigation of the ecological impact of tipping-point methods that dominate the cost term in the example cited in this section.

These are our main contributions in this paper:

1. We propose to utilize the task of feature attribution modelling to efficiently model the attribution maps of expensive explainers.
2. We address feature attribution modelling with trainable explainers that we coin Empirical Explainers.
3. We evaluate their performance qualitatively and quantitatively in the language domain and establish them as an efficient alternative to computationally expensive explainers in applications where an approximation error is tolerable.

2 Framework: Empirical Explainers

Informally, an EMPIRICAL EXPLAINER *is a model that has learned from data to efficiently model the feature attribution maps of an expensive explainer. For training, one collects sufficiently many attribution maps from the expensive explainer and then maximizes the likelihood of these target attributions under the Empirical Explainer.*

An expensive explainer may, for instance, be a costly attribution method such as Integrated Gradients that is used to return attributions for the decisions of a classifier, say, a BERT-based (Devlin et al., 2019) sentiment classifier. The corresponding Empirical Explainer could be a separate neural network, similar in size to the sentiment classifier, consuming the same input tokens as the sentiment model, but instead of predicting the sentiment class, it is trained to predict the integrated gradients for each token.

Whereas the original Integrated Gradients explainer requires multiple passes through the classifier, producing the empirical integrated gradients

[CLS] Although " They Died with their Boots On " is not entirely historically accurate it is a very entertaining western . Not only is Flynn the perfect C ##uster , the character actors are superb . Besides the action portion of the movie Flynn and De ##H ##avi ##lland ' s love scenes are very touching and be ##lie ##vable . (Flynn and De ##H ##avi ##lland were very fond of each other in real life) . Flynn was always so torment ##ed for being not taken seriously if only he knew that there were very few actors who could play the characters he played and play them well ! [SEP]

[CLS] Although " They Died with their Boots On " is not entirely historically accurate it is a very entertaining western . Not only is Flynn the perfect C ##uster , the character actors are superb . Besides the action portion of the movie Flynn and De ##H ##avi ##lland ' s love scenes are very touching and be ##lie ##vable . (Flynn and De ##H ##avi ##lland were very fond of each other in real life) . Flynn was always so torment ##ed for being not taken seriously if only he knew that there were very few actors who could play the characters he played and play them well ! [SEP]

Figure 2: Explanations (attribution maps) for a BERT-based sentiment classification (best viewed digitally) with prominent approximation errors. The input is taken from the test split and was classified into `Positive`. **Top**: Integrated Gradients ($s = 20$, 40 passes through classifier required). **Bottom**: Empirical Integrated Gradients (1 pass through Empirical Explainer required). Attribution scores were normalized on sequence level. Red: positive; blue: negative. Note that contrary to the target explanation (top) the empirical integrated gradients for the token `tormented` are prominently negative (bottom).

requires just one pass through the similarly sized Empirical Explainer. Empirical explanations come with an accuracy-efficiency trade-off that we discuss in the course of a more formal definition of Empirical Explainers.

For the more formal definition, we need to fix notation first. Let $E_f : \mathbb{R}^d \to \mathbb{R}^d$ be the expensive explainer that maps inputs onto attributions. Furthermore, let an Empirical Explainer be a function $e_\theta : \mathbb{R}^d \to \mathbb{R}^d$, parametrized by θ, which also returns attribution maps. Let $||\cdot||$ be a penalty for the inefficiency of a computation, e.g. a count of floating point operations, energy consumption or number of model passes needed. Furthermore, let us assume, without the loss of generality, that $||E_f(x)|| >= ||e_\theta(x)||$ always holds; i.e., the Empirical Explainer – which we develop and train – is never more inefficient than the original, expensive explainer. Let $D : \mathbb{R}^d \times \mathbb{R}^d \to [0, 1]$ be a similarity measure, where $D(l, m) = 0$ if $l = m$, for $l, m \in \mathbb{R}^d$ and $\alpha, \beta \in [0, 1]$ with $\alpha + \beta = 1$. For data $\mathbf{X}$, we define an α-optimal Empirical Explainer by the $\arg\min_{\theta \in \Theta}$

$$\frac{1}{|X|} \sum_{x \in \mathbf{X}} \overbrace{\alpha D(E_f(x), e_\theta(x))}^{\text{accuracy}} + \overbrace{\beta \left(\frac{||e_\theta(x)||}{||E_f(x)||} \right)}^{\text{efficiency}}. \tag{1}$$

2.1 Properties

The first term describes how accurately the Empirical Explainer e_θ models the expensive explainer E_f. The second term compares the efficiency of the two explainers. For $\alpha = 1$, efficiency is considered unimportant and $e_\theta := E_f$ can be set to minimize Eq. 1. $\alpha < 1$ allows to optimize efficiency at the cost of accuracy, which brings about the trade off: One may not succeed in increasing efficiency while maintaining accuracy. In fact, there is generally no exact guarantee for how accurately e_θ models E_f for new data.

Furthermore, while several expensive explainers, such as Integrated Gradients or Shapley Values, were developed axiomatically to have desirable properties, Empirical Explainers are derived from data – empirically. Consequently, the evidence and guarantees Empirical Explainers offer for their faithfulness to the downstream model are empirical in nature and upper-bound by the faithfulness of the expensive explainer used to train them.

We point this out explicitly because we would like to emphasize that we do *not* regard an Empirical Explainer a new explainability method, nor do we argue that it can be used to replace the original expensive explainer everywhere. There are certainly situations for which Empirical Explainers are unsuitable for any $\alpha \neq 1$; critical cases in which explanations must have guaranteed properties.

Nevertheless, we still see a huge potential for Empirical Explainers where approximation errors are tolerable: Consider, for instance, a search engine powered by a neural model in the back-end. Without the need to employ the expensive explainer, Empirical Explainers can efficiently provide the user with clues about what the model probably considers relevant in their query (according to the expensive explainer).

3 Experiments

In this section, we report on the performance of Empirical Explainers that we trained and tested in the language domain. We conducted tests with two prominent and expensive explainers, Integrated

A man in colorful short s is surfing under a wave . sep A man is sun bath ing . sep cls

A man in colorful short s is surfing under a wave . sep A man is sun bath ing . sep cls

Figure 3: Explanations (attribution maps) for an XLNet-based NLI classification (best viewed digitally). The input is taken from the test split and was classified into `Contradiction`. **Top**: Shapley Value Samples ($s = 20$, 380 passes through classifier required). **Bottom**: Empirical Shapley Values (1 pass through Empirical Explainer required). Attribution scores were normalized on sequence level. Red: positive; blue: negative.

Gradients and Shapley Value Samples, varying the experiments across four state-of-the-art language classifiers, trained on four different tasks.

The experiments address the question of whether or not it is feasible – in principle – to train efficient Empirical Explainers while achieving significant accuracy. All experiments, code, models and data are open source and can be retrieved following `https://github.com/DFKI-NLP/emp-exp`. The most important choices are documented in the following paragraphs. Before going into greater detail, it is noteworthy that Eq. 1 provides a theoretical framework which one does not have use directly for explicit optimization. For example, in this work, we address the first objective, accuracy, by fitting Empirical Explainers to the attribution maps of expensive explainers. However, the second objective, efficiency, is addressed implicitly by design, i.e. the Empirical Explainers, in contrast to their expensive counterparts, are designed (and trained) in a way s.t. only a single forward pass is required through a model similar in size to the downstream model. In the future, it would be very interesting to fully incorporate Eq. 1 in a differential setting, i.e. also optimize for efficiency automatically, rather than by manual design.

We trained four Empirical Explainers. All explainers consume only the input tokens to the downstream model and return an attribution score for each token. The first one (EmpExp-BERT-IG) was trained to predict integrated gradients w.r.t. the input tokens to a BERT-based IMDB movie review (Maas et al., 2011) classifier. For the second Empirical Explainer (EmpExp-XLNet-SV), we varied the downstream model architecture, task and target explainer: EmpExp-XLNet-SV predicts the Shapley Values (as returned by the expensive Shapley Value Sampling explainer) for the inputs of an XLNet-based (Yang et al., 2019) natural language inference classifier that was trained on the SNLI (Bowman et al., 2015) dataset. The third (EmpExp-RoBERTa-IG) and fourth (EmpExp-ELECTRA-SV) empirical explainers again approximate IG and SV, but for a RoBERTa-based news topic classifier (Liu et al., 2019) trained on the AG News dataset (Zhang et al., 2015) and an ELECTRA (small)-based model (Clark et al., 2020) that detects paraphrases, trained on the PAWS dataset (subset "labelled_final") (Zhang et al., 2019), respectively.

The Empirical Explainers were trained on target attributions that we generated with IG and SV with $s := 20$ samples. For EmpExp-RoBERTa-IG, we used $s := 25$ due to a slower convergence rate (cf. below). Explanations were generated for the output neuron with the maximal activation. EmpExp-BERT-IG was trained with early stopping using the IG attribution maps for the full IMDB train split (25k). EmpExp-XLNet-SV was trained with around 100k SV attribution maps for the SNLI train split with early stopping, for which we used the 10k attribution maps for the validation split. We did not use all training instances in the split for EmpExp-XLNet-SV, due to the computational costs of Shapley Value Sampling. In case of EmpExp-RoBERTa-IG and EmpExp-ELECTRA-SV it was possible to train with the full train splits again, 108k (12k held out) and around 50k instances, respectively.

As mentioned above, the expensive explainers require user-defined baselines. For the baselines, we replaced all non-special tokens in the input sequence with pad tokens. For the expensive IG, we produced attribution maps for the embedding layer and projected the attribution scores onto tokens by summing them over the token dimension. For the expensive SV, the input IDs were perturbed. During perturbation, we grouped and treated special tokens (CLS, SEP, PAD, ...) in the original input as one feature to accelerate the computation.

In architectural terms, the Empirical Explainers are very similar to the downstream models: We heuristically decided to copy the fine-tuned BERT, XLNet, RoBERTa and ELECTRA encoders from the classifiers and instead of the classification layers on top, we initialized new fully connected layers with T output neurons. T was lower bound

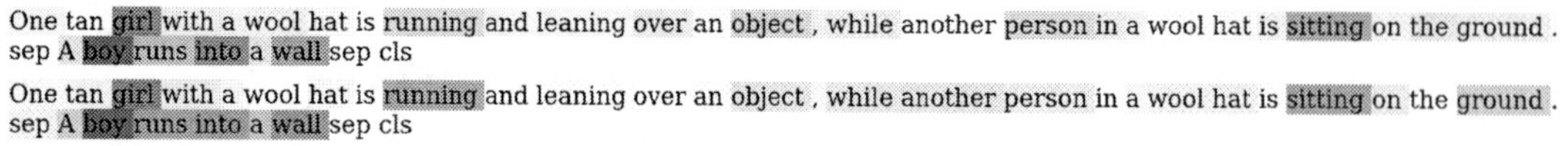

Figure 4: Explanations (attribution maps) for an XLNet-based NLI classification with prominent approximation errors (best viewed digitally). The input is taken from the test split and was classified into `Contradiction`. **Top**: Shapley Value Samples ($s = 20$, 700 passes through classifier required). **Bottom**: Empirical Shapley Values (1 pass through Empirical Explainer required). Attribution scores were normalized on sequence level. Red: positive; blue: negative. Note that, contrary to the target explanation (top), the empirical Shapley Value for the token `running` is in the negative regime (bottom).

by the maximum input token sequence length to the downstream model in the respective dataset: $T = 512$ for BERT/IMDB and RoBERTa/AG News, $T = 130$ for XLNet/SNLI, and $T = 145$ for ELECTRA/PAWS. All input sequences were padded to T and we did not treat padding tokens different from other tokens, when training the Empirical Explainers. Please note that the sequence length has a considerable impact on the runtime of the SV explainer in particular, which is why limiting T increases comparability.

We trained the Empirical Explainers to output the right (in accordance with the expensive explainers) attribution scores for the input tokens, using an MSE loss between $E_f(x_1) \dots E_f(x_T)$ and $e_\theta(x_1) \dots e_\theta(x_T)$ where $x = x_1, x_2, \dots x_T$ is a sequence of input tokens.[2]

To put the performance of an Empirical Explainer into perspective, we propose the following baseline, which is the strongest we can think of: We take the original expensive explainer with a reduced number of samples as the baseline. To position the Empirical Explainer against this alternative energy saving strategy, we compute convergence curves. Starting with $s = 1$, we incrementally increase the number of samples until $s = 19$ ($s = 24$ in the case of EmpExp-RoBERTa-IG) and collect attribution maps from the expensive explainer for the different choices of s. We then compute the MSEs of these attribution maps when compared to the target attributions (with $s = 20$ or $s = 25$). We average the MSEs across the test split. The same is done for the Empirical Explainer.

4 Results & Discussion

In the following, we report the experimental results, divided into the aspects of task performance, explanation efficiency and explanation accuracy.

Task Performance On the test splits, the classifiers we trained achieved weighted F_1 scores of 0.93 (BERT · IMDB), 0.90 (XLNet · SNLI), 0.94 (RoBERTa · AG News) and 0.92 (ELECTRA · PAWS).

Explanation Efficiency Regarding the efficiency term in Eq. 1, in terms of model passes, the Empirical Explainers have a clear advantage over their expensive counterparts. For IG with $s = 20$, 40 model passes are required, for $s = 25$, 50 passes. For SV with $s = 20$, assuming a token sequence length of 100 for the purpose of discussion, 2000 model passes are required. For the empirical explanations, only one (additional) forward pass through a similarly sized model (the Empirical Explainer) is necessary.

Contrary to runtime (and energy consumption) measures, the number of required model passes is largely invariant of available hardware and implementation details. For the sake of completeness, we nevertheless also report our runtimes in appendix A. In summary, generating the expensive explanations for the test splits took between around 02:15 and 48 *hours*, whereas the empirical explanations only required between 02:05 and 07:14 *minutes*.

The runtimes are not definitive, however. We were unable to establish a fair game for the explainers. For example, due to implementation details and memory issues we explained the data instance-wise with the expensive explainers while our Empirical Explainers easily allowed batch processing. We expect that the expensive explainers can be accelerated but due to the larger number of model passes required, they will very likely not outperform their empirical counterparts.

The Empirical Explainers come with additional training costs, which we also report in appendix A. Training took between 02:15 and 07:00 hours. These additional training costs are thus quickly outweighed by the expensive explainers, in particular

[2] Even though we do not solve for Eq. 1 directly, please note that for evaluation we can normalize the attribution scores to $[0, 1]$ prior to computing the MSE and this way force the MSE into the interval $[0, 1]$ to comply with the constraints for Eq. 1.

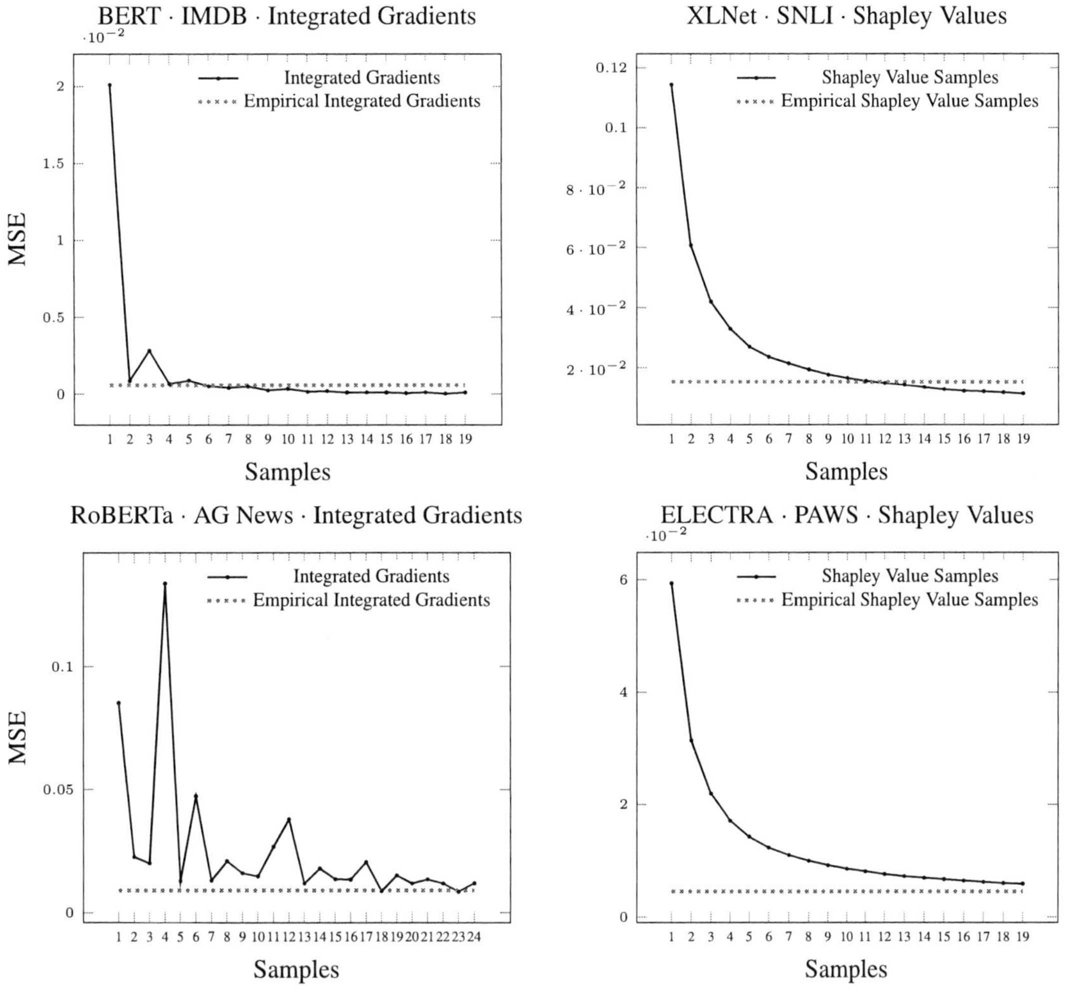

Figure 5: Performance of Empirical Explainers (dashed green lines) and convergence curves of expensive explainers (solid black lines), averaged across test sets. The attribution maps returned by the expensive explainers with $s = 20$ samples in case of BERT, XLNet and ELECTRA and $s = 25$ in case of RoBERTa (slower convergence behaviour), were regarded the target explanations. MSEs were computed on a per-sequence basis and then averaged across the test set.

in a continuous in-production setting.

Explanation Accuracy Regarding the accuracy term in Eq. 1, Figs. 1, 2, 3 and 4 provide anecdotal qualitative evidence that the Empirical Explainers are capable of modelling their expensive counterparts well, with varying degrees of approximation errors. Alongside this paper, we provide four files (see repository) with around 25k (IMDB), 10k (SNLI), 7.6k (AG News) and 8k (PAWS) lines, each of which contains an HTML document that depicts a target attribution and its empirical counterpart from the test set. The heatmaps in the figures mentioned above are taken from the accompanying files.

Figs. 1 and 3 are instances of what we consider surprisingly accurate approximations of the expensive target attribution maps, despite challenging inputs. Let us first consider Fig. 1 in greater detail. Consider the tokens `favorites` and `irritated` that are not attributed much importance by the expensive explainer (IG, top) but could be considered signal words for the positive and negative class, respectively and thus pose a challenge for the Empirical Explainer. Nevertheless, in accordance with the expensive target explainer, the Empirical Explainer (bottom) does not attribute the classifier output primarily to these tokens but instead accurately assigns a lot of weight to `It's overall pretty good`.

A similar phenomenon can be observed in Fig. 2 for the token `love`. The approximation in this figure, however, also contains a prominent approximation error. The Empirical Explainer erroneously attributes a salient negative score to the token `tormented` while the target explainer does not highlight that token. Similarly, in Fig. 4 the Empirical Explainer returns a negative score for `running`, whereas the expensive target explainer has returned a positive score.

We suspect that such errors may result from global priors that the Empirical Explainers have learned and that sometimes outweigh the instantaneous information. For instance, in Fig. 4 the verb `running` in the premise in conjunction with the (conjugated) verb `runs` in the hypothesis may statistically be indicative of an entailment in the training data. This is because to produce a contradiction the verb sometimes is simply replaced by another one (cf. Fig. 3: `surfing` vs. `sun bathing`). In this instance, however, the verb is not replaced. Thus, here the prior knowledge of the Empirical Explainer may outweigh the local information in favor of the error that we observe: The Empirical Explainer may signal that `running` is evidence against the class `Contradiction` since it finds it in the premise and hypothesis. A similar argument can be put forward for the case of `tormented` in Fig. 2.

The above points are rather speculative. A more objective and quantitative analysis of the efficiency/accuracy trade-off is provided in Fig. 5. The left column depicts the MSE lines of IG for an increasing number of samples in x-direction. We observe that IG converges fast in case of BERT/IMDB. (This may be due to saturation effects in Integrated Gradients, reported on by Miglani et al. (2020).) In case of RoBERTa/AG News we found a slower convergence rate, which is why we increased the number of samples for the target explainer. We observe that in both cases, the empirical integrated gradients (dashed lines) perform favourably: To outperform the Empirical Explainer by decreasing s, in case of BERT/IMDB one needs to set $s > 5$ which entails 10 model passes as opposed to the single additional pass through the Empirical Explainer for the empirical explanations. Furthermore, the approximation error is already marginal at the intersection of expensive and empirical line. In case of RoBERTa/AG News, one even needs to set $s := 18$ to be closer to the target than the Empirical Explainer.

A similar trend can be observed for the (empirical) Shapley Values in the right column of Fig. 5. In case of XLNet/SNLI, however, the intersection occurs only after $s = 10$ which means that the Empirical Explainer needs only $\frac{1}{11*100} = 0.9\%$ of model passes (plus the pass through its output layer) when compared to the next best expensive explainer, again assuming 100 input tokens for the purpose of discussion. In case of ELECTRA/PAWS, the Empirical Explainer even beats the expensive explainer with just one sample less than the target.

In summary, we take the experimental results as a strong indication that Empirical Explainers could become an efficient alternative to expensive explainers (in the language domain) where approximation errors are tolerable.

5 Related Work

The computational burden of individual explainability methods was addressed in numerous works. As mentioned above, Integrated Gradients can only be computed exactly in limit cases and for all other cases, the community relies on the approximate method proposed by Sundararajan et al. (2017). Similarly, Shapley Values can rarely be computed precisely which is why Shapley Value Sampling was investigated, e.g. by Castro et al. (2009); Štrumbelj and Kononenko (2010). Shapley Value Sampling was later unified with other methods under the SHAP framework (Lundberg and Lee, 2017) which yielded the method KernelSHAP that showed improved sample efficiency. Covert and Lee (2020) then analysed the convergence behaviour of KernelSHAP and again further improved runtime. Chen et al. (2019) introduced L-Shapley and C-Shapley which accelerate Shapley Value Sampling for structured data, such as dependency trees in NLP.

Thus, computational feasibility appears to be a driving force in the research community, already. To the best of our knowledge, however, we are the first to propose the task of feature attribution modelling to mitigate the computational burden of expensive explainers with Empirical Explainers.

Technically, self-explaining models (Alvarez-Melis and Jaakkola, 2018) are related to our approach in that they also generate explanations in a forward pass (alongside their classification decision). Contrary to self-explaining models, Empirical Explainers can be employed after training for a variety of black box and white box classifiers and explainers.

A source of inspiration for our method was the work by Camburu et al. (2018). The authors train self-explaining models that return a natural language rationale alongside their classification. Thus, they, too, train an explainer. However, their target explanations (natural language) differ substantially from the ones Empirical Explainers are trained with (attribution scores).

Furthermore, related to our work is the technique of gradient matching for which a network's (integrated) gradients are compared to a target attribution, i.e. a human prior, and then the network's parameters are updated, s.t. the gradients move closer to the target, as done e.g. by Ross et al. (2017); Erion et al. (2019); Liu and Avci (2019). Apart from the loss on an alignment with target attributions, our method and goals diverge from theirs significantly.

Human priors and expensive target explanations have recently also been used for *explanatory interactive learning* (XIL). Like Empirical Explainers, XIL is motivated by the expensiveness of a target explainer; in the case of XIL this is a human in the loop. Schramowski et al. (2020) present humans with informative (cf. active learning) instances, the model prediction and an explanation for the prediction The expensive human feedback is then used to improve the model. Apart from the expensive explainer assumption, their approach differs substantially from ours. Very recently, Behrens et al. (2021) contributed to XIL by introducing a method that learns to explain from explanations and in this respect is close to the setting of Empirical Explainers. One fundamental difference between ours and their work is that they propose and focus on a specific class of self-explainable models whereas Empirical Explainers make no assumptions about the underlying predictor and are intended for a variety of model classes, as already mentioned above.

Very recently again, Rajagopal et al. (2021) proposed local interpretable layers as a means to generate concept attributions which in parts aligns with our method, even though their target attributions and task objectives are very different again.

Lastly, Empirical Explainers can be viewed as a form of knowledge distillation (Hinton et al., 2015). However, contrary to the established approach, we do not assume a parametric teacher network that knowledge is distilled from. Very recently we became aware of the work by Pruthi et al. (2020) who boost the accuracy of a student learner with explanations in the form of a subset of tokens that are relevant to the teacher decision, determined by an explainer. In a sequence classification task, the student is trained to identify the relevant tokens and could thus be considered an Empirical Explainer. The task, however, is not to predict the original attribution map and the overall objective differs significantly from ours again.

6 Conclusion & Future Directions

In this paper, we take a step towards greener XAI by again reviving energy efficiency as an additional criterion by which to judge an explainability method, alongside important aspects such as faithfulness and plausibility. In this context, we propose feature attribution modelling with efficient Empirical Explainers. In the language domain, we investigate the efficiency/accuracy trade-off and find that it is possible to generate empirical explanations with significant accuracy, at a fraction of the costs of the expensive counterparts. We take this as a strong indication that Empirical Explainers could be a viable alternative to expensive explainers where approximation errors are tolerable.

Regarding future directions: The Empirical Explainers we trained are our concrete model choices. The framework we propose allows for many other approaches. For instance, one could provide the Empirical Explainers with additional information, such as the gradient w.r.t. the inputs. This would require an additional pass through the model but may possibly further boost accuracy.

We would like to note that we trained and tested our Empirical Explainers only on in-domain data but their behaviour on out-of-domain data should be investigated, too. Fortunately, since we explain the model decision (the maximum output activation), no gold labels are required to train Empirical Explainers which facilitates data collection immensely. Finally, there are some more sample efficient explainers that should be considered, too.

Acknowledgements We would like to thank Christoph Alt, Steffen Castle, Jonas Mikkelsen and David Harbecke for their helpful feedback. This work has been supported by the German Federal Ministry of Education and Research as part of the projects XAINES (01IW20005) and CORA4NLP (01IW20010).

References

David Alvarez-Melis and Tommi Jaakkola. 2018. Towards robust interpretability with self-explaining neural networks. *Advances in Neural Information Processing Systems*, 31:7775–7784.

Freya Behrens, Stefano Teso, and Davide Mottin. 2021. Bandits for learning to explain from explanations. *arXiv preprint arXiv:2102.03815*.

Samuel R. Bowman, Gabor Angeli, Christopher Potts, and Christopher D. Manning. 2015. A large annotated corpus for learning natural language inference. In *EMNLP*.

Oana-Maria Camburu, Tim Rocktäschel, Thomas Lukasiewicz, and Phil Blunsom. 2018. e-snli: Natural language inference with natural language explanations. *Advances in Neural Information Processing Systems*, 31:9539–9549.

Javier Castro, Daniel Gómez, and Juan Tejada. 2009. Polynomial calculation of the shapley value based on sampling. *Computers & Operations Research*, 36(5):1726–1730.

Jianbo Chen, Le Song, Martin J Wainwright, and Michael I Jordan. 2019. L-shapley and c-shapley: Efficient model interpretation for structured data. *International Conference on Learning Representations 2019*.

Kevin Clark, Minh-Thang Luong, Quoc V Le, and Christopher D Manning. 2020. Electra: Pre-training text encoders as discriminators rather than generators. *arXiv preprint arXiv:2003.10555*.

Ian Covert and Su-In Lee. 2020. Improving kernelshap: Practical shapley value estimation via linear regression. *arXiv preprint arXiv:2012.01536*.

J. Devlin, Ming-Wei Chang, Kenton Lee, and Kristina Toutanova. 2019. Bert: Pre-training of deep bidirectional transformers for language understanding. In *NAACL-HLT*.

Kedar Dhamdhere, Ashish Agarwal, and Mukund Sundararajan. 2020. The shapley taylor interaction index. In *ICML 2020*.

Gabriel Erion, Joseph D Janizek, Pascal Sturmfels, Scott Lundberg, and Su-In Lee. 2019. Learning explainable models using attribution priors. *arXiv preprint arXiv:1906.10670*.

Bryce Goodman and Seth Flaxman. 2017. European union regulations on algorithmic decision-making and a "right to explanation". *AI magazine*, 38(3):50–57.

David Harbecke and Christoph Alt. 2020. Considering likelihood in nlp classification explanations with occlusion and language modeling. *ACL 2020 SRW*.

P. Henderson, Jie-Ru Hu, Joshua Romoff, Emma Brunskill, Dan Jurafsky, and Joelle Pineau. 2020. Towards the systematic reporting of the energy and carbon footprints of machine learning. *ArXiv*, abs/2002.05651.

Geoffrey Hinton, Oriol Vinyals, and Jeff Dean. 2015. Distilling the knowledge in a neural network. *arXiv preprint arXiv:1503.02531*.

Alon Jacovi and Y. Goldberg. 2020. Towards faithfully interpretable nlp systems: How should we define and evaluate faithfulness? *ACL 2020*.

Narine Kokhlikyan, Vivek Miglani, Miguel Martin, Edward Wang, Bilal Alsallakh, Jonathan Reynolds, Alexander Melnikov, Natalia Kliushkina, Carlos Araya, Siqi Yan, et al. 2020. Captum: A unified and generic model interpretability library for pytorch. *arXiv preprint arXiv:2009.07896*.

Frederick Liu and Besim Avci. 2019. Incorporating priors with feature attribution on text classification. In *Proceedings of the 57th Annual Meeting of the Association for Computational Linguistics*, pages 6274–6283.

Yinhan Liu, Myle Ott, Naman Goyal, Jingfei Du, Mandar Joshi, Danqi Chen, Omer Levy, Mike Lewis, Luke Zettlemoyer, and Veselin Stoyanov. 2019. Roberta: A robustly optimized bert pretraining approach. *arXiv preprint arXiv:1907.11692*.

Scott M Lundberg and Su-In Lee. 2017. A unified approach to interpreting model predictions. In *Advances in neural information processing systems*, pages 4765–4774.

Andrew L. Maas, Raymond E. Daly, P. T. Pham, D. Huang, A. Ng, and Christopher Potts. 2011. Learning word vectors for sentiment analysis. In *ACL 2011*.

Vivek Miglani, Narine Kokhlikyan, Bilal Alsallakh, Miguel Martin, and Orion Reblitz-Richardson. 2020. Investigating saturation effects in integrated gradients. *arXiv preprint arXiv:2010.12697*.

Danish Pruthi, Bhuwan Dhingra, Livio Baldini Soares, Michael Collins, Zachary C Lipton, Graham Neubig, and William W Cohen. 2020. Evaluating explanations: How much do explanations from the teacher aid students? *arXiv preprint arXiv:2012.00893*.

Dheeraj Rajagopal, Vidhisha Balachandran, E. Hovy, and Yulia Tsvetkov. 2021. Selfexplain: A self-explaining architecture for neural text classifiers. *arXiv preprint arXiv:2103.12279*.

Marco Tulio Ribeiro, Sameer Singh, and Carlos Guestrin. 2016. " why should i trust you?" explaining the predictions of any classifier. In *Proceedings of the 22nd ACM SIGKDD international conference on knowledge discovery and data mining*, pages 1135–1144.

Andrew Slavin Ross, Michael C Hughes, and Finale Doshi-Velez. 2017. Right for the right reasons: Training differentiable models by constraining their explanations. In *IJCAI*.

Patrick Schramowski, Wolfgang Stammer, Stefano Teso, Anna Brugger, Franziska Herbert, Xiaoting Shao, Hans-Georg Luigs, Anne-Katrin Mahlein, and Kristian Kersting. 2020. Making deep neural networks right for the right scientific reasons by interacting with their explanations. *Nature Machine Intelligence*, 2(8):476–486.

Karl Schulz, Leon Sixt, Federico Tombari, and Tim Landgraf. 2020. Restricting the flow: Information bottlenecks for attribution. *ICLR 2020*.

Roy Schwartz, Jesse Dodge, N. A. Smith, and Oren Etzioni. 2020. Green ai. *Communications of the ACM*, 63:54 – 63.

Robert Schwarzenberg and Steffen Castle. 2020. Pattern-guided integrated gradients. *ICML 2020 Workshop on Human Interpretability in Machine Learning (WHI) arXiv preprint arXiv:2007.10685*.

Daniel Smilkov, Nikhil Thorat, Been Kim, Fernanda Viégas, and Martin Wattenberg. 2017. Smoothgrad: removing noise by adding noise. *arXiv preprint arXiv:1706.03825*.

Emma Strubell, Ananya Ganesh, and Andrew McCallum. 2019. Energy and policy considerations for deep learning in NLP. In *Proceedings of the 57th Annual Meeting of the Association for Computational Linguistics*, pages 3645–3650, Florence, Italy. Association for Computational Linguistics.

E. Štrumbelj and I. Kononenko. 2010. An efficient explanation of individual classifications using game theory. *J. Mach. Learn. Res.*, 11:1–18.

Mukund Sundararajan, Ankur Taly, and Qiqi Yan. 2017. Axiomatic attribution for deep networks. In *Proceedings of the 34th International Conference on Machine Learning-Volume 70*, pages 3319–3328.

Z. Yang, Zihang Dai, Yiming Yang, J. Carbonell, R. Salakhutdinov, and Quoc V. Le. 2019. Xlnet: Generalized autoregressive pretraining for language understanding. In *NeurIPS*.

Matthew D Zeiler and Rob Fergus. 2014. Visualizing and understanding convolutional networks. In *13th European Conference on Computer Vision, ECCV 2014*, pages 818–833. Springer Verlag.

Xiang Zhang, Junbo Zhao, and Yann LeCun. 2015. Character-level convolutional networks for text classification. *Advances in neural information processing systems*, 28:649–657.

Yuan Zhang, Jason Baldridge, and Luheng He. 2019. Paws: Paraphrase adversaries from word scrambling. *arXiv preprint arXiv:1904.01130*.

A Runtimes

Generating the expensive target explanations for the official IMDB test split (25k instances, $T = 512$, $s = 25$, BERT, Titan V) with Integrated Gradients took us 7:17 hours (6:22 hours for the 22500 training instances). Generating the expensive Shapley Values for the SNLI test split ($\sim$ 10k instances, $T = 130$, $s = 20$, XLNet, Quadro P5000) took us 48:22 hours (and over 600 GPU hours for under 100k training instances). It took us over 2:15 hours to explain the 7600 instances in the test split of the AG News dataset with IG ($T = 512$, $s = 25$, RoBERTa, RTX2080Ti; over 31 hours for the train split). For the PAWS test split ($T = 145$, $s = 20$, 8k instances, ELECTRA (small), RTX6000) we needed over 18 GPU hours (over 126 GPU hours for the 49401 instances in the train split, using NVIDIA's RTX3090 and RTX2080Ti).

In contrast, generating the empirical explanations took us only 07:14 *minutes* for the IMDB test split on the Titan GPU and only 02:05 *minutes* for SNLI test split on the Quadro P5000 GPU. The AG News test split took 03:16 *minutes* to explain (RTX3090) and the PAWS test split was explained empirically in only 02:19 *minutes* (RTX3090).

The training of EmpExp-BERT-IG terminated after 10 epochs (Titan V), which took less than 4 hours. EmpExp-XLNet-SV (Quadro P5000), EmpExp-RoBERTa-IG (RTX3090), and EmpExp-ELECTRA-SV (RTX3090) terminated after 7, 3, and 8 epochs, respectively (<7 hours, < 2:15 hours, and <1 hours).

Variation and generality in encoding of syntactic anomaly information in sentence embeddings

Qinxuan Wu*
College of Computer Science and Technology
Zhejiang University
wuqinxuan@zju.edu.cn

Allyson Ettinger
Department of Linguistics
The University of Chicago
aettinger@uchicago.edu

Abstract

While sentence anomalies have been applied periodically for testing in NLP, we have yet to establish a picture of the precise status of anomaly information in representations from NLP models. In this paper we aim to fill two primary gaps, focusing on the domain of syntactic anomalies. First, we explore fine-grained differences in anomaly encoding by designing probing tasks that vary the hierarchical level at which anomalies occur in a sentence. Second, we test not only models' ability to detect a given anomaly, but also the generality of the detected anomaly signal, by examining transfer between distinct anomaly types. Results suggest that all models encode some information supporting anomaly detection, but detection performance varies between anomalies, and only representations from more recent transformer models show signs of generalized knowledge of anomalies. Follow-up analyses support the notion that these models pick up on a legitimate, general notion of sentence oddity, while coarser-grained word position information is likely also a contributor to the observed anomaly detection.

1 Introduction

As the NLP community works to understand what is being learned and represented by current models, a notion that has made sporadic appearances is that of linguistic anomaly. Analyses of language models have often tested whether models prefer grammatical over ungrammatical completions (e.g. Linzen et al., 2016), while analyses of sentence embeddings have probed for syntax and semantics by testing detection of sentence perturbations (Conneau et al., 2018). Such work tends to exploit anomaly detection as a means of studying linguistic phenomena, setting aside any direct questions about encoding of anomaly per se. However, models' treatment of anomaly is itself a topic that raises important questions. After all, it is not obvious that we should expect models to encode information like "this sentence contains an anomaly", nor is it obvious which types of anomalies we might expect models to pick up on more or less easily. Nonetheless, anomalies are easy to detect for humans, and their detection is relevant for applications such as automatic error correction (Ge et al., 2018), so it is of value to understand how anomalies operate in our models, and what impacts anomaly encoding.

In the present work we seek to fill this gap with a direct examination of anomaly encoding in sentence embeddings. We begin with fine-grained testing of the impact of anomaly type, designing probing tasks with anomalies at different levels of syntactic hierarchy to examine whether model representations better support detection of certain types of anomaly. Then we examine the generality of anomaly encoding by testing transfer performance between distinct anomalies—here our question is, to the extent that we see successful anomaly detection, does this reflect encoding of a more general signal indicating "this sentence contains an anomaly", or does it reflect encoding of simpler cues specific to a given anomaly? We focus on syntactic anomalies because the hierarchy of sentence structure is conducive to our fine-grained anomaly variation. (Sensitivity to syntactic anomalies has also been studied extensively as part of the human language capacity (Chomsky, 1957; Fodor et al., 1996), strengthening precedent for prioritizing it.)

We apply these tests to six prominent sentence encoders. We find that most models support non-trivial anomaly detection, though there is substantial variation between encoders. We also observe differences between hierarchical classes of anomaly for some encoders. When we test for transferability of the anomaly signal, we find that for most encoders the observed anomaly detection shows little sign of generality—however, transfer performance in BERT and RoBERTa suggests

*This work was done while the first author was a visiting student at the University of Chicago.

Proceedings of the Fourth BlackboxNLP Workshop on Analyzing and Interpreting Neural Networks for NLP, pages 250–264
Online, November 11, 2021. ©2021 Association for Computational Linguistics

that these more recent models may in fact pick up on a generalized awareness of syntactic anomalies. Follow-up analyses support the possibility that these transformer-based models pick up on a legitimate, general notion of syntactic oddity—which appears to coexist with coarser-grained, anomaly-specific word order cues that also contribute to detection performance. We make all data and code available for further testing.[1]

2 Related Work

This paper builds on work analyzing linguistic knowledge reflected in representations and outputs of NLP models (Tenney et al., 2019; Rogers et al., 2020; Jawahar et al., 2019). Some work uses tailored challenge sets associated with downstream tasks to test linguistic knowledge and robustness (Dasgupta et al., 2018; Poliak et al., 2018a,b; White et al., 2017; Belinkov et al., 2017b; Yang et al., 2015; Rajpurkar et al., 2016; Jia and Liang, 2017; Rajpurkar et al., 2018). Other work has used targeted classification-based probing to examine encoding of specific types of linguistic information in sentence embeddings more directly (Adi et al., 2016; Conneau et al., 2018; Belinkov et al., 2017a; Ettinger et al., 2016, 2018; Tenney et al., 2019; Klafka and Ettinger, 2020). We expand on this work by designing analyses to shed light on encoding of syntactic anomaly information in sentence embeddings.

A growing body of work has examined syntactic sensitivity in language model outputs (Chowdhury and Zamparelli, 2018; Futrell et al., 2019; Lakretz et al., 2019; Marvin and Linzen, 2018; Ettinger, 2020), and our *Agree-Shift* task takes inspiration from the popular number agreement task for language models (Linzen et al., 2016; Gulordava et al., 2018; Goldberg, 2019). Like this work, we focus on syntax in designing our tests, but we differ from this work in focusing on model representations rather than outputs, and in our specific focus on understanding how models encode information about anomalies. Furthermore, as we detail below, our *Agree-Shift* task differs importantly from the LM number agreement tests, and should not be compared directly to results from those tests.

Our work relates most closely to studies involving anomalous or erroneous sentence information (Warstadt et al., 2019; Yin et al., 2020; Hashemi and Hwa, 2016). Some work investigates impacts from random shuffling or other types of distortion of input text (Pham et al., 2020; Gupta et al., 2021) or of model pre-training text (Sinha et al., 2021) on downstream tasks—but this work does not investigate models' encoding of these anomalies. Warstadt et al. (2019) present and test with the *CoLA* dataset for general acceptability detection, and among the probing tasks of Conneau et al. (2018) there are three that involve analyzing whether sentence embeddings can distinguish erroneous modification to sentence inputs: *SOMO*, *BShift*, and *CoordInv*. Yin et al. (2020) also generate synthetic errors based on errors from non-native speakers, showing impacts of such errors on downstream tasks, and briefly probing error sensitivity. More recently, Li et al. (2021) conduct anomaly detection with various anomaly types at different layers of transformer models, using training of Gaussian models for density estimation, and finding different types of anomaly sensitivity at different layers. We build on this line of work in anomaly detection with a fine-grained exploration of models' detection of word-content-controlled perturbations at different levels of syntactic hierarchy. Our work is complementary also in exploring generality of models' anomaly encoding by examining transfer performance between anomalies.

3 Syntactic Anomaly Probing Tasks

To test the effects of hierarchical location of a syntactic anomaly, we create a set of tasks based on four different levels of sentence perturbation. We structure all perturbations so as to keep word content constant between original and perturbed sentences, thus removing any potential aid from purely lexical contrast cues. Our first three tasks involve reordering of syntactic constituents, and differ in hierarchical proximity of the reordered constituents: the first switches constituents of a noun phrase, the second switches constituents of a verb phrase, and the third switches constituents that only share the clause. Our fourth task tests sensitivity to perturbation of morphological number agreement, echoing existing work testing agreement in language models (Linzen et al., 2016).

3.1 *Mod-Noun*: Detecting modifier/noun reordering

Our first task tests sensitivity to anomalies in modifier-noun structure, generating anomalous sen-

[1] https://github.com/pepper-w/syntactic_anomalies.

tences by swapping the positions of nouns and their accompanying modifiers, as below:

A man wearing a ***yellow scarf*** *rides a bike.* →
A man wearing a ***scarf yellow*** *rides a bike.*

We call this perturbation *Mod-Noun*. Any article determiner of the noun phrase remains unperturbed.

3.2 *Verb-Ob*: Detecting verb/object reordering

Our second task tests sensitivity to anomalies in English subject-verb-object (SVO) sentence structure by swapping the positions of verbs and their objects (SVO → SOV). To generate perturbed sentences for this task, we take sentences with a subject-verb-object construction, and reorder the verb (or verb phrase) and the object, as in the example below:

A man wearing a yellow scarf ***rides a bike.*** →
A man wearing a yellow scarf ***a bike rides.***

We refer to this perturbation as *Verb-Ob*. Note that *Verb-Ob* and *Mod-Noun* are superficially similar tasks in that they both reorder sequentially consecutive constituents. However, importantly, they differ in the hierarchical level of the swap.

3.3 *SubN-ObN*: Detecting subject/object reordering

Our third task tests sensitivity to anomalies in subject-verb-object relationships, creating perturbations by swapping the positions of subject and object nouns in a sentence. For this task, we generate the data by swapping the two head nouns of the subject and the object, as below:

A ***man*** *wearing a yellow scarf rides a* ***bike.*** →
A ***bike*** *wearing a yellow scarf rides a* ***man.***

We refer to this perturbation as *SubN-ObN*. We target subject-verb-object structures directly under the root of the syntactic parse, meaning that only one modification is made per sentence for this task.

Detecting the anomaly in this perturbation involves sensitivity to argument structure (the way in which subject, verb, and object should be combined), along with an element of world knowledge (knowing that a bike would not ride a man, nor would a bike typically wear a scarf).[2]

[2]For more details about this task, please see Appendix A.7.

3.4 *Agree-Shift*: Detecting subject/verb disagreement

Our fourth task tests sensitivity to anomalies in subject-verb morphological agreement, by changing inflection on a present tense verb to create number disagreement between subject and verb:

A man *wearing a yellow scarf* ***rides*** *a bike.* →
A man *wearing a yellow scarf* ***ride*** *a bike.*

We refer to this perturbation as *Agree-Shift*.[3] This is the only one of our tasks that involves a slight change in the word inflection, but the word stem remains the same—we consider this to be consistent with holding word content constant.

4 Experiments

We generate probing datasets for each of the anomaly tests described above. We then apply these tasks to examine anomaly sensitivity in a number of generic sentence encoders.[4]

Datasets Each of the above perturbations is used to create a probing dataset consisting of normal sentences and corresponding modified sentences, labeled as *normal* and *perturbed*, respectively. Within each probing task, each *normal* sentence has a corresponding *perturbed* sentence, so the label sets for each task are fully balanced. Each probe is formulated as a binary classification task. Normal sentences and their corresponding perturbed sentences are included in the same partition of the train/dev/test split, so for any sentence in the test set, no version of that sentence (neither the perturbed form nor its original form) has been seen at training time. We draw our *normal* sentences from MultiNLI (Williams et al., 2018) (premise only). Perturbations of those sentences are then generated as our *perturbed* sentences.

[3]Note that while this perturbation echoes the popular LM agreement analyses (Linzen et al., 2016; Gulordava et al., 2018; Goldberg, 2019), the fact that we are probing sentence embeddings for explicit detection of this anomaly is an important difference. Performance by LMs on those agreement tasks can indicate that a model prefers a non-anomalous completion, but cannot speak to whether the model encodes any explicit/perceptible awareness that an anomaly is present/absent. For this reason, model performance on our *Agree-Shift* task should not be compared directly to performance on these agreement probability tasks.

[4]Please refer to the Appendix A.5, A.6, A.7 for more details about data generation, probing implementation, as well as descriptions about encoders and external tasks.

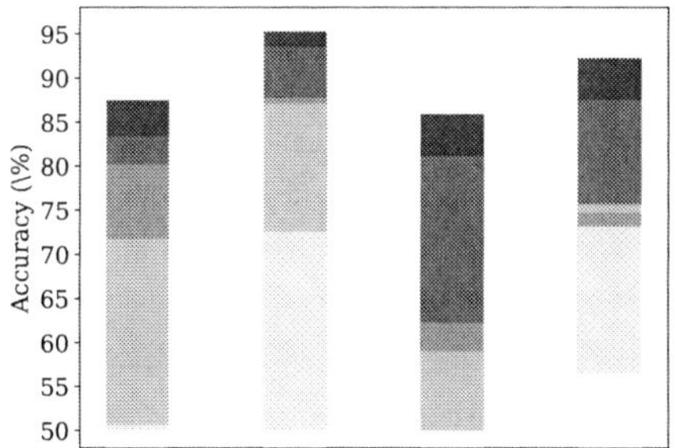

	Mod-Noun	Verb-Ob	SubN-ObN	Agree-Shift
RoBERTa	87.514	95.277	85.943	92.282
BERT	83.453	93.572	81.176	87.536
GenSen	80.132	87.794	62.284	74.736
Skip-thoughts	71.764	87.133	58.975	75.701
InferSent	50.662	72.605	50.0	73.166
BoW	50.0	50.0	50.0	56.518

Figure 1: Anomaly detection performance.

Probing We analyze sentence embeddings from these prominent sentence encoders: InferSent (Conneau et al., 2017), Skip-thoughts (Kiros et al., 2015), GenSen (Subramanian et al., 2018), BERT (Devlin et al., 2019), and RoBERTa (Liu et al., 2019b). The first three models are RNN-based, while the final two are transformer-based.

To test the effectiveness of our control of word content, we also test bag-of-words (BoW) sentence embeddings obtained by averaging of GloVe (Pennington et al., 2014) embeddings. This allows us to verify that our probing tasks are not solvable by simple lexical cues (c.f. Ettinger et al., 2018), thus better isolating effects of syntactic anomalies.

We train and test classifiers on our probing tasks, with sentence embeddings from the above encoders as input. The classifier structure is a multilayer perceptron (MLP) classifier with one hidden layer.[5]

5 Anomaly Detection Results

Fig. 1 shows anomaly detection performance for the tested encoders. We can see first that for three of our four tasks—all reordering tasks—our BoW baseline performs perfectly at chance, verifying elimination of lexical biases. BoW on the *Agree-Shift* task is just above chance, reflecting (expected) slight bias in morphological variations.

Comparing between tasks, we see that *Verb-Ob* yields highest overall performance while *SubN-ObN* yields the lowest. As mentioned above, a particularly informative comparison is between *Verb-Ob* and *Mod-Noun*, which both involve swapping sequentially adjacent content, but at different hierarchical levels. We see that encoders consistently show stronger performance on *Verb-Ob* than *Mod-Noun*, suggesting that the broader hierarchical domain of *Verb-Ob* may indeed make anomalies more accessible for encoding. The only anomaly that affects a broader span of the sentence is *SubN-ObN*—but we see that this is instead one of the most challenging tasks. We suspect that this is attributable to the fact that, as described above, detecting this anomaly may require extra world knowledge and common sense, which certain encoders may have less access to.[6] It is not unexpected, then, that BERT and RoBERTa, with comparatively much larger and more diverse training data exposure, show a large margin of advantage on this challenging *SubN-ObN* task relative to the other encoders. *Agree-Shift* patterns roughly on par with *Mod-Noun*, though notably InferSent (and Skip-thoughts) detects the agreement anomaly much more readily than it does the *Mod-Noun* anomaly.

Comparing between encoders, we see clear stratification in performance. InferSent shows the least anomaly awareness, performing for half of the tasks at chance level with the BoW baseline. GenSen and Skip-thoughts, by contrast, consistently occupy a higher performance tier, often falling not far behind (but never quite on par with) the highest level of performance. The latter distinction is reserved for BERT and RoBERTa, which show the strongest anomaly sensitivity on all tasks. All models show stronger performance on *Verb-Ob* than *Mod-Noun*, but the hierarchical difference between these tasks seems to have particularly significant impact for InferSent and Skip-thoughts, with cues relating to *Verb-Ob* seemingly encoded by InferSent, but cues relating to *Mod-Noun* seeming to be absent. *Mod-Noun* also yields the largest margin of difference between GenSen and Skip-thoughts. Since Skip-thoughts is one objective of GenSen, this suggests that the additional GenSen objectives provide an edge particularly for the finer-grained information needed for *Mod-Noun*.

BERT and RoBERTa emerge soundly as the strongest encoders of anomaly information, with RoBERTa also consistently outperforming BERT. While this is in line with patterns of downstream task performance from these models, it is noteworthy that these models also show superior perfor-

[5]We also train on a logistic regression (LR) classifier. LR results are shown in the Appendix Table 4.

[6]As an encoder trained on semantic reasoning, InferSent nonetheless fails terribly on this task—this may be explained by findings that heuristics can account for much of NLI task learning (Poliak et al., 2018c; McCoy et al., 2020).

mance on these anomaly-detection tasks, as it is not obvious that encoding anomaly information would be relevant for these models' pre-training objectives, or for the most common NLU tasks on which they are typically evaluated.

6 Investigation on Generality of Anomaly Encoding

The above experiments suggest that embeddings from many of these encoders contain signal enabling detection of the presence of syntactic anomalies. However, these results cannot tell us whether these embeddings encode awareness that an "error" is present per se—the classifiers may simply have learned to detect properties associated with a given anomaly, e.g., agreement mismatches, or occurrence of modifiers after nouns. In this sense, the above experiments serve as finer-grained tests of levels of hierarchical information available in these embeddings, but still do not test awareness of the notion of anomaly in general.

In this section we take a closer look at anomaly awareness per se, by testing the extent to which the sensitivities identified above are specific to individual anomalies, or reflective of a more abstract "error" signal that would apply across anomalies. We explore this question by testing transfer performance between different anomaly types.

Transfer Results While in Section 5 we focused on examining anomaly-specific sensitivity in our new tasks—testing variation along fine-grained syntactic hierarchical distinctions and in a word-controlled setting—for examining generality of anomaly encoding it is worthwhile to take into account a broader range of anomaly types and datasets. For this reason we examine transfer between each of our generated probing tasks, as well as transfer to our tasks from established datasets: *SOMO*, *BShift*, and *CoordInv* from Conneau et al. (2018), and the *CoLA* task (Warstadt et al., 2019).

Fig. 2 shows transfer results from each dataset to each of our tasks. For ease of comparison, we also show the test result achieved when training on the same anomaly (the non-transfer result) in the white bars. We see that the majority of encoders show a marked drop in performance relative to the original non-transfer accuracy, and in fact most of the transfer results are approximately at chance performance. This suggests that the embeddings from these models encode information supporting detection of these anomalies, but the signals that enable this detection are anomaly-specific. That is, they may encode some syntactic/semantic signal supporting detection of specific anomalies, but there is no indication that they encode a general awareness that "there is an anomaly".

The notable exceptions to this poor transfer performance are the transformer-based models, BERT and RoBERTa, which by stark contrast to the RNN-based encoders, show non-trivial transfer performance across all four of our generated tasks, regardless of the anomaly that the classifier is trained on. This suggests that to a much greater extent than any of the other encoders, BERT and RoBERTa may encode a more general "error" signal, allowing for generalization across anomalies. Importantly, BERT and RoBERTa do also show some performance drop from non-transfer to transfer settings—so while they may encode a more generalized "error" signal, this is likely in combination with encoding of anomaly-specific information that further aids performance on a given anomaly.

We note that transfer performance from *CoLA* is typically comparable to, or occasionally better than, training on the Conneau et al. tasks–despite the fact that *CoLA* has much smaller training data. *CoLA* is also the only task that contains a variety of anomalies for the model to learn from, rather than a single anomaly type as in all other datasets. This may enable faster, more generalizable learning on this small dataset—but of course, this would only be possible if a generalized anomaly signal is available in the embeddings. Following this reasoning, we also test whether jointly training on multiple anomalies improves transfer performance. The results of these multi-task transfer experiments can be found in Appendix Tables 7-8. These transfer results show overall a small decrease in performance relative to the one-to-one transfer, suggesting that training on single types of anomalies is not creating any major disadvantage for transfer performance. It may also indicate that mixed types of higher-level oddity in natural occurring anomalies from *CoLA* is not trivial to simulate by stacking together data with single type of anomalies as we do here.

The Conneau et al. task that most often shows the best transfer to our tasks (especially *Mod-Noun* and *Verb-Ob*) is *BShift*. This is sensible, given that that task involves detecting a switch in word order within a bigram. Given this similarity, we can expect to see some transfer from this task even in the absence of generalized anomaly encoding.

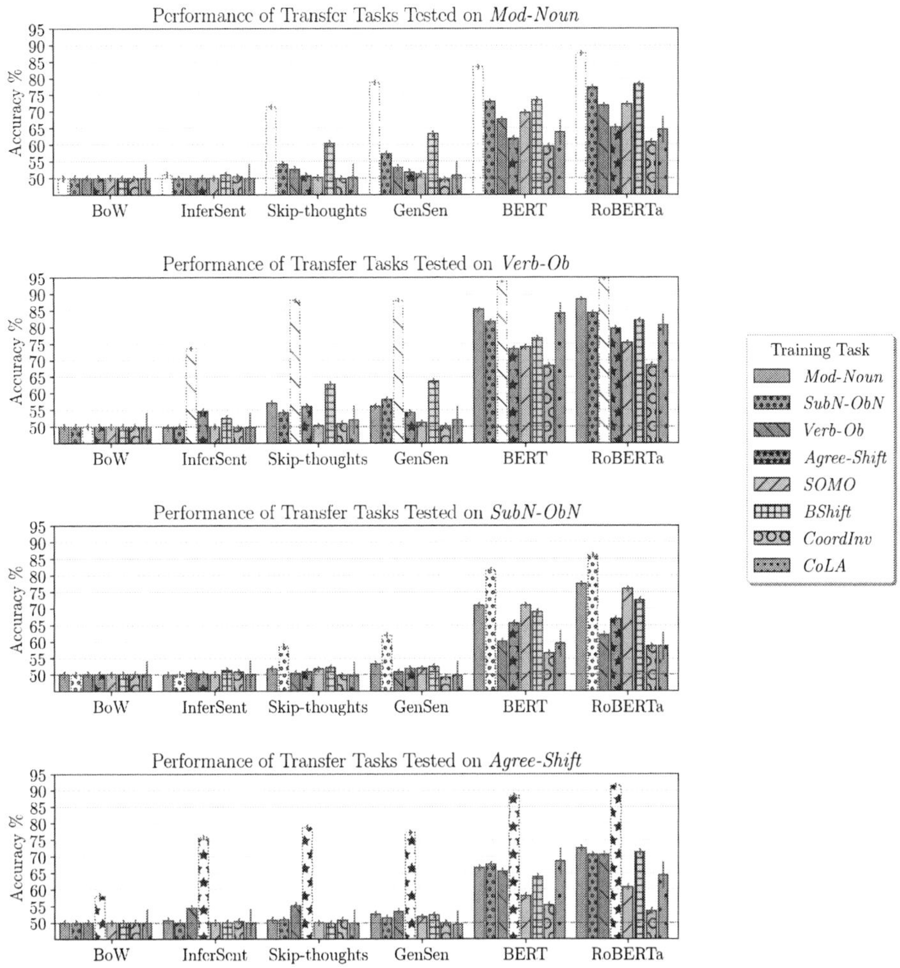

Figure 2: Results on transfer settings, by test tasks. Different patterns/colors represent different training tasks. Results for non-transfer settings (same training and test tasks) are shown in white bars.

As for how our generated anomaly types vary in supporting transfer to other anomaly types, we again note some differences between *Mod-Noun* and *Verb-Ob*. While *Verb-Ob* proved more accessible for detection than *Mod-Noun*, in the transfer setting we find that the broader hierarchical perturbation in *Verb-Ob* is often less conducive to transfer than *Mod-Noun*. Below we explore further to better understand what models are learning when trained on these anomalies.

7 Further analyses

7.1 Exploring false positives

The results above indicate that embeddings from these encoders contain non-trivial signal relevant for specific perturbations, but only BERT and RoBERTa show promise for encoding more general awareness of anomalies. To further explore the anomaly signal learned from these representations, in this section we apply the learned anomaly classifiers to an entirely new dataset, for which no perturbations have been made. For this purpose, we use the *Subj-Num* dataset from Conneau et al. (2018).[7] By default we can assume that all sentences in these data are non-anomalous, so any sentences labeled as *perturbed* can be considered errors. After testing the pre-trained classifiers on embeddings of these unperturbed sentences, we examine these false positives to shed further light on what the classifiers have come to consider anomalies. We focus this analysis on BERT and RoBERTa, as the two models that show the best anomaly detection and the only signs of generalized anomaly encoding.

Error rates for this experiment are shown in Appendix Table 6. We see that in general the false pos-

[7] Dataset size is 10k sentences (test set).

Train task	*Mod-Noun*	*Verb-Ob*	*SubN-ObN*	*Agree-Shift*
BERT	4.9%	2.61%	4.81%	31.98%
RoBERTa	7.73%	3.6%	7.83%	22.13%

Table 1: Error rate on *Subj-Num* data.

itive rates for these models are very low. The highest error rates are found for the classifiers trained on *Agree-Shift*, and examination of these false positives suggests that the majority of these errors are driven by confusion in the face of past-tense verbs (past tense verbs do not inflect for number in English—so past tense verbs were few, and uninformative when present, in our *Agree-Shift* task). This type of error is less informative for our purposes, so we exclude the *Agree-Shift* classifier for these error analyses. For the other classifiers, the error rates are very low, suggesting that the signal picked up on by these classifiers is precise enough to minimize false positives in *normal* inputs.

To examine generality of the anomaly signal detected by the classifiers, we look first to sentences that receive false positives from multiple of the three reordering-based classifiers. We find that within the union of false positives identified across all three classifiers, sentences that are labeled as anomalous by at least two classifiers make up 28.6% and 35.6% for BERT and RoBERTa respectively—and sentences labeled as anomalous by all three classifiers make up 7.3% and 9.6%. Since no two classifiers were trained on the same perturbation, the existence of such overlap is consistent with some generality in the anomaly signal for the representations from these two models.

Table 2 lists samples of false positives identified by all three classifiers. While these sentences are generally grammatical, we see that many of them use somewhat convoluted structures—in many cases one can imagine a human requiring a second pass to parse these correctly. In some cases, as in the "Fireworks" example, there is not a full sentence—or in the "ornaments" example, there appears to be an actual ungrammaticality. The fact that the classifiers converge on sentences that do contain some structural oddity supports the notion that these classifiers may, on the basis of these models' embeddings, have picked up on somewhat of a legitimate concept of syntactic anomaly.

Of course, there are also many items that individual classifiers identify uniquely. We show examples of these in Appendix Table 5. The presence of such anomaly-specific errors is consistent with

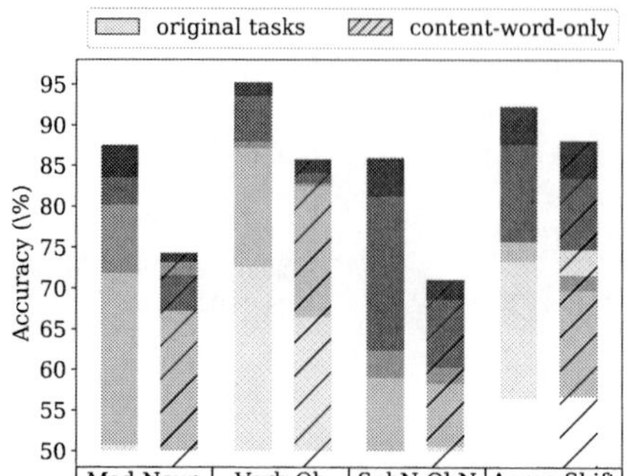

	Mod-Noun	Verb-Ob	SubN-ObN	Agree-Shift
RoBERTa	-13.21	-9.52	-14.85	-4.24
BERT	-11.84	-9.48	-12.6	-4.12
GenSen	-7.03	-5.02	-2.0	-4.08
Skip-thoughts	-4.55	-4.68	-0.69	-6.0
InferSent	-0.66	-6.14	0.58	1.56
BoW	-0.02	0.0	0.0	0.15

Figure 3: Performance of encoders on original tasks vs. "content-word-only" tasks (function words removed). Numbers in embedded table show change in accuracy from original to content-word-only setting.

our findings in Section 6, that even with BERT and RoBERTa the classifiers appear to benefit from some anomaly-specific signal in addition to the potential generalized anomaly signal.

Examining these classifier-specific false positives, we can see some patterns emerging. The *Mod-Noun* classifier seems to be fooled in some cases by instances in which a modifier comes at the end of a phrase (e.g., "a lovely misty gray"). For *Verb-Ob*, the classifier seems at times to be fooled by grammatical sentences ending with a verb, or by fronting of prepositional phrases. For *SubN-ObN*, the false positives often involve nouns that are likely uncommon as subjects, such as "bases". All of these patterns suggest that to some extent, the anomaly-specific cues that the classifiers detect are closely tied to the particulars of our perturbations—some of which may constitute artifacts—and in some cases, they raise the question of whether classifiers can succeed on these tasks based on fairly superficial word position cues, rather than syntax per se. We follow up on this question in the following section.

7.2 Role of content word order

To explore the possibility that classifiers may be succeeding in anomaly detection based on word position cues alone, rather than details of syntactic structure, we run a follow-up test using content-word-only versions of our probes. This serves as a test of how well the models can get by with coarser-grained information about content words positions.

BERT	Dolores asked pointing to a sway backed building made in part of logs and cover with a tin roof . Fireworks* , animals woven of fire and women dancing with flames . There were nice accessible veins there . Three rusty screws down and Beth spoke , making him jump . The pillars were still warming up , but the more powerful they got the more obvious it became to Mac about what was going on . The signals grew clearer , voices , at first faint , then very clear .
RoBERTa	One row , all the way across , formed words connected without spaces . And kidnappers with God only knew what agenda . The slums would burn , not stone nobleman keeps . " " Hull reinforcements are out of power . From inside that pyramid seventy centuries look out at us . The ornaments* she wore sparkled but isn 't noticeable much , as her blissful countenance shined over , surpassing it .

Table 2: Representative false positives shared by all three reordering classifiers.

Fig. 3 shows anomaly detection performance when embeddings reflect only content words, as compared to the original anomaly detection performance. We see that across tasks, anomaly detection performance of Skip-thoughts, GenSen, BERT, and RoBERTa are all reduced as a result of the loss of function words. BERT and RoBERTa in particular show substantial losses for the three reordering tasks, indicating that these models benefit significantly from function words for encoding the information that supports detection of these anomalies. It is also worth noting, however, that the models do retain a non-trivial portion of their original accuracy even with function words absent, supporting the idea that to some extent these perturbations can be detected through coarser position information rather than fine-grained syntax.[8] This is an observation worth keeping in mind, particularly when interpreting anomaly detection as evidence of syntactic encoding (e.g. Conneau et al., 2018).

8 Discussion

In the experiments above, we have taken a closer look at the nature of syntactic anomaly encoding in sentence embeddings. Using fine-grained variation in types of syntactic anomalies, we show differences in patterns of anomaly detection across encoders, suggesting corresponding differences in the types of anomaly information encoded by these models. While the margins of difference in anomaly-specific sensitivity are less dramatic between small RNN-based models and larger transformer models, when we examine the generality of the detected anomaly signal, we find that only BERT and RoBERTa show signs of higher-level anomaly awareness, as evidenced by non-trivial transfer performance between anomalies.

What might be driving the anomaly encoding patterns indicated by our results? Explicit syntactic training does not appear to be necessary. GenSen is the only model that includes an explicit syntactic component in its training (constituency parsing), which could help to explain that model's comparatively strong performance on the individual anomaly detection tasks. However, it is noteworthy that GenSen performs mostly on par with Skip-thoughts, which constitutes just one of GenSen's objectives, and which uses only prediction of adjacent sentences. BERT and RoBERTa, the only models to show signs of more generalized anomaly encoding, have no explicit syntactic training at all. However, various findings have suggested that these types of models do develop syntactic sensitivity as a result of their more generalized training objectives (Goldberg, 2019; Liu et al., 2019a; Alleman et al., 2021; Tenney et al., 2019).

We can imagine various ways in which objectives involving prediction of words in context, as used by BERT and RoBERTa, could encourage learning of a generalized notion of syntactic anomaly. It may be the case that oddities occur together, in which case they could be mutually predictive and therefore of value for optimizing a prediction-based objective. More generally, anomalous sentences are likely identifiable as less probable, or more difficult to generate coherent predictions for. This relationship between anomaly and sentence probability raises a related question: Is this a problem for our conclusions here? Could models simply be identifying anomalous sentences as less probable, without any actual notion of syntactic anomaly? In NLP models, assessment of text probabilities is closely related to assessment of text naturalness and acceptability. For this reason, teasing apart general sensitivity to probability

[8]The notion that coarser position information alone can contribute non-trivially to anomaly identification is further supported by testing on *normal* sentences in *Subj-Num* when training on the content-word-only setting; for these results, see Appendix Table 6.

versus genuine awareness of syntactic grammaticality phenomena is a recurring challenge when testing syntactic knowledge in language models—and these things are similarly potentially entangled in our analyses here. To an extent this entanglement is inevitable and unproblematic: we necessarily expect syntactic anomalies to lower the probability of a string, and we can expect some awareness of syntactic anomaly to be important for assigning lower probability to an ungrammatical string. We can imagine, for instance, a situation in which a language model has no sensitivity to what constitutes good versus anomalous syntax, and thus assigns probability solely on the basis of word co-occurrence or other unrelated indicators of naturalness. In this sense, although it is not difficult to imagine how the close relationship between anomaly and sentence probability could be an explanation for findings that suggest anomaly awareness in these models, this does not change the fact that model representations may end up with genuine, detectable encoding of generalized anomaly information as a byproduct of probabilistic training—and this genuine anomaly encoding may be what we are detecting with our tests here. However, future work can examine further the relationship between syntactic anomaly and model perplexities, to explore whether these embeddings could show signs of anomaly sensitivity while in fact exclusively encoding confounding probabilistic information unrelated to syntactic anomaly.

Our content-word-only analysis provides one source of evidence on the relative importance of genuine syntactic sensitivity in success on our syntactic-related anomaly tasks. This test aims to tease apart the extent to which success on our tasks requires processing of finer-grained syntactic information, versus the extent to which models can succeed based on more superficial content word position information. We find in this analysis that most encoders do benefit from the finer-grained syntactic information provided by function words, supporting an important role for more advanced syntactic sensitivity in these tasks—however, we also find that substantial proportions of the observed detection accuracy can indeed be achieved with content words alone. To the best of our knowledge, we are the first to report this finding. This leaves us with two key takeaways. First, to an extent there is good reason to believe that a reasonable amount of genuine syntactic sensitivity is involved in the highest levels of success on our anomaly tasks. Second, success on syntactic anomaly tasks can also be non-trivially inflated by use of more superficial cues. That is to say, as usual, these datasets have a habit of enabling learning from simpler cues than are intended. This takeaway highlights a need for caution in interpreting detection of reordering anomalies as evidence of deeper syntactic encoding per se (Conneau et al., 2018)—especially in probing datasets that use naturally-occurring data without exerting controls for confounding cues.

While these results have shed light on potential encoding of generalized syntactic anomaly knowledge in pre-trained models, there are many further questions to pursue with respect to these models' handling and understanding of such anomalies. We will leave for future work the problem of understanding in greater detail how model training may contribute to encoding of a generalized awareness of anomalies in text, how a genuine notion of syntactic anomaly could be further disentangled from general probability sensitivity, and how one could exploit models' awareness of anomaly for improving model robustness on downstream pipelines.

9 Conclusion

We have undertaken a direct study of anomaly encoding in sentence embeddings, finding impacts of hierarchical differences in anomaly type, but finding evidence of generalized anomaly encoding only in BERT and RoBERTa. Follow-up analyses support the conclusion that these embeddings encode a combination of generalized and anomaly-specific cues in these embeddings, with models appearing to leverage both finer-grained and coarser-grained information for anomaly detection. These results contribute to our understanding of the nature of encoding of linguistic input in embeddings from recent models. Future work can further explore the relationship between naturalness-oriented training and cultivation of abstract anomaly awareness, and how these insights can be leveraged for more robust and human-like processing of language inputs.

Acknowledgments

We would like to thank several anonymous reviewers for helpful comments and suggestions that have led to improvements on earlier versions of this paper. We would also like to thank the members of the University of Chicago CompLing Lab, for valuable discussions on this work.

References

Yossi Adi, Einat Kermany, Yonatan Belinkov, Ofer Lavi, and Yoav Goldberg. 2016. Fine-grained analysis of sentence embeddings using auxiliary prediction tasks. *arXiv preprint arXiv:1608.04207.*

Matteo Alleman, Jonathan Mamou, Miguel A Del Rio, Hanlin Tang, Yoon Kim, and SueYeon Chung. 2021. Syntactic perturbations reveal representational correlates of hierarchical phrase structure in pretrained language models. *arXiv preprint arXiv:2104.07578.*

Yonatan Belinkov, Nadir Durrani, Fahim Dalvi, Hassan Sajjad, and James Glass. 2017a. What do neural machine translation models learn about morphology? In *Proceedings of the 55th Annual Meeting of the Association for Computational Linguistics (Volume 1: Long Papers)*, pages 861–872.

Yonatan Belinkov, Lluís Màrquez, Hassan Sajjad, Nadir Durrani, Fahim Dalvi, and James Glass. 2017b. Evaluating layers of representation in neural machine translation on part-of-speech and semantic tagging tasks. In *Proceedings of the Eighth International Joint Conference on Natural Language Processing (Volume 1: Long Papers)*, pages 1–10.

Chomsky. 1957. *Syntactic Structures.* The Hague/Paris:Mouton.

Shammur Absar Chowdhury and Roberto Zamparelli. 2018. Rnn simulations of grammaticality judgments on long-distance dependencies. In *Proceedings of the 27th international conference on computational linguistics*, pages 133–144.

Alexis Conneau, Douwe Kiela, Holger Schwenk, Loïc Barrault, and Antoine Bordes. 2017. Supervised learning of universal sentence representations from natural language inference data. In *Proceedings of the 2017 Conference on Empirical Methods in Natural Language Processing*, pages 670–680.

Alexis Conneau, German Kruszewski, Guillaume Lample, Loïc Barrault, and Marco Baroni. 2018. What you can cram into a single vector: Probing sentence embeddings for linguistic properties. In *ACL 2018*, volume 1, pages 2126–2136. Association for Computational Linguistics.

Ishita Dasgupta, Demi Guo, Andreas Stuhlmüller, Samuel J Gershman, and Noah D Goodman. 2018. Evaluating compositionality in sentence embeddings. *arXiv preprint arXiv:1802.04302.*

Jacob Devlin, Ming-Wei Chang, Kenton Lee, and Kristina Toutanova. 2019. Bert: Pre-training of deep bidirectional transformers for language understanding. In *Proceedings of the 2019 Conference of the North American Chapter of the Association for Computational Linguistics: Human Language Technologies, Volume 1 (Long and Short Papers)*, pages 4171–4186.

Allyson Ettinger. 2020. What bert is not: Lessons from a new suite of psycholinguistic diagnostics for language models. *Transactions of the Association for Computational Linguistics*, 8:34–48.

Allyson Ettinger, Ahmed Elgohary, Colin Phillips, and Philip Resnik. 2018. Assessing composition in sentence vector representations. In *Proceedings of the 27th International Conference on Computational Linguistics*, pages 1790–1801.

Allyson Ettinger, Ahmed Elgohary, and Philip Resnik. 2016. Probing for semantic evidence of composition by means of simple classification tasks. In *Proceedings of the 1st Workshop on Evaluating Vector-Space Representations for NLP*, pages 134–139.

Janet Dean Fodor, Weijia Ni, Stephen Crain, and Donald Shankweiler. 1996. Tasks and timing in the perception of linguistic anomaly. *Journal of Psycholinguistic Research*, 25(1):25–57.

Richard Futrell, Ethan Wilcox, Takashi Morita, Peng Qian, Miguel Ballesteros, and Roger Levy. 2019. Neural language models as psycholinguistic subjects: Representations of syntactic state. In *Proceedings of the 2019 Conference of the North American Chapter of the Association for Computational Linguistics: Human Language Technologies, Volume 1 (Long and Short Papers)*, pages 32–42.

Tao Ge, Furu Wei, and Ming Zhou. 2018. Reaching human-level performance in automatic grammatical error correction: An empirical study. *arXiv preprint arXiv:1807.01270.*

Yoav Goldberg. 2019. Assessing bert's syntactic abilities. *arXiv preprint arXiv:1901.05287.*

Kristina Gulordava, Piotr Bojanowski, Edouard Grave, Tal Linzen, and Marco Baroni. 2018. Colorless green recurrent networks dream hierarchically. In *Proceedings of NAACL-HLT*, pages 1195–1205.

Ashim Gupta, Giorgi Kvernadze, and Vivek Srikumar. 2021. Bert & family eat word salad: Experiments with text understanding. *arXiv preprint arXiv:2101.03453.*

Homa B Hashemi and Rebecca Hwa. 2016. An evaluation of parser robustness for ungrammatical sentences. In *Proceedings of the 2016 Conference on Empirical Methods in Natural Language Processing*, pages 1765–1774.

Ganesh Jawahar, Benoît Sagot, and Djamé Seddah. 2019. What does bert learn about the structure of language? In *ACL 2019-57th Annual Meeting of the Association for Computational Linguistics.*

Robin Jia and Percy Liang. 2017. Adversarial examples for evaluating reading comprehension systems. In *Proceedings of the 2017 Conference on Empirical Methods in Natural Language Processing*, pages 2021–2031.

Ryan Kiros, Yukun Zhu, Russ R Salakhutdinov, Richard Zemel, Raquel Urtasun, Antonio Torralba, and Sanja Fidler. 2015. Skip-thought vectors. In *Advances in neural information processing systems*, pages 3294–3302.

Josef Klafka and Allyson Ettinger. 2020. Spying on your neighbors: Fine-grained probing of contextual embeddings for information about surrounding words. In *Proceedings of the 58th Annual Meeting of the Association for Computational Linguistics*, pages 4801–4811.

Yair Lakretz, Cognitive Neuroimaging Unit, German Kruszewski, Theo Desbordes, Dieuwke Hupkes, Stanislas Dehaene, and Marco Baroni. 2019. The emergence of number and syntax units in lstm language models. In *Proceedings of NAACL-HLT*, pages 11–20.

Bai Li, Zining Zhu, Guillaume Thomas, Yang Xu, and Frank Rudzicz. 2021. How is bert surprised? layerwise detection of linguistic anomalies. *arXiv preprint arXiv:2105.07452*.

Tal Linzen, Emmanuel Dupoux, and Yoav Goldberg. 2016. Assessing the ability of lstms to learn syntax-sensitive dependencies. *Transactions of the Association for Computational Linguistics*, 4:521–535.

Nelson F Liu, Matt Gardner, Yonatan Belinkov, Matthew E Peters, and Noah A Smith. 2019a. Linguistic knowledge and transferability of contextual representations. In *Proceedings of the 2019 Conference of the North American Chapter of the Association for Computational Linguistics: Human Language Technologies, Volume 1 (Long and Short Papers)*, pages 1073–1094.

Yinhan Liu, Myle Ott, Naman Goyal, Jingfei Du, Mandar Joshi, Danqi Chen, Omer Levy, Mike Lewis, Luke Zettlemoyer, and Veselin Stoyanov. 2019b. Roberta: A robustly optimized bert pretraining approach. *arXiv preprint arXiv:1907.11692*.

Rebecca Marvin and Tal Linzen. 2018. Targeted syntactic evaluation of language models. In *Proceedings of the 2018 Conference on Empirical Methods in Natural Language Processing*, pages 1192–1202.

R Thomas McCoy, Ellie Pavlick, and Tal Linzen. 2020. Right for the wrong reasons: Diagnosing syntactic heuristics in natural language inference. In *57th Annual Meeting of the Association for Computational Linguistics, ACL 2019*, pages 3428–3448. Association for Computational Linguistics (ACL).

Jeffrey Pennington, Richard Socher, and Christopher Manning. 2014. Glove: Global vectors for word representation. In *Proceedings of the 2014 conference on empirical methods in natural language processing (EMNLP)*, pages 1532–1543.

Thang M Pham, Trung Bui, Long Mai, and Anh Nguyen. 2020. Out of order: How important is the sequential order of words in a sentence in natural language understanding tasks? *arXiv preprint arXiv:2012.15180*.

Adam Poliak, Yonatan Belinkov, James Glass, and Benjamin Van Durme. 2018a. On the evaluation of semantic phenomena in neural machine translation using natural language inference. In *Proceedings of the 2018 Conference of the North American Chapter of the Association for Computational Linguistics: Human Language Technologies, Volume 2 (Short Papers)*, pages 513–523.

Adam Poliak, Aparajita Haldar, Rachel Rudinger, J Edward Hu, Ellie Pavlick, Aaron Steven White, and Benjamin Van Durme. 2018b. Collecting diverse natural language inference problems for sentence representation evaluation. In *Proceedings of the 2018 Conference on Empirical Methods in Natural Language Processing*, pages 67–81.

Adam Poliak, Jason Naradowsky, Aparajita Haldar, Rachel Rudinger, and Benjamin Van Durme. 2018c. Hypothesis only baselines in natural language inference. In *Proceedings of the Seventh Joint Conference on Lexical and Computational Semantics*, pages 180–191.

Pranav Rajpurkar, Robin Jia, and Percy Liang. 2018. Know what you don't know: Unanswerable questions for squad. In *Proceedings of the 56th Annual Meeting of the Association for Computational Linguistics (Volume 2: Short Papers)*, pages 784–789.

Pranav Rajpurkar, Jian Zhang, Konstantin Lopyrev, and Percy Liang. 2016. Squad: 100,000+ questions for machine comprehension of text. In *Proceedings of the 2016 Conference on Empirical Methods in Natural Language Processing*, pages 2383–2392.

Anna Rogers, Olga Kovaleva, and Anna Rumshisky. 2020. A primer in bertology: What we know about how bert works. *Transactions of the Association for Computational Linguistics*, 8:842–866.

Koustuv Sinha, Robin Jia, Dieuwke Hupkes, Joelle Pineau, Adina Williams, and Douwe Kiela. 2021. Masked language modeling and the distributional hypothesis: Order word matters pre-training for little. *arXiv preprint arXiv:2104.06644*.

Sandeep Subramanian, Adam Trischler, Yoshua Bengio, and Christopher J Pal. 2018. Learning general purpose distributed sentence representations via large scale multi-task learning. In *International Conference on Learning Representations*.

Ian Tenney, Patrick Xia, Berlin Chen, Alex Wang, Adam Poliak, R Thomas McCoy, Najoung Kim, Benjamin Van Durme, Samuel R Bowman, Dipanjan Das, et al. 2019. What do you learn from context? probing for sentence structure in contextualized word representations. In *7th International Conference on Learning Representations, ICLR 2019*.

Alex Warstadt, Amanpreet Singh, and Samuel R Bowman. 2019. Neural network acceptability judgments. *Transactions of the Association for Computational Linguistics*, 7:625–641.

Aaron Steven White, Pushpendre Rastogi, Kevin Duh, and Benjamin Van Durme. 2017. Inference is everything: Recasting semantic resources into a unified evaluation framework. In *Proceedings of the Eighth International Joint Conference on Natural Language Processing (Volume 1: Long Papers)*, pages 996–1005.

Adina Williams, Nikita Nangia, and Samuel Bowman. 2018. A broad-coverage challenge corpus for sentence understanding through inference. In *Proceedings of the 2018 Conference of the North American Chapter of the Association for Computational Linguistics: Human Language Technologies, Volume 1 (Long Papers)*, pages 1112–1122.

Yi Yang, Wen-tau Yih, and Christopher Meek. 2015. Wikiqa: A challenge dataset for open-domain question answering. In *Proceedings of the 2015 conference on empirical methods in natural language processing*, pages 2013–2018.

Fan Yin, Quanyu Long, Tao Meng, and Kai-Wei Chang. 2020. On the robustness of language encoders against grammatical errors. In *Proceedings of the 58th Annual Meeting of the Association for Computational Linguistics*.

A Appendix

A.1 Cross-lingual encoders

Our probing tasks focus on anomalies defined relative to English syntax—but of course grammatical properties vary from language to language. Some of our perturbations produce constructions that are grammatical in other languages. We compare Universal Sentence Encoder (Cer et al., 2018) in the variants of both monolingual and cross-lingual (Chidambaram et al., 2019) trained models—Multi-task en-en, Multi-task en-fr, and Multi-task en-de. This allows us to examine impacts of cross-lingual learning, between English and different target languages, on anomaly sensitivity. [9]

From Table 3, we see that the two cross-lingual encoders (Multi-task en-fr and Multi-task en-de) do show slightly stronger anomaly detection relative to the monolingual model (Multi-task en-en) on *Mod-Noun*, *Verb-Ob*, and *Agree-Shift*, while having similar accuracy on *SubN-ObN*. This suggests that to accomplish the cross-lingual mapping from English to French or English to German, these models may carry out somewhat more explicit encoding of syntactic ordering information, as well as morphological agreement information, resulting in encoded embeddings being more sensitive to corresponding anomalies relative to the monolingual model. As we have discussed in the main paper, anomaly detection in the *SubN-ObN* task likely involves understanding extra world knowledge, so it is perhaps not surprising that the cross-lingual component does not provide a boost in sensitivity on that task. For the most part, we find that the difference between the English-to-French and English-to-German mapping does not significantly impact encoding of the tested anomaly types.

(accuracy %)	Multi-task en-en	Multi-task en-fr	Multi-task en-de
Mod-Noun	54.858	57.539	59.109
Verb-Ob	63.204	66.188	66.345
SubN-ObN	56.91	56.372	56.641
Agree-Shift	56.125	61.746	61.33

Table 3: Anomaly detection results on mono-lingual encoder vs. its cross-lingual variants. (MLP)

As for the transferability of the anomaly encoding (especially on the multi-one transfer, see Table 7), we observe non-trivial performance improvement in the multi-task setting for the Multi-task en-en model, relative to the cross-lingual variants. This suggests that Multi-task en-en may result in a somewhat more generalized anomaly encoding, while cross-lingual variants are more sensitive to properties of individual anomalies.

A.2 Logistic regression results

	LR					
	BoW	InferSent	Skip-thoughts	GenSen	BERT	Roberta
Mod-Noun	50	57.595	69.329	79.459	82.903	87.189
Verb-Ob	50	72.078	85.001	87.469	93.033	95.187
SubN-ObN	50	56.451	57.774	61.723	80.48	85.484
Agree-Shift	55.34	72.403	72.93	72.538	83.778	91.676
	MLP					
	BoW	InferSent	Skip-thoughts	GenSen	BERT	Roberta
Mod-Noun	50	50.662	71.764	80.132	83.453	87.514
Verb-Ob	50	72.605	87.133	87.794	93.572	95.277
SubN-ObN	50	50	58.975	62.284	81.176	85.943
Agree-Shift	56.518	73.166	75.701	74.736	87.536	92.282

Table 4: Results (accuracy %) on original anomaly detection tasks, comparing between LR and MLP classifiers. The MLP results are the same as what has been shown in Fig. 1 in the main body.

As seen in Table 4, the results suggest that, for the most part, training with LR yields comparable

[9]We do not discuss this cross-lingual results in the main paper due to that the differences between mono-lingual encoder and its cross-lingual variants are small. But we do think the constant patterns behind the differences here are inspiring.

performance to that with MLP, consistent with the findings of Conneau et al. (2018).[10] We do find, however, that the LR classifier has higher accuracy for InferSent on *Mod-Noun* and *SubN-ObN*. This suggests that, to the extent that these anomalies are encoded (perhaps only weakly) in InferSent, they may in fact be better suited to linear extraction. For the task of *Agree-Shift*, most encoders show large improvements on MLP over LR, suggesting that morphological agreement anomalies are less conducive to linear extraction.

A.3 Error Analysis and the Role of Content Word Order

We show the error analysis results on the out-of-sample *Subj-Num* data in this part. Table 6 shows the error rate in terms of each training task (original and content-word-only), with the top two strongest encoders within our investigation. Table 5 lists sampled false positives identified exclusively by each classifier, along with corresponding initial observations.

As we see in the main paper, BERT and RoBERTa show non-trivial benefits from functional information for improving overall anomaly sensitivity, but the content-word-only setting can account for a substantial proportion of contribution for detecting the anomalies. This is roughly consistent with what we found in Table 6 that training from content word order only can lead to relatively lower error rate for most cases on normal sentences.

A.4 Transferring via Multi-Task Learning

Tables 7-8 list the multi-one transferring results with consistent training size compared to that of one-one transferring. We show the multi-one transfer results along with the performance change relative to the best one-one results obtained on the current test task when training with any one of the joint training tasks. Most of the multi-one transfer results show small amount of decrease from one-one transfer, suggesting that classifiers are still fitting to anomaly-specific properties that reduce transfer of anomaly detection.

A.5 Description of External Tasks for Transfer Training

SOMO *SOMO* distinguishes whether a randomly picked noun or verb was replaced with another noun or verb in a sentence.

BShift *BShift* distinguishes whether two consecutive tokens within a sentence have been inverted.

CoordInv *CoordInv* distinguishes whether the order of two co-ordinated clausal conjoints within a sentence has been inverted.

CoLA *CoLA* tests detection of general linguistic acceptability in natural occurring corpus, using expert annotations by humans.

A.6 Description of Encoders

InferSent InferSent is a sentence encoder optimized for natural language inference (NLI), mainly focusing on capturing semantic reasoning information for general use.

Skip-thoughts Skip-thoughts is a sentence encoder framework trained on the Toronto BookCorpus, with an encoder-decoder architecture, to reconstruct sentences preceding and following an encoded sentence.

GenSen GenSen is a general-purpose sentence encoder trained via large-scale multi-task learning. Training objectives include Skip-thoughts, NLI, machine translation, and constituency parsing.

BERT BERT is a deep bidirectional transformer model, pre-trained on tasks of masked language modeling (MLM) and next-sentence prediction (NSP).

RoBERTa RoBERTa is a variant of BERT, and outperforms BERT on a suite of downstream tasks. RoBERTa builds on BERT's MLM strategy, removing BERT's NSP objective, with improved pre-training methodologies, such as dynamically masking. [11]

A.7 Implementation Details

Hyperparameters Dropout rate is set to be 0.25. Batch size is set to be 64. Early stopping is applied. The optimizer is Adam. The learning rate is explored within $\{0.01, 0.001, 0.0001, 0.00001\}$. The MLP classifier has one hidden layer of 512 units.

[10] Since we observe performance of LR to be mostly on par with one-hidden-layer MLP, we expect benefits of exploration with further classifier complexity to be limited.

[11] We use bert-large-uncased-whole-word-masking, and roberta-large. We take the average of fixed pre-trained embeddings from the last layer for all sentence tokens. Pilot experiments show comparable performance between the average of all token embeddings versus the first/CLS token embedding.

	Exclusive in *Mod-Noun*
BERT	The buildings here were all **a lovely misty gray** , which gave them a dreamlike quality . There are terrible slums in **London Daisy** , places you 'd never want to visit .
RoBERTa	Suddenly , his senses sharpened and he felt **less inebriated** . All the charts are in **drawers below the table** .
observation	Most of the samples involve a construction which is "seemingly a noun followed by a modifier format". For BERT, the samples seem to involve multiple adjectives in a row, where the final word is more frequently to be an adjective generally, and is more clear following the *Mod-Noun*-specific detection rules. For RoBERTa, e.g., "drawers below the table", "drawers" actually belongs to another prepositional phrase "in drawers" which is parallel to the followed by prepositional phrase "below the table".
	Exclusive in *Verb-Ob*
BERT	Slowly , the gatehouse **rose** . **Through their windows** , thick candles spread throughout flickered softly .
RoBERTa	**A satisfactory rate of exchange I feel** . The entire column stretched back almost as far as the eye could **see** .
observation	A clear pattern across both encoders: the error samples involve fronting such as prepositional phrase-fronting or object-fronting, or involve constructions end with a verb/verb phrase (thus not with a standard SVO structure).
	Exclusive in *SubN-ObN*
BERT	The **object** changed as he spoke . The **bases** were wide , and as the buildings climbed into the sky , they became narrower and branched off to connect to other buildings .
RoBERTa	That **joint** will help you sleep . The stealth **assassin** never belonged , but the reason will shatter his every conviction .
observation	For both encoders, the subject word of the sampled sentence is always an uncommon subject word.
	Exclusive in *Agree-Shift*
BERT	Not even the vendors who **stood** at their little shops or at their carts and called out their specials cared that I was there . The Tiger Man , still awake , **regarded** her with groggy eyes .
RoBERTa	My brows **went** up . A humorless laugh **escaped** his mouth and all I could do was stand mute , my heart breaking .
observation	Almost all of the error samples are with past tense main verb, across both encoders.

Table 5: Sampled examples for error analysis, along with some basic observed patterns. We list sampled typical examples for which the sentences are false positives exclusively in each of our four tasks. The bold text highlights words or constructions that possibly relate to what we think as cues that trigger our pre-trained classifier to predict the whole sentence as *perturbed*.

	original			
train task	*Mod-Noun*	*Verb-Ob*	*SubN-ObN*	*Agree-Shift*
BERT	4.9%	2.61%	4.81%	31.98%
RoBERTa	7.73%	3.6%	7.83%	22.13%
	content-word-only			
train task	*Mod-Noun*	*Verb-Ob*	*SubN-ObN*	*Agree-Shift*
BERT	1.82%	3.75%	2.0%	22.86%
RoBERTa	0.96%	1.64%	1.54%	4.92%

Table 6: Error rate on *Subj-Num* data, with a total size of 10,000 sentences (test set). The top rows show the results when the training on original tasks, while the bottom rows show the results when training on content-word-only tasks.

Probing data generation We use the premise sentences from the train, dev-matched, dev-mismatched datasets of MultiNLI, with repeats discarded according to the promptID. [12] [13]

We adopt an approach that we refer to as "exhaustive" perturbation: modifying all instances of a given structure within a sentence, to ensure that sentences have internal structural consistency—e.g., a perturbed sentence in *Mod-Noun* will not contain both "modifier+noun" and "noun+modifier" structures—thus avoiding inconsistency serving as an extra signal for detection. [14]

For each task, we use training data of 71k sentences, and dev and test data of 8.9k sentences.

For the *SubN-ObN* and the *Mod-Noun* tasks,[15]

[12]The following tools are used for our generation: nltk.tree `https://www.nltk.org/_modules/nltk/tree.html`, and spaCy `https://spacy.io`. The transformation tool (along with extra rules) for *Agree-Shift*: https://www.clips.uantwerpen.be/pages/pattern.

[13]The ratio of plural verbs to single verbs (VBP/VBZ) in the original sentences is 1.044/1.

[14]The average number of modifications per sentence is 1.69, 1.97, 1.0, and 1.97 for *Mod-Noun*, *Verb-Ob*, *SubN-ObN*, and *Agree-Shift*), respectively. Note that when we instead restrict perturbations to a single modification per sentence, we see that the same basic patterns across tasks are retained.

[15]For the task of *Mod-Noun*, this could in particular happen

Encoder/Train task	multi-task (*Verb-Ob* + *SubN-ObN* + *Agree-Shift*)		multi-task (*Mod-Noun* + *SubN-ObN* + *Agree-Shift*)		multi-task (*Mod-Noun* + *Verb-Ob* + *Agree-Shift*)		multi-task (*Mod-Noun* + *Verb-Ob* + *SubN-ObN*)	
	Mod-Noun	Δ	*Verb-Ob*	Δ	*SubN-ObN*	Δ	*Agree-Shift*	Δ
BoW	50.0	0.0	50.0	0.0	50.0	0.0	50.0	0.0
InferSent	50.011	**0.011**	54.61	**0.012**	51.369	**0.92**	54.337	-0.1
Skip-thoughts	53.298	-0.83	63.022	**6.001**	51.357	-0.46	55.289	**0.034**
GenSen	55.531	-1.772	60.61	**2.456**	52.984	-0.213	54.729	**1.401**
BERT	73.996	-0.101	83.614	-0.919	72.616	**0.09**	71.257	**0.941**
Multi-task en-en	53.455	**0.123**	54.587	-2.804	52.984	-0.247	51.154	**0.258**
Multi-task en-fr	52.165	-0.797	53.41	-0.28	52.244	-1.054	52.824	-0.258
Multi-task en-de	52.008	-0.381	54.419	**0.179**	52.333	-0.73	52.387	-0.863

Table 7: Transfer results of multi-one transferring among our generated tasks with consistent training size. The amount of training size of multi-task training is consistent with one-one transferring. The columns of Δ show how much the multi-one transferring improves or drops from the best one-one result. The improvements (positive Δ values) are bolded.

Encoder/Train task	multi-task (*SOMO* + *BShift* + *CoordInv*)							
	Mod-Noun		*Verb-Ob*		*SubN-ObN*		*Agree-Shift*	
	acc	Δ	acc	Δ	acc	Δ	acc	Δ
BOW	50.0	0.0	50.033	**0.033**	50.017	**0.017**	50.0	0.0
Infersen	50.067	-0.833	50.217	-2.316	50.1	-1.2	49.933	-0.5
Skip-thoughts	57.767	-2.666	57.733	-5.05	51.3	-0.85	50.383	-0.4
GenSen	58.533	-4.75	58.867	-4.75	50.533	-1.834	50.783	-1.617
BERT	69.883	-3.967	73.683	-5.1	69.317	-0.75	62.367	-1.55
Multi-task en-en	53.283	**0.283**	54.0	-0.533	52.617	**0.134**	51.017	**0.084**
Multi-task en-fr	50.767	-0.933	52.5	-5.467	51.85	-0.45	51.05	**0.117**
Multi-task en-de	49.7	-3.4	50.167	-5.3	50.3	-1.167	50.033	-0.5

Table 8: Transfer tasks jointly trained on multi-task learning with all of Conneau et al. tasks, tested on each of our generated tasks, with consistent training size.

sometimes the case might arise that the resulting perturbed sentences are still normal or acceptable, but perhaps somewhat stranger or less probable to occur in the wild, e.g., "man bites dog". However, this should be a rare case, as the original sentences are long enough to involve adequate context to distinguish normal from perturbed examples.

with noun phrases involving noun-noun compounds.

Enhancing Interpretable Clauses Semantically using Pretrained Word Representation

Rohan Kumar Yadav, Lei Jiao, Ole-Christoffer Granmo, and Morten Goodwin
Centre for Artificial Intelligence Research, University of Agder, 4879, Grimstad, Norway
{rohan.k.yadav, lei.jiao, ole.granmo, morten.goodwin}@uia.no

Abstract

Tsetlin Machine (TM) is an interpretable pattern recognition algorithm based on propositional logic, which has demonstrated competitive performance in many Natural Language Processing (NLP) tasks, including sentiment analysis, text classification, and Word Sense Disambiguation. To obtain human-level interpretability, legacy TM employs Boolean input features such as bag-of-words (BOW). However, the BOW representation makes it difficult to use any pre-trained information, for instance, word2vec and GloVe word representations. This restriction has constrained the performance of TM compared to deep neural networks (DNNs) in NLP. To reduce the performance gap, in this paper, we propose a novel way of using pre-trained word representations for TM. The approach significantly enhances the performance and interpretability of TM. We achieve this by extracting semantically related words from pre-trained word representations as input features to the TM. Our experiments show that the accuracy of the proposed approach is significantly higher than the previous BOW-based TM, reaching the level of DNN-based models.

1 Introduction

Tsetlin Machine (TM) is an explainable pattern recognition approach that solves complex classification problems using propositional formulas (Granmo, 2018). Text- (Berge et al., 2019), numerical data- (Abeyrathna et al., 2019), and image classification (Granmo et al., 2019) are recent areas of application. In Natural Language Processing (NLP), TM has provided encouraging trade-offs between accuracy and interpretability for various tasks. These include Sentiment Analysis (SA) (Yadav et al., 2021; Saha et al., 2020), Word Sense Disambiguation (WSD) (Yadav. et al., 2021), and novelty detection (Bhattarai. et al., 2021). Because TM NLP models employ bag-of-words (BOW) that treat each word as independent features, it is easy for humans to interpret them. The models can be interpreted simply by inspecting the words that take part in the conjunctive clauses. However, using a simple BOW makes it challenging to attain the same accuracy level as deep neural network (DNN) based models.

A key advantage of DNN models is distributed representation of words in a vector space. By using a single-layer neural network, Mikolov et al. introduced such a representation, allowing for relating words based on the inner product between word vectors (Mikolov et al., 2013). One of the popular methods is skip-gram, an approach that learns word representations by predicting the context surrounding a word within a given window length. However, skip-gram has the disadvantage of not considering the co-occurrence statistics of the corpus. Later, Pennington et al. developed *GloVe* – a model that combines the advantages of local window-based methods and global matrix factorization (Pennington et al., 2014). The foundation for the above vector representation of words is the distributional hypothesis that states that "the word that occurs in the same contexts tend to have similar meanings" (Harris, 1954). This means that in addition to forming a rich high-dimensional representation of words, words that are closer to each other in vector space tend to represent similar meaning. As such, vector representations have been used to enhance for instance information retrieval (Manning et al., 2008), name entity recognition (Turian et al., 2010), and parsing (Socher et al., 2013).

The state of the art in DNN-based NLP has been advanced by incorporating various pre-trained word representations such as GloVe (Pennington et al., 2014), word2vec (Mikolov et al., 2013), and fasttext (Bojanowski et al., 2017). Indeed, building semantic representations of the words has been demonstrated to be a vital factor for improved performance. Most DNN-based models utilize the pre-trained word representations to initialize their

Proceedings of the Fourth BlackboxNLP Workshop on Analyzing and Interpreting Neural Networks for NLP, pages 265–274
Online, November 11, 2021. ©2021 Association for Computational Linguistics

word embeddings. This provides them with additional semantic information that goes beyond a traditional BOW.

However, in the case of TM, such word representations cannot be directly employed because they consist of floating-point numbers. First, these numbers must be converted into Boolean form for TM to use, which may result in information loss. Secondly, replacing the straightforward BOW of a TM with a large number of floating-point numbers in fine-grained Boolean form would impede interpretability. In this paper, we propose a novel preprocessing technique that evades the above challenges entirely by extracting additional features for the BOW. The additional features are found using the pre-trained distributed word representations to identify words that enrich the BOW, based on cosine similarity. In this way, TM can use the information from word representations for increasing performance, and at the same time retaining the interpretability of the model.

The rest of the paper is organised as follows. We summarize related work in Section 2. The proposed semantic feature extraction for TM is then explained in Section 3. In Section 4, we present the TM architecture employing the proposed feature extension. We provide extensive experiment results in Section 5, demonstrating the benefits of our approach, before concluding the paper in Section 6.

2 Related Work

Conventional text classification usually focuses on feature engineering and classification algorithms. One of the most popular feature engineering approaches is the derivation of BOW features. Several complex variants of BOW have been designed such as n-grams (Wang and Manning, 2012) and entities in ontologies (Chenthamarakshan et al., 2011). Apart from BOW approaches, Tang et al. demonstrated a new mechanism for feature engineering using a time series model for short text samples (Tang et al., 2020). There are also several techniques to convert text into a graph and sub-graph (Rousseau et al., 2015; Luo et al., 2017). In general, none of the above methods adopt any pre-trained information, hence have inferior performance.

Deep learning-based text classification either depends on initializing models from pre-trained word representations, or on jointly learning both the word- and document level representations. Various studies report that incorporating such word representations, embedding the words, significantly enhances the accuracy of text classification (Joulin et al., 2017; Shen et al., 2018a). Another approach related to pre-trained word embedding is to aggregate unsupervised word embeddings into a document embedding, which is then fed to a classifier (Le and Mikolov, 2014; Tang et al., 2015).

Despite being empowered with world knowledge through pre-trained information, DNNs such as BERT (Devlin et al., 2019) and XLNet (Yang et al., 2019) can be very hard to interpret. One interpretation approach is to use attention-based models, relying on the weights they assign to the inputs. However, more careful studies reveal that attention weights in general do not provide a useful explanation (Bai et al., 2020; Serrano and Smith, 2019). Researchers are thus increasingly shifting focus to other kinds of machine learning, with the TM being a recent approach considered to provide human-level interpretability (Berge et al., 2019; Granmo, 2018; Yadav et al., 2021). It offers a very simple model consisting of multiple Tsetlin Automata (TAs) that select which features take part in the classification. However, despite promising performance, there is still a performance gap to the DNN models that utilize pre-trained word embedding. Yet, several TM studies demonstrate high degree of interpretability through simple rules, with a marginal loss in accuracy (Yadav et al., 2021; Yadav. et al., 2021; Saha et al., 2020).

A significant reason for the performance gap between TM-based and state-of-the-art DNN-based NLP models is that TM operates on Boolean inputs, lacking a method for incorporating pre-trained word embeddings. Without pre-trained information, TMs must rely on labelled data available for supervised learning. On the other hand, incorporating high-dimensional Booleanized word embedding vectors directly into the TM would significantly reduce interpretability. In this paper, we address this intertwined challenge. We propose a novel technique that boosts the TM BOW approach, enhancing the BOW with additional word features. The enhancement consists of using cosine similarity between GloVe word representations to obtain semantically related words. We thus distill information from the pre-trained word representations for utilization by the TM. To this end, we propose two methods of feature extension: (1) using the k nearest words in embedding space and (2) using words within a given similarity threshold, measured as cosine angle (θ). By adopting the two methods, we aim to reduce the current performance gap between interpretable TM and black-box DNN, by achieving either higher or similar accuracy.

3 Boosting TM BOW with Semantically Related Words

Here, we introduce our novel method for boosting the BOW of TM with semantically related words. The method is based on comparing pre-trained word representations using cosine similarity, leveraging distributed word representation. There are various distributional representations of words available. These are obtained from different corpora, using various techniques, such as word2vec, GloVe, and fastText. We here use GloVe because of its general applicability.

3.1 Input Feature Extraction from Distributed Word Representation

Distributed word representation does not necessarily derive word similarity based on synonyms but based on the words that appear in the same context. As such, the representation is essential for NLP because it captures the semantically interconnecting words. Our approach utilizes this property to expand the range of features that we can use in an interpretable manner in TM.

Consider a full vocabulary W of m words, $W = [w_1, w_2, w_3 \ldots, w_m]$. Further consider a particular sentence that is represented as a Boolean BOW $X = [x_1, x_2, x_3, \ldots, x_m]$. In a Boolean BOW, each element $x_r, r = 1, 2, 3, \ldots, m$, refers to a specific word w_r in the vocabulary W. The element x_r takes the value 1 if the corresponding word w_r is present in the sentence and the value 0 if the word is absent. Assume that n words are present in the sentence, i.e., n of the elements in X are 1-valued. Our strategy is to extract additional features from these by expanding them using cosine similarity. To this end, we use a GloVe embedding of each present word $w_r, r \in \{z | x_z = 1, z = 1, 2, 3 \ldots, m\}$. The embedding for word w_r is represented by vector $w_r^e \in \Re^d$, where d is the dimensionality of the embedding (typically varying from 25 to 300).

We next introduce two selection techniques to expand upon each word:

- Select the top k most similar words,
- Select words up to a fixed similarity angle $\cos(\theta) = \phi$.

For example, let us consider two contexts: "very good movie" and "excellent film, enjoyable". Figs. 1 and 2 list similar words showing the difference between top k words and words within angle $\cos(\theta)$, i.e., ϕ. In what follows, we will explain how these words are found.

3.2 Similar Words based on Top k Nearest Words

We first boost the Boolean BOW of the considered sentence by expanding X with $(k-1) \times n$ semantically related words. That is, we add $k-1$ new words for each of the n present words. We do this by identifying neighbouring words in the GloVe embedding space, using cosine similarity between the embedding vectors.

Consider the GloVe embedding vectors $W_G^e = [w_1^e, w_2^e, \ldots, w_m^e]$ of the full vocabulary W. For each word w_r from the sentence considered, the cosine similarity to each word w_t, $t = 1, 2, \ldots, m$, of the full vocabulary is given by Eq. (1),

$$\phi_r^t = \cos(w_r^e, w_t^e) = \frac{w_r^e \cdot w_t^e}{||w_r^e|| \cdot ||w_t^e||}. \quad (1)$$

Clearly, ϕ_r^t is the cosine similarity between w_r^e and w_t^e. By calculating the cosine similarity of w_r to the words in the vocabulary, we obtain m values: ϕ_r^t, $t = 1, 2, \ldots, m$. We arrange these values in a vector Φ_r:

$$\Phi_r = [\phi_r^1, \phi_r^2, \ldots, \phi_r^m]. \quad (2)$$

The k elements from Φ_r of largest value are then identified and their indices are stored in a new set A_r.

Finally, a boosted BOW, referred to as X_{mod}, can be formed by assigning element x_t value 1 whenever one of the A_r contains t, and 0 otherwise:

$$X_{mod} = [x_1, x_2, x_3, \ldots, x_m], \quad (3)$$
$$x_t = \begin{cases} 1 & \exists r, t \in A_r \\ 0 & \nexists r, t \in A_r. \end{cases}$$

In addition, the vocabulary size for a particular task/dataset can be changed accordingly, which is usually less than m. Note that implementation-wise, the GloVe library provides the top k similar words of w_r without considering the word w_r itself, having similarity score 1. Hence, using the GloVe library, w_r must also be added to the boosted BOW.

3.3 Similar Words within Cosine Angle Threshold

Another approach to enrich the Boolean BOW of a sentence is thresholding the cosine angle. This is

excellent film, enjoyable					
excellent	similarity	film	similarity	enjoyable	similarity
good	0.703	movie	0.858	entertaining	0.688
superb	0.680	films	0.839	pleasurable	0.660
terrific	0.656	movies	0.716	exhilarating	0.647
quality	0.603	directed	0.683	fun	0.625
wonderful	0.584	documentary	0.656	exciting	0.619
best	0.550	starring	0.651	amusing	0.605
exceptional	0.550	cinema	0.637	satisfying	0.585
perfect	0.535	screenplay	0.632	engrossing	0.578
impressive	0.534	drama	0.622	enlightening	0.573
decent	0.532	comedy	0.615	informative	0.571

top k similar words; words within ϕ

Figure 1: Similar words for an example "excellent film, enjoyable" using 300d GloVe word representation.

very good movie					
very	similarity	good	similarity	movie	similarity
extremely	0.872	better	0.765	film	0.858
quite	0.858	really	0.736	movies	0.849
so	0.785	always	0.717	films	0.790
pretty	0.738	you	0.707	hollywood	0.679
too	0.731	well	0.704	starring	0.675
really	0.729	excellent	0.703	comedy	0.658
well	0.720	very	0.696	sequel	0.646
always	0.712	things	0.693	remake	0.624
especially	0.709	think	0.689	drama	0.608
but	0.707	way	0.683	actor	0.599

top k similar words; words within ϕ

Figure 2: Similar words for an example "very good movie" using 300d GloVe word representation.

different from the first technique because the number of additional words extracted will vary rather than being fixed. Whereas the first approach always produces $k-1$ new features for each given word, the cosine angle thresholding brings in all those words that are sufficiently similar. The cosine similarity threshold is given by $\phi = \cos(\theta)$, where θ is the threshold for vector angle, while ϕ is the corresponding similarity score.

As per Eq. (2), we obtain Φ_r, which consists of the similarity scores of the given word w_r in comparison to the m words in the vocabulary. Then, for each given word w_r, the indices of those scores ϕ_r^t that are greater than or equal to ϕ ($\phi_r^t \geq \phi$) are stored in the set A_r. Similar to the first technique, the words in W with the indices in A_r are utilized to create X_{mod} as given by Eq. (3).

4 Tsetlin Machine-based Classification

4.1 Tsetlin Machine Architecture

A TM is composed by TAs that operate with literals – Boolean inputs and their negations – to form conjunctions of literals (conjunctive clauses). A dedicated team of TAs builds each clause, with each input being associated with a pair of TAs. One TA controls the original Boolean input whereas the other TA controls its negation. The TA pair selects a combination of "Include" or "Exclude" actions, which decide the form of the literal to include or exclude in the clause.

Each TA decides upon an action according to its current state. There are N states per TA action, $2N$ states in total. When a TA finds itself in states 1 to N, it performs the "Exclude" action. When in states $N+1$ to $2N$, it performs the "Include" action. How the TA updates its state is shown in Fig. 3. If it receives Reward, the TA moves to a deeper state thereby increasing its confidence in the current action. However, if it receives Penalty, it moves towards the centre, weakening the action. It may eventually jump over the middle decision boundary, to the other action. It is through this game of TAs that the TM shapes the clauses into frequent and discriminative patterns.

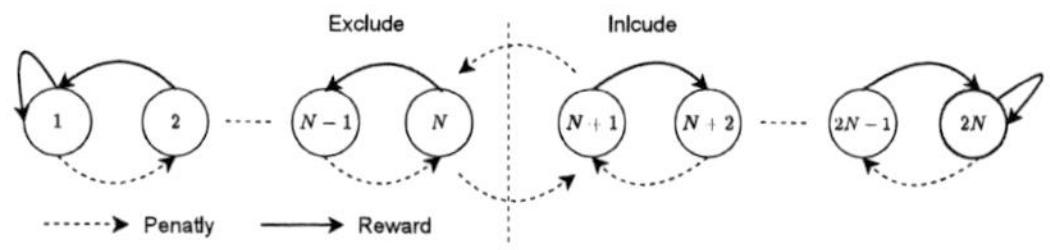

Figure 3: A TA with two actions: "Include" and "Exclude".

With respect to NLP, TM heavily relies on the Boolean BOW introduced earlier in the paper. We now make use of our proposed modified BOW $X_{mod} = [x_1, x_2, x_3, \ldots, x_m]$. Let l be the number of clauses that represent each class of the TM, covering q classes altogether. Then, the overall pattern recognition problem is solved using $l \times q$ clauses. Each clause C_i^j, $1 \leq j \leq q$, $1 \leq i \leq l$ of the TM is given by $C_i^j = \left(\bigwedge_{k \in I_i^j} x_k \right) \wedge \left(\bigwedge_{k \in \bar{I}_i^j} \neg x_k \right)$, where I_i^j and $\bar{I}_i^j$ are non-overlapping subsets of the input variable indices, $I_j^i, \bar{I}_j^i \subseteq \{1, \ldots, m\}$, $I_j^i \cap \bar{I}_j^i = \emptyset$. The subsets decide which of the input variables take part in the clause, and whether they are negated or not. The indices of input variables in I_j^i represent the literals that are included as is, while the indices of input variables in $\bar{I}_j^i$ correspond to the negated ones. Among the q clauses of each class, clauses with odd indexes are assigned positive polarity (+) whereas those with even indices are assigned negative polarity (-). The clauses with positive polarity vote for the target class and those with negative polarity vote against it. A summation operator aggregates the votes by subtracting the total number of negative votes from positive votes, as shown in Eq. (4).

$$f^j(X_{mod}) = \Sigma_{i=1,3,...}^{l-1} C_i^j(X_{mod}) - \Sigma_{i=2,4,...}^{l} C_i^j(X_{mod}). \quad (4)$$

For q number of classes, the final output y is given by the argmax operator to classify the input based on the highest sum of votes, $\hat{y} = \text{argmax}_j \left(f^j(X_{mod})\right)$.

4.2 Distributed Word Representation in TM

Consider two contexts for sentiment classification: "Very good movie" and "Excellent film, enjoyable". Both contexts have different vocabularies but some of them are semantically related to each other. For example, "good" and "excellent" have similar semantics as well as "film" and "movie". Such semantics are not captured in the BOW-based input. However, as shown in Fig. 4, adding words to the BOWs that are semantically related, as proposed in the previous section, makes distributed word representation available to the TM.

The resulting BOW-boosted TM architecture is shown in Fig. 5. Here each input feature is first expanded using the GloVe representation, adding semantically related words. Each feature is then transferred to its corresponding TAs, both in original and negated form. Each TA, in turn, decides whether to include or exclude its literal in the clause by taking part in a decentralized game. The actions of each TA is decided by its current state and updated by the the feedback it receives based on its action. As shown in the figure, the TA actions produce a collection of conjunctive clauses, joining the words into more complex linguistic patterns.

There are two types of feedback that guides the TA learning. They are Type I feedback and Type II feedback, detailed in (Granmo, 2018). Type I feedback is triggered when the ground truth label is 1, i.e., $y = 1$. The purpose of Type I feedback is to include more literals from the BOW to refine the clauses, or to trim them by removing literals. The balance between refinement and trimming is controlled by a parameter called specificity, s. Type I feedback guides the clauses to provide true positive output, while simultaneously controlling overfitting by producing frequent patterns. Conversely, Type II feedback is triggered in case of false positive output. Its main aim is to introduce zero-valued literals into clauses when they give false positive output. The purpose is to change them so that they correctly output zero later in the learning process. Based on these feedback types, each TA in a clause receives Reward, Penalty or Inaction. The overall learning process is explained in detail by Yadav et al. in (Yadav et al., 2021).

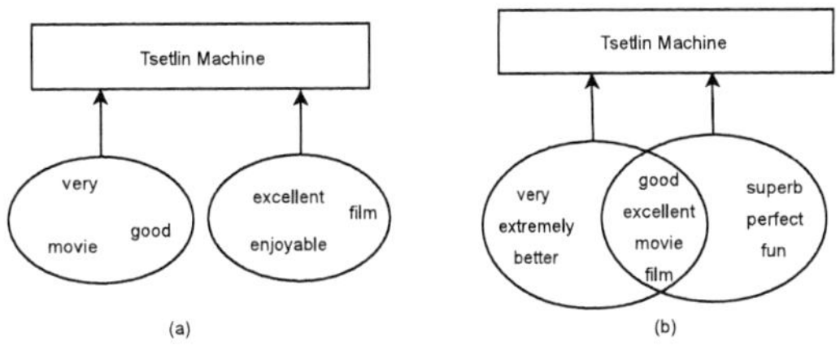

Figure 4: (a) BOW input representation without distributed word representation. (b) BOW input using similar words based on distributed word representation.

5 Experiments and Results

In this section, we evaluate our TM-based solution with the input features enhanced by distributed word representation. Here we use Glove pretrained word vector that is trained using CommonCrawl with the configuration of 42B tokens, 1.9M vocab, uncased, and 300d vectors.

5.1 Datasets

We have selected various types of datasets to investigate how broadly our method is applicable: R8 and R52 of Reuters, Movie Review (MR), and TREC-6. • **Reuters** 21578 dataset include two subsets: R52 and R8 (all-terms version). R8 is divided into 8 sections while there are 52 categories in R52. •**MR** is a movie analysis dataset for binary sentiment classification with just one sentence per review (Pang and Lee, 2005). In this study, we used a training/test split from (Tang et al., 2015)[1]. •**TREC-6** is a question classification dataset (Li and Roth, 2002). The task entails categorizing a query into six distinct categories (abbreviation, description, entity, human, location, numeric value).

5.2 TM Parameters

A TM has three parameters that must be initialized before training a model: number of clauses l, voting target T, and specificity s. We configure these parameters as follows. For R8, we use 2,500 clauses, a threshold of 80, and specificity 9. The vocabulary size is 5,000. For R52, we employ 1,500 clauses, the voting target is 80, and specificity is 9. Here, we use a vocabulary of size 6,000. For MR, the number of clauses is 3,000, the voting target is

[1]https://github.com/mnqu/PTE/tree/master/data/mr.

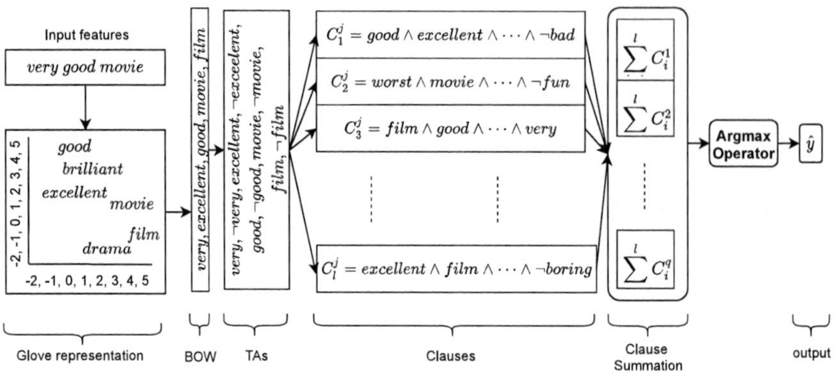

Figure 5: Architecture of TM using modified BOW based on word similarity.

80, and specificity is 9, with a vocabulary of size 5,000. Finally, for TREC, we use 2,000 clause, a voting target of 80, and specificity 9, with vocabulary size 6,000. These parameters are kept static as we explore various k and θ values for selecting similar words to facilitate comparison. The code and datasets are available online [2].

5.3 Performance When Using Top k Nearest Neighbors

Here, we demonstrate the performance on each of the datasets, exploring the effect of different k-values, i.e., 3, 5 and 10. The performance of the proposed technique for selected datasets with various values of k is compared in Table 1. It can be seen that by using feature extension, performance is significantly enhanced. Both $k = 3$ and $k = 5$ outperform the simple BOW ($k = 0$). However, for this particular dataset, $k = 10$ performs poorly because extending each word to its 10 nearest neighbors includes many unnecessary contexts that have no significant impact on the classification. In terms of accuracy, $k = 5$ performs best for the R8 dataset. For the R52 dataset, the feature extension with $k = 5$ and $k = 10$ performs poorly compared to using $k = 0$ and $k = 3$. Here, $k = 3$ is the best-performing parameter. The improvement obtained by moving from a simple BOW to a BOW enhanced with semantically similar features is obvious in the case of the R52 dataset. Similarly, in the case of the TREC dataset, the performance of simple BOW ($k = 0$) is markedly outperformed by the feature extension techniques for all the tested k-values, with $k = 5$ and $k = 10$ being good candidates. The advantage of $k = 10$ over $k = 5$ is that $k = 10$ reaches its peak accuracy in an earlier epoch. Lastly, the performance of the MR is again clear that the feature extension technique outperforms the simple BOW ($k = 0$) with a high margin.

[2] https://github.com/rohanky/Glove-TM

Parameters	R8	R52	MR	TREC
k=0	96.16	84.62	75.14	88.05
k=3	97.08	88.59	75.21	88.72
k=5	96.80	70.60	76.06	89.16
k=10	87.44	66.94	77.51	89.82

Table 1: Comparison of feature extended TM with several parameters for k.

5.4 Performance When Using Neighbors Within a Similarity Threshold

This section demonstrates the performance of our BOW enhancement approach when using various similarity thresholds ϕ for feature extension. Here, ϕ refers to the cosine similarity between a word in the BOW and a target word from the overall vocabulary. Again, similarity is measured in the GloVe embedding space as the cosine of the angle θ between the embedding vectors compared, $\cos(\theta)$. For ϕ, we here explore the values 0.5, 0.6, 0.7, 0.8, and 0.9, whose corresponding angles are 60°, 53.13°, 45.57°, 36.86°, and 25.84°, respectively. The performance of the various ϕ-values for the selected dataset is shown in Table 2. For R8 dataset, feature extension using $\phi = 0.7$, $\phi = 0.8$, and $\phi = 0.9$ outperforms the simple BOW ($\phi = 0$) where $\phi = 0.7$ being the best. In case of the R52 dataset, all of the investigated ϕ-values outperform the simple BOW ($\phi = 0$) where $\phi = 0.5$ and $\phi = 0.8$ performs the best. Similar trend is observed in case of TREC and MR dataset where feature extension outperforms the simple BOW.

Parameters	R8	R52	MR	TREC
$\phi = 0$	96.16	84.62	75.14	88.05
$\phi = 0.5$	88.08	89.14	73.24	90.04
$\phi = 0.6$	90.86	88.05	74.34	87.83
$\phi = 0.7$	96.53	88.51	76.55	89.38
$\phi = 0.8$	96.25	88.94	75.12	88.27
$\phi = 0.9$	96.39	87.50	74.59	87.39

Table 2: Comparison of feature extended TM with several parameters for ϕ.

In most of the cases, however, a too strict similarity threshold ϕ tends to reduce performance because fewer features are added to the BOW. Even though using a looser similarity score thresholds also introduces unnecessary features, these do not seem to impact the formation of accurate clauses. Overall, our experiments show that using ϕ-values from 0.5 to 0.7 peaks performance.

5.5 Comparison with Baselines

We here compare our proposed model with selected text classification- and embedding methods. We have selected representative techniques from various main approaches, both those that leverage similar kinds of pre-trained word embedding and those that only use BOW. The selected baselines are: •**TF-IDF+LR**: This is a bag-of-words model employing Term Frequency-Inverse Document Frequency (TF-IDF) weighting. Logistic Regression is used as a softmax classifier. •**CNN**: The CNN-baselines cover both initialization with random word embedding (CNN-rand) as well as initialization with pretrained word embedding (CNN-non-static) (Kim, 2014). • **LSTM**: The LSTM model that we employ here is from (Liu et al., 2016), representing the entire text using the last hidden state. We tested this model with and without pre-trained word embeddings. • **Bi-LSTM**: Bi-directional LSTMs are widely used for text classification. We compare our model with Bi-LSTM fed with pre-trained word embeddings. •**PV-DBOW**: PV-DBOW is a paragraph vector model where the word order is ignored. Logistic Regression is used as a softmax classifier (Le and Mikolov, 2014). • **PV-DM**: PV-DM is also a paragraph vector model, however with word ordering taken into account. Logistic Regression is used as a softmax classifier (Le and Mikolov, 2014). •**fastText**: This baseline is a simple text classification technique that uses the average of the word embeddings provided by fastText as document embedding. The embedding is then fed to a linear classifier (Joulin et al., 2017). We evaluate both the use of uni-grams and bigrams. • **SWEM** : SWEM applies simple pooling techniques over the word embeddings to obtain a document embedding (Shen et al., 2018b). •**Graph-CNN-C**: A graph CNN model uses convolutions over a word embedding similarity graph (Defferrard et al., 2016), employing a Chebyshev filter. •S^2GC: This technique uses a modified Markov Diffusion Kernel to derive a variant of Graph Convolutional Network (GCN) (Zhu and Koniusz, 2021). •**LguidedLearn**: It is a label-guided learning framework for text classification. This technique is applied to BERT as well (Liu et al., 2020), which we use for comparison purposes here. •**Feature Projection (FP)**: It is a novel approach to improve representation learning through feature projection. Existing features are projected into an orthogonal space (Qin et al., 2020).

From Table 3, we observe that the TM approaches that employ either of our feature extension techniques outperform several word embedding-based Logistic Regression approaches, such as PV-DBOW, PV-DM, and fastText. Similarly, the legacy TM outperforms sophisticated models like CNN and LSTM based on randomly initialized word embedding. Still, the legacy TM falls of other models when they are initialized by pre-trained word embeddings. By boosting the Boolean BOW with semantically similar features using our proposed technique, however, TM outperforms LSTM (pretrain) on the R8 dataset and performs similarly on R52 and MR. In addition to this, our proposed approach achieves quite similar performance compared to BERT, even though BERT has been pre-trained on a huge text corpus. However, it falls slightly short of sophisticated fine-tuned models like Lguided-BERT-1 and Lguided-BERT-3. Overall, our results show that our proposed feature extension technique for TMs significantly enhances accuracy, reaching state of the art accuracy. Importantly, this accuracy enhancement does not come at the cost of reduced interpretability, unlike DNNs, which we discuss below. The state of the art for the TREC dataset is different from the other three datasets, hence we report results separately in Table 4. These results clearly show that although the basic TM model does not outperform the recent DNN- and transformer-based models, the feature-boosted TM outperforms all of

Model	R8	R52	MR
TF-IDF+LR	93.74	86.95	74.59
CNN-rand	94.02	85.37	74.98
CNN-non-static	95.71	87.59	77.75
LSTM	93.68	85.54	75.06
LSTM (pretrain)	96.09	90.48	77.33
Bi-LSTM	96.31	90.54	77.68
PV-DBOW	85.87	78.29	61.09
PV-DM	52.07	44.92	59.47
fastText	96.13	92.81	75.14
fastText (bigrams)	94.74	90.99	76.24
SWEM	95.32	92.94	76.65
LEAM	93.31	91.84	76.95
Graph-CNN-C	96.99	92.74	77.22
S^2GC	97.40	94.50	76.70
BERT	96.02	89.66	79.24
Lguided-BERT-1	97.49	94.26	81.03
Lguided-BERT-3	98.28	94.32	81.06
TM	96.16± 1.52	84.62± 1.8	75.14± 1.2
TM with k	97.50± 1.12	88.59± 1.2	77.51± 0.6
TM with ϕ	96.39± 1.0	89.14± 1.5	76.55± 0.9

Table 3: Comparison of feature extended TM with the state of the art for R8, R52 and MR. Reported accuracy of TM is the mean of last 50 epochs of 5 independent experiments with their standard deviation.

those models except understandably BAE:BERT (Garg and Ramakrishnan, 2020).

Model	TREC
LSTM	87.19
FP+LSTM	88.83
Transformer	87.33
FP+Transformer	89.51
BAE: BERT	97.6
TM (Dragoș et al., 2021)	87.20
TM	88.05± 1.52
TM with k	89.82± 1.18
TM with ϕ	90.04± 0.94

Table 4: Comparison of feature extended TM with the state of the art for TREC. Reported accuracy of TM is the mean of last 50 epochs of 5 independent experiments with their standard deviation.

5.6 Interpretation

The proposed feature extension-based TM does not only impact accuracy. Perhaps surprisingly, our proposed technique also simplify the clauses that the TM produces, making them more meaningful in a semantic sense. To demonstrate this property, let us consider two samples from the MR dataset: S_1="the cast is uniformly excellent and relaxed" and S_2="the entire cast is extraordinarily good". Let the vocabulary, in this case, be [cast, excellent, relaxed, extraordinarily, good, bad, boring, worst] as shown in Fig. 6.

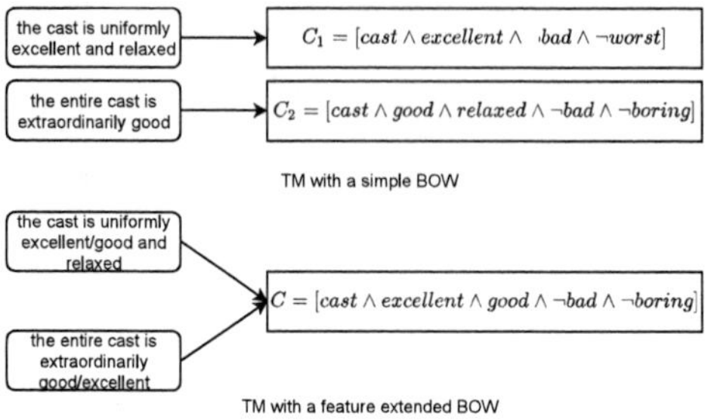

Figure 6: Clause learning semantic for multiple examples compared to simple BOW based TM.

As we can see, that the TM initialized with normal BOW uses two separate clauses to represent two examples. However, augmenting feature on TM uses only one clause that learns the semantic for multiple examples.This indeed makes interpretation of TM more powerful and meaningful as compared to simple BOW based TM.

6 Conclusion

In this paper, we aimed to enhance the performance of Tsetlin Machines (TMs) by introducing a novel way to exploit distributed feature representation for TMs. Given that a TM relies on Bag-of-words (BOW), it is not possible to introduce pre-trained word representation into a TM directly, without sacrificing the interpretability of the model. To address this intertwined challenge, we extended each word feature by using cosine similarity on the distributed word representation. We proposed two techniques for feature extension: (1) using the k nearest words in embedding space and (2) including words within a given cosine angle (θ). Through this enhancement, the TM BOW can be boosted with pre-trained world knowledge in a simple yet effective way. Our experiment results showed that the enhanced TM not only achieve competitive accuracy compared to state of the art, but also outperform some of the sophisticated deep neural network (DNN) models. In addition, our BOW boosting also improved the interpretability of the model by increasing the scope of each clause, semantically relating more samples. We thus believe that our proposed approach significantly enhance the TM in the accuracy/interpretability continuum, establishing a new standard in the field of explainable NLP.

References

Kuruge Darshana Abeyrathna, Ole-Christoffer Granmo, Xuan Zhang, and Morten Goodwin. 2019. A scheme for continuous input to the Tsetlin machine with applications to forecasting disease outbreaks. In *Advances and Trends in Artificial Intelligence. From Theory to Practice*, pages 564–578. Springer International Publishing.

Bing Bai, J. Liang, Guanhua Zhang, Hao Li, Kun Bai, and F. Wang. 2020. Why is attention not so interpretable. *arXiv: Machine Learning*.

Geir Thore Berge, Ole-Christoffer Granmo, Tor Oddbjørn Tveit, Morten Goodwin, Lei Jiao, and Bernt Viggo Matheussen. 2019. Using the tsetlin machine to learn human-interpretable rules for high-accuracy text categorization with medical applications. *IEEE Access*, 7:115134–115146.

Bimal Bhattarai., Ole-Christoffer Granmo., and Lei Jiao. 2021. Measuring the novelty of natural language text using the conjunctive clauses of a tsetlin machine text classifier. In *Proceedings of the 13th International Conference on Agents and Artificial Intelligence - Volume 2: ICAART,*, pages 410–417. INSTICC, SciTePress.

Piotr Bojanowski, Edouard Grave, Armand Joulin, and Tomas Mikolov. 2017. Enriching word vectors with subword information. *Transactions of the Association for Computational Linguistics*, 5:135–146.

Vijil Chenthamarakshan, Prem Melville, Vikas Sindhwani, and Richard D. Lawrence. 2011. Concept labeling: Building text classifiers with minimal supervision. In *IJCAI*, pages 1225–1230.

Michaël Defferrard, Xavier Bresson, and Pierre Vandergheynst. 2016. Convolutional neural networks on graphs with fast localized spectral filtering. In *Advances in Neural Information Processing Systems*, volume 29. Curran Associates, Inc.

Jacob Devlin, Ming-Wei Chang, Kenton Lee, and Kristina Toutanova. 2019. BERT: Pre-training of deep bidirectional transformers for language understanding. In *ACL: Human Language Technologies, Volume 1 (Long and Short Papers)*, pages 4171–4186, Minneapolis, Minnesota. ACL.

Dragoș, Constantin Nicolae, and dragosnicolae. 2021. Question classification using interpretable tsetlin machine. In *International Workshop of Machine Reasoning*. ACM International Conference on Web Search and Data Mining.

Siddhant Garg and Goutham Ramakrishnan. 2020. Bae: Bert-based adversarial examples for text classification.

Ole-Christoffer Granmo. 2018. The tsetlin machine - a game theoretic bandit driven approach to optimal pattern recognition with propositional logic. *ArXiv*, abs/1804.01508.

Ole-Christoffer Granmo, Sondre Glimsdal, Lei Jiao, Morten Goodwin, Christian W. Omlin, and Geir Thore Berge. 2019. The convolutional tsetlin machine. *arXiv*, 1905.09688.

Zellig S. Harris. 1954. Distributional structure. *WORD*, 10(2-3):146–162.

Armand Joulin, Edouard Grave, Piotr Bojanowski, and Tomas Mikolov. 2017. Bag of tricks for efficient text classification. In *EACL: Volume 2, Short Papers*, pages 427–431, Valencia, Spain. ACL.

Yoon Kim. 2014. Convolutional neural networks for sentence classification. In *Proceedings of the 2014 Conference on Empirical Methods in Natural Language Processing (EMNLP)*, pages 1746–1751, Doha, Qatar. ACL.

Quoc Le and Tomas Mikolov. 2014. Distributed representations of sentences and documents. In *Proceedings of the 31st International Conference on Machine Learning*, volume 32 of *Proceedings of Machine Learning Research*, pages 1188–1196, Bejing, China. PMLR.

Xin Li and Dan Roth. 2002. Learning question classifiers. In *COLING*.

Pengfei Liu, Xipeng Qiu, and Xuanjing Huang. 2016. Recurrent neural network for text classification with multi-task learning. In *IJCAI*, page 2873–2879.

X. Liu, Song Wang, X. Zhang, Xinxin You, J. Wu, and D. Dou. 2020. Label-guided learning for text classification. *ArXiv*, abs/2002.10772.

Yuan Luo, Özlem Uzuner, and Peter Szolovits. 2017. Bridging semantics and syntax with graph algorithms - state-of-the-art of extracting biomedical relations. *Briefings in bioinformatics*, 18 1:160–178.

Christopher D. Manning, Prabhakar Raghavan, and Hinrich Schütze. 2008. *Introduction to Information Retrieval*. Cambridge University Press.

Tomas Mikolov, Ilya Sutskever, Kai Chen, Greg S Corrado, and Jeff Dean. 2013. Distributed representations of words and phrases and their compositionality. In *NIPS, Nevada, USA*, volume 26, pages 3111–3119. Curran Associates, Inc.

Bo Pang and Lillian Lee. 2005. Seeing stars: Exploiting class relationships for sentiment categorization with respect to rating scales. In *ACL*, page 115–124, Michigan, USA. ACL.

Jeffrey Pennington, Richard Socher, and Christopher D. Manning. 2014. Glove: Global vectors for word representation. In *EMNLP, Doha, Qatar*, page 1532–1543.

Qi Qin, Wenpeng Hu, and Bing Liu. 2020. Feature projection for improved text classification. In *ACL*, pages 8161–8171, Online. ACL.

François Rousseau, Emmanouil Kiagias, and Michalis Vazirgiannis. 2015. Text categorization as a graph classification problem. In *ACL (Volume 1: Long Papers)*, pages 1702–1712, Beijing, China. ACL.

Rupsa Saha, Ole-Christoffer Granmo, and Morten Goodwin. 2020. Mining interpretable rules for sentiment and semantic relation analysis using tsetlin machines. In *Artificial Intelligence XXXVII*, pages 67–78, Cham. Springer International Publishing.

Sofia Serrano and Noah A. Smith. 2019. Is attention interpretable? In *ACL*, pages 2931–2951, Florence, Italy. ACL.

Dinghan Shen, Guoyin Wang, Wenlin Wang, Martin Renqiang Min, Qinliang Su, Yizhe Zhang, Chunyuan Li, Ricardo Henao, and Lawrence Carin. 2018a. Baseline needs more love: On simple word-embedding-based models and associated pooling mechanisms. In *ACL Volume 1: Long Papers*, pages 440–450, Melbourne, Australia. ACL.

Dinghan Shen, Guoyin Wang, Wenlin Wang, Martin Renqiang Min, Qinliang Su, Yizhe Zhang, Chunyuan Li, Ricardo Henao, and Lawrence Carin. 2018b. Baseline needs more love: On simple word-embedding-based models and associated pooling mechanisms. In *ACL (Volume 1: Long Papers)*, pages 440–450, Melbourne, Australia. ACL.

Richard Socher, John Bauer, Christopher D. Manning, and Andrew Y. Ng. 2013. Parsing with compositional vector grammars. In *Proceedings of the 51st Annual Meeting of the Association for Computational Linguistics (Volume 1: Long Papers)*, pages 455–465, Sofia, Bulgaria. Association for Computational Linguistics.

Jian Tang, Meng Qu, and Qiaozhu Mei. 2015. Pte: Predictive text embedding through large-scale heterogeneous text networks. In *Proceedings of the 21th ACM SIGKDD International Conference on Knowledge Discovery and Data Mining*, KDD '15, page 1165–1174, Sydney, NSW, Australia. Association for Computing Machinery.

Yichen Tang, Kelly Blincoe, and A. Kempa-Liehr. 2020. Enriching feature engineering for short text samples by language time series analysis. *EPJ Data Science*, 9:1–59.

Joseph Turian, Lev-Arie Ratinov, and Yoshua Bengio. 2010. Word representations: A simple and general method for semi-supervised learning. In *Proceedings of the 48th Annual Meeting of the Association for Computational Linguistics*, pages 384–394, Uppsala, Sweden. Association for Computational Linguistics.

Sida Wang and Christopher Manning. 2012. Baselines and bigrams: Simple, good sentiment and topic classification. In *ACL (Volume 2: Short Papers)*, pages 90–94, Jeju Island, Korea.

Rohan Kumar Yadav, Lei Jiao, Ole-Christoffer Granmo, and Morten Goodwin. 2021. Human-level interpretable learning for aspect-based sentiment analysis. In *The Thirty-Fifth AAAI Conference on Artificial Intelligence (AAAI-21)*. AAAI.

Rohan Kumar Yadav., Lei Jiao., Ole-Christoffer Granmo., and Morten Goodwin. 2021. Interpretability in word sense disambiguation using tsetlin machine. In *Proceedings of the 13th International Conference on Agents and Artificial Intelligence - Volume 2: ICAART,*, pages 402–409. INSTICC, SciTePress.

Zhilin Yang, Zihang Dai, Yiming Yang, Jaime Carbonell, Russ R Salakhutdinov, and Quoc V Le. 2019. Xlnet: Generalized autoregressive pretraining for language understanding. In *Advances in Neural Information Processing Systems*, volume 32. Curran Associates, Inc.

Hao Zhu and Piotr Koniusz. 2021. Simple spectral graph convolution. In *International Conference on Learning Representations*.

Analyzing BERT's Knowledge of Hypernymy via Prompting

Michael Hanna and **David Mareček**
Institute of Formal and Applied Linguistics, Faculty of Mathematics and Physics
Charles University, Prague, Czech Republic
hannami@o365.cuni.cz, marecek@ufal.mff.cuni.cz

Abstract

The high performance of large pretrained language models (LLMs) such as BERT (Devlin et al., 2019) on NLP tasks has prompted questions about BERT's linguistic capabilities, and how they differ from humans'. In this paper, we approach this question by examining BERT's knowledge of lexical semantic relations. We focus on hypernymy, the "is-a" relation that relates a word to a superordinate category.

We use a prompting methodology to simply ask BERT what the hypernym of a given word is. We find that, in a setting where all hypernyms are guessable via prompting, BERT knows hypernyms with up to 57% accuracy. Moreover, BERT with prompting outperforms other unsupervised models for hypernym discovery even in an unconstrained scenario. However, BERT's predictions and performance on a dataset containing uncommon hyponyms and hypernyms indicate that its knowledge of hypernymy is still limited.

1 Introduction

Large pretrained language models (Devlin et al., 2019; Radford et al., 2019) have set new standards for performance on NLP tasks. Many of these tasks, such as question answering and natural language inference, might seem to require human-like syntactic and semantic capabilities to perform well, leading to many studies on this topic (Rogers et al., 2020).

However, evidence that LLMs have human-like semantic capabilities is mixed. With respect to polysemy, Wiedemann et al. (2019) find that the sense of a polysemous word can be disambiguated using a k-nearest-neighbor approach on BERT's representation of the word. In contrast, Yenicelik et al. (2020) note that while polysemous words' senses are linearly separable based on their BERT embeddings, these embeddings do not form clusters based on their senses alone.

In terms of BERT's knowledge of lexical semantics, Vulić et al. (2020) find that BERT's embeddings capture useful lexical-type knowledge, performing better than non-contextual embeddings on a lexical relation prediction task. That said, BERT's knowledge of lexical semantics is not equal for all words: it struggles with rare words (Schick and Schütze, 2020).

In this work, we further examine BERT's knowledge of lexical semantics, more specifically that of hypernymy, using a Cloze / prompting methodology. In the most basic form of this framework, we simply run BERT on an input sentence such as "An apple is a `[MASK]`.", and extract the probabilities assigned to each token that could fill in the blank; here, we would expect an answer such as "fruit".

While Ravichander et al. (2020) also approach BERT's lexical semantics using a prompting task, they focus on simple prompts and examine only if BERT can predict a word's canonical hypernym. In contrast, we explore how more complex prompts affect BERT's ability to predict hypernyms, propose new methods of evaluating hypernym discovery that that take into account the fact that a word may have multiple hypernyms, and find effective prompts for hypernym discovery.

2 Background: Prompting

Although fine-tuning is the methodology with which LLMs shattered existing state-of-the-art on many downstream tasks, the use of prompting has also gained interest in recent years. Unlike fine-tuning, prompting involves no further training to solve downstream tasks; instead, a prompt is fed to the language model, which either predicts the continuation of the prompt (autoregressive language modeling) or the identity of one or more masked words (masked language modeling). The output of the language model is then used as the response to the task at hand.

Prompting has seen use for diverse tasks such as

Proceedings of the Fourth BlackboxNLP Workshop on Analyzing and Interpreting Neural Networks for NLP, pages 275–282
Online, November 11, 2021.

knowledge base completion (Petroni et al., 2019) as well as summarization and translation (Radford et al., 2019). While performance on these tasks is not always up to par with supervised state of the art, prompting has the advantage of being unsupervised. However, various studies have found that task performance is highly dependent on the prompt used (Jiang et al., 2020; Reynolds and McDonell, 2021); these same studies propose automatic or hand-made improvements to prompts to improve them. Supervised techniques have also been devised to automatically develop better prompts (Shin et al., 2020).

Beyond downstream tasks, prompting is also useful for investigating language models as a test subject. While probing (Conneau et al., 2018; Tenney et al., 2019), for example, is useful, it involves training an auxiliary model. This auxiliary model can be troublesome; (Hewitt and Liang, 2019) show that the probes themselves can learn tasks independently of whether the model encodes linguistic structure. Moreover, a model can contain information within its internal representations without relying on that information to make predictions. In contrast, prompting requires no auxiliary models that might complicate matters.

Ettinger (2020) uses prompting to compare BERT's linguistic competencies and tendencies to that of humans; among those investigated is hypernymy. They find that BERT easily identifies noun hypernyms, but fails to adapt to negated sentences: given the prompts "A hammer is a `[MASK]`" and "A hammer is not a `[MASK]`", BERT predicts the words "hammer", "tool", and "weapon" for both.

In a follow-up, Ravichander et al. (2020), investigate whether BERT has a systematic understanding of hypernymy. They find that BERT's understanding of hypernymy is not systematic: BERT fails when tasked with finding the hypernym of a hyponym in the plural; it also fails more often when the hyponym in question is uncommon, or has not been seen with its hypernym in Wikipedia. In contrast to the practically-oriented works, these studies that analyze LLMs use primarily simple prompts to extract BERT's predictions.

These two uses of prompting, for downstream tasks and for analysis of LLMs, are somewhat in tension. On one hand, studies searching for knowledge in BERT treat it as a test subject, and use prompting to search for knowledge of hypernymy using very simple prompts. On the other hand, from practically-oriented studies, we know that using simple prompts may lead to BERT underperforming, if only because it is not responding to the task at hand. The use of simple prompts might thus obscure knowledge of hypernymy in BERT.

In this paper, we attempt to balance these two approaches. We explore more complex prompts, in an attempt to reveal knowledge of hypernymy in BERT that might be hidden by challenges with prompting. However, we limit prompts to those which are human-understandable, and can be created without any supervision (excluding, thus, prompt-tuning approaches). Moreover, we compare BERT's performance on a hypernym discovery task to that of other systems, to give context to its hypernym discovery ability.

3 BERT Diagnostics

In this section, we use prompting to determine how well BERT understands hypernymy. In order to predict the hypernym of a word (hyponym) using BERT and prompting, we run BERT on a prompt including a mask token, using it to predict the identity of the masked token. One such prompt might be "An apple tastes good. An apple is a `[MASK]`.", where the hyponym is "apple", and its canonical hypernym is "fruit."

3.1 Dataset

We perform our experiments on a subset of the hypernyms / hyponyms given by Battig and Montague (1969); we call this the Battig dataset. The dataset consists of pairs (x, y) of hyponym word x and canonical hypernym y; these pairs are organized by y, and many words share the same hypernym. Our subset consists of 863 words that have unique 25 hypernyms in total. We select only words where y would be represented by BERT as one token; doing this allows the hypernyms to be guessed by BERT using one `[MASK]` token.

3.2 Experiments

Using the Battig dataset, we conduct a variety of experiments, to determine to what degree BERT is aware of hypernymy. In each experiment, we fix a given prompt, with a slot for a hyponym, as well as a mask token which will be used to obtain the hypernym. Then, for each hyponym in the Battig datset, we use Wolf et al. (2020)'s `bert-base-uncased` BERT model to obtain the probabilities assigned to each word (potential hypernym). Here, we detail the prompts used; in Section 3.3, we discuss how we evaluate our results.

In our first experiment, the **basic** experiment, we extract hypernyms from BERT using the simple prompt "A(n) x is a `[MASK]`.". We use the appropriate article ("a", "an", or none at all) for x, but we always use the article "a" as the determiner for `[MASK]`. This results in difficulties in guessing hypernyms that start with vowels. Although a prompt such as "xs are `[MASK]`." would avoid this issues, using such a prompt is not possible due to tokenization issues: while all hypernyms in the singular are single tokens, hypernyms in the plural are often split into multiple tokens, and cannot be guessed using one `[MASK]` token.

As a follow up, we run the **type-of** experiment, using the prompt "A(n) x is a type[1] of `[MASK]`.". This is intended to allow for vowel hypernyms and clarify that hypernymy is the relation of interest.

We also test two final simple prompts that reflect common real-world situations in which hypernyms might appear. The first, "a `[MASK]`, such as x", is a prompt first proposed as a template using which hypernym-hyponym pairs could be discovered in unlabeled text (Hearst, 1992). This **such-as** prompt is a fragment, rather than a natural sentence. The second prompt is "My favorite `[MASK]` is x.". This "**favorite**" prompt both provides a more natural prompt, and puts the `[MASK]` token in an intermediate position.

Next, we perform a series of contextualized queries, based on the hypothesis that some hypernyms are difficult for BERT to predict because there is insufficient information in the query, and our short, contextless prompts are too different from the training data. To resolve this we generate contexts in two ways. First, we create a **handwritten context** to be used for each hypernym. For example, if the word x is a flower, its context might be "A(n) x smells nice.", followed by the prompt "A(n) x is a `[MASK]`". Note that since there is no training, BERT cannot simply learn a context-hypernym correspondence. However, although we attempted to write prompts that did not hint very strongly at the identity of the hypernym, it is possible that these contexts might have provided clues.

We also experiment with **automatically gathered contexts**, gathered from SemCor 2.0 (Langone et al., 2004). To do this, we first automatically find the WordNet sense of each word in the dataset. We assign to each word the first WordNet sense (if any) that includes the word's hypernym as an inherited hypernym. Then, we choose as the word's context the first SemCor sentence that includes the word used in the appropriate sense.

Additionally we experiment with prompts that include **multiple hyponyms**. Specifically, we use two prompts: "A(n) x is a `[MASK]`. So is a(n) x'." and "My favorite `[MASK]` is either a(n) x or a(n) x'", where x' is another word, in principle another hyponym. These prompts allow us to query the hypernym of polysemous words more clearly: while the word "orange" admits the hypernyms "color" and "fruit", when "orange" is paired with "purple", only the former is acceptable. In the first experiment, we select x' from the actual pool of words that share x's hypernym.

In the **FastText multiple hyponym** experiment, we automatically find values for x'. We represent each word in the dataset as its FastText (Bojanowski et al., 2016) vector, using the `eng-300` pretrained model. Then, we choose as x' the nearest neighbor (using cosine distance) of the word of interest x within the FastText model's vocabulary. Using this method, we can generate x' while keeping the prompting process entirely unsupervised.

Finally, we test an **ensemble** strategy: we take BERT's predictions based on an unweighted average of three prompts: "x is a `[MASK]`", "x is an `[MASK]`", and "x is a type of `[MASK]`". Since the last of the three prompts gives no hint as to the starting letter of the following word, it acts as a tiebreaker between possible vowel / consonant-initial responses.

3.3 Evaluation

We use a variety of metrics to evaluate the hypernyms predicted by BERT. First, we use **precision at 1** (P@1), that is, the proportion of BERT's most-likely predictions that were correct, relative to the canonical hypernym given by the dataset. We also use **mean reciprocal rank** (MRR), which is the mean (taken over examples) of the reciprocal of the rank of the correct answer in BERT's top predictions. We consider only BERT's top 5 predictions, and assign a reciprocal rank of 0 if the answer is not in the top 5.

However, these metrics are flawed, as many words have multiple hypernyms, possibly corre-

[1]We experiment with other words besides "type" that might indicate hypernymy, such as "kind", "category", and "sort", but find no significant difference in results.

sponding to multiple senses of the word. For example, an oak is a type of tree, but also a type of plant; orange, is both a type of fruit and a color. To resolve this, we also create an automated metric, **WordNet P@k**, to determine if a predicted hypernym is valid. In WordNet (Fellbaum, 1998), most nouns have for each word sense a list of inherited hypernyms, including both its direct hypernyms, as well as the inherited hypernyms of the noun's hypernyms. In our WordNet precision at k (P@k) metric, a word w is considered to be a hypernym of a word x if w is an inherited hypernym of x. WordNet P@k is thus the proportion of the top k predicted hypernyms for x that are one of x's inherited hypernyms.

This metric, too, has flaws; because WordNet's word senses are very fine-grained, WordNet's hypernyms do not correspond directly with intuition, penalizing hypernyms that might be valid. Moreover, in some cases, WordNet's hypernyms for a word do not include the hypernym label from the dataset; e.g. WordNet does not include"boat" as a hypernym for "yacht". To partially resolve this issue, we label a prediction correct under WordNet if the prediction is a hypernym from the dataset or an inherited hypernym according to WordNet.

We also notice that in many cases, BERT's most likely prediction for a given word's hypernym is the word itself. In the case of a prompt such as "x is a [MASK]", the tautology "x is x" is not strictly incorrect. Moreover, it is not uncommon that, when x is predicted as its own hypernym, the second most likely prediction is the canonical hypernym of x. So, we report results both including x as a possible prediction, and excluding x when BERT predicts it as its own hypernym.

3.4 Results

For each of our experiments, we use a different set of prompts to predict the top hypernyms of each hyponym in the dataset, and report four metrics: P@1, MRR, WordNet P@1, and WordNet P@5, as defined above. Table 1 reports these metrics as expected, while Table 2 shows the results predicting the hypernyms for a word x with BERT, and deleting x from the list of hypernyms, as BERT often predicts x to be its own hypernym.

3.5 Discussion

The results indicate that the basic experiments, using only prompts of the form "x is a [MASK]" prompt BERT to give the correct answer only 30% of the time. In contrast, explicitly stating the (type-of) relationship intended results in a precision of only 16.2, likely because these constructions are less common in the training data than those without "type-of". This is despite the fact that this prompt avoids the troubles of using "a/an" in the prompt.

The "such-as" prompt is more effective than the prior two: its precision is 18 points higher than the basic prompt, and its MRR is 6 points higher; moreover, its WordNet P@1 is the highest of all prompts using only one hyponym. The "favorite" prompt also performs favorably compared to the first two, although not as well as the "such-as" prompt.

The addition of handcrafted context to the prompt, intended to better replicate BERT's training conditions and disambiguate the meaning of the hyponym in question, improves BERT's hypernym-guessing ability. However, the automatically-found contexts do not yield the same boost; manual analysis reveals that BERT often guesses words that might reasonably continue the text given the context, but these are not necessarily hypernyms.

Adding another hyponym to the prompt in addition to x is the most effective at improving BERT's accuracy. When both hyponyms share the same hypernym, the WordNet P@1 rises to 60%, which is much higher than the baseline basic prompt, but still demonstrates room to improve. Some of the errors (BERT fails to guess the hypernyms "animal" and "instrument") are due to the hypernym's starting with a vowel; others, like the BERT's inability to guess hypernyms "relative" and "cloth", do not admit such an easy explanation. In the case of "cloth", while in the case of "relative", BERT simply guesses wrong.

Although the multiple hyponym method does not allow BERT to perfectly guess the correct hypernym, its MRR of 66.7 (excluding x) is impressive. Moreover, we can use unsupervised methods to find a second hypernym, with only a moderate loss in accuracy.

Finally, the prompt ensemble technique offers no improvement over the basic prompt in terms of accuracy with respect to the canonical hypernym. However, when excluding x from the predicted hypernyms and measuring using WordNet accuracy, the ensemble of prompts performs as well as when multiple hypernyms are given. This reflects the fact that the ensemble of prompts does induce BERT to predict hypernyms starting with a vowel, such as "animal" and "instrument". It is simply that the

Experiment	P@1	MRR	WN P@1	WN P@5
A(n) x is a `[MASK]`.	30.3	44.4	36.2	22.0
A(n) x is a type of `[MASK]`.	16.2	33.7	21.7	21.4
a `[MASK]`, such as a(n) x	48.3	50.4	54.9	25.5
My favorite `[MASK]` is a(n) x.	35.7	44.0	50.8	23.8
`[Handwritten context]`. A(n) x is a `[MASK]`.	42.5	53.0	45.1	18.6
`[SemCor context]`. A(n) x is a `[MASK]`.	29.7	38.2	33.0	15.9
A(n) x is a `[MASK]`. So is a(n) x'.	51.7	63.0	54.1	23.8
A(n) x is a `[MASK]`. So is a(n) x'. (FT)	41.2	52.2	45.7	21.1
My favorite `[MASK]` is either a(n) x or a(n) x'. (FT)	38.5	47.1	55.9	24.7
Ensemble	29.8	44.9	38.6	26.9

Table 1: Diagnostic test performance (Battig dataset) when including the hyponym x in the top k. "WN" denotes WordNet, and "FT" denotes FastText.

Experiment	P@1	MRR	WN P@1	WN P@5
A(n) x is a `[MASK]`.	38.7	49.7	46.6	22.9
A(n) x is a type of `[MASK]`.	31.4	43.4	43.0	22.7
a `[MASK]`, such as a(n) x	50.3	52.7	57.6	26.3
My favorite `[MASK]` is a(n) x.	35.7	44.1	50.8	23.9
`[Handwritten context]`. A(n) x is a `[MASK]`.	44.8	54.7	48.2	19.0
`[SemCor context]`. x is a `[MASK]`.	33.6	41.5	40.3	17.7
A(n) x is a `[MASK]`. So is a(n) x'.	57.4	66.7	61.5	24.2
A(n) x is a `[MASK]`. So is a(n) x'. (FT)	47.2	56.1	53.1	22.0
My favorite `[MASK]` is either a(n) x or a(n) x'. (FT)	38.6	47.4	56.5	24.9
Ensemble	38.2	50.3	53.0	30.0

Table 2: Diagnostic test performance (Battig dataset) when excluding the hyponym x from the top k. "WN" denotes WordNet, and "FT" denotes FastText.

hypernym predicted given this prompt is (in 15% of examples) correct, but not the canonical hypernym.

4 Comparison with other Hypernym Discovery Models

Although the goal of this paper is to learn more about BERT, we also compare BERT to other models used for hypernym discovery, the task of predicting a word's hypernym. To do so, we evaluate on the test split of the Semeval 2018 Task 9 (Camacho-Collados et al., 2018) dataset, which consists of 1500 words, each with a list of valid hypernyms.

This dataset is not very compatible with our approach. The hypernyms listed for each hyponym do not necessarily fit into one token. Moreover, the hyponyms in the dataset are abstract nouns. Many are also not necessarily common knowledge, being instead specific individuals, places, or technical terms. In contrast, the category norms dataset was designed to include only hyponyms that almost anyone would know.

As in the prior experiments, we use the `bert-base-uncased` pretrained BERT model from Huggingface (Wolf et al., 2020). We test the prompts "x is a type of `[MASK]`" and "My favorite `[MASK]` is x", to account for hypernyms starting with either consonants or vowels. We also test the high-performing "such-as" prompt "a `[MASK]`, such as x". We predict the top 15 hypernyms for each hypernym and evaluate using the following metrics: mean average precision (MAP), Mean Reciprocal Rank (MRR), and precision at k (P@k). Mean average precision can be defined as the average over k of P@k; we compute this average for $k = 1, \ldots, 15$. Table 3 shows the results for our BERT model as compared to the highest and lowest scoring (by MAP) supervised and unsupervised models (results from (Camacho-Collados et al., 2018)); our models are "BERT (such as)", "BERT (favorite)", and "BERT (type of)".

For all prompts, BERT outperforms all of the unsupervised models on all metrics, as well as the worst-performing supervised model. The "such-as" prompt even manages to outperform the supervised

Model	S/US	MAP	MRR	P@5
BERT (such as)	US	20.17	12.65	10.49
CRIM_r1	S	19.78	36.10	19.03
SJTU BCMI	S	5.77	10.56	5.96
BERT (favorite)	US	9.17	13.95	7.91
BERT (type of)	US	7.37	22.30	8.81
Team 13	US	2.77	6.07	2.72
Apollo_r1	US	1.40	3.51	1.33

Table 3: Model performance on Semeval 2018 Task 9: Hypernym Discovery (Semeval 2018 Task 9 Dataset). S/US = Supervised or Unsupervised

models with respect to MAP, although its MRR and P@5 put it squarely in the middle of the pack. This is surprising, considering that BERT makes no use of the closed vocabulary of hypernyms that this task has, and other models took advantage of. In fact, with the "such-as" prompt, BERT could not possibly predict many of the hypernyms in this task, including hypernyms that start with vowels, and hypernyms that are represented as multiple tokens. However, its performance is still respectable.

5 Qualitative analysis - does BERT understand hypernymy?

Having quantitatively analyzed BERT's outputs on various prompts, we now turn to qualitatively analyze them. The immediate results—that the quality of BERT's responses depends heavily on the prompt, and none of the prompts are perfect—are not terribly surprising, and follow from those of other works on prompting. However, a closer look reveals that while no prompt was successful at recovering the hypernyms we desired, *certain* prompts were able to most often produce reasonable hypernyms, even if they were not exactly the desired hypernyms.

Past works (Ravichander et al., 2020) have suggested that BERT's answers to hypernym queries show a lack of knowledge of hypernymy. Some of our prompts display the same behavior. For example, the "type-of" prompt yields "wine", "coffee", and "grape" for the hypernyms of the color "mauve". BERT guesses items that may be mauve in color, but are certainly not hypernyms of mauve; this prompt suggests that BERT does not understand the hypernymy relation.

However, the performance of the "such-as" prompt tells a different story. It is, in fact, more accurate than the numbers suggest—it predicts in the Battig dataset, for example, "felony" to be the hypernym of "embezzlement", which is marked wrong, but is in fact correct. Follow-up manual analysis of 100 (out of 419) incorrect predictions from the Battig dataset using this prompt showed that 35% of answers marked as incorrect were actually correct, suggesting a true P@1 of 66.4%. This is also true of the "favorite" prompt, in which the same analysis suggested a true P@1 of 76%, higher than the "such-as" prompt's.

Despite this seemingly-good performance, a closer look at the incorrect answers provided by BERT in response to these prompts complicates the notion that BERT understands hypernymy. When using the "such-as" prompt, a pattern of errors appears with respect to city names: an oft-guessed hypernym is "few". While this makes sense in the context of the prompt—consider a phrase such as "most cities, except for a [few, such as Minneapolis]"—this is not a valid hypernym. However, it is a convenient failure case that BERT can predict for almost any hyponym; it appears in the top 15 predictions for 438 of 1500 entries in the SemEval dataset.

A similar pattern appears with the "favorite prompt". On the Battig dataset, BERT sometimes yields hypernyms that are too generic—for example, as the hypernyms of medicine, it yields "thing", "subject", and "topic". Worse, on the SemEval dataset BERT predicts "word" as the top hypernym for 305 of the 1500 words in the dataset; while "word" is a grammatically and logically correct answer to the prompt, it does not show any understanding of hypernymy. Furthermore, the next 4 top predictions by BERT cover another 427 of the 1500 entries, suggesting that BERT is unable to provide a meaningful hypernym for each word. In contrast, the top hypernym on the Semeval dataset for the "type-of" prompt is assigned to only 37 of 1500 words. So, the "type-of" prompt does not guess the same hypernym for many words.

In light of these phenomena, it is difficult to say whether either of these two high-performing prompts has actually elicited knowledge of hypernymy from BERT. The "such-as" prompt performs well, and if not for vowel / consonant issues, might perform even better. Unfortunately, since the prompt does not specifically ask for the hypernym of x, its incorrect answers leave unclear whether BERT is failing to systematically understand hypernymy, or is simply performing general language modeling when we would prefer that it extract a hypernym.

The "favorite" prompt also performs well, and even its failures are often correct, albeit too-generic, hypernyms. The prompt also implies that "`[MASK]`" is the hypernym of x. Moreover, because some of the hypernyms (e.g. "crime") are rather unlikely to have appeared in BERT's training data in the context of the prompt (i.e. because "My favorite crime is..." is not a common phrase), it seems reasonable to attribute some of BERT's performance to genuine learning of hypernymy, rather than simple memorization of training data. However, this is not true of all hypernyms: it is possible that BERT's use of generic hypernyms like "thing" stems from a memorization of frequent constructions like "my favorite thing" in the training data.

6 Conclusion

In this paper, we conduct a thorough investigation of BERT's knowledge of hypernymy via prompting. Inspired by recent work on prompting, we use a wide variety of prompts to search for knowledge of hypernymy. We find that BERT does have some knowledge of hypernymy, and performs better than other unsupervised models for hypernym discovery. Furthermore, two prompts, "`[MASK]`, such as x" and "My favorite `[MASK]` is x.", often elicit correct hypernyms from BERT. However, even with these prompts, BERT occasionally fails, producing either non-hypernyms or extremely general hypernyms. Moreover, this prompting methodology does not allow us to distinguish between understanding of hypernymy and memorization of hypernyms from training data. Thus, we conclude that while some of the prompts elicited many correct hypernyms, we cannot claim that BERT has fully understood hypernymy.

Acknowledgments

We thank anonymous reviewers for their valuable comments and suggestions for improvement.

This work was supported by the GAČ NEUREM3 grant (Neural Representations in Multimodal and Multi-lingual Modelling, 19-26934X).

Computational resources were supplied by the project "e-Infrastruktura CZ" (e-INFRA CZ ID:90140) supported by the Ministry of Education, Youth and Sports of the Czech Republic.

References

William F. Battig and William E. Montague. 1969. Category norms of verbal items in 56 categories a replication and extension of the connecticut category norms. *Journal of Experimental Psychology*, 80(3p2):1.

Piotr Bojanowski, Edouard Grave, Armand Joulin, and Tomas Mikolov. 2016. Enriching word vectors with subword information. *arXiv preprint arXiv:1607.04606*.

Jose Camacho-Collados, Claudio Delli Bovi, Luis Espinosa-Anke, Sergio Oramas, Tommaso Pasini, Enrico Santus, Vered Shwartz, Roberto Navigli, and Horacio Saggion. 2018. SemEval-2018 task 9: Hypernym discovery. In *Proceedings of The 12th International Workshop on Semantic Evaluation*, pages 712–724, New Orleans, Louisiana. Association for Computational Linguistics.

Alexis Conneau, German Kruszewski, Guillaume Lample, Loïc Barrault, and Marco Baroni. 2018. What you can cram into a single $&!#* vector: Probing sentence embeddings for linguistic properties. In *Proceedings of the 56th Annual Meeting of the Association for Computational Linguistics (Volume 1: Long Papers)*, pages 2126–2136, Melbourne, Australia. Association for Computational Linguistics.

Jacob Devlin, Ming-Wei Chang, Kenton Lee, and Kristina Toutanova. 2019. BERT: Pre-training of deep bidirectional transformers for language understanding. In *Proceedings of the 2019 Conference of the North American Chapter of the Association for Computational Linguistics: Human Language Technologies, Volume 1 (Long and Short Papers)*, pages 4171–4186, Minneapolis, Minnesota. Association for Computational Linguistics.

Allyson Ettinger. 2020. What BERT Is Not: Lessons from a New Suite of Psycholinguistic Diagnostics for Language Models. *Transactions of the Association for Computational Linguistics*, 8:34–48.

Christiane Fellbaum. 1998. *WordNet: An Electronic Lexical Database*. Bradford Books.

Marti A. Hearst. 1992. Automatic acquisition of hyponyms from large text corpora. In *COLING 1992 Volume 2: The 14th International Conference on Computational Linguistics*.

John Hewitt and Percy Liang. 2019. Designing and interpreting probes with control tasks. In *Proceedings of the 2019 Conference on Empirical Methods in Natural Language Processing and the 9th International Joint Conference on Natural Language Processing (EMNLP-IJCNLP)*, pages 2733–2743, Hong Kong, China. Association for Computational Linguistics.

Zhengbao Jiang, Frank F. Xu, J. Araki, and Graham Neubig. 2020. How can we know what language models know? *Transactions of the Association for Computational Linguistics*, 8:423–438.

Helen Langone, Benjamin R. Haskell, and George A. Miller. 2004. Annotating WordNet. In *Proceedings of the Workshop Frontiers in Corpus Annotation at HLT-NAACL 2004*, pages 63–69, Boston, Massachusetts, USA. Association for Computational Linguistics.

Fabio Petroni, Tim Rocktäschel, Sebastian Riedel, Patrick Lewis, Anton Bakhtin, Yuxiang Wu, and Alexander Miller. 2019. Language models as knowledge bases? In *Proceedings of the 2019 Conference on Empirical Methods in Natural Language Processing and the 9th International Joint Conference on Natural Language Processing (EMNLP-IJCNLP)*, pages 2463–2473, Hong Kong, China. Association for Computational Linguistics.

Alec Radford, Jeff Wu, R. Child, David Luan, Dario Amodei, and Ilya Sutskever. 2019. Language models are unsupervised multitask learners.

Abhilasha Ravichander, Eduard Hovy, Kaheer Suleman, Adam Trischler, and Jackie Chi Kit Cheung. 2020. On the systematicity of probing contextualized word representations: The case of hypernymy in BERT. In *Proceedings of the Ninth Joint Conference on Lexical and Computational Semantics*, pages 88–102, Barcelona, Spain (Online). Association for Computational Linguistics.

Laria Reynolds and Kyle McDonell. 2021. *Prompt Programming for Large Language Models: Beyond the Few-Shot Paradigm*. Association for Computing Machinery, New York, NY, USA.

Anna Rogers, Olga Kovaleva, and Anna Rumshisky. 2020. A primer in bertology: What we know about how bert works.

Timo Schick and Hinrich Schütze. 2020. Rare words: A major problem for contextualized representation and how to fix it by attentive mimicking. In *Proceedings of the Thirty-Fourth AAAI Conference on Artificial Intelligence*.

Taylor Shin, Yasaman Razeghi, Robert L. Logan IV au2, Eric Wallace, and Sameer Singh. 2020. Autoprompt: Eliciting knowledge from language models with automatically generated prompts.

Ian Tenney, Patrick Xia, Berlin Chen, Alex Wang, Adam Poliak, R Thomas McCoy, Najoung Kim, Benjamin Van Durme, Samuel R. Bowman, Dipanjan Das, and Ellie Pavlick. 2019. What do you learn from context? probing for sentence structure in contextualized word representations. *ICLR*.

Ivan Vulić, Edoardo Maria Ponti, Robert Litschko, Goran Glavaš, and Anna Korhonen. 2020. Probing pretrained language models for lexical semantics. In *Proceedings of the 2020 Conference on Empirical Methods in Natural Language Processing (EMNLP)*, pages 7222–7240, Online. Association for Computational Linguistics.

Gregor Wiedemann, Steffen Remus, Avi Chawla, and Chris Biemann. 2019. Does bert make any sense? interpretable word sense disambiguation with contextualized embeddings.

Thomas Wolf, Lysandre Debut, Victor Sanh, Julien Chaumond, Clement Delangue, Anthony Moi, Pierric Cistac, Tim Rault, Remi Louf, Morgan Funtowicz, Joe Davison, Sam Shleifer, Patrick von Platen, Clara Ma, Yacine Jernite, Julien Plu, Canwen Xu, Teven Le Scao, Sylvain Gugger, Mariama Drame, Quentin Lhoest, and Alexander Rush. 2020. Transformers: State-of-the-art natural language processing. In *Proceedings of the 2020 Conference on Empirical Methods in Natural Language Processing: System Demonstrations*, pages 38–45, Online. Association for Computational Linguistics.

David Yenicelik, Florian Schmidt, and Yannic Kilcher. 2020. How does BERT capture semantics? a closer look at polysemous words. In *Proceedings of the Third BlackboxNLP Workshop on Analyzing and Interpreting Neural Networks for NLP*, pages 156–162, Online. Association for Computational Linguistics.

An in-depth look at Euclidean disk embeddings for structure preserving parsing

Federico Fancellu* **Lan Xiao*†** **Allan Jepson** **Afsaneh Fazly**
Samsung AI Center, Toronto
{federico.f, allan.jepson, a.fazly}@samsung.com

Abstract

Preserving the structural properties of trees or graphs when embedding them into a metric space allows for a high degree of interpretability, and has been shown beneficial for downstream tasks (e.g., hypernym detection, natural language inference, multimodal retrieval). However, whereas the majority of prior work looks at using structure-preserving embeddings when *encoding* a structure given as input, e.g., WordNet (Fellbaum, 1998), there is little exploration on how to use such embeddings when *predicting* one. We address this gap for two structure generation tasks, namely dependency and semantic parsing. We test the applicability of *disk embeddings* (Suzuki et al., 2019) that has been proposed for embedding Directed Acyclic Graphs (DAGs) but has not been tested on tasks that generate such structures. Our experimental results show that for both tasks the original disk embedding formulation leads to much worse performance when compared to non-structure-preserving baselines. We propose enhancements to this formulation and show that they almost close the performance gap for dependency parsing. However, the gap still remains notable for semantic parsing due to the complexity of meaning representation graphs, suggesting a challenge for generating interpretable semantic parse representations.

1 Introduction

Numerous studies in NLP have focused on embedding linguistic elements into metric spaces, where instances are represented as vectors whose geometric distance reflects the semantic similarity among instances (Mikolov et al., 2013; Baroni et al., 2014; Pennington et al., 2014, *inter alia*). More recently, some have gone beyond embedding words and sequences, and explored the encoding of a hierarchy (e.g., WordNet, Fellbaum, 1998) through modelling its partial order structure (Vendrov et al., 2015; Lai and Hockenmaier, 2017; Vilnis et al., 2018). Consequently, given the size and depth of such structures, attention has shifted to geometric spaces (mostly hyperbolic) that could better represent order and containment relations (Nickel and Kiela, 2017; Ganea et al., 2018; Dong et al., 2018; Suzuki et al., 2019). Methods to embed elements of hierarchies are *structure-preserving*, and therefore interpretable, in that the relative position in the embedding space reflects the relation in the original hierarchy (e.g., parent–child relation). Most of these methods have been shown to be beneficial not only on tasks pertinent to the encoded hierarchy itself (e.g., hyponymy relations), but on downstream tasks including multimodal retrieval (Vendrov et al., 2015) and video understanding (Surís et al., 2021).

However, whereas there is a plethora of studies looking at preserving structure while *encoding* an hierarchy given as input, there is little to no exploration on how to do this while *predicting* one. In this work, we start one such exploration with the quintessential structure generation task in NLP: parsing. Given an input sentence, e.g., 'Anna asked Mary to stop', parsing is the task of transducing a natural language string into a structured linguistic representation (e.g., the AMR graph in Fig. 1(a)) that encodes either syntactic or semantic properties of the string. Recent neural network based approaches have achieved state-of-the-art performance while being able to generalize both across frameworks, as well as across trees and graphs (Zhang et al., 2019; Lindemann et al., 2020; Ozaki et al., 2020; Samuel and Straka, 2020; Procopio et al., 2021, *inter alia*). However, not much can be said about the representations these parsers learn since the parsers are not explicitly trained to preserve any of the geometric properties of their output structure, and as such are not interpretable. We believe that moving to interpretable, structured rep-

*Equal Contribution
†Now at Pinterest

Proceedings of the Fourth BlackboxNLP Workshop on Analyzing and Interpreting Neural Networks for NLP, pages 283–295
Online, November 11, 2021.

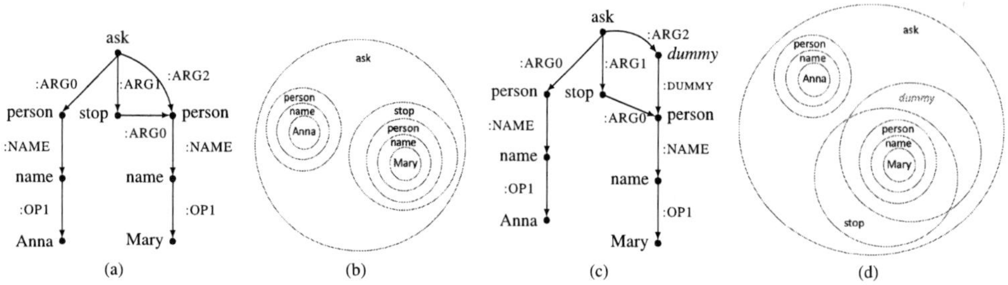

Figure 1: Abstract Meaning Representation (AMR) graph for the sentence 'Anna asked Mary to stop' (a), with a transitive closure between the nodes 'ask' and 'person'; however, given the corresponding disk embedding representation in (b), we cannot reconstruct such a relation. Therefore, we introduce a *dummy* node in every transitive closure (c) so that graph relations and disk embedding containment are bijective (d).

resentations would allow for a better diagnostic of what is learnt by a parser, while at the same time laying the foundations to connect 'deep' natural language understanding to other tasks, especially in the multimodal domain.

How can we build such interpretable representations? Does interpretability impact performance? Kádár et al. (2021) have attempted to answer these questions in the context of parsing into dependency *trees* by means of a structure-preserving loss that forces embedding distances to be isometric to tree distances. Whereas Kádár et al. show that a structure-preserving embedding leads to comparable performance with blackbox methods, their method does not generalize to graphs. This is of particular relevance to semantic parses that are often DAGs, and where it is unclear how to isometrically embed multiple paths between a pair of nodes.

To this end, we turn to a method that allows us to model transitive asymmetrical relations expressible as a DAG: *disk embeddings* (Dong et al., 2018; Suzuki et al., 2019). Disk embeddings represent DAGs as a series of concentric disks, each defined by a center vector and a radius (as the ones in Fig 1(b)), and have been shown to outperform other methods when encoding hypernym relations in the WordNet hierarchy. However, it is not clear whether such a method transfers well to more complex architectures where embeddings are contextualized given an input sentence, and structure prediction often interacts with predicting other elements of the tree or graph (node label, edge label, etc.).

In summary, our work makes the following contributions:

Disk embedding losses for tree and graph generation in parsing: we found the disk embedding loss formulation of Suzuki et al. (2019) to be sub-optimal w.r.t. parsing performance. We found that simply adding a positive margin already provides a large boost in performance, but the best performance is obtained when an auxiliary loss that considers local neighbourhood relations is added, as well as when parent-child relations are oversampled.

Interpretability in parsing (though at the cost of performance): through a comparison with non-interpretable approaches, we found that whereas for dependency trees the price to pay in terms of performance for interpretability is small, for semantic graphs the gap is higher, highlighting where future work should focus its efforts. Importantly, we found that most semantic parsing errors are local and specific to the parser we use, where the lack of explicit alignment between words and graph nodes poses a challenge for disk embeddings, especially in the case of named entity substructures.

2 Disk Embeddings: Background

As discussed above, disk embeddings (Dong et al., 2018; Suzuki et al., 2019) provide an interpretable model for transitive asymmetrical relations (i.e., partially ordered sets or *posets*), such as those represented by a DAG. They are a general framework that allows to embed posets in a (quasi-)metric space. Let's define (X, d) as a quasi-metric space with distance d and a *closed disk* $D(\mathbf{x}, r) = \{p \in X \mid d(p, \mathbf{x}) \leq r\}$, where $\mathbf{x}$ is the *center* and r the radius. We can express the containment relationship for two disks[1] as

$$D(\mathbf{c}_i, r_i) \supset D(\mathbf{c}_j, r_j) \iff d(\mathbf{c}_i, \mathbf{c}_j) < r_i - r_j. \quad (1)$$

[1]Even though multi-dimensional disks are technically balls, we will refer to them as disks throughout the paper.

Given a set of such disks, the ordering provided by this subset relationship provides a poset.[2]

Disk embeddings seek to maintain *order isomorphism* between the posets of a graph G (X_G, $\preceq_G$) and their disk embedding representation (X_ϕ, $\preceq_\phi$). Such an isomorphism exists if there is a bijective function $f : X_G \to X_\phi$ such that $x_G \preceq y_G \iff x_\phi \preceq y_\phi$. In our case the bijective function f is modelled via a neural network architecture introduced in § 3.

To achieve isomorphism, we make use of the *protrusion* ℓ_{ij} of disk $x_j = D(\mathbf{c}_j, r_j)$ with respect to disk $x_i = D(\mathbf{c}_i, r_i)$ as the degree of containment:

$$\ell_{ij} = d(\mathbf{c}_i, \mathbf{c}_j) - r_i + r_j. \tag{2}$$

It follows from Eq. (1) that $\ell_{ij} < 0$ (*negative* protrusion) if and only if $x_j \subset x_i$. Moreover, the protrusion ℓ_{ij} provides a continuous measure of the degree of containment. Specifically it equals the maximum signed distance of points in disk $D(\mathbf{c}_j, r_j)$ from the boundary of disk $D(\mathbf{c}_i, r_i)$. Here $\ell_{ij} < 0$ indicates that $D(\mathbf{c}_j, r_j)$ is entirely contained inside $D(\mathbf{c}_i, r_i)$ (and, indeed, with a margin equal to $-\ell_{ij}$). While $\ell_{ij} > 0$ indicates that some point in $D(\mathbf{c}_j, r_j)$ is outside $D(\mathbf{c}_i, r_i)$ by a distance equal to ℓ_{ij}.

Recovering DAGs from disk embeddings. We wish to be able to represent a DAG with a disk embedding and also be able to recover the edges of that DAG from its disk embedding. However, recovering the edges of the original DAG is not always possible. To see this, suppose we have a disk embedding formed by a 1-1 mapping of the nodes of a DAG to disks.[3] Moreover, suppose the mapping is an order isomorphism, so the partial ordering is preserved.

It is natural to consider an edge from disk x_i to disk x_j if and only if $x_j \subset x_i$ and there is no other intervening node (i.e., there is no x_k such that $x_j \subset x_k \subset x_i$). This process recovers a DAG with the same partial ordering as the original DAG, but it may be missing edges. This issue occurs, for example, for the disk embedding shown in Fig. 1b, which represents the same partial ordering as the DAG in Fig. 1a. However, in decoding this disk embedding, we would not decode the edge from 'ask' to 'person', since 'stop' is an intervening node.

We remedy this problem by adding as many *dummy* nodes as necessary to the original DAG (as illustrated in Fig. 1c and Fig. 1d). Specifically, for any edge (n_i, n_j) in the original DAG that can be removed without changing the partial ordering, we create a new *dummy* node m_{ij}, and replace that edge by the two edges (n_i, m_{ij}) and (m_{ij}, n_j). Every edge in the modified graph is then required to reproduce the implied partial ordering, and this modified DAG is therefore recoverable from an order isomorphism.

3 Disk Embedding: Model

The disk embedding module takes as input the hidden representations of a sentence encoder (LSTM or transformer); we discuss how these representations are obtained in the context of dependency and semantic parsing in § 4.1 and 4.2 respectively. This input undergoes a linear transformation followed by a LeakyReLU activation to obtain X_g, that is then used to learn disk embeddings.

To learn the centers C and the radii R of the disks, we pass X_g through a n-layer MLP (where n=2 in our case) as follows:

$$C = f_a(W_c^{(n)}(X_g^{(n-1)}) + b_c) \tag{3a}$$

$$R = f_a(W_r^{(n)}(X_g^{(n-1)}) + b_r) \tag{3b}$$

where $X_g^{(n-1)}$ are the input representations from the previous layer (X_g^0 is the input representation X_g), $W^{(n)}$ are the weights for the nth MLP layer, b_c and b_r are the biases, and f_a is a non-linearity activation function (LeakyReLU in our case).

Centers and radii C and R are used to compute the *protrusion* values ℓ_{ij} as in Eq. 2. We then use the ℓ_{ij} values in a contrastive loss with a margin α as follows:

$$\mathcal{L}_c = \sum_{(i,j)\in\mathcal{P}} [\ell_{ij}]_+ + \sum_{(i,j)\in\mathcal{N}} [\alpha - \ell_{ij}]_+ \tag{4}$$

where $[x]_+$ is the function max(0,x) and $\mathcal{P}$ and $\mathcal{N}$ represent the sets of positive and negative pairs, respectively, where positives are pairs of nodes in an ancestor–descendant relation, and negatives include all other pairs of nodes. Recall that $\ell_{ij} < 0$ if node i is the ancestor of j, and > 0 otherwise, hence for the positive samples we only incur in a loss if the $\ell_{ij} > 0$.

Given that we have access to both positive and negative instances (node pairs in an ancestor–descendant relationship vs. all the rest), we can

[2]The manner in which individual edges in a DAG are represented in a disk embedding is more subtle and is discussed later.

[3]Note that disk embeddings must necessarily be acyclic due to the subset relations.

also formulate a Maximum Likelihood Estimation (MLE) binary cross-entropy loss, where we directly maximize the probability of a pair of nodes i and j to be either in an ancestor–descendant relationship or not.

$$a_{ij} = \text{sigmoid}(-\ell_{ij}), \tag{5}$$

$$\mathcal{L}_{MLE} = -\sum_{\substack{i,j \in V, \\ i \neq j}} \varrho_{ij} \log a_{ij} + (1 - \varrho_{ij}) \log(1 - a_{ij}), \tag{6}$$

where $a_{i,j}$ is the probability of i and j being in an ancestor–descendant relationship, and is obtained by applying a sigmoid function to ℓ_{ij} over two classes (ancestor–descendant vs. other). ϱ_{ij} is an indicator function that is 1 if i and j are in an ancestor–descendant relationship.

Structure auxiliary loss. A contrastive or MLE loss optimizes a *global* pair-wise containment relationship between nodes; however, this might come at the expense of *local* relations, which we still seek to preserve. In order to incorporate information about local neighbourhood structure, we propose a (local) structure-preserving loss. The goal of this loss is to maximize the probability of correctly predicting the local relation between two nodes out of a class of 6 relations, namely, $\mathcal{C} = \{$parent, grandparent, child, grandchild, sister, other$\}$, where 'other' represents all relations with a path length greater than 2.[4] To predict these relations we start by passing X_g through a biaffine transform to obtain s_{ij}; this is the same as the biaffine function used in dependency and semantic parsing for edge prediction and since our parsers are two such systems, we reuse their implemented biaffine function. During training, we seek to predict the correct relationship between all pairs of nodes using a cross-entropy loss. Computation is as follows:

$$X_b^1, X_b^2 = \text{ReLU}(W_b^{(1)} X_g + b_b^{(1)}) \tag{7}$$

$$s_{ij} = X_b^{1T} U X_b^2 + W_b^{(2)} X_b^1 + W_b^{(3)} X_b^1 + b_b^{(2)} \tag{8}$$

$$\mathcal{L}_{struc} = \sum_{\substack{i,j \in V, \\ i \neq j}} -\log(\text{softmax}(W_b^{(4)} s_{ij} + b_b^{(3)})) \tag{9}$$

where X_b^1, X_b^2 are separate representations for ancestors and descendants respectively, whose dimensionality is half that of X_g, $W_b^{(n)}$ and U are the weight and b_b the bias. s_{ij} is the output of the biaffine transform, on top of which a linear followed by a softmax transform are applied to obtain the probability for the nodes i and j having the relation class $c \in \mathcal{C}$.

When used, the structure auxiliary loss is added to either the constrastive or the MLE loss to obtain the overall loss for a sentence, normalized by a factor T. We use the number of node pairs as T as opposed to the number of nodes, since we observe that the former achieves consistently better performance.

$$\mathcal{L} = \frac{1}{T}(\mathcal{L}_{c/MLE} + \mathcal{L}_{struc}) \tag{10}$$

Decoding into parent–child relations. At test time we recover the parent–child relations from the protrusion values ℓ_{ij} by first using Eq. 5 to get ancestor probabilities a_{ij}. Using this equation, negative protrusion values are transformed to high ancestor probabilities (≥ 0.5) and positive ones to low probabilities (< 0.5). We then identify the direct parent of each node as the ancestor with no intervening node:

$$p_{ij} = a_{ij}[1 - \max_{k \in V \setminus \{i,j\}}[a_{ik} a_{kj}]] \tag{11}$$

Note that for dependency parsing the parent–child probabilities p_{ij} are fed as input to a Maximum Spanning Tree (MST) decoding algorithm to obtain the final tree.

4 Parsing Systems

Our baseline dependency and semantic parsing both determine edge presence between nodes using the biaffine formulation of Dozat et al. (2017) (see Eq. 7-9), which predicts the most likely parent for each node, along with the grammatical relation between each pair of head and dependent, conditioned on an encoded hidden representation. We replace this with the disk embedding module described in § 3, leaving all other modules unchanged.

4.1 Dependency parsing

We use the dependency parser of Kádár et al. (2021),[5] which has been shown to perform on par with SOTA systems while relying on structure-preserving, interpretable representations. To generate the hidden representations $h_1, h_2 ... h_{|S|}$ for a given sentence $S{=}w_1 ... w_{|S|}$, a highway-BiLSTM encoder (Srivastava et al., 2015) takes as input a sequence of $|S|$ embeddings $\mathbf{x}_1, \ldots, \mathbf{x}_{|S|}$, where

[4]We also experimented with maximizing the probability of parent–child relations vs. others ($|\mathcal{C}| = 2$) as well as including sisters relations ($|\mathcal{C}| = 3$) but found that a 6-way classification consistently resulted in the best performance.

[5]The parser of Kádár et al. (2021) is based on the parser of (Qi et al., 2018) whose codebase is provided at `https://github.com/stanfordnlp/stanfordnlp`.

each $\mathbf{x}_i$ is a concatenation of word-level, character-level, part-of-speech and morphological feature embeddings for w_i. We use pre-trained word2vec (Mikolov et al., 2013) and fastText embedding (Bojanowski et al., 2017) to initialize word embeddings, whereas the remaining embeddings are trained from scratch. A BiLSTM decoder then applies an MLP on top of the encoded representation to generate the input to either the biaffine or the disk embedding module.

4.2 Semantic parsing

Unlike dependencies, there is no one-to-one correspondence between words in a sentence and nodes in an AMR graph. A common solution is to use an auto-regressive parser (e.g., Zhang et al., 2019; Bevilacqua et al., 2021) that decodes nodes following an arbitrary graph linearization. However, semantic parses, just like dependency trees, are inherently orderless, which is why we opted for a non-autoregressive parser that predicts all nodes in parallel at once.[6] We use the PERIN parser (Samuel and Straka, 2020) to parse sentences into AMR graphs.[7] The parser generates graphs in two steps: first, a transformer encoder followed by a transformer decoder take pre-trained XLM-R embeddings (Conneau et al., 2019) as input to generate the hidden representations $h_1 ... h_{|S|}$.

Unlike dependency parsing, the alignment between words and nodes in a graph is missing, so the cross-entropy loss w.r.t. node labels cannot be computed directly. The alignments have to be bijective (one hidden state to one node only) but should still accommodate for many-to-many correspondences, as in the case of named entities (e.g., 'Mary') that are mapped to entire subgraphs (e.g., person → name → Mary). To meet both conditions, each h_i is transformed into k representations via a function $\phi : h_i \rightarrow \hat{y}_i$ with $\hat{y}_i \in \mathbb{R}^{dk}$. The parser finds the best alignment between the set of vectors $\hat{\mathcal{Y}} = \{\hat{y}_i\}$, and the set of target nodes $\mathcal{Y}$ by scoring all permutations $\Pi(\hat{\mathcal{Y}})$ and selecting the one, $\pi*$, that maximizes the probability of a vector $\hat{y}_i$ to correspond to the label of a node y, i.e., $p(y^{label})$; see Eq. 12. Note that we require the two sets $\mathcal{Y}$ and $\hat{\mathcal{Y}}$ to be the same size, and as such, we extend the set $\mathcal{Y}$ of target nodes with NULL tokens; in practice this means that the words aligned to NULL are dropped.

[6] Nonetheless, our disk embedding module is parser agnostic and could be applied to auto-regressive models as well.

[7] `https://github.com/ufal/perin`

$$\pi^* = \arg\max_{\pi \in \Pi} \sum_{i=1}^{|S| \times k} \mathbb{1}_{[y^{label} \neq \text{NULL}]} p(y^{label}_{\pi(i)} | \hat{y}_i; \theta) \quad (12)$$

where θ are the model parameters. Given a permutation π^*, the parser then computes the weighted sum of five different losses: the node label, the edge presence, the edge label, the property (see below), and the top node loss. For more detail, we refer the reader to the original paper (Samuel and Straka, 2020).

In our work, we solely focus on the edge presence classifier, that is a biaffine function followed by a cross-entropy loss, as stated at the beginning of this section. Note that there could be multiple nodes with the same label; in particular, this is the case for *properties* that are subgraphs describing named entities containing the same semantic constants (e.g., 'person' and 'name' for the named entities 'Anna' and 'Mary' in Fig. 1). An infelicitous consequence of the formula in Eq. 12 is that 'Anna' (or 'Mary') can be assigned either of the 'name' or 'person' nodes. To solve this problem, the parser decides which mapping is optimal by scoring edge attachments for all permutations of property nodes and selects the argmax. We will refer to this problem as the *edge permutation problem* when analyzing the errors of the parser in § 8.

5 Data and settings

We use the English-EWT section of Universal Dependencies (UD; Nivre et al., 2020) for dependency parsing, and the AMR2.0 dataset (Knight et al., 2017) for semantic parsing.

Ablations. For both tasks, we perform an ablation study on the development data to understand the impact of the choice of the loss function, sampling method, distance function and related settings (see Table 1). Specifically, we consider the following losses: the *original* loss formulation of Suzuki et al. (2019) and an extended version where a margin is added to the positive pairs (*+pos margin*; Eq. 4). Additionally, we report results for the MLE loss (Eq. 6), and for when we add our auxiliary structure loss (*+struct*; Eq. 9) to the contrastive or MLE losses.

In Eq. 3a–3b, centers and radii are computed separately, whereas in the original implementation of Suzuki et al. they are learnt jointly as a single vector in which the radius is the last dimension. To understand whether capturing the interaction between centers and radii helps with learning better disk embeddings, we create a (+*shared*) alternative where we jointly learn the centres and radii as in the original implementation. Finally, we build on the intuition of centers and radii informing each other, and propose an additional option on top of *shared*, (+*iter2* and +*iter3*), where we train an MLP to take C, R and $X_g^{(n-1)}$ as input and iteratively refine the centers and radii k times (where $k \in$ {2,3}).

All the settings described assume that we include all negative instances (node pairs that are not in an ancestor–descendant relation) as part of the loss computation; however this might lead to a class imbalance problem as there are many more negatives than there are positive instances ($\sim$ 10:1 ratio). We therefore experiment with different sampling methods, including removing descendant–ancestor negatives altogether. We found that only one sampling method lead to performance improvement, i.e., oversampling of parent–child nodes (+*sampling*). In practice, we multiply the loss of every parent–child pair by a factor (here 2) in order to penalize errors coming from such pairs. We further test the joint impact of this sampling approach together with the auxiliary structure loss (+*both*).

Eq. 4 uses a constant margin α for negative samples. However, one can formulate a *tailored* lower bound on the margin, σ_{ij}, that depends on the relationship between node i and j. We formally prove the existence of such a lower bound in Appendix B, and provide an algorithm to identify it (Algorithm 1). In practice, however, the use of this tailored margin did not result in a performance improvement for either the dependency or the semantic parsing. For completeness, we include the results in Appendix C, Table 4 (+*tailored*).

For all combinations, we compare two distance functions: ℓ_2 and ℓ_1 norms. We include a list of hyperparameter values in Appendix A.

Comparison with baselines. We then compare the performance of our best systems (on test data) against the dependency parser of parser of Kádár et al. (2021), and the semantic parser of Samuel and Straka (2020), respectively. We found that $\sim 3\%$ of the instances on the test set contain cycles which cannot be modelled by disk embeddings. To assess whether this impacts performance, we also provide results when removing instances containing cycles.

6 Evaluation

For both dependency and semantic parsing tasks, we compare our model output (a tree or a graph) to a reference parse.

For dependency parsing, we report accuracy, calculated using two standard measures: Unlabelled Attachment Score (UAS), that is the percentage of tokens that are assigned the correct head; and Labelled Attachment Score (LAS) that is the percentage of tokens that are assigned the correct head and the correct grammatical relation. We use UAS for model selection.

For semantic parsing, we use Mtool[8] to report a set of fine-grained F1 scores that reflect the performance of each classifier in the PERIN parser. *edge* (presence), (node) *label*, *top* (node) reflect the losses introduced in § 4.2; *prop*(erty prediction) represents a dedicated score on how well we predict named entity subgraphs (the *properties*), as well as how well we connect them to the rest of the graph.[9] Finally, *all* is a weighted average of these F1 scores.[10]

All results are reported as an average of 3 runs, along with standard deviations.

7 Results

The disk embedding loss formulation of Suzuki et al. (2019) performs considerably worse than all other settings. Results in Table 1 show that for both semantic and dependency parsing, adding a margin to positive instances (i.e., pushing positives below a margin $-\alpha$) leads to a considerable boost in performance. Compare the row of results for *original*(ℓ_2) with the rows for different variations of *pos margin*(ℓ_2).

The structure auxiliary loss helps with performance, often in conjunction with oversampling parent–child pairs. Results in Table 1 show that injecting information on the local neighbourhood structure, together with giving more weight to parent–child relations helps both dependency and semantic parsing; see results in the row corresponding to *pos margin*(ℓ_1)+*both*. On top of these settings, we also test whether performance can be further improved by having a shared representation

[8]`https://github.com/cfmrp/mtool`

[9]Property scores can overlap with edge presence scores in that they also assess edge prediction but only for property nodes.

[10]We use Mtool instead of SMATCH scoring (Cai and Knight, 2013) since Mtool provides a more fine-grained evaluation of the parser performance.

	dependency	*semantic*				
system	UAS	edge	label	prop	top	all
Kádár et al. (2021)	91.62(±.33)	-	-	-	-	-
Samuel and Straka (2020)	-	70.14(±.36)	88.15(±.05)	87.34(±.25)	90.37(±.11)	80.28(±.21)
original(ℓ_2)	70(±.94)	46.98(±2.23)	87.70(±.14)	58.36(±4.63)	89.44(±.69)	67.19(±1.85)
pos margin(ℓ_2)	87.64(±.15)	58.29(±1.19)	87.77(±.21)	80.23(±2.92)	90.03(±.35)	73.80(±1.27)
+struct	88.63(±.21)	61.33(±1.07)	86.04(±.07)	81.95(±1.15)	88.12(±1.17)	74.36(±.9)
+sampling	88.79(±.37)	59.58(±.23)	87.76(±.4)	80.78(±.78)	89.59(±.64)	74.38(±.15)
+both	89.63(±.16)	62.47(±.33)	86.15(±.18)	81.57(±2.88)	89.91(±.17)	75.26(±.4)
pos margin(ℓ_1)	87.88(±.21)	58.1(±.28)	87.50(±.09)	80(±2.69)	89.02(±1.14)	73.68(±.18)
+struct	89.23(±.31)	62.14(±.49)	86.2(±.26)	81.58(±2.31)	88.57(±1.32)	75.02(±.52)
+sampling	88.91(±.05)	59.49(±.38)	87.7(±.4)	80.52(±1.43)	89.40(±1.59)	74.36(±.31)
+both	90.08(±.21)	63.78(±.07)	86(±.20)	83.12(±.28)	88.93(±1.1)	75.83(±.02)
+both+shared	90.02(±.01)	63.75(±.5)	86.01(±.12)	83.04(±1.31)	89.88(±.7)	75.89(±.15)
+both+shared(iter2)	**90.27**(±.01)	63.22(±.8)	86.83(±.21)	83.73(±1.46)	88.98(±2.1)	**76.51**(±.6)
+both+shared(iter3)	90.12(±.12)	63.57(±1.6)	86.76(±.13)	83.34(±3.21)	90.61(±.36)	76.24(±1.21)
MLE	85.61(±2.63)	56.52(±.12)	87.71(±.11)	79.15(±2.3)	90.20(±.1)	72.60(±.7)
+struct	87.98(±.46)	59.74(±.08)	85.61(±.16)	80.37(±1.63)	90.57(±.2)	73.42(±.92)

Table 1: Results for dependency and semantic parsing on *dev* set to evaluate the impact of different settings and loss functions.

of radii and centers, as well as by iteratively refining this. Results show that doing so only leads to a slight improvement. Finally, we can see that all our contrastive loss formulations perform better than our MLE loss, and that performance is comparable with ℓ_2 and ℓ_1 distance. Further experiments and analyses use the best setting of *pos margin(ℓ_1)+both+shared(iter2)*.

To have interpretability one has to pay a price in performance. Table 2 shows results on the *test* set for both dependency and semantic parsing, for the SOTA parsers, as well as our best settings. As can be seen, whereas the loss in performance for dependency parsing is rather small, the gap is wider for semantic parsing. We also notice that removing instances with cycles does not change this gap, and as such we can conclude that the fact that disk embeddings cannot model these instances is not responsible for a drop in performance. We investigate this gap in performance for semantic parsing as part of our analysis in the following section.

system	*dependency*		*semantic*	*semantic* (w/o cycles)
	UAS	LAS		
K(2021)	90.93(±.08)	89.91(±.06)	-	-
SS(2020)	-	-	79.89(±.12)	78.86(±.09)
ours	89.17(±.02)	87.69(±.01)	75.21(±.19)	74.54(±.23)

Table 2: Comparison between our best dependency and semantic parsers with a disk embedding loss, *ours*, and the baselines, namely K(2021) (Kádár et al., 2021) and SS(2020) (Samuel and Straka, 2020). Results are on the *test* set.

8 Analysis

Do errors correlate with the (graph) distance and the relation between nodes? Now that we have access to interpetable representations, we can inspect which relations in a parse tree/graph are challenging to embed correctly. We begin by defining two types of errors w.r.t. the protrusion ℓ_{ij} for a predicted edge (i, j): one where $\ell_{ij} > 0$ and one where $-\alpha < \ell_{ij} < 0$ (note that a correct $\ell_{ij} < -\alpha$). We use 0 instead of α as the cutoff point because, although not below the desired margin, the sigmoid in Eq. 5 will still correctly predict the disk for i containing that of j. We plot these errors against the graph distance between all node pairs,[11] and report the % of errors over the total number of node pairs for different values of graph distance. Fig. 2(a) shows that there is an inverse correlation between errors and distance, with parent–child (distance of 1) and grandparent–grandchild relations (distance of 2) displaying the highest numbers of incorrect protrusions; this is particularly striking in the case of semantic parsing and we elaborate more on this when discussing the role of edge permutations below. However, we can see that a large number of incorrect protrusions fall in $(-\alpha, 0)$, especially in the case of dependency parsing, for which the sigmoid will still predict a correct containment.

What makes semantic parsing harder? We

[11] In a graph, where there could be multiple paths between a pair of nodes, we take the length of the longest path as the graph distance.

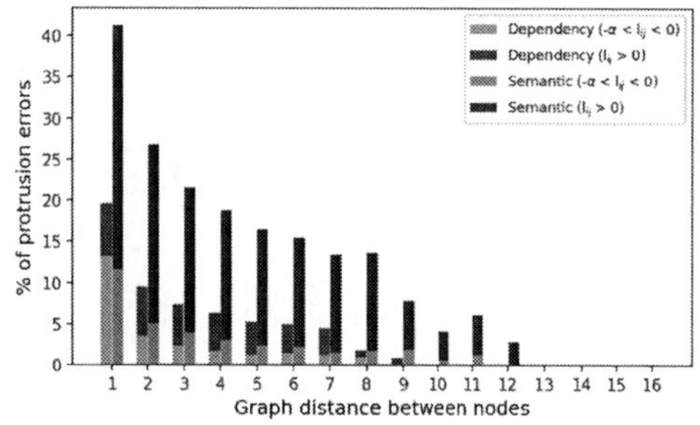

(a)

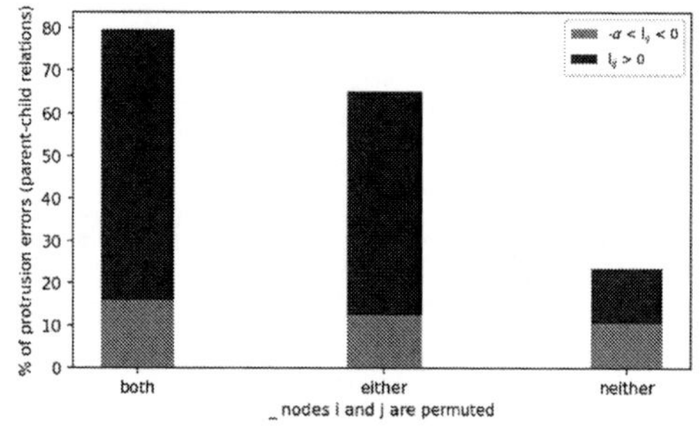

(b)

Figure 2: A detailed breakdown of % protrusion error (i.e., $\ell_{ij} > -\alpha$) for dependency and semantic parsing, for different values of graph distance (a); (b) shows this % for parent–child pairs (pairs with distance 1), categorized according to whether both, either or neither nodes are subjected to edge permutation.

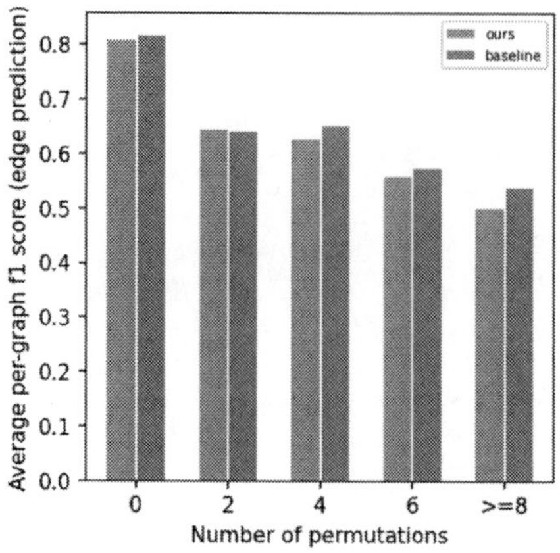

Figure 3: Performance on edge prediction for our disk embedding formulation vs. the baseline semantic parser. Instances are divided based on the number of edge permutations computed (with 1 meaning no permutations), as shown on the X-axis.

start answering this question by looking at the results on the dev set where properties (*prop*) are the ones whose performance is impacted the most. We referred to this in § 4.2 as the *edge permutation* problem for nodes in named entity substructures which pose a challenge in the absence of explicit alignment information; we hypothesize this might cause a drop in performance and if so, we expect performance to drop more when there are more permutations. Fig. 3 shows that there is indeed an effect of the number of permutations on performance, with the baseline system performing better on instances with a large number of permutations. Interestingly, in the absence of permutations, our parser performs comparably to the baseline system.

Edge permutations could also be the main reason behind the large % of local errors in Fig. 2(a). To confirm this, we take a closer look at the breakdown of % protrusion errors for parent–child pairs according to whether both, either or neither node is subjected to permutation. Fig. 2(b) shows that when both or either node is permuted, the containment relationship is usually incorrectly predicted. Note, however, that whereas the number of these incorrect predictions are large, the overall performance is not overly affected, because when matching a predicted and a gold graph, we look at the node label and not at the node id. Using the example in Fig. 1(b), from a matching perspective, we would obtain the same graph swapping the parent node 'name' of 'Anna' with the one of 'Mary'.

We also analyze the difference in performance between trees and graphs, as well as the effect of the number of nodes on performance; due to space limitations we include these results in Appendix D.1. In Appendix D.3, we discuss whether the size of the parses warrants moving to the hyperbolic space.

9 Conclusions and Future Work

We have explored disk embeddings as a means to obtain interpretable representations when training a parser that preduces a tree/graph. We showed that previously proposed disk embedding formulations are sub-optimal for the task of parsing, and accordingnly explored alternatives that improve parsing performance. Nonetheless, our results suggest that we still need to pay a cost in performance to attain interpretability; this cost is small when parsing into trees, but notable for graphs. We also speculate that this cost might be due to properties of the parser we use, especially in cases where the absence of an alignment between words in a sentence and nodes in a graph allows for many permutations.

Our work can be considered as a first attempt to bring parsing and 'deep' natural language understanding into the realm of interpretability and representation learning, so that trees and graphs could be used in downstream tasks (e.g., image retrieval), similarly to how word embeddings have been used.

Acknowledgments

We thank the three anonymous reviewers for their useful comments. Research was conducted at the Samsung AI Centre Toronto and funded by Samsung Research, Samsung Electronics Co.,Ltd

References

Marco Baroni, Georgiana Dinu, and Germán Kruszewski. 2014. Don't count, predict! a systematic comparison of context-counting vs. context-predicting semantic vectors. In *Proceedings of the 52nd Annual Meeting of the Association for Computational Linguistics (Volume 1: Long Papers)*, pages 238–247.

Michele Bevilacqua, Rexhina Blloshmi, and Roberto Navigli. 2021. One spring to rule them both: Symmetric amr semantic parsing and generation without a complex pipeline. In *Proceedings of the Thirty-Fifth AAAI Conference on Artificial Intelligence*.

Piotr Bojanowski, Edouard Grave, Armand Joulin, and Tomas Mikolov. 2017. Enriching word vectors with subword information. *Transactions of the Association for Computational Linguistics*, 5:135–146.

Shu Cai and Kevin Knight. 2013. Smatch: an evaluation metric for semantic feature structures. In *Proceedings of the 51st Annual Meeting of the Association for Computational Linguistics (Volume 2: Short Papers)*, pages 748–752.

Alexis Conneau, Kartikay Khandelwal, Naman Goyal, Vishrav Chaudhary, Guillaume Wenzek, Francisco Guzmán, Edouard Grave, Myle Ott, Luke Zettlemoyer, and Veselin Stoyanov. 2019. Unsupervised cross-lingual representation learning at scale. *arXiv preprint arXiv:1911.02116*.

Tiansi Dong, Chrisitan Bauckhage, Hailong Jin, Juanzi Li, Olaf Cremers, Daniel Speicher, Armin B Cremers, and Jörg Zimmermann. 2018. Imposing category trees onto word-embeddings using a geometric construction. In *International Conference on Learning Representations*.

Timothy Dozat, Peng Qi, and Christopher D. Manning. 2017. Stanford's graph-based neural dependency parser at the CoNLL 2017 shared task. In *Proceedings of the CoNLL 2017 Shared Task: Multilingual Parsing from Raw Text to Universal Dependencies*, pages 20–30, Vancouver, Canada. Association for Computational Linguistics.

Christiane Fellbaum. 1998. *WordNet: An Electronic Lexical Database*. Cambridge, MA: MIT Press.

Octavian Ganea, Gary Bécigneul, and Thomas Hofmann. 2018. Hyperbolic entailment cones for learning hierarchical embeddings. In *International Conference on Machine Learning*, pages 1646–1655. PMLR.

Ákos Kádár, Lan Xiao, Mete Kemertas, Federico Fancellu, Allan Jepson, and Afsaneh Fazly. 2021. Dependency parsing with structure preserving embeddings. In *Proceedings of the 16th Conference of the European Chapter of the Association for Computational Linguistics: Main Volume*, pages 1684–1697.

Kevin Knight, Bianca Badarau, Laura Banarescu, Claire Bonial, Madalina Bardocz, Kira Griffitt, Ulf Hermjakob, Daniel Marcu, Martha Palmer, Tim O'Gorman, et al. 2017. Abstract meaning representation (amr) annotation release 2.0. Technical report, Technical Report LDC2017T10, Linguistic Data Consortium, Philadelphia, PA.

Alice Lai and Julia Hockenmaier. 2017. Learning to predict denotational probabilities for modeling entailment. In *Proceedings of the 15th Conference of the European Chapter of the Association for Computational Linguistics: Volume 1, Long Papers*, pages 721–730.

Matthias Lindemann, Jonas Groschwitz, and Alexander Koller. 2020. Fast semantic parsing with well-typedness guarantees. *arXiv preprint arXiv:2009.07365*.

Tomas Mikolov, Ilya Sutskever, Kai Chen, Greg S Corrado, and Jeff Dean. 2013. Distributed representations of words and phrases and their compositionality. In *Advances in Neural Information Processing Systems*, volume 26, pages 3111–3119. Curran Associates, Inc.

Maximillian Nickel and Douwe Kiela. 2017. Poincaré embeddings for learning hierarchical representations. *Advances in neural information processing systems*, 30:6338–6347.

Joakim Nivre, Marie-Catherine de Marneffe, Filip Ginter, Jan Hajič, Christopher D. Manning, Sampo Pyysalo, Sebastian Schuster, Francis Tyers, and Daniel Zeman. 2020. Universal Dependencies v2: An evergrowing multilingual treebank collection. In *Proceedings of the 12th Language Resources and Evaluation Conference*, pages 4034–4043, Marseille, France. European Language Resources Association.

Hiroaki Ozaki, Gaku Morio, Yuta Koreeda, Terufumi Morishita, and Toshinori Miyoshi. 2020. Hitachi at mrp 2020: Text-to-graph-notation transducer. In *Proceedings of the CoNLL 2020 Shared Task: Cross-Framework Meaning Representation Parsing*, pages 40–52.

Jeffrey Pennington, Richard Socher, and Christopher D Manning. 2014. Glove: Global vectors for word representation. In *Proceedings of the 2014 conference on empirical methods in natural language processing (EMNLP)*, pages 1532–1543.

Luigi Procopio, Rocco Tripodi, and Roberto Navigli. 2021. Sgl: Speaking the graph languages of semantic parsing via multilingual translation. In *Proceedings of the 2021 Conference of the North American Chapter of the Association for Computational Linguistics: Human Language Technologies*, pages 325–337.

Peng Qi, Timothy Dozat, Yuhao Zhang, and Christopher D Manning. 2018. Universal dependency parsing from scratch. In *CoNLL 2018 Shared Task: Multilingual Parsing from Raw Text to Universal Dependencies*.

David Samuel and Milan Straka. 2020. Ufal at mrp 2020: Permutation-invariant semantic parsing in perin. *arXiv preprint arXiv:2011.00758*.

Rupesh Kumar Srivastava, Klaus Greff, , and Jürgen Schmidhuber. 2015. Highway networks. In *Proceedings of the Deep Learning Workshop at the International Conference on Machine Learning*.

Dídac Surís, Ruoshi Liu, and Carl Vondrick. 2021. Learning the predictability of the future. In *Proceedings of the IEEE/CVF Conference on Computer Vision and Pattern Recognition*, pages 12607–12617.

Ryota Suzuki, Ryusuke Takahama, and Shun Onoda. 2019. Hyperbolic disk embeddings for directed acyclic graphs. In *International Conference on Machine Learning*, pages 6066–6075. PMLR.

Ivan Vendrov, Ryan Kiros, Sanja Fidler, and Raquel Urtasun. 2015. Order-embeddings of images and language. *arXiv preprint arXiv:1511.06361*.

Luke Vilnis, Xiang Li, Shikhar Murty, and Andrew McCallum. 2018. Probabilistic embedding of knowledge graphs with box lattice measures. In *Proceedings of the 56th Annual Meeting of the Association for Computational Linguistics (Volume 1: Long Papers)*, pages 263–272.

Sheng Zhang, Xutai Ma, Kevin Duh, and Benjamin Van Durme. 2019. Broad-coverage semantic parsing as transduction. *arXiv preprint arXiv:1909.02607*.

A Hyperparameters

Hyperparameters for the disk embedding modules of both dependency and semantic parsing are listed in Table 3; all hyperparameters *not* related to the disk embedding module are the same as in the original implementations. Both were tuned separately on the *+pos margin(ℓ_2)* system. All models were trained on a single TitanX GPU v100.

	semantic	dependency
batch size	8	5000
accumulation step	4	-
decoder lr	6e-4	1e-3
layers (disk MLP)	2	
center dim.	800	
weight init.	-0.01∼0.01	
activation (Eq. 3a-3b)	leakyReLU	
dropout	0.0	
margin	1	2

Table 3: Hyperparameters used in the disk embedding module for semantic and dependency parsing.

B Tailored bounds on protrusions

Suppose we have a DAG, $G = (V, E)$, with an associated order-isomorphic disk embedding for a given margin of $\alpha > 0$. That is, given any two distinct nodes a and b in the DAG we must have $|\ell_{ab}| \geq \alpha$. Here we prove a stronger lower bound of the form $|\ell_{ab}| \geq \sigma_{ab}\alpha$ where $\sigma_{ab} \geq 1$ depends on the relationship of a and b in the DAG. Moreover, the signs of ℓ_{ab} are such that $\ell_{ab} \leq -\sigma_{ab}\alpha$ when a is an ancestor of b, and $\ell_{ab} \geq \sigma_{ab}\alpha$ otherwise.

Suppose a is an ancestor of b, that is, for some $k > 0$, there is a path $(n_k, n_{k-1}, \ldots, n_0)$ in the DAG with $a = n_k, b = n_0$. If there are several such paths from a to b we choose one that is the longest. Then, since we have assumed the corresponding disk embedding satisfies the margin α, we have that n_i is an ancestor of n_{i-1} and therefore $\ell_{n_i,n_{i-1}} \leq -\alpha$. Therefore

$$\sum_{i=1}^{k} \ell_{n_i,n_{i-1}} \leq -k\alpha. \tag{13}$$

Moreover from the definition of $\ell_{n_i,n_{i-1}}$ in (2), we have

$$\begin{aligned}\sum_{i=1}^{k} \ell_{n_i,n_{i-1}} &= \sum_{i=1}^{k} d(c_i, c_{i-1}) - \sum_{i=1}^{k}(r_i - r_{i-1}) \\ &= \sum_{i=1}^{k} d(c_i, c_{i-1}) - (r_k - r_0) \\ &\geq d(c_k, c_0) - (r_k - r_0) \qquad (14a) \\ &= \ell_{n_k,n_0} \equiv \ell_{a,b}. \qquad (14b)\end{aligned}$$

Here we have used the triangle inequality in (14a). Together (14b) and (13) imply

$$\ell_{a,b} \leq -\sigma_{ab}\,\alpha \text{ with } \sigma_{ab} = k, \tag{15}$$

where k is the maximum length of any path from a to b.

For the protrusion from the descendant b to the ancestor a, namely $\ell_{b,a}$, we use

$$\ell_{b,a} \geq \sigma_{b,a}\,\alpha, \text{ for } \sigma_{b,a} = \sigma_{a,b}. \tag{16}$$

Here (16) is a simple consequence of (15) and the relation

$$\ell_{n_i n_j} + \ell_{n_j n_i} = 2d(\mathbf{c}_i, \mathbf{c}_j) \geq 0, \tag{17}$$

which follows easily from (2).

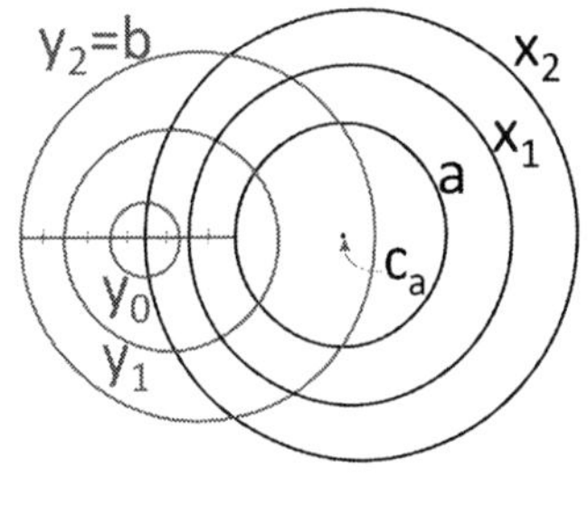

Figure 4: An example of a tight "other" relationship between nodes a and b in the situation described in Theorem B.1. Here $|P_1| = |P_2| = 2$, and $\ell_{a,b}$, is depicted by the length of the red line, where each hash mark denotes a subsegment of length α. Note the lower bound, namely $\ell_{a,b} = [|P_1| + |P_2| + 1]\alpha$, is achieved.

The remaining case is when a and b are in an "other" relationship, that is, they are not in an ancestor–descendant relationship (or vice versa). For this case it is useful to first define a *feasible pair of paths* (see Fig. 4). Define (P_1, P_2) to be a feasible pair of paths for nodes a and b if P_1 is a path $(x_i, x_{i-1}, \ldots, x_0)$ ending at $x_0 = a$, P_2 is a path $(y_j, y_{j-1}, \ldots, y_0)$ starting at $y_j = b$, and where no node in either path is a descendant of a node in the other path. The following theorem provides a lower bound on the protrusion ℓ_{ab} in terms of such a feasible pair (P_1, P_2).

Theorem B.1. Suppose P_1 and P_2 are a feasible pair of paths for nodes a and b, as described above. Then

$$\ell_{ab} \geq [|P_1| + |P_2| + 1]\,\alpha, \tag{18}$$

where $|P|$ denotes the number of edges (i.e., the length) of the path P.

Proof. Since b is an ancestor of y_0, the bound (15) implies $\ell_{b,y_0} \leq -|P_2|\alpha$. Moreover, since x_i is neither an ancestor nor descendant of y_0, we have $\ell_{x_i,y_0} \geq \alpha$. By subtracting these two inequalities we find that

$$\ell_{x_i,y_0} - \ell_{b,y_0} \geq [|P_2| + 1]\,\alpha. \tag{19}$$

From (2) we find

$$\begin{aligned}
[|P_2| + 1]\alpha &\leq \ell_{x_i,y_0} - \ell_{b,y_0} && \text{(20a)}\\
&= d(c_{x_i}, c_{y_0}) - d(c_b, c_{y_0}) - r_{x_i} + r_b && \text{(20b)}\\
&\leq d(c_{x_i}, c_b) - r_{x_i} + r_b && \text{(20c)}\\
&= \ell_{x_i,b}, && \text{(20d)}
\end{aligned}$$

where we have used the triangle inequality in (20c). Similarly, since the path P_1 starts at x_i and ends at $x_0 = a$ we have

$$\ell_{x_i,a} \leq -|P_1|\alpha.$$

Moreover, all the disks x_k, for $k = 0, \ldots, i$ are in the other relationship to node b. Subtracting this inequality from (20) then gives

$$\begin{aligned}
[|P_1| + |P_2| + 1]\alpha &\leq \ell_{x_i,b} - \ell_{x_i,a} && \text{(21a)}\\
&= d(c_{x_i}, c_b) - d(c_{x_i}, c_a) - r_a + r_b && \text{(21b)}\\
&\leq d(c_a, c_b) - r_a + r_b && \text{(21c)}\\
&= \ell_{a,b}, && \text{(21d)}
\end{aligned}$$

where we have again used the triangle inequality in (21c). Eqn. (21) is the desired result. □

We apply Theorem B.1 by defining σ_{ab}, in the case a is neither an ancestor nor descendant of b, to be the maximum lower bound (18) over all feasible pairs, (P_1, P_2), for these nodes a and b. That is

$$\sigma_{ab} = \max_{(P_1,P_2)} \{|P_1| + |P_2| + 1\}. \tag{22}$$

Given a DAG, Algorithm 1 below computes this σ_{ab} for two nodes a and b in an "other" relationship.

Algorithm 1: compute_margin($\mathcal{G}$, n_i, n_j)

```
Input: graph G, nodes n_i and n_j in 'other' relation
Output: maximum lower bound σ_ij
Initialize q with all ancestors of n_i, including n_i;
Initialize σ_i,j = 1;
while q is not empty do
    n_y = q.pop();
    if n_j is reachable from n_y then
        continue;
    else
        G' = copy(G);
        Remove all descendants of n_y in G';
        l_gj = 0;
        for each descendant n_w of n_j in G' do
            if longest_path(n_w, n_j) > l_gj then
                l_gj = longest_path(n_w, n_j);
                n_g = n_w;
        end
        l_yi = longest_path(n_i, n_y);
        σ_ij = max(σ_ij, l_yi + l_gj + 1);
    end
end
```

C Using a tailored bound on protrusion

Eq. 4 can then modified to include σ_{ij} as shown below:

$$\mathcal{L}_c = \sum_{(i,j)\in P} [\sigma_{ij}\alpha + l_{ij}]_+ + \sum_{(i,j)\in N} [\sigma_{ij}\alpha - l_{ij}]_+ \tag{23}$$

Note that in this formulation a margin is used for positive samples as well. Results in Table 4 shows that a tailored margin, even in combination with the auxiliary structure loss as well as parent–child oversampling, does not lead to any gain over our best system (*pos margin(ℓ_1)+both*).

D Analysis

D.1 Is performance worse for larger trees/graphs?

Instances with no permutations might also be easier because they are shallower or contain less nodes. Fig. 5 shows that there is an effect due to the number of nodes. However Fig. 6 shows that performance starts to diverge at more than 25 nodes which doesn't fully explain performance for instance with less than 10 permutations.

D.2 Is there a difference in performance between trees and graphs?

Given the difference in performance between dependency and semantic parsing in Table 1, one can hypothesize that it is easier to preserve the structure of trees than graphs. To answer this question, we

	dependency	*semantic*				
system	UAS	edge	label	prop	top	all
Kádár et al. (2021)	91.62(±.33)	-	-	-	-	-
Samuel and Straka (2020)	-	70.14(±.36)	88.15(±.05)	87.34(±.25)	90.37(±.11)	80.28(±.21)
original(ℓ_2)	70(±.94)	46.98(±2.23)	87.70(±.14)	58.36(±4.63)	89.44(±.69)	67.19(±1.85)
pos margin(ℓ_1)+both	90.08(±.21)	63.78(±.07)	86(±.20)	83.12(±.28)	88.93(±1.1)	**75.83**(±.02)
+tailored (ℓ_2)	88.6(±.65)	52.13(±1.02)	88.79(±.07)	74.09(±2.2)	89.66(±.92)	69.95(±.33)
+struct	89.21(±.05)	61.37(±.35)	86.67(±1.75)	81.86(±1.31)	88.97(±.92)	74.70(±.31)
+sampling	89.14(±.91)	54.47(±1.12)	87.94(±.1)	76(±1.15)	88.93(±1.56)	70.91(±.38)
+both	89.87(±.64)	62.91(±.34)	86.91(±.01)	83.42(±.42)	89.2(±.89)	75.54(±.35)
+tailored (ℓ_1)	88.65(±.16)	52.38(±.58)	88.84(±.25)	73.44(±1.78)	89.81(±.87)	69.72(±.71)
+struct	89.4(±.04)	61.92(±.17)	86.73(±.15)	82.40(±.62)	89.64(±1.62)	75.05(±.06)
+sampling	89.12(±.43)	53.98(±.68)	87.78(±.11)	75.98(±1.92)	89.71(±.34)	70.82(±.18)
+both	89.92(±.4)	62.89(±.65)	86.89(±.11)	82.61(±1.02)	89.11(±.83)	75.60(±.43)

Table 4: Results for the *+tailored* setting for dependency and semantic parsing on *dev* set. Performance of the baseline parsers, the *original* formulation (Suzuki et al., 2019), as well as our best system (*pos margin(ℓ_1)+both*, see Table 1) are also reported for comparison.

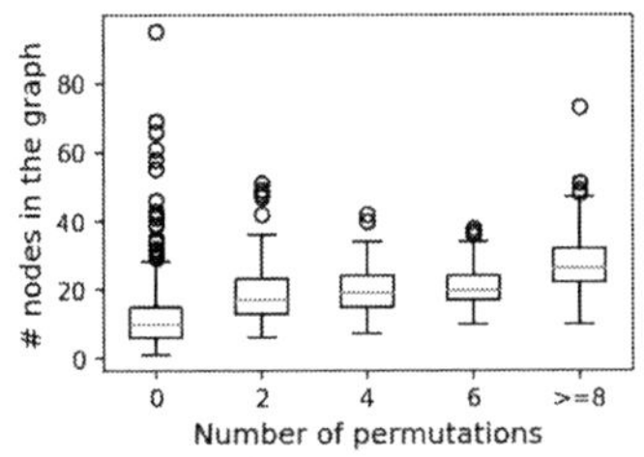

Figure 5: Analysis of number of permutations w.r.t. the number nodes in a graph.

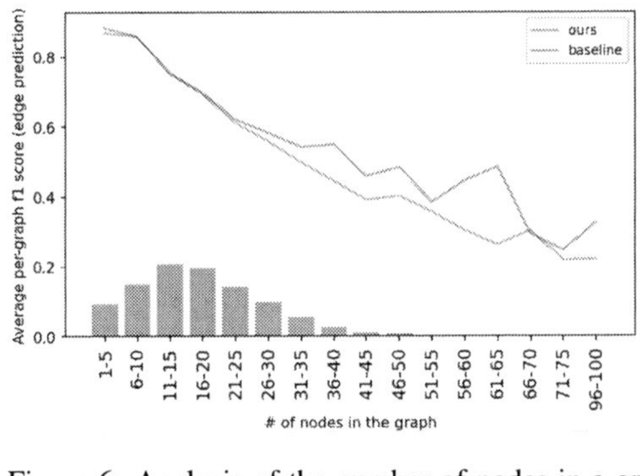

Figure 6: Analysis of the number of nodes in a graph w.r.t. parse prediction performance per instance for the baseline biaffine and the disk embedding system. In orange, an histogram over the proportion of instances in a particular size bin is also reported.

first divide the AMR dev set into instances whose gold parse is a tree vs. those that are graph. We then compare the average of the per-instance F1 scores for edge presence as given by the predictions of the baseline system (Samuel and Straka, 2020) vs. those of our best disk embedding model. We confirm that indeed graphs are harder, and, in line with the results of dependency parsing, the gap between the baseline system and our disk embedding formulation is larger for graphs (Δ =1.95) than trees (Δ =0.77).

D.3 Do we need to move to hyperbolic space?

To answer this question, we plot the difference between the radii for all pairs of ancestor–descendant disks ($|r_i - r_j|$), as well as the norm of the difference between the center of a disk and the mean of all centers of the disks in a graph ($||c_i - \bar{c}||$). We hypothesize that moving to the hyperbolic space is justified if an exponential growth is observed when the graphs get larger. However, Fig. 7 shows that this is not the case.

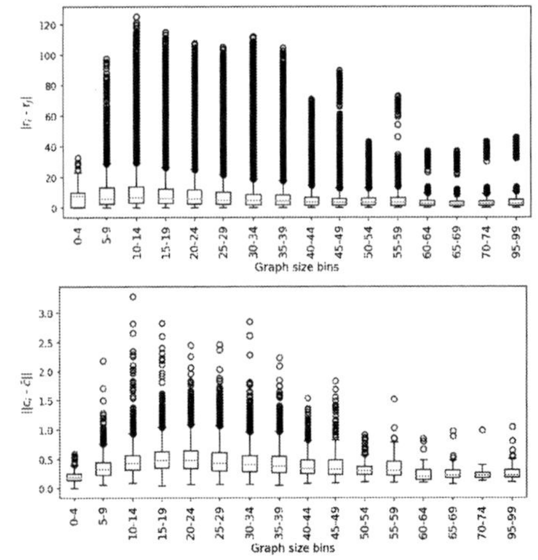

Figure 7: Boxplots analysis the absolute difference between radii of two disks (above) and the norm of the difference between the center of a disk in a graph and the average over the all disk centers in the same graph (below). Both are plotted against the number of nodes in a graph on the x axis.

Training Dynamic based data filtering may not work for NLP datasets

Arka Talukdar* at4786@nyu.edu New York University

Monika Dagar* md4676@nyu.edu New York University

Prachi Gupta* pg1647@nyu.edu New York University

Varun Menon* vk2148@nyu.edu New York University

Abstract

The recent increase in dataset size has brought about significant advances in natural language understanding. These large datasets are usually collected through automation (search engines or web crawlers) or crowdsourcing which inherently introduces incorrectly labeled data. Training on these datasets leads to memorization and poor generalization. Thus, it is pertinent to develop techniques that help in the identification and isolation of mislabelled data. In this paper, we study the applicability of the Area Under the Margin (AUM) metric to identify and remove/rectify mislabelled examples in NLP datasets. We find that mislabelled samples can be filtered using the AUM metric in NLP datasets but it also removes a significant number of correctly labeled points and leads to the loss of a large amount of relevant language information. We show that models rely on the distributional information instead of relying on syntactic and semantic representations.

1 Introduction

Modern deep learning networks are becoming deeper and powerful, and have led to significant advances in Natural Language Processing (NLP) (Devlin et al., 2019), Computer Vision (He et al., 2015), and Speech Processing (Graves et al., 2013). However, these networks rely on large labeled datasets to be effective.

The creation of large labeled datasets has fueled the advances in NLP (Rajpurkar et al., 2016; Bowman et al., 2015). Abundant labeled data increases the likelihood of learning diverse phenomena, which in turn leads to models that generalize well (Linzen, 2020).

Curating expert annotated datasets is very time-consuming and costly (Malik and Bhardwaj, 2011) therefore large language datasets are usually collected through crowd-sourcing, by hiring human annotators (Wang et al., 2019) or by crawling the web. Such methods inherently introduce label noise in the resulting data. Mislabelled training data is particularly problematic for deep neural networks with billions of parameters because they can overfit on the mislabelled data and achieve zero training error even on randomly assigned labels (Zhang et al., 2016). Training models with noisy labels can also lead to misclassification on easy examples during test-time (Beigman and Beigman Klebanov, 2009).

It is prohibitively costly to manually remove mislabeled samples from large datasets. Hence, the need arises to create an automated pipeline to analyze and clean datasets. Area Under the Margin (AUM) metric was designed to identify and eliminate noisy data. It can be used as a plug-and-play method within the training pipeline of any classification network with minimal overhead (Pleiss et al., 2020). AUM shows promising results in identifying mislabelled samples in image classification datasets.

Thus, in this paper, we investigate the applicability of the AUM metric on text classification datasets. We make the following contributions: (i) We show that the AUM metric has lower efficacy for filtering mislabelled data in NLP datasets than image datasets. (ii) We hypothesize that AUM does not work as expected in NLP datasets as it did in image datasets because of the intrinsic nature of the data samples. They have high intra-class and low inter-class feature similarity (Ho et al., 2021), which is usually not the case in NLP datasets. We show samples from NLP datasets to corroborate our hypothesis.

* Equal contribution

2 Related Work

Detecting mislabelled Instances. Pleiss et al. (2020) and Swayamdipta et al. (2020), both use model behavior on each sample over the training process, also known as training dynamics, to identify mislabelled instances in classification datasets but using different metrics. For each sample, Pleiss et al. (2020) finds the difference in logit value of the assigned class (gold label) and the highest other logit value among the non-assigned classes averaged over training epochs called the area under the margin (AUM) metric. They also introduce a fake class with samples having only mislabelled instances by definition to find a threshold AUM value. Samples with low AUM scores are likely to be mislabelled and the threshold AUM value is used to filter out such mislabelled instances. Swayamdipta et al. (2020) uses mean and standard deviation of the gold label probabilities over the training epochs, called confidence and variability scores, respectively, for each sample. They classify samples with low confidence and low variability as either mislabelled or "hard-to-learn" for the model.

Bhardwaj et al. (2010) uses statistical methods to find annotators whose annotations differ considerably from the remaining annotators and use manual inspection to decide the verdict for samples annotated by these annotators. Müller and Markert (2019) classifies training samples with the lowest gold label probabilities on a robust classifier as potentially mislabelled followed by their manual review for final decision. Zhang and Sugiyama (2021) detects samples with erroneous labels using an instance-dependent noise model along with instance-based embedding to capture instance-specific label corruption.

Learning in the Presence of Noisy Labels. Several efforts have been made to account for noise in the data and prevent the model from memorizing wrong examples without actually identifying and removing such examples from the training set. Li et al. (2020) replaces the last layer of models trained on noisy data with a linear layer trained on a small set of clean data, Jindal et al. (2019) adds a non-linear noise-modeling layer on top of the target text-classification model. Kang and Hashimoto (2020) improves faithfulness in text generation by adaptively removing high log loss examples during the training process.

Percentile	Acc. on Unfiltered Data	Acc. on Filtered Data
1	87.91 ± 0.25	88.02 ± 0.79
10	87.79 ± 0.50	87.79 ± 0.61
50	87.87 ± 0.36	87.72 ± 0.48
90	87.79 ± 0.49	87.72 ± 0.48

Table 1: Accuracy on SST-2 dataset at different AUM threshold percentiles; Sieving

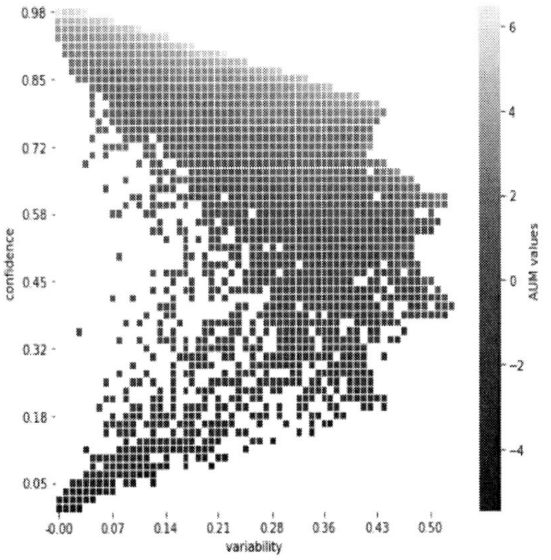

Figure 1: Visualizing AUM values of SST-2 samples along with their Data Map plotted as per Swayamdipta et al. (2020) shows considerable overlap in samples with low AUM values and samples identified as hard-to-learn/mislabelled as per Data map (sampled with low confidence and low variability scores).

Other types of Noise in text data. Depending on the type of supervisory signal and data acquisition method, language datasets can have noise in the form other than labeling errors like spelling errors, grammatical errors (Subramaniam et al., 2009; Malik and Bhardwaj, 2011). Caswell et al. (2021) provides large-scale systematic quality analysis of various web-crawled multilingual datasets and found large amounts of samples with inconsistencies in language codes and mistranslations. Robust-to-noise word embeddings (Malykh, 2019), noisy data classifiers trained on clean data, and synthetically generated noisy data (Xu and Koehn, 2017) are some efforts to deal with non-label noise in language data. In this work, however, we only study label noise.

Relation to annotator disagreement. The work on dealing with noisy labels in classification datasets can also be related to the work on studying annotator disagreements. Previous work (Beigman

Sample Id	Text	Label
390	He I often sees Mary.	1
5766	Heidi believes any description of herself.	1
2801	Paula hit the sticks.	0
1522	That the sun is out was obvious.	0
8332	I wanted Jimmy for to come with me.	1

Table 2: Filtered examples from CoLA dataset (1 = grammatically acceptable; 0 = grammatically unacceptable)

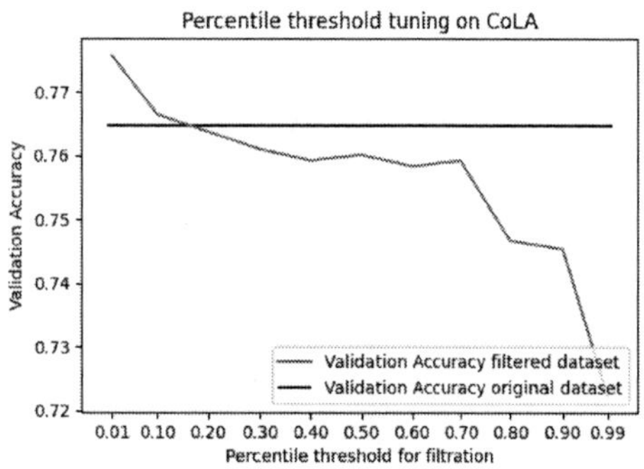

Figure 2: CoLA: Percentile threshold vs Validation accuracy

and Beigman Klebanov, 2009; Beigman Klebanov et al., 2008; Pavlick and Kwiatkowski, 2019) shows that there can be two reasons for disagreements in annotator labels in crowdsourced datasets: difference of opinion and attention slip. Former generally occurs when different groups of people agree with a different assigned label for a sample based on their understanding of the text. Latter generally occurs due to attention slip or genuine mistake during annotation. As a direction of future work, comparing samples identified as mislabelled using the AUM method with samples that get relatively low agreement among crowd worker annotators can provide meaningful insights.

3 Implementation Details

3.1 Filtering data with AUM

We use the AUM metric and methodology from Pleiss et al. (2020) to identify training samples with AUM values below a threshold value as mislabelled. To calculate this threshold, original training data is distributed to make a fake class with equal samples from all the original classes. The classification model is trained on this new dataset configuration to generate the AUM values for all the data points. Samples in fake class are by definition mislabelled hence AUM values of fake class samples can be used as a threshold for the samples in the original classes. This method is repeated to find the mislabelled samples among the samples which were in fake class initially. In the second run, a fake class is created such that it does not have any samples which were in the fake class in the first run.

As discussed in Section 5, we observed that the heuristic-based thresholding technique suggested in Pleiss et al. (2020), wherein they used the AUM value of the 99th percentile threshold sample as the threshold to filter the data, does not show major improvement in NLP datasets. We thus consider the AUM threshold value as a hyperparameter and fine-tune it. We also propose a method to rectify the labels and reuse the data for training (discussed in Section 4).

3.2 Experimental Setup

We finetuned a distillBERT-base model on SST-2 (Socher et al., 2013) and CoLA (Warstadt et al., 2019), pretrained using a masked language modeling (MLM) objective (Sanh et al., 2019) with a default AdamW optimizer (Loshchilov and Hutter, 2017). We selected distillBERT for our experimentation because it is small and fast while preserving over 95% of BERT's performance measured on GLUE benchmark (Sanh et al., 2019).

Zhang and Sugiyama (2021) show the mislabelled samples present in CoLA and SST-2 datasets, and we use these results to validate the efficacy of AUM to identify mislabelled data.

4 Experiments

Following the recommendations from Pleiss et al. (2020), we test the efficacy of AUM on synthetic-noisy and real-world NLP datasets to identify mislabelled samples. To create synthetic-noisy datasets, we injected noise in the real-world datasets by uniformly sampling data points and flipping their labels. We run two experiments on both types of datasets. First, we discard the samples classified by AUM as mislabelled; we will refer to this process as Sieving. Second, instead of discarding samples, we rectify the label and reuse them for training; we will refer to this process as Flipping. Since we train on binary-classification tasks, we flip the label of the samples which are classified as mislabelled.

As noted in Pleiss et al. (2020), the AUM threshold for filtration is dataset dependent. The authors provide a simple heuristic for classifying samples as mislabelled; samples with AUM lower than the

Sample Id	Text	Label
41767	a damn fine and a truly distinctive and a deeply pertinent film	Negative
42407	guts and	Negative
62237	as original and insightful as last week 's episode of behind the music .	Negative
6886	loves the members of the upper class almost as much as they love themselves	Negative
19153	of how horrible we are to ourselves and each other	Positive
19159	he script is n't up to the level of the direction	Positive
62178	though it runs 163 minutes , safe conduct is anything but languorous .	Positive

Table 3: Filtered examples from Stanford Sentiment Treebank (SST2)

Sample Id	Text	Label	AUM
1432	I disliked the boy's playing the piano loudly.	0	-0.501698
1433	The boy whose loud playing of the piano I disliked was a student.	1	0.163168
1434	The piano which I disliked the boy's playing loudly was badly out of tune.	0	-0.349795
1435	The boy's loud playing of the piano drove everyone crazy.	1	0.99208
1436	The boy's playing the piano loudly drove everyone crazy.	1	0.521766
1437	That piano, the boy's loud playing of which drove everyone crazy, was badly out of tune.	1	0.49058
1438	That piano, the boy's playing which loudly drove everyone crazy, was badly out of tune.	0	-0.333451
1439	That piano, which the boy's playing loudly drove everyone crazy, was badly out of tune.	0	-0.628104
1440	Did that he played the piano surprise you?	0	-0.290151
1441	Would for him to have played the piano have surprised you?	0	-0.430419
1442	Is whether he played the piano known?	0	-0.292625
1443	Did his having played the piano surprise you?	1	0.332026

Table 4: Cluster of data points in CoLA with high inter-class similarity; Dominant class - class with samples that have high structural and vocab similarity (This similarity is not quantified numerically but was observed during manual inspection of the data); Class 0 is the major class in this example but the high structural and vocab similarity within class 1 reinforces the modeling process to present it as the dominant class

99th percentile threshold sample's AUM will be classified as mislabelled. Further, they also note that the filtration performance is robust to this hyperparameter (percentile threshold). In our experiments with CoLA and SST-2, we observed that this does not translate well to NLP datasets. Indiscriminately removing samples with AUM less than the 99th percentile threshold consistently had poor performance compared to the unfiltered dataset. As the percentile threshold was reduced, the validation accuracy increases as seen in Figure 2 for CoLA and Table 1 for SST-2. It is because that samples with AUM lower than a high percentile threshold could be a hard-to-learn sample which helps generalization (Swayamdipta et al., 2020). To support this hypothesis, we classified data points using the method (refer to Section 2 for details) suggested by Swayamdipta et al. (2020). We observed significant overlap in samples identified as mislabelled using AUM and samples identified as hard-to-learn using Swayamdipta et al. (2020) which can be seen in Figure 1. As we reduce the percentile threshold, we proportionately filter a larger fraction of truly mislabelled data than hard-to-learn samples. Overfitting is another issue that is facilitated by indiscriminately removing samples with low AUM as the proportion of easy-to-learn samples is increased in the filtered dataset (Swayamdipta et al., 2020).

5 Results & Analysis

Table 1 shows the results for Sieving on the real-world dataset (SST-2). This experiment also shows how increasing the percentile threshold decreases the increase in performance, hinting at the fact that large amounts of relevant language information might be getting filtered. Table 5 shows the result for sieving and flipping on synthetic mislabelled samples (SST-2). We expected to observe a drastic dip in performance with noise injection and a relatively large gain once filtered, but we only observed a marginal dip after injecting noise and a marginal increase after filtering in performance. For the Flipping experiment, we only saw ~1% increase after flipping 68 samples (<0.1 percentile threshold) with the lowest AUM. We considered such a low threshold in an attempt to flip only the truly mislabelled data. Investigating further, we saw that about 60-65% of the noise samples were filtered

Noise %	Accuracy on Unfiltered Data	Accuracy on Filtered Data(Sieving)	Accuracy on Filtered Data(Flipping)
20	85.38	**85.94**	85.83
40	82.70	84.26	**85.96**

Table 5: Accuracy on Synthetic mislabelled Samples (SST-2); Seed: 100; Threshold Percentile: 90

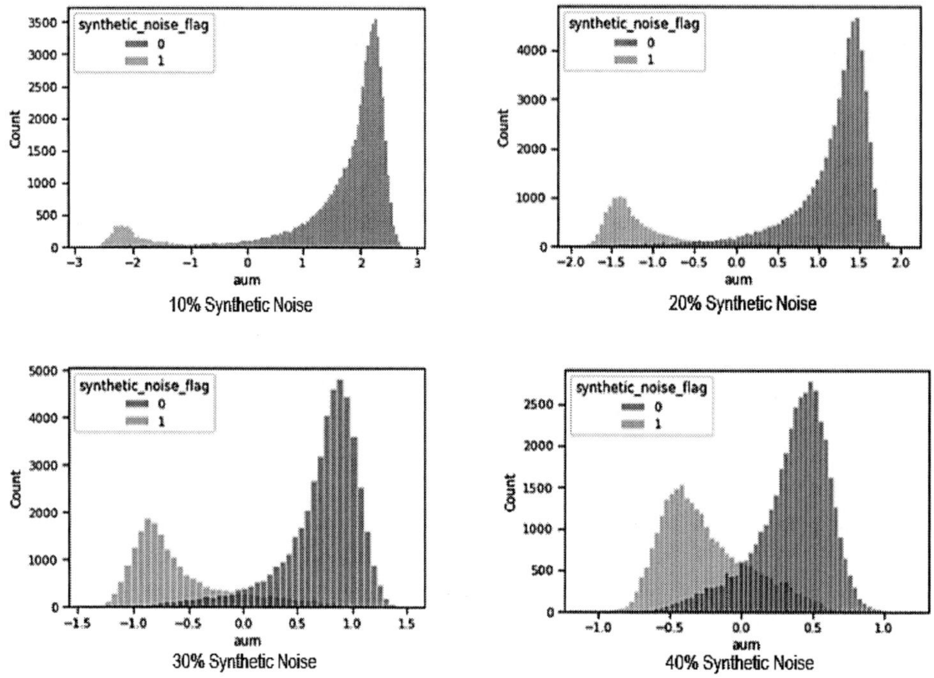

Figure 3: Histogram of AUM values of synthetic noise and unaltered data. (Blue → Unaltered data, Orange → Synthetic noise)

from our experiments. Figure 3 shows the distribution of AUM values of the synthetic noise and clean samples. The graphs clearly show that AUM does help in identifying the mislabelled samples to some extent (Table 2 and Table 3 show the mislabelled samples we detected in SST-2 and CoLA with low AUM values) but a lot of correctly labeled samples also get filtered depending on how noisy the dataset is. Although there is a high correlation between noise and correctly labeled samples being filtered, the amount of noise alone does not explain this behavior. This leads us to question the efficacy of the AUM metric in NLP datasets.

On manual inspection of the CoLA dataset, we found multiple clusters with high feature similarities. Table 4 shows an example of such clusters. We observed that the model is relying on superficial features like word co-occurrence statistics (Sinha et al., 2021), within these clusters and builds a bias for the dominant class label in a particular cluster. Thus the non-dominant class samples (which usually are correctly labeled) get low AUM values instead of the synthetic noise samples. This does not go hand in hand with our previous observations where Figure 3 shows that synthetic noise samples have low AUM, but it is important to note that synthetic noise samples also happen to be a part of the non-dominant class in most cases (noise in an acceptable dataset is non-dominant). Again, we emphasize correlation does not imply causation.

In Table 4, the synthetically introduced noise (marked in red) and members of class 0 (marked in yellow) are both parts of the non-dominant class which gives these samples a negative AUM. While the red labeled samples are legitimate candidates for removal, the removal of yellow samples causes loss of correctly labeled data points. We observed the same pattern through all clusters.

6 Conclusion

We report on the applicability of AUM on NLP datasets. AUM does help in identifying mislabelled samples available to some extent, but sieving these samples indiscriminately removes large amounts of relevant language information. We hypothesize that the reason AUM works well in image datasets is because of the intrinsic nature of the data samples, i.e., data samples in image datasets have high intra-class and less inter-class feature similarity whereas in NLP datasets, data samples have high inter-class feature similarity as seen in Table 4 and this coupled with the model dependency on superficial features results in low AUM values for the non-dominant class samples instead of the mislabelled class samples consequently reducing the efficacy of the AUM metric in NLP datasets.

7 Acknowledgement

We would like to thank Prof. Samuel R. Bowman for his guidance and support. We greatly benefited from the discussions we had with him.

References

Eyal Beigman and Beata Beigman Klebanov. 2009. Learning with annotation noise. In *Proceedings of the Joint Conference of the 47th Annual Meeting of the ACL and the 4th International Joint Conference on Natural Language Processing of the AFNLP*, pages 280–287, Suntec, Singapore. Association for Computational Linguistics.

Beata Beigman Klebanov, Eyal Beigman, and Daniel Diermeier. 2008. Analyzing disagreements. In *Coling 2008: Proceedings of the workshop on Human Judgements in Computational Linguistics*, pages 2–7, Manchester, UK. Coling 2008 Organizing Committee.

Vikas Bhardwaj, Rebecca Passonneau, Ansaf Salleb-Aouissi, and Nancy Ide. 2010. Anveshan: A framework for analysis of multiple annotators' labeling behavior. In *Proceedings of the Fourth Linguistic Annotation Workshop*, pages 47–55, Uppsala, Sweden. Association for Computational Linguistics.

Samuel R. Bowman, Gabor Angeli, Christopher Potts, and Christopher D. Manning. 2015. A large annotated corpus for learning natural language inference. In *Proceedings of the 2015 Conference on Empirical Methods in Natural Language Processing*, pages 632–642, Lisbon, Portugal. Association for Computational Linguistics.

Isaac Caswell, Julia Kreutzer, Lisa Wang, Ahsan Wahab, Daan van Esch, Nasanbayar Ulzii-Orshikh, Allahsera Tapo, Nishant Subramani, Artem Sokolov, Claytone Sikasote, Monang Setyawan, Supheakmungkol Sarin, Sokhar Samb, Benoît Sagot, Clara Rivera, Annette Rios, Isabel Papadimitriou, Salomey Osei, Pedro Javier Ortiz Suárez, Iroro Orife, Kelechi Ogueji, Rubungo Andre Niyongabo, Toan Q. Nguyen, Mathias Müller, André Müller, Shamsuddeen Hassan Muhammad, Nanda Muhammad, Ayanda Mnyakeni, Jamshidbek Mirzakhalov, Tapiwanashe Matangira, Colin Leong, Nze Lawson, Sneha Kudugunta, Yacine Jernite, Mathias Jenny, Orhan Firat, Bonaventure F. P. Dossou, Sakhile Dlamini, Nisansa de Silva, Sakine Çabuk Ballı, Stella Biderman, Alessia Battisti, Ahmed Baruwa, Ankur Bapna, Pallavi Baljekar, Israel Abebe Azime, Ayodele Awokoya, Duygu Ataman, Orevaoghene Ahia, Oghenefego Ahia, Sweta Agrawal, and Mofetoluwa Adeyemi. 2021. Quality at a glance: An audit of web-crawled multilingual datasets.

Jacob Devlin, Ming-Wei Chang, Kenton Lee, and Kristina Toutanova. 2019. BERT: Pre-training of deep bidirectional transformers for language understanding. In *Proceedings of the 2019 Conference of the North American Chapter of the Association for Computational Linguistics: Human Language Technologies, Volume 1 (Long and Short Papers)*, pages 4171–4186, Minneapolis, Minnesota. Association for Computational Linguistics.

Alex Graves, Abdel-rahman Mohamed, and Geoffrey Hinton. 2013. Speech recognition with deep recurrent neural networks. In *2013 IEEE International Conference on Acoustics, Speech and Signal Processing*, pages 6645–6649. IEEE.

Kaiming He, Xiangyu Zhang, Shaoqing Ren, and Jian Sun. 2015. Deep residual learning for image recognition.

Kalun Ho, Janis Keuper, Franz-Josef Pfreundt, and Margret Keuper. 2021. Learning embeddings for image clustering: An empirical study of triplet loss approaches. In *2020 25th International Conference on Pattern Recognition (ICPR)*, pages 87–94. IEEE.

Ishan Jindal, Daniel Pressel, Brian Lester, and Matthew Nokleby. 2019. An effective label noise model for DNN text classification. In *Proceedings of the 2019 Conference of the North American Chapter of the Association for Computational Linguistics: Human Language Technologies, Volume 1 (Long and Short Papers)*, pages 3246–3256, Minneapolis, Minnesota. Association for Computational Linguistics.

Daniel Kang and Tatsunori B. Hashimoto. 2020. Improved natural language generation via loss truncation. In *Proceedings of the 58th Annual Meeting of the Association for Computational Linguistics*, pages 718–731, Online. Association for Computational Linguistics.

Jingling Li, Mozhi Zhang, Keyulu Xu, John P. Dickerson, and Jimmy Ba. 2020. Noisy labels can induce good representations. ArXiv preprint arXiv:2012.12896.

Tal Linzen. 2020. How can we accelerate progress towards human-like linguistic generalization? In *Proceedings of the 58th Annual Meeting of the Association for Computational Linguistics*, pages 5210–5217, Online. Association for Computational Linguistics.

Ilya Loshchilov and Frank Hutter. 2017. Sgdr: Stochastic gradient descent with warm restarts.

Hassan H. Malik and Vikas S. Bhardwaj. 2011. Automatic training data cleaning for text classification. In *2011 IEEE 11th International Conference on Data Mining Workshops*, pages 442–449.

Valentin Malykh. 2019. Robust to noise models in natural language processing tasks. In *Proceedings of the 57th Annual Meeting of the Association for Computational Linguistics: Student Research Workshop*, pages 10–16, Florence, Italy. Association for Computational Linguistics.

Nicolas M. Müller and Karla Markert. 2019. Identifying mislabeled instances in classification datasets. In *2019 International Joint Conference on Neural Networks (IJCNN)*, pages 1–8.

Ellie Pavlick and Tom Kwiatkowski. 2019. Inherent disagreements in human textual inferences. *Transactions of the Association for Computational Linguistics*, 7:677–694.

Geoff Pleiss, Tianyi Zhang, Ethan R. Elenberg, and Kilian Q. Weinberger. 2020. Identifying mislabeled data using the area under the margin ranking.

Pranav Rajpurkar, Jian Zhang, Konstantin Lopyrev, and Percy Liang. 2016. SQuAD: 100,000+ questions for machine comprehension of text. In *Proceedings of the 2016 Conference on Empirical Methods in Natural Language Processing*, pages 2383–2392, Austin, Texas. Association for Computational Linguistics.

Victor Sanh, Lysandre Debut, Julien Chaumond, and Thomas Wolf. 2019. Distilbert, a distilled version of bert: smaller, faster, cheaper and lighter. *arXiv preprint arXiv:1910.01108*.

Koustuv Sinha, Robin Jia, Dieuwke Hupkes, Joelle Pineau, Adina Williams, and Douwe Kiela. 2021. Masked language modeling and the distributional hypothesis: Order word matters pre-training for little. *arXiv preprint arXiv:2104.06644*.

Richard Socher, Alex Perelygin, Jean Y Wu, Jason Chuang, Christopher D Manning, Andrew Y Ng, and Christopher Potts. 2013. Recursive deep models for semantic compositionality over a sentiment treebank. In *Proceedings of the conference on empirical methods in natural language processing (EMNLP)*, volume 1631, page 1642. Citeseer.

L. Venkata Subramaniam, Shourya Roy, Tanveer A. Faruquie, and Sumit Negi. 2009. A survey of types of text noise and techniques to handle noisy text. In *Proceedings of The Third Workshop on Analytics for Noisy Unstructured Text Data*, AND '09, page 115–122, New York, NY, USA. Association for Computing Machinery.

Swabha Swayamdipta, Roy Schwartz, Nicholas Lourie, Yizhong Wang, Hannaneh Hajishirzi, Noah A. Smith, and Yejin Choi. 2020. Dataset cartography: Mapping and diagnosing datasets with training dynamics. In *Proceedings of the 2020 Conference on Empirical Methods in Natural Language Processing (EMNLP)*, pages 9275–9293, Online. Association for Computational Linguistics.

Alex Wang, Amanpreet Singh, Julian Michael, Felix Hill, Omer Levy, and Samuel R. Bowman. 2019. Glue: A multi-task benchmark and analysis platform for natural language understanding.

Alex Warstadt, Amanpreet Singh, and Samuel R. Bowman. 2019. Neural network acceptability judgments. *Transactions of the Association for Computational Linguistics*, 7:625–641.

Hainan Xu and Philipp Koehn. 2017. Zipporah: a fast and scalable data cleaning system for noisy web-crawled parallel corpora. In *Proceedings of the 2017 Conference on Empirical Methods in Natural Language Processing*, pages 2945–2950, Copenhagen, Denmark. Association for Computational Linguistics.

Chiyuan Zhang, Samy Bengio, Moritz Hardt, Benjamin Recht, and Oriol Vinyals. 2016. Understanding deep learning requires rethinking generalization. *CoRR*, abs/1611.03530.

Yivan Zhang and Masashi Sugiyama. 2021. Approximating instance-dependent noise via instance-confidence embedding.

Multi-Layer Random Perturbation Training for Improving Model Generalization

Lis Kanashiro Pereira[1], Yuki Taya[2], Ichiro Kobayashi[3]
Ochanomizu University
kanashiro.pereira@ocha.ac.jp[1], g1620525@is.ocha.ac.jp[2]
koba@is.ocha.ac.jp[3]

Abstract

We propose a simple yet effective Multi-Layer **RA**ndom **P**erturbation **T**raining algorithm (RAPT) to enhance model robustness and generalization. The key idea is to apply randomly sampled noise to each input to generate label-preserving artificial input points. To encourage the model to generate more diverse examples, the noise is added to a combination of the model layers. Then, our model regularizes the posterior difference between clean and noisy inputs. We apply RAPT towards robust and efficient BERT training, and conduct comprehensive fine-tuning experiments on GLUE tasks. Our results show that RAPT outperforms the standard fine-tuning approach, and adversarial training method, yet with 22% less training time.

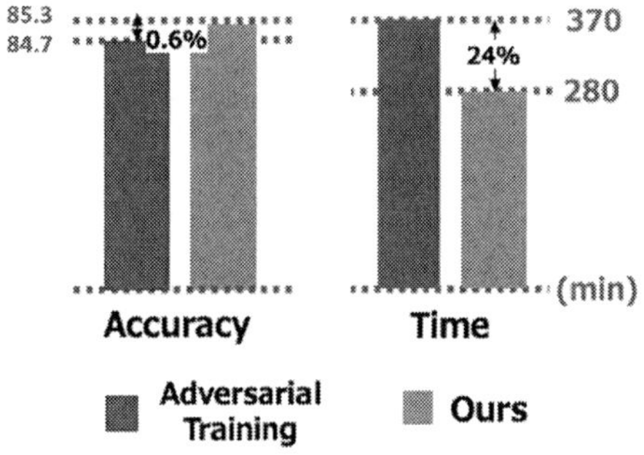

Figure 1: Acurracy and training time comparison between adversarial training (SMART) and RAPT on the MNLI (matched) development dataset. RAPT obains an accuracy gain of 0.6% yet with a training time drop of 24%.

1 Introduction

Although deep learning models have been very successful in various kinds of NLP problems, they are known to be sensitive towards input data distribution change which are pervasive across language tasks. Motivated by this, a recent line of work investigate the adversarial training technique to enhance the model robustness. Adversarial training has proven effective in improving model generalization and robustness in computer vision (Madry et al., 2017; Goodfellow et al., 2014) and natural language processing (NLP) (Zhu et al., 2019; Jiang et al., 2019; Cheng et al., 2019; Liu et al., 2020a; Pereira et al., 2020, 2021; Cheng et al., 2020). It works by augmenting the input with a small perturbation to steer the current model prediction away from the correct label, thus forcing subsequent training to make the model more robust and generalizable. In NLP, the cutting-edge research in adversarial training tends to perform an inner search for the most adversarial direction using gradient steps (Zhu et al., 2019; Jiang et al., 2019; Cheng et al., 2019; Liu et al., 2020a; Pereira et al., 2020, 2021; Cheng et al., 2020). This causes a significant overhead in training time. Moreover, such methods tend to add the adversarial perturbation only to the embedding layer, which might not be optimal.

By contrast, in this paper, we investigate a simpler direction by using only randomly sampled noise to generate label-preserving artificial input points. We thus propose a simple yet effective **RA**ndom **P**erturbation **T**raining algorithm (RAPT) for enhancing model robustness and generalization. For each instance, instead of using gradient steps to generate adversarial examples, RAPT adds randomly sampled noise to the hidden representaions of a randomly chosen layer, among multiple intermediate transformer layers (*i.e.* BERT layers). We hypothesize this might encourage the model to generate more diverse examples, and improve model generalization capability. Our model then regularizes the model posterior difference between clean and noisy inputs.

On the overall GLUE benchmark, RAPT outperforms the standard fine-tuning approach, and

Proceedings of the Fourth BlackboxNLP Workshop on Analyzing and Interpreting Neural Networks for NLP, pages 303–310
Online, November 11, 2021.

matches or improves the performance of strong adversarial training methods such as SMART (Jiang et al., 2019), yet with a significantly reduced training time. Figure 1 shows the accuracy gain and training time drop of RAPT compared to SMART on the MNLI (matched) development dataset.

2 RAPT

In this paper, we focus on fine-tuning BERT models (Devlin et al., 2019), as this approach has proven very effective for a wide range of NLP tasks.

The standard training algorithm seeks to learn a function $f(x;\theta) : x \rightarrow C$ as parametrized by θ, where C is the class label set. Given a training dataset D of input-output pairs (x, y) and the loss function $l(.,.)$ (*e.g.* cross entropy), the standard training objective would minimize the empirical risk:

$$\min_{\theta} \mathbb{E}_{(x,y)\sim D}[l(f(x;\theta), y)].$$

By contrast, in adversarial training, as pioneered in computer vision (Goodfellow et al., 2014; Hsieh et al., 2019; Madry et al., 2017; Jin et al., 2019), the input would be augmented with a small perturbation that maximize the adversarial loss:

$$\min_{\theta} \mathbb{E}_{(x,y)\sim D}[\max_{\delta} l(f(x+\delta;\theta), y)],$$

where the inner maximization can be solved by projected gradient descent (Madry et al., 2017).

Recently, adversarial training has been successfully applied to NLP as well (Zhu et al., 2019; Jiang et al., 2019; Pereira et al., 2020). In particular, SMART (Jiang et al., 2019) regularizes the standard training objective using *virtual adversarial training* (Miyato et al., 2018), by performing an inner loop to search for the most adversarial direction:

$$\begin{aligned}\min_{\theta} \mathbb{E}_{(x,y)\sim D}[l(f(x;\theta), y)+ \\ \alpha \max_{\delta} l(f(x+\delta;\theta), f(x;\theta))]\end{aligned} \tag{1}$$

Effectively, the adversarial term encourages smoothness in the input neighborhood, and α is a hyperparameter that controls the trade-off between standard errors and adversarial errors.

Current adversarial methods for NLP are slower than standard training, due to the inner maximization. SMART, for instance, requires an additional K projected gradient steps to find the perturbation that maximizes the adversarial loss (violation of local smoothness) (Liu et al., 2020a). In practice, $K = 1$ suffices SMART, and it is roughly 2 times slower compared to standard training. By contrast, RAPT completely removes the adversarial steps that use gradient steps from SMART and instead optimizes for stabilizing the model local smoothness using only randomly sampled noise for regularization:

$$\begin{aligned}\min_{\theta} \mathbb{E}_{(x,y)\sim D}[l(f(x;\theta), y)+ \\ \alpha l(f(x+\delta_r;\theta), f(x;\theta))]\end{aligned} \tag{2}$$

RAPT does not require extra backward computations and empirically works as well as or better than SMART. We consider the posterior regularization using the KL-divergence. For all tasks in this work, an input text sequence is divided into subword units w_t, $t = 1, \ldots, T$. The tokenized input sequence is then transformed into embeddings, $\boldsymbol{x}_1, \ldots, \boldsymbol{x}_T \in \mathbb{R}^n$, through a token encoder, which combines a token embedding, a (token) position embedding and a segment embedding (*i.e.* which text span the token belongs to) by element-wise summation. The embedding layer is used as

Algorithm 1 RAPT

Input: N: the number of training epochs, $\mathcal{D}, \{(x_1, y_1), ..., (x_n, y_n)\}$: the dataset, $\mathcal{X}$: the minibatch of the dataset, $f(x;\theta)$: the machine learning model parametrized by θ, σ^2: the variance of the random noise δ, η: the number to controll the size of the noise, L: the number of transformer based model's layers, f^{layer}: the function that computes the hidden representations of a given layer, $\boldsymbol{h}$: the hidden representations of a layer of the model, δ_r: the noise added to the hidden states of layer r , τ: the global learning rate, α: the hyperparameter for balancing the standard loss and the regularization term, max_layer: the number of the maximum layer where the noise can be added during training.

for $epoch = 1, 2, .., N$ **do**
  for $\mathcal{X} \in \mathcal{D}$ **do**
    Generate a random integer $r \in \{1, ..., \text{max\_layer}\}$
    for $(x, y) \in \mathcal{X}$ **do**
      $\delta \sim N(0, \sigma^2 I)$
      $\delta \leftarrow \eta \frac{\delta}{\|\delta\|_\infty}$
      // x : forward pass to the last layer of the model
      for $layer = 1, 2, ..., L$ **do**
        $\boldsymbol{h} \leftarrow f^{layer}(\boldsymbol{h})$
        if $layer$ is r **then**
          $\boldsymbol{h} \leftarrow \boldsymbol{h} + \delta_r \boldsymbol{I}$
        end if
      end for
      $g_\theta \leftarrow \nabla_\theta l(f(x;\theta), y)$
        $+\alpha \nabla_\theta l(f(x+\delta_r;\theta), f(x;\theta))$
      $\theta \leftarrow \theta - \tau g_\theta$
    end for
  end for
end for

Output: θ

the input to multiple transformer layers (Vaswani et al., 2017) to generate the contextual representations, $\boldsymbol{h}_1^{layer}, \ldots, \boldsymbol{h}_T^{layer} \in \mathbb{R}^d$, which are the hidden states of an intermediate layer of the BERT model.

In RAPT, we sample noise vectors $\delta_1, \ldots, \delta_T$ from $\mathcal{N}(0, \sigma^2 I)$, with mean 0 and variation of σ^2. We first set a maximum layer (among all BERT intermediate layers) where the noise vector can be added. In each epoch, for each mini-batch selected, a layer among the first layer and the maximum layer previously set is randomly chosen. The noise input is then constructed by adding the noise vector δ_r (Equation 2) to the hidden state vector of the ramdomly chosen layer ($\boldsymbol{h}^{layer}$). Specifically, the model first performs a forward pass up to the chosen layer, then the noise vector is added to its hidden states, *i.e.* $\boldsymbol{h}_1^{layer} + \eta\delta_{r1}, \ldots, \boldsymbol{h}_T^{layer} + \eta\delta_{rT}$.

The model is then updated according to the task-specific objective for the task. To preserve the semantics, we constrain the noise to be small, and assume the model's prediction should not change after adding the perturbation. The algorithm of RAPT is shown in Algorithm 1.

3 Experiments

3.1 Datasets

We evaluate our model on the GLUE[1] benchmark, a collection of nine natural language understanding (NLU) tasks. It includes question answering (Rajpurkar et al., 2016), linguistic acceptability (Warstadt et al., 2018), sentiment analysis (Socher et al., 2013), text similarity (Cer et al., 2017), paraphrase detection (Dolan and Brockett, 2005), and natural language inference (NLI) (Dagan et al., 2006; Bar-Haim et al., 2006; Giampiccolo et al., 2007; Bentivogli et al., 2009; Levesque et al., 2012; Williams et al., 2018). The diversity of the tasks makes GLUE very suitable for evaluating the generalization and robustness of NLU models. The GLUE tasks used in our experiments are summarized in Table 1.

3.2 Implementation Details

Our model implementation is based on the MT-DNN[2] framework (Liu et al., 2019, 2020b). We use $\text{BERT}_{\text{BASE}}$(Devlin et al., 2019) as the text encoder. We used ADAM (Kingma and Ba, 2015) as our optimizer with a learning rate in the range $\in \{1 \times 10^{-5}, 2 \times 10^{-5}, 8 \times 10^{-6}\}$ and a batch size $\in \{16, 32\}$. The maximum number of epochs was set to 6. A linear learning rate decay schedule with warm-up over 0.1 was used, unless stated otherwise. To avoid gradient exploding, we clipped the gradient norm within 1. All the texts were tokenized using wordpieces and were chopped to spans no longer than 512 tokens. For SMART , we follow (Jiang et al., 2019) and set the perturbation size to 1×10^{-5}. We choose the step size from $\{1 \times 10^{-3}, 1 \times 10^{-2}, 1 \times 10^{-1}, 1, 1.5, 2, 2.5, 3\}$. We set the variance for initializing the perturbation to 1×10^{-5}. The α parameter (Equation 1 and Equation 2) were both set to 1. During RAPT, we select η from $\{0.01, 1.5, 2, 2.3, 2.5\}$. We found that adding the noise to the layers 1 to 3 worked best in our experiments, therefore, the max_layer parameter in Algorithm 1 was set to 3. For more details, please refer to Section 4.

3.3 Main Results

We apply RAPT to $\text{BERT}_{\text{BASE}}$ and evaluate its performance on GLUE. Our results are shown in Table 2. We compare RAPT with the standard fine-tuning approach (Standard) and with the adversarial training method SMART. For our model RAPT, we compare a model that adds the noise to the embedding layer only, RAPT (Embedding), with the model that adds the noise to the other layers. We report the model that uses $\eta = 2$, RAPT ($\eta = 2$), and the model that selects the best η value, RAPT (BEST η).

Overall, we observed that SMART and RAPT were able to outperform standard fine-tuning, without using any additional knowledge source, and without using any additional dataset other than the target task datasets. These results suggest that adding noisy input points during training lead to a more robust model and help generalize better on unseen data. RAPT consistently outperforms standard training (with an average score of 81.9% vs. 81.1% on the test set).

Remarkably, RAPT outperforms SMART on most GLUE tasks, and obtains the highest average score among all tasks on both dev and test sets (85.1% and 81.9%, respectively), yet with a smaller training time (86.7 minutes on average, as shown in Table 3). This indicates that using only randomly sampled noise leads to better results. We also observe pronounced gains of RAPT on the smaller datasets such as RTE (with a test set accuracy of

[1] https://gluebenchmark.com/

[2] https://github.com/namisan/mt-dnn

Corpus	Task	#Train	#Dev	#Test	#Label	Metrics
			Single-Sentence Classification			
CoLA	Acceptability	8.5k	1k	1k	2	Matthews corr
SST	Sentiment	67k	872	1.8k	2	Accuracy
			Pairwise Text Classification			
MNLI	NLI	393k	20k	20k	3	Accuracy
RTE	NLI	2.5k	276	3k	2	Accuracy
QQP	Paraphrase	364k	40k	391k	2	Accuracy/F1
MRPC	Paraphrase	3.7k	408	1.7k	2	Accuracy/F1
QNLI	QA/NLI	108k	5.7k	5.7k	2	Accuracy
			Text Similarity			
STS-B	Similarity	7k	1.5k	1.4k	1	Pearson/Spearman corr

Table 1: Summary information of the GLUE benchmark.

Methods	MNLI-m/mm Acc	QQP Acc/F1	RTE Acc	QNLI Acc	MRPC Acc/F1	CoLA Mcc	SST Acc	STS-B P/S Corr	Average Score
Standard^{dev}	84.1/84.3	90.5/87.3	69.3	90.9	**86.9**/90.7	58.3	92.4	89.9/89.4	84.5
SMART^{dev}	84.7/85.2	90.9/87.9	**70.8**	91.4	86.4/90.5	58.6	92.8	**90.2/89.7**	84.9
RAPT^{dev}(Embedding)	85.2/85.5	**91.2/88.3**	69.5	91.7	86.1/90.1	58.3	**92.9**	90.1/**89.8**	84.9
RAPT^{dev}($\eta = 2$)	85.2/85.5	**91.2**/88.2	70.6	**91.8**	**86.9/90.8**	**58.7**	92.8	89.9/89.6	**85.1**
RAPT^{dev}(BEST η)	**85.3/85.6**	**91.2**/88.2	70.6	**91.8**	**86.9/90.8**	**58.7**	92.8	90.1/89.7	**85.1**
Standard^{test}	84.2/83.2	88.6/70.6	67.9	90.2	**84.0/88.3**	52.1	93.1	86.3/85.0	81.1
SMART^{test}	85.0/84.2	**89.1**/71.8	**68.4**	90.7	83.6/88.1	52.8	93.5	86.9/85.6	81.6
RAPT^{test}(Embedding)	85.3/84.4	89.1/71.8	**68.4**	**91.1**	84.1/88.2	**53.0**	93.7	**87.5/86.4**	**81.9**
RAPT^{test}($\eta = 2$)	85.4/**84.7**	**89.1/71.9**	67.4	**91.1**	**84.0/88.3**	51.1	**93.8**	87.2/86.1	81.7
RAPT^{test}(BEST η)	**85.5/84.7**	**89.1/71.9**	68.0	**91.1**	**84.0/88.3**	52.3	**93.8**	86.8/85.5	81.8

Table 2: Comparison of standard fine-tuning (Standard), adversarial training (SMART) and our methods (RAPT) on GLUE. We use the $BERT_{BASE}$ model as the text encoder for all models. For a fair comparison, all these results are produced by ourselves.Theses scores are the average of each model across 5 random seeds. The GLUE test results are scored using the GLUE evaluation server.

68.4) and STS-B (with a test set Pearson/Spearman correlation scores of 87.5/86.4), which illustrates the benefits of RAPT on improving model generalizability.

Adding the perturbation to multiple intermediate layers leads to better results on the dev set than adding the random perturbation to the embedding layer only (average score of 85.1% vs. 84.9%, respectively). However, on the test set, adding the random perturbation to the embedding layer only leads to slightly better results than adding the random perturbation to multiple intermediate layers (81.9% vs. 81.8%, respectively). Still, both settings outperform SMART and standard fine-tuning.

Regarding the training time, on the overall GLUE benchmark, RAPT takes on average 22% less time to train compared to SMART (86.7 vs 110.9 minutes, respectively), as shown in Table 3.

4 Analysis

Here, we take a closer look at the embeddings and hidden representations of the intermediate layers of BERT using standard fine-tuning (Standard), SMART, and RAPT. After training, we extract the embeddings (for Standard and SMART) and the intermediate layer representations (where noise has been added) of the second intermediate layer (for RAPT) of a sentence. Then, we compute the top most similar words for each word in the sentence. We use the cosine similarity for computing the similarity between the vectors. As shown in Table 4, adding the noise to the intermediate layers using RAPT introduces more diversity. For instance, among the top-10 closest words to the word *country*, SMART shares eight words with the Standard fine-tuning methods, while RAPT shares only five.

Time (min)	MNLI	QQP	RTE	QNLI	MRPC	CoLA	SST	STS-B	Average
Standard	220	175	2.5	40	2.5	4.8	17.5	3.8	69.6
SMART	370	270	4	102	4.1	8	31.5	6	110.9
RAPT	280	220	3	80	3.4	6.5	24.5	4.9	86.7
RAPT/SMART	0.76	0.81	0.75	0.78	0.81	0.79	0.77	0.8	0.78

Table 3: Training time comparison between standard fine-tuning (Standard), SMART, and RAPT. RAPT/SMART denotes the ratio between the training time of RAPT and SMART. We used a A100-PCIE-40GB GPU to measure the training time.

Input: [CLS] by law , mexico can only export half the oil it produces to the united states . [SEP] mexico produces more oil than any other **country** . [SEP]		
Standard	SMART	RAPT
nation	nation	countries
region	county	nation
county	region	region
island	countries	nations
countries	province	cities
state	island	kingdom
territory	state	global
province	territory	city
countryside	homeland	territory
mountain	trade	countryside

Table 4: Top-10 closest words to the vector of the word **country** using standard fine-tuning (Standard), SMART, and RAPT on the RTE development dataset. The words in red are the words not shared with the Standard fine-tuning method. RAPT has five different words, while SMART has only two.

Although having more diversity, the hidden representations are kept meaningful.

To further illustrate the diversity RAPT introduces to the model's hidden representations, Table 5 and Table 6 compare the embeddings produced by SMART before and after adding the perturbation and the hidden reporesentations produced by RAPT before and after adding the noise. For SMART, we can observe that the top-10 similar words to the word *country* do not change after adding the perturbation, and the cosine similarity scores are kept around the same. In our experiments, increasing the perturbation size leads to a drop in accuracy. For RAPT, we extract the hidden representations from the second layer of BERT. As we can see, the cosine similarity scores change and more diversity is introduced. In our development experiments, the accuracy instead increases, indicating that the hidden representations from the intermediate layers might be less sensitive to noise compared to the embedding layer.

Regarding which layer combination setting is best for adding the noise, we found that adding the noise to the layers 1 to 3 worked best in our experiments, as shown in Figure 2 and Figure 3, for the MNLI and MRPC datasets.

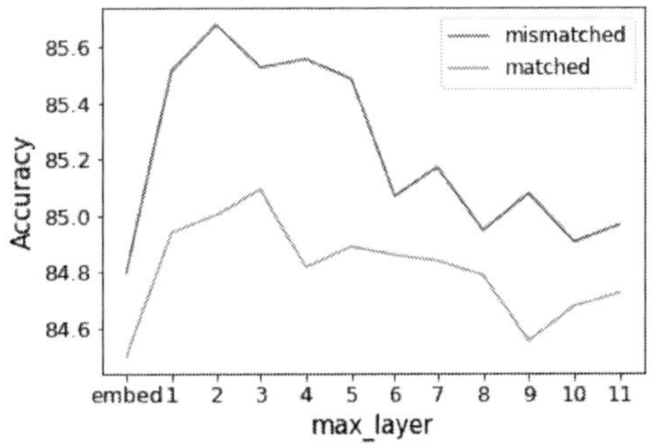

Figure 2: Performance on the MNLI development set as we change the layer combination to add the noise. On the x-axis, max_layer = $embed$ denotes that the noise is added to the embedding layer only. All the other values denote that, for each mini-batch, a layer among the layer 1 up to this layer value is randomly chosen. The model is then updated according to the task-specific objective for the task.

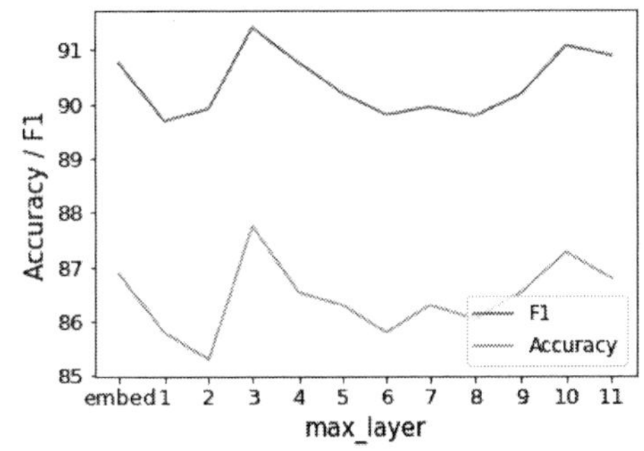

Figure 3: Performance on the MRPC development set as we change the layer combination to add the noise. On the x-axis, max_layer = $embed$ denotes that the noise is added to the embedding layer only. All the other values denote that, for each mini-batch, a layer among the layer 1 up to this layer value is randomly chosen. The model is then updated according to the task-specific objective for the task.

Input: [CLS] by law , mexico can only export half the oil it produces to the united states . [SEP] mexico produces more oil than any other **country** . [SEP]

SMART		SMART (+noise)		RAPT		RAPT (+noise)	
word	similarity	word	similarity	word	similarity	word	similarity
nation	0.2991	nation	0.2992	countries	0.3976	countries	0.3141
county	0.2942	county	0.2945	nation	0.3328	nation	0.2714
region	0.2939	region	0.2941	region	0.3182	region	0.2546
countries	0.2736	countries	0.2738	nations	0.2934	nations	0.2430
province	0.2517	province	0.2515	kingdom	0.2929	cities	0.2337
island	0.2475	island	0.2473	province	0.2880	kingdom	0.2336
state	0.2449	state	0.2445	island	0.2810	global	0.2324
territory	0.2227	territory	0.2227	city	0.2702	city	0.2295
homeland	0.2106	homeland	0.2103	countryside	0.2682	territory	0.2293
trade	0.2090	trade	0.2087	realms	0.2670	countryside	0.2274

Table 5: Top-10 closest words to the vector of the word **country** using SMART and RAPT on the RTE development dataset. SMART (the leftmost column) denotes the embedding of the target vector (**country**) before adding the perturbation using SMART. SMART (+noise) denotes the embedding of the target vector (**country**) after adding the perturbation using SMART. In both cases, we compute the similarity between the embedding of the target word and the embeddings of the other words in the training set. RAPT (the second column from the right) denotes the hidden state vector of the second layer of BERT of the target vector (**country**) before adding the noise using RAPT. RAPT (+noise) denotes the hidden state vector of the second layer of BERT of the target vector (**country**) after adding the noise using RAPT. In both cases, we compute the similarity between the hidden state of the target word and the hidden states of the other words in the training set.

Input: [CLS] by law , mexico **can** only export half the oil it produces to the united states . [SEP] mexico produces more oil than any other country . [SEP]

SMART		SMART (+noise)		RAPT		RAPT (+noise)	
word	similarity	word	similarity	word	similarity	word	similarity
could	0.5857	could	0.5855	could	0.5656	could	0.4580
may	0.3869	may	0.3873	cannot	0.5162	cannot	0.4269
cannot	0.3774	cannot	0.3776	couldn	0.5098	couldn	0.4213
might	0.3736	might	0.3736	allows	0.3445	allows	0.2859
couldn	0.3651	couldn	0.3650	helps	0.3408	must	0.2759
must	0.3388	must	0.3388	shall	0.3218	may	0.2659
will	0.3312	will	0.3314	should	0.3183	doesn	0.2639
should	0.3119	should	0.3121	must	0.3130	sees	0.2531
would	0.2914	would	0.2915	doesn	0.3106	helps	0.2388
shall	0.2624	shall	0.2626	may	0.3083	allow	0.2318

Table 6: Top-10 closest words to the vector of the word **can** using SMART and RAPT on the RTE development dataset. SMART (the leftmost column) denotes the embedding of the target vector (**can**) before adding the perturbation using SMART. SMART (+noise) denotes the embedding of the target vector (**can**) after adding the perturbation using SMART. In both cases, we compute the similarity between the embedding of the target word and the embeddings of the other words in the training set. RAPT (the second column from the right) denotes the hidden state vector of the second layer of BERT of the target vector (**can**) before adding the noise using RAPT. RAPT (+noise) denotes the hidden state vector of the second layer of BERT of the target vector (**can**) after adding the noise using RAPT. In both cases, we compute the similarity between the hidden state of the target word and the hidden states of the other words in the training set.

5 Conclusion

We proposed RAPT, a simple and efficient random perturbation training algorithm for fine-tuning large scale pre-trained language models. Our experiments demonstrated that it achieves competitive results on GLUE tasks, without relying on any additional resource other than the target task dataset. Moreover, our model can significanlty reduce the training time compared to adversarial training. RAPT is model-agnostic, and can also be generalized to solve other downstream tasks as well, and we will explore these directions as future work.

Acknowledgments

We thank the reviewers for their helpful feedback. This work has been supported by the project KAKENHI ID: 21K17802.

References

Roy Bar-Haim, Ido Dagan, Bill Dolan, Lisa Ferro, and Danilo Giampiccolo. 2006. The second PASCAL recognising textual entailment challenge. In *Proceedings of the Second PASCAL Challenges Workshop on Recognising Textual Entailment*.

Luisa Bentivogli, Ido Dagan, Hoa Trang Dang, Danilo Giampiccolo, and Bernardo Magnini. 2009. The fifth pascal recognizing textual entailment challenge. In *In Proc Text Analysis Conference (TAC'09*.

Daniel Cer, Mona Diab, Eneko Agirre, Inigo Lopez-Gazpio, and Lucia Specia. 2017. Semeval-2017 task 1: Semantic textual similarity-multilingual and cross-lingual focused evaluation. *arXiv preprint arXiv:1708.00055*.

Hao Cheng, Xiaodong Liu, Lis Pereira, Yaoliang Yu, and Jianfeng Gao. 2020. Posterior differential regularization with f-divergence for improving model robustness. *arXiv preprint arXiv:2010.12638*.

Yong Cheng, Lu Jiang, and Wolfgang Macherey. 2019. Robust neural machine translation with doubly adversarial inputs.

Ido Dagan, Oren Glickman, and Bernardo Magnini. 2006. The pascal recognising textual entailment challenge. In *Proceedings of the First International Conference on Machine Learning Challenges: Evaluating Predictive Uncertainty Visual Object Classification, and Recognizing Textual Entailment*, MLCW'05, pages 177–190, Berlin, Heidelberg. Springer-Verlag.

Jacob Devlin, Ming-Wei Chang, Kenton Lee, and Kristina Toutanova. 2019. Bert: Pre-training of deep bidirectional transformers for language understanding.

William B Dolan and Chris Brockett. 2005. Automatically constructing a corpus of sentential paraphrases. In *Proceedings of the Third International Workshop on Paraphrasing (IWP2005)*.

Danilo Giampiccolo, Bernardo Magnini, Ido Dagan, and Bill Dolan. 2007. The third PASCAL recognizing textual entailment challenge. In *Proceedings of the ACL-PASCAL Workshop on Textual Entailment and Paraphrasing*, pages 1–9, Prague. Association for Computational Linguistics.

Ian J Goodfellow, Jonathon Shlens, and Christian Szegedy. 2014. Explaining and harnessing adversarial examples. *arXiv preprint arXiv:1412.6572*.

Yu-Lun Hsieh, Minhao Cheng, Da-Cheng Juan, Wei Wei, Wen-Lian Hsu, and Cho-Jui Hsieh. 2019. On the robustness of self-attentive models. In *Proceedings of the 57th Annual Meeting of the Association for Computational Linguistics*, pages 1520–1529.

Haoming Jiang, Pengcheng He, Weizhu Chen, Xiaodong Liu, Jianfeng Gao, and Tuo Zhao. 2019. Smart: Robust and efficient fine-tuning for pretrained natural language models through principled regularized optimization. *arXiv preprint arXiv:1911.03437*.

Di Jin, Zhijing Jin, Joey Tianyi Zhou, and Peter Szolovits. 2019. Is bert really robust? natural language attack on text classification and entailment. *arXiv preprint arXiv:1907.11932*.

Diederik P Kingma and Jimmy Ba. 2015. Adam: A method for stochastic optimization. *ICLR (Poster) 2015*.

Hector Levesque, Ernest Davis, and Leora Morgenstern. 2012. The winograd schema challenge. In *Thirteenth International Conference on the Principles of Knowledge Representation and Reasoning*.

Xiaodong Liu, Hao Cheng, Pengcheng He, Weizhu Chen, Yu Wang, Hoifung Poon, and Jianfeng Gao. 2020a. Adversarial training for large neural language models. *arXiv preprint arXiv:2004.08994*.

Xiaodong Liu, Pengcheng He, Weizhu Chen, and Jianfeng Gao. 2019. Multi-task deep neural networks for natural language understanding. *Proceedings of the 57th Annual Meeting of the Association for Computational Linguistics*, pages 4487–4496.

Xiaodong Liu, Yu Wang, Jianshu Ji, Hao Cheng, Xueyun Zhu, Emmanuel Awa, Pengcheng He, Weizhu Chen, Hoifung Poon, Guihong Cao, and Jianfeng Gao. 2020b. The microsoft toolkit of multitask deep neural networks for natural language understanding. *arXiv preprint arXiv:2002.07972*.

Aleksander Madry, Aleksandar Makelov, Ludwig Schmidt, Dimitris Tsipras, and Adrian Vladu. 2017. Towards deep learning models resistant to adversarial attacks. *arXiv preprint arXiv:1706.06083*.

Takeru Miyato, Shin-ichi Maeda, Masanori Koyama, and Shin Ishii. 2018. Virtual adversarial training: a regularization method for supervised and semi-supervised learning. *IEEE transactions on pattern analysis and machine intelligence*, 41(8):1979–1993.

Lis Pereira, Xiaodong Liu, Fei Cheng, Masayuki Asahara, and Ichiro Kobayashi. 2020. Adversarial training for commonsense inference. *arXiv preprint arXiv:2005.08156*.

Lis Pereira, Xiaodong Liu, Hao Cheng, Hoifung Poon, Jianfeng Gao, and Ichiro Kobayashi. 2021. Targeted adversarial training for natural language understanding. *Proceedings of the 2021 Conference of the North American Chapter of the Association for Computational Linguistics: Human Language Technologies, pages 5385–5393 June 6–11, 2021.*

Pranav Rajpurkar, Jian Zhang, Konstantin Lopyrev, and Percy Liang. 2016. SQuAD: 100,000+ questions for machine comprehension of text. In *Proceedings of the 2016 Conference on Empirical Methods in Natural Language Processing*, pages 2383–2392, Austin, Texas. Association for Computational Linguistics.

Richard Socher, Alex Perelygin, Jean Wu, Jason Chuang, Christopher D Manning, Andrew Ng, and Christopher Potts. 2013. Recursive deep models for semantic compositionality over a sentiment treebank. In *Proceedings of the 2013 conference on empirical methods in natural language processing*, pages 1631–1642.

Ashish Vaswani, Noam Shazeer, Niki Parmar, Jakob Uszkoreit, Llion Jones, Aidan N Gomez, Łukasz Kaiser, and Illia Polosukhin. 2017. Attention is all you need. In *Advances in neural information processing systems*, pages 5998–6008.

Alex Warstadt, Amanpreet Singh, and Samuel R Bowman. 2018. Neural network acceptability judgments. *arXiv preprint arXiv:1805.12471*.

Adina Williams, Nikita Nangia, and Samuel Bowman. 2018. A broad-coverage challenge corpus for sentence understanding through inference. In *Proceedings of the 2018 Conference of the North American Chapter of the Association for Computational Linguistics: Human Language Technologies, Volume 1 (Long Papers)*, pages 1112–1122. Association for Computational Linguistics.

Chen Zhu, Yu Cheng, Zhe Gan, Siqi Sun, Thomas Goldstein, and Jingjing Liu. 2019. Freelb: Enhanced adversarial training for language understanding. *arXiv preprint arXiv:1909.11764*.

Screening Gender Transfer in Neural Machine Translation

Guillaume Wisniewski and **Lichao Zhu**
LLF, Université de Paris & CNRS F-75013 Paris, France
{guillaume.wisniewski,lichao.zhu}@u-paris.fr

Nicolas Ballier
CLILLAC-ARP, Université de Paris
F-75013 Paris, France
nicolas.ballier@u-paris.fr

François Yvon
Université Paris-Saclay & CNRS, LISN
91403 Orsay, France
francois.yvon@limsi.fr

Abstract

This paper aims at identifying the information flow in state-of-the-art machine translation systems, taking as example the transfer of gender when translating from French into English.

Using a controlled set of examples, we experiment several ways to investigate how gender information circulates in a encoder-decoder architecture considering both probing techniques as well as interventions on the internal representations used in the MT system. Our results show that gender information can be found in all token representations built by the encoder and the decoder and lead us to conclude that there are multiple pathways for gender transfer.

1 Introduction

The existence of translation divergences (i.e. cross-linguistic distinctions) raises many challenges for machine translation (MT) (Dorr, 1994): when translating a sentence, some information or constructions are specific to the target language and, consequently, can only be inferred by the decoder from the target context; some are only found in the source language and have to be ignored; finally, some information has to be adapted and transferred from the encoder to the decoder. Contrary to previous generations of MT engines where transfer rules were quite transparent, understanding this *information flow* within state-of-the-art neural MT systems is a challenging task, and a key step for their interpretability.

To illustrate these alternatives and the difficulty they raise, we focus in this work on one specific translation problem: the transfer of gender information from French, where grammatical gender is a property of all nouns, and agreement rules exist within the noun phrase, to English, where gender is only overtly used in rare constructs involving human agents and pronoun coreference.[1] More specifically, we focus on the English translation of French sentences such as "*L'actrice*$_F$ *a terminé son travail.*" (the actress$_F$ has finished her$_F$ job).[2] Translating this kind of sentences is problematic for state-of-the-art MT systems, notably because i) the coreference has to be correctly identified and ii) it can result in gender-biased translations due to stereotypical associations such as *nurses* are always female.

Using a controlled test set, we are able to screen the different information flows at stake when transferring gender information from French into English using two families of methods. The first one relies on linguistic probes to find in which parts of the NMT system gender information is represented; the second one is based on causal models and consists in intervening on the different parts of the source sentence and of the decoder representations in order to reveal their impact on the predicted translations. While this work focuses on one translation phenomenon and on one translation direction only, we believe that our observations shed a new light on how translation systems work and that the methods we describe can be used to analyze other translation divergences.

The rest of the paper is organized as follows. In section 2, we first introduce our controlled dataset and explain how gender is expressed in the two languages. Then, in Section 3 we describe our MT system and evaluate the system outputs in Section 4 its capacity to translate gender information. To explain these results, we then describe two sets of experiments that rely on different ways to analyze neural networks: in Section 5, we use linguistic probes to find out in which source and target tokens gender information is present and in Section 6 we report experiments modifying the token rep-

[1] We follow (Huddleston et al., 2002) presentation of gender in English, mostly grammaticalized in pronouns, as evidenced by *herself, himself, itself.*

[2] In all examples, we tag words either with F or M to indicate a feminine or masculine grammatical gender.

Proceedings of the Fourth BlackboxNLP Workshop on Analyzing and Interpreting Neural Networks for NLP, pages 311–321
Online, November 11, 2021.

resentation to determine when this information is used. Finally, In Section 7, we relate our findings to previous research before summarizing our results in Section 8.

2 A Controlled Test Set to Study Gender Transfer between French and English

Corpus Creation Following (Saunders and Byrne, 2020),[3] we consider parallel sentences with the following pattern to study gender transfer between French and English:

(1) `[DET]` `[N]` a terminé son travail.

(2) The `[N]` has finished `[PRO]` work.

where N is a job noun that can be either masculine or feminine (e.g. in English, actor_M/actress_F; in French, $\textit{acteur}_M$, $\textit{actrice}_F$), DET is the French determiner in agreement with the noun (either the feminine form $\textit{la}_F$, the masculine form $\textit{le}_M$ or the epicene form *l'*[4]) and PRO is the English possessive pronoun '*her*' or '*his*'.

We use the complete list of professions and occupations for French from (Dister and Moreau, 2014) to fill the French `[N]` slot, and select the associated determiner accordingly. This list contains the feminine and masculine forms of each profession, allowing us to create a list of 3,394 sentences, perfectly balanced between genders.[5] Most of these occupational nouns are rare compound nouns unseen in the training corpus: as reported in Figure 1, only 1,707 of the 2,393 occupational nouns used to create the corpus can be found in the training set. This is also reflected in Figure 2, where we see that most occupational nouns are tokenized into multiple BPE units. These sentences were automatically translated and manually verified to produce the corresponding English list.

The motivations for using these fixed syntactic patterns are many. First, they limit the only source of variability between sentences to the `[N]` slots, allowing us to perform controlled experiments. Second, they simplify the analysis and manipulation

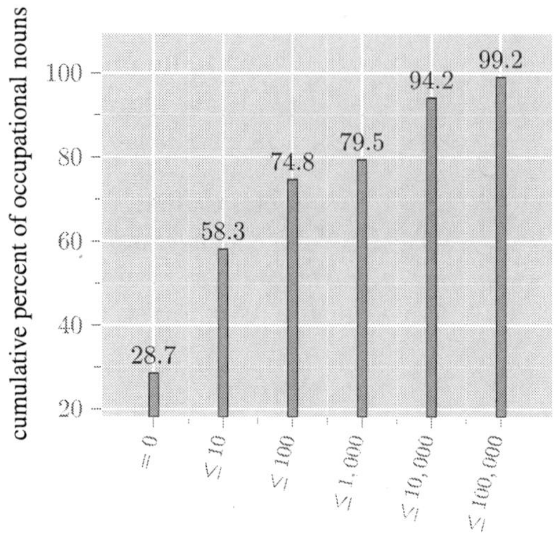

Figure 1: Cumulative frequency of occupational nouns in the training data.

of the trained representations, as the position of each word is almost constant throughout the entire dataset.[6] Despite its simplicity, this dataset enables rich analyses, as the large coverage of the set of nouns enables us to analyze the result with respect to the noun frequency, length, stereotypicality, and also with respect to the amount of gender information available in each language. Furthermore, the asymmetry between the gender carrying words in French and English will be a facilitating factor for generating interesting contrasts. In this paper we focus on French to English translations,[7] using variations in French determiners to generate interesting contrasts in the source. The possessive marker *son* is similarly epicene if the following word begins with a vowel. It should also be noted that there are sociolinguistic implications beyond the remit of this paper, such as a debated preference to refer to women's occupations favouring the masculine form of the occupational noun or exclusive uses of the masculine form to express generic uses (Brauer, 2008).

Expression of Gender When translating from French, four situations can occur:

(i) gender information can be inferred from both determiner DET and noun N, as in $\textit{le}_M$

[3]Using a simplified list from (Prates et al., 2020), Saunders and Byrne (2020) created a "handcrafted" dataset of 388 parallel sentences of the type *The [PROFESSION] finished [his|her] work.* for three translation directions (English-Spanish, English-German and English-Hebrew). In this paper, we adapted this approach for a new translation direction (French to English) using a much larger list of occupational nouns: our corpus contains 3,394 sentences.

[4]The French determiner is *l'* for both genres if the job noun begins with a vowel.

[5]This dataset can be found at `https://github.com/neuroviz/neuroviz/tree/main/blackbox2021`.

[6]Notwithstanding small variations due to the BPE segmentation of the noun N, which can be split into one, two, three, and up to seven subword units.

[7]For a preliminary analysis of the English to French direction, see (Wisniewski et al., 2021).

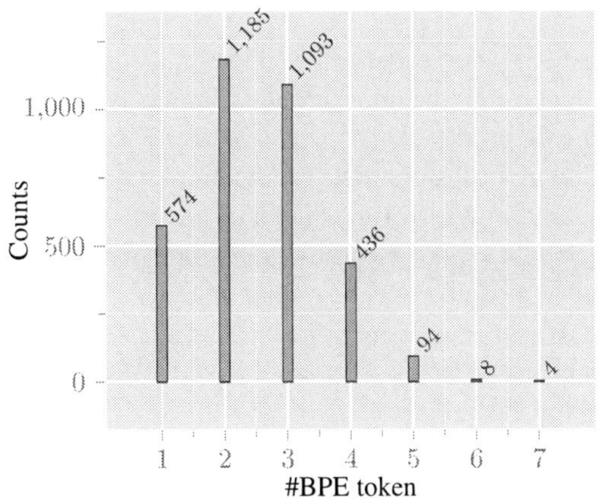

Figure 2: Distribution of the number of tokens in French occupational nouns after BPE tokenization.

determiner	job gender	case	#sentences
l'	fem.	(iii)	251
	epicene	(iv)	272
	masc.	(iii)	251
la	fem.	(i)	895
	epicene	(ii)	415
le	epicene	(ii)	417
	masc.	(i)	893

Table 1: Number of sentences for each way of expressing gender in French sentences.

couturier$_M$/*la*$_F$ *couturière*$_F$ — both translated by 'the stylist' or 'the seamstress' ;

(ii) gender information can be inferred from the determiner `DET` but not from the noun `N`, as in *le*$_M$ *cinéaste*/*la*$_F$ *cinéaste* — 'the film-maker' in both cases;

(iii) gender information can be inferred from the noun `N` but not from the determiner `DET`, as in *l'assistant*$_M$/*l'assistante*$_F$ — 'the assistant' in both cases;

(iv) gender information can not be inferred at all, as in *l'illusioniste* — 'the illusionist'.

Contrary to case (iv), in situations [i-iii], the translation system has the information to predict the right pronoun. Table 1 reports the number of sentences for each of these cases.

Conversely, in English sentences, gender information is always overtly expressed in the English pronoun, and in rare cases, also in the English noun

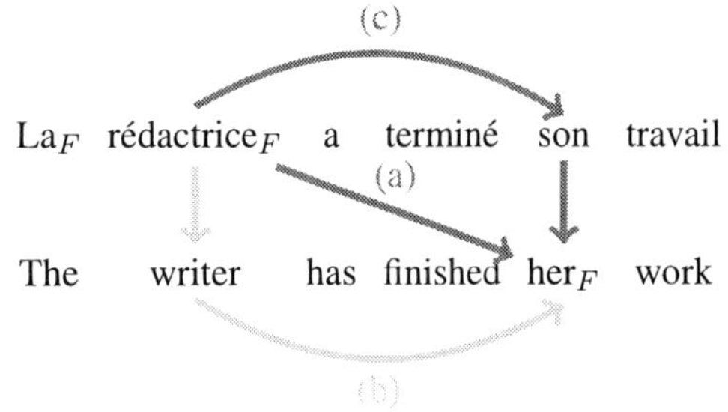

Figure 3: Gender transfer, from French to English: three possible influences on the choice of the gender of the possessive pronoun in English.

`[N]`, as in the *actor/actress* pair of words.[8]

Pathways to Transfer Gender Information Looking at the example in Figure 3, we see that to correctly translate the gender of the French profession into English, three main hypotheses can be entertained:

- (a) a *direct influence* through the cross-lingual attention(s) computed when generating the English pronoun that should attend to the French noun;
- (b) an *indirect influence* through the (monolingual) encoding of gender in the representation of the English noun, the contextualized embedding of which should encode (through cross-lingual projection) the gender of the corresponding French NP;
- (c) an *indirect influence* through the (cross-lingual) attention to the French possessive adjective, the contextualized representation of which should then encode the French Noun gender.

Note that these three possibilities are not mutually exclusive, and gender may well be transferred through a combination of the three influences, and also through the representations computed for the other words in the sentence.

Our main objective in this paper is to explore various ways to assess these hypotheses and try to reach a conclusion regarding the way gender is actually transferred.

[8]Note that two English sentences (one with '*her*' the other with '*him*') were created when the gender of the profession can not be inferred from the French sentence. For instance, the French sentence '*l'artiste a terminé son travail*' appears twice in the parallel corpora: the first time as the translation of 'the artist has finished *her*$_F$ work', the second time as the translation of 'the artist has finished *his*$_M$ work'.

3 Experimental Setting

In all our experiments, we use `JoeyNMT`[9] (Kreutzer et al., 2019), an educational implementation of a translation system based on the `Transformer` model of Vaswani et al. (2017). The simplicity of the codebase, which nonetheless allowed us to achieve near SOTA performance on our data, made it a perfect choice for our endeavor. In our system, encoder and decoder are composed of 6 layers, each with 8 attention heads; the *feed-forward* layers have 2,048 parameters and the dimension of lexical embeddings is 512. Our model comprises a grand total of 76,596,736 parameters. The system was trained with data from the 'News' task of the WMT'2015 evaluation campaign.[10] It includes the `Europarl`, `NewsCommentary` and `CommonCrawl` corpora, and altogether contains 4,813,682 sentences and nearly 141 million French running words. All the corpora were tokenized and segmented into sub-lexical units using the unigram model of `SentencePiece` (Kudo, 2018); the resulting vocabularies contain 32,000 units in each language. The model is trained by optimizing the cross-entropy using the ADAM strategy. This system achieves a BLEU score of 34.0 for the French-English direction.

4 Evaluation of Gender Translation

4.1 Experimental Results

We evaluate the ability of our system to predict the gender of occupational nouns using the corpus described in Section 2 and consider, as a point of comparison, the translations generated by `e-translation`, a translation system developed by the European Commission that is freely accessible for academic research.[11] When translating into English, this evaluation is straightforward and simply amounts to checking the pronoun gender: does the translation hypothesis of a feminine (resp. masculine) occupational noun contains *her* (resp. *his*)? We therefore evaluate the two considered systems by the percentage of sentences for which the possessive pronoun is correct.

It should be noted that the gender information of a translation hypothesis can not always be determined: in some cases, the system produces a correct translation that does not contain *her* nor *his* (e.g. *the programmer has finished working*); in other cases, the translation is completely wrong or the determiner is translated as *its* (901 sentences mostly corresponding to situations in which the job noun was not translated correctly) or as *their* (52 sentences). For the sake of clarity, we do not distinguish these cases in our analyses.

It appears that our system is able to correctly predict the possessive pronoun in only 52.4% of the English sentences (the gender information could not be extracted in 1.4% of the sentences); on the contrary, `e-translation` achieves near perfect results: in 90.9% of the translation hypotheses, the gender of the pronoun is correct, which strongly suggests that this system integrates a specific process to transfer gender information.

Table 2 details these scores for the various situations identified in Section 2. These results show that our system (trained on 'standard' MT corpora) has a clear tendency to favor the translation of *son* by a masculine pronoun even in situations in which there is no ambiguity on the gender of the nominal group (e.g. when both the determiner and the noun both have a form specific to the feminine). Overall, our system achieves a precision of only 26.3% for the feminine pronouns, but correctly predicts the pronoun for 78.5% of masculine sentences. These observations are in line with the conclusions drawn by Saunders and Byrne (2020) on English-German, English-Spanish and English-Hebrew. Similar observations are also reported in (Renduchintala and Williams, 2021) when translating out of English for a larger set of target languages. On the contrary, `e-translation` is able to correctly infer the gender information in almost all cases and most of the errors are due to the French sentences in which the gender is not expressed (case (iv) in the description of Section 2).

4.2 Predicting Failure

We conducted two experiments to better understand the reasons why the gender of the possessive pronoun is not correctly predicted in the translations of `JoeyNMT`.

First, we looked at the number of times the possessive pronoun *son* was translated by *his* or *her* in the training data. For this purpose, we used `eflomal` (Östling and Tiedemann, 2016) to align French and English tokens of the training set[12] and

[9] `https://github.com/joeynmt/joeynmt`

[10] This is the most recent evaluation campaign for English-French organized in the context of the WMT conference (see `http://statmt.org/wmt15`).

[11] `ec.europa.eu/cefdigital/eTranslation`

[12] Alignment was performed after BPE tokenization and

Determiner	Job gender	predicted pronoun	JoeyNMT % sentences	JoeyNMT accuracy	e-translation % sentences	e-translation accuracy
l'	epicene	her	0.7%		4.4%	
		his	80.1%	40.4%	94.1%	49.3%
		other	19.2%		1.5%	
	fem.	**her**	7.2%		91.6%	
		his	59.4%	7.2%	4.0%	91.6%
		other	33.4%		4.4%	
	masc.	her	0.4%		0%	
		his	73.7%	73.7%	96%	96.0%
		other	25.9%		4.0%	
la	epicene	**her**	31.6%		93%	
		his	43.9%	31.6%	0.3%	93.0%
		other	24.5%		6.7%	
	fem.	**her**	33.3%		94%	
		his	18.5%	33.3%	0%	94.0%
		other	48.2%		6%	
le	epicene	her	0.7%		0%	
		his	84.4%	84.4%	95.4%	95.4%
		other	14.9%		4.6%	
	masc.	her	0.2%		0%	
		his	76.8%	76.8%	95.4%	95.6%
		other	21.2%		4.4%	

Table 2: Percentage of translation hypotheses that contain each possessive pronoun according to the way gender is expressed in the French subject. In each case the correct English pronoun is in bold.

translation	frequency
_its	27.94%
_his	**18.28%**
_the	7.24%
_her	**6.42%**
_a	3.34%
_their	2.92%
_it	2.45%
_sound	1.37%
s	1.33%
_he	0.76%
__OTHER__	22.13%

Table 3: Most frequent translation of the French token *son* according to the word alignment links. *son* is aligned with 3,658 different types. Those which do not appear in the table are grouped in the special token `__OTHER__`.

use the alignment link to find all possible translation of the French *son* token.[13] Results reported in Table 3 show that translations of *son* by *his* are three times more frequent than translations by *her*.

Second, we considered a simple logistic regression model that, given a sentence, predicts whether the pronoun gender will be correct or not. We used a small set of surface features to describe a French sentence: the gender of the determiner, the gender of the occupational noun (both can be either masculine, feminine or epicene), a binary feature that is true when both the determiner and the noun have an explicit gender marker, a feature describing the number of BPE units into which the occupational noun has been encoded and three Boolean features to describe the number of occurrences of the occupational noun in the train set. These features are respectively true when the occupational noun does not appear in the training set, when it occurs 10 times or less in the training set and when it occurs 100 times or more in the training set.

This model is trained on 75% of the examples and we evaluate the accuracy of its predictions on the remaining 25% of examples. To assess the stability of the model we consider 100 train-test splits and report the 95% confidence interval.

We report in Table 4 the accuracy achieved using all of these features as well as each of this feature individually.[14] Results show that, overall, the quality of the prediction is pretty high even when considering a single feature. This observation suggests the choice of the possessive pronoun in English is mostly based on surface information and does not result from a 'linguistic' analysis of the input sentence. In particular, the high precision achieved when considering solely the number of

symmetrized using the `grow-diag-final-and` heuristic.

[13]Note that, in French, *son* can either be a possessive pronoun or a noun meaning 'sound'.

[14]Regression models have been computed using `sklearn` (Pedregosa et al., 2011).

feature	accuracy
single features	
occupational noun gender	73.9% ± 0.2
determiner gender	74.5% ± 0.2
number of BPE tokens	74.5% ± 0.2
explicit gender	74.5% ± 0.2
occurrences in train set	74.5% ± 0.2
combination of features	
all gender features	81.5% ± 0.2
all features	82.2% ± 0.2

Table 4: Accuracy achieved when predicting whether the possessive pronoun will be correctly translated. Features are described in Section 4.2; 'all gender features' denotes the combination of three features: occupational noun gender, determiner gender and explicit gender.

BPE tokens, corroborated by the observation reported in Figure 4, shows that the system is not able to correctly predict gender information for occupational nouns that it did not see during training. As expected, the best feature to predict whether the gender of the English pronoun will be correct is the combination between the gender of the determiner and the gender of the job name, a feature that is closely related to the different ways gender is expressed in the French sentence as described in Section 2.

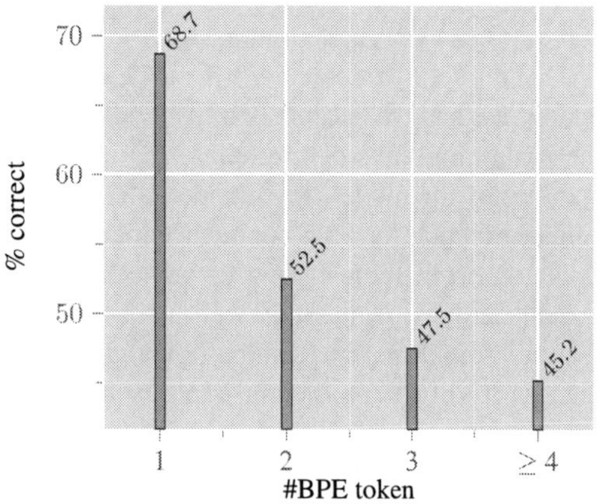

Figure 4: Sentences in which the English possessive pronoun is correctly translated according the number of tokens in the French occupational nouns after BPE tokenization.

layer	decoder	
	the	all tokens
1	89.5% ±0.2	71.6% ±0.6
2	92.0% ±0.1	76.3% ±0.7
3	91.8% ±0.1	78.1% ±0.6
4	90.9% ±0.2	79.1% ±0.6
5	89.3% ±0.2	82.4% ±0.5
6	87.7% ±0.2	84.7% ±0.3

Table 5: Precision of a probe predicting the gender of the French occupational noun given the decoder representation.

5 Probing Representations

In this section, we conduct an analysis of the representations computed by the encoder when translating from French into English. Our goal is to evaluate how well the gender information spreads through the transformer network from the initial French occupational noun (either `DET`, `N` or both of them) to the other French words, as well as to their English counterparts. Following a standard practice, we use probing (Belinkov and Glass, 2019) to analyze which words in the source and target sentence convey gender information: a *probe* (Alain and Bengio, 2017) is trained to predict linguistic properties (here the gender of the French subject) from the representations of language; achieving high accuracy at this task implies these properties were encoded in the representation.

Experimental setup We extract and collect the 512 dimensional hidden representations at the output of each layer of the encoder for all French lexical tokens following the job noun (i.e. *a*, *terminé*, *son*, *travail*, . and `<eos>`), as well as the first token (*the*)[15] of the English sentence in all decoder layers. All these words are frequent enough to correspond to one single BPE unit. We also consider a probe that is trained on all tokens of the target sentence (i.e. we collect the token representations of all translation hypotheses and associate each of them to a label indicating whether occupational name in the French sentence refers to a woman or a man), as the diversity of the translation structures makes it impossible to carry out a position-by-position analysis.

For each word, we randomly split our 3,394 sentences between train (75%) and test (25%), and use

[15]This is the only word that is always predicted correctly.

`scikit-learn` (Pedregosa et al., 2011) to learn a logistic regression model that predicts the gender of the occupational noun using the hidden representation of one single word. We use ℓ_1 penalty to regularize this model. The same data is also used to predict a random binary labeling: this is to control the capacity of our probing model (Hewitt and Liang, 2019). This experiment is repeated on 100 random train/test splits and 95% confidence intervals are computed.

Results Table 6 reports the accuracy achieved by our probes considering the representation of the source tokens as features. It appears that the representation of *son* (the translation of the possessive pronoun in French) is not the same when the occupational noun is masculine as when it is feminine: the representation of the French possessive pronoun encodes gender information even if the form of the word does not. It also appears that this information is more present in the deepest layers of the encoder: the probe achieves an accuracy of 80% when representations from the first layer are considered and of more than 90% when representations are extracted from any of the last three layers of the encoder. This observation confirms that there is actually an information flow between the possessive pronoun *son* and its antecedent the French occupational noun, corresponding to the path denoted (c) in Figure 3.

More surprisingly, accuracies achieved by the probe when the representations of other source tokens are considered are also very high: these accuracies are comparable or only slightly less than the ones achieved with *son*, showing that the gender information has an impact on the representations of all source tokens, even when these tokens have no direct syntactic relations with the subject phrase.

The results of the probe considering the decoder representations of '*the*' (Table 5) show a similar trend: the gender information is encoded in the representation even if the token generated by the decoder does not change with this information. It also appears that the probe is still able to predict the gender of the French occupational noun with a high accuracy when the representation of any token predicted by the decoder is considered as features, showing that, as for the encoder representations, gender information is encoded in all target tokens, even those for which this information is useless.

Results for predicting random labels (column 'random labels' in Table 6) finally show that the information is actually present in the representations and that the probe is not capturing spurious correlations in our data (Hewitt and Liang, 2019).

6 Manipulating Representations

The probing experiments described in the previous section show that gender information is encoded in all tokens representations built by the encoder and the decoder. However, it is not possible to identify from these observations if and when this information is used. To answer this question, the second method we propose to analyze gender transfer in our MT system relies on an *intervention*. It consists in replacing the embedding of the French possessive pronoun (i.e. the *son* token that, intuitively triggers the generation of '*her*' or '*his*') at the output of the encoder by either a *neutral* version of this embedding, obtained by averaging the representations of *son* on the whole test set (it should be borne in mind that the design of our corpus ensures that genders are balanced) or a *prototypical* version of a masculine *son* embedding or a feminine *son* embedding. These embeddings are extracted from the encoder representations of these two sentences:

(3) le facteur a terminé son travail.
the postman has finished his work.

(4) la pharmacienne a terminé son travail.
the pharmacist has finished her work.

These two sentences were chosen because, in both cases, gender information is carried by both the determiner and the noun and the translation of these sentences by our system is correct. After plugging the chosen representation in the last layer of the encoder and keeping the representation of the other tokens of the source sentence unchanged, the rest of the translation proceeds without any further modification.

Results of this manipulation are in Table 7: like in Table 2, we have reported the proportion of translation hypotheses in which the possessive pronoun is feminine, masculine or is neither *her* nor *his*.[16] Contrary to what was expected, changing the representation of the French possessive *son* has little impact (if any) on the choice of the English pronoun. These observations suggest that the representations of *son* built by the MT system are not the only evidence used during the generation of the translation hypothesis, even if the results reported in the

[16]As in Section 4, this last category includes both sentences that cannot be analyzed and those in which the possessive pronoun is *its* or *their*.

layer	encoder						random labels
	a	terminé	son	travail	.	eos	son
1	80.4% ±1.1	75.1% ±0.3	80.6% ±0.3	76.4% ±0.6	59.5% ±1.0	73.3% ±1.0	45,3% ±0.9
2	85.8% ±1.0	80.8% ±0.2	81.6% ±0.3	78.3% ±0.7	87.6% ±0.6	88.3% ±0.7	50,7% ±0.8
3	89.5% ±0.6	88.2% ±0.2	89.2% ±0.2	82.0% ±1.1	86.5% ±1.0	87.6% ±0.6	48,8% ±0.9
4	90.8% ±0.4	89.3% ±0.2	90.6% ±0.2	85.9% ±0.9	85.7% ±1.0	85.6% ±0.7	48,6% ±0.8
5	90.4% ±1.0	89.3% ±0.2	90.4% ±0.2	85.5% ±0.8	86.4% ±0.8	85.2% ±1.2	49,6% ±0.8
6	91.0% ±0.6	89.3% ±0.2	90.0% ±0.2	86.0% ±1.0	86.4% ±1.1	85.1% ±0.8	49,2% ±0.8

Table 6: Precision of a probe predicting the gender of the French subject given the encoder representations.

intervention	English pronoun	% sentences
none	her	13.4%
	his	57.1%
	other	29.5%
feminine	her	17.3%
	his	56.8%
	other	25.9%
gender-neutral	her	13.2%
	other	29.4%
	his	57.4%
masculine	her	13.8%
	other	29.2%
	his	57.0%

Table 7: Intervention on *son* representations: proportion of translation hypotheses in which the English possessive pronoun is *her*, *his* or neither of these two values, depending on the intervention on *son*.

previous section show that these representations are particularly relevant for making the correct prediction. This counter-intuitive result is consistent with several observations made in the literature: the fact that a 'linguistic' information is encoded in the neural representations does not imply that it will be used by the neural network (see, for instance, (Belinkov and Glass, 2019)). This suggests that the information flow along the path denoted (c) in Figure 3 should be small and the choice of the English possessive pronoun is based on other information than the representation of *son*.

7 Related Work

Our work is part of a very active line of research aiming to analyze, interpret, and evaluate neural networks used in NLP. Belinkov and Glass (2019) present a detailed overview of these papers and of the different tools and methods that can be used to uncover the linguistic information represented in the hidden layers of neural networks. Experiments reported in Section 5 are based on the probing approach of Alain and Bengio (2017) and have been used in many works (see (Belinkov and Glass, 2019) for an overview). This approach has also been used in several works to study the information flow within an encoder-decoder architecture: for instance, Belinkov et al. (2020) rely on probes to find which components of a NMT system encode linguistic information when translating morphologically rich languages. However, to the best of our knowledge, this work is the first to use the differences between gender expression in French and English to get insights into the inner representations used in NMT systems based on the Transformer architecture. Experiments reported in Section 6 are inspired by causal analysis, a type of analysis that has been used by Vig et al. (2020) to analyze gender bias in neural monolingual NLP models.

Several studies have investigated gender bias using dedicated datasets, some of them presented at the ACL Workshop on Gender Bias in Natural Language Processing (Costa-jussà et al., 2019, 2020b; Costa-jussa et al., 2021). Savoldi et al. (2021) synthesizes the studies and datasets on gender bias for translation. In particular, the controlled test set considered in our work builds on the works of Stanovsky et al. (2019) and Saunders and Byrne (2020), who both propose challenge test sets to evaluate gender bias in MT systems. The corresponding datasets consider the translation of occupational nouns with an anaphoric reference that makes gender explicit: the former contains instances of difficult translation patterns inspired by the WinoGender dataset of Rudinger et al. (2018); similar to our work, the latter contains a smaller set of simple sentences following a fixed template. Working with a slightly more varied set of sentence templates chosen to unambiguously express the gender of the occupational noun, (Renduchintala and Williams, 2021) also found that a generic multilingual system translating out of English made more errors for feminine than for masculine nouns, a trend that is observed in 20 languages.

Noting the limitations of artificial datasets, (Gonen and Webster, 2020) develop a methodology to mine actual instances of likely biased translations in large corpora: these are found by automatically generating minimal contrasts in English source (e.g. replacing one noun by another) yielding a gender change in the target sentence. For instance, replacing 'doctor' by 'nurse' in the English might trigger a gender change in the corresponding translation in Russian.

Other studies also investigated the influence of socio-professional parameters such as profession types and the importance and the correlation with qualifying adjectives. Using the European multilingual classification of Skills, Competences and Occupations (ESCO) data, Marzi (2021) suggests insufficient biodiversity of the data in the training sets of neural translation systems. Focusing on 73 hypernyms from the 2,942 ESCO occupational nouns, she evidenced a gender gap by comparing the translations from Google Translate, DeepL and Microsoft Translator in the two directions for the French/Italian language pair. She built a dataset with respectively "competence" (i.e. *intelligent*) and "appearance" (i.e. *beautiful*) adjectives (ADJ) in the following pattern <A very `[ADJ]` `[N]` entered the room>. The data was manually analyzed. Adjectives seem to have no influence for the translation of masculine nouns, but competence adjectives affect the translation of feminine nouns more severely than appearance adjectives.

Zhao et al. (2018) studies gender bias in ELMo embeddings using probing techniques. In this study, biases in the embeddings also implied biases in a pronoun reference resolution task using the WinoGender dataset. Balancing data, and using averaged representations, to a certain extend, helped remove this bias.

Analyzing misclassified occupations in terms of gender, Costa-jussà et al. (2020a) investigated the architectural bias for the translation of occupational nouns, suggesting that using language-specific encoders and decoder yields less bias than a shared encoder-decoder architecture. Considering the attention patterns in the first two decoder layers, this paper shows that language-specific systems pay more attention to the determiner and occupational nouns, while bilingual models seem to rely more on the determiner. In the language-specific case, the embeddings are reported to encode more gender information.

Other architectural biases are considered by Renduchintala et al. (2021), who observed that gender bias is amplified when the system is optimised for speed. Using a dictionary of occupations for English to Spanish and English to German, they showed that correct translation rates degrade much faster than BLEU scores when limiting the beam-size to 1 during beam search or using low-bit quantization.

Finally, another line of research focuses on *mitigating* gender bias. This can be either achieved by working on the system's internal represention (Escudé Font and Costa-jussà, 2019), or by creating a more balanced training data where occupational roles are equally distributed between genders via counterfactual data augmentation (Hall Maudslay et al., 2019; Zmigrod et al., 2019). As discussed in (Saunders and Byrne, 2020), a cheaper, yet effective alternative to data augmentation, is to resort to domain adaptation techniques.

8 Discussion and Conclusion

Our paper investigated the different pathways for gender transfer. We created a dataset inspired by previous research to test several hypotheses. Our novel contribution is that we simultaneously mobilized several techniques, probing and manipulating. We extended the scope of the investigation of the locus of gender transfer beyond the determiner/noun analysis of Costa-jussà et al. (2020a) and questioned the role of predicates and epicene determiners for French. Our results show that gender information is present on the representation of all tokens built by the encoder and the decoder and suggest that the choice of the English possessive pronoun is distributed and is not based on the sole information contained in the representation of the French possessive pronoun. In our future research, we plan to identify how information is used to choose the form of the English pronoun and to generalize our observations to other languages and to other syntactic divergences.

Acknowledgements

This work was partially funded by the NeuroViz project (Explorations and visualizations of a neural translation system), supported by the Ile-de-France Region within the DIM RFSI 2020 funding framework.

References

Guillaume Alain and Yoshua Bengio. 2017. Understanding intermediate layers using linear classifier probes. In *5th International Conference on Learning Representations, ICLR 2017, Toulon, France, April 24-26, 2017, Workshop Track Proceedings*. OpenReview.net.

Yonatan Belinkov, Nadir Durrani, Fahim Dalvi, Hassan Sajjad, and James Glass. 2020. On the linguistic representational power of neural machine translation models. *Computational Linguistics*, 46(1):1–52.

Yonatan Belinkov and James Glass. 2019. Analysis Methods in Neural Language Processing: A Survey. *Transactions of the Association for Computational Linguistics*, 7:49–72.

Markus Brauer. 2008. Un ministre peut-il tomber enceinte? L'impact du générique masculin sur les représentations mentales. *L'Année psychologique*, 108(2):243–272.

Marta Costa-jussa, Hila Gonen, Christian Hardmeier, and Kellie Webster, editors. 2021. *Proceedings of the 3rd Workshop on Gender Bias in Natural Language Processing*. Association for Computational Linguistics, Online.

Marta R. Costa-jussà, Carlos Escolano, Christine Basta, Javier Ferrando, Roser Batlle, and Ksenia Kharitonova. 2020a. Gender bias in multilingual neural machine translation: The architecture matters. *arXiv preprint arXiv:2012.13176*.

Marta R. Costa-jussà, Christian Hardmeier, Will Radford, and Kellie Webster, editors. 2019. *Proceedings of the First Workshop on Gender Bias in Natural Language Processing*. Association for Computational Linguistics, Florence, Italy.

Marta R. Costa-jussà, Christian Hardmeier, Will Radford, and Kellie Webster, editors. 2020b. *Proceedings of the Second Workshop on Gender Bias in Natural Language Processing*. Association for Computational Linguistics, Barcelona, Spain (Online).

Anne Dister and Marie-Louise Moreau. 2014. *Mettre au féminin : guide de féminisation des noms de métier, fonction, grade ou titre*, 3e édition edition. Fédération Wallonie-Bruxelles.

Bonnie J. Dorr. 1994. Machine translation divergences: A formal description and proposed solution. *Computational Linguistics*, 20(4):597–633.

Joel Escudé Font and Marta R. Costa-jussà. 2019. Equalizing gender bias in neural machine translation with word embeddings techniques. In *Proceedings of the First Workshop on Gender Bias in Natural Language Processing*, pages 147–154, Florence, Italy. Association for Computational Linguistics.

Hila Gonen and Kellie Webster. 2020. Automatically identifying gender issues in machine translation using perturbations. In *Findings of the Association for Computational Linguistics: EMNLP 2020*, pages 1991–1995, Online. Association for Computational Linguistics.

Rowan Hall Maudslay, Hila Gonen, Ryan Cotterell, and Simone Teufel. 2019. It's all in the name: Mitigating gender bias with name-based counterfactual data substitution. In *Proceedings of the 2019 Conference on Empirical Methods in Natural Language Processing and the 9th International Joint Conference on Natural Language Processing (EMNLP-IJCNLP)*, pages 5267–5275, Hong Kong, China. Association for Computational Linguistics.

John Hewitt and Percy Liang. 2019. Designing and interpreting probes with control tasks. In *Proceedings of the 2019 Conference on Empirical Methods in Natural Language Processing and the 9th International Joint Conference on Natural Language Processing (EMNLP-IJCNLP)*, pages 2733–2743, Hong Kong, China. Association for Computational Linguistics.

Rodney Huddleston, Geoffrey K Pullum, et al. 2002. *The Cambridge Grammar of English*. Cambridge University Press.

Julia Kreutzer, Jasmijn Bastings, and Stefan Riezler. 2019. Joey NMT: A minimalist NMT toolkit for novices. In *Proceedings of the 2019 Conference on Empirical Methods in Natural Language Processing and the 9th International Joint Conference on Natural Language Processing (EMNLP-IJCNLP): System Demonstrations*, pages 109–114, Hong Kong, China. Association for Computational Linguistics.

Taku Kudo. 2018. Subword regularization: Improving neural network translation models with multiple subword candidates. In *Proceedings of the 56th Annual Meeting of the Association for Computational Linguistics (Volume 1: Long Papers)*, pages 66–75, Melbourne, Australia. Association for Computational Linguistics.

Eleonora Marzi. 2021. La traduction automatique neuronale et les biais de genre: le cas des noms de métiers entre l'italien et le français. *Synergies Italie*, 17:19–36.

Robert Östling and Jörg Tiedemann. 2016. Efficient word alignment with Markov Chain Monte Carlo. *Prague Bulletin of Mathematical Linguistics*, 106:125–146.

Fabian Pedregosa, Gaël Varoquaux, Alexandre Gramfort, Vincent Michel, Bertrand Thirion, Olivier Grisel, Mathieu Blondel, Peter Prettenhofer, Ron Weiss, Vincent Dubourg, et al. 2011. Scikit-learn: Machine learning in python. *Journal of machine learning research*, 12(Oct):2825–2830.

Marcelo O. R. Prates, Pedro H. Avelar, and Luís C. Lamb. 2020. Assessing gender bias in machine translation: a case study with Google Translate. *Neural Computing and Applications*, 32(10):6363–6381.

Adithya Renduchintala, Denise Diaz, Kenneth Heafield, Xian Li, and Mona Diab. 2021. Gender bias amplification during speed-quality optimization in neural machine translation. In *Proceedings of the 59th Annual Meeting of the Association for Computational Linguistics and the 11th International Joint Conference on Natural Language Processing (Volume 2: Short Papers)*, pages 99–109, Online. Association for Computational Linguistics.

Adithya Renduchintala and Adina Williams. 2021. Investigating failures of automatic translation in the case of unambiguous gender.

Rachel Rudinger, Jason Naradowsky, Brian Leonard, and Benjamin Van Durme. 2018. Gender bias in coreference resolution. In *Proceedings of the 2018 Conference of the North American Chapter of the Association for Computational Linguistics: Human Language Technologies, NAACL-HLT, New Orleans, Louisiana, USA, June 1-6, 2018, Volume 2 (Short Papers)*, pages 8–14. Association for Computational Linguistics.

Danielle Saunders and Bill Byrne. 2020. Reducing gender bias in neural machine translation as a domain adaptation problem. In *Proceedings of the 58th Annual Meeting of the Association for Computational Linguistics*, pages 7724–7736, Online. Association for Computational Linguistics.

Beatrice Savoldi, Marco Gaido, Luisa Bentivogli, Matteo Negri, and Marco Turchi. 2021. Gender bias in machine translation.

Gabriel Stanovsky, Noah A. Smith, and Luke Zettlemoyer. 2019. Evaluating gender bias in machine translation. In *Proceedings of the 57th Annual Meeting of the Association for Computational Linguistics*, pages 1679–1684, Florence, Italy. Association for Computational Linguistics.

Ashish Vaswani, Noam Shazeer, Niki Parmar, Jakob Uszkoreit, Llion Jones, Aidan N Gomez, Ł ukasz Kaiser, and Illia Polosukhin. 2017. Attention is all you need. In *Advances in Neural Information Processing Systems 30*, pages 5998–6008. Curran Associates, Inc.

Jesse Vig, Sebastian Gehrmann, Yonatan Belinkov, Sharon Qian, Daniel Nevo, Yaron Singer, and Stuart Shieber. 2020. Investigating gender bias in language models using causal mediation analysis. In *Advances in Neural Information Processing Systems*, volume 33, pages 12388–12401. Curran Associates, Inc.

Guillaume Wisniewski, Lichao Zhu, Nicolas Ballier, and François Yvon. 2021. Biais de genre dans un système de traduction automatique neuronale : une étude préliminaire (gender bias in neural translation : a preliminary study). In *Actes de la 28e Conférence sur le Traitement Automatique des Langues Naturelles. Volume 1 : conférence principale*, pages 11–25, Lille, France. ATALA.

Jieyu Zhao, Tianlu Wang, Mark Yatskar, Vicente Ordonez, and Kai-Wei Chang. 2018. Gender bias in coreference resolution: Evaluation and debiasing methods. In *Proceedings of the 2018 Conference of the North American Chapter of the Association for Computational Linguistics: Human Language Technologies, Volume 2 (Short Papers)*, pages 15–20, New Orleans, Louisiana. Association for Computational Linguistics.

Ran Zmigrod, Sabrina J. Mielke, Hanna Wallach, and Ryan Cotterell. 2019. Counterfactual data augmentation for mitigating gender stereotypes in languages with rich morphology. In *Proceedings of the 57th Annual Meeting of the Association for Computational Linguistics*, pages 1651–1661, Florence, Italy. Association for Computational Linguistics.

What BERT Based Language Models Learn in Spoken Transcripts: An Empirical Study

Ayush Kumar, Mukuntha Narayanan Sundararaman and **Jithendra Vepa**
{ayush, mukunthas, jithendra}@observe.ai
Observe.AI
Bangalore, India

Abstract

Language Models (LMs) have been ubiquitously leveraged in various tasks including spoken language understanding (SLU). Spoken language requires careful understanding of speaker interactions, dialog states and speech induced multimodal behaviors to generate a meaningful representation of the conversation. In this work, we propose to dissect SLU into three representative properties: *conversational* (disfluency, pause, overtalk), *channel* (speaker-type, turn-tasks) and *ASR* (insertion, deletion, substitution). We probe BERT based language models (BERT, RoBERTa) trained on spoken transcripts to investigate its ability to understand multifarious properties in absence of any speech cues. Empirical results indicate that LM is surprisingly good at capturing conversational properties such as pause prediction and overtalk detection from lexical tokens. On the downsides, the LM scores low on turn-tasks and ASR errors predictions. Additionally, pre-training the LM on spoken transcripts restrain its linguistic understanding. Finally, we establish the efficacy and transferability of the mentioned properties on two benchmark datasets: Switchboard Dialog Act and Disfluency datasets.

1 Introduction

Language Models (LM) such as BERT, GPT etc., have led to significant advancements in the field of Natural Language Processing (NLP) by learning representations pre-trained on a vast amount of text data. These LMs have shown to perform well on a multitude of downstream tasks such as question answering, intent, entity and sentiment detection, natural language inference etc. (Devlin et al., 2019). Along with NLP, the proliferation of voice-enabled technologies has resulted in the significance of spoken language understanding (SLU) tasks. The general modus-operandi of SLU systems is to convert voice into text using an ASR engine and use natural language understanding (NLU) on the transcribed text by modelling *conversational* and *channel* properties while being robust to *ASR* errors. Since spoken conversation boasts of amalgamation of spontaneous speaker interactions, it has become imperative for model architectures to capture multimodal features from text and speech modalities (Georgiou et al., 2019). The aim of these multimodal systems is to capture acoustic information such as pitch, intonation, rate of speech, etc. along with properties such as pause, disfluency, overtalk and turn shifts to synthesize a complete understanding of what is being spoken and how it is being spoken. While some of these properties rely on speech signals and can only be captured by acoustic systems, properties such as pauses, disfluency, overtalk, turn shifts, speech recognition errors etc. get passed onto the lexical domain in the form of spoken transcripts and meta-information. Few works suggest that the auxiliary tasks such as speaker intent detection (Aldeneh et al., 2018), filler prediction (Hara et al., 2018), pause and speaking-rate (Weiner et al., 2017) help to train a robust model for downstream tasks. Thus, there is a need for a *vigilant* language model capable of encoding the multi-dimensional properties of a SLU dataset to reduce dependence on auxiliary information and/or multimodal inputs. However, in order to come up with such LM for SLU domain, a pre-requisite is to investigate the extent to which an LM already encodes these properties.

In this work, we propose to categorize the spoken language understanding into distinctive properties: 1) *Conversational*: encompass spontaneous speech properties such as pauses, disfluency, overtalk; 2) *Channel*: properties that capture speaker turns such as speaker-type, turn-taking; 3) *ASR*: properties such as error type (insertion, deletion, substitution). While core focus in this work is to not propose a state-of-the-art language model, we believe that unveiling the behavior of LM on these properties

Proceedings of the Fourth BlackboxNLP Workshop on Analyzing and Interpreting Neural Networks for NLP, pages 322–336
Online, November 11, 2021.

will not only help us to understand the encoded information in a pre-trained model, but will also influence architectural designs to build upon the findings. Thus, *we limit our experiments to utilize only lexical tokens present in the spoken transcripts.* Specifically, we aim to answer the following research questions (RQ) in our work:

- **RQ1**: Can language model encode the distinctive properties of SLU datasets in absence of any speech cues?
  - *RQ1a*: Does LM representations capture conversational properties such as disfluency, overtalk, pause?
  - *RQ1b*: How well can LM encapsulate channel understanding: speaker identity of a channel and turn-tasks?
  - *RQ1c*: Can LM identify insertion, substitution and deletion errors in the spoken transcripts and encode word error rate?
- **RQ2**: How much of linguistic understanding is retained by a LM trained on noisy spoken transcripts?
- **RQ3**: Can an LM infused with such properties perform better on an unseen spoken language dataset compared to a vanilla LM?

To answer RQ1, we frame a set of probing tasks (Table 1, Section 2). Probing tasks are a introspection mechanism to unearth the properties encoded in the neural model (LM) (Alain and Bengio, 2017; Tenney et al., 2019). Depending on the task, a probe model can be a classification or a regression setup that is trained on LM-extracted features. The weights of LM are frozen while training the probe model. If the result on a probing task is good enough, we say that the property under the scanner is encoded in the neural model. For RQ2, we evaluate LM on a couple of linguistic properties: dependency relations and entity-value mapping. Finally, we infuse the conversational, channel and ASR properties via a multi-task (MTL) framework trained on probe tasks and evaluate the trained model on unseen spoken language tasks (RQ3). The empirical results and analysis reveal the following insights:

1. LM encodes the conversational properties such as pause and overtalk surprisingly well (*RQ1a*). Channel properties are captured well enough for only speaker role prediction while LM finds itself struggling to encode information relevant for turn-tasks (*RQ1b*). ASR properties are poorly captured in the LM. While the model can detect if a token is erroneous, it is inaccurate in predicting the error type. Interestingly, ASR transcript pre-trained LM detects substitution much better than vanilla LM in comparison to insertion and deletion errors (*RQ1c*).
2. Once trained on spoken transcripts, the LM vastly loses its understanding of dependency relations. Model also scores poorly on entity-value mapping (*RQ2*).
3. An LM fine-tuned on probing tasks with a multi-task learning (MTL) framework results in an improved performance on Switchboard Dialog Act and Disfluency corpus. This shows that language model representations which encode such properties perform better on downstream tasks (*RQ3*).

2 Probing Tasks (RQ1)

In this section, we define probing tasks with respective examples. We also describe the dataset creation methodology in detail in Section A.1.

2.1 Conversational Properties (RQ1a)

2.1.1 Disfluency Detection

An important characteristic of spontaneous speech that makes it distinguishable from a written text or formal speech is the presence of disfluencies. Disfluency can refer to filler words (*um, uh*), repetitions (*this this is just not working*), false starts (*you were okay that's perfectly fine*), discourse markers (*i mean*) etc. that are an integral part of natural conversations. Despite disfluencies considered as noise to downstream NLU tasks, they indicate distinguishing behaviors such as low confidence of the speaker (Dinkar et al., 2020) and non-native speaker of the language. Hence, identification of disfluent text in spoken transcripts is of prime importance to capture auxiliary speaker behaviors.

In this work, we create a disfluency dataset that has the instances categorized into fluent vs disfluent classes. A probe classifier is set up on this dataset for disfluency detection.

2.1.2 Pause Identification

Pauses and silences are natural elements of human interaction. Any spontaneous conversation would contain participants taking pauses and silences indicating situations such as: holds for retrieving

Property Type	Probe Tasks
Conversational	**Disfluency Detection: Is the given spoken utterance disfluent?** *no so no i i don't can i have instead get a refund* *well i don't have a i mean i probably do have a provider there*
	Pause Identification: Does the speaker take long pauses while speaking? *let's see <silence>i see so we haven't tried to go on the website* *okay <silence>so what i see is that your request is already with us*
	Overtalk Detection: Are two speakers talking over each other? *i'm [yes] not [i know] referring to [how] the [it works] transaction* *i [you] thought [want] that [me to] you [do] gotta [that] do [for you]*
	Question Classification: Did the speaker ask any question? *[entity]: and your date of birth please* *[choice]: so you want to go with monthly plan or yearly*
Channel	**Speaker Role: Who is the speaker for a given utterance?** *agent: you can cancel anytime you are not obligated to write to us* *customer: thank you i tried yesterday i was told to call back today*
	Response Length: Is the expected response to current utterance is short or long? *short: <can i get you full name please><it's johnson rest>* *long: <may i know what didn't work><when i came to webpage ...>*
	Turn Taking: Has speaker completed its turn? *turn-break: <appreciate your reply i'll get that done for you><silence>* *turn-continue: <i get that let me verify that for you <silence>okay i've pushed data from my end you should hear back in 48 hours>*
ASR Errors	**Error Type: What category of ASR error does a particular token belong to?** *reference: <customer resolution is our primary motive>* *hypothesis: <customer resolution is hour primary motive>* *hour: substitution error*
	WER Score: What is the word-error-recognition score for the transcript? *reference: <customer resolution is our primary motive>* *hypothesis: <customer resolution is hour primary motive>* *WER: 16.67*

Table 1: Representative examples for each probing task. Special tokens or markers are pruned before running the probe setup.

information, transition to a new topic of discussion, silence to gather thoughts, etc. Identification of pauses can make the language model understand the current dialog state *viz.*, information exchange, call-hold, turn-shifts, topic-change etc.

In this work, we treat silences longer than 5 sec. as a pause and pose pause identification as a binary classification problem with an intent to understand how well an LM encodes the information about the presence or absence pause without taking any speech cues.

2.1.3 Overtalk Detection

Overtalk is a phenomenon that occurs when multiple parties are speaking at the same time. While overtalk is inevitable in a natural conversation, too much overtalk in conversations indicate poor listening skills displayed by the involved parties. Detecting overtalk is straightforward in dual-channel (diarized) calls, but in mono-channel (non-diarized) calls the speaker segmentation is not available. Although diarization is a preferred way to identify speakers, such models are non-trivial to train and would contain margin of errors.

We identify overtalks in dual-channel calls and convert the corresponding spoken transcript in a sequence of time-ordered tokens (mono-channel transcript) for the overtalk detection task (Table 1). Overtalk detection is a binary classification task where one class contains text that contains overtalk between speakers while the other is a turn uttered by single speaker.

2.1.4 Question Identification

An interaction between an agent and a customer hinge around multiple information exchanges often anchored via a question-answer pair. The intent of the question, eg: entity, descriptive, boolean etc. additionally helps to track the anatomy of the call which captures activities such as agent verifying customers (entity questions), agent probing customers to gather complete understanding of the issue (descriptive questions) etc. However, in spoken language, the formal structure of the question is not always followed and often questions are asked in non-surface forms (*and your account number*) instead of *can you provide your account number*). Thus, question identification is a challenging task in SLU domain. We frame question identification as a multi-class setup with four classes: entity, descriptive, boolean and choice based.

2.2 Channel Properties (RQ1b)

2.2.1 Speaker Role

Identity of the current speaker and speaker roles (sender, addressee, observer, etc.) facilitates a better understanding of the dialog state in a conversation (Kim et al., 2020). Speaker roles and identities have also been leveraged in context extraction and response generation in dialog systems (Zhang et al., 2018a). Thus, we formulate a probe task to identify the role of the current speaker in a call. In a call center conversation, there are three speaker roles that co-exist: agent, customer and IVR. We formulate a multiclass classification task to probe the LM on identifying speaker roles.

2.2.2 Turn Tasks

Understanding contexts (turns) in a conversation is a key step to frame a better understanding of the conversation. To probe on how well the LM encode the contexts, we posit two turn-tasks:

- *Response-Length*: We set up a binary classification task where the probe classifier predicts the duration of the next-turn (*short* or *long*) given the current and previous turn. This task is an interesting intersection of spoken and written properties of SLU where a turn that is as short as (*let me see. oh seems you're correct*) in the lexical domain can be as long as a minute in the time domain because of the silence that speaker took while looking-up the information. Hence, we aim to probe LM on not just lexical understanding of tokens but also identify if LM captures such subtleties of spoken transcripts. We consider any turn that lasts up to 30 seconds as a short-response and a turn lasting longer than that as a long-response.
- *Turn-Taking*: In a real-time system, the spoken transcript comes in as a batch of tokens. In such a system, it becomes important to understand if the speaker has completed its turn and is ready to listen. Inspired by (Roddy et al., 2018), we formulate the situation as a binary text classification where the task is to predict if the speaker would continue speaking at the end of the utterance or would it handover the turn to the other party. We use the pause markers in the dataset to identify the discourse segments which is used to generate the dataset for turn-taking.

2.3 ASR Properties (RQ1c)

2.3.1 Error Type Prediction

We formulate this task as a token classification task i.e, a single token of an entire utterance is considered at a time for probing. We define two setups for error type prediction: a) *Binary Classification*: Given a token in spoken transcript, classify if the token is correct or erroneous; b) *Multiclass Classification*: Given an erroneous token in spoken transcript, classify the error type of the token. In case of deletion, the token next to deleted token is probed for the error type. We believe this is an ideal setup as in real scenario, one can only distinguish a deleted token only when next token is predicted in the ASR transcript.

2.3.2 Word Error Rate (WER) Prediction

In downstream tasks such as call summarization, the dialog turns that are highly noisy (contains ASR errors) are undesirable and should not be focused much while generating summaries. To achieve this property, it becomes inevitable for the model to identify such dialog turns with high WERs. Since any such recent summarization system uses language modelling as underlying component, we probe the LM on its ability to predict the WER of a given dialog turn.

3 Linguistic Understanding of LM (RQ2)

Deep language models such as BERT have been shown to encode a range of syntactic and semantic information with more complex structures represented hierarchically in the higher layers of the model (Conneau et al., 2018; Jawahar et al., 2019). Li et al. (2020) emphasize on capturing syntactic structure via syntax aware local attention while Sundararaman et al. (2019) propose injecting structural and syntactic information such as parts-of-speech tags which results in a higher performing machine translation model. Since spoken language transcripts contain spontaneous texts devoid of formal structure and incorrect grammars added with speech to text conversion errors, it becomes imperative to quantify the linguistic structures encoded in the language model. We probe LM for such properties via these setups:

1. ***Dependency Parsing***: Following the work in Clark et al. (2019), we investigate individual attention heads in both directions to probe what aspects of language they have retained after being pre-trained with spoken language transcripts on the benchmark task of dependency parsing. We use Penn Treebank dataset (Marcus et al., 1993) tagged with Stanford's dependencies to report the performance on dependency parsing.
2. ***Entity-Value Mapping***: In an agent-customer conversation, agent usually asks some PII entities to verify the identity of the customer before proceeding further into the call (eg: *can you provide me your date of birth and last name*). The customer replies with a reference to both entities asked by the agent (eg: *sure that would be davis and ninth march ninety four* For an entity extraction system to work in such spoken language transcripts, the model should be able to map *davis* to *last name* and *ninth march ninety four* to *date of birth*. In this work, we pose this problem as a entity-value mapping. Particularly, we compute entity selection accuracy measured by what percent of the time does the head word of a entity value most attend to the head of its entity. For example, if 3 tokens out of *ninth march ninety four* attends maximum to any of the token in *date of birth*, we would say that entity selection accuracy is 75%.

4 Properties Infused LM: A Multi-Task Learning setup (RQ3)

We hypothesize that an LM that better encodes the conversational, channel and ASR properties in its representation performs better on downstream SLU tasks. In order to verify the hypothesis, we follow a two step pipeline:

1. In the first step, we infuse LM with these properties by fine-tuning both LMs on all probe tasks simultaneously using a multi-task learning (MTL) framework.
2. Next, we freeze the weights of the LMs and evaluate the performance of the probe classifier on a couple of external datasets: Switchboard Dialog Act and Switchboard disfluency for dialog act classification and disfluency detection respectively. It should be noted that none of these datasets are utilized in the pre-training step of the two LMs.

Since MTL-trained LMs get explicit supervision to capture properties needed by probing tasks, their performance on downstream tasks would also indicate the relevance of the proposed probing tasks.

5 Experimental Setup

5.1 Language Model

We use BERT (Devlin et al., 2019) as our base language model. Since, RoBERTa (Liu et al., 2019), which is a robustly-optimized version of BERT is also trained on masked language modelling task and has been reported to outperform BERT on several NLP tasks, we extend our probe to RoBERTa. We observe a better result, in general, from RoBERTa-base model. Hence, we run further experiments on variations of RoBERTa-base model. Specifically, we compare following setups:

- ***BERT-base***: We use pre-trained *BERT-base-uncased* model to evaluate out-of-box performance on the probe tasks.
- ***RoBERTa-base***: Since, RoBERTa is a BERT-like model robustly trained with larger dataset, we also utilize pre-trained *RoBERTa-base* model to report the results.
- ***Chat-RoBERTa***: We pre-train RoBERTa on utterances derived from two dialog corpus: PersonaChat (Zhang et al., 2018b) and MultiOz dataset (Budzianowski et al., 2018). The pre-training is done with MLM task to influence the LM with dialog properties, with an aim to establish a competitive baseline trained on a large spontaneous dialog dataset.
- ***ASRoBERTa***: It is imperative to pre-train LM on large domain data for a better performance. ASRoBERTa is pre-trained on in-domain ASR corpus to evaluate the impact of domain pre-

training on the performance on probing tasks (Δ_{domain}).

- ***Oracle***: In an ideal setup, it is suggested to fine-tune the LM on the downstream task for best results. We report results on task fine-tuned model (Oracle) to understand the limits of the LM in an ideal setup compared to in-domain training.

5.2 Dataset

In this work, we focus on evaluating the LM on its ability to encapsulate spoken language understanding in English language with a special focus on real-life spontaneous conversations such as call center interactions. Keeping that in mind, we train ASRoBERTa with transcripts derived from two datasets: a) LibriSpeech (Panayotov et al., 2015) as a general-purpose ASR dataset (960 hrs.); b) real-life proprietary dataset[1] (1000 hrs.). All probing setups are carried out on proprietary datasets. For probing tasks, a total of 10k datapoints are used in the training while validation and test set comprise of 2k datapoints each. The dataset for each probe task is class-balanced. It is to be noted that we use real life dataset with audio of 8-16 kHz. The average word-error-rate (WER) of automatic speech recognition (ASR) system for our dataset is 18.38. The probe task dataset creation methodology is explained in Section A.1.

To evaluate the efficacy of the probing tasks and study the transferability of LM to unseen data, we also evaluate LM fine-tuned with multi-task learning framework on two external datasets: Switchboard Dialog Act (SWDA) (Calhoun et al., 2010) and Switchboard Disfluency dataset (SWDB Disfluency) (Zayats et al., 2019). SWDA consists of utterances categorized into one of 42 dialog act labels, while SWBD disfluency dataset comes with tokens annotated with disfluency tags. We use the already provided train, test and valid splits of the two datasets to run experiments.

5.3 Implementation Details

We use linear probe models (Tenney et al., 2019; Alain and Bengio, 2017) with a cross-entropy loss for classification and mean squared error for regression. The input to probe classifier is the utterance representations derived from <*s*> for all conversational, channel and WER tasks, while we feed contextualized token embeddings for ASR error type detection in the probing model. In line with probing task evaluation, we accumulate layer wise results for each task. Each setup is trained for a total of 20 epochs and the best model on the validation set is used to report the results on the test set (Table 2).

6 Results and Analysis

The results for experiments are presented in Table 2 with the improvements obtained from domain pre-training (Δ_{domain}) and then further with task fine-tuning (*Oracle*).

On Conversation Properties (RQ1a): Properties including disfluency, pause, overtalk are captured surprisingly well by domain LM (ASRoBERTa) without explicit supervision for these tasks in the pre-training step. An LM aware of pauses, disfluency and overtalk can understand discourse and speaker segmentation better and hence it is an encouraging sign to note decent results from probing classifiers on the conversational tasks. The oracle results, although, show that there is a scope for LM to encode these properties even better. A simple downstream task fine-tuning (*Oracle*) provides a considerable boost (2-10%) in F1-score for these tasks.

On Channel Properties (RQ1b): The LM when probed on channel properties performs quite well (83.98%) on speaker role identification. This shows that ASRoBERTa learns to distinguish speaker roles sufficiently in its pre-training step. Although domain pretraining improves the results by 4.5%, the RoBERTa scores for speaker role identification is close to 80% indicating that agents and customers play a disntinctive role easily identifiable by the transcript of the speaker itself. On the other side, the results on turn-tasks are below 70% F1 score. One explanation for this is the inherent difficulty of the turn-tasks which requires a capability to anticipate a turn-transition and response generation properties such as response-length determined by the contextual understanding of the speaker turns and dialog state. Oracle experiment improve over by upto 3% over ASRoBERTa. Relatively lower oracle scores suggest that a robust mechanism is needed to infuse turn-task properties to make LM aware of contextual information.

On ASR Properties (RQ1c): An LM trained on spoken transcripts is able to distinguish tokens that are erroneous from the correct tokens, scoring 73.32% F1 on binary classification probe. How-

[1]We cannot release the datasets or trained models due to privacy reasons.

Probing Task		BERT -base	RoBERTa -base	Chat -RoBERTa	ASRoBERTa	Δ_{domain}	Oracle
Conversational	Disfluency	64.23	65.18	70.52	73.13	2.61	74.18
	Pause	73.67	72.45	77.31	81.29	3.98	85.20
	Overtalk	80.09	81.46	83.75	85.15	1.40	95.45
	Question	69.42	69.94	70.98	75.41	4.43	77.87
Channel	Speaker	79.18	78.45	79.39	83.98	4.59	85.90
	Response-Len	63.28	64.30	65.50	68.11	2.61	70.55
	Turn-Taking	65.26	65.04	66.23	67.45	1.22	70.36
ASR	Binary	67.14	68.58	72.43	73.32	0.89	75.64
	Insertion†	55.66	56.49	58.99	60.87	1.88	61.73
	Deletion†	60.50	58.37	62.49	64.28	1.79	66.17
	Substitution†	48.82	49.96	50.82	55.71	4.89	54.34
	WER$^{\#}$	10.38	10.09	8.50	7.42	-1.08	6.27

Table 2: Probing results on all tasks. WER$^{\#}$ is a regression task while others are classification tasks. Tasks with † are class-wise scores of a multiclass setup. Macro-F1 (higher is better) and MAE (lower is better) are reported for classification & regression respectively. Negative Δ for WER is a welcome change since lower WER is better.

ever, the model is highly inaccurate in distinguishing the error types. The comparisons between ASRoBERTa and RoBERTa on the three error types show that ASRoBERTa is able to identify substitution errors substantially better (55.71%) than RoBERTa (50.82%) while has lower gains on insertion and deletion errors (Δ_{domain} < *2%*). Additionally, ASRoBERTa predicts the WER score of an utterance with a mean absolute error of 7.42 which improves by 1.15 WER once trained with downstream task-finetuning. However, Oracle results are only marginally better than ASRoBERTa on insertion and deletion. The substitution scores drops down at the cost of improving the error type detection. Thus, LM representations are insufficient to capture ASR error types and pre-training mechanism needs to be revisited to make model learn these ASR properties effectively.

Meta-Comments on RQ1: Along with the granular analysis on different properties presented above, the macro-analysis shows some interesting insights:

- Default models (*BERT-base, RoBERTa-base*) perform in close-margins on channel properties, as compared to conversational and ASR properties. We hypothesize that conversational and ASR properties require understanding of spontaneous interactions like pauses, stutters and noisy transcriptions which is not present in the base corpus of BERT-base and RoBERTa-base. On the other hand, channel properties are more generic tasks that require lexical understanding (speaker role) and language generation understanding (turn-tasks) which could still be induced from clean texts.
- A simple pre-training step to induce conversational properties (Chat-RoBERTa) is helpful to realize gains across the tasks. This indicates that we may want to train a better and more suited base-checkpoint for tasks related to dialog systems and spoken language understanding. One of the most simple mechanism would be pre-train a model on publicly available spoken language and/or conversational datasets.
- We observe significant gains in task-finetuning steps for conversational and channel properties. Hoowever, the absolute results on tasks such as response length and turn-taking may note yet be satisfactory. This calls out a need to identify novel pre-training strategies and/or architecture that could lead to a better base-checkpoint across diverse set of generic tasks related to spoken language understanding.
- Weak results on ASR probes suggest that MLM objective is insufficient for the pre-trained language models to effectively distinguish between the erroneous tokens and their error types. It would be interesting to try some ASR-specific language model, such as warped language model (Namazifar et al., 2021) which is trained with two additional training tasks, namely INSERT and DROP where the model is trained to predict where a random token is inserted into or deleted from the input sequence during training.

On Linguistic Understanding (RQ2): The re-

Relations	Chat-RoBERTa	ASRoBERTa	Δ_{r-asr}
all	34.9	31.4	-3.5
	Most frequent relations		
prep	66.6	62.3	-4.3
pobj	71.7	60.9	-10.8
det	87.1	78.8	-8.3
nn	74.0	71.9	-2.1
nsubj	56.4	54.1	-2.3
amod	82.5	79.1	-3.4
dobj	78.9	75.2	-3.7
advmod	51.9	48.8	-3.1
aux	81.4	82.1	0.7
num	78.6	54.2	-24.4
	Relations with highest delta		
num	78.6	54.2	-24.4
ccomp	54.2	35.0	-19.2
poss	83.9	68.4	-15.5
conj	59.0	43.8	-15.2
cc	54.1	41.8	-12.3

Table 3: Results (UAS scores) for attention-based probe on dependency parsing. 10 most frequent dependency relations are reported along with the ones with highest delta (Δ).

Model	Entity-Value Acc.	ISA%
Chat-RoBERTa	7.98	3.78
+NSP Task	38.62	41.98
ASRoBERTa	10.19	3.65
+NSP Task	42.64	46.27

Table 4: Entity-Value mapping accuracy with inter-sentence attention (ISA%).

sults for attention based probe for dependency parsing is reported in Table 3. For the sake of brevity, we present results for 10 most frequent relations in the dataset. We observe that a language model pre-trained on spoken transcripts (ASRoBERTa) worsens the results obtained by a language model trained on clean text chat (Chat-RoBERTa) by 3.5% UAS. Additionally, we note that ASRoBERTa performs poor than Chat-RoBERTa in 81.8% of all dependency relations with *num* relation having the biggest impact on the performance ($\Delta = 24.4\%$). ASRoBERTa performs marginally better only on a couple of relations (*aux:* $\Delta = 0.7\%$, *prt:* $\Delta = 0.5\%$). These results conclusively show that ASRoBERTa does not retain its understanding of dependency relations leading to huge drop in many relations' performance. A reasoning for this could be the fact that ASRoBERTa is trained on grammatically noisy and non-punctuated texts. With a number of ASR errors and incoherent statements, the model may have learnt to not pay attention to dependency links.

Model	SWDA	SWBD Disfluency
Chat-RoBERTa	68.71	68.39
+MTL	**69.72**	**70.27**
ASRoBERTa	67.04	72.01
+MTL	**68.37**	**75.95**

Table 5: Accuracy on SWDA and Switchboard Disfluency dataset in a multi-task learning (MTL) setup

In another experiment of entity-value resolution, it is observed that both RoBERTa and ASRoBERTa performs poorly on the task achieving only 7.98% and 10.19% respectively on attention-based probing method (Table 4). We hypothesize that this could be a result of model's inability to encode the inter-utterance dependencies in a turn-by-turn dyadic conversation. To validate the hypothesis, we perform these steps:

- We compute inter-sentence attention score as a percentage (ISA%) of overall attention that includes self-attention, intra/inter-sentence attention and attention to separator tokens. We observe that the average inter-sentence attention is less than 0.1 except for initial two layers. This shows that model does not put enough emphasis on inter-sentence interactions while encoding the given input. The observation is surprising as model was trained with consecutive dialog turns separated by *</s>* tokens.
- In order to confirm that poor inter-sentence interaction leads to lower attention and consecutively lower entity-value resolution accuracy, we force the model to learn inter-sentence interactions by training it on a binarized next sentence prediction (NSP) task (Devlin et al., 2019). A model would need to understand the input sequence to correctly predict if the last utterance in the input follows the previous utterance. Once the model is trained on NSP task, we run the attention based probing on entity-value resolution once again and note considerable improvements.

The experiment with entity-value resolution task demonstrates that LM poorly encodes inter-sentence interactions and thus provides a scope to model these interactions in an effective manner in future works.

On properties infused LM: MTL Setup (RQ3): We show that an LM fine-tuned on all probe tasks in a multi-task learning (MTL) setup performs better than base LM on an unseen corpus (Table 5). MTL improves the accuracy by 1.35% in SWDA task, while it leads to a gain of 3.94% on the disfluency task for the ASRoBERTa model. Ablation studies across the three categories to train MTL setup show that conversational and channel properties are important for SWDA task while disfluency relies most on conversational properties. The results justify our hypothesis that an LM that encodes the conversational, channel and ASR properties is better equipped for downstream tasks in spoken language understanding. The results also demonstrate that the properties learnt by the LM are transferable to unseen SLU tasks.

Another interesting observation is that ChatRoBERTa outperforms ASRoBERTa on SWDA dataset. Our rationale for this behavior is that SWDA dataset contains majority of utterances in grammatical forms with punctuation, which the real life dataset is devoid of. Higher resemblance of SWDA corpus to chat-dataset could be a reason for difference in performance of the two LMs.

7 Related Works

Recent years have seen a surge of works on the theme of neural network interpretability and understandability. A group of work has focused on unveiling secrets of language models (Clark et al., 2019; Jawahar et al., 2019). While Clark et al. (2019) probe the surface and linguistic patterns in the attention head of BERT through a set of probing tasks, Jawahar et al. (2019) throws light on structural understanding of the language captured by phrase and span representations. Other research works show limitations of LM such as ignoring negation and getting confused by simple distractors (Kassner and Schütze, 2020) in addition to BERT being inexact in encoding numeracy in its representations (Wallace et al., 2019).

There has also been research on probing LM on application specific representations such as question answering (van Aken et al., 2019), information retrieval (Yilmaz et al., 2019), recommendation systems (Penha and Hauff, 2020), dialog systems (Wu and Xiong, 2020) etc. The entire spectrum of these works aims to understand the learning capability and properties encoded in the LM along with discovering their shortcomings. The findings in these works have been utilized by the scientific community to create more robust language models: Zhang et al. (2020) propose Semantics-Aware BERT that performs better than vanilla BERT, while Wang et al. (2020b) demonstrate that incorporating sentence structure in pre-training LM pushes the results on downstream tasks.

However, a major section of work have primarily focused on interpreting LMs trained on clean text. SLU tasks come with their distinctive properties of ASR errors and non-grammatical, ill-punctuated texts. A spoken interaction additionally requires conversational and channel understandability as highlighted in this work. While works have been carried out in understanding disfluency (Wang et al., 2020a; Lin and Wang, 2020) and turn-taking (Aldeneh et al., 2018; Hara et al., 2018), the authors narrowly aim at improving the task specific results by modelling acoustic cues (Aldeneh et al., 2018; Kumar and Vepa, 2020) or training with auxiliary tasks (Aldeneh et al., 2018; Hara et al., 2018; Wang et al., 2020a; Sundararaman et al., 2021). The effort in our work is orthogonal to what has been carried out in the past research. We investigate the representations of language model on real-life and benchmark datasets to identify the strength, limitations and possibility of a generic LM under the lens of conversational, channel and ASR properties.

8 Conclusions and Future Work

We investigate the representations of language model across conversational, channel and ASR properties with probing tasks such as pause, disfluency, overtalk identification, speaker role prediction, turn-tasks and ASR error type. Empirical analysis shows that LM encodes conversational and speaker-type properties to a large extent without external supervision while it has lower performance on turn-tasks and ASR error prediction. Experiments also show that a language model trained on spoken transcripts loses the linguistic understanding of dependency relations. A set of MTL experiments demonstrate the efficacy and transferability of the probe tasks to an unseen SLU dataset that advocates a need and possibility of a domain specific LM. In future, we would like to research along a few directions that originates from this work: benchmarking properties-infused LM against multimodal counterparts and revisiting the pre-training setup to identify advanced mechanisms to infuse such properties. Additionally, we would also like to evaluate on other language models such as XL-Net, GPT etc. to understand the generalizability of the results.

References

Guillaume Alain and Yoshua Bengio. 2017. Understanding intermediate layers using linear classifier probes. In *5th International Conference on Learning Representations, ICLR 2017, Toulon, France, April 24-26, 2017, Workshop Track Proceedings*. OpenReview.net.

Zakaria Aldeneh, Dimitrios Dimitriadis, and Emily Mower Provost. 2018. Improving end-of-turn detection in spoken dialogues by detecting speaker intentions as a secondary task. In *2018 IEEE International Conference on Acoustics, Speech and Signal Processing, ICASSP 2018, Calgary, AB, Canada, April 15-20, 2018*, pages 6159–6163.

Pawel Budzianowski, Tsung-Hsien Wen, Bo-Hsiang Tseng, Iñigo Casanueva, Stefan Ultes, Osman Ramadan, and Milica Gasic. 2018. Multiwoz - A large-scale multi-domain wizard-of-oz dataset for task-oriented dialogue modelling. In *Proceedings of the 2018 Conference on Empirical Methods in Natural Language Processing, Brussels, Belgium, October 31 - November 4, 2018*, pages 5016–5026. Association for Computational Linguistics.

Sasha Calhoun, Jean Carletta, Jason M. Brenier, Neil Mayo, Dan Jurafsky, Mark Steedman, and David Beaver. 2010. The nxt-format switchboard corpus: a rich resource for investigating the syntax, semantics, pragmatics and prosody of dialogue. *Lang. Resour. Evaluation*, 44(4):387–419.

Kevin Clark, Urvashi Khandelwal, Omer Levy, and Christopher D. Manning. 2019. What does BERT look at? an analysis of bert's attention. *ACL Workshop BlackboxNLP: Analyzing and Interpreting Neural Networks for NLP*.

Alexis Conneau, Germán Kruszewski, Guillaume Lample, Loïc Barrault, and Marco Baroni. 2018. What you can cram into a single \$&!#* vector: Probing sentence embeddings for linguistic properties. In *Proceedings of the 56th Annual Meeting of the Association for Computational Linguistics, ACL 2018, Melbourne, Australia, July 15-20, 2018, Volume 1: Long Papers*, pages 2126–2136. Association for Computational Linguistics.

Jacob Devlin, Ming-Wei Chang, Kenton Lee, and Kristina Toutanova. 2019. BERT: pre-training of deep bidirectional transformers for language understanding. In *Proceedings of the 2019 Conference of the North American Chapter of the Association for Computational Linguistics: Human Language Technologies, NAACL-HLT 2019, MN, USA, June 2-7, 2019*, pages 4171–4186.

Tanvi Dinkar, Ioana Vasilescu, Catherine Pelachaud, and Chloé Clavel. 2020. How confident are you? exploring the role of fillers in the automatic prediction of a speaker's confidence. In *2020 IEEE International Conference on Acoustics, Speech and Signal Processing, ICASSP 2020, Barcelona, Spain, May 4-8, 2020*, pages 8104–8108.

Efthymios Georgiou, Charilaos Papaioannou, and Alexandros Potamianos. 2019. Deep hierarchical fusion with application in sentiment analysis. In *Interspeech 2019, 20th Annual Conference of the International Speech Communication Association, Graz, Austria, 15-19 September 2019*, pages 1646–1650.

Kohei Hara, Koji Inoue, Katsuya Takanashi, and Tatsuya Kawahara. 2018. Prediction of turn-taking using multitask learning with prediction of backchannels and fillers. In *Interspeech 2018, 19th Annual Conference of the International Speech Communication Association, Hyderabad, India, 2-6 September 2018*, pages 991–995.

Ganesh Jawahar, Benoît Sagot, and Djamé Seddah. 2019. What does BERT learn about the structure of language? In *Proceedings of the 57th Conference of the Association for Computational Linguistics, ACL 2019, Florence, Italy*, pages 3651–3657.

Nora Kassner and Hinrich Schütze. 2020. Negated and misprimed probes for pretrained language models: Birds can talk, but cannot fly. In *Proceedings of the 58th Annual Meeting of the Association for Computational Linguistics, ACL*, pages 7811–7818.

Jonggu Kim, Yewon Jeong, and Jong-Hyeok Lee. 2020. Speaker-informed time-and-content-aware attention for spoken language understanding. *Computer Speech & Language*, 60:101022.

Ayush Kumar and Jithendra Vepa. 2020. Gated mechanism for attention based multi modal sentiment analysis. In *2020 IEEE International Conference on Acoustics, Speech and Signal Processing, ICASSP 2020, Barcelona, Spain*, pages 4477–4481.

Zhongli Li, Qingyu Zhou, Chao Li, Ke Xu, and Yunbo Cao. 2020. Improving BERT with syntax-aware local attention. *CoRR*, abs/2012.15150.

Binghuai Lin and Liyuan Wang. 2020. Joint prediction of punctuation and disfluency in speech transcripts. In *Interspeech 2020, 21st Annual Conference of the International Speech Communication Association, Virtual Event, Shanghai, China*, pages 716–720.

Yinhan Liu, Myle Ott, Naman Goyal, Jingfei Du, Mandar Joshi, Danqi Chen, Omer Levy, Mike Lewis, Luke Zettlemoyer, and Veselin Stoyanov. 2019. Roberta: A robustly optimized BERT pretraining approach. *CoRR*, abs/1907.11692.

Mitchell P. Marcus, Beatrice Santorini, and Mary Ann Marcinkiewicz. 1993. Building a large annotated corpus of english: The penn treebank. *Comput. Linguistics*, 19(2):313–330.

Mahdi Namazifar, Gökhan Tür, and Dilek Hakkani-Tür. 2021. Warped language models for noise robust language understanding. In *IEEE Spoken Language*

Technology Workshop, SLT 2021, Shenzhen, China, January 19-22, 2021, pages 981–988. IEEE.

Vassil Panayotov, Guoguo Chen, Daniel Povey, and Sanjeev Khudanpur. 2015. Librispeech: An ASR corpus based on public domain audio books. In *2015 IEEE International Conference on Acoustics, Speech and Signal Processing, ICASSP 2015, South Brisbane, Queensland, Australia, April 19-24, 2015*, pages 5206–5210. IEEE.

Gustavo Penha and Claudia Hauff. 2020. What does BERT know about books, movies and music? probing BERT for conversational recommendation. In *RecSys 2020: Fourteenth ACM Conference on Recommender Systems, Virtual Event, Brazil, September 22-26, 2020*, pages 388–397.

Matthew Roddy, Gabriel Skantze, and Naomi Harte. 2018. Investigating speech features for continuous turn-taking prediction using lstms. In *Interspeech 2018, 19th Annual Conference of the International Speech Communication Association, Hyderabad, India, 2-6 September 2018*, pages 586–590.

Dhanasekar Sundararaman, Vivek Subramanian, Guoyin Wang, Shijing Si, Dinghan Shen, Dong Wang, and Lawrence Carin. 2019. Syntax-infused transformer and BERT models for machine translation and natural language understanding. *CoRR*, abs/1911.06156.

Mukuntha Narayanan Sundararaman, Ayush Kumar, and Jithendra Vepa. 2021. PhonemeBERT: Joint Language Modelling of Phoneme Sequence and ASR Transcript. In *Proc. Interspeech 2021*, pages 3236–3240.

Ian Tenney, Patrick Xia, Berlin Chen, Alex Wang, Adam Poliak, R. Thomas McCoy, Najoung Kim, Benjamin Van Durme, Samuel R. Bowman, Dipanjan Das, and Ellie Pavlick. 2019. What do you learn from context? probing for sentence structure in contextualized word representations. In *7th International Conference on Learning Representations, ICLR 2019, New Orleans, LA, USA*.

Betty van Aken, Benjamin Winter, Alexander Löser, and Felix A. Gers. 2019. How does BERT answer questions?: A layer-wise analysis of transformer representations. In *Proceedings of the 28th ACM International Conference on Information and Knowledge Management, CIKM 2019, Beijing, China*, pages 1823–1832.

Eric Wallace, Yizhong Wang, Sujian Li, Sameer Singh, and Matt Gardner. 2019. Do NLP models know numbers? probing numeracy in embeddings. In *Proceedings of the 2019 Conference on Empirical Methods in Natural Language Processing and the 9th International Joint Conference on Natural Language Processing, EMNLP-IJCNLP 2019, Hong Kong, China*, pages 5306–5314.

Shaolei Wang, Wanxiang Che, Qi Liu, Pengda Qin, Ting Liu, and William Yang Wang. 2020a. Multi-task self-supervised learning for disfluency detection. In *The Thirty-Fourth AAAI Conference on Artificial Intelligence, AAAI 2020, The Thirty-Second Innovative Applications of Artificial Intelligence Conference, IAAI 2020, The Tenth AAAI Symposium on Educational Advances in Artificial Intelligence, EAAI 2020, New York, NY, USA, February 7-12, 2020*, pages 9193–9200.

Wei Wang, Bin Bi, Ming Yan, Chen Wu, Jiangnan Xia, Zuyi Bao, Liwei Peng, and Luo Si. 2020b. Structbert: Incorporating language structures into pre-training for deep language understanding. In *8th International Conference on Learning Representations, ICLR 2020, Addis Ababa, Ethiopia*.

Jochen Weiner, Mathis Engelbart, and Tanja Schultz. 2017. Manual and automatic transcriptions in dementia detection from speech. In *Interspeech 2017, 18th Annual Conference of the International Speech Communication Association, Stockholm, Sweden, August 20-24, 2017*, pages 3117–3121.

Chien-Sheng Wu and Caiming Xiong. 2020. Probing task-oriented dialogue representation from language models. In *Proceedings of the 2020 Conference on Empirical Methods in Natural Language Processing, EMNLP 2020, Online, November 16-20, 2020*, pages 5036–5051.

Zeynep Akkalyoncu Yilmaz, Wei Yang, Haotian Zhang, and Jimmy Lin. 2019. Cross-domain modeling of sentence-level evidence for document retrieval. In *Proceedings of the 2019 Conference on Empirical Methods in Natural Language Processing and the 9th International Joint Conference on Natural Language Processing, EMNLP-IJCNLP 2019, Hong Kong, China, November 3-7, 2019*, pages 3488–3494.

Vicky Zayats, Trang Tran, Richard A. Wright, Courtney Mansfield, and Mari Ostendorf. 2019. Disfluencies and human speech transcription errors. In *Interspeech 2019, 20th Annual Conference of the International Speech Communication Association, Graz, Austria, 15-19 September 2019*, pages 3088–3092.

Rui Zhang, Honglak Lee, Lazaros Polymenakos, and Dragomir R. Radev. 2018a. Addressee and response selection in multi-party conversations with speaker interaction rnns. In *Proceedings of the Thirty-Second AAAI Conference on Artificial Intelligence, (AAAI-18), the 30th innovative Applications of Artificial Intelligence (IAAI-18), and the 8th AAAI Symposium on Educational Advances in Artificial Intelligence (EAAI-18), New Orleans, Louisiana, USA, February 2-7, 2018*, pages 5690–5697.

Saizheng Zhang, Emily Dinan, Jack Urbanek, Arthur Szlam, Douwe Kiela, and Jason Weston. 2018b. Personalizing dialogue agents: I have a dog, do you have pets too? In *Proceedings of the 56th Annual*

Meeting of the Association for Computational Linguistics, ACL 2018, Melbourne, Australia, July 15-20, 2018, Volume 1: Long Papers, pages 2204–2213. Association for Computational Linguistics.

Zhuosheng Zhang, Yuwei Wu, Hai Zhao, Zuchao Li, Shuailiang Zhang, Xi Zhou, and Xiang Zhou. 2020. Semantics-aware BERT for language understanding. In *The Thirty-Fourth AAAI Conference on Artificial Intelligence, AAAI 2020, The Thirty-Second Innovative Applications of Artificial Intelligence Conference, IAAI 2020, 10th AAAI Symposium on Educational Advances in Artificial Intelligence, EAAI 2020, New York, NY, USA, February 7-12, 2020*, pages 9628–9635.

A Appendix

A.1 Dataset Creation

In this section, we describe the methodology used to curate the dataset for each probing tasks mentioned in Section 2.

A.1.1 Conversational Properties

- **Disfluency Detection**: To create the dataset for disfluency we follow two-step process: i) candidate retrieval, ii) manual annotation. For candidate retrieval, we have a couple of pipelines, one relying on lexical cues and another taking hints from the speech cues. For lexical cues, we use a simple keyphrase based lookup to identify the candidate speaker utterances containing markers for disfluency such as repetition of words, filler words and discourse markers. We, however, note that lexical cues only forms a subset of all disfluencies. To include speech induced disfluencies, we identify turns that contains multiple intermittent pauses within a short time frame. This candidate extraction ensures that we are probing a lexical model on its capability to understand disfluencies that are not keyword based and hence a greater semantic understanding is needed to locate such disfluent contexts in the spoken transcripts. Once such candidates are obtained, we use manual annotators to label them into fluent and disfluent categories, thus generating a binary classification dataset.

- **Pause Identification**: The dataset for pause identification is generated by retrieving all utterances where speaker takes one or more pauses longer than 5 seconds in an individual turn. Additionally, we exclude all such utterances that could be a disfluent candidate. The rationale behind such decision is to ensure that we not add bias in the pause identification probe setup such that disfluent markers lead to a better pause understanding. In this case, there is no need for manual annotation as the pause duration obtained from the speech information acts as gold label for the utterances. We frame pause identification as a binary classification where one class denotes that speaker takes a pause longer than 5 sec. in a given turn of the conversation while other class denotes the absence of pauses in the turn.

- **Overtalk Detection**: An overtalk in a given dual speaker conversation would like Table 6. These leads to broken and incomprehensible turns compared to their clean versions of transcripts. While it is easy to detect such overtalk when the recording lines itself are unique to speakers, this is an arduous task for monochannel recordings. Thus, we curiously probe the language model to see if it is able to detect transcripts with overtalks. We follow a simple mechanism to curate overtalk dataset: we identify overtalk via rule based system from dual channel call and create corresponding monochannel transcripts (AB-mono in Table 6). These monochannel transcripts are dataset that belong to 'overtalk' label. Any non-overtalk transcript from a single speaker belong to 'non-overtalk' label. Thus, overtalk detection too is a binary classification task.

Speaker	Transcript
A	i'm
B	yes
A	not
B	i know
A	referring to
B	how
A	transaction
B	it works
A - clean	*i'm not referring to transaction*
B - clean	*yes i know how it works*
AB-mono	*i'm yes not i know referring to how transaction it works*

Table 6: An example of a dual channel transcript containing overtalk. A-clean, B-clean refers to rewriting what A and B's transcript would look like if had they not spoken over each other.

- **Question Identification**: Question identification is a non-trivial problem in spoken language transcripts due to inaccurate predictions and non-surface question constructs, such as:

and you would like me to continue. In the example, the speaker intends to actually ask a question if he/she can continue further. To create question dataset, we follow a similar two step process: i) candidate generation; and ii) manual annotation. For candidate generation, we two approaches: a) question keyphrases based lookup; and b) using speaker replies that indicate presence of boolen answers such as *yes that's true* or entities such as *sure, it would be ninety five dollars*. Once candidate turns are collected, we ask manual annotators to mark the question span and the category of the question.

A.1.2 Channel Properties

- **Speaker Role**: We restrict the domain of the dataset to call center conversations with two speaker roles: a) agent and b) customer. These two speakers have distinctive properties as per their role, agent are expected to be fluent while being empathetic and enthusiastic towards the customers. Customers, on the other hand, are calling to raise their concerns or ask for help with many cases of heated engagements with agents. Thus, we create a speaker role binary classification dataset with two classes: agent and customer obtained directly from dual channel calls.

- **Response-Length**: To create dataset for this task, we use the time-duration of an utterance's response to categorize it into a short response if it is is less than 30 seconds of duration. For response lasting longer than 30 seconds are considered to be long response. The utterance is what is taken as consideration in the dataset with the label being short or long depending on the utterance's response length. To arrive at the duration, we discard turns in the initial 5%ile and last 5%ile category based on the turn duration in order to remove outliers. For the remaining dataset, we choose the time period that belongs to the 50th percentile.

- **Turn-Taking**: We pose the task as a binary classification task where a label of 'turn-continue' would mean that with the given utterance, the speaker has not yet finished speaking and hence would add on further, while a label of 'turn-break' would refer to the scenario where speaker has finished its turn of speaking.

A.1.3 ASR Properties

- **Error Type Prediction**: We obtain spoken transcripts from automatic speech recognition system. Additionally, we get manual transcripts for the same set of calls. We run alignment over the parallel corpus to identify the categories of errors for each token in spoken transcripts. We formulate two tasks for error type prediction: binary classification where the model only needs to predict if the token under consideration is erroneous; and multi-class classification in which for any erroneous token, the model needs to predict the error type: insertion, deletion or substitution.

- **WER Prediction**: From the dataset obtained in the above task, we compute the word error rate for the spoken transcript as compared to manual transcripts. A regression model is trained for this task.

A.2 Token Baseline

In addition to the three setups present in Section 5, we also evaluate a ngram based token baseline to contrast the performance observed from language model based probe classifiers. We use ngram features upto quadgrams as input to the model. We use logistic and linear regression for all classification and regression tasks respectively. The results for token baseline is presented in Table 7.

Probe Tasks	Token Baseline
Pause	70.05
Disfluency	66.55
Overtalk	60.94
Question	69.49
Speaker	79.75
Response-Length	65.25
Turn-Taking	58.29
Binary	54.34
Insertion	50.29
Deletion	49.26
Substitution	41.33
WER	10.31

Table 7

A.3 Attention Scores

In this section, we show the variation in average attention scores between a pair of tokens across

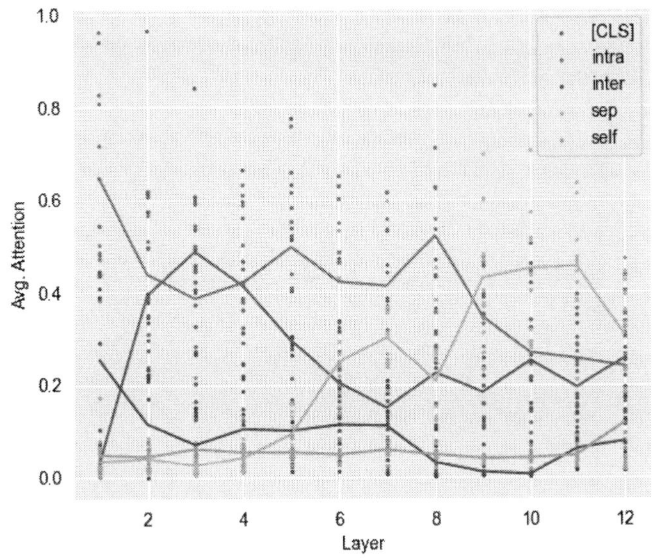

(a) Average attention scores for ASRoBERTa across all layers. The graph shows that inter-sentence attention (ISA) is low for all layers except the initial layer. *[CLS]* and *sep* corresponds to <*s*> and </*s*> in ASRoBERTa.

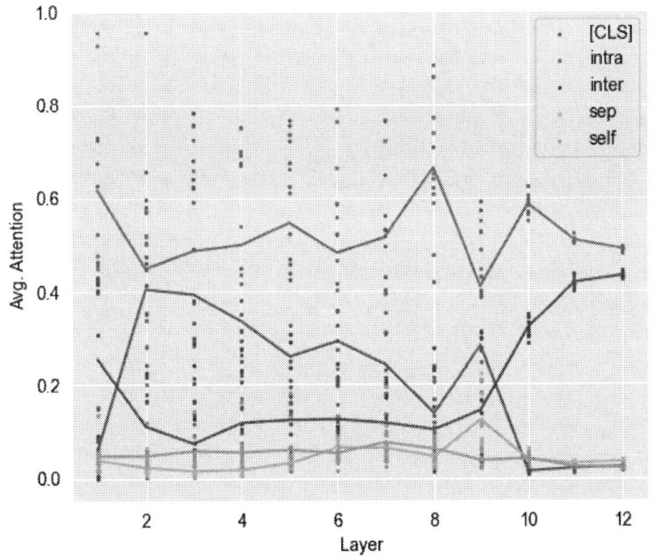

(b) Average attention scores across all layers for ASRoBERTa trained on next-sentence-prediction (NSP) task. The graph shows that inter-sentence attention (ISA) goes up, especially for final layer suggesting that inter-sentence understanding is needed for solving NSP task. *[CLS]* and *sep* corresponds to <*s*> and </*s*> in ASRoBERTa.

all layers for ASRoBERTa model trained only on masked language modelling (MLM) task and ASRoBERTa-NSP model which is further fine-tuned on next-sentence-prediction (NSP) task. The graphs demonstrate that inter-sentence scores rise in final layers (Figure 1b) indicating the need of inter-sentence interaction for solving NSP task. The code for graph generation has been adapted from the paper by Clark et al. (2019).

Assessing the Generalization Capacity of Pre-trained Language Models through Japanese Adversarial Natural Language Inference

Hitomi Yanaka[1] **and Koji Mineshima**[2]
[1]The University of Tokyo, [2]Keio University
hyanaka@is.s.u-tokyo.ac.jp, minesima@abelard.flet.keio.ac.jp

Abstract

Despite the success of multilingual pre-trained language models, it remains unclear to what extent these models have human-like generalization capacity across languages. The aim of this study is to investigate the out-of-distribution generalization of pre-trained language models through Natural Language Inference (NLI) in Japanese, the typological properties of which are different from those of English. We introduce a synthetically generated Japanese NLI dataset, called the Japanese Adversarial NLI (JaNLI) dataset, which is inspired by the English HANS dataset and is designed to require understanding of Japanese linguistic phenomena and illuminate the vulnerabilities of models. Through a series of experiments to evaluate the generalization performance of both Japanese and multilingual BERT models, we demonstrate that there is much room to improve current models trained on Japanese NLI tasks. Furthermore, a comparison of human performance and model performance on the different types of garden-path sentences in the JaNLI dataset shows that structural phenomena that ease interpretation of garden-path sentences for human readers do not help models in the same way, highlighting a difference between human readers and the models.

1 Introduction

Generalization is one of the essential components that account for the understanding of language. In recent years, pre-trained models such as BERT (Devlin et al., 2019) have provided high performance on both English benchmarks (Wang et al., 2019) and multilingual benchmarks (Liang et al., 2020), suggesting that they might have some cross-lingual generalization capacity. Yet, while these models have achieved remarkable performance on an in-distribution test set (i.e., training and test splits are given as the same distribution), several previous studies have pointed out that the models fail on out-of-distribution test sets (i.e., examples drawn from a distribution different from that of the training set) (Marvin and Linzen, 2018; McCoy et al., 2019) and that the models varied widely in terms of the generalization performance (McCoy et al., 2020; Yanaka et al., 2020). It remains an open question to what extent pre-trained models can realize human-like generalization ability.

A standard task for assessing whether pre-trained language models possess human-like language understanding is Natural Language Inference (NLI), which is the task of judging whether a premise sentence entails a hypothesis sentence. Recently, a number of studies have sought to probe the generalization performance of models and detected their fallible heuristics with various NLI datasets (Naik et al., 2018; Glockner et al., 2018; McCoy et al., 2019; Rozen et al., 2019; Goodwin et al., 2020; Yanaka et al., 2021). However, these studies tend to focus on English NLI datasets, and independent analysis in multiple languages would be desirable. In response to this challenge, the study of the out-of-distribution generalization ability of NLI models from cross-lingual perspectives has begun to be explored (Hu et al., 2021) but is not yet fully developed.

The aim of this paper is to investigate to what extent pre-trained language models have generalization capacity in Japanese NLI. For this purpose, we present a Japanese linguistically challenging NLI dataset, called the Japanese Adversarial NLI (JaNLI) dataset.[1] This dataset is inspired by the English HANS dataset (McCoy et al., 2019) and is designed to cover a variety of linguistic phenomena specific to Japanese, a language typologically different from English (Hinds, 1986; Shibatani, 1990). Generating inference examples in a controlled way allows us to analyze whether language models are sensitive to factors such as word order and syntactic

[1]The dataset will be publicly available at https://github.com/verypluming/JaNLI.

Proceedings of the Fourth BlackboxNLP Workshop on Analyzing and Interpreting Neural Networks for NLP, pages 337–349
Online, November 11, 2021.

structure in Japanese.

We present a series of experiments with the JaNLI dataset to evaluate the generalization performance of Japanese and multilingual BERT models. In addition, we compare human performance with model performance. Our experiments shed light on several shortcomings of the models and highlight the following challenges for cross-lingual generalization in NLI:

- Japanese and multilingual NLI models trained on Japanese NLI datasets other than JaNLI behave differently across different classes of sentences. In particular, cross-dataset generalization on non-entailing pairs is weaker on non-entailing pairs than on entailing pairs (Section 4.2).

- Data augmentation with a small subset of the JaNLI dataset can help improve model performance, but the accuracy is not increased for some linguistic phenomena (Section 4.3).

- Whereas humans can achieve near-perfect performance on the JaNLI dataset, there is substantial room for improving the models for Japanese NLI. In addition, structural phenomena that ease the interpretation of garden-path sentences for human readers do not help the models in the same way (Section 4.4).

2 Related Work

Previous studies have probed pre-trained language models on various NLI tasks and discovered that generalization capacity is limited for understanding diverse linguistic phenomena (Naik et al., 2018; Glockner et al., 2018; McCoy et al., 2019; Rozen et al., 2019; Goodwin et al., 2020; Yanaka et al., 2020; Hu et al., 2021; Yanaka et al., 2021) and annotation artifacts (Gururangan et al., 2018) in standard English NLI datasets such as the SNLI (Bowman et al., 2015) and MultiNLI (Williams et al., 2018) datasets. The work most closely related to ours is HANS (McCoy et al., 2019), which is an NLI dataset designed to analyze whether models use structural heuristics to make predictions. Recently, HANS has been used for out-of-distribution evaluation data (Utama et al., 2020; Tu et al., 2020; Yaghoobzadeh et al., 2021; Du et al., 2021) and has been used for data augmentation to improve the generalization performance of models (Min et al., 2020).

Although the generalization capacity of NLI models has been studied mainly in English, non-English NLI datasets (Ham et al., 2020; Hu et al., 2020; Wijnholds and Moortgat, 2021) and multilingual NLI datasets (Conneau et al., 2018) have recently been developed to analyze the performance of pre-trained language models across languages. Several Japanese NLI datasets have been created. The Japanese SNLI dataset (Yoshikoshi et al., 2020) was generated by automatic translation of the English SNLI dataset. The Japanese Realistic Textual Entailment Corpus (Hayashibe, 2020) was created by using realistic texts (hotel reviews) and annotating labels via crowdsourcing. JSeM (Kawazoe et al., 2017) is a Japanese version of the FraCaS test suite (Cooper et al., 1994), which contains manually designed problems involving semantic phenomena that have been well studied in formal semantics. Our dataset is designed to assess whether models capture linguistic structures in Japanese or simply rely on fallible heuristics.

Recent work (Sinha et al., 2021a,b; Gupta et al., 2021; Pham et al., 2021) has shown that shuffled word order has little effect during training or inference with pre-trained language models, which in turn indicates that the models are insensitive to word order in NLI tasks. In English, however, the shuffled data are usually unacceptable and tend to obscure their gold labels. Kuribayashi et al. (2021) have re-analyzed the hypothesis that language models with lower perplexity are more human-like language models in Japanese rather than in English, and their experiments have demonstrated the lack of universality of this hypothesis and the importance of cross-lingual evaluation of models. Japanese word order is fairly free, which enables us to produce grammatically correct sentences even when the word order is shuffled. Analyzing the behavior of models on controlled Japanese inference examples should provide further insights into the sensitivity of the models to word order.

3 Dataset Generation

To analyze the generalization capacity of NLI models, we introduce a synthetically generated Japanese NLI dataset where each pair (P, H) of a premise and hypothesis is tagged with a label for *structural pattern* and *linguistic phenomenon*. Table 1 shows the definition of each pattern and some examples.

Pattern/Description	Example
FULL OVERLAP *P* and *H* share all words and differ only in word order.	Phenomena: Scrambling (Particle-swapping) *P*: ライダー が サーファー を 助け出した **rider ga surfer o rescued** (*The rider rescued the surfer*) *H*: ライダー を サーファー が 助け出した **rider o surfer ga rescued** (*The surfer rescued the rider*)
ORDER-PRESERVING SUBSET All the words in *H* are contained in *P* in an order-preserving way.	Phenomena: NP-coordination (disjunction) *P*: 学生 か 子供 が 遊んでいる **student** or child **ga playing** (*The student or the child is playing*) *H*: 学生 が 遊んでいる **student ga playing** (*The student is playing*)
MIXED SUBSET All the words in *H* are contained in *P* in a mixed (non-order-preserving) way.	Phenomena: Garden-path *P*: 子供 が 泳いでいる 学生 を 助け出した **child ga** swimming **student o rescued** (*The child rescued the swimming student*) *H*: 子供 を 学生 が 助け出した **child o student ga rescued** (*The student rescued the child.*)
SUBSEQUENCE *H* is a contiguous subsequence of *P* but not a constituent of *P*.	Phenomena: Garden-path *P*: 男の子 が 眠っている 女の子 を 見ている **boy ga sleeping** girl o looking (*The boy is looking at the sleeping girl*) *H*: 男の子 が 眠っている **boy ga sleeping** (*The boy is sleeping*)
CONSTITUENT *H* is a constituent of *P*.	Phenomena: Modal *P*: ひょっとしたら 子供 が 眠っている perhaps **child ga sleeping** (*Perhaps the child is sleeping*) *H*: 子供 が 眠っている **child ga sleeping** (*The child is sleeping*)

Table 1: Five patterns of structural relations between premise (*P*) and hypothesis (*H*) sentences: All the examples are *non-entailment*. が(ga) is a nominative case marker; を(o) is an accusative case marker.

3.1 Structural patterns and heuristics

We classify the structural relationship between premise and hypothesis sentences into five patterns, each of which is associated with a type of *heuristic* that can cause incorrect prediction of the entailment relation. For instance, a model that relies on the heuristics of judging an inference as *entailment* when the premise and hypothesis sentences share all the words will make an incorrect prediction for a non-entailment relation. We follow McCoy et al. (2019) for the definitions of the SUBSEQUENCE and CONSTITUENT patterns. McCoy et al. (2019) also proposed the *overlap* heuristics (*H* is constructed from words in *P*), which we divide into three types: FULL-OVERLAP, ORDER-PRESERVING SUBSET (ORDER-SUBSET in short), and MIXED-SUBSET. Note that these five patterns are defined to be mutually exclusive. This fine-grained classification of overlap is suitable for analysis taking into account the characteristics of Japanese that word order is relatively free (Hinds, 1986; Shibatani, 1990). We explore whether language models can perform better on some patterns compared with others.

3.2 Linguistic phenomena

To generate these five patterns of adversarial inferences in a controlled way, we focus on 11 categories of Japanese linguistic phenomena and constructions: garden-path sentences with noun-modifying clauses, scrambling (including particle-swapping), passive, causative, factive adverbs, factive verbs, modal, negation, NP-coordination, sentence-subordination (those corresponding to *because*-clauses and *if*-clauses), and sentence-coordination (sentence conjunction and disjunction).

For each phenomenon, we fix a template for the premise sentence P and create multiple templates for hypothesis sentences H. In total, we produced 144 templates for (P, H) pairs. Each pair of premise and hypothesis sentences is tagged with an entailment label (*entailment* or *non-entailment*), a structural pattern, and a linguistic phenomenon label. Table 2 shows an example template for garden-path sentences with noun-modifying clauses. See Appendix A for examples of templates for each linguistic phenomenon.

To evaluate the performance of NLI models for Japanese, the garden-path construction as shown in Table 2 deserves special attention. In this example, the challenge is to detect the boundary of the noun-modifying clause in the premise sentence P as [child ga [$_{\text{NP}}$ running cat] o chased]. Here the noun *cat* (猫) is the head of the NP with the noun-modifier *running* (走っている); when this noun is processed in the entire sentence, the subject *child* (子供) must be reanalyzed out of the clause so that *running* applies to *cat*, not to *child*. Thus, P entails H_2 (*The cat is running*) but not H_1 (*The child is running*).

Some factors are known to facilitate the interpretation of garden-path sentences (Miyamoto, 2008). We analyze whether the model predicts the entailment labels more accurately when the inference example includes such factors. We categorized problems involving garden-path sentences according to four factors that make it easier for people to interpret them: double-o-constraints (GP-double-o) (Miyamoto, 2002), presence of punctuations (GP-punctuation), selectional preference (GP-selectional) (Inoue, 2006), and presence of the topic marker *wa* (GP-wa) (Inoue, 1991). We also include the construction where the subject and object NPs of a garden-path sentence are swapped so that no garden-path effect can occur (GP-scrambling). Table 3 shows an example of each construction.

In the psycholinguistics literature, it has been observed that the processing of garden-path sentences becomes more difficult when they contain more NP-arguments (Inoue, 1990). Thus, we tagged inference problems with the number of NP-arguments.

3.3 Dataset overview

The JaNLI dataset was automatically generated by instantiating each template 100 times, resulting in a total of 14,400 examples. Table 4 shows the statistics of the linguistic phenomena. We generated the same number of entailment and non-entailment examples for each phenomenon. Table 5 shows the statistics of the structural patterns (heuristics). Note that the ratio of entailment and non-entailment examples is not necessarily $1:1$ for each pattern. This is because we first generated the templates for each linguistic phenomenon and then annotated the structural pattern with the templates.

We used 158 words (nouns and verbs) in total. Nouns and simple verbs were selected from words that occur more than 20 times in the JSICK and JSNLI datasets. Compound verbs were selected from the Compound Verb Lexicon[2]. Each transitive and intransitive verb was selected so that every noun (basically, denoting a human) is a plausible argument of it.

4 Experiments and Analysis

4.1 Experimental setting

One of our aims is to investigate the differences in behavior between monolingual and multilingual pre-trained language models. For this purpose, we conducted experiments with BERT (Devlin et al., 2019), a standard pre-trained language model that is widely used for both multilingual and Japanese texts. We compared the difference in performance between the Japanese and multilingual BERT models, which were implemented by using the transformers framework[3]. In all experiments, we trained each model for 30 epochs with early stopping (patience = 3). We perform five runs and report the average and standard deviation of the accuracy of the models.

Model Japanese BERT is pre-trained on Japanese Wikipedia, and the model processes input texts with word-level tokenization based on a standard Japanese dictionary (ipadic) (Asahara and Matsumoto, 2003), followed by the WordPiece subword tokenization (Schuster and Nakajima, 2012), trained with whole-word masking enabled for the masked language model objective. For multilingual BERT, we used a multilingual-cased model pre-trained on Wikipedia in 104 languages including Japanese, which is more recommended over a multilingual-uncased model in the case of languages with non-Latin alphabets like Japanese.

Training data To see whether the size and quality of training data affect the performance, we

[2]https://db4.ninjal.ac.jp/vvlexicon/en/

[3]https://github.com/huggingface/transformers

Templates for P and H	Sentence Example	Phenomenon/Pattern
P: NP1 ga IV NP2 o TV-o	子供 が 走っている 猫 を 追いかけた child ga running cat o chased *(The child chased the running cat)*	Garden-path sentence
$\nRightarrow H_1$: NP1 ga IV	子供 が 走っている *(The child is running)*	SUBSEQUENCE
$\Rightarrow H_2$: NP2 ga IV	猫 が 走っている *(The cat is running)*	MIXED-SUBSET
$\Rightarrow H_3$: NP1 ga NP2 o TV-o	子供 が 猫 を 追いかけた *(The child chased the cat)*	ORDER-SUBSET
$\nRightarrow H_4$: NP1 o NP2 ga TV-o	子供 を 猫 が 追いかけた *(The cat chased the child)*	MIXED-SUBSET

Table 2: Example templates for premise and hypothesis sentences. The premise P is a garden-path sentence with a noun-modifying clause. "$\Rightarrow$" indicates *entailment* and "$\nRightarrow$" *non-entailment*.

Subcategory	Template	Example
GP-double-o	NP1 ga NP2 o TV-o1 NP3 o TV-o2	子供 が 猫 を 助けた 女の子 を 追いかけた child ga cat o rescued girl o chased *(The child chased the girl who rescued the cat)*
GP-punctuation	NP1 ga , IV NP2 o TV-o	子供 が , 走っている 猫 を 追いかけた child ga PUNCT running cat o chased *(The child chased the running cat)*
GP-selectional	NP-non-human ga IV-human NP2 o TV-o	リス が しゃべっている 女性 を 追いかけた squirrel ga talking woman o chased *(The squirrel chased the woman who was talking)*
GP-wa	NP1 wa IV NP2 o TV-o	子供 は 走っている 猫 を 追いかけた child wa running cat o chased *(The child chased the running cat)*
GP-scrambling	IV NP2 o NP1 ga TV-o	走っている 猫 を 子供 が 追いかけた running cat o child ga chased *(The child chased the running cat)*

Table 3: Example templates for variants of garden-path sentences in the premise sentence.

Linguistic Phenomenon	Examples (Templates)
GP-normal	1,600 (16)
GP-double-o	800 (8)
GP-punctuation	800 (8)
GP-selectional	800 (8)
GP-wa	800 (8)
GP-scrambling	1,600 (16)
Scrambling	1,600 (16)
Passive	400 (4)
Causative	400 (4)
Factive adverb	800 (8)
Factive verb	800 (8)
Modal	600 (6)
Negation	600 (6)
NP-coordination	1,200 (12)
Sentence-subordination	800 (8)
Sentence-coordination	800 (8)
Total	14,400 (144)

Table 4: Statistics of linguistic phenomena.

Pattern (Heuristics)	Entailment	Non-entailment	Total
FULL-OVERLAP	800	1,200	2,000
ORDER-SUBSET	1,600	800	2,400
MIXED-SUBSET	3,400	2,000	5,400
SUBSEQUENCE	200	2,000	2,200
CONSTITUENT	1,200	1,200	2,400
Total	7,200	7,200	14,400

Table 5: Statistics of structural patterns.

use two types of Japanese datasets as basic training datasets: JSICK and JSNLI (Yoshikoshi et al., 2020)[4]. Table 6 shows the data split and examples from the JSICK and JSNLI datasets. We compare the model performance on the in-distribution test sets (JSICK and JSNLI) with that on the out-of-distribution test set (JaNLI). While the JSICK and JSNLI datasets use three labels (*entailment*, *contradiction*, and *neutral*), the JaNLI dataset uses two labels (*entailment* and *non-entailment*), following the HANS dataset (McCoy et al., 2019). To calculate the model accuracy on each test set, we take the highest-scoring label out of *entailment*, *contradiction*, and *neutral* and then collapse *contradiction* and *neutral* into *non-entailment*.

JSICK was created by manually translating SICK (Marelli et al., 2014), an English NLI dataset that targets compositional inference, into Japanese by experts. Marelli et al. (2014) created the original SICK dataset by expanding and normalizing the sentences from Flickr image captions with manual rules to create inference examples involving such linguistically challenging phenomena as negation, disjunction, and active-passive alternation. We ex-

[4]https://nlp.ist.i.kyoto-u.ac.jp/index.php

Dataset	Training	Test	Creation Protocol	Classes	Inference Example	Label
JSICK	5.0K	4.9K	Manual Translation	3	*P*: 水難救助をして救命胴着を着ている人は一人もいない *Nobody is practicing water safety and wearing preservers* *H*: このグループの人々は水難救助を練習していて，救命胴着具を着ている *This group of people is practicing water safety and wearing preservers*	*Contradiction (Non-entailment)*
JSNLI	533K	3.9K	Automatic Translation	3	*P*: 自転車に乗る赤と白のジャケットの女性 *The woman in a red and white jacket riding a bicycle* *H*: 女性が自転車に乗る *The woman is riding a bicycle*	*Entailment*
JaNLI	-	14K	Templates	2	*P*: 走っている猫を子供が追いかけた *The child chased the running cat* *H*: 子供が走っている *The child is running*	*Non-entailment*

Table 6: Overview of the Japanese NLI datasets considered in this study.

Model	Finetuned on	Test-overall		Correct: *Entailment*					Correct: *Non-entailment*				
		In-dist.	JaNLI	Full.	Order.	Mixed.	Subseq.	Const.	Full.	Order.	Mixed.	Subseq.	Const.
Ja	JSICK (5K)	92.1±0.01	51.3±0.01	99.9±0.00	97.8±0.02	79.4±0.10	98.3±0.02	88.6±0.07	0.1±0.00	6.2±0.01	6.7±0.04	32.5±0.11	22.7±0.09
	+JaNLI (0.7K)	92.3±0.01	89.3±0.06	90.8±0.04	98.6±0.01	96.8±0.02	99.2±0.01	97.3±0.02	67.1±0.17	59.1±0.04	84.6±0.23	92.4±0.09	90.4±0.05
	JSNLI (533K)	94.5±0.00	50.4±0.00	98.6±0.02	99.0±0.01	97.2±0.02	97.7±0.02	99.6±0.00	6.8±0.06	4.6±0.04	2.6±0.03	1.1±0.02	0.1±0.00
	+JaNLI (0.7K)	95.5±0.00	72.3±0.01	71.7±0.03	88.4±0.03	81.4±0.07	85.0±0.16	92.5±0.05	53.4±0.07	46.6±0.10	69.2±0.16	48.5±0.03	67.9±0.25
Multi	JSICK (5K)	73.6±0.20	50.2±0.01	66.0±0.57	64.6±0.56	57.1±0.50	62.7±0.55	63.8±0.55	33.9±0.57	34.7±0.57	36.2±0.55	45.1±0.48	43.5±0.49
	+JaNLI (0.7K)	86.5±0.08	56.9±0.06	40.8±0.37	32.9±0.33	38.0±0.35	49.8±0.44	38.8±0.36	64.2±0.33	66.0±0.37	83.3±0.19	77.4±0.32	80.9±0.23
	JSNLI (533K)	94.6±0.01	49.7±0.00	99.0±0.01	99.2±0.01	97.3±0.01	98.8±0.01	99.2±0.01	2.0±0.02	1.6±0.01	0.8±0.01	1.2±0.01	0.8±0.01
	+JaNLI (0.7K)	94.8±0.01	56.3±0.09	26.4±0.46	30.4±0.53	28.0±0.49	26.7±0.46	28.4±0.49	79.4±0.36	76.9±0.40	82.4±0.30	26.7±0.46	79.0±0.36
Human		-	94.0±0.04	94.2±0.05	97.1±0.01	92.7 ±0.04	100.0±0.00	98.3±0.03	97.8±0.01	95.8±0.05	88.7±0.09	94.3±0.08	91.1±0.14

Table 7: Results on the JaNLI test set (average accuracy and standard deviation of five runs). The number in parentheses is the size of the dataset used for finetuning. The accuracy on the in-distribution test set (JSICK/JSNLI test sets) is calculated by translating the *contradiction* and *neutral* labels into *non-entailment*.

Model	Finetuned on	GP	Scramb.	Pass.	Caus.	Fac-adv.	Fac-v.	Modal	Neg.	NP-coord.	Subord.	Sent-coord.
Ja	JSICK	49.3±0.01	50.1±0.00	49.6±0.01	47.7±0.03	49.7±0.00	51.1±0.02	54.8±0.04	63.2±0.03	50.2±0.00	69.3±0.02	46.8±0.02
	+JaNLI	92.8±0.10	79.2±0.06	49.2±0.01	56.1±0.00	75.7±0.10	90.0±0.07	93.7±0.07	98.6±0.02	99.0±0.01	98.4±0.01	97.8±0.01
	JSNLI	50.2±0.01	52.3±0.02	45.9±0.04	49.7±0.01	51.5±0.01	51.2±0.01	49.6±0.00	50.2±0.01	51.4±0.00	50.0±0.00	49.7±0.00
	+JaNLI	70.1±0.06	65.3±0.03	41.2±0.06	50.5±0.01	67.9±0.08	70.2±0.09	71.7±0.19	87.4±0.06	76.6±0.17	88.8±0.11	79.2±0.18
Multi	JSICK	49.3±0.01	49.9±0.00	49.6±0.01	48.6±0.02	49.5±0.01	50.8±0.01	50.5±0.01	49.3±0.01	49.8±0.00	61.0±0.10	49.6±0.01
	+JaNLI	56.3±0.05	52.7±0.03	49.2±0.01	56.0±0.06	53.2±0.04	58.7±0.09	57.6±0.20	62.7±0.24	61.0±0.12	61.5±0.10	60.7±0.10
	JSNLI	49.8±0.00	50.1±0.00	48.1±0.01	49.9±0.00	50.3±0.00	50.3±0.00	49.6±0.01	45.5±0.04	50.5±0.00	49.9±0.00	50.2±0.00
	+JaNLI	54.1±0.07	53.8±0.07	48.9±0.02	50.7±0.01	52.7±0.05	53.3±0.06	55.3±0.09	62.6±0.22	54.4±0.08	54.4±0.08	54.8±0.08
Human		94.2±0.05	93.3±0.03	91.7±0.08	85.0±0.17	95.8±0.05	95.0±0.02	95.6±0.08	94.4±0.05	93.9±0.03	96.7±0.04	92.5±0.09

Table 8: Results on the JaNLI test set for each linguistic phenomenon.

plore whether training on data containing these diverse linguistic phenomena improves the performance of the models. The gold labels of inference examples in JSICK were annotated via crowdsourcing. Given that the gold label of an inference example can be changed as a result of translation due to structural and lexical differences between English and Japanese, the gold labels of JSICK were re-annotated via crowdsourcing.

JSNLI was created by automatically translating the large crowdsourced English NLI dataset SNLI (Bowman et al., 2015), into Japanese. A premise sentence in the original SNLI dataset was sourced from Flickr image captions, and workers were asked to generate a corresponding hypothesis sentence for each of the three labels. Note that the size of the SNLI training set (533K) is around 100 times larger than that of the SICK training set (50K). Thus, we consider whether the quantity of the training data improves the model performance on JaNLI. The gold labels of JSNLI are the same as those of English SNLI.

We hypothesize that even if the models trained on the basic training datasets do not perform well on the JaNLI dataset, data augmentation with a small number of JaNLI examples could help the models to learn how to solve the inferences with diverse linguistic phenomena in the JaNLI dataset. To test this hypothesis, for each baseline setting, we added a small amount of JaNLI data (700 examples)[5] during the finetuning of models and checked whether the performance of the models would be improved.

4.2 Baseline results

Table 7 shows the results for the in-distribution (JSICK and JSNLI) and out-of-distribution (JaNLI) test sets. For the five heuristics, the results on

[5]There is no overlap between the subset of JaNLI and the test set in terms of (P, H) pairs. Only five premise sentences are overlapped between the added subset and the test set, for which the labels are not biased: two of them are *entailment* and three of them are *non-entailment*.

Model	Finetuned on	Scramb.	Pass.	Caus.	Fac-adv.	Scramb.	Pass.	Caus.	Fac-adv.
		Correct: *Entailment*				Correct: *Non-entailment*			
Ja	JSICK	100.0±0.00	94.7±0.05	76.7±0.07	99.4±0.01	0.2±0.00	4.5±0.04	18.7±0.05	0.0±0.00
	+JaNLI	91.5±0.03	94.7±0.03	79.3±0.14	94.8±0.06	66.9±0.12	3.8±0.03	32.8±0.14	56.7±0.25
	JSNLI	98.1±0.03	87.2±0.15	99.0±0.01	99.3±0.01	6.5±0.07	4.7±0.07	0.3±0.00	3.7±0.03
	+JaNLI	71.3±0.03	53.8±0.34	93.0±0.06	94.9±0.02	59.1±0.12	32.0±0.18	7.5±0.08	43,5±0.19
Multi	JSICK	65.9±0.57	65.7±0.57	60.2±0.53	65.2±0.56	33.9±0.57	33.5±0.58	37.0±0.55	33.9±0.57
	+JaNLI	41.8±0.40	47.5±0.44	49.0±0.45	43.9±0.38	63.6±0.34	50.8±0.45	63.0±0.38	62.5±0.34
	JSNLI	98.5±0.02	95.8±0.02	99.8±0.01	99.1±0.01	1.6±0.01	0.3±0.00	0.0±0.00	1.6±0.01
	+JaNLI	71.3±0.03	53.8±0.34	93.0±0.06	94.9±0.02	59.1±0.12	32.0±0.18	7.5±0.08	43.5±0.19

Table 9: Details of performance for problems involving linguistic phenomena for which the model performance was not improved very much by data augmentation.

		Correct: *Entailment*						Correct: *Non-entailment*					
Model	Train	Normal	Double-o	Punct.	Select.	Wa	Scramb.	Normal	Double-o	Punct.	Select.	Wa	Scramb.
Ja	JSICK	90.2±0.09	90.8±0.10	86.8±0.11	82.9±0.15	84.1±0.13	90.6±0.08	9.3±0.07	11.9±0.11	10.2±0.08	14.1±0.13	13.8±0.11	7.2±0.06
	+JaNLI	99.0±0.00	99.2±0.01	99.4±0.01	98.8±0.01	98.6±0.02	98.7±0.01	91.2±0.13	78.3±0.32	83.0±0.27	87.8±0.19	87.8±0.19	86.9±0.14
	JSNLI	98.3±0.01	95.3±0.03	99.4±0.00	98.8±0.02	99.3±0.00	98.6±0.02	2.0±0.03	3.7±0.04	1.8±0.02	0.6±0.01	2.8±0.03	1.5±0.02
	+JaNLI	83.2±0.07	88.2±0.01	86.5±0.08	92.8±0.09	88.8±0.09	82.8±0.07	58.0±0.16	54.8±0.14	53.1±0.20	49.4±0.19	47.7±0.17	55.9±0.09
Multi	JSICK	62.7±0.55	64.0±0.56	59.8±0.53	62.9±0.55	62.4±0.54	62.5±0.55	35.2±0.56	34.2±0.57	35.8±0.56	35.8±0.56	36.2±0.55	37.9±0.54
	+JaNLI	33.8±0.35	34.8±0.39	30.8±0.28	35.4±0.33	32.4±0.33	27.8±0.32	81.2±0.26	74.9±0.36	84.0±0.19	78.7±0.26	82.8±0.20	80.6±0.24
	JSNLI	98.7±0.01	97.1±0.01	99.6±0.01	99.8±0.00	99.2±0.01	98.7±0.02	0.6±0.01	1.8±0.02	0.2±0.00	0.2±0.00	1.1±0.01	0.8±0.01
	+JaNLI	28.3±0.49	29.8±0.52	30.8±0.53	32.2±0.56	30.9±0.54	29.3±0.51	79.8±0.35	79.2±0.36	78.7±0.37	74.2±0.45	77.9±0.38	78.3±0.38
Human		95.0±0.02	96.7±0.06	100.0±0.00	98.3±0.03	98.3±0.03	97.5±0.03	90.8±0.14	96.7±0.12	91.7±0.10	91.0±0.05	95.0±0.22	96.7±0.04

Table 10: Results on the JaNLI dataset for garden-path effects.

		Correct: *Entailment*			Correct: *Non-entailment*		
Model	Train	2	3	4	2	3	4
Ja	JSICK	85.8±0.12	89.4±0.10	95.5±0.04	11.8±0.09	11.0±0.11	5.1±0.05
	+JaNLI	98.9±0.01	98.8±0.01	99.1±0.00	85.2±0.22	88.5±0.14	89.6±0.13
	JSNLI	99.2±0.00	97.1±0.03	96.7±0.02	1.9±0.02	1.5±0.02	2.7±0.03
	+JaNLI	86.3±0.08	85.6±0.04	85.5±0.04	53.0±0.17	55.8±0.08	56.1±0.10
Multi	JSICK	61.5±0.54	63.6±0.55	64.8±0.56	36.8±0.55	35.2±0.56	34.3±0.57
	+JaNLI	33.0±0.33	33.9±0.37	27.4±0.31	80.8±0.23	78.7±0.30	81.3±0.26
	JSNLI	99.5±0.01	97.3±0.02	98.0±0.02	0.4±0.00	1.2±0.02	1.5±0.02
	+JaNLI	30.5±0.53	29.2±0.51	28.4±0.49	78.4±0.37	79.1±0.36	77.2±0.39
	Human	97.7±0.01	96.7±0.10	96.7±0.00	90.0±0.01	94.4±0.05	91.1±0.08

Table 11: Results on problems involving garden-path sentences for different numbers of NPs.

JaNLI are shown for correct *entailment* and *non-entailment* labels. All the models except the multilingual BERT model trained on JSICK achieved high accuracy on their in-distribution test set. They also achieved very high accuracy for the examples where the correct label is *entailment*. By contrast, we can see that regardless of the finetuning data type and model type, BERT performed substantially worse than chance (most accuracies were close to 0% while the chance level is 50%) for the examples where the correct label is *non-entailment*. These results are more or less consistent with the results reported for the English HANS dataset (McCoy et al., 2019), suggesting that the models are fooled by the heuristics in the case of Japanese as well. As explained in more detail in Section 4.4, we also evaluated human performance using a portion of the JaNLI test set. As shown in Table 7, human performance is near perfect for both *entailment* and *non-entailment* cases. Interestingly, the most difficult pattern for humans was the MIXED-SUBSET pattern (92.7 for *entailment* and 88.7 for *non-entailment*) and the same tendency was observed in the BERT models.

Comparing the performance of the multilingual and Japanese BERT models on the JaNLI dataset, we see that the overall performance of multilingual BERT is slightly lower than that of Japanese BERT. Also, comparing the effects of finetuning with JSICK and JSNLI, we see that the performance of the model finetuned with JSICK is slightly better than that of the model finetuned with JSNLI (JSICK: 51.3%; JSNLI: 50.4%). When a portion of JaNLI was added to the training data, the difference became much larger (see Section 4.3). These results suggest that the quality of the training dataset, in particular, the diversity of linguistic phenomena, can be more effective than the quantity of data for solving linguistically challenging inferences.

Table 8 shows detailed results on the JaNLI dataset for each linguistic phenomenon. The performance for each phenomenon is near the chance level (50%) for all baselines. As with the results for the heuristics, the accuracy for *entailment* examples was near 100%, while the accuracy for *non-entailment* examples was close to 0%. When finetuned with JSICK, accuracy tended to be slightly higher for negation and sentence-subordination than for the other phenomena.

4.3 Data augmented with JaNLI examples

As Table 7 shows, when we add a small amount of JaNLI data (700 examples) during finetuning, the performance of the Japanese BERT model improved on *non-entailment* examples, while maintaining its performance on *entailment* examples: the overall accuracy increased from 51.3% to 89.3% on JSICK and 50.4% to 72.3% on JSNLI. On the other hand, the performance of the multilingual model decreased on *entailment* examples and thus failed to consistently improve the performance on JaNLI. This suggests that the training of multilingual BERT is more unstable in learning the Japanese NLI task when compared with Japanese BERT.

For both the Japanese and multilingual BERT models, the degree of performance improvement by the data augmentation was greater when finetuned with JSICK than when finetuned with JSNLI. There are two possible reasons for this result. One is that the effect of adding JaNLI examples is larger when the total size of the dataset is smaller. The other is that the data augmentation is more effective when the linguistic diversity of the original training set is higher. It should be noted that when a portion of the JaNLI dataset was added to the training set during finetuning, both Japanese and multilingual models improved in terms of performance on the in-distribution test set (JSICK/JSNLI). This result seems to support the finding that syntactic data augmentation helps to improve the robustness of models (Min et al., 2020). However, Table 8 also shows that even when JaNLI examples were used for finetuning, the performance of multilingual and Japanese BERT models was not improved on examples involving passive, causative, factive-adverbs, and scrambling. This indicates that some linguistic phenomena are difficult to learn using only data augmentation.

Table 9 shows details of performance for the four types of problems for which the model performance was not improved very much by data augmentation. For these problems, the accuracy on *non-entailment* examples was still worse than that on *entailment* examples, with the exception of the multilingual model finetuned with JSICK. For the problems involving factive adverbs, the model failed to distinguish between non-entailment examples where only the premise contains a non-factive adverb (e.g., *Perhaps the child is sleeping* $\not\Rightarrow$ *The child is sleeping*) and entailment examples where both the premise and hypothesis contain a non-factive adverb of the same type (e.g., *Perhaps the child chased the running cat* $\Rightarrow$ *Perhaps the child chased the cat*). This result is consistent with a previous study (Gupta et al., 2021) showing that the model predictions do not change even when there are repeated phrases in an inference pair.

4.4 Comparison with human judgements

To assess the difficulty of the JaNLI dataset, we collected human judgements on a subset of the JaNLI dataset through the Japanese crowdsourcing platform Lancers[6]. We selected five examples for each of 144 templates, that is, 720 inference problems in total. We collected three annotations per pair and paid annotators $0.10 per labeled pair. The annotators were six native Japanese speakers. The quality of the annotations was maintained by asking the annotators to fully understand the guidelines until they correctly answered all 10 test questions, 5 entailment and 5 non-entailment inference examples sampled from the basic training datasets.

As mentioned in Section 4.2, the overall accuracy of human performance was very high: 94.0% (see Table 7). Also, Table 8 shows that humans can make correct judgements across all types of problems present in the JaNLI dataset, despite the fact that some of them, in particular, garden-path sentences with noun-modifying clauses, are known to be hard to process based on reading time and other tests (Miyamoto, 2008). Compared with the accuracy for other linguistic phenomenon, the accuracy for causative and passive was relatively low (85% and 91.7%, respectively). For example, humans tend to predict the label for the following entailment pair as *non-entailment*.

P: 先生 が 男の子 を 海 で 泳がせた
teacher ga boy o ocean in swim-CAUSE
(*The teacher made the boy swim in the ocean*)

[6] https://www.lancers.jp/

H: 男の子 が 海 で 泳いでいる
boy ga ocean in swimming
(*The boy is swimming in the ocean*)

One possible reason why workers judge this entailment pair as *non-entailment* is that while the hypothesis sentence *H* can be interpreted to mean that the boy is swimming spontaneously of his own will, the premise sentence *P* involving a causative verb in Japanese can be interpreted to mean that the boy is *forced* to swim against his will (Kuroda, 1965; Tsujimura, 2013). A similar additional meaning beyond a simple truth-conditional content (i.e., *affectivity*) is involved in Japanese passive constructions as well (Kuno, 1973; Kuroda, 1979). It is beyond the scope of this work to address the issue of non-truth-conditional meanings.

Garden-path effects Table 10 shows detailed results on sentences with garden-path effects. As expected, the human annotators achieved slightly higher scores on garden-path problems involving factors that make the interpretation of garden-path sentences relatively easy (double-o, punctuation, selectional restriction, the topic marker *wa*, and scrambling) compared with normal garden-path problems. By contrast, there was no consistent tendency in this regard for the predictions of the BERT models. This might indicate that, unlike humans, the models do not distinguish problems involving normal garden-path phenomena from those involving factors that make them easier to interpret.

Number of NP arguments Table 11 shows results on problems involving garden-path sentences for different numbers of NPs. While Japanese psycholinguistic studies have shown that humans tend to struggle with processing garden-path sentences when they contain more NP-arguments (Inoue, 1990), but there seems to be no such trend in the case of NLI for both human judgements and model predictions. This result indicates that the number of NP arguments (at least up to four) does not significantly affect the correctness of entailment judgements.

5 Conclusion

We introduced the JaNLI dataset, which was designed to assess the generalization capacity of pre-trained language models on NLI in Japanese. Experiments showed that both Japanese and multilingual BERT models trained with basic Japanese NLI datasets performed very poorly on the JaNLI dataset. In addition, both Japanese and multilingual models, in particular the latter, struggled with learning some Japanese linguistic phenomena even when augmented with a portion of the JaNLI dataset. This suggests that there is still much room for improving the generalization capacity of pre-trained language models. Lastly, the comparison between human performance and model performance illustrated that whereas the models failed to correctly predict labels for non-entailment examples, human judgement was near perfect. Furthermore, factors that ease the interpretation of garden-path sentences for humans do not help model predictions. Overall, our dataset illuminates the vulnerabilities of the currently standard pre-trained language models and indicate a new challenge for cross-lingual generalization of NLI.

Acknowledgements

We thank the three anonymous reviewers for their helpful comments and suggestions. This work was partially supported by JSPS KAKENHI Grant Number JP20K19868.

References

Masayuki Asahara and Yuji Matsumoto. 2003. ipadic version 2.7.0 User's Manual. Nara Institute of Science and Technology.

Samuel R. Bowman, Gabor Angeli, Christopher Potts, and Christopher D. Manning. 2015. A large annotated corpus for learning natural language inference. In *Proceedings of the 2015 Conference on Empirical Methods in Natural Language Processing*, pages 632–642.

Alexis Conneau, Ruty Rinott, Guillaume Lample, Adina Williams, Samuel Bowman, Holger Schwenk, and Veselin Stoyanov. 2018. XNLI: Evaluating cross-lingual sentence representations. In *Proceedings of the 2018 Conference on Empirical Methods in Natural Language Processing*, pages 2475–2485.

Robin Cooper, Richard Crouch, Jan van Eijck, Chris Fox, Josef van Genabith, Jan Jaspers, Hans Kamp, Manfred Pinkal, Massimo Poesio, Stephen Pulman, et al. 1994. FraCaS–a framework for computational semantics. *Deliverable*, D6.

Jacob Devlin, Ming-Wei Chang, Kenton Lee, and Kristina Toutanova. 2019. BERT: Pre-training of deep bidirectional transformers for language understanding. In *Proceedings of the 2019 Conference of the North American Chapter of the Association for Computational Linguistics: Human Language Technologies, Volume 1 (Long and Short Papers)*, pages 4171–4186.

Mengnan Du, Varun Manjunatha, Rajiv Jain, Ruchi Deshpande, Franck Dernoncourt, Jiuxiang Gu, Tong Sun, and Xia Hu. 2021. Towards interpreting and mitigating shortcut learning behavior of NLU models. In *Proceedings of the 2021 Conference of the North American Chapter of the Association for Computational Linguistics: Human Language Technologies*, pages 915–929.

Max Glockner, Vered Shwartz, and Yoav Goldberg. 2018. Breaking NLI systems with sentences that require simple lexical inferences. In *Proceedings of the 56th Annual Meeting of the Association for Computational Linguistics (Volume 2: Short Papers)*, pages 650–655.

Emily Goodwin, Koustuv Sinha, and Timothy J. O'Donnell. 2020. Probing linguistic systematicity. In *Proceedings of the 58th Annual Meeting of the Association for Computational Linguistics*, pages 1958–1969.

Ashim Gupta, Giorgi Kvernadze, and Vivek Srikumar. 2021. BERT & family eat word salad: Experiments with text understanding. In *Proceedings of the 35th AAAI Conference on Artificial Intelligence, AAAI 2021*, pages 12946–12954.

Suchin Gururangan, Swabha Swayamdipta, Omer Levy, Roy Schwartz, Samuel Bowman, and Noah A. Smith. 2018. Annotation artifacts in natural language inference data. In *Proceedings of the 2018 Conference of the North American Chapter of the Association for Computational Linguistics: Human Language Technologies, Volume 2 (Short Papers)*, pages 107–112.

Jiyeon Ham, Yo Joong Choe, Kyubyong Park, Ilji Choi, and Hyungjoon Soh. 2020. KorNLI and KorSTS: New benchmark datasets for Korean natural language understanding. In *Findings of the Association for Computational Linguistics: EMNLP 2020*, pages 422–430.

Yuta Hayashibe. 2020. Japanese realistic textual entailment corpus. In *Proceedings of the 12th Language Resources and Evaluation Conference*, pages 6827–6834.

John Hinds. 1986. *Japanese: Descriptive Grammar*. Croom Helm.

Hai Hu, Kyle Richardson, Liang Xu, Lu Li, Sandra Kübler, and Lawrence Moss. 2020. OCNLI: Original Chinese Natural Language Inference. In *Findings of the Association for Computational Linguistics: EMNLP 2020*, pages 3512–3526.

Hai Hu, He Zhou, Zuoyu Tian, Yiwen Zhang, Yina Patterson, Yanting Li, Yixin Nie, and Kyle Richardson. 2021. Investigating transfer learning in multilingual pre-trained language models through Chinese natural language inference. In *Findings of the Association for Computational Linguistics: ACL-IJCNLP 2021*.

Masakatsu Inoue. 1990. Kouzou-teki aimai bun-no rikai-ni okeru goku-no nagasa-no kouka (phrasal length effects the comprehension of structurally ambiguous sentences). In *Proceedings of the 54th Japanese Psycholingual Association*, page 678.

Masakatsu Inoue. 1991. Bun-no tougo syori-ni okeru zyosi-wa-no kinou (the funcation of the particle wa in sentence parsing). In *Proceedings of the 33rd Japanese Association of Educational Psychology*, pages 55–56.

Masakatsu Inoue. 2006. Ambiguity resolution or retention in comprehending Japanese sentences. *Cognitive Studies: Bulletin of the Japanese Cognitive Science Society*, 13(3):353–368.

Ai Kawazoe, Ribeka Tanaka, Koji Mineshima, and Daisuke Bekki. 2017. An inference problem set for evaluating semantic theories and semantic processing systems for Japanese. In *New Frontiers in Artificial Intelligence*, pages 58–65.

Susumu Kuno. 1973. *The Structure of the Japanese Language*. MIT Press.

Tatsuki Kuribayashi, Yohei Oseki, Takumi Ito, Ryo Yoshida, Masayuki Asahara, and Kentaro Inui. 2021. Lower perplexity is not always human-like. In *Proceedings of the 59th Annual Meeting of the Association for Computational Linguistics and the 11th International Joint Conference on Natural Language Processing (Volume 1: Long Papers)*, pages 5203–5217.

S.-Y. Kuroda. 1965. Causative forms in Japanese. *Foundations of Language*, 1(1):30–50.

S.-Y. Kuroda. 1979. On Japanese passives. In *Exploration in Linguistics: Papers in Honor of Kazuko Inoue*, pages 305–347. Kenkyusha, Tokyo.

Yaobo Liang, Nan Duan, Yeyun Gong, Ning Wu, Fenfei Guo, Weizhen Qi, Ming Gong, Linjun Shou, Daxin Jiang, Guihong Cao, Xiaodong Fan, Ruofei Zhang, Rahul Agrawal, Edward Cui, Sining Wei, Taroon Bharti, Ying Qiao, Jiun-Hung Chen, Winnie Wu, Shuguang Liu, Fan Yang, Daniel Campos, Rangan Majumder, and Ming Zhou. 2020. XGLUE: A new benchmark datasetfor cross-lingual pre-training, understanding and generation. In *Proceedings of the 2020 Conference on Empirical Methods in Natural Language Processing (EMNLP)*, pages 6008–6018.

Marco Marelli, Stefano Menini, Marco Baroni, Luisa Bentivogli, Raffaella Bernardi, and Roberto Zamparelli. 2014. A SICK cure for the evaluation of compositional distributional semantic models. In *Proceedings of the Ninth International Conference on Language Resources and Evaluation (LREC'14)*, pages 216–223.

Rebecca Marvin and Tal Linzen. 2018. Targeted syntactic evaluation of language models. In *Proceedings of the 2018 Conference on Empirical Methods in Natural Language Processing*, pages 1192–1202.

R. Thomas McCoy, Junghyun Min, and Tal Linzen. 2020. BERTs of a feather do not generalize together: Large variability in generalization across models with similar test set performance. In *Proceedings of the Third BlackboxNLP Workshop on Analyzing and Interpreting Neural Networks for NLP*, pages 217–227.

Tom McCoy, Ellie Pavlick, and Tal Linzen. 2019. Right for the wrong reasons: Diagnosing syntactic heuristics in natural language inference. In *Proceedings of the 57th Annual Meeting of the Association for Computational Linguistics*, pages 3428–3448.

Junghyun Min, R. Thomas McCoy, Dipanjan Das, Emily Pitler, and Tal Linzen. 2020. Syntactic data augmentation increases robustness to inference heuristics. In *Proceedings of the 58th Annual Meeting of the Association for Computational Linguistics*, pages 2339–2352.

Edson T Miyamoto. 2002. Case markers as clause boundary inducers in Japanese. *Journal of psycholinguistic research*, 31(4):307–347.

Edson T. Miyamoto. 2008. Processing sentences in Japanese. In Shigeru Miyagawa and Mamoru Saito, editors, *The Oxford Handbook of Japanese Linguistics*, pages 217–249. Oxford University Press.

Aakanksha Naik, Abhilasha Ravichander, Norman Sadeh, Carolyn Rose, and Graham Neubig. 2018. Stress test evaluation for natural language inference. In *Proceedings of the 27th International Conference on Computational Linguistics*, pages 2340–2353.

Thang Pham, Trung Bui, Long Mai, and Anh Nguyen. 2021. Out of order: How important is the sequential order of words in a sentence in natural language understanding tasks? In *Findings of the Association for Computational Linguistics: ACL-IJCNLP 2021*, pages 1145–1160.

Ohad Rozen, Vered Shwartz, Roee Aharoni, and Ido Dagan. 2019. Diversify your datasets: Analyzing generalization via controlled variance in adversarial datasets. In *Proceedings of the 23rd Conference on Computational Natural Language Learning (CoNLL)*, pages 196–205.

Mike Schuster and Kaisuke Nakajima. 2012. Japanese and Korean voice search. In *2012 IEEE International Conference on Acoustics, Speech and Signal Processing (ICASSP)*, pages 5149–5152.

Masayoshi Shibatani. 1990. *The Languages of Japan*. Cambridge University Press.

Koustuv Sinha, Robin Jia, Dieuwke Hupkes, Joelle Pineau, Adina Williams, and Douwe Kiela. 2021a. Masked language modeling and the distributional hypothesis: Order word matters pre-training for little. *CoRR*, cs.CL/2104.06644. Version 1.

Koustuv Sinha, Prasanna Parthasarathi, Joelle Pineau, and Adina Williams. 2021b. UnNatural Language Inference. In *Proceedings of the Joint Conference of the 59th Annual Meeting of the Association for Computational Linguistics and the 11th International Joint Conference on Natural Language Processing (ACL-IJCNLP2021)*.

Natsuko Tsujimura. 2013. *An Introduction to Japanese Linguistics*. John Wiley & Sons.

Lifu Tu, Garima Lalwani, Spandana Gella, and He He. 2020. An Empirical Study on Robustness to Spurious Correlations using Pre-trained Language Models. *Transactions of the Association for Computational Linguistics*, 8:621–633.

Prasetya Ajie Utama, Nafise Sadat Moosavi, and Iryna Gurevych. 2020. Mind the trade-off: Debiasing NLU models without degrading the in-distribution performance. In *Proceedings of the 58th Annual Meeting of the Association for Computational Linguistics*, pages 8717–8729.

Alex Wang, Yada Pruksachatkun, Nikita Nangia, Amanpreet Singh, Julian Michael, Felix Hill, Omer Levy, and Samuel Bowman. 2019. SuperGLUE: A stickier benchmark for general-purpose language understanding systems. In *Proceedings of Advances in Neural Information Processing Systems 32: Annual Conference on Neural Information Processing Systems (NeurIPS)*, pages 3266–3280.

Gijs Wijnholds and Michael Moortgat. 2021. SICK-NL: A dataset for Dutch natural language inference. In *Proceedings of the 16th Conference of the European Chapter of the Association for Computational Linguistics: Main Volume*, pages 1474–1479.

Adina Williams, Nikita Nangia, and Samuel Bowman. 2018. A broad-coverage challenge corpus for sentence understanding through inference. In *Proceedings of the 2018 Conference of the North American Chapter of the Association for Computational Linguistics: Human Language Technologies, Volume 1 (Long Papers)*, pages 1112–1122.

Yadollah Yaghoobzadeh, Soroush Mehri, Remi Tachet des Combes, T. J. Hazen, and Alessandro Sordoni. 2021. Increasing robustness to spurious correlations using forgettable examples. In *Proceedings of the 16th Conference of the European Chapter of the Association for Computational Linguistics: Main Volume*, pages 3319–3332.

Hitomi Yanaka, Koji Mineshima, Daisuke Bekki, and Kentaro Inui. 2020. Do neural models learn systematicity of monotonicity inference in natural language? In *Proceedings of the 58th Annual Meeting of the Association for Computational Linguistics*, pages 6105–6117.

Hitomi Yanaka, Koji Mineshima, and Kentaro Inui. 2021. Exploring transitivity in neural NLI models through veridicality. In *Proceedings of the 16th Conference of the European Chapter of the Association for Computational Linguistics: Main Volume*, pages 920–934.

Takumi Yoshikoshi, Daisuke Kawahara, and Sadao Kurohashi. 2020. Multilingualization of natural language inference datasets using machine translation (in Japanese). In *Proceedings of the 244th Meeting of Natural Language Processing*.

A Templates

Table 12 shows examples of templates to generate premises and hypothesis sentences for each linguistic phenomenon (except garden-path sentences with noun-modifying clauses, whose example is shown in Table 2). Note that the conjugation of verbs can change for causative and passive forms in Japanese. Thus, when annotating a structural pattern (heuristics) tag, if the verb stems are the same in the premise and hypothesis sentences, we take them to be the same word.

The full list of templates and lexical items can be found at `https://github.com/verypluming/JaNLI`.

Templates for *P* and *H*	Example	Phenomenon/Pattern
P: NP1 ga NP2 o TV-o	子供 が 女性 を 見ている child ga woman o looking (*The child is looking at the woman*)	Scrambling
$\Rightarrow H_1$: NP2 o NP1 ga TV-o	女性 を 子供 が 見ている (*The child is looking at the woman*)	FULL-OVERLAP
$\not\Rightarrow H_2$: NP1 o NP2 ga TV-o	子供 を 女性 が 見ている (*The woman is looking at the child*)	FULL-OVERLAP
$\not\Rightarrow H_3$: NP2 ga NP1 o TV-o	女性 が 子供 を 見ている (*The woman is looking at the child*)	FULL-OVERLAP
P: NP1 ga NP2 ni TV-o passive	男の子 が 若者 に 押された boy ga young-man ni push-passive (*The boy was pushed by the young man*)	Passive
$\not\Rightarrow H_1$: NP1 ga NP2 o TV-o	男の子 が 若者 を 押した (*The boy pushed the young man*)	ORDER-SUBSET
$\Rightarrow H_2$: NP2 ga NP1 o TV-o	若者 が 男の子 を 押した (*The young man pushed the boy*)	MIXED-SUBSET
P: NP1 ga NP2 o IV causative	男の子 が カップル を 笑わせている boy ga couple o laugh-causative (*The boy is making the couple laugh*)	Causative
$\not\Rightarrow H_1$: NP1 ga IV	男の子 が 笑っている (*The boy is laughing*)	ORDER-SUBSET
$\Rightarrow H_2$: NP2 ga IV	カップル が 笑っている (*The couple is laughing*)	ORDER-SUBSET
P: Factive-adverb NP1 ga IV	もしかしたら サーファー が 泳いでいる perhaps surfer ga swimming (*Perhaps the surfer is swimming*)	Factive adverb
$\not\Rightarrow H_1$: NP1 ga IV	サーファー が 泳いでいる (*The surfer is swimming*)	CONSTITUENT
P: NP1 ga IV Factive-verb	サーファー が 眠っている ことは確実だ surfer ga sleeping certain (*It is certain that the surfer is sleeping*)	Factive verb
$\Rightarrow H_1$: NP1 ga IV	サーファー が 眠っている (*The surfer is sleeping*)	CONSTITUENT
P: NP1 ga NP-place de IV MODAL	子供 が 庭 で 泣いている かもしれない child ga garden de crying might (*The child might be crying in the garden*)	Modal
$\not\Rightarrow H_1$: NP1 ga NP-place de IV	子供 が 庭 で 泣いている (*The child is crying in the garden*)	SUBSEQUENCE
$\Rightarrow H_2$: NP-place de NP1 ga IV MODAL	庭 で 子供 が 泣いている かもしれない (*The child might be crying in the garden*)	MIXED-SUBSET
P: NP1 ga NP-place de IV NEG	子供 が 海辺 で 横たわっている わけではない child ga beach de lying negation (*The child is not lying on the beach*)	Negation
$\not\Rightarrow H_1$: NP1 ga NP-place de IV	子供 が 海辺 で 横たわっている (*The child is lying on the beach*)	SUBSEQUENCE
$\Rightarrow H_2$: NP-place de NP1 ga IV NEG	海辺 で 子供 が 横たわっている わけではない (*The child is not lying on the beach*)	MIXED-SUBSET
P: NP1 ga NP2 ka NP3 o TV-o	子供 が 女性 か 男性 を 見ている child ga woman or man o looking (*The child is looking at the woman or the man*)	NP-coordination
$\not\Rightarrow H_1$: NP1 ga NP2 o tv-o	子供 が 女性 を 見ている (*The child is looking at the woman*)	ORDER-SUBSET
$\not\Rightarrow H_2$: NP1 ga NP3 o tv-o	子供 が 男性 を 見ている (*The child is looking at the man*)	ORDER-SUBSET
P: NP1 ga IV reason NP2 ga NP3 o TV-o	カップル が 遊んでいる から 子供 が ライダー を 見ている couple ga playing because child ga rider o looking (*Because the couple is playing, the child is looking at the rider*)	Sentence-subordination
$\Rightarrow H_1$: NP1 ga IV	カップル が 遊んでいる (*The couple is playing*)	CONSTITUENT
$\Rightarrow H_2$: NP2 ga NP3 o TV-o	子供 が ライダー を 見ている (*The child is looking at the rider*)	CONSTITUENT
P: NP1 ga IV ka NP2 ga NP3 o TV-o	女の子 が 走っている か 子供 が ライダー を 追い回している girl ga running or child ga rider o chasing (*The girl is running or the child is chasing the rider*)	Sentence-coordination
$\not\Rightarrow H_1$: NP1 ga IV	女の子 が 走っている (*The girl is running*)	CONSTITUENT
$\not\Rightarrow H_2$: NP2 ga NP3 o TV-o	子供 が ライダー を 追い回している (*The child is chasing the rider*)	CONSTITUENT

Table 12: Example templates for premise and hypothesis sentences for each linguistic phenomenon. "$\Rightarrow$" indicates *entailment* and "$\not\Rightarrow$" *non-entailment*.

Investigating Negation in Pre-trained Vision-and-language Models

Radina Dobreva and **Frank Keller**
Institute for Language, Cognition and Computation
School of Informatics
University of Edinburgh
r.dobreva@ed.ac.uk, keller@inf.ed.ac.uk

Abstract

Pre-trained vision-and-language models have achieved impressive results on a variety of tasks, including ones that require complex reasoning beyond object recognition. However, little is known about how they achieve these results or what their limitations are. In this paper, we focus on a particular linguistic capability, namely the understanding of negation. We borrow techniques from the analysis of language models to investigate the ability of pre-trained vision-and-language models to handle negation. We find that these models severely underperform in the presence of negation.

Figure 1: Examples from the NLVR2 corpus. The input to the model consists of two images and a sentence. The model's task is to predict whether the sentence is true of the images or not. The top example shows an instance where the sentence is true and the bottom one, false. Image from (Suhr et al., 2019).

1 Introduction

Vision-and-language models have made a lot of progress on complex tasks, going beyond recognition and towards reasoning over the two modalities (Zellers et al., 2019; Suhr et al., 2019). Following the success of pre-trained language models such as BERT (Devlin et al., 2019) on a range of language tasks, recent advances in vision-and-language have involved the introduction of pre-trained models (e.g., UNITER, Chen et al. 2020, VisualBERT, Li et al. 2019, ViLBERT, Lu et al. 2019, LXMERT, Tan and Bansal 2019). These models achieve impressive results, topping task leaderboards and improving over previous approaches by a large margin. However, as with pre-trained language models, it is not clear how and why these models perform as well as they do, what information they learn and use in their predictions, or what their limitations are. While a large body of research has focused on the interpretation of pre-trained language models (e.g., Clark et al. 2019; Tenney et al. 2019; Rogers et al. 2020; Elazar et al. 2021), such work has been more limited for vision-and-language models.

This paper focuses on a particular linguistic capability, namely the ability to understand negation. Negation is universal across languages (Zeijlstra, 2007) and is very important for interpreting the meaning and determining the truth value of a statement. Vision-and-language models have applications in real-world scenarios where it is crucial to understand negation, as this is a behaviour expected by humans interacting with them.

For the purposes of this analysis, we focus on a particular vision-and-language task, Natural Language Visual Reasoning for Real (NLVR2) (Suhr et al., 2019). For this task, the model is presented with two images and a sentence and has to predict whether that sentence is true of the images or not (see Figure 1). Since this task involves the prediction of a truth value, it lends itself well to the exploration of negation. We consider two popular pre-trained vision-and-language models, finetuned for the task: LXMERT (Tan and Bansal, 2019) and UNITER (Chen et al., 2020). Details on the data and models are in Section 3.

In order to investigate the performance of these

Proceedings of the Fourth BlackboxNLP Workshop on Analyzing and Interpreting Neural Networks for NLP, pages 350–362
Online, November 11, 2021.

models on examples that contain negation in a controlled manner, we annotated a portion of the original NLVR2 test set to create minimally differing instances. That is, we created pairs of instances where the images remain the same and the sentences only differ in the presence or absence of negation (see Section 3 for details). We show that both models under consideration perform worse on the negated examples, compared to the corresponding non-negated examples (Section 4). We also use causal mediation analysis (Pearl, 2001; Vig et al., 2020) on UNITER to examine the contributions of specific neurons to the final predictions (Section 5). Our results show that the effects of negation are mainly seen in the upper layers of the model. We release the new test set and code for our experiments at `https://github.com/radidd/vision-and-language-negation`.

2 Background

2.1 Negation

Negation is related to the notion of polarity: a clause such as "It is raining" is said to have positive polarity, whereas a clause such as "It is not raining" has negative polarity (Pullum and Huddleston, 2002). Positive polarity is usually structurally simpler, whereas negative polarity is marked by words or affixes. Pullum and Huddleston (2002) categorise negation based on several different properties, but for our purposes we focus on the distinction between verbal and non-verbal negation. In the former, the negation marker is attached to the verb ("I did not see anything at all"), while in the latter, the negation marker is attached to a dependent of the verb ("I saw nothing at all").

Previous analysis of language models has shown that they are not able to handle negation. Pre-trained language models fail to make correct predictions in the presence of negation or even to distinguish between positive and negative sentences (Ettinger, 2020; Kassner and Schütze, 2020). Hossain et al. (2020) finetune several different pre-trained language models for natural language inference and show that performance on instances containing negation deteriorates.

2.2 Vision-and-language models

Following the success of pre-trained language models (Devlin et al., 2019), multimodal tasks such as visual question answering (Antol et al., 2015) and visual commonsense reasoning (Zellers et al., 2019) have also recently been approached using a pretrain-and-finetune method. Pre-trained vision-and-language models fall into two categories: single-stream models (e.g., Li et al. 2019; Chen et al. 2020) and two-stream models (e.g., Lu et al. 2019; Tan and Bansal 2019). While two-stream models have separate encoders for the visual and textual modalities and then jointly process them using a third encoder, single-stream models process both the textual and visual features together from the start.

While these models have been very successful, pushing state-of-the-art results up across tasks, not much is known about their capabilities and limitations. From that perspective, the closest works to ours are by Li et al. (2020) and Cao et al. (2020). Li et al. (2020) analyse attention heads in the model and show that words in the text are correctly mapped to image regions which correspond to them. Cao et al. (2020) probe pre-trained vision-and-language models and report similar observations. Their work focuses more on the grounding aspect of vision-and-language models, whereas our work focuses more on linguistic and reasoning abilities. Cao et al. (2020) also show that multimodal pre-trained models learn some linguistic knowledge, however, they do not analyse this any deeper than providing results on several probing tasks, none of which involves negation.

2.3 Causal mediation analysis

Language-only BERT has been targeted by a lot of recent analysis work focusing on different capabilities of the model (Clark et al., 2019; Tenney et al., 2019; Rogers et al., 2020; Elazar et al., 2021). A recent proposal is the application of causal mediation analysis (Pearl, 2001) to better understand neural NLP models (Vig et al., 2020).

Causal mediation analysis aims to measure the effect of intermediate variables ("mediators") on a response variable. Pearl (2001) defines a natural direct effect (NDE) and a natural indirect effect (NIE), see Figure 2. NDE refers to the direct effect of a particular value of an input variable X on the value of a response variable Y, without the intervention of a mediator Z. More specifically, we can measure the effect of an intervention, or change, of the input variable ($X = x \rightarrow X = x*$), while keeping Z to its value without the intervention. NIE refers to the indirect effect of the input variable X on Y via the intermediate variable Z.

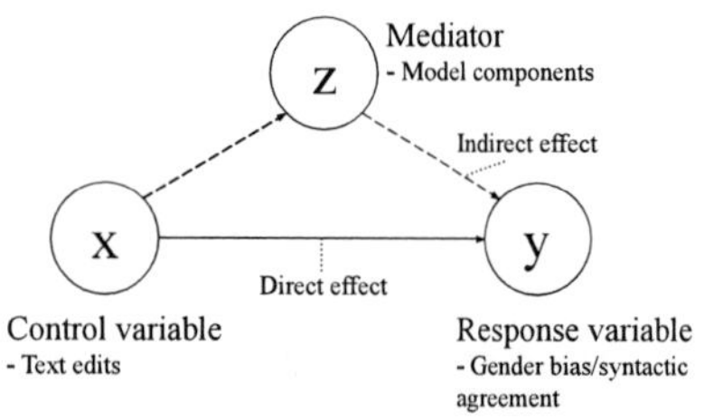

Figure 2: Graphical model of the indirect and direct effect. Figure adapted from Vig et al. (2020).

Specifically, we can fix X to its original value, but change the value of the intermediate variable Z to its value under the intervention $X = x*$.

Vig et al. (2020) apply causal mediation analysis to the study of gender bias in large pre-trained language models. They treat model components – specifically neurons and attention heads – as intermediate variables (Figure 2). They make changes to the input text by switching from gender-ambiguous to gender-unambiguous input and measure the effects of these changes on the amount of bias the model exhibits. This kind of analysis can show whether specific model components are causally responsible for a specific outcome. Indeed, Vig et al. (2020) show that gender bias effects are sparse and concentrated in a handful of attention heads in the middle layers of the model. More recently, Finlayson et al. (2021) apply causal mediation analysis to the problem of subject-verb agreement in language models. They look at neurons in the models and find that some models learn two different mechanisms to resolve agreement for different sentence structures.

3 Data and models

3.1 Models

For our experiments we used two vision-and-language models, both based on the Transformer architecture: LXMERT (Tan and Bansal, 2019) which is a two-stream model and UNITER (Chen et al., 2020), which is a single-stream model. For UNITER, we experiment with two different variants of applying the model to NLVR2: paired with attention and triplet. The paired with attention variant encodes the two images separately and then combines the representations with an additional attention layer, whereas the triplet variant encodes both images together from the start (see Chen et al. (2020) for details).

3.2 NLVR2 dataset

The dataset used for all experiments is NLVR2 (Suhr et al., 2019), which consists of pairs of images, a sentence describing each pair and a True/False tag indicating whether the sentence is true of the image pair. This dataset requires joint reasoning over the two modalities and is more complex than image captioning datasets due to the kind of language it contains – for instance, it requires comparison and counting abilities.

The authors of NLVR2 present statistics of the occurrence of different linguistic phenomena in a portion of their development set. Their analysis shows that 9.6% of the samples they consider contain negation. This statistic is not available for the test and the training set, so we calculated it based on a short list of negation words (see Appendix A). The results are as follows:

- Training set: 7192/86373 samples (8.33%)
- Development set: 630/6982 samples (9.02%)
- Test set: 589/6967 samples (8.45%)

This shows that negation is not very common in the dataset. As a preliminary experiment, we tested the models' performance on the samples identified to contain negation in the original development and test set and compared it to the performance on samples which do not contain negation. Results are shown in Table 1. All three models show a drop in performance on the samples containing negation for both the development and test set, compared to non-negated samples. The drop in performance varies between 1.7 points and 7 points.

There is no more detailed analysis of the types of negation present in the dataset, for example whether it is verbal or non-verbal. This means that there is no way to use the existing data for a more fine-grained analysis of negation. The existing dataset also cannot be used reliably to make performance comparisons between negated and non-negated examples. This is because it is possible that other factors, such as sentence length or complexity of the reasoning required (e.g., counting, comparison between the two images), are influencing performance. Therefore, we manually created a test set of minimally differing pairs by adding negation to the original data.

3.3 Negation test set

In order to investigate whether vision-and-language models perform differently in the presence of negation, we annotated a portion of the NLVR2 test set

	LXMERT		UNITER$_{paired-attn}$		UNITER$_{triplet}$	
	neg.	non-neg.	neg.	non-neg.	neg.	non-neg.
Dev set	71.43	74.92	74.29	77.38	70.00	71.68
Test set	67.74	74.71	74.87	77.89	67.57	73.61

Table 1: Accuracy on samples which contain negation and samples which do not contain negation from the original development and test set.

Negation type	o/n	Example	count
Verbal (content)	o	At least one person is wearing a hat.	91
	n	At least one person is not wearing a hat.	94
Verbal (existential)	o	The left image contains exactly two dogs.	108
	n	The left image does not contain exactly two dogs.	108
NP (nonexistential)	o	All the cars are facing towards the left.	28
	n	Not all the cars are facing towards the left.	29
NP (existential)	o	All the marmots are on rocks.	55
	n	None of the marmots are on rocks.	55
NP (number-to-none)	o	There are a total of four people in the gym.	72
	n	There are no people in the gym.	72
Sentence-wide	o	there are sled dogs moving toward the camera	83
	n	It is not true that there are sled dogs moving toward the camera	83

Table 2: Example negated sentences and counts for each category. "o" stands for original, "n" stands for negated.

to create instances of negation. An important requirement for the annotation was that every negated instance has a flipped label compared to the original.[1] It should also be noted that while negation is a complex phenomenon, here we only consider absolute negators (e.g., *no, not, nobody, nothing*), and we do not consider approximate negators (e.g., *few, little, barely*) or affixal negators (e.g., the prefixes *un-, in-, non-*, see Pullum and Huddleston (2002). The negation categories below are constrained by these two considerations.

First, we identified appropriate samples for negation. We selected the samples in pairs, where both samples belonging to a pair have the same images, but different sentences and True/False labels. This was done so that the labels remain balanced in the new negation test set. See Appendix B for more criteria for sample selection.

Next, we created negated versions of each sample in such a way that the new sample has a flipped label according to the annotator's judgement. It is important to keep in mind that the truth value of an example depends on the images *and* the sentence; if we just look at the sentence on its own, adding negation does not flip the truth value in all cases. The annotator also recorded the type of negation for each example as belonging to one of six categories (see Table 2 and Appendix C for examples):

Verbal negation:

- Content negation: where negation is attached to a verb expressing an action ("is not standing") or a characteristic ("don't have black seats").
- Existential negation: where the negated verb relates to the existence of a predicate ("the image doesn't include ...", "there aren't ... ").

Noun phrase negation:

- Non-existential: the resulting negated NP does not deny the existence of an object, for example "not all birds", "no more than three birds".
- Existential negation: denies the existence of an object in a noun phrase ("no dogs", "neither image").
- Number-to-none negation: similar to existential negation, but the original NP contains a numeral ("at least two dogs", "a total of five birds") and the negated version denies the existence of the object ("no dogs", "no birds").

[1]The flipped label requirement was in place to aid the analysis. It is less straightforward to evaluate pairs with the same label, since we would not be able to tell if the model is doing anything differently with and without the negation. Future work could include analysis of examples where negation does not change the label.

Sentence-wide negation: negating the full sentence by appending "It is not the case that ..." or "It is not true that ..." at the start.

The annotation was done with minimal possible perturbations of the original sentences to allow for a fairer comparison between the original and the negated samples. For some of the original samples it was possible to create several different negated ones. Those were kept to a maximum of three and in practice few samples had more than two possible negations. Table 2 shows the number of samples belonging to each category as well as the number of corresponding original samples. In total there are 441 negated samples created from 400 original samples.

It should be noted that there are some differences between the existing negated examples in the original NLVR2 test set and the examples in our negation test set. Firstly, we had to keep the negated sentences grammatical and minimally different, which restricted the variety of negation structures and types. Second, people likely use negation differently when they are describing images in a natural setting, than when it is added to existing descriptions artificially. See Appendix D for a further discussion of the differences between our test set and negation present in the original NLVR2 test set.

4 Experimental results

4.1 Experimental setup

We followed the instructions in the respective repositories for LXMERT[2] and UNITER[3] to obtain the pre-trained checkpoints and finetune them for the NLVR2 task. For both versions of UNITER we used the UNITER-base pre-trained checkpoint. LXMERT was finetuned for four epochs and achieved an accuracy of 74.61% and 74.12% on the development and test sets respectively. UNITER$_{paired\text{-}attn}$ was finetuned for seven epochs and achieved an accuracy of 77.10% and 77.64% on the development and test sets. UNITER$_{triplet}$ was finetuned for 10 epochs and achieved accuracies of 71.53% on the development and 73.10% on the test set.

4.2 Results on the negation test set

Table 3 shows the results on the negation test set by category. For comparison, we have provided accuracy on the original samples corresponding to the negated samples in each category. As can be seen from the table, all models perform worse on the negation samples, across all categories. The only exception to this is UNITER$_{triplet}$ on the NP (nonexistential) category, where the score for the negative samples is higher than that for the corresponding positive ones. Between the three models, overall the performance of UNITER$_{paired\text{-}attn}$ is highest, followed by UNITER$_{triplet}$ and LXMERT.

Looking at specific categories, LXMERT seems to struggle the most with verbal negation, while both versions of UNITER perform better, achieving scores between 14 and 20 points higher than LXMERT. The scores for the three NP negation types are more varied between models, with UNITER$_{triplet}$ outperforming the others on the number-to-none and nonexistential categories and UNITER$_{paired\text{-}attn}$ outperforming on the existential category. Since the negated forms of the NP (number-to-none) category and the NP (existential) category are very similar, it is surprising that there is such a big gap in performance (around 20 points) for two of the models. All models struggle significantly with sentence-wide negation. One explanation for this could be that the models do not encounter the phrases used to create these samples in the training data and ignore them.

Table 4 shows accuracy of the negated samples, split by whether the model predicts the corresponding original sample correctly or not. A higher score on the originally correct examples indicates that the model is potentially able to handle negation, i.e., it learns that negation inverts the truth value. A higher score on the originally incorrect examples is less clear – since there are only two categories, the model can achieve this by simply ignoring negation and outputting the same prediction as for the original. Looking at the originally correct category, UNITER$_{paired\text{-}attn}$ outperforms both other models across categories, except for the sentence-wide category. For the sentence-wide category, LXMERT outperforms both versions of UNITER by more than 16 points. Turning to the originally incorrect category, here all models perform much better across negation categories, with the exception of NP (existential) negation. The highest score overall is obtained by UNITER$_{triplet}$, followed by LXMERT and UNITER$_{paired\text{-}attn}$.

[2] `https://github.com/airsplay/lxmert`

[3] `https://github.com/ChenRocks/UNITER`

	LXMERT		UNITER$_{paired-attn}$		UNITER$_{triplet}$	
	negative	positive	negative	positive	negative	positive
Verbal (content)	28.72	69.23	43.62	73.63	43.62	71.43
Verbal (existential)	30.56	82.41	50.0	77.77	44.44	66.66
NP (nonexistential)	44.83	67.86	48.28	64.29	55.17	50.0
NP (existential)	34.55	80.0	50.91	85.45	32.73	87.27
NP (number-to-none)	54.17	72.22	51.39	77.77	55.56	76.39
Sentence-wide	38.55	66.27	31.33	69.87	38.55	65.06
Overall	36.96	73.5	45.35	76.5	44.22	71.5

Table 3: Accuracy on the negation test set and the corresponding non-negated (positive) examples.

	LXMERT		UNITER$_{paired-attn}$		UNITER$_{triplet}$	
	o. correct	o. incorrect	o. correct	o. incorrect	o. correct	o. incorrect
Verbal (content)	15.38	58.62	40.58	52.0	30.3	75.0
Verbal (existential)	21.35	73.68	46.43	62.5	29.17	75.0
NP (nonexistential)	30.0	77.78	42.11	60.0	40.0	71.43
NP (existential)	36.36	27.27	55.32	25.0	27.08	71.43
NP (number-to-none)	46.15	75.0	51.79	50.0	47.27	82.35
Sentence-wide	25.45	64.29	8.62	84.0	9.26	93.1
Overall	27.38	63.79	40.54	60.19	29.35	79.39

Table 4: Accuracy for the negated examples for whose original (unnegated) version the model makes a correct/incorrect prediction ("o. correct"/"o. incorrect").

5 Causal mediation analysis

We will now take a closer look at the effect of adding negation and the contributions of specific neurons to model predictions using causal mediation analysis. This type of analysis can help us measure the effect of a change in the input (adding negation) on the output beyond looking at accuracy only. We also apply mediation analysis to find out if specific neurons in the model contribute to a change in the output more than others. We continue to work with the negation categories described previously and aim to discover if the results from this analysis correspond to the observed differences in accuracy between the categories and whether neuron effects differ by category.

Similarly to Finlayson et al. (2021), we are working with a task which has correct and incorrect outputs (in their case continuations, in ours, labels). We therefore follow their definitions. We want to measure the ability of the model to predict the correct True/False label given the images and the sentence. Therefore, we define our response variable as:

$$y(u, l) = \frac{p_\theta(l_{incorrect}|u)}{p_\theta(l_{correct}|u)}$$

where u are the images and the text, which can either match (u_{true}) or not (u_{false}), and l is the label. This equation takes the following form depending on whether the gold label is True or False:

$$y(u_{true}, l) = \frac{p_\theta(l_{false}|u_{true})}{p_\theta(l_{true}|u_{true})}$$

$$y(u_{false}, l) = \frac{p_\theta(l_{true}|u_{false})}{p_\theta(l_{false}|u_{false})}$$

The value for y is small ($y < 1$) when the model assigns the correct label, and large ($y > 1$) when the model assigns the incorrect label.

Following Vig et al. (2020) and Finlayson et al. (2021), we define two *do*-operations: (a) `negate`: negate the original sentence so that the truth value changes, and (b) `null`: no change. We also define $y_x(u, l)$ to be the value of y when we apply the operation x to the context u. This takes the following values under the `negate` operation for each of the possible values of u:

$$y_{\texttt{negate}}(u_{true}, l) = \frac{p_\theta(l_{false}|u_{false})}{p_\theta(l_{true}|u_{false})}$$

$$y_{\texttt{negate}}(u_{false}, l) = \frac{p_\theta(l_{true}|u_{true})}{p_\theta(l_{false}|u_{true})}$$

In order to measure the change in the response variable under the intervention (negation), we define the unit-level (per one original/negated pair) total effect as:

$$TE(\texttt{negate}, \texttt{null}; y, u, l) = \frac{y_{\texttt{negate}}(u,l) - y_{\texttt{null}}(u,l)}{y_{\texttt{null}}(u,l)} = \frac{y_{\texttt{negate}}(u,l)}{y_{\texttt{null}}(u,l)} - 1$$

As Finlayson et al. (2021) state, this quantity measures the margin between the probability of the correct and incorrect answers under an intervention. However, unlike Finlayson et al. (2021), we analyse the originally correct and originally incorrect examples separately. When the model predicts the original example correctly, a larger total effect under the intervention could indicate a better handling of negation, as it suggests a higher probability of the correct label under negation. When the original example is predicted incorrectly, it is less clear what the total effect indicates. While a larger total effect suggests a move towards the correct prediction under negation, this does not necessarily mean negation is handled better. A smaller total effect suggests a move toward the incorrect label, but this means flipping the label, which is desired behaviour.

We calculate the average total effect across all example pairs, for each negation type and for two different sizes of UNITER:

$$\overline{TE}(\texttt{negate}, \texttt{null}; y) = \mathbb{E}_{u,l}\left[\frac{y_{\texttt{negate}}(u,l)}{y_{\texttt{null}}(u,l)} - 1\right]$$

For the mediation analysis, we focus on the effects of individual neurons from the representation of the [CLS] token on the response variable y. In the following definition, z refers to a single neuron. We measure the natural indirect effect (NIE) of a change in the input X on the response variable y, with respect to a mediator z. As mentioned in Section 2.3, this is done by fixing the input to its value without the intervention, but changing the value of the mediator z to its value under the intervention. In this case, we set the input to its value without negation (i.e. the original images-sentence pair which does not contain negation), but set the value of z (the neuron) to the value it would take if the input was the negated version of the images-sentence pair. The population level NIE then is defined as:

$$\overline{NIE}(\texttt{negate}, \texttt{null}; y, z) = \mathbb{E}_{u,l}\left[\frac{y_{\texttt{null}, z_{\texttt{negate}}(u,l)}(u,l)}{y_{\texttt{null}}(u,l)} - 1\right]$$

As we are concerned with the effects of specific mediators (the neurons) on the output, we do not calculate the natural direct effect (NDE) which measures the effect of the input without the intervention of a mediator. We also do not consider intervening on attention heads in this work, as the length of the original and the negated sentences is different.

5.1 Results

For this analysis we use the triplet version of UNITER (Chen et al., 2020). We perform the analysis on the base and large versions of the model (see Appendix E for accuracy results of the large model). We use UNITER-base and UNITER-large to refer to the two sizes of the triplet model.

Total effects We report the total effect for each negation type for both model sizes, separately for the originally correct and originally incorrect examples (Figure 3). Looking at the originally correct examples (left side of Figure 3), we observe that the total effects of UNITER-base are in most cases several orders of magnitude larger than those of UNITER-large. This difference between models could mean that the two models assign probabilities differently, i.e., the base model assigns more extreme probabilities to the correct answers, while the large model assigns more moderate probabilities. Both models show similar patterns, with the lowest total effects being observed for the sentence-wide and the verbal (content) negation categories and the highest for the NP (nonexistential) and verbal (existential) categories. This pattern does not show any apparent correlation with the accuracies reported in the previous section – a higher total effect does not necessarily mean a higher accuracy. It is possible that for categories with higher accuracy but comparatively lower total effects the change in probability is moderate, but meaningful – enough to flip the label. At the same time, it could be that the categories with a high total effect contain examples with extreme probabilities which skew the average.

The right part of the figure shows the total effects of examples for which the model incorrectly predicts the original. A larger total effect indicates a

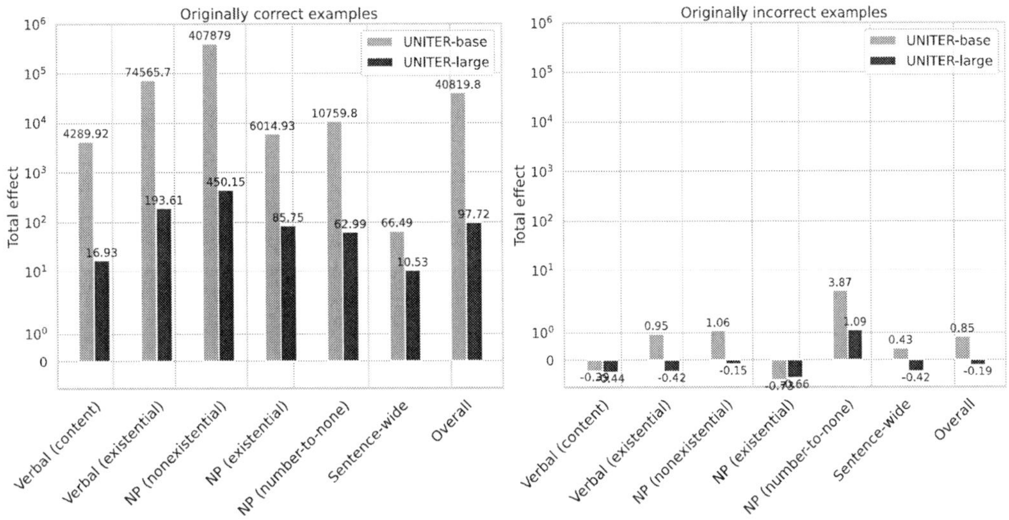

Figure 3: Total effects by correctness of the original (non-negated) example.

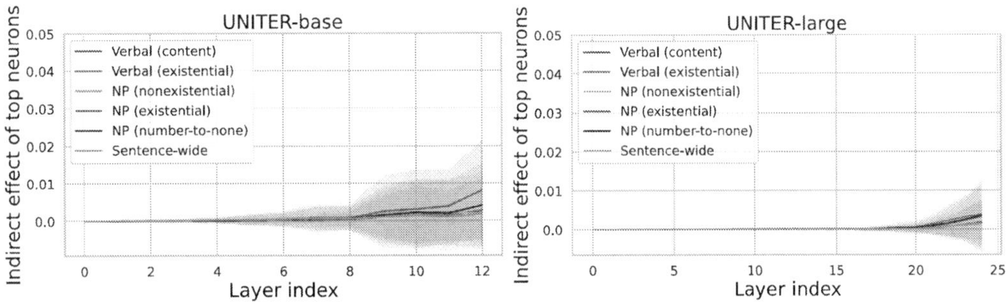

Figure 4: Natural indirect effect of the top 5% of neurons in each layer per negation category. Shaded area represents the standard deviation.

larger change in the probability moving towards the correct prediction for the negated sample, whereas a smaller (negative) total effect indicates a larger change moving in the direction of the incorrect prediction for the negated sample. These changes are more difficult to interpret for the originally incorrect samples. A larger total effect could indicate that the model is handling negation, however, it is not clear why that would be the case if the original sample was incorrectly predicted. A negative total effect indicates that the prediction probability is moving towards the opposite label from the one predicted for the original which could also be interpreted as the model handling the negation, since a change of label is expected. All total effects are smaller than the ones observed for the originally correct examples, which is expected given the observed high accuracies – the model prediction does not change a lot under the intervention and the total effect is closer to zero.

Natural indirect effects Figure 4 shows the NIEs of the top 5% of neurons with the highest NIE in each layer, for each negation category. We observe that for both models, the NIEs are approximately zero in the lower layers and become larger in the upper layers. The NIEs are similar between negation types, however, for both models we observe the highest NIEs for the NP (existential) type. We do not see any differences in patterns based on the negation category, which suggests we do not have evidence for a different treatment of the different categories by the model. We also compared the NIEs of examples split by whether the original/negated one is correctly predicted by the model, however, we do not observe notable differences (Appendix F).

Previous studies on language models have shown

that syntactic information is stored in the middle layers, task-specific information is stored in the upper layers and there are conflicting conclusions regarding semantic information being found in the upper layers, or throughout the model (see Rogers et al. (2020) for an overview). It is unclear whether these patterns hold for vision-and-language models. However, if they do, our results show that the models do not process negation on a syntactic level – at least not in terms of the neurons. The observed effects in the upper layers suggest that negation may be semantically processed in some way. Further investigation is required to draw more definite conclusions.

6 Conclusion

Our work shows that pre-trained vision-and-language models find it difficult to handle negation, which is a finding that is consistent with previous work on pre-trained language models. Using a manually created set of minimally differing pairs we show that two vision-and-language models (LXMERT and UNITER) fail to reach good performance in the presence of negation. We conduct causal mediation analysis on the neurons of one model and find that the main effects of negation are found in the upper layers. However, these effects are small and do not seem to correlate well with model accuracy.

While causal mediation analysis is a useful analysis tool, it is not straightforward to apply it to all models and to the analysis of attention when the input is of different length in the base case and under the intervention. In the future we would like to extend our analysis to other model variations (e.g., the UNITER$_{paired\text{-}attn}$ model which processes the images separately from each other), and to attention heads.

Acknowledgements

This work was supported in part by the UKRI Centre for Doctoral Training in Natural Language Processing, funded by the UKRI (grant EP/S022481/1) and the University of Edinburgh, School of Informatics and School of Philosophy, Psychology & Language Sciences.

References

Stanislaw Antol, Aishwarya Agrawal, Jiasen Lu, Margaret Mitchell, Dhruv Batra, C. Lawrence Zitnick, and Devi Parikh. 2015. VQA: Visual Question Answering. In *2015 IEEE International Conference on Computer Vision (ICCV)*, pages 2425–2433.

Jize Cao, Zhe Gan, Yu Cheng, Licheng Yu, Yen-Chun Chen, and Jingjing Liu. 2020. Behind the scene: Revealing the secrets of pre-trained vision-and-language models. In *Computer Vision – ECCV 2020*, pages 565–580, Cham. Springer International Publishing.

Yen-Chun Chen, Linjie Li, Licheng Yu, Ahmed El Kholy, Faisal Ahmed, Zhe Gan, Yu Cheng, and Jingjing Liu. 2020. UNITER: UNiversal Image-TExt Representation Learning. In *European Conference on Computer Vision*, pages 104–120. Springer.

Kevin Clark, Urvashi Khandelwal, Omer Levy, and Christopher D. Manning. 2019. What Does BERT Look at? An Analysis of BERT's Attention. In *Proceedings of the 2019 ACL Workshop BlackboxNLP: Analyzing and Interpreting Neural Networks for NLP*, pages 276–286, Florence, Italy. Association for Computational Linguistics.

Jacob Devlin, Ming-Wei Chang, Kenton Lee, and Kristina Toutanova. 2019. BERT: Pre-training of deep bidirectional transformers for language understanding. In *Proceedings of the 2019 Conference of the North American Chapter of the Association for Computational Linguistics: Human Language Technologies, Volume 1 (Long and Short Papers)*, pages 4171–4186, Minneapolis, Minnesota. Association for Computational Linguistics.

Yanai Elazar, Shauli Ravfogel, Alon Jacovi, and Yoav Goldberg. 2021. Amnesic Probing: Behavioral Explanation with Amnesic Counterfactuals. *Transactions of the Association for Computational Linguistics*, 9:160–175.

Allyson Ettinger. 2020. What BERT is Not: Lessons from a New Suite of Psycholinguistic Diagnostics for Language Models. *Transactions of the Association for Computational Linguistics*, 8(0):34–48.

Matthew Finlayson, Aaron Mueller, Sebastian Gehrmann, Stuart Shieber, Tal Linzen, and Yonatan Belinkov. 2021. Causal Analysis of Syntactic Agreement Mechanisms in Neural Language Models. In *Proceedings of the 59th Annual Meeting of the Association for Computational Linguistics and the 11th International Joint Conference on Natural Language Processing (Volume 1: Long Papers)*, pages 1828–1843, Online. Association for Computational Linguistics.

Md Mosharaf Hossain, Venelin Kovatchev, Pranoy Dutta, Tiffany Kao, Elizabeth Wei, and Eduardo Blanco. 2020. An Analysis of Natural Language Inference Benchmarks through the Lens of Negation. In *Proceedings of the 2020 Conference on Empirical Methods in Natural Language Processing (EMNLP)*, pages 9106–9118, Online. Association for Computational Linguistics.

Nora Kassner and Hinrich Schütze. 2020. Negated and Misprimed Probes for Pretrained Language Models: Birds Can Talk, But Cannot Fly. In *Proceedings of the 58th Annual Meeting of the Association for Computational Linguistics*, pages 7811–7818, Online. Association for Computational Linguistics.

Liunian Harold Li, Mark Yatskar, Da Yin, Cho-Jui Hsieh, and Kai-Wei Chang. 2019. VisualBERT: A Simple and Performant Baseline for Vision and Language. In *Arxiv*.

Liunian Harold Li, Mark Yatskar, Da Yin, Cho-Jui Hsieh, and Kai-Wei Chang. 2020. What does BERT with vision look at? In *Proceedings of the 58th Annual Meeting of the Association for Computational Linguistics*, pages 5265–5275, Online. Association for Computational Linguistics.

Jiasen Lu, Dhruv Batra, Devi Parikh, and Stefan Lee. 2019. ViLBERT: Pretraining Task-Agnostic Visiolinguistic Representations for Vision-and-Language Tasks. In *Advances in Neural Information Processing Systems*, volume 32. Curran Associates, Inc.

Judea Pearl. 2001. Direct and indirect effects. In *Proceedings of the Seventeenth Conference on Uncertainty in Artificial Intelligence*, UAI'01, page 411–420, San Francisco, CA, USA. Morgan Kaufmann Publishers Inc.

Geoffrey K. Pullum and Rodney Huddleston. 2002. Negation. In *The Cambridge Grammar of the English Language*, page 785–850. Cambridge University Press.

Anna Rogers, Olga Kovaleva, and Anna Rumshisky. 2020. A Primer in BERTology: What We Know About How BERT Works. *Transactions of the Association for Computational Linguistics*, 8:842–866.

Alane Suhr, Stephanie Zhou, Ally Zhang, Iris Zhang, Huajun Bai, and Yoav Artzi. 2019. A Corpus for Reasoning about Natural Language Grounded in Photographs. In *Proceedings of the 57th Annual Meeting of the Association for Computational Linguistics*, pages 6418–6428, Florence, Italy. Association for Computational Linguistics.

Hao Tan and Mohit Bansal. 2019. LXMERT: Learning cross-modality encoder representations from transformers. In *Proceedings of the 2019 Conference on Empirical Methods in Natural Language Processing and the 9th International Joint Conference on Natural Language Processing (EMNLP-IJCNLP)*, pages 5100–5111, Hong Kong, China. Association for Computational Linguistics.

Ian Tenney, Dipanjan Das, and Ellie Pavlick. 2019. BERT Rediscovers the Classical NLP Pipeline. In *Proceedings of the 57th Annual Meeting of the Association for Computational Linguistics*, pages 4593–4601, Florence, Italy. Association for Computational Linguistics.

Jesse Vig, Sebastian Gehrmann, Yonatan Belinkov, Sharon Qian, Daniel Nevo, Yaron Singer, and Stuart Shieber. 2020. Investigating Gender Bias in Language Models Using Causal Mediation Analysis. In *Advances in Neural Information Processing Systems*, volume 33, pages 12388–12401. Curran Associates, Inc.

Hedde Zeijlstra. 2007. Negation in natural language: On the form and meaning of negative elements. *Language and Linguistics Compass*, 1(5):498–518.

Rowan Zellers, Yonatan Bisk, Ali Farhadi, and Yejin Choi. 2019. From recognition to cognition: Visual commonsense reasoning. In *2019 IEEE/CVF Conference on Computer Vision and Pattern Recognition (CVPR)*, pages 6713–6724.

A Negation word list

not, isn't, aren't, doesn't, don't, can't, cannot, shouldn't, won't, wouldn't, no, none, nobody, nothing, nowhere, neither, nor, never, without

B Sample selection

During the annotation samples with the following properties were discarded:

- Samples which already contain negation.
- Samples with inappropriate or unpleasant images.
- Samples which are too similar to already annotated samples. Because of the way NLVR2 was created, there are sample pairs that are very similar to each other – those were discarded to increase the diversity of the negation test set.
- Samples with sentences containing typos and other errors.
- Samples for which there is no way to negate the sentences and flip the label, and at the same time keep them grammatically correct.

C Negation examples with images

See Figure 5.

D Negation types in original data

We annotated the negation types of 100 examples from the NLVR2 training set which were automatically determined to contain negation, as well as 50 from the development and test sets each. Results are shown in Table 5. We do not distinguish between NP (existential) and NP (number-to-none), since there are no "original" examples to compare with. The "Other" category contains mostly negated adjectives. The original negated examples differ from our annotation in several ways. First, the sentence-wide type is not found in the original data. This was confirmed by a simple search across the whole dataset for the phrases which compose this negation type ("It is not the case that ...", "It is not true that ..."). Second, there are very few instances of verbal (existential) negation in the original data, whereas this type is very over-represented in our annotation. Finally, NP (nonexistential) is very under-represented in our annotation compared to the original data.

	Train	Dev	Test
Verbal (content)	20	28	22
Verbal (existential)	3	2	10
NP (existential)	45	40	46
NP (nonexistential)	31	32	26
Other	2	2	4

Table 5: Percentage of examples that contain each of the negation types. Note that some examples contain more than one type, so the percentages do not add up to 100.

E UNITER-large triplet results

See Table 6.

F NIE per correctness category

Figure 6 shows the NIEs of each negation type for UNITER-base, comparing between correctness categories. The four correctness categories reflect the correctness of the original sample without the intervention and the correctness of the negated sample. NIE can be negative, which indicates a change towards the incorrect label. Here, we look at both the top 5% neurons and the bottom 5% neurons to find out if some neurons specifically contribute to incorrect predictions. The patterns we see are largely similar between the six negation types. The largest NIEs are observed in cases where both the original and the negated samples are predicted wrong. However, this result may be unreliable due to the small sample size (recall from Section 4 that a large percentage of the originally incorrect samples are predicted correctly when negated, therefore the number of "i-i" examples is small). The other correctness categories all exhibit similar NIEs with the highest values concentrated in the upper layers (8 to 12). We expected to see higher NIE for the "c-c" category, however, that is not the case.

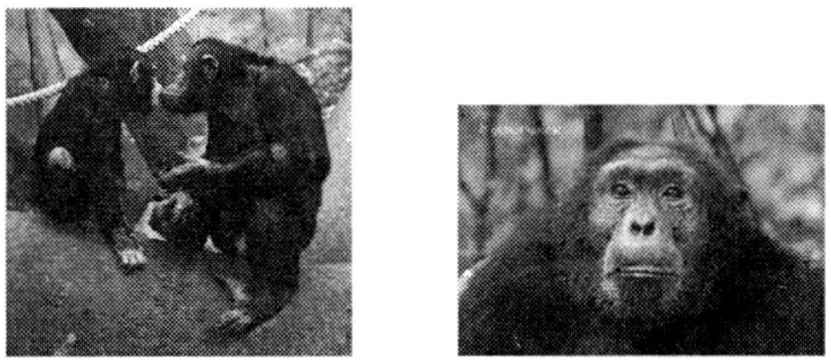

Original: At least one monkey is sitting in a tree in the image on the left. → True

Negated: At least one monkey is not sitting in a tree in the image on the left. → False

(a) Verbal (content)

Original: There are three pandas. → True

Negated: There aren't three pandas. → False

(b) Verbal (existential)

Original: Every dog is wearing a collar. → False

Negated: Not every dog is wearing a collar. → True

(c) NP (nonexistential)

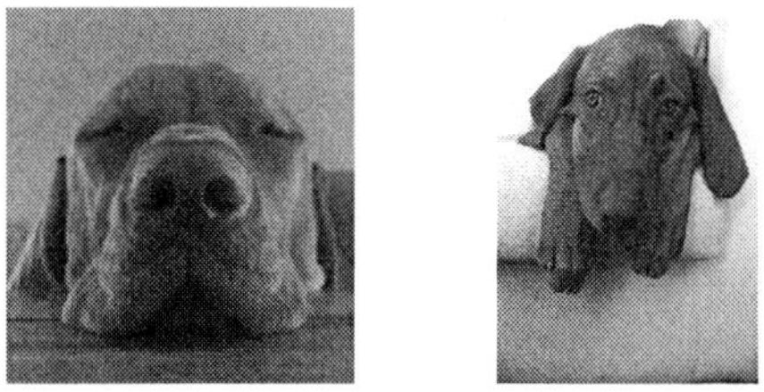

Original: A dog is resting its head on something. → True

Negated: No dog is resting its head on something. → False

(d) NP (existential)

Original: Four or fewer television screens are visible. → True

Negated: No television screens are visible. → False

(e) NP (number-to-none)

Original: Three or fewer goats are visible. → False

Negated: It is not true that three or fewer goats are visible. → True

(f) Sentence-wide

Figure 5: Examples for each negation type with images and labels.

	UNITER$_{triplet-large}$			
	negative	positive	o.correct	o.incorrect
Verbal (content)	43.62	74.76	36.62	65.22
Verbal (existential)	54.63	68.52	51.35	61.76
NP (existential)	56.36	85.46	59.57	37.5
NP (number-to-none)	58.33	76.38	54.55	70.59
NP (nonexistential)	48.28	60.71	33.33	72.73
Sentence-wide	37.35	72.29	21.67	78.26
Overall	49.43	74.0	43.38	66.38

Table 6: Results on the negation test set.

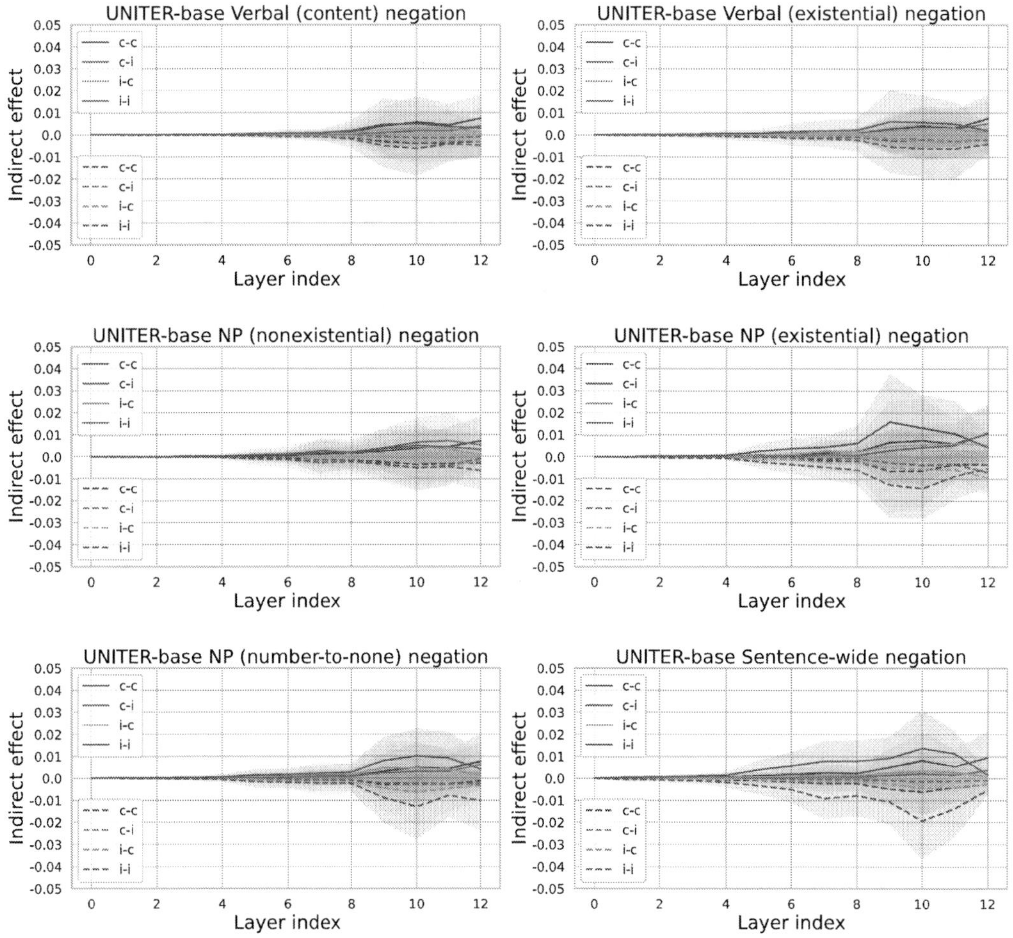

Figure 6: Natural indirect effect of the top (solid line) and bottom (dashed line) 5% of neurons in each layer. The figure shows the NIEs by correctness category: "c-c": both original and negated sample are correctly predicted; "c-i": original is correctly predicted and negated is incorrectly predicted; "i-c": original is incorrectly predicted, negated is correctly predicted; "i-i": both are incorrectly predicted.

Not all parameters are born equal: Attention is mostly what you need

Nikolay Bogoychev
School of Informatics
University of Edinburgh
United Kingdom
n.bogoych@ed.ac.uk

Abstract

Transformers are widely used in state-of-the-art machine translation, but the key to their success is still unknown. To gain insight into this, we consider three groups of parameters: embeddings, attention, and Feed-Forward Neural network (FFN) layers. We examine the relative importance of each by performing an ablation study where we initialise them at random and freeze them, so that their weights do not change over the course of the training. Through this, we show that the attention and FFN are equally important and fulfil the same functionality in a model. We show that the decision about whether a component is frozen or allowed to train is at least as important for the final model performance as its number of parameters. At the same time, the number of parameters alone is not indicative of a component's importance. Finally, while the embedding layer is the least essential for machine translation tasks, it is the most important component for language modelling tasks.

1 Introduction

Bizarrely, we find that a transformer model (Vaswani et al., 2017) for machine translation loses just 1.1–2% BLEU when any one of the three main components (embeddings, attention, and feed-forward) is frozen with randomly initialised parameters. In more extreme cases we see that with just 6% of trainable parameters, we maintain 72% of the baseline BLEU. This suggests that redundancy in the model architecture is able to compensate for poor components. We perform a case study on transformer style models, exploring the built-in redundancy and the limits of what can be achieved when the majority of parameters are frozen after random initialisation. We do this in several different transformer architecture presets for neural machine translation: transformer-big, transformer-base and a transformer-tiny student preset, and one preset for a language modelling task. Our key findings are:

- The majority of the model information is learned by the attention and the Feed-Forward Neural network (FFN), while the embeddings provide complementary but non-essential signals. The attention and the FFN layers are mostly interchangeable.
- Even if it is not essential for some components to be learned, their size (number of parameters) is essential to provide extra expressiveness for the components that are learned: if components are initialised as diagonal matrices as opposed to random matrices, they further lose their effectiveness.
- The overall size of the model does affect the results: Larger models have more built-in redundancy and are able to retain higher performance with fewer trainable components.
- The smaller proportion of trainable parameters the model has, in general, leads to slower convergence in terms of number of epochs, suggesting learning is hampered.
- Our findings are task specific: While machine translation is learned in the attention and the FFN layer, this does not necessarily generalise to other tasks. Language modelling is learned in the embeddings layer.

Our study sheds light on the inner workings of the transformer neural network architecture and examines in detail the relative contribution of each component towards the final performance.

2 Methodology

We perform a parameter-freezing case study on transformer style models. A transformer consists of three basic components: an embeddings layer,

Proceedings of the Fourth BlackboxNLP Workshop on Analyzing and Interpreting Neural Networks for NLP, pages 363–374
Online, November 11, 2021.

attention layers, and FFN, as shown in Figure 1. The embeddings encompass the source, target embeddings and the output layer as they are tied (Press and Wolf, 2017).

We initialise the model with the Glorot distribution (Glorot and Bengio, 2010) and pick a component (or components) to mark as untrainable or "frozen".[1] This effectively means that during training the model will benefit from the extra transformations that those parameters provide, but they are random. It is up to the remaining components to accommodate them. Freezing parameters is frequently performed in transfer learning (Zoph et al., 2016; Thompson et al., 2018; Clinchant et al., 2019) in order to prevent the child model from deviating in an undesired manner from the parent. Through these experiments we identify which components are essential for the model, which are interchangeable and which are complementary. An essential trainable component by itself can achieve high performance with the other components being random, while a non-essential component is not able to achieve good performance by itself. Finally, we exchange the frozen random initialisation of components with frozen diagonal (identity) initialisation to verify how important the transformations of the frozen components are.

In the next few sections, we first train a baseline model with no frozen components. Then we train 3 models with one frozen component: either the embedding layer, the FFN layer or the attention. Finally we perform experiments where two out of the three components are frozen.

3 Transformer-big experiments

For our main experiments we used 1M parallel Turkish-English sentences from the WMT 18 News translation task (Bojar et al., 2018) (200K gold and 800K back-translated (Sennrich et al., 2016a)). Data was preprocessed and tokenised using Moses (Koehn et al., 2007) and a shared vocabulary of 36K byte-pair encoding (BPE) tokens (Sennrich et al., 2016b). For training the model, we used the Marian (Junczys-Dowmunt et al., 2018) implementation of the transformer-big architecture (Vaswani et al., 2017) with tied embeddings and 8 attention heads for a total of 213M parameters. This model, and all subsequent were trained until 10 consecutive stalls on the perplexity of the dev set or 50 consecutive stalls on the BLEU score of the dev set, whichever is sooner. All the BLEU (Papineni et al., 2002) scores are reported on the 2016 dev set provided by the shared task organisers. We present our experiments in Table 1. For reader convenience, each system is also referred to by its number in the result analysis.

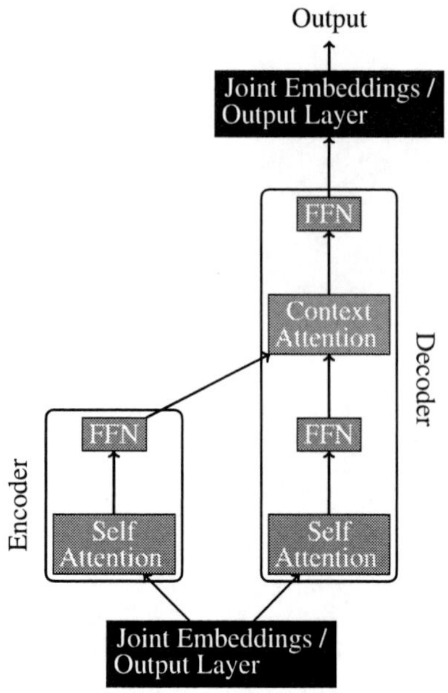

Figure 1: A simplified view of transformer with input, output embeddings, and output layer tied together. The encoder self-attends to the entire input, while the decoder self-attends to the output it has produced thus far.

	Component					Parameter ratio
	EMB	ATT	FFN	BLEU	Epochs	Trainable/All
(0)	✓	✓	✓	24.3	19	1
			One frozen component			
(1)	✗	✓	✓	22.6	26	.82
(2)	✓	✗	✓	22.3	23	.64
(3)	✓	✓	✗	23.2	26	.52
			Multiple frozen components			
(4)	✗	✓	✗	21.5	36	.35
(5)	✗	✗	✓	20.8	37	.47
(6)	✓	✗	✗	4.4	25	.17

Table 1: Trainable and random components for Turkish-English transformer-big. Trainable components are marked with ✓, fixed components with ✗. BLEU is computed on the dev set.

Freezing a subset of the model leads to a tiny increase in the training speed in terms of words processed per second for all models, due to the reduced computational cost when performing the backward

[1] Code available at `https://github.com/XapaJIaMnu/marian-dev/tree/freeze_FFN`

pass. However, this speed benefit is negated by the extra epochs required to achieve convergence, to the point that every single model was slower to converge in terms of real time. The increased training time is likely due to the optimiser running into more saddle points, as there are less parameters that can be pushed into a better model direction (Pascanu et al., 2014; Dauphin et al., 2014). Freezing components also always leads to reduced performance in terms of BLEU compared to the baseline, which is expected and is also observed when transferring pretrained components (Zoph et al., 2016; Clinchant et al., 2019; Aji et al., 2020).

Our results show that when there is one frozen component, all models perform very similarly, with the frozen FFN one (3) being slightly better than the other two. However, when we look at the experiments where we have multiple frozen components, it is evident that the attention and the FFN layer are more essential for the overall model performance: If both of them are initialised randomly and left frozen, the model fails to learn completely (6).

Based on this we can conclude that the embedding layer is the least essential to be learned in the context of the machine translation task and the remaining components can easily learn to work with random embeddings. This result confirms the findings of Aji et al. (2020), who show that transferring the embedding layer during transfer learning is the least important for the overall model performance. In the rest of the transformer-big experiments, we omit the system with just the embedding layer trainable, as the model quality in this setting is very poor.

We also note that a model with trainable embeddings and attention (3) outperforms a model with frozen embeddings (1), despite the FFN and attention being more essential to be learned. This suggests that the embeddings perform a different role from the attention and the FFN in the translation process. Based on the similar performance that the trainable attention and the FFN offer, we hypothesise that they are able to encode the same information and in case that one of them is not trainable, the other one can mostly fulfil its role. Our hypothesis is supported by the work of Geva et al. (2020), who show that feed forward transformer layers are key-value memories. On the other hand, trainable embeddings, while least essential for the model performance likely learn complementary, albeit non-essential, information to the attention and the FFN.

We find a weak correlation between the number of parameters of a component and its importance to the model: The embeddings layer has the least amount of parameters and is the least essential to be trained, however we can't rank the other two components: The FFN has considerably more parameters than the attention, but they both seem to be equally important for the model's performance.

We note that the model with just attention trainable (4) is able to reach competitive performance, despite having just 35% of the model parameters.

3.1 Reducing the embedding layer

Since we found that the embedding layer is the least essential to be trained, we decided to shrink its dimension from the 1024 (default for transformer-big) to 128, set it to trainable and vary the attention layer and FFN layer. By doing this, we implicitly reduce the width of the other components too, because the matrix dimensions need to match. The resulting models have only 18M parameters (Table 2) are markedly worse in terms of BLEU compared to the models with a bigger embedding layer.

	Component EMB	ATT	FFN	BLEU	Epochs	Parameter ratio Trainable/All
	Large baseline			24.3	19	1
(0)	✓	✓	✓	22.9	115	1
	One frozen component					
(1)	✗	✓	✓	18.9	142	.75
(2)	✓	✗	✓	16.2	274	.93
(3)	✓	✓	✗	18.9	132	.31
	Multiple frozen components					
(4)	✗	✓	✗	5.1	227	.07
(5)	✗	✗	✓	7.8	307	.69

Table 2: Turkish-English transformer-big with small, embedding layer dimension. Trainable components are marked with ✓, fixed components are marked with ✗. BLEU is computed on the dev set.

These experiments show larger difference in BLEU between attention and FFN: With this smaller model, when embeddings are trainable, a trainable attention (3) reaches much better BLEU score, and in half of the epochs, compared to trainable FFN (2). In addition to that, the attention layer has a lot fewer parameters compared to FFN, showing that the number of parameters a component has is not a marker for how important it is to have that component trainable for the final model's performance. As the difference between the performance of trainable attention vs trainable FFN is more pronounced in the smaller model setting, we can say that model size can change the conclusions. We also note that in this setting, trainable attention and FFN layer (1) achieve the same performance as (3), despite having more than twice the number of parameters, suggesting again that the embeddings are able to learn complementary information to the attention, even if their dimension is tiny.

Furthermore we note that despite that these models are 12 times smaller then the baseline, they converge slower, requiring up to 10 times more epochs, suggesting learning is more difficult. This further highlights that the attention is a more essential component than the FFN, as it can adapt to the training data with fewer signals.

This model has catastrophic loss of BLEU when there is only one trainable component (4, 5), suggesting that larger models are more robust and have more redundancy between components.

3.2 Reducing the FFN layer size

We perform a similar experiment with the FFN layer, reducing its dimension from 4096 to 1024. The resulting models have 137M parameters and are shown in Table 4.

	Component EMB	ATT	FFN	BLEU	Epochs	Parameter ratio Trainable/All
	trans-big baseline			24.3	19	1
(0)	✓	✓	✓	23.2	22	1
	One frozen component					
(1)	✗	✓	✓	22.0	38	.73
(2)	✓	✗	✓	20.1	36	.55
(3)	✓	✓	✗	23.0	18	.82
	Multiple frozen components					
(4)	✗	✓	✗	21.6	34	.45
(5)	✗	✗	✓	18.0	98	.18

Table 3: Trainable and random components for Turkish-English transformer-big with small FFN layer. Trainable components are marked with ✓, fixed components with ✗. BLEU is computed on the dev set.

This experiment shows similar trends as the one in the previous section: The model requires more epochs to converge compared to the baseline transformer-big and reaches slightly lower quality. As the size of the FFN layer is reduced, we observe that a trainable attention is always better than a trainable FFN layer (Table 3, (2) vs (3), and (4) vs (5)). Finally, when the FFN layer is reduced in size, it matters less whether it is trainable or random and frozen: When it is random (3), we only lose .2 BLEU compared to the baseline system (0). Nevertheless, just the small trainable FFN layer which makes up for 18% of the total model parameters is able to reach 18.0 BLEU (5).

We note that when all of the components of this model are trainable, it achieves the same performance as the baseline system with frozen FFN (Table 1, (3)). This suggests that for certain components, their width may be as important as whether they are trainable or not. In this setting we also see a sharper drop in performance when attention is not trainable, suggesting the capacity of the FFN to take over the attention's function has diminished.

3.3 Reducing the attention layer size

We perform an analogous experiment, where we reduce the size of the second dimension of the keys and queries attention matrices 8-fold, reducing the total model size to 147M parameters. In this setting, all attention matrices make up just 6% of the total model size. We show our experiments in Table 4.

	Component EMB	ATT	FFN	BLEU	Epochs	Parameter ratio Trainable/All
	trans-big baseline			24.3	19	1
(0)	✓	✓	✓	23.4	13	1
	One frozen component					
(1)	✗	✓	✓	22.1	23	.74
(2)	✓	✗	✓	22.1	16	.94
(3)	✓	✓	✗	20.4	23	.31
	Multiple frozen components					
(4)	✗	✓	✗	17.0	196	.06
(5)	✗	✗	✓	21.3	33	.69

Table 4: Trainable and random components for Turkish-English transformer-big with smaller attention matrices. Trainable components are marked with ✓, fixed components with ✗. BLEU is computed on the dev set.

In this setting, our findings are mirroring the results from the previous section: When the size of the attention layer is reduced to that extent, we see that the FFN layer is now more essential for the performance of the model: It outperforms the attention layer in all direct comparisons (Table 4, (2) vs (3), and (4) vs (5)). We note that despite the attention layer having only 6% of the total number of parameters, by itself (4), it manages to retain 72% of the baseline BLEU score.

We note that in this experiment, as well as in the previous where we reduce the dimension of the FFN layer, there is a clear trend that the number of epochs necessary for convergence increases as the number of trainable model parameters decreases.

3.4 Self and context attention

The experiments that we have conducted so far suggest that the attention layer is the most essential for the translation performance. However, attention refers to several different attention modules in a transformer. Attention can be split into self-attention and context attention. Self-attention is present in both the encoder and the decoder. The encoder attends to the full input sequence, while the decoder has masked attention and attends to the output it has produced thus far. Context attention is an attention module that appears only in the decoder and attends to the encoded sequence.

We can also make the split by component, having encoder-only attention and decoder-only attention. The different types of attention and their position in the transformer architecture are shown in Figure 1.

In this experiment, we take the transformer-big model used previously, set the embedding layer to trainable and freeze the FFN layer. We specifically avoid training the FFN layer, because it can take over some of the functionality of our restricted attention layer and this will make our findings less clear. For our experiments, we only train a subset of the attention (the remaining attention parts are left frozen and random), as shown in Table 5.

	Attention	BLEU	Epochs	Parameter ratio Trainable/All
(0)	full	23.2	26	.52
(1)	Self only	10.3	28	.41
(2)	Context only	18.1	40	.29
(3)	Encoder only	18.1	41	.29
(4)	Decoder only	19.8	24	.41

Table 5: tr-en transformer-big with trainable embeddings, fixed FFN and a trainable subset of attention. BLEU is computed on the dev set.

We see significant drop in BLEU when having only subsection of the attention as learnable. Referring back to our initial experiments in Table 1, partially setting the attention to untrainable is more harmful for the model than freezing it completely and having the FFN trainable.

Voita et al. (2019) show that context heads are the most important heads for a model and are the ones that are pruned last when performing head pruning. In our setting however, even if context heads are not learned, the model can still use the random activations with which they are initialised. That is enough for a model with trainable encoder attention to produce a BLEU score similar to that of a model that uses trainable context attention only.

The best result is when we have the full attention on the decoder side, as the decoder is the most involved component in translation (Voita et al., 2019).

In our experiments, trainable encoder attention performs better than self-attention only, despite the former having a superset of the latter's trainable parameters (Figure 1).

Independently from us, Tay et al. (2020) observe that the self-attention component is not essential in the neural machine translation task and can be synthesised on demand. They propose several different functions to do so and achieve smaller quality drop than us, however all of their experiments involve a more advanced synthesisation than simply initialising randomly and not training. Raganato et al. (2020) show that it is possible to replace all but one attention heads with a fixed attentive pattern without impact on translation quality.

Further to this line of work, Liu et al. (2021) show that attention could be replaced with a simple gated MLP network and still achieve competitive results, albeit they only show that for vision tasks.

4 Experiments with smaller models

The transformer-big preset used in the previous experiments is an overly expressive neural network with enough parameters, so that even when preventing a big part of them from being trained, the model likely has enough built-in redundancy to make up for it. In order to avoid this assumption, we performed analogous experiments with a transformer-base model, as well as a knowledge-distilled student transformer model. These experiments aim to reduce the model size in a systematic way in order to see whether our findings in the previous sections are dependent on the overall model size.

4.1 Experiments with transformer-base

We perform the same experiments as the ones in Section 3, but we change the model configuration to transformer-base. In effect this means that the number of attention heads remains the same, but the embeddings' and the FFN's dimension is halved. The overall size of the attention is also reduced implicitly, as its dimension is also dependent on the embeddings. The resulting model has 62.6M parameters. We present our results in Table 6.

	Component EMB	ATT	FFN	BLEU	Epochs	Parameter ratio Trainable/All
	trans-big baseline			24.3	19	1
(0)	✓	✓	✓	23.9	32	1
	One frozen component					
(1)	✗	✓	✓	22.3	62	.71
(2)	✓	✗	✓	20.5	40	.70
(3)	✓	✓	✗	22.7	39	.60
	Multiple frozen components					
(4)	✗	✓	✗	20.0	148	.30
(5)	✗	✗	✓	17.5	76	.40
(6)	✓	✗	✗	3.9	110	.30

Table 6: Trainable and random components for Turkish-English transformer-base. Trainable components are marked with ✓, fixed components with ✗. BLEU is computed on the dev set.

In the transformer-base setting we see similar trends as those with transformer-big (Table 1), except the quality drop when making components untrainable is more severe. We see that the difference between the attention layer and the FFN layer ((2) vs (3), (4) vs (5)) in terms of quality is widening, reaffirming that the attention is the most essential component. The FFN also has more parameters than the attention, showing again that the number of parameters a component has is not indicative of how important it is to have it trainable.

The overall trend we observe is that the smaller the model is, the bigger the gap between the attention and the FFN layer. In a transformer-big, there is more built-in redundancy and when a component is marked as untrainable, it is easy for the other components to step up and make up for it, however as the size of individual components decreases, this is no longer possible.

4.2 Knowledge distilled models

We performed an analogous experiment with a knowledge-distilled, small student model (Kim and Rush, 2016). The student translation models are normally too small to learn a good model from natural data, but given enough synthetic data, they can learn the distribution of a good teacher model. For this setting we trained an ensemble of four transformer-big Estonian-English models on gold and synthetic data from WMT 18 (Bojar et al., 2018). Then, we decoded 142M sentences with the ensemble and used those to train a student model. The student model has 32K shared source and target vocabulary tokens, embedding dimension of 256, 6 encoder layers, 2 decoder layers and 1536 dimensional Feed forward neural network, similar to the student models used in Bogoychev et al. (2020). Just as in the previous experiment, the source embeddings are tied to the target embeddings and to the output layer. This model has 16.9M parameters. We report BLEU scores on the dev set provided by the WMT 18 news task organisers (Bojar et al., 2018). We present our experiments in Table 7.

	Component EMB	ATT	FFN	BLEU	Epochs	Parameter ratio Trainable/All
(0)	✓	✓	✓	24.2	14	1
	One frozen component					
(1)	✗	✓	✓	20.3	15	.51
(2)	✓	✗	✓	21.6	6	.87
(3)	✓	✓	✗	21.3	4	.62
	Multiple frozen components					
(4)	✗	✓	✗	12.5	11	.14
(5)	✗	✗	✓	15.2	8	.39
(6)	✓	✗	✗	3.3	35	.49

Table 7: Trainable and random components for Estonian-English student transformer. Trainable components are marked with ✓, fixed components are marked with ✗. BLEU is computed on the dev set.

In this setting, we observe a few differences from the experiments on bigger transformers: Here, the trainable embedding layer in conjunction with either trainable attention (3), or FFN (2) delivers the best results, outperforming the configuration where it is frozen (1). Despite the embedding layer performing the worst by itself, when it is trainable, it is more valuable to the attention and the FFN. This experiment reaffirms the hypothesis that the attention and FFN layer fulfil the same functionality, and when one of them is frozen, the other is mostly able to compensate for it. However the embedding layer provides a different signal. Again, the embedding layer is unable to learn a meaningful translation model, despite containing nearly half of the model's parameters, clearly showing that the number of parameters is not related to how important a feature is. We also see that this student model is a lot more sensitive to the frozen parameters compared to the bigger transformers, with all results being markedly worse than the baseline, especially the ones with multiple frozen components.

The configuration of this student model differs significantly from the other architectures used, and it also behaves differently when freezing parameters. Therefore, the overall size of the model does affect the behaviour with regards to frozen and random parameters.

5 Language model experiments

In order to verify whether our findings generalise to other tasks, we performed a language modelling experiment. We trained a transformer language model, using 78M sentences taken from newscrawl 2017, 2018 and 2019. Our model is based on the transformer-base preset (Vaswani et al., 2017) with 32K BPE tokens vocabulary and 38M parameters. We show our results in Table 8, where we report perplexity on a dev set, formed by taking the first 1000 lines from each of the three newscrawl datasets. The devset is disjoint from the training set.

	Component					Parameter ratio
	EMB	ATT	FFN	PPL	Epochs	Trainable/All
(0)	✓	✓	✓	37.4	6	1
One frozen component						
(1)	✗	✓	✓	118.4	6	.53
(2)	✓	✗	✓	47.5	6	.81
(3)	✓	✓	✗	50.3	6	.64
Multiple frozen components						
(4)	✗	✓	✗	209.3	6	.18
(5)	✗	✗	✓	157.3	6	.36
(6)	✓	✗	✗	131.7	6	.46

Table 8: Trainable and random components for an English language model. Trainable components are marked with ✓, fixed components are marked with ✗. Perplexity is computed on the dev set.

A neural machine translation system is just a conditional language model, so this task is similar to our previous experiments, except that there is no encoder and no context attention. The transformer components in this case behave differently: the embedding layer is the most essential for the final model performance, capable of delivering the lowest perplexity of any system with multiple frozen components ((2) and (3)), and nearly outperforming by itself (6) a combination of trainable attention and FFN (1). Trainable embeddings and trainable either FFN (2) or attention (3) perform very similarly, suggesting again that they fulfil similar functionality in the model. By itself, however, trainable FFN (5) clearly outperforms trainable attention (4) suggesting that it is more important for this task. It is interesting to note that the number of epochs necessary for convergence does not vary among the different configurations used.

A change in the task can lead to a big change in the overall behaviour of components. For this task, the embedding layer loses the majority of its effectiveness if it is not trainable, unlike in the translation experiments.

6 Randomness and transformations

In order to measure how much the transformations provided by the random parameters help the trainable parameters, we performed an experiment where we initialise either the attention or the FFN layer of a transformer-big model to a diagonal matrix, with zeroes everywhere except at the main diagonal. For the attention this means that all three attention matrices in self and context attention are diagonal and just copy over their input to the output, however since attention is interpreted as different heads, it does mean that the individual heads are very sparse and attend only to a single token. In the case of the FFN layer, since it is not square, the upper part of the matrix is diagonal and the lower part is just zeroes.[2] We present our results on transformer-big model from Section 3 in Table 9.

	Component					Parameter ratio
	EMB	ATT	FFN	BLEU	Epochs	Trainable/All
(0)	✓	✓	✓	24.3	19	1
Random frozen component						
(2)	✓	✗	✓	22.3	23	.64
(3)	✓	✓	✗	23.2	26	.52
Diagonal zeroed frozen component						
(2.1)	✓	✗	✓	19.4	24	.64
(3.1)	✓	✓	✗	22.9	20	.52

Table 9: Trainable and random components for Turkish-English transformer-big contrasting randomly initialised parameters with diagonal matrix parameters. Trainable components are marked with ✓, fixed components with ✗. BLEU is computed on the dev set.

Our results are conflicting. When the attention is diagonal (3), the BLEU score drops significantly from when it is initialised to random (3.1). This suggests that the model indeed makes use of and learns to work with random parameters and the transformations they provide, however it can not adapt to work with diagonal parameter matrices, as they don't provide useful input.

In the case of the FFN layer, we see the opposite results. Making the FFN layer matrices have 1 only across their main diagonal (2.1) seems to marginally improve performance compared to the

[2] We used **numpy.eye** to initialise the matrices.

baseline case (2). Since the FFN layer is bypassed by residual connections which connect the attention to the output layer, we don't lose any information from the attention, and the ones across the main diagonal of the FFN allows for some minimal mixing of the output of the attention. In this case we can clearly see that the random transformations provided by the untrainable FFN are not as important, as the attention can do its job without them.

We conclude that in certain cases the model does benefit from the transformation provided by the random parameters, however this does not generalise to every component of a transformer. We did not perform this experiment with the embedding layer, as it is not square (The shape is (32000,512) or similar) and it is used to encode different vocabulary items. Rendering it diagonal across the main diagonal would leave the majority of the vocabulary items encoded as a 512 zero vector, which is not something that the model can learn from.

7 Discussion

We find that depending on the task, different components of a transformer are essential. Language modelling tasks require the embeddings to be trained, while translation can mostly cope without them. A large amount of research has focused on using BERT (Devlin et al., 2018) or ELMo (Peters et al., 2018) pre-trained embeddings in downstream tasks, but as shown here, embedding representation is not as important as embedding width in a translation task. Furthermore, there is evidence that in some downstream tasks, randomised language models perform competitively (Zhang and Bowman, 2018; Wang et al., 2018). We urge researchers to always evaluate how essential a component is by setting it to random and frozen, before performing transfer learning from pretrained components.

We find that the "width" of a component is at least as important for the final model performance as whether it is trainable or not, but the raw parameter size of a component is not indicative of whether it is essential to have it trained or not. This clearly suggests that when there is a frozen and random component of a model, the rest of the components are able to work around just as if it were an extra activation function. When the attention is rendered completely linear by making it diagonal, we show a more significant drop in the performance compared to when this is done to the FFN layer. This suggests that the transformation that happens in the attention is more important than the transformation that happens in the FFN layer.

We find that the smaller the model is, the more sensitive it is to having some of its components non-trainable. We suspect that transformer-big models have more built-in redundancy into them and adapt better to this situation. Curiously, the less parameters a model has, or the less trainable parameters the model has, the more epochs it takes to train. This is especially visible in the experiments of transformer-base (Table 6) vs transformer-big (Table 1) and the models with reduced embedding layer (Table 2). These effects are explainable by the works of Choromanska et al. (2015); Jacot et al. (2020); Sankararaman et al. (2020) which state that smaller networks are more likely to end up into local minimum and are more sensitive to parameter initialisation compared to bigger networks.

Finally we note how similarly the attention and FFN layers behave: When the attention layer is small, the FFN layer is more essential and vice versa. In a setting where they are trainable by themselves, they achieve similar performance, with the attention having slight edge in larger models. If we decrease the size of the embeddings layer, or use a transformer-base preset, the performance gap between the FFN and the attention widens in favour of the attention. This echoes the findings of Geva et al. (2020) and suggests that the attention and the FFN layer are interchangeable and more essential for the model's performance, however there is a degree of redundancy between them.

8 Related work

Concurrently and independently from us, Garg et al. (2020) perform an ablation study to show how gradually setting different components of an encoder-decoder MT system from random and frozen to trainable increases the BLEU scores from 4 to 39 for an English-French model. Unlike Garg et al. we use a transformer model and we show that wider and deeper models behave differently from small and narrow models. Furthermore we show that depending on the task, the model benefits the most from different components.

Our work follows a long line of research that explores the performance of random (Echo state) neural networks in various tasks (Ramamurthy et al., 2019; Tong et al., 2007; Homma and Hagiwara, 2013; Alhama and Zuidema, 2018).

Enguehard et al. (2019); Wieting and Kiela

(2019) explore random encoders for sentences and evaluate their performance in downstream tasks.

9 Conclusion and Future work

We performed a study of transformer neural machine translation component freezing that identified the attention and the FFN as more essential to be learned, but also interchangeable. The embedding layer can not perform the translation task by itself, but the information it learns is complementary to either the attention or the FFN layer. Our findings do not necessarily generalise over other tasks: In the language modelling setting, the components behave differently.

Our findings could serve as the basis for research into new transformer machine translation architectures for production (Kim et al., 2019; Bogoychev et al., 2020). We have shown that models can retain competitive performance even when the FFN layer, which accounts for up to 48% of the parameters, is just a randomly initialised Glorot distribution. This opens the door for models where part of the parameters are generated on the fly during decoding, as opposed to stored statically on disk, making it particularly suitable to embedded devices with limited memory.

Acknowledgments

We thank the reviewers for their suggestions and comments! We thank Kenneth Heafield, Adam Lopez, Naomi Saphra and the AGORA research group for the discussions and comments that shaped this paper. We thank Maximiliana Benhke for the use of her pretrained models.

This work was conducted within the scope of the Research and Innovation Action *Bergamot*, which has received funding from the European Union's Horizon 2020 research and innovation programme under grant agreement No 825303.

References

Alham Fikri Aji, Nikolay Bogoychev, Kenneth Heafield, and Rico Sennrich. 2020. In neural machine translation, what does transfer learning transfer? In *Proceedings of the 2020 Annual Conference of the Association for Computational Linguistics*, Seattle.

Raquel Alhama and Willem Zuidema. 2018. Pre-wiring and pre-training: What does a neural network need to learn truly general identity rules? *Journal of Artificial Intelligence Research*, 61:927–946.

Nikolay Bogoychev, Roman Grundkiewicz, Alham Fikri Aji, Maximiliana Behnke, Kenneth Heafield, Sidharth Kashyap, Emmanouil-Ioannis Farsarakis, and Mateusz Chudyk. 2020. Edinburgh's submissions to the 2020 machine translation efficiency task. In *Proceedings of the The 4th Workshop on Neural Generation and Translation (WNGT 2020)*, Seattle.

Ondřej Bojar, Christian Federmann, Mark Fishel, Yvette Graham, Barry Haddow, Philipp Koehn, and Christof Monz. 2018. Findings of the 2018 conference on machine translation (WMT18). In *Proceedings of the Third Conference on Machine Translation: Shared Task Papers*, pages 272–303, Belgium, Brussels. Association for Computational Linguistics.

Anna Choromanska, Mikael Henaff, Michael Mathieu, Gérard Ben Arous, and Yann LeCun. 2015. The loss surfaces of multilayer networks.

Stephane Clinchant, Kweon Woo Jung, and Vassilina Nikoulina. 2019. On the use of BERT for neural machine translation. In *Proceedings of the 3rd Workshop on Neural Generation and Translation*, pages 108–117, Hong Kong. Association for Computational Linguistics.

Yann N Dauphin, Razvan Pascanu, Caglar Gulcehre, Kyunghyun Cho, Surya Ganguli, and Yoshua Bengio. 2014. Identifying and attacking the saddle point problem in high-dimensional non-convex optimization. In *Advances in Neural Information Processing Systems*, volume 27, pages 2933–2941. Curran Associates, Inc.

Jacob Devlin, Ming-Wei Chang, Kenton Lee, and Kristina Toutanova. 2018. Bert: Pre-training of deep bidirectional transformers for language understanding.

Joseph Enguehard, Dan Busbridge, Vitalii Zhelezniak, and Nils Hammerla. 2019. Neural language priors. *ArXiv*, abs/1910.03492.

Ankush Garg, Yuan Cao, and Qi Ge. 2020. Echo state neural machine translation.

Mor Geva, Roei Schuster, Jonathan Berant, and Omer Levy. 2020. Transformer feed-forward layers are key-value memories.

Xavier Glorot and Y. Bengio. 2010. Understanding the difficulty of training deep feedforward neural networks. *Journal of Machine Learning Research - Proceedings Track*, 9:249–256.

Yukinori Homma and Masafumi Hagiwara. 2013. An echo state network with working memories for probabilistic language modeling. In *Artificial Neural Networks and Machine Learning – ICANN 2013*, pages 595–602, Berlin, Heidelberg. Springer Berlin Heidelberg.

Arthur Jacot, Franck Gabriel, and Clément Hongler. 2020. Neural tangent kernel: Convergence and generalization in neural networks.

Marcin Junczys-Dowmunt, Roman Grundkiewicz, Tomasz Dwojak, Hieu Hoang, Kenneth Heafield, Tom Neckermann, Frank Seide, Ulrich Germann, Alham Fikri Aji, Nikolay Bogoychev, André F. T. Martins, and Alexandra Birch. 2018. Marian: Fast neural machine translation in C++. In *Proceedings of ACL 2018, System Demonstrations*, pages 116–121, Melbourne, Australia. Association for Computational Linguistics.

Yoon Kim and Alexander M. Rush. 2016. Sequence-level knowledge distillation. In *Proceedings of the 2016 Conference on Empirical Methods in Natural Language Processing*, pages 1317–1327, Austin, Texas. Association for Computational Linguistics.

Young Jin Kim, Marcin Junczys-Dowmunt, Hany Hassan, Alham Fikri Aji, Kenneth Heafield, Roman Grundkiewicz, and Nikolay Bogoychev. 2019. From research to production and back: Ludicrously fast neural machine translation. In *Proceedings of the 3rd Workshop on Neural Generation and Translation*, pages 280–288, Hong Kong. Association for Computational Linguistics.

Philipp Koehn, Hieu Hoang, Alexandra Birch, Chris Callison-Burch, Marcello Federico, Nicola Bertoldi, Brooke Cowan, Wade Shen, Christine Moran, Richard Zens, Chris Dyer, Ondřej Bojar, Alexandra Constantin, and Evan Herbst. 2007. Moses: Open source toolkit for statistical machine translation. In *Proceedings of the 45th Annual Meeting of the Association for Computational Linguistics Companion Volume Proceedings of the Demo and Poster Sessions*, pages 177–180, Prague, Czech Republic. Association for Computational Linguistics.

Hanxiao Liu, Zihang Dai, David R. So, and Quoc V. Le. 2021. Pay attention to mlps.

Kishore Papineni, Salim Roukos, Todd Ward, and Wei-Jing Zhu. 2002. Bleu: a method for automatic evaluation of machine translation. In *Proceedings of the 40th Annual Meeting of the Association for Computational Linguistics*, pages 311–318, Philadelphia, Pennsylvania, USA. Association for Computational Linguistics.

Razvan Pascanu, Yann N. Dauphin, Surya Ganguli, and Yoshua Bengio. 2014. On the saddle point problem for non-convex optimization.

Matthew E. Peters, Mark Neumann, Mohit Iyyer, Matt Gardner, Christopher Clark, Kenton Lee, and Luke Zettlemoyer. 2018. Deep contextualized word representations.

Ofir Press and Lior Wolf. 2017. Using the output embedding to improve language models. In *Proceedings of the 15th Conference of the European Chapter of the Association for Computational Linguistics: Volume 2, Short Papers*, pages 157–163, Valencia, Spain. Association for Computational Linguistics.

Alessandro Raganato, Yves Scherrer, and Jörg Tiedemann. 2020. Fixed encoder self-attention patterns in transformer-based machine translation. In *Findings of the Association for Computational Linguistics: EMNLP 2020*, pages 556–568, Online. Association for Computational Linguistics.

Rajkumar Ramamurthy, Robin Stenzel, Rafet Sifa, Anna Ladi, and Christian Bauckhage. 2019. Echo state networks for named entity recognition. In *Artificial Neural Networks and Machine Learning - ICANN 2019 - 28th International Conference on Artificial Neural Networks, Munich, Germany, September 17-19, 2019, Proceedings - Workshop and Special Sessions*, volume 11731 of *Lecture Notes in Computer Science*, pages 110–120. Springer.

Karthik A. Sankararaman, Soham De, Zheng Xu, W. Ronny Huang, and Tom Goldstein. 2020. The impact of neural network overparameterization on gradient confusion and stochastic gradient descent.

Rico Sennrich, Barry Haddow, and Alexandra Birch. 2016a. Improving neural machine translation models with monolingual data. In *Proceedings of the 54th Annual Meeting of the Association for Computational Linguistics (Volume 1: Long Papers)*, pages 86–96, Berlin, Germany. Association for Computational Linguistics.

Rico Sennrich, Barry Haddow, and Alexandra Birch. 2016b. Neural machine translation of rare words with subword units. In *Proceedings of the 54th Annual Meeting of the Association for Computational Linguistics (Volume 1: Long Papers)*, pages 1715–1725, Berlin, Germany. Association for Computational Linguistics.

Yi Tay, Dara Bahri, Donald Metzler, Da-Cheng Juan, Zhe Zhao, and Che Zheng. 2020. Synthesizer: Rethinking self-attention in transformer models.

Brian Thompson, Huda Khayrallah, Antonios Anastasopoulos, Arya D. McCarthy, Kevin Duh, Rebecca Marvin, Paul McNamee, Jeremy Gwinnup, Tim Anderson, and Philipp Koehn. 2018. Freezing subnetworks to analyze domain adaptation in neural machine translation. In *Proceedings of the Third Conference on Machine Translation: Research Papers*, pages 124–132, Brussels, Belgium. Association for Computational Linguistics.

Matthew H. Tong, Adam D. Bickett, Eric M. Christiansen, and Garrison W. Cottrell. 2007. Learning grammatical structure with echo state networks. *Neural Networks*, 20(3):424 – 432. Echo State Networks and Liquid State Machines.

Ashish Vaswani, Noam Shazeer, Niki Parmar, Jakob Uszkoreit, Llion Jones, Aidan N Gomez, Łukasz Kaiser, and Illia Polosukhin. 2017. Attention is all you need. In I. Guyon, U. V. Luxburg, S. Bengio,

H. Wallach, R. Fergus, S. Vishwanathan, and R. Garnett, editors, *Advances in Neural Information Processing Systems 30*, pages 5998–6008. Curran Associates, Inc.

Elena Voita, David Talbot, Fedor Moiseev, Rico Sennrich, and Ivan Titov. 2019. Analyzing multi-head self-attention: Specialized heads do the heavy lifting, the rest can be pruned. In *Proceedings of the 57th Annual Meeting of the Association for Computational Linguistics*, pages 5797–5808, Florence, Italy. Association for Computational Linguistics.

Alex Wang, Jan Hula, Patrick Xia, Raghavendra Pappagari, R. Thomas McCoy, Roma Patel, Najoung Kim, Ian Tenney, Yinghui Huang, Katherin Yu, Shuning Jin, Berlin Chen, Benjamin Van Durme, Edouard Grave, Ellie Pavlick, and Samuel R. Bowman. 2018. Can you tell me how to get past sesame street? sentence-level pretraining beyond language modeling.

John Wieting and Douwe Kiela. 2019. No training required: Exploring random encoders for sentence classification. In *International Conference on Learning Representations*.

Kelly Zhang and Samuel Bowman. 2018. Language modeling teaches you more than translation does: Lessons learned through auxiliary syntactic task analysis. In *Proceedings of the 2018 EMNLP Workshop BlackboxNLP: Analyzing and Interpreting Neural Networks for NLP*, pages 359–361, Brussels, Belgium. Association for Computational Linguistics.

Barret Zoph, Deniz Yuret, Jonathan May, and Kevin Knight. 2016. Transfer learning for low-resource neural machine translation. In *Proceedings of the 2016 Conference on Empirical Methods in Natural Language Processing*, pages 1568–1575, Austin, Texas. Association for Computational Linguistics.

A The value of training

We measured the benefit of training individual components for a short time before fixing them, as opposed to having them untrainable from the beginning. With experiment we show whether training of certain components is more valuable at the beginning of the model training for the final model performance, or they continue to improve and contribute to the final model performance throughout training. We present our results on transformer-big model from Section 3 in Table 10, where we have a model with one frozen component (attention or FFN), where the component is frozen either at initialisation, or after training for few thousand mini-batches.

	Frozen after Epochs	BLEU	Total Epochs
	Pretrained Attention layer		
(1.0)	0	22.3	23
(1.1)	2	20.5	71
(1.2)	4	20.6	71
(1.3)	7	22.2	34
	Pretrained FFN layer		
(2.0)	0	23.2	26
(2.1)	2	22.6	37
(2.2)	4	22.7	38
(2.3)	7	22.6	21

Table 10: Fixed Attention layer or FNN layer for Turkish-English transformer-big contrasting random initialisation with small amount of pretraining. BLEU is computed on the dev set.

Contrary to our expectations, pretraining the model for a bit before freezing it yields worse overall convergence than having randomly initialised parameters without any pretraining. Pretraining and then freezing either the FFN layer or the attention layer yields similar behaviour. When pretraining is performed for 2 or 4 epochs, we noticed a that the model starts off a bit better than the randomly initialised one, but it quickly catches up in a few epochs. Furthermore convergence time is drastically increased, with small incremental improvements over many more epochs compared to the baseline.

We note that when the component is pretrained for 7 epochs, the final model performance (and convergence time) starts to approach that of a randomly initialised model, but we do not see any improvements over random initialisation. Looking at the attention, model (1.3) performs similar to the baseline model (1.0), but takes more epochs to converge. When we look at the FFN layer, model (2.3) converges faster than the baseline (2.0), but to a lower BLEU score.

Not All Models Localize Linguistic Knowledge in the Same Place: A Layer-wise Probing on BERToids' Representations

Mohsen Fayyaz[1⋆] **Ehsan Aghazadeh**[1⋆] **Ali Modarressi**[2] **Hosein Mohebbi**[2]
Mohammad Taher Pilehvar[3]
[1] University of Tehran, Iran [2] Iran University of Science and Technology, Iran
[3] Tehran Institute for Advanced Studies, Khatam University, Iran
{mohsen.fayyaz77, eaghazade1998}@ut.ac.ir
{m_modarressi, hosein_mohebbi}@comp.iust.ac.ir
mp792@cam.ac.uk

Abstract

Most of the recent works on probing representations have focused on BERT, with the presumption that the findings might be similar to the other models. In this work, we extend the probing studies to two other models in the family, namely ELECTRA and XLNet, showing that variations in the pre-training objectives or architectural choices can result in different behaviors in encoding linguistic information in the representations. Most notably, we observe that ELECTRA tends to encode linguistic knowledge in the deeper layers, whereas XLNet instead concentrates that in the earlier layers. Also, the former model undergoes a slight change during fine-tuning, whereas the latter experiences significant adjustments. Moreover, we show that drawing conclusions based on the *weight mixing* evaluation strategy—which is widely used in the context of layer-wise probing—can be misleading given the norm disparity of the representations across different layers. Instead, we adopt an alternative information-theoretic probing with *minimum description length*, which has recently been proven to provide more reliable and informative results.

1 Introduction

With the impressive success of pre-trained language models, such as BERT (Devlin et al., 2019), and their significant advances in transfer learning, a wave of interest has recently been directed toward understanding the knowledge encoded in their representations (Rogers et al., 2020). One of the analytical tools which is widely used for this investigation is *probing*: training a shallow supervised classifier that attempts to predict specific linguistic properties or reasoning abilities, based on representations obtained from the model (Tenney et al., 2019b,a; Hewitt and Manning, 2019; Talmor et al., 2020; Mohebbi et al., 2021; Ushio et al., 2021; Chen et al., 2021).

However, most of the previous studies have focused on BERT only, neglecting other models in the family. This leaves open the question of how training objectives (which are fundamentally different for some models) and architectural choices would impact the resulting representations and the knowledge encoded in them.

In this work, we carry out an analysis on three popular language models with totally different pre-training objectives: BERT (masked language modeling), XLNet (permuted language modeling, Yang et al., 2019), and ELECTRA (replaced token detection, Clark et al., 2020). We also show that the "weight mixing" evaluation strategy of Tenney et al. (2019a), which is widely used in the context of probing (de Vries et al., 2020; Kuznetsov and Gurevych, 2020; Choenni and Shutova, 2020, *inter alia*), might not be a reliable basis for drawing conclusions in the layer-wise cross model analysis as it does not take into account the norm disparity across the representations of different layers. Instead, we perform an information-theoretic probing analysis using Minimum Description Length proposed by Voita and Titov (2020).

Based on a series of experiments, we find that language models derived from BERT have different behaviors in encoding linguistic knowledge. Specifically, we show that, unlike BERT, XLNet encodes linguistic information in the earlier layers during pre-training, while ELECTRA tends to carry this information to the higher layers. We also extend our probing experiments to the fine-tuned setting to assess the extent of change in the encoded knowledge upon fine-tuning. Using Representation Similarity Analysis (Kriegeskorte et al., 2008, RSA), we show that representations from the higher layers in XLNet—that do not well encode

⋆Equal contribution.

Proceedings of the Fourth BlackboxNLP Workshop on Analyzing and Interpreting Neural Networks for NLP, pages 375–388
Online, November 11, 2021.

specific linguistic knowledge—undergo substantially bigger changes during fine-tuning when compared to the other models. In summary, our main contributions are as follows:

- We point out that the weight mixing evaluation strategy in edge probing does not lead to reliable conclusions in layer-wise cross model analysis studies.
- By relying on an information-theoretic probing method, we carry out a probing analysis across three commonly used pre-trained models.
- We also extend our probing experiments to fine-tuned representations to examine how linguistic information changes during fine-tuning.
- To provide complementary results to validate our findings, we also employ RSA to measure the amount of change in the representations after fine-tuning.

2 Background and Pilot Analysis

In this section, we review BERT and two of its popular derivatives: XLNet and ELECTRA, highlighting their differences as well as two commonly used probing methods that are essential to our discussion. We then conduct a pilot experiment to show the limitations of the evaluation metric used in edge probing and then justify our choice of an information-theoretic alternative.

2.1 Models

There is a wide variety of models derived from BERT, which are generally categorized into *autoencoding* and *autoregressive* models. Here, we focus on the most prominent model in each category. The two models have totally different pre-training objectives and have both shown outstanding performance on standard NLP tasks. BERT[1] is also considered as our baseline.

BERT. BERT (Devlin et al., 2019) has multiple Transformer encoder layers (Vaswani et al., 2017) stacked on top of each other, which are pre-trained with two self-supervised training objectives; Masked Language Model (MLM) and Next Sentence Prediction (NSP). The former predicts randomly masked tokens in the input sentence, whereas the latter checks whether two sentences could be considered consecutive.

XLNet. In contrast to BERT, which attempts to reconstruct the original sentence from corrupted input, XLNet is an auto-regressive model based on the Transformer-XL architecture (Dai et al., 2019) that leverages permutation language modeling to learn from a bi-directional context. This allows the model to consider dependencies between masked tokens in a sentence for prediction. Due to the permuted order of the tokens in this objective, the next predicted token could occur at any position, making it a more difficult task. To address this, XLNet uses a two-stream self-attention mechanism (one for content and one for the query) to autoregressively predict tokens. XLNet has also excluded NSP during pre-training. Though these modifications resulted in better performance than BERT, the costs of pre-training have increased in terms of FLOPs (Clark et al., 2020).

ELECTRA. Another model based on BERT is ELECTRA which falls into the category of autoencoder models. Clark et al. (2020) have introduced the replaced token detection pre-training objective to substitute BERT's objectives. ELECTRA jointly trains two models: generator and discriminator. The generator receives corrupted inputs with masked tokens in the input and tries to reconstruct the input like BERT. The discriminator is trained to predict whether each token was replaced by the generator or not. The authors pointed out that this novel pre-training objective could lead to learning representations that outperform prior models while requiring less computational cost during training.

2.2 Edge Probing

Tenney et al. (2019b) introduced edge probing as a means to measure linguistic knowledge in word representations. This is done by training a simple classifier on top of the representations. The accuracy of this classifier is taken as a representative for the quality of the encoded information about the specific task. Edge probing consists of a set of span-level tasks, where the span is a part of the sentence indicated by the dataset. The probe can only access the representations in that specific span. Eight labeling tasks are considered, including syntactic tasks, such as dependency labeling, and semantic tasks, such as coreference resolution. Before giving the inputs to the classifier, edge probing structure pools the representations across layers to

[1]Due to resource limitations, our evaluations are based on the *base* version (12-layer, 768-hidden size, 12-attention head, 110M parameters) of each model obtained from the HuggingFace's Transformers library (Wolf et al., 2020).

make a fixed size vector for feeding to the classifier. The work of Tenney et al. (2019a) is one of the first studies which leverages edge probing to quantify where linguistic knowledge is captured within BERT.

Scalar Mixing Weights. To estimate the contribution of each layer to a given probing task, Tenney et al. (2019a) used a technique called scalar mixing weights (Peters et al., 2018) which associates a trainable scalar weight with each layer in the model. After learning these weights alongside the probing classifier, they interpret layers with higher weights as those having more information for the particular task.

2.2.1 Mixing Weights Reliability Issues

While Tenney et al. (2019a) made interesting conclusions on BERT using edge probing and the *scalar mixing weights* evaluation strategy, we argue that this procedure is not reliable for layer-wise comparison. Several recent studies have conducted their experiments based on edge probing and *weight mixing* evaluation strategy. In one such study, Toshniwal et al. (2020) concluded that XLNet relies heavily on the input embedding layer in mixing weight evaluation for the coreference arc prediction task (Toshniwal et al., 2020). We show that this conclusion might not be accurate given that the representation norms in XLNet drastically change throughout layers.

Specifically, Figure 1 shows the representation norms across different layers in BERT and XLNet. These norms are computed based on the representations of 500 tokens sampled from the OPUS dataset (Tiedemann, 2012). The results are the average of three runs, and the same tokens are given to both models in each run[2]. In XLNet, the norm of the embedding layer is extremely smaller than that of other layers. This clearly shows that the concentration of edge probing's weight on the embedding layer does not indicate the level of information encoded in that layer. Rather, the model tries to compensate for relatively small representation norms. On the contrary, BERT retains the same level of representation norms across different layers. However, even such minor differences in representation norms might affect the conclusions of edge probing.[3] Given this issue with edge probing, we opted for a theoretically justified method, Minimum Description Length (MDL) probing, in our layer-wise analysis.

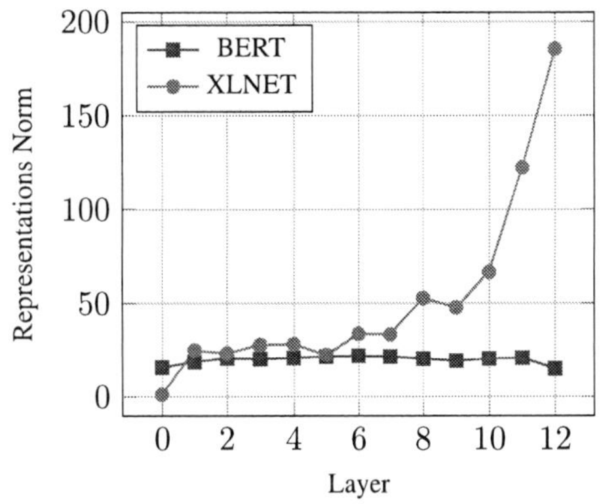

Figure 1: Comparison of the representations norm in different layers of XLNet and BERT when tested on Wikipedia examples. XLNet shows considerable norm disparities across different layers.

2.3 MDL Probing

Conventional probes (such as Conneau et al., 2018; Tenney et al., 2019b; Jawahar et al., 2019) leave unclear whether the classifier identifies linguistic knowledge in the representations or learns the task itself (Hewitt and Liang, 2019). Hence, researchers had to limit the size of the dataset (Zhang and Bowman, 2018) or the probe's complexity (Liu et al., 2019) to make sure the probe is not learning the task itself. However, probes based on information theory enable us to obtain more interpretable and reliable probing results.

The goal of information-theoretic probing is to measure to what extent representations encode a specific linguistic knowledge and how much effort is required to extract it. Voita and Titov (2020) combined the final quality of the probe classifier and the difficulty of achieving it by reformulating probes to a data transmission problem. If N number of representations are given, we plan to send their corresponding labels with a minimum description length, where each label has K classes. In *uniform encoding*, we assume that each representation has a label with a probability of $1/K$ and transmit them as raw information without training, which results in the maximum codelength possible of $N \cdot \log_2(K)$. But suppose the representations

[2]If a word was split into more than one token by the tokenizer, we used the first token of that word.

[3]To mitigate this issue, one can normalize the representations just before applying the scalar mixing weights to obtain more reliable results, especially in XLNet. We reported results with this modification in the appendix (Figure A.1).

Dependencies	I think it will **[help]**$_2$ **[me]**$_1$ very much in my role . → obj (object)
NER	thirty eight years ago founded **[the special Olympics]** . → EVENT
SRL	Their father **[called]**$_1$ later **[to see if they were fine]**$_2$. → ARGM-PRP (Purpose)
Coreference	Thank **[you]**$_1$ very much , **[Tony]**$_2$. → True
Rel. (SemEval)	NASA Kepler mission sends **[names]**$_1$ into **[space]**$_2$. → Entity-Destination(e_1,e_2)

Table 1: Examples of sentences, spans, and target labels for each probing task.

show some degree of regularity with respect to the labels[4]. In that case, instead of sending the labels, we can train a classifier to predict the labels given the representations and transmit the classifier's complexity (classifier codelength). Given that the classifier is usually not optimal, the final cross-entropy of the classifier over the data (data codelength) will be added to the classifier's codelength, resulting in an alternative evaluation metric known as MDL. Also, since the number of targets N will affect the total sum of cross-entropy, and in turn the final codelength (MDL), it is preferred to use the compression evaluation metric, which is defined as:

$$\mathbf{c} = \frac{N \cdot \log_2(K)}{\text{MDL}} \tag{1}$$

where the uniform codelength is divided by the MDL to eliminate the effect of N. Lower MDL indicates that the classifier predicts labels more accurately than a random guessing classifier, leading to higher compression. In contrast, when our classifier makes a random decision, MDL will be equal to the term in the numerator, resulting in no compression ($\mathbf{c} = 1$). We will report compression instead of codelength in our experimental results.

To compute MDL, Voita and Titov (2020) proposed two methods. The first one is *variational coding*, which estimates the complexity of the probe using a Bayesian model. The second method is called *online coding*, which is based on the fact that if the regularity in data is strong, it can be revealed by only a small portion of the data. In this method, the probe will be progressively trained on different amounts of data from small to large portions, and the cross-entropy of each portion will be added together to form the final codelength. Since Voita and Titov (2020) showed that the two compression methods conform in results, we employ the *online coding* method due to its more straightforward implementation.

As the MDL probe is more stable and informative than other conventional probes (Voita and Titov, 2020), one can compare the codelength across layers of the same model or different models for a given probing task. The edge probing method does not allow this comparison since the mixing weights do not necessarily provide an accurate estimate of the richness of linguistic knowledge within each layer. In contrast, in MDL probing, each layer is probed separately, which gives us a direct estimate of the quality of the specific layer itself, rather than that relative to the other layers. MDL probing is, therefore, a better choice to have a layer-wise comparison among different models.

3 Probing Pre-trained Representations

We begin with probing the representations of each pre-trained model on a variety of core NLP tasks, including Dependency Labeling, Named Entity Recognition, Semantic Role Labeling, Coreference Resolution, and Relation Classification (see an example for each task in Table 1). Following Tenney et al. (2019b), we use OntoNotes 5.0 (Weischedel et al., 2011) for NER, SRL, and Coreference arc prediction, English Web Treebank portion of the Universal Dependencies (Silveira et al., 2014) for Dependencies, and SemEval 2010 Task 8 dataset (Hendrickx et al., 2010) for Relation classification. Statistics of the datasets are provided in Table A.1.

For probing evaluation, we perform MDL probing on frozen representations obtained from each model. In order to obtain a fixed-length representation, following Voita and Titov (2020), we project the representations to 256-dimensional vectors, and then apply a self-attention pooling on them.[5]

3.1 Results

For an overall cross-model comparison, we report the MDL probe compression and edge probing F1 score results in Table 2. For each model, the best MDL compression across different layers is reported. ELECTRA consistently achieves

[4]Highly regulated data would result in shorter codelength than weakly regulated ones (Voita and Titov, 2020).

[5]For tasks with two spans, we consider separate trainable weights for projection and attention pooling.

Task	BERT F1 Score	BERT Compression	XLNet F1 Score	XLNet Compression	ELECTRA F1 Score	ELECTRA Compression
Deps.	94.18	15.25	93.93	14.13	**94.77**	**16.15**
NER	95.61	16.87	95.51	15.46	**96.07**	**16.88**
SRL	90.91	13.94	90.56	13.32	**91.69**	**14.44**
Coref.	91.17	4.58	91.34	3.97	**92.94**	**5.88**
Rel.	80.63	3.04	82.07	2.97	**82.41**	**3.37**

Table 2: Cross-model MDL compression and edge probing micro-averaged F1 comparison. For each task we report the highest compression achieved among a model's layers. Bold denotes the best performance on each task. In MDL probing, we employ logarithm with base 2 instead of natural logarithm in the training objective to have the codelength results in bits. Compression is the uniform codelength divided by the model's codelength. F1 scores are obtained by scalar mixing weights similar to Tenney et al. (2019a) which are reported only for further comparison on **overall** probing performances.

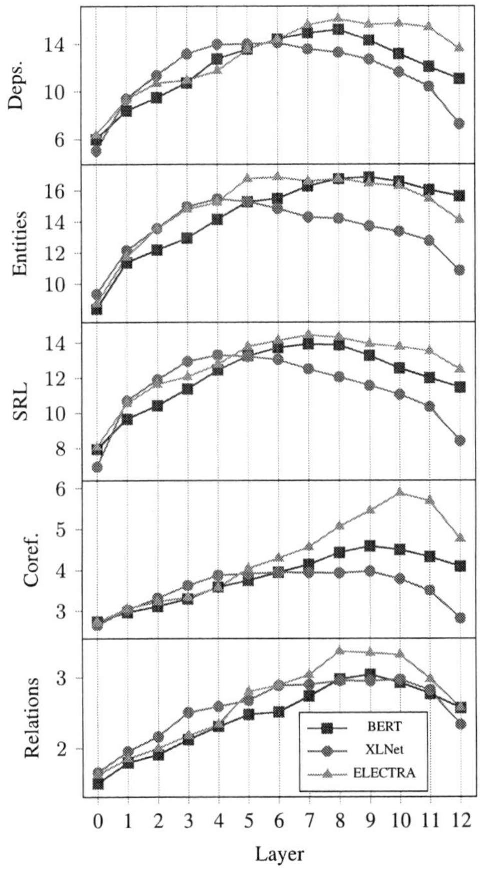

Figure 2: MDL probing compression of BERT, XLNet, and ELECTRA across layers.

the highest compression and edge probing micro-averaged F1[6] according to both metrics. Both results demonstrate how well the five tasks are encoded in the models' representations during pre-training. Table 2 shows that ELECTRA can achieve the best quality in both MDL probing and edge probing compared to BERT and XLNet. Hence, ELECTRA seems to have the best pre-training objective for incorporating linguistic knowledge among the three models. On the other hand, XLNet displays comparable results to BERT, which is interesting given the relatively better fine-tuned performance of the former in a variety of downstream tasks.

Layer-wise analysis. Next, we use MDL probing to investigate how much linguistic knowledge is encoded in different layers in these models. Figure 2 shows layer-wise MDL probing compression results of BERT, XLNet, and ELECTRA on five probing tasks. Higher compression indicates better encoding of the task. As can be seen, ELECTRA attains the highest compression in different layers across most tasks, especially in the deeper layers. Notably, all models start with relatively low compressions and reach higher values in their middle layers. An interesting behavior shared among the three models is the decrease towards the final layer, which can be attributed to their pre-training objectives. The main difference between the models lies in the position in which the maximum amount of linguistic knowledge is accumulated.

To better demonstrate the layer that most captures each task, we compute the center of gravity following Tenney et al. (2019a). The only difference is that we apply it on MDL probing compression, instead of scalar mixing weights, defined as:

$$\bar{E}_{\mathbf{c}}[\ell] = \frac{\sum_{\ell=0}^{L} \ell \cdot \mathbf{c}^{(\ell)}}{\sum_{\ell=0}^{L} \mathbf{c}^{(\ell)}} \tag{2}$$

[6]In relation classification, we ignore the "Other" label for calculating the F1 score.

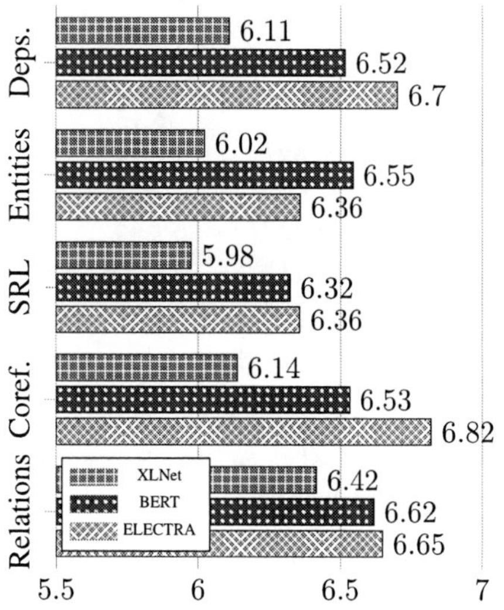

Figure 3: Comparison of the MDL probing compression center of gravity in BERT, XLNet, and ELECTRA.

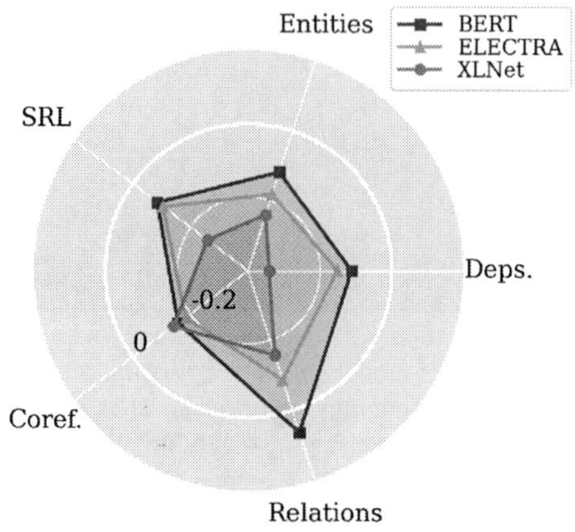

Figure 4: The change in centers of gravity after fine-tuning on MNLI dataset in five linguistic tasks.

where $\mathbf{c}^{(\ell)}$ is the compression score of layer ℓ. Figure 3 shows the center of gravity of compression. The most noticeable distinction among models is that XLNet's linguistic knowledge is concentrated in earlier layers than BERT, while ELECTRA's knowledge is mostly accumulated in deeper layers.

We hypothesize that the difficulty of the objectives has a direct effect on $\bar{E}_{\mathbf{c}}$, which indicates the expected position with the most encoded linguistic knowledge. In particular, recovering input tokens in the final layers of the model in the pre-training objective of BERT and XLNet is a surface task. Some of the linguistic knowledge might diminish in the final layers since highly contextualized representations have to be transformed into a less contextualized level to predict the original inputs (Voita et al., 2019). Whereas the pre-training objective in ELECTRA might be considered as a more semantic task, in which detecting replaced tokens requires more context-aware representations.

4 Probing Fine-tuned Representations

After observing that the amount and distribution of encoded linguistic knowledge can differ in these models, we aim to investigate how this information might be affected after the fine-tuning process. To this end, we repeated MDL probing as described in Section 3 on the fine-tuned representations. Next, to validate our results, we will expand our experiments to complementary analyses and measure the final quality of these representations on downstream tasks at different layers. We opted for the MNLI (Williams et al., 2018) dataset for fine-tuning all models. We used the same hyper-parameters for fine-tuning all three models: 32 as the batch size, max length of 128, the learning rate of 2e-5, and five epochs of training.

Center of Gravity in fine-tuned models. Figure 4 demonstrates the difference in the average layer that most captures the information related to a particular task between the pre-trained and the fine-tuned models. We measure the difference of the two centers of gravity to evaluate the extent to which the concentration of knowledge ($\bar{E}_{\mathbf{c}}$) shifts for each model on a specific probing task after fine-tuning:

$$\Delta\bar{E}_{\mathbf{c}} = \bar{E}_{\mathbf{c}}^{finetuned} - \bar{E}_{\mathbf{c}}^{pretrained} \quad (3)$$

First, we show that the concentration of information in fine-tuned models is usually in earlier layers compared to the pre-trained models. This can be attributed to the significant loss of linguistic knowledge in the final layers of fine-tuned models in favor of the specific information of the fine-tuning task. We show that XLNet in most tasks falls back to earlier layers than the two other models because it forgets the most linguistic knowledge in the final layers. This suggests that XLNet is going through a more extensive change in its representations which we investigate in the following sections. We also indicate that ELECTRA is falling back more than BERT. We hypothesize that since ELECTRA focuses its most capable representations in the final layers, and those are the layers that change the most

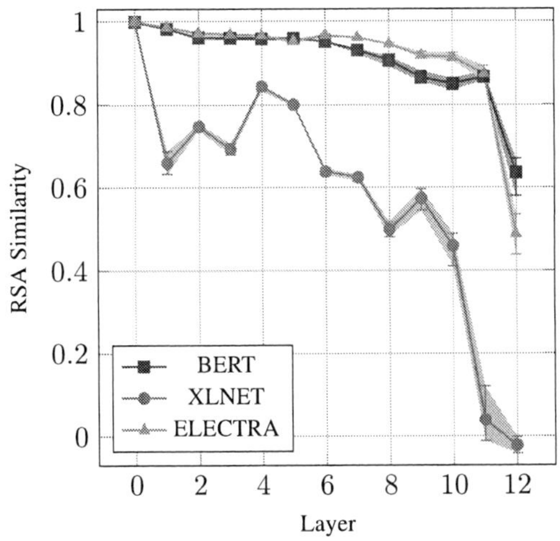

Figure 5: Similarity of the representations of BERT, XLNet, and ELECTRA, before and after fine-tuning on MNLI dataset. Additional plots for CoLA and SST-2 are provided in the appendix (Figures A.3 and A.5).

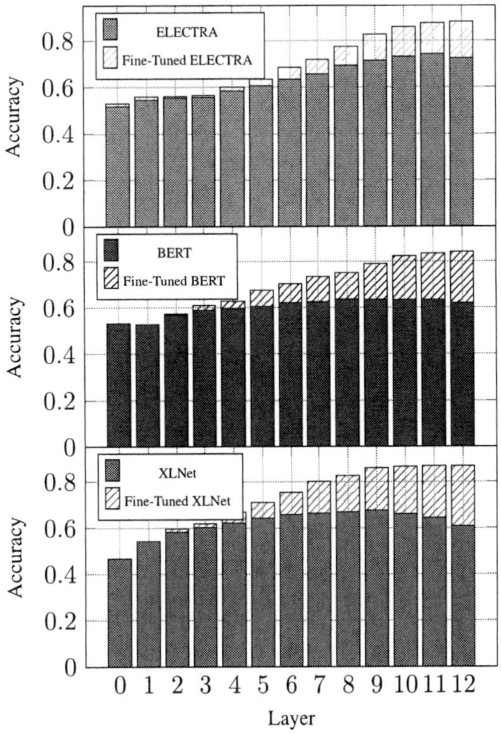

Figure 6: Layer-wise comparison of the performance scores on MNLI dataset across the representations of the pre-trained and fine-tuned models.

in fine-tuning, its center of gravity changes more than BERT. Full MDL compression and codelength results are reported in the appendix (Table A.2).

Global RSA. After fine-tuning each model, we leverage Representational Similarity Analysis (RSA) to investigate the overall amount of changes in the representations of each layer. RSA is a technique borrowed from neuroscience (Kriegeskorte et al., 2008) which is used for comparing two different representation spaces. To be specific, we sampled 5000 English sentences from OPUS dataset (Tiedemann, 2012) and used Global RSA[7], introduced by Chrupała et al. (2020). This is a better choice since we used average pooling in our fine-tuning, discussed next. As a measure of intra- and inter-space similarities, we used cosine similarity and Pearson correlation, respectively.

Figure 5 shows the results of the RSA measure applied to the representations of our models. We observe that XLNet has changed drastically during fine-tuning, while in BERT and ELECTRA, only the top layers are primarily affected. We also see that BERT shows a conservative pattern in the fine-tuning process which is consistent with findings of Merchant et al. (2020). As seen in Figure 2, we hypothesize that higher layers in XLNet are more open to change since they have relatively less specific knowledge. On the contrary, ELECTRA, which enjoys more linguistic information in its representations, especially in the higher layers, does not need to change very much.

Quality of the representations for downstream tasks. With the observations on RSA curves, we were interested in knowing the impact of the extent of these changes on downstream performance. To this end, we evaluated the quality of the representations for downstream tasks in both pre-trained and fine-tuned models. We trained separate classifiers on the unweighted average of representations for each layer.[8] We used Adam optimizer with a learning rate of 5e-4, and binary cross-entropy loss function for optimization.

Results are shown in Figure 6. Based on the performance scores for pre-trained representations, we observe that XLNet encodes most essential information for the downstream task in the shallower layers, BERT in the middle ones, and ELECTRA

[7]Using the average pooled representations as stimuli instead of individual tokens.

[8]Unlike the other two models, BERT involves [CLS] token for NSP objective during pre-training step. Hence, to have a fair comparison between our fine-tuning and feature extraction experiments, we opted for the mean pooling strategy consistently throughout the paper.

in the deeper layers. Interestingly, these patterns are well aligned with the MDL probing curves in Figure 2 which indicates that pre-trained representations with more linguistic knowledge are more suitable for downstream tasks. We also report our results on CoLA (Warstadt et al., 2019) and SST-2 (Socher et al., 2013) datasets in Figures A.2 and A.4. Our results show that the observations are consistent across these downstream tasks. In addition, we show that XLNet significantly improves performance in its second half of layers, while ELECTRA undergoes smaller adjustments. We observe that, before fine-tuning, the last layers of XLNet have fairly similar or even lower performance than BERT. However, when fine-tuned, XLNet compensates for the performance deficit by injecting more task-specific information in those layers, helping the model to outperform BERT. Finally, we demonstrate that the changes in layers and their extent are similar to what we saw in the RSA results in Figure 5, which indicates that the changes in RSA were actually made to achieve higher quality in the fine-tuning task.

5 Related Work

While extensive research has been devoted to probing BERT (Hewitt and Manning, 2019; Tenney et al., 2019a; Merchant et al., 2020), other popular models, such as XLNet and ELECTRA which have significant differences in their pre-training objectives, are less thoroughly investigated. Only a few probing studies similar to our work exist which cover other models within the family. Mosbach et al. (2020) mostly focused on the impact of pooling strategy in probing sentence-level tasks. Based on the accuracy, they found that fine-tuning can affect the linguistic knowledge encoded in the representations. Moreover, Durrani et al. (2020) investigated the distribution of linguistic knowledge across individual neurons. In particular, they found that neurons in XLNet are more localized in encoding individual linguistic information compared to BERT, where neurons are shared across multiple properties. By adopting the method of Hewitt and Manning (2019), Aspillaga et al. (2021) investigated whether pre-trained language models encode semantic information, for instance by checking their representations against the lexico-semantic structure of WordNet (Miller, 1994).

The above studies mainly rely on the accuracy metric for their probing evaluation, which is recently shown to fail in adequately reflecting the differences among representations (Voita and Titov, 2020). To our knowledge, this is the first time that an information-theoretic probing method is employed for conducting a cross-model and layer-wise analytical study.

6 Conclusions

In this paper, we aimed to extend probing studies on BERT to the other models in the family to investigate how training objectives and architectural choices would affect the resulting representations and the linguistic knowledge encoded in them. To this end, we leveraged MDL probing method, which has recently proven to provide more reliable and informative results when compared with conventional probes. To the best of our knowledge, this is the first time MDL probing has been employed to analyze such state-of-the-art pre-trained language models as BERT. By probing three state-of-the-art language models, i.e., BERT, XLNet, and ELECTRA, we found considerable differences in the extent and distribution of the core linguistic knowledge in their representations. Specifically, we demonstrate that XLNet accumulates linguistic knowledge in the earlier layers than BERT, whereas that of ELECTRA is mainly in the final layers.

Moreover, from probing and employing RSA similarity measure on fine-tuned models, we illustrate that XLNet is more susceptible to forgetting linguistic knowledge in final layers and undergoes substantial adjustments to its representations when compared to the other models. Based on differential downstream performance observations for before and after fine-tuning, we confirm that the changes in representations are proportional to the provided gain in the downstream task, which consequently indicates that XLNet injects more information during fine-tuning into its representations than the two other models.

In summary, through probing and measurement tools, we demonstrate that BERT's derivative models, especially those with different objectives and structural choices, express different behaviors in their representations. We hope our analysis helps make more informed choices in the selection and fine-tuning of these state-of-the-art models.

Acknowledgments

Our work is in part supported by Tehran Institute for Advanced Studies (TeIAS), Khatam University.

References

Carlos Aspillaga, Marcelo Mendoza, and Alvaro Soto. 2021. Inspecting the concept knowledge graph encoded by modern language models. In *Findings of the Association for Computational Linguistics: ACL-IJCNLP 2021*, pages 2984–3000, Online.

Boli Chen, Yao Fu, Guangwei Xu, Pengjun Xie, Chuanqi Tan, Mosha Chen, and Liping Jing. 2021. Probing BERT in hyperbolic spaces. In *International Conference on Learning Representations*.

Rochelle Choenni and Ekaterina Shutova. 2020. What does it mean to be language-agnostic? probing multilingual sentence encoders for typological properties. *arXiv preprint arXiv:2009.12862*.

Grzegorz Chrupała, Bertrand Higy, and Afra Alishahi. 2020. Analyzing analytical methods: The case of phonology in neural models of spoken language. In *Proceedings of the 58th Annual Meeting of the Association for Computational Linguistics*, pages 4146–4156, Online.

Kevin Clark, Minh-Thang Luong, Quoc V. Le, and Christopher D. Manning. 2020. ELECTRA: Pre-training text encoders as discriminators rather than generators. In *International Conference on Learning Representations*.

Alexis Conneau, German Kruszewski, Guillaume Lample, Loïc Barrault, and Marco Baroni. 2018. What you can cram into a single $&!#* vector: Probing sentence embeddings for linguistic properties. In *Proceedings of the 56th Annual Meeting of the Association for Computational Linguistics (Volume 1: Long Papers)*, pages 2126–2136, Melbourne, Australia. Association for Computational Linguistics.

Zihang Dai, Zhilin Yang, Yiming Yang, Jaime Carbonell, Quoc Le, and Ruslan Salakhutdinov. 2019. Transformer-XL: Attentive language models beyond a fixed-length context. In *Proceedings of the 57th Annual Meeting of the Association for Computational Linguistics*, pages 2978–2988, Florence, Italy.

Jacob Devlin, Ming-Wei Chang, Kenton Lee, and Kristina Toutanova. 2019. BERT: Pre-training of deep bidirectional transformers for language understanding. In *Proceedings of the 2019 Conference of the North American Chapter of the Association for Computational Linguistics: Human Language Technologies, Volume 1 (Long and Short Papers)*, pages 4171–4186, Minneapolis, Minnesota.

Nadir Durrani, Hassan Sajjad, Fahim Dalvi, and Yonatan Belinkov. 2020. Analyzing individual neurons in pre-trained language models. In *Proceedings of the 2020 Conference on Empirical Methods in Natural Language Processing (EMNLP)*, pages 4865–4880, Online.

Iris Hendrickx, Su Nam Kim, Zornitsa Kozareva, Preslav Nakov, Diarmuid Ó Séaghdha, Sebastian Padó, Marco Pennacchiotti, Lorenza Romano, and Stan Szpakowicz. 2010. SemEval-2010 task 8: Multi-way classification of semantic relations between pairs of nominals. In *Proceedings of the 5th International Workshop on Semantic Evaluation*, pages 33–38, Uppsala, Sweden.

John Hewitt and Percy Liang. 2019. Designing and interpreting probes with control tasks. In *Proceedings of the 2019 Conference on Empirical Methods in Natural Language Processing and the 9th International Joint Conference on Natural Language Processing (EMNLP-IJCNLP)*, pages 2733–2743, Hong Kong, China.

John Hewitt and Christopher D. Manning. 2019. A structural probe for finding syntax in word representations. In *Proceedings of the 2019 Conference of the North American Chapter of the Association for Computational Linguistics: Human Language Technologies, Volume 1 (Long and Short Papers)*, pages 4129–4138, Minneapolis, Minnesota.

Ganesh Jawahar, Benoît Sagot, Djamé Seddah, Samuel Unicomb, Gerardo Iñiguez, Márton Karsai, Yannick Léo, Márton Karsai, Carlos Sarraute, Éric Fleury, et al. 2019. What does BERT learn about the structure of language? In *57th Annual Meeting of the Association for Computational Linguistics (ACL), Florence, Italy*.

Nikolaus Kriegeskorte, Marieke Mur, and Peter Bandettini. 2008. Representational similarity analysis - connecting the branches of systems neuroscience. *Frontiers in Systems Neuroscience*, 2:4.

Ilia Kuznetsov and Iryna Gurevych. 2020. A matter of framing: The impact of linguistic formalism on probing results. In *Proceedings of the 2020 Conference on Empirical Methods in Natural Language Processing (EMNLP)*, pages 171–182, Online.

Nelson F. Liu, Matt Gardner, Yonatan Belinkov, Matthew E. Peters, and Noah A. Smith. 2019. Linguistic knowledge and transferability of contextual representations. In *Proceedings of the 2019 Conference of the North American Chapter of the Association for Computational Linguistics: Human Language Technologies, Volume 1 (Long and Short Papers)*, pages 1073–1094, Minneapolis, Minnesota.

Amil Merchant, Elahe Rahimtoroghi, Ellie Pavlick, and Ian Tenney. 2020. What happens to BERT embeddings during fine-tuning? In *Proceedings of the Third BlackboxNLP Workshop on Analyzing and Interpreting Neural Networks for NLP*, pages 33–44, Online.

George A. Miller. 1994. WordNet: A lexical database for English. In *Human Language Technology: Proceedings of a Workshop held at Plainsboro, New Jersey, March 8-11, 1994.*

Hosein Mohebbi, Ali Modarressi, and Mohammad Taher Pilehvar. 2021. Exploring the role of BERT token representations to explain sentence probing results. *arXiv preprint arXiv:2104.01477.*

Marius Mosbach, Anna Khokhlova, Michael A. Hedderich, and Dietrich Klakow. 2020. On the interplay between fine-tuning and sentence-level probing for linguistic knowledge in pre-trained transformers. In *Proceedings of the Third BlackboxNLP Workshop on Analyzing and Interpreting Neural Networks for NLP*, pages 68–82, Online.

Matthew Peters, Mark Neumann, Mohit Iyyer, Matt Gardner, Christopher Clark, Kenton Lee, and Luke Zettlemoyer. 2018. Deep contextualized word representations. In *Proceedings of the 2018 Conference of the North American Chapter of the Association for Computational Linguistics: Human Language Technologies, Volume 1 (Long Papers)*, pages 2227–2237, New Orleans, Louisiana.

Anna Rogers, Olga Kovaleva, and Anna Rumshisky. 2020. A primer in BERTology: What we know about how BERT works. *Transactions of the Association for Computational Linguistics*, 8:842–866.

Natalia Silveira, Timothy Dozat, Marie-Catherine de Marneffe, Samuel Bowman, Miriam Connor, John Bauer, and Chris Manning. 2014. A gold standard dependency corpus for English. In *Proceedings of the Ninth International Conference on Language Resources and Evaluation (LREC'14)*, pages 2897–2904, Reykjavik, Iceland. European Language Resources Association (ELRA).

Richard Socher, Alex Perelygin, Jean Wu, Jason Chuang, Christopher D. Manning, Andrew Ng, and Christopher Potts. 2013. Recursive deep models for semantic compositionality over a sentiment treebank. In *Proceedings of the 2013 Conference on Empirical Methods in Natural Language Processing*, pages 1631–1642, Seattle, Washington, USA.

Alon Talmor, Yanai Elazar, Yoav Goldberg, and Jonathan Berant. 2020. olmpics-on what language model pre-training captures. *Transactions of the Association for Computational Linguistics*, 8:743–758.

Ian Tenney, Dipanjan Das, and Ellie Pavlick. 2019a. BERT rediscovers the classical NLP pipeline. In *Proceedings of the 57th Annual Meeting of the Association for Computational Linguistics*, pages 4593–4601, Florence, Italy.

Ian Tenney, Patrick Xia, Berlin Chen, Alex Wang, Adam Poliak, R. Thomas McCoy, Najoung Kim, Benjamin Van Durme, Samuel R. Bowman, Dipanjan Das, and Ellie Pavlick. 2019b. What do you learn from context? Probing for sentence structure in contextualized word representations. In *International Conference on Learning Representations.*

Jörg Tiedemann. 2012. Parallel data, tools and interfaces in OPUS. In *Proceedings of the Eighth International Conference on Language Resources and Evaluation (LREC-2012)*, pages 2214–2218, Istanbul, Turkey. European Languages Resources Association (ELRA).

Shubham Toshniwal, Haoyue Shi, Bowen Shi, Lingyu Gao, Karen Livescu, and Kevin Gimpel. 2020. A cross-task analysis of text span representations. In *Proceedings of the 5th Workshop on Representation Learning for NLP*, pages 166–176, Online.

Asahi Ushio, Luis Espinosa Anke, Steven Schockaert, and Jose Camacho-Collados. 2021. BERT is to NLP what AlexNet is to CV: Can pre-trained language models identify analogies? In *Proceedings of the 59th Annual Meeting of the Association for Computational Linguistics and the 11th International Joint Conference on Natural Language Processing (Volume 1: Long Papers)*, pages 3609–3624, Online.

Ashish Vaswani, Noam Shazeer, Niki Parmar, Jakob Uszkoreit, Llion Jones, Aidan N Gomez, Łukasz Kaiser, and Illia Polosukhin. 2017. Attention is All you Need. In *Advances in neural information processing systems*, pages 5998–6008.

Elena Voita, Rico Sennrich, and Ivan Titov. 2019. The Bottom-up Evolution of Representations in the Transformer: A Study with Machine Translation and Language Modeling Objectives. In *Proceedings of the 2019 Conference on Empirical Methods in Natural Language Processing and the 9th International Joint Conference on Natural Language Processing (EMNLP-IJCNLP)*, pages 4387–4397.

Elena Voita and Ivan Titov. 2020. Information-theoretic probing with minimum description length. In *Proceedings of the 2020 Conference on Empirical Methods in Natural Language Processing (EMNLP)*, pages 183–196, Online.

Wietse de Vries, Andreas van Cranenburgh, and Malvina Nissim. 2020. What's so special about BERT's layers? a closer look at the NLP pipeline in monolingual and multilingual models. In *Findings of the Association for Computational Linguistics: EMNLP 2020*, pages 4339–4350, Online.

Alex Warstadt, Amanpreet Singh, and Samuel R. Bowman. 2019. Neural network acceptability judgments. *Transactions of the Association for Computational Linguistics*, 7:625–641.

Ralph Weischedel, Sameer Pradhan, Lance Ramshaw, Martha Palmer, Nianwen Xue, Mitchell Marcus, Ann Taylor, Craig Greenberg, Eduard Hovy, Robert Belvin, et al. 2011. OntoNotes release 4.0. *LDC2011T03, Philadelphia, Penn.: Linguistic Data Consortium.*

Adina Williams, Nikita Nangia, and Samuel Bowman. 2018. A broad-coverage challenge corpus for sentence understanding through inference. In *Proceedings of the 2018 Conference of the North American Chapter of the Association for Computational Linguistics: Human Language Technologies, Volume 1 (Long Papers)*, pages 1112–1122, New Orleans, Louisiana.

Thomas Wolf, Lysandre Debut, Victor Sanh, Julien Chaumond, Clement Delangue, Anthony Moi, Pierric Cistac, Tim Rault, Remi Louf, Morgan Funtowicz, Joe Davison, Sam Shleifer, Patrick von Platen, Clara Ma, Yacine Jernite, Julien Plu, Canwen Xu, Teven Le Scao, Sylvain Gugger, Mariama Drame, Quentin Lhoest, and Alexander Rush. 2020. Transformers: State-of-the-art natural language processing. In *Proceedings of the 2020 Conference on Empirical Methods in Natural Language Processing: System Demonstrations*, pages 38–45, Online.

Zhilin Yang, Zihang Dai, Yiming Yang, Jaime Carbonell, Russ R Salakhutdinov, and Quoc V Le. 2019. XLNet: Generalized autoregressive pretraining for language understanding. In *Advances in neural information processing systems*, pages 5754–5764.

Kelly Zhang and Samuel Bowman. 2018. Language modeling teaches you more than translation does: Lessons learned through auxiliary syntactic task analysis. In *Proceedings of the 2018 EMNLP Workshop BlackboxNLP: Analyzing and Interpreting Neural Networks for NLP*, pages 359–361, Brussels, Belgium.

A Appendices

A.1 Edge Probing Normalized Mixing Weights Results

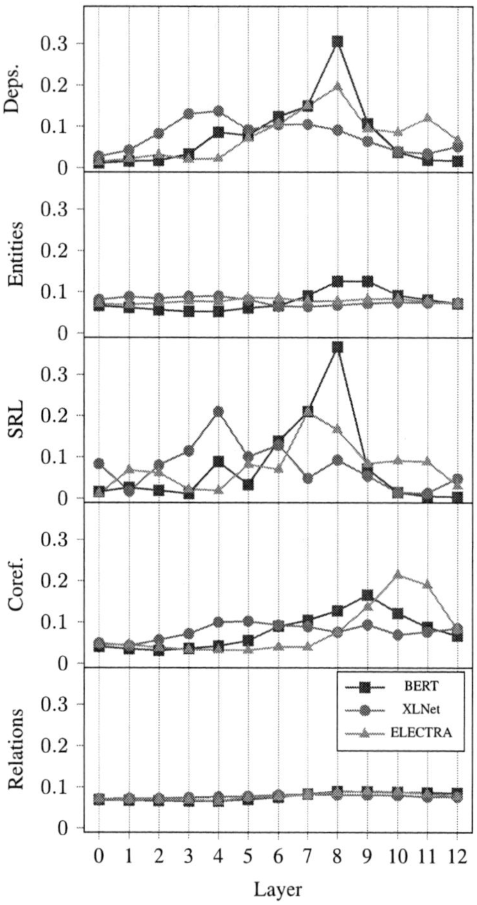

Figure A.1: Edge probing mixing weights results for BERT, XLNet, and ELECTRA. This is a modified version of mixing weights where we normalize the representations before applying mixing weights to eliminate the norms disparity effect.

A.2 Results for CoLA Dataset

Figures A.2 and A.3 report the performance and RSA results before and after fine-tuning on CoLA dataset. The results are consistent with figure 6.

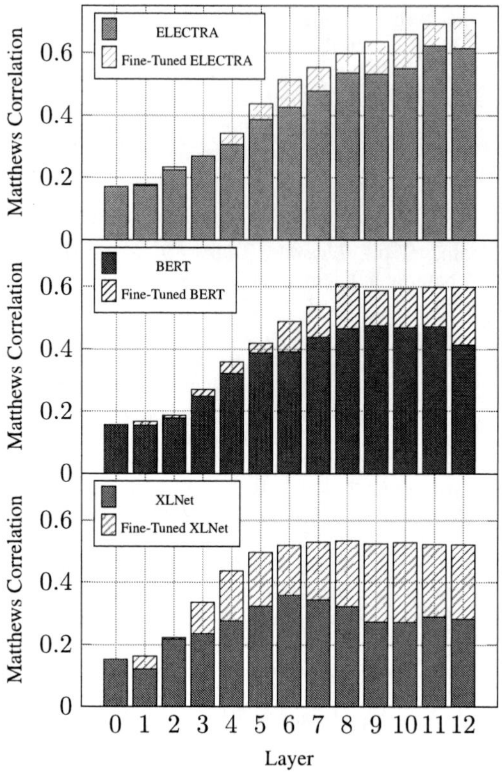

Figure A.2: Layer-wise comparison of the performance scores on CoLA dataset across the representations of the pre-trained and fine-tuned models.

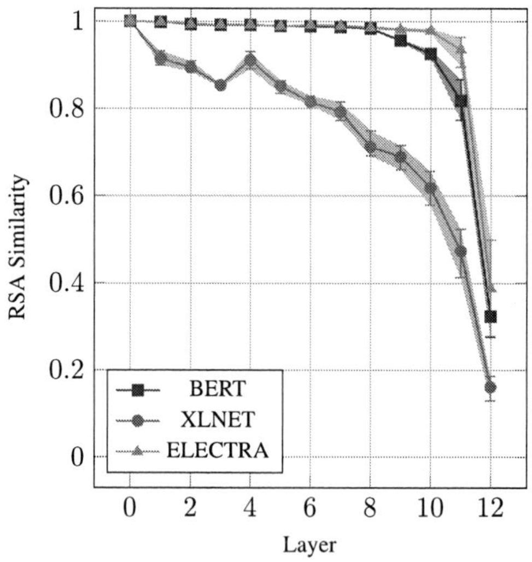

Figure A.3: Comparison of the representations of BERT, XLNet, and ELECTRA base, with their respective fine-tuned model on CoLA dataset.

A.3 Results for SST-2 Dataset

Figures A.4 and A.5 report the performance and RSA results before and after fine-tuning on SST-2 dataset.

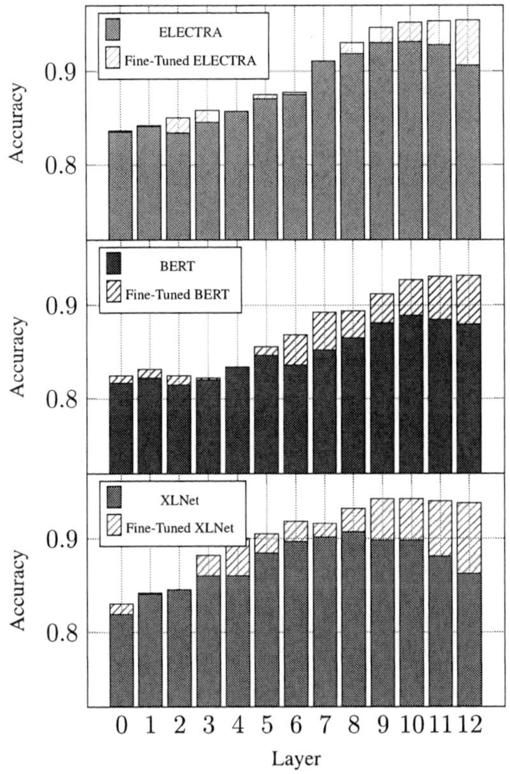

Figure A.4: Layer-wise comparison of the performance scores on SST-2 dataset across the representations of the pre-trained and fine-tuned models.

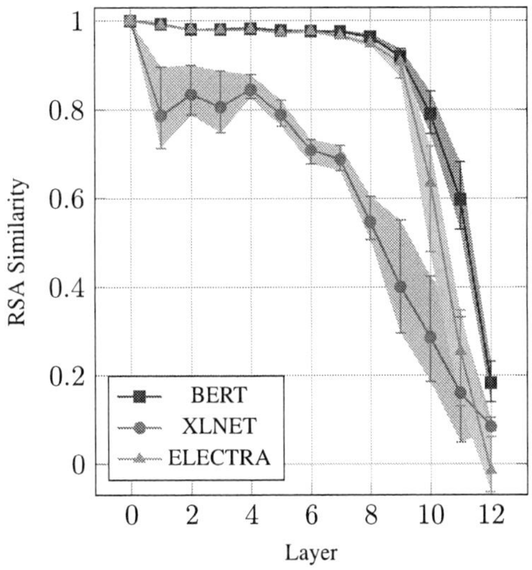

Figure A.5: Comparison of the representations of BERT, XLNet, and ELECTRA base, with their respective fine-tuned model on SST-2 dataset.

A.4 Datasets Statistics

The number of labels and targets of the NLP linguistic tasks we used in probing are reported in table A.1.

Task	Labels	Number of targets
Dependency Labeling	49	203919 / 25110 / 25049
Named Entity Recognition	18	128738 / 20354 / 12586
Semantic Role Labeling	66	598983 / 83362 / 61716
Coreference Resolution	2	207830 / 26333 / 27800
Relation Classification	19	6851 / 1149 / 2717

Table A.1: Dataset statistics for all five core tasks used in probing. Numbers of targets are given for train / dev / test sets.

Tasks	BERT pre-trained	BERT fine-tuned	XLNet pre-trained	XLNet fine-tuned	ELECTRA pre-trained	ELECTRA fine-tuned
	5.99 (186.7)	6.04 (185.1)	5.01 (223.1)	5.03 (222.3)	6.35 (176.0)	6.33 (176.5)
	8.39 (133.3)	7.89 (141.7)	9.39 (119.1)	8.41 (132.9)	9.33 (119.8)	9.26 (120.8)
	9.49 (117.8)	8.92 (125.3)	11.37 (98.3)	10.28 (108.8)	10.71 (104.4)	10.70 (104.5)
	10.75 (104.0)	10.29 (108.7)	13.18 (84.8)	12.44 (89.8)	10.97 (101.9)	10.93 (102.3)
	12.75 (87.7)	12.12 (92.3)	13.98 (80.0)	13.14 (85.1)	11.75 (95.2)	11.55 (96.8)
	13.57 (82.4)	12.88 (86.8)	14.00 (79.9)	13.41 (83.4)	13.54 (82.5)	13.57 (82.4)
Dependencies	14.45 (77.4)	13.45 (83.1)	14.13 (79.1)	13.54 (82.6)	14.42 (77.5)	14.36 (77.9)
	14.95 (74.8)	13.81 (81.0)	13.57 (82.4)	13.11 (85.3)	15.65 (71.5)	15.04 (74.3)
	15.25 (73.3)	13.61 (82.2)	13.30 (84.1)	12.19 (91.7)	16.15 (69.2)	15.15 (73.8)
	14.34 (78.0)	12.46 (89.7)	12.72 (87.9)	10.93 (102.3)	15.67 (71.3)	14.27 (78.3)
	13.17 (84.9)	11.60 (96.4)	11.63 (96.2)	9.32 (120.0)	15.76 (70.9)	14.03 (79.7)
	12.08 (92.5)	10.83 (103.3)	10.42 (107.3)	6.77 (165.1)	15.44 (72.4)	13.89 (80.5)
	11.06 (101.1)	9.76 (114.6)	7.26 (154.1)	3.08 (362.5)	13.62 (82.1)	11.98 (93.4)
	8.37 (62.6)	8.28 (63.3)	9.33 (56.2)	9.41 (55.7)	8.72 (60.1)	8.63 (60.7)
	11.37 (46.1)	10.86 (48.3)	12.14 (43.2)	11.67 (44.9)	11.74 (44.6)	11.47 (45.7)
	12.19 (43.0)	11.77 (44.5)	13.56 (38.7)	13.57 (38.6)	13.55 (38.7)	13.24 (39.6)
	12.95 (40.5)	12.48 (42.0)	14.97 (35.0)	14.92 (35.1)	14.79 (35.4)	14.30 (36.7)
	14.15 (37.0)	13.65 (38.4)	15.46 (33.9)	15.79 (33.2)	15.25 (34.4)	15.02 (34.9)
	15.28 (34.3)	14.76 (35.5)	15.30 (34.3)	15.91 (33.0)	16.77 (31.3)	15.99 (32.8)
Entities	15.50 (33.8)	14.92 (35.1)	14.85 (35.3)	15.63 (33.5)	16.88 (31.1)	15.79 (33.2)
	16.29 (32.2)	15.32 (34.2)	14.29 (36.7)	15.61 (33.6)	16.60 (31.6)	15.63 (33.5)
	16.77 (31.3)	15.58 (33.7)	14.20 (36.9)	15.13 (34.6)	16.76 (31.3)	15.44 (34.0)
	16.87 (31.1)	15.33 (34.2)	13.72 (38.2)	14.09 (37.2)	16.46 (31.9)	14.83 (35.3)
	16.59 (31.6)	14.72 (35.6)	13.36 (39.2)	12.92 (40.6)	16.29 (32.2)	14.22 (36.9)
	16.06 (32.7)	14.55 (36.0)	12.77 (41.0)	10.46 (50.1)	15.47 (33.9)	13.59 (38.6)
	15.64 (33.5)	13.60 (38.5)	10.84 (48.4)	5.38 (97.4)	14.10 (37.2)	11.21 (46.8)
	7.93 (445.7)	7.87 (449.3)	6.91 (511.4)	6.93 (510.3)	8.07 (438.4)	8.03 (440.1)
	9.67 (365.7)	9.44 (374.7)	10.70 (330.5)	10.33 (342.2)	10.55 (335.0)	10.48 (337.4)
	10.42 (339.2)	10.26 (344.6)	11.90 (297.1)	11.68 (302.6)	11.64 (303.7)	11.51 (307.3)
	11.38 (310.8)	11.27 (313.8)	12.95 (273.0)	12.98 (272.5)	12.07 (292.9)	11.94 (296.0)
	12.45 (284.0)	12.40 (285.2)	13.32 (265.5)	13.39 (264.0)	12.77 (276.8)	12.59 (280.8)
	13.25 (266.8)	12.91 (273.8)	13.23 (267.3)	13.36 (264.6)	13.79 (256.4)	13.55 (261.0)
SRL	13.73 (257.6)	13.26 (266.7)	13.05 (270.9)	13.25 (266.8)	14.13 (250.2)	13.91 (254.2)
	13.94 (253.7)	13.30 (265.9)	12.50 (282.8)	12.66 (279.3)	14.44 (244.8)	14.03 (252.1)
	13.88 (254.8)	13.06 (270.7)	12.05 (293.4)	12.13 (291.4)	14.32 (246.8)	13.59 (260.1)
	13.27 (266.5)	12.35 (286.2)	11.57 (305.7)	11.30 (312.8)	13.94 (253.6)	13.09 (270.1)
	12.54 (281.8)	11.64 (303.7)	11.06 (319.8)	10.02 (352.7)	13.78 (256.6)	12.79 (276.4)
	12.00 (294.6)	11.23 (314.8)	10.36 (341.2)	8.16 (433.3)	13.52 (261.4)	12.40 (285.2)
	11.46 (308.5)	10.58 (334.3)	8.40 (420.9)	4.60 (769.0)	12.47 (283.5)	11.32 (312.3)
	2.74 (74.2)	2.75 (73.8)	2.65 (76.6)	2.63 (77.3)	2.73 (74.4)	2.75 (73.8)
	2.96 (68.5)	2.94 (69.0)	3.03 (67.0)	2.91 (69.9)	3.06 (66.4)	3.06 (66.2)
	3.11 (65.2)	3.06 (66.4)	3.31 (61.3)	3.24 (62.6)	3.23 (62.9)	3.22 (63.0)
	3.29 (61.6)	3.31 (61.3)	3.63 (55.9)	3.63 (56.0)	3.33 (60.9)	3.35 (60.5)
	3.59 (56.5)	3.57 (56.8)	3.88 (52.3)	3.87 (52.4)	3.57 (56.8)	3.57 (56.9)
	3.76 (54.0)	3.76 (54.0)	3.92 (51.8)	4.00 (50.7)	4.04 (50.2)	3.93 (51.6)
Coreference	3.95 (51.4)	3.83 (53.0)	3.95 (51.4)	4.03 (50.3)	4.29 (47.3)	4.22 (48.0)
	4.14 (49.1)	3.98 (51.0)	3.94 (51.5)	4.07 (49.9)	4.56 (44.5)	4.43 (45.8)
	4.43 (45.8)	4.18 (48.5)	3.93 (51.6)	4.04 (50.3)	5.06 (40.1)	4.78 (42.4)
	4.58 (44.3)	4.13 (49.2)	3.97 (51.1)	3.95 (51.3)	5.44 (37.3)	4.93 (41.2)
	4.49 (45.2)	4.00 (50.7)	3.78 (53.7)	3.54 (57.3)	5.88 (34.5)	5.09 (39.9)
	4.32 (47.0)	3.85 (52.7)	3.50 (58.0)	3.11 (65.2)	5.68 (35.7)	4.95 (41.0)
	4.09 (49.6)	3.67 (55.3)	2.82 (72.1)	2.01 (101.1)	4.76 (42.7)	4.26 (47.6)
	1.51 (18.9)	1.52 (18.7)	1.66 (17.1)	1.65 (17.2)	1.63 (17.4)	1.61 (17.6)
	1.80 (15.8)	1.73 (16.4)	1.95 (14.5)	1.85 (15.4)	1.85 (15.3)	1.86 (15.3)
	1.91 (14.9)	1.85 (15.4)	2.16 (13.1)	2.04 (13.9)	2.00 (14.2)	2.01 (14.1)
	2.12 (13.4)	2.02 (14.1)	2.51 (11.3)	2.43 (11.7)	2.18 (13.0)	2.15 (13.2)
	2.31 (12.3)	2.29 (12.4)	2.59 (11.0)	2.58 (11.0)	2.34 (12.2)	2.33 (12.2)
	2.48 (11.5)	2.42 (11.8)	2.68 (10.6)	2.67 (10.7)	2.80 (10.1)	2.69 (10.6)
Relations	2.51 (11.3)	2.56 (11.1)	2.89 (9.8)	2.91 (9.8)	2.89 (9.8)	2.83 (10.0)
	2.74 (10.4)	2.76 (10.3)	2.90 (9.8)	3.00 (9.5)	3.04 (9.4)	2.94 (9.7)
	2.98 (9.5)	2.95 (9.6)	2.95 (9.6)	3.07 (9.3)	3.37 (8.4)	3.26 (8.7)
	3.04 (9.4)	3.03 (9.4)	2.95 (9.6)	2.91 (9.8)	3.34 (8.5)	3.19 (8.9)
	2.93 (9.7)	2.93 (9.7)	2.97 (9.6)	2.69 (10.6)	3.32 (8.6)	3.14 (9.0)
	2.77 (10.3)	2.86 (9.9)	2.82 (10.1)	2.36 (12.1)	2.98 (9.5)	2.83 (10.0)
	2.57 (11.1)	2.69 (10.6)	2.33 (12.2)	1.71 (16.6)	2.57 (11.0)	2.30 (12.3)

Table A.2: Cross-model MDL compression in pre-trained and fine-tuned models on MNLI dataset. The corresponding codelengths are presented in the brackets. Layers are 0 to 12 from top to bottom.

Learning Mathematical Properties of Integers

Maria Ryskina*
Language Technologies Institute
Carnegie Mellon University
mryskina@cs.cmu.edu

Kevin Knight
DiDi Labs
kevinknight@didiglobal.com

Abstract

Embedding words in high-dimensional vector spaces has proven valuable in many natural language applications. In this work, we investigate whether similarly-trained embeddings of integers can capture concepts that are useful for mathematical applications. We probe the integer embeddings for mathematical knowledge, apply them to a set of numerical reasoning tasks, and show that by learning the representations from mathematical sequence data, we can substantially improve over number embeddings learned from English text corpora.

1 Introduction

Word vector representations learned by neural models have been shown to capture linguistic knowledge that can be useful for downstream NLP tasks (Belinkov and Glass, 2019). In this work, we look at whether similarly-trained integer embeddings can represent useful mathematical knowledge. As a simple example, a mathematician may look at a few values of the function $2^n - 1$:

n	1	2	3	4	5	6	7	...
$2^n - 1$	1	3	7	15	31	63	127	...

and notice patterns such as *'if n is even, then $2^n - 1$ is divisible by 3'*. This type of reasoning is frequent in the early stages of mathematical work. In order for software to assist people in identifying such patterns, it needs to have an internal representation of the basic properties of integers. Just as learned word representations can capture attributes like the word's part of speech or syntactic dependency label (Köhn, 2015; Belinkov et al., 2017), we would like to develop integer embeddings that capture primality, divisibility by 3, etc.

In this paper, we learn integer embeddings from mathematical resources and probe them for mathematical knowledge. Unlike most natural-language features, many number-theoretic properties are highly regular and often may be easily determined from the integer value itself (e.g. converting an integer to its binary representation instantly reveals whether it is a power of 2). However, our focus is not on building classifiers to predict these properties, but rather on exploring whether this information can be learned from the integer co-occurrence statistics in mathematical data and how it is distributed across the vector's dimensions.

*Research performed at DiDi Labs.

[A000040]: 2, 3, 5, 7, 11, 13, 17, 19, 23, 29, ... (primes)
[A000045]: 0, 1, 1, 2, 3, 5, 8, 13, 21, ... (Fibonacci)
[A000108]: 1, 1, 2, 5, 14, 42, 132, 429, ... (Catalan)
[A005132]: 0, 1, 3, 6, 2, 7, 13, 20, 12, 21, ... (Recamán)

Figure 1: Example sequences and their IDs in the Online Encyclopedia of Integer Sequences (OEIS).

Besides that, we are also interested in whether the integer representations learned from context can capture meaningful mathematical properties without us having to define them explicitly. It is not clear how one would probe for such unspecified features, but we can instead estimate the usefulness of the learned embeddings for downstream numerical reasoning tasks. In this work, we apply several types of integer embeddings to a set of tasks built around mathematical regularities, and show that embeddings learned from integer sequences yield better performance than the ones trained on text.

2 Data: OEIS

Our source of mathematical knowledge is the Online Encyclopedia of Integer Sequences (OEIS), a well-known database of number sequences representing properties that are of interest to mathematicians (Sloane, 2003). Several samples from OEIS are shown in Figure 1. While some OEIS sequences may be recognized by non-mathematicians (e.g. the Fibonacci sequence [A000045]), others are based on complex mathematical regularities and would be extremely difficult for a layperson to interpret (e.g. the greatest possible number of diag-

Proceedings of the Fourth BlackboxNLP Workshop on Analyzing and Interpreting Neural Networks for NLP, pages 389–395
Online, November 11, 2021.

Method	Corpus	Tokens	Types
Ours	OEIS	14M	133,004
GloVe–840B–300D	Common Crawl	840B	64,729
SkipGram–BoW–5	Wikipedia	~2.5B	2,272
FastText–Wiki	Wikipedia, UMBC, `statmt.org`	16B	12,037

Table 1: Training corpus details for the integer embeddings used in this work. OEIS types here only include integers that occur 3 or more times; all others are replaced by UNK.

	Train	Dev	Test
Sequences	302,281	16,793	16,793
Integer tokens	12,979,924	719,808	719,237
Mean sequence length	43	43	43
Integer types	1,531,064	128,488	127,976
Singleton types	1,268,771	–	–
Token OOV rate	0%	10.0%	9.8%

Table 2: Summary of the OEIS data splits used in this work. The development split is used for model selection and the test split is used in the sequence completion experiments. Type statistics are reported without minimum count filtering. Singleton types refer to the integers that occur only once in the training set.

onals of a polyhedron with n faces `[A279015]`).

The sequential structure of OEIS allows us to use it for training NLP models developed for textual data, such as recurrent neural network (RNN) language models and co-occurrence-based word embeddings. Of the 336K sequences in OEIS, we allocate 90% for training and divide the rest into development (used for hyperparameter tuning) and test splits; split statistics are listed in Table 2. Of the 1.5M integer types in the vocabulary, 83% appear in training only once. The sequences are represented by their n first elements ($n = 43$ on average), so the coverage of larger integers in OEIS is sparser, and they make up most of the out-of-vocabulary items in the development and test sets.[1]

3 Integer Embeddings

In our experiments, we compare the integer embeddings learned from OEIS with the representations of integer tokens in the vocabulary of word embedding models trained on English text. Table 1 details the training corpus statistics for all embeddings.

3.1 Embeddings Learned from OEIS

Motivated by the distributional semantics paradigm, we learn multi-dimensional embedding vectors from the contexts in which integers occur in OEIS. We use three training methods, well-known in NLP:

LSTM embeddings: we train a two-layer LSTM language model on the 300K OEIS training sequences and extract the 100-dimensional vectors from the weight matrix of its embedding layer.[2]

LSA embeddings: Latent Semantic Analysis (Hofmann, 1999) performs dimensionality reduction on a "document-term" matrix using truncated singular value decomposition. The rows of the matrix represent the integer sequences (as available in OEIS), the columns stand for the integer types, and the values in the cells are equal to the number of occurrences of each integer in each sequence. The resulting matrix is sparse, and its low rank yields vectors with a maximum of 65 dimensions. This method takes OEIS co-occurrences into account, but not the ordering within the sequences.

FastText: we learn 100-dimensional FastText embeddings (Bojanowski et al., 2017), both with and without the additional subword-level information.

3.2 Pre-trained Embeddings

Prior work has successfully employed word representations that are pre-trained on large text corpora for NLP applications. Naturally, these text corpora include numerical data as well, and some properties of a number can be inferred from the textual context (e.g., if an integer follows the phrase *the year*, it most likely has four digits). While the training data for these embeddings is not designed to encode integer properties, it may contain billions of tokens, compared to only ~13M in OEIS. It has been shown that word embeddings retain some knowledge of the integer properties (Naik et al., 2019), so we exploit these resources as a baseline.

We use three sets of pre-trained embeddings: GloVe (Pennington et al., 2014), SkipGram bag-of-words (Levy and Goldberg, 2014), and FastText (Bojanowski et al., 2017). For all three models, we select the versions that performed best in the numerical knowledge tests of Naik et al. (2019).[3]

Thawani et al. (2021) provide a comprehensive description of prior work on number representations learned from text. Prior work concentrates on basic numeracy (counting, paraphrasing, rela-

[1] For the OEIS data download details, see Appendix A.

[2] For implementation details, see Appendix C.

[3] Specific model versions and links to download them are listed in Appendix B.

Embeddings	Evenness		Divisibility by 3		Divisibility by 4		Primality	
	Single	All	Single	All	Single	All	Single	All
Random baseline	0.50	0.50	0.67	0.67	0.75	0.75	0.87	0.87
GloVe–840B–300D	0.51	0.76	0.67	0.47	0.75	0.71	0.87	0.84
SkipGram–BoW–5	0.50	0.52	0.67	0.67	0.75	0.75	0.87	0.87
FastText–Wiki	0.51	0.61	0.67	0.66	0.75	0.76	0.87	0.62
OEIS–LSTM	0.69	0.93	0.67	0.71	0.76	0.81	0.86	0.95
OEIS–LSA	**0.80**	0.62	0.67	0.67	0.75	0.75	0.87	0.87
OEIS–FastText (with subword units)	0.78	**1.00**	**0.69**	0.94	**0.80**	**1.00**	0.82	**1.00**
OEIS–FastText (no subword units)	0.59	**1.00**	0.68	**0.98**	0.77	0.98	0.86	**1.00**
Concatenate(OEIS–FastText, FastText–Wiki)	0.78	**1.00**	**0.69**	0.94	**0.80**	**1.00**	0.82	**1.00**

Table 3: Accuracies of the logistic regression probing classifiers for three binary properties. The classifiers are trained on integers 1–1000, and results are reported on 1001–2000. "All" uses the entire integer embedding as input, while "Single" uses only the most relevant component of the embedding, chosen by train (1–1000) accuracy. Highest accuracy in each experiment is shown in **bold**, if it is exceeds the random choice baseline.

Embeddings	Value (R^2)		Magnitude (R^2)	
	Single	All	Single	All
GloVe–840B–300D	0.82	**1.00**	0.65	**0.99**
SkipGram–BoW–5	0.79	0.99	0.70	0.97
FastText–Wiki	**0.90**	0.99	**0.76**	0.98
OEIS–LSTM	0.49	0.86	0.31	0.78
OEIS–LSA	0.08	0.55	0.13	0.53
OEIS–FastText (with subword units)	0.38	0.99	0.33	0.96
OEIS–FastText (no subword units)	0.49	0.99	0.39	0.95
Concatenate(OEIS–FastText, FastText–Wiki)	**0.90**	**1.00**	**0.76**	0.98

Table 4: Performance of the linear regression models trained to predict an integer's value and order of magnitude (number of digits). We fit the regression models to integers 1–2000 and evaluate the coefficient of determination R^2 of the fit on the same set (between 0 and 1, higher is better). Best results in each experiment shown in **bold**.

tive magnitude, word problems), while we focus on integer properties relevant to mathematical fields such as number theory.

4 What's in an Integer Embedding?

For the learned vectors to be useful for mathematical applications, they need to contain the information about the important integer properties, and this information can be distributed over one or several neurons. For example, in the LSTM embeddings trained on OEIS, we quickly find an "evenness neuron": the 156th element of the embedding vector v is generally positive for even numbers and negative for odd numbers. This holds for integers from 1 to 50 with only a few exceptions, e.g.:

$$v_{156}(1) = 0.15 \qquad v_{156}(6) = 0.38$$
$$v_{156}(2) = 0.29 \qquad v_{156}(7) = -0.31$$
$$v_{156}(3) = -0.04 \qquad v_{156}(8) = 0.39$$
$$v_{156}(4) = 0.26 \qquad v_{156}(9) = -0.02$$
$$v_{156}(5) = -0.08 \qquad v_{156}(10) = 0.43$$

Probing classifiers. We use probing classifiers to test whether the embeddings learn mathematical properties. To avoid spurious correlations, we keep our classifiers very simple. We start by probing for three binary properties: divisibility by 2, 3, and 4, and primality. We train a logistic regression classifier on integers from 1 to 1000 and evaluate its predictions on integers from 1001 to 2000.

Table 3 shows the prediction accuracies for classifiers trained on each embedding type, using either the entire vector or the single most predictive dimension. Generally speaking, the classifiers trained on LSA vectors and pre-trained word embeddings perform on par with the random baseline, providing no evidence of containing the relevant information. However, the OEIS-trained LSTM and FastText vectors can be reliably used to predict mathematical properties of integers, strongly outperforming the baseline in all cases.

Subword information (in our case, digits) is also useful for inferring mathematical properties: e.g.,

Prompt	Answer	Explanation
0, 2, 4, 6,	8	$a_{n+1} = a_n + 2$ (arithmetic progression)
0, 1, 1, 2, 3, 5,	8	$a_{n+2} = a_n + a_{n+1}$ (Fibonacci numbers)
65536, 256, 16,	4	$a_{n+1} = \sqrt{a_n}$
6, 28, 12, 14, 24, 7,	48	$a_{2n+1} = 2 \cdot a_{2n-1}, a_{2n+2} = a_{2n}/2$ (alternating geometric progressions)
32, 35, 39, 44,	50	$a_{n+1} = a_n + n + 2$ (increments forming an arithmetic progression)

Table 5: Example numerical sequence completion problems used in our experiments, along with the rationales behind the gold answers. All questions shown here are collected from the test preparation website `Nibcode`. In our experimental setup, the language model encodes the prompt and needs to predict the most likely continuation.

a :	b ::	c :	?	Incorrect answer options			Explanation
5 :	36 ::	6 :	49	48	50	56	$x : (x+1)^2$
42 :	56 ::	72 :	90	81	92	100	$x(x+1) : (x+1)(x+2)$
48 :	122 ::	168 :	290	215	225	292	$(x^2-1) : [(x+4)^2+1]$
210 :	380 ::	182 :	342	156	240	272	$(x^2-x) : [(x+5)^2-(x+5)]$
11529 :	7235 ::	152943 :	213549	62034	163044	203448	The sum of the digits in each pair is the same

Table 6: Sample mathematical analogy problems used in our experiments, along with the rationales behind the gold answers; the questions shown here are collected from the test preparation website `LearnFrenzy`. All analogy problems are of the form *a:b :: c:?*, and the task is to choose one of the 3–5 provided options that would most appropriately fill in the blank. The column labeled "?" shows the expected correct answer, and the numbers shaded in grey are the remaining answer options. In our experiments with integer embeddings, we use vector arithmetic to find the projected vector of the answer and then select its nearest neighbor among the presented options.

divisibility by 4 can be determined from the last two digits of a number. The subword-based version of FastText averages vectors for all digit 3-grams to 6-grams, plus the vector for the whole integer. We get further improvements by training classifiers on a concatenation of OEIS–FastText and FastText–Wiki vectors, both trained with subword units.

We also probe for the number's order of magnitude (number of digits) and for the value of the integer itself using a linear regression (Table 4): we fit it on integers 1–2000 and evaluate the coefficient of determination R^2 of the fit. In this case, vectors pre-trained on large text corpora perform well.

Completing integer sequences. The task of predicting the next integer in a given sequence has long been used in aptitude testing as a measure of inductive reasoning skills.[4] We collect 57 sequence completion problems from online test preparation websites offering practice questions. Table 5 shows five sample sequence completion problems from our dataset, annotated with answer explanations.[5]

Most sequences test the subject's ability to recognize common patterns like arithmetic progression (0, 2, 4, 6, ? $\rightarrow$ 8) or well-known sequences like Fibonacci numbers (0, 1, 1, 2, 3, 5, ? $\rightarrow$ 8), but some sequences feature additional distractor patterns such as multiple distinct sequences alternating or the increments themselves forming a sequence following another pattern (32, 35, 39, 44, ? $\rightarrow$ 50).

Table 7 compares the performance of the LSTM model trained on OEIS with two baselines:

Baseline 1: GPT-2. We predict the next token using the OpenAI GPT-2 (Radford et al., 2019) language model.[6] GPT-2 can memorize sequences very well, but it is not specifically trained for mathematical generalization. GPT-2 achieves slightly higher accuracy (Precision@1) than our LSTM model but substantially lower Precision@5.

Baseline 2: Search. We match the prompt directly against the OEIS database and return the most frequent continuation. This is a strong baseline: 56% of the test set questions occur somewhere in OEIS followed by the gold answer at least once.

While human aptitude questions focus on a specific range of patterns that are relatively easy for people to identify, we also want to test the predictive abilities on the OEIS test set sequences which showcase more sophisticated phenomena. The LSTM embeddings yield higher accuracy in that case (lower half of Table 7). The search baseline is not as effective for this task because the

[4]We note the non-uniqueness of solutions is a persistent criticism of these tests (Korossy, 1998).

[5]For the full list of sequence completion problems and their sources, see `https://github.com/ryskina/integer-embedding-tests`

[6]We use the AllenNLP prediction demo: `https://demo.allennlp.org/next-token-lm`

Test set	Method	P@1	P@5
Aptitude tests	OEIS–LSTM	0.05	0.37
	GPT-2	0.07	0.19
	OEIS search	**0.53**	**0.56**
OEIS test set	OEIS–LSTM	**0.14**	**0.26**
	OEIS search (full)	0.02	0.02
	OEIS search (last 5)	0.12	0.17

Table 7: Performance on the sequence completion task. Precision@k measures how often the reference answer is among the top k predicted continuations. For the OEIS search baseline, we sort the possible next tokens by frequency of occurring after the given sequence prefix (using either the full prefix or its last five elements).

prompts are now much longer (42 tokens on average compared to 5). Limiting the search to only the last 5 tokens of the prompt improves accuracy, but it still does not outperform the OEIS–LSTM.

Mathematical analogies. A traditional benchmark for evaluating word representations is word analogy, i.e. answering questions of the form "*a* is to *b* as *c* is to ..." (Mikolov et al., 2013a). We perform a similar mathematical analogy test, collecting 79 questions from numerical aptitude practice tests. All questions are multiple-choice (3 to 5 answer options), to mitigate non-uniqueness of the solution. Table 6 shows five sample analogy problems from our dataset, annotated with the intended analogy explanations.[7]

Following Mikolov et al. (2013b), we use vector arithmetic to solve analogies: out of the given options, for the task *a:b :: c:?* we choose the number whose embedding has the highest cosine similarity to the vector $v(c) - v(a) + v(b)$. Table 8 shows that only the FastText embeddings learned from OEIS outperform the random choice baseline on this task. We believe this is due to the linear regularity encoded in the embeddings by design (lacking in LSA and LSTM), and the training data that highlights mathematical properties useful for the task (as compared to FastText–Wiki).

Expanding integer seed sets. In mathematical exploration, we often have a small set S of integers that exhibit some behavior and aim to find other integers that behave similarly. We test the models' ability to expand a given set by finding the centroid of the embeddings of S's members and sorting candidates by cosine distance to the centroid.

[7]Full list of mathematical analogy problems and their sources can be found at `https://github.com/ryskina/integer-embedding-tests`

Method	Accuracy
Random choice baseline	0.28
OEIS–LSTM	0.25
OEIS–LSA	0.27
OEIS–FastText	**0.34**
FastText–Wiki	0.18

Table 8: Peformance on the multiple-choice numerical analogy questions. The answer to *a:b :: c:?* is chosen by highest cosine similarity to $v(c) - v(a) + v(b)$. OEIS–FastText is trained with subword information.

Seed set	Vectors	Candidate expansions
5 13 29	OEIS–FT	**19, 7, 17, 3,** 9, **23**
	FT–Wiki	26, 12, 28, 14, 27, 15
73 97 83	OEIS–FT	**79, 71, 67, 89,** 77, **103**
	FT–Wiki	82, 81, 78, 84, 76, **79**
729 1024 243	OEIS–FT	**2187, 81, 256, 64, 27, 512**
	FT–Wiki	768, **256**, 640, 840, 384, 216

Table 9: Given a small seed set of integers, we predict other candidate members of the set, ranked by the cosine similarity of their vectors to the centroid of the seed set. Methods include OEIS–FastText and FastText–Wiki, both trained with subword information.

Some qualitative examples are shown in Table 9. Given the seed set **5 13 29**, top results given by the OEIS-trained FastText include small prime numbers, while for **73 97 83** we mostly get prime numbers of similar magnitude. The seed **729 1024 243** returns other powers of 2 and 3. By contrast, embeddings trained on non-OEIS texts mainly just return additional numbers in the same range.

5 Conclusion

We introduce integer embeddings trained on the Online Encyclopedia of Integer Sequences (OEIS) and probe them for mathematical knowledge along with the integer representations found in the vocabulary of pre-trained English word embeddings. We find the OEIS embeddings promising for mathematical applications, as they are able to capture some meaningful mathematical regularities.

Acknowledgements

We thank the DiDi Labs NLP Group members for helpful discussion, and the anonymous reviewers for their valuable feedback.

References

Yonatan Belinkov, Nadir Durrani, Fahim Dalvi, Hassan Sajjad, and James Glass. 2017. What do neural machine translation models learn about morphology? In *Proceedings of the 55th Annual Meeting of the Association for Computational Linguistics (Volume 1: Long Papers)*, pages 861–872, Vancouver, Canada. Association for Computational Linguistics.

Yonatan Belinkov and James Glass. 2019. Analysis methods in neural language processing: A survey. *Transactions of the Association for Computational Linguistics*, 7:49–72.

Piotr Bojanowski, Edouard Grave, Armand Joulin, and Tomas Mikolov. 2017. Enriching word vectors with subword information. *Transactions of the Association for Computational Linguistics*, 5:135–146.

Thomas Hofmann. 1999. Probabilistic latent semantic analysis. In *Proceedings of the Fifteenth Conference on Uncertainty in Artificial Intelligence*.

OEIS Foundation Inc. The on-line encyclopedia of integer sequences. Published electronically at `http://oeis.org`. Retrieved on 2020-07-22.

Arne Köhn. 2015. What's in an embedding? Analyzing word embeddings through multilingual evaluation. In *Proceedings of the 2015 Conference on Empirical Methods in Natural Language Processing*, pages 2067–2073, Lisbon, Portugal. Association for Computational Linguistics.

Klaus Korossy. 1998. Solvability and uniqueness of linear-recursive number sequence tasks. *Methods of Psychological Research Online*, 3(1):43–68.

Omer Levy and Yoav Goldberg. 2014. Dependency-based word embeddings. In *Proceedings of the 52nd Annual Meeting of the Association for Computational Linguistics (Volume 2: Short Papers)*, pages 302–308, Baltimore, Maryland. Association for Computational Linguistics.

Tomas Mikolov, Kai Chen, Greg Corrado, and Jeffrey Dean. 2013a. Efficient estimation of word representations in vector space. *arXiv preprint arXiv:1301.3781*.

Tomas Mikolov, Wen-tau Yih, and Geoffrey Zweig. 2013b. Linguistic regularities in continuous space word representations. In *Proceedings of the 2013 Conference of the North American Chapter of the Association for Computational Linguistics: Human Language Technologies*, pages 746–751, Atlanta, Georgia. Association for Computational Linguistics.

Aakanksha Naik, Abhilasha Ravichander, Carolyn Rose, and Eduard Hovy. 2019. Exploring numeracy in word embeddings. In *Proceedings of the 57th Annual Meeting of the Association for Computational Linguistics*, pages 3374–3380, Florence, Italy. Association for Computational Linguistics.

Jeffrey Pennington, Richard Socher, and Christopher Manning. 2014. GloVe: Global vectors for word representation. In *Proceedings of the 2014 Conference on Empirical Methods in Natural Language Processing (EMNLP)*, pages 1532–1543, Doha, Qatar. Association for Computational Linguistics.

Alec Radford, Jeff Wu, Rewon Child, David Luan, Dario Amodei, and Ilya Sutskever. 2019. Language models are unsupervised multitask learners.

Neil J. A. Sloane. 2003. The on-line encyclopedia of integer sequences. *Notices of the American Mathematical Society*, 50(8).

Avijit Thawani, Jay Pujara, Filip Ilievski, and Pedro Szekely. 2021. Representing numbers in NLP: a survey and a vision. In *Proceedings of the 2021 Conference of the North American Chapter of the Association for Computational Linguistics: Human Language Technologies*, pages 644–656, Online. Association for Computational Linguistics.

Ronald J Williams and Jing Peng. 1990. An efficient gradient-based algorithm for on-line training of recurrent network trajectories. *Neural computation*, 2(4):490–501.

A Data sources

OEIS sequence dump was downloaded from the encyclopedia website: `https://oeis.org/stripped.gz` (accessed on 2020-07-22).

Sequence completion problems were collected from five test preparation websites: `Nibcode`, `Syvum`, `12MinPrep`, `IQTestPrep`, `Hitbullseye`.

Mathematical analogy problems were collected from four test practice websites: `LearnFrenzy`, `Examsbook`, `toppr`, `AllIndiaExams`.

B Pre-trained embeddings

Based on the empirical analysis of numeracy in word embeddings conducted by Naik et al. (2019), we choose three embedding models pre-trained on English text corpora:

- **GloVe–840B–300D:** 300-dimensional GloVe vectors trained on 840B tokens from the Common Crawl corpus. Downloaded from `https://nlp.stanford.edu/projects/glove`
- **SkipGram–BoW–5:** 300-dimensional SkipGram bag-of-words embeddings with window size 5. Downloaded from `https://levyomer.wordpress.com/2014/04/25/dependency-based-word-embeddings`

- **FastText–Wiki:** 300-dimensional FastText vectors with subword information, trained on the 16B tokens from Wikipedia 2017, UMBC webbase corpus and `statmt.org` news dataset. Downloaded from `https://fasttext.cc/docs/en/english-vectors.html`

C LSTM implementation details

We implement our two-layer LSTM language model using the PyTorch toolkit. Our model uses truncated BPTT (Williams and Peng, 1990) and is trained for 40 epochs. Hyperparameters: hidden size 200, dynamically annealed learning rate starting at 20, gradients clipped at 0.25.

Probing Language Models for Understanding of Temporal Expressions

Shivin Thukral and **Kunal Kukreja** and **Christian Kavouras**
Department of Linguistics
University of Washington
{shivin7, kkukreja, cdkavour}@uw.edu

Abstract

We present three Natural Language Inference (NLI) challenge sets that can evaluate NLI models on their understanding of temporal expressions. More specifically, we probe these models for three temporal properties: (a) the order between points in time, (b) the duration between two points in time, (c) the relation between the magnitude of times specified in different units. We find that although large language models fine-tuned on MNLI have some basic perception of the order between points in time, at large, these models do not have a thorough understanding of the relation between temporal expressions.

1 Introduction

While contextualized embeddings obtained from recent transformer-based models such as BERT (Devlin et al., 2019) have proven to contain a lot of semantic and syntactic information about the tokens they encode, recent studies have shown that there are still gaps in their understanding (Rogers et al., 2020). On the semantic side, for instance, BERT struggles with representations of numbers (Wallace et al., 2019) and cannot reason based on its world knowledge (Rogers et al., 2020). Work in NLI has also developed challenge sets showing that the reported performance of these language models on various tasks can be exaggerated (McCoy et al., 2019), and they rely on lexical cues in the dataset instead of actual language comprehension.

Our work explores the grasp of such models on the relation between temporal expressions. Temporal expressions, or time expressions, in text are a sequence of tokens that denote time, such as a point in time (6 May 1980, Monday, 12 PM) or duration (7 minutes, 5 years, 2 months). More specifically, we try to determine whether these models capture the ordering and duration relationships between different points in time. We also analyze if these models can reason about durations specified in different units. Recognition of temporal expressions has had applications in timeline construction (Do et al., 2012; Leeuwenberg and Moens, 2018) and clinical analysis (Bethard et al., 2015) previously, and can be beneficial for dialogue assistants in scheduling reminders and meetings, which shapes our motivation behind conducting such an analysis. We evaluate these models on the above temporal properties by presenting three NLI challenge sets.

Our experiments demonstrate that language models such as RoBERTa (Liu et al., 2019) and DeBERTa (He et al., 2021) fine-tuned on existing large NLI datasets are unable to completely reason about the ordering and duration between temporal expressions. We further analyze the examples and find that while these models recognize whether a point in time lies within an interval, they cannot capture other relations between time instances and durations[1].

2 Related Work

Much work has been done on the extraction of events, temporal expressions (Chen et al., 2019; Ding et al., 2019), and the temporal relations between the two. TimeBank (Pustejovsky et al., 2003b) was one of the first annotated corpora for this task. It utilized the TimeML (Pustejovsky et al., 2003a) standard for annotation. TempEval-1 (Verhagen et al., 2007), TempEval-2 (Verhagen et al., 2010), and TempEval-3 (UzZaman et al., 2013) are shared tasks created for evaluating models on various temporal properties, and most methods used were traditional rule-based (Strötgen and Gertz, 2010; Ning et al., 2018) or grammar-based (Lee et al., 2014) solutions.

Various corpora have been developed that test for different temporal properties. Vashishtha et al. (2019) map events to their fine-grained duration, and event pairs to their relative timelines. Naik et al.

[1]Code and data available on GitHub

Proceedings of the Fourth BlackboxNLP Workshop on Analyzing and Interpreting Neural Networks for NLP, pages 396–406
Online, November 11, 2021.

(2019) create additional annotations in the existing TimeBank-Dense corpus (Cassidy et al., 2014) for discourse-level temporal ordering. Ning et al. (2020) create a reading comprehension dataset that tests for temporal ordering. Zhou et al. (2019) test for various temporal commonsense properties using a multiple-choice question-answering dataset. Vashishtha et al. (2020) recast existing temporal datasets into NLI format to test for temporal ordering and duration.

Our goal is to create similar datasets to probe for a semantic understanding of temporal expressions in pre-trained language models. We create these datasets in an NLI format and use them to evaluate NLI models trained on MNLI (Williams et al., 2018), which is a generic NLI dataset. We choose MNLI because it is large and diverse. The dataset contains time terms in 36% of the development instances, including examples containing temporal expressions like months and days of the week. We investigate whether these examples are sufficient for a general perception of temporal expressions.

To our knowledge, there has been little work investigating the implicit understanding of time expressions in pre-trained large language models. The most similar work to ours is Vashishtha et al. (2020). They produce five NLI datasets recast from existing temporal reasoning corpora and test NLI models for event duration (how long an event lasts) and event ordering (how events are temporally arranged). However, there are some key differences:

- Our focus is to investigate the temporal properties of ordering and duration for explicit *time expressions*, and not for *events* in a sentence.
- We analyze whether language models can reason about more fine-grained duration (e.g., whether an event takes exactly 5 hours) where as they analyze reasoning about more coarse-grained duration (e.g., whether an event takes place in the order of hours or days).
- We also investigate whether language models can figure out commonplace conversions among adjacent units of time.
- We introduce numerous variations in our data creation process about how the time expressions are inserted and draw conclusions from how these variations affect performance.

List Type	**List Range**
hour (12 hr)	*12 AM, ..., 11 PM*
hour (24 hr)	*00:00, 01:00, ..., 23:00*
weekday	*Sunday, ..., Saturday*
month-day	*1st, 2nd, ..., 28th*
month (full name)	*January, ..., December*
month (abbreviated)	*Jan, Feb, ..., Dec*
year	*1900, 1901, ..., 2000*

Table 1: Different lists of temporal expressions

3 Dataset Creation

We construct three NLI datasets that aim to test different relations between temporal expressions. The datasets use templates from a manually curated list of 71 events, labeled with their *temporal occurrence* (when the event is likely to occur) and *temporal duration* (how long the event is expected to last) values. For instance:

Template: I went to Paris
Occurrence: day, month, year
• I went to Paris on Monday.
• I went to Paris in March.
• I went to Paris in 2010.
Duration: hours, days
• I visited Paris from 10 AM to 9 PM.
• I visited Paris from Mon to Wed.

Each temporal unit corresponds to some list(s) spanning different magnitudes of time (Table 1), which are used during NLI pair creation.

3.1 Set I: Temp-Order

We create this NLI challenge set to test whether language models recognize the relationship of ordering between two distinct temporal expressions. We frame this in the NLI format by having the premise mention an event occur at a particular time instance, while the hypothesis mentions the same event but occurring at a different time instance:

Premise : They got married **in March**.
Hypothesis : They got married **before July**.
Label : Entailment

We start constructing a basic NLI pair by choosing a sentence template from the list of events. Based on the *temporal occurrence* label of the event, one of the lists from Table 1 is chosen, and two time instances are sampled from that list with

	Premise	Hypothesis	Label
a)	He left his job *at 12 PM.*	He left his job *before 5 PM.*	E
b)	*At 12 PM*, he left his job.	*Before 5 PM*, he left his job.	E
c)	He will leave his job *at 12 PM.*	He will leave his job *before 5 PM.*	E
d)	He left his job *after 12 PM.*	He left his job *after 9 AM.*	E
e)	He left his job *after 12 PM.*	He left his job *before 5 PM.*	N
f)	He left his job *after 12 PM.*	He left his job *before 9 AM.*	C
g)	He left his job *at 12 PM.*	He left his job *before 17:00.*	E
h)	He left his job *in February.*	He left his job *after Apr.*	C
i)	He left his job *in October 2011.*	He left his job *after Jan 2011.*	E
j)	He left his job *on 21st Sep 2013.*	He left his job *before 23rd Sep 2012.*	C

Table 2: Variations in NLI pairs for ordering of temporal expressions (E $\rightarrow$ entailment, C $\rightarrow$ contradiction, N $\rightarrow$ neutral). *a)* is the basic construction; *b), c)* is with the variation in event template; *d), e), f)* are when premise uses a relative preposition to allow the event to happen in a time interval; *g), h)* are examples of choosing time instances from two different lists; *i), j)* are generation of more specific dates using months and month-days with years.

replacement. For the premise, the first time instance is attached so that the event happens precisely at this time instance. For the hypothesis, we randomly choose a *relative ordering* between *'before'* and *'after'* and attach it to the template event and the second instance. Since the premise claims that the event occurs at an exact point in time while the hypothesis claims that the event happens in a specific time interval, the premise time instance either lies inside the hypothesis time interval or it does not, generating the labels of *entailment* or *contradiction* correspondingly.

During label generation, we have assumed that both time instances lie in the same cycle (e.g., two *weekdays* lie in the same week). However, for cases where the two time instances are close across consecutive cycles, the automated label generated this way might be considered conventionally wrong:

Premise: The concert starts **at 2 AM**.
Hypothesis: The concert starts **before 11 PM**.
Label: Entailment

To reduce the number of such edge cases in the dataset, we do not allow sampling of time instances that are more than half the length of the list far apart (e.g., for within a day, the distance between two *hours* will be at most 12).

We also introduce some variations in the sentence generation process to analyze the sensitivity of the models. Firstly, we tweak the event template by changing its position in the sentence (Table 2 *b*) and by switching it to future tense (Table 2 *c*). Secondly, we allow the premise event to also occur over an interval of time rather than a point in time (Table 2 *d, e, f*). To generate labels for these cases, the criteria we follow is that the pair is an *entailment* if the premise time interval is completely included in the hypothesis time interval (*temporal inclusion*), a *contradiction* if there is no overlap between the two (*temporal precedence*), and *neutral* otherwise. Moreover, we allow the premise and hypothesis to sample points in time from different lists when possible (Table 2 *g, h*). We also generate more specific dates by combining *months* and *month-days* with *years* (Table 2 *i, j*) to see if the language models are still able to reason about the difference in their ordering.

We construct separate train and test datasets, using 53 templates for the train split and 18 templates for the test split. We have 11 different ways of choosing the two time instances: seven ways of choosing both from the same list (Table 1) and four ways of choosing from different lists (Table 2 *g-j*). We choose the two time instances for each template based on its *temporal occurrence* label and run it for five iterations, which results in a train dataset of 16,980 instances and test dataset of 6,140 instances, with the distribution of labels being: 40% *contradiction*, 35% *entailment*, 25% *neutral*.

3.2 Set II: Temp-Duration

The motivation behind this dataset is to test whether language models can reason about fine-grained temporal durations. We frame this in an NLI format by having the premise mention an event occurring between two points in time, while the hypothesis mentions the same event having occurred for a given duration:

Premise : The war lasted **from 1939 to 1945**.

	Premise	Hypothesis	Label
a)	The meeting lasted *from 12 PM to 5 PM.*	The meeting lasted *for 5 hours.*	E
b)	The meeting lasted *from 12 PM to 5 PM.*	The meeting lasted *for 50 hours.*	C
c)	The meeting lasted *from 12 PM to 5 PM.*	The meeting lasted *for less than 5 hours.*	C
d)	The meeting lasted *from 12 PM to 5 PM.*	The meeting lasted *for less than 6 hours.*	E
e)	The meeting *began at 12 PM* and *lasted until 5 PM.*	The meeting lasted *for 5 hours.*	E
f)	The meeting lasted *from 9 PM to 3 AM.*	The meeting lasted *for 6 hours.*	E
g)	The meeting lasted *from 12 PM to 17:00.*	The meeting lasted *for 5 hours.*	E
h)	The spring quarter lasts *from Mar to June.*	The spring quarter lasts *for 3 months.*	E
i)	The war lasted *from July 1914 to Nov 1918.*	The war lasted *for 4 years 4 months.*	E
j)	The war lasted *from July 1914 to Nov 1918.*	The war lasted *for 52 months.*	E

Table 3: Variations in NLI pairs for duration calculation (E$\rightarrow$entailment, C$\rightarrow$contradiction). *a) - d)* are a few examples from the 6 basic pairs; *e)* is with a changed premise structure; *f)* is when the hypothesis time instance crosses over to the next cycle; *g), h)* are examples of choosing time instances from two different lists; *i), j)* are generation of specific dates using months and years in two different formats.

Hypothesis : The war lasted **for 6 years.**
Label : Entailment

We begin forming a basic NLI pair by choosing a sentence template. Based on the event's *temporal duration* label, a list from Table 1 is selected, and two time instances are randomly sampled without replacement. The smaller instance is mentioned in the premise as the event start time and the other instance as the event end time. We construct multiple hypotheses for the same premise. First, we calculate the *gold duration (GOLD)* by finding the difference between the two instances, assuming both the instances are part of the same cycle. Then, the hypothesis mentions the event to have occurred in two different settings *(equal to, less than)* for three different durations *(GOLD, GOLD+1, GOLD*10)*, generating a total of six hypotheses (Table 3 *a-d* are a few examples). We do this to test whether the NLI models can reason for the claimed duration's validity only when they are very distant *(GOLD*10)* or also very close *(GOLD+1)* to the gold duration. Generation of true labels for the pairs is automated, producing an *entailment* or *contradiction* depending on whether the gold duration falls in the duration range specified by the hypothesis.

We again introduce two variations in the dataset creation process. First, we change the wording of the premise sentence (Table 3 *e*). Secondly, while sampling the time instances, we force the ending instance to be picked such that it falls before the starting instance in the list, which implies that the event crossed over to the next cycle. In such cases, the calculation of the gold duration is slightly different (Table 3 *f*). We perform this next cycle calculation for all lists in Table 1 except *month-days* (because gold calculation without specifying the exact month is ambiguous) and *years* (because the list is acyclic). We also allow a similar blend of temporal expressions, like in *Temp-Order* set, combining the two *hours* (Table 3 *g*) and *months* (Table 3 *h*) lists. We construct specific dates by including *months* and *years* and allow the duration to be mentioned in a year-month format (Table 3 *i*) or a months-only format (Table 3 *j*).

We create separate train and test datasets using the same split of 53 and 18 templates as before. For each template, time instances are chosen based on their *temporal duration* label, along with the variations as mentioned above applied (Table 3 *e-j*). Running each template for five iterations produces a train dataset of 13,500 instances and test dataset of 3,540 instances, with the label distribution: 50% *entailment* and 50% *contradiction*.

3.3 Set III: Cross-Unit Duration

The motivation behind the creation of the *Cross-Unit Duration* set is to test whether language models understand the conversion relationship between magnitudes specified in different units of time; for instance, if models are able to interpret that 5 hours are less than 350 minutes but more than 250. Moreover, we investigate if these models are better at

	Premise	Hypothesis	Label
a)	The store will close *in 2 hours.*	The store will close *before 40 minutes.*	C
b)	*In 2 hours*, the store will close.	The store will close *after 84 minutes.*	E
c)	The store will close *in 2 days.*	*After 34 hours*, the store will close.	E
d)	*After 4 days*, the store will close.	The store will close *before 38 hours.*	C
e)	The store will close *before 4 days.*	*Before 174 hours*, the store will close.	E
f)	The store will close *before 6 hours.*	The store will close *after 77 minutes.*	N
g)	*After 3 hours*, the store will close.	The store will close *after 409 minutes.*	N

Table 4: Variations in NLI pairs for cross-unit duration comparison (E $\rightarrow$ entailment, C $\rightarrow$ contradiction, N $\rightarrow$ neutral). *a)* is the basic pair; *b), c)* are variations of basic pair with template position changed; *d) - g)* are variations in which the premise event occurs over a range of time.

certain kinds of conversions. We frame this task in an NLI format in a similar manner to the *Temp-Order* set. In the premise, we mention a future event that will occur after a given duration *(T1)*, while in the hypothesis we mention the same future event to occur before or after a different duration *(T2)*. Apart from varying magnitudes, *T1* and *T2* are also specified in different but adjacent units of time. More specifically, *T1* is specified in the higher adjacent unit of time, i.e., if *T2* is specified in minutes, then *T1* will be specified in hours. Since the premise mentions an event occurring at a future point in time while the hypothesis mention an event occurring over a time interval bounded on just one side, the premise event either lies in the interval or not, leading to the labels *entailment* and *contradiction* respectively. We tried multiple variations similar to *Temp-Order* set, like changing the position of the template in the premise/hypothesis (Table 4 *b, c*) and making the event in the premise also occur over a future interval (Table 4 *d-g*). The labeling procedure of the second variation is again similar to *Temp-Order* set.

To create the challenge set, we first pick a template and look at the list of its *temporal occurrence* values. We then iterate over all adjacent values in this list, e.g., seconds-minutes, hours-days, months-years. For each pair, we iterate over a manually created list of magnitudes for the higher unit of time *(T1)* for the premise. We then pick a magnitude in the smaller unit of time *(T2)* which is either higher or lower than *T1*. *T2*'s value is generated randomly, but a *difference range* parameter controls its absolute difference with *T1*'s value. For each fixed template, fixed duration unit pair, and fixed magnitude of *T1*, we generate twelve different premise-hypothesis pairs, four in which the premise occurs at a future point in time, and eight in which it occurs over a future interval of time. Using a *difference range* parameter of 5, we create a training set of 42,240 rows and a test set of 15,840 rows. Due to the challenge set creation procedure, the resultant dataset is naturally balanced with the same number of samples for each of the three labels.

4 Experimental Setup

We evaluate three different NLI models on each of our challenge sets. The first model is a pre-trained RoBERTa-large model fine-tuned on the MNLI corpus, which reports 90.8% accuracy on the MNLI-matched task. The second model is Microsoft's DeBERTa-large model fine-tuned on the MNLI corpus, which reports 91.9% accuracy on the MNLI-matched task. Both these models are trained on all three labels: *entailment*, *contradiction*, and *neutral*.

The third model comes from Vashishtha et al. (2020), which is a RoBERTa-large model fine-tuned on their temporal NLI datasets. For *Temp-Order* set, we evaluate their model trained on the *UDS-NLI (order)* corpus as it explored ordering relations between events, and we wanted to analyze if any of that knowledge transfers over for determining the ordering between temporal expressions. Similarly, for *Temp-Duration* and *Cross-Unit Duration* sets, we evaluate their model trained on the *UDS-NLI (duration)* corpus, which explored more coarse-grained duration of events. In contrast to the models fine-tuned on MNLI, these models are only trained on binary classification - producing *'entailed'* for the *entailment* label and *'not-entailed'* for the *contradiction* and *neutral* labels. We have a separate majority baseline corresponding to these models.

We report performances of all datasets under

Model	Method	Accuracy	F1 Score
Majority	Ternary Classification	40.29	23.14
	Binary Classification	65.19	51.46
RoBERTa (MNLI)	Direct Evaluation	52.75	45.36
	Hypothesis Only Training	40.29 ± 0	23.14 ± 0
	Train and Evaluate	99.81 ± 0.03	99.81 ± 0.03
DeBERTa (MNLI)	Direct Evaluation	51.57	44.29
	Hypothesis Only Training	40.29 ± 0	23.14 ± 0
	Train and Evaluate	99.76 ± 0.04	99.76 ± 0.04
UDS-NLI (order)	Direct Evaluation	56.36	57.20

Table 5: Evaluating *Temp-Order* set on NLI models

three different settings:

1. **Direct Evaluation**: Evaluating the pre-trained NLI models directly on the test splits of our challenge sets.

2. **Train and Evaluate**: Fine-tuning the NLI models with the train splits and reporting performances on the test splits. We report this to recognize the complexity of the synthetic datasets, and the ceiling performances that various NLI models can achieve on them.

3. **Hypothesis Only Training**: Fine-tuning the NLI models in a hypothesis-only setting (Poliak et al., 2018) with the train splits, and reporting performances on the test splits. We report this as a control for the results achieved in the *Train and Evaluate* setting.

We do not train the models fine-tuned on UDS-NLI corpora, and only report their performance under the *Direct Evaluation* setting, as the architecture of those models is similar to that of the pre-trained RoBERTa-MNLI model and we hypothesize that this may lead to similar results on training. More details on the training process are mentioned in Appendix A.

5 Results & Discussions

We present the results of all three challenge sets separately.

5.1 Set I: Temp-Order

Results of *Temp-Order* set are summarised in Table 5. When evaluating on the RoBERTa and DeBERTa models, there is an improvement of about 10% over the majority baseline. On analyzing the effect of different variations mentioned in Table 2, we find that changing the template position or its tense does not produce any significant difference in performance. However, we find that pairs where the premise event occurred at a fixed time instance (2 *a*) have an average of 75% accuracy, while the pairs where the premise event occurred over a time interval (2 *d-f*) have an average accuracy of 28%. This implies that models trained on MNLI have some basic understanding of temporal ordering, especially in determining whether a fixed time instance is present in another time interval. However, it gets difficult to reason about the ordering between two time intervals, where discerning the label is also not as straightforward.

We further analyze the accuracies for different methods of choosing the two time instances, and the results for DeBERTa are summed up in Figure 1. For pairs where the premise event takes place at a fixed point in time, most methods in which both time instances were sampled from the same list give over 73% accuracy. Among the methods in which time instances are sampled across multiple lists, dates in which *months* are combined with *years* give an average accuracy of 74%, but this drops to 57% when *month-days* are added, signifying that the comparison of specific dates becomes too complicated for the NLI model. The model also has a hard time mapping *hours* between 12 and 24-hour format, giving only 59% accuracy. For pairs where the premise takes place over a time interval, the accuracies of all methods are below 35%.

We also evaluate the RoBERTa model trained on *UDS-NLI (order)* corpus on our challenge set. However, the average performance was only 56%, even below the majority baseline for the corpus, not indicating any significant transfer of knowledge from their task of event-based temporal ordering.

The hypothesis-only baseline for both the RoBERTa/DeBERTa models is exactly the major-

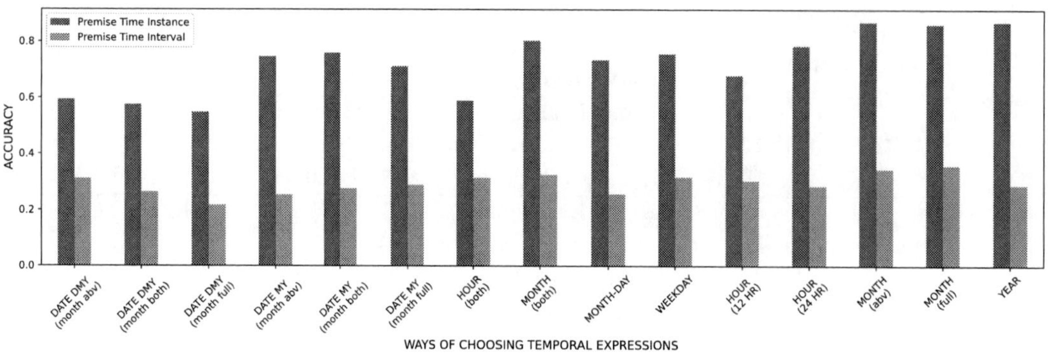

Figure 1: Comparison of accuracies across different ways of choosing temporal expressions when running *Temp-Order* set on DeBERTa fine-tuned on MNLI. Label 'DATE DMY' implies generating dates using all *month-day*, *month* and *year* (Table 2 *j*), while 'DATE MY' uses only *month* and *year* (Table 2 *i*). The added descriptions signify where the month instances are drawn from, where 'month (full)' implies that both months come from the *month (full name)* list, 'month (abv)' implies that they come from *month (abbreviated)* list, and 'month (both)' implies that one month instance comes from each of the two lists. Labels 'MONTH (both)' and 'HOUR (both)' signify similar methods of choosing from multiple lists (Table 2 *h* and *g* correspondingly).

ity baseline, which is not surprising as the true label cannot be determined without knowing the premise time instance. Further fine-tuning the pre-trained MNLI models on our *Temp-Order* set leads to an almost perfect accuracy of 99%. This is despite having separate templates for the train and test split, and having time instances randomly sampled from different lists. Since our method of generating labels was automated and depended on the values of the time instances, we infer that the numerous parameters of a large language model were able to learn this label generation process from the artificial NLI data.

5.2 Set II: Temp-Duration

Results for *Temp-Duration* set are summarized in Table 6. Both the RoBERTa and DeBERTa models fine-tuned on MNLI produce poor accuracies of around 55%, just over the majority baseline. While analyzing the DeBERTa predictions, we found that the model produced *entailment* for 83% of the data points, implying that it is not able to adequately determine durations. The different variations (Table 3) or methods of sampling time instances also did not have any significant effect. We investigated the performances of the six types of hypotheses and found that among the hypothesis types with the *contradiction* gold label, *'equal to GOLD*10'* produced 0.68 F1-score, compared to *'equal to GOLD+1'* and *'less than GOLD'*, which produced 0.15 and 0.07 F1-scores respectively. This might indicate that while the NLI model has difficulty figuring out when the claimed duration is incorrect, it still does better off when it is very distant *(GOLD*10)* from the gold duration compared to when it is very close *(GOLD+1)*. We also find that for the *'equal to GOLD'* hypothesis, pairs of instances far apart in a list tend to be misclassified more than pairs of instances that are closer to each other. This implies that determination of exact duration gets difficult for the NLI model as the distance between instances increases.

We also evaluate the model trained on *UDS-NLI (duration)* corpus on our set, and the results are slightly above the majority baseline. While the predictions by this model were not as skewed, we could not find any significant impact of the variations or the different methods of sampling time instances, not indicating any possible knowledge transfer from their problem of determining coarse-grained event duration.

On fine-tuning our challenge set under the hypothesis-only setting, both MNLI models surprisingly produce at least 15% gains in accuracy over the majority baseline. We investigate and find that the models use lexical cues from the different hypothesis types, producing *entailment* for all *'less than'* hypotheses. For the *'equal'* hypotheses, they predict *contradiction* when the claimed duration is a large value (more likely to be *GOLD*10*) and *entailment* when it is smaller (more likely to be *GOLD*). However, under the standard NLI training

Model	Method	Accuracy	F1 Score
Majority[1]	Binary Classification	50.00	33.33
RoBERTa (MNLI)	Direct Evaluation	54.32	46.64
	Hypothesis Only Training	68.82 ± 0.22	66.84 ± 0.51
	Train and Evaluate	91.86 ± 6.42	91.85 ± 6.42
DeBERTa (MNLI)	Direct Evaluation	56.67	51.53
	Hypothesis Only Training	64.15 ± 0.27	59.64 ± 0.41
	Train and Evaluate	73.72 ± 3.92	73.28 ± 4.50
UDS-NLI (duration)	Direct Evaluation	58.44	57.66

Table 6: Evaluating *Temp-Duration* set on NLI models

Model	Method	Accuracy	F1 Score
Majority	Ternary Classification	33.33	16.67
	Binary Classification	66.67	53.33
RoBERTa (MNLI)	Direct Evaluation	35.47	28.71
	Hypothesis Only Training	49.38 ± 0.71	39.51 ± 0.52
	Train and Evaluate	99.97 ± 0.02	99.97 ± 0.02
DeBERTa (MNLI)	Direct Evaluation	45.02	38.60
	Hypothesis Only Training	49.58 ± 0.79	41.29 ± 0.56
	Train and Evaluate	99.94 ± 0.03	99.94 ± 0.03
UDS-NLI (duration)	Direct Evaluation	52.61	53.54

Table 7: Evaluating *Cross-Unit Duration* set on NLI models

scenario, these cues are not the only factor behind learning, as the RoBERTa MNLI model produces 91.86% average accuracy, which is a gain of 20% over the hypothesis-only setting. Among the various methods of sampling time instances, *years* performs the worst, producing only 66% accuracy, possibly because the lengths of duration can be as large as 100 years. Finally, the hypothesis types *'equal to GOLD*10'* and *'less than GOLD*10'* produce 99% accuracy, while *'equal to GOLD'* and *'less than GOLD'* report below 90%, confirming our speculation that it is easier for the models to reason about the validity of the claimed duration when it is distant from the gold duration.

5.3 Set III: Cross-Unit Duration Set

As shown in Table 7, all the models produce poor performances on direct evaluation, just near the majority baseline. DeBERTa fine-tuned on MNLI manages to perform better when compared to RoBERTa fine-tuned on MNLI by around 10% on overall accuracy. Hence, we can conclude that DeBERTa has a slightly better understanding of cross-unit duration comparison when compared to RoBERTa.

[1]Same majority baseline because no neutral labels.

Similar to *Temp-Order* set, all models performed better compared to their respective majority baselines when the premise event occurs at a future point in time rather than over a time interval. More specifically, we see an improvement in accuracy of around 18% (29.65 to 47.12) for RoBERTa and around 10% (41.77 to 51.52) for DeBERTa when we switch from the premise occurring over a time interval to a point in time.

We analyzed the results on adjacent units to recognize if there are specific pairs for which the models are better able to figure out the conversion relationship. We did not find any significant pair for RoBERTa or DeBERTa models, but we find that the *UDS-NLI (duration)* model does better on bigger unit pairs of duration, i.e., it performs the best on conversion between month-years (56.03% F1), then day-months (55.32% F1), then hours-days (51.02% F1), and then minutes-hours (16.74% F1). This suggests a better transfer of knowledge for bigger time units from the *UDS-NLI (duration)* model to our challenge set.

Similar to *Temp-Duration* set, on fine-tuning under the hypothesis-only setting, both MNLI models produce around 16-17% gains in accuracy over the majority baseline using lexical cues present in the hypotheses due to the challenge set creation process. For the hypotheses that contain *'before'*, the models tend to predict *entailment* if the duration *(T2)* is large, and *contradiction* if it is small. Similarly, for the hypotheses that contain *'after'*, the models mostly predict *contradiction* if the duration is large, and *entailment* if it is small. However, on standard training, the accuracy goes up from around 50% to near perfect 99%, showing that these cues are not the only reason behind the model's performance and that it actually learns the relationship between the premise and hypothesis.

We believe a valuable addition to this challenge set would be introducing more varied phrasing of prepositions. That is, using synonymous ways of denoting a temporal event occurring before, after, or strictly at a point in time. In particular, phrasing like 'after the next 60 minutes' or 'sometime after 60 minutes pass' could be examples of more specific ways to represent that an event occurred 'after 60 minutes' - a phrase which we acknowledge may read to mean 'in exactly 60 minutes', as opposed to some time after.

6 Conclusion

We create three challenge sets that test different kinds of relationships between temporal expressions. We evaluate these challenge sets on popular NLI models like RoBERTa and DeBERTa trained on MNLI, and find that while they can reason about simple cases of ordering between time instances, they fail when presented with more complicated cases or when temporal reasoning requires determining fine-grained duration. Since our challenge sets were synthetically created, training on them helped the NLI models to figure out the label generation process, and they produced near-perfect accuracy for the *Temp-Order* and the *Cross-Unit Duration* sets. A direction for future research could be evaluating and comparing models, trained on other NLI datasets containing temporal expressions, on our challenge sets. Another direction could be to collect naturally occurring sentences that contain temporal expressions from large corpora and recast them into NLI format for similar testing of understanding of temporal expressions.

References

Steven Bethard, Leon Derczynski, Guergana Savova, James Pustejovsky, and Marc Verhagen. 2015. SemEval-2015 task 6: Clinical TempEval. In *Proceedings of the 9th International Workshop on Semantic Evaluation (SemEval 2015)*, pages 806–814, Denver, Colorado. Association for Computational Linguistics.

Taylor Cassidy, Bill McDowell, Nathanael Chambers, and Steven Bethard. 2014. An annotation framework for dense event ordering. In *Proceedings of the 52nd Annual Meeting of the Association for Computational Linguistics (Volume 2: Short Papers)*, pages 501–506, Baltimore, Maryland. Association for Computational Linguistics.

Sanxing Chen, Guoxin Wang, and Börje Karlsson. 2019. Exploring word representations on time expression recognition. Technical report, Microsoft Research Asia.

Jacob Devlin, Ming-Wei Chang, Kenton Lee, and Kristina Toutanova. 2019. BERT: Pre-training of deep bidirectional transformers for language understanding. In *Proceedings of the 2019 Conference of the North American Chapter of the Association for Computational Linguistics: Human Language Technologies, Volume 1 (Long and Short Papers)*, pages 4171–4186, Minneapolis, Minnesota. Association for Computational Linguistics.

Wentao Ding, Guanji Gao, Linfeng Shi, and Yuzhong Qu. 2019. A pattern-based approach to recognizing time expressions. *Proceedings of the AAAI Conference on Artificial Intelligence*, 33(01):6335–6342.

Quang Do, Wei Lu, and Dan Roth. 2012. Joint inference for event timeline construction. In *Proceedings of the 2012 Joint Conference on Empirical Methods in Natural Language Processing and Computational Natural Language Learning*, pages 677–687, Jeju Island, Korea. Association for Computational Linguistics.

Pengcheng He, Xiaodong Liu, Jianfeng Gao, and Weizhu Chen. 2021. Deberta: Decoding-enhanced bert with disentangled attention.

Kenton Lee, Yoav Artzi, Jesse Dodge, and Luke Zettlemoyer. 2014. Context-dependent semantic parsing for time expressions. In *Proceedings of the 52nd Annual Meeting of the Association for Computational Linguistics (Volume 1: Long Papers)*, pages 1437–1447, Baltimore, Maryland. Association for Computational Linguistics.

Artuur Leeuwenberg and Marie-Francine Moens. 2018. Temporal information extraction by predicting relative time-lines. In *Proceedings of the 2018 Conference on Empirical Methods in Natural Language Processing*, pages 1237–1246, Brussels, Belgium. Association for Computational Linguistics.

Yinhan Liu, Myle Ott, Naman Goyal, Jingfei Du, Mandar Joshi, Danqi Chen, Omer Levy, Mike Lewis, Luke Zettlemoyer, and Veselin Stoyanov. 2019. Roberta: A robustly optimized bert pretraining approach.

Tom McCoy, Ellie Pavlick, and Tal Linzen. 2019. Right for the wrong reasons: Diagnosing syntactic heuristics in natural language inference. In *Proceedings of the 57th Annual Meeting of the Association for Computational Linguistics*, pages 3428–3448, Florence, Italy. Association for Computational Linguistics.

Aakanksha Naik, Luke Breitfeller, and Carolyn Rose. 2019. TDDiscourse: A dataset for discourse-level temporal ordering of events. In *Proceedings of the 20th Annual SIGdial Meeting on Discourse and Dialogue*, pages 239–249, Stockholm, Sweden. Association for Computational Linguistics.

Qiang Ning, Hao Wu, Rujun Han, Nanyun Peng, Matt Gardner, and Dan Roth. 2020. Torque: A reading comprehension dataset of temporal ordering questions.

Qiang Ning, Ben Zhou, Zhili Feng, Haoruo Peng, and Dan Roth. 2018. CogCompTime: A tool for understanding time in natural language. In *Proceedings of the 2018 Conference on Empirical Methods in Natural Language Processing: System Demonstrations*, pages 72–77, Brussels, Belgium. Association for Computational Linguistics.

Adam Poliak, Jason Naradowsky, Aparajita Haldar, Rachel Rudinger, and Benjamin Van Durme. 2018. Hypothesis only baselines in natural language inference. In *Proceedings of the Seventh Joint Conference on Lexical and Computational Semantics*, pages 180–191, New Orleans, Louisiana. Association for Computational Linguistics.

James Pustejovsky, José M Castano, Robert Ingria, Roser Sauri, Robert J Gaizauskas, Andrea Setzer, Graham Katz, and Dragomir R Radev. 2003a. Timeml: Robust specification of event and temporal expressions in text. *New directions in question answering*, 3:28–34.

James Pustejovsky, Patrick Hanks, Roser Saurí, Andrew See, Rob Gaizauskas, Andrea Setzer, Dragomir Radev, Beth Sundheim, David Day, Lisa Ferro, and Marcia Lazo. 2003b. The timebank corpus. *Proceedings of Corpus Linguistics*, page 40.

Anna Rogers, Olga Kovaleva, and Anna Rumshisky. 2020. A primer in BERTology: What we know about how BERT works. *Transactions of the Association for Computational Linguistics*, 8:842–866.

Jannik Strötgen and Michael Gertz. 2010. HeidelTime: High quality rule-based extraction and normalization of temporal expressions. In *Proceedings of the 5th International Workshop on Semantic Evaluation*, pages 321–324, Uppsala, Sweden. Association for Computational Linguistics.

Naushad UzZaman, Hector Llorens, Leon Derczynski, James Allen, Marc Verhagen, and James Pustejovsky. 2013. SemEval-2013 task 1: TempEval-3: Evaluating time expressions, events, and temporal relations. In *Second Joint Conference on Lexical and Computational Semantics (*SEM), Volume 2: Proceedings of the Seventh International Workshop on Semantic Evaluation (SemEval 2013)*, pages 1–9, Atlanta, Georgia, USA. Association for Computational Linguistics.

Siddharth Vashishtha, Adam Poliak, Yash Kumar Lal, Benjamin Van Durme, and Aaron Steven White. 2020. Temporal reasoning in natural language inference. In *Findings of the Association for Computational Linguistics: EMNLP 2020*, pages 4070–4078, Online. Association for Computational Linguistics.

Siddharth Vashishtha, Benjamin Van Durme, and Aaron Steven White. 2019. Fine-grained temporal relation extraction. In *Proceedings of the 57th Annual Meeting of the Association for Computational Linguistics*, pages 2906–2919, Florence, Italy. Association for Computational Linguistics.

Marc Verhagen, Robert Gaizauskas, Frank Schilder, Mark Hepple, Graham Katz, and James Pustejovsky. 2007. SemEval-2007 task 15: TempEval temporal relation identification. In *Proceedings of the Fourth International Workshop on Semantic Evaluations (SemEval-2007)*, pages 75–80, Prague, Czech Republic. Association for Computational Linguistics.

Marc Verhagen, Roser Saurí, Tommaso Caselli, and James Pustejovsky. 2010. SemEval-2010 task 13: TempEval-2. In *Proceedings of the 5th International Workshop on Semantic Evaluation*, pages 57–62, Uppsala, Sweden. Association for Computational Linguistics.

Eric Wallace, Yizhong Wang, Sujian Li, Sameer Singh, and Matt Gardner. 2019. Do NLP models know numbers? probing numeracy in embeddings. In *Proceedings of the 2019 Conference on Empirical Methods in Natural Language Processing and the 9th International Joint Conference on Natural Language Processing (EMNLP-IJCNLP)*, pages 5307–5315, Hong Kong, China. Association for Computational Linguistics.

Adina Williams, Nikita Nangia, and Samuel Bowman. 2018. A broad-coverage challenge corpus for sentence understanding through inference. In *Proceedings of the 2018 Conference of the North American Chapter of the Association for Computational Linguistics: Human Language Technologies, Volume 1 (Long Papers)*, pages 1112–1122, New Orleans, Louisiana. Association for Computational Linguistics.

Thomas Wolf, Lysandre Debut, Victor Sanh, Julien Chaumond, Clement Delangue, Anthony Moi, Pierric Cistac, Tim Rault, Rémi Louf, Morgan Funtowicz, Joe Davison, Sam Shleifer, Patrick von Platen, Clara Ma, Yacine Jernite, Julien Plu, Canwen Xu, Teven Le Scao, Sylvain Gugger, Mariama Drame, Quentin Lhoest, and Alexander M. Rush. 2020. Huggingface's transformers: State-of-the-art natural language processing.

Ben Zhou, Daniel Khashabi, Qiang Ning, and Dan Roth. 2019. "going on a vacation" takes longer than "going for a walk": A study of temporal commonsense understanding. In *Proceedings of the 2019 Conference on Empirical Methods in Natural Language Processing and the 9th International Joint Conference on Natural Language Processing (EMNLP-IJCNLP)*, pages 3363–3369, Hong Kong, China. Association for Computational Linguistics.

A Training Details

We use three different NLI models for our experiments. For the RoBERTa and DeBERTa models fine-tuned on MNLI, we use the `roberta-large-mnli` and `microsoft/deberta-large-mnli` models respectively, available under the `transformers` library from HuggingFace (Wolf et al., 2020). For the *UDS-NLI* models, we directly use the saved RoBERTa-large models for *UDS-NLI (duration)* and *UDS-NLI (order)* made publicly available by Vashishtha et al. (2020).

For training, we use an Adam optimizer, with a learning rate of $2 * 10^{-5}$ and 0.1 weight decay. We use a batch size of 16 for training and 128 for testing. We train for 10 epochs, using early stopping with a patience of 2. We run each experiment for three random seeds (3, 5, 7), and use them to calculate the mean and standard deviation for the accuracy and F1 (weighted) score metrics.

How Familiar Does That Sound? Cross-Lingual Representational Similarity Analysis of Acoustic Word Embeddings

Badr M. Abdullah **Iuliia Zaitova** **Tania Avgustinova**
Bernd Möbius **Dietrich Klakow**
Department of Language Science and Technology (LST)
Saarland Informatics Campus, Saarland University, Germany
Corresponding author: babdullah@lsv.uni-saarland.de

Abstract

How do neural networks "perceive" speech sounds from unknown languages? Does the typological similarity between the model's training language (L1) and an unknown language (L2) have an impact on the model representations of L2 speech signals? To answer these questions, we present a novel experimental design based on representational similarity analysis (RSA) to analyze acoustic word embeddings (AWEs)—vector representations of variable-duration spoken-word segments. First, we train monolingual AWE models on seven Indo-European languages with various degrees of typological similarity. We then employ RSA to quantify the cross-lingual similarity by simulating native and non-native spoken-word processing using AWEs. Our experiments show that typological similarity indeed affects the representational similarity of the models in our study. We further discuss the implications of our work on modeling speech processing and language similarity with neural networks.

1 Introduction

Mastering a foreign language is a process that requires (human) language learners to invest time and effort. If the foreign language (L2) is very distant from our native language (L1), not much of our prior knowledge of language processing would be relevant in the learning process. On the other hand, learning a language that is similar to our native language is much easier since our prior knowledge becomes more useful in establishing the correspondences between L1 and L2 (Ringbom, 2006). In some cases where L1 and L2 are closely related and typologically similar, it is possible for an L1 speaker to comprehend L2 linguistic expressions to a great degree without prior exposure to L2. The term *receptive multilingualism* (Zeevaert, 2007) has been coined in the sociolinguistics literature to describe this ability of a listener to comprehend utterances of an unknown but related language without being able to produce it.

Human speech perception has been an active area of research in the past five decades which has produced a wealth of documented behavioral studies and experimental findings. Recently, there has been a growing scientific interest in the cognitive modeling community to leverage the recent advances in speech representation learning to formalize and test theories of speech perception using computational simulations on the one hand, and to investigate whether neural networks exhibit similar behavior to humans on the other hand (Räsänen et al., 2016; Alishahi et al., 2017; Dupoux, 2018; Scharenborg et al., 2019; Gelderloos et al., 2020; Matusevych et al., 2020b; Magnuson et al., 2020).

In the domain of modeling non-native speech perception, Schatz and Feldman (2018) have shown that a neural speech recognition system (ASR) predicts Japanese speakers' difficulty with the English phonemic contrast /l/-/ɹ/ as well as English speakers' difficulty with the Japanese vowel length distinction. Matusevych et al. (2021) have shown that a model of non-native spoken word processing based on neural networks predicts lexical processing difficulty of English-speaking learners of Russian. The latter model is based on word-level representations that are induced from naturalistic speech data known in the speech technology community as acoustic word embeddings (AWEs). AWE models map variable-duration spoken-word segments onto fixed-size representations in a vector space such that instances of the same word type are (ideally) projected onto the same point in space (Levin et al., 2013). In contrast to word embeddings in natural language processing (NLP), an AWE encodes information about the acoustic-phonetic and phonological structure of the word, not its semantic content.

Although the model of Matusevych et al. (2021) has shown similar effects to what has been ob-

Proceedings of the Fourth BlackboxNLP Workshop on Analyzing and Interpreting Neural Networks for NLP, pages 407–419
Online, November 11, 2021.

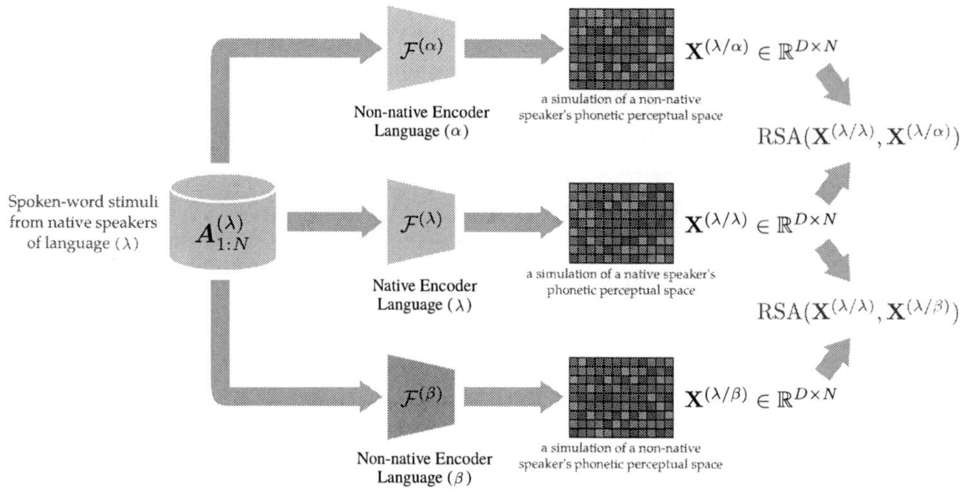

Figure 1: An illustrated example of our experimental design. A set of N spoken-word stimuli from language λ are embedded using the encoder $\mathcal{F}^{(\lambda)}$ which was trained on language λ to obtain a (native) view of the data: $\mathbf{X}^{(\lambda/\lambda)} \in \mathbb{R}^{D \times N}$. Simultaneously, the same stimuli are embedded using encoders trained on other languages, namely $\mathcal{F}^{(\alpha)}$ and $\mathcal{F}^{(\beta)}$, to obtain two different (non-native) views of the data: $\mathbf{X}^{(\lambda/\alpha)}$ and $\mathbf{X}^{(\lambda/\beta)}$. We quantify the cross-lingual similarity between two languages by measuring the association between their embedding spaces using the representational similarity analysis (RSA) framework.

served in behavioral studies (Cook et al., 2016), it remains unclear to what extent AWE models can predict a facilitatory effect of language similarity on cross-language spoken-word processing. In this paper, we present a novel experimental design to probe the *receptive multilingual* knowledge of monolingual AWE models (i.e., trained without L2 exposure) using the representational similarity analysis (RSA) framework. In a controlled experimental setup, we use AWE models to simulate spoken-word processing of native speakers of seven languages with various degrees of typological similarity. We then employ RSA to characterize how language similarity affects the emergent representations of the models when tested on the same spoken-word stimuli (see Figure 1 for an illustrated overview of our approach). Our experiments demonstrate that neural AWE models of different languages exhibit a higher degree of representational similarity if their training languages are typologically similar.

2 Proposed Methodology

A neural AWE model can be formally described as an encoder function $\mathcal{F} : \mathcal{A} \rightarrow \mathbb{R}^D$, where $\mathcal{A}$ is the (continuous) space of acoustic sequences and D is the dimensionality of the embedding. Given an acoustic word signal represented as a temporal sequence of T acoustic events $\boldsymbol{A} = (\boldsymbol{a}_1, \boldsymbol{a}_2, ..., \boldsymbol{a}_T)$, where $\boldsymbol{a}_t \in \mathbb{R}^k$ is a spectral vector of k coefficients, an embedding is computed as

$$\mathbf{x} = \mathcal{F}(\boldsymbol{A}; \boldsymbol{\theta}) \in \mathbb{R}^D \tag{1}$$

Here, $\boldsymbol{\theta}$ are the parameters of the encoder, which are learned by training the AWE model in a monolingual supervised setting. That is, the training spoken-word segments (i.e., speech intervals corresponding to spoken words) are sampled from utterances of native speakers of a single language where the word identity of each segment is known. The model is trained with an objective that maps different spoken segments of the same word type onto similar embeddings. To encourage the model to abstract away from speaker variability, the training samples are obtained from multiple speakers, while the resulting AWEs are evaluated on a held-out set of speakers.

Our research objective in this paper is to study the discrepancy of the representational geometry of two AWE encoders that are trained on different languages when tested on the same set of (monolingual) spoken stimuli. To this end, we train AWE encoders on different languages where the training data and conditions are comparable across languages with respect to size, domain, and speaker variability. We therefore have access to several encoders $\{\mathcal{F}^{(\alpha)}, \mathcal{F}^{(\beta)}, \ldots, , \mathcal{F}^{(\omega)}\}$, where the superscripts $\{\alpha, \beta, \ldots, \omega\}$ denote the language of the training samples.

Now consider a set of N held-out spoken-word stimuli produced by native speakers of language λ: $\boldsymbol{A}_{1:N}^{(\lambda)} = \{\boldsymbol{A}_1^{(\lambda)}, \ldots, \boldsymbol{A}_N^{(\lambda)}\}$. First, each acoustic word stimulus in this set is mapped onto an embedding using the encoder $\mathcal{F}^{(\lambda)}$, which yields a matrix $\mathbf{X}^{(\lambda/\lambda)} \in \mathbb{R}^{D \times N}$. Since the encoder $\mathcal{F}^{(\lambda)}$ was trained on language λ, we refer to it as the *native encoder* and consider the matrix $\mathbf{X}^{(\lambda/\lambda)}$ as a simulation of a native speaker's phonetic perceptual space. To simulate the phonetic perceptual space of a non-native speaker, say a speaker of language α, the stimuli $\boldsymbol{A}_{1:N}^{(\lambda)}$ are embedded using the encoder $\mathcal{F}^{(\alpha)}$, which yields a matrix $\mathbf{X}^{(\lambda/\alpha)} \in \mathbb{R}^{D \times N}$. Here, we read the superscript notation (λ/α) as word stimuli of language λ encoded by a model trained on language α. Thus, the two matrices $\mathbf{X}^{(\lambda/\lambda)}$ and $\mathbf{X}^{(\lambda/\alpha)}$ represent two different views of the same stimuli. Our main hypothesis is that the cross-lingual representational similarity between emergent embedding spaces should reflect the acoustic-phonetic and phonological similarities between the languages λ and α. That is, the more distant languages λ and α are, the more dissimilar their corresponding representation spaces are. To quantify this cross-lingual representational similarity, we use Centered Kernel Alignment (CKA) (Kornblith et al., 2019). CKA is a representation-level similarity measure that emphasizes the distributivity of information and therefore it obviates the need to establish the correspondence mapping between single neurons in the embeddings of two different models. Moreover, CKA has been shown to be invariant to orthogonal transformation and isotropic scaling which makes it suitable for our analysis when comparing different languages and learning objectives. Using CKA, we quantify the similarity between languages λ and α as

$$\mathsf{sim}(\lambda, \alpha) := \mathsf{CKA}(\mathbf{X}^{(\lambda/\lambda)}, \mathbf{X}^{(\lambda/\alpha)}) \quad (2)$$

Here, $\mathsf{sim}(\lambda, \alpha) \in [0, 1]$ is a scalar that measures the correlation between the responses of the two encoders, i.e., native $\mathcal{F}^{(\lambda)}$ and non-native $\mathcal{F}^{(\alpha)}$, when tested with spoken-word stimuli $\boldsymbol{A}_{1:N}^{(\lambda)}$. $\mathsf{sim}(\lambda, \alpha) = 1$ is interpreted as perfect association between the representational geometry of models trained on languages λ and α while $\mathsf{sim}(\lambda, \alpha) = 0$ indicates that no association can be established. Likewise, we obtain another non-native view $\mathbf{X}^{(\lambda/\beta)}$ of the stimuli $\boldsymbol{A}_{1:N}^{(\lambda)}$ using another non-native encoder $\mathcal{F}^{(\beta)}$. We then quantify the cross-lingual representational similarity between languages λ and β as

$$\mathsf{sim}(\lambda, \beta) := \mathsf{CKA}(\mathbf{X}^{(\lambda/\lambda)}, \mathbf{X}^{(\lambda/\beta)}) \quad (3)$$

If $\mathsf{sim}(\lambda, \alpha) > \mathsf{sim}(\lambda, \beta)$, then we interpret this as an indication that the native phonetic perceptual space of language λ is more similar to the non-native phonetic perceptual space of language α, compared to that of language β. Note that while $\mathsf{CKA}(.,.)$ is a symmetric metric (i.e., $\mathsf{CKA}(\mathbf{X}, \mathbf{Y}) = \mathsf{CKA}(\mathbf{Y}, \mathbf{X})$), our established similarity metric $\mathsf{sim}(.,.)$ is not symmetric (i.e., $\mathsf{sim}(\lambda, \alpha) :\neq \mathsf{sim}(\alpha, \lambda)$). To estimate $\mathsf{sim}(\alpha, \lambda)$, we use word stimuli of language α and collect the matrices $\mathbf{X}^{(\alpha/\alpha)}$ and $\mathbf{X}^{(\alpha/\lambda)}$. Then we compute

$$\mathsf{sim}(\alpha, \lambda) := \mathsf{CKA}(\mathbf{X}^{(\alpha/\alpha)}, \mathbf{X}^{(\alpha/\lambda)}) \quad (4)$$

When we apply the proposed experimental pipeline across M different languages, the effect of language similarity can be characterized by constructing a cross-lingual representational similarity matrix (xRSM) which is an asymmetric $M \times M$ matrix where each cell represents the correlation (or agreement) between two embedding spaces.

3 Acoustic Word Embedding Models

We investigate three different approaches of training AWE models that have been previously introduced in the literature. In this section, we formally describe each one of them.

3.1 Phonologically Guided Encoder

The phonologically guided encoder (PGE) is a sequence-to-sequence model in which the network is trained as a word-level acoustic model (Abdullah et al., 2021). Given an acoustic sequence $\boldsymbol{A}$ and its corresponding phonological sequence $\boldsymbol{\varphi} = (\varphi_1, \ldots, \varphi_T)$,[1] the acoustic encoder $\mathcal{F}$ is trained to take $\boldsymbol{A}$ as input and produce an AWE $\mathbf{x}$, which is then fed into a phonological decoder $\mathcal{G}$ whose goal is to generate the sequence $\boldsymbol{\varphi}$ (Fig. 2–a). The objective is to minimize a categorical cross-entropy loss at each timestep in the decoder, which is equivalent to

$$\mathcal{L} = -\sum_{i=1}^{T} \log \mathbf{P}_{\mathcal{G}}(\varphi_i | \boldsymbol{\varphi}_{<i}, \mathbf{x}) \quad (5)$$

[1]We use the phonetic transcription in IPA symbols as the phonological sequence $\boldsymbol{\varphi}$.

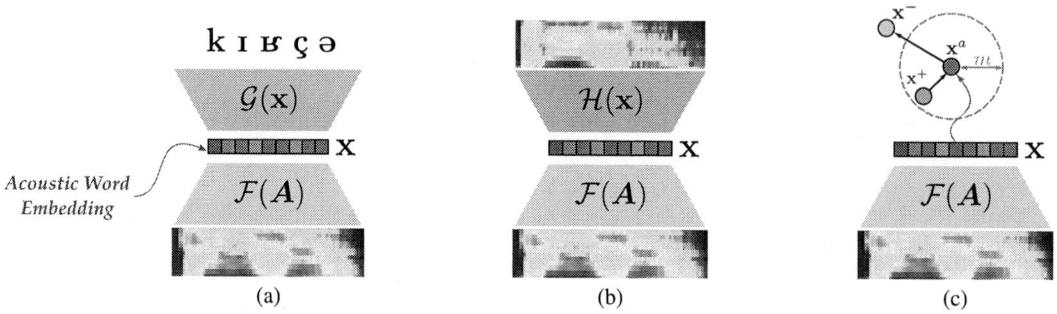

Figure 2: A visual illustration of the different learning objectives for training AWE encoders: (a) phonologically guided encoder (PGE): a sequence-to-sequence network with a phonological decoder, (b) correspondence auto-encoder (CAE): a sequence-to-sequence network with an acoustic decoder, and (c) contrastive siamese encoder (CSE): a contrastive network trained via triplet margin loss.

where $\mathbf{P}_\mathcal{G}$ is the probability of the phone φ_i at timestep i, conditioned on the previous phone sequence $\varphi_{<i}$ and the embedding $\mathbf{x}$. The intuition of this objective is that spoken-word segments of the same word type would have identical phonological sequences, thus they are expected to end up nearby in the embedding space.

3.2 Correspondence Autoencoder

In the correspondence autoencoder (CAE) (Kamper, 2019), each training acoustic segment $\boldsymbol{A}$ is paired with another segment that corresponds to the same word type $\boldsymbol{A}^+ = (\boldsymbol{a}_1^+, \boldsymbol{a}_2^+, ..., \boldsymbol{a}_{T^+}^+)$. The acoustic encoder $\mathcal{F}$ then takes $\boldsymbol{A}$ as input and computes an AWE $\mathbf{x}$, which is then fed into an acoustic decoder $\mathcal{H}$ that attempts to reconstruct the corresponding acoustic sequence $\boldsymbol{A}^+$ (Fig. 2–b). The objective is to minimize a vector-wise mean square error (MSE) loss at each timestep in the decoder, which is equivalent to

$$\mathcal{L} = -\sum_{i=1}^{T^+} ||\boldsymbol{a}_i^+ - \mathcal{H}_i(\mathbf{x})||^2 \quad (6)$$

where $\boldsymbol{a}_i^+$ is the ground-truth spectral vector at timestep i and $\mathcal{H}_i(\mathbf{x})$ is the reconstructed spectral vector at timestep i as a function of the embedding $\mathbf{x}$. It has been hypothesized that learning the correspondence between two acoustic realizations of the same word type encourages the model to build up speaker-invariant word representations while preserving phonetic information (Matusevych et al., 2020a).

3.3 Contrastive Siamese Encoder

The contrastive siamese encoder (CSE) is based on a siamese network (Bromley et al., 1994) and has been explored in the AWEs literature with different underlying architectures (Settle and Livescu, 2016; Kamper et al., 2016). This learning objective differs from the first two as it explicitly minimizes/maximizes relative distances between AWEs of the same/different word types (Fig. 2–c). First, each acoustic word instance is paired with another instance of the same word type, which yields the tuple $(\boldsymbol{A}, \boldsymbol{A}^+)$. Given the AWEs of the instances in this tuple $(\mathbf{x}^a, \mathbf{x}^+)$, the objective is then to minimize a triplet margin loss

$$\mathcal{L} = \max\Big[0, m + d(\mathbf{x}^a, \mathbf{x}^+) - d(\mathbf{x}^a, \mathbf{x}^-)\Big] \quad (7)$$

Here, $d : \mathbb{R}^D \times \mathbb{R}^D \rightarrow [0, 1]$ is the cosine distance and $\mathbf{x}^-$ is an AWE that corresponds to a different word type sampled from the mini-batch such that the term $d(\mathbf{x}^a, \mathbf{x}^-)$ is minimized. This objective aims to map acoustic segments of the same word type closer in the embedding space while pushing away segments of other word types by a distance defined by the margin hyperparameter m.

4 Experiments

4.1 Experimental Data

The data in our study is drawn from the GlobalPhone speech (GPS) database (Schultz et al., 2013). GPS is a multilingual read speech resource where the utterances are recorded from native speakers (with self-reported gender labels) in a controlled recording environment with minimal noise. Therefore, the recording conditions across languages are comparable which enables us to conduct a cross-linguistic comparison. We experiment with seven Indo-European languages: Czech (CZE), Polish (POL), Russian (RUS), Bulgarian (BUL), Brazilian Portuguese (POR), French (FRA), and German

(DEU). We acknowledge that our language sample is not typologically diverse. However, one of our objectives in this paper is to investigate whether the cross-lingual similarity of AWEs can predict the degree of mutual intelligibility between related languages. Therefore, we focus on the Slavic languages in this sample (CZE, POL, RUS, and BUL), which are known to be typologically similar and mutually intelligible to various degrees.

To train our AWE models, we obtain time-aligned spoken-word segments using the Montreal Forced Aligner (McAuliffe et al., 2017). Then, we sample 42 speakers of balanced gender from each language. For each language, we sample ~32k spoken-word segments that are longer than 3 phonemes in length and shorter than 1.1 seconds in duration (see Table 2 in Appendix A for word-level summary statistics of the data). For each word type, we obtain an IPA transcription using the grapheme-to-phoneme (G2P) module of the automatic speech synthesizer, *eSpeak*. Each acoustic word segment is parametrized as a sequence of 39-dimensional Mel-frequency spectral coefficients where frames are extracted over intervals of 25ms with 10ms overlap.

4.2 Architecture and Hyperparameters

Acoustic Encoder We employ a 2-layer recurrent neural network with a bidirectional Gated Recurrent Unit (BGRU) of hidden state dimension of 512, which yields a 1024-dimensional AWE.

Training Details All models in this study are trained for 100 epochs with a batch size of 256 using the ADAM optimizer (Kingma and Ba, 2015) and an initial learning rate (LR) of 0.001. The LR is reduced by a factor of 0.5 if the mean average precision (mAP) for word discrimination on the validation set does not improve for 10 epochs. The epoch with the best validation performance during training is used for evaluation on the test set.

Implementation We build our models using PyTorch (Paszke et al., 2019) and use FAISS (Johnson et al., 2017) for efficient similarity search during evaluation. Our code is publicly available on GitHub.[2]

4.3 Quantitative Evaluation

We evaluate the models using the standard intrinsic evaluation of AWEs: the same-different word discrimination task (Carlin et al., 2011). This task aims to assess the ability of a model to determine whether or not two given speech segments correspond to the same word type, which is quantified using a retrieval metric (mAP) reported in Table 1.

Language	Encoder type		
	PGE	CAE	CSE
CZE	78.3	76.1	**82.9**
POL	67.6	63.5	**73.8**
RUS	64.3	57.7	**71.0**
BUL	72.1	68.9	**78.4**
POR	74.5	72.2	**80.4**
FRA	65.6	64.5	**68.5**
DEU	67.9	70.3	**75.8**

Table 1: mAP performance on evaluation sets.

5 Representational Similarity Analysis

Figure 3 shows the cross-lingual representational similarity matrices (xRSMs) across the three different models using the linear CKA similarity metric.[3] Warmer colors indicate a higher similarity between two representational spaces. One can observe striking differences between the PGE-CAE models on the one hand, and the CSE model on the other hand. The PGE-CAE models yield representations that are cross-lingually more similar to each other compared to those obtained from the contrastive CSE model. For example, the highest similarity score from the PGE model is $\mathsf{sim}(\text{RUS}, \text{BUL}) = 0.748$, which means that the representations of the Russian word stimuli from the Bulgarian model $\mathcal{F}^{(\text{BUL})}$ exhibit the highest representational similarity to the representations of the native Russian model $\mathcal{F}^{(\text{RUS})}$. On the other hand, the lowest similarity score from the PGE model is $\mathsf{sim}(\text{POL}, \text{DEU}) = 0.622$, which shows that the German model's view of the Polish word stimuli is the view that differs the most from the view of the native Polish model. Likewise, the highest similarity score we observe from the CAE model is $\mathsf{sim}(\text{BUL}, \text{RUS}) = 0.763$, while the lowest similarity is $\mathsf{sim}(\text{DEU}, \text{BUL}) = 0.649$. If we compare these scores to those of the contrastive CSE model, we observe significant cross-language differences as the highest similarity scores are $\mathsf{sim}(\text{POL}, \text{RUS}) = \mathsf{sim}(\text{POR}, \text{RUS}) = 0.269$, while the lowest is $\mathsf{sim}(\text{BUL}, \text{DEU}) = 0.170$. This discrepancy between the contrastive model and the

[2]https://github.com/uds-lsv/xRSA-AWEs

[3]The xRSMs obtained using non-linear CKA with an RBF kernel are shown in Figure 6 in Appendix B, which show very similar trends to those observed in Figure 3.

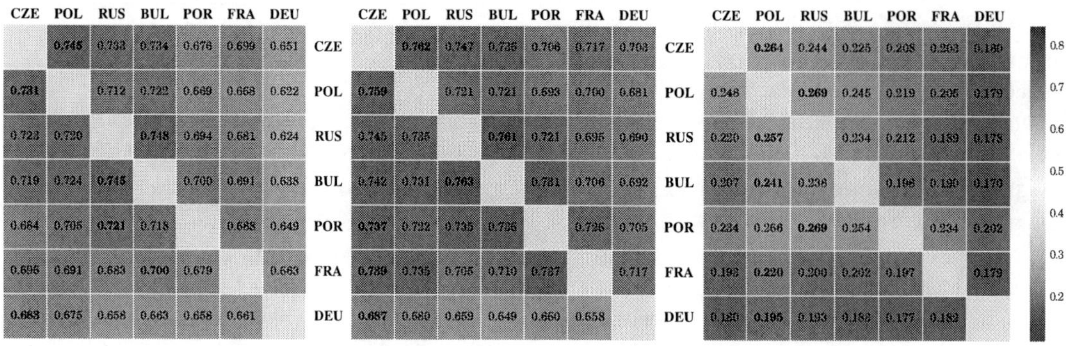

Figure 3: The cross-lingual representational similarity matrix (xRSM) for each model: PGE (Left), CAE (Middle), and CSE (Right). Each row corresponds to the language of the spoken-word stimuli while each column corresponds to the language of the encoder. Note that the matrices are not symmetric. For example in the PGE model, the cell at row CZE and column POL holds the value of $\text{sim}(\text{CZE}, \text{POL}) = \text{CKA}(\mathbf{X}^{(\text{CZE/CZE})}, \mathbf{X}^{(\text{CZE/POL})}) = 0.745$, while the cell at row POL and column CZE holds the value of $\text{sim}(\text{POL}, \text{CZE}) = \text{CKA}(\mathbf{X}^{(\text{POL/POL})}, \mathbf{X}^{(\text{POL/CZE})}) = 0.731$.

other models suggests that training AWE models with a contrastive objective hinders the ability of the encoder to learn high-level phonological abstractions and therefore contrastive encoders are more sensitive to the cross-lingual variation during inference compared to their sequence-to-sequence counterparts.

5.1 Cross-Lingual Comparison

To get further insights into how language similarity affects the model representations of non-native spoken-word segments, we apply hierarchical clustering on the xRSMs in Figure 3 using the Ward algorithm (Ward, 1963) with Euclidean distance. The result of the clustering analysis is shown in Figure 4. Surprisingly, the generated trees from the xRSMs of the PGE and CAE models are identical, which could indicate that these two models induce similar representations when trained on the same data. Diving a level deeper into the cluster structure of these two models, we observe that the Slavic languages form a pure cluster. This could be explained by the observation that some of the highest pair-wise similarity scores among the PGE models are observed between Russian and Bulgarian, i.e., $\text{sim}(\text{RUS}, \text{BUL}) = 0.748$ and $\text{sim}(\text{BUL}, \text{RUS}) = 0.745$, and Czech and Polish, i.e., $\text{sim}(\text{CZE}, \text{POL}) = 0.745$. The same trend can be observed in the CAE models: i.e., $\text{sim}(\text{RUS}, \text{BUL}) = 0.761$, $\text{sim}(\text{BUL}, \text{RUS}) = 0.763$, and $\text{sim}(\text{CZE}, \text{POL}) = 0.762$. Within the Slavic cluster, the West Slavic languages Czech and Polish are grouped together, while the Russian (East Slavic) is first grouped with Bulgarian (South Slavic) before joining the West Slavic group to make the Slavic cluster. Although Russian and Bulgarian belong to two different Slavic branches, we observe that this pair forms the first sub-cluster in both trees, at a distance smaller than that of the West Slavic cluster (Czech and Polish). At first, this might seem surprising as we would expect the West Slavic cluster to be formed at a lower distance given the similarities among the West Slavic languages which facilitates cross-language speech comprehension, as documented by sociolinguistic studies (Golubovic, 2016). However, Russian and Bulgarian share typological features at the acoustic-phonetic and phonological levels which distinguish them from West Slavic languages.[4] We further elaborate on these typological features in §6. Even though Portuguese was grouped with French in the cluster analysis, which one might expect given that both are Romance languages descended from Latin, it is worth pointing out that the representations of the Portuguese word stimuli from the Slavic models show a higher similarity to the representations of the native Portuguese model compared to these obtained from the French model (with only two exceptions, the Czech PGE model and Polish CAE model). We also provide an explanation of why this might be the case in §6.

The generated language cluster from the CSE model does not show any clear internal structure with respect to language groups since all cluster pairs are grouped at a much higher distance compared to the PGE and CAE models. Furthermore, the Slavic languages in the generated tree do not

[4]Note that our models do not have access to word orthography. Thus, the similarity cannot be due to the fact that Russian and Bulgarian use Cyrillic script.

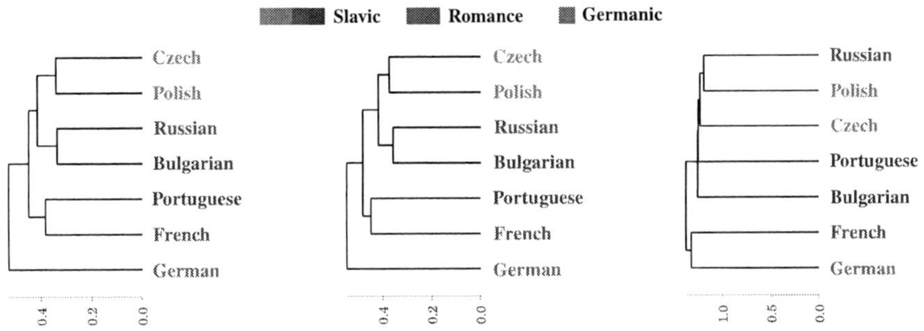

Figure 4: Hierarchical clustering analysis on the cross-lingual representational similarity matrices (using linear CKA) of the three models: PGE (Left), CAE (Middle), and CSE (Right).

form a pure cluster since Portuguese was placed inside the Slavic cluster. We also do not observe the West Slavic group as in the other two models since Polish was grouped first with Russian, and not Czech. We believe that this unexpected behavior of the CSE models can be related to the previously attributed to the poor performance of the contrastive AWEs in capturing word-form similarity (Abdullah et al., 2021).

Moreover, it is interesting to observe that German seems to be the most distant language to the other languages in our study. This observation holds across all three encoders since the representations of the German word stimuli by non-native models are the most dissimilar compared to the representations of the native German model.

5.2 Cross-Model Comparison

To verify our hypothesis that the models trained with decoding objectives (PGE and CAE) learn similar representations when trained on the same data, we conduct a similarity analysis between the models in a setting where we obtain views of the spoken-word stimuli from native models, then compare these views across different learning objectives while keeping the language fixed using CKA as we do in our cross-lingual comparison. The results of this analysis is shown in Figure 5. We observe that across different languages the pairwise representational similarity of the PGE-CAE models (linear $\mathsf{CKA} = 0.721$) is very high in comparison to that of PGE-CSE models (linear $\mathsf{CKA} = 0.239$) and CAE-CSE models (linear $\mathsf{CKA} = 0.230$).[5] Although the non-linear CKA similarity scores tend to be higher, the general trend remains identical in both measures. This finding validates our hypothesis that the PGE and CAE models yield similar representation spaces when trained on the same data even though their decoding objectives operate over different modalities. That is, the decoder of the PGE model aims to generate the word's phonological structure in the form of a sequence of discrete phonological units, while the decoder of the CAE model aims to generate an instance of the same word represented as a sequence of (continuous) spectral vectors. Moreover, the sequences that these decoders aim to generate vary in length (the mean phonological sequence length is ~6 phonemes while mean spectral sequence length is ~50 vectors). Although the CAE model has no access to abstract phonological information of the word-forms it is trained on, it seems that this model learns non-trivial knowledge about word phonological structure as demonstrated by the representational similarity of its embeddings to those of a word embedding model that has access to word phonology (i.e., PGE) across different languages.

6 Discussion

6.1 Relevance to Related Work

Although the idea of representational similarity analysis (RSA) has originated in the neuroscience literature (Kriegeskorte et al., 2008), researchers in NLP and speech technology have employed a similar set of techniques to analyze emergent representations of multi-layer neural networks. For example, RSA has previously been employed to analyze the correlation between neural and symbolic representations (Chrupała and Alishahi, 2019), contextualized word representations (Abnar et al., 2019; Abdou et al., 2019; Lepori and McCoy, 2020; Wu et al., 2020), representations of self-supervised speech models (Chung et al., 2021) and visually-grounded speech models (Chrupała et al., 2020). We take the inspiration from previous work and

[5] CKA scores are averaged over languages.

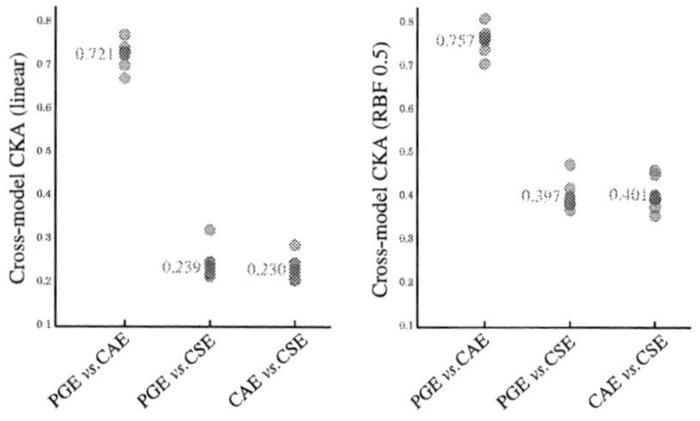

Figure 5: Cross-model CKA scores: linear CKA (left) and non-linear CKA (right). Each point in this plot is the within-language representational similarity of two models trained with different objectives when tested on the same (monolingual) word stimuli. Each red point is the average CKA score per model pair.

apply RSA in a unique setting: to analyze the impact of typological similarity between languages on the representational geometry. Our analysis focuses on neural models of spoken-word processing that are trained on naturalistic speech corpora. Our goal is two-fold: (1) to investigate whether or not neural networks exhibit predictable behavior when tested on speech from a different language (L2), and (2) to examine the extent to which the training strategy affects the emergent representations of L2 spoken-word stimuli. To the best of our knowledge, our study is the first to analyze the similarity of emergent representations in neural acoustic models from a cross-linguistic perspective.

6.2 A Typological Discussion

Given the cross-linguistic nature of our study, we choose to discuss our findings on the representational similarity analysis from a language typology point of view. Language typology is a sub-field within linguistics that is concerned with the study and categorization of the world's languages based on their linguistic structural properties (Comrie, 1988; Croft, 2002). Since acoustic word embeddings are word-level representations induced from actual acoustic realizations of word-forms, we focus on the phonetic and phonological properties of the languages in our study. We emphasize that our goal is not to use the method we propose in this paper as a computational approach for phylogenetic reconstruction, that is, discovering the historical relations between languages. However, typological similarity usually correlates with phylogenetic distance since languages that have diverged from a common historical ancestor inherited most of their typological features from the ancestor language (see Bjerva et al. (2019) for a discussion on how typological similarity and genetic relationships interact when analyzing neural embeddings).

Within the language sample we study in this paper, four of these languages belong to the Slavic branch of Indo-European languages. Compared to the Romance and Germanic branches of Indo-European, Slavic languages are known to be remarkably more similar to each other not only at lexical and syntactic levels, but also at the pre-lexical level (acoustic-phonetic and phonological features). These cross-linguistically shared features between Slavic languages include rich consonant inventories, phonemic iotation and complex consonant clusters. The similarities at different linguistic levels facilitate spoken intercomprehension, i.e., the ability of a listener to comprehend an utterance (to some degree) in a language that is unknown, but related to their mother tongue. Several sociolinguistic studies of mutual intelligibility have reported a higher degree of intercomprehension among speakers of Slavic languages compared to other language groups in Europe (Golubovic, 2016; Gooskens et al., 2018). On the other hand, and even though French and Portuguese are both Romance languages, they are less mutually intelligible compared to Slavic language pairs as they have diverged in their lexicons and phonological structures (Gooskens et al., 2018). This shows that cross-language speech intelligibility is not mainly driven by shared historical relationships, but by contemporary typological similarities.

Therefore, and given the documented phonological similarities between Slavic languages, it is not surprising that Slavic languages form a pure cluster in our clustering analysis over the xRSMs of two of the models we investigate. Furthermore, the grouping of Czech-Polish and Russian-Bulgarian in the Slavic cluster can be explained if we consider word-specific suprasegmental features. Besides the fact that Czech and Polish are both West Slavic languages that form a spatial continuum of language variation, both languages have fixed stress. The word stress in Czech is always on the initial syllable, while Polish has penultimate stress, that is, stress falls on the syllable preceding the last syllable of the word (Sussex and Cubberley, 2006). On the other hand, Russian and Bulgarian languages belong to different Slavic sub-groups—Russian is East Slavic while Bulgarian is South

Slavic. The representational similarity between Russian and Bulgarian can be attributed to the typological similarities between Bulgarian and East Slavic languages. In contrast to West Slavic languages, the stress in Russian and Bulgarian is free (it can occur on any syllable in the word) and movable (it moves between syllables within morphological paradigms). Slavic languages with free stress tend to have a stronger contrast between stressed and unstressed syllables, and vowels in unstressed syllables undergo a process that is known as vowel-quality alternation, or lexicalized vowel reduction (Barry and Andreeva, 2001). For example, consider the Russian word *ruka* ('hand'). In the singular nominative case the word-form is phonetically realized as *ruká* [rʊˈka] while in the singular accusative case *rúku* [ˈrukʊ] (Sussex and Cubberley, 2006). Here, the unstressed high back vowel /u/ is realized as [ʊ] in both word-forms. Although vowel-quality alternations in Bulgarian follow different patterns, Russian and Bulgarian vowels in unstressed syllables are reduced in temporal duration and quality. Therefore, the high representational similarity between Russian and Bulgarian could be explained if we consider their typological similarities in word-specific phonetics and prosody.

The Portuguese language presents us with an interesting case study of language variation. From a phylogenetic point of view, Portuguese and French have diverged from Latin and therefore they are both categorized as Romance languages. The clustering of the xRSMs of the PGE and CAE models groups Portuguese and French together at a higher distance compared to the Slavic group, while Portuguese was grouped with Slavic languages when analyzing the representations of the contrastive CSE model. Similar to Russian and Polish, sibilant consonants (e.g., /ʃ/, /ʒ/) and the velarized (dark) *L*-sound (i.e., /ɫ/) are frequent in Portuguese. We hypothesize that contrastive training encourages the model to pay more attention to the segmental information (i.e., individual phones) in the speech signal at the expense of phonotactics (i.e., phone sequences). Given that contrastive learning is a predominant paradigm in speech representation learning (van den Oord et al., 2018; Schneider et al., 2019), we encourage further research to analyze whether or not speech processing models trained with contrastive objectives exhibit a similar behavior to that observed in human listeners and closely examine their plausibility for cognitive modeling.

6.3 Implications on Cross-Lingual Transfer Learning

A recent study on zero-resource AWEs has shown that cross-lingual transfer is more successful when the source (L1) and target (L2) languages are more related (Jacobs and Kamper, 2021). We conducted a preliminary experiment on the cross-lingual word discrimination performance of the models in our study and observed a similar effect. However, we also observed that cross-lingual transfer using the contrastive model is less effective compared to the models trained with decoding objectives. From our reported RSA analysis, we showed that the contrastive objective yields models that are cross-lingually dissimilar compared to the other objectives. Therefore, future work could investigate the degree to which our proposed RSA approach predicts the effectiveness of different models in a cross-lingual zero-shot scenario.

7 Conclusion

We presented an experimental design based on representational similarity analysis (RSA) whereby we analyzed the impact of language similarity on representational similarity of acoustic word embeddings (AWEs). Our experiments have shown that AWE models trained using decoding objectives exhibit a higher degree of representational similarity if their training languages are typologically similar languages. We discussed our findings from a typological perspective and highlighted pre-lexical features that could have an impact on the models' representational geometry. Our findings provide evidence that AWE models can predict the facilitatory effect of language similarity on cross-language speech perception and complement ongoing efforts in the community to assess their utility in cognitive modeling. Our work can be further extended by considering speech segments below the word-level (e.g., syllables, phonemes), incorporating semantic representations into the learning procedure, and investigating other neural architectures.

Acknowledgements

We thank the anonymous reviewers for their constructive comments and insightful feedback. We further extend our gratitude to Miriam Schulz and Marius Mosbach for proofreading the paper. This research is funded by the Deutsche Forschungsgemeinschaft (DFG, German Research Foundation), Project ID 232722074 – SFB 1102.

References

Mostafa Abdou, Artur Kulmizev, Felix Hill, Daniel M. Low, and Anders Søgaard. 2019. Higher-order comparisons of sentence encoder representations. In *Proceedings of the 2019 Conference on Empirical Methods in Natural Language Processing and the 9th International Joint Conference on Natural Language Processing (EMNLP-IJCNLP)*, pages 5838–5845, Hong Kong, China. Association for Computational Linguistics.

Badr M. Abdullah, Marius Mosbach, Iuliia Zaitova, Bernd Möbius, and Dietrich Klakow. 2021. Do Acoustic Word Embeddings Capture Phonological Similarity? An Empirical Study. In *Proc. Interspeech 2021*, pages 4194–4198.

Samira Abnar, Lisa Beinborn, Rochelle Choenni, and Willem Zuidema. 2019. Blackbox meets blackbox: Representational similarity & stability analysis of neural language models and brains. In *Proceedings of the 2019 ACL Workshop BlackboxNLP: Analyzing and Interpreting Neural Networks for NLP*, pages 191–203, Florence, Italy. Association for Computational Linguistics.

Afra Alishahi, Marie Barking, and Grzegorz Chrupała. 2017. Encoding of phonology in a recurrent neural model of grounded speech. In *Proceedings of the 21st Conference on Computational Natural Language Learning (CoNLL 2017)*, pages 368–378, Vancouver, Canada. Association for Computational Linguistics.

William Barry and Bistra Andreeva. 2001. Cross-language similarities and differences in spontaneous speech patterns. *Journal of the International Phonetic Association*, 31(1):51–66.

Johannes Bjerva, Robert Östling, Maria Han Veiga, Jörg Tiedemann, and Isabelle Augenstein. 2019. What do language representations really represent? *Computational Linguistics*, 45(2):381–389.

Jane Bromley, Isabelle Guyon, Yann LeCun, Eduard Säckinger, and Roopak Shah. 1994. Signature verification using a" siamese" time delay neural network. In *Proc. NIPS*.

Michael A Carlin, Samuel Thomas, Aren Jansen, and Hynek Hermansky. 2011. Rapid evaluation of speech representations for spoken term discovery. In *Proc. Interspeech*.

Grzegorz Chrupała and Afra Alishahi. 2019. Correlating neural and symbolic representations of language. In *Proceedings of the 57th Annual Meeting of the Association for Computational Linguistics*, pages 2952–2962, Florence, Italy. Association for Computational Linguistics.

Grzegorz Chrupała, Bertrand Higy, and Afra Alishahi. 2020. Analyzing analytical methods: The case of phonology in neural models of spoken language. In *Proceedings of the 58th Annual Meeting of the Association for Computational Linguistics*, pages 4146–4156, Online. Association for Computational Linguistics.

Yu-An Chung, Yonatan Belinkov, and James Glass. 2021. Similarity analysis of self-supervised speech representations. In *ICASSP 2021-2021 IEEE International Conference on Acoustics, Speech and Signal Processing (ICASSP)*, pages 3040–3044. IEEE.

Bernard Comrie. 1988. Linguistic typology. *Annual Review of Anthropology*, 17:145–159.

Svetlana V Cook, Nick B Pandža, Alia K Lancaster, and Kira Gor. 2016. Fuzzy nonnative phonolexical representations lead to fuzzy form-to-meaning mappings. *Frontiers in Psychology*, 7:1345.

William Croft. 2002. *Typology and Universals*. Cambridge University Press.

Emmanuel Dupoux. 2018. Cognitive science in the era of artificial intelligence: A roadmap for reverse-engineering the infant language-learner. *Cognition*, 173:43–59.

Lieke Gelderloos, Grzegorz Chrupała, and Afra Alishahi. 2020. Learning to understand child-directed and adult-directed speech. In *Proceedings of the 58th Annual Meeting of the Association for Computational Linguistics*, pages 1–6, Online. Association for Computational Linguistics.

Jelena Golubovic. 2016. Mutual intelligibility in the Slavic language area. *Groningen: Center for Language and Cognition.*

Charlotte Gooskens, Vincent J van Heuven, Jelena Golubović, Anja Schüppert, Femke Swarte, and Stefanie Voigt. 2018. Mutual intelligibility between closely related languages in Europe. *International Journal of Multilingualism*, 15(2):169–193.

Christiaan Jacobs and Herman Kamper. 2021. Multilingual Transfer of Acoustic Word Embeddings Improves When Training on Languages Related to the Target Zero-Resource Language. In *Proc. Interspeech*, pages 1549–1553.

Jeff Johnson, Matthijs Douze, and Hervé Jégou. 2017. Billion-scale similarity search with GPUs. *IEEE Transactions on Big Data*.

H. Kamper, W. Wang, and Karen Livescu. 2016. Deep convolutional acoustic word embeddings using word-pair side information. In *Proc. ICASSP*.

Herman Kamper. 2019. Truly unsupervised acoustic word embeddings using weak top-down constraints in encoder-decoder models. In *Proc. ICASSP*.

Diederik P. Kingma and Jimmy Ba. 2015. Adam: A method for stochastic optimization. In *Proc. ICLR*.

Simon Kornblith, Mohammad Norouzi, Honglak Lee, and Geoffrey Hinton. 2019. Similarity of neural network representations revisited. In *International Conference on Machine Learning*, pages 3519–3529. PMLR.

Nikolaus Kriegeskorte, Marieke Mur, and Peter A Bandettini. 2008. Representational similarity analysis-connecting the branches of systems neuroscience. *Frontiers in systems neuroscience*, 2:4.

Michael Lepori and R. Thomas McCoy. 2020. Picking BERT's brain: Probing for linguistic dependencies in contextualized embeddings using representational similarity analysis. In *Proceedings of the 28th International Conference on Computational Linguistics*, pages 3637–3651, Barcelona, Spain (Online). International Committee on Computational Linguistics.

Keith Levin, Katharine Henry, Aren Jansen, and Karen Livescu. 2013. Fixed-dimensional acoustic embeddings of variable-length segments in low-resource settings. In *Proc. ASRU*.

James S Magnuson, Heejo You, Sahil Luthra, Monica Li, Hosung Nam, Monty Escabi, Kevin Brown, Paul D Allopenna, Rachel M Theodore, Nicholas Monto, et al. 2020. Earshot: A minimal neural network model of incremental human speech recognition. *Cognitive science*, 44(4):e12823.

Yevgen Matusevych, Herman Kamper, and Sharon Goldwater. 2020a. Analyzing autoencoder-based acoustic word embeddings. In *Bridging AI and Cognitive Science Workshop@ ICLR 2020*.

Yevgen Matusevych, Herman Kamper, Thomas Schatz, Naomi Feldman, and Sharon Goldwater. 2021. A phonetic model of non-native spoken word processing. In *Proceedings of the 16th Conference of the European Chapter of the Association for Computational Linguistics: Main Volume*, pages 1480–1490, Online. Association for Computational Linguistics.

Yevgen Matusevych, Thomas Schatz, Herman Kamper, Naomi Feldman, and Sharon Goldwater. 2020b. Evaluating computational models of infant phonetic learning across languages. In *Proc. CogSci*.

Michael McAuliffe, Michaela Socolof, Sarah Mihuc, Michael Wagner, and Morgan Sonderegger. 2017. Montreal Forced Aligner: Trainable text-speech alignment using Kaldi. In *Interspeech*.

Adam Paszke, Sam Gross, Francisco Massa, Adam Lerer, James Bradbury, Gregory Chanan, Trevor Killeen, Zeming Lin, Natalia Gimelshein, Luca Antiga, et al. 2019. Pytorch: An imperative style, high-performance deep learning library. In *Proc. NeuRIPS*.

Okko Räsänen, Tasha Nagamine, and Nima Mesgarani. 2016. Analyzing distributional learning of phonemic categories in unsupervised deep neural networks. *Annual Conference of the Cognitive Science Society (CogSci). Cognitive Science Society (U.S.). Conference*, 2016:1757–1762.

Håkan Ringbom. 2006. *Cross-linguistic similarity in foreign language learning*. Multilingual Matters.

Odette Scharenborg, Nikki van der Gouw, Martha Larson, and Elena Marchiori. 2019. The representation of speech in deep neural networks. In *International Conference on Multimedia Modeling*, pages 194–205. Springer.

Thomas Schatz and Naomi H Feldman. 2018. Neural network vs. hmm speech recognition systems as models of human cross-linguistic phonetic perception. In *Proceedings of the conference on cognitive computational neuroscience*.

Steffen Schneider, Alexei Baevski, Ronan Collobert, and Michael Auli. 2019. wav2vec: Unsupervised Pre-Training for Speech Recognition. In *Proc. Interspeech 2019*, pages 3465–3469.

Tanja Schultz, Ngoc Thang Vu, and Tim Schlippe. 2013. GlobalPhone: A multilingual text and speech database in 20 languages. In *Proc. ICASSP*.

Shane Settle and Karen Livescu. 2016. Discriminative acoustic word embeddings: Recurrent neural network-based approaches. In *Proc. IEEE Spoken Language Technology Workshop (SLT)*.

Roland Sussex and Paul Cubberley. 2006. *The slavic languages*. Cambridge University Press.

Aäron van den Oord, Yazhe Li, and Oriol Vinyals. 2018. Representation learning with contrastive predictive coding. *ArXiv*, abs/1807.03748.

Joe H Ward. 1963. Hierarchical grouping to optimize an objective function. *Journal of the American statistical association*, 58(301):236–244.

John Wu, Yonatan Belinkov, Hassan Sajjad, Nadir Durrani, Fahim Dalvi, and James Glass. 2020. Similarity analysis of contextual word representation models. In *Proceedings of the 58th Annual Meeting of the Association for Computational Linguistics*, pages 4638–4655.

Ludger Zeevaert. 2007. Receptive multilingualism. *JD Ten Thije & L. Zeevaert (Eds.)*, 6:103–137.

Appendices

A Experimental Data Statistics

Table 2 shows a word-level summary statistics of our experimental data extracted from the GlobalPhone speech daabase (GPS).

B Representational Similarity with Non-Linear CKA

We provide the cross-lingual representational similarity matrices (xRSMs) constructed by applying the non-linear CKA measure with a radial basis function (RBF) in Figure 6 below. We observe similar trends to those presented in Figure 3.

Applying hierarchical clustering on the xRSMs in Figure 6 yields the language clusters shown in Figure 7. We observe that the clusters are identical to those shown in Figure 4, except for the CSE model where Portuguese is no longer in the Slavic group. However, Portuguese remains the non-Slavic language that is the most similar to Slavic languages.

Lang.	Language group	#Train spkrs	#Train samples	#Eval samples	#Phones/word (mean ± SD)	Word dur. (sec) (mean ± SD)	Token-Type ratio
CZE	West Slavic	42	32,063	9,228	6.77 ± 2.28	0.492 ± 0.176	0.175
POL	West Slavic	42	31,507	9,709	6.77 ± 2.27	0.488 ± 0.175	0.192
RUS	East Slavic	42	31,892	9,005	7.56 ± 2.77	0.496 ± 0.163	0.223
BUL	South Slavic	42	31,866	9,063	7.24 ± 2.60	0.510 ± 0.171	0.179
POR	Romance	42	32,164	9,393	6.95 ± 2.36	0.526 ± 0.190	0.134
FRA	Romance	42	32,497	9,656	6.24 ± 1.95	0.496 ± 0.163	0.167
DEU	Germanic	42	32,162	9,865	6.57 ± 2.47	0.435 ± 0.178	0.150

Table 2: Summary statistics of our experimental data.

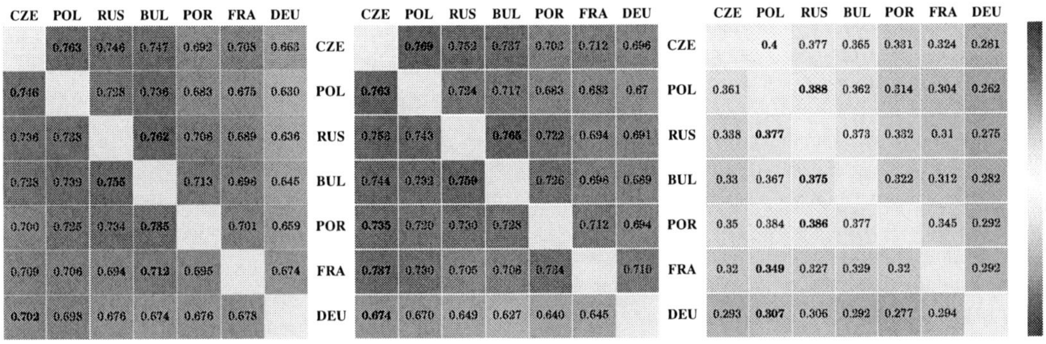

Figure 6: The cross-lingual representational similarity matrix (xRSM) for each model: PGE (Left), CAE (Middle), and CSE (Right), obtained using the non-linear CKA measure. Each row corresponds to the language of the spoken-word stimuli while each column corresponds to the language of the encoder.

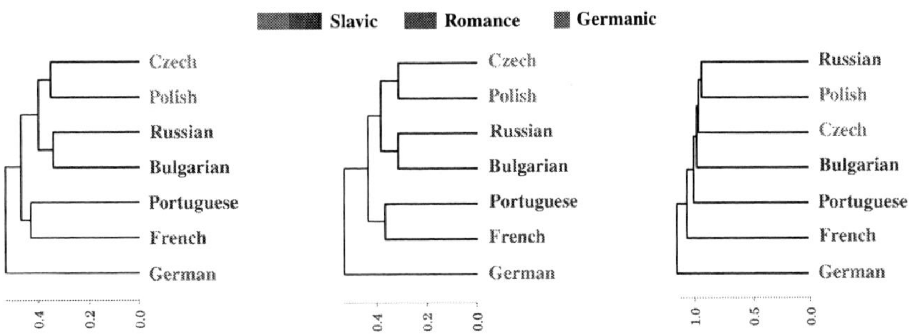

Figure 7: Hierarchical clustering analysis on the cross-lingual representational similarity matrices (using non-linear CKA) of the three models: PGE (Left), CAE (Middle), and CSE (Right).

Perturbing Inputs for Fragile Interpretations in Deep Natural Language Processing

Sanchit Sinha, Hanjie Chen, Arshdeep Sekhon, Yangfeng Ji, Yanjun Qi
Department of Computer Science
University of Virginia
Charlottesville, VA, USA
{ss7mu,hc9mx,as5cu,yangfeng,yq2h}@virginia.edu

Abstract

Interpretability methods like INTEGRATED GRADIENT and LIME are popular choices for explaining natural language model predictions with relative word importance scores. These interpretations need to be robust for trustworthy NLP applications in high-stake areas like medicine or finance. Our paper demonstrates how interpretations can be manipulated by making simple word perturbations on an input text. Via a small portion of word-level swaps, these adversarial perturbations aim to make the resulting text semantically and spatially similar to its seed input (therefore sharing similar interpretations). Simultaneously, the generated examples achieve the same prediction label as the seed yet are given a substantially different explanation by the interpretation methods. Our experiments generate fragile interpretations to attack two SOTA interpretation methods, across three popular Transformer models and on three different NLP datasets. We observe that the rank order correlation drops by over 20% when less than 10% of words are perturbed on average. Further, rank-order correlation keeps decreasing as more words get perturbed. Furthermore, we demonstrate that candidates generated from our method have good quality metrics. Our code is available at: `github.com/QData/TextAttack-Fragile-Interpretations`.

1 Introduction

Recently, the use of natural language processing (NLP) has gained popularity in many security-relevant tasks like fake news identification (Zhou et al., 2019), authorship identification (Okuno et al., 2014), toxic content detection (Jigsaw, 2017), and for text-based automated privacy policy understanding (Harkous et al., 2018). Since interpretations of NLP predictions have become necessary building blocks of the SOTA deep NLP workflow, explanations have the potential to mislead human users into trusting a problematic interpretation. However, there has been little analysis of the reliability and robustness of the explanation techniques, especially in high-stake settings, making their utility for critical applications unclear.

Research has shown that it is possible to disrupt and even manipulate interpretations in deep neural networks (Ghorbani et al., 2019; Dombrowski et al., 2019). The core idea in this literature centers around "fragile interpretations". (Ghorbani et al., 2019) defined that an interpretation is *fragile* if, for a given input, it is possible to generate perturbed input that achieves the same prediction label as the seed, yet is given a substantially different interpretation. Fragility limits how much we can trust and learn from specific interpretations. An adversary for "fragile interpretations" could manipulate the input to draw attention away from relevant words or onto desired features. Such input manipulation might be especially hard to detect because the actual labels have not changed.

The literature includes two relevant groups: (1) to conduct model manipulations (Slack et al., 2019; Wang et al., 2020) (details in Sec. 2), and (2) to manipulate input samples (Ghorbani et al., 2019). There has been little attention studying fragile interpretations via input manipulation in deep NLP.

In this paper, we propose a simple algorithm "ExplainFooler" that can make small adversarial perturbations on text inputs and demonstrate fragility of interpretations. We focus on optimizing two objective metrics - "L2 Norm" or a proposed "Delta LOM", searching for small word-swap-based input manipulation to produce misleading interpretations and using semantic-oriented constraints to constrain the manipulations. Figure 3 provides one example perturbation process. In summary, this paper provides the following contributions:

- Our input perturbation optimizes to increase the objective metric ("L2 Norm" or "Delta LOM") that measures difference between the original and generated interpretations. The LOM score

Proceedings of the Fourth BlackboxNLP Workshop on Analyzing and Interpreting Neural Networks for NLP, pages 420–434
Online, November 11, 2021. ©2021 Association for Computational Linguistics

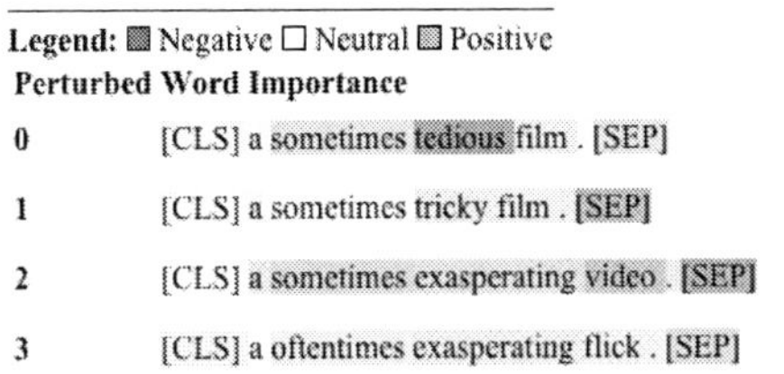

Figure 1: The figure demonstrates the input perturbation process for an increasing number (levels) of word perturbations. The red color depicts negative attribution, and the green shows positive attribution. The saturation of the colors signifies the magnitude of the said attributions. Note: the interpretations gradually become more and more different from the original, although the semantic meaning of the sentence does not change drastically. The model still predicts the correct original output, but the interpretations become senseless as more words get perturbed.[Example taken from the SST-2 dataset. Interpretations calculated using Integrated Gradients on DistilBERT model. Best viewed in color]

captures the approximate center "position" of an interpretation and summarizes it to a scalar.

- We propose an effective algorithm "ExplainFooler" to optimize the objective metric via an iterative procedure. Our algorithm generates a series of increasingly perturbed text inputs such that their explanations are significantly different from the original but preserving predictions.
- Empirically, we show that it is possible to find perturbed text examples to fool interpretations by INTEGRATED GRADIENT and LIME, even on NLP models that are relatively more robust.

The approximate process and results of word perturbation using our approach is detailed in Figure 1.

2 Related Work

Interpretation Methods: Several interpretation methods have been proposed(Shrikumar et al., 2017; Li et al., 2015; Bach et al., 2015; Shrikumar et al., 2017) to calculate feature importance scores. Two well-known methods in this area are Integrated Gradients (IG) (Sundararajan et al., 2017) and Local Interpretable Model Explanations (LIME)(Ribeiro et al., 2016b). IG computes the scores by summing up the gradients along a path from the baseline to the input in a fixed number of steps and subsequently multiplied by the input itself. IG overcomes the saturation problem discussed in (Shrikumar et al., 2017; Sundararajan et al., 2017). On the other hand, LIME is a completely black-box approach which explains the predictions of any classifier in an interpretable and faithful manner, by learning an interpretable model locally around the prediction by training the model on perturbations generated around the input.

Fragile Interpretations More recently, several works have focused on discussing the robustness of the said interpretations. Studies have demonstrated that the interpretations generated are not robust and can be easily manipulated due to high dimensionality of networks. (Ghorbani et al., 2019; Dombrowski et al., 2019; Slack et al., 2019; Wang et al., 2020). Multiple other works have tried to fix the problem by making interpretations robust (Lakkaraju et al., 2020; Rieger and Hansen, 2020).

(Wang et al., 2020) demonstrated that it is possible to introduce a new model over the original and alter gradients, to fool gradient-based interpretation methods. Similarly, (Slack et al., 2019) showed that black-box interpretation methods can also be fooled by allowing an adversarial classifier component. More recently, (Zafar et al., 2021) demonstrated empirically. that interpretability methods produce varying results on the same models but differently initialized.

Adversarial Examples that fool NLP Predictions: Adversarial examples are inputs to a predictive machine learning model that are maliciously designed to fool the model predictions (Goodfellow et al., 2014). Multiple recent works have focused on applying the concept of adversarial examples on language inputs, including (1) attacks by Character Substitution (Ebrahimi et al., 2017; Gao et al., 2018; Li et al., 2018); (2) attacks by Paraphrase (Ribeiro et al., 2018; Iyyer et al., 2018); (c) attacks by Synonym Substitution (Alzantot et al., 2018; Jin et al., 2020; Kuleshov et al., 2018; Papernot et al., 2016); (d) attacks by Word Insertion or Removal (Liang et al., 2017; Samanta and Mehta, 2017); (e) attacks by limiting L_p distance in a latent embedding space (Zhao et al., 2017). Our proposed algorithm is closely connected to the TextFooler algorithm (Jin et al., 2020) that searches for input perturbations to achieve mis-classification. Differently, we optimize the "L2 Norm" and "Location of Mass (LOM)" objective directly on the input space for fragile explanations.

3 Proposed Method

In this section, we present our algorithm to generate perturbed sentences that demonstrate fragile interpretations. First, we propose the metric "Location of Mass (LOM)" and L2 Norm, followed by a discussion on the search strategy to optimize the objective metrics. Subsequently, we discuss the interpretation method choices and end with the final candidates' selection procedure and pseudo-code for our algorithm (Algorithm1). We denote a text input as $\mathbf{x}$ and its word importance score vector (from a specific interpretation strategy on a particular NLP model) using notation I.

3.1 Difference Metrics on Interpretation

To quantify the difference between two interpretations, we propose two objective metrics - "Delta LOM" and "L2 Norm". These metrics are divergent - that is higher the metric, the more different the interpretations.

3.1.1 "Location of Mass (LOM)" Score

First, we propose a metric inspired by (Ghorbani et al., 2019) which provides a quantifiable "position" of the interpretations of a sentence. First, we define the "Location of Mass (LOM)" score as:

$$LOM(I) = \frac{\sum_{t=0}^{t=n-1}(i_t * t)}{\sum_{t=0}^{t=n-1} i_t} \tag{1}$$

Here n is the length of the sentence (along with starting/end special tokens). And i_t is the interpretability score assigned to the token at index 't'. We then propose to calculate the "Delta LOM" metric as: the difference between the LOM scores on the two interpretations I_1 and I_2:

$$\Delta LOM(I_1, I_2) = |LOM(I_1) - LOM(I_2)| \tag{2}$$

The intuition behind this metric comes from the fact that changing the approximate position of the "center" of interpretations changes the relative position and magnitudes of interpretations. This observation is demonstrated in Figure 3.

3.1.2 L2 Norm Metric

We also propose to use a standard L2 Norm to measure difference between two interpretations. Mathematically it is computed as follows:

$$L2Norm(I_1, I_2) = \|I_1 - I_2\|_2 \tag{3}$$

L2 Norm quantifies the extent of difference, higher the L2 Norm- higher the difference in pattern of two interpretations.

3.2 Searching for Word-level Perturbations

Our objective is to perturb a seed input $\mathbf{x}$, into a slightly-modified text $\mathbf{x}_{adv}$, so that ΔLOM or $L2Norm$ is maximized under a set of constraints.

First, we rank each word of an input sentence in the order of their importance to a model's predictions. This is done by the Leave-one-out approach (Li et al., 2016), which removes each word from the sentence one at a time and measures the change in prediction values, ranking the words which produce the greatest change as most important. Subsequently, we start our search in decreasing order of word importance and substituting each word with their k closest nearest-neighbors according to their counter-fitting synonym embeddings (Mrksic et al., 2016). For every subsequent word replacement, interpretation is calculated according to victim interpretation strategy we try to attack.

3.3 Ensuring Constraints

We enforce the following four constraints for each perturbed candidate to ensure candidates do not lose their linguistic structure and approximate semantic meaning of the seed input.

- Repeat Modification: Stops the same word from getting perturbed more than once.
- Stop Word Modification: This excludes pre-defined stop words from getting perturbed.
- Word Embedding Distance: Swaps the original word with words that have less than a particular embedding distance using Counter-Fitting Embeddings.
- Part of Speech: Replaces the original word with only words from the same part of speech.
- Sentence Embedding: Ensure the difference in the Universal Sentence Embedding is less than a pre-defined threshold (Cer et al., 2018).

3.4 Victim Interpretation Choices

Integrated Gradient: We calculate INTEGRATED GRADIENT (Sundararajan et al., 2017) interpretations of NLP models using the open-source package Captum (Kokhlikyan et al., 2020) that provides accurate implementations of various interpretation methods. We use the popular INTEGRATED GRADIENT algorithm to calculate the importance scores on the embedding space of the models. Once the interpretations are calculated, they are summed up along the dimension axis to derive the word importance scores. Subsequently, the ΔLOM and L2 Norm scores of each candidate perturbation are calculated against the original input's interpretation.

LIME: The LIME interpretations are calculated using the official LIME code provided by (Ribeiro et al., 2016a). We normalize the LIME scores by dividing the vector with its L_2-norm. Subsequently, the ΔLOM and L2 Norm scores of each candidate perturbation are calculated against the original input's interpretation.

3.5 Finding the ideal candidate

Once we obtain all the candidates and their metric scores on every candidate achieving the same prediction label as the original, we store those ideal candidates with each 'm' number of words perturbed. This gives us a list of candidates for each level of word perturbation and the associated change in objective metric scores. Next, for each level, the candidate with the highest metric score against the original is chosen. Finally, we convert the number of perturbed words into a ratio with respect to the input's length. This is done to take into account the varying sentence lengths and get a normalized measure. The ratio is limited to 50% because once more than half the words are perturbed, the sentence starts losing its semantic meaning. The complete selection process is schematically detailed in Figure 2

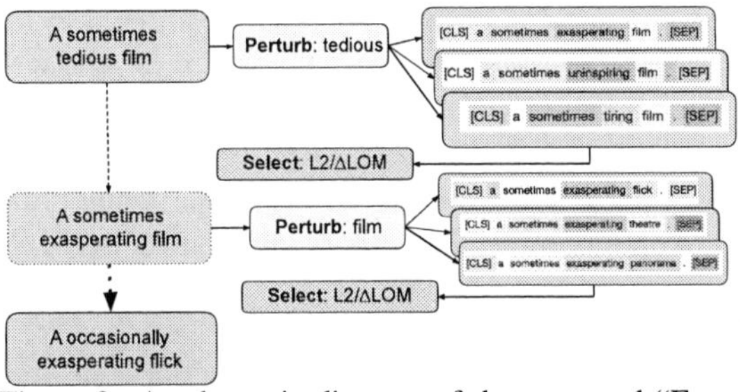

Figure 2: A schematic diagram of the proposed "ExplainFooler" algorithm. In the figure, the "Perturb" step generates a list of all possible perturbations according to the constraints as discussed in Sec. 3.3. The interpretation are generated as discussed in Sec. 3.4. The selection process uses objective metrics explained by Sec. 3.1.

3.6 Algorithm

Algorithm 1 "ExplainFooler" provides pseudocode to compute and select a list of candidates that can induce fragile explanations. Our implementation adapts and builds on top of the open-source package TextAttack (Morris et al., 2020).

Result: A - list of candidate sentences ordered by number of words perturbed from original
For each sentence in dataset
$A \leftarrow$empty
$S \leftarrow$original sentence
$I_0 \leftarrow$ InterpretMethod(S)
$P \leftarrow$ordered list of important words (LOO)
while *<=50% of words perturbed from P* **do**
  $w \leftarrow P[0]$
  $C \leftarrow$empty
  while *Possible perturbations exist* **do**
    $c \leftarrow$Perturb S and get candidate
    if *constraints pass* ***and*** *prediction label is same as S* **then**
      $I \leftarrow$ InterpretMethod(c)
      $\Delta diff \leftarrow diff(I_0, I)$,
      $C \leftarrow C \cup (\Delta diff, c)$
    else
      continue
  $A \leftarrow A \cup$ c where max(diff)
  $P \leftarrow$ remove $P[0]$

Algorithm 1: The "ExplainFooler" algorithm

4 Experiments

4.1 Data Summary

The experiments are conducted on three different datasets for text classification task. Experiments are conducted on the validation set for SST-2(Socher et al., 2013), test set for AG News(Zhang et al., 2015) and test set for IMDB dataset(Maas et al., 2011). We select the first 500 sentences from the SST-2 and AGNews datasets and 100 sentences from the test set from IMDB dataset to run our experiments. We discard sentences with just 2 words or less.

- **SST-2**: The Stanford Sentiment Treebank-2 dataset for movie review classification. It has two classes: positive and negative. Experiments are conducted on the first 500 sentences of the validation set.
- **AG News**: A collection of raw news articles belonging to 4 different classes including World, Sports, Science/Technology and Business. Experiments are conducted on the first 500 sentences of test set.
- **IMDB**: IMDB website dataset for binary sentiment classification containing a set of highly polar movie reviews. Experiments are conducted on first 500 sentences of test set except for LIME where only 100 sentences are used due to very high computation time due to very long average sentence length.

True Label	Predicted Label	Confidence	Predicted Class	Words Perturbed	LOM Score	Word Importance
0	0	0.98	Negative	0	0.00	[CLS] a sometimes tedious film . [SEP]
0	0	0.97	Negative	1	0.82	[CLS] a sometimes exasperating film . [SEP]
0	0	0.86	Negative	2	0.92	[CLS] a sometimes exasperating flick . [SEP]
0	0	0.57	Negative	3	0.95	[CLS] a occasionally exasperating flick . [SEP]

Figure 3: The figure demonstrates the ΔLOM score for an increasing number of word perturbations. The interpretations gradually become more and more different from the original although the semantic meaning of the sentence does not change drastically. We can see that the model still predicts the original output but the interpretations become senseless as the ΔLOM score increases.[Best viewed in color]

4.2 Interpretability Parameters

IG: As integrated gradients is a gradient based approach and requires a reference baseline, we compute the attributions on the embedding space and set the reference baseline to the special token <PAD> which is reserved in transformers as a special character. The step size for Integrated Gradients were chosen as 50 i.e. from reference to baseline, the gradients were summed up in 50 continuous steps.

LIME: The number of perturbations for LIME were chosen as 500 and the maximum number of top-k words were chosen as 512 words - the truncation limit for all the models.

4.3 Perturbation Parameters

We choose the number of nearest neighbours as 50 for swapping the words to limit the number of candidates. The maximum embedding cosine similarity between sentences was set as 0.5 to ensure sentences do not lose their semantic meaning.

4.4 Under the Hood

Pre-processing: All sentences with less than 2 words in all datasets are removed due to word perturbations not existing in some cases. In other cases, the smaller sentence have a very big difference in rank correlation which can spuriously decrease evaluation metrics. Each sentence from all datasets is also converted to lower-case.

Fixing Tokenizations: As pre-trained tokenizers for transformer models contain a ML matching based lookup vocabulary, many words in candidate sentences are tokenized in an unexpected manner. This results in the change of length of the token list which in turn changes the length of interpretations. To alleviate this problem, we test 2 distinct approaches to combine the unnaturally tokenized words into their original form.

- Average: The first approach combines all the tokens prefixed by a set character (## in case of DistilBERT) into one single word and assigns the average value of the tokens to the combined tokens
- Max: The second approach combines all the tokens prefixed by a set character (## in case of DistilBERT) into one single word and assigns the absolute maximum value with sign to the combined word.

Upon careful review, we utilize the second approach for our experiments. This is because, in uncommon cases where tokens hold opposite polarity to the ones in the word result in 'diluted' value of the original token. An example of the effectiveness of the 'Max' approach is given in Figure 4.

[CLS] unflinchingly bleak and desperate [SEP]
[CLS] un ##fl ##in ##ching ##ly bleak and desperate [SEP]

[CLS] unflinchingly bleak and desperate [SEP]
[CLS] un ##fl ##in ##ching ##ly bleak and desperate [SEP]

Figure 4: The figure demonstrates the combining of tokens of a sentence tokenized using DistilBERT's pre-trained tokenizer. The top group of sentences demonstrates averaging approach and the bottom group of sentences are combined using Abs-Max approach detailed in 4.4. [Best viewed in color]

4.5 Evaluation Metrics

4.5.1 Rank Correlation

To compare the correlation between interpretations of 2 sentences, we use the Spearman rank correlation metric. The more the ranks of the interpretations agree with each other, the higher the rank correlations. Importantly, we clip the negative values of the metric to 0. This is done because a negative correlation does not make sense when only comparing the difference in ranks and can spuriously bring down the average scores.

$$R - Correlation = \max(0, Spearman(I_1, I_2)) \quad (4)$$

We report results in Tables 1,3,8,10 and corresponding violin graphs Figures 7,10 of average Spearman rank order correlations and standard deviations versus ratio of words perturbed for 3 datasets (SST-2, AG News and IMDB) across both models (DistilBERT-uncased and RoBERTa-base) using 2 interpretability methods - INTEGRATED GRADIENT and LIME.

4.5.2 Top-50% Intersection

To compare the extent to which the words with highest attributions are correctly predicted by both the interpretation methods, we use the Top-k% intersection metric. To compute the intersection, we first find the words with the maximum absolute value of attributions (most important for prediction). We calculate the intersection of the top 50% highest attribution words.

$$Intersection = \frac{\bigcap(argsort(I_1), argsort(I_2))}{0.5 * length(I_1)} \quad (5)$$

where argsort returns the indices of the top-50% of the words in a sentence with highest attributions.

4.5.3 Candidate Quality

To judge the quality of the candidates generated using "ExplainFooler", we calculate two different commonly used quality metrics from adversarial attack literature - Perplexity and absolute number of grammar errors similar to (Li et al., 2020).

Perplexity We first use perplexity to estimate the fluency of candidates generated using "ExplainFooler". The lower the value, the more fluent the candidates, measured using a small size GPT-2 model (50k vocabulary) (Radford et al., 2019).

Grammatical Errors Estimates the average number of absolute difference in grammatical errors between the original and the candidate sentences. We use the Language Tool (Naber et al., 2003) to compute the errors.

4.6 Model Choices

The robustness concern of interpretation strategies challenges their use in critical applications, raising concerns like lack of trust. However, it is unclear what causes the "fragile explanations", the model or the interpretation? We therefore select three different transformer models namely, DistilBERT-uncased (Sanh et al., 2019), RoBERTa-base (Liu et al., 2019) and BERT-base (Devlin et al., 2018) to conduct our experiments. More importantly, we retrain the BERT-base to obtain the BERT-base-adv model that is an adversarially trained version of the BERT-base model. The rationale behind the choices is to investigate the impact of model's robustness on the robustness of the interpretations. (1) First, a generic transformer model like DistilBERT is relatively smaller and faster but less robust than the other two. (2) Next RoBERTa is extensively better pre-trained and has a far more robust performance. (3) Lastly, BERT-base-adv model is trained from adversarial training. We use the popular TextFooler(Jin et al., 2020) algorithm to generate adversarial examples via the open-source package Textattack. DistilBERT and RoBERTa models were from pre-trained models, fine-tuned on the respective datasets and we take them from the Huggingface's transformer model hub(Wolf et al., 2020) without change. Differently, BERT-base-adv model is adversarially trained by attacking 10000 training examples for the IMDB and AG datasets and attacking all training samples for SST-2 dataset.

5 Empirical Results

5.1 Rank Order and Top-50% Intersection

The results are reported in a tabular manner across 3 datasets (SST-2, AG News and IMDB), 3 models (DistilBERT, RoBERTa and BERT-adv (Section A(Appendix)) and 2 interpretability methods covering both metrics - L2 Norm, "Delta LOM" and compared against random candidate selection independent of both metrics. The first set of tables (Tables 1 and 3) report the average rank-order correlation between interpretations from the perturbed and the original, across different perturbation ratios in buckets of 10%. The second set of tables (Tables 2 and 4) report the average top-50% intersection. The rank correlation results for the IMDB datasets are reported only on IG due to excessive computational constraints. Due to space constraints, the results for both AGNews and IMDB datasets are reported in (Tables 8-11 and Tables 12-13 respectively, Section A.2 (Appendix)) along with a more detailed representation of the intra-bucket distribution in the form of Violin Graphs (Section A.3 (Appendix)).

SST-2									
	DistilBERT			RoBERTa			BERT-adv		
Ratio	L2	ΔLOM	Random	L2	ΔLOM	Random	L2	ΔLOM	Random
0-0.1	0.65	0.78	0.8	0.64	0.76	0.81	0.53	0.6	0.73
0.1-0.2	0.53	0.65	0.64	0.57	0.61	0.69	0.43	0.43	0.52
0.2-0.3	0.42	0.55	0.59	0.51	0.59	0.6	0.3	0.33	0.42
0.3-0.4	0.36	0.48	0.48	0.47	0.47	0.55	0.35	0.3	0.43
0.4-0.5	0.31	0.42	0.47	0.42	0.43	0.48	0.14	0.24	0.36

Table 1: Change in average rank-order correlation using metrics - L2 Norm, LOM and random selection conmputed using the interpretability method: INTEGRATED GRADIENT, for dataset- SST-2 over 3 models - DistilBERT, RoBERTa and BERT-adv.

SST-2									
	DistilBERT			RoBERTa			BERT-adv		
Ratio	L2	ΔLOM	Random	L2	ΔLOM	Random	L2	ΔLOM	Random
0-0.1	0.77	0.78	0.81	0.75	0.76	0.81	0.75	0.76	0.79
0.1-0.2	0.71	0.71	0.73	0.71	0.71	0.74	0.68	0.68	0.7
0.2-0.3	0.67	0.68	0.68	0.68	0.69	0.7	0.63	0.64	0.65
0.3-0.4	0.65	0.65	0.65	0.66	0.67	0.67	0.61	0.61	0.64
0.4-0.5	0.6	0.62	0.62	0.63	0.63	0.65	0.59	0.56	0.63

Table 2: Change in average Top-50% intersection using metrics - L2 Norm, LOM and random selection conmputed using the interpretability method: INTEGRATED GRADIENT, for dataset- SST-2 over 3 models - DistilBERT, RoBERTa and BERT-adv.

SST-2									
	DistilBERT			RoBERTa			BERT-adv		
Ratio	L2	ΔLOM	Random	L2	ΔLOM	Random	L2	ΔLOM	Random
0-0.1	0.64	0.7	0.79	0.59	0.66	0.76	0.57	0.68	0.72
0.1-0.2	0.52	0.58	0.65	0.58	0.63	0.7	0.37	0.52	0.59
0.2-0.3	0.46	0.51	0.56	0.52	0.58	0.62	0.34	0.47	0.54
0.3-0.4	0.39	0.43	0.46	0.48	0.54	0.58	0.31	0.36	0.36
0.4-0.5	0.23	0.29	0.46	0.55	0.55	0.54	0.28	0.2	0.24

Table 3: Change in average rank-order correlation using metrics - L2 Norm, LOM and random selection conmputed using the interpretability method: LIME, for dataset- SST-2 over 3 models - DistilBERT, RoBERTa and BERT-adv.

SST-2									
	DistilBERT			RoBERTa			BERT-adv		
Ratio	L2	ΔLOM	Random	L2	ΔLOM	Random	L2	ΔLOM	Random
0-0.1	0.64	0.7	0.79	0.59	0.66	0.76	0.57	0.68	0.72
0.1-0.2	0.52	0.58	0.65	0.58	0.63	0.7	0.37	0.52	0.59
0.2-0.3	0.46	0.51	0.56	0.52	0.58	0.62	0.34	0.47	0.54
0.3-0.4	0.39	0.43	0.46	0.48	0.54	0.58	0.31	0.36	0.36
0.4-0.5	0.23	0.29	0.46	0.55	0.55	0.54	0.28	0.2	0.24

Table 4: Change in average Top-50% intersection using metrics - L2 Norm, LOM and random selection conmputed using the interpretability method: LIME, for dataset- SST-2 over 3 models - DistilBERT, RoBERTa and BERT-adv.

Perplexity (lower is better)									
	DistilBERT			RoBERTa			BERT-adv		
Dataset	C-avg	ΔLOM	L2	C-avg	ΔLOM	L2	C-avg	ΔLOM	L2
SST-2 (130.85)	352.55	**285.88**	286.62	272.67	**245.55**	248.86	388.99	**237.76**	238.14
AGNews (76.18)	359.13	**239.95**	241.33	275.31	**194.89**	195.29	352.05	230.44	**229.38**
IMDB (39.12)	101.71	**65.04**	65.1	101.3	**62.41**	63.65	84.51	**63.21**	64.58

Table 5: Average values of perplexity calculated using a small GPT-2 model over all candidates generated by "ExplainFooler" (C-avg). The values in columns LOM and L2 denote the perplexity values calculated on the selected sentences using the proposed metrics. The average value of perplexity of original sentences in dataset are given in parentheses. Selection using metrics give more fluent sentences.

		Number of Words Perturbed				
Dataset	Model	0	1	2	3	4
SST-2	DistilBERT	0.97	0.95	0.92	0.88	0.82
	RoBERTa	0.98	0.98	0.98	0.98	0.98
	BERT-adv	0.97	0.96	0.94	0.92	0.91
AGNews	DistilBERT	0.98	0.97	0.93	0.86	0.82
	RoBERTa	0.98	0.98	0.98	0.98	0.98
	BERT-adv	0.97	0.95	0.95	0.94	0.91
IMDB	DistilBERT	0.99	0.97	0.94	0.89	0.84
	RoBERTa	0.98	0.98	0.98	0.98	0.98
	BERT-adv	0.97	0.96	0.94	0.94	0.91

Table 6: Average model confidence for correct prediction values for increasing number of words perturbed over models - DistilBERT, RoBERTa and BERT-adv on datasets - SST-2, AGNews and IMDB

A bucket represents all instances of perturbed candidates in the ratio between that lower and higher range. For example, bucket between "0.1-0.2" contains all rank-order correlations from sentences with a percentage of words perturbed between 10% and 20%. We also provide violin plots in appendix showcasing intra-bucket distribution for the dataset SST-2 (Figures 7-10). We observe that both average rank-order correlation and top-50% intersection scores decrease as the ratio of words being perturbed increases. Observations imply that interpretations of sentences become increasingly dissimilar to the original sentence as more words are perturbed even though the prediction robustness of the models remains high (see Table 6, Figure 12). Similar trends are observed across all models, datasets, and covering both victim interpretability methods. These empirical observations demonstrate interpretations generated by INTEGRATED GRADIENT and LIME are fragile for all models - even models that are adversarially more robust (BERT-adv). To further demonstrate effectiveness of proposed metrics, we plot violin plots on SST-2 dataset for avg. rank correlation versus selection using metrics and random. (Figure 5 - Appendix)

5.2 Quality of candidates

Perplexity The average perplexity values over all models and datasets are reported in Table 5. For each dataset, model pair values corresponding to proposed metrics and random selection are reported. It can be observed that perplexity of candidates selected using proposed metrics have lower perplexity score (implying better fluency) than average of all candidates generated by "ExplainFooler".

Grammatical Errors (lower is better)			
Model	C-avg	L2	ΔLOM
DistilBERT	0.59	0.59	**0.58**
RoBERTa	0.79	0.76	**0.75**
BERT-adv	0.60	**0.51**	0.52

Table 7: Average number of grammatical errors on candidates generated using "ExplainFooler" on the SST-2 dataset (C-avg). The accompanying values in columns ΔLOM and L2 denote the grammar errors calculated on the sentences selected using the proposed metrics.

Grammatical Errors Estimates average number of absolute difference in grammatical errors between the original and candidate sentences. We use Language Tool (Naber et al., 2003) to compute the errors. The results for SST-2 dataset are reported in Table 7.

6 Conclusions

Literature sees a growing emphasis on interpretation techniques for explaining NLP model predictions. Our work demonstrates a novel algorithm that generates perturbed inputs that provide evidence of fragile interpretations. We demonstrate the effectiveness of our approach across three different models, with one of them adversarially trained. Our results show that it is possible to attack interpretations using simple input-level word swaps under certain constraints. We also demonstrate that both black and white-box interpretability approaches (LIME and INTEGRATED GRADIENT) show fragility in their derived interpretations. We hope our findings can pave lights for future studies on defending against problem of fragile interpretations in NLP.

References

Moustafa Alzantot, Yash Sharma, Ahmed Elgohary, Bo-Jhang Ho, Mani Srivastava, and Kai-Wei Chang. 2018. Generating natural language adversarial examples. *arXiv preprint arXiv:1804.07998*.

Sebastian Bach, Alexander Binder, Grégoire Montavon, Frederick Klauschen, Klaus-Robert Müller, and Wojciech Samek. 2015. On pixel-wise explanations for non-linear classifier decisions by layer-wise relevance propagation. *PloS one*, 10(7):e0130140.

Daniel Cer, Yinfei Yang, Sheng-yi Kong, Nan Hua, Nicole Limtiaco, Rhomni St. John, Noah Constant, Mario Guajardo-Cespedes, Steve Yuan, Chris Tar, Yun-Hsuan Sung, Brian Strope, and Ray Kurzweil. 2018. Universal sentence encoder. *CoRR*, abs/1803.11175.

Jacob Devlin, Ming-Wei Chang, Kenton Lee, and Kristina Toutanova. 2018. Bert: Pre-training of deep bidirectional transformers for language understanding. *arXiv preprint arXiv:1810.04805*.

Ann-Kathrin Dombrowski, Maximillian Alber, Christopher Anders, Marcel Ackermann, Klaus-Robert Müller, and Pan Kessel. 2019. Explanations can be manipulated and geometry is to blame. In *Advances in Neural Information Processing Systems*, volume 32, pages 13589–13600. Curran Associates, Inc.

Javid Ebrahimi, Anyi Rao, Daniel Lowd, and Dejing Dou. 2017. Hotflip: White-box adversarial examples for text classification. *arXiv preprint arXiv:1712.06751*.

Ji Gao, Jack Lanchantin, Mary Lou Soffa, and Yanjun Qi. 2018. Black-box generation of adversarial text sequences to evade deep learning classifiers. In *2018 IEEE Security and Privacy Workshops (SPW)*, pages 50–56. IEEE.

Amirata Ghorbani, Abubakar Abid, and James Zou. 2019. Interpretation of neural networks is fragile. *Proceedings of the AAAI Conference on Artificial Intelligence*, 33(01):3681–3688.

Ian J Goodfellow, Jonathon Shlens, and Christian Szegedy. 2014. Explaining and harnessing adversarial examples. *arXiv preprint arXiv:1412.6572*.

Hamza Harkous, Kassem Fawaz, Rémi Lebret, Florian Schaub, Kang G. Shin, and Karl Aberer. 2018. Polisis: Automated analysis and presentation of privacy policies using deep learning. In *Proceedings of the 27th USENIX Conference on Security Symposium*, SEC'18, page 531–548, USA. USENIX Association.

Mohit Iyyer, John Wieting, Kevin Gimpel, and Luke Zettlemoyer. 2018. Adversarial example generation with syntactically controlled paraphrase networks. *CoRR*, abs/1804.06059.

Google Jigsaw. 2017. Perspective api. `https://www.perspectiveapi.com/`.

Di Jin, Zhijing Jin, Joey Tianyi Zhou, and Peter Szolovits. 2020. Is bert really robust? a strong baseline for natural language attack on text classification and entailment. *Proceedings of the AAAI Conference on Artificial Intelligence*, 34(05):8018–8025.

Narine Kokhlikyan, Vivek Miglani, Miguel Martin, Edward Wang, Bilal Alsallakh, Jonathan Reynolds, Alexander Melnikov, Natalia Kliushkina, Carlos Araya, Siqi Yan, and Orion Reblitz-Richardson. 2020. Captum: A unified and generic model interpretability library for pytorch.

Volodymyr Kuleshov, Shantanu Thakoor, Tingfung Lau, and Stefano Ermon. 2018. Adversarial examples for natural language classification problems.

Himabindu Lakkaraju, Nino Arsov, and Osbert Bastani. 2020. Robust and stable black box explanations. In *Proceedings of the 37th International Conference on Machine Learning*, volume 119 of *Proceedings of Machine Learning Research*, pages 5628–5638. PMLR.

Dianqi Li, Yizhe Zhang, Hao Peng, Liqun Chen, Chris Brockett, Ming-Ting Sun, and Bill Dolan. 2020. Contextualized perturbation for textual adversarial attack. *arXiv preprint arXiv:2009.07502*.

Jinfeng Li, Shouling Ji, Tianyu Du, Bo Li, and Ting Wang. 2018. Textbugger: Generating adversarial text against real-world applications. *arXiv preprint arXiv:1812.05271*.

Jiwei Li, Xinlei Chen, Eduard Hovy, and Dan Jurafsky. 2015. Visualizing and understanding neural models in nlp. *arXiv preprint arXiv:1506.01066*.

Jiwei Li, Will Monroe, and Dan Jurafsky. 2016. Understanding neural networks through representation erasure. *arXiv preprint arXiv:1612.08220*.

Bin Liang, Hongcheng Li, Miaoqiang Su, Pan Bian, Xirong Li, and Wenchang Shi. 2017. Deep text classification can be fooled. *arXiv preprint arXiv:1704.08006*.

Yinhan Liu, Myle Ott, Naman Goyal, Jingfei Du, Mandar S. Joshi, Danqi Chen, Omer Levy, Mike Lewis, Luke S. Zettlemoyer, and Veselin Stoyanov. 2019. Roberta: A robustly optimized bert pretraining approach. *ArXiv*, abs/1907.11692.

Andrew L Maas, Raymond E Daly, Peter T Pham, Dan Huang, Andrew Y Ng, and Christopher Potts. 2011. Learning word vectors for sentiment analysis. In *Proceedings of the 49th Annual Meeting of the Association for Computational Linguistics: Human Language Technologies-Volume 1*, pages 142–150. Association for Computational Linguistics.

John X. Morris, Eli Lifland, Jin Yong Yoo, Jake Grigsby, Di Jin, and Yanjun Qi. 2020. Textattack: A framework for adversarial attacks, data augmentation, and adversarial training in nlp.

Nikola Mrksic, Diarmuid Ó Séaghdha, Blaise Thomson, Milica Gasic, Lina Maria Rojas-Barahona, Pei hao Su, David Vandyke, Tsung-Hsien Wen, and Steve J. Young. 2016. Counter-fitting word vectors to linguistic constraints. In *HLT-NAACL*.

Daniel Naber et al. 2003. A rule-based style and grammar checker.

Syunya Okuno, Hiroki Asai, and Hayato Yamana. 2014. A challenge of authorship identification for ten-thousand-scale microblog users. In *2014 IEEE International Conference on Big Data (Big Data)*, pages 52–54. IEEE.

Nicolas Papernot, Patrick McDaniel, Ananthram Swami, and Richard Harang. 2016. Crafting adversarial input sequences for recurrent neural networks. In *Military Communications Conference, MILCOM 2016-2016 IEEE*, pages 49–54. IEEE.

Alec Radford, Jeffrey Wu, Rewon Child, David Luan, Dario Amodei, and Ilya Sutskever. 2019. Language models are unsupervised multitask learners.

Marco Tulio Ribeiro, Sameer Singh, and Carlos Guestrin. 2016a. Model-agnostic interpretability of machine learning. *arXiv preprint arXiv:1606.05386*.

Marco Tulio Ribeiro, Sameer Singh, and Carlos Guestrin. 2016b. Why should i trust you?: Explaining the predictions of any classifier. In *Proceedings of the 22nd ACM SIGKDD international conference on knowledge discovery and data mining*, pages 1135–1144. ACM.

Marco Tulio Ribeiro, Sameer Singh, and Carlos Guestrin. 2018. Semantically equivalent adversarial rules for debugging NLP models. In *Proceedings of the 56th Annual Meeting of the Association for Computational Linguistics (Volume 1: Long Papers)*, pages 856–865.

Laura Rieger and Lars Kai Hansen. 2020. A simple defense against adversarial attacks on heatmap explanations. *arXiv preprint arXiv:2007.06381*.

Suranjana Samanta and Sameep Mehta. 2017. Towards crafting text adversarial samples. *arXiv preprint arXiv:1707.02812*.

Victor Sanh, Lysandre Debut, Julien Chaumond, and Thomas Wolf. 2019. Distilbert, a distilled version of bert: smaller, faster, cheaper and lighter. *arXiv preprint arXiv:1910.01108*.

Avanti Shrikumar, Peyton Greenside, and Anshul Kundaje. 2017. Learning important features through propagating activation differences. In *International Conference on Machine Learning*, pages 3145–3153. PMLR.

Dylan Slack, Sophie Hilgard, Emily Jia, Sameer Singh, and Himabindu Lakkaraju. 2019. How can we fool lime and shap? adversarial attacks on post hoc explanation methods.

Richard Socher, Alex Perelygin, Jean Wu, Jason Chuang, Christopher D Manning, Andrew Ng, and Christopher Potts. 2013. Recursive deep models for semantic compositionality over a sentiment treebank. In *Proceedings of the 2013 conference on empirical methods in natural language processing*, pages 1631–1642.

Mukund Sundararajan, Ankur Taly, and Qiqi Yan. 2017. Axiomatic attribution for deep networks. In *Proceedings of the 34th International Conference on Machine Learning-Volume 70*, pages 3319–3328. JMLR. org.

Junlin Wang, Jens Tuyls, Eric Wallace, and Sameer Singh. 2020. Gradient-based analysis of NLP models is manipulable. In *Findings of the Association for Computational Linguistics: EMNLP 2020*, pages 247–258, Online. Association for Computational Linguistics.

Thomas Wolf, Lysandre Debut, Victor Sanh, Julien Chaumond, Clement Delangue, Anthony Moi, Pierric Cistac, Tim Rault, Rémi Louf, Morgan Funtowicz, Joe Davison, Sam Shleifer, Patrick von Platen, Clara Ma, Yacine Jernite, Julien Plu, Canwen Xu, Teven Le Scao, Sylvain Gugger, Mariama Drame, Quentin Lhoest, and Alexander M. Rush. 2020. Transformers: State-of-the-art natural language processing. In *Proceedings of the 2020 Conference on Empirical Methods in Natural Language Processing: System Demonstrations*, pages 38–45, Online. Association for Computational Linguistics.

Muhammad Bilal Zafar, Michele Donini, Dylan Slack, Cédric Archambeau, Sanjiv Das, and Krishnaram Kenthapadi. 2021. On the lack of robust interpretability of neural text classifiers. *arXiv preprint arXiv:2106.04631*.

Xiang Zhang, Junbo Zhao, and Yann LeCun. 2015. Character-level convolutional networks for text classification. In *Advances in neural information processing systems*, pages 649–657.

Zhengli Zhao, Dheeru Dua, and Sameer Singh. 2017. Generating natural adversarial examples. *arXiv preprint arXiv:1710.11342*.

Xinyi Zhou, Reza Zafarani, Kai Shu, and Huan Liu. 2019. Fake news: Fundamental theories, detection strategies and challenges. In *Proceedings of the twelfth ACM international conference on web search and data mining*, pages 836–837.

A Appendix

A.1 Compare with Baseline

Figures 5,6 show the decrease in average rank correlation when considering random candidates as opposed to selection using the LOM metric.

A.2 Additional Results

In this section we report the average rank order correlation and the average top-50% intersection scores for AGNews and IMDB datasets. The Tables 8,9 correspond to AGNews' rank correlation and top-50% scores using INTEGRATED GRADIENT whereas Tables 10,11 show same values using LIME. Tables 12 and 13 show similar values but for IMDB dataset.

A.3 Violin Plots for intra-bucket distribution analysis

The Violin plots convey more information about the relative distribution of average rank correlations and Top-50% values for various bucket ratios. The following figures are only reported on the SST-2 dataset for each combination of evaluation metric and interpretability methods.

A.4 Visual Results

A few visual results demonstrating the gradual change in interpretations of candidate adversaries is shown in Figure 12. It can be observed that ΔLOM score gradually increases with word perturbations. The examples demonstrate the same 3 sentences from the dataset perturbed under DistilBERT and RoBERTa respectively.

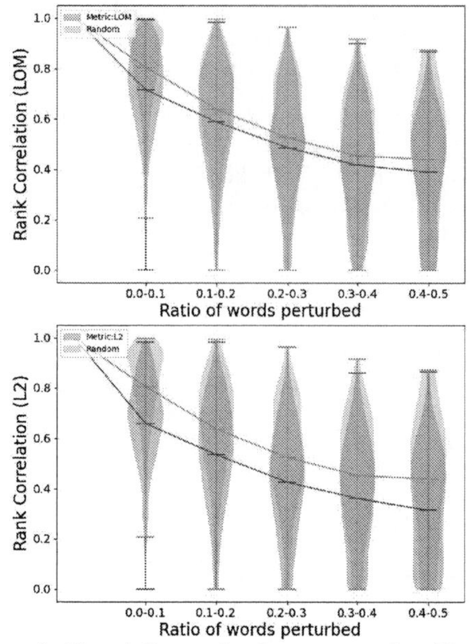

Figure 5: The violin graphs demonstrate the effectiveness of candidate selection based on the proposed metrics LOM and L2 Norm over random selection for SST-2 dataset. As it can be seen that the selection based on the proposed metrics disrupts rank correlation more as compared to randomly selecting candidates.

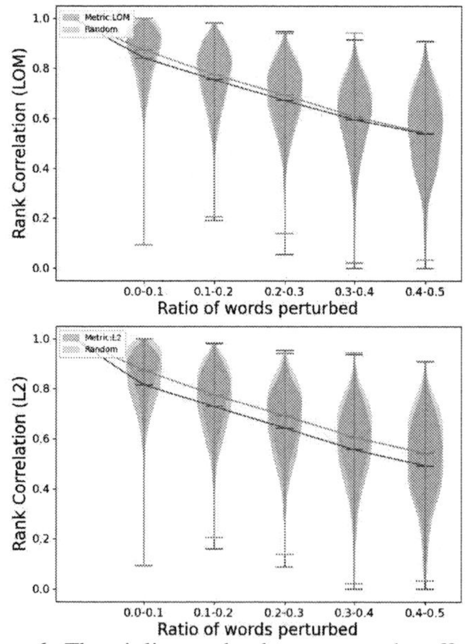

Figure 6: The violin graphs demonstrate the effectiveness of candidate selection based on the proposed metrics LOM and L2 Norm over random selection for AG-News dataset. As it can be seen that the selection based on the proposed metrics disrupts rank correlation more as compared to randomly selecting candidates.

AGNews									
	DistilBERT			RoBERTa			BERT-adv		
Ratio	L2	ΔLOM	Random	L2	ΔLOM	Random	L2	ΔLOM	Random
0-0.1	0.81	0.84	0.86	0.73	0.68	0.82	0.38	0.56	0.63
0.1-0.2	0.72	0.75	0.78	0.65	0.57	0.72	0.32	0.42	0.46
0.2-0.3	0.64	0.66	0.69	0.62	0.52	0.66	0.28	0.32	0.29
0.3-0.4	0.55	0.58	0.58	0.58	0.48	0.62	0.25	0.25	0.26
0.4-0.5	0.49	0.52	0.56	0.52	0.42	0.56	0.18	0.23	0.24

Table 8: Change in average rank-order correlation using metrics - L2 Norm, LOM and random selection conmputed using the interpretability method: INTEGRATED GRADIENT, for dataset- AGNews over 3 models - DistilBERT, RoBERTa and BERT-adv.

AGNews									
	DistilBERT			RoBERTa			BERT-adv		
Ratio	L2	ΔLOM	Random	L2	ΔLOM	Random	L2	ΔLOM	Random
0-0.1	0.64	0.65	0.71	0.7	0.74	0.85	0.48	0.51	0.79
0.1-0.2	0.57	0.58	0.69	0.61	0.64	0.8	0.37	0.4	0.69
0.2-0.3	0.57	0.58	0.62	0.55	0.59	0.77	0.24	0.27	0.64
0.3-0.4	0.53	0.53	0.58	0.52	0.55	0.74	0.22	0.24	0.6
0.4-0.5	0.51	0.52	0.56	0.45	0.5	0.71	0.19	0.24	0.58

Table 9: Change in average Top-50% intersection using metrics - L2 Norm, LOM and random selection conmputed using the interpretability method: INTEGRATED GRADIENT, for dataset- AGNews over 3 models - DistilBERT, RoBERTa and BERT-adv.

AGNews									
	DistilBERT			RoBERTa			BERT-adv		
Ratio	L2	ΔLOM	Random	L2	ΔLOM	Random	L2	ΔLOM	Random
0-0.1	0.65	0.69	0.71	0.58	0.57	0.61	0.7	0.61	0.72
0.1-0.2	0.59	0.6	0.62	0.55	0.54	0.56	0.69	0.45	0.7
0.2-0.3	0.53	0.53	0.58	0.54	0.53	0.48	0.65	0.35	0.66
0.3-0.4	0.48	0.52	0.55	0.51	0.51	0.36	0.65	0.28	0.65
0.4-0.5	0.44	0.38	0.46	0.43	0.42	0.43	0.59	0.26	0.61

Table 10: Change in average rank-order correlation using metrics - L2 Norm, LOM and random selection conmputed using the interpretability method: LIME, for dataset- AGNews over 3 models - DistilBERT, RoBERTa and BERT-adv.

AGNews									
	DistilBERT			RoBERTa			BERT-adv		
Ratio	L2	ΔLOM	Random	L2	ΔLOM	Random	L2	ΔLOM	Random
0-0.1	0.62	0.64	0.66	0.6	0.62	0.61	0.56	0.56	0.55
0.1-0.2	0.58	0.59	0.63	0.58	0.58	0.58	0.53	0.54	0.53
0.2-0.3	0.57	0.57	0.58	0.55	0.57	0.57	0.51	0.51	0.52
0.3-0.4	0.55	0.56	0.58	0.55	0.55	0.57	0.5	0.5	0.52
0.4-0.5	0.53	0.55	0.57	0.54	0.54	0.56	0.51	0.5	0.52

Table 11: Change in average Top-50% intersection using metrics - L2 Norm, LOM and random selection conmputed using the interpretability method: LIME, for dataset- AGNews over 3 models - DistilBERT, RoBERTa and BERT-adv.

IMDB									
	DistilBERT			RoBERTa			BERT-adv		
Ratio	L2	ΔLOM	Random	L2	ΔLOM	Random	L2	ΔLOM	Random
0-0.1	0.69	0.69	0.71	0.75	0.74	0.8	0.45	0.44	0.55
0.1-0.2	0.53	0.55	0.61	0.64	0.59	0.69	0.32	0.32	0.41
0.2-0.3	0.41	0.44	0.5	0.51	0.48	0.58	0.28	0.29	0.39
0.3-0.4	0.42	0.39	0.49	0.45	0.41	0.51	0.27	0.28	0.34
0.4-0.5	0.33	0.31	0.41	0.34	0.37	0.49	0.12	0.17	0.28

Table 12: Change in average rank-order correlation using metrics - L2 Norm, LOM and random selection conmputed using the interpretability method: INTEGRATED GRADIENT, for dataset- IMDB over 3 models - DistilBERT, RoBERTa and BERT-adv.

IMDB									
	DistilBERT			RoBERTa			BERT-adv		
Ratio	L2	ΔLOM	Random	L2	ΔLOM	Random	L2	ΔLOM	Random
0-0.1	0.7	0.71	0.74	0.73	0.75	0.76	0.61	0.63	0.66
0.1-0.2	0.6	0.63	0.66	0.64	0.66	0.69	0.58	0.61	0.63
0.2-0.3	0.59	0.6	0.63	0.57	0.63	0.65	0.57	0.6	0.61
0.3-0.4	0.56	0.57	0.57	0.57	0.58	0.6	0.55	0.57	0.58
0.4-0.5	0.52	0.52	0.52	0.52	0.55	0.57	0.54	0.54	0.54

Table 13: Change in average rank-order correlation using metrics - L2 Norm, LOM and random selection conmputed using the interpretability method: INTEGRATED GRADIENT, for dataset- IMDB over 3 models - DistilBERT, RoBERTa and BERT-adv.

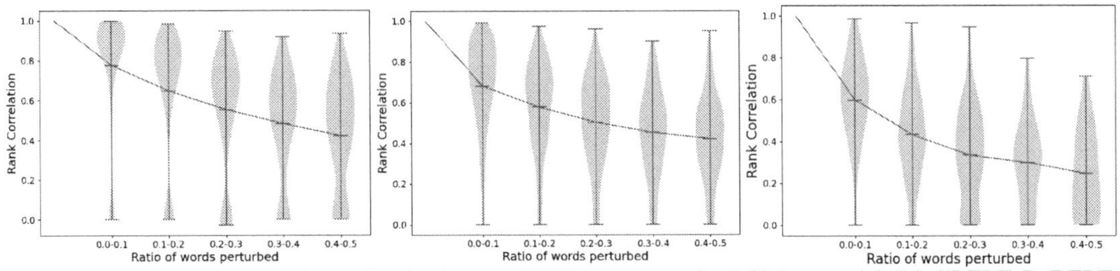

Figure 7: Average Rank-correlation for the dataset: SST-2, using metric: LOM on models DistilBERT, RoBERTa and BERT-adv using interpretability method -INTEGRATED GRADIENT

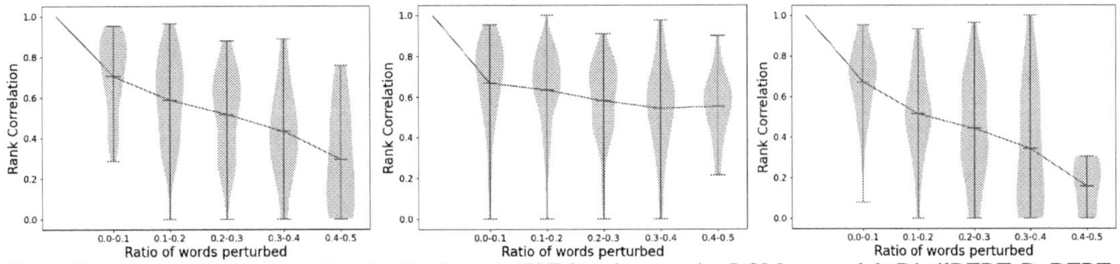

Figure 8: Average Rank-correlation for the dataset: SST-2, using metric: LOM on models DistilBERT, RoBERTa and BERT-adv using interpretability method -LIME

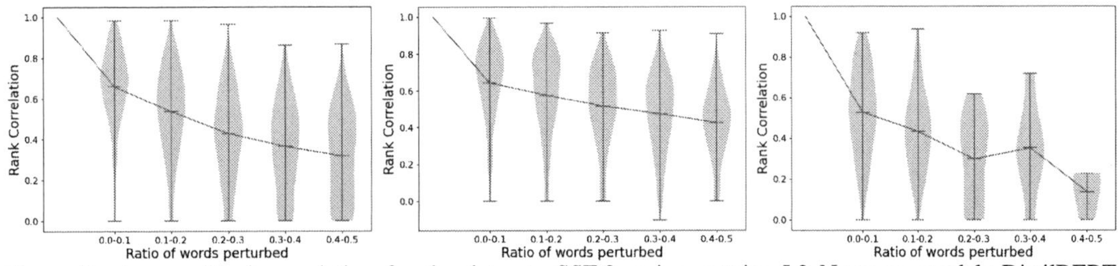

Figure 9: Average Rank-correlation for the dataset: SST-2, using metric: L2 Norm on models DistilBERT, RoBERTa and BERT-adv using interpretability method -INTEGRATED GRADIENT

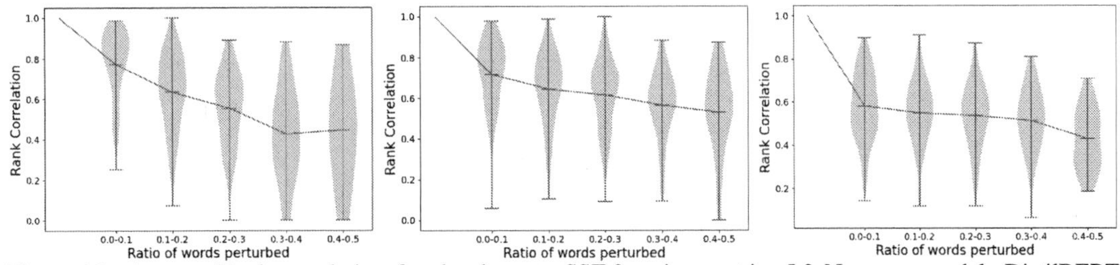

Figure 10: Average Rank-correlation for the dataset: SST-2, using metric: L2 Norm on models DistilBERT, RoBERTa and BERT-adv using interpretability method -LIME

True Label	Predicted Label	Confidence	Predicted Class	Words Perturbed	LOM Score	Word Importance
1	1	1.00	Positive	0	0.00	[CLS] it ' s a charming and often affecting journey . [SEP]
1	1	1.00	Positive	1	0.31	[CLS] it ' s a alluring and often affecting journey . [SEP]
1	1	0.98	Positive	2	0.80	[CLS] it ' s a beautifull and often afflicted journey . [SEP]
1	1	0.72	Positive	3	1.22	[CLS] it ' s a beautifull and often afflicted rook . [SEP]
0	0	0.98	Negative	0	0.00	[CLS] unflinchingly bleak and desperate [SEP]
0	0	0.89	Negative	1	0.72	[CLS] unflinchingly baleful and desperate [SEP]
0	0	0.66	Negative	2	0.86	[CLS] unflinchingly dusky and depressive [SEP]
0	0	0.99	Negative	0	0.00	[CLS] it ' s slow - - very , very slow . [SEP]
0	0	0.99	Negative	1	0.25	[CLS] it ' s slow - - crucially , very slow . [SEP]
0	0	0.99	Negative	2	0.91	[CLS] it ' s slow - - crucially , vitally slow . [SEP]
0	0	0.97	Negative	3	1.44	[CLS] it ' s slow - - crucially , highly lent . [SEP]
0	0	0.91	Negative	4	1.61	[CLS] it ' s sluggish - - crucially , highly lent . [SEP]

Figure 11: A few random sentence explanations from the SST-2 dataset calculated on DistilBERT-uncased using INTEGRATED GRADIENT. [Best viewed in color].

True Label	Predicted Label	Confidence	Predicted Class	Words Perturbed	LOM Score	Word Importance
1	1	1.00	Positive	0	0.00	it 's a charming and often affecting journey . #/s
1	1	1.00	Positive	1	0.73	it 's a mignon and often affecting journey . #/s
1	1	0.99	Positive	2	1.19	it 's a dreamy and often plaguing journey . #/s
1	1	0.98	Positive	3	1.12	it 's a dreamy and often effect nomad . #/s
0	0	1.00	Negative	0	0.00	unflinchingly bleak and desperate #/s
0	0	1.00	Negative	1	0.45	unflinchingly dreary and desperate #/s
0	0	0.90	Negative	2	0.76	unflinchingly sombre and frenetic #/s
0	0	1.00	Negative	0	0.00	it 's slow -- very , very slow . #/s
0	0	1.00	Negative	1	0.78	it 's slow -- very , very lent . #/s
0	0	0.97	Negative	2	0.73	it 's slow -- perfectly , very slowness . #/s
0	0	1.00	Negative	3	0.31	it 's slow -- immeasurably , immeasurably slowness . #/s
0	0	1.00	Negative	4	0.39	it 's slowest -- immeasurably , immeasurably slowness . #/s

Figure 12: The same sentence visualizations calculated on RoBERTa-base. It is clear RoBERTa is much more robust in making predictions but both DistilBERT and RoBERTa are susceptible to such attacks on their interpretations. [Best viewed in color]

An Investigation of Language Model Interpretability via Sentence Editing

Samuel Stevens
The Ohio State University
stevens.994@osu.edu

Yu Su
The Ohio State University
su.809@osu.edu

Abstract

Pre-trained language models (PLMs) like BERT are being used for almost all language-related tasks, but interpreting their behavior still remains a significant challenge and many important questions remain largely unanswered. In this work, we re-purpose a sentence editing dataset, where faithful high-quality human rationales can be automatically extracted and compared with extracted model rationales, as a new testbed for interpretability. This enables us to conduct a systematic investigation on an array of questions regarding PLMs' interpretability, including the role of pre-training procedure, comparison of rationale extraction methods, and different layers in the PLM. The investigation generates new insights, for example, contrary to the common understanding, we find that attention weights correlate well with human rationales and work better than gradient-based saliency in extracting model rationales. Both the dataset and code are available at https://github.com/samuelstevens/sentence-editing-interpretability to facilitate future interpretability research.

1 Introduction

Pre-trained language models (PLMs) (Devlin et al., 2019; Liu et al., 2019; Beltagy et al., 2019) are pervasively used in language-related tasks, but interpreting their predictions is notoriously difficult because of their parameters' complex interdependencies. Given a specific prediction, we want to know *why* a model made that decision, both to further improve performance and to use the model in high-stakes scenarios such as healthcare or bank loan approvals where interpretability is important. This has motivated efforts in extracting model explanations, typically in the form of *rationales*, i.e., subsets of the original input that support a decision (Zaidan et al., 2007). Attention heatmaps (Xu et al., 2015) and gradient-based saliency maps (Simonyan et al., 2014) are common extraction methods.

```
The algorithm <del>descripted</del>
<ins>described</ins> in the previous
sections has several advantages.
```

The algorithm ~~descripted~~ →**described** in the previous sections has several advantages.

```
However, we <del>must note that
we </del>still have no means of
deciding which documents out of _MATH_
deserve to be in _MATH_ and _MATH_,
respectively.
```

However, we ~~must note that we~~ still have no means of deciding which documents out of _MATH_ deserve to be in _MATH_ and _MATH_, respectively.

Figure 1: Two "need edit" examples from AESW in the original data format and a human-readable format. The first example (a) has a spelling error "descripted" and the second (b) is edited for concision.

There have been efforts on developing datasets for interpretability research, for example, the recent ERASER benchmark (DeYoung et al., 2020). However, the majority of ERASER tasks use human rationales highlighted by a different annotator after the original labeling process. Such rationales are not necessarily *faithful*; a rationale highlighted by the second annotator may not have been actually used by the first annotator while labeling. Manual rationale labeling is also difficult and time-consuming; of the six datasets in the ERASER benchmark, only one has more than 200 examples.

Our first contribution is the realization that AESW (Automatic Evaluation of Scientific Writing; Daudaravicius et al., 2016), a sentence editing dataset, contains *thousands* of *faithful human rationales* that can be automatically re-purposed for interpretability research. See Figure 1 for examples. This provides a new, large-scale dataset with truly faithful human rationales for interpretability questions surrounding model rationales.

Our second contribution is investigating multiple factors in PLM rationale plausibility. More plausible rationales are valuable in human-in-the-

Proceedings of the Fourth BlackboxNLP Workshop on Analyzing and Interpreting Neural Networks for NLP, pages 435–446
Online, November 11, 2021.

loop systems where humans use model rationales to make a final decision. We compare (1) pre-training procedures, (2) attention weight- and input gradient-based methods of extracting model rationales, (3) correlation between model rationale plausibility and model confidence, and (4) differences in transformer layers. While previous work (Jain and Wallace, 2019; Serrano and Smith, 2019) has shown that attention weights are not always faithful, we find that they correlate with human rationales better than gradient-based methods.

2 Related Work

Human rationales (as defined by Zaidan et al., 2007) are subsets of input highlighted by human annotators as evidence to support a decision. The same annotator labeling an example might also highlight their rationale (Khashabi et al., 2018; Thorne et al., 2018). In other cases, rationales are collected for an existing dataset by different annotators (Zaidan et al., 2008; Camburu et al., 2018; Rajani et al., 2019). As previously stated, such rationales may not be faithful. Rationale length can vary from sub-sentence spans (Talmor et al., 2019) to multiple sentences (Lehman et al., 2019).

Model rationales can be produced as an explicit training objective (Zaidan et al., 2008) or extracted as a post-hoc explanation. Post-hoc methods typically assign token-level importance scores: attention weights are often used in attention-based models (Bahdanau et al., 2016), gradient-based explanations are typical for differentiable models (Denil et al., 2015; Shrikumar et al., 2017), and LIME is a model-agnostic method (Ribeiro et al., 2016). We follow work using BERT's attention (Clark et al., 2019; Kovaleva et al., 2019) to extract rationales.

A model rationale is evaluated on faithfulness (if it is actually used to make a decision) and plausibility (if it is easily understood by humans). Faithfulness can be measured by perturbing inputs marked as evidence and measuring change in outputs (Jain and Wallace, 2019; Serrano and Smith, 2019). Plausibility can be measured through user studies, wherein users are given a model rationale and asked either to predict the model's decision (Kim et al., 2016) or to rate rationale understandability (Nguyen, 2018; Ehsan et al., 2018, 2019; Strout et al., 2019). Rationale plausibility can also be measured by similarity to human rationales (DeYoung et al., 2020), but this requires faithful human rationales. We use similarity to evaluate rationale plausibility because we gather faithful human rationales from sentence editing annotations.

3 Proposed Task

We propose re-purposing the AESW classification task for measuring model interpretability. We gather examples from AESW from which we can automatically extract faithful and sufficient human rationales, and then use said rationales to investigate factors in PLM rationale plausibility, specifically BERT (Devlin et al., 2019) and its variants. It is worth noting that our rationale dataset can be used for other interpretability topics such as training with rationales or evaluating rationale faithfulness; we will focus on plausibility considering the scope of this paper.

3.1 Human Rationales

Human rationales are substrings used as evidence for a decision (Zaidan et al., 2007). Faithful and sufficient (enough evidence to justify a decision) human rationales can be used as gold labels for evaluating model rationale plausibility.

The original AESW task is to predict if a sentence from a scientific paper needs editing. Daudaravicius et al. extract spans of a sentence before and after professional editing[1] as deleted (`<del>`) or inserted (`<ins>`) and provide 1.1M training, 140K validation and 140K testing examples. Sentences without changes are assumed to not require editing.

We exploit the data format to automatically extract faithful and sufficient human rationales. Delete text (text between `<del>` tags) is always a *faithful* rationale (such text is a source of the error). For edits with arbitrary `<del>` text alone and `<ins>` text, the `<del>` alone is not always a *sufficient* rationale to justify "need edit". Consider a sentence where a verb is incorrectly conjugated and replaced with the correctly conjugated verb. The incorrectly conjugated verb is not sufficient to decide that the sentence needs editing; the surrounding context is required. To find edits where `<del>` text *is* always a sufficient rationale, we use two criteria:

1. A spelling error is corrected. (*spelling error*)
2. Text is only deleted, not added. (*deleted text*)

Spelling errors are always a sufficient rationale to justify editing a sentence (see Figure 1a). In edits with no insertions, removing the `<del>` text leads to an error-free sentence, so the `<del>` text

[1]Native English speaking editors working at VTeX.

is sufficient explanation for editing (see Figure 1b). These criteria lead to both a simple, lexical task (*spelling error*) and a more challenging semantic task (*deleted text*) and constitute a wider range of challenges for future interpretability research. We extract faithful and sufficient human rationales for 1,321 *spelling error* edits and 6,741 *deleted text* edits from the validation set of AESW.[2]

3.2 Model Rationales

Model rationales are substrings provided by a model as evidence for a decision. Given a model, an example x_i and a prediction y_i, we extract three model rationales.

First, we use attention maps (Xu et al., 2015; Kovaleva et al., 2019) to rank word relevance. We measure the total attention weight from BERT's final layer's initial `[CLS]` token to each token t_j across H attention heads. Then we add those totals together for each token t_j in a word w:

$$\text{score}(w) = \sum_{t_j \in w} \sum_{h=1}^{H} \text{Attn}_{h_j}\left([\text{CLS}] \rightarrow t_j\right). \quad (1)$$

Second, we use gradient-based saliency (specifically gradient×input; Denil et al., 2015; Shrikumar et al., 2017) to rank word relevance. We calculate a saliency score for each token t_j in x_i. First, change in model output with respect to t_j's input embedding $\nabla_{e(t_j)} f_{y_i}(x_i)$ captures the sensitivity to token t. The dot product with $e(t_j)$ is then a scalar measure of each token's marginal impact on the model prediction (Han et al., 2020). Finally, we again compute a word-level score by summing over each token t_j in word w:

$$\text{score}(w) = \sum_{t_j \in w} \nabla_{e(t_j)} f_{y_i}(x_i) \cdot e(t_j) \quad (2)$$

In contrast to attention, gradient×input faithfully measures the marginal effect of each input token on the prediction (Bastings and Filippova, 2020). Finally, we extract a third set of rankings using gradient×input's magnitude to rank words.

3.3 Evaluation

We evaluate extracted rationale plausibility using similarity to human rationales (DeYoung et al., 2020). We use the continuous word scores generated in the previous section to rank relevance, then use mean reciprocal rank as an evaluation metric.[3]

4 Experiments

To demonstrate the utility of the AESW task for interpretability research, we present four experiments, each with the goal of understanding factors in PLM rationale plausibility.

For our experiments, we add a linear layer and sigmoid activation function on top of the `[CLS]` token representation, fine-tune BERT-base end-to-end on the AESW training set using the original training objective (classify a sentence as "need edit" or "no edit") and use validation loss to tune hyperparameters. We do not add any interpretability or rationale-related objectives. The classification F1 for the models on *spelling error* and *deleted text* edits is 82.0 and 74.0, respectively.[4] We extract and evaluate model rationales on all *spelling error* and *deleted text* edits, even edits that a model does not correctly predict as "need edit."

Does pre-training procedure affect rationale plausibility? We are interested in how pre-training affects plausibility after fine-tuning (to the best of our knowledge, this is a previously unexplored topic). We compare BERT and two variants, RoBERTa (Liu et al., 2019) and SciBERT (Beltagy et al., 2019). These models have the same architecture but differ in pre-training: RoBERTa is pre-trained for 5x longer with 10x more data than BERT, and SciBERT is pre-trained on a corpus of academic papers. We extract model rationales using attention weights and evaluate their plausibility.

As seen in Figure 2, RoBERTa and BERT generate nearly equally plausible rationales despite differences in pre-training corpus size. We hypothesize that SciBERT generates less plausible rationales because it encodes "need edit" representations in earlier layers (rather than in the final layer), then attends to `[SEP]` as a no-op in later layers, as proposed in Clark et al. (2019) and Kobayashi et al. (2020) and further confirmed in the subsequent experiments.

[2] More details on extracting human rationales, as well as additional examples, can be found in Appendix C

[3] We performed our analyses with additional, similar metrics; our main observations remain consistent independent of the choice of metric. Appendix D contains additional details and complete results.

[4] Appendix B contains more details on fine-tuning procedure and results.

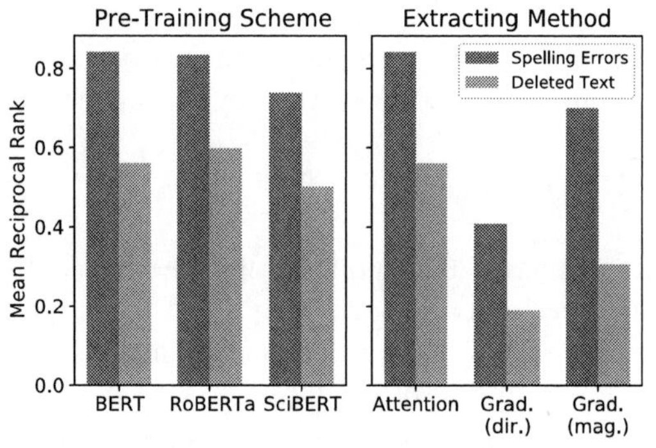

Figure 2: **Left**: BERT, RoBERTa and SciBERT's attention weight rationale plausibility. **Right**: BERT's attention weight, gradient×input and |gradient × input| rationale plausibility (see Section 3.2).

Do attention weights or input gradients produce better rationales? In contrast to attention weights, gradient×input scores are naturally faithful with respect to individual feature importance (Jain and Wallace, 2019; Bastings and Filippova, 2020). However, attention weights can represent word relevance *in context*, potentially leading to more plausible rationales. We extract and evaluate rationales using attention weights and the two gradient×input methods described in Section 3.2.

Figure 2 shows that attention-based rationales are more plausible and that the difference is more pronounced on *deleted text* edits. Using |gradient × input| (right-most) also shows improvements over directional gradient×input (middle-right), in contrast to Han et al. (2020).

Are plausibility and confidence correlated? We are curious if BERT is more confident in its classification decisions when it attends to the original evidence used by editors. We quantify BERT's classification confidence by treating the sigmoid activation function's value as the probability of a "need edit" decision. We only consider examples that BERT correctly classifies as "need edit" and calculate BERT's mean confidence. We find that when human rationales are BERT's most attended-to words, it is 11.7% and 11.9% more confident in its predictions for *spelling error* and *deleted text* edits, respectively.

One possible explanation for such a correlation is that easy-to-classify examples also have easy-to-identify rationales. Because agreement with human rationales is not the training objective, however, we believe this correlation suggests that BERT learns to classify edits similarly to humans.

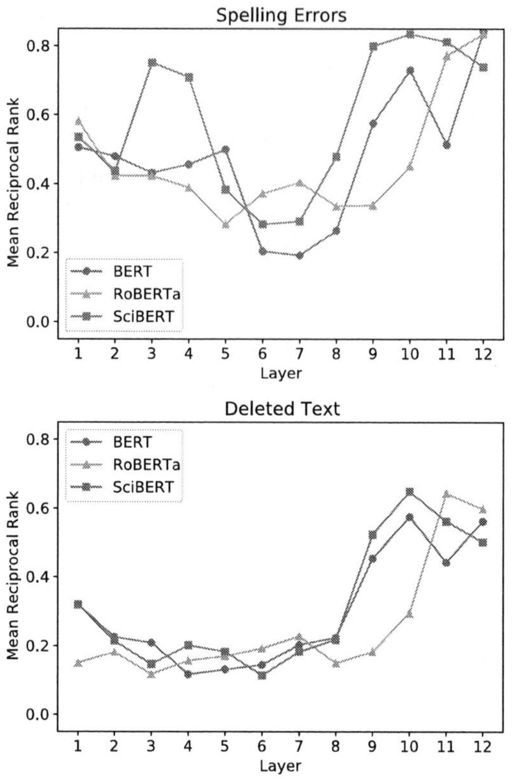

Figure 3: Mean reciprocal rank for each layer (using the *mean* strategy) for each model for *spelling error* and *deleted text* edits.[4]

How does transformer layer affect plausibility? It is widely agreed that BERT's early layers encode more lexical and phrasal information than other layers (Jawahar et al., 2019; Rogers et al., 2020). We hypothesize that rationales extracted from early layers will be more plausible for *spelling error* than *deleted text* edits because it is a more lexical task. We extract rationales from each layer's attention weights and measure their plausibility in Figure 3.

The results confirm the hypothesis and show that early layers in BERT models are indeed more lexically-oriented. We also find that SciBERT strongly attends to spelling errors in earlier layers. We believe it is because that, pre-trained on well-formed academic text, SciBERT is not as well exposed to spelling errors as BERT and RoBERTa so it learns to attend to spelling errors in earlier layers during fine-tuning.

[4]BERT shows a decline in plausibility at layer 11 in both edit types because it attends heavily to periods.

5 Conclusion

We re-purpose the AESW task to gather thousands of inherently faithful human rationales and investigate an array of questions regarding PLM interpretability. We find, among other new insights, that attention weights correlate well with human rationales and produce more plausible rationales than input gradients, which is different from existing understanding. Furthermore, we find that BERT is more confident in its predictions when it attends to the same words that a human did, supporting the idea that while attention is not inherently faithful, attention-based models might rely on the same information as humans when making a prediction.

Future work might expand the subset of examples for which human rationales can be automatically extracted, include human rationales during training or evaluate faithful-by-design model rationales on this dataset.

6 Acknowledgements

The authors would like to extend their thanks to the anonymous reviewers for their insightful feedback.

References

Dzmitry Bahdanau, Kyunghyun Cho, and Yoshua Bengio. 2016. Neural machine translation by jointly learning to align and translate. ArXiv preprint arXiv:1409.0473.

Jasmijn Bastings and Katja Filippova. 2020. The elephant in the interpretability room: Why use attention as explanation when we have saliency methods? In Proceedings of the Third BlackboxNLP Workshop on Analyzing and Interpreting Neural Networks for NLP, pages 149–155, Online. Association for Computational Linguistics.

Iz Beltagy, Kyle Lo, and Arman Cohan. 2019. SciBERT: A pretrained language model for scientific text. In Proceedings of the 2019 Conference on Empirical Methods in Natural Language Processing and the 9th International Joint Conference on Natural Language Processing (EMNLP-IJCNLP), pages 3615–3620, Hong Kong, China. Association for Computational Linguistics.

Oana-Maria Camburu, Tim Rocktäschel, Thomas Lukasiewicz, and Phil Blunsom. 2018. e-snli: Natural language inference with natural language explanations. In Advances in Neural Information Processing Systems, volume 31, pages 9539–9549. Curran Associates, Inc.

Kevin Clark, Urvashi Khandelwal, Omer Levy, and Christopher D. Manning. 2019. What does BERT look at? an analysis of BERT's attention. In Proceedings of the 2019 ACL Workshop BlackboxNLP: Analyzing and Interpreting Neural Networks for NLP, pages 276–286, Florence, Italy. Association for Computational Linguistics.

Vidas Daudaravicius, Rafael E. Banchs, Elena Volodina, and Courtney Napoles. 2016. A report on the automatic evaluation of scientific writing shared task. In Proceedings of the 11th Workshop on Innovative Use of NLP for Building Educational Applications, pages 53–62, San Diego, CA. Association for Computational Linguistics.

Misha Denil, Alban Demiraj, and Nando de Freitas. 2015. Extraction of salient sentences from labelled documents. ArXiv preprint arXiv:1412.6815.

Jacob Devlin, Ming-Wei Chang, Kenton Lee, and Kristina Toutanova. 2019. BERT: Pre-training of deep bidirectional transformers for language understanding. In Proceedings of the 2019 Conference of the North American Chapter of the Association for Computational Linguistics: Human Language Technologies, Volume 1 (Long and Short Papers), pages 4171–4186, Minneapolis, Minnesota. Association for Computational Linguistics.

Jay DeYoung, Sarthak Jain, Nazneen Fatema Rajani, Eric Lehman, Caiming Xiong, Richard Socher, and Byron C. Wallace. 2020. ERASER: A benchmark to evaluate rationalized NLP models. In Proceedings of the 58th Annual Meeting of the Association for Computational Linguistics, pages 4443–4458, Online. Association for Computational Linguistics.

Upol Ehsan, Brent Harrison, Larry Chan, and Mark O. Riedl. 2018. Rationalization: A neural machine translation approach to generating natural language explanations. In Proceedings of the 2018 AAAI/ACM Conference on AI, Ethics, and Society, AIES '18, page 81–87, New York, NY, USA. Association for Computing Machinery.

Upol Ehsan, Pradyumna Tambwekar, Larry Chan, Brent Harrison, and Mark O. Riedl. 2019. Automated rationale generation: A technique for explainable ai and its effects on human perceptions. In Proceedings of the 24th International Conference on Intelligent User Interfaces, IUI '19, page 263–274, New York, NY, USA. Association for Computing Machinery.

Xiaochuang Han, Byron C. Wallace, and Yulia Tsvetkov. 2020. Explaining black box predictions and unveiling data artifacts through influence functions. In Proceedings of the 58th Annual Meeting of the Association for Computational Linguistics, pages 5553–5563, Online. Association for Computational Linguistics.

Sarthak Jain and Byron C. Wallace. 2019. Attention is not Explanation. In Proceedings of the 2019 Conference of the North American Chapter of the Association for Computational Linguistics: Human

Language Technologies, Volume 1 (Long and Short Papers), pages 3543–3556, Minneapolis, Minnesota. Association for Computational Linguistics.

Ganesh Jawahar, Benoît Sagot, and Djamé Seddah. 2019. What does BERT learn about the structure of language? In Proceedings of the 57th Annual Meeting of the Association for Computational Linguistics, pages 3651–3657, Florence, Italy. Association for Computational Linguistics.

Daniel Khashabi, Snigdha Chaturvedi, Michael Roth, Shyam Upadhyay, and Dan Roth. 2018. Looking beyond the surface: A challenge set for reading comprehension over multiple sentences. In Proceedings of the 2018 Conference of the North American Chapter of the Association for Computational Linguistics: Human Language Technologies, Volume 1 (Long Papers), pages 252–262, New Orleans, Louisiana. Association for Computational Linguistics.

Been Kim, Rajiv Khanna, and Oluwasanmi Koyejo. 2016. Examples are not enough, learn to criticize! criticism for interpretability. In Proceedings of the 30th International Conference on Neural Information Processing Systems, NIPS'16, page 2288–2296, Red Hook, NY, USA. Curran Associates Inc.

Goro Kobayashi, Tatsuki Kuribayashi, Sho Yokoi, and Kentaro Inui. 2020. Attention is not only a weight: Analyzing transformers with vector norms. In Proceedings of the 2020 Conference on Empirical Methods in Natural Language Processing (EMNLP), pages 7057–7075, Online. Association for Computational Linguistics.

Olga Kovaleva, Alexey Romanov, Anna Rogers, and Anna Rumshisky. 2019. Revealing the dark secrets of BERT. In Proceedings of the 2019 Conference on Empirical Methods in Natural Language Processing and the 9th International Joint Conference on Natural Language Processing (EMNLP-IJCNLP), pages 4365–4374, Hong Kong, China. Association for Computational Linguistics.

Eric Lehman, Jay DeYoung, Regina Barzilay, and Byron C. Wallace. 2019. Inferring which medical treatments work from reports of clinical trials. In Proceedings of the 2019 Conference of the North American Chapter of the Association for Computational Linguistics: Human Language Technologies, Volume 1 (Long and Short Papers), pages 3705–3717, Minneapolis, Minnesota. Association for Computational Linguistics.

Yinhan Liu, Myle Ott, Naman Goyal, Jingfei Du, Mandar Joshi, Danqi Chen, Omer Levy, Mike Lewis, Luke Zettlemoyer, and Veselin Stoyanov. 2019. Roberta: A robustly optimized bert pretraining approach. ArXiv preprint arXiv:1907.11692.

Dong Nguyen. 2018. Comparing automatic and human evaluation of local explanations for text classification. In Proceedings of the 2018 Conference of the North American Chapter of the Association for Computational Linguistics: Human Language Technologies, Volume 1 (Long Papers), pages 1069–1078, New Orleans, Louisiana. Association for Computational Linguistics.

Nazneen Fatema Rajani, Bryan McCann, Caiming Xiong, and Richard Socher. 2019. Explain yourself! leveraging language models for commonsense reasoning. In Proceedings of the 57th Annual Meeting of the Association for Computational Linguistics, pages 4932–4942, Florence, Italy. Association for Computational Linguistics.

Marco Ribeiro, Sameer Singh, and Carlos Guestrin. 2016. "why should I trust you?": Explaining the predictions of any classifier. In Proceedings of the 2016 Conference of the North American Chapter of the Association for Computational Linguistics: Demonstrations, pages 97–101, San Diego, California. Association for Computational Linguistics.

Anna Rogers, Olga Kovaleva, and Anna Rumshisky. 2020. A primer in bertology: What we know about how bert works. Transactions of the Association for Computational Linguistics, 8:842–866.

Sofia Serrano and Noah A. Smith. 2019. Is attention interpretable? In Proceedings of the 57th Annual Meeting of the Association for Computational Linguistics, pages 2931–2951, Florence, Italy. Association for Computational Linguistics.

Avanti Shrikumar, Peyton Greenside, and Anshul Kundaje. 2017. Learning important features through propagating activation differences. In Proceedings of the 34th International Conference on Machine Learning, volume 70 of Proceedings of Machine Learning Research, pages 3145–3153, International Convention Centre, Sydney, Australia. PMLR.

Karen Simonyan, Andrea Vedaldi, and Andrew Zisserman. 2014. Deep inside convolutional networks: Visualising image classification models and saliency maps. ArXiv preprint arXiv:1312.6034.

Julia Strout, Ye Zhang, and Raymond Mooney. 2019. Do human rationales improve machine explanations? In Proceedings of the 2019 ACL Workshop BlackboxNLP: Analyzing and Interpreting Neural Networks for NLP, pages 56–62, Florence, Italy. Association for Computational Linguistics.

Alon Talmor, Jonathan Herzig, Nicholas Lourie, and Jonathan Berant. 2019. CommonsenseQA: A question answering challenge targeting commonsense knowledge. In Proceedings of the 2019 Conference of the North American Chapter of the Association for Computational Linguistics: Human Language Technologies, Volume 1 (Long and Short Papers), pages 4149–4158, Minneapolis, Minnesota. Association for Computational Linguistics.

James Thorne, Andreas Vlachos, Christos Christodoulopoulos, and Arpit Mittal. 2018.

FEVER: a large-scale dataset for fact extraction and VERification. In Proceedings of the 2018 Conference of the North American Chapter of the Association for Computational Linguistics: Human Language Technologies, Volume 1 (Long Papers), pages 809–819, New Orleans, Louisiana. Association for Computational Linguistics.

Thomas Wolf, Lysandre Debut, Victor Sanh, Julien Chaumond, Clement Delangue, Anthony Moi, Pierric Cistac, Tim Rault, Rémi Louf, Morgan Funtowicz, Joe Davison, Sam Shleifer, Patrick von Platen, Clara Ma, Yacine Jernite, Julien Plu, Canwen Xu, Teven Le Scao, Sylvain Gugger, Mariama Drame, Quentin Lhoest, and Alexander M. Rush. 2020. Huggingface's transformers: State-of-the-art natural language processing. ArXiv preprint arXiv:1910.03771.

Kelvin Xu, Jimmy Ba, Ryan Kiros, Kyunghyun Cho, Aaron Courville, Ruslan Salakhudinov, Rich Zemel, and Yoshua Bengio. 2015. Show, attend and tell: Neural image caption generation with visual attention. In Proceedings of the 32nd International Conference on Machine Learning, volume 37 of Proceedings of Machine Learning Research, pages 2048–2057, Lille, France. PMLR.

Omar Zaidan, Jason Eisner, and Christine Piatko. 2007. Using "annotator rationales" to improve machine learning for text categorization. In Human Language Technologies 2007: The Conference of the North American Chapter of the Association for Computational Linguistics; Proceedings of the Main Conference, pages 260–267, Rochester, New York. Association for Computational Linguistics.

Omar F. Zaidan, Jason Eisner, and Christine Piatko. 2008. Machine learning with annotator rationales to reduce annotation cost. In Proceedings of the NIPS*2008 Workshop on Cost Sensitive Learning.

A AESW Details

The original AESW task is to classify a sentence from an academic paper as "need edit" or "no edit". There is no special markup attached to the sentence when it is given as input to a model. Task participants receive the training and validation sets with `<del>` and `<ins>` tokens for model development, and Daudaravicius et al. provided an automatic test set evaluation through an online portal. Daudaravicius et al. collected these sentences from 9,919 journal articles published by Springer Publishing Company and edited at VTeX. Sentences before and after editing were automatically aligned using a modified diff algorithm.[5] After the challenge, Daudaravicius et al. released the dataset in its entirety (all three datasets with all tokens/spans included).

B Training Details

The AESW task uses scientific papers written in LaTeX, which contains markup characters that impact sentence meaning. The original authors (Daudaravicius et al.) replace these characters with special tokens, as seen in Table 1. We add these four special tokens (_MATH_, _MATHDISP_, _CITE_ and _REF_) to the model vocabulary, fine-tuning the word representations during training.

LaTeX Example	Special Token
`$\beta_{2}$`	_MATH_
`$$2 + 3$$`	_MATHDISP_
`\cite{google2018}`	_CITE_
`\ref{tab:results}`	_REF_

Table 1: Special tokens found in the original AESW data that should not be split further into bytes/tokens.

We train all models for a maximum of 30 epochs with a patience of 5 on a single Tesla P100 GPU.

All models (BERT[6], SciBERT[7], RoBERTA[8]) are based on their HuggingFace (Wolf et al., 2020) implementations.

We list all the key hyperparameters and tuning bounds for reproducibility in Table 3. Our final results for all three BERT-based models along with the top three models from (Daudaravicius et al., 2016) can be found in Table 2. Additionally, we will release code and instructions for reproducing our results.

Model	Dev F1	Test F1
CNN+LSTM	–	0.628
CNN	–	0.611
SVM	–	0.555
BERT$_{base}$	0.654	0.666
RoBERTa$_{base}$	**0.661**	**0.670**
SciBERT$_{scivocab}$	0.658	0.668

Table 2: Performance on the original AESW sentence classification task. Dev set results are not available for models reported in Daudaravicius et al. (2016).

C Gathering Human Rationales

To find *spelling error* edits, we look for sentences with a deleted, misspelled word followed by an inserted, correctly spelled word. The first two examples in Figure 4 are examples of *spelling error* edits, while the third is not.

To find *deleted text* edits, we look for sentences where text is removed but not added. The fourth and fifth examples in Figure 4 are examples of *deleted text* edits.

D Evaluating Model Rationales

Although the main text presents our analyses using mean reciprocal rank, we performed our analyses with multiple metrics. Here we provide specific definitions for our metrics and our complete results for all models with every metric.

Mean reciprocal rank Because human rationales can be made up of multiple words, we need to modify mean reciprocal ranking. For a single sentence, a model's ordered ranking of words M and an unordered human rationale H:

1. Find the top ranked word w in M from H and record the rank.
2. Remove w from M and H.
3. Repeat until H is empty.
4. Use the reciprocal of the mean rank.

If we did not remove words from M, a perfect score for a rationale with multiple words would be impossible. Consider the sentence "The boy ~~ate the~~ **found his** ball." If the rationale ranked 'ate' and 'the' as most important, the mean rationale rank would be $(1 + 2)/2 = 1.5$ and the rationale's reciprocal rank would be $1/1.5 = 0.66$, despite a perfect rationale.

[5] More details can be found in (Daudaravicius et al., 2016)

[6] https://huggingface.co/transformers/v3.0.2/model_doc/bert.html#bertforsequenceclassification

[7] https://github.com/allenai/scibert#pytorch-huggingface-models

[8] https://huggingface.co/transformers/v3.0.2/model_doc/roberta.html#robertaforsequenceclassification

Model	Hyperparameters	Hyperparameter bounds
BERT$_{base}$	learning rate: 1×10^{-6} batch size: 32 model: bert-base-uncased vocab size: 30526 (normally 30522)	learning rate: (2×10^{-7}, 1×10^{-6}, 2×10^{-5}, 1×10^{-4})
RoBERTa$_{base}$	learning rate: 1×10^{-6} batch size: 32 model: roberta-base vocab size: 50269 (normally 50265)	learning rate: (1×10^{-6})
SciBERT	learning rate: 1×10^{-6} batch size: 32 model: allenai/scibert_scivocab_uncased vocab size: 31094 (normally 31090)	learning rate: (1×10^{-6})

Table 3: Hyperparameter options for each model. Note that each model had 4 special tokens added to the vocabulary. BERT was fine-tuned first. Because of compute limitations, RobERTa and SciBERT were both fine-tuned using the same hyperparameters as the optimal BERT configuration (learning rate of (1×10^{-6})).

We take the mean reciprocal ranking across all examples to evaluate rationales.

Mean area under precision-recall curve Using the model relevance scores for words in a sentence, we adjust the threshold for classifying a word as part of the rationale, calculate a precision-recall curve and measure the area underneath. We take the mean AUPRC across all examples.

Mean top 1 match We score a rationale as 1 if the rationale's top ranked word is the human rationale and 0 otherwise. This means that all multiple-word rationales are automatically not a match and scored as 0. We take the mean of these scores across all examples.

Our main observations are consistent across metrics: Table 4 contains all results for models on *spelling error* edits and Table 5 contains all results for models on *deleted text* edits.

Model	F1	Method	Classification	Mean Recip.	AUPRC	Top 1 Match
BERT	82.1	Attention	All	0.841	0.115	0.756
BERT	100.0	Attention	Correct	0.895	0.081	0.824
BERT	0.0	Attention	Wrong	0.717	0.194	0.602
BERT	82.1	gradient×input	All	0.407	0.332	0.325
BERT	100.0	gradient×input	Correct	0.401	0.335	0.322
BERT	0.0	gradient×input	Wrong	0.422	0.325	0.331
BERT	82.1	|gradient × input|	All	0.701	0.201	0.579
BERT	100.0	|gradient × input|	Correct	0.730	0.184	0.615
BERT	0.0	|gradient × input|	Wrong	0.635	0.241	0.498
RoBERTa	81.4	Attention	All	0.834	0.118	0.739
RoBERTa	100.0	Attention	Correct	0.886	0.085	0.811
RoBERTa	0.0	Attention	Wrong	0.721	0.192	0.581
RoBERTa	81.4	gradient×input	All	0.310	0.380	0.231
RoBERTa	100.0	gradient×input	Correct	0.303	0.383	0.229
RoBERTa	0.0	gradient×input	Wrong	0.324	0.375	0.236
RoBERTa	81.4	|gradient × input|	All	0.675	0.219	0.546
RoBERTa	100.0	|gradient × input|	Correct	0.707	0.201	0.583
RoBERTa	0.0	|gradient × input|	Wrong	0.605	0.259	0.463
SciBERT	86.8	Attention	All	0.739	0.203	0.577
SciBERT	100.0	Attention	Correct	0.830	0.138	0.707
SciBERT	0.0	Attention	Wrong	0.442	0.415	0.152
SciBERT	86.8	gradient×input	All	0.475	0.296	0.399
SciBERT	100.0	gradient×input	Correct	0.467	0.296	0.401
SciBERT	0.0	gradient×input	Wrong	0.501	0.295	0.392
SciBERT	86.8	|gradient × input|	All	0.670	0.214	0.557
SciBERT	100.0	|gradient × input|	Correct	0.698	0.197	0.591
SciBERT	0.0	|gradient × input|	Wrong	0.575	0.268	0.447

Table 4: Results for all three models for *spelling error* edits across all methods of selecting rationales (attention, gradient×input and |gradient × input|) and all metrics to evaluate rationales (mean reciprocal ranking, AUPRC and mean top 1 match).

Model	F1	Method	Classification	Mean Recip.	AUPRC	Top 1 Match
BERT	74.0	Attention	All	0.561	0.272	0.411
BERT	100.0	Attention	Correct	0.680	0.211	0.528
BERT	0.0	Attention	Wrong	0.391	0.359	0.244
BERT	74.0	gradient×input	All	0.189	0.447	0.074
BERT	100.0	gradient×input	Correct	0.195	0.442	0.089
BERT	0.0	gradient×input	Wrong	0.181	0.454	0.054
BERT	74.0	|gradient × input|	All	0.306	0.416	0.130
BERT	100.0	|gradient × input|	Correct	0.354	0.399	0.166
BERT	0.0	|gradient × input|	Wrong	0.238	0.440	0.078
RoBERTa	74.8	Attention	All	0.598	0.263	0.426
RoBERTa	100.0	Attention	Correct	0.662	0.230	0.487
RoBERTa	0.0	Attention	Wrong	0.503	0.312	0.335
RoBERTa	74.8	gradient×input	All	0.168	0.456	0.058
RoBERTa	100.0	gradient×input	Correct	0.156	0.458	0.054
RoBERTa	0.0	gradient×input	Wrong	0.187	0.452	0.063
RoBERTa	74.8	|gradient × input|	All	0.321	0.404	0.154
RoBERTa	100.0	|gradient × input|	Correct	0.367	0.384	0.194
RoBERTa	0.0	|gradient × input|	Wrong	0.252	0.434	0.094
SciBERT	73.9	Attention	All	0.501	0.327	0.304
SciBERT	100.0	Attention	Correct	0.605	0.270	0.414
SciBERT	0.0	Attention	Wrong	0.353	0.406	0.148
SciBERT	73.9	gradient×input	All	0.226	0.426	0.111
SciBERT	100.0	gradient×input	Correct	0.260	0.410	0.145
SciBERT	0.0	gradient×input	Wrong	0.178	0.450	0.062
SciBERT	73.9	|gradient × input|	All	0.322	0.400	0.162
SciBERT	100.0	|gradient × input|	Correct	0.356	0.387	0.189
SciBERT	0.0	|gradient × input|	Wrong	0.275	0.418	0.123

Table 5: Results for all three models for *deleted text* edits across all methods of selecting rationales (attention, gradient×input and |gradient × input|) and all metrics to evaluate rationales (mean reciprocal ranking, AUPRC and mean top 1 match).

```
The algorithm <del>descripted</del><ins>described</ins> in the
previous sections has several advantages.
```
A *spelling error* edit; “descripted” is a spelling error and is corrected.

```
For each energy point, the thereby obtained cross-section values
and errors from different experiments have been further averaged
according to the <del>weigthed</del><ins>weighted</ins> average
method used by the Particle Data Group _CITE_, including error
rescaling by _MATH_ in case of large discrepancy.
```
A *spelling error* edit; “weigthed” is a spelling error and is corrected.

```
And the short notations for the denominators are _MATHDISP_,
Furthermore, the following relations are useful to
<del>short</del><ins>shortcut</ins> the expressions:  _MATHDISP_.
```
Not a spelling error edit; “short” is incorrect in this context, but it is not a spelling error.

```
However, we <del>must note that we </del>still have no means of
deciding which documents out of _MATH_ deserve to be in _MATH_ and
_MATH_, respectively.
```
A *deleted text* edit; text is only removed, while no text is inserted.

```
Let _MATH_ be the conjugate Holder<del>'s</del> function of a
Holder<del>'s</del> function _MATH_.
```
A *deleted text* edit; text is only removed, while no text is inserted.

Figure 4: Additional examples of the two types of edits extracted from the original AESW dataset.

Interacting Knowledge Sources, Inspection and Analysis: Case-studies on Biomedical Text Processing

Parsa Bagherzadeh and Sabine Bergler
CLaC Labs, Concordia Univeristy
Montréal, Canada
{p_bagher, bergler}@cse.concordia.ca

Abstract

In this paper we investigate the recently proposed multi-input RIM for inspectability. This framework follows an encapsulation paradigm, where external knowledge sources are encoded as largely independent modules, enabling transparency for model inspection.

1 Introduction

Deep learning with pre-trained language models is widely used in a variety of NLP tasks. Such models are often trained using an end-to-end approach, which assumes that the structure of the network is sufficient to capture the inductive bias from adequate data, using a gradient-descent approach.

Deploying language models for applications such as biomedical text processing, however, poses two main challenges. First, adequate training data is often not available due to the cost of annotation by domain experts and, indeed, the exploratory nature of most biomedical tasks. Second, the biomedical domain uses many terms with a more specialized meaning and language models often cannot demonstrate an understanding of this meaning. For instance, consider Example 1:

(1) *TNFAIP3 is a gene whose expression is induced by the tumor necrosis factor.*

Example 1 defines TNFAIP3 as a *gene* in a copula construction and its *expression* in a relative clause. We mask the token *gene* and ask BioBERT (Lee et al., 2020) (as a masked language model) to predict the masked token. The top 5 predictions are *simulation, coordinates, diffusion, heat,* and *pyramid.* The default solution is to continue the pretraining process of the language models on larger corpora, which is often prohibitive for users with limited access to computational resources. Moreover, biomedical terminologies are always growing and enough textual data might not be available for new concepts. A cheaper option is to use extant quality knowledge sources, in form of ontologies, hierarchies, or specialized gazetteer lists. In the developing field of knowledge injected models, these high-quality, general knowledge sources are expected to work in tandem to address the problem at hand (Søgaard and Goldberg, 2016; Levy and Goldberg, 2014; Tian et al., 2020; Bagherzadeh and Bergler, 2020).

Current knowledge injection models introduce specialized layers to language models or add new training objectives. For instance, (Peters et al., 2019) developed KnowBERT (an extension to BERT), to inject information from WordNet into an intermediate layer of BERT, which requires retraining the BERT model. To leverage medical concepts from the medical knowledge base ULMS, (Hao et al., 2020) added an auxiliary prediction task to the BERT model by training a binary classifier to predict relations between two concepts.

The chosen knowledge source is an integral part of these language models making their contribution difficult to inspect. In precision-oriented applications, users require to understand why and how a prediction is made. Inspection of a system helps developers to detect fallacies in a system and provide insight for the improvement of the system (Verma et al., 2020; Amini and Kosseim, 2019) and users to trust the autonomous system.

Different knowledge sources might include overlapping, contradicting, or differently aimed knowledge,[1] and the wrong components may hamper rather than enhance the learning progress (Glasmachers, 2017). In contrast, if the knowledge sources can adapt to the domain separately and only interact sparingly, the resulting model is expected to be robust (Schölkopf et al., 2012; Goyal et al., 2019)

(Bagherzadeh and Bergler, 2021b) introduced

[1] A *size* feature may encode *height, width,* or *volume*, for instance.

Proceedings of the Fourth BlackboxNLP Workshop on Analyzing and Interpreting Neural Networks for NLP, pages 447–456
Online, November 11, 2021.

the multi-input Recurrent Independent Mechanisms (mi-RIM), which comprise a set of independent and competitive recurrent modules that operate individually on different knowledge embeddings. They report that adding gazetteer and POS tag modules consistently improves performance on a variety of tasks. The mi-RIM architecture injects knowledge in form of different knowledge sources as largely independent modules. They suggest that activation visualizations of each module allow for inspection but do not further probe whether they provide enough insight to explain the system predictions.

This paper offers an in-depth analysis of the contribution of several knowledge sources in several tasks within the mi-RIM framework. We confirm that once modules compete, they specialize to focus on different parts of the input and inspect the competition patterns during processing as a source for explanation and user feed-back.

2 Overview of mi-RIM

Recurrent independent mechanisms (RIM), first introduced by (Goyal et al., 2019), is a modular architecture that models a dynamic system by dividing it into M recurrent units, all of which operate on the same input sequence. The units are selective, i.e they chose to use or ignore their input, and are able to communicate with one another. The standard RIM model was adapted to the language domain and extended by (Bagherzadeh and Bergler, 2021b) to multi-input RIMs (mi-RIM) to allow different modules to operate on different inputs. Since we use mi-RIMs in our case study, a brief overview of their model is provided in the following.

Input selection Each module R_m augments the token input x_t^m to $X_t^m = x_t^m \oplus \mathbf{0}$, where $\mathbf{0}$ is an all-zero vector and $\oplus$ denotes row-level concatenation. Then, using an attention mechanism, unit R_m selects input:

$$A_t^m = softmax\left(\frac{h_{t-1}^m W_m^{query}(K_m)^T}{\sqrt{d_h}}\right) V_m \quad (1)$$

where $h_{t-1}^m W_m^{query}$ is the *query*, $K_m = X_t^m W_m^{key}$ is the *key*, and $V_m = X_t W_m^{val}$ is the *value* in the attention mechanism (Vaswani et al., 2017). If the input x_t is considered relevant to the task, the attention mechanism in Equation 1 assigns more weight to it (selects it), otherwise more weight will be assigned to the null input. The $softmax$ values of Equation 1 determine a ranking for the modules and a subset S_t of the k highest ranked units. Among M units, those with the least attention on the null input are the active units. The selected input A_t^m determines a temporary hidden state $\tilde{h}_t^m$ for the active units:

$$\tilde{h}_t^m = R_m(h_{t-1}^m, A_t^m) \quad m \in S_t \quad (2)$$

where $R_m(h_{t-1}^m, A_t^m)$ denotes one iteration of updating the recurrent unit R_m based on previous state h_{t-1}^m and current input A_t^m. The hidden states of the inactive units R_m $(m \notin S_t)$ remain unchanged:

$$h_t^m = h_{t-1}^m \quad m \notin S_t \quad (3)$$

Communication To obtain the actual hidden states h_t^m, the active units communicate using an attention mechanism:

$$h_t^m = softmax\left(\frac{Q_{t,m}(K_{t,:})^T}{\sqrt{d_h}}\right) V_{t,:} + \tilde{h}_t^m \quad m \in S_t \quad (4)$$

where

$$Q_{t,m} = \tilde{h}_t^m \tilde{W}_m^{query}$$

$K_{t,:}$ is the row-level concatenation of all $K_{t,m}$ $(m = 1, \ldots, M)$ defined as:

$$K_{t,m} = \tilde{h}_t^m \tilde{W}_m^{key}$$

and $V_{t,:}$ is the row-level concatenation of all $V_{t,m}$ $(m = 1, \ldots, M)$ defined as:

$$V_{t,m} = \tilde{h}_t^m \tilde{W}_m^{val}$$

Both the key $K_{t,:}$ and the value $V_{t,:}$ depend on the temporary hidden states of all units, therefore h_t^m in Equation 4 is determined by attending to all units.

As pointed out by (Wiegreffe and Pinter, 2019), the attention-based models can provide explanation when the attention is applied to individual elements in an input sequence, rather than contextualized ones. Similarly, input selection attention for the mi-RIM architecture also operates on raw input encoding. When an input is considered to be relevant to the task, the corresponding module is allowed to be active and to be updated with its additional, specialized input. The activation patterns for each module are traced to inspect what elements in the input sequence were used.

3 Tasks

This paper focuses on the biomedical domain for two reasons. First, effective knowledge components for many biomedical tasks are well-defined and high quality knowledge sources are freely available. Second, model inspection is essential in the biomedical domain, particularly for health related applications. The following four tasks are considered here:

BC7-3 or BioCreative VII Task 3 is a sequence labelling task for detecting spans of drug mentions in tweets.[2] Example 2 shows a tweet with one mention of a drug (*Zantac*), and Example 3 is a tweet with no drug mention. BC7-3 is evaluated by F1 score.

(2) *Sprite and Zantac. was not the best idea.*

(3) *The meds have arrived!!*

BC2-1a or BioCreative II Task 1a concerns extraction of gene mentions in biomedical texts (Smith et al., 2008). Example 4 contains a gene mention (*alpha fetoprotein*) and Example 5 does not contain any gene mentions. The performance is evaluated by F1 score.

(4) *False positive amniotic fluid alpha fetoprotein levels resulting from contamination with fetal blood*

(5) *Teratological study of etoperidone in the rat and rabbit.*

SM21-1a concerns adverse drug event classification of tweets (Klein et al., 2021). Examples 6 and 7 are instances of tweets with and without an adverse drug event respectively. The task is evaluate by F1 score.

(6) *worst was the psychotic episode when starting #paxil*

(7) *need nicotine*

SM21-6 is a three-way classification task of tweets containing CoVID symptom mentions (Klein et al., 2021). In *self-report* tweets (Example 8), posters mention a Covid symptom that they have experienced. *Nonpersonal-reports* however report a symptom for someone else (Example 9), and *News-mentions* are symptom reports that are intended to raise awareness (Example 10). This task is evaluated by the micro-F1 score (μF1) of the *self-reports* and *Nonpersonal-reports* classes.

(8) *I am still breathless upon exertion, but my shortness of breath and cough that used to happen all the time*

(9) my mom was denied a coronavirus test even tho she has a high fever and corona symptoms.

(10) *Many of these patients with post-#COVID19 fatigue will have an abnormal tilt table test and a form of #dysautonomia.*

Note that since the gold labels for BC7-3, SM21-1a, and SM21-6 have not been disclosed, we report the result on a hold out set (20% of the training data).

4 Knowledge sources

For reproducibility, we use off the shelf knowledge sources that are available from standard NLP and deep learning environments, or can be easily accessed from online ontological repositories.

Morphology Drug or gene names often have a specific morphology, favoring certain prefixes, suffixes, etc. The suffix *-statin*, for instance, is observed in drug names of this type, including *torvastatin, lovastatin,* and *pravastatin*. Such morphological information[3] can be used to detect possible mentions of drugs or genes that have not been observed in training data, or those that are not present in drug or gene lists.

Word embeddings BioBERT (Lee et al., 2020) word embeddings provide a meaning representation based on co-occurrence statistics.

POS Part-of-speech tags are the most widely used linguistic feature and are available from many standard NLP environments. POS tags provide useful information such as types of pronouns and tense for verbs, allimportant clues for sequence labeling and text classification.

[2] `https://biocreative.bioinformatics.udel.edu/tasks/biocreative-vii/track-3/`

[3] Note that the subtoken input for BERT models can detect these regularities.

Drug DrugBank includes commercial drug names as well as the scientific names of their active ingredients (Wishart et al., 2018).[4]

Anatomy Body part mentions are important evidence for detection of health experience mentions, in particular adverse drug reactions or disease symptoms. Relevant anatomy terms are extracted from sub-tree A of MeSH (Lipscomb, 2000) into a gazetteer list.

Disease Disease mentions are important evidence for adverse drug event classification and self-reports of disease symptoms. A gazetteer was compiled from subtree C in MeSH which includes terms for *infections, wounds, injuries, pain, etc.*.

Gene To identify mentions of genes, we compile a gazetteer list from the NCBI Gene database. [5]

5 Implementation

Preprocessing We preprocess the data using a GATE pipeline (Cunningham et al., 2002) and use the ANNIE tweet tokenizer as well as the hashtag tokenizer for BC7-3, SM21-6, and SM21-1a data, and the PennBio tokenzier for BC2-1a data. For tweet tasks, we remove URLs and user mentions.

Modules Each module m comprises an embedder E_m (for encoding a knowledge source) and a recurrent unit R_m. For the token at position t, E_m emits its knowledge representation $x_t^m \in \mathbb{R}^{d_{in}^m}$ and $X_t^m = x_t^m \oplus \mathbf{0}$ is used as input to the recurrent layer R_m.

Morph. Following (Kim et al., 2016) we use a character-level Convolutional Neural Network to obtain a morphological representation for each token. We use multiple convolution filters $\mathcal{F}_l$ with different lengths of $l \in \{2, 3, 4, 5\}$. The resulting character-based representations are in a 100-dimensional space.

Word emb. We use the last layer of BioBERT (Lee et al., 2020) to obtain word embeddings. The embeddings are then used as input to a LSTM.

POS Following (Bagherzadeh and Bergler, 2021a), we pre-train POS tags using Word2Vec (Mikolov et al., 2013) to initialize an embedding layer.

Gazetteer modules Each gazetteer list is embedded by two trainable vectors, one corresponding to a match against the gazetteer, and another one for a mismatch. The gazetteer embedings are then used as input to simple RNN units rather than LSTMs.

All NN components are implemented using PyTorch (Paszke et al., 2017), using cross-entropy to calculate loss and the Adam optimizer (Kingma and Ba, 2015).

6 Experiments

We report three sets of experiments. First, we inject different knowledge sources using the mi-RIM model, and evaluate their effectiveness in terms of precision (P), recall (R), and F1 scores. Second, we inspect the activity profiles of the modules for several samples. Third, we provide a quantitative analysis on whether module activity can be used to provide insight into model's predictions using Total Variation Distance (TVD) (Jain and Wallace, 2019) as a measure of change between output distributions.

6.1 Performance

We investigate whether each knowledge source can contribute to each of the different tasks and how different knowledge sources cooperate or whether redundancy or contradicting values decrease performance.

Carefully selected sources Table 1 reports performance when using the four modules *Word Emb., Morph, Drug,* and *POS* on the drug mention detection task BC7-3. Three different competition settings are reported, $k \in \{1, 2, 3\}$. Greater k values are not reported, because performance drops.

Modules	k	P	R	F1
Word Emb.	1	.60	.69	.64
System BC7-3:	3	.67	.68	.67
Word Emb., Morph, Drug, POS	2	.69	**.70**	**.70**
	1	**.70**	.63	.66

Table 1: 4 module mi-RIM system on BC7-3

Table 2 reports performance when using the four modules *Word Emb., Morph, Gene,* and *POS* on the gene mention detection task BC2-1a. Both

[4] https://go.drugbank.com/drugs/DB00863 identifies *Zantac* (Example 2) as a drug mention

[5] *alpha fetoprotein* in Example 4 is identified by https://www.ncbi.nlm.nih.gov/gene/174

BioCreative mention detection tasks show best performance when only two modules can be active at a time.

Modules	k	P	R	F1
Word Emb.	1	.85	.84	.84
System BC2-1a:	3	.86	.86	.86
Word Emb., Morph, Gene, POS	2	**.89**	.85	**.87**
	1	.82	**.89**	.85
SOTA (Lee et al., 2020)	–	.85	.83	.84

Table 2: 4 module mi-RIM system on BC2-1a

Table 3 shows a similar behaviour for five modules on the adverse drug reaction classification task SM21-1a.

Modules	k	P	R	F1
Word Emb.	1	.56	.63	.58
System SM21-1a:	3	.57	.67	.62
Word Emb., Drug,	2	.59	.70	**.64**
Disease, Anatomy, POS	1	**.53**	.74	.63

Table 3: 5 module mi-RIM system on SM21-1a

Modules	k	μP	μR	μF1
Word Emb.	1	92	.93	.92
System SM21-6:	3	.94	.95	.94
Word Emb., Disease,	2	.95	.95	**.95**
Anatomy, POS	1	.92	**.96**	.94

Table 4: 4 module mi-RIM system on SM21-6

The external knowledge sources consistently improve performance across the tasks. Peak performance (F1) is reached for $k = 2$.

This forms a proof of concept that external knowledge sources can be harnessed in fixed configurations tailored to specific tasks. This has been shown in different architectures as well.

Some redundant sources We claim that the mi-RIM architecture can combine redundant and possibly contradicting knowledge sources with no ill effects and offer as justification a seven module system combining all the knowledge sources introduced here and comparing its performance on all the tasks.

Table 5 shows that in fact, the overabundance of these resources slightly lowers performance sometimes (SM21-6), but sometimes improves performance further. We consider this a strong endorsement of the claim.

6.2 Visualization of activation patterns

When $k < M$, only a subset of modules is allowed to contribute and the modules enter into competition mode. As claimed by (Goyal et al., 2019), competition for activity makes the modules to focus on specific parts of the input. We probe activation patterns for varying k.

	BC7-3			*BC2-1a*			*SM21-1a*			*SM21-6*		
k	P	R	F1	P	R	F1	P	R	F1	P	R	μF1
3	.69	.68	.68	.87	.86	.86	.59	.66	.63	.93	.93	.93
2	.70	.70	.70	**.88**	**.87**	**.87**	**.62**	.69	**.66**	.94	**.95**	.94
1	.69	.68	.67	.83	.88	.85	.55	.73	.64	.91	.94	.93

Table 5: Seven module system (Word Emb., Morph, POS, Drug, Disease, Anatomy, Gene) on all tasks

Figures 1–9 show the activation patterns for the four tasks. In each figure's caption, the input is given and the gold spans are indicated as underlined text. Moreover, the correctly tagged tokens are indicated by solid boxes, and the false positives by dashed boxes.

Sequence labeling tasks Figure 1 is an instance of a true-positive classification for BC7-3 (drug mention span detection). When $k = 3$, the *Drug* module is only active when there is a match with the Drug gazetteer; *Fentanyl*. Other modules however are always active which means that they are not focusing on a specific part of the input. On the other hand, when $k = 2$ the *Morph* module is active only for the drug mention, which means that the competition has made the module more focused. For this example, activation patterns of the seven module system for $k = 2$ are identical. Note that for $k = 1$, only the *Drug* module is active for the mention of Fentanyl, indicating that the model prioritizes the high quality drug gazetteer over the general *Morph* module when a choice has to be made.

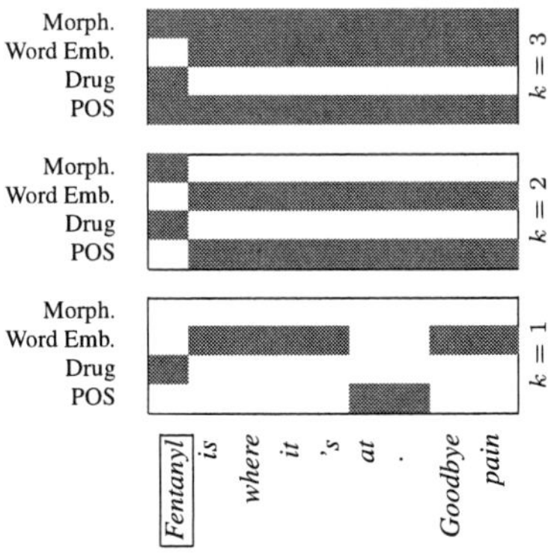

Figure 1: True positive case for BC7-3: Fentanyl *is where it's at. Goodbye pain*

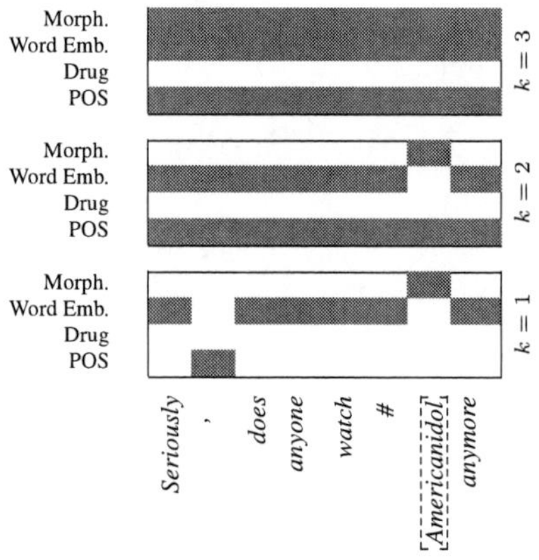

Figure 2: False positive case for BC7-3: *Seriously, does anyone watch #Americanidol anymore*

Figure 2, on the other hand, shows a false-positive case for BC7-3. *Americanidol* has been identified as a drug mention. When $k < 3$, the *Morph* module is active only for the supposed drug mention, suggesting the cause of the misclassification: the token *Americanidol* is a good candidate for a drug name based on its morphological structure: it is capitalized, a composite name, and ends in *ol*. Inspection of such cases using the activation patterns provides valuable insight for users and developers, and allows users to give nuanced feedback to developers capitalizing on their expertise. For instance, expert users might suggest enhancing the tokenizer to split hashtags, for instance, *#Americanidol* into [*#, American, idol*] instead of [*#, Americanidol*]. For this example, activation patterns of the seven module system for $k = 2$ are identical.

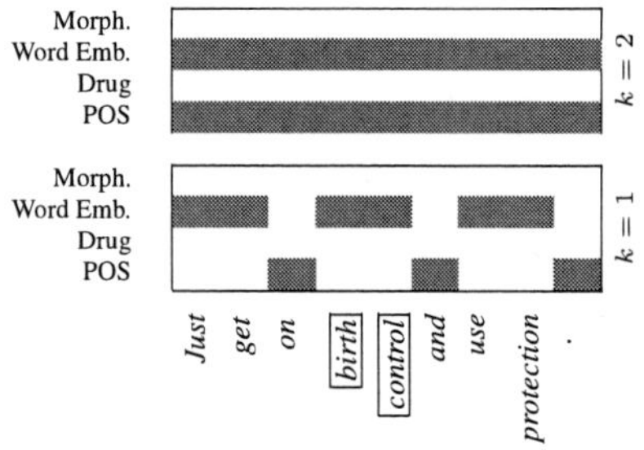

Figure 3: True positive case for BC7-3: *Just get on birth control and use protection*

Figure 3 shows another example of a correctly tagged drug. The term *birth control* is not recognized by the Drug gazetteer, therefore, the *Drug* module is never active. In competition mode ($k = 1$ or $k = 2$), the *Morph* module is also never active, however, the *Word Emb.* module at $k = 1$ is active for the span of *birth control*, and contributes its input.

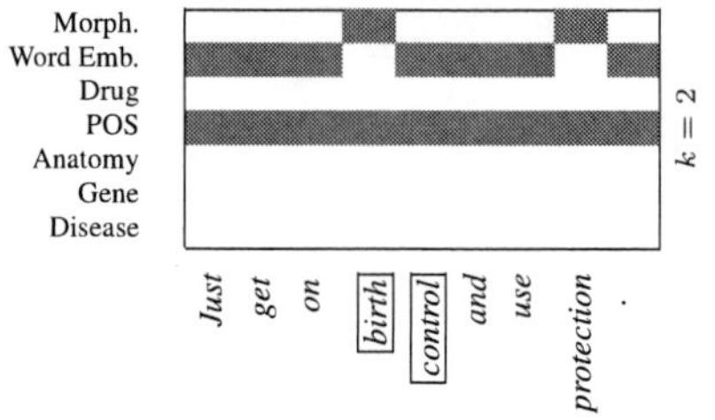

Figure 4: True positive case for BC7-3, 7-modules system: *Just get on birth control and use protection*

This example demonstrates the advantage of redundant capability in a highly competitive context ($k = 1$) and showcases the overgeneralization process for the deep modules *Morph* and *Word Emb.* in the context of redundancy. If a knowledge source (in this case a gazetteer list) has limited expertise, other modules can compensate (capability) but a danger of synchronization exists for fully redundant modes. Figure 4 demonstrates that an abundance of modules can lead to more specialized patterns.

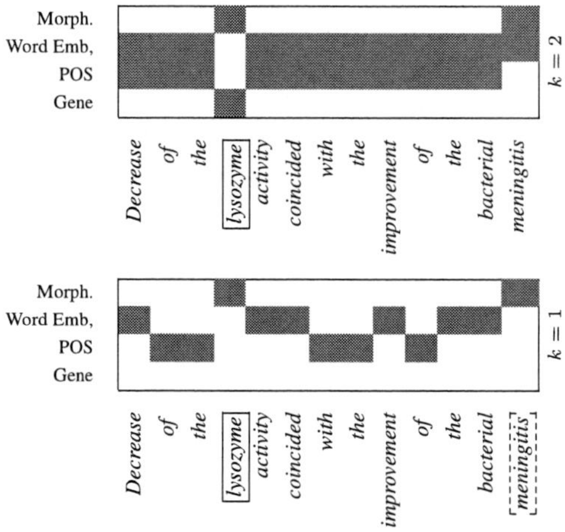

Figure 5: True positive and false positive cases for BC2-1a: *Decrease of the lysozyme activity coincided with the improvement of the bacterial meningitis.*

Figure 5 shows the activation patterns for a sample from BC2-1a. We see a behaviour similar to those for the drug span task; once modules are in competition, they are more focused on specific parts of the input. An interesting observation here is the difference between predictions when k has different values. When $k = 2$ and $k = 3$, the model correctly tags only *lysozyme* as a gene mention. However, when $k = 1$, the model makes a false positive prediction for *meningitis* as well. Note that when $k = 1$, the *Morph* module is active for the token *meningitis*. In this case, the *Morph* module has won the competition and has forced the *Word Emb.* module to be inactive, which is the result of intense competition between modules. This however is not the case when $k = 2$ and both *Morph* and *Word Emb.* modules are active and contribute to a correct prediction.

Document-level tasks Figure 6 shows a true-positive case from SM21-1a. Similar to previous patterns, the more the modules are in competition (smaller k), the more their activities are sparse and focused. The *Anatomy* module is active for the body parts mentions *tendons* and *hands*, and the *Disease* module is active for *pain* and *ruptured*. Note that the *Word Emb.* module is inactive for tokens that are matched with gazetteer lists. On the other hand, the *Word Emb.* module is active for phrases/tokens such as *barely usable* and *damned*, as other evidence for the adverse event classification. The seven modules system again leads to a more specialized pattern in Figure 7.

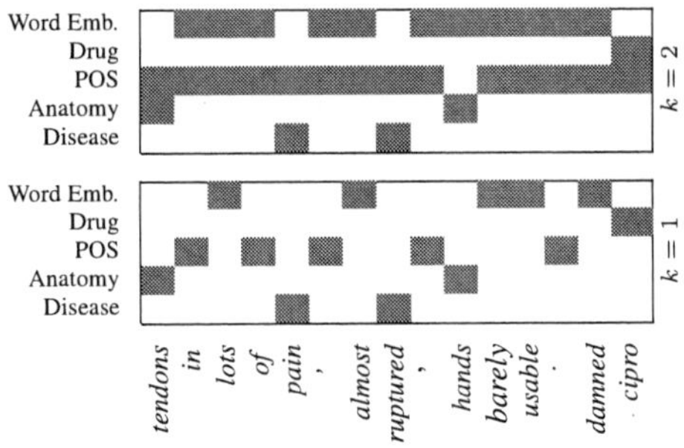

Figure 6: True positive case for SM21-1a: *tendons in lots of pain, almost ruptured & hands barely usable. damned cipro*

Figure 8 on the other hand shows a false-positive case for SM21-1a (adverse drug effect mentions). Note that the tweet is an example of a text with figurative language. When $k = 1$, the *Word Emb.* module is active for the phrases *the marbles made my* and *look pink*. It seems the activity on *look pink* has mislead the model to make a false-positive prediction.

The seven module system shows unfortunately that the abundance of modules is not sufficient to rectify the error, even though the module activations change in certain parts: *Word Emb.* relieves *POS* for *adderall* and *Morph* relieves *Word Emb.* for *marbles*.

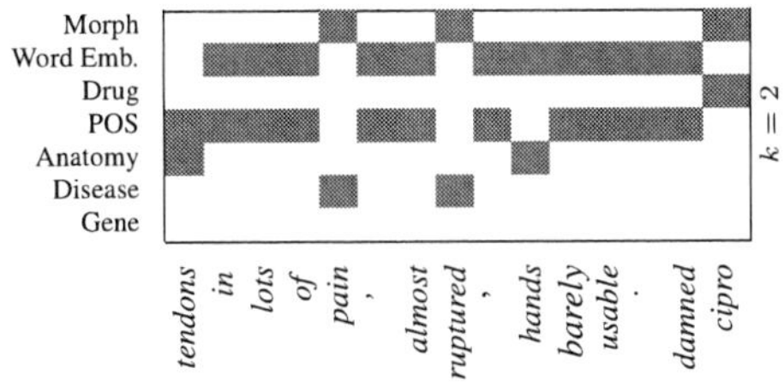

Figure 7: True positive case for SM21-1a, 7 module system: *tendons in lots of pain, almost ruptured & hands barely usable. damned cipro*

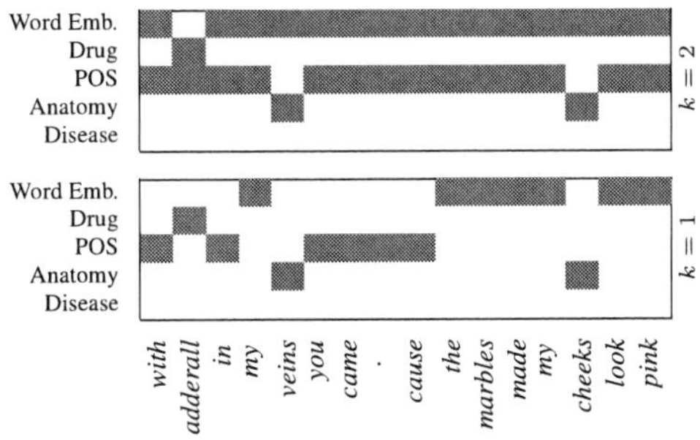

Figure 8: False positive case for SM21-1a: *with adderall in my veins you came. cause the marbles made my cheecks look pink.*

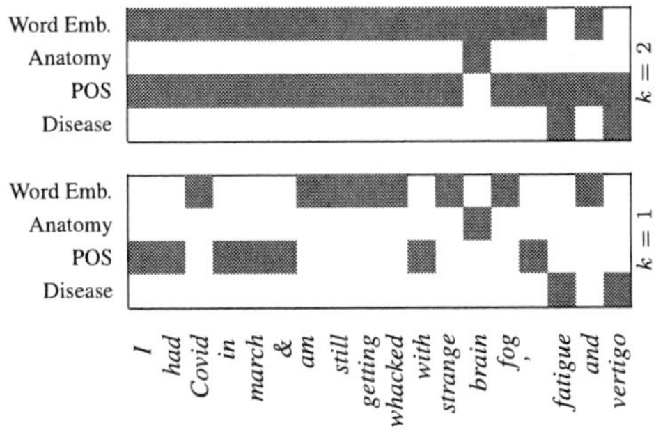

Figure 9: True positive case for SM21-6: *I had Covid in march & am still getting whacked with strange brain fog, fatigue and vertigo*

Finally, an example of a true-positive prediction for SM21-6 (self-reports of CoVID symptoms) is provided in Figure 9. There are three symptom mentions such as *brain fog*, *fatigue*, and *vertigo*, and the *Disease* module is active for the latter two. Interestingly, when $k = 1$, the *Word Emb.* module is active for the token *Covid* and has won the competition against the *Disease* module. Further analysis of the activation patterns revealed that at 77% of the time, the *Disease* module is active only when a token corresponds to a symptom. However, when the actual name of the disease is mentioned, the *Word Emb.* module is active. We surmise, due to the frequent occurrence of terms such as *Covid* and *Corona* in the training set, the *Word Emb.* module has learned to focus on such tokens, and the *Disease* module covers the more lexically-diverse symptom mentions. More module choice in the seven modules system for $k = 2$ leads to three changes: *Morph* is active for *Covid*, *whacked*, and *fatigue*, relieving *Word Emb.* at these time points.

As argued by (Wiegreffe and Pinter, 2019) and (Serrano and Smith, 2019) the attention mechanism fails to provide explanation, since it operates on the contextualized representations. This, however is not the case for the models in the mi-RIM architecture since module activity is the result of the input selection mechanism, assuring that when a module is not active at a particular time-step, it is guaranteed that its input is not used.

6.3 Quantitative analysis of module activity

(Jain and Wallace, 2019) argue that if attention weights provide insight into why a prediction is made, removing a token accorded with a high attention weight has to significantly change the output distribution. In other words, the question is *had we not attended to an element, would we have the same output?* A yes to this question means there is no association between the input with high attention weight and the prediction. A no to this question however shows that the input is crucial for making that prediction. Thus (Jain and Wallace, 2019) perform *leave-one-out* experiments and calculate the Total Variation Distance (TVD) as a measure of change between output distributions, which is defined as:

$$\mathrm{TVD}(\hat{y}(\mathbf{X}), \hat{y}(\mathbf{X}_{-t})) = \frac{1}{2}\sum_{i=1}^{|\mathcal{K}|} |\hat{y}(\mathbf{X})_i - \hat{y}(\mathbf{X}_{-t})_i| \quad (5)$$

where $|\mathcal{K}|$ is the number of classes, $\hat{y}(\mathbf{X})$ is the output distribution when all tokens are in the input, and $\hat{y}(\mathbf{X}_{-t})$ is the output distribution when token at position t is removed from the input. As an example, suppose the initial output distribution for a 3-class problem is:

$$\hat{y}(\mathbf{X})_1 = 0.7\,,\ \hat{y}(\mathbf{X})_2 = 0.1\,,\ \hat{y}(\mathbf{X})_3 = 0.2$$

and the secondary distribution is:

$$\hat{y}(\mathbf{X}_{-t})_1 = 0.1\,,\ \hat{y}(\mathbf{X}_{-t})_2 = 0.8\,,\ \hat{y}(\mathbf{X}_{-t})_3 = 0.1$$

then, the TVD value is 0.7 which is a significant variation in the distribution of the output.

When modules are in competition, they are only active for specific parts of the input that are relevant to the task, and this activity pattern can be inspected to provide some explanation for behavior of the model. To support our claim, we use a similar set of *leave-one-out* experiments as (Jain and Wallace, 2019). Suppose a module is active at time-step t. We manually deactivate the module only for this time-step, and then measure the TVD value. As an example, consider Figure 6, when $k = 2$. The module *Disease* is active for tokens *pain* and *ruptured*. We deactivate the module only at those two time-steps (the rest of the modules keep their activity state) as two *leave-one-out* cases. Note that at time-step t, the inactive modules simply retain their previous hidden states (see Equation 3).

As a consequence, performance of the model is expected to be affected due to changes in output distribution. The performance change can also be used as a measure of the importance of module activity. If the activity of a module is important towards a prediction, deactivating it has to change the performance. When performing leave-one-out experiments, we report these changes by ΔF1. Table 6-8 report the average TVD values,[6] as well as corresponding ΔF1 values.

		Morph		*Word Emb.*		*Drug*		*POS*	
		TVD	ΔF1	TVD	ΔF1	TVD	ΔF1	TVD	ΔF1
	3	.12	-.02	.08	-.02	.14	-.03	.01	.00
k	2	.36	-.16	.16	-.06	.30	-.21	.08	-.01
	1	.42	-.23	.20	-.11	.54	-.32	.14	-.03

Table 6: Mean TVD and ΔF1 on BC7-3

We can assess the overall value of a module for a task by the greatest difference in TVD or ΔF1 values. In Table 6, *Drug* outranks *Morph* followed by *Word Emb.* and *POS*. In fact, *POS* appears to be a marginal module of no great impact on the analyzed examples.

[6]averaged over all leave-one-out experiments

	Morph.		Word Emb.		Gene		POS	
	TVD	ΔF1	TVD	ΔF1	TVD	ΔF1	TVD	ΔF1
3	.18	-.05	.10	-.02	.12	-.02	.06	.00
k 2	.48	-.23	.22	-.09	.26	-.13	.12	-.04
1	.62	-.41	.32	-.18	.54	-33	.16	-.05

Table 7: Mean TVD and ΔF1 on BC2-1a

For Table 7, *Morph* outranks *Drug*, outlining that the results are specific to the tasks and data.

For document-level tasks, changes in the output distribution observed are smaller due to the fact that users often report several symptoms for Covid, and rejecting one of the symptoms as input to the modules does not prevent the model from correct classification, since other evidence still exist. Still, we note that Table 8 for SM21-6 (self-reports of Covid symptoms) shows that for this task *Anatomy* outranks *Word Emb.* followed by *Disease* and finally *POS*, but that the differences are very small.

	Word Emb.		Disease		Anatomy		POS	
	TVD	ΔF1	TVD	ΔF1	TVD	ΔF1	TVD	ΔF1
3	.08	-.01	.04	.00	.06	.00	.02	.00
k 2	.12	-.02	.10	-.02	.14	-.03	.08	-.01
1	.18	-.05	.20	-.07	-.28	-.12	.18	-.05

Table 8: Mean TVD and ΔF1 on SM21-6

The different behaviour of the *Anatomy* module on SM21-a (adverse drug effects) is interesting; deactivation has a greater effect since mentions of body parts are very frequent in reports of adverse drug effects.

	Word Emb.		Drug		Disease		Anatomy		POS	
	TVD	ΔF1	TVD	ΔF1	TVD	ΔF1	TVD	ΔF1	TVD	ΔF1
3	.08	-.02	.06	-.01	.06	-.01	.06	.00	.00	.00
k 2	.12	-.03	.18	-.04	.10	-.03	.09	-.02	.04	.00
1	.22	-.11	.42	-.24	.22	-.10	.16	-.05	.06	-.01

Table 9: Mean TVD and ΔF1 on SM21-1a

7 Conclusion

We have demonstrated the potential of modules for visualizations for inspection: mean TVD values and $\Delta F1$ provide insight into general module importance for tasks, module activation patterns provide some insight into system behavior for individual samples, such as error cases. With the seven module system, we demonstrate that ineffective knowledge sources can be combined without harm in the mi-RIM architecture.

The experiments suggest that the encapsulation approach for leveraging knowledge sources in the mi-RIM architecture is promising but still has to be applied to more modules to gauge complexity implications.

Acknowledgements

We would like to thank Hessam Amini for insightful discussions and comments on explainability and model interpretation.

References

Hessam Amini and Leila Kosseim. 2019. Towards explainability in using deep learning for the detection of anorexia in social media. In *Natural Language Processing and Information Systems*, pages 225–235. Springer International Publishing.

Parsa Bagherzadeh and Sabine Bergler. 2020. CLaC at SMM4H 2020: Birth defect mention detection. In *Proceedings of the Fifth Social Media Mining for Health Applications Workshop & Shared Task.*

Parsa Bagherzadeh and Sabine Bergler. 2021a. Leveraging knowledge sources for detecting self-reports of particular health issues on social media. In *Proceedings of the 12th International Workshop on Health Text Mining and Information Analysis.*

Parsa Bagherzadeh and Sabine Bergler. 2021b. Multi-input Recurrent Independent Mechanisms for leveraging knowledge sources: Case studies on sentiment analysis and health text mining. In *Proceedings of Deep Learning Inside Out (DeeLIO): The 2nd Workshop on Knowledge Extraction and Integration for Deep Learning Architectures*, pages 108–118.

Hamish Cunningham, Diana Maynard, Kalina Bontcheva, and Valentin Tablan. 2002. GATE: A Framework and Graphical Development Environment for Robust NLP tools and applications. In *Proceedings of the 40th Anniversary Meeting of the Association for Computational Linguistics (ACL'02).*

Tobias Glasmachers. 2017. Limits of end-to-end learning. In *Asian Conference on Machine Learning*, pages 17–32.

Anirudh Goyal, Alex Lamb, Jordan Hoffmann, Shagun Sodhani, Sergey Levine, Yoshua Bengio, and Bernhard Schölkopf. 2019. Recurrent independent mechanisms. *arXiv preprint arXiv:1909.10893.*

Boran Hao, Henghui Zhu, and Ioannis Paschalidis. 2020. Enhancing clinical BERT embedding using a biomedical knowledge base. In *Proceedings of the 28th International Conference on Computational Linguistics*, pages 657–661.

Sarthak Jain and Byron C. Wallace. 2019. Attention is not Explanation. In *Proceedings of the 2019 Conference of the North American Chapter of the Association for Computational Linguistics: Human Language Technologies, Volume 1 (Long and Short Papers)*, pages 3543–3556.

Yoon Kim, Yacine Jernite, David Sontag, and Alexander M Rush. 2016. Character-aware neural language models. In *Thirtieth AAAI conference on Artificial Intelligence*.

Diederik P Kingma and Jimmy Lei Ba. 2015. Adam: A method for stochastic optimization. In *Proceedings of the 3rd International Conference on Learning Representations, ICLR'15*.

Ari Z. Klein, Ivan Flores, Arjun Magge, Anne-Lyse Minard, Karen O'Connor, Abeed Sarker, Elena Tutubalina, Davy Weissenbacher, and Graciela Gonzalez-Hernandez. 2021. Overview of the Sixth Social Media Mining for Health applications (SMM4H) shared tasks at NAACL 2021. In *Proceedings of the Sixth Social Media Mining for Health Applications (SMM4H) Workshop & Shared Task*.

Jinhyuk Lee, Wonjin Yoon, Sungdong Kim, Donghyeon Kim, Sunkyu Kim, Chan Ho So, and Jaewoo Kang. 2020. Biobert: a pre-trained biomedical language representation model for biomedical text mining. *Bioinformatics*, 36(4):1234–1240.

Omer Levy and Yoav Goldberg. 2014. Dependency-based word embeddings. In *Proceedings of the 52nd Annual Meeting of the Association for Computational Linguistics (Volume 2: Short Papers)*, pages 302–308.

Carolyn E Lipscomb. 2000. Medical subject headings (MeSH). *Bulletin of the Medical Library Association*, 88(3).

Tomas Mikolov, Wen-tau Yih, and Geoffrey Zweig. 2013. Linguistic regularities in continuous space word representations. In *Proceedings of the 2013 Conference of the North American Chapter of the Association for Computational Linguistics: Human Language Technologies*, pages 746–751.

Adam Paszke, Sam Gross, Soumith Chintala, Gregory Chanan, Edward Yang, Zachary DeVito, Zeming Lin, Alban Desmaison, Luca Antiga, and Adam Lerer. 2017. Automatic differentiation in PyTorch. In *NIPS 2017*.

Matthew E. Peters, Mark Neumann, Robert Logan, Roy Schwartz, Vidur Joshi, Sameer Singh, and Noah A. Smith. 2019. Knowledge enhanced contextual word representations. In *Proceedings of the 2019 Conference on Empirical Methods in Natural Language Processing and the 9th International Joint Conference on Natural Language Processing (EMNLP-IJCNLP)*, pages 43–54.

Bernhard Schölkopf, Dominik Janzing, Jonas Peters, Eleni Sgouritsa, Kun Zhang, and Joris Mooij. 2012. On causal and anticausal learning. In *Proceedings of the 29th International Conference on Machine Learning (ICML 2012)*, pages 1255–1262.

Sofia Serrano and Noah A Smith. 2019. Is attention interpretable? In *Proceedings of the 57th Annual Meeting of the Association for Computational Linguistics*, pages 2931–2951.

Larry Smith, Lorraine K Tanabe, Rie Johnson nee Ando, Cheng-Ju Kuo, I-Fang Chung, Chun-Nan Hsu, Yu-Shi Lin, Roman Klinger, Christoph M Friedrich, Kuzman Ganchev, et al. 2008. Overview of BioCreative II gene mention recognition. *Genome biology*, 9(2):1–19.

Anders Søgaard and Yoav Goldberg. 2016. Deep multi-task learning with low level tasks supervised at lower layers. In *Proceedings of the 54th Annual Meeting of the Association for Computational Linguistics (Volume 2: Short Papers)*, pages 231–235.

Hao Tian, Can Gao, Xinyan Xiao, Hao Liu, Bolei He, Hua Wu, Haifeng Wang, and Feng Wu. 2020. SKEP: Sentiment knowledge enhanced pre-training for sentiment analysis. In *Proceedings of the 58th Annual Meeting of the Association for Computational Linguistics*, pages 4067–4076.

Ashish Vaswani, Noam Shazeer, Niki Parmar, Jakob Uszkoreit, Llion Jones, Aidan N Gomez, Łukasz Kaiser, and Illia Polosukhin. 2017. Attention is all you need. In *Advances in neural information processing systems*, pages 5998–6008.

Tejaswani Verma, Christoph Lingenfelder, and Dietrich Klakow. 2020. Defining explanation in an AI context. In *Proceedings of the Third BlackboxNLP Workshop on Analyzing and Interpreting Neural Networks for NLP*, pages 314–322.

Sarah Wiegreffe and Yuval Pinter. 2019. Attention is not not explanation. In *Proceedings of the 2019 Conference on Empirical Methods in Natural Language Processing and the 9th International Joint Conference on Natural Language Processing (EMNLP-IJCNLP)*, pages 11–20.

David S Wishart, Yannick D Feunang, An C Guo, Elvis J Lo, Ana Marcu, Jason R Grant, Tanvir Sajed, Daniel Johnson, Carin Li, Zinat Sayeeda, et al. 2018. Drugbank 5.0: a major update to the drugbank database for 2018. *Nucleic acids research*, 46(D1):D1074–D1082.

Attacks against Ranking Algorithms with Text Embeddings: A Case Study on Recruitment Algorithms

Anahita Samadi and **Debapriya Banerjee** and **Shirin Nilizadeh**
The University of Texas at Arlington
{anahita.samadi,debapriya.banerjee2}@mavs.uta.edu,
and shirin.nilizadeh@uta.edu

Abstract

Recently, some studies have shown that text classification tasks are vulnerable to poisoning and evasion attacks. However, little work has investigated attacks against decision-making algorithms that use text embeddings, and their output is a ranking. In this paper, we focus on ranking algorithms for the recruitment process that employ text embeddings for ranking applicants' resumes when compared to a job description. We demonstrate both white-box and black-box attacks that identify text items that, based on their location in embedding space, have a significant contribution in increasing the similarity score between a resume and a job description. The adversary then uses these text items to improve the ranking of their resume among others. We tested recruitment algorithms that use the similarity scores obtained from Universal Sentence Encoder (USE) and Term Frequency–Inverse Document Frequency (TF-IDF) vectors. Our results show that in both adversarial settings, on average the attacker is successful. We also found that attacks against TF-IDF are more successful compared to USE.

1 Introduction

Recently some studies have shown that text classification tasks are vulnerable to poisoning and evasion attacks (Liang et al., 2018; Li et al., 2018; Gao et al., 2018; Grosse et al., 2017). For example, some works have shown that an adversary can fool toxic content detection (Li et al., 2018), spam detection (Gao et al., 2018) and malware detection (Grosse et al., 2017) by modifying some text items in the adversarial examples. A recent work (Schuster et al., 2020) showed that applications that rely on word embeddings are vulnerable to *poisoning attacks*, where an attacker can modify the corpus that the embedding is trained on, i.e., Wikipedia and Twitter posts, and modify the meaning of new or existing words by changing their locations in the embedding space. In this work, however, we investigate a new type of attack, i.e., *rank attack*, when the text application utilizes text embedding approaches. In this attack, the adversary does not poison the training corpora but tries to learn about the embedding space, and how adding some keywords to a document can change the representation vector of it, and based on that tries to improve the ranking of the adversarial text document among a collection of documents.

As a case study, we focus on ranking algorithms in a recruitment process scenario. Recruitment process is a key to finding a suitable candidate for a job application. Nowadays, companies use ML-based approaches to rank resumes from a pool of candidates (Sumathi and Manivannan, 2020; Roy et al., 2020). One naive approach for boosting the ranking of a resume can be adding the most words and phrases to his/her resume from the job description. However, this is not the best approach all the time, because: First, the attacker must add a specific *meaningful* word to their resume. For example, they cannot claim they are proficient in some skills while they are not. Second, adding any random keyword from the job description to the resume does not always increase the similarity between the resume and job description. Instead, we demonstrate that the adversary can learn about the influential words and phrases that can increase the similarity score and use this knowledge and decide about the keywords or phrases to be added to their resume.

Therefore, in this work, we investigate: (1) *How can an adversary utilize the text embedding space to extract words and phrases that have a higher impact on the ranking of a specific document (here resume)?* and, (2) *How can an adversary, with no knowledge about the ranking algorithm, modify a text document (here resume) to improve its ranking among a set of documents?*

While we focus on the recruitment application, the same approaches can be employed on

Proceedings of the Fourth BlackboxNLP Workshop on Analyzing and Interpreting Neural Networks for NLP, pages 457–467
Online, November 11, 2021.

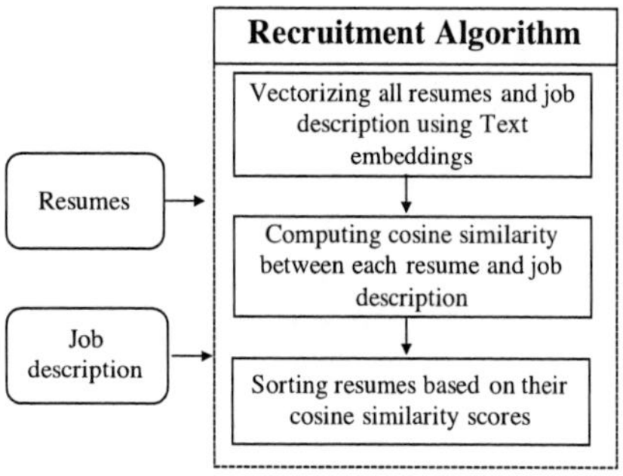

Figure 1: Ranking algorithm for recruitment

other ranking algorithms that use text embeddings for measuring the similarity between text documents and ranking them. For example, such ranking algorithms are applied as part of summarization (Rossiello et al., 2017; Ng and Abrecht, 2015) and question and answering systems (Bordes et al., 2014; Zhou et al., 2015; Esposito et al., 2020).

We consider both white-box and black-box settings, depending on the knowledge of the adversary about the specific text embeddings approach that is used for the resume ranking. In white-box settings, we propose a novel approach which utilizes the text embedding space to extract words and phrases that influence the rankings significantly. We consider both Universal Sentence Encoder (USE) (Cer et al., 2018) and TF-IDF as the approaches for obtaining the word vectors. USE computes embeddings based on Transformer architecture (Wang et al., 2019a), and it captures contextual information while on the other hand TF-IDF does not capture the contextual information. In the black-box setting, we propose a neural network based model that can identify the most influential words/phrases without knowing the exact text embedding approach that is used by the ranking algorithm.

2 System and Threat Model

The recruitment process helps to find a suitable candidate for a job application. Based on Glassdoor statistics, the average job opening attracts approximately 250 resumes (Team), and a recent survey found that the average cost per hire is just over $4,000 (Bika).

To Limit work in progress many companies use Machine Learning to have more efficiency in ranking resumes.A successful approach to rank resumes is calculating similarity among resume and job description leveraging NLP techniques (Excellarate). In this study, the recruitment algorithm is based on a ranking algorithm. This algorithm takes input from the resume and the job description and finds similarities based on their matching score. We use universal sentence encoder (USE) as the text embedding approach to vectorize each resume and the job descriptions. As it is shown in Figure 1, our algorithm includes three steps: (1) all resumes and the job description are vectorized using USE text embedding approach; (2) the similarity between each job description and an individual resume is computed. Cosine similarity is used as a metric to compute the similarity score; and (3) the resumes are sorted based on their similarity scores computed in the second step in such a way that the resume with highest similarity score appears at the top of the list and on the other hand the resume with least similarity score appears at bottom.

Threat Model. Adversaries have a huge motivation to change the rankings provided by some algorithms, when they are used for decision-making, e.g., for recruitment purposes. Adjusting a resume based on the job description is a well-known approach for boosting the chance of being selected for the next rounds of recruitment (Team, 2021). In this work, we show how an adversary can automatically generate adversarial examples specific to a recruitment algorithm and text embeddings. We define this attack as a *rank attack*, where the adversary adds some words or phrases to its document to improve its ranking among a collection of documents. We consider white-box and black-box settings. In a white-box setting, we assume the attacker has complete knowledge about the ranking algorithm. In a black-box setting, however, the attacker has no knowledge of the recruitment process but has limited access to the recruitment algorithm and can test some resumes against the algorithm.

3 Background

USE Text Embedding. This embedding has been used to solve tasks, such as semantic search, text classification, question answering (Rossiello et al., 2017; Ng and Abrecht, 2015; Bordes et al., 2014; Zhou et al., 2015; Esposito et al., 2020). USE uses an encoder to convert given text to a fixed-length 512-dimensional vector. It has been shown that after embedding sentences, sentences that have closer meaning carry out higher cosine similarity (an, 2018). We used USE pretrained model, which is trained on the STS (Semantic Textual Similarity) benchmark (Agirre).

TF-IDF. TF-IDF or term frequency-inverse document frequency is a widely used approach in information retrieval and text mining. TF-IDF is computed as a multiplication of *TF*, the frequency of a word in a document, and *IDF*, the inverse of the document frequency.

4 Data Collection

We collected 100 real public applicant resumes from LinkedIn public job seeker resumes, GitHub, and personal websites. To have an equal chance for applicants and make our experiences closer to real world recruitment procedures, we only considered resumes related to computer science. Resumes are chosen to be in different levels of education (bachelor, master and Ph.D. with equal distribution), skills, experiments (entry level, mid level, senior level), and gender (around fifty percent men and fifty percent women). We also developed a web scraper in python to extract computer science jobs from the Indeed website.[1] Our dataset includes over 10,000 job descriptions, extracted randomly from cities in the USA. We randomly chose 50 job descriptions and used them in our experiments.

For black-box settings, our neural network architecture needs a huge amount of data to be trained on. To have enough training sets we augmented our data for our models. For a simple setting model, we created 5,000 records by concatenating 100 resumes to 50 selected job descriptions to augment our data for recruitment algorithms. Note that the adversary only needs to obtain or create a set of resumes and they do not need to use the job descriptions. For a more complex setting, we split resumes into half, then joined the upper part of each resume to other resumes' lower parts. With this approach, we could maintain the structure of each resume and each resume could have common resume information, such as skills, education, work experince, etc. We did this procedure for all possible combinations and created a database with 10,000 resumes.

5 White-Box Setting and a Recruitment Algorithm that Employs USE

In white-box settings, we assume the adversary has knowledge about the recruitment process and the use of universal sentence encoder (USE) or term frequency–inverse document frequency (TF-IDF) for obtaining the embedding vectors. We propose a novel approach which utilizes the knowledge about the text embedding space, here USE, to identify keywords in the job description that can be added to the adversarial resume and increase its similarity score with the job description. Our approach as it is shown in Figure 2 consists of three phases: in *Phase 1*, the adversary tries to identify the important words in job description; in *Phase 2*, the adversary tries to rank the effectiveness of those words based on its own resume, i.e., identifying those words that can increase the similarity between his/her resume and the job description. After identifying the most effective words, then in *Phase 3*, the adversary modifies its resume based on his/her expertise and skill set and decides to add N of those identified words and phrases. Note that in this attack scenario the adversary does not need to have any knowledge about the other candidates' resumes. The details of phase 1 and 2 in this attack are depicted in Algorithm 1 and Algorithm 2, respectively, and we explain them in the following.

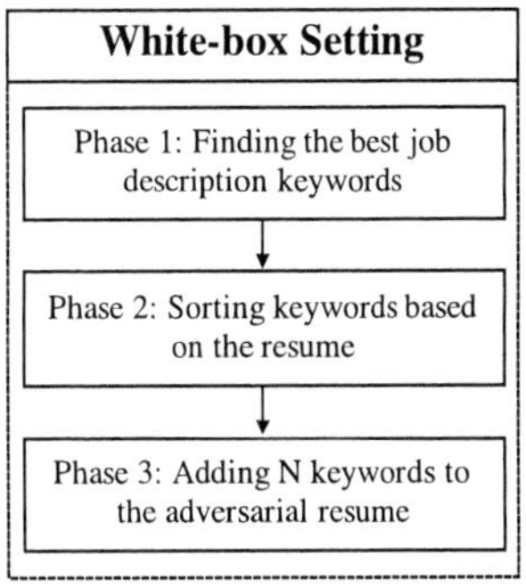

Figure 2: White-box setting

Algorithm 1 Job Description Keywords Extraction

Input: Job Description document

Output: An list of keywords in ascending order based on their similarity score

```
procedure PHASE1(OrginalJob)
    OrginalJob ← FilterStopWords(OrginalJob)
    Tokens ← Tokenize(OrginalJob)
    USE_Job ← USE(OrginalJob)

    Token_Sim ← {}
    for Token_i ∈ Tokens do
        newJob ← DeleteToken(JobDescription, Token_i)
        USE_newJob ← USE(newJob)
        Token_Sim ← Token_Sim + {Token_i, CosSim(USE_Job, USE_newJob)}
    end for

    return AscendingSortByValue(Token_Sim)
```

[1]https://www.indeed.com/

5.1 Phase one: Identifying the Influential Keywords in the Job Description

In this phase, the adversary focuses on identification of the most important keywords from job description. Based on the use of cosine similarity between the vectors of resumes and job descriptions in the recruitment algorithm (depicted in Figure 1), the highest similarity can be achieved if the resume is the same as the job description. We propose to remove words/phrases from the job description and then examine its impact on the similarity score. A substantial decrease in the similarity score when a specific word/phrase is removed demonstrates the importance of the keyword in the word embedding space corresponding to this job description. In the white-box setting, the adversary is aware of the details of algorithms. Therefore, they employ USE text embedding to obtain the vector and use cosine similarity to calculate the similarity scores.

In addition, to examine the importance of phrases instead of individual words, the adversary can try to remove phrases with one word (unigram), two words (bigram), three words (trigram), etc., and then compute the similarity score. Algorithm 1 shows the details of *phase 1* which consists of the following steps: *(1) Text pre-processing:* the keywords of the job description are obtained as a bag of words, and the stop words are removed to lower the dimensional space. *(2) USE embedding:* The embedding vector is obtained for the original job description using universal sentence encoder (USE). *(3) Token removal:* measures the importance of each word in the job description. A single token is deleted from the job description, and the new job description is created. Next, the embedding vector for $NewJob$ is obtained by passing to USE. *(4) Scoring keywords:* Cosine similarity is calculated to measure the similarity between two vectors USE_{newJob} and $USE_{OrginalJob}$. *In this regard, lower cosine similarity expresses the fact that the deleted token has caused an impressive change in the job description content, therefore it might be an important keyword. (5) Repetition:* Steps three and four are repeated for all tokens in the job description. This procedure provides a dictionary, where the keys are tokens, and the values are their corresponding cosine similarity scores. *(6) Sorting keywords:* Finally, extracted keywords are sorted based on the similarity score in ascending order.

N-gram phrases: Moreover, we extended the code in Algorithm 1 so that it can also identify the influential phrases, i.e., bigrams and trigrams. In that case, in each repetition, instead of one individual word, repeatedly 2 or 3 neighbor words are removed from the job description and the similarity score is computed.

5.2 Phase two: Re-sorting the Influential Keywords based on a Specific Resume

The previous phase helps identify the words and phrases in the job description that in USE embedding space have a higher impact on providing a larger similarity score. However, each resume is unique and adding the most influential words obtained from the job description might not have the same impact on all the resumes. In *Phase 2*, we try to identify the best words and phrases that can boost the similarity score between a specific resume and job description. Algorithm 2 shows the details of *phase 2* which consists of the following steps:

(1) Adding Keywords: A keyword from the list of fifty keywords obtained from *phase 1* is added to the adversarial resume. *(2) Obtaining the Embedding Vector*: The embedding vector for the adversarial resume is obtained using USE. *(3) Calculating the Similarity:* The cosine similarity between adversarial and job description is computed. *Higher cosine similarity expresses the fact that the deleted token caused an impressive change in the job description contents, therefore, it might be an important keyword. (4) Repetition:* These steps are repeated for all fifty keywords. This procedure provides a dictionary, where the keys are the fifty keywords, and the values are their corresponding cosine similarity scores. The list of keywords are sorted based on their cosine similarity scores.

N-gram phrases: Algorithm 2 is also extended to get the sorted list of bigrams or trigrams, and added to the adversarial resume.

5.3 Experimental Setup

We implemented the *rank attack* in a white-box setting and tested all combinations of 100 resumes and 50 job descriptions. The attack is shown in Algorithm 3. Then in each experiment, we assumed that a resume is adversarial and therefore the best keywords for that specific resume are added to it. To investigate the impact of the number of keywords on the ranking of the resume, we tested with $n \in (1, 2, 5, 10, 20, 50)$ of keywords. We also repeated these experiments for bigram and trigram

Algorithm 2 Resorting the extracted job description keywords based on a resume

Input: Job description document, Resume document, A list of tokens

Output: An ordered list of keywords

```
procedure PHASE2(JobDescription, Resume, OrderedTokens)
    USE_JobDescription ← USE(JobDescription)
    Keyword_Sim ← {}

    for keyword_i ∈ OrderedTokens do
        adversarialResume ← AddToken(Resume, keyword_i)
        USE_advResume ← USE(adversarialResume)
        Keyword_Sim ← Keyword_Sim + {Keyword_i, CosSim(USE_advResume, USE_JobDescription)}
    end for

    return SortByValue(Keyword_Sim)
```

phrases. Note that in practice, the adversary does not need to, and cannot obtain the ranking of its resume among all other resumes. However, in our experiments we show how using this attack they can improve their position.

Algorithm 3 White Box Adversarial Attack

Input: Job Description documents, Resume documents

Output: Ranking

```
procedure WHITEBOX(Jobs, Resumes)
    for job_i ∈ Jobs do
        Tokens ← Phase1(job_i)
        for resume_j ∈ Resumes do
            Rank ← GetRanking(job_i, resume_j, Resumes)
            words ← Phase2(JobDescription, Resume, Tokens)
            for n ∈ (1, 2, 5, 10, 20, 50) do
                AdvResume ← AddWords(resume_j, n, words)
                Resumes2 ← Resumes − resume_j
                Resumes2 ← Resumes2 + AdvResume
                Rank_new ← Ranking(job_i, Resumes2)
                RankChange_{job_i,resume_j,n} ← Rank_new − Rank
            end for
        end for
    end for

    return RankRankChange
```

5.4 Experimental Results

Figure 3a shows the histogram of average rank improvements for 100 resumes and 50 random job descriptions. All resumes had rank improvement, and in most of them the rank improvement is significant. For example, on average an adversarial resume moved up 16 positions in rank improvement, about 6 resumes had an average of moving up 28 ranking positions, and more than 65 resumes moved up more than 10 ranking positions.

Figure 3b shows the average rank improvement based on the number of words or phrases (bigrams and trigrams) added to the adversarial resume. We see a similar trend when adding unigrams, bigrams, and trigrams, i.e., adding more words and phrases increases the average rank improvement. For example, while adding 2 bigrams improves the ranking of the adversarial resume on average by 6, adding 20 bigrams improves the ranking of the adversarial resume by 30, among 100 resumes. However, interestingly we see that adding too many words/phrases might not have the same effect, e.g., adding 50 bigrams shows a rank improvement by only about 28. This shows there might be an optimal number of words/phrases that can help ranking of a document.

Comparing the addition of unigrams, bigrams, and trigrams, we see that trigrams provide better rank improvement. For example, adding 10 unigrams, bigrams, and trigrams, we see a rank improvement of 12, 21 and 25, respectively. This finding can be explained by USE being a context-aware embedding approach, which takes into account the order of words in addition to their meaning.

6 White-box Setting and a Recruitment Algorithm that Employs TF-IDF

We also investigate the effectiveness of the attacks in white-box setting, when the recruitment algorithm uses TF-IDF vectors to compute the similarity between resumes and job descriptions. The attack is the same. The only difference is in the recruitment algorithm. Since the adversary has the knowledge that the recruitment algorithm uses TF-IDF vectors, then they compute TF-IDF vectors instead of USE vectors.

6.1 Experimental Setup

For these experiments, we implemented the recruitment algorithm that ranks resumes based on the similarity scores that are calculated between the TF-IDF vectors of resumes and the job description. We implemented the rank attack and tested on all combinations of the 100 resumes and 50 job descriptions. For each job description, we first obtained the ranking of the original resumes, and then in each experiment, we assumed that a resume is adversarial and therefore the best keywords for that specific resume are added to it. To investigate the impact of the number of keywords on the ranking of the resume, we tested with $n \in (1, 2, 5, 10, 20, 50)$ of keywords. We also repeated these experiments for bigram and trigram phrases.

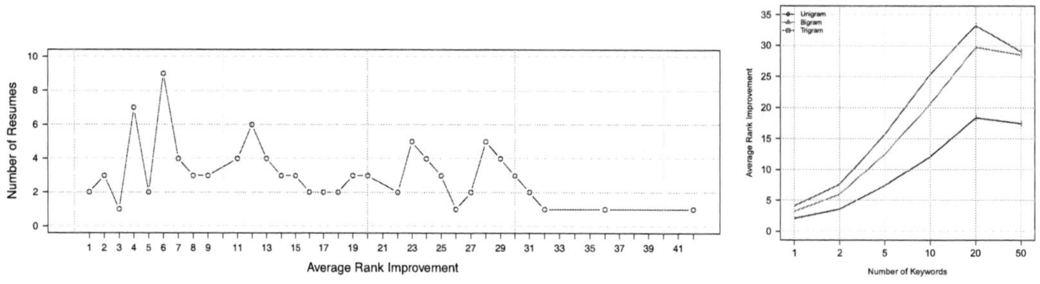

(a) Histogram of average rank improvement

(b) Average rank improvement

Figure 3: Average rank improvement for 100 resumes and 50 job descriptions, in white-box setting when recruitment algorithm employs USE embeddings

6.2 Experimental Results

Figure 4a shows the histogram of average rank improvements for 100 resumes and 50 random job descriptions. Most resumes had rank improvement and in most of them rank improvement was significant. For example, on average, an adversarial resume moved up about 25 ranking positions, and more than 85 resumes moved up more than 10.

In Figure 4b, we investigated the effect of adding bigram and trigram bags of words on average rank improvement. Interestingly, in contrast to our results for recruitment algorithms that employ USE embedding, in these experiments we achieved better results for unigrams compared to bigrams and trigrams. Note that TF-IDF approach is only based on word similarity and does not consider the context. This might explain the results. No matter what n-gram is used, by increasing the number of keywords, the ranks also improve. Comparing results in Figure 3b and Figure 4b also shows that it is easier for the adversary to attack a recruitment algorithm that employs TF-IDF compared to USE, as the rank improvement is larger for attacks against the the recruitment algorithm that employs TF-IDF, specially in the case of unigrams. For example, by adding 20 keywords to attack the recruitment algorithm that employs *USE*, we observe an average rank improvement of 18, 29, and 33 for unigram, bigram and trigram, respectively. However, by adding 10 keywords to attack the recruitment algorithm that employs *TF-IDF*, they are 48, 32, and 37 for unigram, bigram and trigram, respectively.

7 Black-Box Setting

In the back-box setting, an adversary does not have access to the model specification but has access to the recruitment algorithm as an oracle machine, which receives an input, e.g., here a resume, and then generates a response, e.g., here accept/ reject, or the ranking among all the resumes in its pool. Therefore, the adversary is able to send some resumes to the recruitment algorithm and obtain the output for them, which then can be used to train a neural network model. This model then identifies the features (i.e., keywords) that help resumes to be accepted or obtain better ranking. The adversary then can boost its chance of acceptance by adding some or all of the identified keywords.

The input vector of our neural network model is the resumes, and the output is a vector that demonstrates the best keywords. In our experiments, we examine attacks against two recruitment algorithms: a binary classifier, which label a resume as *accept* or *reject*, and a ranking algorithm that provides a ranking based on similarity scores between the job description and the resumes, where they are vectorized by USE embeddings. The attacks against both algorithms have two phases: *phase 1: pre-processing* which prepares the data for the neural network, and *phase 2:* a neural network model.

Phase 1: Pre-processing. To provide an acceptable format for the neural network input, we applied one-hot encoding (Harris and Harris, 2012) following these steps: *(1) Tokenization:* The job description and resumes are tokenized and a dictionary of words is created, where key is the token/word, and value is the frequency of the words in these documents. *(2) Vectorization of Resumes:*

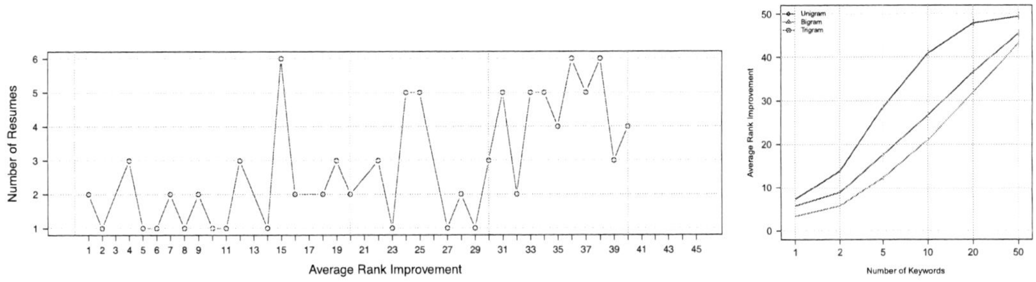

(a) Histogram of average rank improvement

(b) Average rank improvement

Figure 4: Average rank improvement in white-box setting when recruitment algorithm employs TF-IDF vectors

Tokens/words are encoded as a one-hot numeric array, where for each word a binary column is created. As a result, a sparse matrix is returned, which represents the resumes in rows and the words in columns. If a resume includes some word, the entry for that row and column is 1, otherwise it is 0.

Neural Network Architecture. Neural networks have been applied in many real-world problems (Nielsen, 2015; Salakhutdinov, 2014; Hassanzadeh et al., 2020; Ghazvinian et al., 2021; Krizhevsky et al., 2012). We propose a deep neural network architecture which consists of an input layer, three dense layers as hidden layers, and an output layer representing the labels. In the output vector, ones indicate an index of words in the dictionary that adding them to a resume will increase the rank of the resume. For the first two hidden layers we used rectified linear unit (ReLU) (Nair and Hinton, 2010) as the activation function. Due to their unique formulations, ReLUs provide faster training and better convergence relative to other activation functions (Nair and Hinton, 2010). For the output layer we used sigmoid activation function to map the output to lie in the range [0,1], i.e., actual probability values (Han and Moraga, 1995). As our problem was a multilabel problem, we applied binary cross-entropy loss. In contrast to softmax cross entropy loss, binary cross-entropy is independent in terms of class, i.e., the loss measured for every class is not affected by other classes.

For the optimization of loss function (training the neural network), we used a stochastic gradient descent-based optimization algorithm (Adam; (Kingma and Ba, 2015)). For the regularization technique, to avoid over-fitting (Salakhutdinov, 2014), we tested dropout with different rates [0 to 0.5]. Dropout was applied for all hidden layers, and our assessment showed that the dropout rate (0.1) yielded better results.

7.1 Experiments for the Binary Classifier

This is a simpler model, where the recruitment process is defined as a binary classification algorithm, and a resume is accepted based on some rules. In our experiments, we defined simple rules, e.g., if *python* as a skill is in the resume. After tokenization of the resume and the job description, instead of generating the one-hot encoding for all the words obtained, we chose 20 of the most frequent words of all resumes and job descriptions. Also, our proposed neural network will predict a maximum number of 20 keywords that will enhance resume rank. This is to test with a low dimension vector. We then concatenated the vectors of the resume and job description.

Creating the groundtruth dataset. We employed two steps: (1) Xtrain: 5000 records of 40-dimension vectors, each vector is a resume and coded by one-hot format. In Section 4 we explained the method for generating these resumes. (2) Ytrain: 5000 records of 20-dimension vectors. If the value of a word index is set to one then adding this word to resume makes the resume be accepted.

The attack can be more successful if the adversary obtains a larger training dataset. This might be seen as a bottle-neck for this type of attack, since the adversary needs to create/ obtain many resumes and submit them for evaluation without being suspicious. However, this scenario can be practical. First of all, it is easy to obtain resumes online and the attacker can obtain relevant resumes and use them. Also, the adversary does not need to send all the resumes for the target position, but they can divide and send them to multiple positions in the same company assuming that the company uses the same algorithm or set of rules for their recruitment for all their positions.

Model Training. To train our neural network model, we split our data into train and test (70% train set, 30% test set); to evaluate our training results, we used validation set approach (we allocated 30% of training set for validation) and trained on 2,450 samples, validate on 1,050 samples. We also set batch size equal to 50 and number of epochs equal to 100. Our results show that the model is trained well through epochs. After 50 epochs, the recall, precision and F1-score of this model over the validation set reached their maximum, which are 0.6, 0.7 and 0.82, respectively.

We examined the performance of the trained neural network model on test data. We added predicted words in the neural network to each related resume and submitted each resume to the recruitment algorithm and obtained the response from the recruitment oracle in the form of a binary value. Figure 6 shows that the success rate of getting accepted significantly increases by using suggested keywords. While without adding the keywords, the acceptance rate was 20%, after the attack the acceptance rate increased to about 100%.

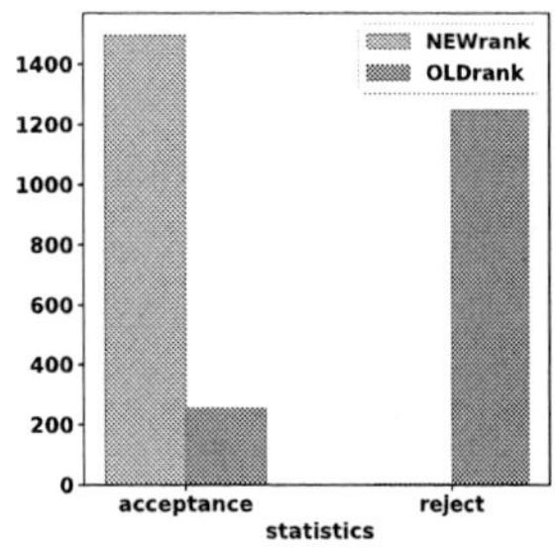

Figure 5: Attack success in black-box simple setting

7.2 Experiments for the Ranking Algorithm

This model is more complicated where the recruitment process is defined as a ranking algorithm. The goal is similar to the previous setup, i.e., identifying the best 50 words that can improve the ranking of a resume. For this setting, we considered higher dimension input vectors with 10,000 words.

Creating the groundtruth dataset. We employed these steps: (1) Xtrain: 10,000 records of 9054-dimension vectors, each vector is a resume that is coded by one-hot format. The 9054-dimension vector represents all the words (after cleaning and removing stop words) in all the resumes. (2) Ytrain: 10,000 records of 50-dimension vectors. For creating the output vectors, we selected a random job description, and employed the same technique proposed in white-box approach (Section 5.1) and identified the 50 most influential words in the job description. We assumed the recruitment algorithm uses the USE embedding, however the attacker can try this approach with other text embedding algorithms, or even choose the most frequent words. Therefore, in practice, the adversary does not need to know about the recruitment algorithm. We used 50 words to be consistent with our white-box attack and have enough choices of words. However, this is a parameter that can be defined during the time of attack. After identifying the influential words for the target job description, the adversary adds each of the words to each of the resumes in the training set, and then queries the black-box algorithm asking if the position of resume is improved. If it is improved then the value for that word and that resume in Ytrain would be 1, otherwise it would be 0. Therefore, the output label is an encoded vector by one-hot format.

Model Training. To train our neural network model, we split our data into 70% train set and 30% test set. To evaluate our training results, we allocated 30% of training set for validation and trained on 4,900 samples, and validated on 2,100 samples. Our results showed that the model is trained well through epochs. After 10 epochs, the recall, precision and F1-score of this model over the validation set reached their maximum values, i.e., 0.62, 0.68 and 0.75, respectively.

To test the performance of our trained neural network model, we ran it on our testing set and obtained the 50-dimention vector for each resume in it. This vector shows which words among the 50 influential words help the resume for this job description. Then, we added the identified words to the resumes, submitted each resume to the recruitment algorithm, and obtained the response in the form of a ranking score. Note that the adversary does not need to obtain these rankings for conducting the attack. Figure 6 shows that most of the resumes have a significant rank improvement. For example, more than 200 resumes out of 3000 resumes in the testing set had a rank improvement of more than 400, while more than 400 resumes had a rank improvement between 150 and 200 after adding the suggested keywords.

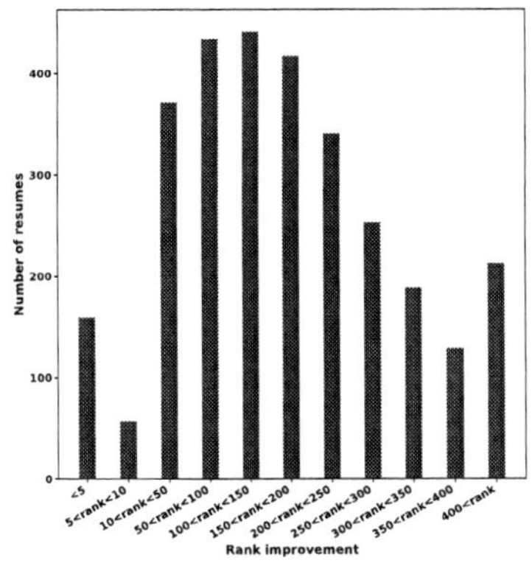

Figure 6: Rank improvement (complex setting)

8 Related Work

Attacks against text retrieval systems. Most of studies attack the deep neural networks for *text classification tasks*, such as sentiment analysis (Li et al., 2018), toxic content detection (Li et al., 2018), spam detection (Gao et al., 2018) and malware detection (Grosse et al., 2017). These works proposed methods for identifying text items that have a significant contribution in text classification task, then generate adversarial text by modifying those text items, e.g., modifying a word's characters (Liang et al., 2018; Ebrahimi et al., 2018b,a), adding or removing words (Liang et al., 2018), replacing words arbitrarily (Papernot et al., 2016; Sun et al., 2018), or substituting words with synonyms (Alzantot et al., 2018; Ren et al., 2019; Wang et al., 2019b; Blohm et al., 2018; Gong et al., 2018).

Adversarial examples for non-classification tasks. There are a couple of articles on crafting adversarial text for non-classification tasks. Jia and Liang (Jia and Liang, 2017) attacked machine comprehension and showed that the Stanford question answering dataset (Rajpurkar et al., 2016) is susceptible to black-box attacks, where adversarial questions are generated by appending distracting sentences at the end of the paragraph. A recent work (Cheng et al., 2020) attacked a text summarization, that is based on seq2seq models. In our paper, however, we propose crafting an adversarial text for ranking algorithms.

Attacks against resume search. A recent work (Schuster et al., 2020) showed that applications that rely on word embeddings are vulnerable to *poisoning attacks*, where an attacker can modify the corpus that the embedding is trained on and modify the meaning of new or existing words by changing their locations in the embedding space. However, our attack is not about poisoning the corpus, but instead it learns the words and phrases, based on some text embedding algorithm. In addition, we focus on the recruitment process that employs cosine similarity for ranking applicants' resumes compared to a job description.

9 Limitations and Future Work

This study examines the recruitment algorithms that use text embeddings and a similarity function to rank the resumes. However, examining more complex ranking algorithms is left for future work. In addition, the analysis can be expanded to other types of text embeddings. In the black-box setting, we did not investigate the trade-off between the number of queries that the adversary needs to send to the recruitment algorithm to create the training set, and the performance of the attack. It might be possible that the adversary can obtain good results using even a smaller training set. We will explore this in the future. We also have not studied the types of words that make it easy to game the system. In the future, we will examine the identified words in experiments in terms of their frequency, semantics, and other linguistic properties. Moreover, investigating the graybox attack remains for future work, when the attacker has this knowledge that the recruitment algorithm uses some kind of text embedding but does not know its type. This attack setting can help us to investigate the use of one text embedding approach for attacking a ranking algorithm that uses another text embedding approach. In other words, we can examine the transferability of one approach for another approach.

10 Conclusion

In this project we found that an automatic recruitment algorithm, as an example of ranking algorithms, is vulnerable against adversarial examples. We proposed a successful adversarial attack in two settings: white-box and black-box. We proposed a new approach for keyword extraction based on USE. We observed the majority of resumes have significant rank improvements by adding more influential keywords. Finally, in a black-box setting, we proposed multilabel neural network architecture to predict the proper keyword for each resume and job description.

References

Eneko Agirre. STSbenchmark. https://ixa2.si.ehu.eus/stswiki/index.php/STSbenchmark.

Moustafa Alzantot, Yash Sharma, Ahmed Elgohary, Bo-Jhang Ho, Mani Srivastava, and Kai-Wei Chang. 2018. Generating natural language adversarial examples. In *Proceedings of the 2018 Conference on Empirical Methods in Natural Language Processing*, pages 2890–2896, Brussels, Belgium. Association for Computational Linguistics.

Melanie Tosik an. 2018. Debunking fake news one feature at a time. *ArXiv preprint*, abs/1808.02831.

N Bika. Recruiting costs FAQ: Budget and cost per hire. https://resources.workable.com/tutorial/faq-recruitment-budget-metrics.

Matthias Blohm, Glorianna Jagfeld, Ekta Sood, Xiang Yu, and Ngoc Thang Vu. 2018. Attention-based convolutional and recurrent neural networks: Success and limitations in machine reading comprehension. Association for Computational Linguistics.

Antoine Bordes, Jason Weston, and Nicolas Usunier. 2014. Open question answering with weakly supervised embedding models. In *Joint European conference on machine learning and knowledge discovery in databases*, pages 165–180. Springer.

Daniel Cer, Yinfei Yang, Sheng-yi Kong, Nan Hua, Nicole Limtiaco, Rhomni St. John, Noah Constant, Mario Guajardo-Cespedes, Steve Yuan, Chris Tar, Brian Strope, and Ray Kurzweil. 2018. Universal sentence encoder for English. In *Proceedings of the 2018 Conference on Empirical Methods in Natural Language Processing: System Demonstrations*, pages 169–174, Brussels, Belgium. Association for Computational Linguistics.

Minhao Cheng, Jinfeng Yi, Pin-Yu Chen, Huan Zhang, and Cho-Jui Hsieh. 2020. Seq2sick: Evaluating the robustness of sequence-to-sequence models with adversarial examples. In *The Thirty-Fourth AAAI Conference on Artificial Intelligence, AAAI 2020, The Thirty-Second Innovative Applications of Artificial Intelligence Conference, IAAI 2020, The Tenth AAAI Symposium on Educational Advances in Artificial Intelligence, EAAI 2020, New York, NY, USA, February 7-12, 2020*, pages 3601–3608. AAAI Press.

Javid Ebrahimi, Daniel Lowd, and Dejing Dou. 2018a. On adversarial examples for character-level neural machine translation. In *Proceedings of the 27th International Conference on Computational Linguistics*, pages 653–663, Santa Fe, New Mexico, USA. Association for Computational Linguistics.

Javid Ebrahimi, Anyi Rao, Daniel Lowd, and Dejing Dou. 2018b. HotFlip: White-box adversarial examples for text classification. In *Proceedings of the 56th Annual Meeting of the Association for Computational Linguistics (Volume 2: Short Papers)*, pages 31–36, Melbourne, Australia. Association for Computational Linguistics.

Massimo Esposito, Emanuele Damiano, Aniello Minutolo, Giuseppe De Pietro, and Hamido Fujita. 2020. Hybrid query expansion using lexical resources and word embeddings for sentence retrieval in question answering. *Information Sciences*, 514:88–105.

Excellarate. Resume Ranking using Machine Learning. https://medium.com/@Excellarate/resume-ranking-using-machine-learning-implementation-47959a4e5d8e.

Ji Gao, Jack Lanchantin, Mary Lou Soffa, and Yanjun Qi. 2018. Black-box generation of adversarial text sequences to evade deep learning classifiers. In *2018 IEEE Security and Privacy Workshops (SPW)*, pages 50–56. IEEE.

Mohammadvaghef Ghazvinian, Yu Zhang, Dong-Jun Seo, Minxue He, and Nelun Fernando. 2021. A novel hybrid artificial neural network - parametric scheme for postprocessing medium-range precipitation forecasts. *Advances in Water Resources*, 151:103907.

Zhitao Gong, Wenlu Wang, Bo Li, Dawn Song, and Wei-Shinn Ku. 2018. Adversarial texts with gradient methods. *ArXiv preprint*, abs/1801.07175.

Kathrin Grosse, Nicolas Papernot, Praveen Manoharan, Michael Backes, and Patrick McDaniel. 2017. Adversarial examples for malware detection. In *European Symposium on Research in Computer Security*, pages 62–79. Springer.

Jun Han and Claudio Moraga. 1995. The influence of the sigmoid function parameters on the speed of backpropagation learning. In *International Workshop on Artificial Neural Networks*, pages 195–201. Springer.

David Harris and Sarah Harris. 2012. *Digital design and computer architecture (2nd ed.)*. Morgan Kaufmann.

Yousef Hassanzadeh, Mohammadvaghef Ghazvinian, Amin Abdi, Saman Baharvand, and Ali Jozaghi. 2020. Prediction of short and long-term droughts using artificial neural networks and hydrometeorological variables.

Robin Jia and Percy Liang. 2017. Adversarial examples for evaluating reading comprehension systems. In *Proceedings of the 2017 Conference on Empirical Methods in Natural Language Processing*, pages 2021–2031, Copenhagen, Denmark. Association for Computational Linguistics.

Diederik P. Kingma and Jimmy Ba. 2015. Adam: A method for stochastic optimization. In *3rd International Conference on Learning Representations, ICLR 2015, San Diego, CA, USA, May 7-9, 2015, Conference Track Proceedings*.

Alex Krizhevsky, Ilya Sutskever, and Geoffrey E. Hinton. 2012. Imagenet classification with deep convolutional neural networks. In *Advances in Neural Information Processing Systems 25: 26th Annual Conference on Neural Information Processing Systems 2012. Proceedings of a meeting held December 3-6, 2012, Lake Tahoe, Nevada, United States*, pages 1106–1114.

Jinfeng Li, Shouling Ji, Tianyu Du, Bo Li, and Ting Wang. 2018. Textbugger: Generating adversarial text against real-world applications. *ArXiv preprint*, abs/1812.05271.

Bin Liang, Hongcheng Li, Miaoqiang Su, Pan Bian, Xirong Li, and Wenchang Shi. 2018. Deep text classification can be fooled. In *Proceedings of the Twenty-Seventh International Joint Conference on Artificial Intelligence, IJCAI 2018, July 13-19, 2018, Stockholm, Sweden*, pages 4208–4215. ijcai.org.

Vinod Nair and Geoffrey E. Hinton. 2010. Rectified linear units improve restricted boltzmann machines. In *Proceedings of the 27th International Conference on Machine Learning (ICML-10), June 21-24, 2010, Haifa, Israel*, pages 807–814. Omnipress.

Jun-Ping Ng and Viktoria Abrecht. 2015. Better summarization evaluation with word embeddings for ROUGE. In *Proceedings of the 2015 Conference on Empirical Methods in Natural Language Processing*, pages 1925–1930, Lisbon, Portugal. Association for Computational Linguistics.

Michael A Nielsen. 2015. *Neural networks and deep learning*, volume 25. Determination press San Francisco, CA.

Nicolas Papernot, Patrick McDaniel, Ananthram Swami, and Richard Harang. 2016. Crafting adversarial input sequences for recurrent neural networks. In *MILCOM 2016-2016 IEEE Military Communications Conference*, pages 49–54. IEEE.

Pranav Rajpurkar, Jian Zhang, Konstantin Lopyrev, and Percy Liang. 2016. SQuAD: 100,000+ questions for machine comprehension of text. In *Proceedings of the 2016 Conference on Empirical Methods in Natural Language Processing*, pages 2383–2392, Austin, Texas. Association for Computational Linguistics.

Shuhuai Ren, Yihe Deng, Kun He, and Wanxiang Che. 2019. Generating natural language adversarial examples through probability weighted word saliency. In *Proceedings of the 57th Annual Meeting of the Association for Computational Linguistics*, pages 1085–1097, Florence, Italy. Association for Computational Linguistics.

Gaetano Rossiello, Pierpaolo Basile, and Giovanni Semeraro. 2017. Centroid-based text summarization through compositionality of word embeddings. In *Proceedings of the MultiLing 2017 Workshop on Summarization and Summary Evaluation Across Source Types and Genres*, pages 12–21, Valencia, Spain. Association for Computational Linguistics.

Pradeep Kumar Roy, Sarabjeet Singh Chowdhary, and Rocky Bhatia. 2020. A machine learning approach for automation of resume recommendation system. *Procedia Computer Science*, 167:2318–2327.

Ruslan Salakhutdinov. 2014. Deep learning. In *The 20th ACM SIGKDD International Conference on Knowledge Discovery and Data Mining, KDD '14, New York, NY, USA - August 24 - 27, 2014*, page 1973. ACM.

Roei Schuster, Tal Schuster, Yoav Meri, and Vitaly Shmatikov. 2020. Humpty dumpty: Controlling word meanings via corpus poisoning. In *2020 IEEE Symposium on Security and Privacy (SP)*, pages 1295–1313. IEEE.

D Sumathi and SS Manivannan. 2020. Machine learning-based algorithm for channel selection utilizing preemptive resume priority in cognitive radio networks validated by ns-2. *Circuits, Systems, and Signal Processing*, 39(2):1038–1058.

Mengying Sun, Fengyi Tang, Jinfeng Yi, Fei Wang, and Jiayu Zhou. 2018. Identify susceptible locations in medical records via adversarial attacks on deep predictive models. In *Proceedings of the 24th ACM SIGKDD International Conference on Knowledge Discovery & Data Mining, KDD 2018, London, UK, August 19-23, 2018*, pages 793–801. ACM.

Glassdoor Team. glassdoor. `https://www.glassdoor.com/employers/blog/50-hr-recruiting-stats-make-think`.

Indeed Editorial Team. 2021. How To Tailor Your Resume To a Job Description. `https://www.indeed.com/career-advice/resumes-cover-letters/tailoring-resume`.

Chenguang Wang, Mu Li, and Alexander J. Smola. 2019a. Language models with transformers.

Xiaosen Wang, Hao Jin, and Kun He. 2019b. Natural language adversarial attacks and defenses in word level. *ArXiv preprint*, abs/1909.06723.

Guangyou Zhou, Tingting He, Jun Zhao, and Po Hu. 2015. Learning continuous word embedding with metadata for question retrieval in community question answering. In *Proceedings of the 53rd Annual Meeting of the Association for Computational Linguistics and the 7th International Joint Conference on Natural Language Processing (Volume 1: Long Papers)*, pages 250–259, Beijing, China. Association for Computational Linguistics.

Controlled tasks for model analysis: Retrieving discrete information from sequences

Ionut-Teodor Sorodoc* **Gemma Boleda*†** **Marco Baroni*†**

*Universitat Pompeu Fabra
†ICREA
Barcelona, Spain
{firstname.lastname}@upf.edu

Abstract

In recent years, the NLP community has shown increasing interest in analysing how deep learning models work. Given that large models trained on complex tasks are difficult to inspect, some of this work has focused on controlled tasks that emulate specific aspects of language. We propose a new set of such controlled tasks to explore a crucial aspect of natural language processing that has not received enough attention: the need to retrieve discrete information from sequences.

We also study model behavior on the tasks with simple instantiations of Transformers and LSTMs. Our results highlight the beneficial role of decoder attention and its sometimes unexpected interaction with other components. Moreover, we show that, for most of the tasks, these simple models still show significant difficulties. We hope that the community will take up the analysis possibilities that our tasks afford, and that a clearer understanding of model behavior on the tasks will lead to better and more transparent models.

1 Introduction

There has been a continuous increase in performance in computational linguistics in recent years. This development correlates with larger and more complex models which are trained on ever bigger datasets. These new characteristics of modelling made it harder to understand which model components are relevant and how they work. This has motivated the NLP community to develop new methods for model analysis.

Given the difficulties analyzing large models, some of this work (Hupkes et al., 2018; Lake and Baroni, 2018; Hewitt and Liang, 2019; Chrupała and Alishahi, 2019; White and Cotterell, 2021) has focused on controlled tasks that emulate specific aspects of language. We propose a new set of such controlled tasks to explore a crucial aspect of natural language processing that has not received enough attention: the need to retrieve discrete information from sequences. [1] Retrieving discrete information from sequences is necessary for natural language processing for instance to track agreement between different constituents of a sentence and to establish coreference relationships (among many other examples). The controlled tasks are built using binary vectors as input in order to exclude the possible inferences of linguistic patterns that are not the focus of our analysis. In particular, we design the tasks such that the models need to emulate four abilities that are crucial for natural language: incremental processing, indirect mappings, contextualization, and order tracking.

We study model behavior on the proposed tasks with simple instantiations of Transformers (Vaswani et al., 2017) and LSTMs (Hochreiter and Schmidhuber, 1997), and show that, for most of the tasks, these models show significant difficulties. Transformers are the state of the art in deep learning for NLP, and LSTMs are a classical architecture that was designed for sequence processing. In the analysis, we aim at understanding the role of the different components of the models, focusing on self-attention and positional encoding for Transformers and decoder attention for LSTMs.

In the Transformer, self-attention turns out to only have a clear beneficial role when the task requires taking token order into account, with decoder attention performing most of the work in other cases. Positional encoding plays a counterintuitive role, helping in tasks that do not involve order by providing beneficial noise, and harming performance when it is redundant with self-attention. The LSTM only compares favorably to the Transformer in short sequence lengths for simple tasks, and decoder attention is highly beneficial for this model.

[1] The associated dataset and code can be downloaded at: https://github.com/sorodoc/DiscreteSeq

Proceedings of the Fourth BlackboxNLP Workshop on Analyzing and Interpreting Neural Networks for NLP, pages 468–478
Online, November 11, 2021.

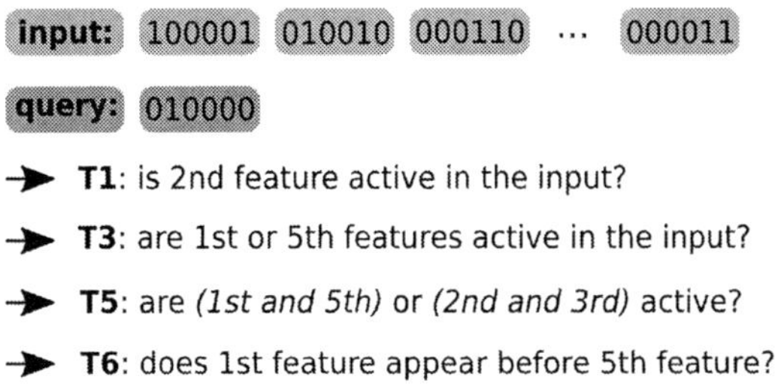

Figure 1: Schematic description of our tasks. Different tasks require different interpretations of the query. The answer is positive for all these instances.

2 Related Work

The current study belongs in the newly developed area of interpretability and explainability of computational linguistics, which seeks to understand how models capture natural language phenomena (Alishahi et al., 2019; Belinkov and Glass, 2019; Rogers et al., 2021).

Much of this literature has focused on model behaviour in complex NLP tasks (Linzen et al., 2016; Conneau et al., 2018; Voita et al., 2019; Abnar and Zuidema, 2020; Sinha et al., 2021; Lakretz et al., 2021). Some other work has used controlled tasks to analyze neural networks regarding specific aspects, such as reasoning skills (Weston et al., 2015), compositionality (Lake and Baroni, 2018; Hupkes et al., 2020), PoS tagging (Hewitt and Liang, 2019), inductive biases (White and Cotterell, 2021) or hierarchical structure (Hupkes et al., 2018; Chrupała and Alishahi, 2019). We follow this latter methodology, and design tasks that highlight one of the core abilities that a model needs to possess in order to process natural language, namely detecting one or more features in a sequence of tokens, possibly in a context- and/or order-sensitive way.

3 Description of the tasks

3.1 Task description

In all tasks, the goal is to perform *feature detection*, that is, to provide a binary response about whether a feature (or feature combination) is present in the input sequence. The tasks are schematically illustrated in Figure 1. The model is always presented with an *input* consisting in a sequence of *tokens*. Each token is a 36-dimensional binary vector with a variable number of dimensions (*features*) activated (set to 1). The model is also given a *query*, which is a single 36-dimensional binary vector with 1 feature activated, except for Task 2 below, where it has 2 activated features.

The tasks are meant to be *incremental*, in the sense that, when processing the input sequence, the model does not know what information it will need to retrieve from it. Some uses of Transformers in the NLP literature instead give access to all the information from the start, such as in BERT (Devlin et al., 2019) and its variants. Arguably, incrementality is necessary in most instances of language understanding "in the wild": For some applications, like Machine Translation for documents, it is realistic to give access to all the input at once, but as we move towards real-time applications such as virtual assistants, models will need to act incrementally.

T1: one-feature detection. T1 asks whether the active feature of the query is present in some token in the sequence. A linguistic example, relevant for syntactic processing, would be: did the plural feature occur in a span of tokens?

In the example in Figure 1, the second input token has feature 2, which is the one the query asks about, so the answer should be positive.

T2: two-feature detection. T2 asks whether two features occur in the sequence, be it in the same or in different tokens. This ability is required, for example, to check agreement between two syntactic units, or to answer a conjoint question.

In T1 and T2, query features and input features coincide: if the query asks about feature 2, then feature 2 needs to be active in some token for the answer to be positive. In the rest of the tasks, the relationship between query and input features is instead indirect. For instance, as illustrated in Figure 1 for T3, a query with feature 2 may ask about features 1 and 5 in the input. Models need to learn this implicit mapping when they are trained. Translation is an example (among many) of an indirect linguistic task, where words in the source language map to different target-language words.

T3: set member detection. In T3, models need to detect whether at least one out of two features is present in the sequence, that is, the task checks for feature disjunction (see Figure 1). This is akin to set member detection because we ask for a positive answer when at least one of the two features (set members) is present.

For example, many question-answering setups require retrieving an *instance* (*Fido, Snoopy, ...*) when prompted with the name of the *class* (*dog*).

T4: contextualized 2-feature detection. T4 asks about a conjunction of two features, like T2 (but with the indirect mapping). A linguistic example could involve a question requiring more than one piece of information to answer (*Who played the 1982 World Cup Final? Italy and Germany*). In addition, we design the mapping such that each feature is part of 2 queries; hence, it is associated only with two other features. This dataset structure should encourage **contextualization**, because a given feature is only ever relevant in the context of one of the other two features it is associated with.

Contextualization is crucial for natural language, where the same feature (e.g., a word) requires different responses depending on other features occurring in the context. A natural hypothesis is that the Transformer is naturally good for contextualization (this should be the strength of self-attention), but as we will see our results are mixed.

T5: contextualized set member detection. Like T3, the task concerns disjunction with indirect mapping, but it consists in checking whether at least one out of two *pairs* of features is present in the input (e.g., $(1 \wedge 5) \vee (2 \wedge 7)$; see Figure 1). Again, in each pair, one feature is only a hit in the context of the other, so this task also requires contextualization.

A linguistic example would be a coreference task where *toy* might refer to *rubber lion* or *plastic truck*, but not to *lion* or *truck* in other contexts.

T6: ordered feature detection. T6 adds order to T4: it asks about a conjunction of two features with the indirect mapping, where the features must be in a specific order. This has many linguistic counterparts, e.g., parsing words in the correct order to determine their syntactic relation.

T7: contextualized ordered set member detection. Finally, T7 adds order to T5: It asks models to check whether at least one out of two pairs of features is present in the input, but now order of context matters (e.g., *(1 before 5)* $\vee$ *(2 before 7)*). An example would be semantic role identification, where *cow* is typically an *agent* if it precedes *eats*, but not if it follows it.

3.2 Dataset construction

All datasets contain 100k training, 10k validation, and 10k test examples. For each datapoint, we sample uniformly at random whether the answer is positive or negative. For each task, we create datasets with sequence lengths 5, 10, 15, 20, 25, and 30. Also, for each datapoint, we exclude between 1 and 6 randomly chosen attributes. We apply this restriction because otherwise, for longer sequences, nearly all positive datapoints would contain all features, whereas negative datapoints must, by construction, miss at least one feature. This would allow models to develop a degenerate guessing strategy ("datapoint is positive if it contains all features").

	Nr. of distinct queries	Nr. of queries containing each feature
T1	36	1
T2	630	36
T3, T4, T6	36	2
T5, T7	36	4

Table 1: Description of the query space.

T1. For each datapoint, we choose a random feature as a query. If the answer is positive, the feature will appear in the sequence. All other features are randomly set to active with $p = 0.2$. During training, the queried feature can appear multiple times (following the 0.2 probability), but it appears only once at test time for 2 main reasons: to facilitate analysis and to avoid having the number of appearances of the queried feature in the sequence as an informative variable.

T2. The 2 queried features are randomly chosen. This is the only task where we have 2 query activations, instead of 1. As is highlighted in Table 1, the query space is much larger for this task, in comparison with all the other tasks (630 possible queries, vs. 36 possible queries for the others). For positive datapoints, we randomly choose whether the features are in the same token. For negative datapoints, we randomly choose whether one of the features appears in the sequence.

For T3-7, we use predefined mappings between query and input features (these mappings will not be accessible to the models, but will need to be learned as part of carrying out the task). The input feature pairs in these tasks consist of a feature between 1 and 18 and one between 19 and 36. Also, we aim for an equal representation of features in the query space, so each feature appears twice in T3, T4 and T6 and four times in T5 and T7 in the input-query mapping (see Table 1).

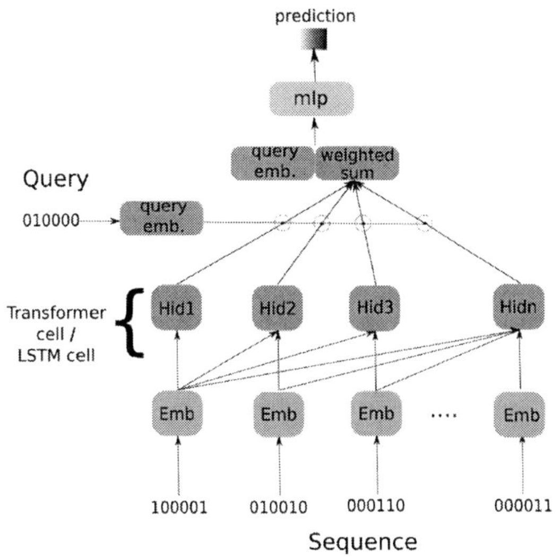

Figure 2: Diagram of the models.

T3. First, we choose a random feature to activate in the query. We then check which are the 2 features associated with the chosen query feature in the predefined mapping. Then, for positive datapoints, we choose randomly whether one or 2 of these features appear in the sequence. If 2 features appear, we randomly choose whether they appear in the same token. For negative datapoints, we ensure that none of these 2 features appear in the input sequence.

T4. The pipeline is similar to T2, the difference being that we randomly choose 1 query and we use its associated features.

T5. We choose one of the 2 pairs of features that are associated with one query. We then apply the same pipeline as in T2 while ensuring that at least 1 feature from the other pair doesn't appear in the sequence.

T6. For positive cases, we randomly choose 2 positions in the sequence and put the 2 tokens on these positions in the correct order. For negative cases, we randomly choose whether the datapoint contains both features in the wrong order or contains at most one of the features.

T7. We choose one of the 2 pairs of features that are associated with one query. We then apply the same procedure as in T6, while ensuring that at least 1 feature from the other pair doesn't appear in the sequence.

4 Models

The general structure of the models is presented in Figure 2. Model equations and training details are provided in the appendix.[2]

Transformer. The Transformer architecture consists of a sequence encoder and a decoder adapted to our tasks. We choose the most basic architecture for interpretability: a single-head, single-layer architecture. To enable incremental processing, the encoder self-attention only looks into the past, as in standard "causal" architectures such as the one of Dai et al. (2019).

The input vectors are mapped to a 100-dimensional space and combined with sine-based positional embeddings, as in Vaswani et al. (2017). Each input token vector then goes through a transformer encoder cell with one attention head and one layer. The query vector is also mapped onto a 100-dimensional space, through a separate embedding matrix. Decoding works as a dot-product-based attention between the query embedding and each token representation (Bahdanau et al., 2015).

The concatenation of the query embedding and the decoded sequence representation is then passed through a multi-layer perceptron (MLP) to generate the answer, a number in the range of [0,1] obtained via the Sigmoid function. The model is optimized with a binary cross-entropy loss. At test time, a result larger than 0.5 is considered a positive answer, as is standard.

We ablate the full Transformer architecture by removing self-attention and skipping positional encoding when embedding the input. The variants solely based on decoder attention are akin to Memory Networks (Sukhbaatar et al., 2015).

LSTM. In order to have a fair comparison with the Transformer model, we do minimal changes to the architecture in the LSTM model, only substituting the transformer self attention block with the LSTM cell.

We experiment with two variants of LSTM:

- (basic) LSTM: the input goes through the LSTM and the output of the last time step is considered the representation of the input and is concatenated with the query embedding to be sent to the MLP.

[2]The models were implemented using the framework Pytorch (Paszke et al., 2019).

Tasks↓ Models→	T-Pos-Att	T+Pos-Att	T-Pos+Att	T+Pos+Att
T1 1 feature	91.3±2.8	96.1±2.9	96.5±1.7	**98.7**±1.1
T2 2 features	83.4±0.2	**84.7**±0.5	83.2±0.2	**84.9**±1.5
T3 set member	98.7±1.2	**100**	99.4±0.9	**100**
T4 context. 2 features	86.2±0.6	**87.7**±0.3	86.4±0.6	**87.7**±0.2
T5 context. set member	77.4±0.4	77.7±1.2	**78.8**±2.5	77.8±1.1
T6 ordered feature	56.6±1	80.2±0.4	**92.1**±0.3	90.7±1.9
T7 ord. context. set member	57.5±0.4	65.8±0.8	**78.6**±0.6	67.6±0.6

Table 2: Results for sequence length 10. Results are averaged over 5 random seeds, with s.d. Best results boldfaced. Models are coded as follows: **+/-Pos** marks absence (-) vs. presence (+) of positional encoding, **+/-Att** marks absence (-) vs. presence (+) of self-attention. The full Transformer is model T+Pos+Att.

- attention LSTM: similarly to the Transformer model, there is an attention mechanism that compares the query embedding to the output from each time step (again using dot product). The input representation that will be concatenated to the query representation is then the weighted sum of the outputs.

5 Results

5.1 Transformer

Since the Transformer surpasses the LSTM in most cases, and the Transformer patterns are quite similar across sequence lengths, we first take a detailed look at the behavior of the Transformer on the tasks for sequence length 10. Table 2 summarizes the results for this sequence length. Recall that datapoints are always uniformly distributed between negative and positive answers, such that a random baseline always averages 50% accuracy.

Task 1 All the models succeed at T1 (single feature detection) with accuracy over 90%. As could be expected, there is a high correlation between the accuracy and the degree of decoder attention on the correct token: This attention is at an average of 0.82 when the answer is correct, vs. 0.17 when it is wrong.

Surprisingly, while this task doesn't involve contextualization nor order, both self-attention and positional encoding bring a boost in performance, from 91.3% accuracy for the base model (T-Pos-Att) to over 96% for the models T+Pos-Att and T-Pos+Att (which add positional encoding and self-attention, respectively). We conjecture that positional embeddings act as a beneficial noising mechanism, akin to regularization: altering a token's embedding depending on the position helps the model not to overfit.

We also find that self-attention triggers an inverse recency effect on accuracy: performance is better when the target feature is towards the beginning of the sequence. Indeed, there is a highly significant Pearson correlation of -0.51 between position and accuracy for models with self-attention vs. no significant correlation for models without it. This recency effect is probably due to the fact that self-attention can copy a feature through the following hidden states, so an earlier feature will tend be more prominent in the weighted sum, and thus easier to detect. We find that this copying mechanism improves results for earlier tokens without significantly harming performance in later tokens.

Thus, the first take-home message from our experiments is that the presence of a component in a Transformer architecture does not imply that the model will learn to use it as expected in a task, even if it puts it to a use that improves performance. In T1, self-attention preserves information and positional encoding possibly adds noise, and both have a serendipitous positive effect. This underscores the need for model analysis.

Task 2 When moving to two-feature detection (T2), there is a predictable drop in accuracy. The models have problems when the queried features are in different tokens (false negatives), with a 25% accuracy drop, and when only one target feature occurs in the sequence (false positives), with a 40% drop. The main reason why features in different tokens are missed is that decoder attention fails to operate distributively, i.e., to focus on two different input tokens at once: On average, the difference between the decoder attention weight of the most attended token and the second most attended token is of 0.6-0.7 across the models, showing that decoder attention indeed focuses on a single token.

Given that the feature combinations are random,

it is not clear how self-attention could help, and indeed using self-attention does not improve results.

Task 3 The T3 results show that all model variants can easily learn to detect a class instance, or feature disjunction, even when using an indirect mapping. Decoder attention suffices, as the models learn to associate a query with both features of its class, and trigger high attention values when either of them is present in a token (average attention on target token between 0.6-0.7 for all variants). Here, model behavior is as expected.

Contextualization Self-attention should help with contextualized feature detection (T4 and T5), by highlighting a specific feature only when it is preceded by one of the other features it is associated with. However, models settle for a degenerate strategy instead, and thus we detect no competitive advantage for models with self-attention (compare models T-Pos-Att and T-Pos+Att in Table 2). In T4, they answer 'yes' if one specific feature is present in the sequence (always the same feature for each query): Average attention for the more attended feature in each query is around 0.9, while the average attention on the other relevant feature is around 0.05. The maximum accuracy for this strategy is 87.5%, which is about what the best models reach in T4.

Thus, the need to contextualize by itself is not enough for models to profit from self-attention; instead, as we will see next, the need to track order does trigger a productive use of self-attention.

Ordered feature detection. In T6 and T7, using self-attention brings accuracy from near chance to 92.1% and 78.6%, respectively (compare models T-Pos-Att and T-Pos+Att in Table 2). We find strong evidence that the models with self-attention use it to record the presence of the first feature in the hidden state of the token containing the second, as we predicted it should do already for tasks requiring contextualization: In both T6 and T7, model T-Pos+Att puts most of the decoder attention on the second feature-carrying token in the sequence, as we show next.

We report in Table 3 the difference between the average decoder attention on the second vs. first feature-carrying token for T6, T7, and T5, which is the unordered version of T7. In models that use self-attention as predicted, this difference will be large and positive. We see in the first column of the table that for T5, where order does not matter, the difference is very low, while it is much larger for T6 and T7. This confirms that there has been a change in strategy, with self-attention being productively used in the order-sensitive tasks.

	T-Pos+Att	T+Pos+Att
T5	0.03±0.02	0.01±0.01
T6	0.79±0.005	-0.14±0.55
T7	0.46±0.03	0.16±0.18

Table 3: Average decoder attention difference (and s.d.) between second and first feature-carrying tokens for the two models with self-attention in the contextualized tasks (T6 and T7), together with T5 for comparison.

Positional encoding is an alternative mechanism to track order, and for T6 and T7 it also improves results substantially with respect to the base models (compare models T-Pos-Att and T+Pos-Att), though much less than self-attention.

However, using both mechanisms actually harms performance (see results for T+Pos+Att). Self-attention and positional encoding seem to get in the way of each other, making it harder, when combined, for the model to converge on a single strategy to track order. We see evidence for this in Table 3, where the full Transformer (T+Pos+Att) has a much smaller difference for T7 compared to model T-Pos+Att, and a negative difference for T6 (meaning that it puts more attention on the first feature-carrying token). Moreover, the full Transformers exhibit a large standard deviation in both order-sensitive tasks, which means that different runs converge on different strategies. In contrast, the models with self-attention show a really low standard deviation; they always converge on the expected strategy.

Impact of sequence length Figure 3 presents average accuracies for sequence lengths from 5 to 30 (in steps of 5; error bars represent standard deviations across 5 random seed initializations). The patterns discussed for length 10 are generally confirmed at other sequence lengths. We further notice that longer sequences are beneficial for "easy" tasks, such as T1 and T3 (perhaps they help models avoiding trivial guessing strategies). On the other hand, when the complexity of the task is higher (Tasks 5, 6 and 7), longer sequences are detrimental to model performance. Accuracies for tasks for which degenerate solutions were found for sequence length 10 (T2 and T4) do not change across sequence length, indicating that the strategy does

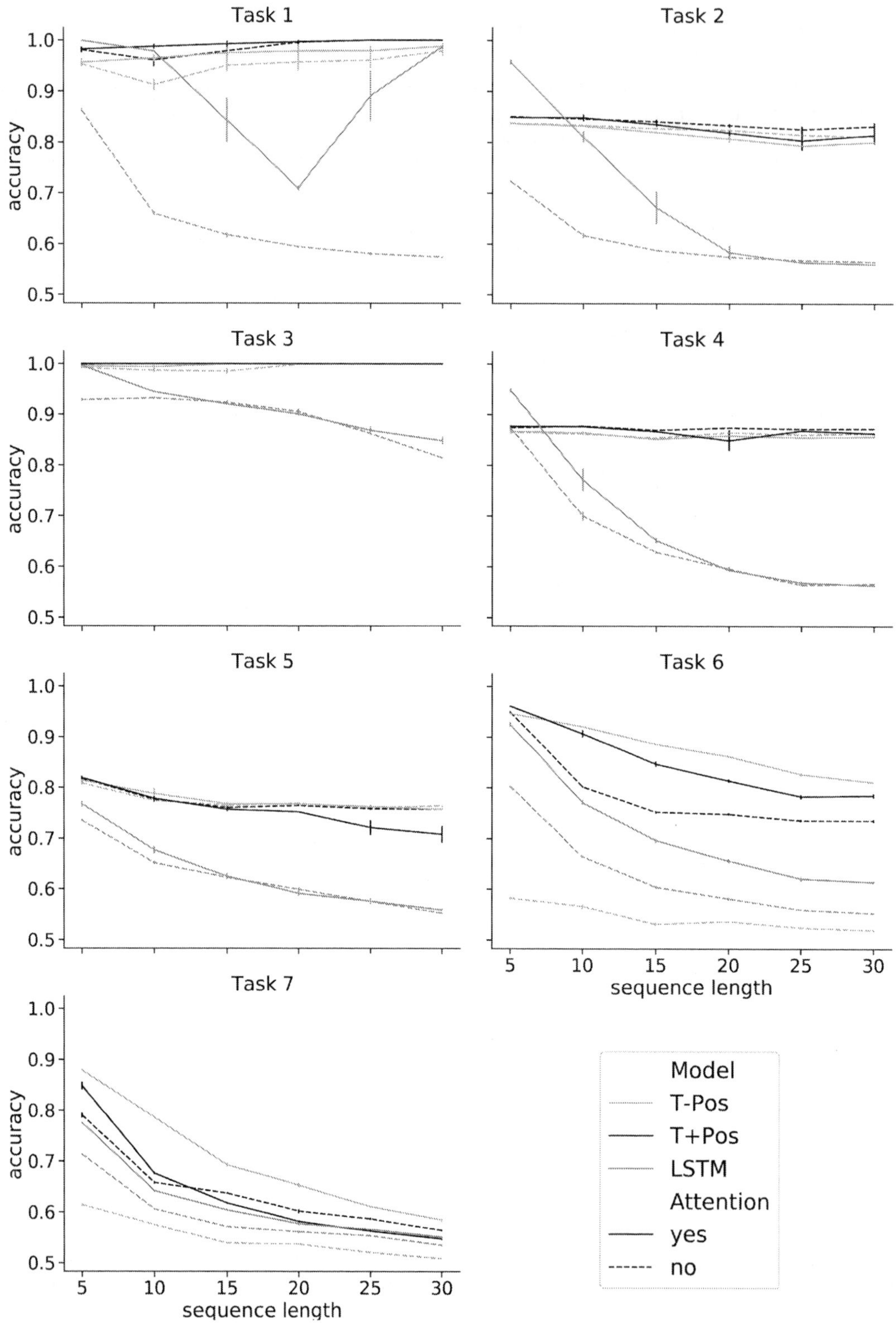

Figure 3: Model performance on multiple sequence lengths for all tasks

not change either. Also note that for the most difficult tasks (T5-T7), model T-Pos+Att is consistently better in longer sequences. Thus, the "getting in the way" effect observed above holds for the three tasks.

5.2 LSTM

In general, the performance of LSTM models on our tasks is markedly worse than that of the Transformer, and they are impacted by sequence length to a much larger extent (see Figure 3). This could be expected given general results on the two architectures (Transformers outperform LSTMs in most computational linguistics tasks, and LSTMs have been shown to have issues with long-distance dependencies). There are two notable exceptions to these general trends.

First, the accuracy of the LSTM with attention in Task 1 shows a characteristic V-shape, dropping at first and recovering for longer sequences (cf. orange solid line in Figure 3).[3] The result is that its performance is on par with that of the Transformer models in sequences of length 5 and 30.

We find that the LSTM changes its behaviour, from a simple recurrent LSTM to an actual attention-based LSTM. Indeed, for short sequences, it does not use decoder attention to identify the target feature (and still performs optimally): for instance, for sequence length 5, the attention is distributed uniformly, with attention values of around 0.2 on all the input tokens. Instead, for long sequences it does use the attention mechanism: the attention values spike on the position of the input that contains the queried feature (e.g., with an average of 0.85 for sequence length 30). This ability to switch behaviours could theoretically help also for other tasks, but it seems that the complexity of the tasks prevents the model from doing so.

Second, the LSTM with attention surpasses all Transformer variants for short sequences in Tasks 2 and 4. Recall that the Transformer models reached a degenerate solution for these tasks (with a maximum accuracy of 87.5%), in which only one of the two relevant features was attended to; instead, the LSTM solves the task correctly, because the information about the previous tokens flows through the recurrent steps in the token representations.

As for the differences between the two model variants of the LSTM, the model enhanced with the decoder attention is consistently better than the classic, basic model. This suggests that the decoder attention mechanism (also present in all the Transformer models) is beneficial independently of the base architecture.

6 Conclusion

Our tasks shed light on how the main model components act and interact regarding the retrieval of discrete information from sequences, uncovering behaviours that would be difficult to detect when the architectures are applied to complex NLP tasks.

A take-home message from our experiments is that the presence of a component in an architecture does not imply that the model will learn to use it as expected in a task. In particular, we found that only the need to track ordered information led the architecture to use self-attention in the predicted way, and that decoder attention can be difficult for LSTMs to use correctly.

On the other hand, the components can assume unexpected functions. Self-attention in transformers can simply serve to blindly propagate information across time, leading to more robust representations of features contained in earlier tokens, that are copied over and over. Also, surprisingly, positional embeddings provide a small but consistent benefit in tasks that do not require order tracking. This suggests that they might have a serendipitous function, possibly adding helpful noise to the representations. Moreover, as both self-attention and positional embeddings can learn to keep track of order, the two mechanisms get in the way of each other, making it harder, when combined, for the Transformer models to converge on a single strategy to track order.

Regarding LSTM, the sequence length is a very big factor. The model has a steep loss in performance when the sequence gets longer. On the simplest task, the model enhanced with decoder attention develops the ability to switch between strategies, but this doesn't generalize to longer sequences.

To conclude, we hope to have shown that the proposed tasks constitute a useful probing mechanism for the ability of models to detect discrete information in sequences, testing in particular four key abilities: incremental processing (in the sense that the query is not known at input processing time), indirect mappings, context-dependence and order tracking. We have shown that most of the tasks are

[3]Instead, the basic LSTM model degrades quickly and monotonically with sequence length; see dashed orange line.

difficult for models even for short sequences; and they can be easily extended to more dimensions and even longer sequences.

Future work should go in two different directions: 1) examining how behavior changes when the probed models are scaled by increasing the number of layers and attention heads, and 2) modify the models to solve some of the problems that we encounter in the current experiments. We hope that the community will take up the analysis possibilities that our tasks afford, and that a clearer understanding of model behavior on the tasks will lead to better and more transparent models.

Acknowledgments

We gratefully acknowledge Laura Aina, Thomas Brochhagen and Sebastian Riedel for the feedback, advice and support. We are also grateful to the anonymous reviewers for their valuable comments. This project has received funding from the European Research Council (ERC) under the European Union's Horizon 2020 research and innovation programme (grant agreement No 715154). We are also grateful to the NVIDIA Corporation for the donation of GPUs used for this research. This paper reflects the authors' view only, and the EU is not responsible for any use that may be made of the information it contains.

References

Samira Abnar and Willem Zuidema. 2020. Quantifying attention flow in transformers. In *Proceedings of the 58th Annual Meeting of the Association for Computational Linguistics*, pages 4190–4197, Online. Association for Computational Linguistics.

Afra Alishahi, Grzegorz Chrupała, and Tal Linzen. 2019. Analyzing and interpreting neural networks for nlp: A report on the first blackboxnlp workshop. *Natural Language Engineering*, 25(4):543–557.

Dzmitry Bahdanau, Kyung Hyun Cho, and Yoshua Bengio. 2015. Neural machine translation by jointly learning to align and translate. In *3rd International Conference on Learning Representations, ICLR 2015*.

Yonatan Belinkov and James Glass. 2019. Analysis methods in neural language processing: A survey. *Transactions of the Association for Computational Linguistics*, 7:49–72.

Grzegorz Chrupała and Afra Alishahi. 2019. Correlating neural and symbolic representations of language. In *Proceedings of the 57th Annual Meeting of the Association for Computational Linguistics*, pages 2952–2962, Florence, Italy. Association for Computational Linguistics.

Alexis Conneau, German Kruszewski, Guillaume Lample, Loïc Barrault, and Marco Baroni. 2018. What you can cram into a single $&!#* vector: Probing sentence embeddings for linguistic properties. In *Proceedings of the 56th Annual Meeting of the Association for Computational Linguistics (Volume 1: Long Papers)*, pages 2126–2136, Melbourne, Australia. Association for Computational Linguistics.

Zihang Dai, Zhilin Yang, Yiming Yang, Jaime Carbonell, Quoc Le, and Ruslan Salakhutdinov. 2019. Transformer-XL: Attentive language models beyond a fixed-length context. In *Proceedings of the 57th Annual Meeting of the Association for Computational Linguistics*, pages 2978–2988, Florence, Italy. Association for Computational Linguistics.

Jacob Devlin, Ming-Wei Chang, Kenton Lee, and Kristina Toutanova. 2019. BERT: Pre-training of deep bidirectional transformers for language understanding. In *Proceedings of the 2019 Conference of the North American Chapter of the Association for Computational Linguistics: Human Language Technologies, Volume 1 (Long and Short Papers)*, pages 4171–4186, Minneapolis, Minnesota. Association for Computational Linguistics.

John Hewitt and Percy Liang. 2019. Designing and interpreting probes with control tasks. In *Proceedings of the 2019 Conference on Empirical Methods in Natural Language Processing and the 9th International Joint Conference on Natural Language Processing (EMNLP-IJCNLP)*, pages 2733–2743, Hong Kong, China. Association for Computational Linguistics.

Sepp Hochreiter and Jürgen Schmidhuber. 1997. Long short-term memory. *Neural computation*, 9(8):1735–1780.

Dieuwke Hupkes, Verna Dankers, Mathijs Mul, and Elia Bruni. 2020. Compositionality decomposed: how do neural networks generalise? *Journal of Artificial Intelligence Research*, 67:757–795.

Dieuwke Hupkes, Sara Veldhoen, and Willem Zuidema. 2018. Visualisation and 'diagnostic classifiers' reveal how recurrent and recursive neural networks process hierarchical structure. *Journal of Artificial Intelligence Research*, 61:907–926.

Brenden Lake and Marco Baroni. 2018. Generalization without systematicity: On the compositional skills of sequence-to-sequence recurrent networks. In *International Conference on Machine Learning*, pages 2873–2882. PMLR.

Yair Lakretz, Dieuwke Hupkes, Alessandra Vergallito, Marco Marelli, Marco Baroni, and Stanislas Dehaene. 2021. Mechanisms for handling nested dependencies in neural-network language models and humans. *Cognition*, page 104699.

Tal Linzen, Emmanuel Dupoux, and Yoav Goldberg. 2016. Assessing the ability of LSTMs to learn syntax-sensitive dependencies. *Transactions of the Association for Computational Linguistics*, 4:521–535.

Adam Paszke, Sam Gross, Francisco Massa, Adam Lerer, James Bradbury, Gregory Chanan, Trevor Killeen, Zeming Lin, Natalia Gimelshein, Luca Antiga, et al. 2019. Pytorch: An imperative style, high-performance deep learning library. *Advances in Neural Information Processing Systems*, 32:8026–8037.

Anna Rogers, Olga Kovaleva, and Anna Rumshisky. 2021. A primer in bertology: What we know about how bert works. *Transactions of the Association for Computational Linguistics*, 8:842–866.

Koustuv Sinha, Robin Jia, Dieuwke Hupkes, Joelle Pineau, Adina Williams, and Douwe Kiela. 2021. Masked language modeling and the distributional hypothesis: Order word matters pre-training for little. *arXiv preprint arXiv:2104.06644*.

Sainbayar Sukhbaatar, Arthur Szlam, Jason Weston, and Rob Fergus. 2015. End-to-end memory networks. In *Proceedings of the 28th International Conference on Neural Information Processing Systems-Volume 2*, pages 2440–2448.

Ashish Vaswani, Noam Shazeer, Niki Parmar, Jakob Uszkoreit, Llion Jones, Aidan N Gomez, Łukasz Kaiser, and Illia Polosukhin. 2017. Attention is all you need. In *Advances in neural information processing systems*, pages 5998–6008.

Elena Voita, David Talbot, Fedor Moiseev, Rico Sennrich, and Ivan Titov. 2019. Analyzing multi-head self-attention: Specialized heads do the heavy lifting, the rest can be pruned. In *Proceedings of the 57th Annual Meeting of the Association for Computational Linguistics*, pages 5797–5808, Florence, Italy. Association for Computational Linguistics.

Jason Weston, Antoine Bordes, Sumit Chopra, Alexander M Rush, Bart van Merriënboer, Armand Joulin, and Tomas Mikolov. 2015. Towards ai-complete question answering: A set of prerequisite toy tasks. *arXiv preprint arXiv:1502.05698*.

Jennifer C White and Ryan Cotterell. 2021. Examining the inductive bias of neural language models with artificial languages. *arXiv preprint arXiv:2106.01044*.

Appendix

Transformer implementation

Each datapoint has **n** 36-dimension binary vectors as input **in** and a 36-dimension binary vector as query **q**. All these vectors are embedded to 100 dimensions using the matrices W_{in} and W_q. Then we apply a sinusoidal positional encoding on the input embeddings and the ReLU function on top of the query embedding:

$$emb_{in_i} = PosEnc(in_i * W_{in})$$

$$emb_q = ReLU(q * W_q)$$

with PosEnc defined for each input position *pos* and for each token dimension *i* similarly to the method used in the main Transformer architecture (Vaswani et al., 2017):

$$PosEnc(pos, 2i) = sin(pos/10000^{2i/d_{model}})$$

$$PosEnc(pos, 2i+1) = cos(pos/10000^{2i/d_{model}})$$

Then, each input embedding goes through the TransformerEncoder cell which has 1 attention head and 1 layer:

$$h_i = TransfEnc(emb_{in_i})$$

as defined in Vaswani et al. (2017), TransfEnc is a scaled dot product attention where *d* is the dimensionality of the input vectors. The dot product is scaled in order to not have regions with very slow gradients.

$$TransfEnc(X) = softmax(\frac{X * X^T}{\sqrt{d}}) * X$$

In order to decode relevant information based on the query we use a dot product attention. α_i represents the attention value that we put on token embedding h_i relative to the query embedding. We then calculate the vector c which is the sum of the token embeddings weighted by α.

$$\alpha_i = \frac{\exp(h_i * emb_q)}{\sum_{k=1}^{n} \exp(h_k * emb_q)}$$

$$c = \sum_{i=1}^{n} \alpha_i h_i$$

We then use a multi-layer perceptron to generate the answer. Firstly, we apply a dimensionality reduction using W_{o1} from 200 to 100 dimensions with ReLU as nonlinearity on top of it. Then the hidden state hid_o is mapped from 100 to 1 dimension. Using the Sigmoid function, we get our result as a number in the range of [0,1]. At test time, if $o \geq 0.5$, then we consider the answer to be positive.

$$hid_o = ReLU((c||emb_q) * W_{o1})$$

$$o = Sigmoid(hid_o * W_{o2})$$

The loss is calculated using binary cross entropy.

LSTM implementation

In order to have a fair comparison with the Transformer model, we do minimal changes to the architecture, only substituting the transformer self attention block and the positional encoding with an LSTM cell.

Learning procedure

All the experiments are optimized with Adam and learning rate 0.0001. We apply 0.2 dropout and gradient clipping at 0.5. We run 100 epochs with batch size 10 and save the model at the epoch with the highest validation accuracy. We experimented with different hyperparameters, but we found the ones we just reported to give the most stable results.

The Acceptability Delta Criterion: Testing Knowledge of Language using the Gradience of Sentence Acceptability

Héctor Javier Vázquez Martínez
Massachusetts Institute of Technology
hjvm@mit.edu

Abstract

Any test that promises to assess Human Knowledge of Language (KoL) for any statistically-based Language Model (LM) must meet three requirements: (1) comprehensive coverage of linguistic phenomena; (2) replicable and statistically-vetted human judgement data; and (3) test the LM's ability to track the gradience of sentence acceptability. To this end, we propose here the LI-Adger dataset: a comprehensive collection of 519 sentence types (4177 sentences) spanning the field of current generative linguistics, accompanied by attested and replicable human acceptability judgements (Sprouse and Almeida, 2012; Sprouse et al., 2013; Sprouse and Almeida, 2017). Finally, we posit the Acceptability Delta Criterion (ADC), an evaluation metric that tests how well a LM can track changes in human acceptability judgements across minimal pairs instead of testing whether the LM assigned a greater likelihood to the expert-labeled acceptable sequence of a minimal pair ($S_1 > S_2$). We benchmark six different BERT (Devlin et al., 2018) models and a baseline trigram model with the ADC. Although the best performing BERT model scores 94%, and the trigram scores 75% classification accuracy under the traditional metric, performance drops precipitously to 38% for BERT and 30% for the trigram model under the ADC. Adopting the ADC reveals how much harder it is for LMs to track the gradience of acceptability across minimal pairs. With this work, we propose and provide the three necessary requirements for a comprehensive linguistic analysis and test of the apparently Human KoL exhibited by LMs that we believe is currently missing in the field of Computational Linguistics.

1 Introduction

Assessing Human Knowledge of Language (KoL) in statistically-based Language Models (LMs) generally involves assuming some fundamental property or computation occurring in the Human Language Faculty and arguing that an often poorly understood, statistical, and typically connectionist model, also encodes that property or uses that computation. This quickly becomes a problematic task because understanding the Human Language Faculty has been conventionally posed as a problem to be solved at a causal level removed from the algorithmic and computational implementation levels. Put in more abstract terms, assessing the KoL of a LM requires inferring some abstract operation inside a human black box based on input-output analysis and determining whether a second, statistical black box is somehow also performing the same operation by some other means.

The issue is made even more challenging by changes in either field that consequently change our assumptions surrounding the Human Language Faculty or the black boxes used in Machine Learning (ML). This, in turn, immediately impacts any claims relating the two by some abstract property, linguistic or otherwise, that is required for the evaluation of LMs. If any concrete progress is to be made when it pertains to KoL in LMs, then the design of the tests we perform and their conclusions must be based on the same empirical data from current input-output analyses of the Human Language Faculty that have subsequently been used to build the linguistic theories that attempt to characterize and explain Human KoL.

We take concrete steps toward designing such a test of KoL for LMs by positing the necessary components required to build upon the same foundation of empirical data as in the field of generative linguistics. First, we posit a gold standard in empirical data: the LI-Adger dataset, a collection of linguistic phenomena representative of the field of linguistics, accompanied by human acceptability judgements in the form of Magnitude Estimation (ME) data, all collected by Sprouse and Almeida 2012 and Sprouse et al. 2013. Altogether, the dataset has an

Proceedings of the Fourth BlackboxNLP Workshop on Analyzing and Interpreting Neural Networks for NLP, pages 479–495
Online, November 11, 2021.

attested maximum False Positive (Type 1 error) rate between 1-12% and is well above the 80% threshold for statistical power (<20% False Negatives, or Type 2 errors) (Sprouse and Almeida, 2017). The reliability of the LI-Adger dataset is such that, if the linguistic theories were somehow proven to be incorrect and reformulated, it would not be because of the data, but because of incorrect theorizing; any tractable theory of linguistics must account for the attested empirical phenomena observed in the LI-Adger dataset (Sprouse and Almeida, 2012). To complement this data, we propose the Acceptability Delta Criterion (ADC), a proof of concept metric that enforces the gradience of acceptability in its evaluation of model performance, and adopts the attested continuous human judgements as the ground-truth labels that LMs must approximate in order to demonstrate KoL. Finally, we use two distinct Bidirectional Encoder Representations from Transformers (BERT; Devlin et al. 2018) models: the out-of-the-box BERT trained using the Masked Language Modeling (MLM) objective (BERT_{MLM}), and $\text{BERT}_{\text{CoLA}}$, which is fine-tuned using the Corpus of Linguistic Acceptability (CoLA; Warstadt et al. 2019). As an additional baseline check, we include a trigram model trained using the British National Corpus (BNC) to test whether the ADC would constitute a meaningful advantage in statistical significance (fewer Type 1 errors) over the traditional method of comparing probabilities over isolated, minimally-differing sequences of words. Henceforth we refer to the traditional metric as the BLiMP criterion[1] (Warstadt et al., 2020), that will be contrasted against the new measure proposed here, the Acceptability Delta Criterion (ADC).

Under the BLiMP criterion, $\text{BERT}_{\text{CoLA}}$, correctly evaluates 2213 out of 2365 ($\sim$94%) minimal pairs in the LI-Adger dataset; that is, for those 2213 minimal pairs, $\text{BERT}_{\text{CoLA}}$ gives a higher score to the sentence in the minimal pair deemed by experts to be the *acceptable* one of the pair. To put the performance of $\text{BERT}_{\text{CoLA}}$ into perspective, the trigram model's output, when normalized for sequence length using the Syntactic Log-Odds Ratio (SLOR; Pauls and Klein, 2012; Lau et al., 2017) is able to correctly evaluate 1781 out of 2365 ($\sim$75%) minimal pairs. Considering the coverage of phenomena in the LI-Adger dataset, we may interpret these results in one of two ways: either metrics such as the BLiMP criterion lead to tests with low levels of statistical significance (with a high rate of false positives), or a basic trigram model using SLOR encodes the KoL necessary to account for 75% of the phenomena in generative linguistics.

Precisely this dilemma is what the ADC is meant to solve. Evaluating the models on how well they track the gradience of acceptability by adopting the ADC at its strictest level (with $\delta = 0.5$, where δ indicates the number of standard deviation units a model's scores are allowed to deviate from the corresponding human judgements) leads to a notable drop in performance, particularly for the trigram model. $\text{BERT}_{\text{CoLA}}$ only correctly scores 726 out of 2365 ($\sim$31%) minimal pairs, whereas the trigram model with SLOR correctly scores 712 out of 2365 ($\sim$30%). The ADC is therefore a much harder task, because the difference in likelihood acceptability score between the two sentences in each minimal pair is what is being evaluated.

2 Related Work

The success of Neural Language Models at different natural language tasks, such as Next Sentence Prediction (NSP), Machine Translation (MT) and Question Answering (QA), among others[2], has made it a popular endeavor to assess the potential KoL encoded in the learned representations of the language models and how that KoL may be contributing to their performance.

Human KoL, due to its abstract, deliberately acomputational nature, can *only* be assessed via proxies, generally by probing language acquisition or use. At present, the studies of LMs' KoL that rely on an input-output analysis of the system tend to focus on probing their weak generative capacity: i.e, testing whether a given LM can discern whether a particular sequence of words is or is not in the set of sentences generated by some presumed corresponding grammar, typically by comparing the probabilities the LM assigns to different but related sequences of words. Contrast this with testing the LM's strong generative capacity by evaluating whether it has assigned the correct syntactic structure, or series of candidate syntactic structures in

[1] Although this has been the traditional metric to test KoL in the literature (Linzen et al., 2016; Marvin and Linzen, 2018; Wilcox et al., 2018; Warstadt and Bowman, 2020; among others), we name this metric with the same acronym as that of the Benchmark for Linguistic Minimal Pairs by Warstadt et al. (2020) mainly for conciseness and ease of use.

[2] For a quick collection of more natural language tasks and how different models perform on them, see the GLUE Leaderboard or the Super GLUE Leaderboard.

the case of ambiguous or homonymous sequences, to a sequence of words (Chomsky, 1956).

Warstadt et al. (2020) have taken seminal steps toward evaluating LMs beyond their weak generative capacity by positing the Benchmark of Linguistic Minimal Pairs for English (BLiMP). They automatically generated 67 datasets of 1000 minimal pairs each from grammar templates that span 12 linguistic phenomena. They designed the templates to contrast in grammatical acceptability by isolating specific phenomena in syntax, morphology or semantics. In doing so, the authors intend to mirror what a working linguist uses to probe KoL in native speakers of a language. Because such principles generally appeal to grammatical constraints, they go beyond simple weak generative capacity.

While the tradition of using minimal pairs in linguistics dates back nearly 100 years (e.g. Bloomfield 1933, among many others), the concept of using minimal pairs to evaluate NN models is not entirely new either (Linzen et al., 2016; Marvin and Linzen, 2018; Wilcox et al., 2018; to name a few). However, the creators of BLiMP take the idea to a much larger scale and propose a single metric for evaluation, which we have named the BLiMP criterion out of convenience. For a given minimal pair m_i consisting of an acceptable sentence $s_{i,1}$ and an unacceptable sentence $s_{i,2}$, if a LM evalutes $P(s_{i,1}) > P(s_{i,2})$, then the LM has met the BLiMP criterion for m_i. The authors of BLiMP thus score a LM on the BLiMP dataset according to the percentage of all the minimal pairs for which it was able to fulfill the BLiMP criterion. This, of course, can be broken down into further analyses of the 12 linguistic phenomena they sought to represent in the dataset.

Because the BLiMP dataset relies on templates, the choice and design of the linguistic phenomena represented in the data is inherently limited, and therefore unrepresentative of syntax or linguistics more broadly. Secondly, the templated approach produces semantically implausible sentences, such as *Sam ran around some glaciers* as noted by Warstadt et al. (2020) in their paper. Sprouse et al. (2018) have shown that semantic implausibility is a very strong confounding factor when eliciting human acceptability judgements, even in a Forced Choice (FC) task such as the one used to collect the human judgement data in BLiMP. Finally, the BLiMP criterion treats sentence acceptability as a functionally categorical phenomenon, which we assert to be gradient by nature.

Our proposed test of Human KoL in LMs takes this minimal pair approach to the next level by addressing the three gaps we have outlined above. We (1) expand linguistic coverage to be representative of the field with the LI-Adger dataset, (2) further control for confounding factors such as semantic implausibility when eliciting human acceptability judgements by using the examples constructed by hand by Sprouse and Almeida 2012 & Sprouse et al. 2013, and (3) enforce the gradient nature of sentence acceptability judgements with the ADC.

3 Why BERT is the benchmark.

We chose BERT as the model to test due to the growing body of research attributing ever greater Human KoL to BERT. Warstadt and Bowman (2019) have shown high Matthews Correlation Coefficient (MCC) scores between the expert acceptability labels for the sentences in the Corpus of Linguistic Acceptability (CoLA; Warstadt et al., 2019) and $\text{BERT}_{\text{CoLA}}$ models' predictions. They have gone on to show with a grammatically annotated CoLA analysis set that $\text{BERT}_{\text{CoLA}}$ models exhibit very strong positive MCC scores on multiple syntactic features. For example, they claim BERT exhibits strong knowledge of complex or noncanonical argument structures such as ditransitives and passives, and has a distinct advantage over baseline performance on sentences with long-distance dependencies such as questions. Finally, Salazar et al. (2019) used the raw pseudo-log-likelihood (PLL; Wang and Cho, 2019; Shin et al., 2019; Salazar et al., 2019) scores from the out-of-the-box BERT_{MLM} to evaluate its KoL using the BLiMP benchmark and found it to correctly predict 84.8% of the minimal pairs in BLiMP, thereby beating GPT-2 by 4.2% and almost reaching the human baseline at 88.6%. We take the information provided here and the overarching body of research surrounding BERT [3] as the baseline level of performance to be expected from the model. We hypothesize that BERT is capable of exhibiting reasonable levels of gradience when it calculates sequence likelihoods or acceptability scores across minimal pairs when compared to the human ME data.

[3]For a recent review of the Knowledge of Language that has been attributed to BERT, see *A Primer in BERTology: What We Know About How BERT Works*, (Rogers et al., 2021)

4 The LI-Adger dataset is the test set.

The LI-Adger dataset is a collection of two separate datasets. The first consists of a randomly selected sample of 150 pairwise phenomena (300 sentence types) from Linguistic Inquiry (LI) 2001-2010 collected by Sprouse et al. (2013). Each pairwise phenomenon includes 8 hand-constructed, semantically plausible and lexically matched minimal pairs such that most of the contribution of lexical information to the acceptability of the sentences would be distributed equally to the pair.

The second set of sentences is an exhaustive selection of 219 sentence types from Adger (2003)'s *Core Syntax* textbook (198 directly from the textbook + 21 as additional controls) that form 105 multi-condition phenomena collected by Sprouse and Almeida (2012). Much like the LI dataset, 8 tokens of each sentence type were created by hand by the original authors such that the structural properties of the condition were maintained but the lexical items varied.

For the purposes of the LI-Adger dataset as a whole, we have split each multi-condition phenomenon into minimal pairs by taking each possible combination of acceptable and unacceptable sentences in the condition as a valid minimal pair, when properly lexically matched. We include an explicit example of the arrangement with a multi-condition phenomenon from Chapter 8 (*Functional Categories III*) of the *Core Syntax* textbook in Appendix A.

The Adger dataset, in virtue of being sampled from the *Core Syntax* textbook, that constructs a theory of syntax from the ground up on the basis of key examples, can be taken to have a reasonably good coverage of the field of syntax. We augment this with the LI dataset, sampled from the 111/114 articles published in Linguistic Inquiry about US English syntax from 2001-2010 (out of the total 308 articles published during that time). Therefore, to the extent that the Adger *Core Syntax* textbook and *LI*2001-2010 are representative of the data in the field, so is the LI-Adger dataset. (Sprouse and Almeida, 2012; Sprouse et al., 2013).

5 The Human Magnitude Estimation (ME) data are the ground truth labels.

Just as important as the coverage of linguistic phenomena represented in the LI-Adger dataset is the foundation of human judgement data built upon it. Sprouse and Almeida (2012) collected Magnitude Estimation (ME) and Yes-No (YN) judgement data from a total of 440 native participants for the 469 data points they sampled from the Adger *Core Syntax* textbook. After conducting three different statistical analyses on the data (standard frequentist tests, linear mixed-effects models, and Bayes factor analyses), they found that the maximum replication failure rate between formal and informal judgements (i.e. formal vs. informal data collection methods) was 2 percent (Sprouse and Almeida, 2012; Schütze and Sprouse, 2013).

Sprouse et al. (2013) took those analyses even further with their sample of 148 pairwise phenomena from *LI*2001-2010. They collected data for the LI sentences using the 7-point Likert Scale (LS) task, ME and Forced Choice (FC) and vetted this dataset via 5 different statistical analyses (Descriptive directionality, one- and two-tailed null hypothesis tests, Bayes factor analysis and linear mixed effect models). They estimated a minimum replication rate for journal data of 95 percent ± 5 (Sprouse et al., 2013; Schütze and Sprouse, 2013.

Finally, Sprouse and Almeida (2017) sampled 50 pairwise phenomena from the LI dataset in a complementary study that determined the statistical power of formal linguistics experiments by task and average effect size and recommend setting the threshold for well-powered experiments at 80% statistical power. They find that the FC task would reach the 80% power threshold and detect 70% of the phenomena published in *LI*2001-2010 with just ten participants, assuming each provides only one judgement per phenomenon. With fifteen participants, FC would detect 80% of the phenomena. Because the ME task has less statistical power than FC, it requires at least thirty to thirty-five participants to reach the same 80% coverage of *LI*2001-2010 as FC (Sprouse and Almeida, 2017; Schütze and Sprouse, 2013). Because the sample sizes for the LI-Adger datsets are much larger (104 participants per condition for the LI sentences and 40 for the Adger sentences), we do not forfeit any statistical power by using ME data in spite of the higher statistical power of the FC task. On the contrary, the ME task will allow us not only to perform the same type of functionally categorical acceptability comparison as the BLiMP criterion, but also allow us to make comparisons between every condition in the dataset.

Taken together, the human ME data that accompany the LI-Adger dataset are therefore reliable, replicable and statistically powerful. This collection of empirical data has the added benefit of being theory-agnostic; if linguistic theories were to fundamentally change in the future, the significance and validity of the data would remain unchanged because this statistically vetted empirical evidence would still remain to be accounted for.

6 The Acceptability Delta Criterion (ADC) is the loss function.

Thanks to the ME data associated with each sentence in the LI-Adger dataset, we can now make direct acceptability comparisons, not just between the two sentences of a minimal pair, but also across minimal pairs, and even across phenomena. The reason why is precisely the gradient nature of acceptability: violations of certain linguistic phenomena elicit much stronger responses from the participants than others, as observed in the differences in ME scores across minimal pairs and across linguistic phenomena in the dataset. We include an example of such a difference in Appendix B.

Acceptability judgement experiments carry as a necessary underlying assumption that acceptability is a *percept* that arises in response to linguistic stimuli. Collecting data about the percept requires then that the subject report that perception of acceptability (Chomsky, 1965; Sprouse and Almeida, 2013; Schütze and Sprouse, 2013; T Schütze, 2016). Consequently, acceptability judgements are a behavioral response that may vary in intensity, much like brightness, loudness, temperature, pain, etc. The degree of this response is inherently informative, in particular because acceptability is the behavioral output of the grammatical system, to which neither speakers nor linguists have direct access. We include one example of this variability in intensity and how it is reflected in the human ME judgements in Appendix B.

To this end, we propose the Acceptability Delta Criterion (ADC). It is founded on the principle that, if we are to ascribe any inferred knowledge of one black box (the Human Language Faculty) to another black box (Neural Language Models) based solely on an input-output analysis of both systems, then the response of both systems must agree both categorically and in magnitude. In other words, for a minimal pair whose change in human acceptability rating is nearly night and day, a language model with comparable KoL must output a similarly drastic change in acceptability rating across the same minimal pair.

To make this example more concrete: Suppose we have a language model L with output function f that takes in a sequence of words $\vec{x}_i$ and outputs a score y_i. The first step in computing the ADC is to understand the range of values output by the language model L over the 4179 LI-Adger sentences: $Y = [y_1, y_2, ..., y_{4179}]$. With the full range of values, we apply a Z-score transformation to each of the values in Y by subtracting the mean of Y from each of the values and then dividing them by the standard deviation of Y. This will yield the set of Z-score transformed predictions $Z = [z_1, z_2, ..., z_{4179}]$. Notice that because this is a purely linear transformation, it preserves the relationships between the data points. In addition, the resulting set of predictions Z represents a standardized form of Y, where each prediction z_i is expressed in standard deviation units of y_i from the mean of Y (Schütze and Sprouse, 2013).

Now that we have grounds for making the comparison[4] and a value for how acceptable the model L finds a sequence of words $\vec{x}_i$ in terms of standard deviation units z_i, we can begin to compare the degree of this acceptability response to the human judgement data, also expressed in standard deviation units. For a given minimal pair m_i consisting of an acceptable sentence $s_{i,1}$ and an unacceptable sentence $s_{i,2}$, we will have 4 pieces of information: two human Z-score transformed acceptability judgements $h_{i,1}$ and $h_{i,2}$, and two language model scores $z_{i,1}$ and $z_{i,2}$. We turn these into two concrete points of comparison: a human acceptability delta $\Delta h_i = h_{i,1} - h_{i,2}$ and a language model acceptability delta $\Delta lm_i = z_{i,1} - z_{i,2}$. In this new formulation, no information has been lost. Recall that the BLiMP criterion is met for the minimal pair m_i when the language model scores the acceptable sentence higher than the unacceptable one, i.e. $\Delta lm_i > 0$.

With the fully defined delta values as well as

[4]We rely on the Z-score transformation as opposed to the log-transformation because the Z-score transformation is linear and therefore preserves the relationships that exist between the data. This transformation also has the added benefit that it assumes the data are continuous, which both the ME data and the LMs' likelihoods are. On the other hand, the log-transformation is generally not recommended for ME data because it introduces distortion to the data by nature of being nonlinear, and is too powerful for simple outlier removal (Sprouse, 2011; Schütze and Sprouse, 2013). The Z-score transformation is therefore the better candidate operation we can reasonably apply to both the human judgement data and the LMs' likelihood scores.

a reformulated BLiMP criterion in terms of the delta values, we may at last proceed to define the ADC. Let δ be a scalar value indicating the number of maximum allowed units of deviation between the human judgement delta Δh_i and the language model delta Δlm_i. Using this δ value, we consider the ADC to be met for the minimal pair m_i when the following two conditions are met:

$$\text{sign}(\Delta h_i) = \text{sign}(\Delta lm_i) \tag{1}$$

$$|\Delta h_i - \Delta lm_i| < \delta \tag{2}$$

The δ parameter in Equation 2 can be adjusted to allow for larger or smaller amounts of deviation between the human and LM acceptability deltas. If δ is set to a large number, the ADC functionally becomes the BLiMP criterion because it is dominated by Equation 1. The main difference would be that, instead of comparing the expert labels to the LM's output, the human judgements would become the ground truth. For example, if δ is set to a very large number, and the human ME data find the expert-labeled *unacceptable* sentence as more acceptable than the expert-labeled *acceptable* counterpart, then the LM is expected to follow the same monotonicity. We include a concrete example of the ADC in action in Appendix C. Because the δ parameter determines how closely the LM's acceptability deltas must track the human judgement deltas, we adopt a first approximation of $\delta = 0.5$, which we believe to be the proper value of δ in order to test for the gradience of acceptability. Additionally, we adopt a value of $\delta = 1$ in order to show how performance under the ADC changes as the δ parameter is relaxed. We include results for both values of δ in the case study to be presented here.

7 The KoL experiment brings everything together.

With the LI-Adger dataset as the test set, the human ME data as the ground truth labels and the ADC as the loss function, this KoL experiment now only requires the model to test.

In order to ensure we observe the best performance by BERT in our benchmarks, we adopt two parallel approaches to the tests: a syntactic probing approach and a MLM approach with a variant of the Cloze task (Taylor, 1953). For the probing approach, we train a linear softmax classifier (probe) on top of BERT's hidden layer outputs using the Corpus of Linguistic Acceptability (CoLA; Warstadt et al., 2019). We use the Huggingface Transformers library (Wolf et al., 2020) to fine-tune three pre-trained versions of BERT in order to be comprehensive in our coverage: 10 random seeds of $\text{BERT}_{\text{base-uncased}}$, 20 random seeds of $\text{BERT}_{\text{large-uncased}}$, and 20 random seeds of $\text{BERT}_{\text{large-cased}}$. For further control we attempt to replicate the mean MCC scores per linguistic phenomenon obtained by Warstadt and Bowman (2019) on their later published CoLA Analysis set. For the purposes of transparency and the replicability of our own experiment, we include the results of our models' performance on the CoLA Analysis set in Appendix D. For each of the three $\text{BERT}_{\text{CoLA}}$ we selected the random restart that yielded the highest MCC score on the CoLA test set as the model to test using the ADC. Finally, we need to adapt the categorical output of the fine-tuned BERT models (c_j where $j \in \{1, 0\}$) to a more gradient form in order to ensure the models have the best chance of tracking sentences through the acceptability gradient. We rely on Sun et al. (2019)'s formulation of the probabilities[5] of the categorical labels as the softmax of BERT's final hidden layer output h_i:

$$P(c_j|h_i) = \text{softmax}(Wh_i) \tag{3}$$

Therefore, the output of the fine-tuned BERT models can be defined as:

$$out_i = \underset{c_j \in \{0,1\}}{\arg\max} \left[P(c_j|h_i) \right] \tag{4}$$

Out of convenience, we will switch the categorical labels from {0, 1} to {-1, 1}. This allows us to multiply the model's confidence in a particular label ($P(c_j|h_i)$) by the label itself, written explicitly below:

$$\begin{aligned} out_i = & \underset{c_j \in \{-1,+1\}}{\arg\max} \left[P(c_j|h_i) \right] * \\ & \max_{c_j \in \{-1,+1\}} \left[P(c_j|h_i) \right] \end{aligned} \tag{5}$$

[5]Guo et al. (2017) among others have found that in order for the softmax output of a neural network to be considered a true probability or confidence, it must be calibrated to the true correctness likelihood via other post-processing methods currently unavailable to us. Because there is currently no complete theory of the gradient nature of acceptability that can produce the gradient acceptability score for a given sentence on demand (Sprouse and Almeida, 2012), we will loosely interpret the output of the softmax in Equation 3 as the model's *confidence* in that particular label.

With this formulation, we can easily retrieve both the predicted categorical label ($\text{sign}(out_i)$) and the model's *confidence* in that label ($|out_i|$).

Reformulations aside, because probing relies on training an additional classifier on top of the latent, albeit poorly understood, representations of neural LMs, it is extremely difficult to control for confounding variables, such as the information being introduced into the system by training the probing classifier in the first place (Warstadt et al., 2020). Additionally, D'Amour et al. (2020) have found substantial evidence indicating that these overparametrized neural LMs by nature exploit different sets of spurious correlations according to their random initialization in spite of exhibiting very similar performance on I.I.D. test sets. This poses a unique set of difficulties for the use of probes for any assessment of KoL in such LMs.

We mitigate these concerns with the second, parallel approach to our experiment: We use the publicly available model checkpoints for $\text{BERT}_{\text{base-uncased}}$, $\text{BERT}_{\text{large-uncased}}$, and $\text{BERT}_{\text{large-cased}}$, which were originally trained using the Masked Language Modeling (MLM) and Next Sentence Prediction (NSP) objectives (Devlin et al., 2018). Because MLM is one of the tasks used to pre-train BERT in the first place, we use it to test the models in their out-of-the-box state. By masking each token in a sentence s_i sequentially and recovering the log likelihood of the original token, we are able to calculate a *pseudo-log-likelihood* (PLL) score for the sentence. Salazar et al. (2020) have shown that BERT's PLL scores are able to outperform GPT-2 on the BLiMP dataset under the traditional metric, as well as on other natural language benchmarks, potentially due to BERT's ability to better leverage the left and right context of each masked token when calculating its likelihood. This altogether strongly favors PLL scores as the ideal metric to test the out-of-the-box BERT models with the ADC.

Now we have 6 distinct BERT models to test: the three best performing random restarts of $\text{BERT}_{\text{base-uncased}}$, $\text{BERT}_{\text{large-uncased}}$, and $\text{BERT}_{\text{large-cased}}$ when fine-tuned using CoLA (collectively $\text{BERT}_{\text{CoLA}}$), and the three unadulterated, publicly available model checkpoints for which we will calculate PLL scores (collectively BERT_{MLM})[6]. To this assortment, we add the trigram model trained by Sprouse et al. (2018) using the British National Corpus (BNC). We will use both its raw negative log-likelihood scores and Syntactic Log-Odds Ration (SLOR; Pauls and Klein, 2012, Lau et al., 2017) scores.

Finally, we test four metrics: the original BLiMP criterion, and the ADC with δ values of 0.5, 1.0 and 5.0. The goal with the last $\delta = 5.0$ is to observe how model performance approaches that of the BLiMP criterion when the ADC is dominated by Equation 1. The results of these tests are presented in Table 1.

8 Results

We summarize the results of our proposed KoL benchmark with the BERT and trigram models in Table 1. We observe extremely good performance across the board under the BLiMP criterion. However, employing the ADC with the stricter δ values ($\delta = 0.5$, $\delta = 1.0$) leads to a precipitous drop in performance. When the distance between the models' output deltas and the human judgement deltas (Equation 2) is no longer considered by the ADC ($\delta = 5.0$), all the models' performances come very close to the performance numbers they obtained under the BLiMP criterion because the models are no longer expected to track the human judgement deltas in magnitude, only monotonicity. The minute differences in performance are primarily accounted for by disagreements between the expert labels and the human judgements in minimal pairs where the human judgements favored the sentence expert-labeled as unacceptable. We include 4 example minimal pairs where the $\text{BERT}_{\text{CoLA}}$ models scored correctly under the BLiMP criterion, but not under the ADC with $\delta = 5.0$ in Appendix E. This is a very encouraging result, suggesting that the ADC is in fact a generalization of the BLiMP criterion, with the difference being explained by the shift to human judgements as the ground-truth labels.

To further compare how each of the models' acceptability deltas (Δlm_i) behave with respect to the ground truth (Δh_i), we plot in Figure 1 a heatmap of the Pearson's Correlation Coefficient (PCC) matrix for all 8 models and the human judgements.

The models that were best able to track the human judgement deltas through the full spectrum of acceptability were the BERT_{MLM} mod-

[6] We make a note here to acknowledge that, due to computational limitations at the time of writing and experimentation, we were unable to add models much larger than $\text{BERT}_{\text{large-cased}}$, such as GPT-2 or GPT-3 to the case study presented here.

Model	BLiMP	ADC, $\delta = 0.5$	ADC, $\delta = 1.0$	ADC, $\delta = 5.0$
$\text{BERT}_{base-uncased;\text{MLM}}$	0.852	0.364	0.631	0.849
$\text{BERT}_{large-uncased;\text{MLM}}$	0.866	0.378	0.658	0.859
$\text{BERT}_{large-cased;\text{MLM}}$	0.871	0.376	0.661	0.868
$\text{BERT}_{base-uncased;\text{CoLA}}$	0.915	0.286	0.538	0.902
$\text{BERT}_{large-uncased;\text{CoLA}}$	0.917	0.311	0.564	0.907
$\text{BERT}_{large-cased;\text{CoLA}}$	0.936	0.307	0.561	0.925
trigram_{SLOR}	0.753	0.301	0.520	0.744
$\text{trigram}_{log-prob}$	0.671	0.165	0.329	0.668

Table 1: Comparison between the models' BLiMP criterion and ADC scores, using δ={0.5, 1.0, 5.0}. We include three BERT_{MLM} models, three $\text{BERT}_{\text{CoLA}}$ models, as well as SLOR and log-likelihood scores from a trigram model trained on the British National Corpus by Sprouse et al. 2018

els with the PLL metric at a moderate positive correlation of 0.38 for $\text{BERT}_{\text{large-cased}}$ and 0.39 for $\text{BERT}_{\text{base-uncased}}$ and $\text{BERT}_{\text{large-uncased}}$. The BERT models fine-tuned using CoLA were only very slightly (0.01) better correlated with the human judgement deltas than the trigram model's SLOR score deltas. Functionally, the 7 models (excluding the trigram's raw log-likelihood scores) perform very closely when tracking the human judgement deltas at the minimal pair level. As an additional resource, we include example minimal pairs of where the $\text{BERT}_{\text{CoLA}}$ models and the trigram model disagree in Appendix F, and plot all six BERT models' deltas (Δlm_i) against the human deltas (Δh_i) in Appendix G.

9 Discussion

The first column of Table 1 (BLiMP) is what first prompted us to formulate the ADC. In particular, note that the performance of the basic trigram model trained using the BNC is at 75.3% when using its SLOR scores. Having discussed how comprehensive the LI-Adger dataset is, this leaves us with the following troubling dichotomy: Either the trigram model encodes approximately 3 quarters of the empirical linguistic phenomena in the LI-Adger dataset, or it is too easy to best the BLiMP criterion with word cooccurrences alone. The dichotomy suggests that the BLiMP criterion has a low significance level as a metric when assessing KoL and thus commits a higher rate of Type 1 errors than would be advisable in order for experiments that rely on it to be conclusive. We believe this to be due to treating sentence acceptability as a functionally categorical metric when it is inherently gradient; we remedy this by testing for the gradience of acceptability using the ADC.

However, the ADC does raise the concern of whether we are fundamentally changing the results by adopting human acceptability judgements as ground-truth instead of the expert labels. We evaluated all 8 models with ever greater δ values in order to observe how much this should concern us, and as observed in the rightmost column of Table 1 (ADC, $\delta = 5.0$), that concern is minimal. The performance of each of the models very closely approximated their original performance under the traditional metric (leftmost column; BLiMP). Adopting the human judgements as the ground truth labels therefore does not inherently cause a steep drop in performance. Furthermore, we believe it a counterproductive effort to compute human performance as compared to the expert labels, or to have LMs competing against human baselines to reach perfect predictive accuracy of expert labels. The expert labels are based on linguistic theories that are firstly subject to change as the theories are either refined or disproven, and secondly built upon the empirical basis of human judgements in the first place. Our belief is as follows: just as any new, tractable theory of linguistics must account for the empirical phenomena observed in the LI-Adger dataset and human judgement data, so must any Language Model account for the linguistic phenomena observed in the dataset, and it must do so by tracking the human data within an established margin (δ).

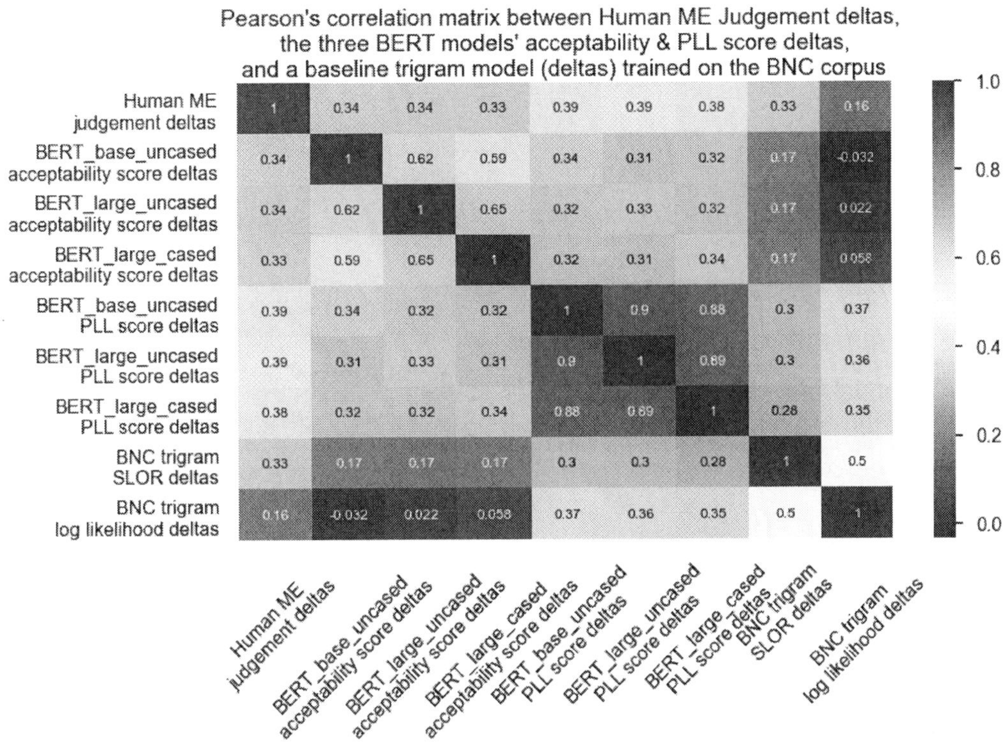

Figure 1: PCC matrix between human judgements and all three $\text{BERT}_{\text{CoLA}}$ & BERT_{MLM} models. As a further baseline we add the SLOR and log likelihood scores of a trigram model trained on the British National Corpus by Sprouse et al. (2018). All correlations shown have a $p < 0.0001$.

10 Contributions

With this work, we have identified three quintessential requirements to a test of Human Knowledge of Language in statistically-based Language Models: It must (1) exhibit comprehensive coverage of linguistic phenomena, (2) support attested and replicable human judgement data, and (3) test LMs' ability to track different linguistic phenomena across the full range of the acceptability gradient. Additionally, we advance a test of KoL for LMs that meets all three requirements.

First, we present the LI-Adger dataset as a gold standard test dataset: a comprehensive, empirically attested collection of 519 pairwise and multi-condition phenomena collected by Sprouse et al. (2013) from Linguistic Inquiry (LI) 2001-2010, and by Sprouse and Almeida (2012) from Adger's (2003) *Core Syntax* textbook. To complement the test dataset, we present statistically powerful, replicable and validated human Magnitude Estimation (ME) data collected by Sprouse and Almeida (2012) and Sprouse et al. (2013) as the ground truth labels we expect LMs with Human KoL to approximate. Finally, in order to tie the LI-Adger dataset and the human ME data together, we present the Acceptability Delta Criterion (ADC), a metric that tests LMs for Human KoL by requiring LMs to track the validated human judgements through the gradient spectrum within a specified margin (δ) as the acceptability values change across minimal pairs.

Our three main contributions with this work when taken together create a comprehensive and powerful input-output analysis of Human KoL for LMs. With further ongoing work, the test will empower us to see a fine-grained analysis of which phenomena a LM is able to account for in its output from how well it predicts the acceptability deltas around them. It is our hope that researchers will rely on the LI-Adger dataset for its coverage of empirically attested linguistic phenomena, embrace the paradigm of human judgements as the ground-truth labels that LMs are expected to approximate, and, beyond that, adopt the ADC as we take our understanding of KoL in LMs to the next level.

References

David Adger. 2003. *Core syntax: A minimalist approach*, volume 20. Oxford University Press Oxford.

N. Chomsky. 1956. Three models for the description of language. *IRE Transactions on Information Theory*, 2(3):113–124.

Noam Chomsky. 1965. Aspects of the theory of syntax. *Cambridge, MA: MIT Press*, (1977):71–132.

Alexander D'Amour, Katherine Heller, Dan Moldovan, Ben Adlam, Babak Alipanahi, Alex Beutel, Christina Chen, Jonathan Deaton, Jacob Eisenstein, Matthew D Hoffman, et al. 2020. Underspecification presents challenges for credibility in modern machine learning. *arXiv preprint arXiv:2011.03395*.

Jacob Devlin, Ming-Wei Chang, Kenton Lee, and Kristina Toutanova. 2018. Bert: Pre-training of deep bidirectional transformers for language understanding. *arXiv preprint arXiv:1810.04805*.

Chuan Guo, Geoff Pleiss, Yu Sun, and Kilian Q Weinberger. 2017. On calibration of modern neural networks. *arXiv preprint arXiv:1706.04599*.

Jey Han Lau, Alexander Clark, and Shalom Lappin. 2017. Grammaticality, acceptability, and probability: A probabilistic view of linguistic knowledge. *Cognitive Science*, 41(5):1202–1241.

Tal Linzen, Emmanuel Dupoux, and Yoav Goldberg. 2016. Assessing the ability of lstms to learn syntax-sensitive dependencies. *Transactions of the Association for Computational Linguistics*, 4:521–535.

Rebecca Marvin and Tal Linzen. 2018. Targeted syntactic evaluation of language models. *arXiv preprint arXiv:1808.09031*.

Adam Pauls and Dan Klein. 2012. Large-scale syntactic language modeling with treelets. In *Proceedings of the 50th Annual Meeting of the Association for Computational Linguistics (Volume 1: Long Papers)*, pages 959–968.

Anna Rogers, Olga Kovaleva, and Anna Rumshisky. 2021. A primer in bertology: What we know about how bert works. *Transactions of the Association for Computational Linguistics*, 8:842–866.

Julian Salazar, Davis Liang, Toan Q. Nguyen, and Katrin Kirchhoff. 2019. Pseudolikelihood reranking with masked language models. *CoRR*, abs/1910.14659.

Julian Salazar, Davis Liang, Toan Q. Nguyen, and Katrin Kirchhoff. 2020. Masked language model scoring. In *Proceedings of the 58th Annual Meeting of the Association for Computational Linguistics*, pages 2699–2712, Online. Association for Computational Linguistics.

Carson T Schütze and Jon Sprouse. 2013. Judgement data. In Robert Podesva and Devyani Sharma, editors, *Research Methods in Linguistics*, pages 27–51. Cambridge University Press.

Joonbo Shin, Yoonhyung Lee, and Kyomin Jung. 2019. Effective sentence scoring method using bert for speech recognition. In *Asian Conference on Machine Learning*, pages 1081–1093.

Jon Sprouse. 2011. A test of the cognitive assumptions of magnitude estimation: Commutativity does not hold for acceptability judgments. *Language*, pages 274–288.

Jon Sprouse and Diogo Almeida. 2012. Assessing the reliability of textbook data in syntax: Adger's core syntax. *Journal of Linguistics*, 48(3):609–652.

Jon Sprouse and Diogo Almeida. 2013. *The Role of Experimental Syntax in an Integrated Cognitive Science of Language*.

Jon Sprouse and Diogo Almeida. 2017. Design sensitivity and statistical power in acceptability judgment experiments. *Glossa*, 2(1):1.

Jon Sprouse, Carson T Schütze, and Diogo Almeida. 2013. A comparison of informal and formal acceptability judgments using a random sample from linguistic inquiry 2001–2010. *Lingua*, 134:219–248.

Jon Sprouse, Beracah Yankama, Sagar Indurkhya, Sandiway Fong, and Robert C Berwick. 2018. Colorless green ideas do sleep furiously: gradient acceptability and the nature of the grammar. *The Linguistic Review*, 35(3):575–599.

Chi Sun, Xipeng Qiu, Yige Xu, and Xuanjing Huang. 2019. How to fine-tune BERT for text classification? *CoRR*, abs/1905.05583.

Carson T Schütze. 2016. *The empirical base of linguistics: Grammaticality judgments and linguistic methodology*. Language Science Press.

Wilson L Taylor. 1953. "cloze procedure": A new tool for measuring readability. *Journalism quarterly*, 30(4):415–433.

Alex Wang and Kyunghyun Cho. 2019. Bert has a mouth, and it must speak: Bert as a markov random field language model. *arXiv preprint arXiv:1902.04094*.

Alex Warstadt and Samuel R Bowman. 2019. Linguistic analysis of pretrained sentence encoders with acceptability judgments. *arXiv preprint arXiv:1901.03438*.

Alex Warstadt and Samuel R Bowman. 2020. Can neural networks acquire a structural bias from raw linguistic data? *arXiv preprint arXiv:2007.06761*.

Alex Warstadt, Alicia Parrish, Haokun Liu, Anhad Mohananey, Wei Peng, Sheng-Fu Wang, and Samuel R. Bowman. 2020. Blimp: The benchmark of linguistic minimal pairs for english. *Transactions of the Association for Computational Linguistics*, 8:377–392.

Alex Warstadt, Amanpreet Singh, and Samuel R Bowman. 2019. Neural network acceptability judgments. *Transactions of the Association for Computational Linguistics*, 7:625–641.

Ethan Wilcox, Roger Levy, Takashi Morita, and Richard Futrell. 2018. What do rnn language models learn about filler-gap dependencies? *arXiv preprint arXiv:1809.00042*.

Thomas Wolf, Lysandre Debut, Victor Sanh, Julien Chaumond, Clement Delangue, Anthony Moi, Pierric Cistac, Tim Rault, Remi Louf, Morgan Funtowicz, Joe Davison, Sam Shleifer, Patrick von Platen, Clara Ma, Yacine Jernite, Julien Plu, Canwen Xu, Teven Le Scao, Sylvain Gugger, Mariama Drame, Quentin Lhoest, and Alexander Rush. 2020. Transformers: State-of-the-art natural language processing. In *Proceedings of the 2020 Conference on Empirical Methods in Natural Language Processing: System Demonstrations*, pages 38–45, Online. Association for Computational Linguistics.

Appendix A

An example of one multi-condition phenomenon from Chapter 8 (*Functional Categories III*) of the Adger (2003) *Core Syntax* textbook is presented in Table 2 below.

Sentence ID	Sentence
ch8.150.*.01	Melissa seems that is happy.
ch8.151.g.01	It seems that Melissa is happy.
ch8.152.g.01	Melissa seems to be happy.

Table 2: Example multi-condition phenomenon from the Adger dataset. Note: the original sentences in the Adger textbook used names from Greek mythology, but were changed to common names in order to avoid inadvertently influencing the native speakers' judgements.

This multi-condition phenomenon would constitute two minimal pairs in the LI-Adger dataset we present as the gold standard test set. The unacceptable sentence (ch8.150.*.01) forms a minimal pair with each of the other two acceptable forms. We include the pairings explicitly in the list below.

1. Minimal pair with ch8.151.g.01
   (a) It seems that Melissa is happy.
   (b) * Melissa seems that is happy.
2. Minimal pair with ch8.152.g.01
   (a) Melissa seems to be happy.
   (b) * Melissa seems that is happy.

Similarly, we form minimal pairs of all multi-condition phenomena in the original LI and Adger datasets by exhaustively enumerating all lexically matched pairs of acceptable & unacceptable sentences in the multi-condition phenomenon.

Appendix B

In order to illustrate the informativeness of adopting gradient acceptability judgements and of being able to make direct comparisons across minimal pairs with the ME data, take as an example the two minimal pairs in Table 3.

It is clear that the difference in acceptability across the Culicover minimal pair is vastly different from the difference across the Bowers minimal pair in Table 3. In fact, the average ME rating for the expert-labeled unacceptable Bowers sentence (33.2.bowers.7b.*.07) is much higher than many other sentences in the data that are expert-labeled as *acceptable*, meaning the 104 participants that were asked to rate this sentence found it *statistically* completely acceptable. This type of information is absolutely crucial when evaluating whether a LM has knowledge of any particular linguistic phenomenon, yet this information is lost when analysing performance according to the BLiMP criterion.

Appendix C

As an example of the ADC in action, consider the minimal pairs from Table 3 (Appendix B), expressed in Table 4 in terms of the Sentence ID of the grammatical sentence. We show the acceptability delta values for the Z-score transformed log probabilities of a simple trigram model trained on the British National Corpus (Sprouse et al. 2018), as well as the human acceptability deltas. We also include two columns indicating whether the BLiMP criterion (BC) or the Acceptability Delta Criterion (ADC) was met.

Appendix D

We recreate in Table 5 an updated version of the table of MCC scores on the CoLA test set presented by Warstadt and Bowman (2019) (W&B). We add a column to indicate the authors responsible for training the model and include our three

Sentence ID	Sentence	ME Z-score
32.3.Culicover.7a.g.01	John tried to win.	1.453262
32.3.Culicover.7b.*.01	John tried himself to win.	-0.86729
33.2.bowers.7b.g.07	Sarah counted the change accurately.	1.230412
33.2.bowers.7b.*.07	Sarah accurately counted the change.	1.20698

Table 3: Two minimal pairs for the Linguistic Inquiry (LI) dataset collected by Sprouse & Almeida, 2012. The ME Z-score is the averaged Z-score transformation of the human Magnitude Estimation scores for each of the shown sentences across the 104 different experimental participants (Sprouse et al., 2013).

Sentence(g) ID	Δh_i	Δlm_i	BC met?	ADC met? ($\delta = 1$)
32.3.Culicover.7a.g.01	2.320552	0.633896671	Yes	No
33.2.bowers.7b.g.07	0.023432	-0.158799029	No	No

Table 4: The two minimal pairs from Table 3 expressed in terms of the Sentence ID of the grammatical sentence with acceptability delta values from the human judgements and Z-score transformed log probability scores from a trigram trained by Sprouse et al. (2018) on the British National Corpus (BNC). The last two columns show whether the BLiMP criterion (BC) or the Acceptability Delta Criterion (ADC) was met.

trained models in the comparison. Additionally, we include two models submitted by Jacob Devlin to the GLUE Leaderboard for additional points of comparison, although we assume the scores presented in the leaderboard are the maximum MCC scores achieved by the models on the CoLA out-of-domain test set. Our mean MCC scores for $\text{BERT}_{\text{CoLA}_{\text{large-cased}}}$ were within error margins of the $\text{BERT}_{\text{CoLA}_{\text{large}}}$ model reported by W&B. Additionally, the maximum MCC score achieved here by $\text{BERT}_{\text{CoLA}_{\text{large-cased}}}$ beat the score posted by Jacob Devlin on the GLUE Leaderboard, and was less than 0.01 away from the maximum MCC score posted by W&B's $\text{BERT}_{\text{CoLA}_{\text{large}}}$. We consider these results to be strongly indicative of successful replication, given the known stochastic variation in such models.

Appendix E

We present in Table 6 four example minimal pairs that the three $\text{BERT}_{\text{CoLA}}$ models evaluated correctly under the BLiMP criterion, but not under the ADC with $\delta = 5.0$. We report the Z-score transformed acceptability scores for $\text{BERT}_{\text{CoLA}_{\text{large-cased}}}$, the best performing out of the three BERT models. In the case of $\text{BERT}_{\text{CoLA}_{\text{large-cased}}}$, the minimal pairs presented are 4 out of the 58 total minimal pairs that it scored correctly under the BLiMP criterion, but not under the ADC with $\delta = 5.0$.

The common factor among the four minimal pairs presented in Table 6, and the other 54 minimal pairs where $\text{BERT}_{\text{CoLA}_{\text{large-cased}}}$ fulfilled the BLiMP criterion but not the ADC with $\delta = 5$, is that the human judgements disagree with the expert categorization. This is, by design, one of the crucial properties of the ADC, because ultimately linguistic theory is developed by probing either language *use* or language *acquisition* and developing grammars that are able to account for the attested empirical phenomena. The paradigm of the ADC is therefore grounded in the empirical data itself, not on the theory built upon it.

Appendix F

We present in Table 7 four example minimal pairs where all three $\text{BERT}_{\text{CoLA}}$ models scored the pair correctly under the ADC with $\delta = 0.5$ but the trigram did not. In Table 8 we present the opposite: four example minimal pairs where the trigram model's SLOR scores evaluated the pair correctly under the ADC with $\delta = 0.5$ but none of the three $\text{BERT}_{\text{CoLA}}$ models did.

Appendix G

In Figure 4 we draw a correlation (scatter) plot with best fit line of the six BERT models' delta scores (Δlm_i) on the x-axis against the human judgement

Model$_{\text{CoLA}}$	**Mean (STD)**	**Max**	**Ensemble**	**Authors**
CoLA baseline	0.320 (0.007)	0.330	0.320	W&B 2019
GPT	0.528 (0.023)	0.575	0.567	W&B 2019
BERT$_{\text{large}}$	**0.582 (0.032)**	**0.622**	**0.601**	**W&B 2019**
Human	0.697 (0.042)	0.726	0.761	Warstadt et al. 2018
BERT$_{\text{base-uncased}}$	0.478 (0.018)	0.514	0.522	HJVM & friends
BERT$_{\text{large-uncased}}$	0.542 (0.019)	0.583	0.578	HJVM & friends
BERT$_{\text{large-cased}}$	**0.574 (0.026)**	**0.613**	**0.588**	**HJVM & friends**
BERT$_{\text{base}}$	0.521* (N/A)	0.521*	0.521*	Jacob Devlin
BERT$_{\text{large}}$	**0.605* (N/A)**	**0.605***	**0.605***	**Jacob Devlin**

Table 5: Replication of Warstadt and Bowman (2019) with our trained BERT$_{\text{CoLA}}$ models for comparison. Performance (MCC) on the CoLA test set, including mean over restarts of a given model with standard deviation, maximum over restarts, and majority prediction over restarts. We include the BERT$_{\text{CoLA}}$ scores on the GLUE leaderboard for the CoLA task submitted by Jacob Devlin for further points of comparison.

deltas (Δh_i) on the y-axis. The figure reveals the BERT$_{\text{CoLA}}$ models' behavior is not gradient despite our reformulation of the BERT$_{\text{CoLA}}$ models' outputs in order to make them more gradient. The BERT$_{\text{CoLA}}$ models consistently predicted sentences to be either more than 90% acceptable or less than 90% unacceptable; the fine-tuning phase on the categorical expert labels in CoLA only seems to cripple the BERT$_{\text{CoLA}}$ models' performance.

The out-of-box BERT$_{\text{MLM}}$ models' PLL output deltas are much more gradient than those of the BERT$_{\text{CoLA}}$ models and seem to better roughly track the best-fit line.

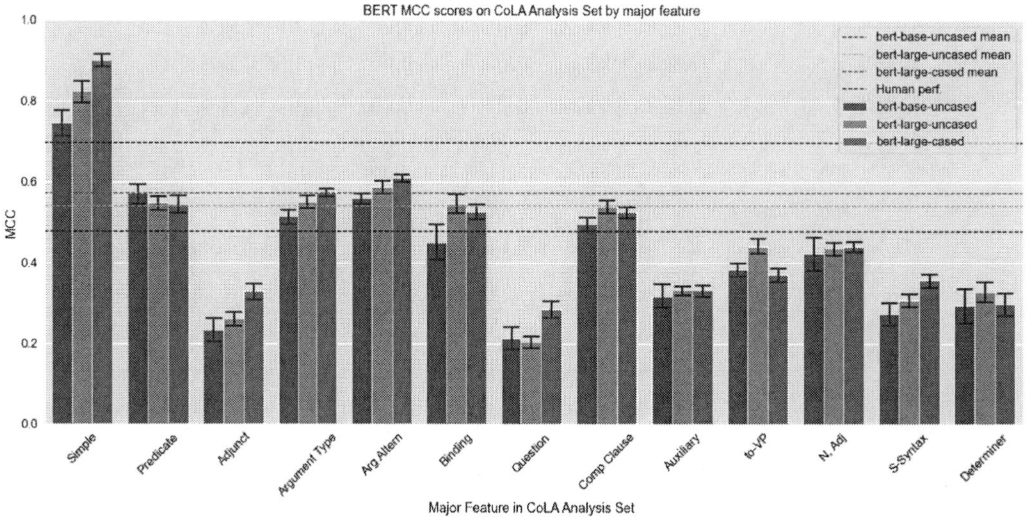

Figure 2: Replication of Warstadt and Bowman (2019) with our $\text{BERT}_{\text{CoLA}}$ models for comparison. Performance (MCC) on CoLA analysis set by major feature. Dashed lines show mean performance on the CoLA out-of-domain test set. From left to right, performance for each feature is given for base-uncased, large-uncased, and large-cased.

Minimal Pair **Top**: Acceptable I **Bottom**: Unacceptable	Human judgement	BERT acceptability
We proved Amelia to the manager to be responsible.	-0.56008	0.732817911
*We proved to the manager Amelia to be responsible.	-0.13864	-1.39757562
There is likely to live a snake in the garden.	-0.6451	-1.02182
*There is likely a snake to live in the garden.	-0.51201	-1.39602
Jenny would accurately have calculated the results.	0.345683	-1.340338319
*Jenny accurately will calculate the results.	0.501494	-1.40060934
The announcer's introduction of Ted was humorous.	0.659471	0.73306608
*The announcer's introduction of Ted's was humorous.	0.748718	-1.335794047

Table 6: Four minimal pairs where the $\text{BERT}_{\text{CoLA}}$ models meet the BLiMP criterion but not the generalized ADC with $\delta = 5.0$. We report the acceptability scores from the large-cased version of $\text{BERT}_{\text{CoLA}}$ The human judgement and BERT acceptability scores are already Z-score transformed. The common factor is that the human judgements disagree with the expert labels.

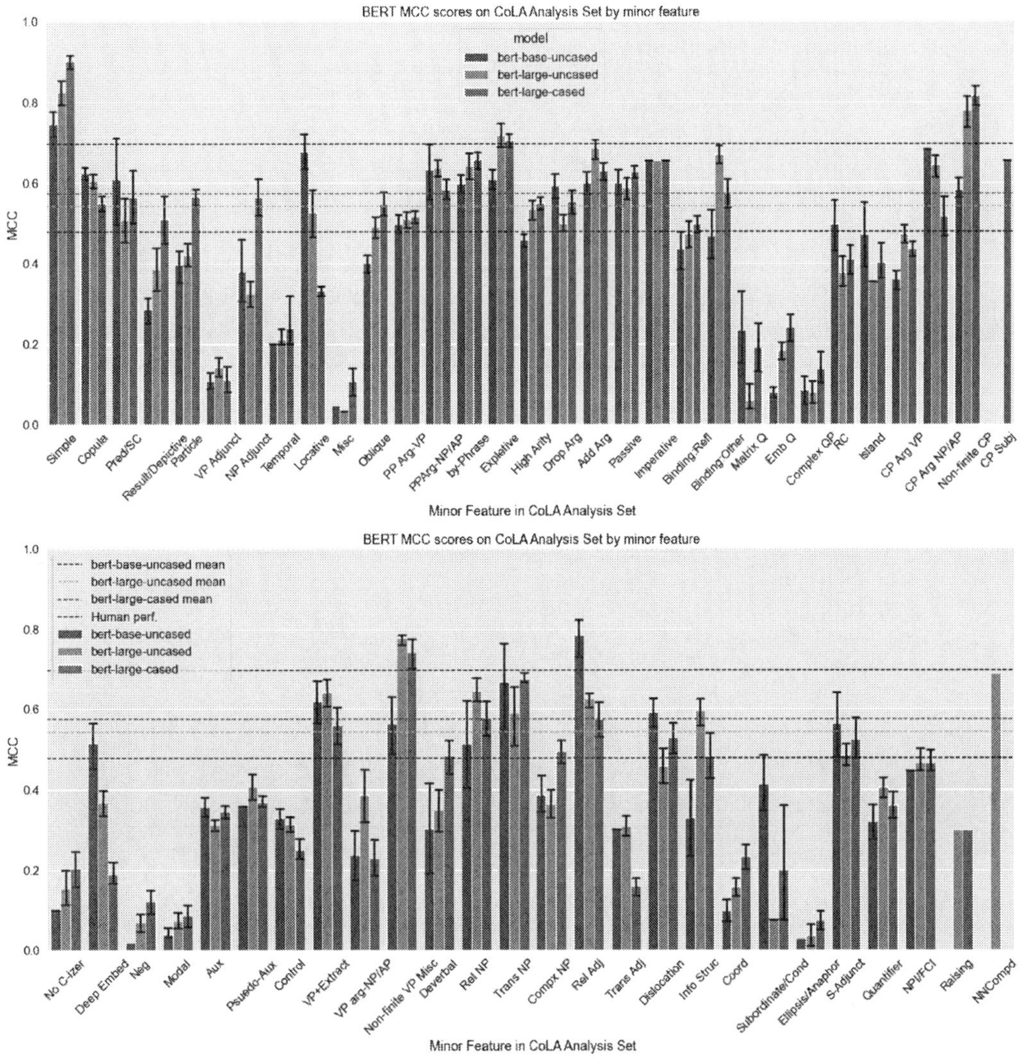

Figure 3: Replication of Warstadt and Bowman (2019) with our trained $\text{BERT}_{\text{CoLA}}$ models for comparison. Performance (MCC) on CoLA analysis set by minor feature. Dashed lines show mean performance on the CoLA out-of-domain test set. From left to right, performance for each feature is given for base-uncased, large-uncased, and large-cased.

Minimal Pair **Top**: Acceptable | **Bottom**: Unacceptable	trigram SLOR	$\text{BERT}_{\text{CoLA}}$ acceptability
She taught the students math.	-0.685949	0.73276
*She taught math the students.	-0.562807	-1.40171
There are linguists available.	-0.337031	0.732224
*There are linguists tall.	-0.512287	-1.41472
Our professor gave no extensions to any students.	-0.728557	0.721394
*Our professor gave any extensions to no students.	-1.33971	-1.3493
What did you address to whom?	0.478869	0.73067
*To whom did you address what?	-0.890322	0.681159

Table 7: Four minimal pairs where all $\text{BERT}_{\text{CoLA}}$ models meet the ADC with $\delta = 0.5$ but the trigram baseline does not. We report the acceptability scores from the large-cased version of $\text{BERT}_{\text{CoLA}}$. The trigam SLOR and $\text{BERT}_{\text{CoLA}}$ acceptability scores are already Z-score transformed.

Minimal Pair **Top**: Acceptable | **Bottom**: Unacceptable	trigram SLOR	$\text{BERT}_{\text{CoLA}}$ acceptability
Michael managed to drive his car.	0.950214	0.733175
*Michael managed to have driven his car.	0.26957	-1.37701
Paul flew to Ireland and Laura sailed to Greece.	0.253906	0.733086
*Paul flew Ireland and Laura sailed to Greece.	-0.779695	0.731989
She ran into Spencer and asked him out.	0.821345	0.73299
*She ran into Spencer and asked out.	-0.194269	-1.38959
The children are almost all sleeping.	0.30149	0.733162
The children almost all are sleeping.	-0.680258	0.729437

Table 8: Four minimal pairs where the trigram baseline meets the ADC with $\delta = 0.5$ but none of the BERT models do. We report the acceptability scores from the large-cased version of $\text{BERT}_{\text{CoLA}}$. The trigam SLOR and $\text{BERT}_{\text{CoLA}}$ acceptability scores are already Z-score transformed.

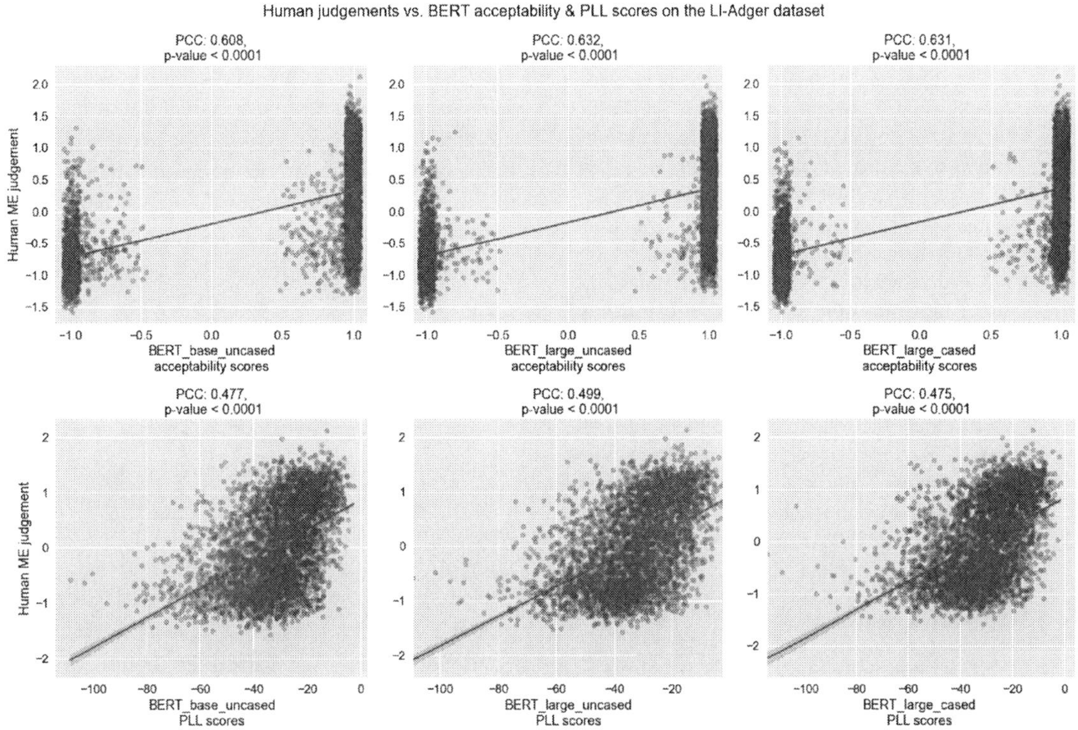

Figure 4: Scatterplot of human judgements (y-axis) vs. $\text{BERT}_{\text{CoLA}}$ acceptability scores, & BERT_{MLM} PLL scores from all three BERT models for each sentence in the LI-Adger dataset with best-fit line in red. We add a jitter of 0.05 along the x-axis and lower the alpha to 0.3 to highlight the density of the points.

How Does BERT Rerank Passages? An Attribution Analysis with Information Bottlenecks

Zhiying Jiang, Raphael Tang, Ji Xin and **Jimmy Lin**
David R. Cheriton School of Computer Science
University of Waterloo
{zhiying.jiang, r33tang, ji.xin, jimmylin}@uwaterloo.ca

Abstract

Fine-tuned pre-trained transformers achieve the state of the art in passage reranking. Unfortunately, how they make their predictions remains vastly unexplained, especially at the end-to-end, input-to-output level. Little known is how tokens, layers, and passages precisely contribute to the final prediction. In this paper, we address this gap by leveraging the recently developed information bottlenecks for attribution (IBA) framework. On BERT-based models for passage reranking, we quantitatively demonstrate the framework's veracity in extracting attribution maps, from which we perform detailed, token-wise analysis about how predictions are made. Overall, we find that BERT still cares about exact token matching for reranking; the [CLS] token mainly gathers information for predictions at the last layer; top-ranked passages are robust to token removal; and BERT fine-tuned on MSMARCO has positional bias towards the start of the passage.

1 Introduction

Pre-trained language models like BERT (Devlin et al., 2019) have achieved prominent improvements in both information retrieval (IR) and natural language processing (NLP). Concurrently, researchers have raised wide awareness about the difficulty of explaining such deep learning models (Guidotti et al., 2018; Robnik-Šikonja and Bohanec, 2018; Fong and Vedaldi, 2017). Recently, many papers scrutinize BERT's behaviors in various tasks (van Aken et al., 2019; Clark et al., 2019; Tenney et al., 2019; Qiao et al., 2019; MacAvaney et al., 2020). When it comes to token-wise analysis, most of the work study intra-layer self-attention and how it relates to various linguistic characteristics. Although these analyses yield unique insights on layer-local behavior across pairs of tokens, they do not take a global perspective of how token-wise representations exactly relate to the prediction. This is crucial for answering a fundamental question in interpretability: what hidden features and tokens contribute the most to the prediction?

To faithfully compute such feature–prediction attribution maps, Schulz et al. (2020) and Jiang et al. (2020) propose to apply information bottlenecks. In this paper, we leverage this model-agnostic method to analyze passage reranking for pre-trained transformers. We first introduce the information bottleneck for attribution (IBA) method (Schulz et al., 2020) in general and elaborate its use in interpreting passage reranking. Afterwards, we compare it with two other widely adopted attribution methods to demonstrate its credibility and justify our choice. We then carry out detailed analyses on the inner mechanisms of passage reranking.

BERT reranking (Nogueira and Cho, 2019) starts a new chapter in information retrieval, as it combines the dual advantages of the speed of sparse representation (BM25) and the deep contextualization of dense representation. To be specific, given a query q, BM25 returns top-1,000 passages D. The label r is 1 if a passage $d \in D$ is relevant to q, and 0 otherwise. For BERT, the input is `[CLS] q [SEP] d [SEP]`, and the output label is r. After fine-tuning, we rerank D based on the output probabilities of relevance. This setting is different from most NLP tasks, where positive and negative labels are provided by the dataset, and only one pair of (input, probability) is required for the final output.

We use IBA to generate attribution maps for BERT-large (Devlin et al., 2019) fine-tuned on the MSMARCO dataset (Bajaj et al., 2016) in this paper. With the attribution maps, we investigate the following questions:

Q1. What are the similarities and differences between BERT and BM25?
For the two-stage pipeline, we wonder how BERT's ranking mechanism is similar to BM25 and what it provides that BM25 doesn't. Through cross-passage examination, we find that BERT still regards lexical matching as important to some extent,

Proceedings of the Fourth BlackboxNLP Workshop on Analyzing and Interpreting Neural Networks for NLP, pages 496–509
Online, November 11, 2021.

similar to BM25. BERT, furthermore, manages to capture deeper-contextualized relationships between the query and the relevant passage.

Q2. How do special tokens contribute to reranking across layers?
In BERT, only the [CLS] token is designed to factor into prediction. Then how do those special tokens collect information across layers to capture a contextualized relationship? We find that, different from what attention analyses show, [CLS] starts to gather the evidence for prediction primarily after layer 16, especially in layer 24.

Q3. How robust is the top-ranked passage?
One of the special settings of ranking is that we do not care about the absolute score, as long as the relevant passage ranks higher than irrelevant ones. We conduct experiments of token removal for the top-1 positive passage to test the robustness. We find that we can truncate up to 22.5% tokens on average, given reasonable attribution scores, of the top-ranked passage without affecting its order.

Q4. Does BERT have positional bias?
We then look deeper into what makes those passages rank higher. We find that BERT, after fine-tuned on MSMARCO, prefers those passages with inverted pyramid structure—that is, passages that put important information at the start. We further confirm that it has positional bias towards the start of the passage through various experiments.

2 Related Work

Generally speaking, interpretability methods are either model specific, applying to only a single architectural family, or model agnostic, covering a broad spectrum of supervised models. Since pretrained transformers represent the state of the art in NLP, for model-specific techniques we discuss those for BERT, the prototypical, most-interpreted transformer model. As this work specifically explores passage reranking, we also provide the necessary literature about recent progress.

2.1 BERT specific

A number of works investigate the inner mechanisms of BERT. Kovaleva et al. (2019); Clark et al. (2019) carefully analyze BERT's attention heads, noting positive correlation between attention heads and linguistic features, as well as special tokens.

Looking at attention, Voita et al. (2018) find that BERT captures anaphora and dependence on position and length in machine translation. Pointing out some shortfalls of these papers, Jain and Wallace (2019); Brunner et al. (2019); Serrano and Smith (2019) argue that attentions often do not reflect how models make predictions.

Another line of work analyzing BERT use probing classifier to draw the connection between vector representation and specific linguistic knowledge (Tenney et al., 2019; Hewitt and Manning, 2019; Liu et al., 2019). Rogers et al. (2020) provide a thorough literature survey about what we already know about how BERT works and they've found different probing methods sometimes lead to contradictory interpretations. A direct remedy is to look into what BERT looks at during inference time (i.e. identify important features for prediction, also known as "attribution methods" in general). That's where our work focuses on.

2.2 Attribution maps

Although more commonly applied to convolutional neural networks in image classification, most attribution methods are model agnostic. They aim to assign weights to input features according to how the model makes predictions, with higher weights corresponding to greater contributions.

The most prevalent methods are gradient-based. Intuitively, gradients reflect how small changes in the input affect the final prediction to some extent. But previous work shows that raw gradients are noisy and limited to capturing only the local "importance" (Smilkov et al., 2017). To remedy this, some of them (Sundararajan et al., 2017; Smilkov et al., 2017) incorporate global importance to mitigate this problem, while others (Binder et al., 2016; Shrikumar et al., 2017; Kindermans et al., 2018) modify or extend the back-propagation algorithms directly to emphasize positive contributions with regard to prediction. However, Sixt et al. (2020) show that most of the modified back-propagation methods fail a basic sanity check: invariance to parameter randomization and label randomization.

LIME (Ribeiro et al., 2016) is not even limited to differentiable models. They use interpretable models like decision trees to approximate deep neural networks, and thus can theoretically interpret any classifier. However, empirically, LIME's high demand on memory may worsen its quality compared to other methods, as we will see in the later section.

Information-theoretic methods are often unconstrained by tasks and models as well, while additionally providing a unified view of how information flows across models. Guan et al. (2019) use mutual information to estimate tokens importance across layers but don't provide quantitative evaluation. Bang et al. (2019) also take advantage of information bottlenecks to interpret predictions, but they restrict the information by sampling tokens, which doesn't generate a complete attribution map for every token and limits the interpretation to be token-wise only. More recently, Schulz et al. (2020) propose the information bottleneck method for attribution, which empirically achieves the best result on multiple evaluation metrics in interpreting images. Jiang et al. (2020) further leverage this method in NLP and also surpass other model-agnostic methods on multiple datasets.

2.3 Neural IR

BERT is a game changer for information retrieval. Lin et al. (2020) even separate neural reranking techniques into "pre-BERT" and "post-BERT" eras. Nogueira and Cho (2019) start the post-BERT era by proposing a two-stage pipeline, using sparse representations like BM25 to generate candidates and then neural models like BERT to rerank them. More recent work explores merging the two-stage pipeline into an end-to-end dense retrieval, like DPR (Karpukhin et al., 2020), which still use BERT as the basic building block for neural information retrieval. Therefore, understanding BERT's behavior for reranking in the original setting still helps.

Toward this, a few previous works specifically analyze BERT for reranking: Qiao et al. (2019) analyze attention to see how BERT attends to stop words and regular words across layers. MacAvaney et al. (2020) does a more thorough study of various reranking models, using carefully designed textual manipulation methods. Different from them, we use a model-agnostic method to generate a token-wise attribution map, as it provides us with the flexibility to carry out a layer-wise analysis. Besides, to the best of our knowledge, no previous work has done a cross-passage analysis to see patterns across the ranks of different passages.

3 IBA Method

3.1 General Introduction to IBA

The starting point of IBA is to keep only the feature-level information that's most helpful toward the final prediction. After a given layer in the target neural network, we insert an information bottleneck, which restricts the total amount of information in the representation. Simultaneously, we maximize the amount of information important toward the final prediction.

To be concrete, given an input $\mathbf{X} \in \mathbb{R}^N$ and output $\mathbf{Y} \in \mathbb{R}^M$, an information bottleneck is an intermediate representation $\mathbf{T}$ that maximizes the following function:

$$\mathrm{I}(\mathbf{Y};\mathbf{T}) - \beta \cdot \mathrm{I}(\mathbf{X};\mathbf{T}), \quad (1)$$

where I denotes mutual information, and β is a hyperparameter that balances the trade-off between reconstruction $\mathrm{I}(\mathbf{Y};\mathbf{T})$ and information restriction $\mathrm{I}(\mathbf{X};\mathbf{T})$. A larger β means a narrower bottleneck and hence less information through the network.

Intuitively, maximizing $\mathrm{I}(\mathbf{Y};\mathbf{T})$ keeps information for accurate prediction, while minimizing $\mathrm{I}(\mathbf{X};\mathbf{T})$ filters out unnecessary information. To obtain the condensed representation $\mathbf{T}$, we construct a loss function based on the intuition above. For $\mathrm{I}(\mathbf{Y};\mathbf{T})$, we can directly use the cross-entropy loss for classification $\mathcal{L}_{\mathrm{CE}}$. For $\mathrm{I}(\mathbf{X};\mathbf{T})$, we will derive it step by step below.

Formally, for a given layer l of a model, let $\mathbf{X} = f_l(\mathbf{H})$, meaning the output of each layer, where $\mathbf{H}$ is the input of layer l. We then restrict the information by injecting noise ϵ into input $\mathbf{X}$, which results in

$$\mathbf{T} = \boldsymbol{\mu} \odot \mathbf{X} + (\mathbf{1} - \boldsymbol{\mu}) \odot \epsilon, \quad (2)$$

where $\odot$ refers to element-wise multiplication, $\mathbf{1}$ is an all-one vector, $\boldsymbol{\mu} \in \mathbb{R}^N$ is the weighting parameter controlling the balance between signal and noise whose dimension is the same as input $\mathbf{X}$. For each dimension, we constrain $\mu_i \in [0, 1]$, setting $\mu_i = \sigma(\alpha_i)$, where σ is the sigmoid function, to simplify the training process. And α_i is the parameter that we are learning for each dimension. From Eq. 2 we can see that when $\boldsymbol{\mu} = 0$, that is, all the information is discarded; only noise is passed through ($\mathbf{T} = \epsilon$). Taking that into account, in order to preserve the magnitude of the input for the next layer, it's desirable to keep ϵ the same mean and variance as $\mathbf{X}$. Therefore, we have $\epsilon \sim \mathcal{N}(\mu_{\mathbf{X}}, \sigma^2_{\mathbf{X}})$. This condition doesn't always ensure $\mathbf{T}$ to have exactly the same mean and covariance with $\mathbf{X}$ though. And the model is recovered after training the bottleneck to ensure the covariance shift doesn't affect interpreting subsequent instances.

After obtaining $\mathbf{T}$, we can now evaluate $\mathrm{I}(\mathbf{X};\mathbf{T})$. By definition,

$$\mathrm{I}(\mathbf{X};\mathbf{T}) = \mathbb{E}_{\mathbf{X}}[D_{KL}[P(\mathbf{T}|\mathbf{X})\|P(\mathbf{T})]], \quad (3)$$

where D_{KL} means Kullback–Leibler (KL) divergence and $P(\mathbf{T}|\mathbf{X})$, $P(\mathbf{T})$ are probability distributions. As $P(\mathbf{T}) = \int P(\mathbf{T}|\mathbf{X})P(\mathbf{X})\mathrm{d}\mathbf{X}$, there is no analytical expression for $P(\mathbf{T})$. We use the standard variational approximation $Q(\mathbf{T}) = \mathcal{N}(\mu_{\mathbf{X}}, \sigma^2_{\mathbf{X}})$ to substitute $P(\mathbf{T})$. Note that we estimate each $\mu_{\mathbf{X}}$ and $\sigma_{\mathbf{X}}$ empirically. The variational approximation assumes that each dimension is distributed independently and normally. The normal distribution comes from the observation that activations after linear and convolutional layers tend to be Gaussian-like (Klambauer et al., 2017; Borovykh, 2018). The independence assumption, on the other hand, does not hold in general, but it just overestimates the mutual information, so it gives an upper bound of mutual information between **X** and **T**:

$$\mathrm{I}(\mathbf{X};\mathbf{T}) \leq \mathbb{E}_{\mathbf{X}}[D_{KL}[P(\mathbf{T}|\mathbf{X})\|Q(\mathbf{T})]]. \quad (4)$$

Proof can be found in Appendix A.

An upper bound means when the approximation between **X** and **T** is 0, their mutual information is guaranteed to be 0, which is a desired property, as we expect $\mathrm{I}(\mathbf{X}, \mathbf{T})$ to be small.

Combining Eq. 4 with the cross entropy for classification, we have our loss function:

$$\mathcal{L} = \mathcal{L}_{\mathrm{CE}} + \beta \cdot \mathbb{E}_{\mathbf{X}}[D_{KL}[P(\mathbf{T}|\mathbf{X})\|Q(\mathbf{T})]]. \quad (5)$$

Note that we negate the sign for minimization. β can be viewed as the gate controlling the relative importance between the two loss components. After getting **T** from above, we calculate how much information **T** still contains about **X** using Eq. 3. This gives us the contribution of each dimension in every token. In order to generate the token-wise attribution map, we sum over the feature–token axis to obtain an attribution score for each token.

3.2 IBA for Passage Reranking Analysis

The procedure of using BERT to rerank passages (Nogueira and Cho, 2019) can be characterized as follows: Given query q, and a list of passages D, $d \in D$ is returned by BM25. BERT then assigns the relevance score $R(q, d)$, the logits for the probability that the passage is regarded as relevant, to each pair of q and d. $\mathcal{L}_{\mathrm{CE}}$ in this case is the same as the cross entropy in Nogueira and Cho (2019). We use BERT-large model fine-tuned on MSMARCO dataset for experiments. In order to get **T**, we optimize the learning parameter α. At the beginning of the training, we start with $\mathbf{T} \approx \mathbf{X}$ to keep the information of **X** in **T** as much as possible. Thus, we initialize $\alpha_j = 5$ for each dimension j as it results in $\mu_j = 0.993$, which is close to 1 as desired. During optimization, we fix the training steps to 10 and repeat a sample 10 times to inject different noise, which altogether requires 100 total steps to generate an attribution map for a single instance. Another important hyperparameter is β. We empirically pick $\beta \approx 10 \times \frac{\mathcal{L}_{\mathrm{CE}}}{\mathcal{L}_{\mathrm{IB}}}$, as suggested in (Jiang et al., 2020).

To compare the effectiveness of IBA with other attribution methods, we carry out a degradation test. The essential idea of a degradation test is to remove the most important $k\%$ tokens, excluding special tokens, identified by different attribution methods and measure the drop of the probability with respect to the given label.

The initial value of k is 11 and we increase k until all the tokens are removed, shown as the x-axis in Figure 1a. y-axis means the normalized average probability drop after removing a certain percentage of tokens: $\frac{\bar{p}(y|x')-m}{o-m}$ where x' represents input with certain tokens removed, o is the original probability before tokens removal, and m is the minimum of the fully degraded instance's probability across all attribution methods. We conduct the experiment across the entire MSMARCO dev set (6980 queries).

We compare the result with two other popular model-agnostic attribution methods, LIME (Ribeiro et al., 2016) and Integrated Gradients (IG) (Sundararajan et al., 2017), each representing a different category of attribution methods: LIME uses interpretable models like decision trees and linear models to approximate the black box, while IG is a variation of using the gradient of the predicted output with respect to given input features. To provide a simple baseline, we also compare the result with "Random," where tokens are removed randomly. We expect a better attribution method will have a steeper slope, meaning removing important tokens identified by the method significantly deteriorates the performance. As shown in Figure 1, IBA outperforms all other three methods with a 61.3% probability drop comparing with second-placed IG, which makes for a 29.0% drop. The absolute probability drop value can be seen in Table 1.

4 Experiments and Analyses

Figure 1c shows an example of important tokens in the query and the passage identified by IBA. Aside from token matching like "pH" and "water", deeper semantic relatedness like "acid" and "neutral" are

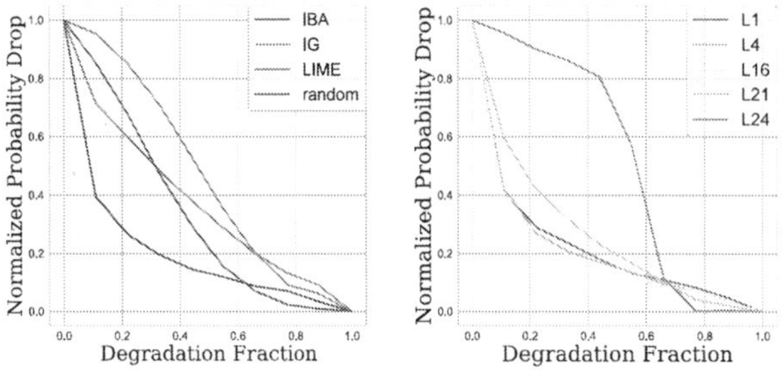

what is the ph of water mean
a ph number measures from 0 to ##14 how acidic or al ##kali ##ne a liquid is - - anything above 7 is al ##kali ##ne and anything below 7 is acid . water has a ph level of 7 - - it ' s neutral , meaning it has the same amount of acids and al ##kali ##s , which balance each other out .

(a) Comparison among attribution (b) Comparison among layers (c) Qualitative example

Figure 1: Degradation test on MSMARCO with BERT-large, followed by an attribution map example.

Methods	$o - \bar{p}(y\|x')$
Random	0.135
LIME	0.043
IG	0.265
IBA	**0.565**

Table 1: Probability drop after removing first $k\%$ important tokens identified by these methods.

also stressed. More examples and analysis are shown in Appendix G.

Given the attribution maps, we are now able to study which tokens BERT looks at for reranking. To be specific, we exploit IBA to extract the top-20 most important tokens $\mathbb{M}$ for each $(q, d), q \in Q, d \in D$, where Q and D represent the query list and the passage list. We carry out our experiment under two different settings:

1. Q consists of 1,000 randomly selected queries from the entire MSMARCO passage reranking dev set. D is composed of the human annotated relevant passages. We then apply IBA to all 24 layers to get top-20 tokens $\mathbb{M}$ for each (q, d).

2. Q consists of 105 queries from a subset of the MSMARCO passage reranking dev set, provided by Pyserini (Lin et al., 2021). D comprises top-50 passages that BERT-large retrieves for each query. For these experiments, we fix the layer l that we insert the information bottleneck after.

For setting 1, we aim at cross-layer analysis for relevant passages. Specifically, we identify if lower layers show different focus from higher layers. This setting is similar to GLUE-like (Wang et al., 2018) classification tasks where we want to find general patterns about BERT. The reason for using the top 20 is that, in our sampled instances, the average tokenized query length is 9.2, and we also want to see the emphasized tokens in passages. For setting 2, we perform cross-passage analysis to investigate different patterns between higher-ranked passages and lower-ranked passages. The choice of the top-50 cutoff is due to frugality: the recall@50 (0.817) is comparable to the recall@1000 (0.848), with much less computation.

4.1 Passage-Level Patterns

It's well known that two-stage ranking pipelines use both exact token matching and semantic relatedness (Lin et al., 2020). As BM25 estimates relevance purely by lexical matching, we wonder if BERT still relies on exact match and what else BERT provides.

Q1. What are the similarities and differences between BERT and BM25?

To answer this question, we first study the correlation between higher ranking scores and higher lexical matching between queries and passages.

To measure the degree of lexical matching, we use the Jaccard index under experimental setting 2: $\mathbf{J} = \frac{|u_i \cap v_j|}{|u_i \cup v_j|}, \{u_i, v_j | u_i \in q \cap \mathbb{M}, v_j \in d \cap \mathbb{M}\}$, where $i \in [1, |q|], j \in [1, |d|]$, remember that $\mathbb{M}$ is the top-20 tokens extracted by IBA.

For each query q, we calculate the Jaccard index for every passage d_i in the top-50 passages. We then average them across all queries. We choose to insert the information bottleneck after layer 16, as it is the most informative one according to our degradation test.

As we see in Figure 2a, the Jaccard index decreases as the rank of the passages becomes lower. In general, the higher[1] the rank is, the more overlapped the important tokens between the query and

[1]"Higher" rank actually means lower order: passages with order 1 have higher rank than passages with order 2, etc.

passages are. We also calculate Spearman's correlation (Spearman, 1961) r_s to gauge the degree of monotonic association. We find that $r_s = -0.98$, indicating a strong monotonic relation between the Jaccard index and passages order. Does this correlation hold among all tokens between the query and passage? Figure 2b shows the Jaccard index $\mathbf{J}' = \frac{|u'_i \cap v'_j|}{|u'_i \cup v'_j|}$, $\{u'_i, v'_j | u'_i \in q, v'_j \in d\}$ across passages. We see it shows a similar trend to $\mathbf{J}$, confirming that even if BM25 returns passages that have higher lexical matching with query, token matching between queries and passages still plays an important role when BERT is reranking. But using all of the tokens between the query and the passage obtains a correlation coefficient of $r_s = -0.71$, which is lower than using important tokens only. We argue that it's because IBA interprets in a way that's more aligned with the specific tokens that BERT looks at when reranking.

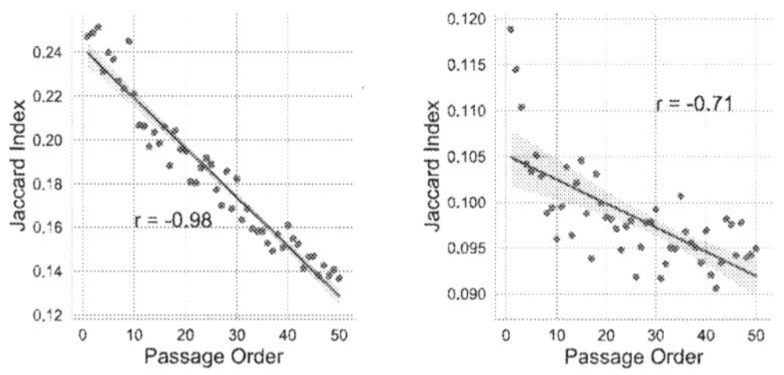

(a) Important tokens. (b) Whole query and passage.

Figure 2: Across top-50 passage analysis.

We further investigate what BERT provides that BM25 doesn't. Specifically, we look into what d_{BERT} gets right but d_{BM25} gets wrong. We notice that BERT captures more contextualized relevance between the query and passage, while the BM25-returned answer has more "superficial" relevance - d_{BM25} seems to talk about the topic but doesn't really answer the question. The example shown in Figure 3 demonstrates that passage returned by BM25 seems highly related to the topic—"cognitive impairment" but instead of explaining what the goal is, it is explaining what "cognitive impairment"'s definition is. On the contrary, BERT not only returns the passage related to "cognitive impairment" but also the goal. More discussions about semantic similarity are in Appendix F.

4.2 Layer-Level Patterns

Downstream tasks often rely on BERT's [CLS] vector at the last layer as input, and that's also true for

Query: what is the goal for the child with a cognitive impairment

BM25 ranked 1st: A cognitive impairment is a condition where your child has some problems with ability to think and learn. Children with a cognitive impairment often have trouble with such school subjects as math and reading. cognitive impairment is a condition where your child has some problems with ability to think and learn. Children with a cognitive impairment often have trouble with such school subjects as math and reading.	**BERT ranked 1st:** Promoting optimum development. The goal for children with cognitive impairment is the promotion of optimum social, physical, cognitive, and adaptive development as individuals within a family and community. Vocational skills are only one part of that goal. The focus must also be on the family and other aspects of development.

Figure 3: Top-1 passage by BM25 and BERT.

reranking. It's intriguing to know the layer at which [CLS] starts to learn the relevance. Clark et al. (2019) thoroughly analyze BERT's self-attention mechanism for each layer. While they provide insight into how tokens attend to one another, the attention weights themselves often do *not* correlate with measures of feature importance (Jain and Wallace, 2019).

Q2. How do special tokens contribute to reranking across layers?

We insert an information bottleneck after each layer for 24-layer attribution maps. First we inspect how the [CLS] token gets emphasized across the layers. Figure 4a shows the attribution score across 24 layers in experimental setting 1, with 95% confidence intervals. Note that the score is normalized between 0 to 1 for each token but it doesn't add up to 1 for each instance. We further normalize the attribution score by dividing the sum of the attribution scores at each layer to account for different layers' scale. As we can see in the plot, the attribution score for [CLS] across layers first decreases from layers 1–7, then goes up and fluctuates between layers 7–16, until finally increasing from layer 16 to 24. This differs from what attention analysis reveals in Kovaleva et al. (2019) and Clark et al. (2019), where they demonstrate that attention heads attend to [CLS] in earlier layers but attend to [SEP] in later layers. It's not contradictory, though, because we inspect feature importance with respect to the predicted output. Since [CLS] at the final layer is treated as a summary representation for the whole sentence to perform classification, it's intuitive that [CLS] is regarded as an important feature in the final layers.

What about the [SEP] tokens? Figure 4b shows the attribution score averaged between the two present [SEP] tokens—recall that BERT inserts two for every input. They become increasingly important with a certain amount of fluctuation from

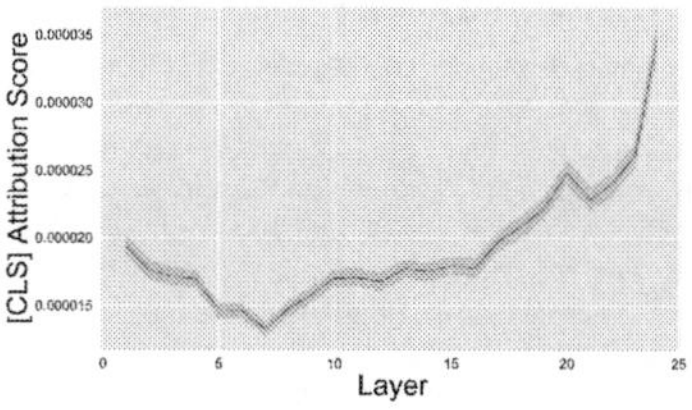

(a) CLS attribution score across layers.

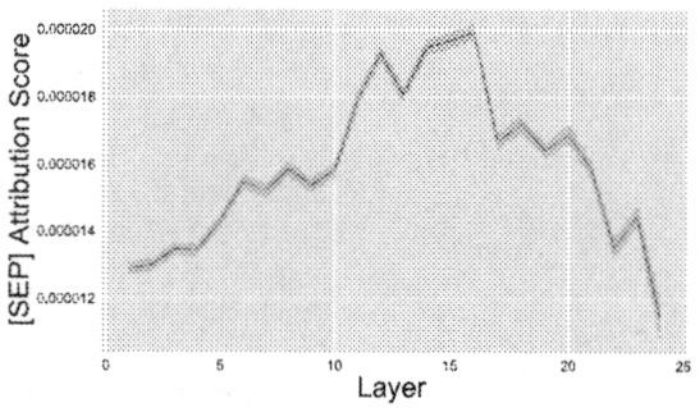

(b) SEP attribution score across layers.

Stats	Query	passage
Avg. Length	9.2	74.8
Med. Length	9.0	69.0
Min. Length	4.0	16.0
Max. Length	44.0	214.0

(c) Stats of 1,000 relevant (q, d).

Figure 4: Normalized attribution scores of special tokens across layers; dataset statistics under setting 1.

layer 1 to layer 16, after which [SEP]'s attribution scores drop, around the point where BERT starts to emphasize [CLS]. We combine the two [SEP] tokens because we find that both of them behave similarly, with the first [SEP] having a slightly higher attribution score. The possible explanation is that the first [SEP] is also responsible for identifying the boundary between the query and the passage, thus more important for reranking than the final [SEP]. Plots for separate [SEP]'s scores and weights can be seen in Appendix D.

Combining the above plots and the degradation tests across layers in Figure 1b, we conjecture that the [CLS] token initially serves as a classification prior to condition the tokens in the early layers (1–7) with [SEP] increasing participation. Then, BERT gathers more general syntactic information (Hewitt and Manning, 2019), until layer 16, after which the [CLS] token slowly aggregates class-specific information and at layer 24 becomes the most important token for classification. Figure 1b (the full 24-layer degradation test is shown in Appendix B) echos the findings from previous work (Liu et al., 2019), demonstrating that the middle layers are the most informative ones for prediction. To be exact, layer 16 ($\frac{2}{3}$ of the total number of layers) is the most informative one in our experiment with BERT-large, the same fraction as what Jiang et al. (2020) find with BERT-base.

	# required	% required
(q, d_1)	8.9	10.39
(d_1)	18.52	22.49

Table 2: Truncation test on top-1 pair/passage.

4.3 Truncation Test

Different from other downstream tasks, passage reranking usually involves scores for 1,000 passages to generate the final result. Instead of absolute scores for passages, we only care if relevant passages have higher scores than irrelevant passages. Recent work (Bai et al., 2020; Formal et al., 2021) starts to incorporate sparse mechanisms (adding and removing tokens) in order to elevate efficiency for the first-stage ranking. We ask how token removal affects those true positive passages.

Q3. How robust is the top-ranked passage?

Specifically, we want to know how many unimportant tokens we can remove before the top-1 passage falls to second place. Once again, we use the IBA-generated attribution map and then remove those tokens with lowest attribution scores, until the ranking score for the top-1 passage drops below the second one. As in the reranking setting, the input is always a query–passage pair (q, d), and we have two experimental settings: (1) removing tokens that appear in both q and d; and (2) removing tokens that appear in only d. We include the result under both settings and report the truncated number, as well as the percentage needed in Table 2.

Surprisingly, even if BERT assigns an extreme score to the passage, making the score close to one another (Qiao et al., 2019), it still takes up to 22.5% tokens on average for top-1 passage to downgrade to the second place.

Obviously, removing tokens from the query quickly deteriorates the ranking score. Passages-only seem to have more redundant tokens that can be safely removed, even though sentences in the passage will become incomplete and broken after token removal. Note that this experiment removes only tokens of the top-1 passage. We attach the comprehensive results and discussion of truncating tokens in all passages in Appendix G.

4.4 Positional Bias

MacAvaney et al. (2020) observe that changing the sentence order has negative effects when reranking with BERT. They suggest that either the model is affected by the discourse-level signal (e.g., topics discussed earlier in passages) or the model encodes positional bias.

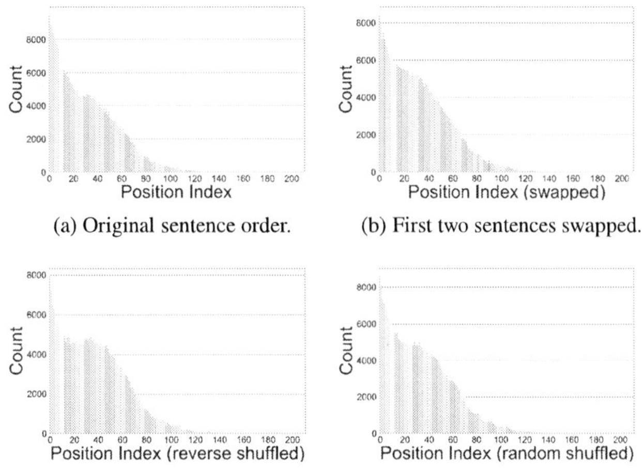

(a) Original sentence order. (b) First two sentences swapped.

(c) Reversed sentence order. (d) Randomized sentence order.

Figure 5: Position index of important tokens in passages; stats of tested passages.

	Precision@1	MRR	MRR@10	Recall@3	Recall@50	Recall 1000
Original	0.276	0.411	0.403	0.427	0.817	0.848
Swapped	0.219	0.362	0.352	0.408	0.813	0.848
Randomized	0.200	0.343	0.332	0.384	0.803	0.848
Reversed	0.181	0.332	0.321	0.390	0.803	0.848

Table 3: Reranking metrics after changing sentence order.

Q4. Does BERT have positional bias?

To investigate if BERT has positional bias, we first plot the position index of x_i where $\{x_i|x_i \in \mathbb{M} \cap d\}$. Specifically, we insert the bottleneck after every layer under experimental setting 1—1000 relevant pairs of (q, d)—and then accumulate the count of each position index for all 24 layers (plots for each layer is also shown in Appendix H). Statistics about randomly selected (q, d) are shown in Figure 4c. As we show in Figure 5a, tokens at the start of passages (e.g., position index from 0 to 20) have significantly higher occurrences than tokens appearing later.

We then conduct three controlled experiments: (1) swapping the first two sentences; (2) reversing the order of all sentences; and (3) randomizing the order of sentences. We maintain the order of within-sentence tokens in order to keep the discourse complete and coherent. The plots are shown in Figure 5. We see that, although changing the order results in more later-appearing tokens emphasized, the start of the passages still have incomparable dominance. To quantify the effect of swapping sentences, randomizing sentences, and reversing sentences, we calculate $p(\text{relevant}|\{\text{original, swap, random, reverse}\})$. We find that $p(\text{relevant}|\text{original}) = 0.939$, $p(\text{relevant}|\text{swap}) = 0.920$, $p(\text{relevant}|\text{random}) = 0.918$, $p(\text{relevant}|\text{reverse}) = 0.897$. The probability drops after every change of sentence order. The more the order changes, the more the probability drops (i.e., the negative effect is reversed order > randomized > swapped). Given that BERT assigns extreme reranking scores to most (q, d) pairs (e.g., scores are mostly either close to 0 or close to 1), it's unclear whether changing the order of sentences affects the final result.

Therefore, we also conduct experiments of changing the order sentence with the subset of the MS-MARCO passage reranking dev set. We present these results in Table 3. Swapping sentences substantially deteriorates the result; randomizing and reversing the sentences further worsens the result.

The above experiments suggest that the sentence order in the passage carries high importance in reranking with BERT. Specifically, passages with the inverted pyramid structure would be preferred, as they present important information at the beginning of the passages. More discussion on positional bias can be found in Appendix E.

5 Conclusions

In this work, we leverage IBA to examine BERT for reranking. We compare ranking mechanisms between BM25 and BERT, finding that BERT still values token matching, and it also learns deeper relevance between queries and passages. We further analyze special tokens across layers and demonstrate patterns that [CLS] aggregate evidence. We then investigate the robustness of top-ranked passages. Finally, we find that BERT fine-tuned on MSMARCO has positional bias towards the start of the passage. In summary, attribution maps can explain models' predictions and serve well as an observation tool that helps us visualize patterns, resulting in improved hypothesis formulation and experimental design.

Acknowledgements

This research was supported in part by the Canada First Research Excellence Fund and the Natural Sciences and Engineering Research Council (NSERC) of Canada; computational resources were provided by Compute Canada.

References

Yang Bai, Xiaoguang Li, Gang Wang, Chaoliang Zhang, Lifeng Shang, Jun Xu, Zhaowei Wang, Fangshan Wang, and Qun Liu. 2020. SparTerm: Learning term-based sparse representation for fast text retrieval. *arXiv preprint arXiv:2010.00768*.

Payal Bajaj, Daniel Campos, Nick Craswell, Li Deng, Jianfeng Gao, Xiaodong Liu, Rangan Majumder, Andrew McNamara, Bhaskar Mitra, Tri Nguyen, et al. 2016. MS MARCO: A human generated machine reading comprehension dataset. *arXiv:1611.09268*.

Seojin Bang, Pengtao Xie, Heewook Lee, Wei Wu, and Eric Xing. 2019. Explaining a black-box using deep variational information bottleneck approach. *arXiv:1902.06918*.

Alexander Binder, Sebastian Bach, Gregoire Montavon, Klaus-Robert Müller, and Wojciech Samek. 2016. Layer-wise relevance propagation for deep neural network architectures. In *Information science and applications (ICISA) 2016*, pages 913–922. Springer.

Anastasia Borovykh. 2018. A Gaussian process perspective on convolutional neural networks. *arXiv:1810.10798*.

Gino Brunner, Yang Liu, Damian Pascual, Oliver Richter, Massimiliano Ciaramita, and Roger Wattenhofer. 2019. On identifiability in transformers. In *International Conference on Learning Representations*.

Kevin Clark, Urvashi Khandelwal, Omer Levy, and Christopher D. Manning. 2019. What does BERT look at? an analysis of BERT's attention. In *Proceedings of the 2019 ACL Workshop BlackboxNLP: Analyzing and Interpreting Neural Networks for NLP*, pages 276–286.

Jacob Devlin, Ming-Wei Chang, Kenton Lee, and Kristina Toutanova. 2019. BERT: Pre-training of deep bidirectional transformers for language understanding. In *Proceedings of the 2019 Conference of the North American Chapter of the Association for Computational Linguistics: Human Language Technologies, Volume 1 (Long and Short Papers)*, pages 4171–4186.

Ruth C. Fong and Andrea Vedaldi. 2017. Interpretable explanations of black boxes by meaningful perturbation. In *Proceedings of the IEEE International Conference on Computer Vision*.

Thibault Formal, Benjamin Piwowarski, and Stéphane Clinchant. 2021. SPLADE: Sparse lexical and expansion model for first stage ranking. In *Proceedings of the 44th International ACM SIGIR Conference on Research and Development in Information Retrieval*, pages 2288–2292.

Chaoyu Guan, Xiting Wang, Quanshi Zhang, Runjin Chen, Di He, and Xing Xie. 2019. Towards a deep and unified understanding of deep neural models in NLP. In *International conference on machine learning*, pages 2454–2463. PMLR.

Riccardo Guidotti, Anna Monreale, Salvatore Ruggieri, Franco Turini, Fosca Giannotti, and Dino Pedreschi. 2018. A survey of methods for explaining black box models. *ACM computing surveys (CSUR)*.

John Hewitt and Christopher D. Manning. 2019. A structural probe for finding syntax in word representations. In *Proceedings of the 2019 Conference of the North American Chapter of the Association for Computational Linguistics: Human Language Technologies, Volume 1 (Long and Short Papers)*, pages 4129–4138.

Sarthak Jain and Byron C. Wallace. 2019. Attention is not explanation. In *Proceedings of the 2019 Conference of the North American Chapter of the Association for Computational Linguistics: Human Language Technologies, Volume 1 (Long and Short Papers)*, pages 3543–3556.

Zhiying Jiang, Raphael Tang, Ji Xin, and Jimmy Lin. 2020. Inserting information bottleneck for attribution in transformers. In *Proceedings of the 2020 Conference on Empirical Methods in Natural Language Processing: Findings*, pages 3850–3857.

Vladimir Karpukhin, Barlas Oguz, Sewon Min, Patrick Lewis, Ledell Wu, Sergey Edunov, Danqi Chen, and Wen-tau Yih. 2020. Dense passage retrieval for open-domain question answering. In *Proceedings of the 2020 Conference on Empirical Methods in Natural Language Processing (EMNLP)*, pages 6769–6781.

Pieter-Jan Kindermans, Kristof T. Schütt, Maximilian Alber, Klaus-Robert Müller, Dumitru Erhan, Been

Kim, and Sven Dähne. 2018. Learning how to explain neural networks: PatternNet and PatternAttribution. In *ICLR (Poster)*.

Günter Klambauer, Thomas Unterthiner, Andreas Mayr, and Sepp Hochreiter. 2017. Self-normalizing neural networks. In *Advances in Neural Information Processing systems*.

Olga Kovaleva, Alexey Romanov, Anna Rogers, and Anna Rumshisky. 2019. Revealing the dark secrets of BERT. In *Proceedings of the 2019 Conference on Empirical Methods in Natural Language Processing and the 9th International Joint Conference on Natural Language Processing (EMNLP-IJCNLP)*.

Jimmy Lin, Xueguang Ma, Sheng-Chieh Lin, Jheng-Hong Yang, Ronak Pradeep, and Rodrigo Nogueira. 2021. Pyserini: An easy-to-use Python toolkit to support replicable ir research with sparse and dense representations. *arXiv:2102.10073*.

Jimmy Lin, Rodrigo Nogueira, and Andrew Yates. 2020. Pretrained transformers for text ranking: BERT and beyond. *arXiv:2010.06467*.

Nelson F. Liu, Matt Gardner, Yonatan Belinkov, Matthew E. Peters, and Noah A. Smith. 2019. Linguistic knowledge and transferability of contextual representations. In *Proceedings of the 2019 Conference of the North American Chapter of the Association for Computational Linguistics: Human Language Technologies, Volume 1 (Long and Short Papers)*, pages 1073–1094.

Sean MacAvaney, Sergey Feldman, Nazli Goharian, Doug Downey, and Arman Cohan. 2020. ABNIRML: Analyzing the behavior of neural IR models. *arXiv preprint arXiv:2011.00696*.

Rodrigo Nogueira and Kyunghyun Cho. 2019. Passage re-ranking with BERT. *arXiv preprint arXiv:1901.04085*.

Yifan Qiao, Chenyan Xiong, Zhenghao Liu, and Zhiyuan Liu. 2019. Understanding the behaviors of BERT in ranking. *arXiv:1904.07531*.

Nils Reimers and Iryna Gurevych. 2019. Sentence-BERT: Sentence embeddings using siamese BERT-networks. In *Proceedings of the 2019 Conference on Empirical Methods in Natural Language Processing*. Association for Computational Linguistics.

Marco Tulio Ribeiro, Sameer Singh, and Carlos Guestrin. 2016. "Why should I trust you?" explaining the predictions of any classifier. In *Proceedings of the 22nd ACM SIGKDD International Conference on Knowledge Discovery and Data Mining*.

Marko Robnik-Šikonja and Marko Bohanec. 2018. Perturbation-based explanations of prediction models. In *Human and machine learning*. Springer.

Anna Rogers, Olga Kovaleva, and Anna Rumshisky. 2020. A primer in BERTology: What we know about how BERT works. *Transactions of the Association for Computational Linguistics*, 8:842–866.

Karl Schulz, Leon Sixt, Federico Tombari, and Tim Landgraf. 2020. Restricting the flow: Information bottlenecks for attribution. In *International Conference on Learning Representations*.

Sofia Serrano and Noah A. Smith. 2019. Is attention interpretable? In *Proceedings of the 57th Annual Meeting of the Association for Computational Linguistics*, pages 2931–2951.

Avanti Shrikumar, Peyton Greenside, and Anshul Kundaje. 2017. Learning important features through propagating activation differences. In *International Conference on Machine Learning*, pages 3145–3153. PMLR.

Leon Sixt, Maximilian Granz, and Tim Landgraf. 2020. When explanations lie: Why many modified BP attributions fail. In *International Conference on Machine Learning*, pages 9046–9057. PMLR.

Daniel Smilkov, Nikhil Thorat, Been Kim, Fernanda Viégas, and Martin Wattenberg. 2017. SmoothGrad: removing noise by adding noise. *arXiv preprint arXiv:1706.03825*.

Charles Spearman. 1961. The proof and measurement of association between two things.

Mukund Sundararajan, Ankur Taly, and Qiqi Yan. 2017. Axiomatic attribution for deep networks. In *International Conference on Machine Learning*, pages 3319–3328. PMLR.

Ian Tenney, Dipanjan Das, and Ellie Pavlick. 2019. BERT rediscovers the classical NLP pipeline. In *Proceedings of the 57th Annual Meeting of the Association for Computational Linguistics*, pages 4593–4601.

Betty van Aken, Benjamin Winter, Alexander Löser, and Felix A Gers. 2019. How does BERT answer questions? a layer-wise analysis of transformer representations. In *Proceedings of the 28th ACM International Conference on Information and Knowledge Management*, pages 1823–1832.

Elena Voita, Pavel Serdyukov, Rico Sennrich, and Ivan Titov. 2018. Context-aware neural machine translation learns anaphora resolution. In *Proceedings of the 56th Annual Meeting of the Association for Computational Linguistics (Volume 1: Long Papers)*, pages 1264–1274.

Alex Wang, Amanpreet Singh, Julian Michael, Felix Hill, Omer Levy, and Samuel R. Bowman. 2018. GLUE: A multi-task benchmark and analysis platform for natural language understanding. In *International Conference on Learning Representations*.

A Proof of Variational Upper Bound

$$
\begin{aligned}
\mathrm{I}(\mathbf{X};\mathbf{T}) &= \mathbb{E}_{\mathbf{X}}[D_{KL}[P(\mathbf{T}|\mathbf{X})\|P(\mathbf{T})]] \\
&= \int_{\mathbf{X}} p(x)(\int_{\mathbf{T}} p(t|x)\log\frac{p(t|x)}{p(t)}dt)dx \\
&= \int_{\mathbf{X}}\int_{\mathbf{T}} p(x,t)\log\frac{p(t|x)}{p(t)}\frac{q(t)}{q(t)}dtdx \\
&= \int_{\mathbf{X}}\int_{\mathbf{T}} p(x,t)\log\frac{p(t|x)}{q(t)}dtdx \\
&+ \int_{\mathbf{X}}\int_{\mathbf{T}} p(x,t)\log\frac{q(t)}{p(t)}dtdx \\
&= \int_{\mathbf{X}}\int_{\mathbf{T}} p(x,t)\log\frac{p(t|x)}{q(t)}dtdx \\
&+ \int_{\mathbf{T}} p(t)(\int_{\mathbf{X}} p(x|t)dx)\log\frac{q(t)}{p(t)}dt \\
&= \mathbb{E}_{\mathbf{X}}[D_{KL}[P(\mathbf{T}|\mathbf{X})\|Q(\mathbf{T})]] \\
&- D_{KL}[Q(\mathbf{T})\|P(\mathbf{T})] \\
&\leq \mathbb{E}_{\mathbf{X}}[D_{KL}[P(\mathbf{T}|\mathbf{X})\|Q(\mathbf{T})]]
\end{aligned}
$$

B All 24 Layer Degradation Result

Figure 6 shows the degradation test result for all 24 layers. As we can see, middle layers show the steepest slope at first, indicating they are the most capable ones of capturing important tokens. The reason why layer 24 gets a slow probability drop is because special tokens like [CLS] and [SEP] are not removed in degradation test while [CLS] is regarded as the most important token in layer 24.

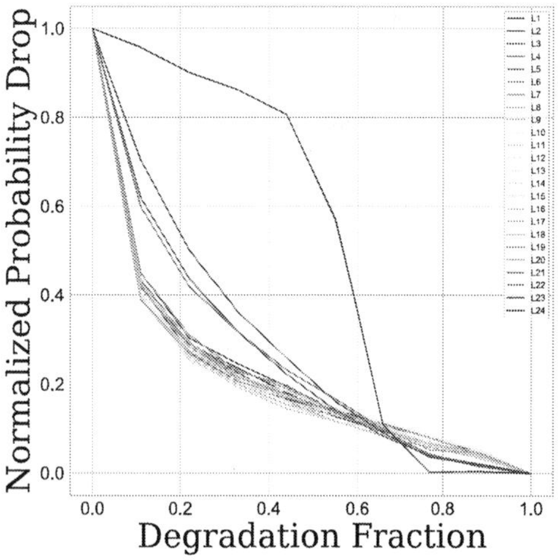

Figure 6: 24-layer degradation test result

C Qualitative Anlysis

Table 4 shows a few examples with highlighted important tokens. We can see top-10 most important tokens across query and passage not only show the token matching but also capture semantic relatedness. For example, "much" in the query of the first example is highlighted. "number", "million" and "$" sign, which are highly related to the concept of "much", are also highlighted. Similarly, in the second example, BERT identifies that the core of the question – "same document". In the corresponding passage, it emphasizes "or" as well as "mortgage" before that and "trust" after that. In the third example, the query is about "stronger", which is again, captured by BERT, and related tokens like "vs" and "roughtly equivalent" are highlighted.

D Detailed [SEP] Attribution Score across Layers

Figure 7 contains plots showing [CLS] weight and two [SEP] scores as well as weights across layers. As we've discussed in Section 4.2, Figure 7c shows how important [CLS] is compared with other tokens across layers—that is, we divide the attribution score by the sum of all of the tokens' attribution scores. It's even more clear that the [CLS] token aggregates all tokens' information in the final layer and becomes the most important token for prediction. The first [SEP] has slightly higher weight than the second one. It's probably because the first [SEP] indicates the boundary between query and document, which is an important information to learn for reranking. But in general they show similar patterns.

E Further Discussion on Positional Bias

We find that BERT prefers passages with important information emphasized at the beginning. But is this preference a real "bias"? Will it cause misjudgement because of emphasizing too much on the start of the passages? To answer this question, we design an experiment to see if passages with higher reranked scores (than the ground truth passages) also happen to get key tokens emphasized earlier. Concretely, for those instances that have incorrectly ranked negative passages higher than the positive one, we regard each token u_i in q as a query, and we find the position of corresponding token v_j that appears in d where $u_i = v_j$. Then, we calculate the mean reciprocal rank for

Query	Document
how much did nr ##a give to congress	m ##em ##bers of congress pay attention to these numbers , and they know that in the last election cycle the nr ##a spent $ 18 . 6 million on various campaigns , a says lee dr ##ut ##man , who has studied the role of gun money in politics for the sunlight foundation .
is mortgage and deed of trust the same document	the mortgage or deed of trust is recorded in the county land records , usually shortly after the borrow ##ers sign it . if the loan is fully paid off , the lend ##er will record a release (or satisfaction) of mortgage or a rec ##on ##vey ##ance of deed (which is used in conjunction with deeds of trust) in the county land records .
which is stronger hydro ##co ##don ##e or ox ##y ##co ##don ##e	dos ##age conversion : hydro ##co ##don ##e vs . ox ##y ##co ##don ##e , in terms of strength , 5 ##mg of ox ##y ##co ##don ##e is roughly equivalent of 7 . 5 of hydro ##co ##don ##e . that is the conversion required to bring about the same effects . hydro ##co ##don ##e would work better if you happen to be a lightweight person with a weak stomach .

Table 4: Top-10 most important tokens identified by IBA in three examples. '[CLS]' and '[SEP]' are ignored.

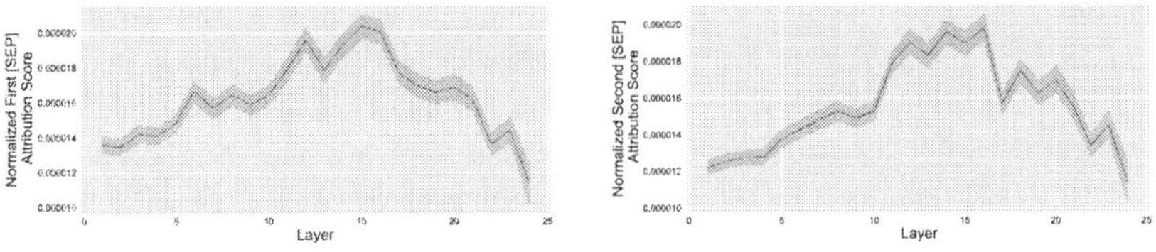

(a) Firt [SEP] Normalized Score (b) Second [SEP] Normalized Score

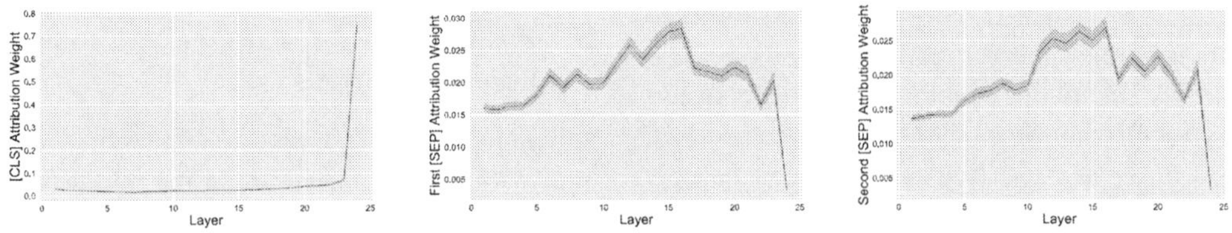

(c) CLS attribution weight. (d) Firt [SEP] Weight (e) Second [SEP] Weight

Figure 7: Special tokens attribution scores and weights.

	USE	sent-bert(p)	sent-bert(n)
BM25 top-1	0.540	0.593	0.578
BERT top-1	0.483	0.731	0.563

Table 5: Cosine similarity between query and top-1 passage returned by different methods. "p" refers to pretrained model paraphrase-MiniLM-L6-v2", "n" refers 'bert-base-nli-mean-tokens'

all v_j — $\text{MRR} = \frac{1}{|q \cap d|}\sum_{j=1}^{|q \cap d|}\frac{1}{\text{position}(v_j)}$. We then aggregate the MRR for all higher-ranked negative passages (HRNPs) and compare it with the MRR for the lower-ranked positive passages (LRPPs). When we aggregate by the "max" function, we find that, in 86.2% of cases, HRNPs have higher MRR than LRPPs. Averaging all MRRs for HRNPs gives us 0.191, while it's 0.103 for averaging LRPPs. These numbers are 63.8%, 0.129, and 0.103, respectively if we aggregate by the arithmetic mean. We cannot say that the reason for those negative passages ranking higher is due to matched tokens appearing earlier, but we do note a correlation between HRNPs and early-appearing matched tokens.

Driven by this positional bias, we are also curious about how positional index correlates with the passages' ranks. We compute the average positional index p_i for each document's top-20 most important tokens, and then average p_i for each query. As we show in Fig. 8, higher-ranked passages do have earlier tokens emphasized, meaning that passages with important tokens stressed earlier are preferred. When comparing the top-1 document returned by BERT d_{BERT} with the top-1 document returned by BM25 d_{BM25}, this preference also exists. We compute the MRR across all tokens in the query and passages like we do

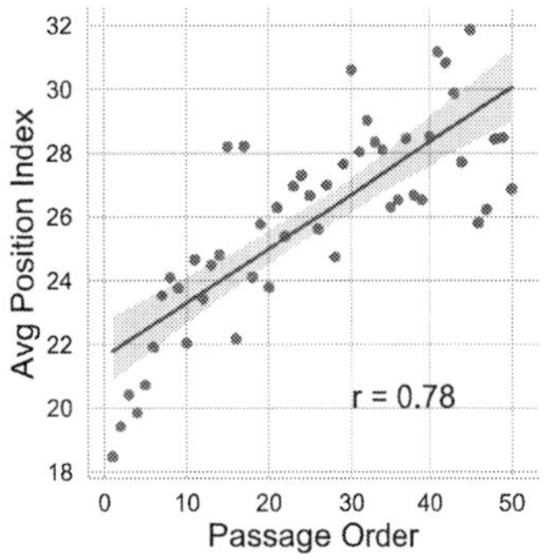

Figure 8: Positional index.

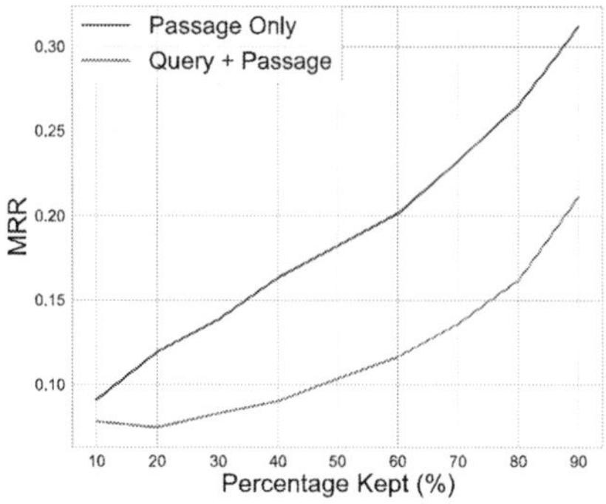

Figure 9: Average truncation MRR.

in Section 4.4 for those passages $d_{\text{BERT}} \neq d_{\text{BM25}}$ and d_{BERT} makes the correct prediction. We find that even BM25 is almost all about term matching, with $\mathbf{J}(q, d_{\text{BERT}}) = 0.062$, $\mathbf{J}(q, d_{\text{BM25}}) = 0.074$, considering the position, $\text{MRR}(q, d_{\text{BERT}}) = 0.127$ is still higher than $\text{MRR}(q, d_{\text{BM25}}) = 0.099$.

F Note on Semantic Similarity Measurement

We also find that it is hard to measure the contextualized relevance between query and passages by simply calculating cosine similarity ϕ between query vectors and document vectors. We encode q, d_{BERT}, d_{BM25} and don't find that $\phi(\eta(q), \eta(d_{\text{BERT}}))$ is higher than $\phi(\eta(q), \eta(d_{\text{BM25}}))$ when using the Universal Sentence Encoder or Sentence-BERT (Reimers and Gurevych, 2019), denoted as η, pre-trained on an NLI dataset. However, if using a Sentence-BERT pre-trained on a paraphrase corpus (specifically the model "paraphrase-MiniLM-L6-v2") to measure semantic similarity, $\phi(\eta(q), \eta(d_{\text{BERT}}))$ is significantly higher than $\phi(\eta(q), \eta(d_{\text{BM25}}))$ as "paraphrase-MiniLM-L6-v2's" pretrained corpus includes MSMARCO triplet. Tempting as it is to conclude that BERT has indeed captured semantic similarity that BM25 hasn't, it's unfair to use a pre-trained model with prior knowledge on MSMARCO to measure the semantic similarity. Therefore, we think BERT has learned a deeper relevance between the query and document, but it cannot be simply measured by vaguely defined semantic similarity.

G Truncation Test across All Passages

To further measure the trade-off between compression and quality, we do truncation test for all passages. Specifically, given a $g\%$ of tokens kept for every single document, we measure final ranking performance—MRR score. The result is shown in Figure 9. From the result, we can see that truncating doc only is more robust than truncating both query and doc. On average, with 90% tokens of passage kept, we have MRR = 0.311. But for the maximum, we can get MRR = 0.392 with 90% tokens, which is very close to the original score, and that depends on what tokens we remove.

H Position Index for Important Tokens across 24 Layers

Shown in Figure 10, layer 24 is the outlier, where most tokens emphasized are in the middle of the document. For other layers, it's still the start of passages that is emphasized.

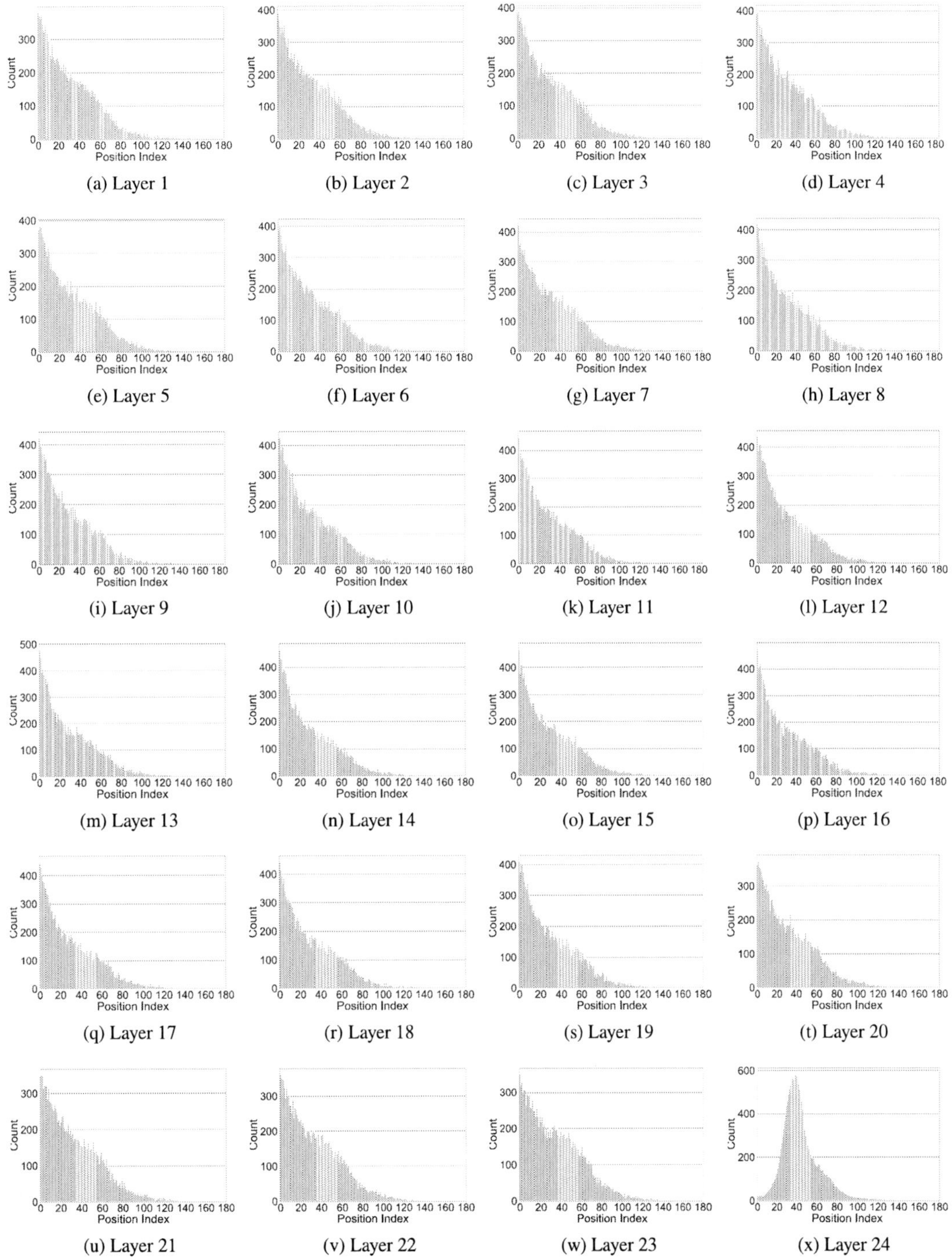

(a) Layer 1 (b) Layer 2 (c) Layer 3 (d) Layer 4

(e) Layer 5 (f) Layer 6 (g) Layer 7 (h) Layer 8

(i) Layer 9 (j) Layer 10 (k) Layer 11 (l) Layer 12

(m) Layer 13 (n) Layer 14 (o) Layer 15 (p) Layer 16

(q) Layer 17 (r) Layer 18 (s) Layer 19 (t) Layer 20

(u) Layer 21 (v) Layer 22 (w) Layer 23 (x) Layer 24

Figure 10: Positional index across 24 layers

Do Language Models Know the Way to Rome?

Bastien Liétard
University of Lille
bastien.lietard.etu
@univ-lille.fr

Mostafa Abdou and Anders Søgaard
University of Copenhagen
{madbou,soegaard}@di.ku.dk

Abstract

The global geometry of language models is important for a range of applications, but language model probes tend to evaluate rather local relations, for which ground truths are easily obtained. In this paper we exploit the fact that in geography, ground truths are available beyond local relations. In a series of experiments, we evaluate the extent to which language model representations of city and country names are isomorphic to real-world geography, e.g., if you tell a language model where Paris and Berlin are, does it know the way to Rome? We find that language models generally encode limited geographic information, but with larger models performing the best, suggesting that geographic knowledge *can* be induced from higher-order co-occurrence statistics.

1 Introduction

Language models (LMs) are fundamental building blocks in state-of-the-art natural language processing. These models are trained to predict words in context, and as a side product, they learn to compress higher-order co-occurrence statistics to represent the distributional properties of words and phrases.

It is well-documented that the representations of modern language models encode some syntactic (Tenney et al., 2019) and semantic knowledge ((Reif et al., 2019)), as well as some real-world knowledge (Davison et al., 2019; Petroni et al., 2019; Jiang et al., 2020; Roberts et al., 2020), i.e., some knowledge base relations can be extracted directly from language models. Much of this information was available in older language models such as Word2Vec, too (Mikolov et al., 2013).

The probes that have been designed for the above studies, however, only probe for one-dimensional information (e.g., part of speech or semantic class) or very local relations (e.g., is Daniel Kehlmann a writer?). It is an open question whether higher-order co-occurrence statistics found in textual corpora can induce representations show isomorphism to human mental representations of entities and relations. To test this we operationalize a dataset of geographic information. Geographic knowledge is a domain in which we can go beyond local relations, since we can access global representations of geographic knowledge (to the extent it is isomorphic to the physical world).

Cross-lingual language model alignment provides additional motivation for probing for geographic knowledge: We know that language models of different languages are sometimes near-isomorphic (Søgaard et al., 2018; Vulić et al., 2020), and it is tempting to think that this is because language models reflect real-world structures, and that the (occasional) near-isomorphism of language models is simply the result of the fact that we use language(s) to talk about the same world. Is the isomorphism of language models a result of them being in part isomorphic to the physical world?

Why would language models potentially encode physical geometry? Higher-order co-occurrence statistics can be surprisingly informative. Copenhagen and Malmö are in different countries, but connected by a bridge, often referred to as *the bridge between Copenhagen and Malmö*. Other cities belong to the same municipalities and their names therefore co-occur with the name of the municipality. Other cities were, for instance, potentially impacted by the same natural disaster or part of the same development project. By distilling thousands, or maybe hundreds of thousands, of such co-occurrences, we conjecture that language models might be able to induce somewhat fine-grained maps of physical geometry.

In this work, we study the extent to which geographical information is encoded by language models. Based on geographic information from multiple sources, we train probing models on language

Proceedings of the Fourth BlackboxNLP Workshop on Analyzing and Interpreting Neural Networks for NLP, pages 510–517
Online, November 11, 2021. ©2021 Association for Computational Linguistics

model representations and evaluate their ability to predict the locations of cities and countries, as well as their ability to predict (one-dimensional) population numbers and (local) neighbor relations, relative to control probe performance levels.

Contributions We collect geographic information from multiple sources and design experimental protocols to probe language models for such information. We evaluate two BERT models (Devlin et al., 2019) of different sizes, two RoBERTa models (Liu et al., 2019) of different sizes, as well as GPT-2 (Radford et al., 2019) and Word2Vec (Mikolov et al., 2013) across three different tasks and various protocols. Our results show that modern language models do not encode much more geographic information than Word2Vec, but that larger (non-autoregressive) language models encode more information than their smaller counterparts, suggesting that such information is nevertheless available through higher-order co-occurrence statistics.

2 Related Work

Word representations based on distributional statistics have been theorised to capture a wide range of information (Schütze, 1992). To evaluate this, a considerable body of literature has made use of semantic similarity, relatedness, and analogy datasets (Agirre et al., 2009; Bruni et al., 2012; Baroni et al., 2014; Faruqui et al., 2014; Hill et al., 2015; Drozd et al., 2016; Abdou et al., 2018). Asking a broader question, Rubinstein et al. (2015) investigated the types of semantic information which are encoded by different classes of word embedding models, finding that taxonomic properties (such as animacy) are well-modelled. In a similar direction, Collell Talleda and Moens (2016) and Lucy and Gauthier (2017) draw on semantic norm datasets to test how well these models can encode a range of perceptual and conceptual features.

In the context of the neural language models, several recent works such as Davison et al. (2019) and Petroni et al. (2019) have attempted to extract factual and commonsense knowledge from them by posing knowledge base triplets as close statements which are used to query the models. Most related to this work, Forbes et al. (2019) investigate whether LMs can learn physical commonsense through language. They find that LM representations do indeed encode information regarding object properties (e.g., *bananas are yellow*), and affordances (e.g. *bananas can be eaten*) but they do not to capture the more subtle interplay between the two.

Studies investigating the geometry of word representations have focused on intrinsic dimensionality and subspaces (Yaghoobzadeh and Schütze, 2016; Coenen et al., 2019), embedding concentration in narrow cones and anisotropy (Mimno and Thompson, 2017; Ethayarajh, 2019), and comparisons to the geometry of cognitive measurements or perceptual spaces (Abnar et al., 2019; Abdou et al., 2021). In this work we investigate the degree of isomorphism between language model representations of geographic location names and their real-world counterparts. See Vulić et al. (2020) for a general discussion of isomorphism across language models, what explains this, and what it depends on.

3 Methodology

We probe language model representations of city and country names. Below, we propose three classification/regression probing tasks, as an well as an analysis based on (relational) similarity.

3.1 Probing tasks

Task 1: Predicting geo-coordinates We probe LMs' representation about whether they convey information about the actual position of the location. To this extent, we train a model to predict GPS coordinates (latitude and longitude) given the location's representation through language models. We evaluate prediction error by computing the distance in kilometers between the predicted GPS point and the expected point, and compute the average of error distances. Since we use linear models (Lasso[1]) to predict geo-coordinates, we effectively evaluate the isomorphism of language model representations to the physical world. Our target variable is two-dimensional, and we evaluate non-local relations.

Task 2: Predicting population sizes In the physical world, cities are characterized not only by their location, but also by their size and population. There is indeed a major difference between Shanghai (27M people) and Worcester (101K people). Given the representation of a country name or a city name, we train a probe to predict the population living in the location. We evaluate the performance by computing the *mean squared error*.

[1] We also include an MLP regressor for comparison.

This is a one-dimensional attribute included here for comparison.

Task 3: Predicting neighboring countries Borders between countries are also an important geographic relation that is closely related to a country's international policy. It also provides information about the continental situation ; indeed, a country with no land borders must be an island. To probe language models for neighboring relations, we train an classifier to predict whether two countries share a border or not, given the pair of representations. We report the probe accuracy. Neighboring relations are local and included here for comparison.

3.2 Control tasks and scores

Hewitt and Liang (2019) have shown the importance of a control task to balance the probe accuracy. We construct our control tasks by randomly permuting the target variables and train the model on this randomly-permuted dataset. We repeat this control task 10 times and take the mean error/accuracy.

Probe classifier selectivity For the country borders classification task, we define the *probe selectivity* as the difference between the probe accuracy on the original task and the accuracy on the control task (Hewitt and Liang, 2019).

Probe error reduction Similarly, we define the *probe error reduction*, which measures how well the probe performs on the original task compared to the control task, by comparing positive error measures of both tasks through error reduction, i.e., the proportion of control task error that is reduced in our probe.

$$PER = 1 - \frac{\textit{Probing task error}}{\textit{Control task error}}$$

Less formally, if the PER is between 0 and 1, its upper bound, it indicates to what extent the probe is doing better on the original task than on the control task ; a negative PER indicates the probe is doing worse on the original task than on the control task. We use PER for regression tasks rather than absolute error or MSE, because figures are more easily interpretable when properly baselined. Note that if absolute error is 0, PER is 1; if absolute error is as high as the random baseline, PER is 0. Under the assumption performance is better than random, PER thus ranges between 0 and 1.

3.3 Similarity Analysis

For each language models, we compute the cosine similarity between each pair of cities. Our hypothesis is that cities belonging to the same country will be more similar than two cities from different countries. We report both average similarities (cities in the same country and cities in different countries) and also compute the histogram of the distribution of these two sets of similarities.

4 Experimental Settings and Data

Language models We compare three different state-of-the-art contextualized LMs, namely BERT (Devlin et al., 2019), RoBERTa (Liu et al., 2019) and GPT-2 (Radford et al., 2019). A major difference between GPT-2 and the two other models is that it is trained to be unidirectional (*i.e.* using next-token language modelling), whereas BERT and RoBERTa are trained to be bidirectionnal (*i.e.* using masked language modelling). For BERT and RoBERTa, we used both `base` ($L = 12$ layers and $D = 768$ output dimensions) and `large` ($L = 24$ layers and $D = 1024$ output dimensions) version, so we can study the influence of the model's size. We probe widely-used pre-trained versions of these models, as they have been trained in their respective original papers. Both versions of BERT and RoBERTa have been pre-trained on the BookCorpus (800M words) and English Wikipedia (2.5B words). GPT-2 is also trained on the Book Corpus.

Geographic data We get a list of names of cities around the world having a population of 100K or more people, with their GPS coordinates (Latitude and Longitude), their country and their population, from a MaxMind database[2]. Country geocoordinates correspond to the centroid of each country. We obtain population size data from the United Nations' Human Development Data Center[3], given in millions of inhabitants. Our datasets are then composed of 3527 cities and 249 countries and territories.

Representations extraction Since the LMs provide *contextualised* token representations, we provide three linguistically-basic contexts : *He lives in* X, *She moved to* X and *I come from* X, replacing X with either a city name or a country name.

[2]`https://www.kaggle.com/max-mind/world-cities-database`

[3]`http://hdr.undp.org/en/data`

For each context, we extract the representation corresponding to the name by averaging the hidden states of the last 4 layers of the LMs. Following Bommasani et al. (2020), we use a mean pooling of subwords' representations when necessary.

Word2Vec To compare static and contextualized models, we also use pre-trained Word2Vec *static* representations learned over the Google News dataset (150B words), provided by the `gensim`[4] library. The representational vectors are in 300 dimensions.

Probe models For the classification problem (task 3), we use a 100-units single-layered MLP as a classifier. As a probe for regression task (1 and 2), we train both a Lasso regressor with a L2-penalty of α and a single hidden layer MLP with 100 units. We arbitrarily choose $\alpha = 1$, except for task 1 for which we remarked that $\alpha = 0.5$ significantly decreased the training time without affecting to much the error ratio. No other hyperparameters-tuning was done, since we are not interested in designing the best task-specific models. Probes are trained on a random split of 80% of the dataset, and evaluate on the 20% remaining.

5 Results

In Table 1, probe error reduction scores are displayed for both regression tasks, namely Task 1 and 2. The full list of performances (error distances in kilometers) for Task 1 is provided in the appendix A.1. In Appendix A.2, error values for population prediction with countries are reported. Since the number of countries is relatively small, we perform a *5-fold cross-validation* with this dataset.

When predicting a location's GPS coordinates, all models have an error reduction score significantly larger than 0, across both families of regressors and across cities and countries. The Word2Vec model especially has often the lowest error and a high PER, showing no real weakness compared to contextualised models. GPT-2 has the lowest PER and the worst error value, across almost all tasks and probes. The two regressors globally lead to the same error values, even though MLP allows a slightly bigger error reduction than Lasso. We can also note that, for both BERT and RoBERTa, increasing model size (moving from `base` models to `large`), one increases the gap between the performance on the task and on the random control, reducing overall error. Finally, we can also see that the models are generally not very accurate for predicting GPS coordinates, leading to an average error of 2'500-5'000 kilometers. It is relatively accurate continent-wise, but not precise.

In sum, we can conclude that it is non-trivial to learn linear maps from language models to physical world geo-coordinates, presumably because representations are non-isomorphic. On the other hand, the improvements from larger models seem to suggest that geographical knowledge is available from higher-order co-occurrence statistics. Static model also provide a strong baseline compared to contextualised models.

In Task 2, the gap between the two regressors is more noticeable compared to Task 1: MLP exhibits much higher error reductions between the original task and the random control, and generally allow for lower error numbers. We remark that our Lasso model is particularly ineffective for country population prediction, leading only to low PER and high errors. On this task and dataset, GPT-2 random control error is high, leading to an outlying PER for this LM, even if its probing-task error is still the biggest. The scheme observed in Task 1 between `base` and `large` version of BERT and RoBERTa seems to hold, with only an exception for countries with MLP. This overall indicates that a one-dimensional attribute is easier to learn than a two-dimensional space, giving more expressive models an upper hand.

Table 2 shows the probe's accuracy and selectivity on Task 3, predicting country borders. This is a local relation, included for comparison. Probe accuracy scores exhibit little variance, and control accuracies are almost identical, close to **0.5**, which is expected for random binary classification. All language models allow exhibit probe accuracies above 80%. This indicates the insufficiency of probing only for local relations.

The results of the similarity analysis on city names are displayed in Table 3 and in Figure 1. It is to be observed that representations are highly similar in contextualized LMs, especially compared to those from Word2Vec, which is in accordance with Ethayarajh (2019) results about anisotropy in higher layers of LMs. On the other hand, we observe that representations of cities in the same country are always more similar than cities in dif-

[4] `https://radimrehurek.com/gensim/`

Task	Probe	Dataset	Word2Vec	BERT	BERT-L	GPT-2	RoBERTa	RoBERTa-L
GPS	MLP	city	**0.666**	0.479	0.585	0.424	0.466	0.517
		country	0.57	0.424	**0.58**	0.422	0.405	0.468
	Lasso	city	0.498	0.454	**0.555**	0.364	0.398	0.466
		country	0.395	0.394	**0.465**	0.349	0.378	0.454
Population	MLP	city	0.507	0.694	0.704	0.624	0.696	**0.707**
		country	0.618	0.59	**0.63**	0.568	0.528	0.505
	Lasso	city	**0.628**	0.539	0.55	0.447	0.403	0.531
		country	-0.242	0.116	0.276	**0.372**	0.078	0.116

Table 1: Probe error reduction. "BERT-L" and "RoBERTa-L" denote `large` versions of BERT and RoBERTa. Column name "Probe" designates the different regression architectures used for probing. For GPS coordinates, error reduction is computed with average error in kilometers, whereas it is computed using MSE for Population. Control tasks are performed on $n = 10$ trials, and the control error is obtained by averaging all trials errors.

Model	Accuracy Prb.	Accuracy Ctrl.	Probe Selectivity
Word2Vec	0.849	0.49	0.36
BERT	0.856	0.51	0.34
BERT-L	**0.873**	0.51	**0.37**
GPT-2	0.808	0.51	0.3
RoBERTa	0.817	0.51	0.31
RoBERTa-L	0.843	0.52	0.32

Table 2: Probe accuracy (Prb.), control accuracy (Ctrl.) and probe selectivity for country borders prediction.

Model	intra	inter	gap
Word2Vec	0.51	0.24	0.27
BERT	0.83	0.77	0.06
BERT-L	0.77	0.65	0.12
GPT-2	0.90	0.89	0.01
RoBERTa	0.92	0.89	0.03
RoBERTa-L	0.94	0.93	0.01

Table 3: Average representational similarities between cities in the same country (`intra`), in different countries (`inter`) and the gap between them.

ferent countries, even if the gap is small for some models. Finally, we can note that no conclusion can be made about the effect of increasing the LM's size in this analysis: the gap is bigger in large version of BERT than in the base version, but this relation does not hold for RoBERTa.

6 Discussion

Tasks 1 to 3 suggest that the amount of geographic knowledge learned by the language models is limited. On the one hand, trained predictors for both GPS coordinates and population are of poor quality, making average errors of thousands of kilometers or hundreds of millions of people. On the other hand, the probes are doing significantly better on these tasks than during random control, and information about country borders have been shown by results of Task 3 to be embedded in pre-trained language models' representations. This suggests that approximate geographic positions and their neighborhood are learned during training by these models. Similarity analysis also indicates that pre-trained models have learned to associate representations of cities in the same country.

In the end, language models, whether they are static or contextualized, seem to be able to extract limited geographical knowledge from higher-order co-occurrence statistics. The size of the language models, as well as the amount of data they were trained on, seem to be important for how well they encode this information. Increasing the model's size leads to best performances and error reduction scores, indicating a better learning of geographic knowledge. Overall, context-sensitive language models do not show significantly better performances than Word2Vec. Finally, our experiments demonstrate the importance of probing for global, multi-dimensional relations that require near-isomorphism and are not easily saturated.

In the future, it would be of interest to test models finetuned on corpora which contain a wealth of geographic information (e.g. a corpus of atlases) in order to evaluate a) whether representational alignment to real-world geography can be affected by seeing factual expressions such as *"Italy, France, and Switzerland share borders."* and b) how exactly representations of entities (e.g. *France*) alter when the model sees factual statements as the one above.

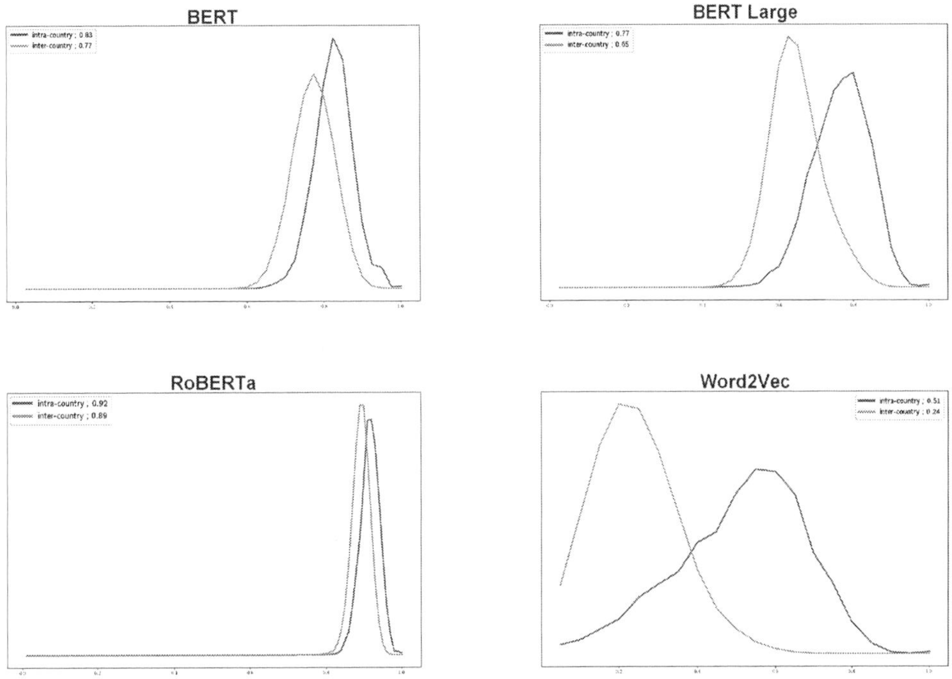

Figure 1: Representational similarity histograms for BERT, BERT `large`, RoBERTa and Word2Vec. The similarity is computed through cosine similarity. Blue is the curve of *intra-country* (same country) similarity ; orange is the one for *inter-countries* (different countries) similarity.

Acknowledgements

We thank the anonymous reviewers. Mostafa Abdou was funded by a Google Focused Research Award. We used data created by MaxMind, available from `http://www.maxmind.com/`.

References

Mostafa Abdou, Artur Kulmizev, Daniel Hershcovich, Stella Frank, Ellie Pavlick, and Anders Søgaard. 2021. Can language models encode perceptual structure without grounding? a case study in color.

Mostafa Abdou, Artur Kulmizev, and Vinit Ravishankar. 2018. Mgad: Multilingual generation of analogy datasets. In *Proceedings of the Eleventh International Conference on Language Resources and Evaluation (LREC 2018)*.

Samira Abnar, Lisa Beinborn, Rochelle Choenni, and Willem Zuidema. 2019. Blackbox meets blackbox: Representational similarity and stability analysis of neural language models and brains. *arXiv preprint arXiv:1906.01539*.

Eneko Agirre, Enrique Alfonseca, Keith Hall, Jana Kravalova, Marius Pasca, and Aitor Soroa. 2009. A study on similarity and relatedness using distributional and wordnet-based approaches.

Marco Baroni, Georgiana Dinu, and Germán Kruszewski. 2014. Don't count, predict! a systematic comparison of context-counting vs. context-predicting semantic vectors. In *Proceedings of the 52nd Annual Meeting of the Association for Computational Linguistics (Volume 1: Long Papers)*, pages 238–247.

Rishi Bommasani, Kelly Davis, and Claire Cardie. 2020. Interpreting Pretrained Contextualized Representations via Reductions to Static Embeddings. In *Proceedings of the 58th Annual Meeting of the Association for Computational Linguistics*, pages 4758–4781, Online. Association for Computational Linguistics.

Elia Bruni, Gemma Boleda, Marco Baroni, and Nam-Khanh Tran. 2012. Distributional semantics in technicolor. In *Proceedings of the 50th Annual Meeting of the Association for Computational Linguistics (Volume 1: Long Papers)*, pages 136–145.

Andy Coenen, Emily Reif, Ann Yuan, Been Kim, Adam Pearce, Fernanda Viégas, and Martin Wattenberg. 2019. Visualizing and measuring the geometry of bert. *arXiv preprint arXiv:1906.02715*.

Guillem Collell Talleda and Marie-Francine Moens. 2016. Is an image worth more than a thousand words? on the fine-grain semantic differences between visual and linguistic representations. In *Proceedings of the 26th International Conference on Computational Linguistics*, pages 2807–2817. ACL.

Joe Davison, Joshua Feldman, and Alexander Rush. 2019. Commonsense knowledge mining from pretrained models. In *Proceedings of the 2019 Conference on Empirical Methods in Natural Language Processing and the 9th International Joint Conference on Natural Language Processing (EMNLP-IJCNLP)*, pages 1173–1178, Hong Kong, China. Association for Computational Linguistics.

Jacob Devlin, Ming-Wei Chang, Kenton Lee, and Kristina Toutanova. 2019. Bert: Pre-training of deep bidirectional transformers for language understanding.

Aleksandr Drozd, Anna Gladkova, and Satoshi Matsuoka. 2016. Word embeddings, analogies, and machine learning: Beyond king-man+ woman= queen. In *Proceedings of coling 2016, the 26th international conference on computational linguistics: Technical papers*, pages 3519–3530.

Kawin Ethayarajh. 2019. How contextual are contextualized word representations? comparing the geometry of BERT, ELMo, and GPT-2 embeddings. In *Proceedings of the 2019 Conference on Empirical Methods in Natural Language Processing and the 9th International Joint Conference on Natural Language Processing (EMNLP-IJCNLP)*, pages 55–65. Association for Computational Linguistics.

Manaal Faruqui, Jesse Dodge, Sujay K Jauhar, Chris Dyer, Eduard Hovy, and Noah A Smith. 2014. Retrofitting word vectors to semantic lexicons. *arXiv preprint arXiv:1411.4166*.

Maxwell Forbes, Ari Holtzman, and Yejin Choi. 2019. Do neural language representations learn physical commonsense? *arXiv preprint arXiv:1908.02899*.

John Hewitt and Percy Liang. 2019. Designing and interpreting probes with control tasks. In *Proceedings of the 2019 Conference on Empirical Methods in Natural Language Processing and the 9th International Joint Conference on Natural Language Processing (EMNLP-IJCNLP)*, pages 2733–2743, Hong Kong, China. Association for Computational Linguistics.

Felix Hill, Roi Reichart, and Anna Korhonen. 2015. Simlex-999: Evaluating semantic models with (genuine) similarity estimation. *Computational Linguistics*, 41(4):665–695.

Zhengbao Jiang, Frank F Xu, Jun Araki, and Graham Neubig. 2020. How can we know what language models know? *Transactions of the Association for Computational Linguistics*, 8:423–438.

Yinhan Liu, Myle Ott, Naman Goyal, Jingfei Du, Mandar Joshi, Danqi Chen, Omer Levy, Mike Lewis, Luke Zettlemoyer, and Veselin Stoyanov. 2019. Roberta: A robustly optimized bert pretraining approach.

Li Lucy and Jon Gauthier. 2017. Are distributional representations ready for the real world? evaluating word vectors for grounded perceptual meaning. *arXiv preprint arXiv:1705.11168*.

Tomás Mikolov, Kai Chen, Greg Corrado, and Jeffrey Dean. 2013. Efficient estimation of word representations in vector space. In *1st International Conference on Learning Representations, ICLR 2013, Scottsdale, Arizona, USA, May 2-4, 2013, Workshop Track Proceedings*.

David Mimno and Laure Thompson. 2017. The strange geometry of skip-gram with negative sampling. In *Empirical Methods in Natural Language Processing*.

Fabio Petroni, Tim Rocktäschel, Sebastian Riedel, Patrick Lewis, Anton Bakhtin, Yuxiang Wu, and Alexander Miller. 2019. Language models as knowledge bases? In *Proceedings of the 2019 Conference on Empirical Methods in Natural Language Processing and the 9th International Joint Conference on Natural Language Processing (EMNLP-IJCNLP)*, pages 2463–2473, Hong Kong, China. Association for Computational Linguistics.

Alec Radford, Jeff Wu, R. Child, David Luan, Dario Amodei, and Ilya Sutskever. 2019. Language models are unsupervised multitask learners.

Emily Reif, Ann Yuan, Martin Wattenberg, Fernanda B Viegas, Andy Coenen, Adam Pearce, and Been Kim. 2019. Visualizing and measuring the geometry of bert. In *Advances in Neural Information Processing Systems*, volume 32. Curran Associates, Inc.

Adam Roberts, Colin Raffel, and Noam Shazeer. 2020. How much knowledge can you pack into the parameters of a language model? *arXiv preprint arXiv:2002.08910*.

Dana Rubinstein, Effi Levi, Roy Schwartz, and Ari Rappoport. 2015. How well do distributional models capture different types of semantic knowledge? In *Proceedings of the 53rd Annual Meeting of the Association for Computational Linguistics and the 7th International Joint Conference on Natural Language Processing (Volume 2: Short Papers)*, pages 726–730.

Hinrich Schütze. 1992. Dimensions of meaning. In *SC*, pages 787–796.

Anders Søgaard, Sebastian Ruder, and Ivan Vulić. 2018. On the limitations of unsupervised bilingual dictionary induction. In *Proceedings of the 56th Annual Meeting of the Association for Computational Linguistics (Volume 1: Long Papers)*, pages 778–788, Melbourne, Australia. Association for Computational Linguistics.

Ian Tenney, Dipanjan Das, and Ellie Pavlick. 2019. BERT rediscovers the classical NLP pipeline. In *Proceedings of the 57th Annual Meeting of the Association for Computational Linguistics*, pages 4593–4601, Florence, Italy. Association for Computational Linguistics.

Ivan Vulić, Sebastian Ruder, and Anders Søgaard. 2020. Are all good word vector spaces isomorphic? In *Proceedings of the 2020 Conference on Empirical Methods in Natural Language Processing (EMNLP)*, pages 3178–3192, Online. Association for Computational Linguistics.

Yadollah Yaghoobzadeh and Hinrich Schütze. 2016. Intrinsic subspace evaluation of word embedding representations. *arXiv preprint arXiv:1606.07902*.

A Appendices

A.1 Task 1 performances

On the following tables, *Prb.* stands for "probing task" and *Ctl.* for "control task".

Model	MLP		Lasso	
	Prb.	Ctl.	Prb.	Ctl.
Word2Vec	**2612**	7825	3447	6870
BERT	4195	8057	3780	6920
BERT-L	3315	7997	**3077**	6911
GPT-2	4613	8011	4498	7070
RoBERTa	4278	8007	4148	6894
RoBERTa-L	3876	8029	3686	6903

Mean error distances in kilometers for GPS prediction of **cities**

Model	MLP		Lasso	
	Prb.	Ctrl.	Prb.	Ctrl.
Word2Vec	3738	8695	**4379**	7234
BERT	4950	8598	4944	8152
BERT-L	**3603**	8578	4488	8394
GPT-2	5111	8840	5658	8684
RoBERTa	5522	9275	5036	6091
RoBERTa-L	4764	8960	4433	8125

Mean error distances in kilometers for GPS prediction of **countries**

A.2 Task 2 performances on countries

Reported results are *mean squared errors*. Therefore, mean absolute errors are at most of the magnitude of few hundreds (of millions) of people.

Model	MLP		Lasso	
	Prb.	Ctrl.	Prb.	Ctrl.
Word2Vec	12142	31815	22112	17810
BERT	16382	39952	26583	30063
BERT-L	17166	46365	22559	31174
GPT-2	15264	3566	32130	51171
RoBERTa	15266	32338	26375	28592
RoBERTa-L	16390	33112	22927	25923

Mean squared error distances (in millions of people) for prediction of country's population.

Exploratory Model Analysis Using Data-Driven Neuron Representations

Daisuke Oba
The University of Tokyo

Naoki Yoshinaga
Institute of Industrial Science,
The University of Tokyo

Masashi Toyoda
Institute of Industrial Science,
The University of Tokyo

{oba,ynaga,toyoda}@tkl.iis.u-tokyo.ac.jp

Abstract

Probing classifiers have been extensively used to inspect whether a model component captures specific linguistic phenomena. This top-down approach is, however, costly when we have no probable hypothesis on the association between the target model component and phenomena. In this study, aiming to provide a flexible, exploratory analysis of a neural model at various levels ranging from individual neurons to the model as a whole, we present a bottom-up approach to inspect the target neural model by using neuron representations obtained from a massive corpus of text. We first feed massive amount of text to the target model and collect sentences that strongly activate each neuron. We then abstract the collected sentences to obtain neuron representations that help us interpret the corresponding neurons; we augment the sentences with linguistic annotations (*e.g.,* part-of-speech tags) and various metadata (*e.g.,* topic and sentiment), and apply pattern mining and clustering techniques to the augmented sentences. We demonstrate the utility of our method by inspecting the pre-trained BERT. Our exploratory analysis reveals that i) specific phrases and domains of text are captured by individual neurons in BERT, ii) a group of neurons simultaneously capture the same linguistic phenomena, and iii) deeper-level layers capture more specific linguistic phenomena.

1 Introduction

Deep neural networks (DNNs) learn to induce internal feature representations or neurons[1] for a given input, which are optimized for the target task. The success of DNNs in the field of natural language processing (NLP) is underpinned by this flexibility to induce internal vector representations of input. It is, however, difficult for humans to interpret their roles and properties, which hinders us from leveraging DNNs in practical applications.

Researchers have therefore investigated what linguistic aspects of input text are captured by the internal representations of DNNs optimized for NLP tasks (§ 2). Most of the existing methods inspect a pre-specified model component (*e.g.,* individual BERT layers) in a top-down manner. A typical approach first takes aim at specific linguistic phenomena that would be captured by the target components, and then trains a probing classifier that predicts the chosen linguistic phenomena from the target components (Bau et al., 2018; Giulianelli et al., 2018; Dalvi et al., 2019; Lakretz et al., 2019; Kovaleva et al., 2019; Goldberg, 2019; Petroni et al., 2019; Hewitt and Manning, 2019; Jawahar et al., 2019; Durrani et al., 2020; Zhou and Srikumar, 2021; Cao et al., 2021; Jumelet et al., 2021).

Although this top-down approach based on probing classifiers has provided thought-provoking insights into the target model components, it becomes costly when we want to inspect many combinations of model components and linguistic phenomena. This is because the probing requires us to train machine-learning classifiers for each combination of model component and linguistic phenomenon. Although there are a few bottom-up approaches to inspect DNNs by examining the response of the neurons towards (perturbed) inputs that represent the target linguistic phenomenon (Karpathy et al., 2016; Shi et al., 2016; Qian et al., 2016), these approaches are labor intensive since they require manual intervention.

This study aims at efficiently inspecting neural NLP models at various levels of granularity ranging from individual neurons to the model as a whole, and presents a bottom-up approach to inspecting what kind of concrete linguistic phenomena each neuron of the model responds to, without presupposing the target linguistic phenomenon to be examined (§ 3). Given a massive amount of text, we first feed individual sentences to the target model, and collect sentences to which each neuron strongly

[1] **Neurons** refer to numerical values of each dimension of internal representations such as hidden states.

Proceedings of the Fourth BlackboxNLP Workshop on Analyzing and Interpreting Neural Networks for NLP, pages 518–528
Online, November 11, 2021.

responds (§ 3.1).[2] We next annotate the collected sentences with the linguistic annotations (*e.g.*, part of speech tags) and various metadata (*e.g.*, topic and sentiment). With the help of these annotations, we then apply text mining techniques such as frequent pattern mining to extract common patterns as *the linguistic signatures*[3] that exist repeatedly and intricately in the sentences collected for the target neurons (§ 3.2). We finally investigate relationships between multiple neurons by comparing and clustering continuous neuron representations induced from the collected sentences.

We apply our method to the pre-trained BERT (base-uncased) (Devlin et al., 2019) to demonstrate how much insight into BERT the method can actually provide. Our exploratory model analysis have confirmed that it is possible to identify, without any prior assumptions, a wide variety of specific linguistic phenomena to which each neuron responds (§ 4.2). Furthermore, by comparing the linguistic phenomena and sentences corresponding to individual neurons, we revealed the existence of neurons that work cooperatively for the same purpose. We finally revealed the impact of optimizing BERT to the target task (here, the pre-training task and sentiment classification) by comparing neurons of randomly initialized BERT with neurons of the pre-trained and the fine-tuned BERT (§ 4.3).

The contribution of this study is threefold:

- We present a method of **exploratory model analysis to understand neural NLP models.** We investigate concrete linguistic phenomena (*e.g.*, skip n-grams) captured by the neurons of the target model, without any prior assumptions about the phenomena to be examined.
- We revealed **concrete linguistic phenomena captured by various BERT's neurons** and layers, whereas existing approaches reported coarse linguistic phenomena that are indicated by high performance in probing tasks.
- We confirmed that **neurons in deeper BERT layers capture more specific linguistic phenomena, and fine-tuning facilitates this tendency** in a sentiment classification task.

[2]For simplicity, we hereafter assume that input to the target model is a single sentence, although our method can be applied to models that takes input in shorter or larger linguistic units.

[3]This term is named after topic signatures (Agirre et al., 2001), which are supplemental data-driven representations of word senses whose representations are extracted from external language resources.

2 Related Work

In order to clarify what kind of linguistic phenomena are captured by neural NLP models, researchers have analyzed the internal representations of the models at various levels of granularity such as neurons (Karpathy et al., 2016; Shi et al., 2016; Qian et al., 2016; Bau et al., 2018; Lakretz et al., 2019; Vig et al., 2020; Cao et al., 2021), layers (Hewitt and Manning, 2019; Liu et al., 2019; Tenney et al., 2019a; Goldberg, 2019; Jawahar et al., 2019; Miaschi and Dell'Orletta, 2020), attentions (Kovaleva et al., 2019; Clark et al., 2019; Brunner et al., 2020; Kobayashi et al., 2020), and the model as a whole (Petroni et al., 2019; Broscheit, 2019; Roberts et al., 2020). In what follows, we start by reviewing probing methods that investigate the classifier performance of external tasks based on the target model components. We next describe some microscopic methods that focus on individual neurons. We then discuss a method of inspecting each neuron using text generated for that neuron.

Most of the recent methods adopt a top-down approach called *probing*, which takes target component (*e.g.*, layer) as inputs, trains a classifier that predicts the linguistic phenomena of interest such as syntactic information (Jawahar et al., 2019; Miaschi and Dell'Orletta, 2020; Wu et al., 2020) , agreement information (Giulianelli et al., 2018; Goldberg, 2019), and semantic knowledge (Tenney et al., 2019b; Ettinger, 2020), and evaluates the properties of the internal representation with reference to the accuracy of the classifier. To reduce the cost of training a classifier, Zhou and Srikumar (2021) indirectly predict the performance of probing classifiers by analyzing how the labeled data is represented in the vector space. Some studies identify neurons which make a huge contribution to solving the desired task, by looking at the performance of the task when the activation of neurons is forcibly controlled (Bau et al., 2018; Lakretz et al., 2021; Cao et al., 2021).

These probing methods are inductive in that they examine whether the target model component captures the target linguistic phenomenon. It is costly to inspect various pairs of model components and phenomena. Our approach does not presuppose linguistic phenomena to be examined and gives information that differs from the above methods; we show concrete linguistic phenomena each neuron responds to strongly, in a form that can be easily understood by humans (*e.g.*, skip n-grams) (§ 4.2).

Datasets	#sent.	domain	metadata	avg. length	distribution of simplified POS tags
BookCorpus (Zhu et al., 2015)	40M	book	author	16.3	noun: 21.4%, verb: 17.6%, adj.: 5.1%
English Wikipedia[4]	40M	wikipedia	entity	22.0	noun: 32.5%, verb: 11.7%, adj.: 6.0%
Sentiment140 (Go et al., 2009)	2M	social media	sentiment	10.3	noun: 23.4%, verb: 18.4%, adj.: 5.8%
IMDB (Maas et al., 2011)	0.3M	review	sentiment	23.8	noun: 22.9%, verb: 15.3%, adj.: 7.4%
20Newsgroups (Lang, 1995)	0.2M	news	topic	23.6	noun: 29.0%, verb: 13.0%, adj.: 5.3%
Reuters[5]	39K	news	category	28.9	noun: 38.2%, verb: 11.7%, adj.: 6.2%
Total	82M	-	-	18.9	noun: 27.7%, verb: 14.2%, adj.: 5.7%

Table 1: Datasets used to collect sentences to which individual neurons of the target model strongly activate. Among the PTB annotations obtained by the POS tagger described in § 4.1, we here defined those POSs whose letters begin with N, V, and J as "noun," "verb," and "adj," respectively.

There are several studies that have investigated the roles of neurons – the finest components of models such as a cell state in a long short term memory – by observing interactions between their values and (perturbed) input sentences (Karpathy et al., 2016; Shi et al., 2016; Qian et al., 2016; Vig et al., 2020; Lakretz et al., 2021). However, these methods are tailored to analyze a few pre-defined particular phenomena such as sequence length, or need to perform the analysis per phenomenon. Our method, on the other hand, allows for a wide range of analytical perspectives in that it uses a massive amount of raw text to collect sentences in which individual neurons show strong interest and leverages pattern mining to highlight linguistic phenomena contained in the collected sentences.

As the most similar to our approach, Poerner et al. (2018) proposed a gradient-based method that generates input text which strongly activates neurons, inspired by work in computer vision (Simonyan et al., 2014). Their method differs from the probing methods in that it embodies the information captured by the neurons as text, which is similar to our study. However, their method can generate only text of pre-fixed length, and requires hyper-parameter tuning (*e.g.*, annealing temperature) to generate natural text, making it costly to apply to massive neurons in the models. Moreover, it is difficult for humans to interpret properties of the generated text just by observing them. In contrast, we propose an example-based method for collecting human-written sentences from a huge text corpora, determining which each neuron finds interesting, without any parameter tuning. By exploiting text mining techniques, we can reveal various linguistic phenomena as long as they appear in the source raw text.

[4] 12/20/2020 ver. https://dumps.wikimedia.org/enwiki

[5] http://kdd.ics.uci.edu/databases/reuters21578

3 Data-Driven Inspection of Neurons

This section describes our methodology for providing a deeper insight into a neural model at the finest level of granularity (i.e., neurons[1]). Our approach abstracts the sentences retrieved from a massive amount of text such as the BookCorpus (Zhu et al., 2015). The whole process is as follows.

Step 1: Collecting sentences activating neurons This step finds which neurons consider what text to be interesting. Feeding a massive amount of raw text such as Wikipedia and BookCorpus (Zhu et al., 2015) to the target model, we collect a large number of sentences that are strongly associated with each neuron in the model (§ 3.1).

Step 2: Abstracting the collected sentences This step finds what concrete linguistic phenomena each neuron finds interesting. We associate the collected sentences with linguistic annotations such as part-of-speech tags and available metadata such as topic and sentiment (Table 1). We then abstract a wide range of linguistic phenomena that exist in the retrieved sentences using data mining techniques such as frequent pattern mining, utilizing the associated information (§ 3.2). We call the resulting patterns as *linguistic signatures* of neurons.

3.1 Collecting Sentences Activating Neurons

We first feed a massive amount of text to the target model, and then extract sentences which strongly activate each neuron. In other words, we look for sentences that each neuron finds interesting. For this purpose, the size of the corpus can be reduced if there is a large diversity in the linguistic phenomena and domains contained in the corpus.

Since it is impractical to record the neurons' values for all the sentences, we use a priority queues to maintain only the top-N sentences that strongly activate each neuron.

3.2 Abstracting the Collected Sentences

Although the collected sentences embody various linguistic phenomena, it is difficult to induce the types of covered linguistic phenomena due to the diversity and redundancy of language. We therefore exploit data-mining techniques such as frequent pattern mining to obtain common patterns as *linguistic signatures*, which represent abstract properties of the sentences, for neurons. To help the pattern mining sum up sentences, we augment the collected sentences with linguistic annotations (here, part-of-speech tags) and metadata in advance.

Single-neuron analysis To understand which types of phenomena are captured by each neuron, we first rely on frequent (skip) n-grams obtained by using sequential pattern mining (Han et al., 2001).[6] We used relative frequency to find n-grams specific to individual neurons. We can also observe the distribution of the linguistic annotations (*e.g.*, part-of-speech tags) and metadata which capture traits of the sentences (*e.g.*, domain). By encoding the sentences collected for each neuron into vectors and clustering them, we can find the typical sentence which strongly activates the target neuron.

Cross-neuron analysis We compare the linguistic signatures (*e.g.*, common n-grams and distribution of metadata) obtained for individual neurons. We also extract groups of neurons that work together to capture the same linguistic phenomena by clustering continous neuron representations induced from the sentences collected for the neurons.

4 Experiments

Taking the pre-trained BERT (base-uncased) (Devlin et al., 2019) as an example, we demonstrate that our methodology can perform similar analysis to that obtained by existing approaches. We also provide novel findings on how and what aspects of language each neuron captures.

4.1 Settings

Data We use six English corpora in various domains to mine neuron-sentence interactions (Table 1). We split each corpus into sentences with a sentence tokenizer[7], and normalize repetitions of symbols[8] to a single symbol (*e.g.*, from +++ to +). We then tokenize the resulting sentences with FastTokenizer,[9] and exclude sentences less than three tokens in length. In addition to metadata associated with text in the corpora, we annotate the sentences with part-of-speech (POS) tags using a POS tagger.[10] The statistics of the resulting corpora are summarized in Table 1.

Models We adopt the pre-trained BERT (base-uncased, 12 layers, and 768 dimensions of hidden states)[11] as the target for inspection (**pre-trained**). To investigate the effect of representation learning (*e.g.*, masked language modeling and fine-tuning) on the properties of neurons, we also examine two models: one with parameters randomly initialized (**random**) and the other with parameters fine-tuned on sentiment classification task (**fine-tuned**).

To fine-tune BERT, we use the training set in Sentiment140 (Go et al., 2009) that annotates the sentences with polarity labels (positive and negative). We passed the CLS token's output vector through a fully-connected layer, and updated the parameters of pre-trained with a learning rate of 10^{-5}, dropout rate of 0.3, batch size of 32, and 5 epochs. To obtain the **random** model, we randomly re-initialized only the parameters of the **pre-trained** model other than the word embedding layer since this paper conducts the analysis of 12-layer encoder's neurons excluding the embedding layers.

In experiments, we treat each hidden state as a neuron to be analyzed (i.e., 12×768 neurons in total in each model). Here we take the average over the hidden states of each token in the sentence for quantifying how strongly the neuron responds to the input. This is to find interesting "sentences" first, and then to find interesting words and phrases exploiting well-established pattern mining methods as described in § 3. Interesting future work will associate with each token the value of the hidden states after processing that token, and use the values to amplify the frequency of n-grams.

To find typical sentences among the sentences collected for each neuron by clustering the 10K sentences for each neuron (single-neuron analysis) and to find a group of neurons that capture similar linguistic phenomena by clustering continuous neuron representations induced from the 10K sentences (cross-neuron analysis), we represent each

[6] Although here we use only part-of-speech taggers for annotation, we can exploit syntactic parsers and FREQT (Asai et al., 2004) to obtain common syntactic structures.

[7] nltk sentence tokenizer ver. 3.2.4

[8] !@#$%^&*()_+-=[]{};:?,.

[9] https://github.com/huggingface/tokenizers

[10] https://www.logos.ic.i.u-tokyo.ac.jp/ tsuruoka/lapos

[11] https://github.com/huggingface/pytorch-pretrained-BERT

Noun neuron; 740th hidden state in 3rd layer	
words	william, john, roBERT, de, edward
word pattern	(Sir William), (Sir John)
POS pattern	(NNP NNP NNP), (NNP IN NNP), (NNP NNP IN)
ratio of POS	noun: 91.7%, verb: 0.9%, adj.: 0.4%
avg. length	3.8
typical sent.	*The architects of the Square Mile included RoBERT Findlay, Bruce ...*

Verb neuron; 462nd hidden state in 6th layer	
words	going, got, help, need, get, know
word pattern	(going to have), (we have to)
POS pattern	(PRP TO VB), (VBP TO VB), (VBG TO VB)
ratio of POS	noun: 16.6%, verb: 29.8%, adj.: 1.1%
avg. length	6.4
typical sent.	*Something was going to have to give, and it wasn't going to be him.*

Social Media neuron; 200th hidden state in 6th layer	
Words	lol, im, u, twitter, haha, ur, like, miss
word pattern	(I my), (i it), (i i), (I was), (i lol)
POS pattern	(NN NN NN), (NN NN), (PRP NN)
ratio of POS	noun: 29.8%, verb: 18.3%, adj.: 6.3%
avg. length	7.6
typical sent.	*nooo I got so many tho That sucks I finished the boook and now I'm ...*

Short sentence neuron; 169th hidden state in 1st layer	
words	war, party, revolutionary, ibn
word pattern	(of the), (the of), (Giovanni Battista)
POS pattern	(NNP NNP NNP), (NNP IN NNP), (DT NNP NNP)
ratio of POS	noun: 67.5%, verb: 5.5%, adj.: 5.3%
avg. length	3.5
typical sent.	*The Tale of Loyal Knights and ...*

Science neuron; 705th hidden state in 9th layer	
words	species, family, genus, found, sea
word pattern	(is in the), (is of the), (is a the)
POS pattern	(IN NNP), (DT IN), (IN DT)
ratio of POS	noun: 34.4%, verb: 11.5%, adj.: 7.0%
avg. length	16.7
typical sent.	*Pachliopta polyphontes is a species of butterfly from the family Papilionidae...*

Positive neuron; 43rd hidden state in 7th layer	
words	chapter, love, welcome, good, ha
word pattern	(Chapter Chapter Chapter), (the of the)
POS pattern	(DT JJ NN), (PRP DT NN), (PRP RB JJ)
ratio of POS	noun: 42.3%, verb: 7.7%, adj.: 4.2%
avg. length	8.1
typical sent.	*doing great sweetie, about to take my dog for a walk in the park (while ...*

United States neuron; 203rd hidden state in 7th layer	
words	freyja, united, states, house, election
word pattern	(is going be), (was going be)
POS pattern	(DT JJ NN), (PRP DT NN), (PRP RB JJ)
ratio of POS	noun: 63.3%, verb: 1.6%, adj.: 2.8%
avg. length	8.0
typical sent.	*1912 United States House of Representatives election in Wyoming ...*

Olympic neuron; 69th hidden state in 6th layer	
words	olympics, summer, games
word pattern	(United States in), (United States of)
POS pattern	(NNP NNP NNP), (NNP IN NNP)
ratio of POS	noun: 36.2%, verb: 7.4%, adj.: 3.6%
avg. length	17.4
typical sent.	*In the 5000 metres she competed at the 1995 World Championships and the ...*

Table 2: Examples of neurons and their linguistic signatures extracted from the top-10K sentences to which they strongly responded. The neurons were manually named to highlight the linguistic phenomena they capture (§ 4.2). The "word" and "word/POS pattern" rows show the most frequent patterns in the 10K sentences. The "typical sent." is that is closest to the average vector of the collected 10K sentences when they are vectorized (§ 4.1).

sentence as vectors, and take average over the 10K sentence vectors to obtain neuron representations. Specifically, we represent each sentence with an average of 300-dimensional fastText embeddings (Bojanowski et al., 2017)[12] of the tokens.

4.2 Single-Neuron Analysis

We collected 10K sentences corresponding to each neuron, and identified the common linguistic phenomena in those sentences by using frequent pattern mining. We found interpretable neurons from several perspectives. As inspired by Quiroga et al. (2005) that reports the existence of a "Halle Berry neuron" in a human brain analysis, we gave distinguished names to represent the roles of neurons (*e.g., Science neuron* is activated by text in science domain), and showed some of the linguistic phenomena they captured in Table 2.

With the help of the automatic linguistic annotations, we found neurons that responded only to nouns or verb-rich sentences (*Noun* or *Verb neuron*), and neurons that responded only to short sentences (*Short-length neuron*). Digging deeper into what kind of text *Noun neuron* is actually responding to, we can see another aspect; it responds to names of people such as "william" and "john." It would be very interesting to investigate the relationship between the existence of neurons corresponding to these fundamental linguistic annotations and the task performance of the model.

By looking at the metadata distribution for the collected sentences, we also found neurons that responded to specific domains/concepts. For example, 82.2% of the 10K sentences corresponding to one neuron were taken from the social media domain in Table 1 (*Social Media Neuron*), 80.2%

[12]https://github.com/facebookresearch/fastText

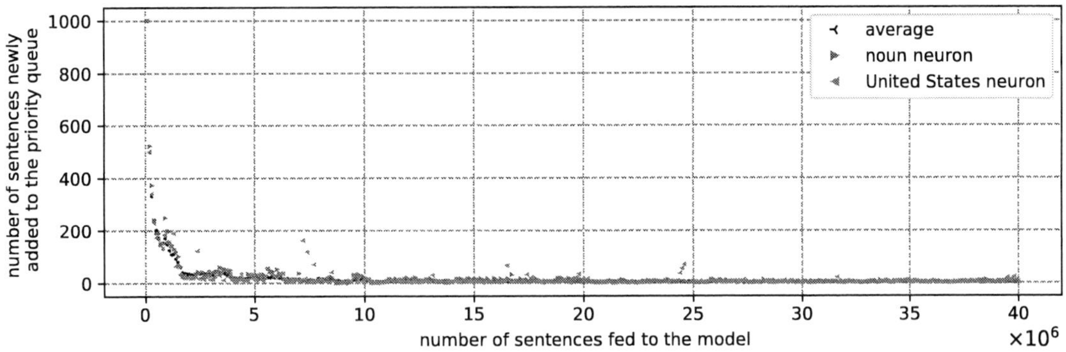

Figure 1: The average number of sentences that were newly added to top-1000 of the priority queues of each neuron for every 100K input sentences when we apply our method to the sentences taken from Wikipedia (Table 1).

of the 10K sentences for another neuron consist of positive sentiment documents[13] (*Positive Neuron*), and 45.3% of the 10K sentences for a third neuron are scientific documents[14] (*Science Neuron*). Moreover, digging deeper into the abstracted linguistic phenomena in Table 2, we can see that *the Social Media neuron* actually responds to informal words such as "lol" and "haha," and *Science neuron* has a role in responding strongly to relatively uncommon words such as "species" and "genus." It is an interesting direction to investigate the relationship between the robustness of the model to the domain and the existence of these domain-specific neurons.

We can also reveal the topic-specific neurons by using a list of words that represent particular topics. For example, we have found neurons that are strongly activated by the words "united states, us, u.s., u.s.a, america" (*United States neuron*) and neurons that strongly respond to the words "olympic" (*Olympic neuron*). It would be interesting to investigate the relationship between the existence of such topic-specific neurons and the knowledge possessed by the model (Petroni et al., 2019).

As we have demonstrated so far, the proposed method can find characteristic neurons from various perspectives in a bottom-up manner. It can also reveal information about the properties of neurons (i.e., specific text and linguistic phenomena) that are not covered by the probing task performance (i.e., numerical value). By comparing neurons based on the collected sentences and the linguistic signatures (abstracted phenomena), we can gain insight into the target model components at any level of granularity, as we will demonstrate in the next section.

[13]Sentences of *positive* class in Sentiment140 dataset.

[14]Sentences of *sci* class in 20Newsgroups dataset.

On the frequency in updating top-N sentences With the datasets in Table 1 and our server with two Intel® Xeon® E5-2680 v4 2.40-GHz CPUs and eight NVIDIA Quadro P6000 GPUs, analysis of BERT by our method took about 10 hours for Step 1, and about five minutes per neuron for Step 2. The computation time in Step 1 can be reduced if we stop feeding sentences to the target model when the elements of priority cues for neurons become stable.

To confirm this, we performed the Step 1 using the 40M sentences in the Wikipedia corpus in Table 1 with a single GPU on the same server, and checked how many sentences were newly added to the priority queues on a neuron-average basis for every 100K sentences input. Figure 1 shows that after feeding about 2M sentences into the model, 96% of the sentences in the priority queues have already been fixed. This indicates that we can truncate the computation in Step 1 by monitoring the frequency in updates on the priority cues.

We should mention that priority queues for a few neurons are frequently updated even after feeding the model with millions of sentences. This happens if the neurons capture very specific phenomenon, such as *the United States neuron* in Table 2. This suggests that we should diversify the feeding sentences to include various linguistic phenomena as possible when we want to reduce the amount of the corpus fed to the model.

4.3 Cross-Neuron Analysis

Clustering neuron vectors induced from the collected sentences We leverage the collected 10K sentences for individual neurons to obtain example-based neuron representations (vectors), and then cluster the obtained neuron vectors to identify co-

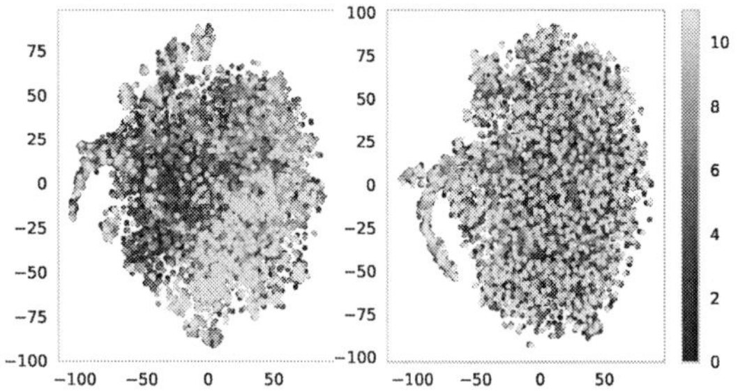

(a) pre-trained (b) random

Figure 2: Clustering neurons in both models. Each neuron is represented by the average of the sentence vectors of the corresponding 10K sentences. The color indicates the layer in which the neuron is located.

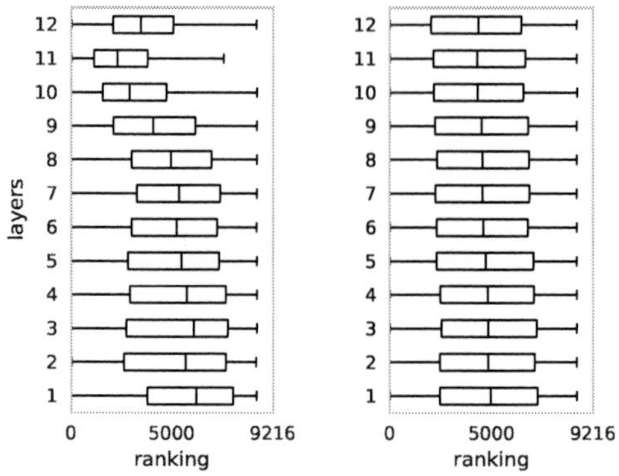

(a) pre-trained (b) random

Figure 3: Ranking neurons in the models in terms of how selectively the neuron responds to a specific part-of-speech. The box-and-whisker diagrams show where the neurons in each layer are distributed in the ranking.

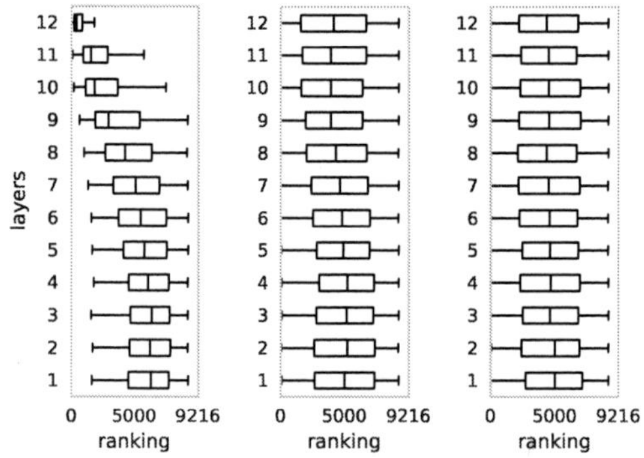

(a) fine-tuned (b) pre-trained (c) random

Figure 4: Ranking neurons by standard deviation of sentiment polarity of the collected sentences. The box-and-whisker diagrams show the distribution of each layer's neurons in the ranking.

operating neurons. Here we verify a hypothesis that neurons in the same layer are cooperating. First, we represent each neuron with an average of the vectors for the corresponding 10K sentences. Next, we perform k-means clustering of these 12×768 neuron vectors. The number of clusters is set to 12, which is identical to the number of layers. We report the accuracy of the clustering using the Hungarian algorithm (Kuhn, 1955).

The clustering accuracy is 15.9% for the **pre-trained** model compared to 9.6% for the **random** model. This result suggests that although the overall performance is low, the pre-training made the neurons in each layer capture similar linguistic phenomena, reconfirming results of the existing studies that explore each layer in a top-down manner (§ 2) had a reasonable point of view.

Figure 2 visualizes the neuron vectors using t-SNE (van der Maaten and Hinton, 2008). The heatmap shows which layer the neurons (vectors) belong to. We can see that the pre-trained BERT's neurons in the shallower and deeper layers form different clusters.

Ranking neurons by the skewness of captured linguistic phenomena By ranking (sorting) the neurons by the frequency of each linguistic phenomenon and the deviation of their distribution, we can examine where the neurons that represent each linguistic phenomenon are distributed in the model. Here, we take the simplified version of the PTB part-of-speech tags for nouns, verbs, and adjectives (Table 1) and binary sentiment polarity as the target linguistic phenomenon.

For part-of-speech tags, we find neurons that selectively respond to a specific part-of-speech tag. First, we normalize the frequency of each part of speech tag in the 10K sentences collected for each neuron using the frequency obtained from the original corpus (Table 1). The maximum relative frequency (percentage) among all the part-of-speech tags is then used as a measure of how selectively the neuron responds to a particular part of speech tag. For sentiment polarity, we find the neurons that selectively respond to a particular polarity (i.e., positive and negative). First, we calculate the standard deviation of the binary sentiment polarity distribution of the 10K sentences collected for each neuron, and then use this as a measure of how much the neuron responds to a particular sentiment.

Figure 3 and 4 show the results of ranking the neurons in each layer for their selective responsive-

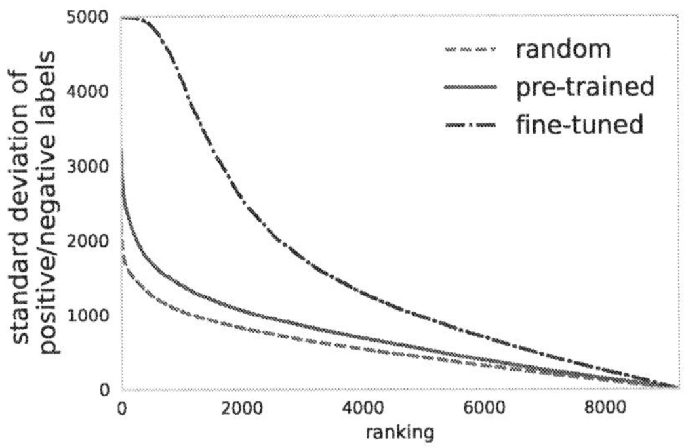

Figure 5: Ranking neurons in the three models by standard deviation of sentiment polarity of the collected sentences.

ness to part-of-speech and sentiment polarity. The box-and-whisker diagrams show where the neurons in each layer are distributed in the ranking. From the figures, we can see that **random** model results in a ranking of neurons that is independent of the layer, while the **pre-trained** model tends to show that neurons in deeper layers are more selectively responsive to both phenomenon.

Interestingly, for the POS tagging task, it has been reported that neurons in the lower layers are better able to handle the probing task (Tenney et al., 2019a). This suggests that, for POS tagging, the presence of neurons that respond uniformly to part-of-speech tags has a significant influence on POS tagging performance. For sentiment polarity, we also calculated the ranking of the neurons in the **fine-tuned** model. Figure 4 shows that the neurons of the **fine-tuned** model in the deeper layers become more capable of capturing the sentiment of the text, while the neurons in the shallower layers are kept insensitive to the polarity of the text.

Figure 5 depicts the results of ranking the neurons in each model, where the y-axis represents the standard deviation of sentiment polarity of the collected sentences for the ranked neurons. We can see that the models have increased the percentage of neurons that show a certain degree of selective response to specific sentiment polarity by pre-training and by fine-tuning. It will be interesting to utilize this standard deviation to measure the distance between the two tasks.

5 Conclusions

This study aims to provide a method of exploratory model analysis for a neural NLP model at various levels of granularity ranging from individual neurons to the model as a whole, and proposed a bottom-up methodology for revealing what kind of concrete linguistic phenomena each neuron of the model strongly responds to. We take advantage of large-scale text data and data mining techniques to extract linguistic signatures (common patterns) that characterize the individual neurons.

Taking BERT (base-uncased) as an example, we first showed that specific phrases such as those related to United States are captured by individual neurons in BERT (*e.g., United States Neuron* in Table 2). By comparing neurons in terms of the collected sentences they strongly respond to, we then revealed that neurons in the same layer of BERT have similar properties. Lastly, in comparing the corresponding linguistic phenomena with those of neurons in randomly initialized and fine-tuned models, we found that neurons in deeper BERT layers capture more linguistic phenomena specific to language modeling and sentiment classification.

In the future, we plan to investigate models with different architectures. For example, our method can be used to compare the differences of encoder and decoder neurons in end2end models; there is a debate in the field of neural machine translation as to whether modifying the encoder or the decoder contributes more to domain adaptation (Wang et al., 2021).

Our method enables us to find non-apriori linguistic phenomena the neurons may capture, so that it is possible to assist in the construction of a novel training/evaluation dataset for the probing-based evaluation methods. In addition, our method provides information of a different nature, i.e., the concrete linguistic phenomena to which the internal representations respond, as opposed to numerical information such as accuracy of probing tasks.

As mentioned in § 4.2, our method has the potential to perform with less time complexity by reducing the corpus size fed to the target model in Step 1. Therefore, we plan to study how to select a text corpus of such a small size that it reproduces the analysis results obtained when using a very large corpus as the one used in this study.

Acknowledgements

This work was supported by JST CREST Grant Number JPMJCR19A4 including AIP challenge program, Japan and JSPS KAKENHI Grant Number 21H03494. We thank Joshua Tanner and the anonymous reviewers for their valuable comments.

References

Eneko Agirre, Olatz Ansa, David Martinez, and Eduard Hovy. 2001. Enriching WordNet concepts with topic signatures. In *Proceedings of the NAACL workshop on WordNet and Other Lexical Resources: Applications, Extensions and Customizations*.

Tatsuya Asai, Kenji Abe, Shinji Kawasoe, Hiroshi Sakamoto, Hiroki Arimura, and Setsuo Arikawa. 2004. Efficient substructure discovery from large semi-structured data. *IEICE TRANSACTIONS on Information and Systems*, 87(12):2754–2763.

Anthony Bau, Yonatan Belinkov, Hassan Sajjad, Nadir Durrani, Fahim Dalvi, and James Glass. 2018. Identifying and controlling important neurons in neural machine translation. In *Proceedings of the sixth International Conference on Learning Representations*.

Piotr Bojanowski, Edouard Grave, Armand Joulin, and Tomas Mikolov. 2017. Enriching word vectors with subword information. *Transactions of the Association for Computational Linguistics*, 5:135–146.

Samuel Broscheit. 2019. Investigating entity knowledge in BERT with simple neural end-to-end entity linking. In *Proceedings of the 23rd Conference on Computational Natural Language Learning*, pages 677–685.

Gino Brunner, Yang Liu, Damian Pascual, Oliver Richter, Massimiliano Ciaramita, and Roger Wattenhofer. 2020. On identifiability in transformers. In *Proceedings of the eighth International Conference on Learning Representations*.

Steven Cao, Victor Sanh, and Alexander Rush. 2021. Low-complexity probing via finding subnetworks. In *Proceedings of the 2021 Conference of the North American Chapter of the Association for Computational Linguistics: Human Language Technologies*, pages 960–966.

Kevin Clark, Urvashi Khandelwal, Omer Levy, and Christopher D. Manning. 2019. What does BERT look at? an analysis of BERT's attention. In *Proceedings of the 2019 ACL Workshop BlackboxNLP: Analyzing and Interpreting Neural Networks for NLP*, pages 276–286.

Fahim Dalvi, Nadir Durrani, Hassan Sajjad, Yonatan Belinkov, Anthony Bau, and James Glass. 2019. What is one grain of sand in the desert? Analyzing individual neurons in deep NLP models. In *Proceedings of the 33th AAAI Conference on Artificial Intelligence*, pages 6309–6317.

Jacob Devlin, Ming-Wei Chang, Kenton Lee, and Kristina Toutanova. 2019. BERT: Pre-training of deep bidirectional transformers for language understanding. In *Proceedings of the 2019 Conference of the North American Chapter of the Association for Computational Linguistics: Human Language Technologies, Volume 1*, pages 4171–4186.

Nadir Durrani, Hassan Sajjad, Fahim Dalvi, and Yonatan Belinkov. 2020. Analyzing individual neurons in pre-trained language models. In *Proceedings of the 2020 Conference on Empirical Methods in Natural Language Processing*, pages 4865–4880.

Allyson Ettinger. 2020. What BERT is not: Lessons from a new suite of psycholinguistic diagnostics for language models. *Transactions of the Association for Computational Linguistics*, 8:34–48.

Mario Giulianelli, Jack Harding, Florian Mohnert, Dieuwke Hupkes, and Willem Zuidema. 2018. Under the hood: Using diagnostic classifiers to investigate and improve how language models track agreement information. In *Proceedings of the 2018 EMNLP Workshop BlackboxNLP: Analyzing and Interpreting Neural Networks for NLP*, pages 240–248.

Alec Go, Richa Bhayani, and Lei Huang. 2009. Twitter sentiment classification using distant supervision. *CS224N project report, Stanford*, 1(12).

Yoav Goldberg. 2019. Assessing BERT's syntactic abilities. *arXiv preprint arXiv:1901.05287*.

Jiawei Han, Jian Pei, Behzad Mortazavi-Asl, Helen Pinto, Qiming Chen, Umeshwar Dayal, and Meichun Hsu. 2001. Prefixspan: Mining sequential patterns efficiently by prefix-projected pattern growth. In *Proceedings of the 17th International Conference on Data Engineering*, pages 215–224.

John Hewitt and Christopher D. Manning. 2019. A structural probe for finding syntax in word representations. In *Proceedings of the 2019 Conference of the North American Chapter of the Association for Computational Linguistics: Human Language Technologies, Volume 1*, pages 4129–4138.

Ganesh Jawahar, Benoît Sagot, and Djamé Seddah. 2019. What does BERT learn about the structure of language? In *Proceedings of the 57th Annual Meeting of the Association for Computational Linguistics*, pages 3651–3657.

Jaap Jumelet, Milica Denic, Jakub Szymanik, Dieuwke Hupkes, and Shane Steinert-Threlkeld. 2021. Language models use monotonicity to assess NPI licensing. In *Findings of the Association for Computational Linguistics: ACL-IJCNLP 2021*, pages 4958–4969.

Andrej Karpathy, Justin Johnson, and Li Fei-Fei. 2016. Visualizing and understanding recurrent networks. In *Proceedings of the fourth International Conference on Learning Representations – Workshop Track*.

Goro Kobayashi, Tatsuki Kuribayashi, Sho Yokoi, and Kentaro Inui. 2020. Attention is not only a weight: Analyzing transformers with vector norms. In *Proceedings of the 2020 Conference on Empirical Methods in Natural Language Processing*, pages 7057–7075.

Olga Kovaleva, Alexey Romanov, Anna Rogers, and Anna Rumshisky. 2019. Revealing the dark secrets of BERT. In *Proceedings of the 2019 Conference on Empirical Methods in Natural Language Processing and the 9th International Joint Conference on Natural Language Processing*, pages 4365–4374.

Harold W Kuhn. 1955. The Hungarian method for the assignment problem. *Naval research logistics quarterly*, 2(1-2):83–97.

Yair Lakretz, Dieuwke Hupkes, Alessandra Vergallito, Marco Marelli, Marco Baroni, and Stanislas Dehaene. 2021. Mechanisms for handling nested dependencies in neural-network language models and humans. *Cognition*, page 104699.

Yair Lakretz, Germán Kruszewski, Théo Desbordes, Dieuwke Hupkes, Stanislas Dehaene, and Marco Baroni. 2019. The emergence of number and syntax units in lstm language models. In *Proceedings of the 2019 Conference of the North American Chapter of the Association for Computational Linguistics: Human Language Technologies, Volume 1*, pages 11–20.

Ken Lang. 1995. Newsweeder: Learning to filter netnews. In *Proceedings of the Twelfth International Conference on Machine Learning*, pages 331–339.

Nelson F. Liu, Matt Gardner, Yonatan Belinkov, Matthew E. Peters, and Noah A. Smith. 2019. Linguistic knowledge and transferability of contextual representations. In *Proceedings of the 2019 Conference of the North American Chapter of the Association for Computational Linguistics: Human Language Technologies, Volume 1*, pages 1073–1094.

Andrew L. Maas, Raymond E. Daly, Peter T. Pham, Dan Huang, Andrew Y. Ng, and Christopher Potts. 2011. Learning word vectors for sentiment analysis. In *Proceedings of the 49th Annual Meeting of the Association for Computational Linguistics: Human Language Technologies*, pages 142–150.

Alessio Miaschi and Felice Dell'Orletta. 2020. Contextual and non-contextual word embeddings: an in-depth linguistic investigation. In *Proceedings of the 5th Workshop on Representation Learning for NLP*, pages 110–119.

Fabio Petroni, Tim Rocktäschel, Sebastian Riedel, Patrick Lewis, Anton Bakhtin, Yuxiang Wu, and Alexander Miller. 2019. Language models as knowledge bases? In *Proceedings of the 2019 Conference on Empirical Methods in Natural Language Processing and the 9th International Joint Conference on Natural Language Processing*, pages 2463–2473.

Nina Poerner, Benjamin Roth, and Hinrich Schütze. 2018. Interpretable textual neuron representations for NLP. In *Proceedings of the 2018 EMNLP Workshop BlackboxNLP: Analyzing and Interpreting Neural Networks for NLP*, pages 325–327.

Peng Qian, Xipeng Qiu, and Xuanjing Huang. 2016. Analyzing linguistic knowledge in sequential model of sentence. In *Proceedings of the 2016 Conference on Empirical Methods in Natural Language Processing*, pages 826–835.

R. Quian Quiroga, Leila Reddy, Gabriel Kreiman, Christof Koch, and Itzhak Fried. 2005. Invariant visual representation by single neurons in the human brain. *Nature*, 435(7045):1102–1107.

Adam Roberts, Colin Raffel, and Noam Shazeer. 2020. How much knowledge can you pack into the parameters of a language model? In *Proceedings of the 2020 Conference on Empirical Methods in Natural Language Processing*, pages 5418–5426.

Xing Shi, Kevin Knight, and Deniz Yuret. 2016. Why neural translations are the right length. In *Proceedings of the 2016 Conference on Empirical Methods in Natural Language Processing*, pages 2278–2282.

Karen Simonyan, Andrea Vedaldi, and Andrew Zisserman. 2014. Deep inside convolutional networks: Visualising image classification models and saliency maps. In *Proceedings of the second the International Conference on Learning Representations – Workshop Track.*

Ian Tenney, Dipanjan Das, and Ellie Pavlick. 2019a. BERT rediscovers the classical NLP pipeline. In *Proceedings of the 57th Annual Meeting of the Association for Computational Linguistics*, pages 4593–4601.

Ian Tenney, Patrick Xia, Berlin Chen, Alex Wang, Adam Poliak, R. Thomas McCoy, Najoung Kim, Benjamin Van Durme, Samuel R. Bowman, Dipanjan Das, and Ellie Pavlick. 2019b. What do you learn from context? Probing for sentence structure in contextualized word representations. In *Proceedings of the seventh International Conference on Learning Representations.*

Laurens van der Maaten and Geoffrey Hinton. 2008. Visualizing data using t-SNE. *Journal of Machine Learning Research*, 9:2579–2605.

Jesse Vig, Sebastian Gehrmann, Yonatan Belinkov, Sharon Qian, Daniel Nevo, Yaron Singer, and Stuart M Shieber. 2020. Investigating gender bias in language models using causal mediation analysis. In *Advances in Neural Information Processing Systems 33*, pages 12388–12401.

Yue Wang, Cuong Hoang, and Marcello Federico. 2021. Towards modeling the style of translators in neural machine translation. In *Proceedings of the 2021 Conference of the North American Chapter of the Association for Computational Linguistics: Human Language Technologies*, pages 1193–1199.

Zhiyong Wu, Yun Chen, Ben Kao, and Qun Liu. 2020. Perturbed masking: Parameter-free probing for analyzing and interpreting BERT. In *Proceedings of the 58th Annual Meeting of the Association for Computational Linguistics*, pages 4166–4176.

Yichu Zhou and Vivek Srikumar. 2021. DirectProbe: Studying representations without classifiers. In *Proceedings of the 2021 Conference of the North American Chapter of the Association for Computational Linguistics: Human Language Technologies*, pages 5070–5083.

Yukun Zhu, Ryan Kiros, Rich Zemel, Ruslan Salakhutdinov, Raquel Urtasun, Antonio Torralba, and Sanja Fidler. 2015. Aligning books and movies: Towards story-like visual explanations by watching movies and reading books. In *Proceedings of the IEEE International Conference on Computer Vision*, pages 19–27.

Fine-Tuned Transformers Show Clusters of Similar Representations Across Layers

Jason Phang[1], **Haokun Liu**[2], **Samuel R. Bowman**[134]

[1]Center for Data Science, New York University
[2]Dept. of Computer Science, University of North Carolina at Chapel Hill
[3]Dept. of Linguistics, New York University
[4]Dept. of Computer Science, New York University

Correspondence: `jasonphang@nyu.edu`

Abstract

Despite the success of fine-tuning pretrained language encoders like BERT for downstream natural language understanding (NLU) tasks, it is still poorly understood how neural networks change after fine-tuning. In this work, we use centered kernel alignment (CKA), a method for comparing learned representations, to measure the similarity of representations in task-tuned models across layers. In experiments across twelve NLU tasks, we discover a consistent block diagonal structure in the similarity of representations within fine-tuned RoBERTa and ALBERT models, with strong similarity within clusters of earlier and later layers, but not between them. The similarity of later layer representations implies that later layers only marginally contribute to task performance, and we verify in experiments that the top few layers of fine-tuned Transformers can be discarded without hurting performance, even with no further tuning.

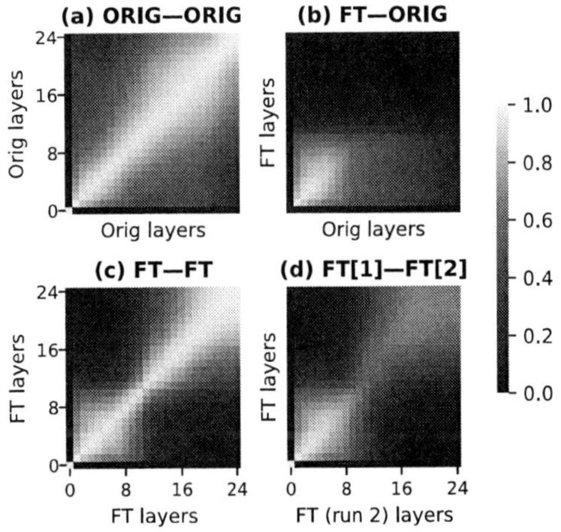

Figure 1: CKA similarity scores of `CLS` (classifier token) representations of ORIG (untuned ALBERT) and FT (fine-tuned) models on RTE, across different layers of the model. FT[1]–FT[2] compares two RTE models with different random restarts. ORIG–ORIG and FT–FT are symmetric by construction. Fine-tuned models exhibit a block-diagonal structure in the representation similarities. The same color scale is used in all plots.

1 Introduction

Fine-tuning pretrained language encoders such as BERT (Devlin et al., 2019) and its successors (Liu et al., 2019b; Lan et al., 2020; Clark et al., 2020; He et al., 2020) has proven to be highly successful, attaining state-of-the-art performance on many language tasks, but how do these models internally represent task-specific knowledge?

In this work, we study how learned representations change through fine-tuning by studying the similarity of representations between layers of untuned and task-tuned models. We use centered kernel alignment (CKA; Kornblith et al., 2019) to measure representation similarity and conduct extensive experiments across three pretrained encoders and twelve language understanding tasks.

We discover a consistent, block diagonal structure (Figure 1c,d) in the similarity of learned representations for almost all task-tuned RoBERTa and ALBERT models, where early layer representations and later layer representations form two distinct clusters, with high intra-cluster and low inter-cluster similarity.

Given the strong representation similarity of later model layers, we hypothesize that many of the later layers only marginally contribute to task performance. We show in experiments that the later layers of task-tuned RoBERTa and ALBERT can indeed be discarded with minimal impact to performance, even without any further fine-tuning.

2 Experimental Setup

Models For the majority of our experiments, we consider three commonly used language-encoding models: RoBERTa (Liu et al., 2019b), ALBERT (Lan et al., 2020) and ELECTRA (Clark et al., 2020). Because of the large number of exper-

Proceedings of the Fourth BlackboxNLP Workshop on Analyzing and Interpreting Neural Networks for NLP, pages 529–538
Online, November 11, 2021.

iments being performed, we use RoBERTa$_{\text{BASE}}$, ALBERT$_{\text{LARGEV2}}$ and ELECTRA$_{\text{BASE}}$ rather than the largest available versions of these models.

Tasks We use the tasks included in the GLUE benchmark (Wang et al., 2018) excluding the data-poor WNLI, namely: CoLA (Warstadt et al., 2019), MNLI (Williams et al., 2018), MRPC (Dolan and Brockett, 2005), QNLI (Rajpurkar et al., 2016), QQP,[1] RTE (Dagan et al., 2005), SST-2 (Socher et al., 2013), and STS-B (Cer et al., 2017). We include four additional tasks to cover a more diverse set of task formats and difficulties: BoolQ (Clark et al., 2019) and Yelp Review Polarity (Zhang et al., 2015) classification tasks, and HellaSwag (Zellers et al., 2019) and CosmosQA (Huang et al., 2019) multiple-choice tasks.

Optimization The representations learned over the course of training and similarity of representations may be sensitive to the number of steps used in training. To control for this, and to avoid task-specific hyperparameter tuning, we fine-tune on each task for up to 10,000 steps. We use the Adam (Kingma and Ba, 2014) optimizer with batch size of 4, a learning rate of 1e-5, and 1,000 warmup optimization steps.

We use the `jiant` (Phang et al., 2020) library, built on Transformers (Wolf et al., 2020) and PyTorch (Paszke et al., 2019), to run our experiments.

3 Representation Similarity with CKA

To analyze how learned representations change via fine-tuning, we use centered kernel alignment (CKA; Kornblith et al., 2019) to measure representation similarity. CKA is invariant to both orthogonal transformation and isotropic scaling of the compared representations, making it ideal for measuring the similarity of neural network representations, and has applied to BERT-type models in prior work (Wu et al., 2020; Sridhar and Sarah, 2020). Given two sets of representations $X \in \mathbb{R}^{N \times d_1}$ and $Y \in \mathbb{R}^{N \times d_1}$ where N is the number of examples and d_1, d_2 the hidden dimensions, CKA computes a similarity score between 0 and 1, where a higher score indicates greater similarity. Further details on CKA are provided in Appendix A.

Using CKA, we can compare the similarity of representations between different layers of the same model or even different models. For our analysis, we use the representations of the `CLS` token, i.e. the token whose final layer representation is fed to the task output head.[2] We compute CKA over the validation examples of each task.

To provide intuition for CKA scores, we first show in Figure 1 an example of the comparison formats using ALBERT fine-tuned on RTE.

ORIG–ORIG The top left plot shows the similarity of representations across the layers of the untuned ALBERT model on RTE inputs. Adjacent layers have high similarity scores, only gradually decreasing as more distant layers are compared.

FT–ORIG We show layers of the task-tuned model on the Y-axis and untuned model on the X-axis. The `CLS` representations of the later layers in the task-tuned model appear highly dissimilar to any of the untuned model: In other words, the representations differ starkly from those used for ALBERT's masked language modeling (MLM) and sentence order prediction (SOP) pretraining. This coheres with prior work showing that representations of later layers are most likely to change during fine-tuning (Kovaleva et al., 2019; Wu et al., 2020).

FT–FT Next, we compare layers within a single fine-tuned model. We observe a block-diagonal structure in the representation similarities—two distinct clusters of earlier (approx. first 10) and later (approx. last 14) layers that have high inter-cluster but low intra-cluster similarity. When considered together with FT-ORIG, we can infer that the earlier layer representations resemble those used for pretraining, whereas the later layers encode a representation suitable for tackling the task. The high internal similarity between the top few layers and the sharp block diagonal structure of the similarity matrix imply that the representations starkly differ.

FT[1]–FT[2] Finally, we compare fine-tuned ALBERT models across two random restarts. We observe a similar block diagonal structure. In particular, the similarity of the `CLS` representations in the later layers indicates that CKA is able recover the similarity of representations for tackling the same task across random restarts. This likely arises as the models are fine-tuned from the same initial pretrained parameters.

[1] `https://quoradata.quora.com/First-Quora-Dataset-Release-Question-Pairs`

[2] RoBERTa uses a `<s>` token instead, but for brevity and consistency, we will refer to it as `CLS` as well.

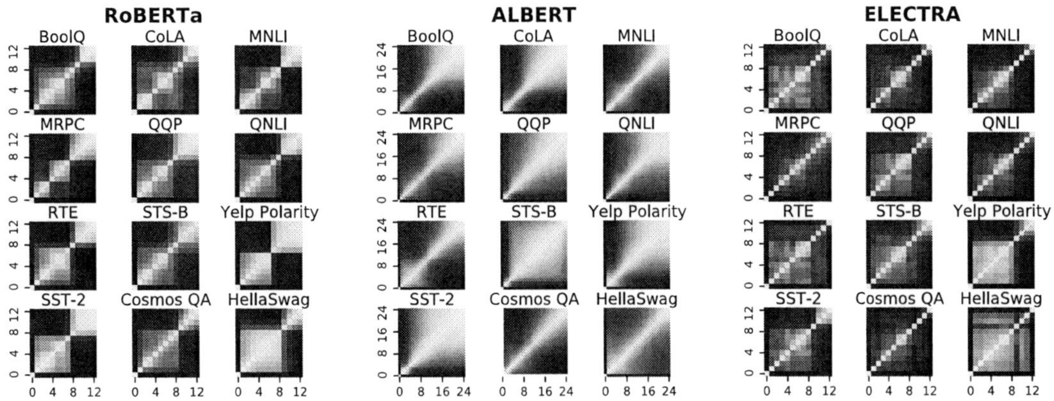

Figure 2: Representation similarity between layers for task-tuned models (FT–FT). RoBERTa and ALBERT task models exhibit a 'block diagonal' structure in the representation similarity of CLS tokens across nearly all tasks.

3.1 Results

We extend our CKA analysis to all twelve tasks and all three pretrained models, showing the FT-FT results in Figure 2. We observe that the block diagonal structure of representation similarity identified in Section 3 appears in almost every RoBERTa and ALBERT model, sharply delineating the earlier and later clusters of representations. In fact, RoBERTa often has even more distinct clusters than ALBERT. We hypothesize that since ALBERT shares parameters across layers, it is more difficult for representations to sharply change across a single layer, whereas RoBERTa, which has no parameter sharing, has no such constraint.

The significant similarity of the later layers suggests that many of the later layers may not contribute much to the task. Given residual connections between Transformer layers, later layers could learn a 'no-op' or only slightly adjust the output representation if the task can be adequately 'solved' at an earlier layer. If this is true, we should be able to feed an intermediate representation from later layers to the output head with no further fine-tuning and retain most of the task performance. We investigate this hypothesis in Section 4.

In contrast, we do not see the same pattern in the ELECTRA models. The representations of the later layers are generally highly dissimilar even up to the penultimate layer in many tasks. A few tasks do exhibit a minor block diagonal structure, such as STS-B, Yelp Polarity and SST-2, but it is far less apparent compared to the other two models. ELECTRA has a very different pretraining task from the other two models (replaced token detection), which may explain this difference.

We see complementary results for FT–ORIG and FT[1]–FT[2] in Figure 5 and Figure 6. For RoBERTa and ALBERT, while the earlier layers of the task models have similar CLS representations to the untuned models, the later layers are largely dissimilar to any layer in the base model.

4 Truncating Fine-tuned Models

To test our hypothesis that the later layers of tuned task-models only marginally contribute to task performance, we propose a simple experiment where we feed the representations from an intermediate layer directly to the task output head, effectively discarding the later layers. We refer to these as *truncated* models. We test three different configurations: (a) UNTUNED , where we feed intermediate representations from a fine-tuned model to the tuned task output head *without any further fine-tuning*, (b) TUNED , where we fine-tune only the output head, and (c) TUNEDORIG , where we use representations from the base model (not fine-tuned on the task), but we fine-tune the output head. Performance of the UNTUNED trunated models indicates the extent to which an intermediate representation can be directly substituted for the final layer's representation; the TUNED and TUNEDORIG models provide an upper-bound of performance using the CLS representation of a given layer of a fine-tuned and non-fine-tuned encoder respectively.

Our results are shown in Figure 3. For RoBERTa and ALBERT, we find that the UNTUNED truncated models perform comparably to the Tuned truncated and full fine-tuned models[3] at the later layers. For

[3]An UNTUNED model using the final layer representation

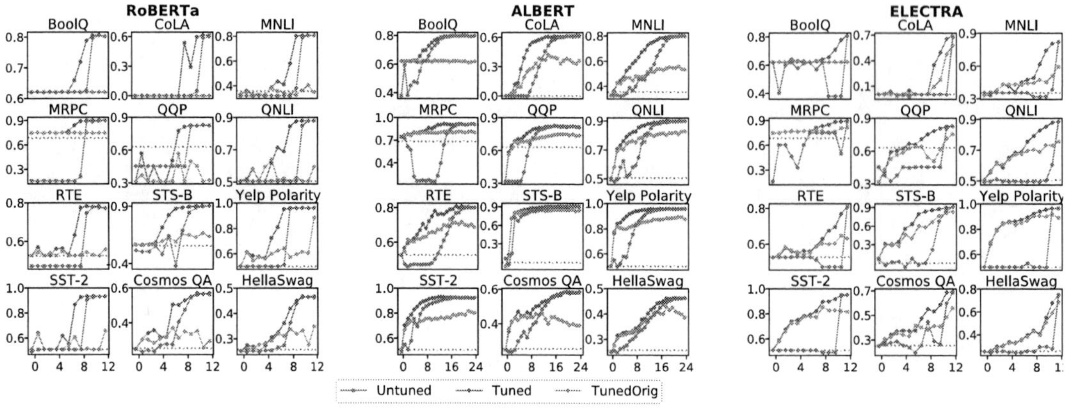

Figure 3: Model Truncation Experiments: Task performance (Y-axis) when feeding representation from an intermediate layer (X-axis) directly to the task output head, equivalent to discarding the top layers of the model. UNTUNED (green), uses a task-tuned encoder, but no further fine-tuning of the task-tuned output head. TUNED (blue), involves further fine-tuning the output head on the intermediate representation. TUNEDORIG (yellow) uses the pretrained encoder, but the output head is fine-tuned. For RoBERTa and ALBERT, the top few layers bcan e discarded for many tasks in either TUNED or UNTUNED configurations without hurting performance. The majority class baseline is shown with a red dotted line, while the rightmost data-point corresponds to a full model with no truncation.

instance, the top 4 layers of the RoBERTa for Yelp Polarity model can be discarded with no further tuning and minimal impact to performance (95.5 vs 96.1). On the other hand, TUNEDORIG models perform very poorly compared to the TUNED models across all layers, showing that task-tuned intermediate representations are crucial for good performance, even when fine-tuning the output head. For ALBERT, which shares parameters between layers, a larger fraction of layers can be discarded with minimal impact to performance for both UNTUNED and TUNED truncated models.

On the other hand, we do not find a similar pattern in ELECTRA models. The UNTUNED truncated models perform extremely poorly when discarding almost any number of layers, and even the TUNED truncated models quickly drop in performance with even one or two layers discarded. These results are consistent with our CKA analyses that showed that the learned and task-tuned representations for ELECTRA do not share the same structure as those of RoBERTa and ALBERT. We speculate that this differences stems from the different pretraining objectives—replaced token detection is a binary prediction problem, whereas masked language modeling involves predicting a distribution over a large number of tokens—leading to differences in learned representations that propagate even to fine-tuned models. We leave further investigation these differences to future work.

is equivalent to a regular fine-tuned model.

4.1 Skipping Layers

We perform a smaller set of experiments on skipping intermediate layers in a model and measuring the impact on performance. We use fully fine-tuned RoBERTa models on a subset of the tasks we considered above, and evaluate task performance of the tuned models when we skip over contiguous spans of layers in the model without any further fine-tuning. We show the results for skipping every possible span of layers in Fig 4. Performance tends to drop as larger spans of layers are skipped, although in many cases skipping any single layer seems to make little to no impact to performance. The primary exception to this is the very first layer, where we observe that skipping just the first layer can heavily impact task performance, such as in CoLA, STS-B and Cosmos QA. On the other hand, we find that skipping multiple of the later layers can have minimal impact on performance, consistent with our results above. The profile of performance drops given the number of intermediate layers skipped also differs greatly across tasks: For instance, dropping more than two contiguous layers in the middle of the model seems to heavily impact MNLI and RTE performance, whereas for SST-2 the impact is not as large until 3-4 layers are skipped.

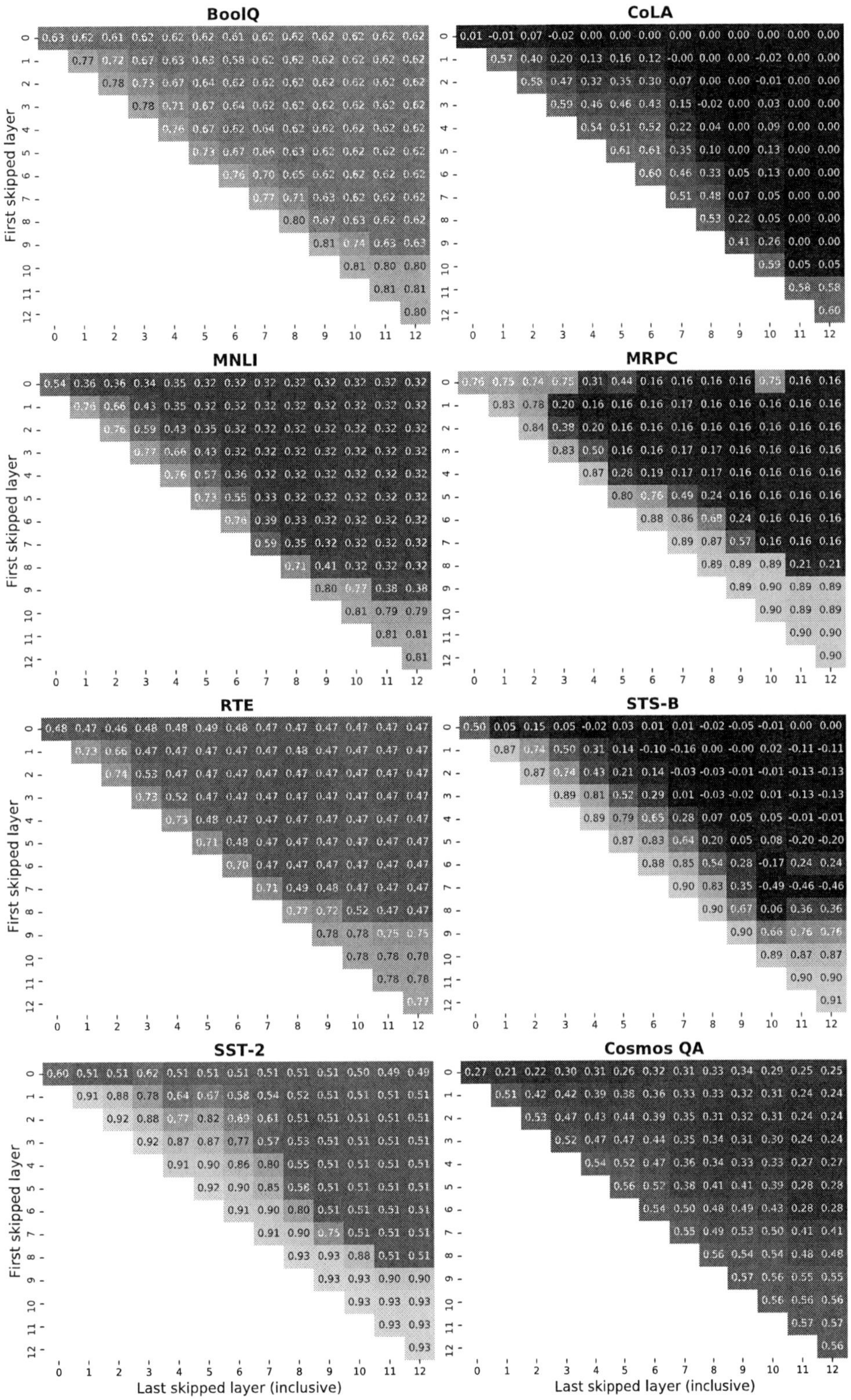

Figure 4: Layer Experiments: Task performance when skipping contiguous spans of Transformer layers, with the Y-axis and X-axis indicating the first and last (inclusive) skipped layers, with no further fine-tuning. Performance tends to drop as more layers are skipped, but in many cases skipping any single layer makes little to no impact to performance, except for the first layer. Consistent with results above, many of the higher layers can be skipped with minimal impact to performance.

5 Related Work

While CKA (Kornblith et al., 2019) was initially proposed as an interpretability method for computer vision models, it has more recently seen application to NLP models. Wu et al. (2020) applied CKA to pretrained Transformers models such as BERT and GPT-2, focusing on cross-model comparison—our analysis builds on their findings, with greater focus on layer-wise comparisons and implications for fine-tuning and discarding layers. Sridhar and Sarah (2020) use CKA to measure the impact of a proposed model architecture change on the learned representations. Voita et al. (2019) and Merchant et al. (2020) apply similar representation similarity analyses to Transformers, with the latter also investigating freezing and dropping layers from models.

More broadly, significant work has been done on better understanding and interpreting the capabilities of BERT-type models—Rogers et al. (2020) offers a thorough survey of this line of work. Of particular relevance to our work: Work on model probing (Tenney et al., 2019b; Liu et al., 2019a; Tenney et al., 2019a) has studied the extent to syntactic and semantic features are represented at different layers of BERT-type models.

Our results on model truncation also cohere with existing work on early exit in BERT models(Xin et al., 2020a,b; Zhou et al., 2020), wherein models are explicitly fine-tuned to dynamically skip the later layers of a BERT encoder and directly to the output head, often to reduce inference times of models. Our results somewhat differ as we show that models can also be truncated or exited early without any explicit tuning. It has also been shown in the computer vision domain that models with residual networks work akin to an ensemble of deep and shallow models (Veit et al., 2016).

6 Conclusion

We show a consistent pattern to the structure of representation similarity in task-tuned RoBERTa and ALBERT models, with strong representation similarity within clusters of earlier and later layers, but not between them. We further show that the later layers of task-tuned RoBERTa and ALBERT models can often be discarded without hurting task performance, verifying that the later layers of these models truly have similar representations. However, we find that ELECTRA models exhibit starkly different properties from the other two models, which prompts further investigation into how and why these models differ.

Acknowledgments

We would like to thank Kyunghyun Cho for his invaluable feedback on this work. This project has benefited from financial support to SB by Eric and Wendy Schmidt (made by recommendation of the Schmidt Futures program), Samsung Research (under the project *Improving Deep Learning using Latent Structure*), Apple, and Intuit, and from in-kind support by the NYU High-Performance Computing Center and by NVIDIA Corporation (with the donation of a Titan V GPU). This material is based upon work supported by the National Science Foundation under Grant Nos. 1922658 and 2046556. Any opinions, findings, and conclusions or recommendations expressed in this material are those of the author(s) and do not necessarily reflect the views of the National Science Foundation.

References

Daniel Cer, Mona Diab, Eneko Agirre, Iñigo Lopez-Gazpio, and Lucia Specia. 2017. SemEval-2017 task 1: Semantic textual similarity multilingual and crosslingual focused evaluation. In *Proceedings of the 11th International Workshop on Semantic Evaluation (SemEval-2017)*, pages 1–14, Vancouver, Canada. Association for Computational Linguistics.

Christopher Clark, Kenton Lee, Ming-Wei Chang, Tom Kwiatkowski, Michael Collins, and Kristina Toutanova. 2019. BoolQ: Exploring the surprising difficulty of natural yes/no questions. In *Proceedings of the 2019 Conference of the North American Chapter of the Association for Computational Linguistics: Human Language Technologies, Volume 1 (Long and Short Papers)*, pages 2924–2936, Minneapolis, Minnesota. Association for Computational Linguistics.

Kevin Clark, Minh-Thang Luong, Quoc V. Le, and Christopher D. Manning. 2020. ELECTRA: Pre-training text encoders as discriminators rather than generators. In *ICLR*.

Ido Dagan, Oren Glickman, and Bernardo Magnini. 2005. The pascal recognising textual entailment challenge. In *Machine Learning Challenges Workshop*, pages 177–190. Springer.

Jacob Devlin, Ming-Wei Chang, Kenton Lee, and Kristina Toutanova. 2019. BERT: Pre-training of deep bidirectional transformers for language understanding. In *Proceedings of the 2019 Conference of the North American Chapter of the Association for Computational Linguistics: Human Language Technologies, Volume 1 (Long and Short Papers)*, pages 4171–4186, Minneapolis, Minnesota. Association for Computational Linguistics.

William B. Dolan and Chris Brockett. 2005. Automatically constructing a corpus of sentential paraphrases. In *International Workshop on Paraphrasing*.

Pengcheng He, Xiaodong Liu, Jianfeng Gao, and Weizhu Chen. 2020. Deberta: Decoding-enhanced bert with disentangled attention.

Lifu Huang, Ronan Le Bras, Chandra Bhagavatula, and Yejin Choi. 2019. Cosmos QA: Machine reading comprehension with contextual commonsense reasoning. In *Proceedings of the 2019 Conference on Empirical Methods in Natural Language Processing and the 9th International Joint Conference on Natural Language Processing (EMNLP-IJCNLP)*, pages 2391–2401, Hong Kong, China. Association for Computational Linguistics.

Diederik P. Kingma and Jimmy Ba. 2014. Adam: A method for stochastic optimization. In *3rd International Conference for Learning Representations, San Diego, 2015*.

Simon Kornblith, Mohammad Norouzi, Honglak Lee, and Geoffrey E. Hinton. 2019. Similarity of neural network representations revisited. *CoRR*, abs/1905.00414.

Olga Kovaleva, Alexey Romanov, Anna Rogers, and Anna Rumshisky. 2019. Revealing the dark secrets of BERT. In *Proceedings of the 2019 Conference on Empirical Methods in Natural Language Processing and the 9th International Joint Conference on Natural Language Processing (EMNLP-IJCNLP)*, pages 4365–4374, Hong Kong, China. Association for Computational Linguistics.

Zhenzhong Lan, Mingda Chen, Sebastian Goodman, Kevin Gimpel, Piyush Sharma, and Radu Soricut. 2020. ALBERT: A lite BERT for self-supervised learning of language representations. In *8th International Conference on Learning Representations, ICLR 2020*.

Nelson F. Liu, Matt Gardner, Yonatan Belinkov, Matthew E. Peters, and Noah A. Smith. 2019a. Linguistic knowledge and transferability of contextual representations. In *Proceedings of the 2019 Conference of the North American Chapter of the Association for Computational Linguistics: Human Language Technologies, Volume 1 (Long and Short Papers)*, pages 1073–1094, Minneapolis, Minnesota. Association for Computational Linguistics.

Yinhan Liu, Myle Ott, Naman Goyal, Jingfei Du, Mandar Joshi, Danqi Chen, Omer Levy, Mike Lewis, Luke Zettlemoyer, and Veselin Stoyanov. 2019b. RoBERTa: A robustly optimized bert pretraining approach. Unpublished manuscript available on arXiv.

Amil Merchant, Elahe Rahimtoroghi, Ellie Pavlick, and Ian Tenney. 2020. What happens to BERT embeddings during fine-tuning? In *Proceedings of the Third BlackboxNLP Workshop on Analyzing and Interpreting Neural Networks for NLP*, pages 33–44, Online. Association for Computational Linguistics.

Adam Paszke, Sam Gross, Francisco Massa, Adam Lerer, James Bradbury, Gregory Chanan, Trevor Killeen, Zeming Lin, Natalia Gimelshein, Luca Antiga, Alban Desmaison, Andreas Kopf, Edward Yang, Zachary DeVito, Martin Raison, Alykhan Tejani, Sasank Chilamkurthy, Benoit Steiner, Lu Fang, Junjie Bai, and Soumith Chintala. 2019. PyTorch: An Imperative Style, High-Performance Deep Learning Library. In H. Wallach, H. Larochelle, A. Beygelzimer, F. d' Alché-Buc, E. Fox, and R. Garnett, editors, *Advances in Neural Information Processing Systems 32*, pages 8024–8035. Curran Associates, Inc.

Jason Phang, Phil Yeres, Jesse Swanson, Haokun Liu, Ian F. Tenney, Phu Mon Htut, Clara Vania, Alex Wang, and Samuel R. Bowman. 2020. `jiant` 2.0: A software toolkit for research on general-purpose text understanding models. `http://jiant.info/`.

Pranav Rajpurkar, Jian Zhang, Konstantin Lopyrev, and Percy Liang. 2016. SQuAD: 100,000+ questions for machine comprehension of text. In *Proceedings of the 2016 Conference on Empirical Methods in Natural Language Processing*, pages 2383–2392, Austin, Texas. Association for Computational Linguistics.

Anna Rogers, Olga Kovaleva, and Anna Rumshisky. 2020. A primer in BERTology: What we know about how BERT works. *Transactions of the Association for Computational Linguistics*, 8:842–866.

Richard Socher, Alex Perelygin, Jean Wu, Jason Chuang, Christopher D. Manning, Andrew Ng, and Christopher Potts. 2013. Recursive Deep Models for Semantic Compositionality Over a Sentiment Treebank. In *Proceedings of the 2013 Conference on Empirical Methods in Natural Language Processing*, pages 1631–1642, Seattle, Washington, USA. Association for Computational Linguistics.

Sharath Nittur Sridhar and Anthony Sarah. 2020. Undivided attention: Are intermediate layers necessary for bert?

Ian Tenney, Dipanjan Das, and Ellie Pavlick. 2019a. BERT rediscovers the classical NLP pipeline. In *Proceedings of the 57th Annual Meeting of the Association for Computational Linguistics*, pages 4593–4601, Florence, Italy. Association for Computational Linguistics.

Ian Tenney, Patrick Xia, Berlin Chen, Alex Wang, Adam Poliak, R Thomas McCoy, Najoung Kim, Benjamin Van Durme, Sam Bowman, Dipanjan Das, and Ellie Pavlick. 2019b. What do you learn from context? probing for sentence structure in contextualized word representations. In *International Conference on Learning Representations*.

Andreas Veit, Michael J. Wilber, and Serge J. Belongie. 2016. Residual networks are exponential ensembles of relatively shallow networks. volume abs/1605.06431.

Elena Voita, Rico Sennrich, and Ivan Titov. 2019. The bottom-up evolution of representations in the transformer: A study with machine translation and language modeling objectives. In *Proceedings of the 2019 Conference on Empirical Methods in Natural Language Processing and the 9th International Joint Conference on Natural Language Processing (EMNLP-IJCNLP)*, pages 4396–4406, Hong Kong, China. Association for Computational Linguistics.

Alex Wang, Amanpreet Singh, Julian Michael, Felix Hill, Omer Levy, and Samuel Bowman. 2018. GLUE: A multi-task benchmark and analysis platform for natural language understanding. In *Proceedings of the 2018 EMNLP Workshop BlackboxNLP: Analyzing and Interpreting Neural Networks for NLP*, pages 353–355, Brussels, Belgium. Association for Computational Linguistics.

Alex Warstadt, Amanpreet Singh, and Samuel R. Bowman. 2019. Neural network acceptability judgments. *Transactions of the Association for Computational Linguistics (TACL)*, 7:625–641.

Adina Williams, Nikita Nangia, and Samuel Bowman. 2018. A broad-coverage challenge corpus for sentence understanding through inference. In *Proceedings of the 2018 Conference of the North American Chapter of the Association for Computational Linguistics: Human Language Technologies, Volume 1 (Long Papers)*, pages 1112–1122. Association for Computational Linguistics.

Thomas Wolf, Lysandre Debut, Victor Sanh, Julien Chaumond, Clement Delangue, Anthony Moi, Pierric Cistac, Tim Rault, Remi Louf, Morgan Funtowicz, Joe Davison, Sam Shleifer, Patrick von Platen, Clara Ma, Yacine Jernite, Julien Plu, Canwen Xu, Teven Le Scao, Sylvain Gugger, Mariama Drame, Quentin Lhoest, and Alexander Rush. 2020. Transformers: State-of-the-art natural language processing. In *Proceedings of the 2020 Conference on Empirical Methods in Natural Language Processing: System Demonstrations*, pages 38–45, Online. Association for Computational Linguistics.

John Wu, Yonatan Belinkov, Hassan Sajjad, Nadir Durrani, Fahim Dalvi, and James Glass. 2020. Similarity analysis of contextual word representation models. In *Proceedings of the 58th Annual Meeting of the Association for Computational Linguistics*, pages 4638–4655, Online. Association for Computational Linguistics.

Ji Xin, Rodrigo Nogueira, Yaoliang Yu, and Jimmy Lin. 2020a. Early exiting BERT for efficient document ranking. In *Proceedings of SustaiNLP: Workshop on Simple and Efficient Natural Language Processing*, pages 83–88, Online. Association for Computational Linguistics.

Ji Xin, Raphael Tang, Jaejun Lee, Yaoliang Yu, and Jimmy Lin. 2020b. DeeBERT: Dynamic early exiting for accelerating BERT inference. In *Proceedings of the 58th Annual Meeting of the Association for Computational Linguistics*, pages 2246–2251, Online. Association for Computational Linguistics.

Rowan Zellers, Ari Holtzman, Yonatan Bisk, Ali Farhadi, and Yejin Choi. 2019. HellaSwag: Can a machine really finish your sentence? In *Proceedings of the 57th Annual Meeting of the Association for Computational Linguistics*, pages 4791–4800, Florence, Italy. Association for Computational Linguistics.

Xiang Zhang, Junbo Zhao, and Yann LeCun. 2015. Character-level convolutional networks for text classification. In *Advances in Neural Information Processing Systems*, volume 28. Curran Associates, Inc.

Wangchunshu Zhou, Canwen Xu, Tao Ge, Julian McAuley, Ke Xu, and Furu Wei. 2020. Bert loses patience: Fast and robust inference with early exit. In *Advances in Neural Information Processing Systems*, volume 33, pages 18330–18341. Curran Associates, Inc.

A Centered Kernel Alignment

Given two sets of representations $X \in \mathbb{R}^{N\times d}$ and $Y \in \mathbb{R}^{N\times d}$ where N is the number of examples and d the hidden dimension (for instance the `CLS` vector representations of a set of examples from two different layers of the same model), CKA computes a similarity score between 0 and 1. :

$$\text{CKA}(K, L) = \frac{\text{HSIC}(K, L)}{\sqrt{\text{HSIC}(K, K)\text{HSIC}(L, L)}}$$

with

$$\text{HSIC}(K, L) = \frac{1}{(n-1)^2}\text{tr}(KHLH)$$

and $H = I_n - \frac{1}{b}\mathbf{1}\mathbf{1}^T$ $K = XX^T$, $L = YY^T$ when using a linear kernel. We refer the reader to the original work (Kornblith et al., 2019) for more details and properties of CKA.

B Additional Results

Figure 5 shows the FT–ORIG plots for all tasks and models.

Figure 6 shows the FT[1]–FT[2] plots for all tasks and models.

Figure 7 computes representation similarity *between* models.

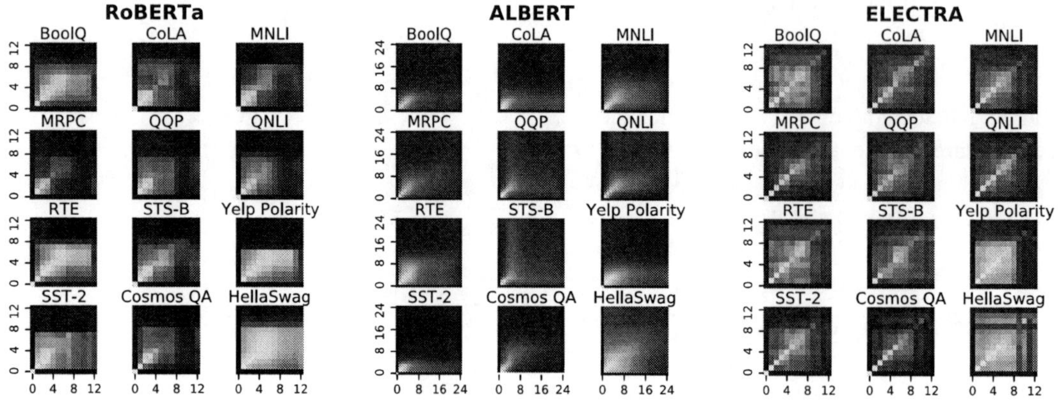

Figure 5: CKA representation similarity for FT–ORIG. Task-tuned layers are on the Y-axis, untuned layers in the X-axis. `CLS` representations of the top few layers RoBERTa and ALBERT models are highly dissimilar to those of the pretrained model at any layer.

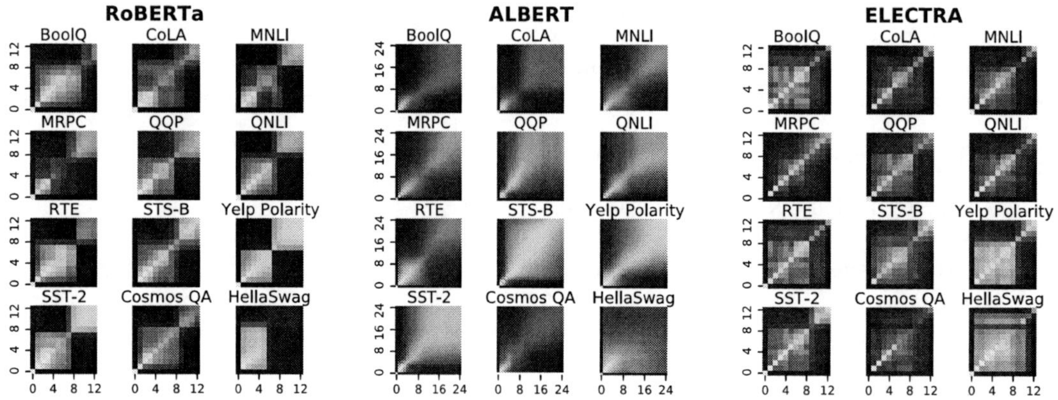

Figure 6: CKA representation similarity for FT[1]–FT[2]. RoBERTa and ALBERT task models exhibit a 'block diagonal' structure to representation similarity of `CLS` tokens, indicating in particular that the representations of the top few layers are highly similar. Plots for tasks that do not use the `CLS` token are dimmed.

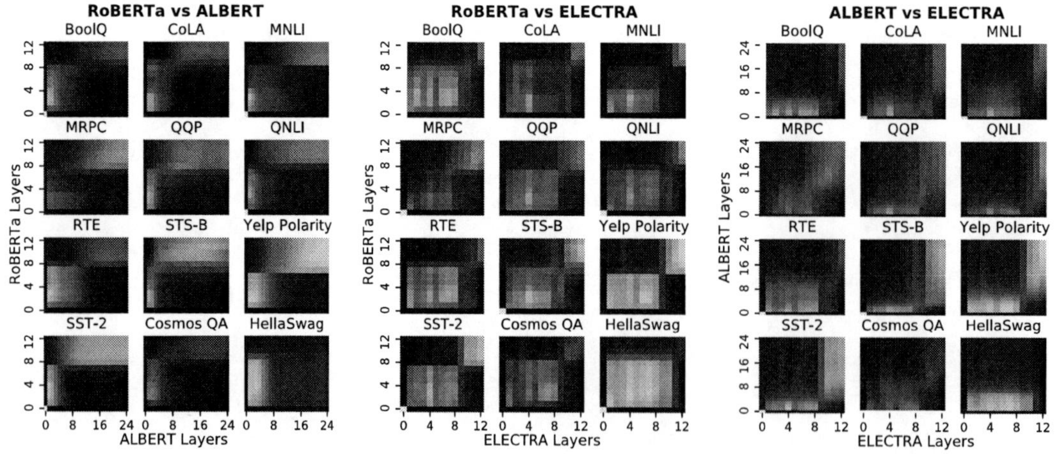

Figure 7: CKA representation similarity comparing `CLS` representations cross models. The upper right blocks indicate the representations in the earlier and the later layers are similar even across models.

BERT Has Uncommon Sense: Similarity Ranking for Word Sense BERTology

Luke Gessler **Nathan Schneider**
Georgetown University
{lg876, nathan.schneider}@georgetown.edu

Abstract

An important question concerning contextualized word embedding (CWE) models like BERT is how well they can represent different word senses, especially those in the long tail of uncommon senses. Rather than build a WSD system as in previous work, we investigate contextualized embedding neighborhoods directly, formulating a query-by-example nearest neighbor retrieval task and examining ranking performance for words and senses in different frequency bands. In an evaluation on two English sense-annotated corpora, we find that several popular CWE models all outperform a random baseline even for proportionally rare senses, without explicit sense supervision. However, performance varies considerably even among models with similar architectures and pretraining regimes, with especially large differences for rare word senses, revealing that CWE models are not all created equal when it comes to approximating word senses in their native representations.

1 Introduction

Contextualized word embedding (CWE) models such as BERT (Devlin et al., 2019), which were enabled by Transformers (Vaswani et al., 2017), have yielded great improvements in a variety of NLP tasks. However, because BERT and other CWE models are deep neural networks with complicated architectures and very high parameter counts, it is not easy to understand exactly which aspects of linguistic form and meaning contextualized word embeddings are able to capture.

In response to these difficulties, much work has been done attempting to interpret CWE models, most notably in the field of BERTology. Over 100 BERTological studies have been published since BERT was introduced in 2018, covering a diverse range of linguistic phenomena (Rogers et al., 2020) such as POS tags, constituency, and event factuality (Liu et al., 2019a). The methods developed in this area are usually applicable to other CWE models.

An important question for CWE models is how well they can represent rare word senses. Word sense disambiguation systems have been observed to be most lacking in the long tail of rare word senses (Blevins and Zettlemoyer, 2020; Blevins et al., 2021), and sense-awareness is of fundamental importance for many NLP applications. Thus a better understanding of how well CWE models understand senses, and especially rare senses, would aid the interpretation of NLP systems.

To address this question, we perform an evaluation we call CWE similarity ranking on two sense-annotated English corpora using several popular CWE models. We find that while all models outperform a random baseline on the evaluation, models differ substantially in their performance on rare word senses, with significant differentiation even between models which are closely related.[1]

2 Previous Work

2.1 Word Senses

The task of word sense disambiguation (WSD) introduced the notion of a *word sense* into NLP (Navigli, 2009; Bevilacqua et al., 2021). The WSD task is typically formulated as labeling words in context with their senses as defined by a dictionary or other lexical resource.

Many resources exist to support work on word senses. WordNet (Miller, 1992) has been a crucial resource for work on word senses, providing a fine-grained and comprehensive inventory of words and their senses for English. Several large annotated corpora have been constructed using WordNet senses, including SemCor (Miller et al., 1993; Landes et al., 1998) and OntoNotes (Hovy et al., 2006). More recently, WSD systems

[1] All code for this work is available at `https://github.com/lgessler/bert-has-uncommon-sense`.

Proceedings of the Fourth BlackboxNLP Workshop on Analyzing and Interpreting Neural Networks for NLP, pages 539–547
Online, November 11, 2021.

have been able to achieve human-like performance on WSD tasks, but performance on rare senses remains comparatively poor (Blevins and Zettlemoyer, 2020), leading to the construction of corpora tailored for assessing systems on rare senses (Blevins et al., 2021).

2.2 Word Sense BERTology

Few studies have focused narrowly on the question of how well BERT and other CWE models capture word senses. In one such study, Wiedemann et al. (2019) evaluate CWE models by using the CWE models' embeddings as representations for a kNN classifier: the predicted sense of a word is the one most represented among by the word's k nearest neighbors (via cosine distance). Despite the simplicity of this WSD system, it is able to achieve results that are competitive with state-of-the-art systems, even achieving new SOTA scores on the SensEval-2 and SensEval-3 datasets. Reif et al. (2019) construct a similar WSD system, relying not on kNN but closest sense-centroids (centroids are constructed using a labeled training set) to decide on a label.

Other studies have approached the question by modifying BERT's training scheme. Tayyar Madabushi et al. (2020) train a BERT variant where the next sentence prediction task has been replaced with a same construction prediction task and find mixed results on downstream tasks. Levine et al. (2020) train a BERT variant by adding a new supersense prediction task, wherein the masked token's WordNet supersense is to be predicted, and find performance gains on a variety of meaning-related tasks, which shows that BERT's representations do not perfectly capture word senses.

Some recent approaches have developed specialized methods for exploring CWE models' embedding spaces. Karidi et al. (2021) present an iterative method for surveying the "topography" of BERT's embedding space, finding that word senses often form cohesive regions.

3 CWE Similarity Ranking

We formulate a query-by-example task in which a word in sentence context is used to query for similar usages of the same word in other sentences. In a process we call **contextualized word embedding (CWE) similarity ranking**, we will assume some embedding function f and two corpora of sense-labeled text segmented into sentences: a larger "database" corpus $\mathcal{D}$, and a smaller "query" corpus $\mathcal{Q}$. We will use sentences from $\mathcal{Q}$ to rank sentences in $\mathcal{D}$, as detailed below.

1. Select a query sentence from $\mathcal{Q}$ consisting of tokens $w_1^{(q)}, \ldots, w_n^{(q)}$, where a token $w_i^{(q)}$ has been designated as the *target token* and has sense s_i.
2. Find embeddings for the query sentence, $\mathbf{h}_1^{(q)}, \ldots, \mathbf{h}_n^{(q)} = f\left(w_1^{(q)}, \ldots, w_n^{(q)}\right)$.
3. For every instance $w_j^{(d)}$ with its context $w_1^{(d)}, \ldots, w_m^{(d)}$ in $\mathcal{D}$, and sense s_j, find embeddings $\mathbf{h}_1^{(d)}, \ldots, \mathbf{h}_m^{(d)} = f\left(w_1^{(d)}, \ldots, w_m^{(d)}\right)$.
4. Rank instances in $\mathcal{D}$ in descending order by cosine similarity between embeddings of the two tokens, $w_i^{(q)}$ and $w_j^{(d)}$: $\text{COS-SIM}\left(\mathbf{h}_i^{(q)}, \mathbf{h}_j^{(d)}\right)$.
5. Evaluate the ranking, e.g. with precision at k.

CWE similarity ranking consists of much of the same work that a CWE-based kNN system would do,[2] with the difference that the kNN WSD evaluation will only reward a model if the gold sense is held by a plurality of the neighbors, whereas CWE similarity ranking is less stringent and will award "partial credit" for retrieving any gold instances, even if they do not form a majority. This provides a clearer view of how coherent rare word senses are in CWEs' representations. See Figure 1 for query examples.

4 Experimental Setup

We use the CWE similarity ranking method to evaluate several popular pretrained CWE models retrieved from `huggingface.co` (Wolf et al., 2020).

Corpora Our two corpora are OntoNotes 5.0 (Hovy et al., 2006), which has sense annotations for nouns and verbs,[3] and the Pattern Dictionary of English Prepositions (PDEP) corpus (Litkowski, 2014), which has sense annotations for prepositions.[4] For OntoNotes, we discard instances labeled with "none-of-the-above" senses, as we expect them to be heterogeneous. For PDEP, we

[2] Indeed, the basic method of finding embeddings that are nearest to a target embedding has been widely used both before and after the rise of CWEs (cf. Wiedemann et al. 2019, which we describe in §2.2, and Schnabel et al. 2015).

[3] Specifically, we use the OntoNotes English noun and verb *sense groupings*, whose sense inventory was formulated by merging WordNet senses for each lemma until an acceptable level of interannotator agreement was reached. Our preliminary experiments with WordNet senses in another corpus, SemCor (Langone et al., 2004), were difficult to interpret because annotations often seemed to be inconsistent.

[4] We use a copy of PDEP obtained from a SQL dump dated 2019-04-19. Original data is available with our code.

Query: But with all the money and glamour of high finance come the relentless pressures to do well; pressure to **pull**$_4$ off another million before lunch [...]
1: "Sometimes," he says, "we'll **pull**$_3$ someone off phones for more training."
2: Hence, they have never lacked their own stately or amusing charms to **pull**$_2$ in wealth and keep it within a household.
3: I can't **pull**$_4$ it off.
4: Bulatovic says Kostunica was able to **pull**$_4$ off the balancing act because he is not really anti-American.

(a) A sample of a single query on OntoNotes for the verb *pull*. Sense 4, glossed as 'commit, do', is rare, comprising just 5 of the 78 occurrences of *pull* in the OntoNotes training set. Here, the first two results are incorrect: sense 3 means 'eliminate from a situation', and sense 2 means 'steer something in a certain direction'. All 5 correct instances are retrieved in the top 50 results, at ranks 3, 4, 5, 6, and 41.

Query: These days I take five pills a day, but at one point I was **on**$_{20}$ about 20.
1: I'm happier than I was three years ago, when I was drinking and I was **on**$_{20}$ cocaine.
2: I was **on**$_{20}$ about sixty cigarettes a day.
3: I was **on**$_{20}$ heavy duty painkillers for 48 hours.
4: He had been put **on**$_{20}$ prescription drugs to help him cope with coming off crack.
5: Recorded in 21 days in a Mitcham garage, the fact that it is **on**$_2$ Chrysalis is a mere coincidence.
6: You can phone now **on**$_{12}$ o-five-hundred , four-o-four , treble zero to put your views to Tory MP Phil Gallie .

(b) A sample of a single query on PDEP for the preposition *on*. Sense 20, glossed as 'regularly taking (a drug or medicine)', is very rare, comprising 14 of the 1728 occurrences of *on* in the PDEP training set. The 5th and 6th results are incorrect: sense 2 has to do with location, and sense 12 a medium of communication. Only 6 of the 14 total occurrences in $\mathcal{D}$ make it into the top 50 for this query.

Figure 1: Query samples using `bert-base-cased`.

use only instances of 48 common English prepositions. For both corpora, we use only single-word targets, and use pre-existing train–validation–test splits. We treat the training split of each as our $\mathcal{D}$, and the combined validation and test split of each as our $\mathcal{Q}$, and discard any senses in $\mathcal{Q}$ that did not occur at least 5 times in $\mathcal{D}$, as these senses are so rare in $\mathcal{D}$ that performance on them is liable to be overtaken by noise. For OntoNotes, $|\mathcal{D}| = 229{,}989$, $|\mathcal{Q}| = 50{,}395$. For PDEP, $|\mathcal{D}| = 33{,}090$, $|\mathcal{Q}| = 8{,}020$.

Inoculation by Fine-Tuning In addition to the base models, we also evaluate versions of the models that have been fine-tuned with a small number of instances from another dataset, a method called *inoculation by fine-tuning* (Richardson et al., 2020; Liu et al., 2019b). Inoculation by fine-tuning allows model to surface more domain-relevant information in its output embeddings, while using only a small amount of data so as to avoid teaching the model anything entirely new. We use STREUSLE 4.4 (Schneider and Smith, 2015; Schneider et al., 2018) to fine-tune, sampling supersense annotations of single-word nouns, verbs and prepositions in equal numbers for total counts of 100, 250, 500, 1000, and 2500. See Appendix A for full details.

Layer Choice In this work, we use embeddings from the last layer of every model we assess. Preliminary experiments showed that many models show no improvement past the middle layers, and using the last layer is also of interest because many systems freeze their CWE models' weights and use embeddings from their final layers.

Lemma Restriction In all cases, neighbors are restricted to instances that have the same lemma.

Evaluation To assess the quality of a ranking, we use mean average precision[5] for the top 50 ranked instances.[6] Since there can be very few gold-labeled instances, it may be impossible for a model to achieve a perfect score. To make these metrics more interpretable for a given dataset, we also include a baseline score obtained by randomly ranking results, and an oracle upper bound, i.e. the score that would be obtained by a perfect model.[7]

5 Results

Main results are given in Table 1. Instances are bucketed by two parameters: ℓ is the instance's lemma's frequency in $\mathcal{D}$, and r is the proportion of all instances of the lemma that have the same sense in $\mathcal{D}$. Recall that each cell in Table 1 is *mean* average precision over precision at k for 50 instances, and see Figure 2 for a sample of what the P@K curves look like for each cell in Table 1.

Two example queries and top results appear in Figure 1. Consider the results for the "on" query at right: out of a large haystack (1728 available tokens of "on"), the system has correctly retrieved 6 of the 14 relevant needles, featuring 4 at the top of the list! Interestingly, even though the complement of *on* in the query instance is just "20" (a fused-head construction; Elazar and Goldberg, 2019) instead

[5]Recall is omitted here—see Appendix B.

[6]Average precision is defined for a single query as the average of precision calculated for every result from 1 to some k, where k ranges from 1 to a maximum of 50 for the present study. Mean average precision in turn is the average of this quantity across all instances in $\mathcal{Q}$.

[7]Note that this is not always 100%: for queries with fewer than 50 gold instances that can be retrieved in all of $\mathcal{D}$, the oracle's performance will be under 100%.

Model	$\ell < 500$ $r < 0.25$	$\ell < 500$ $r \geq 0.25$	$\ell > 500$ $r < 0.25$	$\ell > 500$ $r \geq 0.25$
Baseline	11.55	62.41	9.55	76.08
Oracle	82.02	93.89	100.00	100.00
bert-base-cased	41.60	81.89	48.48	88.53
distilbert-base-cased	39.80	81.32	48.17	88.50
roberta-base	32.87	78.39	45.16	88.37
distilroberta-base	29.33	76.48	43.69	86.86
albert-base-v2	40.44	81.81	51.58	89.56
xlnet-base-cased	28.72	75.07	36.16	84.29
gpt2	18.34	69.56	33.53	82.74

(a) Performance for OntoNotes, no fine-tuning. Buckets respectively contain 6,949, 30,694, 1,649, and 11,123 query instances.

Model	$\ell < 500$ $r < 0.25$	$\ell < 500$ $r \geq 0.25$	$\ell > 500$ $r < 0.25$	$\ell > 500$ $r \geq 0.25$
Baseline	11.56	56.34	18.25	49.88
Oracle	96.41	100.00	100.00	100.00
bert-base-cased	59.59	83.54	66.34	89.39
distilbert-base-cased	58.06	83.15	65.09	88.10
roberta-base	39.84	76.79	47.65	80.01
distilroberta-base	32.42	72.22	42.29	70.81
albert-base-v2	56.53	82.22	66.64	88.44
xlnet-base-cased	35.76	74.08	37.68	75.16
gpt2	21.75	63.41	33.33	61.00

(b) Performance for PDEP, no fine-tuning. Buckets respectively contain 4,970, 1,618, 733, and 699 query instances.

Model	$\ell < 500$ $r < 0.25$	$\ell < 500$ $r \geq 0.25$	$\ell > 500$ $r < 0.25$	$\ell > 500$ $r \geq 0.25$
Baseline	11.55	62.41	9.55	76.08
Oracle	82.02	93.89	100.00	100.00
bert-base-cased	43.42	82.37	49.81	89.45
distilbert-base-cased	41.62	81.98	50.31	89.43
roberta-base	37.87	80.68	53.65	89.43
distilroberta-base	34.74	79.27	48.50	88.74
albert-base-v2	39.26	81.50	51.65	89.31
xlnet-base-cased	37.53	79.12	51.40	87.97
gpt2	18.12	68.92	32.99	82.08

(c) Best performance across all fine-tuning trials for each model on OntoNotes.

Model	$\ell < 500$ $r < 0.25$	$\ell < 500$ $r \geq 0.25$	$\ell > 500$ $r < 0.25$	$\ell > 500$ $r \geq 0.25$
Baseline	11.56	56.34	18.25	49.88
Oracle	96.41	100.00	100.00	100.00
bert-base-cased	60.37	83.49	67.87	89.28
distilbert-base-cased	58.33	82.91	67.27	87.52
roberta-base	48.99	80.32	60.04	85.72
distilroberta-base	42.25	77.25	53.37	79.19
albert-base-v2	53.75	81.85	65.57	86.97
xlnet-base-cased	49.46	80.50	56.19	84.53
gpt2	21.53	63.00	35.57	61.08

(d) Best performance across all fine-tuning trials for each model on PDEP.

Table 1: Mean average precision performance broken down by corpus and model. Performance was further measured on different buckets of instances, as indicated in column headers: ℓ is a query instance's lemma frequency in $\mathcal{D}$, and r is the proportional frequency of a query instance's sense across all instances of the lemma in $\mathcal{D}$.

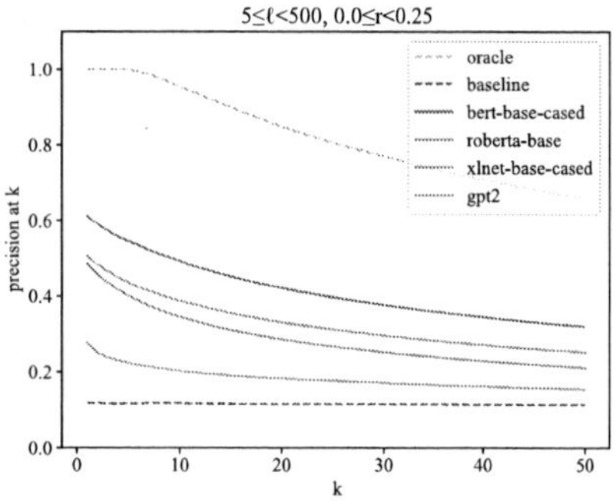

Figure 2: A sample of averaged precision at k curves, showing performance of several models on OntoNotes for the bucket with lemmas occurring fewer than 500 times in $\mathcal{D}$ and senses with proportional frequencies lower than 0.25. Mean average precision, as shown in each cell in Table 1, is obtained by averaging every point along one of these lines.

of the name of a drug or substance, the first four results are still relevant. From examining the top 50 results as well as the 8 false negatives (which include "high on drugs", "drunk on Scotch", etc.), it appears that BERT is prioritizing syntactic criteria ("on" following a verb, especially a copula), possibly because the information following the query preposition is semantically impoverished. In fact, the top 3 results have a trigram match ("I was **on**").

All models perform well above the random baseline across all buckets, and show little differentiation for buckets with only non-proportionally-rare senses $r \geq 0.25$. Dramatic differences emerge, however, for buckets with proportionally rare senses $r < 0.25$, with GPT-2 (Radford et al., 2019) showing the poorest performance. In line with general trends, the distilled variants of models (Sanh et al., 2020) generally track only a few points behind their undistilled variants. Overall, `bert-base-cased` performance is best. ALBERT (Lan et al., 2020) usually performs similarly, and RoBERTa (Liu et al., 2019c) and XLNet (Yang et al., 2019) show noticeably worse performance on rare senses.

It is especially surprising that RoBERTa performs so much worse than BERT on rare senses (cf. Table 1a, column 1), even though RoBERTa outperforms BERT on GLUE (Wang et al., 2019), and RoBERTa is more closely related to BERT than XLNet or ALBERT: whereas XLNet and ALBERT differ architecturally from BERT, RoBERTa is architecturally identical and differs only in details of training. (For example, it implements dynamic masking, does not perform next sentence prediction, and uses an order of magnitude more data.) Fine-tuning allows RoBERTa to close much of this gap but not all of it (cf. Table 1c). This indicates that word sense information is less readily accessible in RoBERTa embeddings compared to BERT embeddings, and that fine-tuning cannot draw out this information to the extent that it already is in BERT. Taken together, these results call into the question how conclusively a model can be judged based just on performance on downstream task benchmarks: RoBERTa performs better on GLUE, which has led many to prefer it as generally superior to BERT, but we have seen here it seems to be inferior within the domain of lexical semantics.

6 Conclusion

We have presented an evaluation method for probing the word sense content of contextualized word embeddings and applied it to several popular CWE models. We find that their ability to capture rare word senses using their representations is variable and not easily explained by each model's training and architectural characteristics. Moreover, we find that performance of models on this word sense evaluation is not directly proportional to their performance on downstream task benchmarks like GLUE. We view these differences between models as reason for further evaluation of CWE models to investigate their word sense representations, and inquiry into factors that affect word sense content of contextualized word embeddings.

Acknowledgments

We thank Ken Litkowski for providing us with the PDEP corpus and for allowing us to distribute it with our code.

References

Michele Bevilacqua, Tommaso Pasini, Alessandro Raganato, and Roberto Navigli. 2021. Recent trends in word sense disambiguation: A survey. In *Proceedings of the Thirtieth International Joint Conference on Artificial Intelligence, IJCAI-21*, pages 4330–4338. International Joint Conferences on Artificial Intelligence Organization. Survey Track.

Terra Blevins, Mandar Joshi, and Luke Zettlemoyer. 2021. FEWS: Large-scale, low-shot word sense disambiguation with the dictionary. In *Proceedings of the 16th Conference of the European Chapter of the Association for Computational Linguistics: Main Volume*, pages 455–465, Online. Association for Computational Linguistics.

Terra Blevins and Luke Zettlemoyer. 2020. Moving down the long tail of word sense disambiguation with gloss informed bi-encoders. In *Proc. of ACL*, pages 1006–1017, Online. Association for Computational Linguistics.

Jacob Devlin, Ming-Wei Chang, Kenton Lee, and Kristina Toutanova. 2019. BERT: Pre-training of deep bidirectional transformers for language understanding. In *Proc. of NAACL-HLT*, pages 4171–4186, Minneapolis, Minnesota. Association for Computational Linguistics.

Yanai Elazar and Yoav Goldberg. 2019. Where's my head? Definition, data set, and models for numeric fused-head identification and resolution. *Transactions of the Association for Computational Linguistics*, 7:519–535.

Eduard Hovy, Mitchell Marcus, Martha Palmer, Lance Ramshaw, and Ralph Weischedel. 2006. OntoNotes: The 90% solution. In *Proceedings of the Human Language Technology Conference of the NAACL, Companion Volume: Short Papers*, pages 57–60, New York City, USA. Association for Computational Linguistics.

Taelin Karidi, Yichu Zhou, Nathan Schneider, Omri Abend, and Vivek Srikumar. 2021. Putting words in BERT's mouth: Navigating contextualized vector spaces with pseudowords. In *Proc. of EMNLP*, Punta Cana, Dominican Republic. Association for Computational Linguistics.

Zhenzhong Lan, Mingda Chen, Sebastian Goodman, Kevin Gimpel, Piyush Sharma, and Radu Soricut. 2020. ALBERT: A lite BERT for self-supervised learning of language representations. In *Proc. of ICLR*. OpenReview.net.

Shari Landes, Claudia Leacock, and Randee I. Tengi. 1998. Building semantic concordances. In Christiane Fellbaum, editor, *WordNet: An Electronic Lexical Database*, pages 199–216. MIT Press, Cambridge, MA.

Helen Langone, Benjamin R. Haskell, and George A. Miller. 2004. Annotating WordNet. In *Proceedings of the Workshop Frontiers in Corpus Annotation at HLT-NAACL 2004*, pages 63–69, Boston, Massachusetts, USA. Association for Computational Linguistics.

Yoav Levine, Barak Lenz, Or Dagan, Ori Ram, Dan Padnos, Or Sharir, Shai Shalev-Shwartz, Amnon Shashua, and Yoav Shoham. 2020. SenseBERT: Driving some sense into BERT. In *Proc. of ACL*, pages 4656–4667, Online. Association for Computational Linguistics.

Ken Litkowski. 2014. Pattern dictionary of English prepositions. In *Proc. of ACL*, pages 1274–1283, Baltimore, Maryland. Association for Computational Linguistics.

Nelson F. Liu, Matt Gardner, Yonatan Belinkov, Matthew E. Peters, and Noah A. Smith. 2019a. Linguistic knowledge and transferability of contextual representations. In *Proc. of NAACL-HLT*, pages 1073–1094, Minneapolis, Minnesota. Association for Computational Linguistics.

Nelson F. Liu, Roy Schwartz, and Noah A. Smith. 2019b. Inoculation by fine-tuning: A method for analyzing challenge datasets. In *Proc. of NAACL-HLT*, pages 2171–2179, Minneapolis, Minnesota. Association for Computational Linguistics.

Yinhan Liu, Myle Ott, Naman Goyal, Jingfei Du, Mandar Joshi, Danqi Chen, Omer Levy, Mike Lewis, Luke Zettlemoyer, and Veselin Stoyanov. 2019c. RoBERTa: A Robustly Optimized BERT Pretraining Approach. *arXiv:1907.11692 [cs]*. ArXiv: 1907.11692.

Ilya Loshchilov and Frank Hutter. 2019. Decoupled weight decay regularization. In *Proc. of ICLR*. OpenReview.net.

George A. Miller. 1992. WordNet: A lexical database for English. In *Speech and Natural Language: Proceedings of a Workshop Held at Harriman, New York, February 23-26, 1992*.

George A. Miller, Claudia Leacock, Randee Tengi, and Ross T. Bunker. 1993. A semantic concordance. In *Human Language Technology: Proceedings of a Workshop Held at Plainsboro, New Jersey, March 21-24, 1993*.

Roberto Navigli. 2009. Word sense disambiguation: A survey. *ACM Computing Surveys*, 41(2):1–69.

Alec Radford, Jeff Wu, Rewon Child, David Luan, Dario Amodei, and Ilya Sutskever. 2019. Language models are unsupervised multitask learners.

Emily Reif, Ann Yuan, Martin Wattenberg, Fernanda B. Viégas, Andy Coenen, Adam Pearce, and Been Kim. 2019. Visualizing and measuring the geometry of BERT. In *Proc. of NeurIPS*, pages 8592–8600, Vancouver, BC, Canada.

Kyle Richardson, Hai Hu, Lawrence Moss, and Ashish Sabharwal. 2020. Probing natural language inference models through semantic fragments. *Proc. of AAAI*, 34:8713–8721.

Anna Rogers, Olga Kovaleva, and Anna Rumshisky. 2020. A primer in BERTology: What we know about how BERT works. *Transactions of the Association for Computational Linguistics*, 8:842–866.

Victor Sanh, Lysandre Debut, Julien Chaumond, and Thomas Wolf. 2020. DistilBERT, a distilled version of BERT: smaller, faster, cheaper and lighter. *arXiv:1910.01108 [cs]*. ArXiv: 1910.01108.

Tobias Schnabel, Igor Labutov, David Mimno, and Thorsten Joachims. 2015. Evaluation methods for unsupervised word embeddings. In *Proc. of EMNLP*, pages 298–307, Lisbon, Portugal. Association for Computational Linguistics.

Nathan Schneider, Jena D. Hwang, Vivek Srikumar, Jakob Prange, Austin Blodgett, Sarah R. Moeller, Aviram Stern, Adi Bitan, and Omri Abend. 2018. Comprehensive supersense disambiguation of English prepositions and possessives. In *Proc. of ACL*, pages 185–196, Melbourne, Australia. Association for Computational Linguistics.

Nathan Schneider and Noah A. Smith. 2015. A corpus and model integrating multiword expressions and supersenses. In *Proc. of NAACL-HLT*, pages 1537–1547, Denver, Colorado. Association for Computational Linguistics.

Harish Tayyar Madabushi, Laurence Romain, Dagmar Divjak, and Petar Milin. 2020. CxGBERT: BERT meets construction grammar. In *Proc. of ICCL*, pages 4020–4032, Barcelona, Spain (Online). International Committee on Computational Linguistics.

Ashish Vaswani, Noam Shazeer, Niki Parmar, Jakob Uszkoreit, Llion Jones, Aidan N. Gomez, Lukasz Kaiser, and Illia Polosukhin. 2017. Attention is all you need. In *Proc. of NeurIPS*, pages 5998–6008.

Alex Wang, Amanpreet Singh, Julian Michael, Felix Hill, Omer Levy, and Samuel R. Bowman. 2019. GLUE: A multi-task benchmark and analysis platform for natural language understanding. In *Proc. of ICLR*. OpenReview.net.

Gregor Wiedemann, Steffen Remus, Avi Chawla, and Chris Biemann. 2019. Does BERT Make Any Sense? Interpretable Word Sense Disambiguation with Contextualized Embeddings. *arXiv:1909.10430 [cs]*. ArXiv: 1909.10430.

Thomas Wolf, Lysandre Debut, Victor Sanh, Julien Chaumond, Clement Delangue, Anthony Moi, Pierric Cistac, Tim Rault, Remi Louf, Morgan Funtowicz, Joe Davison, Sam Shleifer, Patrick von Platen, Clara Ma, Yacine Jernite, Julien Plu, Canwen Xu, Teven Le Scao, Sylvain Gugger, Mariama Drame, Quentin Lhoest, and Alexander Rush. 2020. Transformers: State-of-the-art natural language processing. In *Proc. of EMNLP*, pages 38–45, Online. Association for Computational Linguistics.

Zhilin Yang, Zihang Dai, Yiming Yang, Jaime G. Carbonell, Ruslan Salakhutdinov, and Quoc V. Le. 2019. Xlnet: Generalized autoregressive pretraining for language understanding. In *Proc. of NeurIPS*, pages 5754–5764, Vancouver, BC, Canada.

A Fine-tuning Setup

For the fine-tuning step, a simple linear projection layer is added to the end of the CWE model. HuggingFace's implementation of AdamW (Loshchilov and Hutter, 2019) is used as the optimizer with a learning rate of `2e-5` for 40 epochs. Prepositions in STREUSLE are annotated with two supersenses, but only the first one is used for fine-tuning.

B Full Results, Main Experiment

B.1 OntoNotes, $\ell < 500$, $r < 0.25$

Model	# FT Instances	Precision	Recall
random baseline	0	11.55	3.63
oracle	0	82.02	23.92
roberta-base	0	32.87	9.28
roberta-base	100	34.38	9.80
roberta-base	250	37.87	10.80
roberta-base	500	35.75	10.20
roberta-base	1000	36.88	10.48
roberta-base	2500	35.09	9.96
bert-base-cased	0	41.60	11.79
bert-base-cased	100	42.88	12.20
bert-base-cased	250	43.04	12.24
bert-base-cased	500	42.02	11.93
bert-base-cased	1000	43.42	12.37
bert-base-cased	2500	43.37	12.34
distilroberta-base	0	29.33	8.30
distilroberta-base	100	32.87	9.32
distilroberta-base	250	34.74	9.88
distilroberta-base	500	33.99	9.63
distilroberta-base	1000	32.24	9.16
distilroberta-base	2500	32.92	9.33
distilbert-base-cased	0	39.80	11.26
distilbert-base-cased	100	41.62	11.84
distilbert-base-cased	250	41.42	11.78
distilbert-base-cased	500	41.11	11.70
distilbert-base-cased	1000	40.70	11.55
distilbert-base-cased	2500	41.55	11.83
gpt2	0	18.34	5.37
gpt2	100	16.92	4.99
gpt2	250	18.08	5.30
gpt2	500	18.12	5.32
gpt2	1000	17.59	5.18
gpt2	2500	17.39	5.11
albert-base-v2	0	40.44	11.50
albert-base-v2	100	39.26	11.22
albert-base-v2	250	37.24	10.66
albert-base-v2	500	36.72	10.51
albert-base-v2	1000	38.01	10.86
albert-base-v2	2500	38.48	10.98
xlnet-base-cased	0	28.72	7.93
xlnet-base-cased	100	36.38	10.05
xlnet-base-cased	250	37.53	10.44
xlnet-base-cased	500	34.42	9.55
xlnet-base-cased	1000	37.38	10.36
xlnet-base-cased	2500	36.95	10.31

B.2 OntoNotes, $\ell < 500$, $r \geq 0.25$

Model	# FT Instances	Precision	Recall
random baseline	0	11.55	3.63
oracle	0	82.02	23.92
roberta-base	0	32.87	9.28
roberta-base	100	34.38	9.80
roberta-base	250	37.87	10.80
roberta-base	500	35.75	10.20
roberta-base	1000	36.88	10.48
roberta-base	2500	35.09	9.96
bert-base-cased	0	41.60	11.79
bert-base-cased	100	42.88	12.20
bert-base-cased	250	43.04	12.24
bert-base-cased	500	42.02	11.93
bert-base-cased	1000	43.42	12.37
bert-base-cased	2500	43.37	12.34
distilroberta-base	0	29.33	8.30
distilroberta-base	100	32.87	9.32
distilroberta-base	250	34.74	9.88
distilroberta-base	500	33.99	9.63
distilroberta-base	1000	32.24	9.16
distilroberta-base	2500	32.92	9.33
distilbert-base-cased	0	39.80	11.26
distilbert-base-cased	100	41.62	11.84
distilbert-base-cased	250	41.42	11.78
distilbert-base-cased	500	41.11	11.70
distilbert-base-cased	1000	40.70	11.55
distilbert-base-cased	2500	41.55	11.83
gpt2	0	18.34	5.37
gpt2	100	16.92	4.99
gpt2	250	18.08	5.30
gpt2	500	18.12	5.32
gpt2	1000	17.59	5.18
gpt2	2500	17.39	5.11
albert-base-v2	0	40.44	11.50
albert-base-v2	100	39.26	11.22
albert-base-v2	250	37.24	10.66
albert-base-v2	500	36.72	10.51
albert-base-v2	1000	38.01	10.86
albert-base-v2	2500	38.48	10.98
xlnet-base-cased	0	28.72	7.93
xlnet-base-cased	100	36.38	10.05
xlnet-base-cased	250	37.53	10.44
xlnet-base-cased	500	34.42	9.55
xlnet-base-cased	1000	37.38	10.36
xlnet-base-cased	2500	36.95	10.31

B.3 OntoNotes, $\ell \geq 500$, $r < 0.25$

Model	# FT Instances	Precision	Recall
random baseline	0	11.55	3.63
oracle	0	82.02	23.92
roberta-base	0	32.87	9.28
roberta-base	100	34.38	9.80
roberta-base	250	37.87	10.80
roberta-base	500	35.75	10.20
roberta-base	1000	36.88	10.48
roberta-base	2500	35.09	9.96
bert-base-cased	0	41.60	11.79
bert-base-cased	100	42.88	12.20
bert-base-cased	250	43.04	12.24
bert-base-cased	500	42.02	11.93
bert-base-cased	1000	43.42	12.37
bert-base-cased	2500	43.37	12.34
distilroberta-base	0	29.33	8.30
distilroberta-base	100	32.87	9.32
distilroberta-base	250	34.74	9.88
distilroberta-base	500	33.99	9.63
distilroberta-base	1000	32.24	9.16
distilroberta-base	2500	32.92	9.33
distilbert-base-cased	0	39.80	11.26
distilbert-base-cased	100	41.62	11.84
distilbert-base-cased	250	41.42	11.78
distilbert-base-cased	500	41.11	11.70
distilbert-base-cased	1000	40.70	11.55
distilbert-base-cased	2500	41.55	11.83
gpt2	0	18.34	5.37
gpt2	100	16.92	4.99
gpt2	250	18.08	5.30
gpt2	500	18.12	5.32
gpt2	1000	17.59	5.18
gpt2	2500	17.39	5.11
albert-base-v2	0	40.44	11.50
albert-base-v2	100	39.26	11.22
albert-base-v2	250	37.24	10.66
albert-base-v2	500	36.72	10.51
albert-base-v2	1000	38.01	10.86
albert-base-v2	2500	38.48	10.98
xlnet-base-cased	0	28.72	7.93
xlnet-base-cased	100	36.38	10.05
xlnet-base-cased	250	37.53	10.44
xlnet-base-cased	500	34.42	9.55
xlnet-base-cased	1000	37.38	10.36
xlnet-base-cased	2500	36.95	10.31

B.4 OntoNotes, $\ell \geq 500$, $r \geq 0.25$

Model	# FT Instances	Precision	Recall
random baseline	0	11.55	3.63
oracle	0	82.02	23.92
roberta-base	0	32.87	9.28
roberta-base	100	34.38	9.80
roberta-base	250	37.87	10.80
roberta-base	500	35.75	10.20
roberta-base	1000	36.88	10.48
roberta-base	2500	35.09	9.96
bert-base-cased	0	41.60	11.79
bert-base-cased	100	42.88	12.20
bert-base-cased	250	43.04	12.24
bert-base-cased	500	42.02	11.93
bert-base-cased	1000	43.42	12.37
bert-base-cased	2500	43.37	12.34
distilroberta-base	0	29.33	8.30
distilroberta-base	100	32.87	9.32
distilroberta-base	250	34.74	9.88
distilroberta-base	500	33.99	9.63
distilroberta-base	1000	32.24	9.16
distilroberta-base	2500	32.92	9.33
distilbert-base-cased	0	39.80	11.26
distilbert-base-cased	100	41.62	11.84
distilbert-base-cased	250	41.42	11.78
distilbert-base-cased	500	41.11	11.70
distilbert-base-cased	1000	40.70	11.55
distilbert-base-cased	2500	41.55	11.83
gpt2	0	18.34	5.37
gpt2	100	16.92	4.99
gpt2	250	18.08	5.30
gpt2	500	18.12	5.32
gpt2	1000	17.59	5.18
gpt2	2500	17.39	5.11
albert-base-v2	0	40.44	11.50
albert-base-v2	100	39.26	11.22
albert-base-v2	250	37.24	10.66
albert-base-v2	500	36.72	10.51
albert-base-v2	1000	38.01	10.86
albert-base-v2	2500	38.48	10.98
xlnet-base-cased	0	28.72	7.93
xlnet-base-cased	100	36.38	10.05
xlnet-base-cased	250	37.53	10.44
xlnet-base-cased	500	34.42	9.55
xlnet-base-cased	1000	37.38	10.36
xlnet-base-cased	2500	36.95	10.31

B.5 PDEP, $\ell < 500$, $r < 0.25$

Model	# FT Instances	Precision	Recall
random baseline	0	11.56	1.85
oracle	0	96.41	15.19
roberta-base	0	39.84	5.90
roberta-base	100	42.09	6.29
roberta-base	250	47.86	7.21
roberta-base	500	45.20	6.78
roberta-base	1000	48.99	7.37
roberta-base	2500	46.63	6.99
bert-base-cased	0	59.59	8.99
bert-base-cased	100	60.00	9.07
bert-base-cased	250	60.23	9.11
bert-base-cased	500	60.07	9.07
bert-base-cased	1000	59.94	9.07
bert-base-cased	2500	60.37	9.13
distilroberta-base	0	32.42	4.80
distilroberta-base	100	39.20	5.84
distilroberta-base	250	42.25	6.34
distilroberta-base	500	41.75	6.26
distilroberta-base	1000	40.09	6.02
distilroberta-base	2500	39.89	5.96
distilbert-base-cased	0	58.06	8.75
distilbert-base-cased	100	58.06	8.77
distilbert-base-cased	250	58.02	8.76
distilbert-base-cased	500	57.96	8.75
distilbert-base-cased	1000	58.03	8.75
distilbert-base-cased	2500	58.33	8.79
gpt2	0	21.75	3.24
gpt2	100	18.34	2.76
gpt2	250	21.53	3.17
gpt2	500	19.77	2.93
gpt2	1000	19.42	2.90
gpt2	2500	20.58	3.08
albert-base-v2	0	56.53	8.55
albert-base-v2	100	53.75	8.14
albert-base-v2	250	52.56	7.95
albert-base-v2	500	51.63	7.80
albert-base-v2	1000	51.97	7.86
albert-base-v2	2500	53.10	8.03
xlnet-base-cased	0	35.76	5.12
xlnet-base-cased	100	48.28	7.02
xlnet-base-cased	250	48.47	7.08
xlnet-base-cased	500	45.99	6.68
xlnet-base-cased	1000	48.80	7.13
xlnet-base-cased	2500	49.46	7.25

B.6 PDEP, $\ell < 500$, $r \geq 0.25$

Model	# FT Instances	Precision	Recall
random baseline	0	11.56	1.85
oracle	0	96.41	15.19
roberta-base	0	39.84	5.90
roberta-base	100	42.09	6.29
roberta-base	250	47.86	7.21
roberta-base	500	45.20	6.78
roberta-base	1000	48.99	7.37
roberta-base	2500	46.63	6.99
bert-base-cased	0	59.59	8.99
bert-base-cased	100	60.00	9.07
bert-base-cased	250	60.23	9.11
bert-base-cased	500	60.07	9.07
bert-base-cased	1000	59.94	9.07
bert-base-cased	2500	60.37	9.13
distilroberta-base	0	32.42	4.80
distilroberta-base	100	39.20	5.84
distilroberta-base	250	42.25	6.34
distilroberta-base	500	41.75	6.26
distilroberta-base	1000	40.09	6.02
distilroberta-base	2500	39.89	5.96
distilbert-base-cased	0	58.06	8.75
distilbert-base-cased	100	58.06	8.77
distilbert-base-cased	250	58.02	8.76
distilbert-base-cased	500	57.96	8.75
distilbert-base-cased	1000	58.03	8.75
distilbert-base-cased	2500	58.33	8.79
gpt2	0	21.75	3.24
gpt2	100	18.34	2.76
gpt2	250	21.53	3.17
gpt2	500	19.77	2.93
gpt2	1000	19.42	2.90
gpt2	2500	20.58	3.08
albert-base-v2	0	56.53	8.55
albert-base-v2	100	53.75	8.14
albert-base-v2	250	52.56	7.95
albert-base-v2	500	51.63	7.80
albert-base-v2	1000	51.97	7.86
albert-base-v2	2500	53.10	8.03
xlnet-base-cased	0	35.76	5.12
xlnet-base-cased	100	48.28	7.02
xlnet-base-cased	250	48.47	7.08
xlnet-base-cased	500	45.99	6.68
xlnet-base-cased	1000	48.80	7.13
xlnet-base-cased	2500	49.46	7.25

B.7 PDEP, $\ell \geq 500$, $r < 0.25$

Model	# FT Instances	Precision	Recall
random baseline	0	11.56	1.85
oracle	0	96.41	15.19
roberta-base	0	39.84	5.90
roberta-base	100	42.09	6.29
roberta-base	250	47.86	7.21
roberta-base	500	45.20	6.78
roberta-base	1000	48.99	7.37
roberta-base	2500	46.63	6.99
bert-base-cased	0	59.59	8.99
bert-base-cased	100	60.00	9.07
bert-base-cased	250	60.23	9.11
bert-base-cased	500	60.07	9.07
bert-base-cased	1000	59.94	9.07
bert-base-cased	2500	60.37	9.13
distilroberta-base	0	32.42	4.80
distilroberta-base	100	39.20	5.84
distilroberta-base	250	42.25	6.34
distilroberta-base	500	41.75	6.26
distilroberta-base	1000	40.09	6.02
distilroberta-base	2500	39.89	5.96
distilbert-base-cased	0	58.06	8.75
distilbert-base-cased	100	58.06	8.77
distilbert-base-cased	250	58.02	8.76
distilbert-base-cased	500	57.96	8.75
distilbert-base-cased	1000	58.03	8.75
distilbert-base-cased	2500	58.33	8.79
gpt2	0	21.75	3.24
gpt2	100	18.34	2.76
gpt2	250	21.53	3.17
gpt2	500	19.77	2.93
gpt2	1000	19.42	2.90
gpt2	2500	20.58	3.08
albert-base-v2	0	56.53	8.55
albert-base-v2	100	53.75	8.14
albert-base-v2	250	52.56	7.95
albert-base-v2	500	51.63	7.80
albert-base-v2	1000	51.97	7.86
albert-base-v2	2500	53.10	8.03
xlnet-base-cased	0	35.76	5.12
xlnet-base-cased	100	48.28	7.02
xlnet-base-cased	250	48.47	7.08
xlnet-base-cased	500	45.99	6.68
xlnet-base-cased	1000	48.80	7.13
xlnet-base-cased	2500	49.46	7.25

B.8 PDEP, $\ell \geq 500$, $r \geq 0.25$

Model	# FT Instances	Precision	Recall
random baseline	0	11.56	1.85
oracle	0	96.41	15.19
roberta-base	0	39.84	5.90
roberta-base	100	42.09	6.29
roberta-base	250	47.86	7.21
roberta-base	500	45.20	6.78
roberta-base	1000	48.99	7.37
roberta-base	2500	46.63	6.99
bert-base-cased	0	59.59	8.99
bert-base-cased	100	60.00	9.07
bert-base-cased	250	60.23	9.11
bert-base-cased	500	60.07	9.07
bert-base-cased	1000	59.94	9.07
bert-base-cased	2500	60.37	9.13
distilroberta-base	0	32.42	4.80
distilroberta-base	100	39.20	5.84
distilroberta-base	250	42.25	6.34
distilroberta-base	500	41.75	6.26
distilroberta-base	1000	40.09	6.02
distilroberta-base	2500	39.89	5.96
distilbert-base-cased	0	58.06	8.75
distilbert-base-cased	100	58.06	8.77
distilbert-base-cased	250	58.02	8.76
distilbert-base-cased	500	57.96	8.75
distilbert-base-cased	1000	58.03	8.75
distilbert-base-cased	2500	58.33	8.79
gpt2	0	21.75	3.24
gpt2	100	18.34	2.76
gpt2	250	21.53	3.17
gpt2	500	19.77	2.93
gpt2	1000	19.42	2.90
gpt2	2500	20.58	3.08
albert-base-v2	0	56.53	8.55
albert-base-v2	100	53.75	8.14
albert-base-v2	250	52.56	7.95
albert-base-v2	500	51.63	7.80
albert-base-v2	1000	51.97	7.86
albert-base-v2	2500	53.10	8.03
xlnet-base-cased	0	35.76	5.12
xlnet-base-cased	100	48.28	7.02
xlnet-base-cased	250	48.47	7.08
xlnet-base-cased	500	45.99	6.68
xlnet-base-cased	1000	48.80	7.13
xlnet-base-cased	2500	49.46	7.25